Living in the Environment
Third Edition

G. Tyler Miller, Jr.
St. Andrews Presbyterian College

Wadsworth Publishing Company
Belmont, California
A Division of Wadsworth, Inc.

Science Editor: Jack Carey
Production Editor: Jeanne Heise
Designer: Patricia Dunbar
Copy Editors: Paul Monsour and Carol Reitz
Cover photograph: Douglas Faulkner

1 2 3 4 5 6 7 8 9 10—86 85 84 83 82

Library of Congress Cataloging in Publication Data
Miller, G. Tyler (George Tyler), 1931-
  Living in the environment.

  Bibliography: p.
  Includes index.
  1. Human ecology.   2. Environmental policy.
I. Title.
GF41.M54   1981   304.2   81-4878
ISBN 0-534-00994-8   AACR2

Books in the Wadsworth Biology Series

Biology: The Unity and Diversity of Life, 2nd, Starr and Taggart
Energy and Environment: Four Energy Crises, 2nd, Miller
Replenish the Earth: A Primer in Human Ecology, Miller
Oceanography: An Introduction, 2nd, Ingmanson and Wallace

Biology books under the editorship of William A. Jensen, University of California, Berkeley

Biology, Jensen, Heinrich, Wake, Wake
Biology: The Foundations, Wolfe
Biology of the Cell, 2nd, Wolfe
Botany: An Ecological Approach, Jensen and Salisbury
Plant Physiology, 2nd, Salisbury and Ross
Plant Physiology Laboratory Manual, Ross
Plant Diversity: An Evolutionary Approach, Scagel et al.
An Evolutionary Survey of the Plant Kingdom, Scagel et al.
Plants and the Ecosystem, 3rd, Billings
Plants and Civilization, 3rd, Baker

The environmental crisis is an outward manifestation of a crisis of mind and spirit. There could be no greater misconception of its meaning than to believe it to be concerned only with endangered wildlife, human-made ugliness, and pollution. These are part of it, but more importantly, the crisis is concerned with the kind of creatures we are and what we must become in order to survive.

Lynton K. Caldwell

Foreword

In trying to find words for the changes that now take place within a single lifetime, we speak of the great "speed" of history—but what a lame expression that is! Mere speed can be reckoned with. No matter how fast we may be moving, by measuring the speed (and perhaps the acceleration), we can predict where we will be tomorrow or next year. But can we predict the future? Sometimes we succeed fairly well by merely assuming that present trends will continue. But every now and then human affairs undergo a shocking transformation, at which time the tone of the world shifts radically almost overnight. History then seems to pass through a sharp discontinuity not at all predicted by extending major trends. Saying that the speed of change changes tells us nothing about the feeling of people who live through such a time.

We went through such a discontinuity during the 1960s when civilization entered the Age of Ecology—just when all the media agreed that we had entered the Space Age. They were right—but only in an ironic sense. By the end of the decade it was obvious that the most crucial space was not outer space, but *inner* space, where we build our conceptions of the world and of how humanity fits into it—the space of ecological insights.

Until we entered the Age of Ecology, almost no one knew the word *ecology*, although it was already 100 years old. Now it would be hard to find an alert citizen who does not have a rough working knowledge of what ecology is about. Most of us realize that no single action that we take—no single cause—has only a single effect. It has many effects. We have also learned that it is unwise to belittle the unwanted effects by labeling them *side effects*.

Effects are effects, and we must try to foresee them. We can never do merely one thing. Once we recognize this truth, our burden of responsibility becomes far greater. Ecology is a responsible science.

The world is an unimaginably complex system of systems; if we are to live well, this is what we must try to understand. The nature of their work makes ecologists different from experts in other fields. It is often sarcastically said of specialists that "they know more and more about less and less." This cannot be said of ecologists. They may have other faults, but not this one. Their job compels them to know more and more about more and more, and they do the best they can. Searching for the general principles that run through many disciplines, ecologists are inescapably generalists.

Rachel Carson's *Silent Spring* ushered in the ecological age in 1962. Since that time a dazzling array of articles and books has appeared. One hardly has time to read even just the best of them. We need sound guidance, and we get it in this text by Professor Miller. It is not the "last word" on ecology: It will be a long time before that is written (if ever). But it is a splendid first word, filled with knowledge and with questions that challenge you to carry the work further.

It is a marvelous frontier, this ecology frontier. It abounds in first-rate intellectual puzzles and opportunities for improving the quality of human life. There is more than enough work for all. Jump in!

Garrett Hardin
Chairman of the Board and Chief Executive Officer,
The Environmental Fund

Foreword

The past few decades have seen an unprecedented accumulation of knowledge concerning humans and their environment. Unfortunately, the very mass of this "information explosion" has created problems for those concerned with disseminating the material. College and university courses, initially structured to meet the growing demand for "environmental awareness," became an uphill struggle for teacher and student alike. Instructors, invariably specialists in any one of a number of disciplines, had to garner information from journals quite remote from their own fields. Such accounts, often couched in terms unknown to all but a privileged few, became time-consuming hazards that many instructors would rather avoid. Even after relevant information was gathered, the rational organization of the material for presentation in a meaningful course became a massive logistical problem. For the student, tracing cited papers became an unenviable task and, in many cases, the reading base for a course became dog-eared photocopies of offprints that inevitably disappeared at the time they were most needed. Evidence that such suffering was widespread is seen in the spate of "environmental-ecology readers" that became available. Although many excellent volumes were published, none quite seemed to fit one's own needs.

It was against such a background that Professor Miller's text first appeared. To meet the demands of an audience having many different specializations, he organized a mass of diverse information into a meaningful whole. In order to keep this information within the bounds of realistic utility, the novel two-book approach permits maximum classroom flexibility, a high priority of most instructors.

Of major significance to anyone using an environmental-ecology text is that the book maintain a sound factual basis. To this end, Professor Miller has drawn upon the best possible sources. A glance at the list of reviewers of the text shows that each subject area has been read by a foremost authority in the field. Beyond that, experts of international repute have actually contributed original articles to the text. Not only has the factual base been verified, but here too are comments by individuals who were instrumental in formulating the building-blocks on which modern interpretations are based.

One aspect of study in the environmental sciences is that often there is no simple answer to any given problem. Controversy is an integral part of the study. It is gratifying to see that within this text controversial issues are raised and that no valid viewpoint is overlooked. Fortunately, and it is certainly not true of all recent publications, the author maintains an objective intellectual style in his presentation of varying interpretations and the controversy they generate.

Living in the Environment appears at a most apt time. The great surge in "ecology" of the late sixties has leveled off, the heady feeling perhaps being tempered by the discovery that all of our problems cannot be solved in a single semester. Scholars now participating in human-environment studies are serious about their responsibilities, and are well aware that ultimate solution of human-ecologic problems requires a solid foundation of fact and rational opinion. Such people will find that *Living in the Environment* provides a splendid base for their studies.

John E. Oliver
Professor of Geography
Indiana State University

Preface

An Introductory Course in Environmental Studies The purposes of this book are (1) to cover the diverse material of an introductory course on environmental studies in an accurate, balanced, and interesting fashion, (2) to enable teachers and students to use the material in a flexible way, and (3) to use basic ecological concepts to show the relationships between environmental problems and possible ways of dealing with them.

Two Texts in One *Living in the Environment* is really two texts in one (see the brief table of contents). The **basic text** of 20 chapters provides a balanced coverage of major environmental concepts, problems, and possible solutions to the problems. To add more depth or to adapt the course to your students' needs and interests, you can use any desired combination of the 17 **enrichment studies** that follow the basic text.

One of the difficulties in writing for or teaching a course in environmental studies is that the information needs almost constant revision. In this third edition, I have extensively updated every chapter and enrichment study. No major changes have been made in organization, since surveys indicated that users desired no such changes. A number of users of the second edition indicated that the extensive documentation of most material in the text interrupted the flow of the reading and was unnecessary for an introductory text—especially since most of the introductory environmental concepts and data have become more firmly established since the 1960s and early 1970s. For these reasons—along with a desire to keep the text length and price down—I have eliminated the detailed documentation from the third edition. The very extensive list of readings suggested for each chapter and enrichment study, however, has been retained in this edition. They provide the reader with over 650 references that can be used to document and amplify the material in each chapter and enrichment study.

Material New to the Edition The rapidly changing nature of environmental concerns demands that new material be added to each edition. However, I'm equally aware of the importance to limit the length of the text. Through careful editing and pruning of the second edition I was able to add new material and still shorten the book by 30 pages. *Some* of the topics new to this edition are: Acid rain, environmental policy of the Reagan Administration, The Council of Environmental Quality's *Global 2000 Report*, loss of the world's tropical forests, the dilemma of whether to grow grain for food or for conversion to alcohol to fuel cars, the snail darter and the revised Endangered Species Act, indoor air pollution, the Love Canal episode and toxic wastes, deep and shallow ecology (environmental ethics), and organic farming.

Emphasis on Basic Concepts The third edition continues to use basic ecological concepts to show how environmental facts, problems, and possible solutions are related, and it continues to emphasize energy as a major integrating concept. Five short introductory chapters cover important ecological concepts without involving math, chemistry, or other technical details that often confuse beginning students.

Balanced Treatment The third edition continues to offer a balanced and unbiased discussion of the opposing sides of the major environmental issues, and strives to provide an objective analysis of proposed solutions to environmental problems. A superficial coverage of the opposing sides of issues cannot provide a good basis for making the informed decisions that are so urgently required. I have also included the 650 most important references so that students can probe even deeper into the controversial issues that face us. To further assist students in coming to their *own* conclusions, I have suggested major principles that may be used in developing detailed plans for dealing with the major environmental problems that confront us. These suggestions are presented to stimulate critical thinking and debate, and are not offered as "the" answer to our complex environmental problems.

Documentation Although references are not specifically cited, the material in this third edition is backed up by about 5,500 references—almost three times as many as the first edition. The extensive list of readings found at the end of each chapter and enrichment study can be used to document and amplify most topics.

Extensive Manuscript Review Because this course covers such a wide range of topics, no author or small group of authors can provide the necessary expertise. Thus, I have used 99 reviewers from many fields to improve the quality and accuracy of the book and to ensure that it is up to date. Each chapter has been reviewed in detail by at least two recognized experts in that area. In addition, a number of instructors who used the first and second editions in a wide range of colleges and universities evaluated the entire manuscript.

Sustainable Earth World View The third edition continues to focus on the importance of moving from our present frontier and spaceship world views to a sustainable earth world view over the next 50 years. Such a world view recognizes the interdependence, diversity, and vulnerability of the earth's life-support systems and our own responsibility to work with, not against, nature to safeguard these systems for present and future generations.

Guest Editorials Twenty-three prominent environmentalists have written short guest editorials for this book (see the list of guest editorialists). The third edition includes 9 new Guest Editorials. To avoid breaking up the logical flow of the chapter, Guest Editorials are boxed and appear at the end of each chapter in a different type face from the text.

Illustrations I have tried especially hard to find or commission attractive and useful illustrations, designed to clarify complex relationships. In the third edition figures have been modified to make them even more useful, and some new figures have been added.

A Realistic Hopeful View The necessity of avoiding the opposing but equally immobilizing traps of gloom-and-doom pessimism and technological optimism continues to be an important theme in the third edition. I have tried to present a realistic but hopeful view that shows how much has been done since 1965 (when the public was first made aware of many environmental problems) as well as how much more we need to do over the next 50 years.

As you and your students deal with the crucial and exciting issues discussed in the book, I hope you will take the time to correct errors and suggest improvements for future editions.

Acknowledgments I wish to thank all of the teachers who responded to the detailed questionnaires evaluating the first and second editions. My thanks also go to the students and teachers who responded so favorably to the first two editions and offered suggestions for improvement. I am deeply indebted to the prominent environmentalists who wrote Guest Editorials for this book and to the 99 reviewers (see the list) who pointed out errors and suggested many important improvements. Any deficiencies remaining are mine, not theirs.

One of the pleasures of writing the three editions of this book has been the opportunity to work with the talented people at Wadsworth Publishing Company. I am particularly indebted to Autumn Stanley for reading the entire manuscript and making many improvements; to Mary Arbogast for coordinating the editing and publishing activities for the first two editions with her usual dedication, talent, and good humor in times of stress; to Jeanne Heise for the superb job she did in coordinating the editing and publishing of the third edition; to Paul Monsour for his careful copy-editing; to Darwen Hennings, Vally Hennings, and John Waller for their innovative art work in the first edition; to John Dawson, Flo Fujimoto, Tim Keenan, and Larry Jansen for continuing this tradition of artistic excellence in the second and third editions; and to Patricia Dunbar for designing the book.

Above all, I wish to thank Jack Carey, science editor at Wadsworth. Besides designing and managing a superb reviewing system, he has provided many key ideas for the organization and format of the three editions of this book. It has been a rare pleasure to work closely with such a talented, creative, and dedicated editor and to count him as one of my closest friends.

G. Tyler Miller, Jr.

Guest Editorialists

Hannes Alfvén
Professor of Applied Physics, University of California, San Diego, and Nobel Laureate in Physics

Barbara Blum
Former Deputy Administrator, Environmental Protection Agency

Kenneth E. Boulding
Professor Emeritus of Economics, University of Colorado

Herman E. Daly
Professor of Economics, Louisiana State University

J. Clarence Davies III
Executive Vice-President, Conservation Foundation

Richard A. Falk
Albert E. Milbank Professor of International Law and Practice, Princeton University

John H. Gibbons
Director, Office of Technology Assessment

Garrett Hardin
Chairman of the Board and Chief Executive Officer, The Environmental Fund

Denis Hayes
Former Director, Solar Energy Research Institute

Carol A. Jolly
U.S. Department of Energy

Edward J. Kormondy
Provost and Professor of Biology, University of Southern Maine

Amory B. Lovins
Friends of the Earth and international energy policy consultant

L. Hunter Lovins
Energy policy consultant

V. E. McKelvey
U.S. Geological Survey

Eugene P. Odum
Director, Institute of Ecology, University of Georgia

Howard T. Odum
Graduate Research Professor of Environmental Engineering Sciences and Director of the Center for Wetlands, University of Florida

William Ophuls
Writer and lecturer on politics and ecology

Stephen H. Schneider
Deputy Director, Advanced Study Program, National Center for Atmospheric Research

Gus Speth
Former Chairman, Council on Environmental Quality

Geraldine Watson
Naturalist and environmental activist

Kenneth E. F. Watt
Professor of Zoology, University of California, Davis

Alvin M. Weinberg
Director, Institute for Energy Analysis

Harvey Wheeler
Director, Institute of Higher Studies

Reviewers

Brief Contents

Detailed Contents

Enrichment Studies

Prologue

Passengers on *Terra I,* the only true spacecraft, it is time for the annual State of the Spaceship report. As you know, we are hurtling through space at about 107,200 kilometers (66,600 miles) per hour on a fixed course. Although we can never take on new supplies, our ship has a marvelous set of life-support systems that use solar energy to recycle the chemicals needed to provide a reasonable number of us with adequate water, air, and food.

Let me summarize the state of our passengers and of our life-support system. There are over 4.6 billion passengers on board, distributed throughout 165 nations that occupy various sections of the ship. One-quarter of you are in the more developed nations, occupying the good to luxurious quarters in the first-class section. You used about 80 percent of all supplies available this past year.

Unfortunately, things have not really improved this year for the 75 percent of you in the so-called less developed nations traveling in the hold of the ship. Over one-third of you are suffering from hunger, malnutrition, or both, and three-fourths of you do not have adequate water and shelter. More people starved to death or died from malnutrition-related diseases this year than at any time in the history of our voyage. This number will certainly rise as long as population growth continues to wipe out gains in food supply and economic development.

With the limited supplies and recycling capacity of our craft, many of you are now wondering whether you will ever move from the hold to the first-class section. Even more important, many of you are asking why you had to travel in the ship's hold in the first place.

The most important fact molding our lives today is that we have gone around the bend of three curves shaped like the letter *J* that represent the global increases in population, resource use, and pollution over the past hundred years. Population growth rates have decreased slightly in recent years, partially because of tragic increases in the death rates of the desperately poor countries, home to a billion of you. At the present growth rate, our population will probably grow to 6.1 billion by the year 2000 and could double to over 9 billion passengers in the next 41 years.

But we don't have to maintain our present rate of population growth. We must come to grips with an important question: What is the population level that will let all passengers live with freedom, dignity, and a fair share of *Terra I's* re-sources? Some experts put this ideal level at about 2 billion passengers, a figure that we reached in 1930.

But the overpopulation of the hold, serious though it is, may be less of a threat to our life-support system than the overpopulation in the first-class section. Both consumption and pollution rise sharply with even a slight increase in the wealthier population. For example, the 228 million Americans, who make up only 5 percent of our total population, used about 35 percent of all our supplies and produced over one-third of all our artificial pollution last year. Each first-class passenger has about 25 times as much impact on our life-support system as each passenger traveling in the hold. The first-class passengers must continue to reduce their rate of population growth and at the same time change their patterns of consumption, which squander many of our limited supplies. Failure to do so will continue to strain and damage the life-support systems for everyone. Efforts to conserve resources in the rich nations are still grossly inadequate. Pollution control in these nations, however, continues to improve, although there is a long way to go.

In spite of the seriousness of the interlocking problems of overpopulation, dwindling resources, and pollution, the single greatest human and environmental threat is that of war—especially a nuclear holocaust. It is discouraging that so little progress has been made in reducing the extravagant waste of resources and human talent devoted to the arms race. During the past year we spent 200 times more on military expenditures than on international cooperation for peace and development. Each year more nations develop the ability to produce nuclear weapons.

Some say that our ship is already doomed, while other technological optimists see a glorious future for everyone. Our most thoughtful experts agree that the ship's situation is serious but certainly not hopeless. They feel that if we begin now, we have about 50 years to learn how to control our population and consumption and to learn how to live together in cooperation and peace on this beautiful and fragile lifecraft that is our home. Obviously, more of us must start to act like members of the crew rather than like passengers. This particularly applies to those of you traveling first class, who have the most harmful impact on our life-support system and who have the greatest financial and technological resources to help correct the situation.

Just what is spaceship *Terra I*? Where are we going? What

problems and opportunities do we face? What is our individual responsibility for the other passengers and for preserving our life-support systems? We must look more deeply into these complex questions so that we may convert our understanding into effective individual and group action.

1. Two college students spending the weekend at a Colorado ski resort caught the State of the Spaceship report on the lodge's color TV. "I'm sick of hearing about the environmental crisis," said John as he ripped the tab from his third can of beer. "It's already too late. My motto is 'Eat, drink, and have a good time while you can.' What's the world done for me?"

    "I don't think it's too late at all," observed Susan. "If we can put astronauts on the moon, we can certainly solve our pollution problems. Sure it's going to cost some money, but I'm willing to pay my share. The whole thing is just a matter of money and technology. By the way, John, during Christmas break let's fly to Switzerland to ski. There are too many people here. We always have to wait in line, and all these hideous new ski lodges have spoiled the view. Besides, I want to shop for a new ski outfit."

2. In a rotting tenement room in Harlem, Larry angrily switched off the TV, even though he usually kept it on to drown out the noises around him—particularly the rats scratching. A high school dropout, he's given up looking for work. "This ecology crap is just another whitey trick to keep us from getting a piece of the action. Every summer some liberal college kids come down to help the social workers show us blacks how to use IUDs. Sounds like a new way to keep us down. What do I care about pollution when my little sister was bitten by a rat last night, my ma's got emphysema, and we haven't had any heat in this firetrap for months? Tell it to my uncle in Florida who's paralyzed from the waist down from some chemical they used on the fruit he was picking. Give me a chance to pollute and then I might worry about it."

3. In Calcutta, Mukh Das, his wife, and their seven children did not hear the broadcast in the streets where they live. As Mukh, who is 36, watched his 34-year-old wife patting dung into cakes to be dried and used for fuel, he was glad that 7 of his 12 children were still alive to help now that he and his wife were in their old age. He felt a chill, and he hoped his children would soon be returning from begging and gathering dung and scraps of food. Perhaps they had been lucky enough to meet another rich American tourist today.

4. In a Connecticut suburb, Bill and Kathy Farmington and their three children, David, Karen, and Linda, were discussing the broadcast. David, a college senior, turned away from the TV in disgust. "This ecology thing is just a big cop-out by people who don't really know what it's all about. In the commune I'm moving into we're going to get back to nature and away from this plastic, racist society of people who don't care."

    "That's the biggest cop-out of all," said Karen, a college sophomore. "The only reason you have the freedom to drop out is that you live in a rich country. Why don't you help rather than trying to escape? The real problem is with the poor Americans in the ghetto who keep having all those children. Why don't you work on family planning in the slums this summer like I'm going to do? I'm even going to get college credit for it."

    Bill Farmington, chief engineer for Monarch Power Company, looked at his children irritably. "The problem with all of you back-to-the-woods dropouts and misguided liberals is that you don't understand what hard work it takes to keep the world going. If you're so fired up about pollution, David, why don't you walk to your commune rather than driving the car I gave you? Karen, you might consider turning in that snowmobile you use to recuperate from your hot summer in the ghetto. How do you think I paid for all those things you wanted? I'm all for clean air and water, but we can't stop the economic progress our American way of life is built on. Remember last year when we had a lot of ecofreaks and liberal professors trying to stop us from building the new nuclear power plant? In spite of all this talk about conservation, Americans are going to use more and more energy, and we have to give our customers the power they want. You're as bad as those college professors who go around making speeches and writing books on ecology, but don't change their own life-styles and don't know what hard physical work is all about. David, cut off that TV and the one in the kitchen, too. I'm sick of hearing about pollution, corruption in government, and rioting in India. Linda, it's getting hot in here. Would you please turn up the air conditioning?"

    Kathy, Bill's wife, was slowly shaking her head. "I just don't know. This ecology crisis is bad and we have to do something. The problem is I don't know what to do. One scientist says we shouldn't build nuclear power plants, another says we should. One says ban DDT and another says if we do many will die from diseases and starvation. How can we know what to do when experts disagree? I recognize that the population problem is bad in India, Africa, and South America. Remember how horrid it was in Calcutta on our trip last summer? I just couldn't wait to leave. I'm glad we don't have an overpopulation problem in the United States. At least we can afford to have children."

    As Linda, a college freshman, got up, she was thinking that no one really listened to the speech. "Don't they realize that we are all connected with one another and that our primary goal must be to preserve—not destroy—the life support systems that keep us and other species alive? Can't they see that everyone on *Terra I* is a unique human being entitled to a share of our ship's basic resources? I'm afraid for all of us too, but I really don't think it's too late. When I become a public service lawyer, I plan to devote my life to environmental reform."

This book is dedicated to the growing number of Lindas on Terra I *and to Larry, the Das family, and others whose right to human dignity, freedom, and a fair share of the world's resources must be respected.*

PART ONE

Humans and Nature: An Overview

Kennecott Copper Corporation

It is only in the most recent, and brief, period of their tenure that human beings have developed in sufficient numbers, and acquired enough power, to become one of the most potentially dangerous organisms that the planet has ever hosted.

John McHale

Humankind still has the time and option to make it. But it's absolutely touch and go whether we are going to make it on this planet.

R. Buckminster Fuller

1

Population, Resources, and Pollution

1-1 A Crisis of Crises

The prospect for humanity is both brighter and darker than at any other time in history. Caught between the prophets of doom and the prophets of technological salvation, we live in a world that often seems absurd. We spend billions to transport a handful of humans to the moon only to learn the importance of protecting the diversity of life on this beautiful blue ball that is our home. The richest fourth of the world's population tries to consume more and more of the world's resources, but the resulting waste products erode the position of the rich and the hopes of the poor. With mass communication, many of us know more about national and world affairs than about the uniqueness of our neighbors. We use modern medicine and sanitation to lower death rates from disease, only to be faced with a population explosion. Pesticides and fertilizers help us grow more food than ever before, but they also kill birds and fish and pollute our food and water. When we burn coal, oil, and natural gas to provide us with electricity, to cool and warm our buildings, to run our industries, and to move us from place to place we also pollute our air, water, and land, threaten our health, and possibly change the global climate. If we replace fossil fuels with nuclear power, we risk catastrophe from accidents, proliferation of nuclear weapons, thefts of nuclear fuel by terrorists to make atomic bombs, and leakage of radioactive nuclear wastes, which must be stored for thousands of years.

The problems of increasing population, decreasing resources, and increasing pollution are all interrelated.

Water, rich soil, and fossil fuels are needed to grow, process, and transport food for the human population. Electrical energy cannot be generated without copper, aluminum, and other metal resources. Motor vehicles, buildings, and other items we use require water, metals, plastics, and energy to make and maintain. When we grow food, generate electricity, and make useful (and not-so-useful) products, we always produce some pollution. As more and more people try to use more and more resources, we place increasing stresses on the forests, fisheries, grasslands, croplands, and on the air and water systems that support all life on earth. Each of these systems has a limit that is essentially fixed by nature. To exceed these limits is to invite disease and death, and there is growing evidence that we are reaching these limits, as discussed by Gus Speth in his Guest Editorial at the end of this chapter.

This avalanche of complex interlocking problems can be described as a crisis of crises. But a crisis is also an opportunity to change how we think and act. *The primary aim of this book is to describe our major environmental problems, present the ecological concepts that connect them, and use these concepts to evaluate the exciting opportunities we have to deal with these problems in coming decades.*

Let us begin with a brief overview of the related problems of population growth, resource depletion, and pollution. In later chapters we will look at these problems and proposed solutions in greater depth.

1-2 Population

The J Curve One of the most important facts affecting our lives today is that we have gone around the bend on a **J curve,** or *exponential curve*, of rising population. What is a J curve? Any system that grows by doubling—that is, 1, 2, 4, 8, 16, 32, and so on—experiences **exponential growth,** or *geometric growth*. If you graph these numbers, you get a curve shaped like the letter *J:* For a few dou-

---

Enrichment Study 1 is related to this chapter.

blings, nothing much seems to happen. Then suddenly the bend in the J is rounded, and the curve takes off.

Let me take you around the bend on a J curve. Let us start doubling the thickness of a page of this book. If we assume that the page is about 0.1 millimeter (about 1/254 inch) thick, after the first doubling the thickness is 0.2 millimeter, then 0.4, 0.8, 1.6, 3.2, and so on. After 8 doublings, the paper is 25.6 millimeters (about 1 inch) thick. After 12 doublings it is about 410 millimeters (1.34 feet) thick, and after 20 doublings about 105 meters (340 feet). Still very little has happened; we are on the lower part, or the *lag phase,* of the J curve.

However, if we double our page slightly over 35 times, its thickness would equal the distance from New York to Los Angeles. Doubling the page 42 times would create a mound of paper reaching from the earth to the moon, some 386,400 kilometers (240,000 miles) away. Double it just over 50 times and the thickness reaches the sun, 149 million kilometers (93 million miles) away.

The Population J Curve   Unfortunately, the human population on earth (Figure 1-1) has rounded the bend on a J curve.* *The net birth rate on this planet is now about 235 babies per minute, or approximately 338,000 per day, while the net death rate is only about 92 persons per minute, or 133,000 per day. In other words, the net birth rate is about 2.5 times the net death rate.* Population growth for the entire planet is determined by the difference between these two figures:

population increase = net birth rate − net death rate

In 1981 this difference meant that the world's population grew by about 1.7 percent. Although this seems like a small rate of increase, it means that we are now adding about 205,000 more passengers each day, 1.4 million each week, and 75 million each year to the decks of *Terra I*. At this rate, it takes less than 3 days to replace all Americans killed in all U.S. wars, only 6 months to replace all battlefield casualties in all wars fought in the world during the past 500 years, and only 13 months to replace the more than 75 million people killed in the world's largest single disaster, the bubonic plague epidemic of the fourteenth century (Table 1-1). Thus, not even disaster, except perhaps global nuclear war, can control the world's population.

*The J curve is a useful image, but by expanding, contracting, or distorting the scale of a graph, you can make almost any curve a J curve. The scales in the J curves used in this text were chosen to present facts realistically.

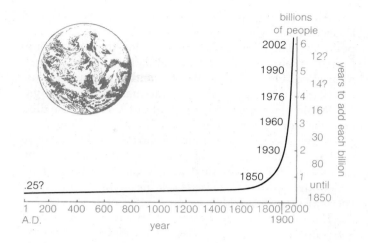

Figure 1-1   J curve of the world's population growth (future projections based on the present growth rate of 1.7 percent).

Table 1-1   Implications of Exponential Population Growth

Disasters	Approximate Number Killed	Time Needed to Replace Number Killed*
Pakistan tidal wave, 1970	200,000	1 day
All U.S. wars (Americans killed)	600,000	3 days
Great flood, Hwang Ho River, 1887	900,000	4½ days
U.S. automobile deaths through 1979	2,000,000	1½ weeks
India famine, 1769–1770	3,000,000	2½ weeks
All major global disasters†	6,500,000	5 weeks
China famine, 1877–1878	9,500,000	7 weeks
Annual global famine today	4,400,000–20,000,000	3 weeks to 3⅓ months
Influenza epidemic, 1918	21,000,000	3½ months
All wars in the past 500 years (about 280 wars)	35,000,000	6 months
Bubonic plague (Black Death), 1347–1351	75,000,000	13 months

*At present world population growth rate.

†This includes deaths from all recorded major earthquakes, avalanches, volcanic eruptions, tornadoes, floods, typhoons, fires, explosions, shipwrecks, and railroad and aircraft accidents to 1979.

All these new passengers must be fed, clothed, and housed. Each will use some resources and add to global pollution. The United Nations estimates that at least one-fourth of our passengers are already hungry or malnourished. One out of three has neither adequate housing (Figure 1-2) nor a safe and adequate water supply.

While you ate dinner today, about 1,400 people died of starvation, malnutrition, or diseases resulting from these conditions. By this time tomorrow, 41,000 will have died from starvation or starvation-related diseases; by next week, 287,000; by next year, about 15,000,000. Half are children under five. *Those who died were human beings, not numbers or things!*

If it makes you feel better, use the lower estimate of 4.4 million starvation or starvation-related deaths per year. But this doesn't change the reality of the problem. Comparing the present starvation and malnutrition death rate of 4.4 to 20 million each year with previous major famines (see Table 1-1), we see that the greatest famine in human history is occurring now. To avoid facing this reality, officials often classify mass starvation as a famine only if it is concentrated in a particular country—not if it is diffused around the world.

It is very encouraging that between 1970 and 1981 the world's yearly population growth rate slowed down from 1.9 to 1.7 percent. But this very hopeful trend should not lull us into a false sense of security. It is somewhat encouraging when the driver of a car slows down from 190 kilometers per hour (119 miles per hour) to 170 kilometers per hour (106 miles per hour), but obviously the car is still going dangerously fast. The important point is that we still add about 75 million people a year—a rate that will double the world's population in about 41 years.

By 2000 the world's population will probably be about 6 billion—50 percent more people to feed, clothe, and house than in 1976. At that time the world's population will increase by an estimated 90 million people each year (compared with 75 million per year in 1981) even assuming that the annual rate of population growth will drop further to 1.5 percent. Over the next 30 to 50 years, we must decrease this growth rate to zero so that each year the average number of births is equal to the average number of deaths (**zero population growth,** or *ZPG*).

Population growth, however, is not our only problem. We are also faced with the environmental problems of resource depletion and pollution. Let's look briefly at these problems and their relationship to population growth.

Figure 1-2 One-third of the people in the world do not have adequate housing. These lean-to shelters are homes for several families in Dacca, Bangladesh.

1-3 Natural Resources

Resource Use and Depletion Another J curve confronts us. Affluent nations, such as the United States, have gone around the bend on a J curve of increasing resource consumption. For example, *the Western affluent nations plus Japan and the U.S.S.R. account for only about one-fourth of the world's population but use 80 percent of its natural resources. The United States alone, with about 5 percent of the world's population, uses about one-third of the world's resources* (Table 1-2) *and produces at least one-third of the world's pollution.* Furthermore, the United States unnecessarily wastes about half of the matter and energy resources it uses.

Resource use by the affluent nations is expected to rise sharply in coming decades. At the same time, the poor and moderately affluent nations of the world hope to become more affluent, which will increase resource use still further. Nobel Prize-winning economist Wassily Leontief projects that in order for even moderate economic growth to occur between 1975 and 2020, production of food must increase fourfold and that of common minerals fivefold.

These combined pressures on food, energy, timber, metals, and other key resources have led some to speculate that resource depletion might limit population and economic growth.

What Is a Resource?   Whether we run out of a particular resource depends in part on how we define *resource*. In broad terms, a **resource,** or *natural resource*, is anything needed by an organism or group of organisms. In other words, a resource is something useful. But for humanity what is useful or useless can change because of technology, economics, and the environmental effects of getting and using a resource, as discussed in greater detail in Chapter 12.

Technology cannot bring back an extinct animal resource or a paved-over wilderness area, but it can extend the supply of some resources by improving them, using them more efficiently, or recycling them. For example, a unit of today's steel provides 43 percent more structural support than it did a decade ago. Today we get 7 times more electrical power from 907 kilograms (1 ton) of coal than we did in 1900. Similarly, the energy needed to produce 907 kilograms (1 ton) of pig iron has fallen eightfold since 1800. In the United States in 1900, only 10 percent of the copper was recycled. Today about 40 percent is recycled. However, *while many matter resources, such as copper, lead, and silver, can be recycled, we can never recycle energy resources. Once a fossil fuel resource, such as coal, oil, or natural gas, is burned, it is gone forever as a useful energy source.* The concentrated energy in the fossil fuel is released as heat, which is eventually dispersed into the earth's atmosphere. From there it flows back into space.

Sometimes technology can solve the problem of a scarce resource by finding a substitute or replacement. For instance, as a structural material bronze replaced stone, iron replaced bronze, steel replaced iron, and now aluminum and reinforced plastics are replacing steel for some structural uses. As an energy source, animals replaced human muscle power, coal (to produce steam) replaced animals, and oil replaced coal for many uses (although this may be revised soon). There is a vigorous debate over whether a combination of coal-derived energy and nuclear power (obtained from uranium) or a combination of solar, wind, and plant (biomass) energy may soon replace petroleum and natural gas.

In addition to technology, resource use is tied to economics. *Something is useful as a resource only if it can be made available at a reasonable cost.* For example, once we

Table 1-2   Average Lifetime (70-Year) Resource Use and Pollution per American

Resource Consumption	Waste
566,000 kilograms (623 tons) of coal, oil, and natural gas	764,000 kilograms (840 tons) of agricultural wastes
557,000 kilograms (613 tons) of sand, gravel, and stone	748,000 kilograms (823 tons) of garbage, industrial, and mining wastes
98,000 cubic meters (26 million gallons) of water	26,000 cubic meters (7 million gallons) of polluted water
80 cubic meters (21 thousand gallons) of gasoline	64,000 kilograms (70 tons) of air pollutants
46,000 kilograms (51 tons) of metals	19,250 bottles
45,000 kilograms (50 tons) of food	19,000 cans
44,000 kilograms (48 tons) of wood	7 automobiles
19,000 kilograms (19 tons) of paper	
4,700 kilograms (5.2 tons) of synthetic plastics, rubber, and fibers	
4,500 kilograms (5 tons) of fertilizer	

Figures assume constant 1975 consumption rates. If average consumption goes up as projected, the figures will be much higher. Figures include direct and indirect uses.

deplete the easily available supplies of a resource, we have to look harder and dig deeper to find remaining supplies. If the costs of finding and making a scarce resource available rise, the resource will eventually become too expensive for most people. Higher costs may stimulate a search for new supplies or make mining and processing lower-grade deposits economically feasible. But regardless of what we are willing and able to pay, we can't get a resource out of the earth if it isn't there.

There can also be an economic limit to recycling. Typically, recycling is cheaper than mining virgin materials, but only if the material to be recycled is not too widely dispersed. For example, if products made from iron and steel, such as cars and toys, are thrown away, buried, and widely scattered through use, labor and energy costs for finding and collecting the objects may be too expensive to make recycling feasible.

The continued use of a resource may also depend on the impact its mining, processing, and use has on the environment. Even if affordable supplies of a resource

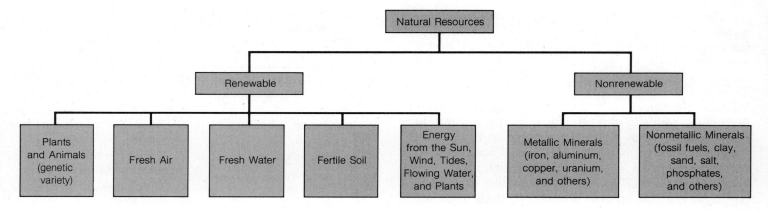

Figure 1-3 Major types of natural resources.

are available, its use (at least for certain purposes) may have to be abandoned if this use seriously threatens humans and other forms of life. Sometimes the environmental effects of resource use can be minimized and cleaned up. But this costs money, and in some cases the costs may be so high that we can no longer afford to use the resource.

Types of Resources Resources are usually classified as renewable or nonrenewable, as summarized in Figure 1-3. **Renewable resources** can theoretically last forever. Either they come from an essentially inexhaustible source (such as solar energy), or they can be renewed and replenished by natural or artificial cyclical processes. For example, food crops and animals, wildlife, forests, and other living things, as well as fresh air, fresh water, and fertile soil, can be renewed again and again if they are managed wisely. The main problem is that we may use renewable resources faster than they can be renewed or in such a way that the environmental side effects endanger or degrade life. These renewable resources are then in effect converted to nonrenewable resources.

Genetic (inheritable) variety is an important example of a renewable resource that can become nonrenewable due to human abuse or ignorance. The genetic variety found in different wild strains of plants can be crossbred to develop new strains of food crops (as has been done with wheat and rice). But if human activity clears off, paves over, or pollutes too much of the earth's surface, many wild strains of plants and animals become extinct, and genetic diversity is depleted.

Nonrenewable resources can be used up or at least depleted to such a degree that further recovery is too expensive. Most nonrenewable resources are *mineral re-*

sources that either exist on earth in a fixed supply (such as iron and copper) or are only renewable after such a long period of time that they cannot be renewed as fast as they are used (such as fossil fuels). A **mineral** is either a chemical element or chemical compound (combination of chemical elements), and it can be classified as either metallic or nonmetallic (see Figure 1-3).

1-4 Pollution

What Is Pollution? **Pollution** can be defined as an undesirable change in the physical, chemical, or biological characteristics of the air, water, or land that can harmfully affect health, survival, or activities of humans or other living organisms. Note that according to this definition pollution does not have to cause physical harm. It may merely interfere with human activities. For example, a lake may be considered polluted if it cannot be used for boating activities.

The problem with defining pollution is specifying what constitutes "undesirable change," which requires value judgments. For example, chemicals spewed into the air or water from an industrial plant may be harmful to humans and other organisms living near the plant. However, if expensive pollution controls are required, the plant may be forced to shut down. Thus, workers who would lose their jobs may feel that the risks to them from contaminated air and water are not as serious as the benefits of having jobs.

Value judgments about short-term versus long-term risks can also cause controversy. Building a worldwide network of nuclear power plants may provide electricity for the present human generation, but it compels future generations to handle and store the radioactive wastes produced for thousands of years, even if nuclear power is abandoned or exhausted as an energy source.

Thus, we see that the determination of desirable versus undesirable effects of an environmentally altering activity is a very difficult and highly controversial process. The nature of tragedy, as the philosopher Hegel pointed out long ago, is the conflict not between right and wrong but between right and right. Nevertheless, although defining pollution is a difficult, controversial process, it must be done in order to control pollution.

Types of Pollution   From a biological viewpoint, we can recognize two major types of pollutants: degradable and nondegradable. A **degradable pollutant** can be decomposed, removed, or consumed and thus reduced to acceptable levels either by natural processes or by human-engineered systems (such as sewage treatment plants), as long as the systems are not overloaded. There are two classes of degradable pollutants: rapidly degradable (nonpersistent) and slowly degradable (persistent). *Rapidly degradable pollutants,* such as human sewage and animal and crop wastes, can normally be decomposed rather quickly if the system is not overloaded. For example, a rapidly flowing river can normally cleanse itself of some human sewage fairly quickly, but this natural cleansing process can be overwhelmed by too much raw sewage from a large city or a number of small cities or farms.

Slowly degradable pollutants, such as DDT and some radioactive materials, decompose slowly but eventually are either broken down completely or reduced to harmless levels. Some radioactive materials that give off harmful radiation, such as iodine-131, decay to harmless levels in a few minutes or hours and are rapidly degradable pollutants. Others, such as strontium-90 (produced by nuclear bomb blasts), can persist at harmful levels for decades; plutonium-239, produced by nuclear power plants, can remain at harmful levels for many thousands of years. Slowly degradable pollutants are often synthetic compounds, such as DDT and plastics. Because they are artificial substances, nature usually has not evolved processes for breaking them down. Potentially harmful pollutants that break down slowly must either be prevented from reaching the environment or controlled so that they do not build up to harmful levels.

Nondegradable pollutants are not broken down by natural processes. Examples of nondegradable pollutants are mercury, lead, and some of their compounds (Enrichment Study 5) and some plastics. Like slowly degradable pollutants, nondegradable pollutants must be either prevented from entering the air, water, and soil or kept below harmful levels by removal from the environment.

Concentration and Threshold Levels   The amount of a chemical or pollutant in a particular volume or weight of air, water, soil, or other medium is called its **concentration.** Concentrations are often expressed as parts per million or parts per billion. *Parts per million* (ppm) is the number of parts of a chemical or pollutant found in 1 million parts of a particular gas, liquid, or solid mixture. One part per million is equivalent to one drop of vermouth in 80 fifths of gin (a very dry martini), 28 grams (1 ounce) of salt in 28,118 kilograms (31 tons) of potato chips, or 1 mouthful of food out of all the food consumed during a 70-year lifetime. *Parts per billion* (ppb) is the number of parts of a chemical or pollutant found in a billion parts of a particular gas, liquid, or solid mixture. One part per billion corresponds to 1 drop of vermouth in 80,000 fifths of gin.*

One part per million and one part per billion may seem very small, but for some organisms and with some pollutants they can represent dangerous levels of pollution. Some substances, called **nonthreshold pollutants,** are harmful to a particular organism in any concentration (Figure 1-4). Examples include some radioactive substances and mercury, lead, cadmium, and some of their compounds (Enrichment Study 5). Other substances, called **threshold pollutants,** are harmful only above a certain concentration, or *threshold level* (Figure 1-4). For these latter pollutants (DDT is an example), the concentration can increase with no effect until the threshold is crossed, which triggers a harmful or even fatal effect—much like the straw that broke the camel's back.

Threshold levels and damage vary widely, depending on the pollutant, the organism, and the environment involved. For example, 1 ppm of phenol in water is lethal to some fish species, 0.2 ppm of sulfur dioxide in the air can increase the human death rate, and 1 ppb of hydrogen fluoride in the atmosphere can injure some plants, such as peaches. In addition, an organism's sensitivity to a particular pollutant often varies at different times in its life cycle. For most animal species, threshold levels are much lower during the juvenile stage (when body

---

*In gas mixtures, the parts are usually units of *volume;* for liquids and solids, the parts are usually units of *mass.* Another common way to express the concentration of gaseous pollutants and particulate matter in the air is in micrograms of pollutant per cubic meter of air ($\mu g/m^3$).

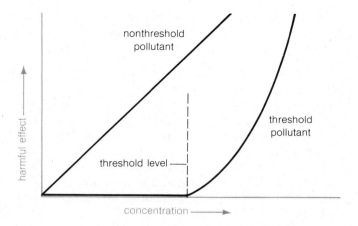

Figure 1-4 Effects of nonthreshold and threshold pollutants.

defense mechanisms may not be fully developed) than during the adult stage.

To further complicate matters, some harmful effects of pollution may not show up for many years, making it difficult to discover which chemical or chemicals are the villains. For example, it is estimated that 80 to 90 percent of all human cancer is caused by environmental factors (see Enrichment Study 6). Since many forms of cancer do not show up for several decades, it is extremely difficult to identify which chemicals are involved.

Sources of Pollution Polluting substances can enter the environment as a result of natural inputs (such as volcanoes) or human activities (such as burning coal). Several examples of natural and human-generated pollutants are given in Table 1-3.

The fact that nature is sometimes a polluter does not justify our adding extra pollutants that can cause threshold-level concentrations to be approached or exceeded. For example, we are exposed to small amounts of radiation from cosmic rays entering the atmosphere and from some radioactive minerals in the earth's crust. Nevertheless, this does not mean that it is safe to increase the radiation we are exposed to through atomic bomb tests and nuclear power plants. In addition, most natural pollution (except that from volcanic eruptions) is not concentrated in a particular area and is normally diluted or degraded to harmless levels. In contrast, the most serious human pollution problems occur in or near urban and industrial areas, where large amounts of pollutants are concentrated in relatively small volumes of air, water, and soil. In addition, many pollutants from human activities are synthetic chemicals that cannot be decomposed by natural processes.

The biggest overall threat to humans and all other forms of life is *war*—especially nuclear war—as discussed by Nobel Prize-winning physicist Hannes Alfvén in his Guest Editorial at the end of this chapter. In spite of these conditions, in 1980 the world spent about $500 billion for military purposes—about $1 million a minute. Annual world military spending is equal to the total annual income of the 2 billion people who make up the poorer half of the world's population.

Concern over nuclear power plant safety is an important environmental issue, but there are only about 70 nuclear power plants in the United States and about 35,000 nuclear weapons, each of which poses a greater hazard than a serious nuclear reactor accident. *Today the nuclear weapons in the world's arsenals have a total explosive power of about 1 million Hiroshima-type atomic bombs— enough to kill every person in the world 12 times.*

1-5 Relationships Between Pollution, Population, Resources, Technology, and Society

The Roots of Pollution What causes pollution? The obvious answer is people. Thus, we could conclude that pollution increases with population growth. But population growth is not the only cause. Pollution occurs when people use matter and energy resources. But the situation is even more complicated. The use of some types of resources creates more pollution than the use of other types. For example, a throwaway aluminum can wastes more resources and creates more pollution than a returnable glass bottle (since making the can requires about 3 times as much energy as making the bottle). In other words, pollution also depends on the type of technology used.

A crude model has been proposed to estimate the pollution, or harmful environmental impact, caused by people and their consumption activities. Total pollution depends on the product of three factors: the number of people, the amount of resources each person uses, and the pollution resulting from each unit of resource used.

$$\begin{array}{c} \text{pollution or} \\ \text{environmental} \\ \text{impact} \end{array} = \begin{array}{c} \text{population} \\ \text{size} \end{array} \times \begin{array}{c} \text{resource} \\ \text{use per} \\ \text{person} \end{array} \times \begin{array}{c} \text{pollution per} \\ \text{unit of} \\ \text{resource used} \end{array}$$

Two Kinds of Overpopulation We can use this three-factor model to distinguish between two kinds of overpopulation. One kind is the result of too many mouths to feed. This kind of overpopulation is called **Malthusian overpopulation,** after Thomas Robert Malthus, who in

Table 1-3 Pollutants Generated by Natural and Human Activities

Type of Pollutant	Text Discussion
Class 1: Almost completely generated by human activities	
DDT, PCBs, and other chlorinated hydrocarbon compounds	Enrichment Study 11
Lead in the air (from burning leaded gasoline)	Enrichment Study 5
Solid wastes and litter	Enrichment Study 15
Class 2: Primarily generated by human activities	
Radioactive wastes	Chapter 14
Oil in the oceans	Chapter 16
Sewage (animal and plant wastes)	Chapter 16
Phosphates in aquatic systems	Enrichment Study 16
Waste heat in rivers, lakes, and oceans	Chapter 16
Photochemical smog in the air (from burning gasoline)	Chapter 17
Sulfur dioxide in the air (from burning coal and oil)	Chapter 17
Noise	Enrichment Study 13
Class 3: Primarily generated by natural sources	
Hydrocarbons in the air	Chapter 17
Carbon monoxide and carbon dioxide in the air	Chapter 17 Enrichment Study 3
Solid particles in the air	Chapter 17; Enrichment Study 3
Mercury in the ocean	Enrichment Study 5

1803 warned that population size tends to outrun food production until poor health and death from starvation and disease restore the balance. In this type of overpopulation, the population size factor tends to be much more important than the other two factors. In the poor nations of the world, Malthusian overpopulation already means death for an estimated 4.4 to 20 million human beings each year and bare subsistence for hundreds of millions more.

In affluent and technologically advanced countries, such as the United States and Russia, we encounter a second type of overpopulation, called **neo-Malthusian overpopulation.** In this type the resource use and pollution factors are most important. This type of overpopulation occurs when a relatively small number of people use resources which produce relatively high levels of pollution at a fast rate. In this type of overpopulation, people do not get sick or die from a lack of food. Instead, they can sicken and die from contaminated air, water, and soil. From this perspective the United States and the Soviet Union can be considered the two most overpopulated nations in the world followed closely by other heavily industrialized nations.

The Soviet Union may be the world's biggest polluter. Of the two-thirds of the U.S.S.R. land area that is inhabitable, an estimated 10 percent already suffers serious erosion and poisoning of the land and water from logging, mining and farming. The Soviet economy produces twice as much air pollution per unit of goods manufactured as the United States.

During a 70-year lifetime, an American uses, directly or indirectly, an enormous quantity of resources (Table 1-2). For example, the average American consumes 50 times as much steel, 56 times as much energy, 170 times as much synthetic rubber and newsprint, 250 times as much motor fuel, and 300 times as much plastic as the average citizen of India. The pollution that results from this very high rate of resource use means that *the average American has from 25 to 50 times as great an impact on the world's life-support system as a peasant in a less developed country.*

The idea that in neo-Malthusian terms the United States and Russia are the most overpopulated countries in the world, however, is hotly debated. Critics of this idea feel either that the United States and Russia have no serious population problem or that population size is not a key factor in their environmental problems. Other critics accuse people who warn of the dangers of overpopulation and pollution of being alarmists and doomsday prophets who are oversimplifying and overdramatizing the problems.

These critics also argue that the benefits of rapid economic growth in the affluent nations outweigh the harmful side effects. Such growth may deplete resources and produce pollution, but it also produces most of the world's industrial products, technology, and knowledge, which in turn can be used to control pollution and help the poor nations become economically developed. But opponents of these critics argue that rapid resource depletion by the rich nations makes it extremely difficult—perhaps impossible—for most poor nations to become affluent or even moderately affluent. This complex debate cannot be analyzed here, but throughout the rest of this book both sides of this and other major environmental controversies will be examined.

Is Technology the Culprit? Environmentalist Barry Commoner argues that the most important factor in the

Table 1-4 Some Synthetic Products Substituted for Natural Products in Industrialized Nations Since World War II

Natural Product	Modern Substitute
Natural fibers (cotton, silk, and wool), synthetic fibers based on natural cellulose	Synthetic fibers (noncellulose)
Lumber	Plastics, aluminum
Soap	Detergent
Natural food	Food with additives
Natural fertilizer	Synthetic fertilizer
Natural predators	Pesticides
Natural rubber	Synthetic rubber
Dyes of plant origin	Synthetic dyes

three-factor model is the pollution per unit of resource used. He suggests that the introduction of environmentally harmful technologies since World War II has been the major cause of pollution in industrialized, affluent nations. These countries have shifted much of their production and consumption from *natural products* that can be broken down, diluted, or absorbed by natural cleansing processes to *synthetic products* that in some cases cannot be degraded by natural processes (Table 1-4).

The idea that technology is the primary cause of pollution, however, is much too simplistic. New technologies are not always harmful. Since World War II, technologies have been introduced that provide important environmental and resource supply benefits. These benefits include: (1) substitutes for scarce natural resources, such as rubber; (2) improved efficiency and reduced waste in the use of resources such as wood, mercury, and coal; (3) the development of processes to control and clean up many forms of pollution; and (4) the substitution of less harmful products for those previously used. For example, in the early 1900s the major insecticide was lead arsenate—a substance much more toxic and persistent than DDT and most modern insecticides. Decades ago the major red food coloring in the United States was lead chromate—an environmental horror compared with the recently banned red dye no. 2.

Our problem and challenge is not to eliminate technology but to decide how to use it more carefully and humanely. As Stuart Chase reminds us, "To condemn technology *in toto* is to forget gardens made green by desalinization of seawater, while to idealize technology is to forget Hiroshima."

Appropriate Technology One attempt to use technology wisely is the increased global emphasis on appropriate technology.* It was made popular by the late E. F. Schumacher's important book *Small Is Beautiful: Economics As If People Mattered.*

High technology (or *hard technology*) is big, complex, centralized, and expensive and tends to replace people with machines. **Appropriate technology** (or *soft technology*) is small, simple, decentralized, and inexpensive and preserves meaningful work for people, as summarized in Table 1-5. Appropriate technology emphasizes (1) the use of small-to-medium sized machines that are easy to use and repair, (2) production methods that conserve matter and energy resources and produce little pollution, and (3) helping people, communities, and nations become more self-sufficient by using nationally and locally available materials to produce needed goods.

The use of a tractor to plow fields in a poor rural village in India is an example of inappropriate and destructive technology. In such villages the most plentiful resource is human labor. The tractor deprives a number of people of their only means of survival and forces them to migrate to already overpopulated cities to look in vain for jobs. The tractor also makes the people dependent on industrialized nations for expensive gasoline and parts and is too complex to be repaired by local people. Instead of a tractor, a well-designed metal plow could be used. It could be pulled by locally available oxen and made and repaired by a local blacksmith.

The increased use of appropriate technology in less developed nations, however, is controversial. Government officials in India have called it a Western plot to keep India and other less developed nations perpetually backward by the use of inferior or outdated technology. Appropriate technology, like high technology, can also have unanticipated and harmful side effects. For example, in India many farmers have begun using biogas generators to generate energy. These simple and inexpensive forms of appropriate technology generate methane gas (the major component of natural gas) by the bacterial decomposition of animal wastes. This use had an unexpected consequence for many of India's poorest peasants who used dried animal manure as a fuel for cooking. When larger farmers began using the manure to produce biogas, not enough manure was available as a cooking fuel for the poor.

However, *appropriate technology does not mean the use of outdated or inferior methods. Nor are its advocates op-*

---

*It is also known as intermediate, careful, gentle, alternative, frugal, and humane technology.

Table 1-5 Characteristics of High and Appropriate Technology

High Technology	Appropriate Technology
Involves big machines that displace many people	Involves small to medium size machines that don't displace very many people
Is complex and understandable only to highly trained workers	Is simple and understandable to nonspecialized workers
Provides meaningless and uncreative (assembly line) work roles	Provides meaningful and creative (whole product) work roles
Requires much capital to build and maintain	Requires small amounts of capital to build and maintain
Involves machinery that is difficult and expensive to repair	Involves machinery that is easy and cheap to repair
Depends on imported materials	Emphasizes self-sufficiency and use of local materials
Creates products designed for export	Creates products designed for use in local area
Requires centralized production and control in urban areas	Involves decentralized production under local or regional control in rural areas
Disrupts local culture	Is compatible with local culture
Produces standardized, short-lasting products that are soon thrown away	Produces unique, often handcrafted products that are durable and easily reused and recycled
Emphasizes use of synthetic materials	Emphasizes use of natural materials
Requires large input of matter and energy resources	Requires small input of matter and energy resources
Creates much pollution	Creates little pollution
Emphasizes use of nonrenewable energy resources (fossil fuels, nuclear fuels)	Emphasizes use of renewable energy resources (sun, wind, water flow, wood)
Is efficient only on a large scale	Is efficient on a small scale
Attempts to disrupt and dominate nature	Attempts to maintain and cooperate with nature

posed to the use of high technology—they are only opposed to its use in situations where people would be better served by soft technology. The use of communications satellites to improve global communication and genetic engineering to eliminate birth defects are examples of the beneficial uses of high technology. Appropriate technology and high technology can also be mixed. For example, a homeowner might use an efficient wood stove (a form of appropriate technology) to reduce the use of fossil fuels for heating and to save money and a microwave oven (a form of high technology) to conserve energy and save money.

The use of appropriate technology is not confined to less developed nations. There are also efforts to scale down some forms of high technology in industrialized nations. For example, small wind and solar power systems in communities and neighborhoods might replace large, centralized fossil fuel and nuclear power plants (Chapters 13 and 14). Waterless toilets that convert human sewage to fertilizer might be used in place of large sewage systems and sewage treatment plants (Chapter

16). Other examples include solar greenhouses, geodesic domes, passive solar homes, compost heaps, and methane (biogas) generators. The state of California has an Office of Appropriate Technology, and in 1977 the U.S. government established a National Center for Appropriate Technology in Butte, Montana. In addition, a growing number of Americans are adopting a more self-sufficient, intermediate-technology life-style based on voluntary simplicity. Appropriate technology is not a panacea for all of our environmental problems, but it marks an encouraging trend that should be nurtured.

The Myth of Single Causes for Complex Problems In the three-factor model presented earlier, no single factor can be ignored. When a group of factors are multiplied, no factor is insignificant in producing the final result.*

---

*In addition or subtraction, one number may be so large that the others can be ignored. For example, (193,000 + 2 + 3) is about 193,000. But leaving out the 2 and 3 in (193,000 × 2 × 3) makes the final answer one-sixth of its actual value.

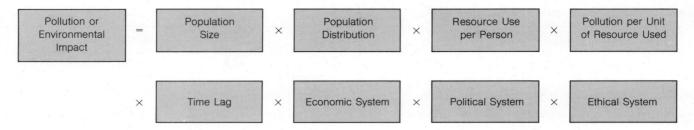

Figure 1-5 Crude model of the major factors causing pollution.

The three-factor model, though useful, is itself far too simple. A number of other factors need to be considered. One such factor is the *time-lag factor.* The amount of time needed to change each of the three factors varies. Unless we have nuclear war or catastrophic famines, it will take 50 to 70 years for world population to level off, even if every family in the world from now on has only two children. This long time lag occurs because a large portion of the people in the world today are under age 15. This means that the total number of people having babies will increase for many decades, even if each couple decides to have fewer children (as discussed in more detail in Chapter 7). Average per capita resource use can be reduced in only 1 to 5 years, but this would probably require an economic recession or depression. A more gradual and planned reduction in resource use, emphasizing reuse, recycling, and longer-lasting products, can take place in 10 to 20 years. The time lag for reducing the pollution impact of harmful types of technology is about 5 to 10 years in many instances but is a few decades for slowly degradable pollutants such as radioactive wastes and fluorocarbons from aerosols.

Still other factors need to be added to the three-factor model. Pollution is caused not only by population size but also by *population distribution.* The most severe air and water pollution problems occur when a large number of people are concentrated in an urban area. Conversely, spreading people out can have a more devastating effect on the land. Economic, political, and ethical factors must also be added. By including the costs of pollution control in the price of a product, we can use the economic system to control pollution (Chapter 18). Similarly, pollution can be controlled politically by enacting and enforcing pollution control laws (Chapter 19). However, efforts to control pollution by modifying economic and political systems will not occur until a politically active group of people (probably 5 to 10 percent of

the population) realizes that it is both unwise and unethical to abuse the world's life-support systems (Chapter 20).

Figure 1-5 presents a more realistic but still simplistic model of the major factors causing pollution. This model is incomplete but it does remind us that the complex environmental problems and challenges that we face are all related and cannot be understood in purely scientific terms. *As we examine major environmental problems and their possible solutions in this book, we should be guided by Alfred North Whitehead's motto "Seek simplicity and distrust it."*

1-6 Moving from a Frontier Society to a Sustainable Earth Society

The Transition to a Sustainable Earth Society We live in exciting times. We face a crisis of interlocking problems, but every crisis is also an opportunity for change. We have been living by *frontier,* or *throwaway, rules,* and over the next 50 years we must change to a new set of *sustainable earth rules* designed to maintain the earth's vital life support system.

The frontier mentality sees the earth as a place of unlimited room and resources, where ever increasing production, consumption, and technology inevitably lead to a better life for everyone. If we pollute one area, we merely move to another or eliminate or control the pollution through technology.

The frontier mentality is an attempt to dominate nature. Frontier rules can be useful for a population in the initial stages of J-curve growth, but once population size and resource use go around the bend of the J curves, such rules become obsolete and dangerous.

In contrast, a sustainable earth mentality sees that the earth is a place of limited room and resources and that ever increasing production and consumption put severe stress on the natural processes that renew and maintain the air, water, and soil upon which we depend. Sustaining the earth calls for cooperation with nature, and it recognizes that there are no frontiers left. We must clean up the damage we have done to our home and develop rules to sustain the earth that will prevent future damage.

The Space Myth   But, some say, isn't space a new frontier? Even if we make a garbage dump out of this spaceship, can't we solve our problems by shipping people off to other planets or to space colonies? Physicist Gerard K. O'Neill and others have developed a detailed plan for putting 10,000 people in a self-sufficient orbiting space colony by 1990 at an estimated initial cost of about $100 billion. By 2050 they envision a number of these colonies with a combined population of 1 million people; each colony will have green land, hills, streams, and wildlife.

Before spending trillions of dollars and using much of human creativity on such a visionary project, let's look at some sobering facts. To inhabit other planets or space colonies, we would have to develop total life-support systems. We have the technology to do this temporarily for a few astronauts at incredible expense. But it is the height of technological arrogance to think that we can create and maintain a diverse life-support system in space for millions of people when we have yet to understand the complex interactions that maintain life in a small pond or a patch of forest.

But let's wave a magic technological wand and assume that starting today we can build a series of livable space colonies. According to Hitch's rule, any new project always costs from 2 to 20 times as much as the most careful original estimate. Thus, the first colony could easily cost $200 billion to $2 trillion. This latter figure is more than the total annual U.S. gross national product. By 1990 this colony might provide sanctuary for only 10,000 people—equal to the population increase on earth during the first 1½ hours of implementing the project. After about 70 years and hundreds of trillions of dollars, we *might* be able to provide a space habitat for a million people—equal to the world's population increase during the first 5 days of the project. Just to stay even with today's world population growth, we would have to ship away about 75 million passengers a year, or 8,500 persons each hour.

It seems clear that space colonies will not solve the world's population, resource, and pollution problems. Nor will they provide freedom for the new colonists. Survival on a space colony requires that each person's actions be rigidly controlled by a centralized authority. Although O'Neill envisions these colonies as creating little pollution, the garbage we have already discarded on the moon and in space casts doubt on this expectation. The vastness of space merely encourages the throwaway mentality.

It would be tragic to spend trillions of dollars to create our solar system's most expensive habitats for a few people while billions of people are left to lead wretched lives on an earth drained of investment capital. The real challenge of the next few decades is to make the earth a better place to live for everyone. Ironically, the need for a sustainable earth society was revealed by our present space program. As TV cameras looked back at earth from space, they showed us that we do indeed live on a fragile spaceship, and we had better treat it right. This realization is an important step in making the transition from a frontier to a sustainable earth society.

Some Hopeful Signs   Is the achievement of a sustainable earth society over the next few decades a hopeless, idealistic goal? Fortunately, the answer to this important question is no. There are growing signs that we can make such a transition. *In 1965 only a few specialists had ever heard of the words* ecology, pollution, *and* environment. *Today in affluent nations there is sophisticated awareness of these problems, and this knowledge is spreading to poor nations.*

Even more important, this awareness has been translated into action. Today there are over 3,000 organizations worldwide devoted to environmental issues. Most affluent nations have passed laws designed to protect the air, water, land, and wildlife. Environmental concern is not confined to the rich nations. By 1980, 102 less developed countries had environmental protection agencies (compared with only 11 countries in 1972). Nations are also getting together to begin dealing with global environmental problems. Between 1965 and today, 70 U.S. rivers, lakes, and streams were cleaned up; levels of many air pollutants in most U.S. cities have decreased. Smog in London has decreased sharply since 1952, and the river Thames is returning to life. *The amazing thing is not a lack of progress but that so much progress has been made since 1965.*

Nevertheless, we shouldn't get carried away with rosy optimism. We have only started to deal with the complex problems facing us, but we have made an important beginning. Nurturing this hope into a new sustainable earth society requires that we avoid several traps that prevent people from becoming involved.

First, we must avoid the "gloom and doom" trap, which merely paralyzes us with fear. Second, we must avoid the technological optimism trap. Believing that technology will always save us and lead to a land of plenty makes people feel that they don't need to be concerned or involved. Even if technology could theoretically solve every problem, it is unlikely that such technology would always be developed. We must remember that 40 percent of all world expenditures for research and development, employing over half the scientists and engineers in the world, are devoted to improving our ability to kill one another (see the Guest Editorial by Hannes Alfvén at the end of this chapter).

Third, we must avoid the "good old days" trap—the romantic idea that all we need to do is to return to the past when life was simpler and better. In the United States the good old days were not so good for most people. Today the average U.S. life expectancy is between 68 and 73. In 1850 it was only about 35, and in 1900 it was about 45. Around 1800 the workweek in the United States averaged 72 hours for men and 98 hours for women. There were no fresh vegetables during the winter, and vitamin-deficiency diseases were common. In 1793 one-fifth of the population of Philadelphia died in a typhoid fever epidemic caused by polluted water. Between 1800 and 1900, epidemics of yellow fever, smallpox, typhus, cholera, and other infectious diseases were common in most U.S. cities.

The fourth trap we must avoid is believing that we merely have to go back to nature. We do need to control harmful technology and rely more on appropriate technology, but the idea of a return to nature is based on false romanticism. Nature can be harsh. When people put their down sleeping bags and freeze-dried food into a well-designed van and head for the woods, they are not getting back to nature. Instead, they are using modern technology to insulate themselves from some of nature's harsh realities.

We don't yet know all of our new rules for sustaining the earth, nor how to change some of our present political, economic, technological, and ethical rules and systems. But we are beginning to ask the right questions. What makes life worthwhile? Who are we in relationship to our fellow passengers, and what should we do with our lives? A major goal of this book is to explore the meaning of and to suggest ways to achieve a sustainable earth society during your lifetime. Working together, we can make this exciting transition in history so that we preserve rather than destroy the only home we and our descendants will ever have.

What is the use of a house if you don't have a decent planet to put it on?

Henry David Thoreau

Guest Editorial: War: The Worst Environmental Threat

Hannes Alfvén

Hannes Alfvén has been professor of applied physics at the University of California, San Diego, since 1967. Prior to that he was professor of plasma physics at the Royal Institute of Technology in Stockholm, Sweden. He has been science advisor to the Swedish government and member of the Swedish Atomic Energy Commission. In 1970 he received the Nobel Prize in physics. In recent years he has used his expert knowledge to warn the world of the grave dangers of nuclear war and nuclear power plants.

The environmentalist movement is now a major factor in the political life of the United States and of the whole world.

It started long ago as a protest against the factory around the corner that stinks or fouls the water in the river you used to swim in, or mars the scenic view from your window. Two or three decades ago it was found that in many cases industry had much more serious effects: It made the spring "silent," its waste killed fish and wildlife and was also dangerous to human beings. The processes by which this damage happens are sometimes very complicated and cannot be understood without careful studies of how nature works and how it is affected by industrial wastes.

This introduced a second phase in the environmentalist movement: It was obvious that unless environmentalists acquired at least the same competence in these problems as the industrialists, their fight against industrial pollution was hopeless. This challenge has given rise to the new interdisciplinary field of human ecology, which is introduced in this book.

A third phase in this movement began with the controversy over nuclear energy. The nuclear industry presented nuclear energy as a perfectly clean, cheap, and inexhaustible supply of energy, a wonderful result of the most sophisticated science and technology: no smoke, no dirty water. When some environmentalists objected to it, they were denounced as ignoramuses: They would understand that nuclear energy was a savior of humanity if only they studied the matter closer.

The environmentalists followed this advice. Guided by a few very competent biologists, they learned how radioactivity induces cancer and produces genetic damage, and they discovered that the methods to keep the radioactive substances isolated from the air, water, and soil might work in a technological paradise but are unlikely to work in the real world. Now an increasing number of environmentalists have the same knowledge as the nuclear insiders. They can now judge nuclear energy without the unavoidable bias of those who have devoted a lifetime to the development of nuclear power or invested $100 billion in this development. The result of this spread of knowledge seems to be catastrophic to the nuclear industry: It is increasingly difficult to claim that the radioactive substances are under control, it is increasingly dubious that nuclear energy is cheap, and it is quite clear that there are several other and better ways of solving the energy problem.

The environmentalists have also learned that the most serious objection to nuclear energy is its coupling to nuclear arms. It is now generally admitted that any country—large or small—that can build nuclear reactors will eventually get a nuclear arms capability. The peaceful atom and the militant atom are Siamese twins. This fact has led the environmentalist movement into its fourth phase, which is likely to be the most difficult but also the most important.

Everybody knows that war is more destructive to the environment—and to the human beings living in it—than anything else. Still this is very seldom mentioned by environmentalists. (Perhaps many people consider this to be a mil-

itary secret?) Everybody knows that the destruction caused by nuclear arms is enormous compared with that by conventional arms, and that both the United States and the U.S.S.R. have enough nuclear arms to destroy the whole world. But most people prefer not to think about such horrible things, much less talk about them. They hope that war is something that takes place in Europe or Vietnam and that it cannot be a threat to *our* environment. But this hope is false and dangerous in the thermonuclear missile age.

In order to protect national security, there are a large number of underground silos in the United States, each containing a missile with a hydrogen bomb warhead. In each of them, four young officers, relieved every morning, are ready round the clock to launch their missiles at the order of the president. Once launched, such a missile will undoubtedly reach its target and very likely kill a million innocent people. This is a threat to the rest of the world, but not to Americans. However, the Russians have similar silos that they claim are necessary for their national security—to deter the United States from blackmailing and killing them. In order to increase the "security" of the world still more, there are many nuclear submarines and planes carrying nuclear arms. Furthermore, when the sales drive of the nuclear industry spreads nuclear power plants to an increasing number of countries, a similar spread of nuclear arms capability is unavoidable.

Political and military leaders in the United States have certainly attempted to analyze in detail what will happen if a nuclear war breaks out. Considering that no political or military leadership was able to predict how World War I, World War II, or the Vietnam war would develop, we have little reason to suppose that present predictions—which, moreover, are top military secrets—have very much to do with reality. Many people outside the establishment believe that the first few nuclear bombs released will create such political tension that a number of irrational actions will follow, and that after a few hours the result will be a nuclear holocaust. It is not certain that the whole human race would be eliminated, but there would be such destruction of ourselves and our environment that our concern for the stinking factory around the corner, the silent spring, and even the nuclear power plant would seem trivial.

What can the environmentalists do about this? I think the key to the fourth phase of our struggle for a new and better world is the same as in the earlier phases: more knowledge and more concern. We must realize now that our legitimate demand for national security cannot be satisfied through nuclear armament. Instead, the enormous increase in destruction capability results in a global "insecurity" both for this and for all nations.

As long as the environmentalists were ignorant, there could be no efficient opposition against nuclear energy. As long as the environmentalists know next to nothing about the global destructive power that the political and military leaders of the world have prepared and are perfecting, there will be no popular movement strong enough to avert the approaching catastrophe. But if we all learn about the real situation in the world and act accordingly, there might still be time to stop the "race to oblivion."

Guest Editorial Discussion

1. Have you seen much information or discussion in the media about nuclear war as a fatal environmental hazard? Why or why not?

2. Do you think or talk about the possibilities of nuclear war? Why or why not? What causes most people to ignore this subject?

3. What is the connection between the peaceful use of nuclear energy in nuclear power plants and the possible spread of nuclear weapons?

4. Should we ban nuclear power plants in the United States? Why or why not? Should the United States ban the export of nuclear power plants and technology to other nations? Why or why not?

Guest Editorial: The Global 2000 Report

Gus Speth

Gus Speth served as chairman of the President's Council on Environmental Quality (CEQ) between 1979 and 1981, after serving as a member of the council from 1977 to 1979. During his tenure, he served as chairman of the Carter administration's Toxic Substances Strategy Committee and as a member of the interagency groups that developed the administration's policies on solar energy, nuclear waste management, water conservation, and water resource development. Before his appointment to CEQ, Speth was a staff attorney for the Natural Resources Defense Council, a public interest group which he helped found in 1970. In 1981, he assumed an administrative position with the Conservation Foundation.

During the past decade a number of disturbing studies and reports have been issued by the United Nations, the Worldwatch Institute, the World Bank, and other organizations. These reports have sounded a persistent warning: International efforts to stem the spread of human poverty, hunger, and misery are not achieving their goals; the staggering growth of the human population, coupled with ever increasing human demands, are beginning to cause permanent damage to the earth's resource base.

The most recent such warning was issued in July,1980, by the Council on Environmental Quality and the U.S. State Department. Called *The Global 2000 Report to the President,* it was the result of a 3-year effort by more than a dozen agencies of the U.S. government to make long-term projections concerning various population, resource, and environmental concerns. Given the obvious limitations of such projections, the report can best be seen as a reconnaissance of the future. And the results of that reconnaissance are disturbing.

The conclusions of *The Global 2000 Report* indicate the potential for deepening global problems over the next two decades if policies and practices around the world continue as they are today. The next 20 years will see an increasingly crowded world, containing more than 6 billion human beings by 2000. It *could* be a world where growing numbers of people suffer hunger and privation; where losses of croplands and forests mount while human numbers and needs increase; where per capita supplies of fresh water, timber, and fish are diminished; where deterioration of the earth's air and water accelerates; and where plant and animal species vanish at unprecedented rates.

These findings confront the United States and the other nations of the world with one of the most difficult challenges facing our planet during the next two decades. Disturbing as these findings are, however, it is important to stress what the report's conclusions represent: not *predictions* of what will occur, but *projections* of what *could* occur if we do not change our ways. I believe that as the people and governments of the world come to realize the full dimensions of the challenge before us, we *will* take the actions needed to meet it.

The first thing we must do is to get serious about the conservation of resources—renewable and nonrenewable alike. We can no longer take for granted the renewability of our renewable resources. We must realize that the natural systems—the air and water, the forests, the land—that yield food, shelter, and other necessities of life are susceptible to disruption, contamination, and destruction.

In some parts of the world, particularly in the less developed countries, the ability of biological systems to support human populations is being seriously damaged by human demands for grazing land, firewood, and building materials. Nor are these stresses confined to the less developed countries: In recent years, the United States has been losing annually about 3 million acres of rural land—one-third of prime agricultural land—due to the spread of housing developments, highways, shopping malls, and the like. We are also losing the equivalent, in terms of production capability, of about 3 million more acres a year due to soil degradation, erosion, and salinization.

Achieving the necessary restraint in the use of renewable resources will require new ways of thinking by the peoples and governments of the world. It will require the widespread adoption of a "conserver society" ethic—an approach to resources and environment that, while attuned to the needs of each society, recognizes not only the importance of resources and environment to our own sustenance, well-being, and security, but also our obligation to pass this vital legacy along to future generations.

Fortunately, we are beginning to see signs that people in the United States and in other nations *are* becoming aware of the limits to our resources and the importance of conserving them. Energy problems, for example, are pointing the way to a future in which conservation is the password. As energy supplies go down and prices go up, we are learning that conserving—getting more and more out of each barrel of oil or ton of coal—is the cheapest and safest approach. Learning to conserve nonrenewable resources like oil and coal is the first step toward building a conserver society that values, nurtures, and protects *all* of its resources. Such a society appreciates economy in design and avoidance of waste. It realizes the limits to low-cost resources and to the environment's carrying capacity. It insists that market prices reflect all costs, social as well as private, so that consumers are fully aware in the most direct way of the real costs of consumption.

But the conserver society ethic by itself is not enough. It is unrealistic to expect people living at the margin of existence—people fighting desperately for their own survival—to think about the long-term survival of the planet. When people need to burn wood to keep from freezing, they will cut down trees.

For this reason, an equally important element in an effective strategy to deal with global resource problems must be the *sustainable development* of the less developed nations of the world. Development, far from being in conflict with resource conservation and environmental protection, is essential to achieving these goals. It is only through sound, sustainable economic development that real progress can be made in alleviating hunger and poverty and in erasing the conditions that contribute so dangerously to the destruction of our planet's carrying capacity.

It is clear that the trends discussed in *The Global 2000 Report,* especially the growing disparity in income between the rich and poor peoples of the world, greatly heighten the chances for global instability—for exploitation of fears, resentments, and frustrations; for incitement to violence; for conflicts based on resources. While the humanitarian reasons for acting generously to alleviate global poverty and injustice are compelling enough in themselves, we must also recognize the extent to which poverty and resource problems can threaten the security of nations throughout the world.

These growing tensions can only be defused through a much greater emphasis on *equity*—on a fair sharing of the means to development and the products of growth, not only among nations but also within nations. It should be obvious that the interests of all nations of the world, more developed and less developed alike, are inextricably linked. In helping others, we help ourselves; and in providing generous but effective assistance—grants, loans, technical aid—to nations that are in need, we can make a national investment that will yield important dividends in the future.

Guest Editorial Discussion

1. What specific obligations, if any, do you feel we should have to future generations?

2. How would you define *sustainable development* for the less developed nations of the world? If this goal is adopted, what effects might it have on your life and life-style?

3. Do you agree that the means to economic development and the products of economic growth must be shared more fairly not only among nations but also within nations? How would you bring about this greater emphasis on equity?

Discussion Topics

1. How many people would have to die from famine and disease this year in order for world population to stabilize? Compare this with the figures in Table 1-1.

2. Debate the following resolution: High levels of resource use by the United States are necessary because they mean purchases of raw materials from poor nations and U.S. economic growth that will produce money for foreign aid to poor nations.

3. Should resource use in rich nations be restricted? Which resources, if any, should be restricted? How?

4. Debate the following resolution: The world will never run out of resources because technological innovations will either find substitutes or allow us to mine lower and lower grades of scarce resources.

5. What is zero population growth? Explain how zero population growth in the world could allow average per capita income to rise.

6. What factors could limit the absolute size of the human population on earth? How are these factors related? Which of these factors are probably the most important?

7. Should economic growth in the United States and in the world be limited? Why or why not? Is all economic growth bad? Which types, if any, do you believe should be limited? Which types, if any, should be encouraged?

8. Distinguish between the two types of overpopulation. Is the world overpopulated? Why or why not? Is the United States overpopulated? Why or why not?

9. Why is pollution so hard to define? Why must it be defined?

10. On the whole, are the substitutions shown in Table 1-4 desirable or undesirable? Which ones would you eliminate? Why? How would these eliminations affect your life?

11. Is harmful technology a main cause of pollution? Why or why not? If so, would you be willing to give up automobiles, stereos, central heating, air conditioning, electricity, airplanes, refrigeration, ski lifts, and other conveniences, all of which pollute either in their use or in their making, or both?

12. What might happen to pollution levels if U.S. population size stabilizes but average per capita consumption doubles? What might happen if per capita consumption stabilizes but population size doubles?

13. What forms of existing technology, if any, do you believe should be eliminated? Why? What existing technologies should be reduced from hard to soft forms in the United States? Why?

14. You have been appointed to a technology assessment board. What drawbacks and advantages would you list for the following: (1) IUDs; (2) snowmobiles; (3) sink garbage disposal units; (4) trash compactors; (5) pocket transistor radios; (6) televisions; (7) electric cars; (8) abortion pills; (9) effective sex stimulants; (10) drugs that would retard the aging process; (11) drugs that would enable people to get high but are harmless; (12) electrical or chemical methods that would stimulate the brain to remove anxiety, fear, and unhappiness; and (13) genetic engineering (manipulation of human genes)? In each case, would you recommend that the technology be introduced?

15. In terms of environmental improvement and the possibility of achieving a sustainable earth society within the next 50 years, would you classify yourself as a pessimist, an optimist, or an optimistic pessimist? Why?

Readings

Asimov, Isaac. 1979. *A Choice of Catastrophes: The Disasters That Threaten the World.* New York: Simon & Schuster.

Brown, Harrison. 1978. *The Human Future Revisited: The World Predicament and Possible Solutions.* New York: Norton. Excellent analysis of the interrelated problems of population, resources, pollution, affluence, and weaponry.

Brown, Lester R. 1978. *The Twenty-Ninth Day: Accommodating Human Needs and Numbers to the Earth's Resources.* New York: Norton. Brilliant analysis of the world's environmental problems and their interrelationships by one of our best multidisciplinary thinkers. Highly recommended.

Callahan, Daniel, ed. 1971. *The American Population Debate.* Garden City, N.Y.: Doubleday. Superb collection of articles on whether the U.S. is overpopulated.

Commoner, Barry. 1971. *The Closing Circle: Nature, Man and Technology.* New York: Knopf. Well written presentation of Commoner's view that the misuse of technology is the cause of most pollution. See the critique of this view by Holdren and Ehrlich (1974).

Council on Environmental Quality. 1980. *The Global 2000 Report to the President,* vols. 1–2. Outstanding and up-to-date summary of global population, resource, and pollution problems with projections to the year 2000.

Echols, James R. 1977. "Population vs. Environment: A Crisis of Too Many People." *American Scientist,* vol. 64, 165–173. Excellent analysis of relationships between population growth and environmental problems.

Edberg, Rolf. 1969. *On the Shred of a Cloud.* Alabama University: University of Alabama Press. Eloquent and compassionate statement of our problems.

Esfandiary, F. M. 1970. *Optimism One: The Emerging Radicalism.* New York: Norton. Superb antidote for pessimism, although he gets carried away at the end.

Gardner, John W. 1970. *The Recovery of Confidence.* New York: Norton. Moving analysis of hope and how to bring about change by one of our more important thinkers and leaders.

Holdren, John P., and Paul R. Ehrlich. 1974. "Human Population and the Global Environment." *American Scientist,* vol. 62, 282–292. Excellent analysis of the relationships between population size, resource use, and harmful technology and an answer to Commoner's (1971) view that harmful technology is the key factor in producing pollution.

Lapp, Ralph E. 1973. *The Logarithmic Century.* Englewood Cliffs, N.J.: Prentice-Hall. Superb summary of J curves in the world today.

Maddox, John. 1972. *The Doomsday Syndrome.* New York: McGraw-Hill. Attacks environmentalists as being alarmists and doomsday prophets who are oversimplifying and overdramatizing the problems. Maddox makes some important points but oversimplifies many issues far more than do the people whom he is attacking.

Meadows, Donella H., et al. 1972. *The Limits to Growth.* New York: Universe Books. Nontechnical summary of a computer model of the interrelationships between population, food, resource use, economic growth, and pollution. One of the most important books published in the last decade (see Enrichment Study 1 for more details).

Mesarovic, Mihajlo, and Eduard Pestel. 1974. *Mankind at the Turning Point.* New York: Dutton. Another computer model of world and regional population, resource, and pollution problems (see Enrichment Study 1 for more details).

Murdoch, William W., ed. 1975. *Environment: Resources, Pollution and Society.* 2nd ed. Sunderland, Mass.: Sinauer. Best single collection of in-depth essays by noted experts on environmental problems.

O'Neill, Gerard K. 1978. *The High Frontier: Human Colonies in Space.* 2nd ed. New York: Bantam. Well-thought-out proposal for building self-sufficient colonies in space. A fascinating idea that we should consider only after we have eventually made the earth a better place to live for everyone.

Platt, John R. 1969. "What We Must Do." *Science,* vol. 116, 115. Overview listing our planetary crises in order of their importance and including a plan for action.

Schumacher, E. F. 1973. *Small Is Beautiful: Economics as if People Mattered.* New York: Harper & Row. Eloquent presentation of the need for appropriate technology. One of the most important books published in the last decade.

2

Human Impact on the Earth

Three Billion Years plus a Few Minutes

ooze
cohesion, opulence
twinges, space, undulations
slithering, boring, hatching, germination
increase, complexity, blooming, coordination, cooperation
predation, parasitism, migration, competition, adaptation, selection
crowding, starvation, disease, populations, diversity, camouflage, mimicry
specialization, reduction, exclusion, conversion, blight, drouth
pressure, defeat, decline, smoke, decimation
explosion, abuse, ignorance, teeming
contamination, residual, choking
silence, stillness
ooze

William T. Barry*

As humans, we are one of nature's most recent evolutionary experiments. Are we really headed for ooze as William Barry's poem suggests? Apparently we are the only species capable of bringing about our own extinction. Unlike dinosaurs and other extinct species, we can ponder this possibility and make cultural changes in our behavior to meet environmental threats. But to make the necessary cultural changes, we must have both a sense of our cultural past and a concern for the future survival of our species.

Our role in changing the face of this planet began as soon as we appeared approximately 4 million years ago. During most of human history, however, our impact was fairly small or at least localized. This was because humans lived in small groups, each of which obtained its subsistence resources from the local environment. Today

*Reprinted by permission from *Reflection*. Gonzaga University, Spokane, Washington.

Enrichment Studies 6 and 12 are related to this chapter.

we have over 4 billion people on earth who increasingly depend on a global subsistence system for their survival.

It is important to realize that during 99 percent of humanity's time span on earth, it has had a single occupation—hunting and gathering food. The J curves of increasing population, consumption, and pollution (Chapter 1) are merely symptoms of the more fundamental J curve of rapid cultural change from hunter-gatherer to tiller of the soil to industrial worker.

This chapter will briefly review the five major phases in sociocultural evolution: (1) early hunter-gatherer society, (2) advanced hunter-gatherer society, (3) agricultural society, (4) industrial society, and (5) the new sustainable earth society needed for future survival. Although each phase is presented separately, they overlap so that today we find all phases—except sustainable earth—at various places on earth.

2-1 Humans in Nature: Early Hunter-Gatherers

Without claws, fangs, great strength, or great speed, humans have survived and multiplied because of three major cultural adaptations, all related to increased intelligence: (1) using tools for hunting, gathering, and preparing food and protective clothing; (2) learning to live in the environment through social organization and cooperation with other human beings; and (3) using language to aid in cooperation and to pass on knowledge of previous survival experiences. This increased capacity for learning has been enhanced by having the fairly rare biological feature of an opposing thumb. Because the thumb can be pressed against our other fingers, we can grasp objects. This has allowed us to use tools to expand our ability to survive and reduce environmental stress.

Cultural knowledge teaches us what we must do to survive in a particular habitat and social group. Early human groups survived by hunting animals and gathering plants. Much of their cultural knowledge was ecological knowledge of the environment in which they lived—how to find drinkable water and how to locate edible plants and animals. Elton tells us, "The Arawak of the South American equatorial forest knows where to find every kind of animal and catch it, and also the names of the trees and the uses to which they can be put."

Early hunter-gatherers lived in small bands. Each band of several families usually consisted of no more than 50 persons. This form of social organization promoted cooperation in the hunting and gathering of food needed for survival. Hunting also made sharing a must. Meat rotted so quickly that a killed animal had to be divided and eaten before it decayed.

Because the bands of hunters had to move around to find food, people had few material possessions. These consisted primarily of simple tools, such as digging sticks, scrapers, and crude hunting weapons. These widely scattered bands of people rarely had fixed homes or habitats. They moved around their territory to find the plants and animals that they needed to exist.

The first hunters probably used their hands to kill small animals or clubbed their prey after running them down. Later, spears and bows and arrows were developed, but these hunters couldn't kill a large number of animals with such unsophisticated weapons. Modern studies of Bushmen, Pygmies, and other hunter-gatherer cultures reveal that the women's less dramatic collecting of plants, fruits, eggs, mollusks, reptiles, and insects actually provides most of the food.

These early groups of humans depended completely on their local natural environment for survival. Population size was limited directly and quickly by the availability of food. If the group became too large, it could split up, and part could move to another area. These early human groups undoubtedly produced many small, localized ecological imbalances. But these imbalances in the long run limited and controlled the number of people, creating a new equilibrium with the local environment. Our early ancestors thus responded to the environment, rather than controlling and manipulating it. They were an example of humans *in* nature—not *against* nature.

2-2 Humans in Nature: Advanced Hunter-Gatherers

Human groups slowly learned to cooperate more effectively, to make more sophisticated tools, and to use fire. As they passed this cultural knowledge on to their off-spring, their numbers grew slowly and they began to exert greater pressure on their environment. With improved stone axes they could chop down shrubs and trees. Using more sophisticated projectiles and projectile points, they became highly skilled hunters who could cooperate to kill herds of big game.

Advanced hunter-gatherer groups improved the quality and quantity of their food supply by specializing in hunting herds of large animals and in collecting the more abundant wild grains, nuts, fruits, and roots. This increased their understanding of the nature of the animals and plants on which they had to rely. It also required greater social organization and human cooperation. Sharing of food, tools, and other goods was an important aspect of many of these societies.

During the ice ages that occurred from about 1 million to 11,000 years ago, some of the larger game animals became extinct. Although climatic changes were undoubtedly a major cause of extinction, some scholars think groups of advanced hunters hastened this process by overhunting many big-game species. About 70 percent of the large North American mammals, such as the mammoth, mastodon, ground sloth, giant buffalo, and musk ox, disappeared. These advanced hunters discovered many methods for mass killing. They probably used fire to flush and chase game, and they drove entire herds over cliffs. One layer of ground uncovered at Solutré, France, reveals the remains of more than 100,000 horses. Endangered species are not new.

In observing natural fires, people must have discovered that fire radically changes vegetation. The plants that repopulate an area after a fire are more favorable for gathering and provide pasture land for game. Indians in North America learned that fire in a brush field creates vegetation that attracts deer. Some major types of world vegetation such as African savanna and the Mediterranean chaparral are believed to have been created or at least expanded by repeated and deliberate burning.

Thus, advanced hunter-gatherers were the first humans to make broad-scale changes in their local and regional environment. They did not have direct control of it, but they affected it significantly. The gradual change from humans in nature to humans against nature had begun. Because of their small numbers, however, the impact of these hunter-gatherers was still insignificant on a global or even a regional scale.

We tend to believe that advanced hunter-gatherer societies led a harsh life devoted almost totally to the struggle to keep alive. But recent research shows that some advanced hunter-gatherer cultures can be considered as the original "affluent societies." For example,

Richard B. Lee has shown that the Kung San, a small group of hunters and gatherers who still live in the Kalahari Desert in southern Africa, work an average of 20 hours a week. Because hunting is so unpredictable, they might work for a week and then rest for a month. During the leisure periods they visit neighbors in other camps, dance, and celebrate. In other words, these "primitive" people spend half their time on vacation, have no bosses, and live much freer from anxiety than most "modern" people.

Contrary to popular opinion, people in contemporary hunter-gatherer societies are among the healthiest in the world—living into their 60s without the aid of modern medicine. The Bushman diet includes at least 23 species of vegetables and 17 species of meat—a more varied diet than many of their agricultural neighbors have. They also have a welfare system that respects and cares for the aged and handicapped. Many hunter-gatherer societies are built on sharing and cooperation rather than aggression against one another or outside groups.

According to some, malnutrition, starvation, and chronic disease were rare among early advanced hunter-gatherers. But recent studies indicate that this might be an overly romanticized view. Life expectancy was probably around 30, and infant mortality was high, primarily due to infectious diseases. These facts, coupled with high levels of infanticide (killing the young), geronticide (killing the old), and war, kept population in balance with food resources. Such forms of population control were essential for the groups' survival. Because their populations tended to be small and widely scattered, these early societies put relatively little stress on their environment.

2-3 Humans Against Nature: Agricultural Societies

Around 10,000 to 12,000 years ago, we began what is perhaps the most significant change in human cultural evolution—*agriculture*. Although this change is sometimes called the "agricultural revolution," it was probably a slow, gradual process that took place over several thousand years.

Although no one really knows how and why agriculture started, hunter-gatherers likely changed to an entirely new life-style because their survival depended on it. Game and edible plants upon which they depended may have become scarce due to overhunting and climatic changes, and the hunter-gatherers may not have

been able to find new areas to support themselves. Survival thus required staying put and trying out new ideas. In the first stage people may have domesticated the dogs, chickens, and pigs found as pets and scavengers around human campsites. Sheep and goats were probably domesticated next, followed by donkeys, horses, reindeer, camels, and elephants. Although we have improved livestock through selective breeding, we still depend on essentially the same animals that early peoples did.

People became shepherds after domesticating herd animals. The pastoral societies of the early shepherds had far more impact on their habitats than hunter societies.

Although natural changes in climate played an important role, shepherds and farmers helped transform the landscape from forest to open habitats. They destroyed some of these new grasslands by allowing their close-grazing animals to remain in one place too long. This destruction and the resulting erosion were repeated in many areas, with shepherds responsible for destroying vast areas of the Mediterranean region and the Near East long before the ravages of industrial civilization. The recent drought and famine in the Sahel area in western Africa shows that even today we have to keep relearning the drastic price of overgrazing when it is accompanied by climatic changes and increased population.

Another form of food production resulted from *horticulture*, or "hoe culture." Women are generally credited with inventing both the digging stick and hoe. People found that they could grow some of their favorite food plants by digging a hole with a stick and placing the roots and tubers of desired plants in the ground. Horticulture let people grow specific plants near home, rather than gathering plants over a large territory. Early horticulture had relatively little effect on the local environment, but it brought about major social changes. Mobility and a varied diet began to be replaced by permanent settlements and a diet based on only a few foods.

In tropical and subtropical areas, **slash-and-burn agriculture** was developed. In this shifting land technique, part of a forest is cleared and burned before planting (Figure 2-1). The ash left after the leaves and branches are burned forms a rich fertilizer. Torrential rains, however, can leach out many of the vital plant nutrients, and the hot sun can harden the soil into an infertile crust. Slash-and-burn agriculture yields abundant harvests for 2 to 5 years, but then the soil is useless for further cultivation. At this point the plots must be abandoned for about 10 years in order to restore soil fertility and new plots cleared and burned.

Figure 2-1 Slash-and-burn technique for growing food in Indonesia.

This slash-and-burn technique is still used today in parts of Southeast Asia, Africa, and South America by an estimated 150 to 200 million people (Figure 2-1). It is an efficient and environmentally sound method for cultivating tropical forest lands as long as the human population is low and the cleared land is allowed to revert to forest. Because of these limitations of soil and climate, we cannot provide most of the food for the world by clearing the world's lush tropical forests and making large-scale modern farms like those in industrialized nations.

The next stage of cultivation involved the planting of seed crops (probably barley and wheat). People started with the basic food plants, such as wheat, barley, peas, lentils, rice, corn, and potatoes (in South America). More than 3,000 years ago, we were cultivating all of the major seed crops used today. With only a few exceptions, we have domesticated no new major food plants in the last 2,000 years, although we have improved strains through genetic breeding.

True *agriculture* (as opposed to horticulture) began with plows pulled by domesticated animals. Other improvements in agriculture, such as irrigation (Figure 2-2), terraced hillsides, strip and contour cropping, and restoring or improving soil fertility by using animal and synthetic fertilizers, allowed farmers to harvest more than one crop per year and made much more land cultivable.

Humans thus became advanced food producers, and for the first time they had not only a constant food supply but a regular food surplus. This surplus had several major environmental and social effects: (1) Without the threat of starvation, populations began to rise; (2) people cleared off more and more land and began trying to control and shape the surface of the earth to suit their needs, with greatly increased environmental problems and a sharp decrease in societies based on hunting; (3) new economic, political, and social patterns emerged as farming villages began trading surplus products, ideas of property and inheritance developed, and increased theft and warfare forced settlements to cooperate and develop strong political authority systems to protect their food and water supplies; and (4) urbanization began as villages, then towns, and eventually cities slowly formed because some people had the leisure to develop skills and specialties other than farming.

By 5,000 B.C., village farming communities of 200 to 500 people had developed in parts of the Near East. The first urban civilization apparently developed in Sumer, but these Sumerian towns were small by our standards, with 5,000 to 20,000 people. As late as 600 B.C., the largest city in Babylon had no more than 80,000 people, and Athens in the classical period had a population of only about 20,000.

The period from 5,000 B.C. to A.D. 200 is known for its great civilizations—Sumeria, Babylonia, Assyria,

Figure 2-2 Irrigation as a means of increasing agricultural productivity. An irrigation canal in the Coachella Valley of California separates irrigated and nonirrigated areas.

Phoenicia, Crete, Egypt, Greece, Rome, India, and China. We study their important contributions in art, literature, science, and government, but we fail to note the devastating impact that their increased use of agriculture had on the land. Not only was this an important factor in their downfall, but it left a ravaged land for future generations.

As agriculture took over, significant social and cultural changes occurred. Land and water rights became valuable. People began to fight over them and conflict became a way of life. Armies and war leaders rose to power, and organized aggression became a force in human life.

To survive in an urban-industrial environment, people had to give up some of their individual freedom and identify with their group. Specialized work became necessary, and the strong forced or persuaded others to work for them. The average workweek increased dramatically, and what we call the "rat race" had begun.

Agriculturalists deliberately use much larger amounts of energy from animals and fossil fuels to change the environment. The landscape is altered drastically with forests, grasslands, and other habitats converted to vast stretches of land planted with single crops or covered with concrete and asphalt for urban settlements.

As advanced food producers grew in numbers and spread out over the face of the earth, a new set of ecological problems appeared. The list of species made extinct or endangered by humans (Enrichment Study 12)

grew as habitats were destroyed or changed. Irrigation without proper drainage built up salts in the topsoil and lowered productivity. Great forests were cleared, and the unprotected topsoil washed away into streams, rivers, and lakes. Forest clearance upset other natural ecological balances and some insects became pests (Enrichment Study 11). Urban life provided centers that spread parasites and disease (Enrichment Study 6). The invention of agriculture thus radically shifted the relationship between humans and their environment. Although they made vast changes in nature, agriculturalists knew much less about the earth as a natural system than hunter-gatherers. In attempting to shape and dominate nature, humans began shifting from hunter-gatherers *in* nature to agriculturalists *against* nature, with little knowledge of how this would affect the earth.

2-4 Humans Against Nature: Industrial Societies

Humanity's history of attempting to change and control the environment is basically a history of using more and more energy per person. Primitive peoples had to rely on muscle power. Agricultural peoples added animal power. But during the eighteenth century, humans made a gigantic leap by inventing more powerful machines and discovering how to unlock the chemical energy stored in coal, oil, and natural gas and to take ores from the earth more efficiently. Like the agricultural revolution, this industrial revolution was not a dramatic shift but a gradual process of technological and social change.

Industrial societies led to a new catalog of ecological problems. New forms of air pollution, water pollution, and strip mining arose, and the loss of grasslands accelerated. Indeed, according to Carl Sauer it was the plowing up of the nontropical grasslands of the world that made the industrial revolution possible. As we learned to build industries that put chemicals together in new ways, we produced a series of useful products, but pollution also increased. Industrial societies have also decreased the need for much of the population to engage in agriculture. This has caused massive shifts of population from rural to urban areas, with a new array of social, political, and economic problems.

The benefits of the industrial revolution are great, but this phase of human cultural history has also cost us dearly. As we have tried to impose our technologies on the natural environment, we have had to work more and more to keep our gains. Increasingly our new technologies are designed not to enhance life but merely to clean up after the last technology that we introduced.

Very few would propose that we should return to the simple life, with little or no dependence on the technological achievements of the past several hundred years. A certain amount of naive romanticism and cultural bias creeps into our glib put-downs of today's city smells, sights, and sounds. But we are beginning to discover the limits of our control over the environment. Ironically, near these limits, the more we try to control nature, the less control we seem to have. Until we consciously control the factors that we can control—population growth, levels of consumption, and allocation of resources—it is we who will be controlled in a drastic and unnecessary manner.

2-5 Humans and Nature: A Sustainable Earth Society

There are important glimmerings that more and more people may be ready to move into a new phase of cultural evolution. For the first time since the industrial revolution, significant numbers of people are beginning to accept the limits to our control over nature. Humans are rediscovering that we are part of rather than apart from nature and that to protect ourselves we must protect nature. In only a few short years many people have begun to see the world as an interconnected whole. Our survival seems to depend on adopting this holistic world view. In other words, we must change from an agricultural-industrial society based on humans against nature to a sustainable earth society based on humans and nature (Figure 2-3). This means that we must cooperate with nature rather than blindly attempt to control it.

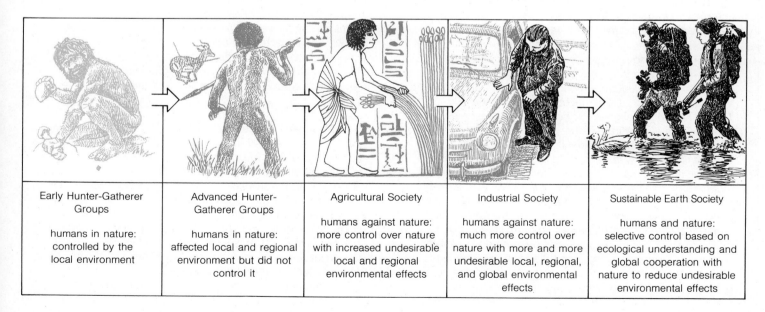

Early Hunter-Gatherer Groups	Advanced Hunter-Gatherer Groups	Agricultural Society	Industrial Society	Sustainable Earth Society
humans in nature: controlled by the local environment	humans in nature: affected local and regional environment but did not control it	humans against nature: more control over nature with increased undesirable local and regional environmental effects	humans against nature: much more control over nature with more and more undesirable local, regional, and global environmental effects	humans and nature: selective control based on ecological understanding and global cooperation with nature to reduce undesirable environmental effects

Figure 2-3 Cultural and ecological stages of humanity.

"Survival of the fittest" does not mean survival of the strongest or the most aggressive. It simply means that the species or member of a species best adapted to its environment (or most able to change with changing circumstances) has the best chance to survive and reproduce successful offspring. In times of slow change, the most specialized organism has the best chance of survival, but under conditions of rapid change the generalist organism has the best chance. The rate of technological change today is so great that survival of the fittest has shifted from a biological evolution to a cultural evolution. Such cultural evolution will require human cooperation, not aggression. *During 99 percent of our time on this planet, we have survived only because we cooperated intelligently with nature and with other humans in defending against predators, hunting and gathering and growing food, rearing the helpless young, and helping one another in endless ways.*

Thus, in cooperating with nature and one another on a global scale, the emerging breed of men and women who seek to sustain the earth will not be starting a new trait, but renewing and strengthening a basic human urge. A growing number of earth's inhabitants are beginning to see themselves as members of a global tribe whose cooperative efforts with one another and with the earth are necessary for survival, as illustrated by Geraldine Watson's Guest Editorial found at the end of this chapter. We must nurture and coax this sharing and cooperation so that they burst forth again as we enter a new and more rewarding relationship with our environment. This social evolution must be fast, for time is too short for biological evolution to come up with an answer. A major purpose of this book is to outline the problems and exciting opportunities that we face in making this cultural transition to a sustainable earth society.

A continent ages quickly once we come.
Ernest Hemingway

Guest Editorial: Caring for the Earth and Its Inhabitants

Geraldine Watson

Geraldine Watson is an environmental and social activist who for over 15 years has played a major role in saving some of the Big Thicket—an incredibly diverse array of plant and animal communities in southeast Texas—from being ravaged by lumber companies. Her efforts—along with those people she worked with and inspired—helped lead to a federal law in 1974 that set aside about 20 percent of the Thicket area as the Big Thicket National Preserve. For her efforts to preserve a small portion of the land she grew up on and loved, she was forced to become a social outcast in her lifelong community, which was dominated by the forest products industry; a pro-Thicket newspaper for which she wrote was firebombed; she was ordered out of the houses of former friends at gunpoint; and her teenage children couldn't drive down the highway without being stopped by the police, humiliated, and insulted. She has no formal training in biology, yet by self-training she has become one of the best field ecologists in the United States, according to the national president and members of the board of directors of the Audubon Society, whom she led on one of her famous tours of the Big Thicket area. She is author of Big Thicket Plant Ecology *and serves as a consultant to the National Park Service on a vegetational survey of the Big Thicket National Preserve. She declined to become a permanent employee of the federal government because she would not have been permitted to engage in political activism. She and one of her sons have a pleasure barge, the* Bayou Queen, *which they use to give visitors a tour of the cypress swamps of the Big Thicket National Preserve.*

For 57 years, I have lived in the Big Thicket area of southeast Texas—a land of lush forests, flowing streams, and a pioneer way of life. The cultural systems I have known range from the independent, horse-power family farm to the pure capitalism of the sawmill town, the post-World War II Gulf Coast petrochemical megalopolis, and a university campus. An obsessive curiosity and a conviction that truth lies in all things relating to humans, morals, and matter made a searcher of me. So I am searching, by examination and comparison of the past, present, and apparent future, for the ideal way for humans—for myself—to live on this earth.

In the naiveté of childhood, adequate necessities—food, clothing, shelter, and someone to care for me—were sufficient for happiness. Early adulthood was bewildering and traumatic as I learned what the world ought to be like and was not. At middle age, I was appalled at the waste of my early years and how little time I had left to do something about what I saw happening to my world and to my fellow humans.

I saw the by-products of the "good life" pollute and poison the land and water; I saw all the beautiful scenes I loved devastated; I saw America squandering its natural resources and refusing to conserve. So I became an activist for the environment.

I saw an increasing unwillingness of less developed nations to supply our gluttony without equal benefit, and I watched my government sacrifice morality for political, economic, and military expediency in order to acquire these natural resources. So I became an activist for peace, human rights, and international understanding.

I saw the churches of "Christian" America exchange the simple Way of Christ, "Love thy neighbor as thyself," for either cold, formal ritualism or wild hysteria with a veil of priest and demagogue between God and humans, playing the ages-old game of manipulating the minds of the simple for power and profit. So, after a cycle of blind faith, agnosticism, atheism, and back to agnosticism, I acquired a reasoning faith and became a teacher of Christ's Way.

I saw the dawning of an age of terror as nuclear power plants were built on known earthquake fault zones, a quarter of a million years worth of radioactive wastes accumulating with no safe storage place and enough nuclear weapons made to annihilate worlds without end. So I organized an anti-nuke group.

After my twenty years of fanatic activism, it seems that little has changed. Alienation between humans and between humans and their God and their natural world is widening; the environment is in even greater peril because of the energy crunch; we are still on the brink of war—jostling, shoving, and lining up for the big scramble for the last of the world's fuels. That suicide, insanity, and depression are epidemic shows that our system based on super abundance, pleasure, and ease has not brought health and happiness.

So I have chosen to walk away.

I have come full circle back to the simple life, to three acres of land and a house that I designed and built with my own hands and that is independent of the oil and power industries. That I do not choose to participate in the American way of life does not admit to hopelessness. I still believe that one person, sufficiently motivated and totally oblivious of his or her own welfare, can turn the world upside down. There is a power in believing that you have Right and Truth on your side that is absolutely invincible. But one reaches a time and place for a change in strategy.

In the entrance hall of my house hangs a scroll with the words of the prophet Micah:

And they shall beat their swords into plowshares
And their spears into pruning hooks;

Nation shall not lift up sword against nation
Neither shall they learn war anymore;
But they shall sit every man under his vine
And under his fig tree;
And none shall make them afraid;
For the mouth of the Lord has spoken it.

Surely, reason assures us, with universal education, humans will learn from history the advantages of cooperation and the futility of war. If we each dedicate our lives to the possibility of peace, justice, and human rights, our own eyes might see that One World where all humans can cooperate with one another and with nature and live out their lives in peace.

We must learn to be satisfied with enough rather than greedily grasping for more; but to state that human survival rests on our willingness to eliminate the nonessentials and return to a simple life means nothing unless that statement is backed up by example. It is my intention to prove that anyone, even a 57-year-old woman, can provide for themselves food, clothing, shelter, and a comfortable and happy life with little help from the self-destructive elements of our society.

My first concession to reality is that we, as a nation, cannot go back to the Jeffersonian idyllic rural life—not without cataclysmic social, political, and economic changes and redistribution of land. Most of the arable land in the United States is owned by business conglomerates—ranch industry in the West, agribusiness in the Midwest, and the forest products industries in the Southeast and Northwest. Small tracts are available, however, and there are numerous popular books on the subject of living well on two to five acres of land. Sufficient land for all is contingent, of course, on a strict control of population growth.

My tract of land is located by a small lake with two acres of hillside and one acre of flat ground in a longleaf pine–bluestem grass habitat. Under nature, this is a Pyrrhic association, so periodic burning maintains a parklike ground cover of native grasses and wildflowers without need for a noisy, gas-consuming lawnmower.

The lakeside site was chosen for reasons both practical and aesthetic—an occasional fish to add to a largely vegetarian diet, a source of cool breezes in summer and future wind power, and a scene of tranquillity to inspire serenity of spirit.

On the flat ground, I have 4 × 8 foot frames filled with organic matter for intensive gardening. All household wastes are disposed of here. Our mild winters permit year-round gardening, and the frames can be covered in winter during the few freezes. A flock of bantam chickens, which are great foragers, provide eggs for food and manure for the garden; beehives produce honey; dried beans, corn meal, and rice are brought from the town three miles distant on my three-wheel carryall bicycle. They could be grown if I had sufficient time and ambition. This simple diet is not only economical but healthy. Those in this country who are not dying of stress-related illnesses are dying of too much too rich food. On two separate occasions, I have dined with a prince and a president. What I remember best is that at both these sumptuous feasts, someone complained about the food.

Ninety percent of the clothing we own could be classed as nonessential. We have different garments for work, play, the street, lounging, sleeping, partying, business, and church. Much of our time and money goes into being appropriately attired. Even if permanent press does pass away, never again will I stand all day in the heat of summer over a hot wood cook stove heating irons to press starched khaki suits for my husband to wear while plowing the field. Sheer insanity! Whatever is handy, clean, and does not violate the local laws of decency serves me for any of the above purposes. In fact, *no* clothing suits me better at times. The freedom and ease with which one can work unhampered by the restraint of sweat-soaked garments is marvelous. I have considered posting a sign: "Warning! Naked woman at work!" to avoid accidentally offending the mores of some chance visitor, but concluded it might attract rather than repel.

My house is on a south slope facing the lake. There are two and a half levels; each is one room, 18 × 20 feet. The lower is of concrete blocks and has three sides underground; the upper is an A-frame with the entrance at ground level, and the end facing the lake has a 12 × 18 foot deck that extends into the branches of dogwood trees, which are understory to the towering pines. Here, I paint wildflower portraits, write poetry, or watch water birds on the lake. The deck provides a roof for the stone terrace below. An upper half of the A-frame is a railed loft where sleeping pads are stored. There is no conventional furniture—just built-ins—and anyone may carry their pad anywhere they wish to sleep. One wing at ground level serves as an entrance hall and another, a bathroom. Water is supplied by an underground reservoir. It operates on the same principle as the spring house where we kept milk and butter cold in the early days. The fireplace in the lower room has vents to take heat to the upper levels and serves as a cooking place in winter. For summer cooking, there is a stone grill and oven on the terrace. Solar stoves will soon be available, but in the meantime one can pick up enough twigs and downwood about the place for cooking fuel.

The entire front of all levels facing south is glass. In winter, when the sun is on the south horizon, full sun warms the interior; in summer, when the sun is on the north horizon, the glass front is shaded. The lower, underground level is delightfully cool in summer and easy to warm in winter.

Objections most often raised are: "What do you do for light at night?" and "What on earth do you do for entertainment—for music—with no TV or radio?" I do have a battery-powered tape player, for I love classical music. There is nothing grander than a thundering symphony to accompany a storm roaring in off the lake into the tall pines. In addition, there is a drum, tambourine, violin, guitar, flute, and harmonica so I and anybody else who happens to be in the mood can make any amount and quality of music. Other than these instruments, there are no valuables here to tempt anyone to steal. The door is never locked. People come and go—stay as long as they wish—whether I am home or not.

As for illumination: If I get up in the morning as soon as it is light enough to work, I am quite ready to rest by nightfall. Then, I can sit before the fireplace in winter, or on the deck under the stars in summer and practice tai chi chuan in the moonlight, or play music, or sing, or meditate, or engage in long, meaningful conversations with all those interesting people who come to share the love and peace, their own fears and hopes for our world, and to know that, at least in this one place, they need not be afraid.

Guest Editorial Discussion

1. After 20 years of social activism, the author believes that little has changed. Does this mean that what she did was unimportant? Explain.

2. Do you believe that "one person, sufficiently motivated and totally oblivious of his or her own welfare, can turn the world upside down"? Why or why not?

3. What is the importance of the author's present strategy "to prove that anyone can provide for themselves food, clothing, shelter, and a comfortable and happy life with little help from the self-destructive elements of our society"? Is this a way of life you plan to choose? Why or why not?

Discussion Topics

1. You may hear the argument that "humans have always been polluters and despoilers of the planet, so why all the fuss over ecology and pollution? We've survived so far." Explain the kernel of truth in this statement and then discuss its serious deficiencies.

2. Imagine that we could assemble representatives from five of our cultural phases to offer an ecology course. Briefly summarize the ecological lesson that each would give.

3. Humans have been hunter-gatherers for 99 percent of their time on earth. Which traits of this occupation are useful to us today and which are harmful?

4. Are people basically evil and aggressive or basically good and compassionate? What evidence do we have for each position? Over the entire span of human history, which view seems more reasonable? During the rise of Western civilization in the past few thousand years, which view seems more reasonable?

5. Debate the following statement: War is inevitable because the human species has inherited the basic characteristic of aggressiveness from its ancestors.

6. Why can some societies of advanced hunter-gatherers be described as affluent societies? Contrast this kind of society with modern, leisure-oriented affluent societies.

7. Would we be better off if fire had never been discovered? What about dynamite, pesticides, the automobile, and atomic energy?

8. Do you believe that we may be entering a new phase of cultural evolution based on cooperation and an ecological world view? Cite evidence for your position. How would you promote the development of this new cultural phase?

Readings

Bennett, Charles F. 1975. *Man and Earth's Ecosystems.* New York: Wiley. Excellent survey of human impact on the earth with a geographic emphasis.

Bronowski, Jacob, Jr. 1974. *The Ascent of Man.* Boston: Little, Brown. Outstanding overview of cultural evolution.

Dasmann, Raymond F. 1976. *Environmental Conservation.* 4th ed. New York: Wiley. Superb overview of human environmental impact, past and present.

Dubos, René. 1971. *Man Adapting.* New Haven, Conn.: Yale University Press. Good discussion of cultural evolution.

Glasser, William. 1972. "The Civilized Identity Society." *Saturday Review,* September 19, pp. 26–31. Excellent article used as a basis for many ideas in this chapter.

Harris, Marvin. 1971. *Culture, Man and Nature.* New York: Crowell. Excellent introduction to anthropology. See especially chaps. 3, 4, 5, 9, and 10.

Howells, William W. 1967. *Mankind in the Making.* New York: Doubleday. Well-written layperson's account of human evolution.

Hyams, Edward. 1976. *Soils and Civilization.* New York: Harper & Row. Splendid discussion of the human impact on the earth.

Levine, Norman D., ed. 1975. *Human Ecology.* North Scituate, Mass.: Duxbury Press. Excellent introduction.

Livingston, John A. 1973. *One Cosmic Instant.* Boston: Houghton Mifflin. Highly readable account of cultural evolution.

Morris, Desmond. 1969. *The Human Zoo.* New York: McGraw-Hill. Interesting and provocative view of human nature.

Mumford, Lewis. 1962. *The Transformations of Man.* New York: Collier. Superb analysis of cultural evolution.

Pfeiffer, J. E. 1972. *The Emergence of Man.* Rev. ed. New York: Harper & Row. Highly recommended introduction to human evolution.

Sears, Paul B. 1980. *Deserts on the March.* Norman: University of Oklahoma Press. Probably the best account of how human activities have contributed to the spread of deserts.

Spencer, J. E., and W. L. Thomas. 1977. *Introducing Cultural Geography.* 2nd ed. New York: Wiley. Highly recommended evolutionary account of human changes of earth's surface and its resources.

Tiger, Lionel, and Robin Fox. 1971. *The Imperial Animal.* New York: Delta. Magnificent analysis of human behavior.

Watson, Richard A., and Patty Jo Watson. 1969. *Man and Nature: An Anthropological Essay in Human Ecology.* New York: Harcourt Brace Jovanovich. Excellent discussion with the same organization as this chapter.

PART TWO

Some Concepts of Ecology

USDI/National Park Service/George Grant

Some Environmental Principles*

1. Everything must go somewhere, or we can never really throw anything away. (Law of conservation of matter)   2. You can't get something for nothing, you can only break even, or there is no such thing as a free lunch. (First law of energy, or law of conservation of energy)   3. You can't even break even, or if you think things are mixed up now, just wait. (Second law of energy)   4. Everything is connected to everything else, but how?   5. A thing is right when it tends to preserve the integrity, stability, and beauty of the biotic community. It is wrong when it tends otherwise.   6. In some cases, the greater the diversity of a biotic system, the greater its stability, or don't put all of your eggs in one basket.   7. Natural systems can take a lot of stress and abuse, but there are limits.   8. In nature you can never do just one thing, so always expect the unexpected.   9. Nature usually knows best.   10. Humans are just ordinary citizens of nature.   11. Up to a point, the bigger the better; beyond that point, the bigger the worse. (Brontosaurus principle)

*Based primarily on statements by Kenneth Boulding, Barry Commoner, Garrett Hardin, Aldo Leopold, and Kenneth E. F. Watt.

3

Some Matter and Energy Laws

Look at a beautiful flower, drink some water, eat some food, or pick up this book. The two things that connect these activities and other aspects of life on earth are matter and energy. **Matter,** or anything that has mass and occupies space, is of course the stuff you and all other things are made of. **Energy** is a more elusive concept. Formally it is defined as the ability or capacity to do work or produce change by pushing or pulling some form of matter. Energy is what you and all living things use to move matter around and to change it from one form to another. Energy is used to grow your food, to keep you alive, to move you from one place to another, and to warm and cool the buildings in which you work and live. The uses and transformations of matter and energy are governed by certain scientific laws, which, unlike legal laws, cannot be broken. In this chapter we begin our study of ecological concepts with a look at one fundamental law of matter and two equally important laws of energy. These laws will be used again and again throughout this book to help you understand many environmental problems and to aid you in evaluating solutions to these problems.

3-1 Law of Conservation of Matter: Everything Must Go Somewhere

We always talk about consuming or using up matter resources, but actually we don't consume any matter. We only borrow some of the earth's resources for a while—taking them from the earth, carrying them to another part of the globe, processing them, using them, and then discarding, reusing, or recycling them. In the process of using matter, we may change it to another form, such as burning complex gasoline molecules and breaking them down into simpler molecules of water and carbon dioxide. But in every case we neither create nor destroy any measurable amount of matter. Ultimately, all of the goods we think we have "consumed" are still here in some form. This results from the **law of conservation of matter:** In any ordinary physical or chemical change, matter is neither created nor destroyed but merely changed from one form to another.

This law tells us that we can never really throw any matter away. In other words, there is no such thing as either a consumer or a "throwaway" society. *Everything we think we have thrown away is still here with us in some form or another.* Everything must go somewhere, and all we can do is to reuse or recycle some of the matter we think we have thrown away. Unfortunately, the false idea that we can throw "away" anything we want makes it difficult for people to get excited about recycling, reusing, and trying to use less matter.

Furthermore, we can collect dust and soot from the smokestacks of industrial plants, but these solid wastes must then go somewhere. Cleaning up smoke is a misleading practice, because the invisible gaseous and very tiny particle pollutants left are often more damaging than the large solid particles that are removed. We can collect garbage and remove solid wastes from sewage, but they must either be burned (creating air pollution), dumped into rivers, lakes, and oceans (creating water pollution), or deposited on the land (creating soil pollution and water pollution if they wash away).

We can reduce air pollution from the internal combustion engines in cars by using electric cars, but since electric car batteries must be recharged every day, we will have to build more electric power plants. If these are coal-fired plants, their smokestacks will add additional and even more dangerous air pollutants to the air; more

---

Enrichment Studies 1 and 3 are related to this chapter.

land will be scarred from strip mining, and more water will be polluted by the acids that tend to leak out of coal mines. We could use nuclear power plants to produce the extra electricity needed, but then we risk greater heat or thermal pollution of rivers and other bodies of water used to cool such plants. Further, we also risk releasing dangerous radioactive substances into the environment through plant or shipping accidents, hijacking of nuclear fuel to make atomic weapons, and leakage from permanent burial sites for radioactive wastes.

Although we can certainly make the environment cleaner, talk of cleaning up the environment and pollution-free cars, products, or industries is a scientific absurdity. The law of conservation of matter tells us that we will always be faced with pollution of some sort. Thus, we are also faced with the problem of *trade-offs*. In turn, these frequently involve subjective and controversial scientific, political, economic, and ethical judgments about what is a dangerous pollutant level, to what degree a pollutant must be controlled, and what amount of money we are willing to pay to reduce a pollutant to a harmless level. Now let's look at energy and the two energy laws that tell us more about what we can and cannot do on this planet.

3-2 First Law of Energy: You Can't Get Something for Nothing

Types of Energy You encounter energy in many forms: mechanical, chemical (food or fuel), electrical, nuclear, heat, and radiant (such as light). Doing work involves changing energy from one form to another. In lifting this book, the chemical energy stored in chemicals obtained from your digested food is converted into the mechanical energy that is used to move your arm and the book upward and some heat energy that is given off by your body.

In an automobile engine, the chemical energy stored in gasoline is converted into mechanical energy, used to propel the car, and heat energy. A battery converts chemical energy into electrical energy and heat energy. In an electric power plant, chemical energy from fossil fuels (coal, oil, or natural gas) or nuclear energy from nuclear fuels is converted into mechanical energy, which is used to spin a turbine, and heat energy. The turbine then converts the mechanical energy into electrical energy and more heat. When this electrical energy passes through the filament wires in an ordinary light bulb, it is converted into light and still more heat. In all of the energy

transformations discussed in this section, we see that some energy always ends up as heat energy that flows into the surrounding environment.

Scientists have found that all forms of energy can be classified either as potential energy or kinetic energy, as shown in Figure 3-1. **Kinetic energy** is the energy that matter has because of its motion. Heat energy is a measure of the total kinetic energy of the molecules in a sample of matter. The amount of kinetic energy that a sample of matter has depends both on its mass and its velocity (speed). Because of its higher kinetic energy, a bullet fired at a high velocity from a rifle will do you more damage than the same bullet thrown by hand. Similarly, an artillery shell (with a larger mass) fired at the same velocity as the bullet will do you considerably more harm than the bullet.

Stored energy that an object possesses due to its position, condition, or composition is known as **potential energy.** A rock held in your hand has stored or potential energy that can be released and converted to kinetic energy (in the form of mechanical energy and heat) if the rock is dropped. Coal, oil, natural gas, wood, and other fuels have a form of stored or potential energy known as chemical energy. When the fuel is burned, this chemical potential energy is converted into a mixture of heat, light, and the kinetic energy of the molecules moving in the air and in other nearby materials.

With this background on the types of energy, we are prepared to look at the two scientific laws that govern what happens when energy is converted from one form to another.

First Energy Law What energy changes occur when you drop a rock from your hand to the floor? Because of its higher position, the rock in your hand has a higher potential energy than the same rock at rest on the floor. Has energy been lost or used up in this process? At first glance it seems so. But according to the **law of conservation of energy,** also known as the **first law of thermodynamics,** in any ordinary physical or chemical process, energy is neither created nor destroyed but merely changed from one form to another. The energy lost by a *system,* or collection of matter under study (in this instance, the rock), must equal the energy gained by the *surroundings,* or *environment* (in this instance, the air). This energy law holds for all systems, both living and nonliving. Thus, no organism can create its own food supply. Green plants require light energy to produce food energy, and animals must get their energy by eating either plants or other animals.

Type of Energy	Potential	Kinetic
Mechanical	firewood being held above ground	firewood dropped, which does work on experimenter's toe
Chemical		
Electrical	charged battery	battery being discharged through a wire
Nuclear	Nuclear power plant potential energy in nuclei of certain atoms	electricity produced (kinetic energy)

light bulb

Radiant energy is always kinetic energy

wood stove

Heat energy is always kinetic energy.

Figure 3-1 The two major types of energy are potential and kinetic.

Let's look at what really happens. As the rock drops, its potential energy is changed into kinetic energy (energy of motion)—both its own kinetic energy and that of the air through which it passes. The dropping rock causes the air molecules to move faster so that their temper-

ature rises. This means that some of the rock's original potential energy has been transferred to the air as heat energy. The energy lost by the rock (system) is exactly equal to the energy gained by its surroundings. In studying hundreds of thousands of mechanical processes (such as the rock falling) and chemical processes (such as the burning of a fuel), scientists have found that no detectable amount of energy is either created or destroyed. Energy input always equals energy output.

Although most of us know this first energy law, we sometimes forget that it means that, regarding energy quantity, we can't get something for nothing; at best we can only break even. In the words of environmentalist Barry Commoner, "There is no such thing as a free lunch." For example, we usually hear that we have so much energy available from oil, coal, natural gas, and nuclear fuels (such as uranium). The first law of thermodynamics, however, tells us that we really have much less energy available than these estimates indicate. *It takes energy to get energy.* We must use large amounts of energy to find, remove, and process these fuels. The only energy that really counts is the *net energy* available for use after we have subtracted from the total energy made available to us the energy used to obtain it, as discussed further in Chapter 13.

3-3 Second Law of Energy: You Can't Break Even

Second Energy Law and Energy Quality Energy varies in its *quality* or ability to do useful work. For useful work to occur energy must move or flow from a level of high-quality (more concentrated) energy to a level of lower quality (less concentrated) energy. The chemical potential energy concentrated in a lump of coal or a liter of gasoline and concentrated heat energy at a high temperature are forms of high-quality energy. Because they are concentrated, they have the ability to perform useful work in moving or changing matter. In contrast, dispersed or less concentrated heat energy at a low temperature has little remaining ability to perform useful work. Since energy quality flows downhill, the supply of concentrated, usable energy available to the earth is being continually depleted. In investigating hundreds of thousands of different conversions of heat energy to useful work, scientists have found that some of the energy is always degraded to a more dispersed and less useful form, usually heat energy given off at a low temperature

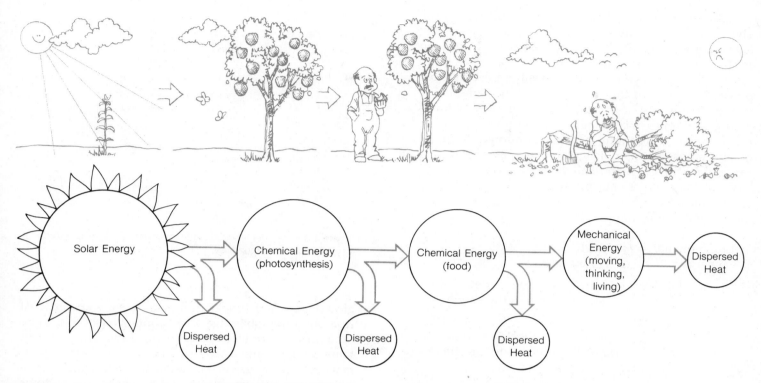

Figure 3-2 The second energy law. In all energy changes, some energy is degraded to low-quality heat energy that is dispersed throughout the environment.

to the surroundings. This is a statement of the *law of energy degradation*, also known as the **second law of thermodynamics.**

Let's look at an example of the second energy law. In an internal combustion automobile engine, the high-quality potential energy available in gasoline is converted to a combination of high-quality heat energy, which is converted to the mechanical work used to propel the car, and low-quality heat energy. Only about 20 percent of the energy available in the gasoline is converted to useful mechanical energy; the remaining 80 percent is released into the environment as degraded heat energy. In addition, about half of the mechanical energy produced is also degraded to low-quality heat energy through friction, so that 90 percent of the energy in gasoline is wasted and not used to move the car. Most of this loss is an energy-quality tax automatically exacted as a result of the second law. Frequently the design of an engine or other heat-energy conversion device wastes more energy than that required by the second law, but the second law ensures that some energy quality will be lost or wasted.

Another example of the degradation of energy involves the conversion of solar energy to chemical energy

in food. Photosynthesis in plants converts radiant energy (light) from the sun into high-quality chemical energy (stored in the plant in the form of sugar molecules) and low-quality heat energy. If you eat plants, such as spinach, the high-quality chemical energy is transformed within your body to high-quality mechanical energy, used to move your muscles and to perform other life processes, and low quality heat energy. As shown in Figure 3-2, in each of these energy conversions, some of the initial high-quality energy is degraded into low-quality heat energy that flows into the environment.

The first energy law governs the *quantity* of energy available from an energy-conversion process, whereas the second energy law governs the *quality* of energy available. In a heat-to-work conversion, we can get out no more energy than we put in. But according to the second law, the quality of the energy available from a heat-to-work conversion will always be lower than the initial energy quality. Not only can we not get something for nothing (the first law), we can't even break even in terms of energy quality (the second law). As Robert Morse put it, "The second law means that it is easier to get into trouble than to get out of it."

The second energy law also tells us that high-grade energy can never be used over again. *We can recycle matter but we can never recycle high-quality energy.* Every time you think, move your arm, light a fire, drive a car, or move any type of matter, you are automatically and irreversibly decreasing some of the world's supply of high-quality energy. There is no choice in this matter. Fuels and foods can be used only once to perform useful work. Once a piece of coal or a tank of gasoline is burned, its high-quality potential energy is lost forever. This means that the net useful, or high-quality, energy available from coal, oil, natural gas, nuclear fuel, geothermal, or any concentrated energy source is even less than that predicted by the first energy law.

$$
\begin{aligned}
\text{net high-quality} \;=\;& \text{total high-quality} \\
\text{energy} & \quad \text{energy available} \\
& -\;\text{high-quality energy needed to find,} \\
& \qquad \text{get, and process the energy} \\
& \qquad\qquad \text{(first law)} \\
& -\quad \text{energy quality lost in finding,} \\
& \qquad \text{getting, and processing the energy} \\
& \qquad\qquad \text{(second law)}
\end{aligned}
$$

From this equation we see that both the first and second energy laws must be used to evaluate our energy options, as discussed further in Chapter 13.

Second Energy Law and Increasing Disorder   The second energy law can be stated in a number of ways. Another expression of this law results from realizing that energy tends to flow or change spontaneously from a compact and ordered form to a dispersed and random, or disordered, form. Heat always flows spontaneously from hot to cold. You learned this the first time that you touched a hot stove. A cold sample of matter has its heat energy dispersed in the random, disorderly motion of its molecules. This is why heat energy at a low temperature can do little if any useful work.

Let's look at other spontaneous changes in the world around us. A vase falls to the floor and shatters into a more disordered state. A dye crystal dropped into water spontaneously dissolves, and the fact that color spreads is evidence that its molecules spontaneously tend toward a more dispersed and disordered state throughout the solution. A woman dies and the highly ordered array of molecules in her body decays to many smaller molecules that are dispersed randomly throughout the environment. Your desk and room seem spontaneously to become more disordered after a few weeks of benign ne-

Figure 3-3   The spontaneous tendency toward increasing disorder of a system and its surroundings.

glect (Figure 3-3). Smoke from a smokestack and exhaust from an automobile disperse spontaneously to a more random or disordered state in the atmosphere. Pollutants dumped into a river or lake tend to spread spontaneously throughout the water. Indeed, until we discovered that the atmosphere and water systems could be overloaded, we assumed that such spontaneous dilution solved the problem of pollution.

These observations all suggest that a *system* of matter spontaneously tends toward increasing randomness or disorder. But is this hypothesis valid? You may have already thought of some examples that contradict this hypothesis. As its temperature decreases to 0°C, liquid water spontaneously increases its order and freezes into ice. What about living organisms with their highly ordered systems of molecules and cells? You are a walking, talking contradiction to the idea that systems tend spontaneously toward disorder. We must look further.

The way out of our dilemma is not to look at changes in disorder or order only in the system but in both the system *and its environment.* Look at your own body. To form and preserve its highly ordered arrangement of molecules and its organized network of chemical reactions, you must continually obtain high-quality energy and raw materials from your surroundings. This means that disorder is created in the environment—primarily in the form of low-quality heat energy. Just think of all the disorder in the form of heat that is added to the environment to keep you alive. Planting, growing, processing, and cooking foods all requires energy inputs that add heat to the environment. The breakdown of the chemicals in food in your body gives off more heat to the environment. Indeed, your body continuously gives off heat equal to that from a 100-watt light bulb—which explains why a closed room full of people gets hot.

Measurements show that the disorder, in the form of low-quality heat energy, that is added to the environment to keep you alive is much greater than the order maintained in your body. This does not even count the enormous amounts of disorder added to the environment when concentrated deposits of minerals and fuels are extracted from the earth and burned or dispersed to heat the buildings you use, to move you around in vehicles, and to make roads, clothes, shelter, and other things that you use.

Thus, all forms of life are merely tiny pockets of order maintained by creating a sea of disorder around themselves. The primary characteristic of modern industrial society is an ever increasing use or flow of high-quality energy to maintain the pockets of order we call civilization. As a result, today's industrialized nations are creating more environmental disorder than any society in human history. The second energy law tells us that this cannot go on indefinitely. The increasing signs of environmental stress on the world's forests, fisheries, grasslands, and croplands and serious pollution are early warnings that we are beginning to produce disorder faster than it can be absorbed by the environment.

In considering the system and surroundings as a whole, scientists find that there is *always* a net increase in disorder with any spontaneous chemical or physical change. For any spontaneous change, either (1) the disorder in both the system and the environment increases, (2) the increase in disorder in the system is greater than the increase in order created in the environment, or (3) the increase in disorder in the environment is greater than the order created in the system. Experimental measurements have demonstrated this over and over again. Thus, we must modify our original hypothesis to include the surroundings. *Any system and its surroundings as a whole spontaneously tend toward increasing randomness or disorder*, or, in other words, if you think things are mixed up now, just wait. This is another way of stating the second energy law, or **second law of thermodynamics.**

Scientists frequently use the concept of **entropy,** a measure of relative randomness or disorder. A random system has high entropy, and an orderly system has low entropy. Using this concept, we can state the second energy law as follows: Any system and its surroundings as a whole spontaneously tend toward increasing entropy. If you have the feeling that each day the world gets more disordered, you are exactly right. The second law tells us that this is the most fundamental thing that is going

on in the world, and we cannot do a thing about it. The only thing we can do is to use matter and energy at a slower rate so that the rate at which disorder or entropy builds up in the environment is slowed down.

No one has ever found a violation of this law. In most apparent violations, the observer fails to include the greater disorder (entropy) increase in the surroundings when there is an increase in order in the system.

3-4 Matter and Energy Laws and the Environmental Crisis

As we shall see throughout this book, the law of conservation of matter and the first and second laws of energy (see the summary box) give us keys for understanding and dealing with the environmental crisis. These laws tell us why any society living on a finite planet must eventually become a *low-entropy or sustainable earth society* based on recycling and reusing matter and reducing the rate at which matter and energy are used. Energy flows to the earth from the sun and then goes back into space, but for all practical purposes little matter enters or leaves the earth. We have all of the supply of matter that we will ever have. Romantic and technological dreams that we can get new supplies of matter from space and other planets fail to consider that these efforts, even if the supplies were available on inhospitable planets, might require more resources from earth than we could bring back from space. Since we won't get any large amounts of new matter from beyond the earth, and since the law of conservation of matter tells us that no breakthrough in technology will create any new matter, we must learn to live with the matter we now have.

Our present one-way or "throwaway society" is based on using more and more of the earth's resources at a faster and faster rate (Figure 3-4). To sustain such growth rates requires an essentially infinite and affordable supply of mineral and energy resources. Technology can help us stretch these supplies and perhaps find substitutes, but sooner or later we must face up to the finiteness of the earth's supplies (as discussed further in Enrichment Study 1). The present environmental crisis and rising prices of key resources are warnings that these built-in entropy limits to growth may be closer than we like to think.

We have been taught that technology creates more and more order in the world but the truth is that it does just the opposite. Technology is merely a more effective way to harness high-quality energy for human use and

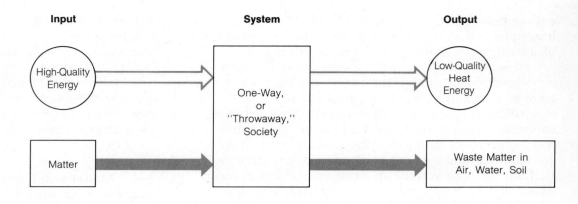

Figure 3-4 Today's one-way, or throwaway, society is based on maximizing the rates of energy flow and matter flow. This results in a conversion of the world's mineral and energy resources to trash, pollution, and waste heat at a very fast rate. It is sustainable only with essentially infinite supplies of mineral and energy resources and an infinite ability of the environment to absorb the resulting heat and matter wastes.

thus to degrade it to low-quality energy. The more we use energy-intensive high technology (such as cars, power plants, skyscrapers, and factories), the faster we use up the world's supply of high-quality energy and the faster disorder or entropy builds up in the environment. This does not mean that we should abandon all technology, but it does mean that we must depend more and more on appropriate technology (Section 1-5), which uses less energy and matter resources.

Some say we must become a *matter-recycling society* so that growth can continue without depleting matter resources. As high-grade and economically affordable matter resource supplies dwindle, we must, of course, recycle more and more matter. But there is a catch to such recycling. In using resources such as iron, we dig up concentrated deposits of iron ore (because they are the cheapest). Then we disperse this concentrated iron over much of the globe as we fashion it into useful products, discard it, or change it into other chemical substances. To recycle such widely dispersed iron, we must collect it, transport it to central recycling centers, and melt and purify it so that it can be used again. This is where the two energy laws come in. *Recycling matter always requires high-quality energy.*

However, if a resource is not too widely scattered, recycling often requires less high-quality energy than that needed to find, get, and process virgin ores. In any event, a recycling society based on ever increasing growth must have an essentially inexhaustible and affordable supply of high-quality energy. And high-quality energy, unlike matter, can never be recycled. Although experts disagree on how much usable energy we have, it is clear that supplies of fossil fuels and nuclear fuels are finite. Indeed, affordable supplies of oil, natural gas, and nuclear fuel may last no longer than several decades.

"Ah," you say, "but don't we have an essentially infinite supply of solar energy flowing into the earth?"

Sunlight reaching the earth is high-quality energy, but the quantity reaching a particular area of the earth's surface each minute or hour is low and nonexistent at night. Thus, solar energy is a flow limited renewable energy source. Using solar energy to heat a house to relatively moderate temperatures makes sense. However, in order to use it to heat water to high temperatures, to melt metals, or to produce electricity, it must be collected and concentrated. This requires high-quality energy—lots of it. This means that to have an almost total solar-energy society we must have an almost infinite supply of some other high-quality energy source, such as nuclear or fossil fuels, to mine, process, and transport the large amounts of matter needed to make solar collectors, focusing mirrors, pipes, and other materials. We are apparently in a vicious circle.

For the moment, however, let's assume that nuclear fusion energy (still only a faint technological dream) or some other energy breakthrough comes to our rescue. Even with such a technological miracle, the *second energy law tells us why continued growth on a finite planet is not possible. As we use more and more energy to transform matter into products and then recycle these products, the disorder in the environment will automatically increase.* We will have to disrupt more and more of the earth's surface and add more and more low-quality heat energy and matter pollutants (many of which are small gaseous molecules created by breaking down larger, more ordered systems of matter) to the environment. Low-quality heat energy flows back into space, but if we create it at a faster rate than that at which it can flow back, the earth's atmosphere could heat up and create unknown and possibly disastrous ecological and climatic changes, as discussed in Enrichment Study 3. Thus, paradoxically, the more we try to order, or "conquer," the earth, the greater the stress we put on the environment. *From a physical standpoint, the environmental crisis is a disorder or entropy crisis, and the second energy law tells us why.* Failure to accept that no technological breakthrough can repeal the second energy law can only result in more and more damage to the quality of life on this planet. It means that to reduce waste we must cut down on haste.

Why do many think we can ignore or repeal the second energy law? Part of the problem is ignorance. Most people have never heard of the second law, let alone understood its significance. In addition, this law has a cumulative rather than individual effect. You accept the law of gravity because it limits you and everyone else on a personal level. However, though your individual activities automatically increase the disorder in the environment, this effect seems small and insignificant. But the cumulative impact of the disorder-producing activities of billions of individuals trying to convert all of the world's resources to trash and garbage as fast as possible can have a devastating impact on the life-support systems that sustain us all. *The second energy law tells us that we are all interconnected, whether we like it or not.*

This may seem like a rather gloomy situation, but it need not be. The second energy law, along with the first energy law and the law of conservation of matter, tells us what we *cannot* do. But even more important and hopeful, these laws tell us what we *can* do. These matter and energy laws show us that the way out is to shift to

a *low-entropy* or *sustainable earth society* (Figure 3-5), which is based on reducing the rate of using matter and high-quality energy so that the entropy limits of the environment are not exceeded and resources are not depleted. This requires matter recycling, but more important it requires reusing matter (which takes less high-quality energy than recycling), making products that last, increasing pollution control, and emphasizing conservation of matter and high-quality energy (which cannot be recycled). Only by conserving and not wasting matter and high-quality energy supplies can we conserve and preserve life and life quality. In other words, we must go on an "entropy diet" by shifting to life-styles that walk as lightly on the earth as possible. This is the key to a sustainable earth society.

Our actions are based consciously and unconsciously on our world view—the way we think the world works. *The reason that nothing seems to work anymore is that the world view most of us have bears little resemblance to the way the world really works.* The world view that most people in industrialized societies have been taught for over 400 years is that all economic growth is good and that we can use technology to provide us with an ever increasing abundance of matter and high-quality energy resources. But as we have seen, the matter and energy laws tell us that the more we use technology to run matter and energy resources through our economic machine, the more

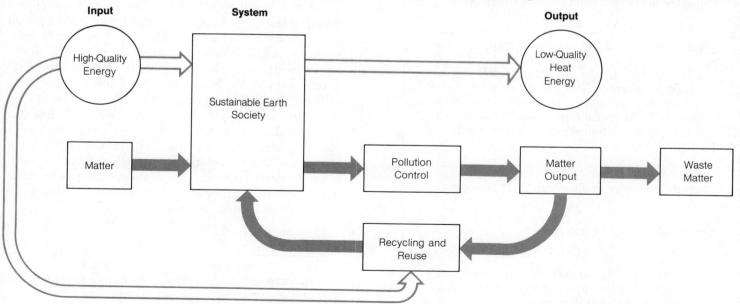

Figure 3-5 A sustainable earth society is based on energy flow and matter recycling. It requires reusing and recycling finite mineral resources, conserving energy (since it can't be recycled), increasing pollution control, and deliberately lowering the rate at which we use matter and energy resources so that the environment is not overloaded and resources are not depleted.

disorder we create in the environment. The real world operates on the basis of the matter and energy laws—not on any economic or political laws that we choose to dream up. In the words of Nobel Prize-winning chemist Frederick Soddy, "The laws of thermodynamics control the rise and fall of political systems, the freedom or bondage of nations, the movements of commerce and industry, the origins of wealth and poverty, and the general physical welfare of the human race."

There is increasing evidence that we have only about 50 years—or one generation—to rid ourselves of our present high-entropy, throwaway world view and adopt and live by a low-entropy or sustainable earth world view. We don't really have any choice in this matter. We will either make this crucial transition by voluntarily reducing the rate at which we produce entropy, or the laws of matter and energy operating through nature will do it for us. The automatic backlash from stretching nature to its entropy limits could result in a sharp drop in food, energy, and other vital resources—thus causing the death of billions of people—along with the extinction of many other living species. The more matter and energy that a person, city, industry, or nation is using, the more vulnerable it is to nature's backlash. Thus, the first people to succumb could be those in a society using energy and matter at a high rate who don't know how to adjust quickly to a sudden drop in available matter and energy resources. People in less developed societies will have a better chance of survival because they have been forced to learn how to survive without using much energy and matter.

A new world view based on the laws of matter and energy is the best way to avoid catastrophe in the difficult years ahead. To make the exciting and necessary transition to a sustainable earth society, we must stop thinking of earth as a spaceship that we can pilot—and resupply—at will. Far from "seizing the tiller of the world," as Teilhard de Chardin would have us do, we must stop trying to steer completely. Somehow we must tune our senses and hearts to nature, though we will never completely understand its marvelous complexity. We must learn anew that we belong to the earth and not the earth to us. As part of nature, we will always attempt to shape it to some extent for our own benefit, but we must do so with ecological wisdom, care, and restraint.

Matter and Energy Laws

Law of conservation of matter: In any ordinary physical or chemical change, matter is neither created nor destroyed but only transformed from one form to another.

Or:

We can never really throw matter away.

Or:

Everything must go somewhere.

First law of energy (law of conservation of energy): In any ordinary physical or chemical change, energy is neither created nor destroyed but merely changed from one form to another.

Or:

Regarding energy quantity, you can't get something for nothing—you can only break even.

Or:

There is no such thing as a free lunch.

Second law of energy (law of energy degradation): In all conversions of heat energy to work, some of the energy is always degraded to a more dispersed and less useful form, usually heat energy given off at a low temperature to the surroundings.

Or:

Regarding energy quality, you can't break even.

Or:

Energy can never be recycled.

Or:

Any system and its surroundings (environment) as a whole spontaneously tend toward increasing randomness, disorder, or entropy.

Or:

If you think things are mixed up now, just wait.

The law that entropy increases—the second law of thermodynamics—holds, I think, the supreme position among laws of nature. . . . If your theory is found to be against the second law of thermodynamics, I can give you no hope; there is nothing to do but collapse in deepest humiliation.

Arthur S. Eddington

Discussion Topics

1. Explain why we don't really consume anything and why there is no such thing as a throwaway society.

2. A tree grows and increases its mass. Explain why this isn't a violation of the law of conservation of matter.

3. Explain why removing odors and large particles from the smoke emitted from smokestacks could be a misleading and even dangerous long-term pollution control strategy. Does this mean it shouldn't be done? Explain.

4. Discuss the line in Genesis 3:19 "You are dust and to dust you shall return" in relation to the law of conservation of matter and the second law of thermodynamics.

5. Describe the energy transformations involved in the flow of water over a dam. How could some of the energy released be used to generate electricity?

6. List six different types of energy that you have used today and classify each as either kinetic or potential energy.

7. Use the first and second energy laws to explain why the usable supply of energy from coal, oil, natural gas, and uranium (nuclear fuel) is considerably less than that given by most official estimates.

8. What does it mean to say that electricity is high-quality energy? What is low-quality energy?

9. Use the second energy law to explain why a barrel of oil can only be used once as a fuel.

10. Criticize the statement "Any spontaneous process results in an increase in the disorder of the system."

11. Criticize the statement "Life is an ordering process, and since it goes against the natural tendency for increasing disorder, it breaks the second law of thermodynamics."

12. Explain how the environmental crisis can be considered an entropy crisis.

13. Using the first and second energy laws and the law of conservation of matter, explain the idea "To exist is to pollute." Does this mean that increasing pollution is inevitable? Why or why not? Does it apply to all types of pollution or only to some?

14. a. Use the law of conservation of matter to explain why a matter-recycling society is necessary.

    b. Use the second energy law to explain why there must be more emphasis on reusing than on recycling matter and why we must move to a sustainable earth society.

    c. Use the second energy law to explain why energy can never be recycled.

Readings

Angrist, S. W., and L. G. Hepler. 1967. *Order and Chaos*. New York: Basic Books. Excellent nontechnical introduction to thermodynamics emphasizing its fascinating historical development.

Bent, Henry A. 1971. "Haste Makes Waste: Pollution and Entropy." *Chemistry*, vol. 44, 6–15. Excellent and very readable account of the relationship between entropy (disorder) and the environmental crisis.

Boulding, Kenneth E. 1964. *The Meaning of the 20th Century*. New York: Harper & Row. Penetrating discussion of our planetary situation by one of our foremost thinkers. See especially chaps. 4, 6, and 7 on the war, population, and entropy (disorder) traps.

Cook, Earl. 1976. *Man, Energy, Society*. San Francisco: Freeman. Superb discussion of energy and energy options.

Cottrell, F. 1955. *Energy and Society*. New York: McGraw-Hill. Survey of the development of energy sources.

Miller, G. Tyler, Jr. 1971. *Energetics, Kinetics and Life: An Ecological Approach*. Belmont, Calif.: Wadsworth. Attempt to show the beauty and wide application of thermodynamics to life. Amplifies and expands the material in this chapter at a slightly higher level.

Odum, Howard T. 1971. *Environment, Power and Society*. New York: Wiley-Interscience. Important and fascinating higher-level discussion of human energy use.

Odum, Howard T., and Elisabeth C. Odum. 1980. *Energy Basis for Man and Nature*. New York: McGraw-Hill. Outstanding discussion of energy principles and energy options at a somewhat higher level.

Rifkin, Jeremy. 1980. *Entropy: A New World View*. New York: Viking Press. Superb nontechnical description of the sustainable earth world view based on the second law of energy.

Steinhart, Carol E., and John S. Steinhart. 1974. *Energy: Source, Use, and Role in Human Affairs*. North Scituate, Mass.: Duxbury Press. Excellent treatment of energy principles and options.

Thirring, Hans. 1958. *Energy for Man*. New York: Harper & Row. Informative overview of the use of energy.

4

Ecosystem Structure: What Is an Ecosystem?

Walk into a forest on a warm summer day and look, listen, smell, and feel. A gentle breeze flows over your skin and the air feels cool and slightly damp. The sounds of the urban world you just left are excluded by magnificent oak and hickory trees that surround you with their beauty. Glimmering sunlight cascades through the canopy of leaves to reveal a varied tapestry of shrubs and herbs growing at your feet. A squirrel scampers noisily up a tree trunk. Looking down you see the tracks of a deer. Turning over a rotting log in your path, you uncover a frenzy of activity as worms, beetles, ants, termites, centipedes, cockroaches, and other unidentified insects move in all directions to escape your intrusion into their world. You pick up a handful of soil looking for further signs of life, but you can only imagine that it teems with millions of bacteria and other microorganisms.

What types of plants and animals live in this forest? How do they get the matter and energy that they need to stay alive? How do these plants and animals interact with one another and with their physical environment? What changes will this dynamic system of life undergo with time? Ecology is the branch of science that attempts to answer such questions. Ernest Haeckel coined the term *ecology* from two Greek words: *oikos*, meaning "house" or "place to live," and *logos*, meaning "study of." Literally, then, **ecology** is a study of organisms in their home; it is a study of the structure and function of nature or of the organisms and groups of organisms found in

nature and their interactions with one another and with their environment. Ecologists call the forest just described and other dynamic systems of living things and their environment *ecosystems*. These next three chapters will be devoted to a study of ecosystems. In this chapter we will look at the structure and types of ecosystems. In Chapter 5 we will look at ecosystem function, or what happens in them, and Chapter 6 will examine some changes that can occur in ecosystems as a result of natural and human activities.

4-1 What Is an Ecosystem?

Levels of Organization Looking at earth from space, we see mostly a blue sphere with irregular green, red, and white patches on its surface. As we zoom closer, these colorful patches become deserts, forests, grasslands, mountains, seas, lakes, oceans, farmlands, and cities. Each subsection is different, having its own characteristic set of organisms and climatic conditions. Yet, as we shall see, all of these subsystems are related. As we move in even closer, we can pick out a wide variety of living organisms. If we could magnify these plants and animals, we would see that they are made up of cells, which in turn are made up of molecules, atoms, and subatomic particles. All matter, in fact, can be viewed as being organized in identifiable patterns, or levels of organization, ranging in complexity from subatomic particles to galaxies (Figure 4-1).

The Realm of Ecology As Figure 4-1 shows, ecologists are concerned with five levels of organization of matter—*organisms, populations, communities, ecosystems,* and the *ecosphere.* A group of individual organisms (such as squirrels or oak trees) of the same kind (species) is called a **population.** A population may be local or global, de-

---

Enrichment Studies 2 and 3 are related to this chapter.

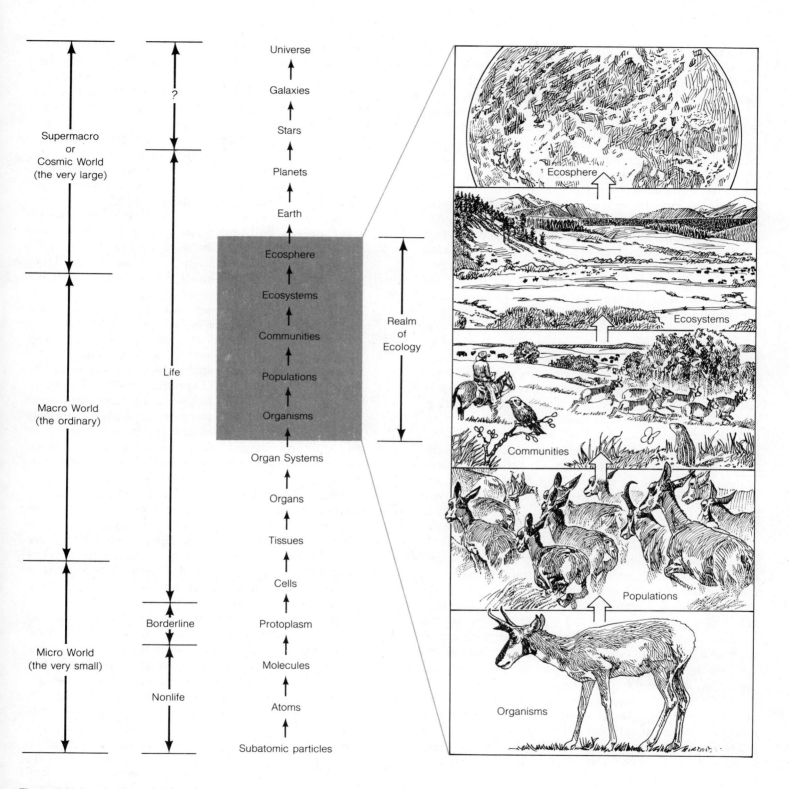

Figure 4-1 Levels of organization of matter.

pending on the size of the geographic system under study. It may include all of the squirrels and oak trees on earth or all of the squirrels and oak trees in the oak-hickory forest described in the opening of this chapter.

In nature we find several populations of different organisms living in a particular area. The populations of plants and animals living and interacting in a given locality are called a **community,** or *natural community*. Each organism in such a community has a **habitat,** the place where it lives. Habitats vary widely in size from an entire forest to the intestine of a termite. A community, such as an oak-hickory forest, is not just a collection of squirrels, trees, plants, bacteria, and other populations living together in the same place. The important aspect of a natural community is that its animals and plants interact with one another. In many communities one or two organisms dominate. For example, in an oak-hickory forest community, oak and hickory trees are the dominant species. They provide habitats and protection from the harsh sun so that certain plants and animals can survive. They also serve as the largest single source of food for a number of organisms, such as squirrels and rodents.

Any natural or biological community also has an environment. A community of living things interacting with one another and with their physical environment (solar energy, air, water, soil, heat, wind, and their chemical environment) is called an *ecological system,* or **ecosystem,** a term first introduced by A. G. Tansley. An ecosystem can be a planet, a tropical rain forest, a pond, an ocean, a fallen log, or a puddle of water in a rock. An ecosystem is any area with a boundary through which an input and output of energy and matter can be measured and related to one or more environmental factors. The boundaries drawn around ecosystems are arbitrary and are selected for convenience in studying each system. It is easy to think of a pond, lake, desert, or forest as an ecosystem, because each tends to have recognizable geographic boundaries. But it is often just as useful to treat a patch of an oak-hickory forest or a clump of grass in a field as an ecosystem. In studying an ecosystem, we are interested in the interactions between the organisms and between the organisms and their environment. (The ecosystem approach is not the only way of studying ecology. Some ecologists prefer to approach ecology from the standpoint of biological evolution. Because the evolutionary approach requires a fairly detailed and technical background in biology, we will use the ecosystem approach.)

All of the various ecosystems on the planet, along with their interactions, make up the largest life unit, or planetary ecosystem, called the **ecosphere** or **biosphere** (see Figure 4-2 on page 47). the ecosphere includes all forms of life and every relationship that binds them together. As shown in Figure 4-2, the earth can be divided into three intersecting regions—the **atmosphere** (air), the **hydrosphere** (water), and the **lithosphere** (soil and rock). The ecosphere, or sphere of life, is found at the intersection of these three areas. It consists of three life zones: (1) above us, a thin layer of usable atmosphere no more than 11 kilometers (7 miles) high; (2) around us, a limited supply of life-supporting water in rivers, glaciers, lakes, oceans, and underground deposits as well as in the atmosphere; and (3) below us, a thin crust of soil, minerals, and rocks extending only a few thousand meters into the earth's interior. This intricate film of life contains all of the water, minerals, oxygen, carbon, phosphorus, and other chemical building blocks necessary for life. Because essentially no new matter enters or leaves the earth (Section 3-4), these vital chemicals must be recycled again and again for life to continue.

If the earth were an apple, the ecosphere would be no thicker than the skin. Everything in this skin of life is interdependent: Air helps purify water and keep plants and animals alive, water keeps plants and animals alive, plants keep animals alive and help renew the air and soil, and the soil keeps plants and many animals alive and helps purify the water. The ecosystems that make up the ecosphere also help to moderate the weather, recycle vital chemicals needed by plants and animals, dispose of many of our wastes, control more than 95 percent of all potential crop pests and causes of human disease, and maintain a gigantic genetic pool that we use to develop new food crop strains, and medicines. The beautiful thing is that nature provides us with all of these services for free as long as we don't disrupt these natural processes.

The ecosphere, then, is a remarkably effective and enduring system—and endure it must, or life will become extinct. We are beginning to understand that disrupting or stressing the ecosphere in one place can often create unpredictable and sometimes undesirable effects elsewhere. This ecological backlash effect has been eloquently summarized by the English poet Francis Thompson: "Thou canst not stir a flower, without troubling of a star." *The goal of ecology is to find out just how everything in the ecosphere is related.* Using this knowledge, humans can work as partners within nature rather than as conquerors of nature.

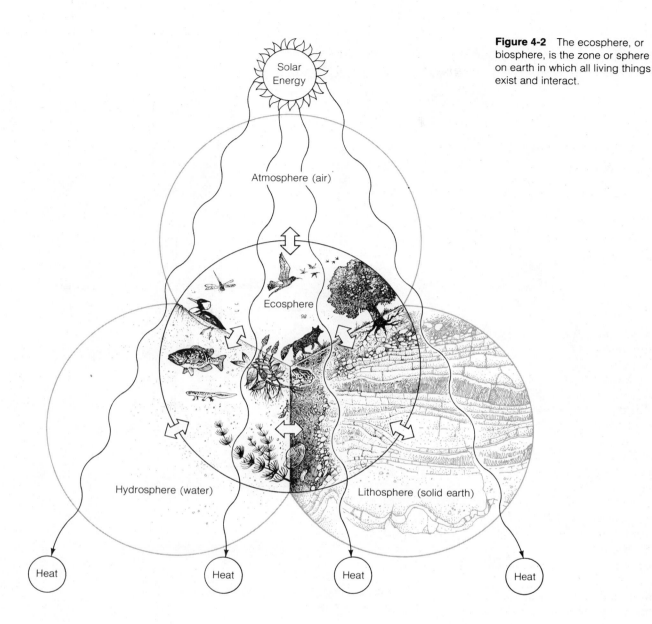

4-2 Ecosystem Structure

Let's take a closer look at the structure of an ecosystem. As mentioned earlier, an ecosystem always has two major parts or components: nonliving and living. The *nonliving*, or **abiotic**, part includes an outside energy source (usually the sun), various physical factors such as wind and heat, and all of the chemicals essential for life. The living, or **biotic**, portion of an ecosystem can be divided into food **producers** (plants) and food **consumers**. Consumers are usually further divided into *macroconsumers* (animals) and **decomposers**, or *microconsumers* (chiefly bacteria and fungi). More detailed descriptions are given

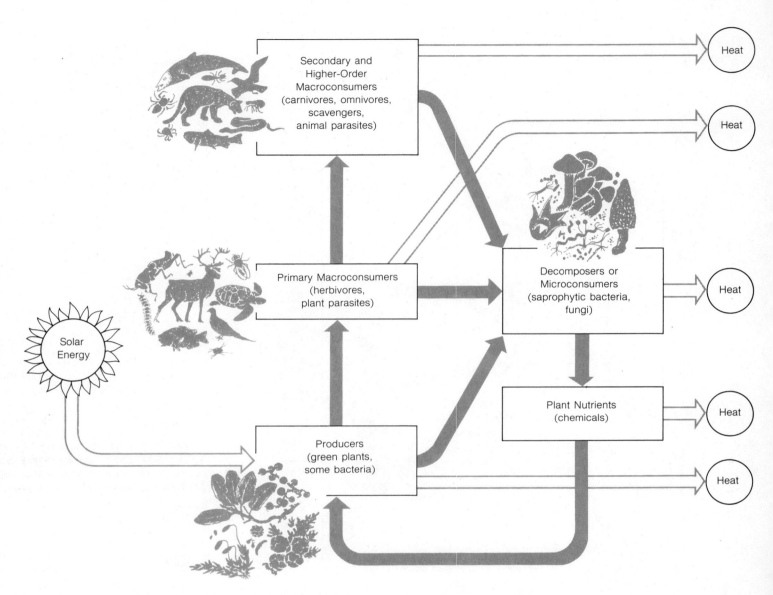

Figure 4-3 The basic components of an ecosystem. Solid lines represent the cyclical movement of chemicals through the system, and unshaded lines indicate one-way energy flows.

in Figures 4-3, 4-4, and 4-5 (page 50) and in the box on ecosystem structure (page 51).

4-3 Limiting Factors in Ecosystems: Climate and Soil

Organisms and Limiting Factors What determines whether a given plant or animal species can exist and thrive in a given ecosystem? An organism's survival depends on certain *chemical factors*, such as the availability of carbon dioxide, oxygen, nitrogen, phosphorus, and sodium, and certain *physical factors*, such as temperature, light, precipitation, and humidity. Every living thing is affected by the combined action of many such factors. Each organism has a certain range of tolerance to variations in these factors. However, too much or too little of any single factor may destroy an organism or limit its

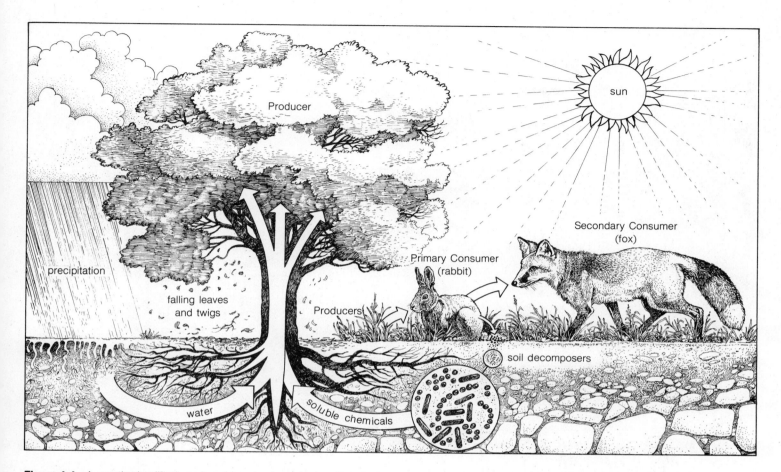

Figure 4-4 A greatly simplified version of the structure of a forest ecosystem.

numbers and distribution. There may be too much moisture or not enough; too high a temperature or too low; too much light or not enough; too many minerals dissolved in the soil or too few. This is summarized in the **limiting factor principle,** which combines ideas put forth by Justus Liebig and V. E. Shelford: The existence, abundance, or distribution of an organism can be determined by whether the levels of one or more limiting factors fall above or below the levels required by the organism.

A single factor can limit the growth of an organism. For example, suppose a farmer plants wheat in a field containing too little nitrogen. Even if the wheat's requirements for solar energy, water, and other chemical nutrients are met, the wheat will stop growing when it has used up the available nitrogen. In this case, nitrogen is the limiting factor.

Plants and animals vary widely in their range of tolerance to different environmental factors. For example, white-tailed deer, starlings, and deer mice are very adaptable and are found in a wide range of climates and types of ecosystems. Conversely, Kirtland's warbler, a small insect-eating bird, is found in only a few jack pine forests in Michigan, and the North American mountain goat is found only from Alaska to Washington.

Limiting Factors and Biomes The ecologist is concerned not just with organisms but also with communities and ecosystems. The variation in ecosystems, especially those on the land, is essentially infinite. But since many plant and animal species are often found together, it is useful to classify ecosystems according to their similarities in structure or composition. On this basis, the terrestrial portion of the ecosphere can be viewed

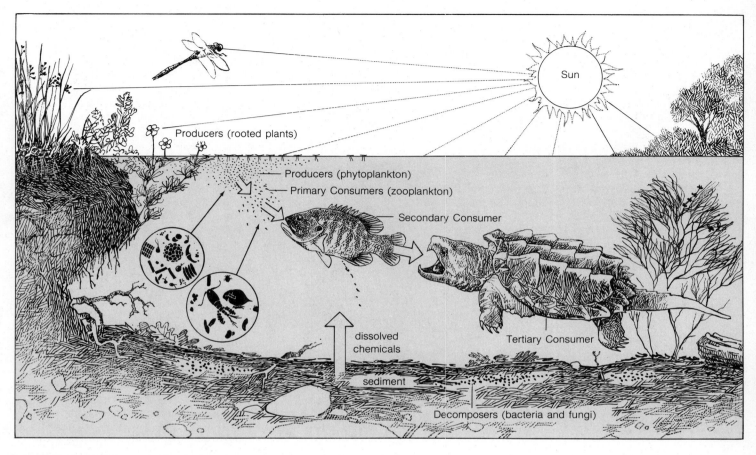

Producers (rooted plants)

Producers (phytoplankton)

Primary Consumers (zooplankton)

Secondary Consumer

Sun

Tertiary Consumer

dissolved chemicals

sediment

Decomposers (bacteria and fungi)

Figure 4-5 A greatly simplified version of the structure of a freshwater pond ecosystem.

as consisting of about a dozen different *biomes*, or major life zones. Each **biome** is a large terrestrial ecosystem consisting of similar groupings of plants and animals. Among the major types of biomes are the tundra, grassland, chaparral, and several types of forest. The ecological map of the world shown in Figure 4-6 on pages 52–53 is a much more natural representation of the globe than the political maps that we are so used to seeing. (For more details on biomes, see Enrichment Study 2.)

But why is one area of the world a desert, another a grassland, and another a forest? We might expect that such large collections of plants and animals would not be controlled by only one limiting factor, but by *groups of factors* acting together. For example, physical factors such as average temperature, light, precipitation, and humidity can be grouped together as climate. Similarly,

a large number of chemical and physical factors can be grouped together as soil. Let's look more closely at the climates and soils that cause the plants and animals in major world biomes to differ.

Climate Many people confuse climate with weather. You can have a good climate and poor weather, and vice versa. **Climate** is the average of atmospheric conditions over a relatively long period of time; **weather** is the day-to-day variation in atmospheric conditions. In other words, climate is the average weather over a relatively long period. The major factors that make up climate are average annual quantity and seasonal distribution of light, temperature, precipitation, and humidity. Expressed very simply, climatic patterns result when solar

Ecosystem Structure

Nonliving (Abiotic) Portion

Energy: Solar energy normally drives the ecosystem by helping to create climate, to recycle essential chemicals, and to support plant life. Green plants use a tiny fraction of incoming solar energy plus water and carbon dioxide to make carbohydrates and other food substances that store chemical energy. Plants and animals that consume plants or other animals break down (oxidize) these fuel molecules to obtain energy. In accordance with the second law of thermodynamics, energy flows one way through an ecosystem, is degraded to heat, and passes into the environment and eventually back into space.

Physical factors: These include conditions such as temperature, light, wind, humidity, water currents, and rainfall, which are created when solar energy interacts with the organic and inorganic chemicals in the ecosystem and with structural features of the earth's surface.

Chemicals: These include inorganic substances (water, oxygen, carbon, nitrogen, carbon dioxide, and essential minerals) and organic substances (proteins, carbohydrates, lipids, vitamins, and other complex chemicals necessary for life). The critical inorganic and organic chemicals found in the air, water, and soil must be continually recycled through the ecosphere.

Living (Biotic) Portion

Producers (plants, or autotrophs): These are plants, ranging in size from tiny floating phytoplankton (algae, diatoms, and so on) in water ecosystems to giant trees; producers also include some types of bacteria. Plants are **autotrophic** (self-producing) **organisms** because they use solar energy to photosynthesize organic food substances and other organic chemicals from carbon dioxide and water.

Macroconsumers (animals or heterotrophs): These organisms, called **heterotrophic organisms,** cannot manufacture their own food and must consume the organic food compounds found in plants or other animals. **Herbivores** (plant eaters), such as whales, deer, cows, rabbits, mice, grasshoppers, zebras, sheep, plant lice, and zooplankton, are the primary consumers that feed on plants. They may, like caterpillars, feed on only one species of plant, or they may, like rabbits and goats, feed on a variety of plant species. **Carnivores** (meat eaters), such as ladybugs, small birds, coyotes, frogs, lizards, snakes, cats, and fish, are secondary consumers that feed on herbivores. Higher-level carnivores, such as lions, hawks, fleas, and large fish, feed on these meat eaters. **Omnivores** (generalists), such as pigs, rats, and humans, can feed on both plants and other animals.

Decomposers (microconsumers, or saprotrophs): These are tiny organisms, such as bacteria, fungi (including molds and mushrooms), termites, and maggots, that break down the bodies and complex compounds in dead animals and plants into simpler substances. This process releases these chemicals for reuse by producer species, completing the cycle of chemicals through the ecosystem. The nutrition of decomposers is said to be **saprophytic**—pertaining to the absorption of the products of organic breakdown and decay.

energy produces thermal patterns. When these patterns are coupled with the earth's rotation and revolution around the sun, they produce ocean currents and the prevailing winds. These air and water currents, in turn, are major factors in the distribution of precipitation and heat over various parts of the earth.

Climate is modified locally by a number of factors, especially mountains and the proximity of a land mass to a large body of water. Because of their higher altitudes, mountains tend to be cooler and windier than adjacent valleys. In addition, mountains directly affect precipitation patterns. The air sweeping up a mountainside cools and tends to release some of its water content as precipitation before it goes over the mountain. Thus, the windward slopes of a mountain tend to be relatively wet, while the slopes on the other side of the mountain and the land beyond these slopes tend to be much drier. Oceans, lakes, and other large bodies of water tend to modify the climate because water absorbs large quantities of heat and releases this heat slowly. This alters and moderates the temperatures of nearby land areas. For example, coastal cities (such as New York and Boston) are warmer in winter, and cooler in summer than inland areas.

Figure 4-6 World biomes.

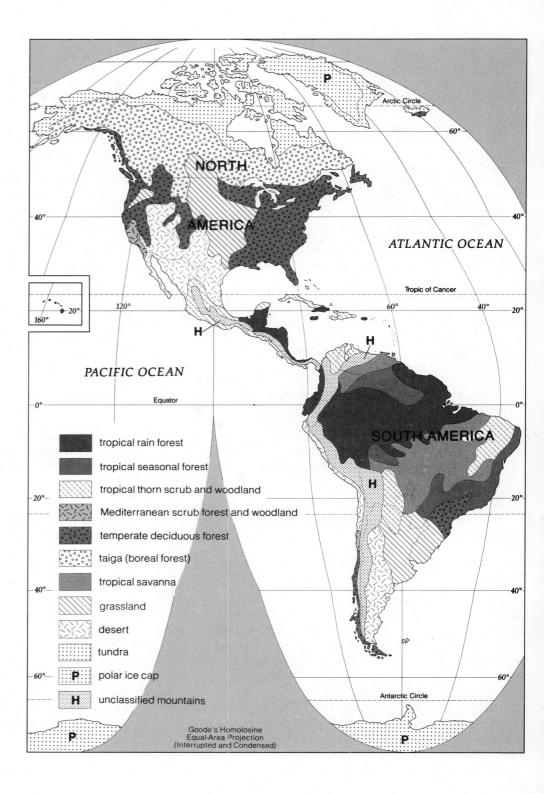

legend:
- tropical rain forest
- tropical seasonal forest
- tropical thorn scrub and woodland
- Mediterranean scrub forest and woodland
- temperate deciduous forest
- taiga (boreal forest)
- tropical savanna
- grassland
- desert
- tundra
- **P** polar ice cap
- **H** unclassified mountains

NORTH AMERICA

SOUTH AMERICA

ATLANTIC OCEAN

PACIFIC OCEAN

Arctic Circle

Tropic of Cancer

Equator

Antarctic Circle

Goode's Homolosine
Equal-Area Projection
(Interrupted and Condensed)

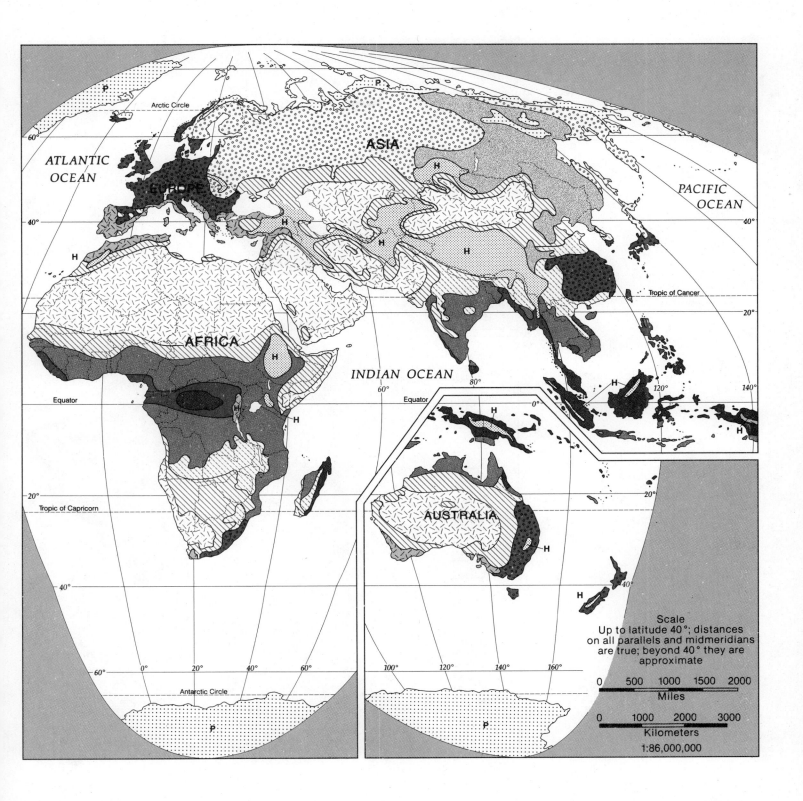

Figure 4-7 World climates (Köppen-Geiger classification).

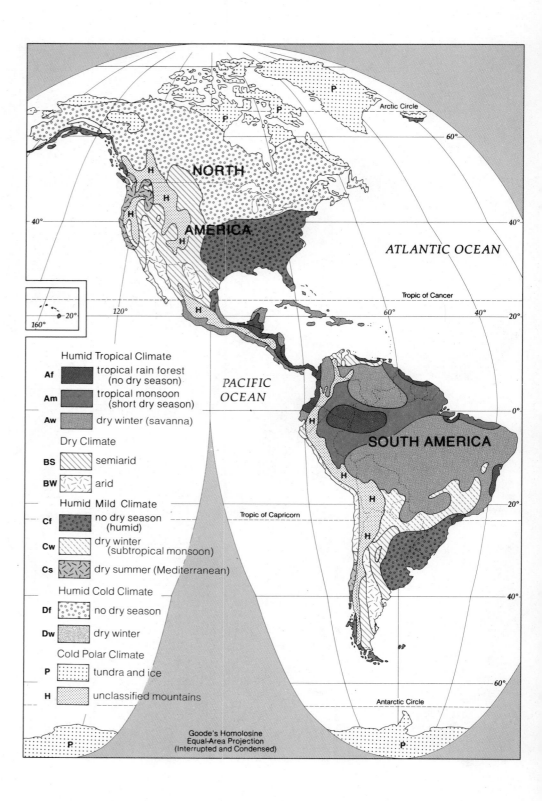

Humid Tropical Climate

Af tropical rain forest (no dry season)

Am tropical monsoon (short dry season)

Aw dry winter (savanna)

Dry Climate

BS semiarid

BW arid

Humid Mild Climate

Cf no dry season (humid)

Cw dry winter (subtropical monsoon)

Cs dry summer (Mediterranean)

Humid Cold Climate

Df no dry season

Dw dry winter

Cold Polar Climate

P tundra and ice

H unclassified mountains

Goode's Homolosine
Equal-Area Projection
(Interrupted and Condensed)

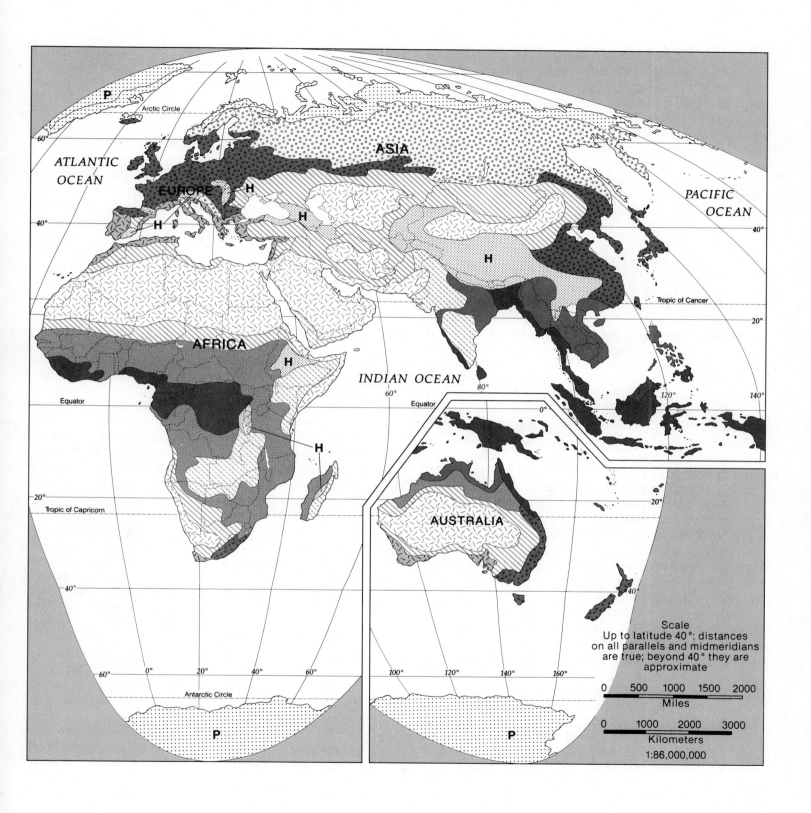

A widely used method for classifying different types of climate, called the Köppen-Geiger method, uses the two climatic elements of temperature and precipitation to characterize five major climatic types: (1) humid tropical climate, (2) dry climate, (3) humid warm climate, (4) humid cold climate, and (5) cold polar climate. The overall world distribution of these five climatic types is shown in Figure 4-7 on pages 54–55. By comparing Figure 4-7 with Figure 4-6, we can see how climate is the major factor determining the plant life that exists in a given biome. A more detailed discussion of climate is given in Enrichment Study 3.

Soil Unless you come from a farming family, you may not realize that soil is one of our most vital and most abused resources. Soil, the uppermost layer of the earth's crust, is the crucial interface between the lithosphere and all living plants that grow on its surface. Almost all of our supplies of vegetables, fruit, meat, wool, cotton, lumber, paper, and many other resources come, directly or indirectly, from this astonishingly thin carpet of life.

Many people think of soil as dirt, something to be gotten rid of—an idea that sends shudders through soil scientists. **Soil** is a complex mixture of small pieces of inorganic rock, gravel, and minerals, organic compounds, living organisms, air, and water. It is a dynamic body, always changing in response to climate, vegetation, local topography, parent rock material, age, and human use and abuse.

Matter continually circulates from the soil to plants and back to the soil. Plants obtain water and various nutrient chemicals or minerals from the soil. When leaves and branches die, they fall to the ground. Then millions of bacteria, fungi, worms, tiny arthropods, millipedes, termites, and other organisms that live in the surface layers of the soil decompose the leaves and twigs and release their minerals for reuse by plants.

We tend to think of soil as a single layer, but it is really made up of several layers called **soil horizons** (Figure 4-8 on page 57). By digging a ditch, you can see a cross section, or *soil profile*, of these layers. Most mature soils have three layers. The top layer, called the *A-horizon, consists of freshly fallen plant litter, some leaves and twigs, a sublayer of* **humus** (made up mostly of decaying organic material and some inorganic material), and another sublayer containing insoluble minerals. The A-horizon is sometimes called the *zone of leaching*, because

as water percolates through this layer, it leaches out, or dissolves, most of the soluble inorganic materials. When rain falls on fertile soil, much of the water is held in place by the humus. The quantity and type of organic and inorganic compounds in the A-horizon determine the fertility of the soil. When trees or plants are cleared away, this valuable layer of topsoil can be washed or blown away.

Below the A-horizon we find the *B-horizon*, or subsoil. It contains fine particles of inorganic materials, such as clay, that have washed from the A-horizon and some finely divided minerals from the parent rock below. Because it receives inorganic material from the A-horizon, the B-horizon is also called the *zone of deposition*. Since the B-horizon contains little organic material, it cannot support plant life if the A-horizon is eroded away or removed by strip mining or other human earth moving activities. The bottom, or *C-horizon*, contains pieces of rock broken down from the parent rock (bedrock) by repeated freezing and other weathering processes.

Soils in different biomes of the world (Enrichment Study 2) vary widely in color, physical and chemical characteristics, and depth of the three horizons, as shown in Figure 4-8. We can use these differences to classify soils throughout the world according to several major groups. World soils can be divided into two major classes: pedalfers and pedocals. **Pedalfers** are soils found in the hot, wet rain forest and in biomes such as temperate rain forest, deciduous (leaf dropping) forest, taiga or coniferous (evergreen and cone bearing) forest, and tundra, which have cool to very cold climates with moderate to high precipitation. The major types of pedalfers are laterite, red and yellow podzol, gray-brown podzol, podzols, and tundra soils. **Pedocals** are soils found in biomes such as grassland, shrubland (savanna), and desert, which have climates with moderate to low precipitation (semiarid to arid) and moderate to high temperatures. The major types of pedocals are the prairie, chernozem, chestnut, brown, and desert soils. A third group of soils found in mountains and mountain valleys is so varied that the soils cannot be easily classified. The soils that are best suited for raising crops and grazing livestock are the brown, chestnut, and chernozem pedocals found in grasslands and, to a lesser extent, the gray-brown podzol pedalfers found in temperate deciduous forests. Figure 4-9 on pages 58–59 shows a highly generalized soil map of the world. It can be correlated with the world biomes (Figure 4-6 and the major types of world climates (Figure 4-7).

Relationships Between Climate, Soil, and Biomes As seen from Figures 4-6, 4-7, and 4-9, climate is the major factor determining the plant life in a biome. Climate and plants together are the primary factors determining the soil type. Climate, plants, and soil then interact to determine the types, numbers, and distribution of animals in a given biome. More details on the climate and types of plants and animals found in the major biomes are found in Enrichment Study 2.

In this chapter we have seen how various physical and chemical factors, such as climate and soil, can influ-ence the number, kinds, and distribution of plants and animals in an ecosystem. With this background in ecosystem structure, we are ready to learn more about how these plant and animal species interact with one another and with their environment.

No ecosystem is an island.

Anonymous

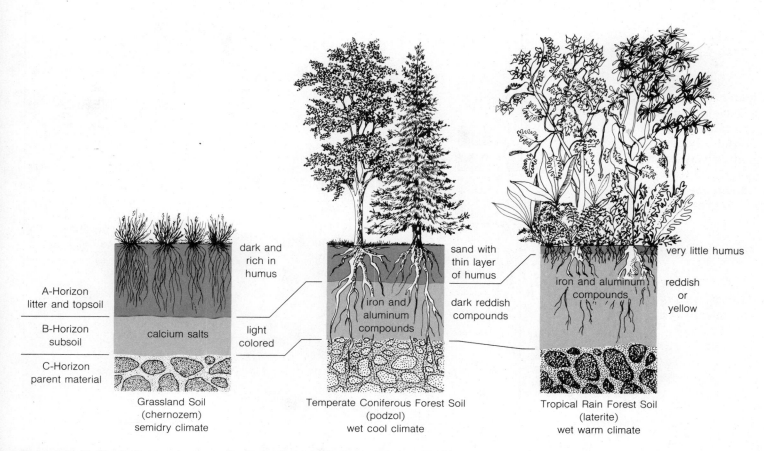

A-Horizon
litter and topsoil

B-Horizon
subsoil

C-Horizon
parent material

dark and rich in humus

light colored

calcium salts

Grassland Soil (chernozem) semidry climate

sand with thin layer of humus

iron and aluminum compounds

dark reddish compounds

Temperate Coniferous Forest Soil (podzol) wet cool climate

very little humus

iron and aluminum compounds

reddish or yellow

Tropical Rain Forest Soil (laterite) wet warm climate

Figure 4-8 Profiles for three major types of soil: grassland, coniferous forest, and tropical forest.

Figure 4-9 World distribution of major soil types. The best soils for agriculture are brown, chestnut, and chernozem pedocals, which are found in grasslands; and podzol and gray-brown podzol pedalfers, which are found in temperate deciduous forests.

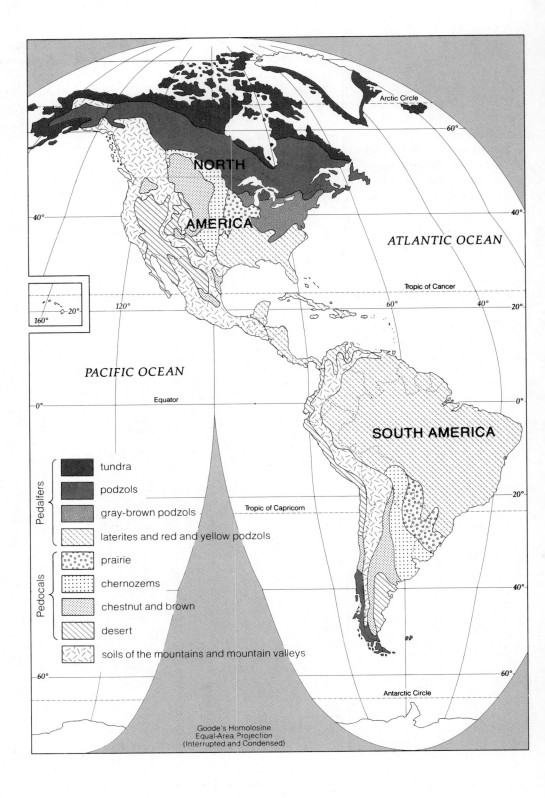

Pedalfers
- tundra
- podzols
- gray-brown podzols
- laterites and red and yellow podzols

Pedocals
- prairie
- chernozems
- chestnut and brown
- desert

soils of the mountains and mountain valleys

Goode's Homolosine
Equal-Area Projection
(Interrupted and Condensed)

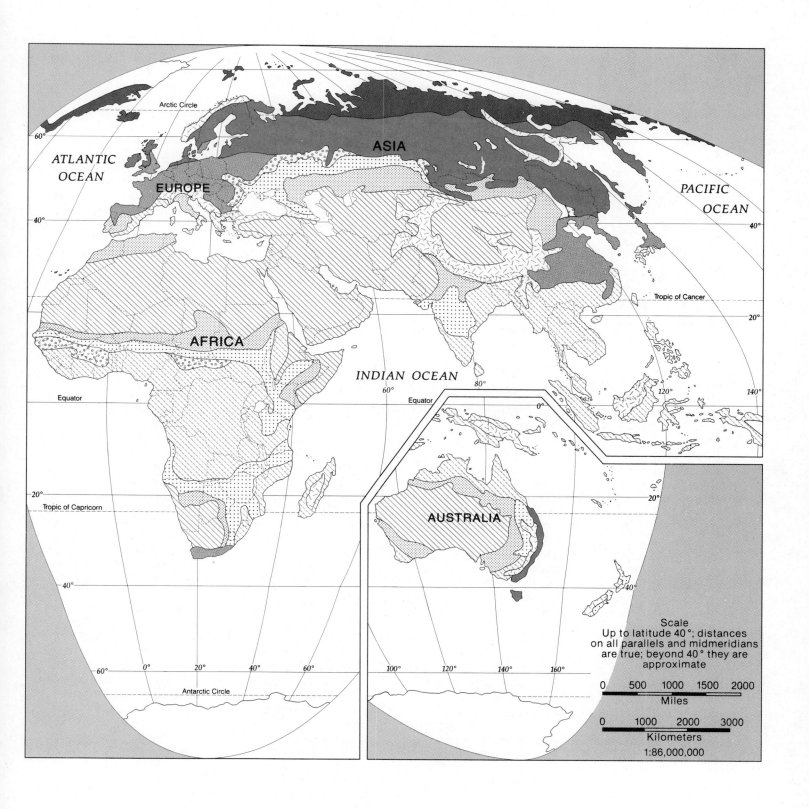

Guest Editorial: Climate and the Human Predicament

Stephen H. Schneider

Stephen H. Schneider is deputy director of the Advanced Study Program at the National Center for Atmospheric Research in Boulder, Colorado. He is editor of the interdisciplinary, international journal Climate Change. *He has testified before various congressional committees on the issues of climatic change, food production, energy use, water supply, and weather control, and has served on the Carter-Mondale task force on science policy and on the Colorado Drought Council, which coordinated responses to the drought in Colorado in 1977. In addition to publishing scores of scientific articles, he is co-author of* The Genesis Strategy: Climate and Global Survival *(1976, New York: Plenum Press) and* The Primordial Bond: Exploring Connections Between Man and Nature Through the Humanities and Sciences *(1981, New York: Plenum Press). Stephen Schneider is one of the new breed of highly competent scientists who combine humane concern with the ability to tackle important interdisciplinary problems.*

Climatic change is an important component of the human predicament—the problems of food, population, resources, and environment. But what really is the climate problem and what should we be doing about it? Some talk about famine from climatic change, while others speak of wheat gluts from good weather. Much has also been written recently about such conflicting possibilities as the melting of the ice caps due to the "greenhouse effect," caused by air pollution and the triggering of a new ice age from dust and smoke. All this climatic confusion makes it very difficult to sort out a real message.

However, there is no single underlying climatic problem or message, but a series of them. In the short term, the main problem is to insure that our society is not too vulnerable to the fluctuations in climate that have wreaked havoc on our crops, water supply, and energy demand in the past. For example, in 1972 dramatic fluctuations in food prices and dwindling food reserves took place because of a shortened monsoon season in India, failure of much of the Russian wheat harvest, and failure of the Peruvian anchovy catch. Again in 1974 we suffered from a severe reduction in U.S. food productivity and another shortened monsoon season in India. Food reserves were cut in half, and bloated bodies of spindly-legged children in Africa and India were pictured on the covers of major magazines. "Excess deaths" in Asia were estimated in the millions.

Since 1974 some modest gains in food reserves—mostly in the United States—have led to talk of a "wheat glut." Then in 1979 and 1980 bad harvests once again raised danger signals. It must be recognized that the way to cope with short-term variations in climate is to maintain adequate food reserves and a distribution system that can cope with several climatic "lean years." This is what I have called "the Genesis strategy," after the biblical story of Joseph's advice to the pharaoh to stockpile food after seven fat years as a margin of safety against the possibility of a food shortage. As with food, we also need sufficient water reserves to prevent the kind of rationing that occurred in much of the drought-stricken western United States in 1976 and 1977. Finally, adequate reserves of energy, in particular natural gas, are essential to prevent sharp jumps in temporary unemployment, such as occurred when industrial concerns in a number of states were forced to shut down for lack of natural gas during the winter of 1977.

Another climate problem relates to long-term trends. In particular, the use of fossil fuels—coal, oil, and natural gas—generates pollution by-products such as carbon dioxide (CO_2). For decades carbon dioxide has been building up in the atmosphere, and this buildup can be expected to accelerate over the next several decades as more and more people use more and more fossil fuels. What does this mean climatically? According to theoretical models, the well-known greenhouse effect would lead to a planetary warming, which could be as great as any warming in the last 5,000 years. In the next century, this warming could move grain belts, redistribute rain patterns, and perhaps even change the volume of glacial ice, thus altering the sea level and changing the coastline geography.

The interesting question here is, How do we verify the predictions of the climatic models that suggest such drastic outcomes? Since we have never before experienced such a carbon dioxide buildup, theoretical models are the only way we can estimate the potential effect of this environmental insult. If the models are correct, then it seems urgent that we either slow down the growth rates of industrial society or shift away from fossil fuels to other—preferably renewable—energy sources (all of which have other problems, even if they prove to be economically feasible). Unfortunately, such drastic decisions rest uneasily on climatic models that are far from certain.

We face a difficult choice. We can proceed along the current path merely collecting data by studying the events (as many scientists have suggested we should), or we can begin to implement hedging policies, such as dramatic curbs on the growth rate of energy, strong efforts to increase the efficiency of energy use, and a major attack on the engineering problems that hinder the rapid deployment of one of the safest energy sources, the sun. These are not just technical issues but issues that involve value judgments of whether the risks posed by present climatic trends are justified by the benefits of continuing to use fossil fuels. Clearly, these value judgments must travel through the political process—the choice of what to do in the face of these uncertainties must not be made by technical committees of scientific "experts" but by all those affected, which is everybody.

From this brief discussion, it is clear that our climate problems cannot be divorced from the other human problems of population, food, resources, and environment. The pressures to pollute and thus possibly to change the climate are in direct proportion to population size and life-style demands. The economic and social costs of suddenly slowed growth have to be weighed against the economic and social costs of accelerated growth, which leads to a degraded environment. Perhaps reduced economic growth in the richer countries and temporary economic expansions in the poorer ones—what I have referred to as the "global survival compromise" in *The Genesis Strategy*—would be appropriate.

Whatever growth strategy is chosen, it must be recognized that solutions to the human predicament lie not in one discipline or in one approach. Instead, solutions require a massive interdisciplinary effort that examines global systems as an interconnected group of subsystems and subproblems. Certainly, specialization has its place. Knowledge cannot be integrated into a realistic interdisciplinary approach if that knowledge has not first been obtained from rigorous work by disciplinary experts. Yet the very institutions at the forefront of new knowledge, the universities and academic laboratories, have been among the most resistant to interdisciplinary efforts. While we all face grave potential dangers, we find too many of the very people to whom society often looks for intellectual leadership and nonpartisan advice squabbling over the purity of disciplinary originality rather than looking for ways out of the human predicament. In the meantime, it is my hope that those of you who will make up the next generation of scholars will get your priorities straight in time to make a difference.

Guest Editorial Discussion

1. Stephen Schneider urges that we stockpile large reserves of food to aid starving people in times of famine, while some other scientists argue that we should stop giving away food since it only encourages population growth that in the long run leads to even greater famines. Which of these views do you support? Why?

2. Do you believe that we should shift away from fossil fuels and drastically curtail energy use in order to prevent the potential heating up of the atmosphere several decades from now? Why? How would this affect your life?

3. How would you change the educational process to prepare you to tackle interdisciplinary problems and still provide you with the disciplinary base needed to deal with such problems?

Discussion Topics

1. Distinguish among *ecosystem, ecosphere, population,* and *community,* and give an example of each. Rank them by increasing complexity or level of organization of matter.

2. List the major components of all ecosystems.

3. **a.** How would you set up a self-sustaining aquarium for tropical fish?

   b. Suppose you had a balanced aquarium with a transparent glass top used to seal it. Can life continue in the aquarium indefinitely as long as the sun shines regularly on it?

   c. Which of the following will probably be the limiting factor—the oxygen supply in the air above the water, the original oxygen supply dissolved in the water, or the supply of nitrogen in soil at the bottom?

4. A friend cleans out your aquarium and removes all of the

soil and plants, leaving only the fish and water. What will happen?

5. **a.** A popular bumper sticker asks, "Have you thanked a green plant today?" Give two reasons for thanking a green plant.

   b. Trace back the materials comprising the sticker and see whether the sticker itself represents a sound application of the slogan.

6. **a.** What is a limiting factor?

   b. Give the limiting factor for each of the following: a desert, the open ocean, the arctic tundra, and a tropical rain forest.

7. What might be the limiting factor for the human population on earth? Defend your choice.

8. How can an area have poor weather and a good climate?

9. Explain why lands just beyond some mountain ranges tend to be dry.

10. Explain how plants depend on soil and soil depends on plants.

11. Why is the A-horizon of soil sometimes called the zone of leaching and the B-horizon sometimes called the zone of deposition? What is leached out and what is deposited?

12. What kind of climate, soil, and biome is best for growing wheat? What is best for slash-and-burn agriculture?

Readings

Billings, W. D. 1970. *Plants, Man, and the Ecosystem.* 2nd ed. Belmont, Calif.: Wadsworth. See especially the discussion of biomes in chap. 7.

Clapham, W. B., Jr. 1973. *Natural Ecosystems.* New York: Macmillan. Introduction to ecology at a slightly higher level.

Colinvaux, Paul A. 1973. *Introduction to Ecology.* New York: Wiley. Excellent basic text using the evolutionary approach.

Commoner, Barry. 1970. "The Ecological Facts of Life." In H. D. Johnson, ed., *No Deposit—No Return.* Reading, Mass.: Addison-Wesley. Excellent simplified summary of ecological principles.

Darnell, Rezneat M. 1973. *Ecology and Man.* Dubuque, Iowa: Wm. C. Brown. Outstanding introduction to ecological principles.

Ehrlich, Paul R., Anne H. Ehrlich, and John P. Holdren.

1977. *Ecoscience: Population, Resources and Environment.* San Francisco: Freeman. Superb, more detailed text at a higher level.

Emmel, Thomas C. 1973. *An Introduction to Ecology and Population Biology.* New York: Norton. Another superb introduction.

Kormondy, Edward J. 1976. *Concepts of Ecology.* 2nd ed. Englewood Cliffs, N.J.: Prentice-Hall. First-rate introduction at a slightly higher level.

Krebs, Charles J. 1978. *Ecology.* 2nd ed. Splendid basic text using the evolutionary approach to ecology.

McHale, John. 1970. *The Ecological Context.* New York: Braziller. Superb diagrams and summaries of ecosphere data.

Miller, G. Tyler, Jr. 1972. *Replenish the Earth—A Primer in Human Ecology.* Belmont, Calif.: Wadsworth. Abbreviated version of some of the key material in this book.

Odum, Eugene P. 1971. *Fundamentals of Ecology.* 3rd ed. Philadelphia: Saunders. Probably the outstanding textbook on ecology by one of our most prominent ecologists.

Odum, Eugene P. 1975. *Ecology.* 2nd ed. New York: Holt, Rinehart and Winston. Superb short introduction.

Reid, Keith. 1970. *Nature's Network.* Garden City, N.Y.: Natural History Press. Beautifully done introduction to ecology.

Richardson, Jonathan L. 1977. *Dimensions of Ecology.* Baltimore: Williams & Wilkins. Excellent brief introductory text.

Ricklefs, Robert E. 1976. *The Economy of Nature.* Portland, Ore.: Chiron Press. Beautifully written introduction to ecology at a slightly higher level.

Smith, Robert L. 1976. *The Ecology of Man: An Ecosystem Approach.* 2nd ed. New York: Harper & Row. Probably the best collection of ecological articles with excellent introductory commentaries.

Smith, Robert L. 1980. *Ecology and Field Biology.* 3rd ed. New York: Harper & Row. An excellent basic text in ecology using the ecosystem approach.

Southwick, Charles H. 1976. *Ecology and the Quality of the Environment.* 2nd ed. New York: Van Nostrand Reinhold. Very readable introduction to human ecology.

Sutton, David B., and N. Paul Harmon. 1973. *Ecology: Selected Concepts.* New York: Wiley. Superb self-study guide for the material in this chapter and Chapters 5 and 6.

Watt, Kenneth E. F. 1973. *Principles of Environmental Science.* New York: McGraw-Hill. Outstanding discussion of ecological principles at a higher level.

5

Ecosystem Function: How Do Ecosystems Work?

5-1 Energy Flow and Chemical Cycling

What keeps you, an oak tree, a squirrel, a termite, and other living organisms alive on this relatively small planet hurtling through space at about 107,200 kilometers (66,600 miles) per hour? To survive, you and every other form of life must have an almost continuous *input* of both energy and matter. An oak tree gets its energy directly from the sun, while you and other animals get energy from certain chemicals in your food supply. Merely receiving energy and matter, however, will not keep an organism alive. An *output* of degraded energy (heat) and waste matter must flow from an organism—otherwise it will be drowned in its own waste heat and waste matter. To remain alive, the input and output of energy and matter must be in balance. Thus, *life at the organism level depends on a balanced flow of both matter and energy through the organism.*

Organisms, however, don't live in isolation, as we saw in the previous chapter on ecosystem structure. To get the matter and energy they need, living things must interact with their physical environment and with other organisms. For animals like you this is called breathing, drinking, eating, and reproducing. At the ecosystem and ecosphere levels (Section 4-1), life still depends on energy flow, because according to the second law of energy (Section 3-3), *energy can never be recycled.* As energy flows through an organism, community, ecosystem, or the ecosphere, it is always degraded in quality to less useful heat energy.

Enrichment Studies 2, 3, 4, and 12 are related to this chapter.

Life at the ecosystem and ecosphere levels depends on matter cycling, not on one-way matter flow. The one-way flow of energy through the ecosystem and ecosphere is used to cycle these essential chemicals, as summarized in Figure 5-1. Thus, *while life at the organism level depends on energy flow and matter flow, at the ecosystem and ecosphere levels it depends on energy flow and matter cycling.*

Chemicals must cycle in the ecosphere because no significant amounts of matter enter or leave the earth and because, according to the law of conservation of matter (Section 3-1), we cannot create any new matter or destroy what we have. This means the overall survival of the collection of species in an ecosystem and in the ecosphere requires that certain essential forms of matter, such as water, carbon, oxygen, nitrogen, and phosphorus, be converted from one form to another and thus be cycled.

At the ecosphere level, the chemicals essential for life must be completely cycled. But since the various ecosystems on earth are connected, some matter flows from one ecosystem to another. Considerable chemical cycling, however, must occur in any ecosystem for it to survive. Indeed, in an ecosystem there is almost no such thing as waste matter. One organism's waste or death is another organism's food. If vital chemicals in an ecosystem and in the ecosphere are not cycled or if they are cycled at rates that are too fast or too slow, then individual organisms, groups of organisms, or even all organisms will die.

Thus, we can generally answer the question "What happens in an ecosystem?" by saying that energy flows and matter cycles. These two major ecosystem functions connect the various structural parts of an ecosystem (Section 4-2) so that life is maintained. This relationship between ecosystem structure and ecosystem function is summarized in Figure 5-2.

In the remainder of this chapter we will examine these two functional processes occurring in ecosystems. We will examine energy flow first at the ecosphere level

Figure 5-1 Life on earth depends on the cycling of critical chemicals and the one-way flow of energy through the ecosphere. Dotted lines represent energy flow and solid lines represent chemical cycling.

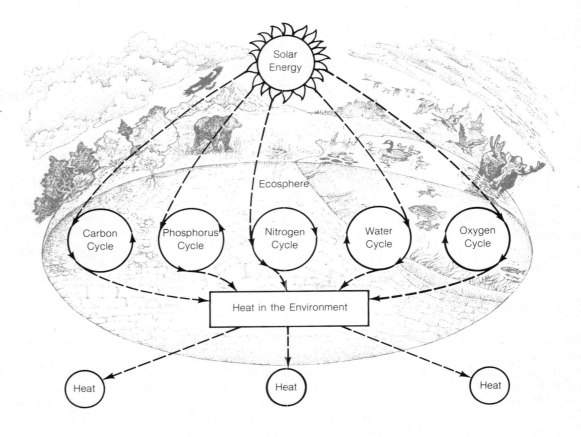

and then at the ecosystem level. This will be followed by a look at how carbon, oxygen, nitrogen, and phosphorus are cycled through ecosystems and the ecosphere in what are called **biogeochemical cycles** (*bio-* for living, *-geo-* for water, rocks, and soil, and *-chemical* for the matter changes involved). Then we will look at an organism's *ecological niche*—a concept that summarizes how an organism participates in energy flow and chemical cycling in an ecosystem. Some of the ways organisms interact with one another as they carry out the processes of energy flow and chemical cycling are discussed in Enrichment Study 4.

5-2 Solar Energy and Global Energy Flow

Solar Electromagnetic Radiation Just as an economy runs on money, an ecosystem, community, or individual organism runs on energy. The source of the energy that sustains all life on earth is the sun. The sun warms the earth and provides energy for photosynthesis in plants, which in turn provides the carbon compounds that feed

all life. Solar energy also powers the water cycle, which purifies and desalinates ocean water to provide the fresh water upon which land life depends.

Only about half of one-billionth of the sun's total radiated energy is intercepted by the earth, a minute target in the vastness of space. The sun's energy comes to us as *radiant energy,* traveling through space at a speed of 300,000 kilometers (186,000 miles) per second. At this speed the light striking your eyes made the 150-million-kilometer (93-million-mile) trip from the sun to earth in about 8 minutes. The visible light we call sunlight is only a tiny part of the wide range, or spectrum, of energies given off by the sun, which is known as the **electromagnetic spectrum** (Figure 5-3). This spectrum of energy ranges from high-energy gamma rays, X rays, and ultraviolet radiation to lower-energy visible, infrared (heat), and radio waves. Each different type of energy in the spectrum can be treated as a wave with a different **wavelength,** the distance between the crest of one wave and the next. High-energy radiation has a short wavelength, whereas low-energy radiation has a long wavelength. The higher-energy, shorter-wavelength rays—gamma rays, X rays, and most ultraviolet rays—are harmful to

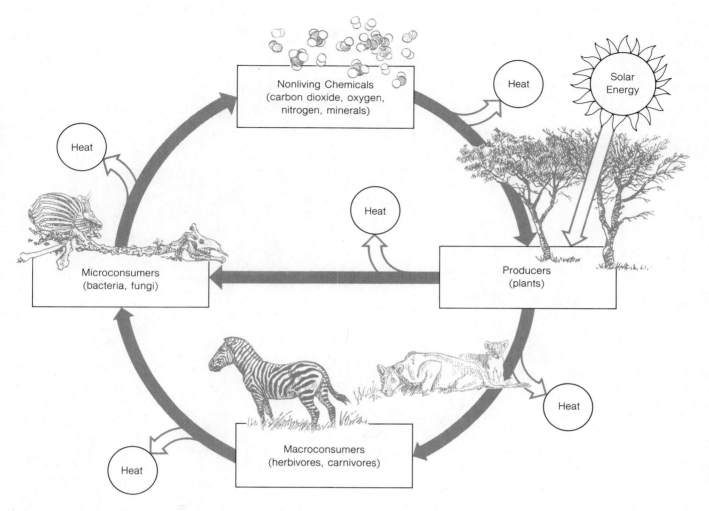

Figure 5-2 A summary of ecosystem structure and function. The major structural components (energy, chemicals, and organisms) of an ecosystem are connected through the functions of energy flow (unshaded lines) and chemical cycling (solid lines).

living organisms. Luckily, most of this harmful radiation is screened out by chemicals in the atmosphere, such as ozone and water vapor. Without this screen almost all life on this planet would be destroyed.

Global Energy Flow   Let's see what happens to the tiny fraction of the sun's total energy output that is intercepted by the earth. As shown in Figure 5-4, about 34 percent of the incoming solar radiation is immediately reflected back to space by clouds, chemicals in the air, dust, and the earth's surface. This reflectivity of the earth and its atmosphere is called the planetary **albedo.** The

remaining 66 percent of the incoming radiation is absorbed by the atmosphere, lithosphere, hydrosphere, and ecosphere systems of the earth (Figure 4-2).

About 42 percent of the incoming solar energy is used to heat the land and warm the atmosphere. Another 23 percent regulates the cycling of water through the ecosphere. Solar energy evaporates water on land, in lakes and rivers, and in the ocean. As this warm, moist air rises in the atmosphere, it expands and cools. This forms clouds, which can release their water as rain, snow, or hail. A tiny fraction (1 percent) of the incoming solar energy is used to generate air currents or winds, which in turn move the clouds and form waves in the

Figure 5-3 The electromagnetic spectrum. The sun radiates a wide range of energies with different wavelengths. Much of this incoming radiation is reflected and absorbed by the earth's atmosphere so that mostly moderate- to low-energy radiation actually reaches the earth's surface.

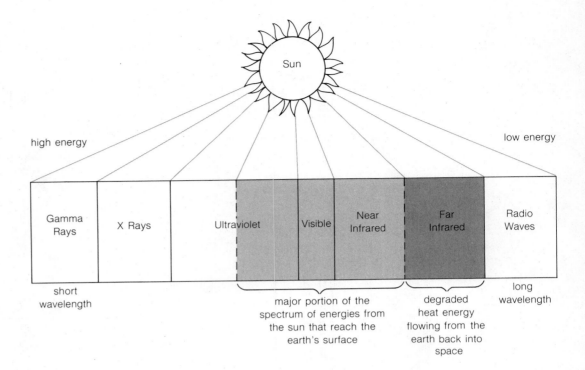

Figure 5-4 The flow of energy to and from the earth.

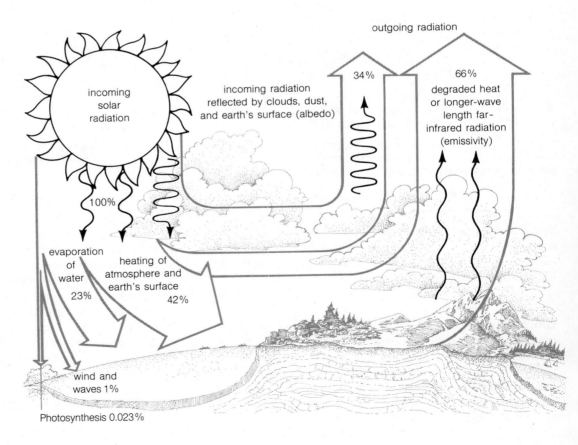

ocean. An even tinier fraction of only 0.023 percent is captured by green plants and converted by photosynthesis to chemical energy in the form of carbohydrates, proteins, and other molecules needed for life.

Almost all of the 66 percent of the solar energy entering the earth's atmosphere, hydrosphere, lithosphere, and ecosphere is degraded into longer-wavelength heat or infrared radiation, in accordance with the second law of thermodynamics (Section 3-3). This heat flows back into space, and the total amount returning to space is called the **emissivity** of the earth. Emissivity is affected by various chemical molecules (such as water, carbon dioxide, and ozone) in the atmosphere. These molecules act as gatekeepers either to allow heat energy to flow back into space or to absorb and reradiate some of the heat back toward the earth's surface.

Usually the amount of heat or infrared radiation emitted by the earth is approximately equal to the 66 percent of incoming solar energy absorbed by the earth. This balance, along with the albedo of the earth, determines the average global temperature. Should something change either the albedo or the emissivity of the earth, the average global temperature would drop or rise to correct the imbalance. For example, a rise of only 2°C in the average global temperature could cause major changes in global weather patterns, and a 3°C to 6°C rise could eventually melt the polar ice caps, thus flooding a large portion of the world. Similarly, a drop of only a few degrees in the average global temperature could trigger an ice age.

Increasing the albedo of the atmosphere could lead to global cooling, whereas decreasing the atmosphere's emissivity could lead to global heating. We know that volcanic eruptions and dust storms can disturb the albedo by injecting tiny particles into the atmosphere. Such particles normally increase the reflectivity of the atmosphere and lead to a drop in average global temperature. There is concern that land-clearing activities and smoke-emitting power and industrial plants may be adding significant amounts of dust and soot particles to the atmosphere.

The atmosphere's emissivity is affected by a number of factors, including the total amount of carbon dioxide gas present. There is concern that the large amounts of carbon dioxide that we add to the atmosphere by burning wood and fossil fuels (oil, coal, and natural gas) could lead to a gradual warming of the atmosphere (the greenhouse effect). A more detailed discussion of whether human activities may be altering global climate is given in Enrichment Study 3.

With this overview of global energy flow, we are now ready to look more closely at how energy flows through ecosystems.

5-3 Energy Flow in Ecosystems: Food Chains, Food Webs, and Energy Productivity

Food Chains   All organisms, alive or dead, are potential sources of food for other organisms. A caterpillar eats a leaf; a robin eats the caterpillar; a hawk eats the robin. When the plant, caterpillar, robin, and hawk die, they are in turn all eaten by decomposers (Figure 5-5). In general, the flow of energy through an ecosystem is the study of who eats or decomposes whom. The general sequence of who eats or decomposes whom is called a **food chain,** or *energy chain.* A food chain involves the transfer of food energy from one organism to another when one organism eats or decomposes another (Figure 5-5). This flow of energy always moves in one direction— from producers to consumers. The various feeding levels of producers and consumers in a food chain are called **trophic levels** (from the Greek *trophikos* for "nourishment" or "food").

The first trophic level in an ecosystem always consists of *producers,* or green plants (and some photosynthesizing bacteria). *Herbivores,* or plant eaters, represent the second trophic level. Because they are the first organisms to feed on other organisms, they are sometimes called *primary consumers.* The third trophic level is composed of *carnivores,* who feed on herbivores. They are often called secondary consumers. The *top carnivores* in a food chain are animals that feed on other carnivores. They represent the fourth and sometimes even the fifth trophic levels and are often called *tertiary* and *quaternary consumers,* respectively. When plants and animals at all trophic levels die, their bodies are broken down by *decomposers,* or *microconsumers.* The early stages of decomposition may be accomplished by millipedes, earthworms, wood lice, and other invertebrates, but the final breakdown of organic compounds into inorganic compounds is accomplished by microorganisms such as fungi, bacteria, and yeast. Some organisms eat from more than one trophic level and are called *omnivores.* When you eat a bacon, lettuce, and tomato sandwich, you are eating three types of producers (lettuce, wheat, and tomato) and one consumer (pig).

Ecologists sometimes distinguish between two major types of food chains in an ecosystem: the grazing

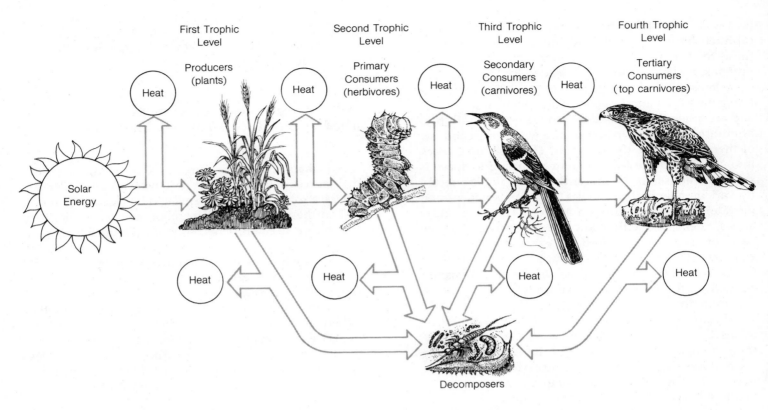

First Trophic Level

Second Trophic Level

Third Trophic Level

Fourth Trophic Level

Producers (plants)

Primary Consumers (herbivores)

Secondary Consumers (carnivores)

Tertiary Consumers (top carnivores)

Heat

Solar Energy

Decomposers

Figure 5-5 A food chain. The arrows show how energy in food chemicals flows through various trophic levels, with some of the energy being degraded to heat in accordance with the second law of thermodynamics.

food chain and the decomposer, or detritus, food chain. In the **grazing food chain,** producers or green plants are eaten by herbivores, which in turn may be eaten by carnivores. In the *decomposer* or **detritus food chain,** plant material from producers is converted to dead organic matter, or *detritus*. Figure 5-6 shows several examples of grazing and decomposer food chains, along with mixed grazing-decomposer food chains. Eventually, of course, all organisms die and become part of the decomposer food chain. Detritus food chains are more common in terrestrial ecosystems (such as forests) and in aquatic ecosystems (such as rivers, streams, and marshes) than in other ecosystem types.

In a land or terrestrial ecosystem, such as a mature forest, only about 10 percent of the living matter produced by trees and plants is eaten by herbivores. The remaining 90 percent of this matter falls to the forest floor as food for decomposers. In aquatic or water ecosystems (Figure 5-6), where phytoplankton (free-floating plants) are the major producers, about 90 percent of the energy flows through the grazing food chain. Figure 5-6 also shows that aquatic food chains often have a larg-

er number of trophic levels, or links, than land-based food chains. Humans can eat plants or animals, but most humans function as herbivores in grazing food chains—getting a worldwide average of 89 percent of their food energy (64 percent in the United States) from vegetables, cereals, and fruits. For more details on how species interact in food chains, see Enrichment Study 4.

Food Chains and the Second Energy Law Because of the second law of thermodynamics (Section 3-3), no transfer of energy from one trophic level to another is 100 percent. In fact, *only about 10 percent of the chemical energy available at one trophic level gets transferred and stored in usable form in the bodies of the organisms at the next trophic level.* In other words, about 90 percent of the chemical energy is degraded and lost as heat to the environment.* This is some-

_____

*Actual percentages vary from 5 to 30 percent with species. Some sulfur bacteria have an energy transfer of only 2 percent. Typically, only 10 percent of the energy entering the plant population is available to herbivores. For warm-blooded carnivores, the conversion efficiency is usually lower than 10 percent, whereas for cold-blooded ones it may be 20 or 30 percent. Ten percent seems a fair average.

times called the **ten percent law.** The percentage transfer of useful energy between trophic levels is called **ecological efficiency,** or *food chain efficiency*. For a striking picture of this loss of usable energy at each step in food chains, look at the **energy pyramid** in Figure 5-7. The size of each compartment shows the usable energy available at each trophic level, and the resulting shape of the trophic levels is that of a pyramid.

We get the same picture if we look at the number of organisms of a particular type that can be supported at

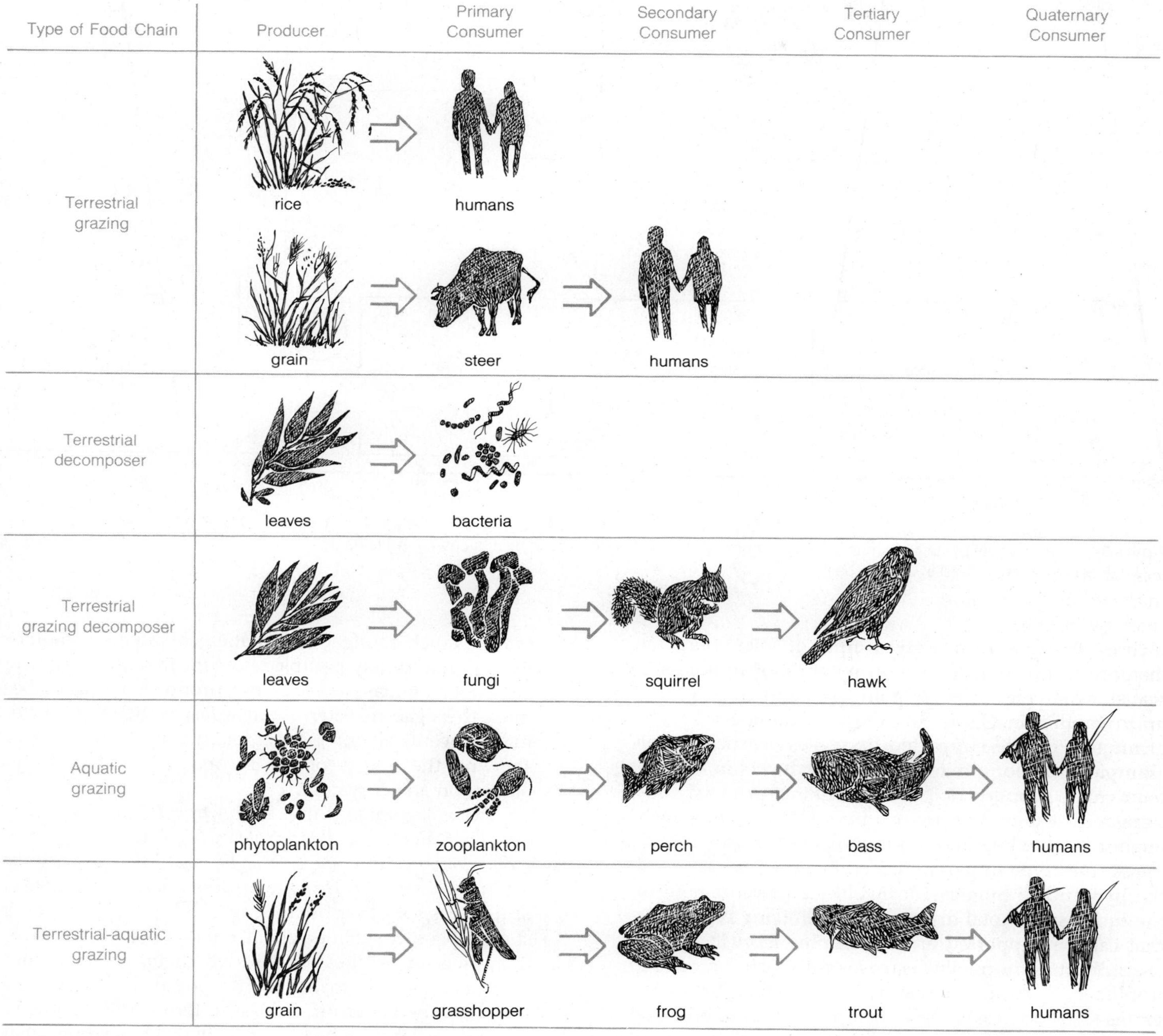

Type of Food Chain	Producer	Primary Consumer	Secondary Consumer	Tertiary Consumer	Quaternary Consumer
Terrestrial grazing	rice	humans			
	grain	steer	humans		
Terrestrial decomposer	leaves	bacteria			
Terrestrial grazing decomposer	leaves	fungi	squirrel	hawk	
Aquatic grazing	phytoplankton	zooplankton	perch	bass	humans
Terrestrial-aquatic grazing	grain	grasshopper	frog	trout	humans

Figure 5-6   Some typical food chains. Upon their death, the plants and macroconsumer animals shown in these simplified chains are broken down by decomposers.

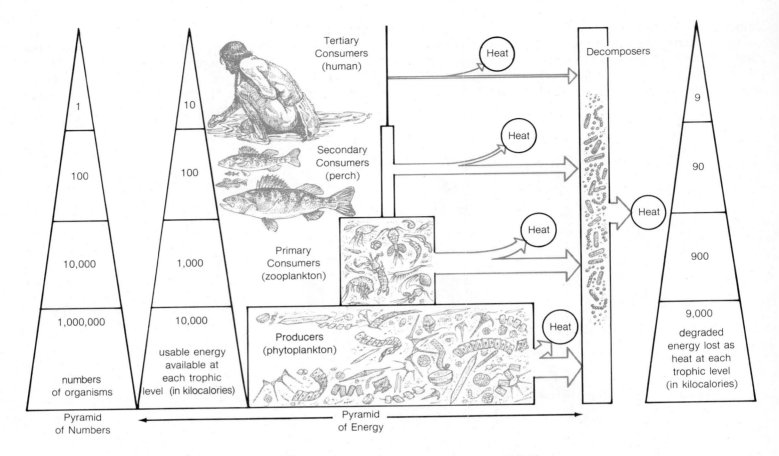

Figure 5-7 Hypothetical pyramids of energy and numbers showing the decrease in usable energy available at each succeeding trophic level in a food chain.

each trophic level from a given input of solar energy at the producer trophic level. This **pyramid of numbers** is also shown in Figure 5-7. In going from one trophic level up to another in Figure 5-7, the total number of organisms that can be supported decreases drastically. For example, a million phytoplankton producers in a small pond may support 10,000 zooplankton primary consumers. These in turn may support 100 perch, which might feed one human for a month or so (Figure 5-7).

A third type of pyramid used by ecologists is called the **pyramid of biomass.** It involves a measurement of the **biomass,** or total dry weight of all living organisms that can be supported at each trophic level in a food chain. Biomass normally decreases with each succeeding trophic level. A plot of pasture may produce 1000 kilograms (2203 pounds) of hay, that can be used to produce 100 kilograms (220 pounds) of cattle meat. This in turn can be used to add 10 kilograms (22 pounds) to a person. But in some ecosystems where tiny producers grow very

rapidly (such as algae in aquatic ecosystems), the biomass pyramid may be upside down. In such cases, the consumer biomass exceeds the producer biomass, because the algae are eaten about as fast as they reproduce. In any event, all three types of pyramids are ways of showing the effects of the second law of thermodynamics on an ecosystem.

Two important principles emerge from the food chain concept. First, all life and all forms of food begin with sunlight and green plants. Second, the shorter the food chain, the less the loss of usable energy. This means that a larger population of humans (or other organisms) can be supported by a shorter plant-based food chain, such as rice ⟶ human, than by a longer meat-based food chain, such as grain ⟶ steer ⟶ human. An overpopulated country or world will be better off, at least in terms of total energy intake, by eating wheat or rice than by feeding such plants to herbivores (with a 90 percent energy loss) and then eating the herbivores (with another 90 percent en-

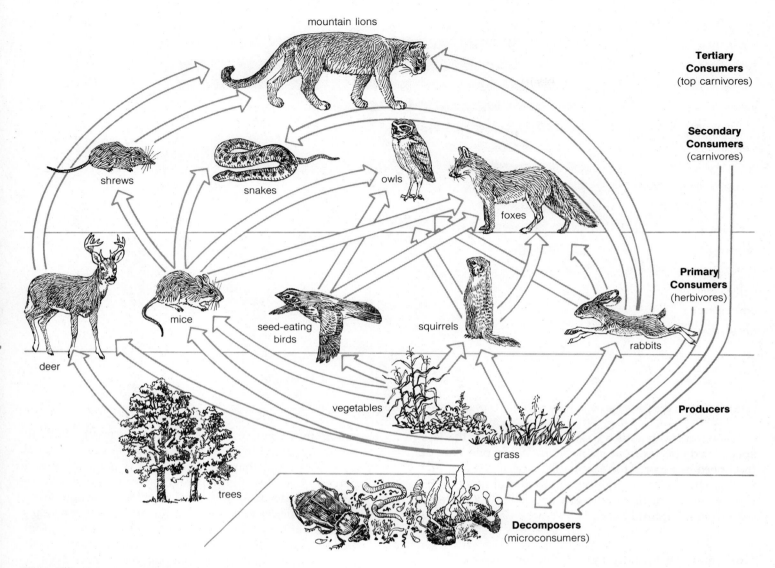

mountain lions

**Tertiary
Consumers**
(top carnivores)

shrews

snakes

owls

foxes

**Secondary
Consumers**
(carnivores)

**Primary
Consumers**
(herbivores)

deer

mice

seed-eating
birds

squirrels

rabbits

vegetables

grass

Producers

trees

Decomposers
(microconsumers)

Figure 5-8   A greatly simplified land food web.

ergy loss). But a diet based on only one or two plants lacks some of the proteins essential for good health, as will be discussed in Chapter 9.

Food Webs   The food chain concept is a very useful tool for tracing out who eats or decomposes whom in an ecosystem. In reality, however, simple food chains, such as those shown in Figure 5-6, rarely exist by themselves. Many animals feed on several different types of food at the same trophic level. In addition, omnivores, such as humans, bears, and rats, can eat several different kinds of plants and animals at several trophic levels. For example, birds that normally eat seeds may switch to in-

sects in the spring. Foxes may gorge themselves on mice when they are abundant, go after rabbits when mice become scarce, eat berries when they are ripe, and switch to grasshoppers and fallen apples in the fall.

Because of these more complex feeding patterns, natural ecosystems consist of complex networks of many interconnected food chains. When we diagram the types of organisms that each kind of organism eats, we get a **food web** (Figure 5-8) instead of a series of linear food chains lying side by side. The real situation in nature is much more complex than that shown in Figure 5-8: We would have to add thousands of other species to Figure 5-8 to show its actual complexity.

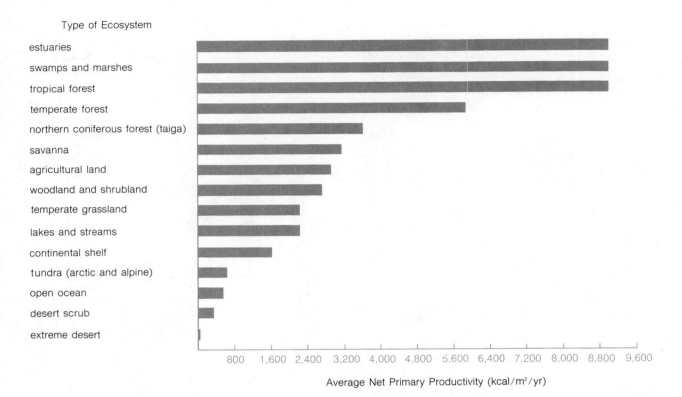

Type of Ecosystem

estuaries
swamps and marshes
tropical forest
temperate forest
northern coniferous forest (taiga)
savanna
agricultural land
woodland and shrubland
temperate grassland
lakes and streams
continental shelf
tundra (arctic and alpine)
open ocean
desert scrub
extreme desert

800   1,600   2,400   3,200   4,000   4,800   5,600   6,400   7,200   8,000   8,800   9,600

Average Net Primary Productivity (kcal/m²/yr)

Figure 5-9   Estimated average net primary productivity by plants in major types of ecosystems.

The food web adds a degree of stability for the less specialized species in an ecosystem. When one type of food becomes scarce for a generalist species, it can survive by shifting to another type of food. For more information on interactions between species in food webs, see Enrichment Study 4.

Gross and Net Primary Energy Productivity by Plants
Green plants use solar energy to make carbohydrates and other organic material. The *rate* at which green plants convert solar energy by photosynthesis into chemical energy or biomass is called the **gross primary productivity**. This is the total rate of photosynthesis and is usually reported in kilocalories of energy produced per square meter per year.* It is also reported in terms of the grams of biomass (plant material) produced per

---

*The joule (abbreviated J and pronounced *jool*) is the standard unit of heat in the metric system of measurement. Other widely used energy units are the kilojoule (kJ), calorie (cal), and kilocalorie (kcal):

1 kJ = 1,000 or 10^3 J
1 cal = 4.186 J
1 kcal = 1,000 or 10^3 cal = 4,186 J

square meter per year. The efficiency of green plants in capturing and converting solar energy to plant material is seldom more than 3 percent and is usually about 1 percent. Even this figure is high, since it applies to ecosystems under favorable conditions. The average gross primary efficiency for the entire ecosphere over a year's time is estimated at only about 0.2 percent. In other words, *about 99.8 percent of the solar energy striking plants each year through the world is not captured by them. Even so, the total amount of energy captured and converted to chemical energy by plants each year is over 400 times the total amount of fossil fuel and nuclear energy used by humans each year.*

Gross primary productivity, however, is not an accurate measure of the amount of energy available to a consumer organism that eats a green plant. Plants and animals must continually break down some of their chemicals to get the energy that they need to stay alive. This process of chemical breakdown to maintain life is called **respiration.** As chemical energy is used for respiration, it is degraded to heat energy, which flows into the environment. Thus, the energy an organism uses for respiration is not available as usable food or chemical energy to an animal that consumes the plant. The *rate* at which plants produce usable food or chemical energy

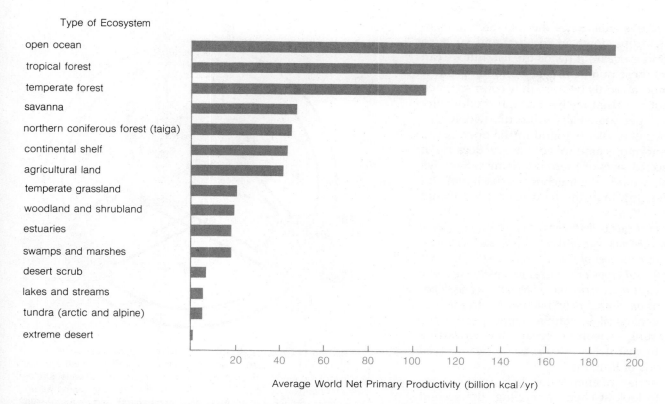

Type of Ecosystem

open ocean
tropical forest
temperate forest
savanna
northern coniferous forest (taiga)
continental shelf
agricultural land
temperate grassland
woodland and shrubland
estuaries
swamps and marshes
desert scrub
lakes and streams
tundra (arctic and alpine)
extreme desert

20   40   60   80   100   120   140   160   180   200

Average World Net Primary Productivity (billion kcal/yr)

Figure 5-10 Estimated average world net primary productivity by plants in major types of ecosystems.

(or usable biomass) is called the **net primary productivity** (usually expressed in kilocalories per square meter per year). It is obtained by subtracting the rate at which plants use energy to stay alive (rate of respiration) from the total rate at which they produce energy (gross primary production):

$$\frac{\text{net primary}}{\text{productivity}} = \frac{\text{gross primary}}{\text{productivity}} - \frac{\text{rate of}}{\text{respiration}}$$

Note that both gross and net primary productivity represent rates at which a certain amount of materials that store chemical energy are produced. They should not be confused with the total amount or yield of energy material.

Ecologists have estimated the average annual net primary production per square meter for different major land and water ecosystems throughout the world, as summarized in Figure 5-9 (see Enrichment Study 2 for a description of the major land ecosystems). From Figure 5-9 we see that the highest net productivities are found in estuaries (the zones where land and ocean meet when rivers flow into the ocean), swamps and marshes, and tropical forests, and the lowest are found in tundra, open ocean, and desert ecosystems.

From Figure 5-9 you might conclude that we should harvest the estuaries, swamps, and marshes and clear the tropical forests and plant there in order to grow more food for the world's growing human population. Such a conclusion is incorrect for two reasons. First, the net primary productivities shown are for the plants normally found in such ecosystems. The plants (mostly grasses) in estuaries, swamps, and marshes are not very useful for direct human consumption, although they are extremely important as food sources and spawning areas for many types of fish, shrimps, and other forms of aquatic life that are important sources of protein for humans. Filling in estuaries, swamps, and marshes destroys a major source of protein that is produced for us free of charge. Similarly, we saw in Figure 4-8 that most of the nutrients in tropical forests are contained in the trees and vegetation rather than in the relatively infertile soil, which has very little humus. Clearing such forests and planting them with crops destroys the high natural net productivity of these systems.

The second reason for caution in evaluating the data in Figure 5-9 is that these numbers do not tell us how much of each ecosystem is available throughout the world. Figure 5-10 shows the world net productivity for major types of ecosystems. Since the total area of estuaries is small, it drops down in the list, and since so much of the world is ocean, it heads the list. But we can also misinterpret these numbers. The world net productivity is high for oceans only because they cover so much of the globe—not because they have a high productivity per square meter per year. Harvesting the widely dispersed algae and other plants found in the open ocean would require enormous amounts of energy. Because of the first and second laws of thermodynamics (Sections 3-2 and 3-3), this would take much more fossil fuel and other types of energy than the food energy we would get.

A basic ecological rule is that crops can normally be grown productively in ecosystems that in their natural state can support a relatively large number of plants similar to the food crop plants. Since most food crops are grasses or closely related to grasses, most agriculture is carried out on temperate grasslands and to some extent on cleared temperate forests. In spite of this important ecological limitation, some people still talk about harvesting algae in the oceans and converting tropical forests to vast fields of corn and wheat to feed the world's billions of humans.

With this overview of energy flow in ecosystems, we are now ready to look at chemical cycling, the second major functional process occurring in ecosystems.

5-4 Chemical Cycling in Ecosystems: The Carbon, Oxygen, Nitrogen, and Phosphorus Cycles

Types of Biogeochemical Cycles   In chemical terms, life can almost be summed up in six words—*carbon, oxygen, hydrogen, nitrogen, phosphorus,* and *sulfur.* Although about 40 of the 92 naturally occurring chemical elements are essential for life, these 6 elements make up over 95 percent of the mass of all living organisms. These 6 plus a few others required in relatively large quantities are called **macronutrients.** Iron, manganese, copper, iodine, and other elements needed in only minute quantities are called **micronutrients.**

Because we have a fixed supply of these six macronutrient elements, they must continuously cycle from their reservoirs of air, water, and soil through the food webs of the ecosphere and back again to their reservoirs. As mentioned earlier, these cyclical movements of materials are called **biogeochemical cycles.** A generalized view of a biogeochemical cycle is given in Figure 5-11.

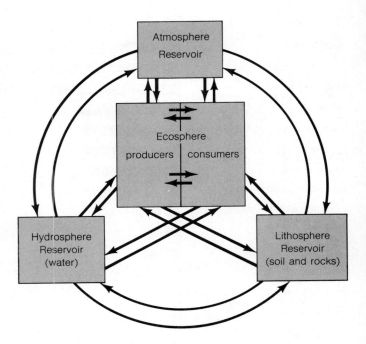

Figure 5-11   A generalized model of a biogeochemical cycle. Various forms of essential life chemicals are stored in the atmosphere, lithosphere, and hydrosphere reservoirs and circulate at various rates from one reservoir to another and through the food chains and webs of plants (producers), animals (macroconsumers), and decomposers (microconsumers) in the ecosphere.

There are three types of these biogeochemical cycles: gaseous, sedimentary, and hydrological (water). The **gaseous cycles,** in which the atmosphere is the primary reservoir, include the *carbon, oxygen,* and *nitrogen cycles.* The **sedimentary cycles** move materials from land to sea and back again. They include the *phosphorus, sulfur, calcium, magnesium,* and *potassium cycles.* The *hydrological cycle*—representing the cycling of water through the ecosphere—is discussed in Chapter 15.

In this section we will look at the carbon, oxygen, nitrogen, and phosphorus cycles. In all chemical cycles, both the nature of the cycling process and the rate at which critical chemicals are cycled are important. For example, all water on earth eventually goes through the photosynthesis process in plants, but at a rate estimated to be once every 2 million years. Similarly, the oxygen gas produced by green plants through photosynthesis cycles about every 2,000 years, and the gaseous carbon dioxide given off by all plants and animals when they break down food molecules by respiration cycles about once every 300 years. Thus, vast quantities of critical chemicals usually remain in their major reservoirs. In contrast, these chemicals flow fairly rapidly from organism to organism. Some effects of human activities on these natural cycles will be discussed in the next chapter.

Gaseous Carbon and Oxygen Cycles   Carbon is the basic building block of the large organic molecules necessary for life. Plants get carbon from the carbon dioxide (CO_2)* that makes up 0.03 percent of the atmosphere and the much larger amount of carbon dioxide dissolved in the waters that cover two-thirds of the earth's surface. Plants use solar energy to combine carbon dioxide with water (H_2O) to form organic carbon, hydrogen, and oxygen food substances such as glucose ($C_6H_{12}O_6$).

---

*Each chemical element is given a symbol, such as C for carbon, O for oxygen, N for nitrogen, and P for phosphorus. Elements exist as **atoms,** which can combine with atoms of other elements to form **molecules.** For example, two oxygen atoms can combine to form an oxygen molecule (O_2), two nitrogen atoms can form a nitrogen molecule (N_2), and two hydrogen atoms can form a hydrogen molecule (H_2). The number of atoms of each kind in a molecule is represented by a subscript. Thus, when one atom of carbon (C) combines with a molecule of oxygen (O_2) to form carbon dioxide, we can represent it in chemical shorthand as CO_2. Similarly, two hydrogen atoms and one oxygen atom can combine to form a water, or H_2O, molecule.

Molecules have no overall electrical charge. But atoms can also combine to form charged species called **ions,** which can have either negative ($-$) or positive ($+$) charges. For example, one nitrogen atom and four hydrogen atoms can combine to form the positively charged ion NH_4^+, which is called the ammonium ion. One nitrogen atom can also combine with three oxygen atoms to form a negatively charged nitrate ion, NO_3^-. Similarly, one phosphorus atom and four oxygen atoms can combine to form a phosphate ion with three negative charges (PO_4^{3-}).

Molecules that contain atoms of carbon and hydrogen (such as the methane, or CH_4, in natural gas), or carbon, hydrogen, and oxygen (such as the sugar glucose, $C_6H_{12}O_6$), or of carbon, hydrogen, oxygen, and nitrogen (such as various complex protein molecules) are called **organic compounds.** All other substances are called **inorganic compounds.**

We also use chemical symbols to represent the substances involved in a chemical reaction. Because of the law of conservation of mass (Section 3-1), we can't create or destroy any new atoms in a chemical reaction. Thus, the number of atoms of each element used as a starting chemical, or reactant, must equal the number of atoms of each element in the products of the reaction. To balance the atoms on each side of a chemical reaction, we must sometimes put numbers in front of one or more of the chemicals. For example, we balance the shorthand version of the reaction of molecular hydrogen and molecular oxygen to form water as follows:

$$H_2 + O_2 \longrightarrow H_2O \text{ (unbalanced)}$$

Two hydrogen atoms plus two oxygen atoms does not equal two hydrogen atoms and one oxygen atom.

$$2H_2 + O_2 \longrightarrow 2H_2O \text{ (balanced)}$$

Four hydrogen atoms plus two oxygen atoms does equal four hydrogen atoms plus two oxygen atoms.

The ultimate source of energy used by all organisms is the sun. A tiny amount (0.023 percent) of the sun's energy flows into food webs through the process of **photosynthesis** that takes place in green plants. This process can be summarized as follows:

$$\text{carbon dioxide} + \text{water} + \text{solar energy} \longrightarrow \text{sugars, such as glucose} + \text{oxygen}$$

$$6CO_2 + 6H_2O + \text{solar energy} \longrightarrow C_6H_{12}O_6 + 6O_2$$

Producers and consumers then transform a portion of the carbon in food back into carbon dioxide and water by the respiration process. The carbon dioxide is then released to the atmosphere. Carbon that is tied up in dead plants and animals is also converted to carbon dioxide by the respiration process in detritus decomposers. This **respiration** process, which provides the energy plants and animals need to live, can be summarized as follows:

$$\text{sugars, such as glucose} + \text{oxygen} \longrightarrow \text{carbon dioxide} + \text{water} + \text{energy}$$

$$C_6H_{12}O_6 + 6O_2 \longrightarrow 6CO_2 + 6H_2O + \text{energy}$$

The photosynthesis and respiration processes both consist of a large number (80 to 100) of different chemical reactions operating in a sequence. However, from the equations just given, we see that the net or overall reaction for the reaction sequence involved in respiration is the opposite of that for the photosynthesis process. Thus, photosynthesis and respiration operate together as a cycle to circulate carbon and oxygen in various chemical forms through ecosystems. By stripping away some of the details, as done in Figure 5-12, we can see more clearly how photosynthesis and respiration work together to cycle carbon and oxygen.

For over 600 million years a small fraction of the organic material from decayed plants and animals has been taken out of the primary cycling path and converted by heat and compression in the earth's crust to fossil fuels (coal, oil, and natural gas) and carbonate rock formations (such as limestone and coral reefs). These fossil fuels, which took millions of years to form, represent a temporary storage of solar energy in concentrated and thus very useful chemical form. Since the industrial revolution, we have been burning fossil fuels at an increasing

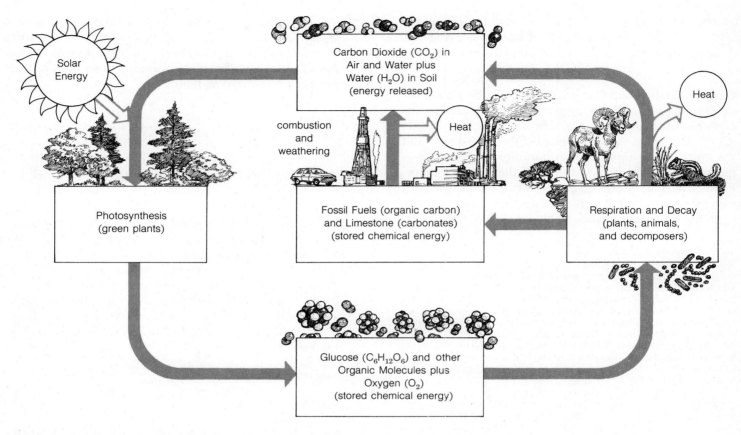

Figure 5-12 A greatly simplified version of the carbon and oxygen cycles, showing chemical cycling (solid lines) and one-way energy flow (unshaded lines).

rate and releasing their carbon, hydrogen, and oxygen back into the atmosphere as carbon dioxide and water. Once used, these concentrated forms of energy are gone forever. Although remaining coal deposits may last several hundred years, affordable supplies of oil and natural gas may be depleted within only a few decades (Chapter 13). The carbon and oxygen tied up in carbonate rock formations are also eventually returned to the normal carbon cycle as carbon dioxide and water as these rocks slowly weather away. The potential impact of human activities on the carbon and oxygen cycles is discussed in the next chapter and in Enrichment Study 3.

Gaseous Nitrogen Cycle As the human population continues to grow, the supply and particularly the distribution of nitrogen become major limiting factors. Many of the body's essential functions require nitrogen-

containing molecules, such as proteins, nucleic acids, vitamins, enzymes, and hormones.

Although molecular nitrogen (N_2) makes up about 78 percent of the earth's atmosphere by volume, most plants and animals can't use it in this gaseous form. Fortunately, over millions of years a natural cycle for converting nitrogen to the right form and circulating it at the right place has evolved. A greatly simplified version of this gaseous biogeochemical cycle is shown in Figure 5-13. Most of the nitrogen in living organisms is not obtained directly from the atmosphere as molecular nitrogen. Instead, nitrogen-fixing bacteria in the soil, blue-green algae in water, and bacteria on pealike nodules on alfalfa, clover, and other legumes (members of the pea family) can convert, or fix, gaseous molecular nitrogen to solid nitrate salts (containing nitrate, or NO_3^-, ions). These nitrate salts dissolve easily in soil water and are taken up by plant roots. The plants then convert the

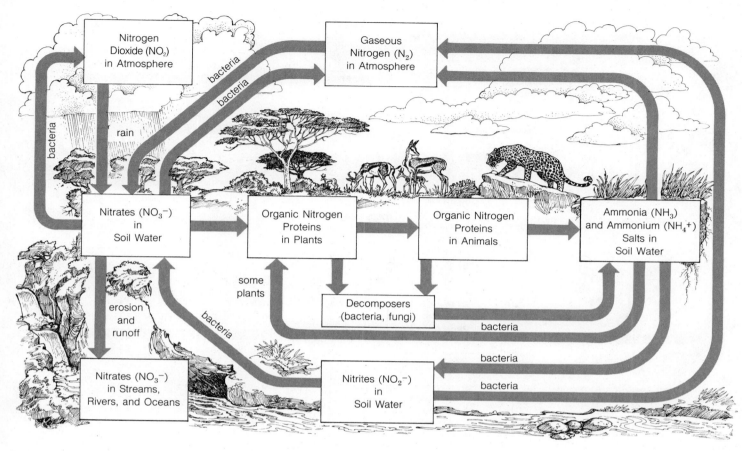

Figure 5-13 A greatly simplified version of the nitrogen cycle (energy flow not shown).

nitrates to large nitrogen-containing protein molecules and other organic nitrogen molecules necessary for life.

When animals eat plants, some of these nitrogen-containing protein molecules are transferred to these animals and eventually to other animals that feed on them. When plants and animals die, decomposers break down these large organic nitrogen molecules into ammonia gas (NH_3) and water-soluble salts containing ammonium ions (NH_4^+). Ammonia and ammonium are then converted by other groups of soil bacteria either into water-soluble nitrite ions (NO_2^-) or back to atmospheric molecular nitrogen or another gas called nitrous oxide (N_2O). Some plants can absorb the ammonium ions from salts dissolved in soil water and convert them to nitrogen-containing protein molecules. Another group of bacteria can add a third oxygen atom to nitrite ions and convert them to nitrate ions, which can be taken up by plants to begin the cycle again. A very small amount of

nitrogen is lost from the cycle when soluble nitrate salts are washed from the soil into rivers and streams and eventually into the oceans.

Ecosystems differ in the amounts of nitrogen retained in the soil. For example, deciduous forests tend to have relatively large amounts of organic nitrogen in their soil because of the large amount of decomposing leaves and other material on the forest floor. In contrast, approximately 70 percent of the nitrogen in deserts is lost to the atmosphere as gaseous ammonia and is not available for plant growth.

Because nitrogen is essential for photosynthesis, the amount of nitrogen, primarily as nitrate and ammonium ions, in the soil can regulate crop growth. During World War I, Fritz Haber, a German chemist, developed an industrial process to convert molecular nitrogen gas by reacting it with hydrogen gas to produce ammonia gas. The ammonia can then be converted to ammonium salts

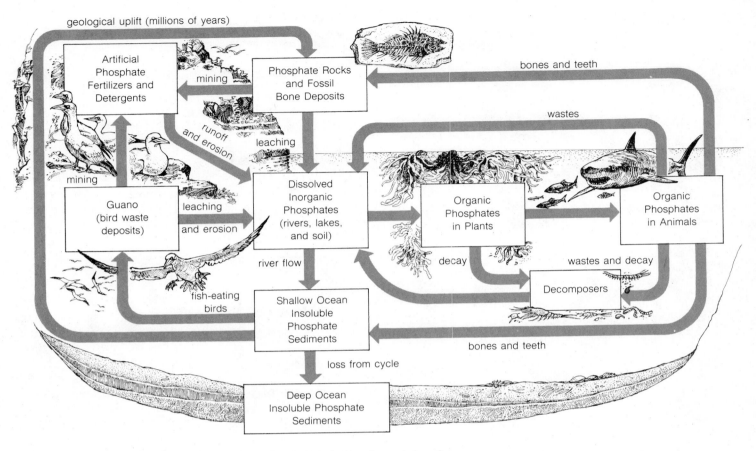

Figure 5-14 A greatly simplified version of the phosphorus cycle (energy flow not shown).

and used as artificial fertilizer. Nitrate salts can also be mined and used along with ammonium salts as artificial fertilizer to increase crop yields in areas with nitrogen-poor soil.

Sedimentary Phosphorus Cycle The phosphorus cycle is a sedimentary cycle in which the earth's crust is the major reservoir (Figure 5-14). Phosphorus is cycled rather rapidly through living organisms (Figure 5-14), where it is an important genetic material (in molecules such as DNA and RNA) and a component of cell membranes, bones, and teeth. Some phosphate rock (containing PO_4^{3-} ions) is dissolved in water in the soil. The roots of plants can absorb the phosphate ions and when the plant is eaten the phosphorus is passed on to animals. It eventually returns to the soil, rivers, and oceans as animal wastes and decay products.

Phosphorus is cycled slowly from the land to the sea and back to the land. The major reservoirs of phospho-

rus are phosphate rock formations in the earth's crust. Slowly, through weathering and erosion, phosphorus washes into rivers and eventually to the oceans. Most of this phosphorus forms insoluble deposits on the bottom of shallow ocean areas near the coast. After millions of years of buildup, these deposits are raised into mountains by geological uplifting, and the cycle can begin again. Unfortunately, some phosphorus is also deposited in deep ocean sediments. For all practical purposes, these phosphorus deposits represent permanent leaks from the phosphorus cycle.

Because geological uplifting is so slow, phosphorus is being washed into the sea faster than it is being returned to land. Our fish catches return some 54 million kilograms (60,000 tons) of phosphorus per year, and the phosphorus-rich waste deposits of fish-eating birds, such as pelicans, gannets, and cormorants, return another 3,100 million kilograms (350,000 tons) of phosphate wastes, called *guano*, to the land each year. But the returns of phosphorus to the land are small compared with the larger amounts of phosphorus that erode from the land to the oceans each year. The cutting of forests and other human land-clearing activities accelerate these natural erosion losses.

About 1.8 billion kilograms (2 million tons) of phosphorus are mined each year in the United States (especially Florida) to produce fertilizer to replace phosphates lost from farmland and lawns. In turn, some of this is eroded away, further hastening the loss of phosphorus to the oceans. Phosphorus, more than any other element, can become the limiting factor (Section 4-3) for plant growth in a number of ecosystems. The world as a whole will not run out of phosphorus for a long, long time, but local and regional shortages already exist and could get worse unless we learn how to work with rather than against this vital chemical cycle.

5-5 Ecological Niches

The Niche Concept Now that the overall patterns of energy flow and chemical cycling in an ecosystem have been described, let's look more closely at the role that individual species or populations of organisms play in carrying out these processes. The **ecological niche** is a description of a species' total structural and functional role in an ecosystem. It includes not only the habitat or physical space where a species lives, but also what the species does in the ecosystem—how it transforms matter and energy, and how it responds to and modifies its physical and biotic environment. A common analogy is that habitat refers to an organism's "address" in an ecosystem and that the ecological niche is an organism's "life-style" in an ecosystem.

The ecological niche, then, includes all of the physical, chemical, and biological factors that a species needs to survive and reproduce in an ecosystem. To describe a species' niche we must know what it eats and what eats it, where it leaves its wastes, the ranges of temperature, wind, shade, sunlight, and various chemicals it can tolerate, the nature and range of its habitat, its effects on other species and on the nonliving parts of its environment, and what effects other species have on it. Obviously, we can never know everything about the niche of any plant or animal.

Different species may live together in the same habitat yet have quite different ecological niches. If you examine a tidal pond near the ocean, you may find species of microscopic algae, starfish, and other organisms all living together. Yet the algae act as producers and the starfish as consumers—thus they occupy different niches.

Some niches, such as those occupied by producers or green plants, are so basic that they are found in every major ecosystem. Others, especially those for some animal and decomposer species, may be highly specialized. For example, the niche of some birds involves eating various parasites and ticks that are found on or near animals. In Africa, egrets catch insects near elephants, and in England, the starling picks ticks off of sheep and deer. Other niches are limited by physical conditions. In moist soils, earthworms mix humus, and their burrowing loosens and aerates the soil. In dry soils, where earthworms can't exist, this ecological niche is taken over by burrowing ants.

In general, no two species in the same ecosystem can occupy *exactly* the same ecological niche indefinitely. Generally, the more similar the niches of two species are, the more they will compete for the same food, shelter, space, and other critical resources. When two species try to occupy the same niche, one of the species will probably have to move, switch its habits, or become extinct, as discussed in more detail in Enrichment Study 4. Different species, however, can occupy the same or similar ecological niches in similar ecosystems located in different parts of the world. Such species are called **ecological equivalents.** Grasslands, for example, are found all over the world. The niche of grassland grazers can be occupied by bison and pronghorn antelope in North America, wild horses and the saga antelope in Eurasia, kangaroos in Australia, and antelope and zebras in Africa. In many regions, a number of these ecologically equivalent herbivores have been replaced by domesticated cattle and sheep.

Knowing the niches of species can help ecologists predict what might happen if some new factor is added to or eliminated from a given ecosystem—if heated water from a nuclear power plant is added to an aquatic ecosystem, for example, or if a new species is introduced or an existing species eliminated or driven out.

Ideally, in any ecosystem, no foreign species or new physical or chemical factor should be introduced or purposefully eliminated without careful study of how the change could affect the various niches in that ecosystem. Even careful study is not always enough, for in its new habitat an organism may change its nesting or feeding habits. If it has no predators or parasites, its population could explode and it could become a pest. In practice, however, many organisms have been carried from continent to continent and to and from various islands, some intentionally and some accidentally. Many of these have become pests or unwanted species, but a few are beneficial (see Enrichment Study 12). For more information on interactions of species, see Enrichment Study 4.

Our Ecological Niche What niche do human beings occupy? Most plants and animals are limited to specific habitats in the ecosphere because they can tolerate only a narrow range of climatic and other environmental conditions. But some species, such as flies, cockroaches, mice, and humans, are very adaptable and can live over much of the planet and eat a wide range of foods.

Thus, humans occupy a generalist niche. In addition to an array of food energy sources, humans have also been able to tap into solar energy stored millions of years ago as chemical energy in deposits of coal, oil, and natural gas. With this fossil fuel energy subsidy, as well as other forms of energy such as draft animals and nuclear and geothermal energy, humans have been able to great-

ly expand their habitat and niche on a global scale. This has led to many benefits. At the same time, this ever increasing use and flow of energy through industrialized societies is a major factor in today's environmental crisis (Section 3-4).

In this chapter and the preceding one, we have seen that the essential feature of the living and nonliving parts of an ecosystem is their interdependence. In the next chapter we shall see that this interdependence is a key to understanding how ecosystems can change in response to stresses from natural and human sources. In the Guest Editorial that follows Eugene P. Odum discusses the importance of ecology.

We cannot command nature except by obeying her.
Sir Francis Bacon

Guest Editorial: Ecology: A New Integrative Discipline

Eugene P. Odum

Eugene P. Odum is director of the Institute of Ecology; Alumni Foundation Distinguished Professor of Zoology; and Callaway Foundation Professor of Ecology at the University of Georgia. Dr. Odum has served as president of the Ecological Society of America (1964–1965) and received its Eminent Ecologist Award in 1974. In 1975 he and his brother Howard T. Odum (see his Guest Editorial at the end of Chapter 13) jointly received the international scientific prize awarded by the French L'Institut de La Vie—a prize considered equivalent to a Nobel Prize. In 1977 he

received ecology's highest honor, the Tyler Ecology Award, and then gave the entire $150,000 stipend to the University of Georgia's Institute of Ecology for use in training young ecologists. His textbook, Fundamentals of Ecology, *has been one of the most widely used introductory ecology texts since it was first published in 1953. He was one of the first professional ecologists to integrate scientific, sociological, political, economic, and ethical factors.*

During the 1970s the discipline of ecology emerged from its roots in biology to become a new integrative discipline that links the natural and social sciences. This transformation comes in part from an increasing general public awareness that the major problems of society must now be assessed and managed on a more holistic and a more global basis rather than piecemeal, as has been the custom for so long. In other words, to cope with today's real world of energy and resource shortages, an increasing gap between the rich and the poor, and other dilemmas, we must consider the whole forest, not just the individual trees.

Another factor responsible for the emergence of a new ecology is the increase in research at the ecosystem level of organization, which has benefited from new technology drawn from both the biological and physical sciences. Also, attempts to deal with atomic energy made bedfellows of ecologists, geologists, chemists, and physicists and resulted in exchanges of ideas, philosophies, and technology to the benefit of all. Thus, although the problems of harnessing atomic energy are very far from being solved, the interplay of different disciplines has contributed considerable vigor to the entire field of environmental science.

Perhaps the greatest need and thus the greatest challenge for the next decade or so is to build a bridge between ecology and economics. The terms *ecology* and *economics* come from the same Greek root *oikos* (meaning "household"); *ecology* literally translates as the "study of households" and *economics* as the "management of households." Accordingly, the two disciplines should be complementary, but as we all know, the public views them as poles apart at best.

And there is a deep philosophical gap between professional economists and ecologists that hampers attempts to achieve long-range solutions to our most recalcitrant problems. Economists have concentrated their attention in both theory and practice on human-made goods and services while largely classing the equally important life-support goods and services of nature (such as air and water purification and recycling) as "externalities" not to be included in the mainstream of economic benefits and costs. Economists too often assume that new technology can always find a substitute for any depleted resources. Ecologists, on the other hand, have too often retreated behind a kind of wilderness ethic that assumes that all human activities are detrimental to the environment. Ecologists also often underestimate the capacity of humans to repair and improve the biosphere.

The credibility gap here is essentially one between market values (that is, priced goods and services) and nonmarket values (unpriced goods and services)—or, in other words, between the private and the public good. Fortunately, some economists are now trying to build a bridge from their side of the bank by considering ways to internalize the externalities. At the same time, some ecologists are seeking to find common denominators (such as energy) that can be used to assess both market and nonmarket values so that preservation of the earth's life-support system (for which there is no technological substitute) can be an integral part of economic decision making.

It will be up to the coming generations of students of the *oikos*—the whole household of humans and nature—to complete this difficult bridge if the quality of future life is to be preserved.

Guest Editorial Discussion

1. What is an externality (see Section 18-3)? List some externalities not included in the price of an automobile.

2. What are some of the dangers of not building a bridge between economics and ecology? Why hasn't this been done sooner?

3. Professor Odum states that ecologists "often underestimate the capacity of humans to repair and improve the biosphere." Can you give any examples illustrating the repair and improvement of the biosphere by humans?

Discussion Topics

1. Explain how the survival of an individual organism depends on energy flow and matter flow, whereas the ecosystem in which it lives is able to survive only by energy flow and matter cycling.

2. Why can't energy be recycled in an ecosystem?

3. What effect, if any, can each of the following activities have on the global heat balance, or average temperature of the earth's atmosphere?

   a. air conditioning operated by electricity

   b. driving a car

   c. using aerosols that contain fluorocarbons

   d. a nuclear power plant

4. Would you rather be exposed to electromagnetic radiation with a short or long wavelength? High or low frequency? Explain why people who spend a lot of time getting suntans may get skin cancer.

5. Draw a diagram showing the major features of the heat or energy budget of the earth. List four human activities that can upset this balance.

6. Using the second law of thermodynamics, explain why there is such a sharp decrease in usable energy along each step of a food chain. Doesn't an energy loss at each step violate the first law of thermodynamics? Explain.

7. Using the second law of thermodynamics, explain why people in the poorer nations of the world must exist primarily on a vegetarian diet. (A detailed discussion of this topic is found in Chapter 9.)

8. Explain why a balanced vegetarian diet is sound ecological practice. Trace the effects of vegetarianism on the carbon, oxygen, and phosphorus cycles and on global heat balance.

9. Distinguish between a pyramid of numbers, a pyramid of biomass, and a pyramid of energy. How does the inefficiency of energy transfer affect the number of humans that can be supported in a more developed country such as the United States? In a less developed country?

10. What did you have for lunch or supper today? Trace each of these foods back through the food chain and through the carbon and oxygen cycles. What effect does growing and eating these foods have on the global heat balance?

11. Explain why you should thank the sun and green plants every day.

12. Explain the usefulness of food chains and food webs in understanding ecosystems.

13. Why is the net primary productivity of a forest lower than its gross primary productivity? Give the two types of ecosystems with the highest net primary productivity and the two with the lowest.

14. a. It has been proposed that we clear the lush tropical rain forests and convert them to modern farmlands. What might happen?

    b. Explain how the extensive draining, filling, dredging, building, and polluting of estuaries, marshes, and swamps can decrease the ability of the planet to support its human population.

    c. Criticize the statement that we can farm the sea to feed our increasing population. (See Chapter 9 for a detailed discussion of this question.)

15. What effect does each of the following have on the carbon and oxygen cycles?

    a. using fossil fuels to provide air conditioning

    b. using a light or any electrical appliance (trace electricity from the wall plug back to its source)

    c. driving an automobile or motorcycle

    d. making an automobile

16. When you "throw away" your trash, where does it go? Trace it through the carbon, oxygen, and nitrogen cycles.

17. What effect does fertilizing a lawn or eating a meat-based diet have on the carbon, oxygen, nitrogen, and phosphorus cycles?

18. Explain how the carbon and oxygen cycles are linked together.

19. Why is phosphorus more often a limiting factor in ecosystems than oxygen, nitrogen, or carbon?

20. How does a species' habitat differ from its ecological niche? Give four examples of ecological equivalents.

21. Compare the ecological niches of humans in a small town and in a large city; of humans in a more developed country and in a less developed country.

Readings

See Readings for Chapter 4.

6

Changes in Ecosystems:
What Can Happen to Ecosystems?

When we try to pick out anything by itself we find it hitched to everything else in the universe.
John Muir

Many people think "balance of nature" means that ecosystems do not change. Nothing could be further from the truth. *Ecosystems are dynamic.* They contain organisms that, by their very presence, change local conditions. The organisms may then be forced to change or die in response to the new conditions that they themselves have created. Or their environment may change because of fires, floods, drought, volcanic eruptions, erosion, climatic shifts, earthquakes, or human influences (farming, industrialization, pollution, or urbanization). Although ecosystems are always changing, they do show a certain stability—the ability to tolerate or resist changes by outside influences or to restore themselves after an outside disturbance. If Robin Hood were alive today, he would still find a Sherwood Forest (though much smaller), and he would still recognize most if not all of the kinds of plants and trees growing there. This ability to adapt and yet maintain an overall stability if not pushed too far is truly a remarkable feature of ecosystems. Indeed, if most ecosystems were not so adaptable, we would not be here today. In this chapter we will look first at how ecosystems evolve and change normally without human influence and then at some human influences on ecosystems.

6-1 Ecological Succession:
Immature and Mature Ecosystems

Succession: Immature and Mature Ecosystems A tropical rain forest, an oak-hickory forest, or a coral reef ecosystem does not spring full-blown from the ground or sea bottom. It develops over decades or centuries, starting when a simple community of pioneer species (such as lichens or weeds) takes over a patch of the earth's surface. These pioneers are slowly joined and then mostly replaced by other species to form a new community as the ecosystem matures. This repeated replacement of one kind of community of organisms by another, usually more diverse community of organisms over a period of time is called **ecological succession.**

If not severely disrupted by natural disasters or by human activities, most ecosystems eventually reach a stage that is much more stable than those that preceded it. This is sometimes called a **climax ecosystem,** or *climax community,* although many ecologists prefer the term *mature* to *climax.* With a more diverse array of species and ecological niches, a mature ecosystem can use energy and cycle critical chemicals more efficiently than simpler, more immature ecosystems. A mature ecosystem is thus able to absorb or tolerate a number of stresses that would destroy a younger ecosystem. Consequently, mature ecosystems tend to be self-perpetuating and may last for centuries so long as climate and other major environmental factors remain essentially the same. But natural disasters and human intrusions are always happening. Thus no place on earth supports a climax ecosystem forever, and some places never even reach a mature stage.

Immature and mature ecosystems have strikingly different characteristics, as summarized in Table 6-1. Note from Table 6-1 that in a young ecosystem the emphasis is on rapid growth or high productivity at the expense of efficiency. Large amounts of energy flow through the system and are used inefficiently with very little matter being recycled. The young, pioneering ecosystem spreads out rapidly to fill up existing space and contains fairly simple food webs made up mostly of producers. By contrast, a mature ecosystem has low productivity and high efficiency in the use of energy and recycling of matter. Matter and energy go primarily into maintaining existing structures and connecting the dif-

Enrichment Studies 1, 3, 5, 6, 11, 12, and 16 are related to this chapter.

Table 6-1 Characteristics of Ecosystems at Immature and Mature Stages of Ecological Succession

Characteristic	Immature Ecosystem	Mature Ecosystem
Ecosystem Structure		
Plant size	Small	Large
Gross primary productivity	High and rapidly increasing	Low and stable
Net primary productivity	High and rapidly increasing	Zero
Species diversity	Low	High
Living organic matter (biomass)	Small	Large
Nonliving organic matter (detritus)	Small	Large
Plant growth pattern	Dispersed	Crowded
Community diversity (ecological niches)	Few, mostly generalized	Many, mostly specialized
Trophic structure	Mostly producers	Balance of producers, consumers, and decomposers
Community organization (number of interconnecting links)	Low	High
Energy Flow		
Plant growth rate	Rapid	Slow
Net primary productivity	High	Low
Efficiency of energy use	Low	High
Food webs	Simple, mostly grazing	Complex, mostly detritus
Chemical Cycling		
Type of cycle	Open	Closed
Rate of matter cycling	Rapid	Slow
Efficiency of matter cycling	Low	High
Role of decomposers	Unimportant	Important

ferent parts of the system instead of going into high productivity. Mature ecosystems also have a greater variety of producers, consumers, and decomposers interconnected by elaborate food webs than immature ecosystems.

An immature ecosystem operates on the principle of haste makes waste. The emphasis is on taking over an area and filling it up with rapidly growing pioneer species. By contrast, in a mature ecosystem haste is reduced in order to cut down on waste. This is the principle that human society must use to make the transition from the present frontier (or haste makes waste society) to a sustainable earth society built on reducing the haste or rates of matter and energy flow through society to reduce the rate of waste or entropy buildup in the environment (Section 3-4).

Types of Succession Ecologists recognize two types of ecological succession—primary and secondary. The type that takes place depends on the soil conditions present at the beginning of the process. **Primary succession** occurs in a soilless area where no living community has existed before or where there are no remaining traces of organic matter in the soil or rock from an earlier living community. In other words, the community must start from scratch. Examples of such areas are newly exposed bare rocks from retreating glaciers, cooled volcanic lava, and newly exposed sand dunes. On such barren surfaces, primary succession from bare rock to a mature forest may take hundreds of thousands of years. A more common form of succession is **secondary succession,** which occurs when an ecosystem at some stage of succession is removed or partially destroyed and thus set back to an earlier stage of succession. In this case soil is present so that new vegetation can sprout within a few weeks. Examples include succession on abandoned farmland, forests that have been burned or cut, new ponds that are abandoned, and heavily polluted streams. Let's look at some examples of primary and secondary succession.

exposed rocks   lichens and mosses   small herbs and shrubs   heath mat   jack pine, black spruce, and aspen   balsam fir, paper birch, and white spruce climax community

Figure 6-1 Primary ecological succession on Isle Royale in northern Lake Superior over several hundred years.

Primary Succession During the early part of this century, William S. Cooper was able to trace the stages of primary succession from bare rock to a mature ecosystem on Isle Royale in northern Lake Superior (Figure 6-1).

First, retreating glaciers exposed bare rock. Wind, rain, and frost weathered the rock surfaces to form tiny cracks and holes. Water collecting in these depressions slowly dissolved minerals out of the rock's surface. These minerals were able to support hardy pioneer plants, such as lichens and mosses. Gradually these early invaders covered the rock surface, dissolving additional minerals from the rock and depositing organic matter from their dead bodies. Decomposer organisms then moved in to feed on the dead lichens and mosses and were followed by a few small animals such as ants, mites, and spiders. This first combination of plants, animals, and decomposers is called the *pioneer community*.

After many years, the pioneer community built up enough organic matter in the thin soil to support the roots of small herbs and shrubs such as bluebell, yarrow, bearberry, blueberry, and juniper. These newcomers slowed down the loss of moisture and provided food and cover for new plants, animals, and decomposers. Under these new conditions, the pioneer species were crowded out. This illustrates a major feature of terrestrial succession: Organisms at one stage of succession change the environment so that it becomes less favorable for them and more favorable for a different type of community.

As this new community thrived, it added further organic matter to the slowly thickening crust of soil. This led to the next stage of succession, a compact layer of vegetation called a heath mat. This mat, in turn, provided a thicker and richer soil needed for the germination and growth of trees such as jack pine, black spruce, and oc-

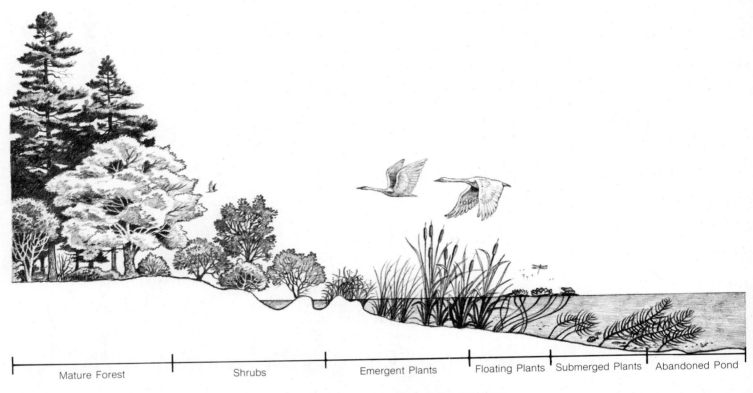

Figure 6-2 Secondary ecological succession on an abandoned farm pond over several hundred years.

casionally aspen. Over several decades these trees increased in height and density, and the plants of the heath mat were crowded out. The shade and other conditions created by these trees allowed the germination and growth of other taller trees such as balsam fir, paper birch, and white spruce. These trees grew through the earlier forest and created shade and other conditions that eliminated most of the earlier trees. After several centuries, what was once bare rock became a mature or climax ecosystem. It has a variety of plant and animal life and can make such efficient use of matter and energy that it is stable and self-perpetuating if not severely disturbed.

Secondary Succession Suppose a farmer creates a pond and then later abandons it. Figure 6-2 shows one way in which such a pond undergoes succession. Succession begins with open water and a community of plankton (tiny floating plants). As time passes, the pond slowly fills with dead plankton and with sediment or silt, which erodes from the surrounding land. The decrease in water depth and the increase in bottom sediments first allows submerged plants (such as musk grass) and then floating plants (such as water lilies) to colonize the pond. Note that these new stages of succession in an aquatic ecosystem are not brought about by organisms primarily but by the physical change of erosion. This is a typical difference in succession between aquatic ecosystems and terrestrial ecosystems. The pond continues to fill with sediment and dead organic matter and is eventually shallow enough to support emergent plants, such as cattails, sedges, and rushes. What was once a pond becomes a swamp. In a moist, temperate climate, alders and willow shrubs can then take hold as sediments build above the water level. This changes the soil and other conditions so that taller silver maples, red maples, white pines, and elms take over. In a drier climate the result might be a prairie rather than a forest.

Figure 6-3 shows a secondary succession that occurs when land in an oak-hickory forest in the eastern United States is cleared, used to grow corn, and then abandoned

canopy

lower
canopy trees

understory
trees

tall shrub
understory

low shrub
ground layer

Annual
Weeds

Perennial Weeds
and Grasses

Shrubs

Young Pine Forest

Mature Oak-Hickory
Forest Ecosystem

Figure 6-3 Secondary ecological succession on an abandoned farm field over about 150 years.

after harvesting. The abandoned field already has a thick layer of soil so that the early stages of primary succession are not necessary. The bare field is quickly covered with crabgrass in the fall. In the spring horseweed takes over. During the summer the field is invaded by white aster plants. After 2 or 3 years, enough organic matter in the soil has built up to support a perennial grass such as broom sedge. As dead plants and other debris accumulate, decomposers thrive and build up the rich layer of soil needed for pine trees to germinate. Pine seedlings invade the broom sedge, grow within 5 or 10 years to the low-shrub stage, and begin to shade out the broom sedge. Over the years the pines grow, and the shade that they provide does not allow new pine seedlings enough light to survive. In time hardwood species such as red gum, red maple, black oak, and hickory begin growing under the pines. These new species have long tap roots and can obtain moisture unavailable to the shallow-rooted pines. Over about 150 years these hardwoods, especially oak and hickory, grow up through the pines; eventually the pines die out in the shade. Other shade-

tolerant trees and shrubs, such as dogwood, sourwood, and redbud, fill in the understory below the canopy of oak and hickory trees. We now have a mature oak-hickory deciduous forest.

6-2 Stability in Living Systems

What Is Stability? Organisms, populations, communities, and ecosystems all have some ability to withstand or to recover from externally imposed changes or stresses. In other words, they have some degree of **stability.** It is useful to distinguish between two aspects of stability—inertia and resilience. **Inertia** refers to the ability of an ecosystem (or any system) to resist being disturbed or altered. **Resilience** refers to the ability of an ecosystem (or any system) to restore its structure and function following a natural or human-induced stress. Nature is remarkably resilient. For example, (1) human societies have survived natural disasters and devastating wars; (2)

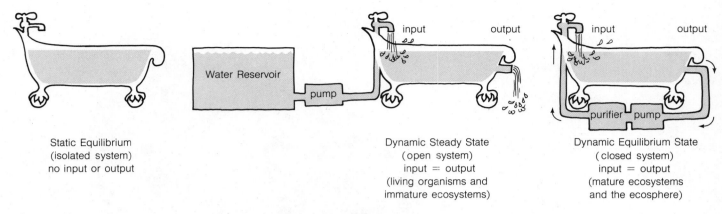

Static Equilibrium
(isolated system)
no input or output

Dynamic Steady State
(open system)
input = output
(living organisms and
immature ecosystems)

Dynamic Equilibrium State
(closed system)
input = output
(mature ecosystems
and the ecosphere)

Figure 6-4 Three possible states of a bathtub (or any system)—static equilibrium, dynamic steady state, and dynamic equilibrium state.

insect populations can alter their genetic structure to survive massive doses of deadly pesticides; and (3) plants can eventually recolonize areas devastated by volcanoes, nuclear explosions, and paved parking lots.

Stability in a system implies persistence of structure over time. This stability is maintained, however, only by constant change. You are continually adding and losing matter and energy, but your body maintains a fairly stable structure over your life span. Similarly, the oak-hickory forest ecosystem in Figure 6-3 will still be recognizable as a deciduous forest 50 years from now (unless it is cut or burned down). Some trees will die, others will take their place. Some species may also disappear, and the numbers of individual species may change. But you will still recognize it as a deciduous forest.

Dynamic Steady States   In real life there are two types of systems, closed and open. In a **closed system,** such as the earth,* energy but not matter is exchanged between the system (earth) and its environment (space). In an **open system,** both matter and energy are exchanged between the system and its environment. You (along with all other forms of life) are a walking, talking, breathing example of an open system. You take energy and matter into your body and then transform and use them to stay alive. At the same time, you put waste matter and degraded heat energy (Section 3-4) into the environment. You remain alive only if your input of matter and energy is balanced by an output of matter and energy.

---

*Some people mistakenly call the earth an open system because it receives energy from the sun. They confuse a closed system with an **isolated system,** in which neither matter nor energy is exchanged between the system and its environment.

When input and output are balanced by a steady flow in a system, we say that the system is in a **dynamic steady state.** Thus we can describe life as an open system maintained in a dynamic steady state.

Other terms used to describe a dynamic steady state are *stationary state* and *zero-growth state.* These are unfortunate terms, since they give the totally false impression that a steady state is static and dull with no forms of growth present. *The most important thing to remember about a steady state is that it is a very dynamic system. Some things are increasing, some are decreasing, and some remain fairly constant.* All of these ups and downs help keep the system from being destroyed or harmed by exceeding one or more of its limits of tolerance. In your body, some tissues are growing, and the rates of flow of certain chemicals are increasing. At the same time, other tissues are dying, and the flow rates of other chemicals are decreasing.

Immature ecosystems also tend to be in a dynamic steady state if not disturbed too severely. This occurs because their chemical cycles are fairly open (Table 6-1), with much of their matter flowing or leaking out of the system. Rapidly flowing inputs of matter and energy are needed to keep the system intact. Mature ecosystems also can be found in a dynamic steady state. Their steady state, however, is maintained by a much lower rate of flow of new matter into the system, because the system internally cycles most of its matter with only small leaks. It is essentially a closed system, and instead of reaching a dynamic steady state, it can achieve a **dynamic equilibrium state** based on matter cycling and energy flow rather than matter flow and energy flow.

We can use a bathtub (Figure 6-4) to compare a static equilibrium or true no-growth state (not represented by

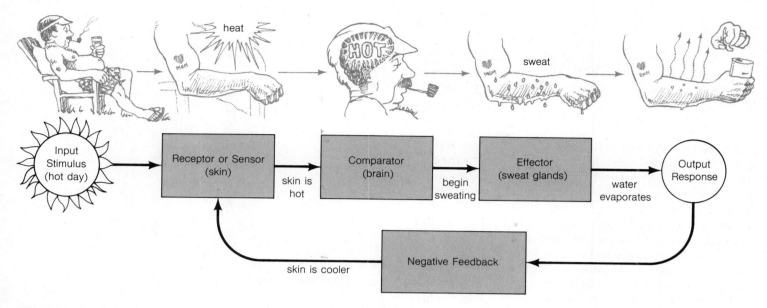

Figure 6-5 Keeping cool on a hot day—a simple homeostatic system based on negative feedback (arrows show flow of information).

any form of life) with a dynamic steady state (living organisms and immature ecosystems) and a dynamic equilibrium state (mature ecosystems and the ecosphere). A tub filled with water is a static equilibrium system. There is no input or output. By attaching an overflow pipe to the tub, we can convert it to a dynamic steady state system. By running water in as fast as it flows out, we can keep the water level in a dynamic steady state somewhere below the top of the tub. A number of different steady state levels or different water levels are possible as long as we don't exceed the limits of the tub. A number of flowthrough or throughput rates are also possible, depending on the sizes of input and output pipes, the supply of water, the capacity of the input water pump, and the supply of energy to run the pump. The steady state is a dynamic balance of these variables.

But this open system is still linear, or one way; water is flowing through the system and presumably being wasted. If water is a scarce item, we can run the overflow pipe back into the tub and recycle the water to get a *closed* system in a dynamic equilibrium state. Now we're getting somewhere. We no longer need to worry about running out of water. We just have to get enough energy to run the recycling pump and water purifier. It will take much less energy to pump the water the length of the bathtub than to pump it from the nearest reservoir or river. This system is analogous to a mature ecosystem, where solar energy is used to recycle water and decom-

posers are used to break down and purify matter for reuse.

Stability and Negative Feedback Just how does an organism or ecosystem maintain a dynamic steady state despite environmental stresses, changes, and shocks? The dynamic steady state is maintained or restored because parts of the system are connected to one another by a flow of signals, or *information*. A more formal way of saying this is that living organisms and ecosystems are *homeostatic* (or *cybernetic*) *systems*. A **homeostatic system** is one in which control and adaptability are maintained by feeding information back into the system. It is a self-regulating system based on **information feedback.**

The most common type of information feedback in a homeostatic system is **negative feedback,** which is a flow of information that causes a system to counteract the effects of an input or change in external conditions. For example, negative feedback keeps your body temperature at approximately 37°C (98.6°F) (Figure 6-5). If the temperature of the environment rises, sensory devices detect the change and send a message to your brain. This negative feedback causes your brain to send a message to cause sweating, a cooling mechanism. As the sweat evaporates, it takes heat from your skin. Once your body is cool, your skin sensors feed this new information back in to slow or stop the sweating process.

Conversely, if the environment is too cold, a similar mechanism stops the sweating, slows blood flow, and may start a shivering or exercise mechanism so that your body will produce more heat. Thus, negative feedback regulates a system so that it remains fairly constant or stable.

Tolerance Levels and Feedback Any feedback system can be overloaded. Organisms have a limited **range of tolerance** (Section 4-3 and Figure 6-6). Conditions must be maintained within this range for an organism to stay alive and grow, develop, and function normally. The wider an organism's tolerance range for a given factor, the greater the chance that the organism will survive changes in that factor. Through technology, humans have broadened their range of tolerance to many environmental factors. As a result, we can survive almost anywhere on the planet as long as there are enough matter and energy resources to provide us with a means of tolerance.

Organisms of the same species have the same general range of tolerance to various stresses (such as temperature), as shown in Figure 6-7. Few species, however, can exist for a long time at temperatures below 0°C (32°F) or above 54°C (130°F). There are some individual differences within a large population of organisms because of genetic variability. It may take a little more heat or a little more of a poisonous chemical to kill one cat or one human than another. This is why Figure 6-6 is plotted for a large number of organisms of the same species rather than for a single organism.

Normally an organism's sensitivity to a particular stress also varies with its physical condition and with its life cycle. Organisms already weakened by fatigue or disease are almost always more sensitive to stresses than healthy individuals. For most animal species, tolerance levels are also much lower in the juvenile (where body defense mechanisms may not be fully developed) than in the adult stages. For example, adult blue crabs can tolerate fresh water, whereas blue crab larvae cannot.

When environmental conditions exceed the tolerance limits of the system, the system can go out of control as another type of feedback, called positive feedback, takes over. **Positive feedback** reinforces change rather than counteracts it. It can drive a system to higher and higher or lower and lower values. For example, if disease or external conditions cause your body temperature to exceed 42°C (108°F) or fall below 32°C (90°F), your thermostatic control mechanisms break down and begin to operate by positive feedback. As it gets hotter, your body

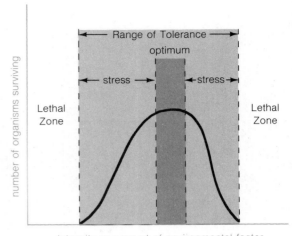

Figure 6-6 Ranges of tolerance for a large number of organisms of the same species to an environmental factor, such as temperature.

activates a warming process rather than a cooling one, and you will eventually die of heat stroke. Conversely, as it gets colder, positive feedback can activate a cooling process instead of a warming one, and you will freeze to death.

Organism Responses to Stress Organisms (especially humans) have a number of responses to stress: (1) they may move away (some birds fly south for the winter), (2) wait out the stress period in a less active physiological state (chipmunks, bears, and ground squirrels hibernate in winter), (3) change their metabolism to meet or counteract the stress (arctic hares are white during the snowy winter season but shed their white coat and become brown during the spring to blend in with the brown tundra vegetation), or (4) slowly become used to the new conditions. You are not able to jump into a cold swimming pool without considerable shock, but you can wade in little by little.

This ability to adapt slowly to new conditions is a useful protective device, but it can also be dangerous. Many changes in pollution levels, for instance, occur so gradually that we "tolerate" them. But with each change we come closer to our limit of tolerance without any warning signals. Suddenly we cross a threshold that triggers a harmful or even fatal effect. This **threshold effect**—the straw that broke the camel's back—partly ex-

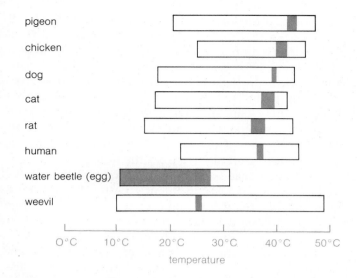

pigeon
chicken
dog
cat
rat
human
water beetle (egg)
weevil

0°C 10°C 20°C 30°C 40°C 50°C
temperature

Figure 6-7 Limits of tolerance for temperature vary among different species. Shaded areas represent the normal temperature range, and unshaded areas represent the range of tolerance.

plains why so many ecological problems seem to pop up suddenly, even though they have been incubating for a long time (Figure 1-4).

Population Responses to Stress Populations also have a number of responses to stress. Death rates may increase or birth rates may decrease, thus reducing the population size to one that can be supported by available resources. Also, the structure of the population may change. The old, very young, and weak members may die and leave a population more capable of surviving stress, such as a more severe climate or an increase in predators.

Populations are also capable of evolutionary change. **Evolution** is the process by which the population of a species (a group of plants or animals that breed or are bred together but cannot breed successfully with members outside their group) changes its genetic makeup over the course of time. Note that populations evolve—not individuals. The different combinations of genetic material that offspring inherit from their parents, along with mutations or changes in genetic material brought about by outside influences such as radiation and certain chemicals, guarantee that the individuals in a single population will vary slightly. Individuals who are unable to tolerate a new stress die off. Others whose genetic traits allow them to cope with the stress tend to survive and

pass these beneficial adaptive traits on to their offspring. This sequence of events in which a specific genetic characteristic is favored or "selected" by environmental conditions is called **natural selection**. In the long run this process leads to a population that is better adapted to a particular stress.

Species with short generation times and large numbers of offspring, such as bacteria, insects, and rats, can make adaptive evolutionary changes in a relatively short time. For example, in only a few years a number of species of mosquitoes have become genetically resistant to DDT, as discussed in Enrichment Study 11. Similarly, species of bacteria can evolve new strains that are genetically resistant to widely used bacteria-killing drugs, such as penicillin. In marked contrast, humans and many other species cannot reproduce a large number of offspring rapidly. For these species, adaptation to an environmental stress by natural selection takes hundreds of thousands and in some cases millions of years. To survive new environmental stresses that last for several decades or centuries, the human race must rely on cultural evolution (see Chapter 2)—not biological evolution.

Time Delays and Synergy Another characteristic of homeostatic systems, especially complex ones containing a number of interacting negative feedback loops, is **time delay.** This is the delay between the time a signal or stimulus is received and the time when the system makes a corrective action by negative feedback. Different feedback loops in a complex system have different response times. Time delays can protect a system for a while, but a time delay between a cause and its effect often means that corrective action is not effective by the time the symptoms finally appear. A pollutant released into the environment may not affect human health or other organisms for years. For example, workers exposed to a cancer-causing (carcinogenic) chemical may not get cancer for 20 to 30 years. By then it is too late.

Another property of complex homeostatic systems is *synergy.* You were taught that 2 plus 2 always equals 4. But in homeostatic systems, it may equal 1 or 5 or 20. In such systems two or more factors can interact so that the net effect is greater or less than the sum of the factors acting independently. This phenomenon of wholes being less than or greater than the sum of their parts is known as **synergy.** In other words, a **synergistic effect** occurs when two or more substances or factors interact to produce effects that they could not produce by acting separately.

If two or more factors interact so that the net effect is less than that from adding their independent effects, we call this **negative synergy,** or an *antagonistic effect.* This happens when one factor partially counteracts or cancels the effect of another. For example, by themselves the two air pollutants nitrogen dioxide (NO_2) and particulates (tiny particles of matter, such as soot in the air) can harm the lungs, but when they act together, the effect on the lungs is less than when each acts alone. The concept of negative synergy helps explain one reason why complex ecosystems can absorb or counteract stresses.

Positive synergy involves the interaction of two or more factors so that the net effect is greater than that from adding their independent effects. This means that an intrusion (such as pollution) into an organism or ecosystem is magnified. For example, particulates and sulfur dioxide do some damage alone in the air, but together they may greatly increase the chance of contracting lung cancer. Another well-known example involves the positive synergistic interaction between alcohol and sleeping pills. Taken alone, each slows down one's reflexes, but taken together, the two can be fatal.

Positive synergy, however, can also be beneficial. It can mean that the positive effects of vital chemicals in an organism or ecosystem can be amplified. We could use this principle to magnify or increase the amounts of a chemical found to counteract some form of pollution in the ecosystem. Unfortunately, we still know very little about this use of positive synergy.

Biological Magnification   Often pollutants are diluted to harmless levels in the air or water, or they are degraded or broken down to harmless forms by decomposers and other natural processes. But this does not always happen. Some synthetic chemicals, such as DDT (Enrichment Study 11), some radioactive materials (Chapter 14), and some mercury compounds (Enrichment Study 5) are not diluted or broken down by natural processes. Instead, they can become more and more concentrated as they pass up through various food chains or webs (Section 5-3) in an ecosystem. As a result, organisms at high trophic levels can receive large dosages of such chemicals even though relatively small amounts are found in the air, water, or soil. Figure 6-8 illustrates this phenomenon of **biological magnification** in an estuarine ecosystem on Long Island Sound.

Biological magnification in the food chain depends on three factors: the second law of thermodynamics (Section 3-3), chemicals that are soluble in fat but insoluble in water, and chemicals that are slowly degraded or bro-

ken down in the environment. Since energy transfer at each link in the food chain shown in Figure 6-8 is so inefficient (Section 5-3), a small fish must eat a great deal of plankton, larger fish must eat a great many small fish, and a pelican must eat a great many larger fish to survive. Anything that is not degraded or excreted as it moves through this chain—like DDT—will become more concentrated, especially if it can dissolve in and remain in the fatty tissues of organisms. If each phytoplankton concentrates 1 unit of DDT from the water, then a small fish eating thousands of phytoplankton will store thousands of units of DDT in its fatty tissue. If DDT were water soluble, the fish would excrete it at each level, but it is not. A large fish that eats ten of these smaller fish will receive and store tens of thousands of units of DDT. A bird or human that feeds on several large fish can get hundreds of thousands of units of DDT. For more details on pesticides, see Enrichment Study 11.

Ecosystem Stability   How do ecosystems maintain their stability? Frankly, ecologists do not have a very complete answer to this question, although there are a number of controversial hypotheses. The reason for this lack of knowledge is that ecosystem stability is extremely complex—it represents all of the structural components and the maze of interactions between all parts of the ecosystem.

Until recently it was widely believed that the diversity and complexity found in mature ecosystems always increase their stability. Intuitively it seems that species diversity (the number of different species and their relative abundance) and food web complexity should help stabilize ecosystems. With so many different species and ecological niches, risk is widely spread; the system should have more ways to respond to environmental stress, and it should be more efficient in capturing and using matter and energy. A complex food web should also promote stability. If one species is eliminated, many predators can shift to another food source. In other words, it seems intuitively obvious that it is better not to have all of one's eggs in the same basket. A parallel to this idea is the fact that a country or city that has a variety of natural resources and industries is more stable economically than a country or city where the economy is based on only one or a small number of products. In other words, following the old saying "variety is the spice of life" makes sense.

But does diversity always increase stability? This appealing idea has a number of problems. First, because of the complexity of most ecosystems, it is very hard to find tangible evidence that this idea is correct. Second, most

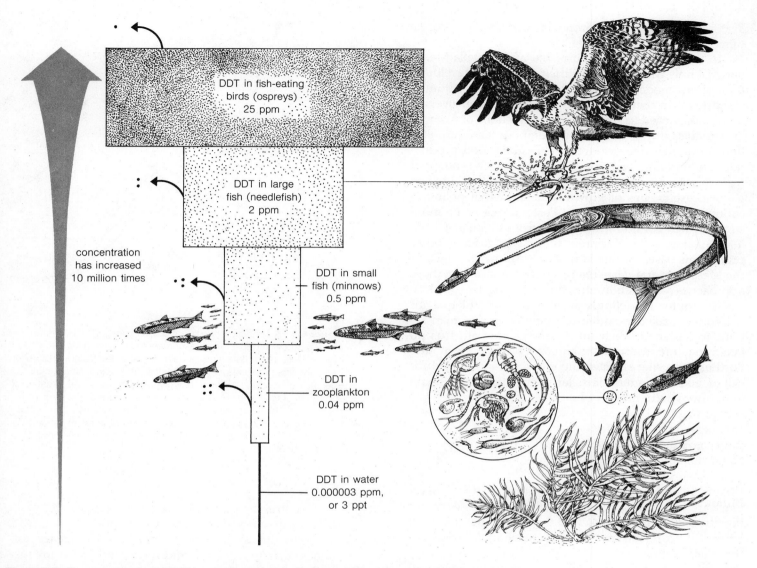

concentration
has increased
10 million times

DDT in fish-eating
birds (ospreys)
25 ppm

DDT in large
fish (needlefish)
2 ppm

DDT in small
fish (minnows)
0.5 ppm

DDT in
zooplankton
0.04 ppm

DDT in water
0.000003 ppm,
or 3 ppt

Figure 6-8 The concentration of DDT in organisms is magnified approximately 10 million times in a food chain on Long Island Sound. Dots represent DDT, and arrows show small losses through respiration and excretion.

tests of this hypothesis have been on aquatic ecosystems and simple ecosystems created in the laboratory rather than in terrestrial ecosystems. Some evidence supports the idea that diversity increases stability. Other studies indicate that it may not apply to all types of ecosystems, especially grasslands and savannas.

Part of the problem is that, like *stability*, the term *diversity* is hard to define. It can refer to species diversity, food chain diversity, genetic diversity, the diversity of ecological niches, and the ways in which various populations are distributed in an ecosystem. *The idea that di-versity leads to ecosystem stability may be valid in some types of ecosystems, especially if a stress is not enough to wipe out the dominant species. But we should be wary of applying this idea to all situations.* Everything is connected to everything else in ecosystems, but we still know relatively little about these connections.

Ecological Modeling We may get a fuller understanding of ecosystems and of the relationships between diversity and stability by increasing our use of cybernetics, systems analysis, and computer modeling of ecosystems.

In the early 1970s Jay Forrester, and Donella Meadows, Dennis Meadows, and their associates developed a simplified model of the world ecosystem from a human standpoint. In their widely publicized and controversial model, they tried to simulate the interactions of five major variables in the world ecosystem: population, pollution, nonrenewable resources, per capita food production, and industrial output. Figure 6-9, which is adapted from the Meadowses' work, shows one possible outcome if the present rates of growth and industrial pollution continue. Later Mesarovic and Pestel developed a more sophisticated computer model to project similar trends in the major geographic areas of the world. Some other projections based on the Forrester-Meadows model and the Mesarovic and Pestel model and evaluations of these approaches are given in Enrichment Study 1.

Computer modeling can be a very useful tool for helping us project possible consequences of human actions in the ecosphere, but it is not a cure-all. It is no better than the assumptions and data put into the model. Furthermore, like all scientific ideas, it can be used for evil or good—to guide missiles or to guide us in living in harmony with nature. The choice is ours.

6-3   What Can Go Wrong in an Ecosystem?

Effects of Environmental Stress   Since mature ecosystems are self-maintaining and self-repairing, why not just drop all of our wastes into the environment and let nature take care of them? By now you should realize that there are serious problems with this idea. First, as we have seen, organisms, populations, and ecosystems all have certain limits of tolerance. Second, ecosystems do not have the decomposers and other mechanisms for coping with many of the synthetic chemicals produced by humans. Third, populations could evolve so that ecosystems could digest these new chemicals and absorb many of today's environmental insults—but for most populations (especially the human population) these evolutionary changes would take hundreds of thousands if not millions of years, and many people would have to die.

Thus we are left with the problem of trying to understand just how various environmental stresses affect ecosystems. Table 6-2 summarizes what can happen to organisms, populations, and ecosystems if one or more limits of tolerance are exceeded.

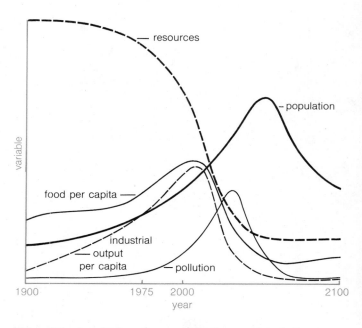

Figure 6-9   A projection of present growth curves into the future shows worldwide depletion of resources and declining industrial growth. Because of time lags, population (age structure) and pollution (retention time) continue to grow after the peak of industrialization. Eventually population declines sharply as death rates rise because of shortages of food and medical services. *These are projections, not predictions.* The variables are plotted on different vertical scales but are combined on the same graph to emphasize modes of behavior. (Source: D. H. Meadows et al., *The Limits to Growth.* New York: Universe Books, 1972. Used by permission.)

The stresses that can cause the changes shown in Table 6-2 may result from natural or geological hazards, such as earthquakes, volcanic eruptions, hurricanes, tornadoes, drought, floods, and forest and brush fires ignited by lightning. Stresses also come from human activities such as industrialization, urbanization, transportation, agriculture, and other land-clearing activities. Let's examine how such human activities can disrupt energy flow and chemical cycling and simplify ecosystems.

Disrupting Energy Flow: SSTs, Fertilizers, Fluorocarbons, and the Ozone Layer   Take a deep breath of air. You probably know that about 20 percent of the air is made up of oxygen molecules in a two-atom form (O_2). Another very important molecule in the atmosphere is *ozone*, the three-atom form of oxygen (O_3). Ozone is a strange chemical. Inhaling a tiny amount of it will kill you. Yet this poisonous chemical is essential to your life and health.

Table 6-2 Some Effects of Environmental Stress

Organism Level

Physiological and chemical changes
Psychological disorders
Fewer or no offspring
Genetic defects (mutagenic effects)
Birth defects (teratogenic effects)
Cancers (carcinogenic effects)
Death

Population Level

Population decrease
Excessive population increase (if natural predators are eliminated or reduced)
Change in age structure (old, young, and weak may die)
Natural selection of genetically resistant individuals
Loss of genetic diversity and adaptability
Extinction

Community-Ecosystem Level

Disruption of energy flow
   changes in solar energy input
   changes in heat output
   changes in food webs and patterns of competition

Disruption of chemical cycles
   leaks (shifts from closed to open cycles)
   introduction of new synthetic chemicals

Simplification
   lower species diversity
   loss of sensitive species
   fewer habitats and ecological niches
   less complex food webs
   lowered stability
   partial or total collapse of structure and function of the ecosystem
   return to an earlier stage of succession

A few parts per million of ozone are found in the lower stratosphere—a portion of the atmosphere about 20 to 50 kilometers (12 to 31 miles) above the earth's surface. If all the ozone in the stratosphere was compressed by ordinary atmospheric pressure, it would form a layer only about as thick as a dime. Yet this thin shell of ozone far above you, called the **ozone layer,** has profound effects. It acts as a shield for life on earth by filtering out about 99 percent of the harmful, high-energy ultraviolet radiation from the sun (Figure 5-3). This absorption of ultraviolet radiation by ozone also helps keep the stratosphere warmer than it would be otherwise.

In recent years a number of scientists have proposed that some human activities could deplete the ozone layer. Large-scale nuclear war would probably destroy most of it. In addition, three other potential threats have been

identified: (1) direct injection of nitrogen oxides (NO and NO_2) into the ozone layer by a worldwide fleet of supersonic transport planes (SSTs), (2) upward diffusion of fluorocarbons (Freons) from aerosol spray cans and refrigeration and air conditioning equipment into the ozone layer, and (3) upward diffusion of nitrous oxide (N_2O) from the bacterial decomposition of nitrogen fertilizers into the ozone layer.

In each case, when these chemicals (or other chemicals formed from them) come under the influence of high-energy ultraviolet radiation, they can be converted to highly reactive forms that can destroy ozone in a complicated sequence of at least 125 different chemical reactions.

Depletion of this ozone layer could have the following major effects: (1) an increase in malignant melanoma, an often fatal form of skin cancer; (2) an increase in normally nonfatal types of skin cancer that already affect about 300,000 persons each year in the United States; (3) influence on the growth of animals and plants, including plants important to agriculture (such as tomatoes, corn, and sugar beets); and (4) unpredictable changes in world climate patterns.

The potential effect of SSTs on the ozone layer, along with the excessive noise pollution that the airplanes create and the fact that they are extremely expensive to build and operate, led Congress to halt their development in the United States. There is continuing pressure, however, to revive the program, especially since more recent studies indicate that the effect of SSTs on the ozone layer may not be as great as originally projected. Even if they prove to be environmentally acceptable, fuel-guzzling SSTs appear to be economic disasters. In 1979, after years of economic losses, the British and French governments stopped producing their Concorde SSTs.

The use of fluorocarbons has been growing very rapidly in recent years. At least 8 billion kilograms (18 billion pounds) have already been released into the atmosphere and will slowly diffuse into the stratosphere in coming decades, even if all use of fluorocarbons is immediately halted. The best estimates are that over the next 50 to 100 years, the ozone layer could be depleted primarily by fluorocarbons by 5 to 28 percent—with the most likely figure being 17 percent if fluorocarbon emissions continue at the 1977 rate. In the United States alone, this would probably cause several hundred thousand more cases of skin cancer a year—with several thousand of these cases being malignant melanoma, an untreatable and usually fatal type of skin cancer. Because we know so little about the physics and chemistry of the atmosphere, these predicted effects are based on theoretical models, not direct experimental measurements. Direct measurements can't be accurate enough to confirm or deny the models because the amount of ozone in the stratosphere varies naturally by as much as 20 percent between seasons and up to 7 percent due to the sunspot cycle. It would take from 10 to 15 years for the maximum ozone depletion to occur after the release of the harmful chemicals was stopped, and by then much damage could already have been done.

In 1978 the Environmental Protection Agency banned the use of fluorocarbon propellants in spray cans in the United States. Fluorocarbons are still used for a few purposes, such as (1) refrigerants in home and auto air conditioners and in refrigerators and freezers; (2) the manufacturing of various plastic foams; and (3) in industrial processes for fast-freezing foods and for cleaning metals, clothes, and surgical instruments. Canada, Sweden, and Denmark have imposed similar bans, but other countries had refused to follow suit by 1981. This banning (along with that of the SST) causes little hardship, since fluorocarbons and SSTs are not vital for survival or life quality. Furthermore, alternatives are available, such as very high speed (but subsonic) aircraft and spray cans with hand pumps or other propellant chemicals (although any new propellants must also be carefully checked before being widely used).

Beyond spray cans, most of the fluorocarbons produced in the United States are used for refrigeration and air conditioning units. The banning of fluorocarbons for these uses poses much more serious problems and trade-offs. Refrigeration is essential for food preservation, and air conditioning is widely used in warm climates. Automobile air conditioners might be redesigned to reduce fluorocarbon leaking, but a new design would not affect the millions of auto air conditioners already in use.

The *potential* threat to the ozone layer from the worldwide use of synthetic nitrogen fertilizer poses extremely serious scientific, political, and moral problems. If nitrous oxides released from nitrogen fertilizer affect the ozone layer, we are forced to choose between banning or reducing fertilizer use (and thus allowing millions to die from starvation) or continuing to use fertilizer, with an increase in skin cancer and potentially adverse effects on food crops and global climate. Fortunately, the evidence so far indicates that nitrous oxides do not pose a serious threat to the ozone layer, but more studies are necessary to evaluate conflicting data and claims.

SSTs, fluorocarbons, and fertilizers were all developed to help people. At the time of their development, their potential environmental effects were unknown. They serve as dramatic warnings that blundering into the ecosphere, even with good intentions, can have serious long-range consequences. Hopefully, these early warnings will cause us to survey all present (and future) chemicals released into the atmosphere. Ozone depletion could be caused by any widely used chemicals that are volatile (existing as a gas in the atmosphere), chemically inert (unreactive and tending to remain in the atmosphere), and insoluble in water (not washed out of the atmosphere by rain).

Additional examples of the potential disruption of global and regional energy flow from burning fossil fuels, land clearing, and other human activities are discussed in Enrichment Study 3.

Disrupting the Oxygen, Nitrogen, and Phosphorus Cycles Let's begin with some good news. In the late 1960s, an ecological story was widely circulated that we might run out of oxygen by using it up to burn fossil fuels. We have a large number of serious ecological problems, but global suffocation from lack of oxygen is not one of them. The oxygen content of the atmosphere remains essentially constant, with the oxygen consumed by all animals, bacteria, and respiration processes roughly balanced by the oxygen released by land and sea plants during photosynthesis.

We will not run out of oxygen. But this is not the case for some fish and other oxygen-consuming organisms in a number of lakes and slow-moving rivers and streams. This breakdown of the oxygen cycle is caused by overloading the nitrogen and phosphorus cycles in some aquatic ecosystems. Some nitrogen and phosphorus compounds naturally erode and run off from the land into lakes in a process called **eutrophication,** which creates an excess of plant nutrients. But this natural eutrophication can be greatly accelerated by artificial enrichment from a number of human activities, leading to what is called **cultural eutrophication** (Figure 6-10). The key sources of nutrient overload include runoff of synthetic fertilizer and animal wastes (manure) from the land; increased runoff from agriculture, mining, construction, and poor land use; discharge of municipal sewage and detergents; and to a much lesser extent the dissolving of nitrogen oxides from the burning of fossil fuels in cars, power plants, and home furnaces (Figure 6-10).

Nitrogen and phosphorus are plant nutrients, and when present in excessive amounts they can set off an explosive growth of water plants, such as green and blue-

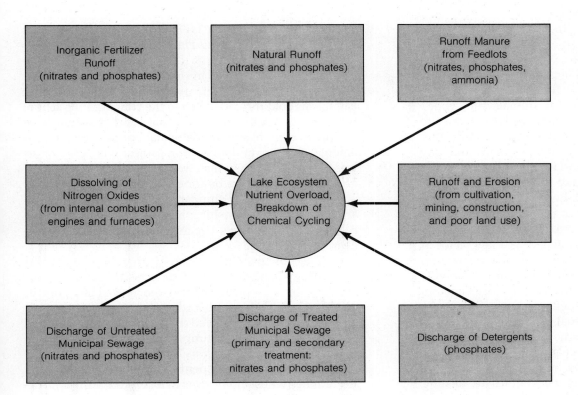

Boxes in figure:

Inorganic Fertilizer Runoff (nitrates and phosphates)

Natural Runoff (nitrates and phosphates)

Runoff Manure from Feedlots (nitrates, phosphates, ammonia)

Dissolving of Nitrogen Oxides (from internal combustion engines and furnaces)

Lake Ecosystem Nutrient Overload, Breakdown of Chemical Cycling

Runoff and Erosion (from cultivation, mining, construction, and poor land use)

Discharge of Untreated Municipal Sewage (nitrates and phosphates)

Discharge of Treated Municipal Sewage (primary and secondary treatment: nitrates and phosphates)

Discharge of Detergents (phosphates)

green algae. This excess growth dies and falls to the bottom of the lake. Oxygen-consuming bacteria decompose these masses of dead algae and in the process deplete dissolved oxygen from water at the bottom of the lake. This kills most oxygen-consuming fish and causes further oxygen depletion as more bacteria decompose the dead fish. If nutrient overload continues, the entire chemical cycling system in the lake can break down and the water can become foul and almost devoid of life. Further details on this process of *cultural eutrophication* are given in Enrichment Study 16.

Disrupting Chemical Cycles and Food Chains with Synthetic Chemicals Malaria once infected 9 out of 10 people on the island of North Borneo, now a state of Indonesia. In 1955, the World Health Organization began spraying dieldrin (a pesticide similar to DDT) to kill malaria-carrying mosquitoes.* The program was very suc-

*Most versions of this episode report that DDT was the insecticide used. According to a personal communication from A. J. Beck (at one time a medical zoologist at the Institute for Medical Research in North Borneo), dieldrin, not DDT, was used.

cessful and all but eliminated this dreaded disease. But other things began happening. Besides killing mosquitoes, the dieldrin killed other insects, including flies and cockroaches that inhabited the houses. The islanders applauded. But then small lizards that also lived in the houses died after gorging themselves on dead insects. Then cats began dying after feeding on the dead lizards. With the cats dead, the large rat population in the nearby jungles began overrunning the villages. Now people were threatened by typhus carried by fleas on the rats. Fortunately, this situation was brought under control.

But on top of everything else, the thatched roofs of some houses began to fall in. The dieldrin also killed wasps and other insects that fed on a particular type of caterpillar that either avoided or was not affected by dieldrin. With most of their predators eliminated, the caterpillars had a population explosion and proceeded to munch their way through one of their favorite foods, the leaves that made up the thatched roofs. On balance the Borneo episode was a success story, in that the terrible disease of malaria and the unexpected side effects of the spraying program were brought under control. But it shows the unpredictable results that we can encounter when we interfere in an ecosystem. More details on the dilemma of using pesticides are found in Enrichment Study 11.

Simplifying an Ecosystem by Eliminating and Introducing Species We tend to divide animals into "good" and "bad" species and assume that we have a duty to wipe out the villains. Consider the American alligator. Its marsh and swamp habitats are destroyed to make way for agriculture and industry, and it is illegally hunted for its hide, which is used to make expensive purses and shoes. Between 1950 and 1960, Louisiana lost 90 percent of its alligators, and the alligator population in the Florida Everglades was also threatened.

Why should we care? The alligator is a key factor in the ecological balance of the Everglades—a balance on which much of the urbanizing state of Florida depends for water. The deep pools, or "gator holes," that alligators dig collect water during dry spells and provide a sanctuary for the birds and animals that repopulate the glades after a drought. The large nesting mounds that alligators make are popular nest sites for herons, egrets, and other birds essential to the life cycle in the glades. As alligators move from their gator holes to nesting mounds, they also help keep the waterways open. In addition, they preserve a balance of game fish by consuming large numbers of predator fish, such as the gar.

In 1968 the U.S. government placed the American alligator on the endangered species list. Protected from hunters, the alligator population made a comeback in many areas by 1975. Indeed, they made too much of a comeback. People began finding alligators in their backyards and swimming pools. Now the American alligator has been removed from the endangered species list in most areas, and limited hunting is allowed in some areas to keep the alligator population from becoming too large.

Ecological backlash can also occur when a new species is introduced to an ecosystem. In 1948 five cats were brought to an isolated Antarctic island to control the rat population. Today the island still has rats along with about 2,500 feral (wild) cats, who gobble up about 600,000 of the island's birds each year. For more details on the effects of species on ecosystems, see Enrichment Study 12.

The Love Canal Episode "Out of sight, out of mind" does not always apply. Hazardous industrial wastes buried decades ago can bubble up to the surface, find their way into groundwater supplies, or end up in backyards and basements, as residents of a suburb of Niagara Falls,

New York, discovered in 1977. Between 1947 and 1952, the Hooker Chemicals and Plastics Corporation dumped over 19 million kilograms (21,000 tons) of chemical wastes (mostly contained in steel drums) into an old canal and then covered them with dirt. In 1953, Hooker Chemicals sold the canal area to the Niagara Falls school board for $1 on the condition that Hooker would have no future responsibility for the state of the land. An elementary school and a housing project with 239 homes was built in the area, which was called Love Canal. Later, 710 more homes were built nearby. In 1977, heavy rains and snows turned the dumpsite into a muddy quagmire, and topsoil began washing away. Chemicals from the badly corroded barrels began oozing into gardens and nearby basements.

Studies of Love Canal residents then revealed an unusually high incidence of birth defects (3.5 times the normal rate); miscarriages (2.5 times the normal rate); nerve, respiratory, and kidney disorders; and assorted cancers. Later investigations revealed that at least 200 compounds were leaking from the dump site. When the danger of this chemical time bomb was finally recognized in 1978, New York State officials spent $37 million relocating the 239 families whose homes were closest to the dump. Anxiety began to mount among the 710 families still living in the area. In 1980, after protests from the outraged families still living in the area, President Carter declared Love Canal a federal disaster area and had the 710 families temporarily relocated in hotels, motels, and nearby army barracks (at a cost that may exceed $30 million). In late 1980, tests were still being run to see if the residents can ever go back to their homes.

Today the site looks like a war zone. Houses are boarded up, and the area is surrounded by a high fence to keep tourists and looters away. A fire engine and ambulance stand by as workers attempt to seal off the flow of chemicals. Even if the effects of exposure to these chemicals should prove to be less harmful than expected, the psychological damage to the evacuated residents is enormous. They will spend the rest of their lives wondering whether some disorder will strike and worrying about the possible effects of these chemicals on their children and grandchildren.

Faced with over $2 billion in lawsuits from the federal government, New York State, and Love Canal residents, Hooker Chemicals contends that: (1) It only sold the land to the Niagara Falls school board after the School Board threatened to condemn and take over the site; (2) The Niagara Falls school board knowingly and willfully built on the land after being warned by Hooker Chemicals not to construct any buildings over the canal site; (3) The dumping was legal at the time; (4) There is no absolute proof that its chemicals are responsible for the illnesses among Love Canal residents; and (5) It was relieved from all legal responsibility when it sold the property to the Niagara Falls school board for $1. Regardless of the final outcome, the Love Canal episode is a vivid reminder that we can never really throw anything away. It is even more frightening when we realize that the Environmental Protection Agency estimates that there are from 1,200 to 2,000 other chemical dump sites in the United States that could pose similar problems in the future. Today or in the future, you could be living near one of these chemical time bombs. For more details, see Enrichment Study 15.

The small number of cases described in this section show that the careless use of technology can cause unexpected side effects, as discussed by L. Hunter Lovins in her guest editorial at the end of this chapter. These undesirable effects don't mean that we have to abandon technology, but they do mean that we must learn to anticipate possible side effects before introducing a technology on a large scale. In many cases this will mean using gentler, simpler appropriate technology (Section 1-5).

6-4 Humans and Ecosystems

Simplifying Ecosystems In modifying ecosystems for our own use we simplify them. Every dam, cornfield, highway, pipeline and irrigation project, and use of insecticides makes ecosystems simpler. We bulldoze fields and forests containing thousands of interrelated plant and animal species and cover the land with buildings, highways, or fields containing single crops, such as wheat, rice, or corn, that sometimes stretch as far as the eye can see. Modern agriculture consists of deliberately keeping ecosystems in early or immature states of succession (Table 6-1), where net productivity of one or only a few plant species (such as corn or wheat) is high. But due to their simplicity, such fast-growing, single-crop systems (monocultures) are highly vulnerable. Weeds and just a single disease or pest can wipe out an entire crop unless we protect the crop with chemicals such as pesticides (pest-killing chemicals) and herbicides (weed-killing chemicals) and support the crop's growth with chemicals such as water and synthetic fertilizers.

Modern agriculture also requires large amounts of fossil fuel energy to make fertilizers, pesticides, and other agricultural chemicals and to run the tractors and other machines used to plant, protect, and harvest the

Table 6-3 Comparison of Properties of a Mature Natural Ecosystem and a Simplified Human System

Mature Ecosystem (marsh, grassland, forest)	Human System (cornfield, factory, house)
Captures, converts, and stores energy from the sun	Consumes energy from fossil or nuclear fuels
Produces oxygen and consumes carbon dioxide	Consumes oxygen and produces carbon dioxide
Creates fertile soil	Depletes or covers fertile soil
Stores, purifies, and releases water gradually	Often uses and contaminates water and releases it rapidly
Provides wildlife habitats	Destroys wildlife habitats
Filters and detoxifies pollutants and waste products free of charge	Produces pollutants and waste materials, much of which must be cleaned up at our expense
Capable of self-maintenance and self-renewal	Requires continual maintenance and renewal at great cost

crops. When quickly breeding insects develop genetic resistance to some pesticides, we often use stronger and stronger pesticides. This can kill other species that prey on the pests, thus simplifying the ecosystem even further and allowing the pest population to grow even larger and to become more genetically resistant (see Enrichment Study 11).

There is nothing wrong with converting a reasonable number of mature ecosystems into immature ecosystems in order to provide food for the human population. But the price we must pay for simplifying mature ecosystems includes matter and energy resources, time, and money needed to maintain and protect these vulnerable systems, as summarized in Table 6-3.

It is not only cultivation that simplifies ecosystems. The sheep rancher doesn't want bison competing with the sheep for grass, so the bison must be eliminated. So must the wolf, coyote, eagle, and other predators that occasionally kill sheep. We also tend to overfish and overhunt some species to extinction or near extinction. A living species is a nonrenewable resource that carries valuable genetic information developed over thousands or millions of years of evolution. Once extinct, it is gone forever. Species become extinct naturally, but we often deliberately or accidentally kill off species.

Achieving a Balance Between Simplicity and Diversity
The comparison in Table 6-3 does not mean we should not simplify complex ecosystems, but there is the danger

that as the human population grows, we will convert too many of the world's mature ecosystems to young, productive, but highly vulnerable ecosystems. These immature systems depend on the existence of nearby mature ecosystems. For example, simple farmlands on the plains must be balanced by diverse forests on nearby hills and mountains. These forests hold water and minerals and release them slowly to the plains below. If the forests are cut for short-term economic gain, then the water and soil will wash down the slopes in a destructive rush instead of a nourishing trickle. Thus, forests must be valued not only for their short-term production of timber but also for their vital long-term role in maintaining the young productive ecosystems that supply our food. In addition, almost half of all modern drugs originate from plants, and to date only a tiny fraction of the world's plants have been screened for possible medical uses.

What we must do, then, is to preserve a balance between young and mature ecosystems. Some progress has been made, but deciding on this balance is difficult, since we still know so little about how ecosystems work. Biologist Paul Ehrlich has likened the ecosphere to a massive and intricate computer cross-linkng a vast array of transistors and other electrical components. Even though we do not really understand it, and even though our lives depend on it, we are busy simplifying this complex network by randomly pulling out transistors and by overloading and disconnecting various parts and circuits. Removing certain species or altering parts of an ecosystem may not be lethal to the system, but we do not know which parts of the system can safely be altered.

As Lewis Mumford put it most eloquently at a conference in 1965:

> When we rally to preserve the remaining redwood forests or to protect the whooping crane, we are rallying to perserve ourselves, we are trying to keep in existence the organic variety, the whole span of natural resources upon which our own future development will be based. If we surrender this variety too easily in one place, we shall lose it everywhere; and we shall find ourselves enclosed in technological prison, without even the hope that sustains a prisoner in jail—that someday we may get out.

In addition to preserving biological diversity, we also need to preserve human cultural diversity. This can help us maintain our mental health, keep life from being boring, and provide us with wisdom for dealing with environmental changes. Culture, the nongenetic information possessed by individuals and societies, is the raw material of cultural evolution (Chapter 2)—just as genes are the raw material of biological evolution. Each cultural system in the world has insights to help us deal with the problems we face. Since we know even less about cultural evolution than about biological evolution, it would be dangerous to put all of our cultural eggs in one basket by attempting to convert the world to the Western—or any other—culture.

Some Lessons from Ecology   What can we learn from the brief overview of ecological principles presented in the past few chapters? It should be clear that ecology forces us to recognize five major features of all life: *interdependence, diversity, stability, adaptability,* and *limits*. Its message is not that we should avoid change, but that we should recognize that human-induced changes can have far-reaching and often unpredictable consequences and that there are important limits to what we can and cannot do to ecosystems. Ecology is a call for wisdom, care, and restraint as we alter the ecosphere.

What has gone wrong, probably, is that we have failed to see ourselves as part of a large and indivisible whole. For too long we have based our lives on a primitive feeling that our "God-given" role was to have "dominion over the fish of the sea and over the fowl of the air and over every living thing that moveth upon the earth." We have failed to understand that the earth does not belong to us, but we to the earth.

Rolf Edberg (1969)

Guest Editorial: We Propose and Nature Disposes

Edward J. Kormondy

Edward J. Kormondy is provost and professor of biology at the University of Southern Maine, in Portland. He has taught at the University of Michigan, Oberlin College, The Evergreen State College, and the University of Pittsburgh's summer field station, and conducted research at several of these institutions, the Savannah River Atomic Energy Plant, and the Center for Bioethics at Georgetown University. His research has concerned the ecology of dragonflies, primary productivity in ecological succession, the nutrient cycle of zinc, and environmental ethics. Among his numerous research articles and books are Concepts of Ecology *(1976, Englewood Cliffs, N.J.: Prentice Hall) and* Readings in Ecology *(1965, Englewood Cliffs, N.J.: Prentice-Hall). He has been a major force in biological education and for several years was director of the Commission on Undergraduate Education in the Biological Sciences (CUEBS).*

Energy flows—but downhill only; minerals circulate—but some stagnate; populations stabilize—but some go wild; communities age—but some age faster. These processes are as characteristic of ecosystems as are thermonuclear reactions of solar systems and feedback loops in hormonal systems. They are also every bit as dynamic and relentless.

Thinking one can escape the operation of these laws of nature is like thinking one can stop the earth from rotating and revolving or thinking that rain can fall up. Yet we have consciously peopled the earth only to endure starvation and malnutrition, deliberately dumped wastes only to ensure contamination, purposefully simplified agricultural systems only to cause complete crop loss. Such actions suggest that we believe that energy increases as people multiply, that things stay where they are put, that simplification aids management and maintenance. Such actions indicate that we have ignored basic, unbreakable laws of ecological systems. We have proposed, but nature has disposed.

We proposed more people, more mouths to be fed, more space to be occupied. Nature disposed by placing an upper limit on primary productivity, by using and degrading energy at and between all trophic levels, by imposing an upper limit on the total space that is available and which can be occupied. Ultimately, the only way there can be more and more people is for each person to have less and less energy and less and less space. Absolute limits to growth are imposed both by thermodynamics and by space. We may argue what those limits are and when they will be reached, but there are limits and they will be reached. The more timely question then becomes a qualitative one. What quality of life within those limits? What kind of life do you want?

We proposed exploitive use of natural resources and indiscriminate disposal of the wastes generated by people and technology. Nature disposed, and like a boomerang, the consequences of our acts came back and hit us. On the one hand, coal, oil, and mineral reserves are significantly depleted—some are near exhaustion. On the other hand, air, water, and land are contaminated, some beyond restoring. Nature's law limits each resource; some limits are more confining than others, some more critical than others. The earth is finite, and its resources are therefore finite. Yet another of nature's laws is that fundamental resources—elements and compounds—circulate, some fully and some partially. They don't stay where they are put. They move from the land to the water and the air, just as they move from the air and the water to the land. Must not our proposals for using resources and discharging wastes be mindful of ultimate limits and the givens of cycling processes? What about your own patterns of resource use and waste disposal?

We proposed simplification of our agricultural and to some extent our aquatic food producing systems to ease the admittedly heavy burden of cultivation and harvest. Nature disposed otherwise, however. Simple systems are youthful ones, and like our own youth, are volatile, unpredictable, and unstable. Young ecological systems do not conserve nutrients, and agricultural systems in such a stage must have their nutrients replaced artificially and expensively by fertilization. Young systems essentially lack resistance to pests and disease and have to be protected artificially and expensively by chemical means. These systems are more subject to the whims of climate and have to be expensively irrigated. Must not our proposals for managing agricultural systems be mindful of nature's managerial strategy of stability in complex ecosystems? What of your own lawn?

The take-home lesson is a rather straightforward one: We cannot propose without recognizing how nature is disposed. We are not free agents. We are shackled by basic ecological laws of energetics, mineral cycling, population growth, and community aging processes. We have plenty of freedom within the limits of these laws, but we are bounded by them. You are bounded by them. What do you propose be done? What do you propose to do yourself?

Guest Editorial Discussion

1. Using the laws of thermodynamics, explain why energy does not increase simultaneously with population increase.

2. Edward Kormondy suggests that the quality of life is a more important concern than numbers of people. What is quality of life? What does it mean to you? To other members of your class? To a poor person living in a ghetto? To a rich person living on an estate?

3. List the patterns of your own life that are in harmony with the laws of energy flow and chemical cycling and those that are not.

4. Can you think of other examples of "we propose" and "nature disposes"?

5. Set up a chart with examples of "we propose" and "nature disposes" but add a third column based on ecological principles titled "we repropose."

Guest Editorial: Surprises

L. Hunter Lovins

L. Hunter Lovins is a lawyer, forester, sociologist, political scientist, energy policy consultant, and cowboy. Presently, she spends most of her time working as an energy policy consultant with her husband Amory B. Lovins (see his Guest Editorial at the end of Chapter 13). From 1974 to 1979 she served as assistant director of the California Conservation Project ("Tree People"), which she co-founded in Los Angeles. She supervised the planting of thousands of smog-tolerant trees in forest and urban areas of Southern California, designed and implemented the project's environmental and energy education projects, coordinated community participation in urban forestry, and wrote and edited the project's many publications. She has lectured and consulted widely on energy policy, community energy education and participation. Ms. Lovins has also co-authored and edited recent publications with her husband including two very important books: Energy/

War: Breaking the Nuclear Link *(San Francisco: Friends of the Earth, 1980) and* Energy Unbound: Your Invitation to Energy Abundance *(San Francisco: Friends of the Earth, 1982).*

In 1974, my husband and colleague, Amory Lovins, made a list of the twenty most likely surprises in energy policy over the next decade or so. Near the top of the list were "a major nuclear reactor accident" and "a revolution in Iran." Number twenty on the list, of which no examples could be given, was "surprises we haven't thought of yet."

It is remarkable how energy policy analysts who spend their professional lives coping with the effects of the unexpected OPEC oil embargo in 1973 go on to assume a surprise-free future. It isn't going to be like that at all. We need to prepare for a *surprise-full* future and plan accordingly for resilience in dealing with these surprises.

Three traps lie in wait for people who try to devise ever more powerful and intrusive technologies to alter the natural course of events but who do not expect any unpleasant and dangerous surprises. *The first trap is believing that we know what we are doing.* The past decade alone shows many examples of newly discovered side-effects obvious only in hindsight. In addition to the ones already discussed in this chapter they include:

● Krypton-85, a radioactive gas released by nuclear reactors and nuclear fuel reprocessing plants, can apparently alter atmospheric ionization with unknown—but potentially large—effects on nimbus rainfall and other processes important to global climate. This may become important at levels of krypton-85 several orders of magnitude below those of public-health concern, possibly including present levels.

• An oil spill in the Beaufort Sea (where drilling is now under way) could spread under the fragile Arctic sea-ice, work its way to the surface as the ice melts on top and refreezes at the bottom, make the ice surface gray, and increase its solar absorptivity. This could lead to probably irreversible melting of the sea-ice, with dramatic effects on hemispheric weather patterns.

• Current standards for allowed levels of highly toxic plutonium-239 (a radioactive substance produced in conventional and breeder reactors) in water assume that it is very poorly absorbed by the gut. If the absorption tests upon which this idea is based are rerun with chlorinated city water rather than distilled water, the plutonium chemistry changes and its absorption coefficient rises by several orders of magnitude.

• Most of what we thought we knew about the environmental pathways of plutonium and transplutonic elements is turning out to be wrong. For example, plutonium-239 that was thought to remain innocently fixed in the soil was found to be selectively incorporated into the aerial spores of a soil fungus. This makes it ideal for inhalation into human lungs, where only a tiny speck of the plutonium-239 could cause lung cancer.

Thus, as René Dubos says, "the worst environmental problems may be the ones we haven't discovered yet."

The second trap is that the world is not as simple as we like to think. As discussed in this chapter (and in Enrichment Study 1), the world is full of nonlinear, threshold, delayed, and irreversible behavior that we are not used to in everyday life. That is, a system under stress may not respond at all for a while; then may respond suddenly and out of proportion to normal expectations; and when the stress is removed, the system may not bounce back to the way it started. The world is full of enormously intricate *connections* which continue working away whether we notice them or not. An example of this second trap is presented in this chapter in the discussion of the unexpected side effects that occurred when the World Health Organization sprayed dieldrin (a pesticide to kill malaria-carrying mosquitoes) on the island of North Borneo (Section 6-3).

The third trap is that the cause of many problems is solutions. If we don't know what we are doing because of our lack of understanding about how nature really works, then often even the most "expert" actions to solve a problem make things much worse. Or, if we define a problem too narrowly, we can make it into someone else's problem. For example, many experts urge us to solve our energy problem by relying more on nuclear power and burning more coal. But even if these two energy alternatives could temporarily "solve" the energy problem (which is not even possible, as discussed by Amory Lovins in his guest editorial at the end of Chapter 13), the increased use of nuclear power would greatly increase the risk of nuclear war through the proliferation of bomb-usable knowledge and materials to make nuclear weapons throughout much of the world. Similarly, by relying more on coal we release enormous amounts of carbon dioxide and particulates that could alter global climate patterns (see Enrichment Study 3) and large quantities of sulfur dioxide that can seriously degrade the air, water, and soil upon which we depend. The easiest, quickest, and cheapest solution to our energy problem is to concentrate on improving energy efficiency by reducing the enormous amounts of energy we waste and to rely more on renewable energy resources such as the sun, wind, water (hydropower), and biomass wastes, as discussed in Chapters 13 and 14. The challenge before us is to try to solve the energy problem (or any other problem) without, at the same time, making other problems worse.

However, we don't yet seem to have learned this lesson. We are making in water policy the same mistakes we have been making in energy. We are trying to supply more water before we efficiently use that which we already have. We are treating all uses of water as being alike rather than determining the quality needed for each task. The analogy to heating houses with electricity is flushing toilets with drinking-quality water, purified by expensive processes. We are also encouraging water waste by pricing water at a tenth or a hundredth of the true cost of getting more of it. It is not surprising then that much of the farming in the United States is based on unsustainable mining of groundwater. The Ogallala Aquifer, underlying the High Plains states, is being drawn down 1 to 3 meters per year and being recharged at less than 1 centimeter per year. This vital supply of groundwater is already half gone. During the four dry months of the year alone, more water is pumped up from this underground formation than the full annual flow of the Colorado River through the Grand Canyon.

At the same time, much of the farming and forestry in the United States is based on unsustainable mining of the soil. American farmland is losing an average of 18,000 to 27,000 kilograms (20 to 50 tons) of soil per hectare per year—many times the maximum rate of soil formation [short tons] and more than the nation was losing per year at the peak of the Dust Bowl disaster in the 1930s. A dumptruckload of precious topsoil is washed away in the Mississippi River every *second*. In Iowa, one of the world's richest farming areas, a third of the topsoil is gone.

These water and soil problems are connected. Two-fifths of America's feedlot cattle are raised on grain irrigated with water from the shrinking Ogallala Aquifer. To grow enough corn to add enough weight on a feedlot steer to put an extra 1 kilogram of meat on your table results in a loss of about 100 kilograms of topsoil and the mining of over 8,000 kilograms of unrecharged groundwater. Enjoy your hamburger while you still can.

It is in this already overstressed land-water-food system in the Rocky Mountain and High Plains states that some people are proposing to strip-mine coal, dig up and process oil shale, build giant synfuel plants to convert mined coal to synthetic gas and oil, and mine uranium to supply nuclear reactors. In addition, others propose that some of this land be planted with crops such as corn (which with present agribusiness farming practices typically erodes two bushels of soil for each bushel of corn) to be converted inefficiently into ethanol to run our inefficient cars. All of these schemes, each of which requires enormous amounts of water, are to be carried out simultaneously in an area that is already seriously short of water (as discussed in Section 13-5). People with such a small sense of interconnections, if not checked by those with a greater sense of how the world works, can lead the nation into some of the most unpleasant and irreversible surprises in human history.

If the earth were the size of an egg, all the water on it, gathered together, would be just a drop. All the air, condensed to the density of water, would be a droplet about a fortieth as big. All the arable land would be a not-quite visible speck. That drop, droplet, and speck are what make the earth enduringly different from the moon. The stewardship that can help these unique, lifegiving features of the earth to endure must be founded not only on foresight but on humility: not only on subtle understanding of how the world works but on willingness to let well enough alone.

Guest Editorial Discussion

1. Can you think of examples not discussed in this editorial and in this chapter where the cause of one problem was the solution to another problem?

2. If solutions are the cause to problems, what do we do? Does this mean we shouldn't attempt to solve the problems that confront us? If we should attempt solutions, how should we go about it?

3. Make a list of three political, environmental, or resource supply surprises that might occur within the next 10 years and try to see how they might affect your life.

Discussion Topics

1. Explain how organisms can change local conditions so that they become extinct in a given ecosystem. Could humans do this to themselves?

2. Explain how the "balance of nature" is dynamic, not static.

3. If the energy use in an immature agricultural system is so inefficient (see Table 6-1), why is its net primary productivity so high? Similarly, if a mature ecosystem uses energy so efficiently, why is its net primary productivity so low?

4. How can an immature ecosystem have high net primary productivity but only small amounts of living organic matter, or biomass? How can a mature ecosystem have low net primary productivity and a large biomass?

5. Give two examples each of closed systems and open systems not discussed in this chapter. Why is the earth a closed system?

6. Explain why a steady state is so exciting and important. Develop an explanation of this idea for a typical growth-oriented economist who insists that a steady state or no-growth economy would be stagnant and undesirable.

7 What does it mean to say that modern farming consists of keeping an ecosystem at an early stage of succession? Why is this necessary? What undesirable effects can it have?

8. Draw a homeostatic diagram (see Figure 6-5) for (a) stopping your car and (b) picking up a pencil.

9. Give several examples of negative feedback control in your body, in your room, in your school, and in your community. Analyze a riot with a homeostatic diagram in which the limits of tolerance have been disrupted by positive feedback.

10. Explain to your younger brother or sister why and how 2 plus 2 does not always equal 4 in an ecosystem. Cite specific examples of positive and negative synergy to back up your explanation. How can positive synergy be used to bring about political change?

11. Someone tells you not to worry about air pollution because we will all develop lungs that can detoxify pollutants. How would you reply? What types of species can do this?

12. Give two examples of time delays not discussed in this chapter. How can time delays be harmful? How can they be helpful?

13. What characteristics must a chemical have before it can be biologically magnified in a food chain or web?

14. Does diversity in an ecosystem always increase stability? Why or why not?

15. It has been said that people live in cities because a city offers more diversity, excitement, and challenge. If so, then does this diversity add stability? How do you explain the fact that many of our cities seem unstable? How is the term *stability* being used here?

16. Discuss the building of Howard Johnsons, Holiday Inns, McDonalds, and the like throughout the United States. Do such chains increase or decrease stability? Diversity? Why do you think they are so popular? Should these chains be the only eating and lodging places available?

17. Should we preserve all species somewhere in their natural habitats? Why would you want to preserve the dinosaur? How many? Where?

18. Could the instances of ecological backlash discussed in this chapter have been predicted and avoided? How? Analyze each case separately. Do you think we are learning from these past mistakes? Cite specific evidence, pro or con.

19. Should the United States reactivate its SST program? Why or why not? Should we ban all commercial flights of SSTs into the United States from other countries? Why or why not?

20. Should the use of fluorocarbons in all aerosol spray cans be banned? Why or why not? Should fluorocarbons be banned from use in refrigeration and air conditioning units? Why or why not?

21. Should we ban the use of synthetic fertilizers if it is established that they would deplete the ozone layer over the next 150 years? Why or why not?

22. Should all coyotes and eagles be exterminated from lands where sheep graze? Why or why not? What are the alternatives?

23. Rachel Carson has written, "Most of us walk unseeing through the world, unaware alike of its beauties, its wonders, and the strange and sometimes terrible intensity of the lives that are being lived about us." Relate this sentiment to your own life and the increasing urbanization of the planet. Can you think of moments in your life when nature has suddenly impinged on the plastic bubble that surrounds you?

24. What could happen if we simplify too many ecosystems? Explain to a younger child why we must preserve forests and swamps.

25. Who is most likely to survive a major nuclear or ecological catastrophe—city dwellers or poor dirt farmers, suburbanites or ghetto residents, people in the more developed or less developed countries? Why? Relate your answer to the biblical statement that "the meek shall inherit the earth." Look up the literal meaning of the word *meek*.

26. How does species diversity in an ecosystem differ from diversity in the human population? Is human cultural diversity really necessary? Why? Could we have too much cultural diversity? Could cultural diversity lead to stability or instability in the human population? Relate this to war.

Readings

See also Readings for Chapter 4.

Dale, M. P. 1970. "Systems Analysis and Ecology." *Ecology*, vol. 51, 2–16. Good introductory article.

Edberg, Rolf. 1969. *On the Shred of a Cloud*. University: University of Alabama Press. A beautifully written book about humans and the ecosphere.

Ehrenfeld, D. W. 1970. *Biological Conservation*. 2nd ed. New York: Wiley. Outstanding introduction to conservation.

Ehrlich, Paul R. 1980. "Variety Is the Key to Life." *Technology Review*, March/April, pp. 59–68. Very important article showing the need for preserving diversity.

Farvar, M. Taghi, and John P. Milton, eds. 1972. *The Careless Technology: Ecology and International Development*. Garden City, N.Y.: Natural History Press. Describes and documents numerous cases of ecological backlash described at a major conference.

Foin, Theodore C., Jr. 1976. *Ecological Systems and the Environment*. Boston: Houghton Mifflin. A fine textbook at a slightly higher level than this book. Emphasis is on a systems approach.

Meadows, Donella H., et al. 1972. *The Limits to Growth*. New York: Universe Books. Description of a slightly revised version of Forrester's cybernetic model of the world ecosystem.

Meeker, Joseph W. 1972. "The Comedy of Survival." *North American Review*, Summer, pp. 11–17. Discussion of the relationship between literature and ecology with emphasis on diversity.

Mesarovic, Mihajlo, and Eduard Pestel. 1974. *Mankind at the Turning Point*. New York: Dutton. A computer model that analyzes the world in terms of different regions. Read along with the book by Meadows et al. (1972).

Odum, Eugene P. 1969. "The Strategy of Ecosystem Development." *Science*, vol. 164, 262–270. Excellent summary of succession.

Parsegian, V. L. 1972. *This Cybernetic World of Men, Machines and Earth Systems*. Garden City, N.Y.: Doubleday. Probably the best introduction to cybernetics.

Stumm, Werner, and Elisabeth Stumm-Zollinger. 1972. "Concepts of Pollution and Its Control." *Technology Review*, October/November, pp. 19–26. Introduction to diversity, stability, succession, and the ecological effects of pollution.

Whittaker, Robert H., and George M. Woodwell. 1972. "Evolution of Natural Communities." In John A. Wiens, ed., *Ecosystem Structure and Function*. Corvallis: Oregon State University Press. Good summary of diversity and succession.

Woodwell, G. M. 1970. "Effects of Pollution on the Structure and Physiology of Ecosystems." *Science*, vol. 168, 429–433. Superb analysis by a highly respected ecologist.

7

Human Population Dynamics

We'll all be a doubling, a doubling, a doubling.
We'll all be doubling in thirty-two years.

From "A Population Ballad"
Words and music by Pete Seeger, 1969

In this chapter we will look at the major factors affecting changes in the size of the human population. In the next chapter we will discuss the control of the size and growth rate of the human population.

7-1   Birth Rate and Death Rate

Crude Birth Rate and Crude Death Rate   In Section 1-2 we saw that the human population has gone around the bend when plotted as a J curve (Figure 1-1). Each new billion human beings is being added faster than the last billion. It took 2 to 5 million years to get the first billion humans on earth by 1800. It took 130 years to add another billion by 1930, and only 30 years more to add a third billion by 1960. But it took only 16 years to add the fourth billion by 1976. We may add the fifth billion by 1990, and the sixth billion only 10 years later, by 2000. One billion is about 4 times the present population of the United States. Lined up side by side, 1 billion people would stretch 914,800 kilometers (568,200 miles), or more than 200 times the distance between New York City and Los Angeles. Each 1 billion newcomers will need food, housing, water, medical care, and other necessities of life.

Has a soaring birth rate caused this dramatic increase in the rate of population growth? At first glance this is what you might expect. However, average worldwide birth rates have stayed about the same over most of the past 200 years; they have sharply declined in the more

Enrichment Studies, 1, 7, 8, 9, and 10 are related to this chapter.

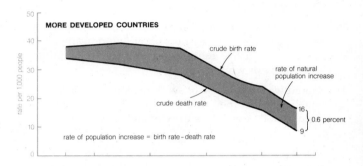

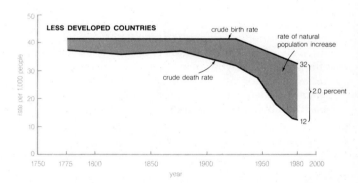

Figure 7-1   Estimated crude birth and death rates and rates of natural population increase in more developed and less developed countries between 1775 and 1980.

developed nations during the past 100 years and slightly declined in the less developed nations during the past 50 years (Figure 7-1).* How, then, can we possibly have the present population explosion?

*This statement must be qualified in two ways. First, births and deaths have not been (and still are not) well recorded in most less developed countries. This is why birth and death rates are often called crude birth and death rates. Second, this statement refers to an average of many countries, which individually may have had increases or decreases in birth rates.

First, you must realize that global population growth (or decline) is not determined only by birth rate. You must look at death rate, too. *Net population growth (or decline) for the world over a period of time is the difference between the total number of live births and the total number of deaths during that time period.* If there are more births than deaths, the world's population will increase.

Demographers, or population specialists, normally use the crude birth rate and crude death rate (often called birth rate or death rate) rather than total births and deaths to describe population growth or decline. The **crude birth rate** and **crude death rate** are the number of births and deaths per 1,000 persons in the population at the midpoint of a given year. To find the crude birth or death rate, we divide the total number of births or deaths per year by the total population at midyear and multiply the result by 1,000. The difference between the crude birth and death rates is known as the **rate of natural increase** (or **decrease**),* which is a measure of the change in population size.

Thus, population change on this planet is the difference between the crude birth rate and the crude death rate. As long as the birth rate is greater than the death rate over a given time period, there will be a net growth in population. Sometimes the population growth (or decline) rate is expressed as a percentage, as follows:

$$\frac{\text{percent annual}}{\text{growth rate}} = \frac{\text{crude birth rate} - \text{crude death rate}}{10}$$

For example, in 1981 the crude birth rate for the world was 28 and the crude death rate was 11. Then,

$$\text{percent annual growth rate} = \frac{28 - 11}{10} = \frac{17}{10} = 1.7\%$$

---

*For example, in 1980 the world population at midyear was 4,414,-000,000, or 4.414 billion. During the year there were about 123 million births and 48.5 million deaths. From these figures we can find the crude birth rate, crude death rate, and the rate of natural increase:

$$\text{crude birth rate} = \frac{\text{births per year}}{\text{midyear population}} \times 1,000 =$$

$$\frac{123,498,000}{4,414,000,000} \times 1,000 = 28 \text{ births per 1,000 population}$$

$$\text{crude death rate} = \frac{\text{deaths per year}}{\text{midyear population}} \times 1,000 =$$

$$\frac{48,554,000}{4,414,000,000} \times 1,000 = 11 \text{ deaths per 1,000 population}$$

rate of natural increase = crude birth rate − crude death rate = 28 − 11 = 17 persons per 1,000 population

For the planet as a whole, migration is not a factor. But people can leave (*emigrate* from) or enter (*immigrate* into) a given country or region. Thus, for a given country or region, population change is the difference between crude birth rate and crude death rate plus the crude migration rate. The **crude migration rate** is the difference between the number of people leaving and the number entering a given country or area per 1,000 persons in its population at midyear. If more persons immigrate than emigrate, the crude migration rate is positive. If more leave than enter, it is negative. The box on population change indicators shows the equations for calculating the figures discussed above.

World population growth is thus the result of an excess of births over deaths. Every time a person dies, an average of 2.5 babies are born. Birth and death rates for the planet are now so far out of balance (Figure 7-1) that world population is increasing by about 205,000 persons each day, or 75 million each year (this information is presented in the box on world population growth).* This means that every 3 years a population equal to the present U.S. population is being added to the world. The total world population is expected to increase from 4.6 billion in 1981 to about 6.1 billion by 2000.†

Words like *million* or *billion* often make little impression on us. But suppose you decided to take only 1 second to say hello to each of the 75 million persons added during the past year. Working 24 hours a day, you would need 2⅓ years to greet them, and during that time 163 million more persons would have arrived.

What has happened is that gradual declines in world birth rates have been offset by sharp decreases in death rates—especially in the less developed nations, which contain about 75 percent of the world's population. There are a number of interrelated reasons for this general decline in death rates, including improved agricultural production, better food distribution due to improved transportation, better nutrition, improved sanitation and water supplies, and improvements in medicine. Thus,

---

*All birth rate, death rate, and population growth figures are estimates, because births and deaths are registered incompletely or not at all in most less developed nations. To show this uncertainty, organizations such as the United Nations usually give low, medium, and high estimates. The figures quoted here are official medium UN estimates. Another example of uncertainty involves the controversy over the population of the People's Republic of China, the world's largest country. No one knows what the actual population of China is, and estimates range from 800 million to 1.2 billion, with the best estimate for 1980 being 975 million.

†Estimates range from 5.8 billion to 6.3 billion, with the average around 6.1 billion. The projections differ primarily because different estimates are used for the world's two most populous countries, China and India.

Population Change Indicators

World

net birth rate = total births per year

net death rate = total deaths per year

net population increase or decrease = net birth rate − net death rate

$$\text{crude birth rate} = \frac{\text{births per year}}{\text{midyear population}} \times 1{,}000$$

$$\text{crude death rate} = \frac{\text{deaths per year}}{\text{midyear population}} \times 1{,}000$$

rate of natural increase (or decrease) = crude birth rate − crude death rate

$$\text{percent annual growth rate} = \frac{\text{crude birth rate} - \text{crude death rate}}{10}$$

$$\text{approximate doubling time (years)} = \frac{70}{\text{percent growth}}$$

Country or Regional

$$\text{crude migration rate} = \frac{\text{immigrants per year} - \text{emigrants per year}}{\text{midyear population}} \times 1{,}000$$

rate of natural increase (or decrease) = crude birth rate − crude death rate + crude migration rate

$$\text{percent annual growth rate} = \frac{\text{crude birth rate} - \text{crude death rate} + \text{crude migration rate}}{10}$$

the explosive growth of the world's population over the past 100 years was not the result of a rise in birth rates but of a decline in death rates.

Annual percent population growth rates vary widely throughout the world, as shown in Figures 7-2 and 7-3. Since they are often confused, it is important to distinguish between *net population growth* and *population growth rate*. In the late 1970s, a series of newspaper headlines, such as "Population Time Bomb Fizzles," "Another Non-Crisis," and "Population Growth May Have Turned a Historic Corner," falsely implied that world population growth had stopped or almost stopped. What actually happened, as shown in Figure 7-4 on page 113, is that the annual percentage population growth rate had declined from 1.9 to 1.7 percent between 1970 and 1980. Despite this encouraging slowdown in the rate of population growth, annual births exceeded annual deaths by such a larger number (75 million) in 1980 than in 1970 (69 million), as shown in Figure 7-4. By 2000, it is projected to be growing at 100 million persons a year. Thus, the ticking of the world's population time bomb is still loud.

Figure 7-3 also shows how what appear to be only small annual percentage increases in population growth rates lead to very large increases in population. The **doubling time** is the time it takes for a population to double in size. Doubling time can be calculated by the *rule of 70*. The approximate doubling time in years can be found by dividing the annual percentage growth into 70. Hence, a population growing at 1 percent per year would double in size in 70 years (70/1 = 70); with a 2 percent annual growth rate, it would double in 35 years (70/2 = 35). Other examples are shown in Figure 7-3. In 1980 the doubling time for the world's population was about 41 years (70/1.7 = 41). If 1980 growth rates should continue, the population would double in only 18 years in Kenya, 22 years in Mexico, 36 years in India, 82 years in the U.S.S.R., 88 years in Canada, 99 years in the United States, and 385 years in Denmark.

We can also use doubling times to illustrate the dramatic increase in the rate of population growth on earth. During almost all of the time humans have inhabited the earth, the human population grew at an annual rate of only about 0.002 percent and thus doubled about every 35,000 years. Between 1650 and 1980, the annual growth rate increased almost by a factor of 1,000 to 1.7 percent, and the doubling time has decreased by a similar factor to 41 years.

The United States   In the 1970s a wave of newspaper headlines, editorials, and articles declared "U.S. Population Explosion Over," "Birth Rates at All-Time Low," "ZPG Has Been Attained," and "U.S. Headed for Population Decline—Sociologist Calls for More Births." Because such misleading stories will probably appear again and again, let us examine them.

It is true that the crude birth rate in the United States has made a significant decline from a high of 26.6 per 1,000 population in 1947 to a low of 14.7 in 1976, followed by a rise to 16.2 in 1980 (Figure 7-5 on page 113). During this same period, annual death rates remained nearly constant at about 9 deaths per 1,000 population.

Thus, although the rate of natural population growth (excluding migration) has declined since 1947 except for the slight upturn since 1976, the U.S. population continues to grow. This is because the birth rate (around 16) is considerably larger than the death rate (around 9). In 1980 the natural increase in the U.S. population was about 1.6 million persons. To this natural increase we have to add a net legal immigration of about 400,000 persons per year (or a crude migration rate of 0.96 per 1,000 persons per year), so that the total official growth in 1980 was about 2.2 million or an average of about 5,500 new Americans each day (see box on U.S. population growth).

Average World Population Growth in 1980

    338,000 babies were born each day
− 133,000 persons died each day
    205,000 people were added each day

or

1.4 million people per week

or

75 million people per year

Average U.S. Population Growth in 1980

    9,849 babies were born each day
− 5,402 persons died each day
    4,447 people were added each day
+ 1,100 legal immigrants
    5,547 new Americans each day

or

38,829 per week

or

2.2 million per year (without counting illegal immigration)

Actually the total population growth in 1980 was probably 2.5 to 2.8 million, since the U.S. Immigration and Naturalization Service estimates that 460,000 to 800,000 illegal immigrants enter the United States each year, with 80 to 90 percent of them from Mexico. However, accurate estimates of illegal immigrants are very difficult to make. For example, many Mexicans go back and forth across the border several times a year in order to find temporary work in the United States. Figure 7-5 illustrates why we should not confuse a decline in the rate at which a population is growing with an actual decrease in population size.

Figure 7-2 Rate of natural population increase (excluding migration) throughout the world in 1980.

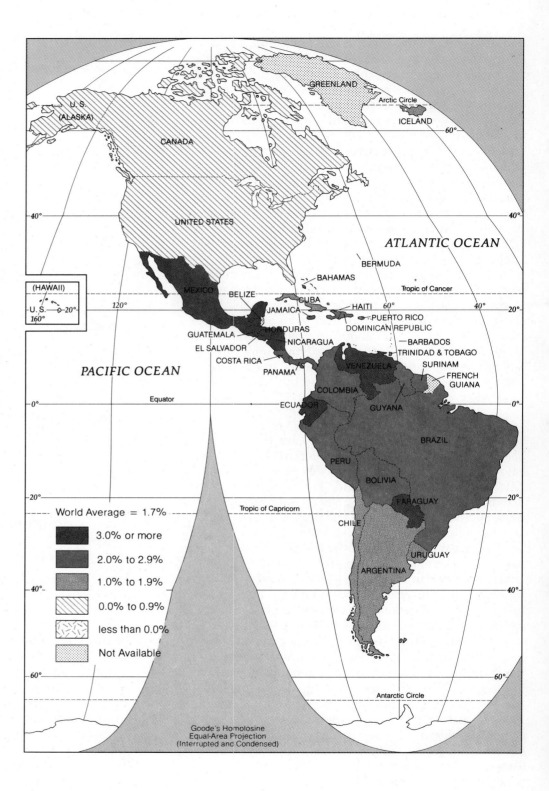

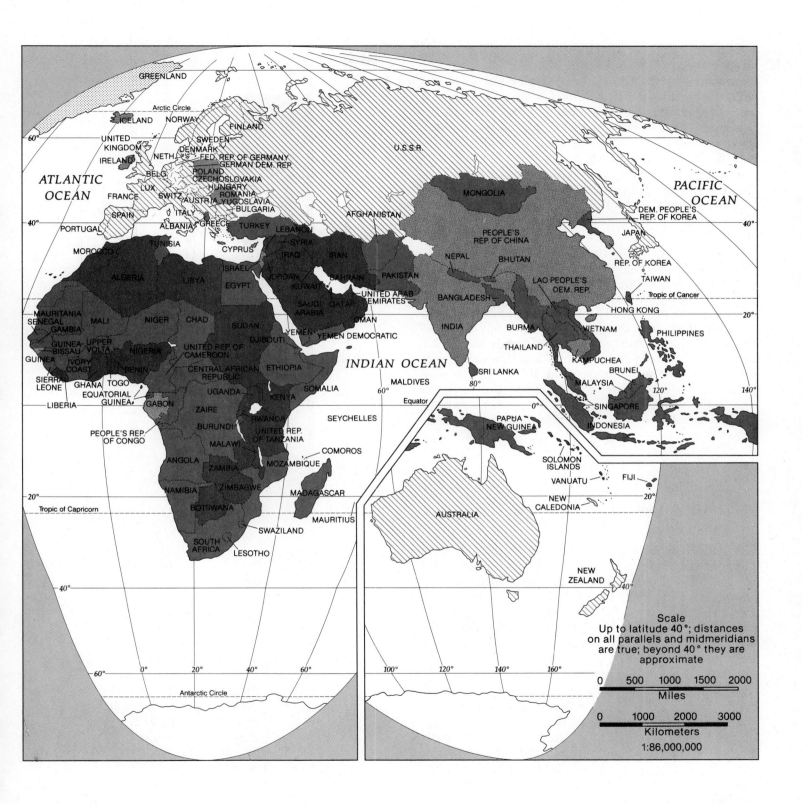

ATLANTIC
OCEAN

PACIFIC
OCEAN

GREENLAND

Arctic Circle

ICELAND   NORWAY
UNITED   SWEDEN   FINLAND
KINGDOM   DENMARK
IRELAND   NETH.   FED. REP OF GERMANY
          BELG.   GERMAN DEM. REP
          LUX   POLAND
FRANCE   SWITZ   CZECHOSLOVAKIA
          AUSTRIA HUNGARY
SPAIN   ITALY   ROMANIA   YUGOSLAVIA
      ALBANIA GREECE   BULGARIA
PORTUGAL

MOROCCO   TUNISIA   TURKEY   LEBANON
                          CYPRUS   SYRIA
ALGERIA   LIBYA   ISRAEL   IRAQ   IRAN
                    EGYPT   JORDAN KUWAIT   BAHRAIN
MAURITANIA   SAUDI   QATAR   UNITED ARAB
SENEGAL   ARABIA   EMIRATES
GAMBIA   MALI   NIGER   CHAD   SUDAN   OMAN
GUINEA UPPER   DJIBOUTI YEMEN
BISSAU VOLTA   NIGERIA   YEMEN DEMOCRATIC
GUINEA   IVORY   UNITED REP OF
          COAST BENIN   CAMEROON
SIERRA   CENTRAL AFRICAN   ETHIOPIA
LEONE GHANA TOGO   REPUBLIC
      EQUATORIAL   UGANDA   SOMALIA
LIBERIA GUINEA   GABON
PEOPLE'S REP.   ZAIRE   KENYA
OF CONGO   BURUNDI   UNITED REP.
              RWANDA   OF TANZANIA
                MALAWI
ANGOLA   ZAMBIA   MOZAMBIQUE   COMOROS
NAMIBIA   ZIMBABWE   MADAGASCAR
      BOTSWANA
              SWAZILAND   MAURITIUS
SOUTH
AFRICA LESOTHO

AFGHANISTAN

MONGOLIA

PEOPLE'S
REP. OF CHINA

NEPAL   BHUTAN

PAKISTAN   BANGLADESH   LAO PEOPLE'S
                    DEM. REP.
INDIA   BURMA   VIETNAM
      THAILAND
                KAMPUCHEA
SRI LANKA   MALAYSIA
MALDIVES   SINGAPORE
                BRUNEI
                INDONESIA

DEM. PEOPLE'S
REP. OF KOREA

JAPAN

REP. OF KOREA

TAIWAN

HONG KONG

PHILIPPINES

Tropic of Cancer

INDIAN OCEAN

SEYCHELLES

Equator

PAPUA
NEW GUINEA

SOLOMON
ISLANDS

VANUATU   FIJI

NEW
CALEDONIA

AUSTRALIA

NEW
ZEALAND

Tropic of Capricorn

Antarctic Circle

Scale
Up to latitude 40°; distances
on all parallels and midmeridians
are true; beyond 40° they are
approximate

0   500   1000   1500   2000
Miles

0   1000   2000   3000
Kilometers
1:86,000,000

In 1980, the official U.S. population was about 228 million—an 87-fold increase in 200 years. Actually, the population was probably somewhere between 236 and 241 million, since the U.S. Bureau of the Census missed an estimated 5 to 7 million people in the 1980 census, and there were an estimated 3 to 6 million illegal immigrants in the United States by 1981. Even in a country with sophisticated record keeping, it is hard to get accurate population figures.

But with birth rates declining, shouldn't the U.S. population stabilize soon? The answer to this question is a resounding no, unless the crude birth rate declines to about 9 to equal the crude death rate or the crude death rate rises sharply to about 16 to equal the crude birth rate. No one expects either of these events to happen in the near future. *The United States is a long way from zero population growth, or ZPG.* Indeed, the U.S. Bureau of the Census projected that the U.S. population would be about 260 million by the year 2000 and still be growing, assuming an average completed family size of 2.1 children per woman and an annual legal immigration of 400,000 persons per year (see Figure 7-7). To see why population will continue to grow in the United States and in the world for many years to come, we have to look at several other factors that affect future population growth.

7-2 Fertility Rate

General and Total Fertility Rates We have seen the importance of birth rate minus death rate in population dynamics. Most population experts have consistently been wrong in their projections of world and U.S. population growth in this century. They missed not only the postwar baby boom between 1945 and 1960 in the United States but also the dramatic fall in the U.S. birth rate between 1957 and 1976. Why?

The answer to this question is not fully known. In some cases, no reliable data are available. But the main reason seems to be that during the approximately 30-year period that women are fertile, many changes in attitudes toward children, ideal family size, use of birth control methods, women's roles, and life-styles take place. In addition, a decline in the crude birth rate (assuming crude death rates remain constant) does not tell us whether women are having fewer children on the average or whether there is simply a lower percentage of

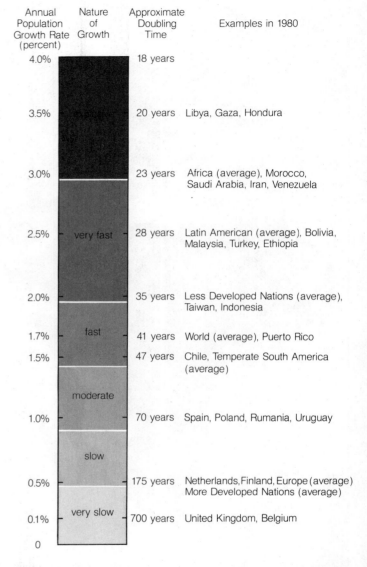

Figure 7-3 Population growth rate and doubling time (70 ÷ annual percent population growth).

women in the population who are in their most reproductive years.

To improve their ability to understand and project population changes, demographers use another factor in population dynamics called the *fertility rate*. There are two types of fertility rates in common use—the *general fertility rate* and the *total fertility rate*. The **general fertility rate** is the number of live births per 1,000 women in the reproductive age group (15 to 44 in the United States and 15 to 49 in most other countries). The general fertility rate in the United States has fallen sharply from a high

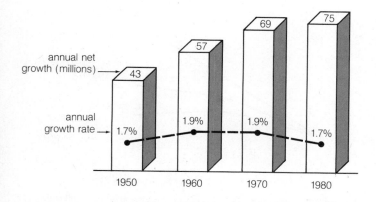

annual net growth (millions)

annual growth rate

| 43 | 57 | 69 | 75 |

1.7% 1.9% 1.9% 1.7%

1950   1960   1970   1980

Figure 7-4 Comparison of annual net population growth and annual percent population growth rate.

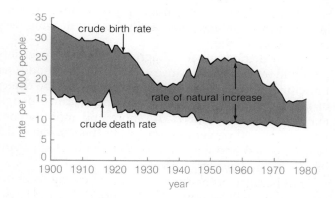

Figure 7-5 Crude birth and death rates and the rate of natural population increase (migration excluded) in the United States between 1900 and 1980.

of about 123 in 1957 to a low of about 66 in 1976, followed by a slight rise in 1980 to about 67 (Figure 7-6). From Figure 7-6 we can see that the general fertility rate has oscillated rather wildly during the past 50 years. Figure 7-6 also shows why crude birth rates dropped so sharply between 1957 and 1976. The average American woman simply had fewer children during her reproductive years. No one understands exactly why this drop occurred, but sociologist Charles Westoff believes that a major factor for the drop in the 1960s was the reduction in the number of unwanted and mistimed births because of the widespread use of effective birth control methods and the availability of legal abortion. Other factors include the rising cost of raising a family, the increasing number of women working outside the home, and the greater social acceptance of childless couples.

In order to make better projections of future population changes, demographers use the **total fertility rate**, which is a *projection* of the average number of children a woman will have during her entire reproductive period (ages 15 to 44 in the United States and ages 15 to 49 in most countries), if she continues the same reproductive rate as women in their reproductive years do today. In 1980 the average total fertility rate in the world was 3.8 children per woman. The average rate was 4.4 in the less developed nations and 2.0 in the more developed nations. This shows very clearly why the world is a long way from zero population growth. Note from Figure 7-6 that the peak of the postwar baby boom occurred in 1957, when the average total fertility rate reached 3.7 children per woman. This was followed by a sharp drop to an average of 1.8 children per woman in 1980. This baby boom was apparently caused by a mix of factors, including better economic conditions (good jobs and

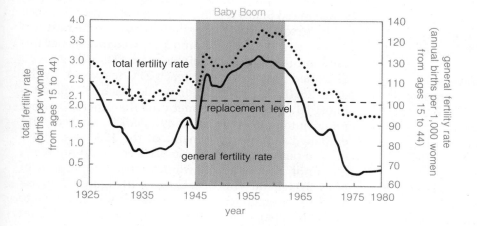

Figure 7-6 General fertility rate and total fertility rate for the United States between 1925 and 1980. The shaded area shows the peak years of the baby boom.

earnings along with mortgage guarantees for housing and college education grants for World War II veterans), an increase in preferred family size, early marriage, and rapid parenting of 2 to 3 children.

Logic suggests that two children should suffice to replace two parents. The actual average number of children needed for replacement, however, is slightly higher than two. In more developed countries the replacement level is 2.1 children per woman (Figure 7-6), and in the less developed nations it is about 2.7. The reasons that both these numbers are above two are that some female children die before reaching their reproductive years (especially in less developed nations) and that there is a slightly higher percentage of male children than female. In other words, if females in the United States had an average of 2.1 children and females in less developed nations had an average of 2.7 children, one female would survive and could replace each mother.

Possibilities for Stabilizing U.S. Population How close is the United States to ZPG? Since 1957 the average total fertility rate in the United States dropped from a peak of 3.76 children per woman to a record low of 1.75 in 1976 and then rose slightly to 1.8 by 1980 (Figure 7-6)—well below replacement level. Some newspapers incorrectly reported that the United States had reached ZPG because the total fertility rate had fallen below replacement level. It is very important to realize that a total fertility rate at or even below replacement level does not necessarily mean zero growth of the population. ZPG occurs (neglecting net migration) only when the birth rate equals the death rate. Since the crude birth rate in 1980 (16 births per 1,000 persons) is still much greater than the crude death rate (9 deaths per 1,000 persons) (Figure 7-5), the U.S. population continues to grow by about 2.0 million per year (including net legal immigration) and at about 2.5 to 2.8 million per year if net illegal immigration is included. The United States is a long way from ZPG in spite of the dramatic drop in the total fertility rate.

It is true, however, that if the total fertility rate stays at or below replacement level, a population will eventually stabilize (excluding migration) or decrease. No one knows whether U.S. fertility rates will remain below replacement level—something that Figure 7-6 shows has not happened in the past 50 years. Indeed, between 1976 and 1980 the total fertility rate showed a slight rise from 1.75 to 1.8 births per woman. Some demographers believe that the total fertility rate will continue to rise. They argue that couples who have deferred parenthood may

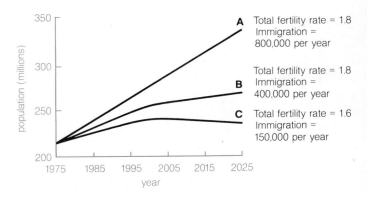

Figure 7-7 Projections of U.S. population size assuming different constant total fertility rates and annual immigration rates.

decide to start having children and make up for their late start. In addition, the present delay in childbearing by women aged 25 to 34 may not apply to younger women in their teens and early 20s. Attitudes could swing back to having more children.

Other demographers disagree. They believe fertility rates will remain low because birth control methods (see Enrichment Study 8) now allow most women the choice of not having unwanted children and because people may want fewer children. As more and more women work (about 60 percent of women in their prime childbearing years) and get married later or not at all, many don't want to have large families.

But because of the uncertainty in knowing what human beings will do, population expert Philip M. Hauser has said that anyone who claims to be able to predict future population change is either a fool or a charlatan. This does not mean, however, that projections (as opposed to predictions) based on clearly defined assumptions are not useful. The U.S. Bureau of the Census has made several projections for future population growth in the United States (Figure 7-7). From Figure 7-7 we see that if the total fertility rate should rise over the next few years from 1.8 to 2.1 children per woman and net immigration (legal plus illegal) averages 800,000 per year, the United States can never reach ZPG (curve A). By the year 2025, the U.S. population would reach 337 million—almost 50 percent more Americans than in 1980. If net annual immigration totals only 400,000 per year and completed family size remains at the 1980 rate of 1.8 children per woman, the United States would not reach ZPG until 2035, when it would have a population of about 270 million (curve B). Curve C in Figure 7-7 shows that if the average total fertility rate should decrease to 1.6 children per woman over the next few years and net immigration is decreased to 150,000 a year, the United States would reach ZPG by the year 2007, when it would have a population of 241 million. After that the population size would slowly decrease.

The transition from a growing to a stationary population in the United States can only be achieved in three ways: The death rate can be increased (a morally unacceptable solution), the birth rate can be decreased, and immigration can be reduced or eliminated. It seems unlikely that the United States, itself a nation of immigrants, will stop legal immigration, although it could take steps to drastically reduce illegal entry.

A reasonable goal for the United States is to attain ZPG within the next 50 years, with a population near 250 million. As mentioned before, this would require a total fertility rate of 1.7 children per woman (only slightly below the 1980 level of 1.8), allow 400,000 immigrants to enter each year, and sharply curtail illegal entry.

In the next chapter we will look at some of the implications of living in such a ZPG, or dynamic steady state (Section 6-2), society.

Possibilities for World Population Stabilization By 1980 Great Britain, Sweden, and Belgium had attained ZPG and population was even declining in Austria, East and West Germany, and Luxembourg, where deaths now exceed births. If present trends continue, several other more developed European nations should reach ZPG by 1990. Achieving ZPG in the world, however, is more difficult than in the United States and other more developed nations because poor nations have a much higher average total fertility rate. For world population to even begin the transition to ZPG, the average world total fertility rate would have to drop from 3.8 in 1980 to about 2.5 children per woman (2.7 in the less developed nations and 2.1 in the more developed nations). Once this world replacement level is reached and maintained, population would still grow for 70 to 100 years before stabilizing (Figure 7-8). Figure 7-8 shows that the year in which this world replacement level is reached has an important effect on the overall stationary population size. From Figure 7-8, *it appears that between now and 2050 world population is likely to grow to at least 8 billion and possibly to 12 billion unless death rates rise.* World population could stabilize eventually at about 10 to 15 billion, with 8 billion being the likely minimum.

From Figure 7-8 we can see why plans to control population growth must be made and put into effect 70 to 100 years in advance. In the next chapter we will look at some of the ways that world population growth can be brought under control.

7-3 Average Marriage Age

The average fertility rate of women is influenced by a number of economic, social, and psychological factors. One important factor is the *average age of women at the time of their first marriage*, or, more precisely, *the average age at which women give birth to their first child.* This seems

Table 7-1   Situation of the World's Children in 1980

Item	Number of World's Children Affected (millions)	Percentage of World's Children Affected
Expected life span less than 60 years	693	48
No access to effective medical care	604	42
No access to safe water	590	41
No adequate housing	417	29
Living in countries with average per capita income less than $200 per year	396	28
Not in school (ages 5–14)	250	17
Inadequate food (undernourished)	230	16
Living in slums and squatter settlements	156	11
Death each year from six major infectious diseases	5	0.3

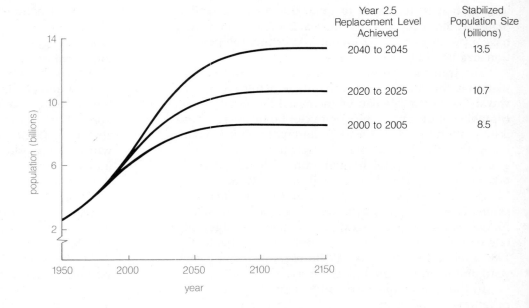

Figure 7-8 Projections of world population growth with different assumptions about when average replacement-level fertility of 2.5 children per woman is reached.

Year 2.5 Replacement Level Achieved	Stabilized Population Size (billions)
2040 to 2045	13.5
2020 to 2025	10.7
2000 to 2005	8.5

to hold true in both less developed nations with high birth rates and young marriage ages and more developed nations with low birth rates and late marriage ages. Increasing age at marriage has been an important factor in reducing fertility in countries such as Indonesia, the Philippines, Malaysia, and China.

If society uses special pressure to raise the marriage age, as in Ireland, India, and China, the fertility rate normally drops, because older brides tend to have fewer children. By raising the average marriage age (or age at which the first child is born, whether the woman is married or not) to 24, the reproductive period is changed from 15–44 to 24–44 and the prime reproductive period is cut almost in half from 20–29 to 24–29. This will almost certainly lead to fewer children per family and is probably one of the fastest and surest ways to attain ZPG. In the United States, Great Britain, and Australia, women who marry before age 20 have an average of one child more than those who marry after age 25. To employ increasing the marriage age as a key factor in attaining ZPG will be difficult, since the worldwide median age for marriage is 15, although it is rising in some less developed nations (such as China). Setting the marriage age higher by law, as several less developed nations (such as China) have done in recent years, is often hard to enforce because of political, cultural, and religious barriers. An easier and more effective approach may be to provide free or very low cost contraceptives and to provide more education and employment opportunities for young women.

Since 1955 the average marriage age in the United States has been increasing and is now near 23 years of age. At the same time, however, a lower percentage of women are now getting married. In addition, a higher percentage of women are getting divorced—with the divorce rate more than doubling between 1960 and 1980. According to the U.S. Bureau of the Census, 48 percent of American women from ages 20 to 24 were still single in 1978, compared with 29 percent in 1960. Many American women who plan to marry do not do so until they are almost 30 and often opt for a career in place of child raising.

7-4 Age Structure

Number of Women of Childbearing Age Why will world population keep growing for 50 to 100 or more years (assuming death rates don't rise) even after replacement fertility levels are reached (Figure 7-8)? Why do many demographers expect the U.S. birth rate to rise between now and 1993, even though fertility rates may drop or stay at low levels? To answer these questions we must consider a fourth factor in population dynamics. It is the **age structure,** or *age distribution,* of a population—the number or percentage of persons at each age level in a population. A major factor in population growth is the number or percentage of women of childbearing age and especially the number in the prime reproductive years of

20 to 29. If a large number of women are of childbearing age, births can rise even when women on the average have fewer children. *Any population with a large number of people below age 29, and especially below age 15, will have a powerful built-in momentum to maintain population growth.*

One of the most alarming statistics is that in 1980 about 35 percent of the people on this planet were under 15 years of age (Figure 7-9). As shown in Table 7-1, many of these young people live threatened and degraded lives. These young people constitute the broad base of the age structure of the world population and represent the great explosion of births that is likely to come—especially in less developed nations—unless death rates rise sharply. In fact, there are now about 800 million women capable of reproducing—more than at any time in history.

Population age structure also explains why it will probably take at least 50 years for the United States to reach ZPG, even if present historically low fertility rates are maintained at 1.7 to 2.0 births per woman (Figure 7-6). It also explains why the number of births each year in the United States will probably rise between 1977 and 1993. From 1947 to 1964 the United States had a baby boom (Figure 7-6). Women born in 1947 entered their peak reproduction years of 20 to 29 in 1966 and stayed there until 1976, whereas those born in 1963 will enter this phase in 1984 and stay there until 1993. Thus, the postwar baby boom has an echo effect that becomes the potential "mother boom" of the 1980s. Between 1960 and 1985, the number of women between 20 and 29 in the United States will almost double from 11 million to 20 million. Sharp increases in population growth thus affect the future growth and structure of society for 20 to 40 years, as the population bulge moves through an entire generation. Thus, *even though many American couples are now having smaller families, the number of births could easily rise during the 1980s—not because women will have more babies but because there are more women who can have babies.*

Age Structure Diagrams We can obtain an age structure diagram for the world or for a given country or region by plotting the percentages of the total population in three age categories: preproductive (ages 0 to 14), reproductive (ages 15 to 44 with prime reproductive ages 20 to 29), and postproductive (ages 45 to 75), as shown in Figure 7-10 on page 120. *The shape of the age structure diagram is a key to whether a population might expand, decline, or stay the same.* A rapidly expanding population has a very broad base with a large number already in the reproductive category and an even larger percentage of children ready to move into this category during the fol-

lowing 15 years. This is the general shape of the age structure diagrams for most less developed nations—a shape that is not expected to change between today and 2000. A declining population has a small base, and a stable population with a zero growth rate has a shape with vertical sides rather than pyramidal sides. In such a stabilized age structure, all generations and age groups are about the same size.

Now that we have seen the general shapes of age structure diagrams, let us look at a few actual examples. Figure 7-11 on page 121 compares the age structure diagrams in 1977 for Mexico, a country with very fast population growth; the United States, which had slow population growth; and Sweden, which was approaching ZPG. (By 1980 Sweden had reached ZPG.)

Making Future Projections from Age Structure Diagrams In Figure 7-12 on page 122 we can see that the baby boom in the United States between 1947 and 1964 (Figure 7-6) caused a bulge in the age structure, which will be moving through the prime reproductive ages of 20 to 29 between 1970 and 1987 and through older age groups in later years. As this large baby boom group passes through succeeding age groups, it creates a need for rapid expansion of schools, housing, employment opportunities, medical services, and eventually social security. As economist Robert Samuelson put it, "You cannot understand economics or politics in the United States today without understanding the impact of the baby boom."

By looking at these diagrams, we can make some projections of the age, social, and economic structures of the United States. The 1960s and 1970s have been called the "generation of youth," with the number of elementary and high shool children jumping 70 percent between 1950 and 1970. For the same reasons the period between 1975 and 1990 could be called the "age of the young adult"; after 1990 there will be an increase in the number of middle-aged adults.

Between 2010 and 2030, the United States will have the largest number and percentage of older persons in its history (assuming the death rates don't rise). The burden of caring for so many older people will fall on the shoulders of the much smaller group of babies born in the 1960s, 1970s, and 1980s. By 2030 there will be nearly 60 million Americans aged 65 and over, compared with only 25 million in 1980. This increase in older persons could put a severe strain on the U.S. social security system. Under this system, payments made by the current work force are used to make payments to retired persons. In 1980 three workers were paying into the system

Figure 7-9 Percentage of the population under 15 years of age in 1980.

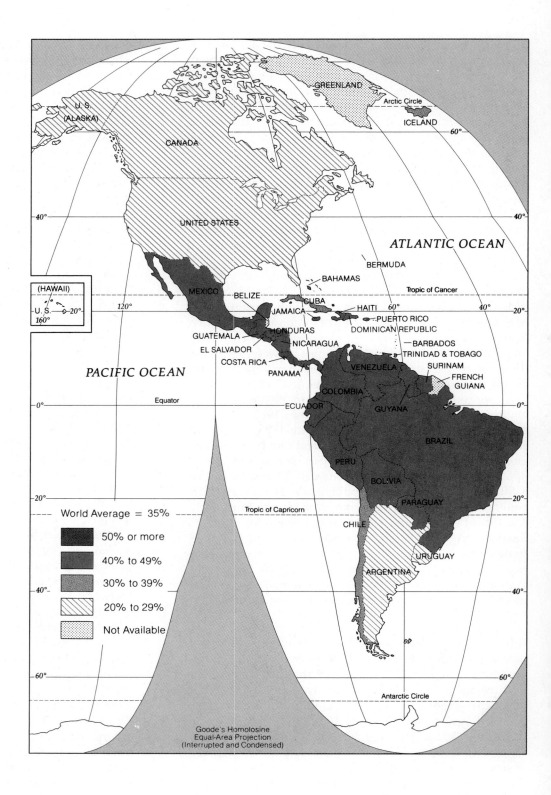

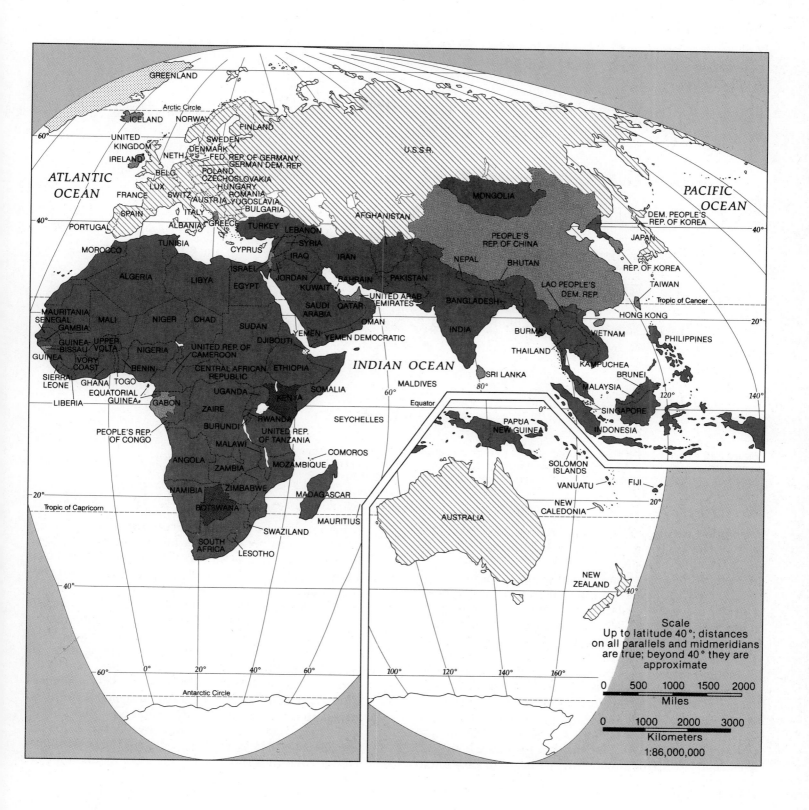

GREENLAND

Arctic Circle

ICELAND NORWAY
FINLAND
60°
UNITED SWEDEN
KINGDOM
IRELAND DENMARK FED. REP OF GERMANY
NETH. GERMAN DEM. REP
BELG. POLAND
LUX. CZECHOSLOVAKIA
FRANCE HUNGARY
SWITZ. AUSTRIA ROMANIA
40° YUGOSLAVIA
SPAIN ITALY BULGARIA
PORTUGAL ALBANIA GREECE TURKEY LEBANON
SYRIA
MOROCCO TUNISIA CYPRUS
IRAQ IRAN
ISRAEL
ALGERIA LIBYA JORDAN BAHRAIN PAKISTAN
EGYPT KUWAIT
SAUDI QATAR UNITED ARAB
MAURITANIA ARABIA EMIRATES
SENEGAL MALI NIGER CHAD OMAN
GAMBIA SUDAN YEMEN
GUINEA- UPPER DJIBOUTI YEMEN DEMOCRATIC
BISSAU VOLTA NIGERIA
GUINEA IVORY UNITED REP. OF
COAST CAMEROON ETHIOPIA
SIERRA CENTRAL AFRICAN
LEONE GHANA TOGO REPUBLIC
EQUATORIAL SOMALIA
LIBERIA GUINEA UGANDA
GABON ZAIRE KENYA
RWANDA
PEOPLE'S REP. BURUNDI UNITED REP.
OF CONGO OF TANZANIA
MALAWI
ANGOLA ZAMBIA
ZIMBABWE MOZAMBIQUE
NAMIBIA
BOTSWANA
SWAZILAND
SOUTH LESOTHO
AFRICA

ATLANTIC
OCEAN

U.S.S.R.

MONGOLIA

AFGHANISTAN

PEOPLE'S
REP. OF CHINA

NEPAL BHUTAN

BANGLADESH LAO PEOPLE'S
DEM. REP.

INDIA BURMA VIETNAM

THAILAND

SRI LANKA KAMPUCHEA

MALAYSIA

SINGAPORE

INDONESIA

PACIFIC
OCEAN

DEM. PEOPLE'S
REP. OF KOREA

JAPAN

REP. OF KOREA

TAIWAN

Tropic of Cancer

HONG KONG

PHILIPPINES

BRUNEI

INDIAN OCEAN

MALDIVES 80°

SEYCHELLES Equator 0°

COMOROS

MADAGASCAR

MAURITIUS

Tropic of Capricorn

Antarctic Circle

PAPUA
NEW GUINEA

SOLOMON
ISLANDS

VANUATU FIJI

NEW
CALEDONIA

AUSTRALIA

NEW
ZEALAND

120° 140°

20°

Scale
Up to latitude 40°; distances
on all parallels and midmeridians
are true; beyond 40° they are
approximate

0 500 1000 1500 2000
Miles

0 1000 2000 3000
Kilometers

1:86,000,000

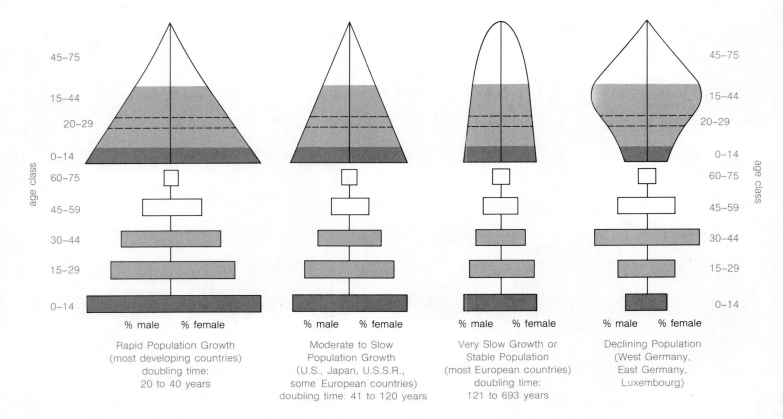

Figure 7-10 Major types of age structure diagrams for human populations. Dark portions represent preproductive periods (0–14), shaded portions represent reproductive years (15–44), clear portions are postproductive years (45–75), and dotted lines show prime reproductive years (20–29).

to support each of the 25 million retirees. By 2030 only two workers will be paying for each of the estimated 60 million retired persons.

We can also use the age structure diagrams in Figure 7-12 to project answers to other interesting and important questions. For instance, what type of job opportunities will you have? Which businesses will grow and which will decline over the next two decades? Between 1947 and 1964, about 68 million children were born—a fifth of the present U.S. population. This means that the overloaded classrooms of the 1950s and 1960s were replaced in the 1970s by high unemployment rates for teenagers and adults under 25, as large numbers of baby boom adults flooded the job market. Almost half of all unemployed people in the United States in 1977 were between ages 20 and 25. This situation won't begin to ease until after 1988, when the last of the baby boom cohorts (a term for all those born in a given year) turn 25. This pressure of "baby boomers" on the job market will become even more intense in the 1980s because of the enor-

mous increase in working women, many of whom are deciding to postpone childbearing or to remain childless. In 1960, 35 percent of all American women 16 and over were working or actively looking for work. By 1981, this figure had increased to over 50 percent.

By 1980 there were 40 million more baby boomers between ages 20 and 29 than there were in 1960. This is creating large housing demands and rapidly rising housing costs. In addition, older houses coming onto the market, which were built for larger families, may be too expensive to heat and maintain for smaller families. There will also probably be a rise in demand for furniture, appliances, adult clothing, adult education, travel, and entertainment over the next two decades. Job advancement will be much slower than in the present generation, and there may be cutthroat competition for the few upper-level jobs. Many well-educated people will be working in jobs far below their level of training and expectations. As a result, mental health problems may increase.

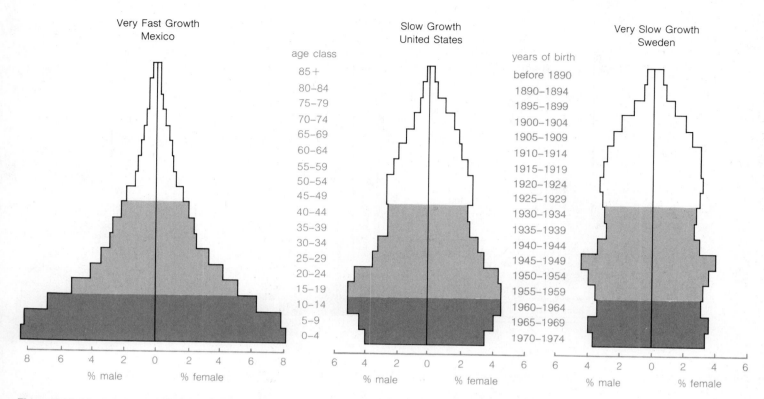

Figure 7-11 Age structure diagrams in 1977 for Mexico, which has very fast population growth; the United States, which has slow population growth; and Sweden, a country that reached ZPG in 1980.

The smaller number of teenagers in the 1980s will make recruiting more difficult for the military services. As a result, there could be increased pressure to start up the peacetime drafting of men between the ages of 18 and 24. Women may also be drafted to compensate for the drop in the number of people in this age group.

In the 1990s the baby boom generation will be settling into middle age. These adults may face relatively little opportunity for advancement unless they somehow force those aged 45 to 59 to retire early. This may cause a new surge in adult education in the 1990s as people go back to school to change to less competitive careers or to improve their skills in order to compete more effectively for the small number of advancement opportunities. We should also see more young leaders in government, politics, and private industry. Also during the 1990s the U.S. divorce rate—which was among the world's highest in 1980—is likely to remain high as baby boomers pass through their 30s and early 40s, the ages when divorce is most likely.

This bulge in the age structure will also cause changes in the work force. The work force of a popula-tion is drawn primarily from those of age 20 to 65, who support children and retired people. The ratio of old and young dependents to the work force is called the **dependency load.** One problem of the 1960s was that a relatively small work force had a large dependency load, particularly of children. If present trends continue, by 2030 a relatively small work force will have to support a large number of retired people.

The declining birth and fertility rates of the 1960s and 1970s will also have important effects. Enrollments in elementary schools began dropping in the 1970s. In the late 1970s the decline moved into the high schools, and in the 1980s it began affecting college enrollments. College enrollments may remain steady or even rise slightly, however, if a larger percentage of high school graduates with poor job prospects go to college or if more unemployed young adults return to college. The decrease in elementary and high school enrollments reduces the need to build new schools, which in turn reduces the tax burden on adults. But it also means a flood of unemployed teachers. The lower number of teenagers over the next decade should also mean lower sales of

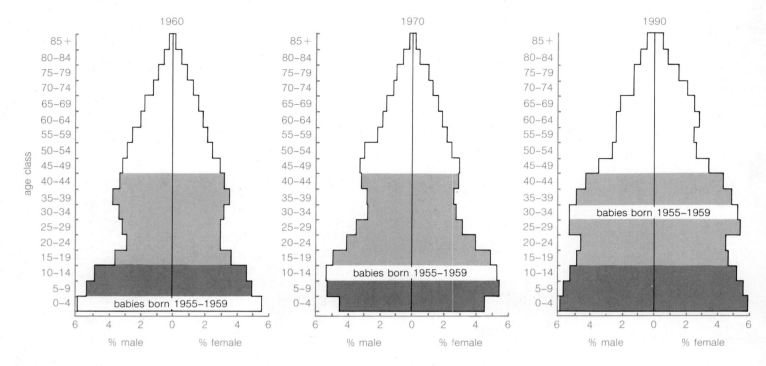

Figure 7-12   Age structure of the U.S. population in 1960, 1970, and 1990 (projected). The population bulge of babies born in 1955 to 1959 will slowly move upward.

teenage clothing, record albums, stereo equipment, bicycles, and other youth-oriented items.

The people born during a *baby bust* period of low birth and fertility rates have significant social and economic effects. Such a period occurred in the early 1930s during the Depression (Figures 7-5 and 7-6). The relatively few people born in those years have been called the "good times" cohorts. They found uncrowded classrooms, ample job opportunities, and no housing shortage, and by the time they retire, the large baby boom generation they parented should be able to help support them.

The latest baby bust cohort of people born in the 1970s, when fertility rates were low, should have a much easier time than the baby boom generation that preceded them. Fewer of them will be competing for education, jobs, and services. In addition, public services will have increased to support the larger baby boom generation. The baby bust cohort, however, may find it hard to get job promotions as they reach middle age because upper-level positions will be filled by the baby boom group.

From these few projections, we can see that any bulge or indentation in the age structure of a population can create a number of important social and economic changes that ripple through a society for 70 years.

In summary, we have seen that there are four major factors in human population dynamics.* They are:

1. *Birth and death rate* (as long as the birth rate is greater than the death rate, the population will grow).

2. *Total fertility rate* (the average number of children that a woman in the reproductive age group has) and *general fertility rate* (the number of live births per year per 1,000 women in the reproductive age group).

3. *Average first marriage age* or *average age when first child is born* (normally the later the marriage age, the fewer children per average family).

4. *Age structure* (of particular importance is the number of women in the reproductive ages and the percentage of the population under age 15).

We must be wary of any population projection unless it considers all of these factors. Knowing the unpredictability of human beings, we should be cautious even then. Macbeth's challenge could be the demographer's motto: "If you can look into the seeds of time / And say

---

*There are other factors not covered in this introductory presentation.

Table 7-2 Major Characteristics of Less Developed and More Developed Countries in 1980

Less Developed Countries	More Developed Countries
High crude birth rates (25–50 births per 1,000 population, average 32)	Low crude birth rates (10–20 births per 1,000 population, average 16)
Low to high crude death rates (9–25 deaths per 1,000 population, average 12)	Low crude death rates (9–10 deaths per 1,000 population, average 9)
Low to fairly high average life expectancy (average 57 years)	High average life expectancy (average 72 years)
Rapid population growth (average 2%)	Slow population growth (average 0.6%)
Large fraction of population under 15 years old (average 39%)	Moderate fraction of population under 15 years old (average 24%)
Moderate to high infant mortality rate (40–200 deaths of infants under 1 year old per 1,000 live births, average 110)	Low infant mortality (8–20 deaths of infants under 1 year old per 1,000 live births, average 20)
Moderate to high total fertility rate (average 4.4 children per woman)	Low total fertility rate (average 2 children per woman)
Low to moderate per capita daily food supply (1,500–2,700 calories per person per day)	High per capita daily food supply (3,100–3,500 calories per person per day)
High illiteracy level (25%–75%)	Low illiteracy level (1%–4%)
Mainly rural, farming population (33% to 80% labor force in agriculture)	Mainly urban, industrial population (5%–30% of labor force in agriculture)
Low per capita energy use (average 3 million kilocalories per person per year)	High per capita energy use (average 30 million kilocalories per person per year)
Low to moderate average per capita income (widespread poverty) ($90–$3,000 per person per year, average $560)	High average per capita income (widespread affluence) ($3,000–$12,000 per person per year, average $6,260)

which grain will grow and which will not, / Speak then to me."

7-5 The Geography of Population: The Rich-Poor Gap

Comparison of Less Developed and More Developed Nations The world has polarized into two major groups—one rich and one poor; one literate, the other largely illiterate; one overfed and overweight, one hungry and malnourished; one with a moderate to low rate of population growth, the other with a very high rate. About one-fourth of the world's population is found in the more developed or rich countries, such as the United States, the U.S.S.R., Japan, most European nations, Australia, and New Zealand. These nations account for about 85 percent of the gross world product (or total expenditures) and use about 80 percent of the world's

resources. In sharp contrast, about three-fourths of the world's population is found in less developed or poor nations,* found mostly in Asia, Africa, and Central and South America. These nations account for only about 15 percent of the gross world product (GWP) and use only 20 percent of the world's resources.

The rate of population growth is beginning to decrease slightly in the poor nations, but it is decreasing even more in the rich nations. As a result, both the population gap and the economic gap between these two groups of nations is widening and is expected to widen even more by the year 2000. In 1960 the gap in average per capita income between the rich and poor countries was $1,240. By 1980 this gap had widened to $5,700, and by 2000 it is projected to be about $7,900.

*The terms *less developed nations, developing nations, poorer nations, "Third World" nations,* and *"South"* are used to describe nations with non-industrial economies and average per capita gross national products below $3,000 per year.

Figure 7-13 Average life expectancy at birth throughout the world in 1980.

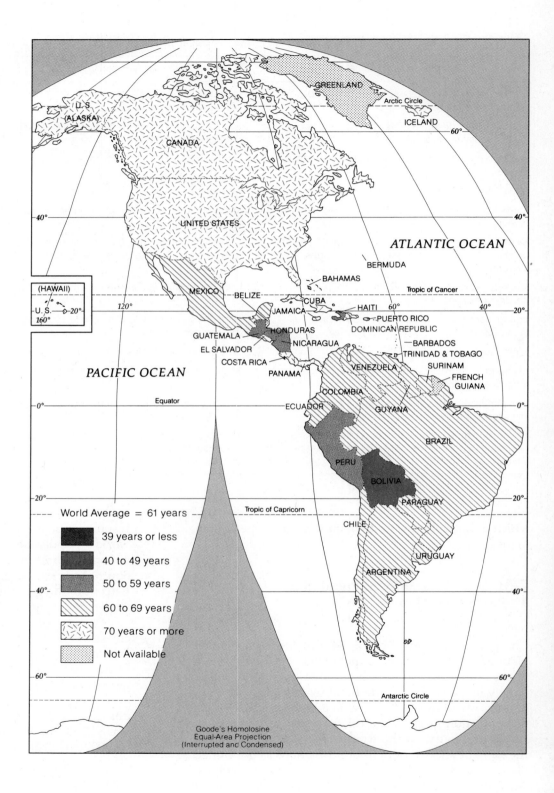

ATLANTIC OCEAN

PACIFIC OCEAN

World Average = 61 years

■	39 years or less
▓	40 to 49 years
▒	50 to 59 years
╱	60 to 69 years
·	70 years or more
⋯	Not Available

Goode's Homolosine
Equal-Area Projection
(Interrupted and Condensed)

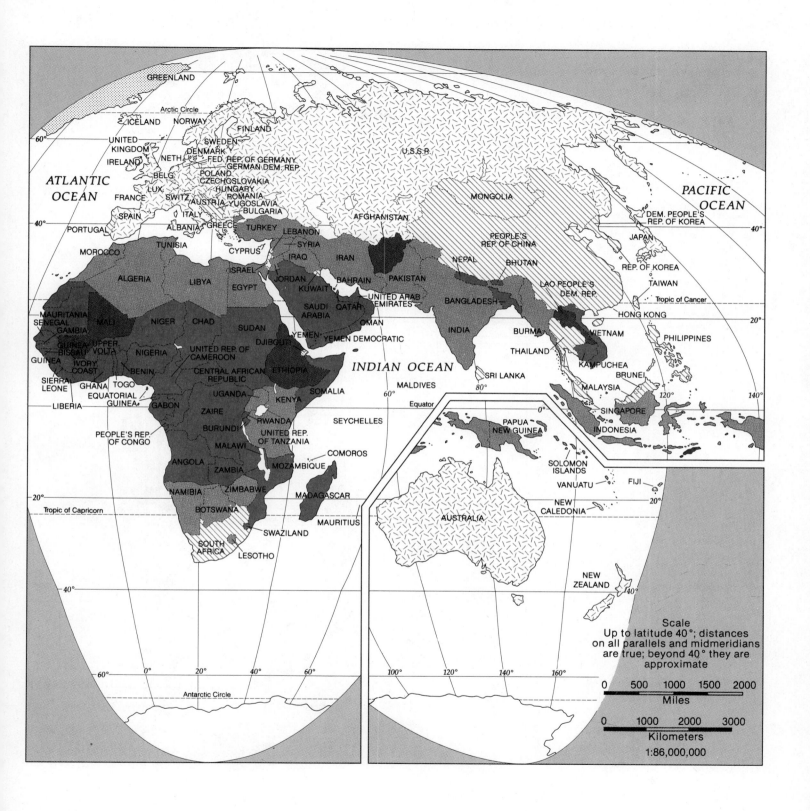

Figure 7-14 Average infant mortality rates throughout the world in 1980.

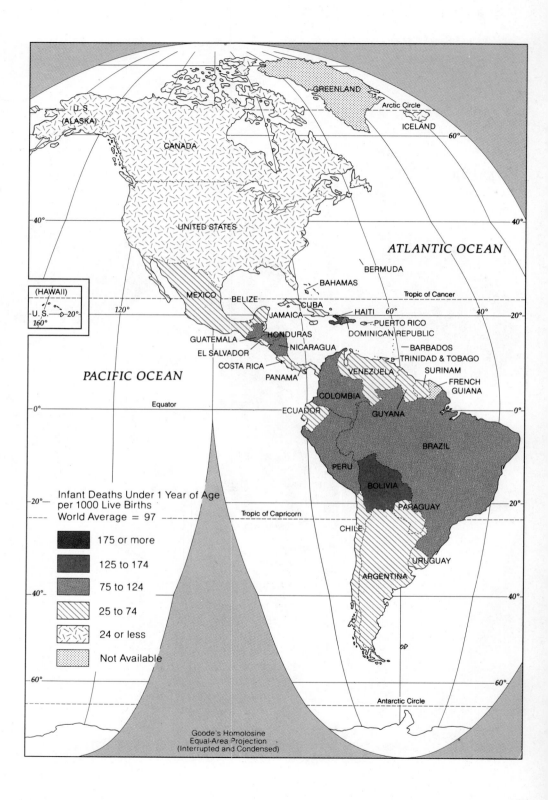

Infant Deaths Under 1 Year of Age
per 1000 Live Births
World Average = 97

- 175 or more
- 125 to 174
- 75 to 124
- 25 to 74
- 24 or less
- Not Available

Goode's Homolosine
Equal-Area Projection
(Interrupted and Condensed)

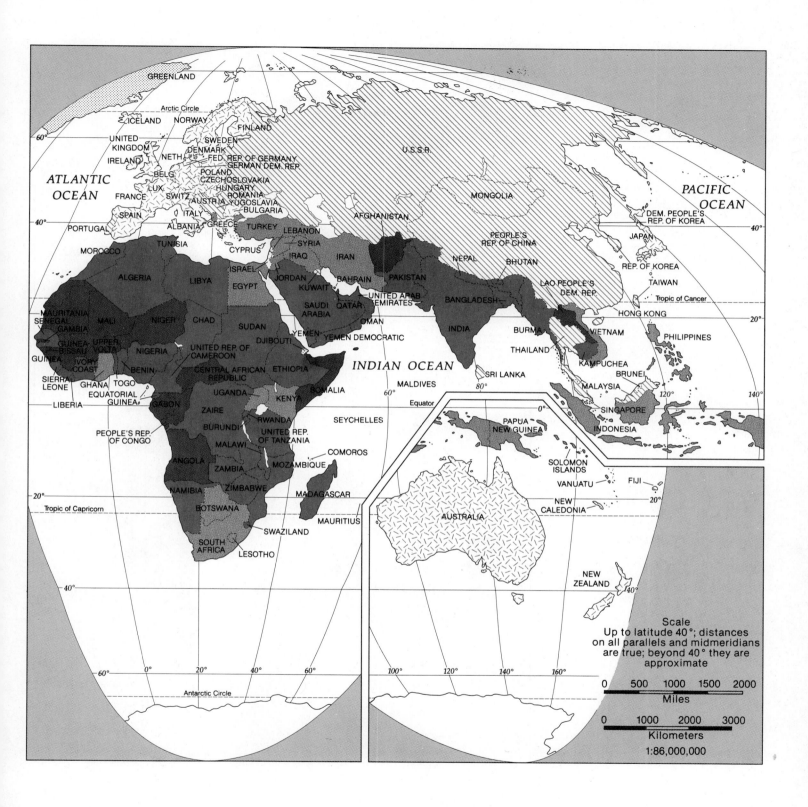

GREENLAND

Arctic Circle

ICELAND   NORWAY
60°   FINLAND
UNITED
KINGDOM   SWEDEN
IRELAND   DENMARK
NETH.   FED. REP OF GERMANY
BELG.   GERMAN DEM. REP.
LUX.   POLAND
ATLANTIC   CZECHOSLOVAKIA
OCEAN   FRANCE   SWITZ.   HUNGARY
AUSTRIA   ROMANIA
SPAIN   ITALY   YUGOSLAVIA
40°   BULGARIA
PORTUGAL   ALBANIA   GREECE   TURKEY   LEBANON
                                        CYPRUS   SYRIA
MOROCCO   TUNISIA   IRAQ
                        ISRAEL
ALGERIA   LIBYA   EGYPT   JORDAN
                                         KUWAIT
MAURITANIA   SAUDI   QATAR
SENEGAL   MALI   NIGER   CHAD   ARABIA
GAMBIA   OMAN
GUINEA-   UPPER   SUDAN   YEMEN
BISSAU   VOLTA   DJIBOUTI   YEMEN DEMOCRATIC
GUINEA   IVORY   NIGERIA
          COAST   UNITED REP. OF
SIERRA   GHANA   TOGO   CAMEROON
LEONE   EQUATORIAL   CENTRAL AFRICAN   ETHIOPIA
LIBERIA   GUINEA   REPUBLIC
              GABON   UGANDA   KENYA
PEOPLE'S REP.   ZAIRE
OF CONGO   BURUNDI   RWANDA
                  MALAWI   UNITED REP.
                           OF TANZANIA
ANGOLA   ZAMBIA   MOZAMBIQUE   COMOROS
NAMIBIA   ZIMBABWE
20°   MADAGASCAR
Tropic of Capricorn
         BOTSWANA   MAURITIUS
         SOUTH
         AFRICA   SWAZILAND
              LESOTHO

U.S.S.R.

MONGOLIA

AFGHANISTAN

PEOPLE'S
REP. OF CHINA

NEPAL
                BHUTAN
PAKISTAN
BANGLADESH   LAO PEOPLE'S
                   DEM. REP.
INDIA   BURMA
                   VIETNAM
         THAILAND
                   KAMPUCHEA
INDIAN OCEAN
                   MALAYSIA
MALDIVES   80°
         SRI LANKA   SINGAPORE
Equator   INDONESIA
SEYCHELLES   60°

PACIFIC
OCEAN

DEM. PEOPLE'S
REP. OF KOREA
                        40°
JAPAN

REP. OF KOREA

TAIWAN
Tropic of Cancer
HONG KONG   20°

PHILIPPINES

BRUNEI
         120°   140°

40°

20°

Scale
Up to latitude 40°; distances
on all parallels and midmeridians
are true; beyond 40° they are
approximate

0   500   1000   1500   2000
          Miles

0   1000   2000   3000
        Kilometers
1:86,000,000

PAPUA
NEW GUINEA
              SOLOMON
              ISLANDS
VANUATU   FIJI
              NEW
              CALEDONIA

AUSTRALIA

NEW
ZEALAND

0°

20°

40°

100°   120°   140°   160°

40°

Antarctic Circle

0°   20°   40°   60°

Figure 7-15 The five worlds and their 1980 per capita gross national products (GNP) in U.S. dollars in 1980.

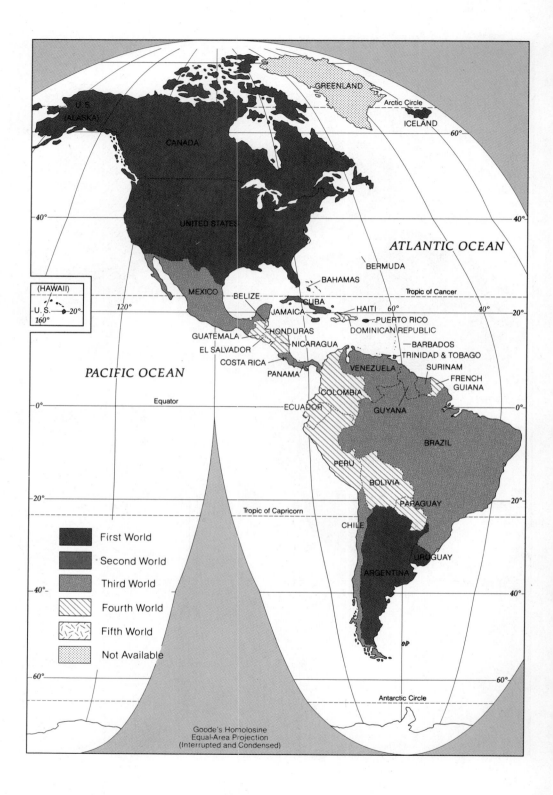

First World

Second World

Third World

Fourth World

Fifth World

Not Available

Goode's Homolosine
Equal-Area Projection
(Interrupted and Condensed)

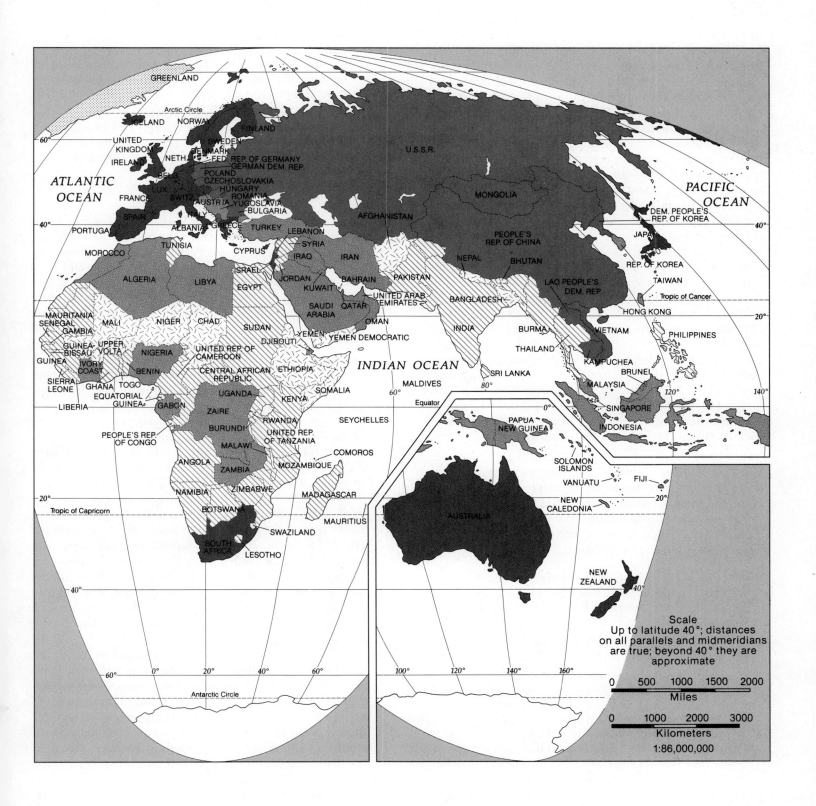

GREENLAND

Arctic Circle

ICELAND   NORWAY
60°   FINLAND
UNITED   SWEDEN
KINGDOM   DENMARK
IRELAND   NETH.   FED. REP. OF GERMANY
BELG.   GERMAN DEM. REP.
LUX.   POLAND
ATLANTIC   CZECHOSLOVAKIA
OCEAN   HUNGARY
FRANCE SWITZ. AUSTRIA ROMANIA
40°   ITALY YUGOSLAVIA
SPAIN   ALBANIA GREECE BULGARIA
PORTUGAL   TURKEY   LEBANON

U.S.S.R.

PACIFIC
OCEAN

MONGOLIA

AFGHANISTAN

DEM. PEOPLE'S
REP. OF KOREA
40°
JAPAN

PEOPLE'S
REP. OF CHINA

REP. OF KOREA

MOROCCO   TUNISIA   CYPRUS   SYRIA
                                         IRAQ   IRAN
ALGERIA   LIBYA   ISRAEL   NEPAL   BHUTAN
                    EGYPT   JORDAN BAHRAIN   PAKISTAN
                            KUWAIT   LAO PEOPLE'S
MAURITANIA   SAUDI QATAR   DEM. REP.
SENEGAL   ARABIA UNITED ARAB   BANGLADESH
GAMBIA   MALI   NIGER CHAD SUDAN   EMIRATES
                                   OMAN   INDIA   BURMA
GUINEA- UPPER   YEMEN
BISSAU   VOLTA   DJIBOUTI YEMEN DEMOCRATIC   THAILAND
GUINEA   NIGERIA UNITED REP. OF
SIERRA   IVORY   CAMEROON
LEONE   COAST   CENTRAL AFRICAN   INDIAN OCEAN
GHANA TOGO BENIN   REPUBLIC   ETHIOPIA   MALDIVES
LIBERIA EQUATORIAL   UGANDA   SOMALIA
         GUINEA GABON   KENYA
PEOPLE'S REP.   ZAIRE   SEYCHELLES
OF CONGO   BURUNDI RWANDA
                  MALAWI   UNITED REP.
         ANGOLA   OF TANZANIA   COMOROS
                  ZAMBIA MOZAMBIQUE
NAMIBIA ZIMBABWE   MADAGASCAR
20°
Tropic of Capricorn   BOTSWANA   MAURITIUS
         SOUTH   SWAZILAND
         AFRICA LESOTHO

Tropic of Cancer

HONG KONG
20°
VIETNAM   TAIWAN
          PHILIPPINES
KAMPUCHEA
          BRUNEI
MALAYSIA
          SINGAPORE   120°   140°
          INDONESIA

Equator

PAPUA
NEW GUINEA

SOLOMON
ISLANDS
VANUATU   FIJI

NEW
CALEDONIA
20°
AUSTRALIA

NEW
ZEALAND   40°

80°

60°

40°

0°   20°   40°   60°

100°   120°   140°   160°

40°

60°
Antarctic Circle

Scale
Up to latitude 40°; distances
on all parallels and midmeridians
are true; beyond 40° they are
approximate

0   500   1000   1500   2000
Miles

0   1000   2000   3000
Kilometers
1:86,000,000

The term *rich-poor gap* is helpful in dramatizing the difference between nations but is an oversimplification. The fact that a country is classified as a less developed or poor nation does not always mean that living conditions are hopelessly bad. Many people in less developed nations are well fed and live reasonably comfortable lives. At the same time, these regions contain at least 800 million people living in dire poverty, characterized by malnutrition, disease, illiteracy, squalid shelter and surroundings, high infant mortality, and low life expectancy. People living under such conditions do not enjoy even the most basic requirements for a decent life. One measure of the degree of poverty in a country is the average per capita gross national product (GNP). Although it is a very crude and sometimes misleading indicator, it is the only one that we have at this time. In Africa and Asia, almost half of the population exists on an average per capita gross national product of less than $300 per person. Up to 80 percent of this is spent on food.

A crude comparison of less developed and more developed countries is given in Table 7-2 on page 123, and Figures 7-2, 7-9, 7-13 (pages 124–125), and 7-14 (pages 126–127). Study this table and these figures carefully in order to get some idea of the significant differences between the rich and poor countries.

The Five Worlds Table 7-2 shows some general differences between less developed and more developed nations. But there are some important differences between various less developed nations that it does not reveal. It is more useful to divide the nations of the world into five categories (Figure 7-15 on pages 128–129):

1. The *first world* indicates the more advanced industrial nations: the United States, Canada, Japan, most noncommunist nations of Europe, Australia, and New Zealand.

2. The *second world* includes the communist nations: the U.S.S.R., China, and eastern Europe.

3. The *third world* is made up of a number of poor states that have one or more major resources which should allow them to become more developed nations without significant foreign aid. These include the oil-rich nations in the Organization of Petroleum Exporting Countries (OPEC), Morocco (with reserves of phosphates), Malaysia (tin, rubber, and timber), and Zaire and Zambia (copper).

4. The *fourth world* consists of nations that have some raw materials and could eventually become more developed, but only with a combination of aid from

today's more developed nations and strong government programs for population control and increased self-reliance. This group includes Peru, Liberia, Jordan, and Egypt.

5. The *fifth world* is made up of countries such as Chad, Ethiopia, Somalia, Rwanda, and Bangladesh, which have few if any resources and poor climates and soils. These countries face mass starvation and continuing poverty.

Life in the Fourth and Fifth Worlds Tables and maps comparing the rich and poor countries of the world are very useful for giving us overall patterns, but these abstract statistics translate into hunger, drudgery, and early death for almost half of the human beings on this planet. When you walk into a typical rural village or urban slum in one of the fourth and fifth world countries, you are greeted with the stench of refuse, open sewers, and smoke. Groups of malnourished children may be sitting around wood fires eating breakfasts of bread and coffee. Children and women have to carry jars or cans of water from a muddy, disease-infested river, canal, or single village water faucet. At night some people may sleep on the street in the open or under makeshift canopies. Other families of 10 and 12 may crowd into single-room shacks, often made from straw, reeds, cardboard, or rusting corrugated sheet metal. Three or four people may be in one or two beds, but most sleep on the dirt floor.

The father and perhaps most of the children may work in the fields or beg for food in the city. If lucky, the father may make about $200 a year—giving him an average of 55¢ a day to feed his family of eight or nine. The parents, who themselves may die by age 45, know that three or four of their seven children may die as infants from hunger or routine childhood diseases. The children that survive add to the flood of people in the slums or to those who leave their farms and head for urban slums, hoping to find jobs that do not exist.

When members of affluent societies actually see such conditions, they sometimes experience cultural shock and try to blot the grim picture out of their minds. Others consider these people ignorant for having so many children. However, from the parents' viewpoint, their very survival depends on having six, seven, or more children—especially boys—to help them beg or work in the fields and to help them in their old age. It is estimated that a couple in India would have to bear an average of 6.3 children to have a 95 percent chance of one son surviving. People in affluent nations rationally invest in life insurance, social security, and pension plans to help them in their old age. Many parents in poor nations have a number of children for the same carefully thought-out reasons. When you live near the edge of survival, having too many children may cause problems, but having too few can cause death at an even earlier age. Clearly, there is an urgent need to control population growth in the rich and poor nations, as discussed by John H. Gibbons in the Guest Editorial at the end of this chapter.

In the past five chapters on ecological principles we have seen that much of ecology can be understood from four major viewpoints: *energy flow, matter cycling, communities and ecosystems,* and *populations.* Each approach gives us vital information, but in studying natural systems we must integrate all four points of view. To deal with the problems of the human population, especially those affecting ecosystems, we must take an even broader or more holistic view. Throughout the rest of this book we will shift increasingly from classical or scientific ecology to human ecology. **Human ecology** is the study of the relations between the human community and its en-

vironment. Because humans are social and cultural animals, human ecology crosses traditional academic and scientific boundaries and seeks to integrate scientific, behavioral, sociological, political, economic, and ethical factors in our relationship to the environment.

In this more complex realm, principles are fewer and less understood. But it is the arena in which we must work if we are to interpret and seek solutions to the growing list of environmental problems. Human ecology involves making decisions when we have insufficient information and little understanding to guide us. But the world's problems won't wait. In the next chapter we will begin this emphasis on human ecology by looking at some possibilities and methods for bringing world population growth under control.

Not to decide is to decide.

Harvey Cox

Guest Editorial: Building a Sustainable Future

John H. Gibbons

John H. Gibbons has served as director of the U.S. Congressional Office of Technology Assessment since 1979. Between 1973 and 1979 he was director of the Environmental Center at the University of Tennessee. In 1973 and 1974, Dr. Gibbons directed the energy conservation program for the Federal Energy Administration (FEA) and received the FEA's Distinguished Service Award. Prior to his work at FEA, he spent 19 years *with the Oak Ridge National Laboratory, beginning as a research physicist and rising to direct its program of studies on environmental quality.*

In one of my favorite anecdotes, two briefcase-bearing business executives stand on the corner of a busy city street. One says to the other, "The way I see it, there's a trade-off for everything—if you want a high standard of living, you settle for a low quality of life."

That brief comment seems to sum up the paradox we have found ourselves increasingly and inextricably caught in over recent years: that beyond some point of material affluence, added material gains seem to have increasingly deleterious effects on total well-being. But old notions do not die easily. And if we have come to understand that growth is not always synonymous with progress, we also have a hard time fully accepting that fact.

The growing and related problems of pollution, energy and water shortages, food scarcities, and crowding that grip our planet—affecting all countries and peoples, whether affluent or not—are clear signals that the days of constant growth and free resources are over. We continue, although we know better, to cling to the familiar and comforting idea that "our" world is infinite and that the destiny of humans is to consume that world's resources and fill it with more people.

This country has spawned some counterideas to this consumerist vision, some far older than the American Revolution. The original Americans, for example, viewed their relationship with the rest of nature as a "oneness." In the words of a nineteenth-century Indian chief who spurned a white man's offer to buy land, "The land does not belong to man—man belongs to the land." We have typically believed, instead, that "this land was made for you and me." We find for that belief a rationalization—in the biblical charge that humans should have "dominion over the earth," to subdue and conquer it. But we conveniently ignore what biblical scholars have understood for many years: that the word *dominion* as used by the Old Testament writers meant stewardship, not exploitation.

Stewardship does not mean keeping everything just like it was—pristine and undisturbed by humans. Rather, it means wise and thoughtful use—a custodial relationship. It means making use of the resources of the earth with a clear understanding and a healthy respect for its laws and limits. In my view, it is absolutely impossible to be a steward over the earth and simultaneously advocate indefinite population growth. Similarly, it is a betrayal of future generations—of our own children and grandchildren—for our generation to exhaust what remains of the planet's whole inheritance of oil, gas, and other nonrenewable resources. Even at present rates, we consume amounts of fossil fuel *in a single year* that it took the ancient sun *a million years* to make in the earth's forests, swamps, and seas.

What can and should we do?

First, we must recognize and understand the nature and the intensity of the problem as greater populations press upon limited resources and an already overstressed environment. Ecological, geological, atmospheric, and oceanographic studies conducted over the past several decades are beginning to give us a clear picture both of what our environment and resources are and of how they are affected by human activity. Recognition must be followed by positive action to slow population growth and to reduce demands on natural resources.

Second, we need to take fuller advantage of the one resource base, often overlooked, that is filled with potential new options for humankind: human ingenuity. Technology is one of the most important manifestations of that ingenuity and, largely for that reason, it mirrors humankind, reflecting at once the best and the worst of human creation. Used wisely, technology can enable us to provide the goods and services we need and desire in ways that require far fewer resources and do far less environmental harm than we might have imagined even a decade ago. Technology can be the wellspring of our highest hopes and a key mechanism in our stewardship of the earth, or it can serve as the instrument that, by our own hand, dashes our hopes and destroys our society. The choice is up to us.

Most importantly, we must recognize the mounting imperative to halt population growth. In most parts of the world, we are already overpopulated—populated beyond the point of long-term sustainability. I even doubt that the present U.S. population can be sustained over the next century without erosion of economic and environmental conditions unless we are willing to commit ourselves to an indefinite dependence on nuclear power and other massive, complex technologies that will *inescapably* entail greater regulation and more centralized authority. If this is the course we want to choose for ourselves and our descendants, then so be it; but we should make that choice consciously and explicitly, not implicitly and by default.

Can we conserve our way out of troubles? As an early advocate of energy efficiency, I must emphasize that conservation, too, has its price. One price is the requirement for much greater technical sophistication throughout our society to produce, properly use, and service the technologies that substitute for energy. Another price is the increased interdependence among various units of our economy—such as links between cogenerating industries and utilities, and farms that produce not only food but also chemicals and energy.

So, even for conservation, there's no free lunch. As Ralph Waldo Emerson once observed, "Nature never gives anything to anyone. Everything is sold at a price. It is only in the ideals of abstraction that choice comes without consequences." But we need not assume the specter of a crowded society, growing poorer, and freezing in the dark. There are several options to deal with our difficulties if we would but commit to them. Perhaps a good start would be to deliberately sort out actions that are sustainable for a long time from those that aren't. Contrary to its aura of being a renewable resource, current agriculture is largely unsustainable in many parts of the world, including the United States. We probably will have to continue to borrow on the future, but at least we should begin to be more explicit about it and to give more attention to setting out on the long path toward a just and sustainable future.

Guest Editorial Discussion

1. Why do you think that many Americans cling to the notion that the world is infinite and the destiny of humans is to indefinitely consume its resources and fill it with more people? Do you hold this belief?

2. List some examples of wise and unwise uses of technology.

3. List some energy and matter resource options that are sustainable and some that are not. How might we shift over to greater dependence on sustainable resources? What role should controlling population growth play in this shift? Why?

Discussion Topics

1. Why are falling birth rates not necessarily a reliable indicator of future population growth trends?

2. Discuss the pros and cons of introducing DDT and modern health and sanitation practices into less developed nations. On balance, did the introduction of these practices save more lives? Why? What might be the population situation in poor countries today if DDT and antibiotics had never been discovered? How might this have changed present world politics? (See Enrichment Study 11.)

3. Why do the deaths of millions of human beings by starvation and famine make little impression on many of us, while the deaths of individual human beings by murder, drowning, or being trapped in a coal mine receive nationwide attention and sympathy? Analyze this response in terms of dealing with our ecological crisis.

4. Suppose modern medicine finds cures for cancer and heart disease. What effects would this have on population growth in more developed and less developed countries? On age structure? On social problems?

5. Explain the difference between achieving replacement level and ZPG. Why is the replacement level in less developed countries higher than in more developed countries?

6. What must happen to the total fertility rate if the United States is to attain ZPG in 40 to 60 years? Why will it take so long? Explain why instant ZPG is for all practical purposes not possible.

7. Explain how the U.S. population has the potential to grow rapidly again through 1993.

8. What is the dependency load? Explain why it is high in most less developed nations. How does it limit economic growth? Why is the dependency load in the United States relatively high now? Why should it be low when you reach middle age? What are some possible implications of a lower dependency load for the ecological crisis?

9. Project what your own life may be like at ages 25, 45, and 65 on the basis of the present age structure of the U.S. population or that of the country in which you live. What changes, if any, do such projections make in your career choice and in your plans for marriage and children?

10. Explain why raising the average first marriage age is an effective means of reducing population growth rates.

11. Criticize each of the following headlines or statements. Be specific.
    a. "Baby Boom Replaced by Bust—U.S. in Danger of Instant ZPG."
    b. "Birth Rates Falling—Prophets of Doom Wrong Again."

12. List some basic characteristics of more developed and less developed countries. Which of the characteristics of less developed nations do you believe could be changed most rapidly? How? Explain how fast population growth can lock a country into continued poverty despite an increasing GNP.

13. Explain why it may be rational for a couple in India to have six or seven children. What changes would have to take place for them to perceive such behavior as irrational?

Readings

Bouvier, Leon F. 1976. "On Population Growth." *Intercom*, July, pp. 8–9. Excellent discussion of the misuse of population data.

Bouvier, Leon F. 1980. "America's Baby Boom Generation: The Fateful Bulge." *Population Bulletin*, April, pp. 1–35. Superb discussion of the implications of the baby boom for American society.

Campbell, Arthur H. 1973. "Three Generations of Parents." *Family Planning Perspectives*, vol. 5, no. 2, 106–112. Excellent analysis of changes in U.S. fertility patterns.

Commission on Population Growth and the American Future. 1972. *Population and the American Future*. Washington, D.C.: Government Printing Office. Also available in paperback (Signet, New American Library). Important document in U.S. history. Hopefully, most of its recommendations will be implemented.

Davis, Kingsley, 1973. "Zero Population Growth: The Goal and Means." *Daedalus*, vol. 102, no. 2, 15–30. Superb analysis of ZPG.

Ehrlich, Paul R., et al. 1977. *Ecoscience: Population, Resources, and Environment*. 3rd ed. San Francisco: Freeman. Excellent and very comprehensive text on human ecology at a somewhat higher level.

Frejka, Tomas. 1973. "The Prospects for a Stationary World Population." *Scientific American*, vol. 228, no. 3, 15–24. Superb analysis and projections.

Hapke, Rodelia. 1973. "The United States: Future Population Alternatives." *Equilibrium*, April, pp. 26–32. Excellent analysis and computer projections of future U.S. population changes.

Haupt, Arthur, and Thomas T. Kane. 1978. *The Population Handbook*. Washington, D.C.: Population Reference Bureau. Superb introduction to demographic terms and concepts.

Keyfitz, Nathan. 1975. "The Numbers and Distribution of

Mankind." In William W. Murdoch, ed., *Environment: Resources, Pollution and Society.* 2nd ed. Sunderland, Mass.: Sinauer. Excellent summary of population dynamics by an expert.

Mauldin, W. Parker. 1980. "Population Trends and Prospects." *Science,* vol. 209, 148–157. Outstanding overview.

Population Reference Bureau. 1976. *Sourcebook on Population, 1970–1976.* Washington, D.C.: Population Reference Bureau. Detailed, annotated list of key 1970 to 1976 references on population.

Population Reference Bureau. 1976. *World Population Growth and Response, 1965–1975: A Decade of Global Action.* Washington, D.C.: Population Reference Bureau. Superb analysis.

Population Reference Bureau. 1980. *1980 World Population Data Sheet.* Washington, D.C.: Population Reference Bureau. A concise summary of world population data that is published each year. It is the source for most of the population data used in this chapter.

Trewartha, Glenn T. 1969. *A Geography of Population: World Patterns.* New York: Wiley. Outstanding analysis from a geographic point of view. Contains many useful maps.

Trewartha, Glenn T. 1978. *The More Developed Realm: A Geography of Its Population.* New York: Pergamon Press. Excellent geographic analysis.

van der Tak, Jean, et al. 1979. "Our Population Predicament: A New Look." *Population Bulletin,* vol. 34, no. 5, 1–46. One of the best overviews of world population problems.

PART THREE

Population, Resources, and Pollution

EPA Documerica/Bob Smith

Humans of flesh and bone will not be much impressed by the fact that a few of their contemporaries can explore the moon, program their dreams, or use robots as slaves, if the planet Earth has become unfit for everyday life. They will not long continue to be interested in space acrobatics if they have to watch them with their feet deep in garbage and their eyes half-blinded by smog.

René Dubos

8

Human Population Control

In mature ecosystems, population control is the rule rather than the exception. Through species interactions (Enrichment Study 4) and negative feedback mechanisms (Section 6-2), populations of various plant and animal species are normally kept from becoming too large or too small. When you walk into a forest, you don't expect to be trampled to death by a million deer. In immature ecosystems (Section 6-1) and those altered by human activities, however, populations of some plants and animals can become so large or so small that they can affect human well-being. Large swarms of locusts can periodically wipe out crops, and a decline in the numbers of predators, such as hawks, owls, and foxes, can allow populations of rabbits, mice, and rats to grow dangerously large.

What factors affect human population size? What methods are available for controlling the size of the human population? How can we develop a plan for controlling population growth in the world and in the United States? These important questions and some possible answers are the subjects of this chapter. Let's begin with a general discussion of the factors that can limit the population of any species and then relate these ideas to the human population.

8-1 Factors Affecting Maximum Population Size

J Curves and S Curves The population story for a species can usually be told with two very simple curves—a

J curve and an S curve. With unlimited resources and ideal environmental conditions, a population can reproduce at its maximum rate, called its **biotic potential,** or **reproductive potential.** Such growth starts off slowly but then increases rapidly to produce an exponential or J curve of population growth (see Figure 8-1). Biotic potential varies widely among species. Bacteria, insects, mice, and rats tend to have high biotic potentials, while larger species, such as lions, elephants, and humans, have relatively low biotic potentials. Since environmental conditions are usually not ideal, a population rarely reproduces at its biotic potential.

In the world or in an ecosystem with finite resources, J-curve population growth cannot go on forever. The maximum population size that a given ecosystem can support indefinitely under a given set of environmental

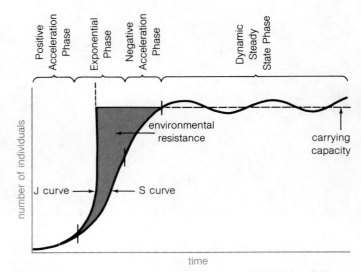

Figure 8-1 The J curve of population growth is converted to an S curve when a population encounters environmental resistance caused by one or more limiting factors.

Enrichment Studies 1, 4, 7, 8, 9, and 10 are related to this chapter.

conditions is called the ecosystem's **carrying capacity.** This size is determined by the level of resources needed by the population, the existing environmental conditions, and the population's upper and lower limits of tolerance (Section 6-2) to various environmental factors.

All of the limiting factors that act together to regulate the maximum allowable size of a population (carrying capacity) are called the population's **environmental resistance.** As a population encounters environmental resistance, the J curve of population growth bends away from its steep incline and eventually levels off at a size that fluctuates above and below the carrying capacity (Figure 8-1). In other words, environmental resistance converts a J curve into an S curve.

As seen from Figure 8-1, the S curve can be divided into four distinct phases: the *positive acceleration* (or *lag*) *phase* (representing the initial slow growth), the steep *exponential* (or *logarithmic*) *phase* (representing very rapid growth), the *negative acceleration phase* (as the curve bends after encountering environmental resistance), and the *dynamic steady state* (or *plateau*) *phase,* in which the population fluctuates above and below the carrying capacity level. This final phase shows that population stabilization does not mean that the population is fixed exactly at a particular level.

Because of a slow time delay, some populations (especially those of insects, bacteria, and algae) may temporarily overshoot their carrying capacity size by a wide margin and then undergo a **population crash,** or *dieback* (Figure 8-2). A dieback can also occur when a change in environmental conditions lowers the carrying capacity level for a population. A simplified homeostatic diagram of the interactions between biotic potential and environmental resistance is shown in Figure 8-3.

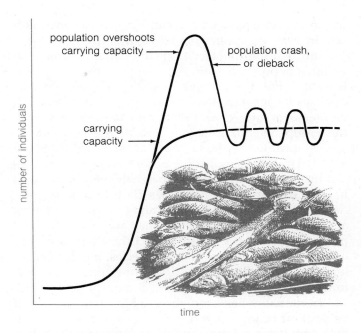

Figure 8-2 A population crash, or dieback, can occur either when a population temporarily overshoots its carrying capacity due to a time lag in negative feedback controls or when a change in environmental conditions lowers the carrying capacity.

Extrinsic and Intrinsic Limiting Factors Two types of limiting factors can regulate population growth and size: extrinsic and intrinsic. **Extrinsic limiting factors** are those that operate from outside a population. Plant populations tend to be controlled by such extrinsic factors as available nutrients, climate, light, and disease; animal populations tend to be controlled by such extrinsic fac-

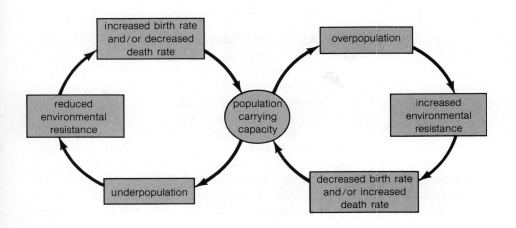

Figure 8-3 A simplified homeostatic diagram of population control. As environmental conditions change, negative feedback causes population size either to increase or decrease.

tors as available food supply, climate, disease, and interactions between species (Enrichment Study 4).

Intrinsic limiting factors are those that are generated within a population itself. An example for some species is *territoriality*. For instance, a group of lions typically confines its activities to a *home range,* an area in which its members interact and search for food. Each lion in the group defends a certain area of the home range against intruders of the same species who are not in the group. This area is called the lion's **territory.** Some species that move periodically, such as baboons and humans in some hunter-gatherer societies (Section 2-2), have *nucleated territories.* Instead of defending a fixed geographic area, they defend the area that they are currently occupying. Organisms will also defend their territory from intrusion by individuals of other species, but this behavior is not normally included under the concept of territoriality.

Territoriality has been observed in many species of fishes, lizards, mammals, birds, and social insects. It can limit population size from within by restricting the access of individual members of a group to food supplies, sexual partners, and certain habitats. Individuals not strong enough to hold a territory cannot get a mate and are forced to live in poorer habitats with a lower chance of reproduction and survival. When food is abundant, territory size tends to be small, thus allowing more individuals to live in a given area. When food becomes scarce, territory size usually increases, thus reducing the population size. When territories are disrupted, social order breaks down and there is an increase in aggression.

Some social biologists have attempted to apply the concept of territoriality to human society. They suggest that humans have an innate "territorial imperative" that can account for increased levels of aggression in high-density urban environments. Other investigators, however, conclude that territoriality is a learned behavior, not an innate or inherited behavior, and that it is not found among all animals, least of all primates.

Another intrinsic factor that can limit population growth is *social stress.* Every organism apparently has a certain amount of *personal space.* It is the area around an organism's body, into which intruders are not welcome. The amount of personal space needed by an organism varies with situation, age, status, sex, and cultural and social norms. When one organism intrudes inside the personal space of another organism of the same species, certain physiological changes can occur in both organisms. The number of such social interactions between individuals of the same species in a given area is called **social density.** This is in contrast to the *arithmetic population density,* which is the total number of organisms in a given area regardless of whether they interact socially. As population density increases, however, social density also increases. When the social density gets too high, the organisms experience *overcrowding.* As their personal space is violated more and more, they are put under an increasingly high degree of stress.

Most animal species have optimal levels of crowding, above or below which undesirable effects occur. For example, in some animal populations overcrowding can cause a number of disorders, including hypertension, gastric ulcers, arteriosclerosis, and increased susceptibility to infectious diseases.

Behavioral changes have also been observed in crowded experimental animals. John Calhoun demonstrated this effect in his study of extreme overcrowding among Norway rats. He confined the rats to pens, gave them plenty of food, and protected them against their normal predators. As the rat population increased, death rates increased, especially among the very young and among pregnant females during delivery. Miscarriages also increased, fertility rates dropped, and aggression and conflict increased as dominant males occasionally went on rampages. Some rats become cannibals, even though there was plenty of food. Mothers often abandoned their young, some rats became sexually deviant, and others pathologically withdrew from social contact. Similar results have been seen in other species of crowded animals, but the effect is not uniform for all species.

Some observers have applied these observations of rats to human behavior, suggesting that overcrowding may be a major factor in increased crime, drug abuse, mental illness, and stress in urban areas. It is tempting to make such comparisons, but the data presently available on humans and crowding are conflicting and ambiguous, and what is thought of as crowding varies with different cultures.

Factors Controlling Human Population Size and Growth Rate Most animal species experience fluctuations in their population size. However, the human species has so far generally experienced only a long upward trend (Figure 8-4). Supposedly human population size is controlled by famine, disease, and war, but so far these factors have had relatively little effect on overall human population growth, as summarized earlier in Table 1-1. In early times, famine and disease reduced the population in certain geographic areas. Within a relatively short time, however, the population again began to grow. Today world population is growing so rapidly that 75 mil-

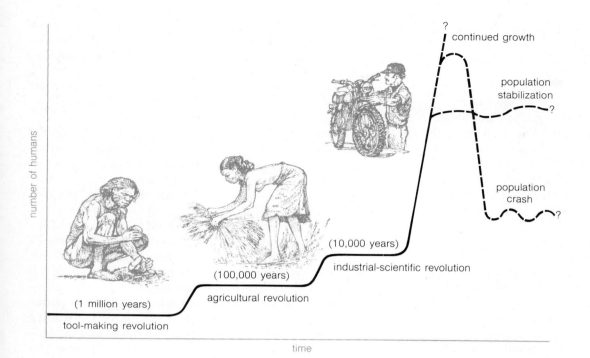

number of humans

? continued growth

population stabilization ~?

population crash ~?

(10,000 years)

industrial-scientific revolution

(100,000 years)

agricultural revolution

(1 million years)

tool-making revolution

time

Figure 8-4 So far humans have extended the earth's carrying capacity by technological innovation. After each major technological revolution, the population has grown rapidly and then, with the exception of the industrial-scientific revolution, leveled off for a long period of time. Dotted lines represent different projections for the human population: continued growth, population stabilization, and continued growth followed by a population crash and population stabilization at a much lower level. All curves are suggestive and are not drawn to scale.

lion people are added each year—the same number that were killed by bubonic plague in Europe between 1347 and 1351. Similarly, the number of all people that were killed in all wars during the past 500 years are born in only 6 months at today's rate of population growth (Table 1-1).

The human population has continued to grow in size because of human cleverness, technological and social adaptations, and other forms of *cultural evolution*. Thus, we have been able to postpone the action of the mechanisms that would otherwise control our population. We invented clothing, spears, axes, and the bow and arrow; learned to build and heat shelters; domesticated animals; cultivated plants; selectively bred both plants and animals; and developed machines to do work for us, such as the steam engine, the internal combustion engine, and nuclear reactors. Soon we may learn how to use and modify DNA to tailor ourselves and other forms of life to our specific needs and whims—an idea that excites some people and frightens others. Through these and other forms of cultural evolution, we have been able to expand into various parts of the earth and to raise the human carrying capacity of the environment.

Does this mean that the human species does not face limits to growth as do other species? No—sooner or later we must face the limits to our own growth. No amount

of technological or cultural intervention can change the fact that the earth and its resources are finite, and the rate at which they can be extracted and used is governed by the law of conservation of matter and the first and second laws of energy (Chapter 3). There are increasing signs that we may be approaching the entropy limits of growth on planet earth (see Section 3-4 and Enrichment Study 1 for more details), so that the most recent J curve of human population growth may move toward a new dynamic steady state, or an S curve (dashed lines in Figure 8-4).

There are several important differences between our present situation and past periods of cultural transition. For the first time we have no new place to which to migrate in significant numbers. We are using most of the inhabitable land on earth, and the idea that we can use space colonies to solve the earth's population problems over the next few decades is a misleading and dangerous myth, as discussed in Section 1-6. Also for the first time, people in the more developed nations are using energy and mineral resources at such incredible rates that the new limiting factor may be widespread environmental disruption (entropy) rather than the depletion of one or more vital resources (Section 3-3). Making the transition in Figure 8-4 will depend on humans—especially those in the rich nations—learning how to use and waste less matter and energy resources. If we do not do this voluntarily, nature will do it for us by drastically cutting back the world's population size. The choice is ours.

Projections for the Future The dashed lines in Figure 8-4 show three projections for the human population based on our present understanding. We could be much further from the earth's carrying capacity than some seem to think, or perhaps some technological breakthrough will again raise the earth's carrying capacity for humans. If there is such a breakthrough, population may continue to grow rapidly, perhaps reaching 50 billion or more within the next 100 years.

No one, of course, knows what *maximum human population* can be supported by the earth or what the limiting factors might be—food, air, water, pollution, or lack of space. Many scholars have made crude estimates of such a maximum. In terms of oxygen, space, and energy, the population limit is hypothesized at 100 billion people. If we properly distribute people and cultivate every inch of arable land, the National Academy of Sciences estimates that we could produce enough food to support 30 billion people living an anthill existence barely above starvation. Roger Revelle put this same anthill existence level at 38 to 48 billion. Herman Kahn claims the earth could support 20 billion people with an average annual income of $20,000 (in U.S. dollars) each. An even rosier picture is given by agricultural economist Colin Clark, who sees a world in which 45 billion people could have a U.S.-type diet by cultivating all arable land, using nuclear power for energy, and mining much of the earth's crust to a depth of 1.6 kilometers (1 mile). If the human diet was based on grain rather than a mixture of grain and meat, he estimates that the earth could support 157 billion people.

A limit that could be exceeded long before these optimistic population levels are reached is the ability of the earth to radiate heat back into space. With too many people using too much energy, the earth's atmosphere could begin to heat up and possibly cause changes in world climate and food-growing capacity (see Enrichment Study 3). The population limit at which heat build-up could become serious is put at 15 to 20 billion people, a figure we could easily reach by 2050 at present growth rates. Other observers feel that we could support the world's projected equilibrium population of 7 to 12 billion (Figure 7-8) at a decent standard of living by distributing the world's food supply more equitably and by shifting from less abundant resources (such as lead, tungsten, tin, oil, and natural gas) to more abundant resources (such as aluminum, glass, cement, and various forms of solar energy). However, even if some or all of these optimistic estimates become technologically, ecologically, and climatically possible, it seems unlikely that our social and political structures could adapt to such a crowded and stressful world without resorting to mass destruction through nuclear warfare.

A second possibility shown in Figure 8-4 is continued growth past the carrying capacity, followed by a dieback of billions (perhaps 50 to 80 percent of the population) through a combination of famine, disease, war, and widespread ecological disruption. Some think that this, unfortunately, may be the most likely path to ZPG. A third possibility, based on present estimates, involves gradual stabilization of the population over the next 75 to 100 years at a size between 8 and 15 billion. A fourth possibility not shown in Figure 8-4 is stabilization of the world population at some level (say 8 to 15 billion) followed by a gradual decline to a lower **optimum population** that would allow most, if not all, of the world's population to live with reasonable comfort and individual freedom. However, asking how many people the earth could support is asking the wrong question. Instead, we should be asking how many people the earth could support at a decent standard of living. Again, no one knows what this optimum population is. Some consider it a meaningless question, some put it at 20 billion, others at 8 billion, and others at a level below today's population level.

It seems clear that something must give during the next few decades. By controlling deaths but not births on earth, we now face the possibility of either a massive population increase or a massive dieback. We can avoid both of these events by sharply reducing birth rates so that the population stabilizes before the limits to growth are temporarily exceeded. If we do not reduce the birth rate, population will be controlled sooner or later by a tragic rise in the death rate. As the *Whole Earth Catalog* put it, "We are as Gods and we had better become good at it." With this in mind, let's look at some of the ways that we can control the growth rate and size of the human population.

8-2 Methods for Controlling Human Population Growth

A government can alter the size and growth rate of its population by encouraging a change in any of the three basic demographic variables: births, deaths, and migration. All governments throughout the world are presum-

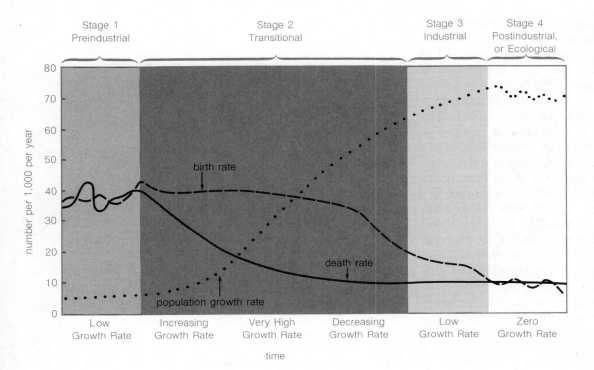

Figure 8-5 A generalized model of the demographic transition.

ably committed to reducing death rates as much as possible. In addition, most governments restrict emigration and immigration so that migration is a significant factor in only a few countries, including the United States. Thus, *controlling the birth rate is the key to controlling human population growth in the world.* There are two general approaches to controlling the size and growth rate of the human population: *economic development* and *family planning.* Let's look at these two approaches more closely.

Economic Development and the Demographic Transition Between 1929 and 1950, demographers began to examine the birth rates and death rates in the western European nations that became industrialized during the nineteenth century. From this analysis they formed an hypothesis of population change and control known as the **demographic transition.** Simply put, this hypothesis states that economic development through industrialization eventually leads to both falling birth rates and falling death rates; overall, a country's population growth slows down significantly (Figure 8-5). In other words, according to this hypothesis, population growth can be decreased through industrialization and modernization.

Based on analysis of industrialized western European nations, the demographic transition appears to

have three distinct phases. In the first *preindustrial stage,* harsh living conditions lead to high birth rates (to compensate for high infant mortality) and high death rates, with the population stable or growing slowly. In the second *transitional stage,* as industrialization spreads and living conditions improve, birth rates remain high but death rates fall sharply. This leads to a temporary but prolonged period of very rapid population growth. In the third *industrial stage,* industrialization is widespread. Birth rates fall and approach death rates as "upwardly mobile" couples (especially in cities) see too many children as hindering them from taking advantage of job opportunities in an expanding economy. Population growth continues but at a slow and perhaps fluctuating rate, depending on economic conditions. It is now believed that the United States, Japan, the U.S.S.R., Canada, Australia, New Zealand, and most of the remaining European nations are in this third phase. It has been suggested that a fourth *postindustrial* (or, as I call it, *ecological) phase* be added to this model. It would correspond to ZPG, where birth rates decline even further to equal death rates (Figure 8-5).

Supposedly the less developed nations of Africa, Asia, and Latin America can control their populations by becoming *industrialized* and making a similar transition. According to this hypothesis, an important factor in a world population control program is for the wealthy nations to provide the poor nations with food, money, and technical advice to help them become industrialized as soon as possible. Using this model, most less developed nations today are considered to be in the transitional phase with high population growth rates (Figure 8-6).

There is considerable debate, however, over whether the demographic transition model is valid for today's less developed nations. A number of important differences between the less developed nations today and the western European nations when they were in the transitional phase are given in Table 8-1. In addition, historical demographers, using new methods and information, have developed a better picture of how the fertility decline began in western Europe that may modify the classical demographic transition theory. This new evidence suggests that improved and expanded family planning programs may bring about a more rapid decline in the birth rate than economic development alone. Furthermore, economic development will be more difficult for today's poor nations than it was for the nations that developed a century ago because many of the resources needed for development are less available and their prices are higher.

The large number of powerful inhibiting factors shown in Table 8-1 could prevent most poor nations from completing the demographic transition; they could become caught in the transitional stage (Figure 8-5) or be forced back to the preindustrial stage if death rates should rise. Their present high population growth rates could slow, if not wipe out, economic gains and lead to a rise in death rates.

The positive factors shown in Table 8-1, however, could help these nations make the transition. This depends, however, on the more developed nations' willingness to give more money and technical aid designed to help poor nations learn to help themselves. This argument in behalf of many less developed nations was summed up at the 1974 World Population Conference in Bucharest: "Development is the best contraceptive" (see Enrichment Study 9). Table 8-1 also indicates that economic development associated with the demographic transition must be combined with family planning in order to reduce birth rates directly. Thus, it seems clear that both approaches are needed.

Family Planning and Beyond Family Planning Basic **family planning** is a purely voluntary approach whereby information is provided and contraceptives are distributed to help parents have the number of children they

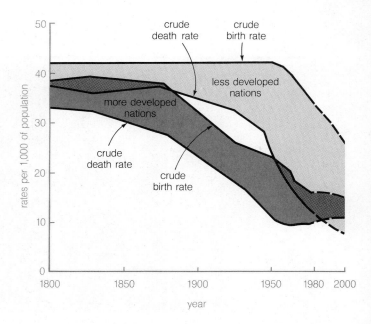

Figure 8-6 Comparison of crude birth rates and crude death rates for more developed and less developed nations between 1800 and 2000 (projected). The less developed nations have yet to reach the last stage of the demographic transition and are not expected to do so by 2000.

want at the time that they want them. *Beyond family planning* is a more deliberate attempt to reduce birth rates by the use of one or more voluntary, economically motivated, or involuntary methods. These methods are summarized in the box on population control.

Selecting a Method In selecting a course of action for population control, Bernard Berelson suggests that we evaluate each proposal according to several criteria:

1. *Scientific readiness.* Is the scientific and medical technological base ready or can it be developed in time?

2. *Political feasibility.* Can the proposal gain enough government and public support?

3. *Administrative feasibility.* Can the proposal be administered effectively? Will it use existing administrative machinery or require new organizations?

4. *Economic feasibility.* How much will it cost? Can society afford this cost?

5. *Ethical acceptability.* Is the proposal ethically and morally acceptable?

Table 8-1 Less Developed Nations Today and Western European Nations at the Transitional Stage of the Demographic Transition

Less Developed Nations	Western European Nations
Factors Hindering Less Developed Nations	
Very high birth rates (25 to 50 per 1,000 people, average = 32)	Moderately high birth rates (8 to 14 per 1,000 people, average = 12)
Sharp decline in death rates within 25 years due to rapid importation of modern agricultural, medical, and other technologies from more developed nations	Gradual decline in death rates over 100 to 150 years
Very high population growth rates (2 to 3.5 percent, average = 2 percent)	Moderate population growth rates (-0.4 to 0.3 percent, average = 0.1 percent)
Large-scale migration not available	Large-scale migration from Europe to North and Latin America and Oceania
Very young age structure (very strong momentum for further population growth)	Less youthful age structure (allowed more rapid decrease in population growth rate)
Moderate degree of urbanization (average 29 percent) and low degree of industrialization (10 to 17 percent) (tends to raise unemployment and poverty levels in cities and to slow economic growth)	Moderate degree of urbanization (average 23 percent) and moderate degree of industrialization (25 to 35 percent) (provided jobs in the cities and accelerated economic growth)
Slow spread of universal education (particularly among women) and low percentage of women in the labor force (tends to keep birth rates at high levels)	More rapid spread of universal education among women and moderate percentage of women in the labor force (helped decrease birth rates)
Most arable land already in use	Large areas of land brought under cultivation
Factors Helping Less Developed Nations	
Increased monetary and technical aid from more developed nations (can allow more rapid industrial and agricultural growth and a decline in birth rates)	International aid not available
More awareness of undesirable effects of rapid population growth and more (but varied) support of family planning programs	Relatively little awareness of consequences of rapid population growth and opposition of governments and other institutions to family planning
Availability of improved methods of birth control	Modern methods of birth control not available; fertility declines based primarily on abortion and coitus interruptus
Communication techniques (radio, telephone, TV) to educate couples and persuade them to reduce fertility rates	Modern, rapid communication techniques not available
Governmental ability for central planning and administration	Less central planning and administration
Use of labor-intensive appropriate technology (can ease unemployment) and slow migration rate from rural to urban areas (can reduce environmental impact)	Intermediate and advanced technologies widely used, resulting in increased pollution and environmental impact

6. *Effectiveness*. Will it work?

7. *Overall rating*. A weighted average of the above factors used to rank various methods.

To these criteria I would add a ninth factor, *short- and long-range consequences:* What might be the social, psychological, political, economic, and ecological consequences of the proposal for the individual, the nation, and the world?

These various population control methods are evaluated in Enrichment Study 7.

Motivations for Childbearing   No plan will be effective in controlling population unless it takes into account the culture of the country and what motivates people to have (or not to have) children. Do they have children because women are conditioned from childhood to believe that raising a family is the only way to find fulfillment? Because they love children? Because of religious traditions? To prove their masculinity or femininity? Because their friends have children and they feel left out? To please their parents? To support themselves in their old age? Because children are seen as economic assets who can

Approaches to Population Control

Basic Voluntary Family Planning

Strictly speaking, basic family planning is not a population control policy, because its goal is to help parents have the number of children they want when they want them.

Extended Voluntary Family Planning

1. Open access to contraceptive information, devices, and counseling, regardless of age, marital status, or economic situation.

2. Open access to voluntary abortion and sterilization.

3. Intensive education campaigns using schools and media to alter cultural values and to inform and convince people to practice contraception, to have fewer children, to see reproduction (not the sex act) as having important social and ecological consequences, and to avoid migration from rural to urban areas where jobs are not available.

4. Changes in social institutions by increasing the choices open to people. Goals include eliminating narrow stereotyped roles (especially of women as mothers and of male machismo or virility), instituting women's rights and unbiased work opportunities, encouraging women to work, encouraging changes in family structure that would reduce the number of children desired, and promoting later marriage ages.

Economic Motivation: Incentives and Deterrents

1. Further extension of voluntary programs by using economic inducements or penalties to increase an individual's motivation for reducing fertility.

2. Possible incentives include direct cash payments, tax breaks, savings certificates, transistor radios (an incentive used in India), and providing free or low-cost contraceptives, abortion, sterilization, maternity care, and child care. Other methods include health plans, old-age pensions, and education for individuals or couples who agree to use contraceptives, to delay marriage or childbearing, to limit their number of children, to become sterilized, or to move from crowded urban areas to rural areas.

3. Possible deterrents include elimination of income tax deductions for some or all children; elimination of welfare, health, and maternity benefits after two children; limitations on

---

help the parents in the fields or in their work? To add happiness, affection, love, novelty, creativity, or fun to a household? To relive or remold their own childhood? To provide companions for existing children or to relieve the loneliness of one or both parents? To have a child of a certain sex (especially males in less developed nations)? To save a marriage? To get attention? To have power and influence over another person? To fulfill a natural biological urge to reproduce? Because of an unplanned accident? The answers for any couple and for any culture are varied, complex, and personal.

Studies have indicated that poor parents in many less developed countries tend to place a high economic value on children, particularly sons. Yet the work contribution of children is not large enough to offset the economic burden that they place on the family—a fact that most of these parents apparently do not realize.

In contrast, middle class couples in more developed countries do not expect economic benefits from their children, and they show only a slight preference for males. These couples emphasize the emotional benefits of children—happiness, love, companionship, the parents' personal development, and child-rearing satisfaction. Their most common reason for not wanting more than a certain number of children is the financial burden, even though most people underestimate the cost of raising a child.

In 1980 the cost of raising one child in the United States, including college education at a public university, was estimated at about $58,000 for a low-income family ($8,000 to $12,000 per year) and $85,000 for a middle-income family ($15,000 to $25,000 per year). Widespread dissemination of such information can be an important factor in population control, especially in more devel-

government housing, scholarships, and loans for families with more than the allowed number of children; and taxes on marriage, children, and child-related goods and services.

Involuntary Population Control

1. Limiting couples to one or two children.

2. Licenses or certificates, which can be sold, that allocate the number of children a couple can have.

3. Compulsory reversible sterilization for all. A time capsule contraceptive could be implanted at birth or after a couple had the allotted number of children, or reversible sterilants could be added to the drinking water or to staple foods. Sterilization could be reversed by physicians so that couples could have their allotment of children.

4. Compulsory abortion for women exceeding the allotted number of children.

5. Reducing or eliminating immigration.

6. Limiting food rations so that a family can eat adequately with three or four members but not with five or more.

7. Banning, restricting, or forcing movement within

a country in order to obtain a more favorable population distribution.

8. Death control by euthanasia (mercy killing) and infanticide.

Political, Scientific, and Administrative Support for All Methods

1. Population stabilization as an official national and world goal.

2. Private and governmental population planning and control agencies at local, national, and world levels.

3. Population control as a condition for foreign aid.

4. Improvement of health standards so that parents need fewer children to aid them in their old age.

5. Expanded basic research in human reproduction and applied research to improve contraceptive methods.

6. Increased social and psychological research on the relation of population to other problems; on the consequences of various population control policies; and on methods to increase the motivation to have fewer children, to move from urban areas, and to adjust to a society with a stabilized population.

oped nations. Already more and more Americans apparently are finding that they can't afford to raise a large number of children.

8-3   Efforts at Human Population Control

Types of Population Policies   In 1960 only two countries—India and Pakistan—had official policies to reduce their birth rates. *By 1980 some 93 percent of the world's population and 96 percent of the people in less developed nations lived in countries where governments had either adopted family planning programs or permitted the operation of private programs.*

Of course, having a policy to control population growth and providing the financial support and orga-

nized efforts to implement such a policy are two different things. Few governments spend more than 1 percent of their national budgets on family planning services. Some nations without an official policy, especially more developed ones, have been more successful in reducing their birth rates than other nations with official policies but little actual support. In more developed nations such as the United States, birth rates have declined without an official policy presumably because of economic well-being, high literacy, and an increased number of women in the work force.

Most efforts at controlling population involve abortion and family planning. In 1980, about 70 percent of the world's population lived in countries where abortion was legal during the first 3 months of pregnancy. Another 16 percent lived in countries where abortions were permitted for medical, eugenic, and humanitarian reasons, such as in cases of rape or incest. In other words, over three-fourths of the world's population have some access to legal abortion. Where legal abortion is not available, illegal abortion is widespread. *In spite of religious proscriptions and antiabortion groups and laws, it appears that abortion has been and still is one of the most widely used methods of birth control.* (For more details, see Enrichment Studies 7 and 8.)

Because of the controversy surrounding abortion, most governments prefer family planning as their official form of population control. The effectiveness of family planning programs in less developed nations is hotly debated and has been rated from relatively unsuccessful to moderately successful to very successful. Between 1965 and 1980, family planning successes were claimed in China (the world's most populous nation) and in some small less developed countries, such as Singapore, Hong Kong, Barbados, Taiwan, Mauritius, Costa Rica, Fiji, and Jamaica. However, only moderate to poor results have been claimed in other populous, less developed nations, such as India, Indonesia, Brazil, Bangladesh, Pakistan, Nigeria, and Mexico, and in 79 less populous, poor nations.

Part of the problem is that record keeping has been poor. Probably a more significant factor is that many family planning programs have not been in effect long enough to evaluate their effectiveness. Most programs were started in the 1960s or early 1970s. Even when data show a drop in the birth rate, it is difficult to establish what fraction of the decrease was due to family planning efforts rather than economic development. To some observers, a combined program of vigorous family planning efforts and economic development offers the best chance of success. Other observers feel that family planning, even coupled with economic development, cannot bring birth rates in less developed countries down fast enough because most couples apparently still want large families. These observers consider family planning to be very important but point out that its official goal is not to lower the birth rate, but rather to help couples have the number of children they want when they want them.

To get some idea of the success and failure of population control programs, let's look briefly at what has happened in the world's two largest countries—India and the People's Republic of China, which together contain about 37 percent of the world's population.

India India's population problems are staggering. It is the world's second most populous country, with a population of almost 676 million in 1980. This is one-seventh of all the people in the world and is more people than there are in the Western Hemisphere, Middle Africa, and Oceania combined. Yet this mass of humanity lives in a country only about one-third the size of the United States.

Each year about 10 million Indians die—but 23 million are born. This means that there are about 13 million new Indians to feed, clothe, and house each year. Because 41 percent of the population is under 15 years of age, India's population could easily reach 926 million by 2000 and eventually 1.6 billion. Yet at least one-third of its population has an annual per capita income of no more than $70 a year, and average per capita income in 1980 was only $180. India had an estimated 309 million people living in poverty in 1980—nearly half of its population. Average per capita food supplies are one-third below the levels needed for good health and have been that way for over a decade, despite an almost 30 percent increase in agricultural production. To add to the problem, nearly half of India's labor force is either unemployed or underemployed. Furthermore, each *week* 100,000 more people enter the job market, looking mostly for nonexistent jobs.

Recognizing its problem, India started the world's first official population control policy. Its program began in 1952, when its population was near 400 million and it had a doubling time of 53 years. After 28 years of effort at population control, in 1980 it had a population of 676 million and a doubling time of only 36 years. In 1951 India added 5 million persons to its population each year—today it adds 13 million.

Without its population control program, India's population would be growing even faster today. But overall the program has been considered a failure for a number of reasons, including poor planning and bureaucratic inefficiency and the fact that the program did not have much administrative and financial support until 1965— 13 years after it was started.

But the problem is deeper than that. For one thing, 79 percent of India's people live in 560,000 rural villages, where birth rates are still close to about 40 per thousand. The economic and administrative task of delivering contraceptive services and education to this population is overwhelming. This is further complicated by the fact that the illiteracy rate is about 67 percent, with 80 to 90 percent illiteracy among rural women. In spite of years of government propaganda about having fewer children, the ordinary couple in an Indian village is convinced that children are economic assets. Children can help parents with household chores, work in the fields, and care for the parents in their old age. Because of this belief and the cultural traditions of early marriage and a desire for male children, rural Indian couples have an average of 5.3 children. Population control is also hindered by India's kaleidoscopic diversity. India has 14 major languages, over 200 dialects, a number of social castes, and 11 major religions.

To improve the effectiveness of its program, in 1976 Indira Gandhi's government instituted a mass sterilization program, primarily for males with two or more children. One state passed a compulsory sterilization bill, although it was never signed into law. With a target of 4.6 million sterilizations, the campaign actually produced 6 million during 1976. The program was supposedly voluntary and based on financial incentives, but coercion was used in many areas. Males who could not produce a sterilization certificate were often denied government jobs and salary increases, ration cards, land, reduced interest rates, and other privileges. The backlash from this overzealous and coercive program was an important factor in Gandhi's election defeat in 1977, although she was later reelected. In addition, this unsuccessful attempt at coercive birth control may set back family planning efforts in India for years—during 1979 voluntary sterilizations had fallen to about 1.5 million. In 1978 a new approach was taken, when the legal minimum age for marriage was raised from 18 to 21 years for males and from 15 to 18 years for females.

China   Reports from the People's Republic of China, the world's largest nation, present a far more hopeful picture than reports from India. Although accurate information is hard to get, it is estimated that in 1980 China had a population of about 975 million—one-fifth of humanity—a crude birth rate of 18 per thousand, a crude death rate of 6 per thousand, and a doubling time of 58 years, compared with 36 years for India. At these rates China adds about 13 million persons each year. But these figures may be too low, and at least one population expert believes that the crude birth rate in 1980 may have been as high as 22 and the crude death rate as high as 8.

If any of these estimates are correct, China's drop from an estimated birth rate of 32 per thousand in 1970 may be the world's greatest population control and health care success story—accomplishing in only 10 years a demographic transition that took Europe almost 150 years.

China's program goes far beyond mere family planning. It is an integrated and highly organized program that is incorporated into the governmental, social, educational, political, and economic structures of the entire nation. Its official goal is to achieve ZPG by the year 2000 in order to stabilize its population at 1.2 to 1.3 billion. Such a program, however, would require a very rapid drop from a total fertility rate of 2.3 children per woman in 1980 to 0.8 by 1985—much lower than any country in the world has today.

China's population control program is built around a number of practices: (1) strongly encouraging couples to marry at a late age (typically 24 to 28 for women and 26 to 30 for men); (2) indoctrinating couples in family planning techniques at the time of marriage; (3) strongly encouraging couples to have only one child by providing salary bonuses, larger pensions, and better housing for one-child couples and by imposing a baby tax and wage and pension reductions on couples with three or more children; (4) providing free contraceptives to married couples (sales are forbidden) either at their place of work or, in rural areas, via home deliveries by "barefoot doctors" (paramedics); (5) making abortion freely available; (6) compensating women and men for time lost from work due to sterilizations, abortions, and IUD insertions; (7) using mobile units to bring sterilization and family planning education to rural areas; (8) training local people to carry on the program; (9) pressuring mothers to get an IUD after the first child is born and providing free sterilization of men and women; (10) using motivational techniques by showing goals and contraceptive acceptance rates on clinic walls and factory bulletin boards; and (11) expecting all leaders to set an example.

Most countries can't exert the same degree of social and political pressure on its population that China can, but some elements of China's program can be transferred to other less developed countries. Especially useful is the practice of bringing contraceptives and family planning to the people at little or no cost to them, rather than making the people come to special centers. With this brief overview of population control efforts throughout the world, let's look at how and when world population growth might be brought under control.

8-4   Controlling World Population Growth

Some Signs of Hope   Based primarily on China's apparent (but still unsubstantiated) success, some observers see encouraging signs that world population growth may be controlled over the next 50 years. They point to the following indications: (1) The majority of nations now have population control policies; (2) survey after survey has shown that women in developing countries allegedly would have fewer children if family planning services were available; (3) the World Population Year in 1974, the 1974 World Population Conference in Bucharest, the World Population Plan of Action approved by 136 nations (which calls for making family planning information and means available to all individuals and couples), and the International Women's Year Conference in Mexico City in 1975 have greatly increased awareness and acceptability of population control programs; (4) fertility control methods have improved and their use has become more widespread; (5) recent successes in less developed countries indicate that when family planning is readily available, the resulting large decreases in fertility can contribute to economic development; and (6) most more developed nations are either at or nearing ZPG or could reach it within several decades.

Some Discouraging Signs Before we get carried away with these hopeful trends, it is necessary to point out some discouraging signs. First, we must remember that about 35 percent of the people in the world are under 15 years old. This provides strong momentum for continued growth. If everyone in the world miraculously decided only to replace themselves, world population would still continue to grow for about 125 years and level off at about 6 billion. If replacement-level fertility is achieved throughout the world in 2005, world population would not level off until about 2100 at about 8 billion—twice today's population. Second, some 300 million couples, or half of the world's couples, still do not practice any form of family planning.

Third, poor weather and a lack of world food reserves could cause catastrophic famines in the next few decades. Indeed, part of the population decrease in 1974 and 1975 was due to rising death rates in some poor countries—hardly a desirable way to reduce the world's population growth. Fourth, although many countries have official population control policies, they often rely almost exclusively on either the economic development or the family planning approach. The real hope lies in a carefully planned and implemented program that combines the economic development, family planning, and beyond family planning approaches.

Finally, the success of all types of population control programs may depend on significantly increased foreign aid for the less developed nations from the more developed nations. However, the reverse has been occurring. Since 1960 the amount of development foreign aid (excluding military aid) from rich to poor countries, expressed as a percentage of the annual GNP of more de-

veloped countries, has been declining. In 1979 the United States gave only 0.19 percent of its GNP as foreign aid and the Soviet bloc only 0.04 percent of their GNP. By contrast, the OPEC nations gave about 3 percent of their GNP as aid in 1979 and the average aid of all industrialized nations, excluding the United States, was 0.42 percent of their GNP. In 1980 the more developed countries gave less than one-third of 1 percent of their total GNP in the form of aid to the less developed countries. The United Nations estimates that this level of giving should be increased to 1 percent. This would cost each U.S. citizen an average of $100 per year.

In spite of recent declines in giving, the United States has been and still is by far the largest donor of foreign aid—giving $7 billion of nonmilitary aid in 1979. Between the end of World War II and 1980, the United States provided $162 billion in nonmilitary economic assistance to over 140 different nations.

Despite the importance of foreign aid, it must not be viewed as a cure-all for the world's population problems. Much foreign aid has been in a form that makes a poor nation dependent on industrialized nations for goods rather than helping to make it more self-reliant. For example, for every dollar the United States contributes to the World Bank or other international financial institutions that lend or give aid to poor nations, the recipients spend two dollars to buy goods and services in the United States. Another problem is that because of internal corruption in some less developed nations, much of the aid never reaches the people who need it. Thus, foreign aid should be given only to countries whose policies insure that most of it actually benefits the poor. Furthermore, such aid should be designed to help poor nations help themselves rather than to become more dependent on the rich nations.

In summary, we find both promising and discouraging trends in controlling world population growth.

Goals of a World Population Plan There is considerable debate over whether we have a world population problem and over the desirability of achieving ZPG. Some argue that world population stabilization is neither practical nor desirable, saying that it would not allow the poor nations to achieve economic development and would lead to an older, less resilient and innovative society for each country achieving ZPG. Others argue that world population will soon stabilize anyway, so there is no urgent need to institute a world population plan. Still others contend that population control is a severe threat to individual freedom.

At the 1974 UN World Population Conference, a number of less developed nations and even a few more developed nations actively opposed ZPG, although they generally favored reducing the rate of world population growth. They argued that more developed nations like the United States are pushing for ZPG so that they can continue to use and waste a large share of the world's resources and keep the poor nations from developing and becoming industrially competitive (see Enrichment Study 9 for more details). These countries urged that less developed nations should receive more economic development aid from the rich nations—not more family planning experts, IUDs, and birth control pills. They see population growth as either a false or irrelevant issue compared with other world problems such as peace, poverty, racism, and health.

Most observers, however, favor stabilizing the size of the world population. World population control is urgently needed because the built-in momentum from the youthful age structure will cause world population to grow for at least 50 to 100 years, even if a stringent population control policy is put into effect now. Population growth is also seen as intensifying other social and environmental problems (Section 1-5). The problems of peace, poverty, racism, health, pollution, urbanization, ecosystem simplification, and resource depletion won't be solved by population stabilization. But without it each of these problems will become much worse.

Assuming that leaders throughout the world decide that the world population should be stabilized, what would be a realistic population size to aim for and how long would it take to reach? Supporters of population stabilization disagree on the optimum population size and the rate at which ZPG could or should be reached.

To avoid large-scale death from famine and disease, Lester Brown calls for world population stabilization at 6 billion within 50 years. But Tomas Frejka has shown that in order for this to occur by 2070, the average world fertility rate would have had to be 2.5 children per woman in 1980 and the average world crude birth rate 19 per thousand. Instead, by 1980 the average world total fertility rate was 3.8 children per woman and the average crude birth rate 28. Although 6 billion may be a desirable goal for world population, it is unrealistic—unless death rates rise sharply.

A realistic but still very difficult goal would be to stabilize world population at around 8 billion by about 2100 (Figure 7-8). This would require a replacement-level fertility of 2.5 children per woman throughout the world by 2000, with a total fertility level of 2.1 in the more developed nations by 1985 (which had already been achieved by 1980) and 2.7 in the less developed nations by 2000 (compared with 4.4 in 1980).

Major Principles of a World Population Plan There is no single best solution for controlling world population growth. The particular mix of economic development, family planning, and beyond family planning methods to be used must be designed specifically for each country or region and should take into account the wide diversity of customs, religious beliefs, values, and other cultural and political factors. The accompanying box lists some principles upon which a world population plan might be based. These principles could be used to develop more detailed plans to be implemented over the next 50 years.*

Goals of a U.S. Population Plan Should the United States attempt to stabilize its population? At present the United States has no official population control policy, although it provides financial support for family planning, population education, and contraceptive and reproductive research, primarily because population control is a controversial issue. As a result, most politicians have been unwilling to push for an official U.S. population control policy.

Yet a very strong case can be made for attaining ZPG in the United States or at least greatly slowing the rate of growth. One of the best reasons is that even if today's low fertility rates are maintained and illegal immigration is eliminated, the United States would not reach ZPG until 2020, with a population of about 253 million (Figure 7-7). Another very good reason for stabilizing population is that adding millions to the American population intensifies most other environmental problems. Energy, water, and minerals would be in shorter supply. Pollution levels would rise unless extremely expensive pollution control devices were employed. Land abuse and pressure on recreation facilities would increase and rebuilding the cities would be much harder.

Some have argued that population growth is necessary for continued economic growth and that a ZPG society would be dull and less innovative. But studies have shown that the health of the economy, the vitality of business, and individual welfare are not dependent on

---

*I have offered suggestions to be used in developing detailed short-range, intermediate-range, and long-range proposals for most of our major environmental problems. In no way do I offer these as final solutions to our complex problems. They are merely suggestions based on my necessarily limited view and analysis of the suggestions of numerous experts and thinkers. The purpose in presenting them is to provoke debate, hard thinking, and action.

A Suggested Plan for Stabilizing World Population

1. Blend different economic development, family planning, and beyond family planning approaches to population control, instead of relying on only one approach.
2. Design a specific program for each country or region based on its cultural, demographic, economic, political, ecological, and ethical characteristics.
3. Use voluntary and positive incentive methods coupled with education to help motivate families to limit the number of children. In addition to important ethical concerns, strongly coercive and involuntary methods are often impractical (as shown by the backlash that they produced in India) except in nations such as China, which have strong government control.
4. Emphasize the following: free or low-cost health care; reduced infant mortality; good nutrition; old-age social security; widespread availability of free contraceptives; sterilization with legalized abortion (a less desirable, secondary approach); increased literacy and birth control education in rural areas (especially for women between 13 and 30); improved and decentralized delivery systems of health, birth control, and education services (especially in rural areas); work opportunities for women; raising the social, economic, and political status of women; raising the average marriage age; and more equitable distribution of income.
5. Reduce and reverse the flow of people from farms to overurbanized areas in most less developed nations by land reform and land redistribution, and provide funds and loans for rural economic development for small farmers using labor-intensive (not machine-intensive) appropriate technology methods.
6. More developed nations should set an example by adopting population stabilization goals and plans.
7. More developed nations should commit 1 to 2 percent of their annual GNP for economic and family planning aid to less developed nations and for worldwide research on population control. This aid should be designed to help poor nations become more self-reliant, rather than making them dependent on rich nations. Aid should not be given to nations that do not make most of it available to the poor.
8. More developed nations should liberalize trade between themselves and less developed nations by eliminating tariff barriers and import quotas and by paying higher prices for resources imported from less developed nations.
9. More developed nations should increase private and government funding of population control research with emphasis on designing population control plans tailored for each nation, developing new contraceptive methods, determining factors that affect fertility and population distribution, and predicting the effects of living in a country and world with longer life expectancies and a stabilized age structure.
10. Carefully integrate population policies with those for economic development, agriculture, energy and mineral resources, land use, and pollution control.

continued U.S. population growth. Indeed, ending population growth should help reduce high unemployment levels, raise average per capita income, and lower taxes.

The idea that a ZPG, or dynamic steady state, society would be dull and conservative is not necessarily valid for several reasons. First, as discussed in Section 6-2, a steady state society is dynamic, diverse, and exciting—not static, monotonous, and dull. Some things would be growing, some declining, and some remaining about the same; in this way the system does not exceed the carrying capacity of the environment.

Second, the fear that a dynamic steady state society with more older people would be conservative and less innovative is not borne out by the facts. Sweden has achieved ZPG, and it is considered to be one of the most energetic and innovative societies in the world. The supposed link between a stabilized and thus older population and conservatism has not been established. Instead, the more conservative societies tend to be those in rural, poor nations with a youthful age structure. South Africa and Portugal have young populations, but they are more conservative than the older populations of Sweden and West Berlin.

Adopting an official population policy and a goal of ZPG in the United States should also help control world population growth. Without setting such an example, the United States will have little success in persuading other nations to adopt such goals.

A Suggested Plan for Stabilizing the U.S. Population

1. Establish an official national goal to attain ZPG by 2015 with a stationary population of about 250 million.
2. Use voluntary and positive incentive methods coupled with education to help people of any age, sex, race, or economic status to control their own reproductive behavior and to be aware of the advantages of achieving a stabilized population.
3. Emphasize greatly expanded reproductive education, recognition and protection of women's rights, increased work opportunities for women, and voluntary and open access to sterilization, contraceptive devices, counseling, and abortion (as a less desirable backup method), with all these services being free to those unable to pay.
4. Place equal emphasis on reducing births among middle- and upper-class Americans, rather than focusing primarily on the poor. This will do more to actually slow population growth and environmental disruption and will also decrease minority group concern over genocide (Enrichment Study 9).
5. Remove tax discrimination against single people and childless couples.
6. Attack poverty through annual income support for those unable to work and through increased job training and opportunities for others.
7. Support large-scale research programs on improved contraceptives, basic reproductive biology, incentives that would be successful in reducing family size, motivational psychology to reduce family size, migration away from cities, living in a society with a stabilized population, and the effects of genetic engineering and intervention.
8. Develop a program for reducing illegal immigration to no more than 100,000 per year by 1985. Emphasize greatly increased border security, large fines and possibly jail sentences for employers who repeatedly hire illegal immigrants, a national identification card system, enforcement of minimum wage laws so that employers cannot hire illegal immigrants at low wages, and economic aid to countries based at least partially on their help in controlling illegal emigration to the United States.
9. Reduce legal immigration from 400,000 to 200,000 per year by 1985 if illegal immigration cannot be held below 200,000 per year. Immigration of trained and skilled persons from poor nations should be halted, since this robs less developed nations of one of their most valuable resources.
10. Carefully integrate population policies with those for agriculture, land use, energy, mineral resources, and pollution control by creating a cabinet-level Department of Population, Natural Resources, and Environment.

How soon and at what level should the U.S. population be stabilized? If between 1980 and 1985 the total fertility rate is reduced from 1.8 to 1.7 and held at this level, and illegal and legal immigration is reduced to about 400,000 per year, the United States could stabilize its population by 2015 at about 250 million (Figure 7-7). This would probably reduce legal immigration from its present value of 400,000 to about 200,000 per year by 1985 if illegal immigration cannot be reduced below 200,000 per year.

Reducing legal and illegal immigration into the United States, however, is a difficult and controversial goal, since the United States was built by immigrants. As a result, the United States will probably emphasize trying to reduce the number of illegal immigrants. Some argue that illegal immigrants take jobs away from Americans, undermine the wage scale by providing a source of cheap and nonunionized labor that can easily be exploited by employers, and take advantage of welfare, the food stamp program, and other services to which they are not legally entitled. But others point out that many illegal immigrants take primarily menial jobs that most American workers won't take (mostly because of low pay and worker exploitation). They also argue that the social security, income taxes, and other payments made by illegal immigrants far exceed the payments made to some of them by social service organizations. The accompanying box lists some principles upon which a program to stabilize U.S. population might be based.

We have little to fear from trying to achieve ZPG in the world and in the United States over the next few decades and much to fear from continuing our present pattern of growth. The transition to a dynamic steady state society will not be without its problems, and much research and much planning are needed. But not making this crucial transition will create even more serious problems.

Short of thermonuclear war itself, rampant population growth is the gravest issue the world faces over the decades immediately ahead.

Robert S. McNamara

Discussion Topics

1. What is an S curve? Carrying capacity? Distinguish between maximum and optimum population. Do you think we have passed the world's maximum population limit? Have we passed the world's optimum population? Cite evidence. What do you think the optimum population for the United States is? Why?

2. Is war an effective means of population control? (See Table 1-1.) Does this apply to global nuclear war?

3. Explain how the United States could be considered the most overpopulated country in the world. Give pro and con arguments.

4. The average middle class American is estimated to have 50 to 150 times the environmental impact of an Indian peasant and 30 to 50 times the impact of a typical poor American (see Section 1-5). How was this estimate made? Try to find data to show that it is valid. Relate the data to your own life-style.

5. Debate the following resolution: The United States has a serious population problem and should adopt an official policy for stabilizing its population.

6. Is concern about the "population explosion" diverting attention from other problems, such as war, civil rights, and poverty? Give evidence pro and con (see Enrichment Study 9). How would you resolve this problem?

7. Explain why population policy, unlike most other policies, requires a 50- to 70-year plan.

8. Debate the following resolution: Voluntary family planning is the best and only major approach we should use in controlling world population (see Enrichment Study 7).

9. Debate the following resolution: Economic development is the best and only major approach we should use in controlling family planning.

10. Describe the demographic transition and give reasons why it may or may not apply to less developed nations today.

11. Debate one of the following two resolutions: (1) Each woman should have the freedom to use abortion as a means of birth control; (2) abortion should not be legal because it is an act of murder and denies the unborn child its right to live (see Enrichment Study 7).

12. Is the U.S. population problem serious enough to justify using compulsory measures? Why or why not? What forms of compulsory measures? What types of coercion are already being used directly or indirectly to stimulate U.S. population growth (pronatalist policies)? (See Enrichment Study 7.)

13. Debate the following resolution: Population control in the United States should be directed mostly at middle and upper class Americans (see Enrichment Studies 7 and 9).

14. Make a list of restrictions (for example, stoplights), laws, and other losses in individual freedom that occur as a result of an increase in population and population density. What individual and group freedoms do you gain? (See Enrichment Study 7.)

15. Debate the idea that eliminating poverty in the United States and increasing foreign aid to less developed countries should be an essential part of any U.S. population stabilization plan.

16. Should foreign aid be given to the United Nations or some other international organization for distribution to less developed countries? What are the advantages and disadvantages of this ploy?

17. Debate the following resolution: No foreign aid should be given to any country judged to have a hopeless population growth situation or any country that refuses to adopt a policy for stabilizing its population.

18. Debate the following resolution: The U.S. military budget should be cut by 40 to 50 percent, and the money should be spent on U.S. and world population control, reducing poverty, and pollution control.

19. What problems are likely if the number of elderly increases as a result of a stabilizing U.S. population? Compare these problems with those the United States will have if its population is not stabilized.

20. Debate the suggestions that immigration into the United States should be halved or stopped and that trained or skilled persons from less developed countries should not be admitted. What implications might such changes have for the United States? For less developed countries? (See Enrichment Study 7.)

21. How would you go about stopping illegal immigration into the United States? (See Enrichment Study 7.)

22. Debate the following resolution: A world population level of 8 billion by 2070 is too high; more drastic measures should be taken now to ensure that we don't reach that level.

23. Debate the following resolution: A U.S. population level of 250 million by 2015 is too high, and more drastic measures should be taken now to ensure that this level is not reached.

24. Debate the following resolution: The United States should set an example for the world by stabilizing its own population.

25. Survey members of your class and another class or dorm group about what incentives would lead them to limit their family to zero, one, or two children. It is important to know the following about each person: age, number of children in his or her family, religious background, number of children he or she already has (if any), and number of children he or she wants.

Readings

See also Readings for Chapter 7 and Enrichment Studies 7, 8, and 9.

Ahmed, W. 1974. "Population Policy and the Peasant." *Bulletin of the Atomic Scientists,* June, pp. 29–35. Superb article showing how what can seem rational to you and me can seem irrational to a peasant.

Berelson, Bernard. 1969. "Beyond Family Planning." *Science,* vol. 163, 533–543. Excellent overview and evaluation of all methods suggested for population control. Should be read with caution, however, since he does weight the evaluation to make family planning seem to be the only desirable and feasible alternative.

Brown, Lester R. 1978. *The Twenty-Ninth Day: Accommodating Human Needs and Numbers to the Earth's Resources.* New York: Norton. Superb discussion of the need to control world population growth.

Callahan, Daniel, ed. 1971. *The American Population Debate.* Garden City, N.Y.: Doubleday. Outstanding collection of pro and con arguments on America's population problem.

Callahan, Daniel. 1972. "Ethics and Population Limitation." *Science,* vol. 175, 487–494. Superb analysis of ethical implications of various population policies.

Day, Lincoln H. 1978. "What Will a ZPG Society Be Like?" *Population Bulletin,* vol. 33, no. 3, 1–42. Superb description of life in a ZPG society.

Ehrlich, Paul R., and John P. Holdren. 1971. "Impact of Population Growth." *Science,* vol. 171, 1212–1217. Answer to Barry Commoner's charge that population growth is not a very important factor in the environmental crisis.

Hardin, Garrett. 1974. "Living on a Lifeboat." *BioScience,* vol. 24, 561–568. Argues that the population situation is already so serious that giving food and other forms of aid to most poor nations would only cause a larger number to die at a later time.

Jones, Landon Y. 1980. *Great Expectations: America and the Baby Boom Generation.* New York: Coward, McCann and Geoghegan. Very readable discussion of the impact of the baby boom generation.

Kahn, Herman, et al. 1976. *The Next 200 Years: A Scenario for America and the World.* New York: Morrow. Excellent presentation of the technological optimism view. In his earlier books projecting the future of the world, Kahn didn't even mention the population and pollution problems. In this book he dismisses them as being easily solved. Read this book and see if you can find any fallacies and hidden assumptions.

Maddox, John. 1972. *The Doomsday Syndrome.* New York: McGraw-Hill. Attack on prophets of ecological doom by a British scientist and editor. He makes a few valid points, but Maddox deliberately distorts positions of some environmentalists and demonstrates the type of naiveté and extremism that he is criticizing.

Oakley, Deborah, and Leslie Corsa. 1979. *Population Planning.* Ann Arbor, Mich.: University of Michigan Press. Superb textbook on population issues and population control.

Pohlman, Edward, ed. 1973. *Population: A Clash of Prophets.* New York: New American Library. Excellent collection of articles on both sides of the population debate.

Polgar, Stephen. 1972. "Population History and Population Policies from an Anthropological Perspective." *Current Anthropology,* vol. 13, no. 2, 203–241. Outstanding analysis showing how most solutions ignore the anthropology of the particular culture involved and thus are often doomed to failure from the start.

Scientific American. 1974. *The Human Population.* San Francisco: Freeman. Very good collection of articles about the world population problem.

Silverman, Anna C., and Arnold Silverman. 1971. *The Case Against Having Children.* New York: McKay. Exposes traditional motherhood myths and explores alternative roles for women.

Teitelbaum, Michael S. 1975. "Relevance of Demographic Transition Theory for Developing Countries." *Science,* vol. 188, 420–425. Excellent summary of why demographic transition may or may not work today.

Zero Population Growth. 1977. *The Benefits of Zero Population Growth.* Washington, D.C.: Zero Population Growth. Superb summary.

9

Food Resources and World Hunger

Hunger is a curious thing: at first it is with you all the time, working and sleeping and in your dreams, and your belly cries out insistently, and there is a gnawing and a pain as if your very vitals were being devoured, and you must stop it at any cost. . . . Then the pain is no longer sharp but dull, and this too is with you always.

Kamala Markandaya

In a refugee camp in Bangladesh, several thousand starving Bengalis are near death. Most sit almost motionless—too weak to even brush away the flies collecting on the sores on their faces. An emaciated 35-year-old woman, who looks 60, clutches an infant whose withered body and peeling skin reveal the telltale signs of severe malnutrition. Most of *Terra I*'s passengers spend most of their waking hours and 50 to 70 percent of their meager incomes trying to keep themselves and their children from starving. In sharp contrast, the affluent one-fourth of *Terra I*'s passengers typically spend a small fraction of their waking hours buying foods from a dazzling variety in air conditioned supermarkets. Many of these more fortunate passengers complain because they must spend 14 to 30 percent of their income on food, and many others who are overnourished go from one diet fad to another in an attempt to lose weight.

Each day there are 205,000 new mouths to feed. Can the world grow enough food to feed its increasing population and thus prevent large-scale famines in the next few decades? If so, how can it be done and what might be the environmental consequences? Even if enough food can be grown, how can it be made available to the world's poor, who desperately need it for their survival? In this chapter we will examine these questions and see how the problems of food, land, water, fossil fuels, and fertilizer and those of population growth and pollution are all interwoven.

Enrichment Studies 1, 3, 6, 9, 10, 11, and 16 are related to this chapter.

9-1 Food Supply, Population Growth, and Malnutrition

Population Growth and Food Production   Total world food production in both more developed and less developed countries except those in Africa has increased sharply since 1961 (Figure 9-1). Indeed, since 1961 the less developed countries have improved their total food production at a faster rate than the more developed nations, where average per capita food production has also risen significantly. But in the less developed nations, average *per capita* food production increased only slightly between 1961 and 1970 and remained about the same or declined between 1970 and 1979 (Figure 9-1). In other words, in the less developed nations, where three-fourths of the world's people live, food production has barely kept up with population growth. Thus, despite the dramatic increase in global food production since 1960, there are more hungry and malnourished people today than ever before. Most of these people are in the poor nations, especially in Africa and Asia.

Extent of World Hunger and Malnutrition   Estimating the total number of people who are underfed is a difficult and controversial process for several reasons: (1) It is very difficult to gather adequate data, especially in poor countries; (2) hunger may be hidden when people suffer from **undernutrition** (insufficient quantity or calorie intake of food) or **malnutrition** (inadequate quality of diet) and therefore not show visible symptoms until the deficiency becomes extreme;* (3) the minimum daily input of calories varies with climate, sex, body weight, individual physiology, and daily physical activity; and (4) there is controversy over the minimum level of protein that people need.

---

*Undernutrition and malnutrition are collectively called **protein-calorie malnutrition**.

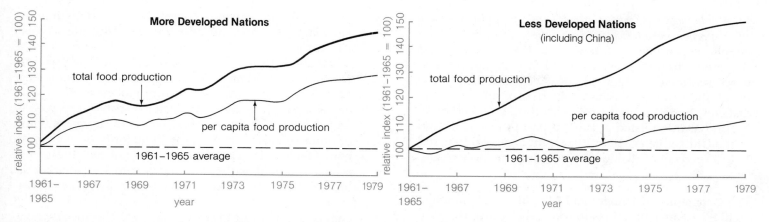

Figure 9-1 Total and per capita food production in more developed and less developed nations from 1961 to 1979.

The problem is further complicated by the fact that protein deficiency results not only from a lack of protein but also from a lack of high-quality protein, as is found in animal products (meat, milk, and eggs) and pulses (peas, beans, and soybeans). The millions of different proteins we need for growth and good health are made in the bodies of plants and animals as their natural living processes link together 19 or 20 different amino acids in different sequences. Our bodies can only make 10 of the amino acids we need. We must get the other 8 (9 for children) from proteins in the food we eat. If one or more of these **essential amino acids** are missing or found in small quantities in a food, as is the case with most plants, that food is a low-quality source of protein (see Table 9-1). The problem is that most people in the world, especially the poor, are forced to live primarily on plants because meat is too expensive.

Of the estimated 350,000 species of plants in the world, perhaps 80,000 are edible. Yet over the course of history, people have used only about 3,000 plant species for food. Today only 16 plants feed the world and provide the poor with almost all of their food calories and over three-fourths of their protein. These plants consist of five cereals (rice, wheat, maize [corn], sorghum, and barley), two sugar plants (sugar cane and sugar beet), three root crops (potato, sweet potato, and cassava), three legumes (bean, soybean, and peanut), and three tree crops (coconut, banana, and nuts). Three of these plants—wheat, rice, and maize—provide people in less developed nations with about two-thirds of their daily supply of calories and 55 percent of their protein. From Table 9-1, we can see these plants are low in protein quantity or quality, or both.

People who live on plants can upgrade protein quantity and quality by combining wheat, corn, or rice with legumes (such as peanuts or soybeans). Affluent vegetarians can afford such a combined diet, but for the poor, legumes are sometimes too expensive.

Because of the difficulties in making accurate food and health surveys, it is not surprising that estimates of the number of people in the world who are underfed vary widely. For 1974, estimates (excluding China) ranged from the admittedly conservative figure of 483 million, or 17 percent of the world's population, to 1.6 billion, or 40 percent of the world's population.

Table 9-1 Protein Content and Quality of Selected Foods

Food	Protein by Weight (percent)	Relative Protein Quality (percent)*
Wheat, white flour	11	32
Potato, white	2	34
Beans	22	34
Cassava (manioc)	2	41
Maize (corn), whole grain	10	41
Peanuts	26	43
Wheat, whole grain	12	44
Soybeans	38	47
Rice, polished white	7	56
Rice, brown	8	57
Cow's milk, whole	3.5	60
Beef	18	69
Fish	19	70
Hen's egg	13	100

*A relative scale based on the number and amount of the essential amino acids present.

While most poor people in the world are underfed, many affluent people in both rich and poor nations are overfed. Many people, especially in affluent countries, exist on diets that are high in calories, saturated fats, salt, sugar, and processed foods and low in vegetables and fruits. As a result, these individuals have high risks of suffering from diabetes, hypertension, stroke, heart disease, and other health hazards related at least in part to **overnutrition.** In the United States, 10 to 12 percent of all children and 35 to 50 percent of all middle-aged adults are overweight.

The Geography of Hunger and Malnutrition Although Figure 9-1 is useful, it fails to reveal the widespread differences in protein-calorie malnutrition and vitamin and mineral deficiencies throughout the world. For example, Bolivia has a very low calorie supply, while its next-door neighbor Brazil has an adequate supply.

In addition there are regions within countries where *average* per capita food intake is far below the minimum, even though the average for the country is adequate or even high. For example, in more fertile and urbanized southern Brazil, the average daily per capita food supply is high (above 3,000 Calories). But in Brazil's semiarid and less fertile northeastern interior, much of the population is badly underfed. As you would expect, it is the poor in a country who are the most underfed. The urban poor, who cannot grow their own food, normally have the lowest food intake.

Food is also poorly distributed within families. In poor families, young children (ages 1 to 5), pregnant women, and nursing mothers are the most likely to be severely underfed. This occurs because these groups require more of certain nutrients per kilogram of body weight and because the largest portion of the family food supply normally goes to working males.

Even in rich nations there are pockets of hunger and malnutrition, although this hunger is less visible than the horrors of starvation seen on the streets of Calcutta and in the countryside of Bangladesh. In the early 1970s an estimated 10 to 15 million Americans, mostly poor, were suffering from protein-calorie malnutrition.

Nutritional Deficiency Diseases Protein-calorie malnutrition can have a devastating effect, especially on children. The two most widespread nutritional deficiency diseases are *marasmus* and *kwashiorkor*. **Marasmus** (from the Greek "to waste away") occurs when a diet is low in both calories and protein. A child suffering from severe marasmus (see Figure 9-3) has a bloated belly, a thin body, shriveled skin, wide eyes, and the face of an old

person. With marasmus comes diarrhea, dehydration, anemia, and a ravenous appetite. **Kwashiorkor** (a West African word meaning "displaced child") occurs with a diet that is relatively high in calories but deficient in protein. It occurs primarily in infants and very young children when they are weaned from mother's milk—usually when they are displaced by a new baby—and placed on a starchy diet, usually based on cassava, maize flour, or other cereals with low protein quantity or quality, or both (Table 9-1). The entire body—not just the stomach—of a child suffering from severe kwashiorkor is bloated because liquids collect under the skin. Other symptoms include skin rash and discoloration and a change in hair color to reddish-orange. This disease normally leads to brain damage, anemia, irritability, apathy, and a loss of appetite.

Kwashiorkor and marasmus are the most widespread threats to malnourished humans, but other diseases caused by deficiencies in specific vitamins and minerals (such as iron, iodine, calcium, phosphorus, and zinc) are also found. The most widespread of these is *iron-deficiency anemia*, which affects 5 to 15 percent of adult men, a third of adult women, and more than half of the children in many less developed countries. Anemia saps one's energy, makes infection more likely, and increases a woman's chance of dying in childbirth. Every year 200 million people in the poor nations go deaf or mute because of a lack of iodine. Another serious disease results from *vitamin A deficiency*, which is the leading cause of partial or total blindness in children in many less developed countries, especially in parts of Asia, Latin America, and Africa. In India alone there are at least 1 million cases, and an estimated 20,000 to 250,000 children worldwide become blind each year because of vitamin A deficiency.

Effects of Protein-Calorie Malnutrition Infants and children under 5 need about twice as much protein and energy in relation to body weight as do adults. If children are deprived of calories, high-quality protein, or both, they will grow and develop poorly, be sick, and, if deprived long enough, die. If the children survive past age 5 in spite of malnutrition and related diseases, their ability to learn and work will probably be impaired, and their life expectancy will be lowered because of poor health. Poverty, malnutrition, and disease interact to produce a tragic cycle of human misery and despair (Figure 9-2).

Protein-calorie malnutrition affects from half to two-thirds of the children under age 5 in poor countries. An

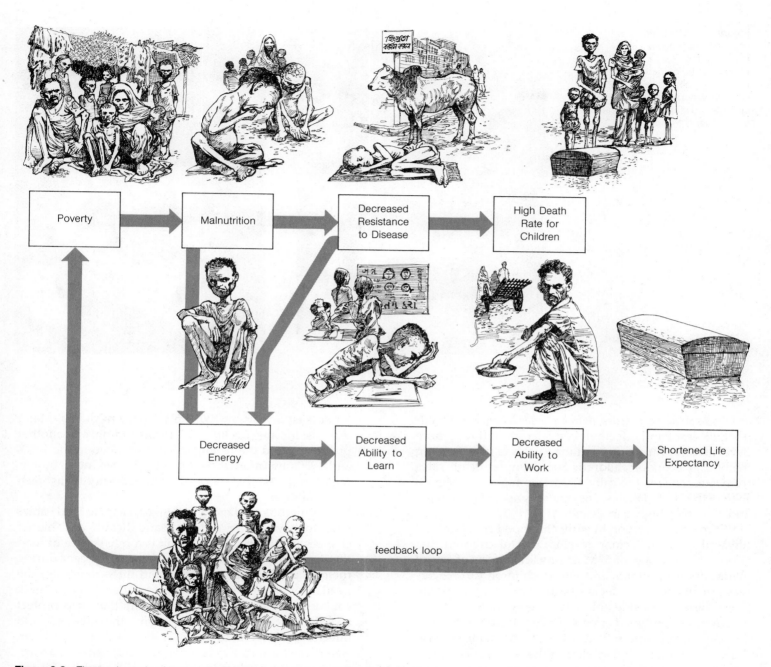

Figure 9-2 The tragic cycle of interactions between poverty, malnutrition, and disease.

estimated 10 to 20 million people, mostly children, die each year from protein-calorie malnutrition and its associated diseases—approximately 41,000 deaths each day if we assume 15 million deaths per year. Other estimates put the average number of malnutrition-related deaths at 12,000 per day, or about 4.4 million each year. In 1980 the average death rate among infants under 1 year of age (the most dangerous year in life) in less developed nations was over 5 times that in the more developed nations. Regardless of the estimate, it is clear that we now have the largest annual global famine in history (see Table 1-1).

Most victims of malnutrition do not starve to death. They die because they become more vulnerable to minor infections

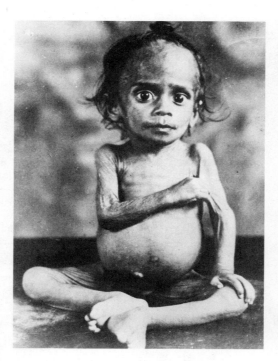

Figure 9-3 Most effects of severe protein-calorie malnutrition or marasmus (left photo) can be corrected (right photo). The pictures show a 2-year-old Venezuelan girl before and after 10 months of treatment and proper nutrition.

UN Food and Agriculture Organization

and diseases such as measles, diarrhea, and chicken pox. Childhood diseases and infections considered routine in more developed countries are common causes of death among malnourished poor children. For example, death rates from measles are typically 180 times higher in Mexico than in the United States, 268 times higher in Guatemala, and 480 times higher in Ecuador.

Severe malnutrition in early childhood can stunt the physical and intellectual development of children that survive past the age of 5. Most physical effects of severe malnutrition in infants and young children can be corrected if an adequate diet is administered in time (Figure 9-3). There is considerable controversy, however, over whether the combined effects of malnutrition, infection, and poverty (Figure 9-2) can lead to permanent brain damage and mental retardation. Whether the damage to a malnourished mind is permanent or not, it is clear that most infants and young children in poor families throughout the world today are not receiving a diet that would reduce or reverse these effects.

Decline in Breast-Feeding *A tragic cause of increased malnutrition and infection of infants in less developed nations is the sharp decline in breast-feeding since 1960.* In 1949 about 95 percent of Chilean mothers breast-fed their children for at least a year; by 1969 only 6 percent did so. Major reasons for the decline in breast-feeding are another pregnancy and the feeling (often promoted in the 1950s and 1960s by international companies selling baby formula products) that modern women do not breast-feed their children.

Numerous studies have shown that breast-fed babies tend to have better nutrition and health and higher chances of survival. Breast milk is a free source of food that can supply all of an infant's nutritional needs during the critical first 4 to 6 months, and three-fourths of the needs from 6 months to a year. In addition, breast milk contains antibodies and other factors that help protect an infant from diarrhea and many other diseases and infections. Most poor mothers lack a source of clean water, can't afford the fuel needed to sterilize baby formula and often dilute the formula milk because it is too expensive. As a result, babies are fed contaminated formula and typically suffer from malnutrition, severe diarrhea, and sometimes death.

Besides raising the infant death rate in less developed countries, the decline in breast-feeding can raise the birth rate. Strong and prolonged suckling can suppress ovulation in mothers—protecting them from pregnancy for 10 weeks to 26 months after a birth, depending on the individual's health and diet and on the intensity of suckling. This safe period is an important form of birth control in some countries.

In response to pressures from churches and other groups, most international companies selling baby formulas had eliminated or greatly reduced promotional advertising in less developed countries by the mid-1970s. By this time, however, the damage had already been done.

9-2 World Food Problems and Proposed Solutions: An Overview

Is There a World Food Shortage? With an estimated 15 million people dying each year from malnutrition and malnutrition-related diseases, this may seem like a strange question. Yet some observers like to point out that there really is no food production crisis in the world: We have enough food to feed everyone, and we can use modern technology to produce much more food in the future. If all the grain produced in the world each year was distributed equally among the world's population, everyone would have a modest but adequate diet.

Although the previous statement is true, it is highly misleading for a number of reasons. First, it specifies that everyone in the world would exist on a diet made up almost entirely of grain (mostly rice, wheat, and corn). Little or no meat would be allowed except from animals grazing on land that is either not needed or not suitable for crops. Grain could no longer be used to feed livestock, poultry, and pets. *In addition to the 4.6 billion humans on the planet, we must feed the world's livestock, poultry, and pets, which require enough food to feed 16 billion people.*

Second, we saw in the previous section that a diet based only on grains can lead to malnutrition unless it is carefully balanced with animal products for children and legumes for adults. Third, although a more equal distribution of the world's grain supply among the rich and poor nations is desirable, it is highly unlikely that the more prosperous nations and peoples will forgo their plenty.

Fourth, it is assumed that all of the grain produced each year gets to consumers before it spoils or is eaten by pests. However, about 43 to 48 percent of the annual grain production is destroyed by pests, crop disease, and spoilage (see Enrichment Study 11). Fifth, even if everyone agreed to distribute the world's annual grain production equally, there are not enough ships, planes, trains, trucks, storage facilities, roads, and marketing systems to store, distribute, and sell the food. These deficiencies are especially acute in the less developed nations, where food needs are the most critical.

Sixth, even if the food could somehow be distributed, the poor people of the world couldn't buy enough for an adequate diet. Most people become hungry and malnourished because they no longer grow food themselves and do not have the money to buy the food they need. Seventh, even if people have the money to buy food, they won't buy and eat it unless they find it culturally acceptable. People living near the edge of starvation can't afford to risk their lives and the little money they have on a strange-looking or strange-tasting food. The United States once sent wheat to feed starving people in India, but they did not eat it because they were used to rice.

Eighth, even if the world's annual grain production was distributed equally, bought, and found acceptable, projected world population growth (Chapter 7) indicates that world food production must almost *double* between 1970 and 2000 to meet minimum needs. In the less developed nations, where the bulk of the world's population growth is occurring, minimum food needs will almost *triple* between 1970 and 2000. Ninth, doubling the world's food supply in this period will require massive increases in use of cropland, water (Chapter 15), fertilizer, pesticides (Enrichment Study 11), fossil fuels (Chapter 14), and other agricultural resources.

Tenth, producing food even at today's levels assumes that world climate patterns and local weather patterns will not change (Enrichment Study 3). Eleventh, providing, processing, and trying to distribute food to today's world population is already degrading the world's soil, water (Enrichment Study 16), and air (Chapter 17), as well as the world's forests, estuaries, and other diverse ecosystems (Chapter 10). Doubling the world's food production over the next few decades could greatly intensify these environmental problems.

World Food Problems: Producing More Food Is Not Enough From this discussion, we see that there is not one but many food and food-related problems—all of which are related in a complex manner (see the accompanying summary box).

Any world food plan must deal with all of these problems simultaneously. Since many of these problems are discussed in other chapters and enrichment studies (see references in the summary box), the rest of this chapter will be devoted to (1) evaluating proposals for

World Food and Food-Related Problems

1. *Quantity.* Producing enough calories.

2. *Quality.* Producing food with enough fats, vitamins, critical minerals, and high-quality protein.

3. *Crop protection.* Protecting food from pests, diseases, and spoilage before and after harvesting (Enrichment Study 11).

4. *Distribution.* Transporting, storing, marketing, and distributing the food to people who need it.

5. *Poverty.* Making sure people can afford to grow or buy the quantity and quality of food they need (Chapters 18, 20; Enrichment Study 9).

6. *Cultural acceptance.* Providing types of food that people with different cultural backgrounds and preferences will buy and eat.

7. *Resource supply.* Having enough land (Chapter 10), water (Chapter 15), fertilizer, pesticides (Enrichment Study 11), fossil fuels (Chapter 14), and other resources (Chapter 12) to grow and distribute enough food for the world's human and animal populations.

8. *Climate and weather.* Hoping that natural and human-related activities will not adversely change global climate and local weather patterns (Enrichment Study 3).

9. *Population growth.* Trying to control population growth (Chapter 8; Enrichment Study 7) so that world food production and distribution won't have to be doubled every 30 to 40 years; at present growth rates we must try to feed 205,000 new people each day.

10. *Ecological effects.* Trying to produce, process, and distribute more and more food without seriously degrading soil, water (Enrichment Study 16), air (Chapter 17), wildlife, and forests, estuaries, and other ecosystems (Chapters 6, 10).

---

producing more food, (2) reviewing the ecological effects of food production, and (3) listing the major principles of a world food plan.

World Agricultural Systems To see how food production might be increased in the future, we must first understand how food is produced today. Agriculture is the world's largest solar energy system; it is a way of converting the sun's rays into chemical energy stored in plants (Section 5-3). Most of the world's food for humans and domestic animals is produced by cultivating plant crops and using pasture and rangeland to provide most of the food for livestock. The three major agricultural systems in the world today involve supplementing the input of solar energy with other forms of energy. These systems are (1) *simple (subsistence) agriculture* (based on an energy supplement from human labor), (2) *animal-assisted agriculture* (based on energy supplements from human labor and draft animals), and (3) *industrialized agriculture* (based on an energy supplement from fossil fuels with an emphasis on replacing human labor with machines).

The first two types of agricultural systems are still widely used in less developed nations. More developed nations, however, depend primarily on industrialized agriculture, which has greatly increased crop yields and productivity per farm worker. In a more developed country that relies primarily on industrialized agriculture, only 4 to 10 percent of the labor force is directly engaged in agriculture, in contrast to 50 to 80 percent in less developed countries.

The success of industrialized agriculture when coupled with a favorable climate has been demonstrated by the dramatic increase in food production in the United States. In 1820 about 72 percent of the U.S. labor force worked on farms; by 1980 this figure had dropped to only 3 percent, with half of the remaining farmers holding second jobs off the farm (Figure 9-4). Agriculture is far and away the biggest industry in the United States, with assets of $790 billion in 1979. It is also the nation's largest employer, if we include all the people in farming, farm machinery, fertilizer production, food processing, and retailing who help get food from the farm to the table; it accounts for about one-fifth of all jobs in private enterprise.

Between 1920 and 1980, total U.S. food production approximately doubled, and the relative output per farm worker increased eightfold (Figure 9-4). In 1980 each U.S. farm worker fed about 61 people, although this figure drops to about 15 if we include all of the other agricultural workers involved in the production of farm machinery and fertilizer and in the processing and marketing of food. In addition to feeding the U.S. population, in 1979 the American agricultural system accounted for almost 42 percent of the world's wheat exports—an amount nearly equal to that needed to feed all of India's 635 million people. These and other food exports—totaling $47 billion in 1981—partially offset the cost of U.S. oil imports. Today only the United States, Canada, Argentina, Australia, and New Zealand regularly export more grain than they import. As the world's largest grain exporter, the United States has unrivaled power over the world food distribution system—similar to the power OPEC commands over world oil distribution. A number of components of modern industrialized agriculture (see the accompanying summary box) have helped make such spectacular increases in food productivity possible.

Because most Americans no longer farm and thus are away from the soil, their view of how the natural world really works is distorted. As Aldo Leopold reminded us in 1949, "There are two spiritual dangers in not owning a farm. One is the danger of supposing that breakfast comes from the grocery, and the other that heat comes from the furnace."

Research is under way to increase the efficiency with which agricultural plants use solar energy, but so far modern industrialized agriculture does not use solar energy any more efficiently than unindustrialized agriculture. Instead, industrialized agriculture merely supplements solar energy with massive inputs of fossil fuel energy (Figure 9-5). Yet, none of this supplementary energy in the fuel ends up in the food. Instead, it merely replaces energy once derived from human and animal muscle power.

The energy used to grow food in the United States is about 6 percent of its total energy use and about 17 percent if we include the energy used to process and distribute food. Most plant crops in the United States (especially grains and legumes) still provide more calories in food energy than they use from the fossil fuel energy used to grow them, although the energy return has been decreasing as farmers become more and more dependent on fossil fuels. Raising animals for food, however, requires more calories of fossil fuel energy than the animals provide as food. The energy input needed to produce a given amount of animal protein is summarized in Table 9-2. Note that for animal and animal products, the best energy efficiencies per unit of protein produced are found in milk, chickens, and turkeys, with drastically lower efficiencies for beef, pork, and sheep.

This situation is much worse if we look at the entire food system in the United States. If one counts the fossil fuel energy input used to grow, process, package, transport, refrigerate, and cook all plant and animal food in the United States, *it takes about 9 calories of fossil fuel energy to put 1 calorie of food energy on the table*—an energy loss of 8 calories per calorie of food energy. The U.S. food-processing industry alone is the nation's fourth-largest energy user—after the metals, chemicals, and oil industries. To feed the entire world using the same energy-intensive agriculture practiced in the United States would greatly increase environmental pollution, consume 80 percent of all energy used in the world each year, and deplete the world's known oil reserves in only 13 years.

Americans like to boast of the efficiency of their large-scale food production system. Industrialized agriculture is very efficient in terms of the food produced per unit of human labor, but in terms of energy efficiency it is the most inefficient food production system in the world. One farmer in India with an ox and a plow can

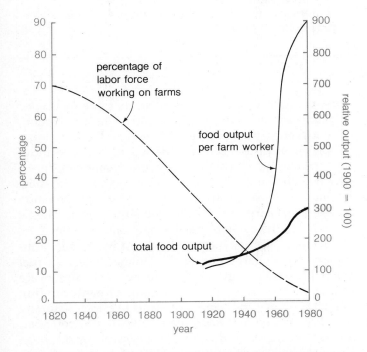

Figure 9-4 Effects of increased use of industrialized agriculture in the United States.

Components of Modern Industrialized Agriculture

1. *Mechanization.* Substituting fossil-fuel-powered machines for manual labor and draft animals (at least two-thirds of the world's cropland is tilled with mechanical power).

2. *Artificial fertilizers.* Using commercially produced plant nutrients (such as nitrogen) to increase crop yields (one-fourth of the world's annual food output is based on the use of artificial fertilizers). This practice is simple and convenient, but requires large amounts of fossil fuel energy to make the fertilizer.

3. *Irrigation.* Building dams and canals and using fossil-fuel-powered machines to pump water to cropland (Chapter 15).

4. *Pesticides.* Using synthetic chemicals to reduce crop losses due to pests, disease, and weeds (Enrichment Study 11).

5. *Soil conservation.* Establishing sound land-use practices to reduce soil erosion (see Section 16-6).

6. *Animal feedlots.* Shifting from pastures and open ranges to feedlots, where hundreds to thousands of animals are concentrated in a small space for more efficient production. (In this practice, the animals stand in front of a feed bin and eat hay or grain to which have been added various chemicals to encourage rapid weight gain. This practice requires large amounts of fossil fuel.)

7. *Genetic selection and hybridization.* Using research to select and develop high-yield and disease-resistant crops, livestock, and poultry.

8. *Large-scale and specialized production.* Shifting from small, diversified farms to large, specialized farms. (For example, the number of U.S. farms dropped from 6.8 million in 1935 to 2.8 million in 1976, but the average farm size increased significantly. To start an industrialized farm today in the United States would require an investment of about $500,000 in land and equipment.)

9. *Storage, processing, distribution, and marketing.* Developing storage facilities and extensive transportation, processing, and marketing networks.

10. *Agricultural training and research.* Establishing a system of agricultural schools and research centers and using extension services to bring new developments to farmers.

---

produce more food energy per unit of energy put into the system than the largest, most mechanized farm in America. Chinese farmers using intensive organic farming can get a food energy output 40 times larger than their energy input by making use of human and animal dung and crop residues as fertilizer. A typical home garden in the United States has a food energy output 2 to 4 times the energy put into it.

In spite of its energy inefficiency, however, today's industrialized agriculture supplies much of the world's food supply. If fossil fuels should become scarce or too expensive, the present agricultural system in industrialized nations would collapse, causing a sharp drop in world food production and a sharp rise in malnutrition and famine. Without energy to produce synthetic fertilizers, many sandy and unproductive soils now made fertile by almost continuous doses of synthetic fertilizer would not be worth farming. Desert areas that now pro-

duce two or three crops per year because energy is used to pump water to the fields would cease production. With less energy available to transport and process food, people in industrialized nations would begin to move back to areas with fertile soil—creating tremendous pressures on the land. The high crop yields made possible by intensive use of artificial fertilizers and irrigation would drop sharply until American farmers learned how to return to the age-old practice of organic farming.

There is already increased interest in organic farming and home gardening in the United States. As fuel prices have risen, a growing number of U.S. farmers are calling for a return to organic farming. **Organic farming** is a method of producing crops and livestock naturally by using organic fertilizer (manure, legumes, compost, and crop residues) and natural pest control ("good" bugs that eat "bad" bugs, plants that repel bugs, and crop rotation) instead of synthetic chemical pesticides and

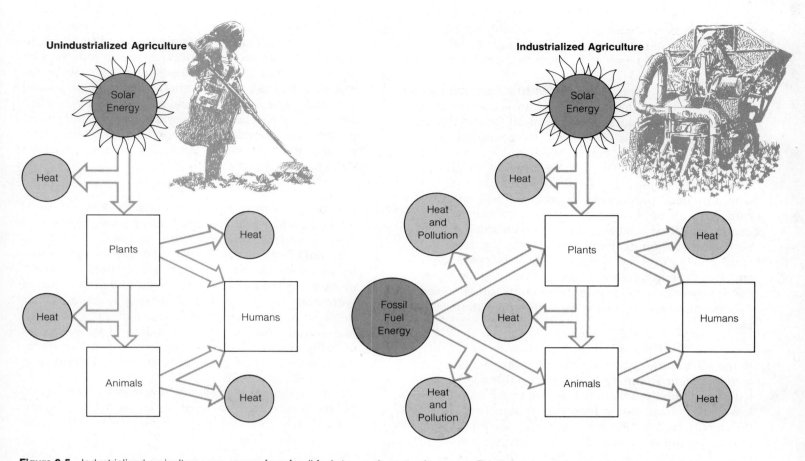

Uninstrialized Agriculture

Industrialized Agriculture

Figure 9-5 Industrialized agriculture uses energy from fossil fuels to supplement solar energy. This increases crop yields and productivity per worker, but it also increases pollution and the heat load on the environment because of energy losses required by the second law of energy (Section 3-3).

Table 9-2 Energy Inputs Needed to Produce 1 Kilogram (2.2 lbs.) of Selected Plant and Animal Proteins in the United States

Crop or Animal Production System	Energy Input (millions of calories)
Soybeans	6
Corn	12
Wheat	14
Milk (grass fed)	29
Chickens (grain fed)	39
Milk (grain fed)	47
Turkeys (grain fed)	54
Eggs (grain fed)	71
Beef (grass fed)	86
Beef (grain fed)	87
Pork (grain fed)	171
Sheep (grass fed)	254
Sheep (grain fed)	392

herbicides (see Enrichment Study 11). Scientific studies comparing organic and chemical farming have shown: (1) Organic farming provides adequate nitrogen for plant growth, but it is not clear whether it provides adequate phosphorus and potassium; (2) pest control without pesticides has been moderately successful and should become more successful as we learn more about integrated pest management (see Enrichment Study 11); (3) some organic farms have 5 to 15 percent higher yields than chemical farms, but this varies by crop and region; (4) the financial returns for both types of farms are about equal per unit area, but the indebtedness of organic farmers is usually lower; and (5) organic farms use 15 to 50 percent less energy per unit of food produced than conventional farms. A U.S. Department of Agriculture study indicated that a total shift to organic farming in the United States could meet U.S. food needs, but there would be some decrease in the food available for export. Political opposition to such a shift by the powerful pesticide and fertilizer industries, however, would be intense.

Higher food prices have also led to a significant increase in home gardens throughout Europe and America in recent years—a practice that is crucial for survival in less developed nations. Half of all Americans now grow some of their own vegetables, which had a retail value of $14 billion in 1977. The U.S. Department of Agriculture estimates that a family of four could be well fed without animal products by using high-yield intensive gardening on only one-sixth of an acre. Increasingly, manicured lawns are being replaced with small garden plots, and rooftop gardens, window box planters, and small greenhouses are being used to help save money and energy. Furthermore, home gardens require fewer (if any) chemical pesticides because crops can be mixed to provide a less appetizing and convenient target for pests.

Proposed Solutions   A number of proposals (see the accompanying summary box) have been made to deal with world food problems. These are based on wasting less food and increasing food production (proposals 1 through 7), distributing more equitably the food that is grown (proposals 8 and 9), and stabilizing the world population (proposals 10 and 11).

Let's look more closely at the first six of these proposals. (The last five are discussed in other chapters and in the Enrichment Studies.)

9-3   Fortified, Fabricated, and Unconventional Foods

Over the next several decades, most of the increase in the world's food supply will result from expanding the supplies of traditional foods, such as wheat, rice, and maize. A very promising approach is cultivating new crops to supplement or replace heavy dependence on these traditional foods in the poor nations. Examples of these new crops include the winged bean (a crop that contains as much protein as soybeans), cocoyam (native plant of West Africa and Central and South America that is as nutritious as the potato), *Ye-ed* (a small bush native to East Africa whose seeds alone contain a nutritionally balanced diet), and a number of other little-known beans, grains, and gourds.

Food quality can also be upgraded by fortifying existing foods with missing vitamins, minerals, and essential amino acids and by fabricating protein food supplements and new high-protein foods from leaves, soybeans, cottonseeds, trash fish, grasshoppers, trash, oil, natural gas, and other unconventional sources. Many of these new food sources are already available, but it remains to be seen whether people will be willing to eat them and whether the foods can be produced cheaply enough so that poor people can buy them.

Fortifying Existing Foods   Adding missing vitamins, minerals, and essential amino acids to conventional food sources, such as flour, bread, rice, and salt, is a relatively easy and often inexpensive way to upgrade protein quality and eliminate many mineral- and vitamin-deficiency diseases. In the United States, bread and flour enriched with vitamins, minerals, and missing amino acids has helped eliminate many nutritional deficiency diseases, and adding small amounts of iodine to table salt has virtually wiped out goiter. Similarly, Japan has essentially eradicated beriberi since World War II by enriching its rice with vitamin B_1.

A major advantage of enriching existing foods is that people don't have to change their eating habits. A major disadvantage, however, is that these processed foods are not normally available to the rural poor who don't buy their food.

New Protein Supplements and Fabricated Foods   In the 1960s there was talk that *fish protein concentrate* (FPC) would solve the protein malnutrition problems of the poor. FPC is a powder with an extremely high protein content that can be added to conventional foods. It is made by processing inedible trash fish (such as hake, skate, and dogfish) that are normally tossed back into the sea. Unfortunately, it is difficult to remove the fishy taste from FPC and to produce it at a reasonable price. Because of these problems the idea of using FPC has largely been abandoned.

In recent years some have talked of using **single-cell protein** (SCP) as a protein supplement for humans and livestock. SCP is a high-protein powder that can be produced from oil, natural gas, alcohol, sewage, waste paper, and other organic materials by the action of single-cell organisms such as yeast, fungi, and bacteria. SCP produced from yeast can contain 50 percent protein, and that produced from bacteria can contain as high as 80 percent protein—compared to 40 to 45 percent protein

Proposals for Solving World Food Problems

1. *Using new foods* (such as winged beans, Ye-ed, and insects), *fabricated foods* (such as simulated meat products made from soybeans), *and unconventional foods* (such as fish protein concentrate and single-cell protein).

2. *Simplifying diets.* Shortening the food chain by reducing the use of meat and meat products in more developed nations.

3. *Using and wasting less food and energy.* Reducing use and waste of food and fossil fuel energy in industrialized agriculture.

4. *Food from the ocean.* Trying to increase the world seafood catch and harvesting ocean plants (algae).

5. *Adding new farmland.* Cultivating more land by clearing forests, plowing pastures, draining wetlands, and irrigating arid land.

6. *Improving crop yields.* Increasing yields by transferring or adapting industrialized agriculture to less developed nations.

7. *Applying agricultural appropriate technology.* Helping less developed nations learn how to grow more food using appropriate agricultural technology (Section 1-5), thus making them less dependent on more developed nations for food and aid.

8. *Increasing foreign aid.* Having rich nations give more aid and money to poor nations that is designed to help these nations grow more of their own food (Chapter 18; Enrichment Study 9).

9. *Instituting land ownership reform.* Distributing more land to the poor in less developed nations so they can grow their own food.

10. *Controlling population.* Limiting world population growth and size (Chapter 8; Enrichment Study 7).

11. *Establishing space colonies.* Decreasing the population size and food needs of earth by shipping people to colonies in space. (See Section 1-6 for a discussion of why this is an impractical approach.)

---

in soybeans. Theoretically, 227 grams (½ pound) of newspaper or junk mail could provide your daily protein need. A few small-scale pilot factories, mostly in Europe, are producing SCP, but there are still a number of problems to be overcome. For instance, the high ribonucleic acid (RNA) content of SCP can cause urinary stones to form in humans. In addition, the walls of the cells are indigestible for humans and can cause diarrhea, nausea, and gastric distress.

In 1975 consumer and government protests over the safety of SCP halted plans to produce it commercially in Japan and Europe. A number of pilot plants in Europe have been closed but by 1980 one plant in England was running continuously. Scientists, however, think that SCP could be made sufficiently pure for human consumption, but this might add considerably to its projected cost, which is already so high that poor people wouldn't be able to afford foods supplemented with or fabricated from SCP.

Even if the safety of SCP can be established, consumers may not accept the supplement in their foods. Some argue that it makes no sense economically or eco-logically to use increasingly expensive and dwindling petroleum and natural gas resources to produce SCP. SCP might be produced from agricultural wastes in less developed nations, but these wastes might be better used for fertilizer to grow conventional crops, since the poor can't afford to buy fertilizer.

Another approach is to supplement the protein in foods with meal or flour made from soybeans, cottonseed, peanuts, coconuts, sunflower seeds, rape seeds, and other oil seeds. There are problems in making these meal supplements tasteless and in removing toxic compounds, although progress is being made. Soybean meal has been used as a protein supplement for decades. Vitasoy, a soybean-based soft drink, has been marketed with great success in Hong Kong for over three decades and now has one-fourth of the soft drink market there. Other soybean-based beverages are being marketed with varying degrees of success in Asia and Latin America.

In the United States, oleomargarine and vegetable oils (from soybeans, sunflower seeds, and other plants) have greatly reduced the use of the animal products butter and lard. Another recent development is the production of simulated meat products (such as imitation bacon, eggs, chicken, ham, and meat extenders) that contain spun vegetable protein fibers (SVP), made primarily from soybean concentrate and wheat gluten. In this process soybean protein is extracted and concentrated and then either spun into fibers or extended into meat-textured nuggets. If these products become widely accepted, they could reduce U.S. meat consumption. Since SVP contains no cholesterol, it could also reduce the incidence of heart disease. But to make these products look and taste like meat, food processors must add a number of dyes, flavors, and other food additives, which some fear might increase the risks of cancer and other health hazards (Enrichment Study 10).

Producing SVP requires sophisticated, high-cost, energy-intensive technology. Less developed nations, however, have had low-cost, low-technology meat analogues, such as Indonesian tempeh, for hundreds of years. To produce tempeh, soybeans are soaked, hulled, partially cooked, and then overgrown with an edible mold that binds the soybean material into a compact cake that can be deep-fat fried or cut into meatlike chunks.

In the future we may be able to extract protein from the leaves and stalks of forage crops (such as alfalfa), shrubs, and trees, but so far these processes are still in the experimental stage. Another source of protein is the insects that compete with us for the food we grow. In parts of Africa and Latin America, ants, termites, crickets, beetles, and grasshoppers are eaten as a food source, and chocolate-covered ants are sold in many gourmet food stores. Indeed, the protein content of these insects ranges from 30 to 60 percent by weight—2 to 4 times that of beef, fish, or eggs (Table 9-1). Perhaps in the future you may eat a gourmet meal consisting of fried termites as an appetizer, grasshopper soup, salad with moth sauce, beetle patties as the main course, a side order of algae with caterpillar sauce, and bumblebee pie for dessert.

If supported by research and development, a number of the fortified, fabricated, and unconventional foods discussed in this section could make important contributions to human nutrition in the future. But they are not a cure-all for the serious food problem (Section 9-2) that the world faces during the next few decades.

9-4 Simplifying Affluent Diets

Human Diets and Food-Chain Losses When we eat meat, about 90 percent of the energy available in the meat is degraded and lost to the environment as low-temper-
ature heat because of the second law of energy (Figure 9-6). This loss of usable food energy, however, is only important when livestock and poultry animals eat grains or other plants that could be eaten by humans or when these animals are grazing on land or being fed from forage crops (such as hay and alfalfa) grown on land that could be used to grow food crops for humans. This food-chain loss of usable energy (Section 5-3) explains why meat is more expensive than grain and why poor people are forced to live primarily on a diet of grain rather than meat.

As their incomes rise, people began to substitute meat and meat products for grain in their diets. For example, average per capita meat consumption in the less developed countries is only about 4.5 to 9 kilograms (10 to 20 pounds) annually, whereas in more developed nations the figure is about 114 kilograms (250 pounds). As a result of the trend toward meat-based diets, in 1975 about one-third of the world's annual grain production was fed to livestock and poultry to produce meat, eggs, and milk for the affluent, rather than being used to decrease hunger and malnutrition among the poor.

This situation is aggravated by the increased use of animal feedlots, especially in the United States. Typically, beef cattle are fed forage crops until they reach a certain weight. Then they are moved to a feedlot, and for 2 to 6 months before slaughtering they are fed a rich diet of grain concentrations with growth stimulating chemicals and antibiotics added. This fattens the cattle quickly, increases beef production with fewer cattle, and produces the high-cholesterol, fatty (marbled), choice beef that many consumers seem to prefer. Indeed, the average person in the United States consumes about 273 kilograms (600 pounds) of meat, eggs, and dairy products each year.

There is growing concern however that the antibiotics added to animal feed promote the rise of antibiotic-immune bacteria in meat-eating humans, which would decrease the humans' protection against infectious diseases. Animal feedlots also require large inputs of fossil fuel energy. About 12 to 20 calories of fossil fuel energy are needed to produce 1 calorie of food energy in grain-fed beef. In contrast, beef fed totally on forage (grass-fed beef) require about 9 to 15 calories of fossil fuel energy, and range-fed beef need only about 0.5 calorie (used mostly by pickup trucks to round the animals up) to produce 1 calorie of food energy.

Altering Affluent Diets and Reducing Energy Waste Representatives from less developed nations at the 1974 UN Food Conference in Rome and a number of

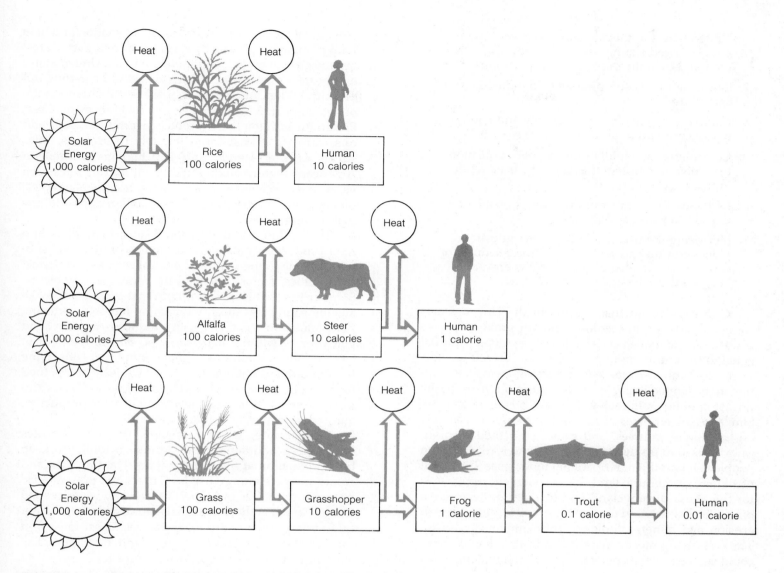

Figure 9-6 In a food chain only about 10 percent of the energy available is transferred from one trophic level to another. Because of the second law of energy, the other 90 percent is degraded to heat and lost to the environment. (Actual energy transfer values vary somewhat from the average values shown.)

environmentalists and food experts have called for affluent nations to alter their diets in order to make more food available for export to feed the poor. Suggestions include the following:

1. Reducing beef consumption by at least one-half and slightly increasing the consumption of fish, chicken, eggs, dried beans, potatoes, and vegetables that can be grown locally or in home gardens.

2. Substituting vegetable oils (such as oleomargarine) for animal fats (such as butter).

3. Substituting vegetable protein for animal protein.

4. Replacing grain-fed (feedlot) animals with animals eating grass on ranges and eating forage crops grown on marginal agricultural land.

5. Using fertilizer only on food crops and eliminating or sharply reducing its use on lawns, golf courses, and cemeteries, and replacing suburban lawns with home gardens and orchards.

6. Reducing food waste (estimated to be 30 to 40 percent of all food consumed in the United States with enough food thrown away each day in the

United States to theoretically feed over 100 million people) by educating people to throw away less food and by reducing the size of portions served.

7. Reducing the use of fossil fuels in industrialized agriculture.*

8. Using the sun instead of electricity and natural gas to dry corn and other crops before storage.

9. Controlling the rapidly growing pet populations that consume protein that could be used to feed humans.

10. Reducing the number of overweight people to improve health and save energy.

11. Increasing the use of no-tillage agriculture (no plowing or disking and leaving crop residues for cover) to reduce soil erosion, save energy, and increase the soil's ability to hold water.

Critics point out that if cattle in the United States were not fattened in feedlots, enough grain would be made available to feed about 400 million people—almost equal to the entire population of Africa. Even if feedlots were not eliminated, merely decreasing meat consumption in the United States by 10 percent could theoretically release enough grain each year to feed 60 million people. Similarly, the fertilizer that Americans spread each year on lawns, golf courses, and cemeteries could theoretically be used to produce enough grain to feed 65 million people. The production of animal foods uses 95 percent of all U.S. agricultural land. It is also largely responsible for the abuse of rangeland and forestland, destruction of wildlife habitat, and for the loss of soil fertility through erosion and mineral depletion (Enrichment Study 16). Thus, reducing meat consumption in the United States could significantly decrease the environmental impact of agriculture.

In addition, the pet foods consumed in the United States each year could theoretically provide enough protein to feed 21 million people. The $2.8 billion that Americans spend on pet food annually could buy enough food to feed one-third of the world's hungry people. Pets can help offset feelings of loneliness and alienation and help limit population growth by serving as child substitutes, but the growth of the pet population in the United States and in many European nations seems to be getting out of control. The United States has the world's highest ratio of pets to people—followed closely by France and Great Britain. In addition to their food consumption, dogs and cats carry 65 diseases transmittable to humans, litter streets with feces and urine, bite humans (1.5 million Americans require medical treatment for dog bites each year), and create noise. Furthermore, taxpayers pay $600 million a year to dispose of the 20 million dogs and cats that owners throw away annually.

That affluent nations should alter their diets and food production patterns is a highly controversial subject, revealing the complex environmental, economic, and political factors involved in world food problems. Some critics of this idea point out that grain made available by eating less meat, eliminating feedlots, reducing pet populations, and not using fertilizer on lawns and golf courses will not necessarily be sent to the poor in less developed countries. Others argue that conserving food in affluent nations could actually lead to less food for the poor, because it would lead to food surpluses and price declines, thus causing farmers to cut production and reduce exports to other nations.

Furthermore, without feedlots the United States would need additional land planted in forage to keep beef production at the present level. Planting this land would increase energy use by 5 times the present level because of the large inputs of fertilizer and water needed to make much of these marginal lands usable for grazing. In addition, hogs and poultry cannot digest grass and thus can't be fed grass on rangeland or forage. The amount of fossil fuels used to produce food crops and livestock can be reduced, but energy savings in one area of food production sometimes increase energy use in another area. For example, little fossil fuel would be saved by substituting animal manure for artificial fertilizer unless forage pastures and feedlots were fairly close to the crop fields. Otherwise, most of the fossil fuel not used to produce fertilizer would be needed to haul the manure long distances.

In summary, altering affluent diets and reducing the waste of food and energy in industrialized nations can help ease the world food situation. But this will happen only if such changes are coupled with political, economic, and ethical factors so that the food and money made available are either given to the poor or preferably used to help them grow their own food.

---

*Ways to accomplish this include increasing the use of animal wastes as fertilizers, rotation of nitrogen-producing legumes to reduce the need for artificial fertilizer, moving feedlots and forage-fed animals closer to crop fields so that it is more economical to collect and use the animal wastes as fertilizer, substituting crops that require low fossil fuel inputs (corn, wheat, soybeans, peanuts, potatoes, rice, and apples) for crops that require large fossil fuel inputs (tomatoes, lettuce, broccoli, grapefruit, melons, and green beans), using returnable containers, and eliminating the excess packaging of food (often the container requires more fossil fuel energy to make than the energy value of the food) (Enrichment Study 15).

9-5 Food from the Ocean

Trends in the World Fish Catch For decades some have talked of solving world food problems by harvesting the fish, shellfish, and the tiny floating plants (phytoplankton) found in the oceans, which cover 71 percent of the earth's surface. Unfortunately, there is increasing evidence that this vision is an illusion.

Until recently the number of fish we could get from the ocean seemed unlimited. Between 1950 and 1970, the marine fish catch more than tripled—an increase greater than that occurring in any other human food source during the same period (Figure 9-7). To achieve such large catches, modern fishing fleets use sonar, helicopters, aerial photography, and temperature measurement to locate schools of fish and lights and electrodes to attract them. Large, floating factory ships follow the fleets to process the catch. In spite of this technological sophistication, the steady rise in the marine fish catch halted abruptly in 1971. Between 1971 and 1976 the annual catch leveled off and rose only slightly between 1976 and 1980 (Figure 9-7). A major factor in this leveling off was the sharp decline of the Peruvian anchovy catch, which at one time made up 20 percent of the global ocean harvest. A combination of overfishing and a shift in the cool, nutrient-rich currents off the coast of Peru were apparently the major factors causing this decline.

Some observers now fear that the global catch may be at or near the maximum sustainable yield. Meanwhile, world population has continued to grow, so that between 1970 and 1980 the average per person in the world marine fish catch declined by 15 percent and is projected to decline even further back to the 1960 level by the year 2000 (Figure 9-8).

The annual aquatic catch provides only about 0.8 percent of the world's calorie intake and about 5 percent of the intake of protein. But for hundreds of millions of the world's poor—in China and in other less developed Asian, African, and Latin American countries—fish is virtually the only source of high-quality animal protein. Many poor nations cannot afford expensive fishing fleets and have been effectively priced out of a fair share of the ocean's food resources although some less developed nations are beginning to develop modern fishing fleets. In 1978 the less developed nations got only about one-fourth of the edible protein in the world's marine catch, with the remaining three-fourths going to the more developed nations. About two-thirds of this was consumed directly in the more developed nations, and the remaining third (mostly trash fish) was ground into meal and

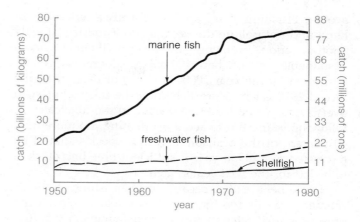

Figure 9-7 World aquatic catch, 1950 through 1980. Between 1950 and 1970, the annual world marine fish catch tripled, but since 1970 the catch has leveled off.

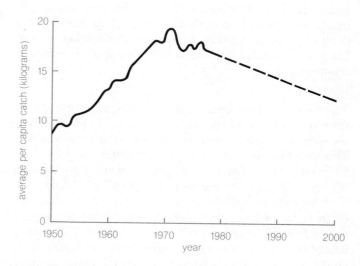

Figure 9-8 Average per capita world fish catch from 1950 to 1980, with projections to 2000.

used as a feed supplement for poultry and hogs (95 percent) and pets (5 percent).

During the 1980s a larger share of the world's fish catch may go to the less developed nations. Under international law, poor nations bordering the sea have been able to extend their legal boundaries to 320 kilometers (200 miles) offshore; other countries cannot fish within these waters without permission.

Has the ocean fish catch leveled off permanently or can it be increased? J. H. Ryther estimates that if we do everything right—expand the fishing fleets 5 to 6 times, avoid overfishing of key species (already a serious problem), and not pollute the oceans and estuaries (already another serious problem)—then we could get an annual sustainable yield of about 100 billion kilograms (110 million tons) by the year 2000—43 percent more than the record 1970 catch. More fish could be taken, but such **overfishing** would lead to a decline in the total catch in following years. But to avoid overfishing, no more than 40 percent of the available fish in a species should be harvested in a given year if sufficient breeding stock is to be left for the next year's catch.

Some believe that because of overfishing, Ryther's estimate may be too high, and they fear that even the present annual catch may not be sustainable. By 1976 it was estimated that overfishing was causing declines in the annual yields of 30 of the leading species of table fish. Some species have been so overfished that they are in danger of extinction, as discussed in Enrichment Study 12. Even if 1975 yields could be doubled to 150 billion kilograms (165 million tons) by 2020, average per capita fish consumption would still decline because of the projected doubling of the world's population during this period.

The Sea as a Biological Desert Why can't the yields from ocean fish and shellfish be increased indefinitely if we can somehow control overfishing internationally? The basic reason is that *the open sea, which makes up about 90 percent of the ocean, has such low net primary productivity (Figure 5-9) that it is sometimes called a biological desert.*

Only about 0.06 percent of the annual marine fish catch is taken from the open ocean. About 50 percent comes from the relatively shallow coastal zone. The other half of the world's fish catch comes from the coastal wetlands and estuaries (Section 10-6), which make up only 0.1 percent of the total ocean area. Unfortunately, these coastal waters and estuaries are receiving massive loads of pollutants (see Section 10-6).

Ocean Food Chains There is another reason why the food yield from the sea is limited. The most favored food fish tend to be high in the ocean food chain—typically in the fourth or fifth trophic level. A typical chain is phytoplankton → zooplankton → mackerel → tuna fish → humans.

Since 80 to 90 percent of the energy available at each trophic level is lost as heat (Figure 9-6), eating fish at the end of a long food chain is very inefficient due to the second law of energy (Section 3-3). Commercial fishing operations merely use large quantities of fossil fuel to carry out a hunting-and-gathering operation taking place over a large area of the world's oceans. As a result, it takes a lot of expensive fossil fuel energy to catch fish and shellfish. Typical inputs of fossil fuel energy for each calorie of food energy caught are 75 for shrimp, 34 for lobster, 20 for king salmon, 5.3 for flounder, and 1.3 for perch.

Why not go to the base of the marine food chain and harvest phytoplankton, the grass of the sea? Problems of taste and smell aside, the second energy law gets us again. Phytoplankton are so widely dispersed that 3.8 million liters (1 million gallons) of water would have to be filtered to yield 454 grams (1 pound) of phytoplankton. In addition, like all forms of SCP, they have to be processed to remove RNA impurities and to break their cell walls so that they will be digestible for humans. The extremely large fossil fuel input needed to do all this makes them far costlier than they are worth as a food source.

However, we may be able to increase the protein yield of the sea by going one step above plants in the food chain and harvesting Antarctic krill—tiny, shrimp-like crustaceans that are plentiful in Antarctic waters. Krill might be particularly useful as a livestock feed supplement. Soviet and Japanese scientists believe that we can harvest enough krill each year to about equal the total current annual marine fish catch. By 1978 at least eight nations were harvesting krill, but some scientists warn that extensive harvesting could cause ecological problems. The already threatened baleen whales (such as the blue whale) feed on krill, along with several kinds of fish, seabirds, seals, and penguins. Furthermore, harvesting krill in distant Antarctic waters requires a large fossil fuel input.

Fish Farming: Aquaculture and Mariculture If we have trouble catching more fish and shellfish using our present hunting-and-gathering approach, then why not grow and harvest crops of them in land-based ponds **(aquaculture)** or in coastal lagoons and estuaries **(mariculture)?** Fish farming is not new. In Asia it has been done in ponds, canals, and rice paddies for several thousand years. In 1979 fish farming supplied about 10 percent of the total world aquatic catch—about equal to the annual catch of freshwater fish (Figure 9-7). But in some countries aquaculture supplies a significant proportion of the fish (such as carp and milkfish) and shellfish (such as oysters and shrimp) consumed. A number of scientists believe that aquaculture and mariculture yields can be increased eightfold between 1975 and 2000 and thus provide an important source of high-quality protein for

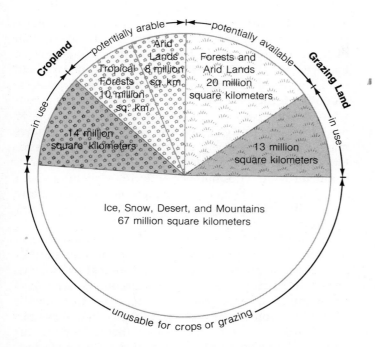

Figure 9-9 Classification of the earth's land. Theoretically, the world's cropland could be doubled in size by clearing tropical forests and irrigating arid lands. But converting this marginal land to cropland would destroy valuable forest resources and cause serious environmental problems, and it could cost far more than it is worth.

people in all nations. This might not happen, however, if the less developed nations use the expensive and energy-intensive fish-farming methods now used in the United States and other more developed nations.

In land-based aquaculture, a complete ecosystem is set up in a pond or small lake. Artificial fertilizers, protein concentrates, animal wastes, or fish wastes are used to produce phytoplankton, which are eaten by zooplankton and bottom animals, which in turn are eaten by fish. There is no doubt that aquaculture can be an important and growing source of low-cost, high-quality protein for local consumption in many poor countries—especially those with many lakes, ponds, and marshes. But to increase this important source of food will require education of farmers, funds for research and development to improve techniques, and care that such food supplements rather than substitutes for crops grown on land. One serious problem is that aquaculture is very vulnerable to runoff of fertilizer and pesticides from nearby cropland. This has already reduced fish production in farm ponds in the Philippines, Indonesia, and Malaysia.

Japan, the Soviet Union, and the United States have used mariculture to raise fish and shellfish—especially

shrimp and oysters. Because estuaries are natural sinks for nutrients flowing from the land to the sea, they could be used with controlled fertilization to produce large yields of desirable marine species in fenced-off bays, large tanks, or floating cages. Although mariculture could become a fairly important source of protein within 20 to 30 years, this seems unlikely. The growing pollution of the sea, particularly in coastal and estuarine zones, threatens both cultivated and natural fish and shellfish, as discussed in more detail in Sections 10-6 and 16-5. Many natural coastal shellfish operations in the United States and Japan have already been shut down because of poisoned waters.

In summary, *we can increase the global supply of protein by increasing the fish catch, harvesting krill, and increasing the practices of aquaculture and mariculture. However, instead of increased yields, we may end up with yields lower than we have today because of the global problems of overfishing and ocean pollution.* These problems are classic examples of the "tragedy of the commons." Each nation takes as much as possible from the ocean and then uses it as a free dump for its wastes—a process that will eventually ruin this common resource for everyone.

9-6 Cultivating More Land

Availability of Arable Land   If the sea has limited potential for expanding the world food supply, then what about the land? Why not convert more land to cropland? Since 71 percent of the planet is covered with water, only 29 percent, or 132 million square kilometers (32 billion acres),* is land surface. Figure 9-9 gives a rough classification of this land. About half consists of permanent ice and snow, deserts, and mountains that cannot be used for grazing or for growing crops. One-fourth of the total is classified as rangeland potentially suitable for grazing. In 1975 only about 38 percent of this land was actually used for grazing, but two-thirds of this rangeland was already suffering from overgrazing. The remaining fourth of the world's land is classified as potentially arable (farmable). In 1975 about 44 percent of this potential cropland was under cultivation, with only about 60 to 70 percent actually harvested each year. The remaining 56 percent of the world's potential cropland consists primarily of tropical forests that could be cleared and planted and arid land that could be irrigated and cultivated.

---

*Another widely used unit for land area is the hectare (ha) (1 hectare = 2.47 acres = 0.01 square kilometer).

Using this classification in Figure 9-9, a number of observers have suggested that we could at least double the world's cropland. Others believe this optimistic projection will probably never be realized for several reasons: (1) Most of the soils under the tropical forests to be cleared are not suitable for high-intensity cultivation; (2) there is not enough water in the arid lands for extensive irrigation (Chapter 15) except at great expense; (3) converting this marginal land to cropland by extensive use of fertilizer and large-scale irrigation projects would cost too much compared with other options, such as increasing crop yields on existing cropland; and (4) cutting down a large portion of the world's tropical forests to grow food will have serious environmental effects.

Another problem is that much of the land that might be converted to cropland is not where it is needed. Essentially all available land is being farmed in Europe and Asia, which together contain 69 percent of the world's population. Some land is available in temperate North America and parts of the U.S.S.R., but the vast amounts theoretically available in Africa, South America, and Australia are limited by lack of water or poor soil, or both. In addition to these problems, 83 percent of the potential cropland is in the Amazon and Orinoco river basins in South America and the rain forests in parts of Africa. This land, however, is far away from population centers. Furthermore, this tropical jungle land requires farming techniques very different from those developed in temperate zones. Since techniques for the intensive farming of cleared jungle land are not well developed, a lot of research and development must be carried out before this land could become cropland. In West Africa potential cropland equal to 5 times the area now farmed in the United States cannot be used for grazing or farming because it is infested with the tsetse fly. This carrier of sleeping sickness is very difficult and expensive to eradicate.

In the United States, about 81 percent of the potentially arable land is being used to grow crops. An additional 304,000 square kilometers (75 million acres) are potentially arable, but developing this marginal land would require draining swamps, irrigating deserts, and converting some valuable forest, pasture, and recreation land (Chapter 10) to cropland.

Loss of Arable Land   The trend in the United States and in many less developed countries (such as overcrowded Egypt) is to take over high-quality farmland for urbanization and transportation. Between 1975 and the year 2000, the world will probably lose about 6.1 million square kilometers (1.5 billion acres) of cropland to erosion and urbanization—an amount almost equal to half of the cultivated land in the world today (Figure 9-9). Each year the United States loses enough prime farmland to highways, shopping centers, housing developments, and other forms of urbanization to equal a 0.8-kilometer-wide (0.5-mile-wide) strip stretching from New York to San Francisco. Between 1980 and 2000, the United States may lose up to 7 percent of its present prime farmland. Each year an additional area of farmland equal to a 2.4-kilometer-wide (1.5-mile-wide) strip stretching from New York to San Francisco is abandoned because of low soil fertility and terrain that is unsuited for modern farm machinery.

By 1978, about one-third of all the topsoil had been lost from U.S. cropland, and each year at least another 2.7 trillion kilograms (3 billion tons) are lost by erosion. This reduces crop productivity and requires larger and larger inputs of energy-intensive fertilizer to maintain soil fertility. Some marginal land in the United States can be converted to farmland to replace that lost by urbanization and erosion, but this conversion represents a loss in soil fertility and requires a great deal of energy and money.

Loss of cropland and soil fertility is taking place just as rapidly or even more rapidly in many less developed nations. This is the result of (1) clearing forests (especially tropical forests) for firewood and wood products, with the resulting soil erosion and water runoff flooding croplands; (2) growing urbanization; and (3) the burning of crop residues for fuel instead of returning them to the soil as fertilizer.

A new threat to the use of cropland to produce food in the United States and in other nations, such as Brazil, is the increasing interest in growing grain or other crops for conversion to ethyl alcohol to make gasohol (gasoline that contains about 10 percent ethyl alcohol) to run cars. In this choice between feeding people or feeding cars, the poor of the world may lose out because affluent people can afford to pay more for the grain to be used as fuel. This will drive world grain prices up and make what grain is available to feed the poor even more expensive.

The Tropical Agriculture Myth: Soil as a Limiting Factor   About 56 percent of the land in the world that can theoretically be converted to cropland (Figure 9-9) exist as lush, moist jungles and tropical rain forests in Latin America (especially Brazil) and Africa (mostly West Africa) (see Enrichment Study 2).

Although blessed with plentiful rainfall and long or

continuous growing seasons, these tropical rain forests have poor soils that are quite low in humus and critical plant nutrients. Most of the nutrients are in the vegetation, not in the soil. As a result, one ecologist has called the tropical forests "a desert covered with trees." Once the vegetation is stripped away, the heavy rainfall rapidly washes remaining nutrients out of the thin soil. In addition to the severe erosion problem, some tropical soils (perhaps 5 to 10 percent) have a high content of iron and aluminum (Figure 4-8). After clearing, such soils bake under the tropical sun into brick-hard surfaces called laterites (from the Latin for "brick") and are useless for farming. These limitations explain why for centuries tropical forest residents have used slash-and-burn (or shifting) cultivation of small plots (Figure 2-1) rather than the extensive clearing found in other areas of the world with more fertile soils. Instead of being backward, shifting agriculture is an ecologically sound system well adapted to the conditions found in tropical rain forests. But unfortunately it cannot be used to support a large population.

The tropical climate in these areas also hinders the use of industrialized agriculture. Soil erosion is more rapid because of the frequent rainfall. In addition, the warm temperatures, high moisture, and year-round growing season are ideal conditions for the proliferation of various kinds of pests. Even if farmers can afford to use pesticides, the chemicals are washed away by the rains.

Researchers are looking for methods to grow more crops in tropical ecosystems, but this biome is less understood than any other. However, others argue that intensive agriculture should never be introduced on a large scale into these areas. Not only does cutting down the tropical forests destroy valuable and diverse ecosystems, but it could also affect global climate patterns in an unpredictable manner (Enrichment Study 3). Instead, production in these areas should rely primarily on tree and forest products (for example, rubber trees, oil palms, and bananas) that are already adapted to the tropical climate and soils. Already more than 2 percent of the Amazon basin's rain forests are being cleared for agriculture and wood products each year. At this rate, these valuable world ecosystems could disappear forever within 35 years.

Irrigation: Water as a Limiting Factor More than half of the remaining potentially arable land lies in very dry areas (Figure 9-9), where water is the limiting factor (Section 4-3) for growing more food.

Irrigation has played a key role in opening up new agricultural lands. Between 1950 and 1970, the amount of irrigated cropland in the world doubled, with much of this irrigation occurring in China, where 80 percent of the irrigated land depends on gravity-fed or animal-powered systems, in sharp contrast to the energy-intensive, gasoline-powered and electricity-powered systems used in more developed nations. Today between 30 and 40 percent of the world's annual food production is dependent on irrigation and 88 percent of the water used throughout the world each year is for irrigation. Between 1975 and 2000, it is estimated that the amount of irrigated land will have to at least double for food production to keep up with population growth.

It is doubtful that such an increase can be accomplished. Water shortages are already serious in many parts of the world—especially in the arid lands people dream of irrigating (Chapter 15). We have already dammed most of the world's accessible rivers (Section 15-4). Those remaining, such as the Mekong and Amazon, tend to be where the need is least. The Amazon's vast width also makes it almost impossible to harness. In addition, dams provide only a temporary solution (Section 15-4) and can cause a number of undesirable ecological and economic effects. To complicate matters even further, many of the lands being irrigated are becoming unproductive because of waterlogging and salt buildup (salinization) of the soil (Section 15-4). Some people talk of desalinating ocean water for irrigation, but it takes so much energy to remove the salt and to pump the water inland where it is needed that the method would not be cheap enough for agriculture (Section 15-5).

Money as the Limiting Factor From a technical standpoint, we can farm remote Amazon jungles and irrigate arid lands to grow more food. But the real problem is cost. "The people who are talking about cultivating more land," comments Lester Brown, an authority on world food problems, "are not considering the cost. If you are willing to pay the cost, you can farm the slope of Mt. Everest. Thus, the real question is how much will it cost, and how does the cost relate to the ability of the poorest people in the world to pay."

9-7 Increasing Crop Yields

The Green Revolutions Most experts agree that the quickest and usually the cheapest way to grow more food is to raise the yield per square kilometer on existing cropland. This can be done by developing varieties of crops that are better adapted to climate, soil conditions, and fertilizer use in an area and by improving yields of existing and new crop varieties through the use of fertilizers, irrigation, and pest and disease control. When such methods produce a significant increase in the yield per square kilometer over relatively large areas, we often call the result a **green revolution.** Such a revolution occurred in 1967 when new high-yield dwarf varieties of rice and wheat, especially selected and bred for tropical and subtropical climates, were introduced into less developed countries such as Mexico, India, Pakistan, the Philippines, and Turkey. These new varieties give higher yields than conventional varieties, primarily because they respond better to much larger applications of fertilizer and water than conventional varieties. In conventional varieties of wheat and rice, heavy doses of fertilizer produce tall plants that topple over. The shorter, stiffer stalks of the new dwarf varieties allow them to take up to 3 times as much fertilizer without toppling over as long as enough water is available to keep the high levels of fertilizer used from killing the crops (Figure 9-10). In addition, the new varieties can be grown in a wide range of climates, are less prone to wind damage, have more plant nutrients going into grain instead of stalks and leaves, and with adequate water can be grown and harvested two or more times a year (multiple cropping) because they have a shorter growing season than conventional varieties.

"Green evolution" is probably a more accurate term for the latest green revolution, since it resulted from 30 years of painstaking genetic research and trials. These activities were conducted under the joint sponsorship of the Ford and Rockefeller Foundations at two major research centers, the International Maize and Wheat Improvement Center in Mexico and the International Rice Research Institute in the Philippines. The work in Mexico was led by Norman E. Borlaug, who in 1971 won the Nobel Peace Prize for his contribution to humanity.

Limitations of the Latest Green Revolution By the early 1970s much of the heady optimism of the late 1960s had been replaced by a more realistic analysis of the limits of the green revolution. Disillusionment surfaced as famine continued to stalk the poor regions of the world and the increase in crop yields from the new seeds began to level off. Droughts and floods struck frequently in 1972, 1973, and 1979, and the projected food production did not increase as much as expected. Without large

Figure 9-10 The latest green revolution. Scientists compare for two Indian farmers a full, older variety of rice (left) and a new, high-yield dwarf variety (right). The dwarf variety can accept much larger amounts of fertilizer without toppling over than the older variety.

doses of fertilizer and water or with too much water, the new crop varieties actually produce a lower yield than traditional grains. In addition, rapidly rising oil and natural gas prices have driven up the two things that are essential to green revolution high yields: irrigation and fertilizer.

Even when the weather is good, there are limitations to the latest green revolution. First, it can only happen in areas with adequate water. As Georg Borgstrom points out, the green revolution could just as easily be called a hydrological feat—a water festival. To treble or quadruple yields using the new seeds requires 4 to 7 times as much water per square kilometer as conventional seeds. The only areas that can turn green, then, are those blessed with enough rainfall or irrigation water.

Lack of fertilizer can also be a limiting factor in less developed countries. Without massive doses of fertilizer and water, the new varieties of crops won't yield any more food per square kilometer than conventional varieties. To meet the food needs of the world between 1970 and 2000, it is estimated that annual world fertilizer production must be tripled, and in less developed countries it must increase more than sevenfold. The limiting factor in increasing world fertilizer production is the investment capital needed to build expensive fertilizer plants.

Even if less developed nations could raise such enormous amounts of capital, subsistence farmers in these countries could not afford to buy the fertilizer produced. Thus, even with good weather, a lack of fertilizer, water, or money can limit the spread of the latest green revolution in less developed countries.

Reducing Genetic Diversity   A very dangerous side effect of the green revolution is the loss of genetic variability in crop plants throughout the world. If we continue to clear fields of natural varieties and replace them with only one or a few crossbred varieties, much of the natural genetic diversity that is essential for new hybrids could be reduced or lost forever. We would then have no way to develop crops in the future that would be resistant to climate changes and to the new strains of diseases and pests that always arise. For example, one part of the green revolution was launched with a variety of high-yield rice called IR-8. When this became susceptible to disease, a new, more disease-resistant strain, IR-20, was bred. When this was also hit by disease, IR-26 rice was developed. When it couldn't stand up to high winds, plant breeders found a new strain in Taiwan that had almost become extinct because it had been replaced with the original IR-8.

Indeed, biologist Paul Ehrlich has warned that "aside from nuclear war, there is probably no more serious environmental threat than the continued decay of the genetic variability of crops." Vast stands of only one or a few crop varieties (monocultures) are also very vulnerable to pests, diseases, and climate change. Between 1845 and 1850, 1 million people died in Ireland and another million emigrated to other countries when potato blight (a fungal disease) destroyed the potato crop, which fed most of the population. This disaster and the corn blight that destroyed one-fifth of the corn crop in the United States in 1970 should serve as brutal reminders of the fragility of vast monocultures.

There is nothing wrong with breeding new high-yield strains and planting them widely. Modern agriculture is based on taking this risk to feed growing populations. But it is folly to do this without protecting and preserving natural reserves of native plants throughout the world, gathering diverse strains of food crops, and maintaining them in genetic storage banks.

Crop Protection and the Pesticide Dilemma   All crops are vulnerable to pests and disease, but the large monoculture stands in green revolution fields are especially vulnerable. The multiple cropping allowed by the faster-maturing new seeds also gives pests a year-round food supply and can keep their populations at high levels. Although some of the new strains are more resistant to disease and pests, the primary emphasis has been on high yields. In addition, according to the U.S. Department of Agriculture, disease, germs, and insects adapt and mutate to attack a new plant variety in only about 5 years. In the hot and wet tropics, insects and diseases can adapt and mutate even faster.

Worldwide, about 33 percent of the food crops are destroyed by insects (13%), crop diseases (12%), and weeds (8%); another 10 to 15 percent are lost to pests and spoilage after harvest. Thus, *each year pests and disease consume or destroy about 43 to 48 percent of the world's food supply.* Insects and diseases destroy nearly half of all rice before it reaches the table, and rodents destroy from 10 to 30 percent of the yearly crops in India. Rats and mice consume enough food each year to feed about 130 million people. Even in the United States, which uses vast amounts of pesticides and has sophisticated food storage and transportation networks, the total loss due to pests and disease each year is estimated at 42 percent—33 percent before harvest and 9 percent after.

Between 1945 and 1962, the answer to the problem of preharvest pests and diseases seemed clear: Blanket the fields with pesticides. DDT and many other synthetic pesticides were remarkably successful in protecting crops from disease, pests, and weeds. But with the publication of Rachel Carson's *Silent Spring* in 1962 and from more recent evidence (see Enrichment Study 11), we began to realize that all was not well. With the benefits of pesticides came some important ecological and human risks.

When heavy doses of pesticides are used over and over, the insects and disease organisms adapt and mutate so that later generations are more resistant to the chemical. Then either stronger doses must be used or another chemical must be found. Thus, we can end up using more and more chemicals and still have greater crop losses than before. For example, the Environmental Protection Agency estimates that in 1945 U.S. farmers used 23 million kilograms (50 million pounds) of pesticides and lost 7 percent of their crops to insects before harvest. In 1975 U.S. farmers used 12 times more pesticides but lost twice as much (14 percent) of their crops to insects before harvest.

The use of pesticides is highly controversial. On the one hand, we hear that human life and the stability of the ecosphere are seriously threatened unless we limit (not ban) and closely control their use. On the other hand, we hear that if the use of pesticides and herbicides is severely limited, world food production will drop by at least one-third and lead to massive famines, malaria and other diseases will again go out of control and kill or

Table 9-3 Environmental Effects of Food Production

Effect	Text Discussion
Overfishing	Section 9-5; Enrichment Study 12
Overgrazing	Chapter 2
Soil erosion	Section 16-6
Loss of soil fertility (leaching of soil nutrients and laterization)	Section 9-6
Spread of deserts (desertification)	Chapter 2
Loss of forests (deforestation)	Section 10-4
Endangered wildlife from loss of habitat	Section 10-7; Enrichment Study 12
Salt buildup in irrigated soil (salinization)	Section 15-4
Waterlogging of irrigated soil	Section 15-4
Waterborne diseases from irrigation	Section 6-3; Enrichment Study 6
Water pollution from runoff of fertilizers	Section 16-3; Enrichment Study 16
Water pollution from runoff of animal wastes	Section 16-3; Enrichment Study 16
Water and food pollution from pesticides	Enrichment Study 11
Loss of genetic diversity	Sections 1-3, 6-3, 9-7
Ecosystem simplification	Section 6-3
Climate change from land clearing	Enrichment Study 3
Disruption of ozone layer from use of fertilizer (nitrous oxide emissions)	Section 6-3
Air pollution from use of fossil fuels	Chapter 17
Health dangers from food additives	Enrichment Study 10

weaken millions more, and food prices will rise 50 to 100 percent. What are the advantages and disadvantages of using pesticides? Must we limit them? Are there other ways to control pests? These important and controversial questions are discussed in Enrichment Study 11.

Social Consequences of the Latest Green Revolution
The green revolution is not responsible for the social, economic, and political ills of poor countries. But by offering the false hope that it can eliminate hunger, it gives governments an excuse for not dealing with the difficult and controversial problems of poverty, unjust land distribution, and population control.

One major problem is that only large landowners and wealthy farmers can afford the fertilizer, irrigation water, pesticides, and equipment that the new seeds require. Most farmers in less developed nations are subsistence farmers—barely producing enough food on

their tiny plots to feed themselves and their families. If they can borrow the money (which is very rare) to plant the new seeds and the crop fails, they can lose the little land they have (usually to the wealthy landowner) and join the unemployed, unfed masses.

The latest green revolution has been a very important factor in helping the world feed more people. Without it the world hunger situation would be much worse. But because of its limitations it was never intended to solve world food problems—only to buy some time to get population growth under control. Even where it has been successful, it does not provide enough food for the hungriest people because they can't afford to buy it. For example, in 1978 India produced more grain than needed to feed its population a subsistence diet, but many millions of Indians were too poor to pay for this grain. In a 1979 address, Norman Bourlag, father of the green revolution, noted that to feed the 4 billion people who are supposed to be added over the next 40 years and the 4.6

A Suggested Plan for World Food

1. Stabilize world population by a combination of economic development, family planning, and beyond family planning approaches (Chapter 8 and Enrichment Study 7).

2. Design a specific food production and distribution program for each country or region based on cultural, demographic, economic, political, ecological, and ethical factors.

3. Increase world food supplies primarily by increasing yields on existing farmland by employing appropriate technology (Section 1-5) in agriculture in less developed nations. These efforts should include (a) greatly increased research on tropical agriculture; (b) development of disease-, pest-, and drought-resistant crop varieties; (c) carefully planned small-scale irrigation projects; (d) building of fertilizer plants in less developed countries; (e) increased use of animal wastes as fertilizer instead of burning them for fuel; (f) using waste water to irrigate and help fertilize fields; (g) research to develop crop varieties that produce their own nitrogen and thus require less fertilizer; (h) use of a mix of biological, ecological, and chemical methods to control pests (integrated pest control) rather than the exclusive use of chemical pesticides (Enrichment Study 11); (i) making loans available to small farmers; (j) more extensive global crop forecasting; (k) extensive replanting of trees in less developed nations; and (l) making more efficient use of grazing animals in less developed nations.

4. Protect existing cropland from being taken over by urbanization (Chapter 11) rather than emphasizing the cultivation of new marginal cropland. Additional land should be cultivated only when it will not lead to greatly increased soil erosion, to the destruction of forests, wetlands, or wildlife habitats, or to the salinization or waterlogging of irrigated soil.

5. Greatly increase the use of labor-intensive, low-energy aquaculture and mariculture in less developed nations.

6. To increase food production from the ocean, establish global cooperation and control efforts to prevent overfishing and extensive ocean pollution.

7. Decrease food and energy waste in more developed nations by (a) reducing meat consumption; (b) substituting vegetable protein and simulated meat products for animal protein; (c) reducing the grain feeding of animals in feedlots; (d) reducing the use of fertilizer on nonagricultural land (such as lawns and golf courses); (e) using animal wastes as fertilizer; (f) reducing food waste; (g) reducing pet populations; (h) encouraging a partial switch to home gardens and small, intensively cultivated organic farms instead of large, energy-intensive farms owned by large corporations; (i) reducing wasteful packaging of food products; (j) preventing significant amounts of prime farmland from being used for growing grain to produce gasohol for cars; and (k) encouraging the development of local farmers' markets to give farmers a better price and reduce consumer costs by eliminating expensive food processing and retailing; and (l) encouraging farms where consumers can save money by picking the food they wish to buy.

8. More developed nations should help less developed nations learn how to grow their own food and become more self-reliant rather than giving them food and money that often does not reach the poor and that destroys local incentives to grow food. Slowing down and reversing some of the flow of people from farms to cities should be stressed by providing funds and loans to small farmers, by using labor-intensive appropriate technology to grow food, by encouraging land reform and land redistribution, by eliminating trade barriers so that poor nations can sell excess food or trade other resources for food, and by paying less developed nations more for their resources.

9. Set up a network of genetic storage banks throughout the world to preserve the genetic diversity of crop plants.

10. Establish a massive educational campaign in less developed nations to encourage mothers to breast-feed their children.

11. Maintain an international system of 60-day food reserves to prevent large fluctuations in food and feed prices and to provide a source of emergency aid with the more developed nations taking the lead in promoting food security as a basic human right.

12. Carefully integrate the world food plan with plans for population control, economic development, energy and mineral resources, land use, and pollution control.

billion already here will require increasing world food production more than it has increased during the entire 12,000 years since the beginning of agriculture. By 1980 some governments had used the first 10 years of the latest green revolution to develop effective family planning programs and population control policies, but most nations had failed to do so (Enrichment Study 7).

9-8 Environmental Effects of Producing More Food

One limitation on increasing the world food supply—especially for the poor—may be the environmental effects from trying to produce more and more food. As agricultural expert Lester R. Brown puts it, "The central question is no longer 'Can we produce enough food?' but 'What are the environmental consequences of attempting to do so?' "

The major environmental effects of food production are summarized in Table 9-3 on page 176.

More detailed information on these environmental threats from agriculture is found throughout much of this text, as shown in Table 9-3. To deal with these problems, we need to emphasize (1) land-use control to reduce erosion, loss of soil fertility, loss of wildlife habitats, and deforestation (Chapters 10 and 11); (2) careful control and use of fertilizers (Enrichment Study 16) and pesticides (Enrichment Study 11); (3) improved sanitation and higher-quality water supplies in less developed nations to reduce the spread of waterborne diseases (Enrichment Study 6); and (4) the preservation of genetic diversity by setting up a worldwide network of storage banks for natural varieties of food crops. Control of agricultural pollution in less developed nations will be particularly difficult because of population pressures, lack of money and technical skills, and the fact that the struggle to get enough food and fuel for survival reduces concern about pollution and hinders the adoption of long-range solutions.

9-9 Principles of a World Food Plan

There is no single best solution to the complex mix of world food problems (see the related summary box in Section 9-2). A world food plan must consist of a combination of efforts to stabilize population, to grow more food, and to insure that the poor have more access to food supplies and food production. The accompanying box contains a list of suggested basic principles upon which a world food plan might be based and implemented over the next 50 years.

Not devoting ourselves and our resources to dealing with the world's food problems will make this planet a risky habitat for everyone, including ourselves. We dare not hesitate.

I was hungry and you circled the moon.
I was hungry and you told me to wait.
I was hungry and you set up a commission.
I was hungry and you talked about bootstraps.
I was hungry and you told me I shouldn't be.
I was hungry and you had napalm bills to pay.
I was hungry and you said, "Machines do that kind of work now."
I was hungry and you said, "The poor are always with us."
I was hungry and you said, "Law and order come first."
I was hungry and you blamed it on the Communists.
I was hungry and you said, "So were my ancestors."
I was hungry and you said, "We don't hire over 35."
I was hungry and you said, "God helps those. . . ."
I was hungry and you said, "Sorry, try again tomorrow."

Anonymous (Printed in the November-December issue of These Days)

Discussion Topics

1. Explain how total world food production can keep rising while average per capita food available drops or rises only slightly in many countries and regions.

2. Explain how both of these statements can be true: "We averted the threat of famine in the 1970s" and "We now have the largest annual global famine in history." How should the word *famine* be defined?

3. Why is it so difficult to estimate the number of hungry and malnourished people in the world?

4. What are legumes? Why are they important to soil fertility and to the diets of people eating little if any meat?

5. Explain why most people who die from lack of food do not starve to death.

6. Explain how a decline in breast-feeding can lead to an increase in infant deaths from diarrhea and to a rise in the birth rate in poor countries.

7. Can you get adequate amounts and types of proteins if you don't eat meat and meat products? What precautions would you have to take? Explain why persons in an affluent country can get a balanced diet from plant sources alone and why most people in poor countries cannot.

8. Debate the following statement: "There really is no world food shortage because if the grain produced each year was distributed equally among the world's population, everyone would have a modest but adequate diet."

9. Explain why trying to grow more food is necessary but will not solve world food problems.

10. Modern agriculture depends on mechanization, irrigation, fertilizers, chemical control of pests and weeds, and a large input of fossil fuel energy. Explain how each of these technologies has made it possible to feed more people. How has each caused ecological disruption?

11. Debate the proposition that we should abandon modern industrialized agriculture and return to agriculture based primarily on organic farming.

12. Why will fortified, fabricated, and unconventional foods not solve the food problems of the rural poor? What are the benefits, if any, of such foods?

13. Explain why most people in the world are forced to live primarily on a diet of grain rather than meat. What contribution, if any, do you make to this problem?

14. Explain why the elimination of all livestock animals is not desirable from an ecological and human health standpoint. What changes in the production of livestock animals could be helpful in providing more food for the world?

15. Debate the following resolution: The pet population in the United States and other more developed nations should be drastically reduced, and birth control for all pets should be mandatory.

16. How can more beef be raised on a feedlot than on an open range? Should we do away with animal feedlots? Why or why not?

17. Explain why the use of tractors, combines, and other forms of mechanized farm machinery raises the food output per hour of human labor but sharply decreases the energy efficiency for producing crops. Should we do away with the use of such machinery? Why or why not?

18. Summarize the advantages and limitations of each of the following proposals for increasing world food supplies over the next 30 years: (a) cultivating more land by clearing tropical jungles and irrigating arid lands, (b) catching more fish in the open sea, (c) harvesting algae and krill from the ocean, (d) harvesting fish and shellfish by using aquaculture and mariculture, (e) increasing the yield per square kilometer of cropland, and (f) shipping the world's excess population to space colonies (see Section 1-6).

19. Should farmland be converted to suburban housing and shopping centers? How? What are the alternatives?

20. Discuss some of the potential ecological, political, economic, and social side effects of the green revolution and project their consequences in the future. Does this mean we should abandon the green revolution? Explain.

21. Should we abandon or sharply decrease the use of pesticides? Explain. What might be the consequences for the less developed nations? For the United States? For you? See Enrichment Study 11 for an in-depth discussion of this issue.

22. In responding to the problems of hunger in America, Senator Strom Thurmond of South Carolina stated: "There has been hunger since the time of Jesus Christ, and there always will be." Evaluate this position.

23. Debate the following resolution: The more developed nations should not give food aid or technical advice to any less developed nation that has not instituted a strict program for population control.

Readings

American Chemical Society. 1980. *Chemistry and the Food System*. Washington, D.C.: American Chemical Society. Technical overview.

Berg, Alan. 1973. "Nutrition, Development, and Population Growth." *Population Bulletin*, vol. 29, no. 1. Excellent summary.

Berry, Wendel. 1977. *The Unsettling of America*. San Francisco: Sierra Club Books. Superb presentation of an alternative to industrialized agriculture.

Brown, Lester R. 1974. *By Bread Alone*. New York: Praeger. Excellent overview of world food problems.

Brown, Lester R. 1980. *Food or Fuel: New Competition for the World's Cropland*. Washington, D.C.: Worldwatch Society. Thought-provoking analysis of the dangers of running our cars on alcohol or gasohol.

Brown, Lester R., and Erik P. Eckholm. 1975. "Man, Food, and Environment." In William W. Murdoch, ed., *Environment: Resources, Pollution and Society*. 2nd ed. Sunderland, Mass.: Sinauer. Superb overview.

Campbell, Keith D. 1979. *Food for the Future*. Lincoln: University of Nebraska Press. Useful overview of world food problems and possible solutions.

Crosson, Pierre R., and Kenneth D. Frederick. 1977. *The World Food Situation*. Washington, D.C.: Resources for the Future. Excellent overview emphasizing the environmental impact of agriculture.

Eckholm, Erik P. 1976. *Losing Ground: Environmental Stresses and World Food Prospects*. New York: Norton. Outstanding survey of environmental problems associated with agriculture throughout the world.

Eckholm, Erik P. 1979. *The Dispossessed of the Earth: Land Reform and Sustainable Development*. Washington, D.C.: Worldwatch Institute. Discussion of how land ownership by the wealthy in less developed nations contributes to world poverty and hunger.

Eckholm, Erik P., and Frank Record. 1976. *The Two Faces of Malnutrition*. Washington, D.C.: Worldwatch Institute. Superb summary of the undernutrition of the poor and the overnutrition of the rich.

Ehrlich, Paul R., et al. 1977. *Ecoscience: Population, Resources, and Environment*. San Francisco: Freeman. See chap. 7 for an excellent summary of world food problems and possible solutions.

Food and Agriculture Organization. 1977. *The Fourth World Food Survey*. Rome: Food and Agriculture Organization. Very useful UN survey of food supplies and the extent of hunger and malnutrition.

Gilland, Bernard. 1979. *The Next Seventy Years: Population, Food, and Resources*. Forest Grove, Ore.: ISBS. Excellent overview.

Hardin, Garrett. 1977. *The Limits of Altruism: An Ecologist's View of Survival*. Bloomington: Indiana University Press. Argument that the rich nations should not provide food aid to poor nations but instead help them become self-reliant.

Huessy, Peter. 1978. *The Food First Debate*. San Francisco: Institute for Food and Development Policy. Pros and cons of the proposals made by Lappé and Collins (1977).

Lappé, Frances M., and Joseph Collins. 1977. *Food First*. Boston: Houghton Mifflin. Provocative discussion of world food problems that runs counter to some of the ideas in this chapter.

Paddock, William, and Paul Paddock. 1976. *Time of Famines: America and the World Food Crises*. Boston: Little, Brown. Excellent summary of world food problems with suggestions for solutions.

Pimentel, David, and Marcia Pimentel. 1979. *Food, Energy, and Society*. New York: Wiley. One of the best discussion of food problems and possible solutions with an emphasis on energy use and food production.

Pimentel, David, et al. 1975. "Energy and Land Constraints in Food Protein Production." *Science*, vol. 190, 754–761. Excellent summary of factors that limit food production.

Todd, Nancy J., ed. 1977. *The Book of the New Alchemists*. New York: Dutton. Description of experiments in developing a decentralized, self-sufficient agricultural system at the New Alchemy Institute in Woods Hole, Massachusetts.

Wortman, Sterling, and R. W. Cummings, Jr. 1978. *To Feed the World: The Challenge and the Strategy*. Baltimore: Johns Hopkins University Press. Optimistic view of how to solve world food problems.

10

Nonurban Land Use: Wilderness, Parks, Forests, Surface Mines, Estuaries, and Wildlife

We abuse land because we regard it as a commodity belonging to us. When we see land as a community to which we belong, we may begin to use it with love and respect.

Aldo Leopold, Sand County Almanac

10-1 Use and Misuse: Land Ethics

How Is Land Used? Vast as the earth is, only a small percentage of its land surface can be occupied and cultivated by humans. Only about 1 to 2 percent of the world's land is devoted to towns and cities and about 11 percent to crops. Most of the land on earth is too cold, too dry, too hot and wet, or too high and rugged for human habitation (Figure 10-1), but this land is not useless. It supports animals and plants, helps renew the air and water, absorbs some of our wastes, provides recreation, offers wilderness experiences, and serves as an ecological reserve and a laboratory for studying nature.

In the United States, land is divided into three major categories: forest (32 percent), pasture and rangeland (31 percent), and cropland (17 percent). Deserts, tundra, marshes, swamps, and other forms of land with little direct human use make up about 12 percent of the land area, with much of this land located in Alaska. Towns and cities occupy about 2.7 percent of U.S. land, and 3.6 percent is preserved for parks, wilderness, and recreation areas. About one-third of the land in the United States is owned by the federal government. Most of this is grazing land and forest in the West and in Alaska, where 97 percent of the land is federally owned.

As land is used in the United States and throughout the world, it is changed. Often these changes are beneficial in the short run—at least for us. We simplify ecosystems to grow food for the world's increasing population, and large areas of once-barren land have been

made livable and more productive. But some of our changes can be ecologically harmful. Simplifying ecosystems to grow crops can make them more productive, but it can also make them more vulnerable to pests, disease, and climate changes (Section 6-4). Precious soil has eroded from millions of overgrazed and intensively cultivated acres, converting productive land to barren desert. Forests are a renewable resource, but often they have been cut for fuel and building materials with no efforts to replant them. To satisfy our increasing needs for mineral and fuel resources, we surface mine vast land areas, often neglecting to repair the resulting scars and ecological disruption.

Land is a finite and vulnerable resource, but many of its services are eternal and renewable if the land is not abused. As world population and ecological understanding grow, we are beginning to realize that all types of land and land uses are related. For example, urban areas may cover only a tiny fraction of the earth's surface, but they are not self-sustaining ecosystems. They must be supported by vast farmlands, pastures, watersheds, forests, estuaries, and other ecosystems. Converting too much renewable forest and agricultural land to nonrenewable urban land may eventually threaten the existence of an urban area. Fortunately, more and more people are calling for the development of ecological land-use plans that consider these interrelated uses and demands. But ecological land-use planning by itself is not enough—our plans must be guided by a *land-use ethic.*

Land-Use Ethics Opinions on how land should be used generally fall into three categories: the *economic ethic,* the *conservationist ethic,* and the *ecological ethic* (see the box on land-use ethics). According to the economic, or "use it," ethic, every parcel of land should be used or developed so as to bring its owner the highest profit. The emphasis is on ownership and profit. According to the conservationist, or "preserve it," ethic, large portions of undeveloped land should stay undeveloped. The em-

Enrichment Studies 2, 11, 12, 14, 15, and 16 are related to this chapter.

Figure 10-1 Lands attractive and hostile to humans. Some hot and wet regions, especially in the Old World tropics, are densely populated, but most of the unoccupied or sparsely occupied lands are too hot and wet, too cold, too dry, or too high and rugged.

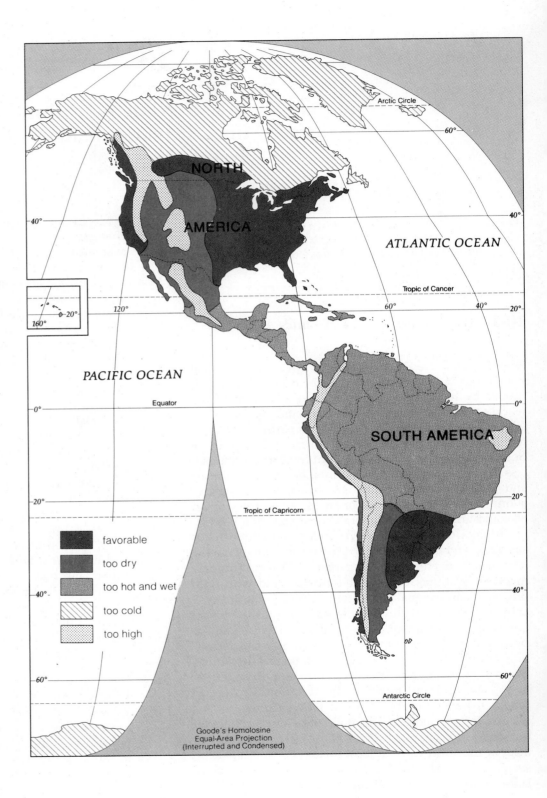

favorable

too dry

too hot and wet

too cold

too high

Goode's Homolosine
Equal-Area Projection
(Interrupted and Condensed)

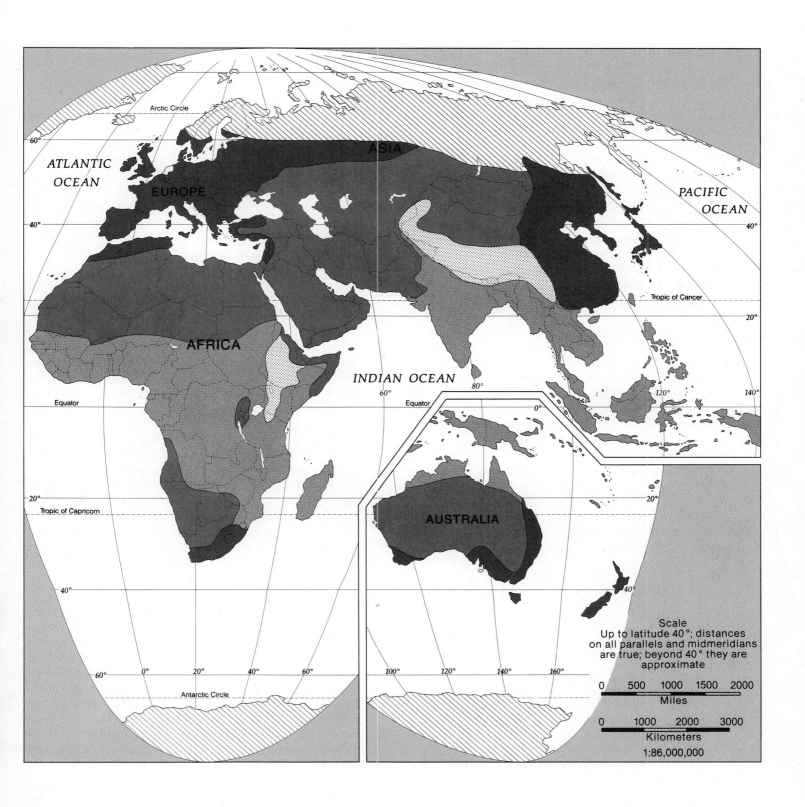

ATLANTIC
OCEAN

PACIFIC
OCEAN

Arctic Circle

60°

40°

ASIA

EUROPE

Tropic of Cancer

AFRICA

Equator

INDIAN OCEAN

Equator

60°

80°

40°

120°

140°

20°

Tropic of Capricorn

AUSTRALIA

20°

60°

0°

20°

40°

60°

100°

120°

140°

160°

40°

Antarctic Circle

Scale
Up to latitude 40°; distances
on all parallels and midmeridians
are true; beyond 40° they are
approximate

0   500   1000   1500   2000

Miles

0   1000   2000   3000

Kilometers

1:86,000,000

phasis is on trusteeship to preserve the beauty and ecological health of the land.

According to the ecological, or *sustainable earth*, ethic, all economic, ecological, and social factors should be considered both on a short-term and a long-term basis, with the goal of preserving the capacity of large amounts of land for self-renewal. The emphasis is on treating the land with love and respect and on achieving a balance between strictly human needs and the needs of all other living species, with the primary goal being to preserve the integrity, stability, and beauty of the world's ecosystems. This ethic attempts to balance the often conflicting goals of the economic and conservationist viewpoints, and it challenges us to recognize that we are merely members, not lords, of the living land ecosystems. The ecological ethic is based on a sustainable earth world view (Section 3-4), which recognizes the effect of the second law of energy—the more we attempt to order and control the world, the more disorder (entropy) we create in the environment.

Very few people adopt only the "use it" or the "preserve it" philosophy. Recognizing the need for trade-offs and compromises, many people instead call for *balanced multiple use*—an approach that combines economic and conservationist ethics. At first glance, this philosophy appears to be the same as the ecological ethic, but in practice the balanced multiple use approach has often resembled the economic view. This has occurred because of the political influence of business interests and because of the difficulty in placing a monetary value on ecological self-renewal, clean air, pure water, and natural beauty. The multiple use approach also fails to recognize

that in some cases good ecological land management might call for a "dominant use." In such a case, a certain area is designated to be used for a single purpose only. Garrett Hardin discusses the conflict between the economic and ecological viewpoints in his Guest Editorial at the end of this chapter.

In the remainder of this chapter, we will look at some of the conflicts in the use of nonurban land. In the next chapter we will consider urban land use and discuss approaches to ecological land-use planning for both urban and nonurban areas. Because of limited space, the emphasis is on land use in the United States. The principles developed, however, are applicable to land areas throughout much of the world.

10-2 Wilderness

The U.S. National Wilderness Preservation System In wilderness lands we find one of the few pure examples of the conservationist ethic in practice. The United States was settled and exploited rapidly. As a result, in the late 1800s conservationists began to urge that large tracts of federally owned land be set aside and protected from all forms of development.

After a century of debate, Congress created a National Wilderness System with the passage of the Wilderness Act of 1964. This act requires that key tracts of federal wildlands be set aside forever as undeveloped areas. In this act, **wilderness** is defined as an area where the earth and its community of life are undisturbed by humans and where humans themselves are temporary visitors. Roads, timbering, commercial activities, human structures, and motor vehicles are all prohibited. Grazing is permitted only where it was already established before the law was passed. As a political compromise, mining is allowed and new claims may be filed only through 1983.

Wilderness areas are open to humans for fishing, hiking, camping, canoeing, and, in some cases, hunting and horseback riding. However, all these activities are strictly controlled. Nevertheless, the greatly increased interest in hiking and camping has raised the question of how much visiting a wilderness area can withstand before it is harmed. This is difficult to answer, since wilderness ecosystems vary so widely in their carrying capacities.

The 1964 act immediately designated 54 national forest wilderness, wild, and canoe areas, totaling about 36,000 square kilometers (9.1 million acres). Congress has designated additional acres under this act, the En-

---

Major Ethical Views on Land Use

Economic, or "use it," ethic. Land should be used or developed so as to bring its owner the highest profit.

Conservationist, or "preserve it," ethic. Large portions of land should not be used or developed in order to preserve their beauty and ecological health.

Ecological, or sustainable earth, ethic. Land should be treated with love and respect by balancing strictly human needs with the needs of other living creatures so as to preserve other living species and the self-renewing capacity of considerable amounts of land.

dangered American Wilderness Act of 1978, and the Alaska Lands Act of 1980. By the end of 1980 designated federal wilderness lands amounted to about 308,000 square kilometers (76 million acres). The Alaska Lands Act of 1980 alone quadrupled the amount of U.S. land officially designated and protected as wilderness. In spite of these important gains, wilderness makes up only about 8 percent of government-owned lands and 3 percent of all the land in the United States.

Since 1964 the major battle has been over how much more land should be added to the wilderness system. Timber and mining industries operating on public lands have opposed wilderness preservation, while environmentalists have urged Congress to add more wilderness areas.

Another law protecting natural systems is the Wild and Scenic River Act of 1968. Its purpose is to prevent the construction of dams and other water developments on some of the remaining free-flowing rivers and to restrict riverbank development. Rivers chosen for the system must have outstanding scenic, recreational, geological, fish and wildlife, historic, or other cultural values. The act recognizes three types of rivers as suitable for protection: *wild rivers* that are primitive and inaccessible except by trail, *scenic rivers* that are still largely undeveloped, and *recreational rivers* that are accessible and already developed. By 1980, 27 rivers were in the system and 75 others were under consideration. This act is an important first step, but it remains to be seen whether the system will provide much protection.

Why Do We Need Wilderness? Opponents of preserving wilderness and wild species often accuse conservationists of trying to lock up the woods for the exclusive use of a few nature lovers. They also argue that it really doesn't make any difference whether we have any passenger pigeons, dodo birds, whooping cranes, or other exotic species left.

Such views show a lack of understanding of the web of life connecting all living species and of the many important reasons for preserving wild places and species. One argument for wilderness is that we need places where we can experience majestic beauty and natural diversity, breathe clean air, drink pure water, and get away from it all. Others argue on ethical or religious grounds that we have no right to exterminate any forms of life. Wallace Stegner argues philosophically:

> Save a piece of country . . . intact and it does not matter in the slightest that only a few people every year will go into it. This is precisely its value . . . we simply need

that wild country available to us, even if we never do more than drive to its edge and look in. For it can be a means of reassuring ourselves of our sanity as creatures, a part of the geography of hope.

Still others see important biological and ecological reasons for preserving wild areas and species. By preserving wilderness we maintain diverse ecosystems and species that serve as ecological buffers or reserves, which are protected from the ravages of an increasingly populated and urbanized world. When a species is exterminated, ecosystems throughout the world lose a functioning part; as a result, their biological complexity is reduced. Such ecological simplification may lead to irreparable harm that cannot be discovered until it is too late. Wilderness also serves as an ecological laboratory where we can study the natural processes that maintain life on earth. By studying undisturbed ecosystems, we may learn how to prevent and repair ecological damage in ecosystems that we use.

Wilderness is also a genetic reservoir of diverse strains of plant and animal life. Each species is a storehouse of genetic information; once a species is destroyed, this information is lost forever. We cannot predict how such genetic information may someday be valuable to us or other species. What if all the cinchona (a South American tree) had been cut down before anyone discovered that the quinine obtained from its bark was a remedy for malaria? Or what if all the cobras of the world had been killed off before anyone discovered that their venom could be used to treat certain types of heart disease? Or what if native grasses had been crowded out so that nothing was left to breed the new hybrids of wheat used in the latest green revolution (Section 9-7)?

The real question, then, is not why we should preserve wilderness but how we can preserve more of it. We do not know how much wilderness should be preserved, but since it is irreplaceable, it is best to protect very large and diverse areas. In the words of Henry D. Thoreau: "In wildness is the preservation of the world."

10-3 Parks

Park System in the United States National, state, and local parks are preserved lands that get considerably more use than wilderness areas, usually because they are less fragile. Parks vary widely in size, terrain, usage, and purpose. They range from a small local street park to a nearby state park to a large national park such as

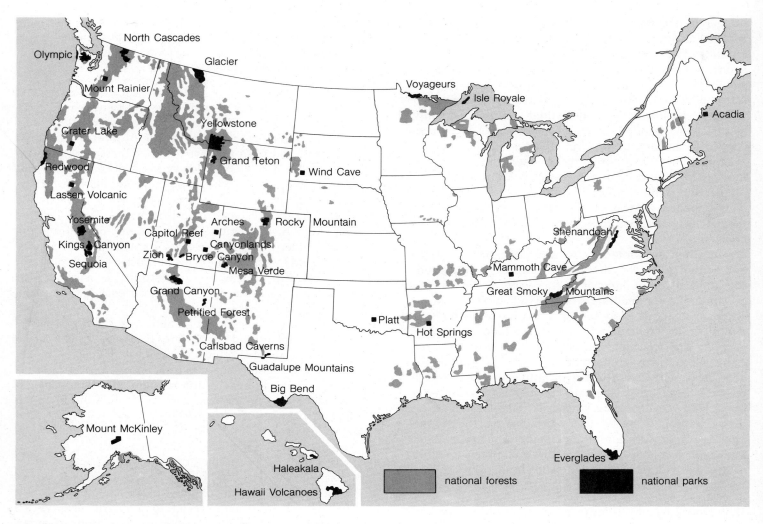

Figure 10-2 The national parks and national forest lands of the United States.

Yellowstone. Most people think of parks as forested areas, but they also include deserts, seashores, zoos, public beaches, monuments, and historic sites.

The National Park System in the United States was established over 100 years ago (1872) with the creation of Yellowstone, the world's first national park. The purpose of this system is to preserve natural areas of public lands considered unique because of their scenery, historical significance, wildlife resources, and recreational potential. They provide spectacular scenery on a large scale not usually found in state or local parks, preserve wildlife that can coexist with limited human contact, and serve as buffer zones for some wilderness areas. In 1916 the National Park Service was created to administer the

entire system. Camping, fishing, and on-road motorized vehicles are permitted in the national parks, but hunting, timbering, mining, and off-road vehicles are banned.

Since 1872 the National Park System has grown to include 302 thousand square kilometers (76 million acres), consisting of 37 parks (Figure 10-2) and 285 national monuments, historic sites, recreational areas, near-wilderness areas, national seashores, and lakeshores. Most of the major, large parks are in Alaska and in the western United States, in large, mountainous areas of spectacular beauty. The system could double in size if Congress approves proposed parkland in Alaska. The national park concept in the United States has been so successful that over 100 nations have adopted it.

Stresses on National and State Parks   The major problems of the national and state parks come from their spectacular success. With more money, leisure time, and mobility, visitors have swamped many of the more desirable parks. Between 1950 and 1980, annual visitors to the hundreds of state parks increased from about 100 million to almost 650 million. During the same period, annual visitors to the 37 national parks increased from about 40 million to about 283 million. In addition, there are an estimated 1.5 billion visits to county and city parks each year.

This trend will probably continue—increasing stress on the already overburdened parks—unless fuel shortages decrease travel. While visits have soared, park budgets have been reduced, causing a noticeable decline in services, maintenance, and equipment. Many improvements for the older parks as well as plans to add new areas to the system have been postponed.

Under the onslaught of people during the peak summer season, some parks resemble the cities that their visitors are trying to escape. Many parks are overcrowded with cars and trailers and plagued by trail bikes, noise, traffic jams, litter, pollution, vandalism, crime, and drugs. Reservations are required for some campgrounds, and campers sometimes wait in a parking lot for two days to get a campsite. Some visitors treat the Grand Canyon as our biggest wastebasket. Arriving in air conditioned $35,000 motor homes, they spend most of their time looking at TV; others take more advantage of what the parks have to offer. Backpackers are afoot in such numbers that they beat fragile trails into powder. Some of the most remote trails in the Rockies are so heavily traveled that the National Park Service has begun paving them to prevent erosion.

The press of visitors is not the only problem. Some people want to turn the most popular and beautiful parks into highly developed recreation and convention centers with luxury hotels, fancy restaurants, golf courses, ski villages, and other recreation and amusement facilities. A large corporation was barely prevented from building a large convention center in the middle of Yosemite National Park.

Suggested Solutions   The basic problem is how to preserve the parks and still use them intensively for recreation, as required by federal and state laws. Following are suggested ways to meet these conflicting demands:

1. Develop free recreation and camping facilities near most major urban areas, especially in nonwestern states that have few national parks (Figure 10-2). This would make it unnecessary to visit a national park just to go camping and thus ease the stress on these parks. In 1971 Congress established two urban national areas on government-owned land around New York harbor and San Francisco Bay. The expansion of this promising urban parks program has been curtailed because the National Park Service doesn't have enough funds and personnel to maintain existing national parks, much less new ones. Public transit systems should also be planned that will make urban parks available to inner-city residents. Ninety percent of the visitors to the Gateway National Recreation Area near New York City arrive by automobile—in a city where one-half of the households have no car.

2. Require advance reservations for campgrounds, restrict the number of hikers and climbers by establishing quotas and issuing permits, and close some trails for a year or two to allow them to recover. Such practices are already being tried in some parks. Entrance fees should be raised considerably for anyone bringing a car, motor home, or trailer into a park.

3. Phase out hotels, trailer camping areas, and other such facilities located in parks and locate them beyond the park boundaries.

4. Prohibit or severely limit cars and motorized vehicles in heavily used national parks and use quiet, low-polluting, electric- or butane-powered vehicles to carry visitors from satellite parking lots to the park interior. Some intensely used parks such as Yosemite have already used such an approach with great success. Provide bicycles and low-polluting shuttle buses for visitors within parks.

5. Use favorable tax advantages and other rewards to encourage private landowners to buy or donate land to be used for outdoor recreation. Half of the outdoor recreation areas in the United States are privately owned. Private groups such as the Nature Conservancy and the Audubon Society have bought threatened wildlands in 47 states and held them in trust until they could be purchased by the slower-moving machinery of the state and federal governments.

6. Greatly increase land acquisition and operating budgets for national and state parks. Annual operating and acquisition appropriations for the national park system in recent years have totaled less than $1 per citizen.

7. Develop an ecologically sound policy for federal, state, and local parks in conjunction with a national land-use plan.

8. Support the UN World Heritage Trust set up to expand the national park concept to a global level.

Steps such as these should enable the United States to continue its development of a park system that serves as a model for the rest of the world. In 1981, however, James G. Watt, an opponent of environmentalists, was appointed Secretary of the Interior. He pledged a review of the national park system with the goal of turning some federal parklands over to the states, and, possibly selling some to private interests.

10-4 Forests

The Importance of Forests Unprotected forests tend to be heavily used for a variety of purposes, including recreation, mining, and obtaining firewood, lumber, and paper products (Figure 10-3). In the future when oil supplies dwindle, wood may be used to produce methyl alcohol to run the world's cars (see Section 14-8) and to produce plastics, pesticides, drugs, and other petrochemical products now produced from natural gas and oil. Fortunately, forests are renewable resources if they are managed wisely and not overharvested. Forests vary widely (see Enrichment Study 2) and take from 30 to 200 years to regenerate, depending on the species and the environment.

Forests also have other very important functions. As René Dubos reminds us, "Trees are the great healers of nature." They help control climate by influencing the wind, temperature, humidity, and rainfall, and keep soil from washing off mountainsides and sand from blowing off deserts. They assist in the global recycling of water, oxygen, carbon, and nitrogen (Section 5-4). Forests absorb, hold, and slowly release water, thus reducing erosion and flooding and helping recharge springs, streams, and underground waters. They also help keep topsoil (and thus plant nutrients) on croplands and reduce the amount of sediment washing into rivers and dam reservoirs. Forests also provide wildlife habitats and rangelands for livestock, help absorb some air pollutants and noise, serve as the home of a variety of organisms that make up much of the bank of genetic diversity the earth has left, and nourish the human spirit by providing solitude and beauty. As Ogden Nash remarked, "I think that I shall never see a billboard lovely as a tree." All of these crucial functions are done with solar energy on a self-sustaining basis at no cost to us.

Status of the World's Forests Unfortunately, the human race has not taken very good care of the world's forests. So far human activity has reduced the original forested area by at least one-third and perhaps one-half. Cutting trees for timber has contributed to deforestation,

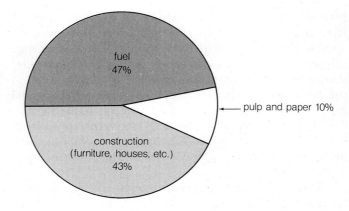

Figure 10-3 Worldwide uses of wood.

but the two most important factors have been land clearing for agriculture and wood gathering for fuel.

Today about one-third of the world's land is classified as forest land. Much of the Middle East, North Africa, continental Asia, Central America, and the Andean region of South America is treeless. Only about 18 percent of India's land and 9 percent of China's can be described as forested. Table 10-1 shows the distribution of closed forest areas and open woodlands in the world.* The four countries with the largest remaining forests are, in order, the U.S.S.R., Brazil, Canada, and the United States. By 2000, it is estimated that the world's closed forest areas will have decreased by 20 to 40 percent. This is expected to cause large-scale flooding, followed by droughts, loss of soil nutrients, silting of rivers and dams, groundwater depletion, reduced food production, and could change global climate (see Enrichment Study 3).

The greatest loss of forests is occurring in the world's tropical moist forests (tropical rain forests and tropical moist deciduous forests)—the world's most diverse, most productive, and least understood terrestrial ecosystems (see Enrichment Study 2). The major areas affected are shown in Table 10-2. The major direct causes of tropical forest losses are, in order of importance, (1) clearing for agriculture and cattle ranches (Section 9-6), (2) firewood gathering, and (3) industrial timbering. But the indirect causes of this ecological tragedy are poverty, inequalities in land ownership, rising unemployment, and rapidly growing populations in less developed nations with large forest areas. Thus, the destruction of the

*Forests, or closed forests, are areas where trees provide a crown that covers 20 percent or more of the ground. Open woodlands are wooded areas in which a scattering of trees provides a crown cover of 5 to 20 percent.

Table 10-1 Amount of Closed Forest and Open Woodland Areas of the World

Region	Area (millions of square kilometers)	Percentage of Total Land Area
World	42.3	32
Latin America	9.6	47
U.S.S.R.	9.2	41
Africa	8.3	27
North America	6.5	34
Asia (excluding U.S.S.R.)	5.1	19
Oceania and Australia	1.9	22
Europe (excluding U.S.S.R.)	1.8	36

world's tropical moist forests is ultimately related to the global problems of food production, population growth, and increased use of resources.

In Latin America, most of the tropical moist forests are being cleared for timber and cattle ranches. Most of the resulting products—beef and timber—are then shipped to Japan, European nations, and the United States. Thus, when people in these rich nations eat hamburgers made from beef raised in Latin America or use Latin American wood to build furniture and houses, they indirectly have their hands on the chain saws that are leveling these irreplaceable tropical forests. Forests in the rich nations are often replanted, but the pressures for quick profit from timber without reforestation is much greater for poor countries. After timber companies cut roads into vast virgin forest areas, they are followed by hordes of poor and hungry people looking for firewood or land to cultivate. The tropical soils are so poor (Figure 4-8) that they can only be cultivated in small patches for a few years by slash-and-burn agriculture (Figure 2-1). With too many people attempting to use the land, the tropical soil doesn't get the 10-year rest it needs to rebuild

soil fertility after being cultivated for 2 or 3 years. Eventually the soil loses its fertility and there are even more hungry people than before.

The tropical moist forests are the world's richest gene banks, with a wider variety of plants and animals than any other terrestrial ecosystem. Half of the world's animals live in these forests. Losing the incredible genetic diversity that these forests contain means the extermination of at least 500,000 different species of plants and animals (see Section 10-7). In addition to the important moral issue involved, this destruction could have serious consequences for humanity. Our ability to develop new hybrids of food to support future green revolutions (Section 9-7) and new medicines to fight disease will be greatly decreased. The 16 plants that produce 90 percent of the world's food today (Section 9-1) were domesticated from plants found in the tropics. Likewise, about 50 percent of the drug prescriptions written in the United States contain a drug of natural origin, with most of these substances extracted from tropical plants. Examples include morphine (from the poppy tree), quinine (from the cinchona tree), and cocaine (from the coca tree). Recently it was found that rosy periwinkle, which grows in many parts of the tropics, contains a drug that (when combined with other drugs) can cause an 80 percent remission rate for Hodgkin's disease (compared to 19 percent before its use), 99 percent for acute lymphocytic leukemia, and 50 to 80 percent remission for several other types of cancer. So far, only about 1 percent of the world's plant species have been thoroughly screened for possible value to humanity.

Tropical plants can also have industrial uses. In 1975 researchers found that oil extracted from the jojoba bean could be used as a high-grade industrial oil. In addition, because the jojoba oil is similar to sperm whale oil, its widespread use could help save an endangered whale species (see Enrichment Study 12).

Table 10-2 Estimates of Tropical Deforestation

Severity of Deforestation	Countries
Very critical (lowland forests mostly gone, hill forests being removed; average forest life 10 years at most)	Ghana, Guatemala, Haiti, India, Ivory Coast, Nigeria, Panama, Penisular Malaysia, Philippines, Queensland (Australia), Thailand, West Indies
Critical (shifting cultivation and logging increasing rapidly; average forest life 15-20 years)	Brazil, Honduras, Kalimantan, Mexico, Sabah, Sarawak, Sumatra, Venezuela
Potentially critical (logging and shifting cultivation increasing but not yet a major problem)	Cameroon, Colombia, Congo (Brazzaville), Ecuador, Gabon, Irian Barat, Liberia, Papua New Guinea, Peru, Sierra Leone, Zaire

The World Firewood Crisis Another major factor in the destruction of the world's forests is the world firewood crisis. While people in the more developed nations worry about the end of the oil age and argue about the benefits and dangers of nuclear power, most of the world's poor are still in the wood age. For one-third of the human race—and 90 percent of the people in poor countries—firewood is the principal fuel. As shown in Figure 10-3, this use alone accounts for almost half of the timber cut in the world and 80 percent of the wood cut in poor countries. This is not surprising, since the average villager burns about 909 kilograms (1 ton) of firewood a year. By the year 2000, world firewood needs will probably exceed available supplies by 25 percent. The rising price of oil has increased this assault on the world's forests, leading to a deadly vicious circle. Not only is a vital resource depleted, but the loss of forest cover expands deserts, which allows water to flood croplands and human habitats, which reduces soil fertility. In 1978, India had its largest flood in 100 years when the Ganges River overflowed and killed 2,000 people, washed away 40,000 cattle, and destroyed at least $750 million of crops. The deforestation of the Himalayan hillsides, primarily to obtain firewood, was believed to be a factor in the flood's severity.

Forests that are cleared to replace poor land are often on steep terrain where erosion is a significant problem. Soil fertility is further decreased as families who run out of firewood burn dried cow dung instead of returning it as manure to the soil. Thus, the food problems of many poor countries (Chapter 9) are intensified by firewood scarcity and increasing oil prices. Again we see that in ecological matters, everything is connected.

The solution to this serious environmental problem lies in taking the following measures: (1) population control (Chapter 8); (2) wise forest management with emphasis on rural people growing trees to meet their own needs, as is being done very successfully in China and South Korea; (3) planting fast-growing trees on vacant lands near and in villages and cities; (4) raising trees, crops, and livestock together as a mutually beneficial system; (5) obtaining better information on world forest losses; (6) increasing funding for forestry planning and reforestation; (7) encouraging less developed nations that export timber to more developed nations to form a trade block (like OPEC) to get a better price for their valuable resources and to slow down deforestation; and (8) conserving or replacing wood by more widespread use of cheap, simple devices such as efficient wood stoves, solar cookers, pressure cookers, and small biogas plants that produce methane gas fuel from organic wastes and

leave behind a fertilizer for use on village fields. We can learn more about replenishing and managing the world's forests by looking at forest conservation and management in the United States.

Forest Conservation in the United States When the first European settlers arrived in the United States, they found a country richly blessed with forests. But by the beginning of the twentieth century, about one-third of these virgin forests had disappeared. This early ravaging of virgin forests for timber left stripped hillsides, extensive erosion, muddy streams, and flooding.

In the late 1800s Gifford Pinchot, John Muir, Henry David Thoreau, and other conservationists began efforts to halt this "mining" of the forests. In 1891 Congress set aside Yellowstone Timberland Reserve, surrounding Yellowstone Park, as the first federal forest reserve. Additional national forests were designated, and in 1905 Congress created the U.S. Forest Service to manage and protect them. Today about one-third of the land area is still forested, thanks in part to the activities of the U.S. Forest Service under Gifford Pinchot. About two-thirds of these forests are classified as commercial forest land, which is available and suitable for growing continuous crops of wood. About 59 percent of this commercial forest land is privately owned, 27 percent is owned by federal, state, or local governments, and the remaining 14 percent is owned by forest industries (Figure 10-4).

Today the National Forest System consists of 155 national forests (Figure 10-2) and 19 national grasslands, which encompass nearly a tenth of the land surface of the United States and about 17 percent of all U.S. forest lands.

The national forests are managed under the Multiple Use Sustained Yield Act of 1960 and the 1974 and 1976 Forest Reserves Management Acts. These laws require that these forests be managed according to the principles of sustained yield and multiple use. **Sustained yield** means that there should be a balance between new planting and growth and the amount of wood removed by cutting, pests, disease, and fire so that the national forests are not depleted. **Multiple use** requires that the forests not be used for a single purpose but for a variety of purposes, including timbering, mining, recreation, grazing, wildlife preservation, and soil and water conservation. Unlike wilderness areas and national parks, the national forests have relatively few restrictions on their use except in certain areas. They receive about 200 million visits a year—more than double the use of the purely recreational national parks. They are especially used in

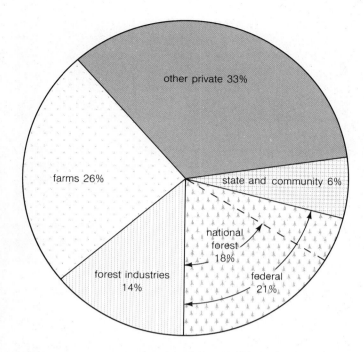

Figure 10-4 Ownership of commercial forest land in the United States in 1978.

the East, where they are often the only large natural areas open to the public (Figure 10-2).

Multiple use is supposed to allow a finite resource to be used wisely by many different groups, but it does not always work well in practice because the users have conflicting goals. Timber industries see the national forests as hordes of trees waiting to be made into newspapers and houses. Campers, hikers, and hunters want to enjoy diverse, uncut forests with varied scenery and wildlife. Campers and hikers don't want to be shot by hunters, so hunting and camping seasons normally do not overlap. Farmers and towns don't want timbering because they depend on nearby forests to prevent flooding and to fill reservoirs. Nor do they want campers because forest fires and fecal contamination might reduce the quality of their water supply.

The U.S. Forest Service is charged by law with balancing such conflicting uses and demands. In recent years conservationists have accused the service of allowing the cutting of timber to become the dominant use as a result of political pressure from the lumber industry. Conservationists also charge that lumber companies have been using privately owned forests to supply wood to overseas customers in order to create an artificial shortage and then demand that national forests be cut

to satisfy U.S. demands. Charges and countercharges fly back and forth in this familiar conflict between the economic ethic and the conservationist ethic. As is usually the case when an issue becomes polarized, the truth probably lies somewhere between the two extremes. To better understand this conflict and some possible solutions, we need to look at some methods of forest management and protection.

Forest Management   Just as *agriculture* is the cultivation of fields, **silviculture** is the cultivation of forests. Forests are usually harvested by either *selective cutting, clear-cutting,* or *shelter-wood cutting.* In **selective cutting,** or *thinning,* a few mature trees scattered throughout a stand are cut every few years, while young trees are left to grow to maturity (Figure 10-5). This creates a forest of uneven-aged trees and is particularly useful in forests with trees of different species and ages. Also, this method does not significantly alter the natural appearance of the forests. It is the method favored by those wishing to use forests for various purposes and those wishing to preserve the ecological diversity found in mature climax forests (Section 6-1). However, selective cutting can be harmful when only the most desired species are removed and just commercially undesirable species are left for reseeding.

Most commercial tree species do best in sunlight, and for economic reasons are usually grown and cut in stands of even age. These trees are usually harvested either by clear-cutting or shelter-wood cutting. **Clear-cutting** means removing all trees from an area (Figure 10-6). When done properly, the resulting debris and litter are removed or burned, and the area is reseeded so that a new crop of trees, all necessarily of the same age, can be clear-cut decades later. Age diversity of trees in a large forest can be preserved by clear-cutting a number of areas over a long period of time. This method creates a checkerboard of patches, each patch comprising trees of the same age (Figure 10-7). In the southeastern United States, many diverse climax oak-hickory forests have been clear-cut and replaced with row after row of pine trees. Forest managers then often set controlled ground fires to prevent oak and hickory seedlings from invading the farms of more fire-resistant pines.

Clear-cutting is a controversial form of forest management. The timber companies like clear-cutting; it is relatively quick, and it saves money because the cutting activity occupies a limited area, thus reducing the number of logging roads needed at any one time. Also, clear-cut forests grow back faster because the seedlings get

Figure 10-5 Selective cutting of old trees in a diverse climax forest.

Figure 10-6 Clear-cutting of redwoods and the resulting erosion.

more sunlight than in selectively cut forests, a fact that enables more frequent harvesting. Some foresters argue that clear-cutting is also the best way to grow species that need direct sunlight and space to grow, such as Douglas fir, yellow poplar, oak, cherry, and walnut. Clear-cutting can also benefit some wildlife species if the clear-cut areas are relatively small and spaced over time. It can even help to control disease when used to remove infected trees.

Opponents argue that clear-cutting creates ugly scars (Figure 10-7) that take years to heal and that it replaces a diverse stand of trees with a monoculture of even-aged trees that are much more susceptible to insects, disease, wind, and fire. Clear-cutting, especially in large patches and on steep slopes, can destroy wildlife habitats, lead to extensive soil erosion, deplete soil nutrients, lower water tables, and degrade water quality—as well as reduce the recreational values of the forest for many years. Some foresters argue that no tree species appears to require large-scale clear-cutting and that clear-cutting is done purely for economic, not ecological, reasons. They also argue that many tree species now being clear-cut should be selectively cut. Species that do grow best with plenty of sunlight should only be clear-cut in very small, widely spaced patches to protect the soil and watershed. An alternative for such species is **shelter-wood cutting,** where only a small group of trees (not exceeding 0.04 square kilometer, or 10 acres) is removed at one time for light penetration, with the entire area to be cut removed in 2 or 3 stages over a period of 10 to 15 years.

Environmentalists have charged that large-scale clear-cutting violates the multiple use concept by degrading soil and water quality and by making national forests unsuitable for recreation. When confronted with clear-cut areas, hikers, hunters, and campers are reminded of Gertrude Stein's remark, "When you get there, there is no there there." The argument is not whether clear-cutting should be banned in national forests, but to what degree it should be allowed and under whose control.

Fortunately, Congress has eased the controversy by passing the National Forest Management Act of 1976. This law allows some clear-cutting in national forests but only under strictly controlled conditions and after trees have reached a minimum age. Clear-cutting is not allowed in large-scale cuts, on steep slopes, on unstable soils, or on lands where the cuts do not blend with the natural terrain. If this law is strictly enforced, it should go a long way toward protecting U.S. national forests. These advances, however, may be eroded by James G. Watt who was appointed Secretary of the Interior by President Ronald Reagan in 1981. Secretary Watt has vowed to open up more federal land to mining and logging.

Protecting Forests Protecting forests from fire, diseases, and insects is an important part of forest management. These three threats destroy about one-fourth of the net annual growth of commercially usable saw timber in the United States.

Fires are the best-known threat to forests. According

Figure 10-7 A patchwork of clear-cut areas, which will take decades to heal.

to the U.S. Forest Service, about 85 percent of all forest fires are started accidentally or deliberately by humans. The remaining 15 percent, which cause about half of all forest fire damage, are triggered by natural causes, such as lightning.

Most forest fires should be prevented or extinguished. But since the 1930s Americans have been taught by Bambi and Smokey the Bear that *all* forest fires are bad. In recent years people have been startled to learn that *many ecologists and foresters consider carefully controlled, low-level fires to be an important tool in the management of many forests,* especially giant sequoia, Douglas fir, longleaf pine, ponderosa pine, redwood, and some other conifers. Fires in some forests are allowed to burn; more and more frequently, small fires are deliberately started and carefully controlled. These occasional surface fires burn away the dense accumulation of forest litter and undergrowth without harming the large trees. Preventing these low-level fires allows highly combustible material to build up for decades, thus increasing the possibility of devastating crown fires that destroy wildlife, burn all trees, and accelerate erosion.

Intermittent small fires in some forests also help to release and recycle valuable nutrients tied up in litter and undergrowth. They also increase the activity of nitrogen-fixing bacteria and prepare the soil for the germination of some seeds, such as those of the redwood. Some trees cannot grow at all without a fire. The cones of the jack pine, for instance, will not release their seeds unless exposed to the intense heat of a forest fire. Such fires can also wipe out infestations of insects that kill trees over wide areas.

As children we learned that forest fires are harmful to wildlife. They do kill many animals and can destroy the nuts and berries on which surviving birds, squirrels, and rabbits depend. But many other species, such as deer, moose, elk, muskrat, woodcock, and quail, depend on periodic fires to maintain their habitats and to provide them with food from the vegetation that sprouts after such fires. Many water birds, songbirds, and even the endangered California condor depend on fire to provide open and treeless spaces for feeding and nesting.

Forest fires get the most publicity, but diseases and insects cause much more forest destruction in the United States and throughout the world. Parasitic fungi cause most diseases that damage trees. These diseases include chestnut blight, Dutch elm disease, white pine blister rust, dwarf mistletoe, and oak wilt. Chestnut blight, which was accidentally introduced from China around 1900, has made the once abundant and highly valued chestnut almost extinct in the United States. Dutch elm disease, a fungus that is carried by insects from tree to tree, has killed more than two-thirds of the elm trees in the United States. It was probably brought to the United States accidentally on a shipment of elm logs from Europe. The best methods for controlling forest diseases include (1) banning or inspecting imported timber that might carry alien parasites; (2) treating diseased trees with antibiotics; (3) developing disease-resistant species; (4) removing dead, infected, and susceptible trees; (5) reducing air pollution (especially sulfur dioxide, ozone, and fluorine) that damages trees and makes them susceptible to disease; and (6) maintaining forest diversity by decreasing clear-cutting, since diseases spread rapidly in stands of even-aged trees.

Destruction by insects is also a serious problem. Some highly destructive insect pests are the spruce budworm, the gypsy moth, the pine weevil, the pinebark beetle, and the larch sawfly. Pest control methods include isolating and removing infested trees, introducing other insects that prey on the pests, using sex attractants to lure and kill insects, releasing sterilized male insects to reduce the population growth of pest species, and preserving forest diversity. For more details on pest control, see Enrichment Study 11.

Suggestions for Managing U.S. Forests How can the United States meet its timber demands, which are expected to double between 1970 and 2000, and at the same time renew its forests and preserve them for other

Figure 10-8 A giant shovel used for strip mining coal. Note the size of the cars behind the shovel.

4. Provide the U.S. Forest Service with greatly increased funding to help it accomplish multiple use management of national forests.

5. Decrease demand for new timber by wasting less wood in the forest, in manufacturing, and in packaging and throwaway paper items (see Enrichment Study 15); using wood substitutes; and greatly increasing the recycling of wood wastes and paper. The average annual paper consumption in the United States is almost 273 kilograms (600 pounds) per person. Much of this use is unnecessary and does not improve the quality of life.

6. In conjunction with a national land-use plan (see Section 11-5), develop an ecologically sound policy for the use of national, state, and private forests.

10-5   Surface Mines

Types and Extent of Surface Mining   Imagine a shovel 32 stories high, with a boom as long as a football field, that is capable of gouging out 152 cubic meters (200 cubic yards) of land every 55 seconds and dropping this 295,000-kilogram (325-ton) load a block away. This is a description of Big Muskie, a $25 million power shovel now used for surface mining coal in the United States (Figure 10-8).

Surface mining (of which strip mining is one form) is the process of removing the overburden of topsoil, subsoil, rock, and other strata so that underlying mineral deposits can be removed. There are several types of surface mining: (1) **open pit mining** (used primarily for stone, sand and gravel, and copper); (2) **area strip mining,** in which trenches are cut out of flat or rolling terrain (used primarily for coal and phosphate) (Figure 10-9); (3) **contour strip mining,** in which a series of contour bands are cut out of the side of a hill or mountain (used primarily for coal); and (4) **dredging** of seabeds (used primarily for sand and gravel). Of these types, contour strip mining is usually the most destructive.

An estimated 52,000 square kilometers (13 million acres) of land in the United States have been disrupted by surface mining of all types, and only about half of this land has been reclaimed. By the year 2000 an estimated 60,000 additional square kilometers (15 million acres) of land will be torn up by surface mining. If these disrupted lands are not reclaimed, the resulting wasteland will equal the combined land area of Connecticut, Delaware, New Hampshire, Rhode Island, New Jersey, Vermont,

uses? Following are suggestions for meeting these often conflicting objectives:

1. Improve forest management and stimulate production on privately owned, nonindustrial forest lands. About 59 percent of the forests in the United States are in small tracts owned by over 4 million farmers and other private owners (Figure 10-4). Most of these tracts are poorly stocked and unmanaged, and the trees are often cut at will without regard to reforestation and other sound forestry practices. Methods for improving management of privately owned forest lands include: cooperative professional management; leasing tracts; providing state and federal loans and subsidies for management and reforestation; increasing free technical advice and research; discouraging premature cutting through liberalized tax assessments; and establishing strict federal standards for harvesting timber, constructing logging roads, mandatory reforestation, and water and soil protection.

2. Prohibit harvesting in large areas of public forests and raise output on other productive public forest lands, in keeping with the National Forest Management Act of 1976.

3. Increase control of destructive fires, forest diseases, and pests by means of improved management, integrated pest control rather than the use of herbicides and pesticides (see Enrichment Study 11), increased research, and development of faster-growing trees that are more resistant to disease, insects, fire, and drought.

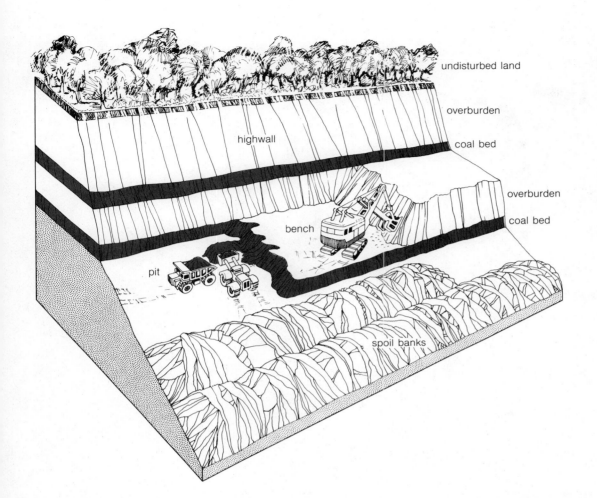

undisturbed land

overburden

highwall

coal bed

overburden

coal bed

bench

pit

spoil banks

Figure 10-9 How area strip mining of coal works: Bulldozers and power shovels clear away trees, brush, and overburden (topsoil and subsoil). Explosive charges loosen the coal deposits, and power shovels or auger drills load the coal into trucks in the pit area. Strip mining exposes cross sections of the earth's crust (the highwalls), and the discarded overburden is piled into long rows called spoil banks.

and Washington, D.C. Not surprisingly, this form of land use is a major point of conflict between proponents of the economic and of the conservationist ethic.

Strip Mining of Coal: A Land-Energy Trade-off Today coal is the source of about 20 percent of all energy and about half of the electricity used in the United States. It will probably provide much more energy in the future as oil and natural gas get scarcer and more expensive (Chapter 13). About 45 percent of all surface mining in the United States is for coal. Strip mining has rapidly replaced the underground mining of coal, because coal companies find it much faster, cheaper, safer, and more efficient. The percentage of coal obtained from strip mines has been rising steadily, increasing from about 9 percent to over 63 percent between 1940 and 1980.

Many people associate strip mining with West Virginia, Kentucky, and Pennsylvania, but as Figure 10-10 shows, it already affects about half of the states. The

newest and largest battleground over strip mining is in the Great Plains—primarily the coal-rich states of Montana, South Dakota, North Dakota, Wyoming, Colorado, and New Mexico. Under these vast grasslands and high plateaus lie more than 40 percent of the nation's coal supply and 77 percent of the coal that can be strip mined at reasonable cost. Much of this western coal is on federally owned land.

Strip mining can have a severe impact on land, water supplies, wildlife, and humans. These effects have been graphically described by Rep. Ken Hechler (Democrat, West Virginia) in testimony before Congress in 1973:

> Strip mining has ripped, torn, and scarred our land. It has polluted our streams with acid, silt, and sediment. It has destroyed valuable topsoil and seriously disturbed or destroyed wildlife habitats. It has created miles of ugly highwalls. Strip mining has left a trail of utter fear and despair for thousands of honest and hard-working people whose only fault is that they have their homes near the strip mines.

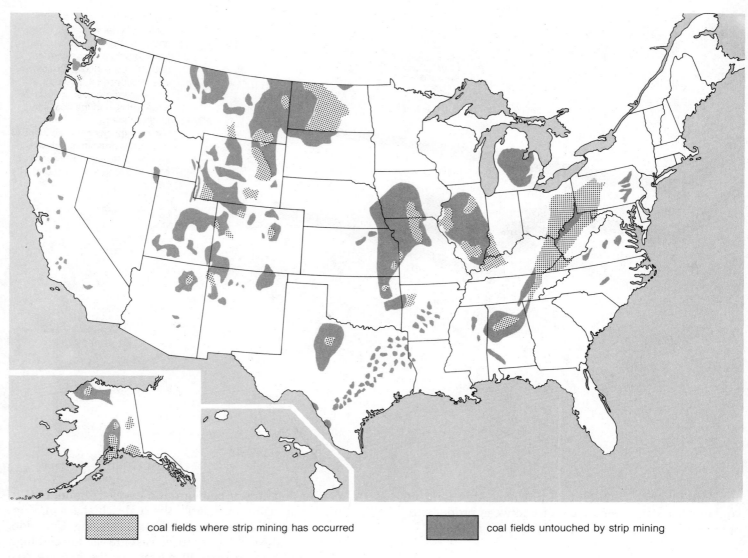

coal fields where strip mining has occurred   coal fields untouched by strip mining

Figure 10-10   Major coal reserves in the United States.

The problems of strip mining and land reclamation vary throughout the United States. In the East, especially Appalachia, contour surface mining carried out on steep slopes causes massive land disruption and acid runoff into nearby streams. Much of this coal contains sulfur compounds, which, when exposed to air, are converted into sulfuric acid. Rainfall washes this acid down the slopes, contaminating streams and rivers. Almost 18,000 kilometers (11,000 miles) of U.S. waterways have been polluted from acid runoff and silting caused by strip and underground coal mining.

In the Midwest, especially in Illinois, strip mining destroys prime farmland. In the West, strip mining de-

stroys valuable rangeland and depletes underground water supplies in the arid regions where most of the coal is located. Much of this western land can probably never be fully reclaimed.

The arguments for and against strip mining are summarized in Table 10-3.

Some Solutions   The argument over strip mining is not whether it should be banned, but to what degree and under what controls it should be allowed. Many states have attempted to control surface mining, especially the strip mining of coal, by passing laws. But it has been a difficult political battle, and enforcement of the laws has

Table 10-3 The Strip Mining Controversy

Arguments in Favor	Arguments Against
The maximum amount of strip mining of coal projected by the year 2000 would disturb only about 0.2 percent of the total land area of the United States.	Comparing the total amount of strip mined area to the total land area of the United States is misleading. Strip mining affects the people, land, and wildlife of large sections of the United States very intensely.
Strip mining produces short-term environmental damage that can be repaired with available technology. Surface mining and reclamation often improve the land.	Surface mining destroys land, forests, soil, and water. It scars the landscape, disrupts wildlife habitats and recreational areas, can cause landslides and soil erosion, and may pollute nearby rivers and streams with silt and acid runoff. Some land can be reclaimed, but without strictly enforced regulations, the coal companies do not restore it. In addition, reclamation costs are very high, ranging from $741,000 to $2,471,000 per square kilometer ($3,000 to $10,000 per acre).
Strip mining is the cheapest and best way to produce coal and meet growing energy demands. A ban on or severe restriction of strip mining would disrupt energy supplies and damage the economy by raising the price of coal.	The nation's energy needs could be met by greater development of underground coal reserves, which are 8 times more plentiful than surface coal reserves. The only reason strip mining is cheaper than underground mining is that coal companies are not paying the environmental and social costs of their ecological disruption of land and water resources.
Coal companies cannot convert to deep mining quickly enough to replace the surface coal that is now used for electric power generation.	More than 1,500 deep mines have been closed since 1969. Many of these mines still contain coal that could replace the supplies lost due to a restriction of strip mining.
It takes 5 years to bring an underground mine to full production.	New underground mines could start production within 18 months with more efficient technology and management.
Surface mining recovers nearly 100 percent of the coal, compared with 55 percent for underground mining. New technology that permits a higher recovery of underground coal cannot be used in all mines.	Recovery in most deep mines could be increased significantly by using new mining technology.
Underground miners who have been laid off are too old to return to the mines, and their skills are outdated because of new technology.	Underground mining requires 20 times more workers than strip mining and thus reduces unemployment and improves the economy. Enough miners can be trained to greatly increase the amount of underground mining.
Surface mining is safer than underground mining by a ratio of 1.5 to 1.	Although underground mining is one of the nation's most hazardous occupations, it can be made as safe as surface mining by enacting and enforcing more stringent safety standards. The injury rate in the safest mines is lower than injury rates for real estate, higher education, and the wholesale and retail trade, and black lung disease could be almost eliminated if existing dust-level regulations were enforced.

varied widely from state to state. In the early 1970s environmentalists began campaigning for strict federal regulations on the strip mining of coal. In 1977, after years of work and debate and two presidential vetoes, such a federal law, the Surface Mining Control and Reclamation Act of 1977, was enacted.

Some major features of this law are the following:

1. In order to get a mining permit, mine operators are required to prove beforehand that they can reclaim the land.

2. Land must be restored so that it can be used for the same purposes as it was used before mining. Such restoration includes filling in holes, contouring the land to its original shape, preserving all soil, removing all wastes, and replanting the land with grass and trees.

3. Strip mining is banned on some prime agricultural lands in the West, and farmers and ranchers have the right to veto mining under their lands, even though they do not own the mineral rights.

4. Mining companies must minimize the effects of their activities on local watersheds and water quality by using the best available technology, and they must prevent acid from entering local streams and groundwater.

5. A $4.1 billion fund is provided for restoring strip-mined land that has never been reclaimed. The fund is financed by a fee of 35¢ per ton of strip-mined coal and 15¢ per ton of underground-mined coal;

the fees will be collected until 1993. Responsibility for enforcement of this law is delegated to the states, with enforcement by the Department of the Interior where the states fail to act.

If interpreted and enforced strictly and adequately funded, this law should go a long way to protect valuable ecosystems from the effects of the strip mining of coal. Since this law was passed, however, there have been growing pressures from the coal industry (much of which is now owned by the major oil companies), some members of Congress, and the courts to have this act weakened or declared unconstitutional. Intense citizen pressure will be necessary to insure that this act will not be weakened, and that Congress will enact similar laws governing the surface mining of all other materials. In 1981, the newly appointed Secretary of the Interior James G. Watt fired most dedicated environmentalists serving in managerial positions in the Department of Interior and promised to ease strip mining rules and end the visits of state and federal inspectors to mine sites.

10-6 Estuaries and Wetlands

Importance of Estuarine Zones Among the most important, most misunderstood, and most abused natural resources in the United States are estuaries and wetlands. **Estuaries** are thin, fragile zones along coastlines where freshwater streams and rivers meet and mix with salty oceans. **Coastal wetlands** are shallow shelves that are normally wet or flooded and that extend back from the freshwater-saltwater interface. They consist of a complex maze of marshes, bays, lagoons, tidal flats, and mangrove swamps. Coastal wetlands and estuaries together are called **estuarine zones.** Beyond the coastal saltwater wetlands we find **inland freshwater wetlands,** which consist of swamps, marshes, and bogs.

According to the economic land ethic, these desolate, mosquito-infested estuarine zones are worthless lands that should be eliminated by draining, dredging, and filling or used as sinks for municipal and industrial wastes. Far from being worthless, however, estuarine zones have the highest average net primary productivity of any ecosystem (see Figure 5-9). This high productivity occurs because most estuarine zones are at the end of rivers flowing into the ocean. As a result, they receive and trap the rich silt and organic matter that rivers wash down from the land, and then hold and use these nutrients to produce an extraordinary bloom of plant life (phytoplankton and marsh and sea grasses) and large populations of detritus feeders.

The plants (mostly grasses) growing in estuaries, swamps, and marshes are not very useful for human consumption, but the nutrient-rich habitats they provide are very important food sources, homes, and spawning grounds for many types of shellfish and commercial and sport saltwater fish that are vital sources of protein for humans. An estimated 65 percent of the commercial and recreational U.S. harvests of saltwater fish, clams, oysters, crabs, shrimp, and lobsters depend on the estuarine zone. At some stage of their life, these valuable species depend on estuaries for food, spawning grounds, or nurseries for their young. Thus, filling in or damaging the productivity of estuaries, marshes, and swamps destroys a major source of protein and affects the livelihood of the 260,000 Americans involved in the $7-billion-a-year commercial fishing industry. According to one controversial hypothesis, however, most estuarine species could learn to survive in other niches if the estuaries disappeared. This may be true because in order to survive in the harsh estuarine environment, the species must have wide ranges of tolerance to temperature, salinity (dissolved salts), and high concentrations of suspended sediment.

In addition, estuarine zones feed and shelter wading marsh birds (herons, egrets, ibis, and cranes), birds of prey (ospreys, marsh hawks, and bald eagles), and other waterfowl (cormorants, pelicans, grebes, and loons). Also, migratory birds (ducks, geese, snipes, and rail) rest in estuarine zones.

Furthermore, estuarine zones and adjoining sand dunes are two of our most important natural flood-control devices. The estuarine zones block and absorb damaging waves caused by violent storms and serve as a kind of giant sponge to help protect human coastal habitats.

Under natural conditions the area behind any beach is protected by two sets of sand dunes, which are held together by sea oats and other grasses and shrubs. For free and effective flood protection, buildings should be placed behind these primary and secondary dunes (Figure 10-11), with walkways built over both dunes to the beach. In this way the dunes and the grasses that hold them together are protected.

When coastal developments remove these protective dunes or build behind the first set of dunes, minor hurricanes and sea storms can sweep away the cottages, homes, and buildings. Some people then call such events "natural" disasters and insist on insurance payments and loans so that they can build again and wait for the next disaster. As a result, government disaster agencies and the National Flood Insurance Program help rebuild what will almost surely be destroyed again someday.

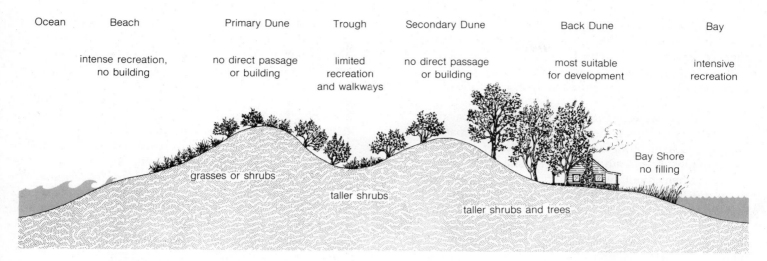

Ocean	Beach	Primary Dune	Trough	Secondary Dune	Back Dune	Bay
	intense recreation, no building	no direct passage or building	limited recreation and walkways	no direct passage or building	most suitable for development	intensive recreation

grasses or shrubs

taller shrubs

taller shrubs and trees

Bay Shore no filling

Figure 10-11 Primary and secondary dunes offer natural protection from flooding. Ideally, construction and development should be allowed only behind the double system of dunes, with walkways built over the dunes to the beach.

If they are not overloaded, estuaries and wetlands provide another important, free service by removing large amounts of pollutants from coastal waters. It is estimated that 0.004 square kilometer (1 acre) of tidal estuary substitutes for a $75,000 waste treatment plant and is worth a total of $83,000 when sport and fish food production is included.

Stresses on Estuarine Zones Estuarine zones comprise only 0.0005 percent of U.S. land area. Because these zones are limited and highly desirable, they have been subjected to enormous stress. Besides providing recreation, wildlife habitats, and scenic beauty, coastal regions also are in heavy demand for homesites, industrial sites (especially oil refineries and nuclear power plants), ship channels, harbors, superports for oil supertankers, oil and natural gas rigs, and mining. These areas are often crowded with motels, hotels, condominiums, mobile home parks, businesses, and marinas to satisfy the rush of Americans who wish to experience the poetry, joy, and advantages of this limited type of land.

About 53 percent of the American population live within 81 kilometers (50 miles) from the ocean or the Great Lakes (estimated at 75 percent by 1990), and millions more vacation in these areas. Nine of the nation's largest cities and about 40 percent of the nation's manufacturing plants are located in coastal counties. In addition, about two-thirds of the operating nuclear and fossil-fuel electric power plants in the United States are in the coastal zone, and more than 100 new power plants are scheduled to be built there by 1995. Furthermore, about 75 percent of the phosphate rock mined in the United States comes from the estuarine zones of Florida and North Carolina. The National Sand and Gravel Association testified before Congress that much of the construction material needed between 1970 and 2000 would be mined and dredged from estuarine zones. Thus, the fate of the coastal environment directly or indirectly affects every U.S. citizen.

Because of these multiple uses and stresses, over 40 percent of the U.S. coastal estuaries have been destroyed or damaged, primarily by dredging and filling, and an additional 1,200 square kilometers (300,000 acres) of coastal and inland wetlands are lost or damaged each year. Between 1947 and 1967, California lost over two-thirds of its original estuaries. Fortunately, since 1967 this destructive trend has been slowed and in some cases reversed.

Coastal Zone Management The use of estuarine zones is one of the major battlegrounds between economic and conservationist ethics. Fortunately, about two-thirds of the nation's estuaries and wetlands remain. But trying to protect these lands while still allowing reasonable use is a difficult task, especially since more than 90 percent of the coastline (excluding Alaska) is privately owned.

First, there are many different types of estuarine systems. Plans for protecting and using one system may not be applicable to another. Second, even when there is an ecologically sound plan, there is tremendous economic and political pressure to use estuarine areas primarily for economic purposes. Third, designs for controlled use and protection are hampered because of the conflicting goals of many coastal municipalities, counties, and states.

Although Congress has been unable to pass any comprehensive laws governing land use, it did pass the National Coastal Zone Management Act of 1972. This law provides federal aid to the 35 coastal states and territories to help them develop voluntary, comprehensive programs for protecting and managing their coastlines. It also provides matching funds for states with approved plans to establish estuarine sanctuaries and pledges that the U.S. government will abide by state programs for managing coastal resources. Although this law is an important step, it has been hindered by inadequate funding and the fact that plans drawn up and approved for funding do not have to be implemented because the program is voluntary.

Coastal zone problems, then, are entrusted to the states. Before the new law some states, such as Delaware and California, had already passed laws regulating coastal development. The 1972 federal law prompted other coastal states and territories to decide how they wanted to use their coastal lands. By 1980, 19 of the 35 coastal states had federally approved coastal management plans, and most others were in advanced stages of program development. Although it is too early to evaluate state programs, so far North Carolina and California have the strictest plans for control—however, both states failed to protect endangered farmland. Furthermore, since 1979 the powers of California's Coastal Commission have been weakened by the California legislature and by the appointment of more pro-development commission members. Unfortunately, many of the voluntary state plans are vague and lack sufficient legal authority to protect coastal lands adequately. The Chesapeake Bay, the largest estuarine zone in the United States, was continuing to deteriorate in 1980 because the two states involved, Virginia and Maryland, had either failed to enact a strong program (Maryland) or had no federally approved program at all (Virginia).

Environmentalists successfully pressured Congress to declare 1980 the "Year of the Coast" and to renew and strengthen the 1972 National Coastal Zone Management Act, especially by providing additional incentive grants to states making good progress in protecting coastal resources. Suggestions for further improving the act in the future, while still balancing economic and ecological uses of coastal areas, include the following: (1) making maintenance of coastal ecology the most important goal; (2) allowing new development only in already developed areas; (3) protecting cultural, historic, aesthetic, and scenic sites; (4) prohibiting irrelevant uses of coastal areas (such as warehouses and drive-in theaters); (5) carefully evaluating the short- and long-term effects of all types of economic development and encouraging developments that are not environmentally destructive; (6) ensuring that the public has free and unrestricted access to shorelines and beaches; (7) letting citizens have a voice in deciding how coastal lands are to be used; (8) terminating all federal funds provided under the National Coastal Zone Management Act if a state fails to meet minimum standards; and (9) having the federal government establish a coastal program for states that fail to enact and enforce adequate coastal protection programs.

There will continue to be tremendous pressures from developers and manufacturers to build marinas, condominiums, resorts, and power plants on coastal land without adequate environmental protection. Perhaps the only way to protect these areas quickly enough is to support federal, state, and private foundation efforts to buy up the most critical areas and hold them in ecological reserve. We had enough foresight to do this for some of our forest land 100 years ago. Because of their ecological value and their scarceness, estuarine zones are in even greater need of protection. Hopefully, the United States will follow the example of Sweden, which has protected large amounts of its shoreline for free public use.

10-7 Wildlife

Extinction, Extermination, and Rare and Endangered Species Some species adapt to climatic change, competition with other species, natural disasters, and other environmental changes, but other species do not. Those that don't adapt ultimately disappear and become **biologically extinct.** Of the estimated 500 million species of plants and animals that have existed since life began on earth, only about 2 to 4 million are here today. This means that *about 80 to 90 percent of all species have become extinct.*

Although biological extinction is a natural evolutionary process, it has been greatly accelerated by human activities. Such human-related extinction is sometimes called **biological extermination.** Biological extermination typically occurs in several phases. First, a species may become *regionally exterminated,* disappearing from part of its normal range. Next it may become *ecologically exterminated* when too few individuals are left to have a significant impact on the ecology of their habitat. If not protected

Figure 10-12 The whooping crane (left) and the California condor (right) are two critically endangered species in the United States.

so that it can reproduce and replenish its numbers, an ecologically exterminated species can eventually become biologically exterminated. Because of the accelerated destruction and pollution of the world's tropical moist forests (Section 10-4) and other wildlife habitats, it is estimated that at least 500,000 species of insects, plants, and animals may be biologically exterminated between 1980 and 2000—representing 13 to 25 percent of all the estimated species in the world. This includes not only highly publicized animals like whales, tigers, and condors, but also nameless plant species, many with the potential to be the source of the next miracle drug or miracle food strain.

Species heading toward extermination (or extinction) are classified by the International Union for the Conservation of Nature and Natural Resources (IUCN) according to four categories: *endangered, critically endangered, threatened,* and *rare.* An **endangered species** is one in immediate danger of extermination (extinction). Examples are the Everglades kite, the black-footed ferret, and the blue whale. A **critically endangered species** is one that will not survive without direct human intervention and protection. Two examples in North America are the whooping crane and the California condor (Figure

10-12). **Threatened species,** such as the grizzly bear, sandhill crane, and green turtle, are still abundant in their range but are threatened because of a decline in numbers. **Rare species,** such as the Galapagos tortoise and Komodo dragon, are not presently in danger but are subject to risk because of their low numbers in widely separated populations.

Since 1600, when record keeping began, about 300 species of animals have become extinct as a direct or indirect result of human activities. In 1976 the IUCN listed 903 species or subspecies of animals and 20,000 species, subspecies, and varieties of the world's flowering plants, representing 10 percent of these plants, as endangered, rare, or threatened. By 1980 the Department of the Interior's Office of Endangered Species listed 276 plant and animals in the United States as endangered, and hundreds of others were being evaluated. In addition, approximately 3,200, or 16 percent, of the 200,000 species, subspecies, and varieties of native U.S. plants are considered endangered or threatened. For case studies of endangered species, see Enrichment Study 12.

Causes of Extermination The major causes of extermination, in decreasing order of importance, are: (1) habitat disturbance and elimination; (2) commercial hunting; (3) introduction of competing or predatory species; (4) sport hunting; (5) pest and predatory control for protection of livestock and crops; (6) hunting for food; (7) collecting specimens for pets, medical research, and zoos; and (8) pollution (Figure 10-13). Most species are not driven to extermination or near extermination by a single cause but by a combination of factors.

The most important cause of extermination and the greatest threat to wildlife is the destruction or alteration of habitat, which is aided by the ax, chain saw, bulldozer, and tractor. This category alone accounts for about 30 percent of the presently endangered species, and in combination with other factors it probably affects over two-thirds of all endangered species, especially in the tropical moist forests of Africa, Asia, and Latin America (Section 10-4). Thus, the basic problem of preserving wildlife is the problem of preserving land, since any species must have a habitat. Habitat loss usually means extermination because there is too little time for species to adapt and too few unfilled new habitats. Habitat disturbance has been a major factor in the disappearance of some of America's most magnificent bird species, such as the trumpeter swan and the ivory-billed woodpecker, and the near extermination of the whooping crane and the California condor, the largest land flying bird in North America (see Figure 10-12). By 1980 there were probably about 126 whooping cranes and 20 to 30 California condors left.

Hunting for commercial products, sport, and food accounts for about 39 percent of today's endangered species (Figure 10-13). Commercial hunting for furs, hides, tusks, feathers, and other animal products has decreased somewhat because of the development of synthetic substitutes. But hunting still threatens species such as the jaguar, cheetah, tiger, and snow leopard (which are hunted for their furs), alligators (skins), elephants (ivory tusks), and rhinoceroses, which are hunted because many Chinese believe that powdered rhinoceros horn is a powerful aphrodisiac. Wildlife preservation expert Norman Myers says that we could solve two problems simultaneously if we could persuade the Chinese and others throughout the world that rats—not rhinos—have aphrodisiac properties. By 1980, nearly half of China's 130 species of rare birds and animals were nearing extermination, primarily as a result of hunting for sport and for export to other nations.

Game hunting has been and is still a threat to a number of species, such as the elephant, Bengal tiger, rhinoceros, and oryx. It was also a factor in the extermination of the American passenger pigeon and the near extermination of the American bison, as discussed in

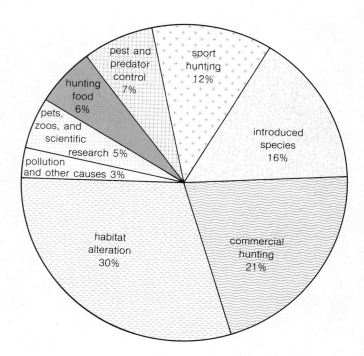

Figure 10-13 Human causes of extermination and extinction of species.

more detail in Enrichment Study 12. Today game hunting in the United States is closely regulated and does not greatly threaten game species, although it is a controversial issue. In the 1600s hunting for food was the major cause of extermination. Today such hunting has declined sharply in most areas except for hunting of certain fish and whales (see Enrichment Study 12).

Introducing new species into an ecosystem, either accidentally or deliberately, can often have unpredictable and undesirable effects, not only on a particular species but also on entire ecosystems. Introduced species may affect other species by preying on them, competing with them for food, destroying their habitat, or upsetting the ecological balance. One classic disaster was the deliberate introduction of mongooses into Hawaii in 1883 to control the rodent population, which was destroying much of the valuable sugar cane crop. Unfortunately, mongooses hunt by day and rats tend to hunt by night; thus the two species rarely met. The mongoose population continued to grow, attacking amphibians, reptiles, and some birds that helped keep the rat population down. With fewer predators, the rat population rose, and the sugar cane crop was in worse trouble than before. Island species are especially vulnerable. For example, the dodo bird, which lived only on the small island of Mauritius in the Indian Ocean, became extinct

Table 10-4 Damage Caused by Imported Plants and Animals in the United States

Name	Origin	Mode of Transport	Type of Damage
Mammals			
European wild boar	Russia	Intentionally imported (1912), escaped captivity	Destruction of habitat by rooting; crop damage
Nutria (cat-sized rodent)	Argentina	Intentionally imported, escaped captivity (1940)	Alteration of marsh ecology; damage to levees and earth dams; crop destruction
Birds			
European starling	Europe	Intentionally released (1890)	Competition with native songbirds; crop damage; transmission of swine diseases; airport interference
House sparrow	England	Intentionally released by Brooklyn Institute (1853)	Crop damage; displacement of native songbirds
Fish			
Carp	Germany	Intentionally released (1877)	Displacement of native fish; uprooting of water plants with loss of waterfowl populations
Sea lamprey	North Atlantic Ocean	Entered via Welland Canal (1829)	Destruction of lake trout, lake whitefish, and suckers in Great Lakes
Walking catfish	Thailand	Imported into Florida	Destruction of bass, bluegill, and other fish
Insects			
Argentine fire ant	Argentina	Entered via coffee shipments from Brazil? (1891)	Crop damage; destruction of native ant faunas
Camphor scale insect	Japan	Accidentally imported on nursery stock (1920s)	Damage to nearly 200 species of plants in Louisiana, Texas, and Alabama
Japanese beetle	Japan	Accidentally imported on irises or azaleas (1911)	Defoliation of more than 250 species of trees and other plants, including many of commercial importance
Plants			
Water hyacinth	Central America	Intentionally introduced (1884)	Clogging waterways; shading out other aquatic vegetation
Chestnut blight (a fungus)	Asia	Accidentally imported on nursery plants (1900)	Destruction of nearly all eastern American chestnut trees; disturbance of forest ecology
Dutch elm disease *Cerastomella ulmi* (a fungus, the disease agent)	Europe	Accidentally imported on infected elm timber used for veneers (1930)	Destruction of millions of elms; disturbance of forest ecology
Bark beetle (*Scolytus multistriatus*, the disease vector)		Accidentally imported in unbarked elm timber (1909)	

From *Biological Conservation* by David W. Ehrenfeld. Copyright © 1970 by Holt, Rinehart and Winston, Inc. Modified and reprinted by permission.

by 1681 after pigs brought to the island consumed its eggs.

Some harmful species that were accidentally introduced into North America are the European corn borer, the Japanese beetle, the cotton boll weevil, the Dutch elm fungus, the piranha, and other examples shown in Table 10-4 and discussed in Enrichment Study 12.

Not all alien species have been disastrous. The ring-necked pheasant from Asia and the brown trout from England are important game species in the United States, and most major U.S. food crops were deliberately imported from other areas. Nevertheless, the disasters far outnumber the successes.

Government-sponsored pest and predator control has also exterminated or nearly exterminated some species. The Carolina parakeet was exterminated in the United States because it fed on fruit crops. The populations and ranges of mountain lions and wolves have been greatly reduced because the animals threaten livestock. Trying to exterminate particular species by poisoning sometimes poisons their predators. This can upset the food chains in ecosystems and allow species whose populations were controlled naturally to become pests. For example, poison campaigns against prairie dogs and pocket gophers in order to protect rangeland for grazing livestock have just about eliminated their natural predator, the black-footed ferret. Unsuccessful attempts to exterminate the coyote in the southwestern United States constitute another highly controversial program.

In 1972, a presidential executive order stopped the poisoning of all predators on government lands or by government employees anywhere. Shortly thereafter the Environmental Protection Agency canceled the use of several (but not all) of the poisons commonly used against predators, even on private land. Although these are important steps, they still leave many dangerous poisons in use, such as "1080." Meanwhile, the search continues to find effective and ecologically sound methods for animal control. One of the most inventive tricks so far is the use of tabasco sauce on samples of mutton to condition coyotes against killing sheep.

Collecting wild animals for pets, scientific research, and zoos can also threaten certain species. A number of endangered animals, such as Gila monsters and various species of fish, lizards, parakeets, and parrots, are sold as pets, especially in pet-loving nations such as the United States, the United Kingdom, and Germany. Many of these exotic animals die during capture or shipment or after purchase. Medical research is an important activity, but it is also a serious threat to endangered wild primates, such as the chimpanzee and orangutan. At one time zoological parks and aquariums also contributed to the decline of some species. Since 1967 most zoos and aquariums have agreed to control their acquisition of endangered species, although there are still some abuses.

Chemical pollution is a relatively new but growing threat to wildlife. Industrial wastes, mine acid, and excess heat from electric power plants have wiped out some species of fish in local areas, such as the humpbacked chub. Chlorinated hydrocarbon pesticides, especially DDT and dieldrin, have been magnified in food chains (Section 6-3) and have caused reproductive failure and eggshell thinning of important birds of prey, such as the peregrine falcon, brown pelican, osprey, and bald eagle. See Enrichment Study 11 for more details.

Characteristics of Endangered Species For good reasons the plight of endangered species is emphasized.

But some species are less susceptible to extermination than others. Some characteristics of susceptible species are given in Table 10-5.

One factor that enhances the probability that many larger animals may become endangered is a low reproductive rate. The near extinction of the California condor, shown in Figure 10-12, is largely a result of this factor. A pair of condors may produce only one offspring every two years, and the new chicks don't mate until they are 7 years old. Furthermore, when disturbed by human activities, the condors may abandon their nests and chicks. Despite being treated as an endangered species since 1949, the population of this largest bird in North America continues to decline. By 1980 only 20 to 30 of these huge birds were believed to exist solely in the mountains north of Los Angeles. In 1980, a controversial $2 million (and perhaps futile) effort to save this species was mounted by using radio tracking to capture and breed some of the birds in captivity. Some conservationists have argued against this program since they believe the condor is almost certainly headed for extinction. They have made the controversial suggestion that we concentrate limited funds on those species that have the best chance for survival and that have the most ecological value to an ecosystem or are potentially useful for agriculture, medicine, or industry.

Normally a species is susceptible to extermination because of a combination of factors—not just one factor. Much more research is needed to identify these combinations so that it will be easier to identify and protect vulnerable species before—not after—they become endangered.

Wildlife Protection and Management The reasons for preserving wild species and places have already been discussed (Section 10-2). Fortunately, wildlife protection and management have made headway throughout the world in spite of opposing economic and political pressures. The IUCN, International Council for Bird Preservation (ICBA), and the World Wildlife Federation have led worldwide efforts.

Europe and the United States have been world leaders in wildlife conservation. In the United States, the federal government and the state governments have established extensive programs of wildlife management, supplemented (and watched over) by private groups such as the Audubon Society and the National Wildlife Federation (see the appendix at the end of this book for a more complete list of such organizations). The world's largest system of wildlife habitats is in the United States. States and private groups have established hundreds of

Table 10-5 Characteristics of Species Susceptible to Extermination or Extinction

Characteristic	Examples
Natural Factors	
Large size and visibility	Lion, Bengal tiger, elephant, blue whale, American bison
Low reproductive rate	Blue whale, polar bear, California condor, passenger pigeon, human
Limited or vulnerable habitats	Kirtland's warbler (nests only in jack pine trees that are from 6 to 15 years old), orangutan (found only on islands of Sumatra and Borneo), whooping crane (depends on marshes for food and nesting)
Specialized breeding grounds	Green sea turtle (lays eggs on only a few beaches)
Very specialized diet	Ivory-billed woodpecker (beetle larvae in recently dead trees), Everglades kite (apple snail of southern Florida), blue whale (krill in polar upwelling zones)
Inability to adapt behavior to different environmental conditions	Redheaded woodpecker (flies in front of cars), Carolina parakeet (when one member of flock was shot, rest of flock hovered over its body)
Human-Related Factors	
Susceptibility to pollution and pesticides	Peregrine falcon, brown pelican, osprey, bald eagle
Use as game animal	Whooping crane, great auk, passenger pigeon, grizzly bear, elephant, tiger, lion
Economic value	Blue whale (oil), American alligator (hide), elephant (tusks), snow leopard (fur), South American parrot (pet), orangutan (zoos and medical research)
Feeding on crops, livestock, or game animals	Carolina parakeet, lion, wolf

wildlife refuges, and the U.S. Bureau of Sport Fisheries and Wildlife administers the National Wildlife Refuge System. The primary purpose of these national refuges is to protect and provide breeding grounds for wildlife, particularly migrating birds and endangered species.

Although the refuges preserve many types of habitats and wildlife, environmentalists argue that the emphasis has been on managing game species for the approximately 45 million Americans who hunt and fish and who support the program by buying hunting and fishing licenses. Under careful control, hunting can be used to check rapidly growing populations of deer, squirrels, and rabbits, although sometimes too much killing is allowed.

The federal government has been increasing its efforts to protect all native game and nongame endangered species with the passage of the Endangered Species Conservation Act of 1966, the Marine Mammal Protection Act of 1972, and the Endangered Species Act of 1973. With adequate funding and strict enforcement, the Endangered Species Act of 1973 may be one of the toughest

and most controversial environmental laws ever passed by Congress. It extends endangered species protection to plants as well as animals, requires protection of threatened as well as endangered species by using *all* necessary methods and procedures, allows any group or individual to bring suit in any federal court to halt any action by anyone alleged to be in violation of the act, permits the court to award all court costs (including attorney's fees) to any party regardless of who wins the case, and prohibits federal projects that would jeopardize endangered species or destroy or modify habitats critical to their survival.

This last provision has been most controversial. In 1978 a battle over the Endangered Species Act resulted in amendments that may have weakened the original act. These amendments resulted primarily from the court action that stopped the $116 million Tellico Dam project in Tennessee because the area to be flooded by the dam reservoir threatened the survival of an endangered species, the snail darter (a tiny minnow 8 centimeters [3 inches] long). In 1978 the Supreme Court stated that the

Endangered Species Act of 1973, as written by Congress, prohibited the construction of any federally funded project if the project threatened the survival of any species on the official list of endangered or threatened species.

After an intense debate between conservationists (who wanted to preserve the act as originally written) and developers (who wanted to have all federally funded projects exempted from the act), a compromise was reached. In 1978, Congress amended the act so that exemptions could be granted for federally declared major disaster areas, for national defense, or by a seven-member Endangered Species Review Committee if they found that the economic benefits of the project outweighed the harmful ecological effects. At their first meeting, the review committee denied the request to exempt the Tellico Dam project on the grounds that it was economically unsound. In 1979, however, Congress overruled that decision and the dam's reservoir is now full of water. The snail darters that once dwelled there were transplanted to nearby rivers, and by 1981 they were apparently making a slow comeback.

The review committee has apparently acted in good faith so far, but environmentalists are not convinced that this will continue should future administrations appoint people more sympathetic to economic interests. The new amendments also weaken the ability of the government to add new species to the endangered and threatened lists. Now before a species can be listed, the boundaries of its critical habitat must be determined, an economic impact study must be prepared, and public hearings must be held—all within two years of the proposal of the listing. Some scientists have also called for increased emphasis on evaluating the endangered status of microorganisms such as bacteria, fungi, algae, and protozoa and insects, earthworms, and nematodes—rather than concentrating primarily on some of the larger and aesthetically appealing animals. Microorganisms are crucial for the breakdown of organic wastes (Section 16-6), detoxification of pollutants, nitrogen fixation (Section 5-4), and biological pest control (Enrichment Study 11). Invertebrates (including insects, earthworms, and nematodes) are vital for organic waste degradation, soil formation, pollination, and biological pest control.

In addition to the Endangered Species Act, other major approaches to protecting wildlife and restoring endangered species are the following: (1) laws to protect and regulate hunting, fishing, and commercial use of threatened species; (2) acquisition, preservation, and management of wildlife refuges and other natural habitats; (3) stricter control of pesticides, herbicides, and predator poisons (see Enrichment Study 11); (4) better con-

trol over the introduction of species that upset balanced predator-prey relationships; and (5) the captive breeding and reintroduction of endangered species into selected wild habitats.

Control of killing and commercial harvesting has allowed endangered animals such as the sea otter, wild turkey, Alaskan seal, and American alligator to make comebacks. In 1977 the American alligator was removed from the endangered species list in most parts of the United States and reclassified as a threatened species. Wildlife refuges have helped the endangered Key deer of southern Florida and the trumpeter swan to recover. The bald eagle, peregrine falcon, and osprey may be making modest recoveries because of protection and restrictions on the use of pesticides. Breeding in captivity, along with protection, has so far saved the whooping crane and the Hawaiian goose (nene) from biological extermination. Special gardens and arboretums are also being set up to preserve and study endangered plants so that they might be eventually reestablished in the wild. In addition, regional seed banks are being established throughout the world to collect and preserve existing crop strains for breeding new crop strains.

In spite of these and other important successes, much needs to be done to protect American wildlife. Here are some suggestions:

1. Greatly increase funding to protect wildlife.

2. Acquire and develop more wildlife refuges and improve their management. Special attention should be given to the 85 percent of U.S. hunting lands that are privately owned.

3. Use a much broader ecological approach to wildlife conservation. Emphasis should be on programs to keep species from becoming endangered, ecological pest and predator control that uses several methods rather than relying almost exclusively on pesticides and poisons that can kill a variety of organisms (Enrichment Study 11), and looking at wildlife conservation in terms of preservation of ecosystems rather than preserving a particular endangered species.

4. Adapt and enforce an ecological approach to land use at the federal, state, and local levels (see Section 11-5). This will require a national plan for land use and a single centralized authority of all land and wildlife management at both the federal and state levels. Having agencies in different and often conflicting departments leads to chaos, unnecessary conflicts, and delays, and prevents problems from being dealt with from a broad ecological viewpoint.

5. Help protect wildlife at the international level by

imposing a tax on all imported wildlife products, with the revenue being given to the International Wildlife Fund.

This chapter has been devoted to the problems and management of nonurban lands. In the next chapter we will look at urban land use and some approaches to ecological land-use planning.

If we love our children, we must love our earth with tender care and pass it on, diverse and beautiful, so that on a warm spring day 10,000 years hence they can feel peace in a sea of grass, can watch a bee visit a flower, can hear a sandpiper call in the sky, and can find joy in being alive.

Hugh H. Iltis

Guest Editorial: Why Plant a Redwood Tree?

Garrett Hardin

Garrett Hardin is professor emeritus of human ecology at the University of California, Santa Barbara, and one of the foremost human ecologists in the United States. Presently he is chairman of the board and chief executive officer of the Environmental Fund. His 1968 essay "The Tragedy of the Commons" (Science, vol. 162, 1243–1248) is recognized as one of the most important ecological articles and has been widely reprinted in anthologies. His books include Population, Evolution, and Birth Control *(1969, San Francisco: W. H. Freeman);* Exploring New Ethics of Survival *(2nd ed. 1978, New York: Viking); and* The Limits to Altruism *(1977, Bloomington, Ind.: Indiana University Press). Few people have contributed more important insights to the meaning of the environmental crisis. He has the rare ability to make us think beyond the superficial level about important and controversial ideas.*

"Would you plant a redwood tree in your backyard?" the ecologist asks the economist. "I mean, assuming that you had a large backyard and suitable soil and climate?"

The economist smiles wanly and says no.

"Well, I would," says the ecologist. "In fact, I did."

"Then you're an economic fool."

The economist is right, of course. A tree can hardly be planted for less than $1. To mature to the stage the ecologist has in mind takes some 2,000 years, by which time the tree will be about 91 meters (300 feet) high. How much is the tree worth then? An economist will insist, of course, on evaluating the forest giant as lumber. Measured 1.8 meters (6 feet) above the ground, the diameter of the tree will be about 3 meters (10 feet), and the shape of the shaft from there upward is essentially conical. The volume of this cone is 94,248 board feet. At a "stumpage" price of 25 cents a board foot—the approximate price a lumberer must pay for a standing tree—the redwood would be worth some $23,500.

This may sound like a large return on an investment of only $1, but we must not forget how long the investment took to mature: 2,000 years. Using the exponential formula to calculate the rate of compound interest, we find that the capital earned slightly less than 0.5 percent per year. Yes, a person would be an economic fool to put money into a redwood seedling when so many more profitable opportunities are at hand.

Is that all there is to say about the matter? If it is, then sooner or later we will have no great groves of redwood trees for our delight. It is the groves of trees that we are interested in. A single redwood tree, remarkable though it may be for its size, is not enough to evoke these religious feelings that seize sensitive people in the hush of a forest of towering trees. But how can we assign a value to religious feelings? Confined by the prejudices of the marketplace, the economist must advise us not to plant a forest of redwoods.

(A tree farm is something else. Depending on the price of land and lumber and discounting future uncertainties, economic analysis may justify planting an aesthetically sterile, disciplined array of trees that will be harvested in less than a century for lumber. But that is not our problem.)

Among contemporaries, rationality demands that there be a quid pro quo in every exchange. But what if the exchange is between generations? This logical sticking point was brutally laid bare two centuries ago by the American poet John Trumbull, who wrote scornfully of those who would have us act

As though there were a tie
And obligation to posterity.
We get them, bear them, breed, and nurse:
What has posterity done for us?

By asking that question do we prove that all redwood forests must go? Is this the best that rationality has to offer? Or is it true, as Pascal said, that "the heart has reasons that Reason knows not of"? Can we delve deep into the abyss of the heart and expose the reasons that Reason sometimes denies?

I think we can. A clue is given us by the great English voice of conservatism Edmund Burke: "People will not look forward to posterity who never look backward to their ancestors." His aphorism asserts a sort of symmetry to the psyche. If people are so brought up that they feel a tie to the past, by symmetry they can perceive and acknowledge a similar tie to the future. By contrast, hard-headed rationalists live only in the present. To them, the remembrance of things past as well as concern for the distant future bespeaks a sort of mental corruption. It is not easy to refute this view, which tragically is shared by some of the most radical as well as some of the most reactionary people in our time.

Must we be concerned with posterity? It is always tempting to try to get others to do our will by bringing in the word *must*. Rationally it is more useful to point out the ecological implications of Burke's insight. If we want a community to care for the future, we must raise its members with a strong sense of place, of ancestry—with a pervasive feeling of connectedness with their origins. The managers of great enterprises, seeking the maximum economic "efficiency," are quite willing to treat people as objects, moving them around like so many pieces on a chessboard. The resulting mobility erodes the sense of place and past connectedness. When the past disappears, the future soon follows. Make a society fully mobile and you can kiss the redwood trees—and all that they stand for—goodbye.

A few years ago a journalist coined the phrase "the now generation." He intended it to be laudatory. Edmund Burke would surely view it in another light. So also must his spiritual descendants, people now called conservationists, environmentalists, and ecologists. Pure "nowness" to them indicates a spiritual poverty that should be deprecated. To such people the world is richer if the psyche has an enduring awareness both of the unalterable past and of a future that can, with effort and intelligence, be molded nearer to the heart's desire.

Guest Editorial Discussion

1. List some things other than redwood trees to which Garrett Hardin's analysis applies.

2. Why must we be concerned about posterity? Are you concerned? What actions are you taking now to show that your concern is real?

Discussion Topics

1. How does the ecological land-use ethic differ from the idea of a balanced multiple use of land and from the conservationist ethic?

2. Distinguish between wilderness and national parks in terms of purpose and allowed uses. Why should vast areas of wilderness be preserved?

3. Explain why few backpackers are getting back to nature in a fundamental sense. (Hint: Take a look at the technology involved in freeze-dried foods and Dacron-filled sleeping bags.) Should backpacking be encouraged?

4. Conservationists want people to know and appreciate wilderness, but they don't want wilderness areas intruded on by large numbers of people. How can this dilemma be resolved?

5. Discuss the pros and cons of each of the following suggestions for the use of national parks: (a) Charges should be made for use; (b) reservations should be required; (c) a quota system should be established; (d) all cars and other private vehicles should be kept out; and (e) campgrounds, lodges, and other facilities should be moved to nearby areas outside the parks.

6. Discuss the pros and cons of bringing "parks to the people" by establishing new parks around and in urban areas.

7. Argue for and against: (a) selling national forests to private interests, (b) selling national forests to state and local governments, (c) selling public lands for intensive agriculture, and (d) eliminating future purchases of new land by the federal government. In each case relate your decision to your own life-style and consumption habits.

8. Discuss some dangers of selective cutting and clear-cutting of forests. Outline a program for the management of the small tracts of privately owned woodlands, which make up 59 percent of the forests in the United States. Try to consult a local forester and visit nearby tracts.

9. Would you expect clear-cutting to increase or decrease the probability of large-scale destruction by wildfires? Explain.

10. How are fires both useful and damaging to a forest and its wildlife?

11. What would probably be major characteristics of trees that should be (a) clear-cut, (b) selectively cut, and (c) controlled by occasional ground fires?

12. What are some possible solutions to the firewood crisis, which is a major threat to the world's forests?

13. Because of the rising costs of oil, coal, and natural gas, more and more Americans are switching to wood stoves for heating and cooking. Discuss the pros and cons of this trend.

14. Should trail bikes, dune buggies, snowmobiles, and other off-road vehicles be banned from all national forests, national parks, and wilderness areas? Why?

15. Should regulations for the strip mining of coal be relaxed so that the United States can mine more coal to relieve its dependence on nuclear power and imported oil? Why?

16. Why should an urban dweller worry about clear-cutting? About estuary filling? About strip mines? About preserving wildlife?

17. Make a log of your own consumption for a single day and relate it to the increased demand for (a) clear-cutting, (b) destruction of wildlife, (c) surface mining, and (d) draining, filling, and dredging of estuarine areas.

18. What is the value of the Florida Everglades to us? The redwood forests? An estuary? An alligator? A whooping crane? A coyote? How would you explain this to a child? To a land developer? To a legislator? To a slum dweller?

19. Use Table 10-5 to predict a species that may soon be endangered. What, if anything, is being done for this species? What pressures is it being subjected to? Try to work up a plan for protecting it.

20. Give the pros and cons of hunting. Find out how much revenue your state fish and game department receives each year from taxes and from the sale of fishing and hunting licenses, and find out how this money is used.

21. Discuss each of the following statements:

   a. "We are not exploiters of a resource, we are harvesters of a resource at the behest of public demand." James R. Turnbull, executive vice-president of American Plywood Association.

   b. "We have the directive from God: Have dominion over the earth . . . replenish and subdue it . . . God has not given us these resources so we can merely watch their ecological succession." H. D. Bennett, executive vice-president of Appalachian Hardwood Manufacturers, Inc.

   c. "Preservationists are a selfish lot. Only a few are physically able or really want to have a wilderness experience. Ninety-nine percent of the people in New York City are never going to see it." Bernard L. Orell, vice-president of Weyerhauser Company.

   d. "If you've seen one redwood, you've seen them all." Ronald Reagan, President of the United States.

   e. We should not use public funds for buying up and preserving forests, wilderness areas, and estuaries when the less developed nations and the poor in this country are in such great need.

   f. "Reclamation of strip-mined land is like putting lipstick on a corpse." Representative Ken Hechler (Democrat, West Virginia).

22. Explain how you indirectly contribute to the destruction of tropical moist forests. What difference, if any, could the loss of these forests have on your life or on any child you might bring into the world?

23. Criticize the idea that since 80 to 90 precent of the species that have existed on earth have become extinct by natural selection, we should not be concerned about the several hundred species that have become extinct because of human activities.

Readings

Allen, Robert L. 1980. *How to Save the World*. London: Kogan Page. Superb presentation of a strategy to preserve more of the world's vanishing wildlife and land ecosystems.

Barlowe, Raleigh. 1972. *Land Resource Economics*. 2nd ed. Englewood Cliffs, N.J.: Prentice-Hall. Excellent basic reference on land use and land resources.

Brooks, Paul. 1980. *Speaking for Nature: How Literary Naturalists from Henry Thoreau to Rachel Carson Have Shaped America*. New York: Houghton Mifflin. Excellent overview.

Caldwell, Lynton K., et al. 1976. *Citizens and the Environment: Case Studies in Popular Action*. Bloomington: Indiana University Press. See chaps. 1, 2, and 5.

Clawson, Marion. 1975. *Forests for Whom and for What?* Baltimore: Johns Hopkins University Press. Excellent discussion of forest uses and policy.

Conservation Foundation. 1972. *National Parks for the Future*. Washington, D.C.: Conservation Foundation. Task force report outlining policy suggestions for national parks.

Dasmann, Raymond F. 1976. *Environmental Conservation*. 4th ed. New York: Wiley. One of the better books on land use and conservation. See chaps. 4, 7, 8, and 9.

Dasmann, Raymond F. 1981. *Wildlife Biology*. 2nd ed. New York: Wiley. Excellent introductory text.

Eckholm, Erik. 1975. *The Other Energy Crisis: Firewood*. Washington, D.C.: Worldwatch Society. Outstanding discussion of the cutting of the world's forests to provide firewood.

Eckholm, Erik. 1978. *Disappearing Species: The Social Challenge.* Washington, D.C.: Worldwatch Institute. One of the best overviews of the need for wildlife conservation.

Eckholm, Erik. 1979. *Planning for the Future: Forestry for Human Needs.* Washington, D.C.: Worldwatch Institute. Excellent suggestions for preserving and renewing more of the world's forests.

Ehrenfeld, David W. 1970. *Biological Conservation.* New York: Holt, Rinehart and Winston. One of the best introductions to conservation of land and wildlife.

Hardin, Garrett. 1968. "The Tragedy of the Commons." *Science*, vol. 162, 1243–1248. Classic environmental article describing how land and other resources are abused when they are shared by everyone.

Hendee, John, et al., eds. 1977. *Principles of Wilderness Management.* Washington, D.C.: Government Printing Office. Very useful collection of articles.

Iltis, Hugh H. 1972. "Wilderness: Can Man Do Without?" In David J. Allan and Arthur J. Hanson, eds., *Recycle This Book.* Belmont, Calif.: Wadsworth. An eloquent summary of why we need wilderness.

Joffe, Joyce. 1970. *Conservation.* Garden City, N.Y.: Natural History Press. Outstanding layperson's introduction to conservation of wildlife and resources.

Lang, Reg, and Audrey Armour. 1980. *Environmental Planning Resourcebook.* Montreal: Lands Directorate, Environment Canada. Excellent overview of resource and pollution problems with an emphasis on Canada.

Myers, Norman. 1979. *The Sinking Ark.* New York: Pergamon Press. Try to read this very important book on the disappearance of the world's tropical moist forests.

Nash, Roderick. 1973. *Wilderness and the American Mind.* 2nd ed. New Haven, Conn.: Yale University Press. The best book on American attitudes toward wilderness.

Nash, Roderick. 1979. "Problems in Paradise: Land Use and the American Dream." *Environment*, vol. 20, no. 6, 25–40. Excellent discussion of environmental problems that could arise if a large number of Americans move back to rural areas to farm the land.

National Academy of Sciences. 1980. *Conversion of Tropical Moist Forests.* Washington, D.C.: National Academy of Sciences. Authoritative discussion of the loss of the world's tropical moist forests and what can be done about it.

Owen, Oliver S. 1980. *National Resource Conservation: An Ecological Approach.* 3rd ed. New York: Macmillan. Outstanding basic text for the reader wanting more details.

Pimentel, David, et al. 1980. "Environmental Quality and Natural Biota." *BioScience*, vol. 30, no. 11, 750–755. Makes a strong case for evaluating the endangered status of microorganisms and invertebrates.

Simon, Anne W. 1978. *The Thin Edge: Coast and Man in Crisis.* New York: Harper & Row. Superb discussion of stresses on estuarine zones and possible solutions.

Smith, Robert Leo. 1976. "Ecological Genesis of Endangered Species: The Philosophy of Preservation." *Annual Reviews of Ecology and Systematics*, vol. 7, 33–56. Excellent discussion of how some species are vulnerable to extinction.

Spurr, Stephen H., and Burton V. Barnes. 1980. *Forest Ecology,* 3rd ed. New York: Ronald Press. Very good forestry text.

Surface Mining Research Library. 1972. *Energy and the Environment: What's the Strip Mining Controversy All About?* Charleston, W. Va.: Surface Mining Research Library. Balanced analysis and pictures showing both sides of the strip mining controversy.

Teal, J., and M. Teal. 1969. *Life and Death of a Salt Marsh.* New York: Ballantine. Superb description of estuaries.

Utetz, George, and Donald L. Johnson. 1974. "Breaking the Web." *Environment*, vol. 16, no. 10, 31–39. Excellent overview of wildlife extermination.

11

Urban Land Use: Urbanization, Urban Growth, and Land-Use Planning

Modern cities are centers of employment, education, and culture. But they are also centers of poverty, delinquency, crime, prostitution, alcoholism, and drug abuse. As a rule, cities offer less space, less daylight, less fresh air, less greenery, and more noise.

Georg Borgstrom

11-1 Urbanization and Urban Growth

The World Situation At the beginning of this century almost everyone on earth lived in the country. *By 1980 about 39 percent of the world's population lived in towns and cities. If present trends continue, by the close of this century at least half of the people in the world will live in urban areas, with perhaps half of these people unemployed or unable to earn a living wage.* To accommodate these new urban dwellers, between 1980 and 2000 the world will need housing, utilities, schools, hospitals, and commercial enterprises equivalent to building 1,600 cities of a million people each—an average of 80 such cities each year. This does not even include the rebuilding and revitalizing of today's cities. Clearly, such a task will be monumental.

Such figures, however, can be deceiving. We need to distinguish between urbanization and urban growth. **Urbanization** is the proportion of the total population concentrated in an urban area. An **urban area** is typically defined as any place with a population of 20,000 or more. **Urban growth** is the increase in size of the urban population.

By comparing Figures 11-1 and 11-2, we can see how the concepts of urbanization and urban growth differ. In 1980 the more developed nations were 69 percent urbanized and less developed nations were only 29 percent urbanized (Figure 11-1). By the year 2000 the urban population in the poor countries should be about twice that

in the rich countries (Figure 11-2), even though the degree of urbanization in the rich nations is expected to be about twice that in the poor nations (Figure 11-1). This difference is occurring because the less developed nations are simultaneously experiencing high population growth and a rapid migration of people into urban areas. Because poor nations are experiencing more urban growth (Figure 11-2), by the year 2000 they should contain about 2 billion, or two-thirds, of the world's urban dwellers. India and China alone should account for 60 percent of this urban growth.

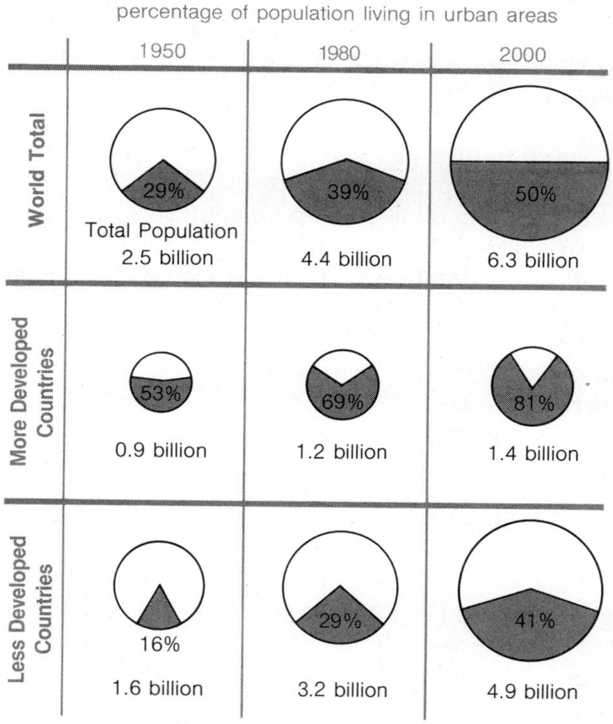

Figure 11-1 Percentage of world population living in cities in 1950, 1980, and 2000. Figures below pie graphs indicate total population.

Enrichment Studies 1, 3, 6, 9, 13, 14, and 15 are related to this chapter.

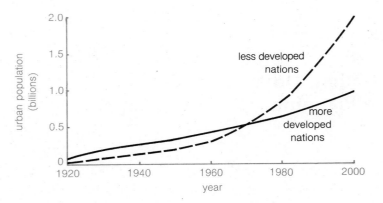

Figure 11-2 Urban population growth in more developed and less developed nations.

In 1980, 20 cities had populations greater than 7 million, with 11 of these in poor countries. By 2000 the world's largest cities will probably be in the less developed nations. By then, Mexico City (with 31 million people) should be the world's largest city, followed by Tokyo (24 million), Shanghai (23 million), São Paulo (21 million), and New York (21 million). Indeed, urban planner C. A. Doxiadis has predicted that if the world population continues to grow, cities will spread until they meet and form one large world city, separated only by physical barriers. This world city would have 20 to 30 billion inhabitants, a figure that is 5 to 8 times the present world population.

These figures obscure the great increase in human misery and despair that will result. Today at least one-third of the city dwellers in poor countries live in slums and shantytowns. The population of large cities in poor countries is doubling every 10 to 15 years, but the population of many of the urban slums in these cities is doubling in only 5 to 7 years. Adding 1.3 billion mostly poor and unskilled people to these already bloated centers of poverty between 1975 and 2000 could create unthinkable human suffering and death.

The U.S. Situation   In 1800 only 5 percent of the U.S. population lived in towns larger than 2,500. By 1980, 74 percent—three out of four Americans—lived in urban regions (Figure 11-3). By the year 2000 it is projected that 80 to 90 percent of all Americans will be living in urban regions. To appreciate this important shift, we need to define terms such as *urban area, rural area, metropolitan area, nonmetropolitan area,* and *urban region.*

The terms **rural area** and *country* refer to areas containing up to 2,500 people. In the United States, popu-

lation centers have decentralized into suburbs so much that these definitions are inadequate. A suburb or other area near a city may look rural because it is sparsely settled, when in fact most of its inhabitants commute to the city and participate in its economic and social life.

To remedy this semantic problem, the U.S. Bureau of the Census uses the terms *metropolitan area* and *nonmetropolitan area.* A **metropolitan area** is a city of 50,000 or more people plus surrounding counties or suburbs that are an integral part of the city's economic and social life. For example, in 1980 the city of New York had about 7.0 million people, but the city plus surrounding areas had about 23 million. A **nonmetropolitan area** is any area in which most inhabitants are not an integral part of the economic and social life of a city of at least 50,000 people. It may consist of one or several cities with less than 50,000 people, or it may be a rural area with no urban population.

Metropolitan areas can merge to form an **urban region** or *megalopolis*, a large zone of metropolitan areas separated only by occasional topographical barriers and containing at least 1 million people. In the United States the most heavily populated urban region is a 725-kilometer (450-mile) strip that stretches from Boston to Washington, D.C. (Figure 11-4). Sometimes called "BoWash," it includes 45 metropolitan areas that contained 42 million people in 1978—about one of every five Americans.

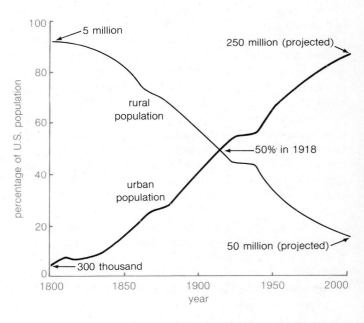

Figure 11-3 Percentage of the U.S. population in rural and urban regions between 1800 and 2000.

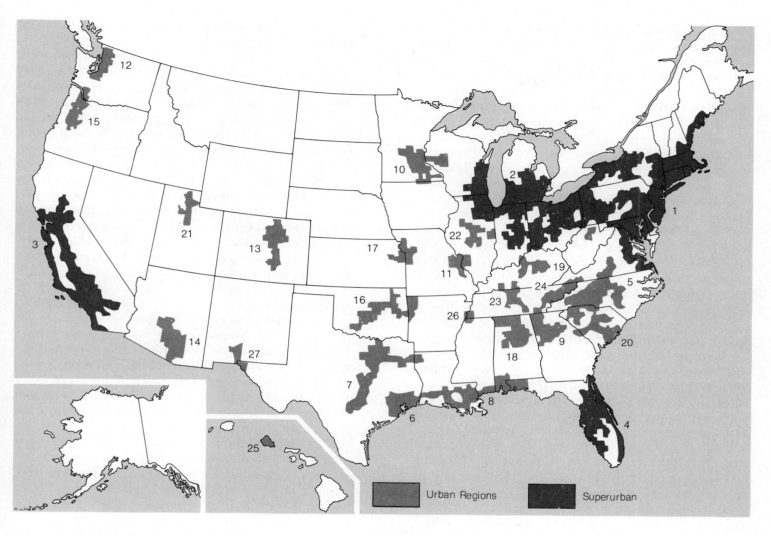

Figure 11-4 U.S. urban regions in order of decreasing population size. The five superurban regions are shown in a darker shade.

1. Atlantic Seaboard (BoWash)

2. Lower Great Lakes (ChiPitts or Midlands)

3. California Region (SanSan or Pacific)

4. Florida Peninsula (JaMi or Sunland)

5. Southern Piedmont (GrRa or Western Carolinas)

6. Gulf Coast West (Houston-Galveston Bay)

7. Mid-Texas (Dallas-San Antonio)

8. Gulf Coast East (New Orleans-Florida)

9. Central Dixie (Atlanta-Chattanooga)

10. Twin Cities (Minneapolis-St. Paul)

11. St. Louis (Missouri-Illinois area)

12. Puget Sound (Western Washington)

13. Colorado Piedmont

14. Metropolitan Arizona

15. Willamette Valley

16. Central Oklahoma-Arkansas Valley

17. Missouri-Kaw Valley

18. Northern Alabama

19. Blue Grass

20. Southern Coastal Plain

21. Salt Lake Valley

22. Central Illinois

23. Nashville Region

24. East Tennessee

25. Oahu Island

26. Memphis

27. El Paso-Ciudad Juarez

Its average population density in 1978 was 349 people per square kilometer (805 per square mile), compared with an average 19 people per square kilometer (49 per square mile) for the rest of the country.

Figure 11-4 also shows five other major urban regions: (1) "ChiPitts" or "Midlands," a belt from Chicago to Pittsburgh containing 36 million people, or 16 percent of the U.S. population, (2) "SanSan," stretching from San Francisco to San Diego, which has about 20 million people, or 9 percent of the U.S. population; (3) "JaMi" or "Sunland," which stretches along Florida's eastern coast from Jacksonville to Miami, which has 7.1 million people, or 3 percent of the U.S. population; (4) "HoGa" or Gulf Coast West region around Houston, with 3.3 million people or 1.5 percent of the U.S. population; and (5) "GrRa" or "Southern Piedmont," which stretches from Greenville, S.C., to Raleigh, N.C., and contains 3.1 million people, or 1.4 percent of the U.S. population. In 1978, 48 percent of the U.S. population lived in these 5 urban regions. The 27 urban regions shown in Figure 11-4 contained about 72 percent of the population in 1980.

Between 1800 and 1970, urban growth took place in two major phases: the *country-to-city shift* and the *central-city-to-suburbs shift*. From 1800 to 1950, about 70 percent of the U.S. population moved from rural areas to cities. Then, between 1950 and 1970, large numbers of middle and upper class citizens began moving from central cities to suburbs to form what are now called metropolitan areas. Suburbanites outnumbered central city residents for the first time in the 1970 census. This second shift occurred because of several factors: (1) the building of roads and freeways made possible by the National Highway Act; (2) the GI housing bill that subsidized single-family dwellings for middle class Americans; (3) the rapidly expanding economy of the 1950s and 1960s, which allowed people to buy homes outside the city; (4) dissatisfaction with high living costs, increased crime, poor schools, and deteriorating conditions in central cities; and (5) the desire of most Americans to live in a small town or suburban setting and still have the economic and cultural advantages of a large city.

During the 1970s three new shifts began to take place: (1) The growth rate of metropolitan areas slowed, and some of the largest areas, such as New York, Chicago, and Philadelphia, lost population; (2) people in metropolitan and nonmetropolitan areas began moving from the north central and northeastern regions to the southern and western regions sometimes called the "Sun Belt" (between 1970 and 1980, population increased 20 percent in the West, 15 percent in the South, and 3.4 percent in the Midwest; it declined 0.3 percent in the Northeast); and (3) people began moving from metropolitan to nonmetropolitan areas.

This third metropolitan-to-nonmetropolitan shift may have the greatest impact on land use. Between 1970 and 1980, about 3 million more people moved from metropolitan to nonmetropolitan areas than from nonmetropolitan to metropolitan. The apparent reasons for this new shift include: (1) disenchantment with deteriorating conditions and high living costs in cities; (2) more jobs in rural areas and small cities (especially jobs related to retirement settlements, recreation, and energy resources) as cities lost factories; and (3) advanced communications technology and the interstate highway system, which make it easier and often advantageous for a firm or family to locate outside of a metropolitan area.

There is talk of a shift back toward the central city in the 1980s as a result of (1) rising energy costs, which make commuting to the city for work too expensive; (2) the increasing number of young, childless working couples who wish to be near their work and the excitement of big cities; (3) "empty nesters" wishing to move from the suburbs back to the cities after raising their children; and (4) the increasing use of federal funds and tax breaks to help redevelop businesses in selected parts of many major cities. It remains to be seen whether these factors will be powerful enough to reverse or slow down the present shift to rural areas.

The long-range effects of this metropolitan-to-nonmetropolitan shift are hard to predict. Some nonmetropolitan counties, especially those not too far from large cities, will merely become metropolitan areas—often against the wishes of most residents. The influx of people to some rural counties will strain local governments' ability to provide schools, houses, sewage disposal, and other services. Indeed, an increasing number of small towns and rural areas have been so alarmed by this "rural urbanization" that they have tried to discourage or halt further growth.

11-2 The Urban Environment: Benefits and Stresses

Benefits of Cities Throughout history, people have flooded into cities to find jobs. Cities bring together people with many different skills and talents who set up factories to produce the countless number of manufactured goods used by all people.

However, a city is not just an economic center; it can also be a physical and social center. Those who get good jobs and do well are often enthusiastic about living in the city. It provides them with pleasant places to live, an incredible variety of goods and services, and an exciting diversity of social and cultural activities. In addition, these social and cultural activities enrich the lives of people who live far from city boundaries.

Urban Problems and Stresses Cities also concentrate a wide range of social and environmental problems, such as poverty, crowding, crime, inadequate transportation and housing, unsanitary conditions, poor mental and physical health, ethnic tensions, noise, air pollution, water pollution, and solid wastes (Table 11-1). Such problems are not peculiar to cities, but cities intensify them. Cities also have harmful effects on land areas and people beyond their boundaries (Table 11-1), fouling the air and water of surrounding areas and gobbling up valuable farmland, forests, wetlands, and estuaries as they expand (Chapter 10).

Urban Problems in Poor Countries In the more developed nations, urbanization and urban growth have traditionally been an index of industrialization and modernization. As the industrial revolution progressed, people were drawn to cities to take advantage of job opportunities. In poor countries today, people are being *pushed* rather than *pulled* into the cities. Uncontrolled population growth and a decrease in available jobs in overpopulated rural areas are forcing millions of people to migrate from the countryside into cities, where most cannot find jobs. For this rapidly growing number of urban poor, the city becomes a trap of poverty and misery—not an oasis of economic opportunity and cultural diversity. They are forced to live on the streets or crowd into the *callampas* (mushroom cities) of Chile, the *favelas* of Brazil, the *gourbivilles* of Tunisia, the *barriadas* of Peru, and the *gecekindu* (meaning "built between dusk and dawn") of Turkey.

The names of these human anthills may vary, but their inhabitants all face poverty, grubbing for food and fuel, overcrowded housing, open sewers, untreated drinking water taken from filthy sources, intestinal and other contagious diseases, and little access to schools and hospitals. Ironically, expanded services may do little to improve conditions, since they merely attract even more of the rural poor to the city.

In the past, cities have helped rural areas by exchanging goods and services for food, energy, and mineral resources. Today, more and more cities are beginning to

Table 11-1 Problems of Urban Growth and Urbanization

Problem	Text Discussion
Inside the Cities	
Inadequate water supply	Chapter 15
Inadequate energy supply	Chapters 13, 14
Inadequate housing	Sections 11-2, 11-3
Inadequate transportation	Section 11-4
Lack of recreation and open space	Chapter 10; Enrichment Study 14
Damage from floods and earthquakes	Chapter 15
Air pollution	Chapter 17; Enrichment Study 5
Water pollution	Chapter 16; Enrichment Studies 5, 16
Solid wastes	Enrichment Study 15
Climatic change	Chapter 17; Enrichment Study 3
Potential for disease epidemics	Enrichment Study 6
Noise	Enrichment Study 13
Crowding	Section 8-1
Poverty	Sections 7-5, 8-4, 11-2; Enrichment Study 9
Crime	Section 11-2
Racial tensions	Section 11-2; Enrichment Study 9
Mental stress and drug abuse	Enrichment Study 6
Outside the Cities	
Loss of agricultural land	Section 9-6
Threats to wilderness, forests, parks, estuaries, and wildlife	Chapter 10; Enrichment Studies 12, 14
Surface mining	Section 10-5
Use of pesticides and herbicides	Enrichment Study 11
Ecosystem simplification	Chapters 6, 10

exchange more of their goods and services (except for food) with one another rather than with nearby rural areas. Thus, many cities in poor countries suck resources from the rural areas and give little in return.

Urban growth in poor nations, however, is not a total disaster. Although it does not provide enough jobs, the city usually offers its residents more opportunities than do rural areas. In spite of urban horrors, shantytown residents cling to life with incredible resourcefulness, tenacity, and hope. Most of them are convinced that the city can offer, possibly for themselves and certainly for their children, the only chance of a better life. Urban dwellers also tend to have fewer children and can be more readily reached by family planning and population control programs. In the long run, this can help prevent population growth from swamping economic growth.

Coping with Urbanization in Poor Countries The urban and rural problems of poor countries constitute some of the most complex economic, political, social, and ecological challenges in the world. The governments of all nations tend to believe that these problems can be solved by urban economic development—an attempt to follow the demographic transition model of the rich nations (Section 8-2). This belief is based on four assumptions: (1) Population growth will be brought under control within the next 30 years; (2) the people in cities will be fed by food surpluses created by the green revolution; (3) cheap energy will be available to allow energy-intensive urban development; and (4) rapid industrialization in the cities will provide enough jobs.

Unfortunately, recent trends indicate that none of these assumptions are valid. The rate of population growth in poor nations has only decreased slightly (Chapter 8); the ability of rural land to grow food is being decreased by erosion, cutting trees for fuel (Section 10-4), and other abuses; energy is becoming too expensive for most poor nations; and most rich countries are decreasing foreign aid as a percentage of their GNP.

Instead of concentrating on urban development, the major emphasis should be on rural development. This effort should include reforestation, water supply development, solar energy for cooking, population control, better health services and education, land ownership by each family rather than by large landowners, and loans to small farmers and businesses rather than to large businesses. The rich countries should liberalize trade for agricultural and light industrial products, and increase their aid to poor countries for rural development. These actions should attract people back to the countryside, make poor individuals and countries more self-reliant in producing their own food (Chapter 9), and require less use of expensive and scarce energy resources. *The guiding principle for helping poor countries to deal with the related problems of food, poverty, water, energy, and housing should be to help them to help themselves.*

Within the cities, governments should provide shantytown residents with food, safe water supplies and sewerage, schooling, and hospitals. Instead of building fancy housing projects, governments should provide slum residents with the materials to build or expand their own homes, according to their own designs.

11-3 Urban Systems and Natural Ecosystems

Is an Urban System an Ecosystem? A number of ecologists and urban experts treat cities and urban regions as ecosystems. Other ecologists argue that while an urban system has some characteristics of a natural ecosystem, it is not a true ecosystem.

Much of this disagreement depends on how we define an ecosystem. In Section 4-1 an ecosystem was defined as a community of plants and animals interacting with one another and with their environment. Technically, a city meets the requirements of this definition, but there are some important differences between natural ecosystems and urban ecosystems.

Unlike natural ecosystems, cities do not have enough producers (green plants) to support their inhabitants. Cities may have a few trees, lawns, and parks, but these are not used as food for humans. As an unknown observer remarked, "Cities are places where they cut down the trees and then name the streets after them." Some cities are even replacing their shrubs and grass with plastic plants and Astroturf. This is unfortunate, since urban plants, grasses, and trees absorb some air pollutants, give off oxygen, help cool the air by evaporating water from their leaves, muffle noise, and satisfy an important psychological need for urban dwellers, whose artificial environment cuts them off from nature. The lack of producers in cities also means that the input of solar energy is largely wasted, in sharp contrast to its use for photosynthesis in natural ecosystems (Chapter 5).

Cities also lack animals or consumers that can be used as food for their human population. Without enough producers and consumers, urban systems survive only by importing food from external plant-growing ecosystems located throughout the world.

Cities must also obtain fresh air, water, minerals, and energy resources from outside areas. At the same time, they must export their solid, liquid, and gaseous waste products and waste heat (Figures 11-5 and 11-6). The massive matter and energy inputs required to sustain life in a city result in intensified levels of pollution (entropy) in accordance with the second energy law (Section 3-3). As the entire urban system begins to break down from entropy overload, more and more money and energy are put into maintenance, repair, and health care. This in turn creates even more environmental disorder and de-

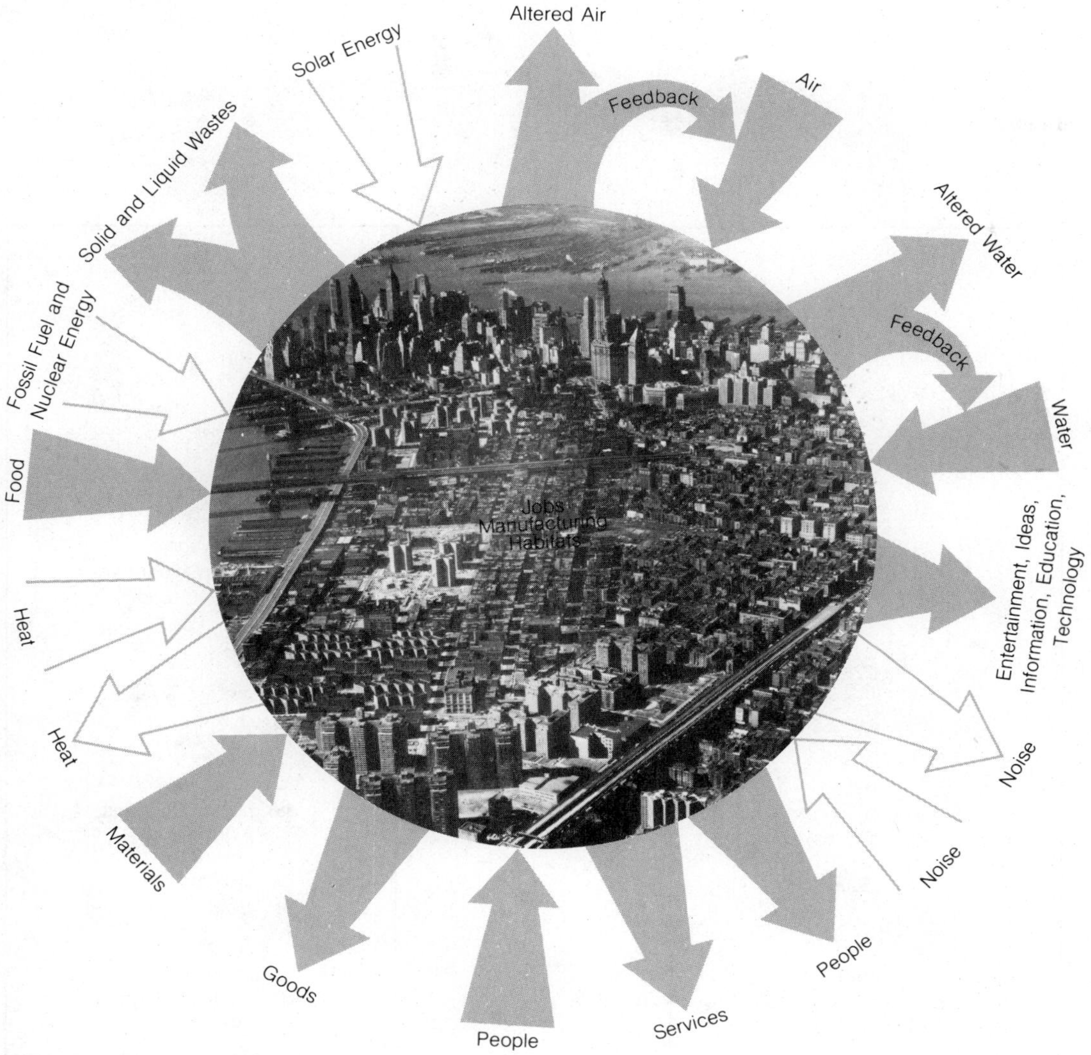

Figure 11-5 Some major matter (shaded arrows) and energy (unshaded arrows) inputs and outputs for a city.

Labels around the figure: Altered Air, Solar Energy, Feedback, Air, Solid and Liquid Wastes, Altered Water, Fossil Fuel and Nuclear Energy, Feedback, Water, Food, Entertainment, Ideas, Information, Education, Technology, Heat, Jobs, Manufacturing, Habitats, Heat, Noise, Materials, Noise, Goods, People, People, Services, People

Department of Housing and Urban Development

pletes high-quality energy resources even faster. For example, the construction and maintenance of America's buildings (most of which are in urban areas) require about 57 percent of all the electricity produced in the United States each year.

Without such inputs and outputs of matter and energy a city collapses, as shown by occasional electrical power failures and air pollution alerts in New York City and water shortages in San Francisco. In exchange for such life supports, cities provide goods, services, information, manufacturing, technology, and entertainment for outlying towns and farms (Figure 11-5). Future shortages of energy and matter resources (especially water and some metals) may force cities to use matter more

efficiently, to make better use of solar energy, and to reduce the flows of matter and energy through them (Enrichment Study 15).

Urban Habitats, Niches, and Spatial Structure By analogy, we can apply the ecosystem characteristics of habitat, niche (Section 5-5), and spatial structure (Enrichment Study 2) to urban systems. A city has habitats where its dominant population of humans lives and works. These inhabitants also have various structural and functional roles, or niches. In a natural ecosystem we usually find many different species, each occupying different roles or niches. By contrast, urban systems have

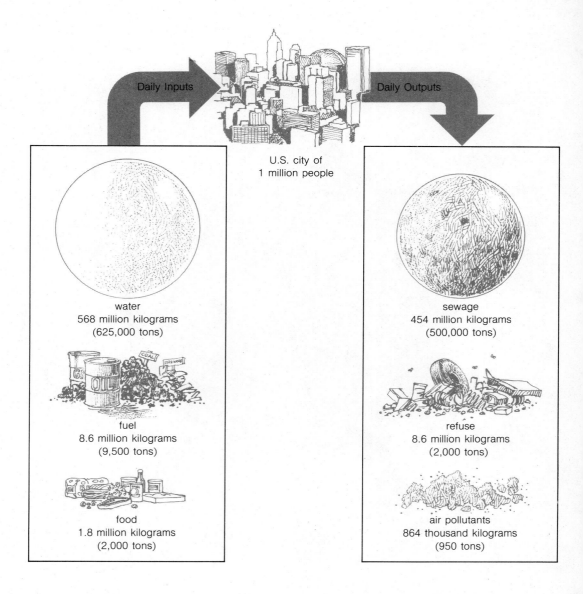

Figure 11-6 Typical daily inputs and outputs for a U.S. city of 1 million people.

Daily Inputs

Daily Outputs

U.S. city of
1 million people

water
568 million kilograms
(625,000 tons)

fuel
8.6 million kilograms
(9,500 tons)

food
1.8 million kilograms
(2,000 tons)

sewage
454 million kilograms
(500,000 tons)

refuse
8.6 million kilograms
(2,000 tons)

air pollutants
864 thousand kilograms
(950 tons)

one major species whose individuals occupy many different niches.

Like natural ecosystems, cities have a recognizable spatial and physical structure—they are not just random accumulations of buildings, roads, and people. The spatial organization includes places of production, commerce, residence, education, and leisure.

Three classic models of city spatial structure are the concentric circle model, the sector model, and the multiple nuclei model (Figure 11-7). A city resembling the *concentric circle model* develops outward from its center in a series of rings. The industries and businesses in the center zone are surrounded by zones of housing that improve as we move outward. These zones are not static; as the city grows, the entire system spreads out. A city resembling the *sector model* is a system of pie-shaped wedges, or sectors, that are formed when high-, intermediate-, and low-rent districts push out from the center along major transportation routes. In the *multiple nuclei model*, a large city develops around a number of independent centers, or nuclei, rather than a single center. Although no city perfectly matches any of these simplified models, the models can be used to identify key structural characteristics. If you should fly over or visit a city, see which (if any) of these models best describes its spatial form.

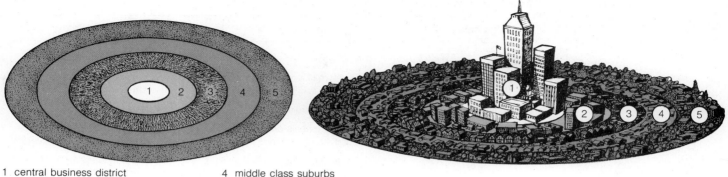

1 central business district
2 deteriorating transition zone
3 workers' homes
4 middle class suburbs
5 commuters' zone

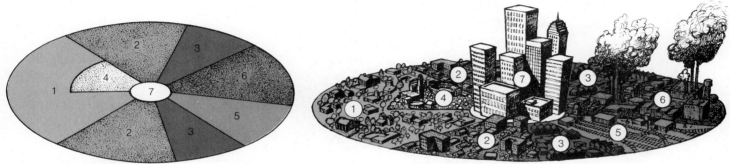

1 high-rent residential
2 intermediate-rent residential
3 low-rent residential
4 education and recreation
5 transportation
6 industrial
7 core

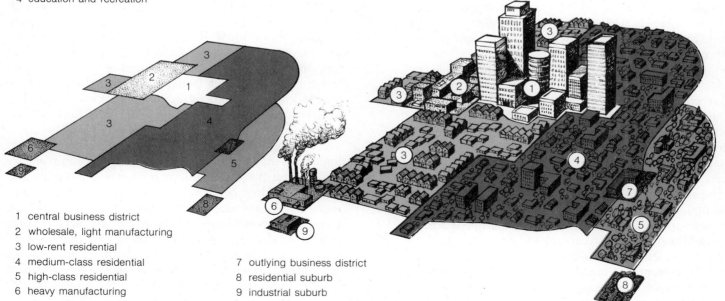

1 central business district
2 wholesale, light manufacturing
3 low-rent residential
4 medium-class residential
5 high-class residential
6 heavy manufacturing
7 outlying business district
8 residential suburb
9 industrial suburb

Figure 11-7 Some models of urban spatial structure. (Modified with permission from Harm J. deBlij, *Human Geography,* 1977, New York: Wiley.)

Table 11-2 Characteristics of Immature and Mature Urban Systems

Characteristic	Immature	Mature
Structure		
Structural diversity	Low (small low-rise structures)	High (large high-rise and small low-rise structures)
Productivity	High and rapidly increasing	Moderate and stable
Business diversity	Low (emphasis on production to build structures and profits)	High (diverse mix of production, manufacturing, and services)
Population	Small and rapidly growing	Moderate to fairly large with stabilized growth
Spatial diversity (population distribution)	Dispersed	Compact
Spatial efficiency	Low	High
Energy Flow		
Economic growth rate	High	Low to moderate
Energy efficiency	Low	High
Community organization	Low	High
Matter Cycling		
Rate of matter flow through system	High	Low to moderate
Amount of matter recycling	Low	High

Urban Succession and Diversity Natural ecosystems tend to evolve and change in response to environmental changes; this phenomenon is called ecological succession (Section 6-1). Urban systems also respond to economic and social change. By analogy, we can describe such urban development as economic and social succession. A city, like a biological community undergoing secondary succession (Section 6-1), begins as an immature pioneer settlement when land is cleared.

Just as undisturbed natural ecosystems often evolve toward biological maturity, diversity, and stability, so can cities evolve toward economic and social maturity, diversity, and stability. Table 11-2 compares some of the properties of immature and mature urban systems (as was done earlier in Table 6-1 for immature and mature ecosystems). Note from Table 11-2 that the early stages of city development are characterized by high productivity (to build the necessary structures and products), few services, inefficient use of matter and energy resources, very little community organization, and a rapid outward spread of small structures. By contrast, mature cities have a diverse mix of businesses, use matter and energy resources efficiently, and tend to be fairly compact with a mix of large (high-rise) and small (low-rise) structures.

Unfortunately, no major cities in the world today appear to have reached the mature stage shown in Table 11-2, although many cities have a few aspects of such maturity. With their emphasis on productivity or economic growth, most of today's cities seem locked in a pattern of immaturity that wastes vast amounts of matter and energy resources and produces high levels of pollution (entropy). This is happening in a world where survival now depends on maintaining a more healthful environment and on using increasingly scarce and expensive matter and energy resources more efficiently.

The solutions to many of the world's urban and ecological ills may lie in the development of urban maturity by (1) using matter and energy resources to maintain and renovate existing city structures and to develop interconnections within the community rather than blindly trying to increase economic growth at all costs; (2) promoting economic stability by making sure there is a diverse mix of production, manufacturing, and service businesses; (3) using organic waste matter as a resource by either burning organic garbage to produce electricity or, better yet, using it (along with sewage plant effluents) as fertilizer for urban gardens on vacant lots and on farmlands on the outskirts of the cities (see Enrichment Study

16); (4) recycling inorganic resources such as metals, paper, and water (see Enrichment Study 15); (5) reducing the waste of matter and energy resources by emphasizing matter and energy conservation (see Section 14-1); (6) increasing spatial efficiency to reduce matter and energy waste by making cities more compact (but with planned open spaces); (7) increasing emphasis on mass transit, bicycling, and walking instead of allowing uncontrolled urban sprawl based on the widespread use of energy-wasting automobiles; (8) promoting cultural diversity through a mix of educational, artistic, and entertainment opportunities that allow the human creative potential to develop fully; and (9) developing a better community organization to open lines of communication between industry, business, agriculture, and services as well as between races, ages, and social strata in order to help prevent strife, exploitation, and injustice.

As an urban area continues to spread out, it can become unstable, and its services can begin to break down, especially in the central city. Let's look at one way in which this can happen. In the early stages of urban growth, housing, industry, and employment increase rapidly. As the original central city housing deteriorates, middle and upper class residents leave and build residences in new rings, wedges, or nuclei beyond the city core (Figure 11-7). Since economic growth and diversity require specialized skills, the unskilled poor that are left in the central city are unable to find work. Rising unemployment generates the need for welfare, housing, and other expenditures. More poor people may be drawn to the central city to take advantage of these benefits. Since there are no new tax revenues to absorb this new financial load, the city government raises business and private property taxes. More landowners and businesses flee the city to avoid the high taxes; deteriorating schools, services, and public transportation; crime; and social tension. Central city unemployment levels and tax rates continue to rise, and more people and businesses leave as the vicious cycle continues.

Freeways and mass transit systems are built so that suburbanites can commute to their city jobs. This encourages the flight to the suburbs. Since the freeways and mass transit systems are usually built through poor neighborhoods, the poor suffer loss of housing, increased air pollution, noise, and other environmental insults. Also, as freeways grow, the transit system within the city usually deteriorates, and the poor (who still have jobs) have a hard time getting to and from work. Since the young, more affluent residents tend to move out of the central city, it becomes a dumping ground and trap for poor minority groups and elderly persons.

Crime increases, unemployment rises, and the city is forced to spend even more to keep down the disorder, as one would predict from the second law of energy (Section 3-3). This model of urban growth and decay is typical for cities in the rich nations. By contrast, in most poor nations the middle class and affluent tend to live in the central city with the poor living in surrounding slums.

Sometimes cities in the more developed nations try to improve the slums by urban renewal, which often tears down old buildings and replaces them with poorly planned high-rise public housing projects. A few of these projects have been successful, but many have been disasters. They disrupt families and the protective and useful neighborhood structure and often have high rents that the poor can't afford. In St. Louis, a $36 million urban renewal project of 43 high-rise apartment buildings became an urban jungle. Much of it had to be abandoned, demolished, and rebuilt on a smaller scale at a cost of $39 million.

The outlook for high-rise housing developments, however, need not be totally bleak. Some of the abandoned developments have been converted to play schools and commercial buildings, where a group of small businesses can share receptionists, restaurants, and maintenance and other operating costs. In Jersey City, a rundown high-rise project with a high crime rate was turned around by a tenant committee. The tenants themselves replaced broken-out windows with unbreakable plastic glass, installed indoor and outdoor lights that could not be broken and easily removed, repaired broken elevators and rubbish chutes, repainted the entire building, and planted grass and flowers; they also found employment for some tenants in building managerial and service jobs. Dozens of other projects have formed successful tenant-management groups in other cities.

Cities as Incomplete Ecosystems We have seen that urban systems are essentially like ecosystems. But as they exist today, urban systems are artificial, immature, and inefficient ecosystems that waste matter and energy. Also, since they depend on outside areas for their matter and energy inputs and outputs, they are not self-sustaining. In the words of Theodore Roszak:

The supercity . . . stretches out tentacles of influence that reach thousands of miles beyond its already sprawling perimeters. It sucks every hinterland and wilderness into its technological metabolism. It forces rural populations off the land and replaces them with vast agroindustrial combines. Its investments and technicians bring the roar of the bulldozer and oil derrick into the most uncharted quarters.

Table 11-3 Major Forms of Urban Transportation

Type	Advantages	Disadvantages
Individual Transit		
Automobile and taxi	Allows freedom of movement (door-to-door service) Convenient Usually not crowded Can carry one or several people	Requires much land (highways, parking areas, etc.) Wastes energy and matter resources Pollutes air Promotes urban sprawl Increasingly expensive to buy and operate or to hire
Motorcycle and moped	Allows freedom of movement Convenient Less expensive to buy and operate than car Uses and wastes less matter and energy resources than car Requires relatively little land Pollutes less than car	Rider not sheltered from weather, noise, and air pollution Carries only 1 or 2 persons Less protection from injury
Bicycle	Allows freedom of movement Convenient As fast as car in urban trips less than 8 km (5 mi) Very inexpensive to buy and operate Provides exercise Conserves energy and matter resources Requires little land Nonpolluting	Does not shelter rider from weather, noise, and air pollution Carries only 1 or 2 persons Provides less protection from injury Slow for trips greater than 8 km (5 mi)
Walking or running	Allows freedom of movement Convenient for short trips Free Provides exercise Conserves energy and matter resources Requires very little land Nonpolluting	Slow and difficult for long trips Does not protect from weather, noise, and air pollution
Mass Transit		
Railroad and subway (heavy rail systems)	Handles large number of passengers Rapid once boarded and if on time Safer than car Fairly inexpensive for rider Uses fewer matter and energy resources than car Requires much less land than car Pollutes less than car	Very expensive to build and operate Economically feasible only along heavily populated routes Lacks door-to-door service Requires fixed routes Can be crowded and noisy
Trolley and streetcar (light rail systems)	Handles large number of passengers Fairly rapid once boarded and if on time Safer than car Fairly inexpensive for rider Uses fewer energy and matter resources than car Requires less land than car Pollutes relatively little if electric Cheaper to build and operate than railroad and subway	Expensive to build and operate Economically feasible only along heavily populated routes Lacks door-to-door service Requires fixed routes Can be crowded and noisy
Bus	Handles large number of passengers Has more flexible routes than railroad and trolley Safer than car Fairly inexpensive for rider Uses fewer energy and matter resources than car Requires less land than car Normally cheaper to build and operate than railroads	Fairly expensive to build and operate Lacks door-to-door service Fairly fixed routes Often not on time Can be crowded and noisy Pollutes air

Table 11-3 Major Forms of Urban Transportation

Type	Advantages	Disadvantages
Para Transit		
Carpools and vanpools	Carries small group of people Saves money Wastes fewer energy and matter resources than car Provides social interaction	Fairly inconvenient Promotes urban sprawl Requires much land Pollutes air Wastes matter and energy resources
Dial-a-ride (minibuses, vans, jitneys, and shared taxicab systems)	Handles small to moderate number of passengers Safer than car Moderately inexpensive for rider Usually provides door-to-door service Uses fewer energy and matter resources than car Requires less land than car Cheaper to build and operate than railroad Very useful for the poor, young, elderly, and handicapped	Fairly expensive to operate Can require long waits Can be crowded and noisy Pollutes air

It runs its conduits of transport and communication, its lines of supply and distribution through the wildest landscapes. It flushes its waste into every river, lake, and ocean or trucks them away into desert areas. The world becomes its garbage can.

Urban systems can be classified as self-sustaining ecosystems only if we expand their boundaries to include (1) the farmlands, forests, mines, watersheds, and other areas throughout the world that provide their input materials and (2) the air, rivers, oceans, and soil that absorb their massive output of wastes. This should remind us that *none of the world's cities can completely sustain themselves, even if they should become more ecologically mature* (Table 11-2).

11-4 Urban Transportation

Transportation Options   People in urban systems move from one place to another by three major types of transportation: *individual transit* (private automobile, taxi, motorcycle, moped, bicycle, and walking); *mass transit* (railroad, subway, trolley, and bus), which moves large groups of people; and *para transit* (carpools, vanpools, and dial-a-ride systems), which moves small groups of people. Each type has certain advantages and disadvantages, as summarized in Table 11-3.

Effects of Automobiles on Cities   By providing almost unlimited mobility, the automobile has been a major factor in the urban sprawl that characterizes most American

cities. Most suburbanites and many people living in nonmetropolitan areas now depend almost completely on the private automobile to get to work, schools, and shopping centers, which are sprawled over vast areas of land. In the United States the car is used for about 90 percent of all personal travel, 97.5 percent of all urban travel, and 85 percent of the travel between cities. Despite the world energy crisis, the average American family now travels an average of 15,000 kilometers (9,500 miles) a year and spends more on transportation than on food. For the typical American, the automobile provides privacy and freedom of movement, and for many it is also a status symbol. In 1979, there were about 140 million motor vehicles in the United States—half of all those in the world.

The automobile provides many advantages, as shown in Table 11-3. In addition, the U.S. economy is built around the car. One out of every five dollars spent in the United States is related directly or indirectly to the automobile industry or related industries (oil, steel, rubber, plastics, and highway construction). This giant industrial complex accounts for about 31 percent of all energy used and 20 percent of the annual gross national product (GNP), provides about 18 percent of all federal taxes, and employs about 22 percent of the total U.S. work force. It is no wonder that British author J. B. Priestly remarked, "In America, the cars have become the people."

In spite of its advantages, the automobile has a number of harmful effects on human lives and on air, water, and land. By fostering urban sprawl, the automobile has been a key factor in the decline of mass transit systems in the central cities, where up to 60 percent of the population does not own a car. Forty years ago most people lived close enough so that they could walk or take a trolley to work. Today most people are so spread out in the suburbs that they must often drive their cars 32 kilometers (20 miles) or more to work. Without cars and adequate public transportation, almost 100 million poor, young, elderly, and handicapped Americans do not enjoy the freedom of travel for work and pleasure that other Americans have. In addition, each year about 51,000 mostly poor Americans are displaced from their homes to make way for highways that most of them don't use. Motor vehicles also kill about 50,000 Americans and injure about 2 million each year at a cost of about $45 billion annually in lost income, insurance, and administrative and legal expenses.

Since the automobile was introduced, almost 2 million Americans have been killed on the highways—about twice the number killed in all U.S. wars. Automobile accidents are the leading cause of death among Americans under age 35 and the sixth leading cause of death for the entire U.S. population. The world's 302 million cars kill an average of 170,000 people, permanently maim 500,000, and injure 7 million each year.

Motor vehicles also use vast amounts of mineral and energy resources, including 56 percent of the petroleum, 72 percent of the rubber, 30 percent of the zinc, and almost 20 percent of the aluminum used each year in the United States. But cars are so inefficient (Section 3-3) that they waste 90 percent of the energy available in gasoline. Automobiles also produce about 85 percent (by weight) of the air pollution in many cities (Chapter 17) and about 85 percent of all urban noise (Enrichment Study 13). Furthermore, over 6 million junked cars litter the countryside (Enrichment Study 15).

Motor vehicles also have a horrendous appetite for land. Roads and parking spaces take up over half the land in Dallas and Los Angeles and over a third of New York City and Washington, D.C. Highways cover about 9 million square kilometers (3.5 million square miles) of land in the United States, an area equal to Vermont, New Hampshire, Connecticut, Massachusetts, and Rhode Island. This system also gobbles up money. Between 1956 and 1973, the United States spent over $200 billion to build local, state, and federal highways, and between 1973 and 1985 an estimated $294 billion will be needed to maintain existing roads and to build new ones.

Building more highways and freeways encourages more automobiles and travel, and the resulting congestion decreases the average automobile speed in many urban areas. According to former New York Transportation Director Arthur E. Palmer, "In 1907, the average speed of horse drawn vehicles through New York City's streets was 18.5 kilometers per hour [11.5 miles per hour]. In 1966 the average speed of motor vehicles (with the power of 200 to 300 horses) through the central business district was 13.7 kilometers per hour [8.5 miles per hour]—and during the midday crushes slower still." Like energy-intensive agriculture (Section 9-2), the American transportation system has become more and more energy inefficient. During the past 35 years, Americans have switched from reliance on energy-efficient railroads to inefficient cars, trucks, and airplanes. As a result, the automobile industry and related industries are together the single greatest producer of entropy in American society.

There are three basic methods for reducing the problems created by the automobile: (1) Encourage the use of bicycles and develop urban mass and para transit systems; (2) discourage automobile use; and (3) reduce pollution and energy and matter waste in automobiles. Let's look more closely at these options.

Bicycles and Mopeds The leg-powered bicycle won't replace cars in urban areas, but its use could be greatly increased. Indeed, between 1969 and 1979, more bicycles were sold in the United States than cars. The bicycle uses no fossil fuels and only small amounts of resources, and is very useful for trips under 8 kilometers (5 miles), which make up about 43 percent of all urban trips. In traffic, cars and bicycles both travel at about the same average speed, 21 kilometers per hour (13 miles per hour). To increase the use of bicycles, city governments should build bicycle paths. In 1975, only 470,000 people—roughly 0.6 percent of all commuters—biked to work in the United States. But with more bike paths and secure bike parking (to prevent theft), the U.S. Department of Transportation believes that the number of bike commuters could be increased to over 2 million by 1985. Davis, California, setting an example for the rest of the United States, has 28,000 bicycles, wide bicycle lanes, and some streets closed to automobiles for its population of 35,000. As a result, cycling accounts for about one-fourth of all travel in Davis.

Mass Transit Because of the switch to cars since 1950, the number of riders on all forms of mass transit (buses, subways, and trolleys) declined from about 19.5 billion passengers in 1950 to about 6.6 billion passengers in 1975. By 1979, ridership had climbed back up to about 8 billion per year.

In many cities mass transit systems have either gone

out of business or cut back their services. A vicious circle sets in. As the number of riders decreases, operating costs and fares rise. Service deteriorates, causing the number of riders to decline even further.

Urban mass transportation is a complex and controversial problem. Some see *fixed-rail rapid transit systems* as the key to urban transportation problems. Others argue that such technological solutions are extremely expensive and do not serve many people in today's spread-out cities. They are primarily useful where many people live along a narrow corridor, and even then their high construction and operating costs may outweigh their benefits.

Problems with the new Bay Area Rapid Transit (BART) system in San Francisco and the METRO system in Washington, D.C., support the latter argument. With its sleek, air conditioned, 129-kilometer-per-hour (80-mile-per-hour) cars, the $1.6 billion BART system was supposed to be a model for future rapid mass transit systems. However, since its opening in 1974, BART has been plagued with breakdowns, massive financial losses, and worst of all, far too few riders. Part of the problem may be that BART is too rapid. Its stations are widely spaced so that the trains can run at high speeds. Since many passengers have to take a bus or car to the nearest BART station, they don't bother to use BART at all. In addition, this expensive, tax-supported system primarily benefits affluent suburban commuters and does little to help the poor. A whole fleet of new buses that would carry all of BART's passengers would have cost only 2.5 percent of BART's original cost.

Washington, D.C.'s METRO system is better planned than BART and has the advantage of serving a concentrated urban area. But it has also had problems, including building costs that were twice the original estimate. Atlanta, Baltimore, Miami, Munich, Rotterdam, and Milan are also building expensive mass transit systems.

Because of these problems, mass transit planners in other cities have been "thinking small" and are switching back to the use of trolleys (also called streetcars or light rail systems) and buses. Fixed rails limit the flexibility of trolleys, but trolleys have several important advantages: (1) By moving on a median strip between traffic lanes, trolleys can move much faster than buses; (2) by linking several cars together, one operator can carry a large number of passengers during rush hours; (3) electric-powered cars cause relatively little direct pollution; and (4) construction costs are relatively low—from $2.5 million to $5 million per 1.6 kilometers (1 mile) compared with $15 to $20 million for urban highways and $30 to $45 million for underground subways.

Buses are cheaper and much more flexible than trolleys. They can be routed to almost any area in today's widely dispersed cities. To attract more riders and to help buses avoid traffic congestion, more than 50 urban areas in the United States and 30 European cities have set aside bus express lanes. However, when Los Angeles tried bus express lanes, outraged car commuters, restricted to lanes that were more jammed than ever, protested loudly even though it tripled bus ridership and increased carpool riders by 65 percent.

Bus systems require less capital and have lower operating costs than most light and heavy rail mass transit systems, but by offering low fares they usually lose money. To be successful and effective, most bus systems must be subsidized by government funds. Other experiments indicate that ridership of buses and other forms of mass transit increases most when service is improved and when vehicles are well-engineered, quiet, and comfortable.

The argument that rail and bus systems use less energy than cars is being challenged. With low average daily loads (typically only 25 percent of their seats are occupied), trains, trolleys, and buses use about the same amount of energy per passenger as the private automobile. There is much talk about high-speed trains, but Japan's trains that whiz along at 193 kilometers per hour (120 miles per hour) consume much energy (because of wind resistance), produce vibrations that have cracked buildings, and make a horrendous noise.

Para Transit Para transit, which includes carpools, vanpools, and dial-a-ride systems, attempts to combine the advantages of the private automobile and mass transit. Carpools and vanpools have been most successful when large employers have made intense efforts to establish and support them.

Dial-a-ride systems are in operation in about 40 American cities in 22 states. Users call a central exchange, and small buses, vans, or tax-subsidized taxis are routed to pick them up at their doorsteps, usually about 20 to 50 minutes after they call. These systems are fairly expensive to operate, but compared with most large-scale mass transit systems, they are a bargain. They are one of the best ways to provide transportation for the poor, the young, the elderly, and the handicapped.

One cheaper and simpler approach to dial-a-ride systems is to use tax dollars to subsidize taxi fares. In El Cajon and La Mesa, California, the local taxicab company offers fairly cheap, citywide dial-a-ride services, with city taxes paying the company a subsidy for each trip. Some cities can offset this subsidy by reducing or eliminating little-used bus routes.

In cities such as Mexico City, Caracas, and Cairo, large fleets of *jitneys*—taxis or minibuses that travel along fixed routes but stop on demand—carry millions of passengers each day. Perhaps this is an idea that the United States and other rich nations should borrow from less developed nations.

Discouraging Automobile Use   Proposals for reducing automobile use in cities include: (1) refusing to build new highways into and out of the city; (2) setting aside express lanes for buses, streetcars, bicycles, and carpools during peak traffic hours (used in London, Paris, and Washington, D.C.); (3) charging higher road and bridge tolls during peak hours; (4) eliminating or reducing road and bridge tolls for cars with three or more passengers; (5) raising parking rates by taxing parking lots; (6) eliminating some downtown parking lots; (7) charging automobile commuters high taxes or fees; (8) staggering work hours to reduce rush hour traffic; and (9) prohibiting cars on some streets or in entire areas. A combination of these approaches can greatly reduce car use. In Singapore, the number of automobiles entering the business district has decreased 75 percent since 1975 as a result of a commuter fee of $50 to $90 per month and an increased parking rate of $6 a day. As a result, automobile traffic during the morning rush hour has dropped by two-thirds and there has been a large increase in bus ridership. Since the 1960s scores of European cities have banned cars from downtown areas to reduce congestion and revive the inner city. In the United States, elected officials are usually unwilling to risk the wrath of commuters and voters by imposing such coercive measures.

Improving the Automobile   In spite of attempts to increase the use of mass and para transit systems, the private automobile will likely remain the primary means of transportation in today's widely dispersed urban areas. Such areas do not lend themselves to regular bus and mass transit routes, so the only possibility for most trips is the automobile. Americans are not about to give up their love affair with the car. Even if a rapid shift away from automobiles was possible, the resulting economic decline of the giant automobile industry and its supporting industries could upset the entire economy and lead to unemployment and economic hardship for millions.

Since we can't get most Americans out of their cars, the next best goal is to reduce energy and matter wastes and pollution caused by automobiles. Methods include: (1) modifying existing internal combustion engines so that they burn less fuel and produce less pollution, (2) shifting to more energy-efficient and less-polluting engines, (3) reducing car weight by using more plastics and lightweight metals, and (4) discouraging the use or improving the efficiency of gas-guzzling options such as air conditioning and automatic transmissions. These options are discussed in more detail in Section 17-5.

A Suggested Plan for Urban Transportation   The four major goals of any urban transportation plan should be (1) to provide cheap and efficient transportation within an urban area for the poor, the elderly, the young, and the handicapped; (2) to allow suburban commuters to move efficiently into and out of the central city; (3) to conserve matter, energy, and land resources; and (4) to reduce pollution. The best way to accomplish the first goal is to increase para transit and express lane bus services with tax dollars. The second goal can be accomplished by improving highways and mass transit services. The third and fourth goals require more energy-efficient and less-polluting cars, improved traffic flow, less automobile use, more bicycle use, and compact cities rather than sprawling ones.

Any successful urban transportation plan will require a mix of individual, mass transit, and para transit methods that is designed to fit the needs of the particular urban area. We need greatly increased federal, state, and local aid and coordination to develop such integrated plans. So far, billions of federal and state dollars have been spent on highways, parking lots, and other facilities to encourage automobile use, while alternatives such as buses, trains, mopeds, and bicycles have received little support.

Most of the funds for improving urban transportation will have to come from the federal government. Ironically, the Public Highway Act of 1956 was a major factor in causing our present transportation mess. It established the Highway Trust Fund, which by 1980 was receiving about $10 billion a year from taxes on gasoline, trucks, buses, tires, and parts. Since 1956 these funds have been used to finance 90 percent of the costs of the interstate highways and freeways, which have encouraged urban sprawl. After a long battle by environmentalists, the Federal-Aid Highway Acts of 1973 and 1976 allowed more money from this fund to be used for other purposes. States can use funds approved for interstate highways for mass transit, para transit, and other transportation programs, but this alternate use is discouraged because the federal government puts up 90 percent of the cost of highway projects and only 80 percent of substitute projects.

There has been pressure to set up a separate trust fund for mass transit, but such an approach could be disastrous. It would separate planning for highways from planning for mass transit and emphasize expensive, highly technological mass transit projects that don't solve many urban transportation problems. The United States needs to eliminate the Highway Trust Fund and create a Transportation Fund. Revenues from this new fund would be used to plan and finance balanced, integrated transportation programs rather than programs that overemphasize highway or mass transit schemes that waste money, energy, and matter resources.

11-5 Land-Use Planning and Control

Need for Comprehensive Land-Use Planning The interlocking problems of population, food, water, pollution, and resource consumption are all related to patterns of land use. Thus, land use planning that integrates economic, political, social, ethical, and ecological goals on a local, regional, and national scale is one of the most urgent needs in the United States. Comprehensive land-use planning will not solve all of the social, economic, and environmental problems in the United States, but without it these problems could intensify.

The basic problem of ecological land-use planning is how to achieve a balance among the four major types of ecosystems: (1) *unmanaged natural ecosystems* (wilderness, deserts, and mountains), (2) *managed multiple use ecosystems* (parks, estuaries, and managed forests), (3) *managed productive ecosystems* (farms, cattle ranches, and strip mines), and (4) *managed urban ecosystems* (cities and towns). At the root of this problem we find the conflict between the economic ethic and the conservationist ethic, as discussed in Section 10-1. To resolve this conflict, we must deal with some key questions. How many unmanaged natural ecosystems should remain? How can we protect prime cropland from urban sprawl? Should we encourage urban sprawl or design more compact cities? How can we build cities that provide for human needs while being ecologically sound?

Urban Sprawl or Compact Cities? In poor nations a main problem is how to keep rural people from flooding into the cities. But in more developed nations the problem may be how to slow down urban sprawl and the increasing movement of people from urban to rural areas. The question of whether urban sprawl and deurbanization should be encouraged in the United States is complex and controversial.

As long as jobs are available, suburbanization, deurbanization, and controlled city size can have a number of advantages. Movement to the suburbs or rural areas can raise the quality of life for the migrants and decrease noise, crowding, congestion, and air and water pollution in the city. In 1934 Frank Lloyd Wright proposed a model for decentralized cities, and in 1898 English planner Ebenezer Howard urged that new towns be built to lure Londoners. Since that time Great Britain, Finland, the Netherlands, Venezuela, Brazil, Sweden, the United States, and several other countries have experimented with building new towns and satellite cities on the periphery of large cities, as discussed in more detail in Enrichment Study 14.

Some people have proposed a model for small, self-sufficient cities surrounded by farms, greenbelts, and community gardens. Homes and marketplaces would be built close together, and most local transportation would be by bus and bicycle and on foot. Buildings would be cooled and heated by sun and wind, and wastes would be recycled. Food would be grown locally, and huge factories would be rare. Others have urged Americans to move out of the cities and reinhabit the countrysides.

But suburbanization and deurbanization create a number of problems and can prevent a city from maturing ecologically (Table 11-2). They rob central cities of jobs and financial support; as a result, the quality of life for the poor, who often remain trapped there, may decrease. As people spread out, they also use more land and put more stress on forests, parks, estuaries, wilderness, wildlife, and agricultural lands. Urban sprawl, with its emphasis on single-unit housing and automobiles, also wastes more energy and mineral resources than do compact cities. It also hinders the development of mass transit systems. As environmentalist Peter Newman puts it, "To continue planning cities as though the cheap energy extravaganza is still possible, with huge freeways and a drive-in culture, just brings the world closer to the brink of disaster only hinted at by the recent energy crisis."

In 1974 a study prepared for the Council on Environmental Quality and the Environmental Protection Agency compared the costs of urban sprawl with those of building clusters of high-density, six-story dwellings. They found that clustering would: (1) use 75 percent less land for houses and thus give more space for parks and recreation; (2) generate 45 percent less air pollution because of less need for private cars; (3) cut energy use by 44 percent, mostly because of fewer cars; and (4) cost 44 percent less to build because housing, sewers, streets, and other public facilities would be concentrated.

Other planners and environmentalists have concentrated on urbanization rather than deurbanization. Some have developed grandiose designs that expand large cities upward. R. Buckminster Fuller believes that technology can be used to overcome and completely control nature. He envisions cities of 1 million people each that are inside gigantic, climate-controlled geodesic domes. Since these cities would be insulated from nature, they could be built on the oceans or in inhospitable areas, such as the polar regions and deserts. Unfortunately, his technological designs pay little attention to the social, human, and ecological relationships within cities and to the ecological relationships between cities and the rest of the ecosphere. He also assumes that advances in technology will give us infinite supplies of water, food, energy, and mineral resources and take care of wastes without serious ecological disruption.

C. A. Doxiadis and Paolo Soleri would emphasize highly centralized cities to preserve natural ecosystems. Like Fuller, however, both make no attempt to preserve nature within cities. Doxiadis has developed a world land-use plan, in which a network of cities comprising a single world supercity would accommodate 20 to 30 billion people on only 2.5 percent of the world's land. Soleri has concentrated on the design of smaller cities that combines architecture and ecology in what he calls "archology." At present, he is building Arcosanti in the Arizona desert with a crew of about 100 mostly college-educated volunteers who accept his architectural philosophy. Arcosanti, which is being built without public or private funding, is designed to be a self-sufficient city for 5,000 people. When completed, it will occupy only 0.06 square kilometer (15 acres) and be housed under an enormous glass roof. There will be shopping centers, open space (including parks), and a 25-story complex that will contain apartments and light industries (such as furniture and textiles). A 0.002-square-kilometer (4.5-acre) complex of greenhouses attached to the city's southern exposure will supply solar heat and food for a primarily vegetarian diet. The concrete that makes up most of the city's structure will act as a heat sink for storing solar heat, releasing the heat when the surrounding air cools. No cars, prisons, or cemeteries will be permitted. By 1980, after 10 years of work, the city was only about 2 percent finished, and it may take from 20 to 200 years to complete. Its budget is only about $250,000 a year, most of which comes from Soleri's books and lectures, the $300 fee paid by the volunteers who come to learn and work, and sales at the project's visitor center.

Despite the fact that Fuller, Doxiadis, and Soleri all use phrases such as *ecology* and *humane design* extensively, their schemes have been criticized as being inhumane and antiecological. They have apparently paid little attention to the functional and human relationships within their cities and have not shown why their cities would not repeat the disasters of high-rise urban renewal projects. Also, these men have not shown how the rest of the world's ecosystems can provide the massive input of resources and absorb the continuous output of wastes that their megacities would require.

Instead of designing new cities, other planners have concentrated on redesigning existing cities. Some have emphasized the expansion and use of open space, as discussed in more detail in Enrichment Study 14. Others have emphasized the need for humanizing cities by finding out what people need by allowing the people to direct the planners and architects and by building and maintaining small, socially cohesive neighborhoods instead of replacing them with high-rise urban renewal projects. These designers have made an important contribution by stressing human needs, but so far they have not analyzed the ecological impact of their ideas.

Methods of Land-Use Planning Four major methods are used for urban planning and land-use planning: (1) extrapolation, (2) reaction to crisis, (3) systems analysis and modeling, and (4) ecological planning. Planning by extrapolation is the most widely used approach but one of the least effective. It is based on projecting (extrapolating) existing trends into the future. For a 1- or 2-year period this method can be useful, but for longer terms it can be disastrous. Another widely used and usually ineffective approach is planning by reaction to crisis. Little long-range planning is done, and programs and agencies are set up only when problems become critical.

Systems analysis and modeling simulates cities and land areas. Data are collected, goals are set, mathematical models are constructed based on different assumptions, and a computer is used to project and compare these different models. If goals can be agreed on and weighted, computer techniques can also be used to find an optimal plan.

A computer model, like any model, is no better than the data and assumptions on which it is based (see Enrichment Study 1). Far too often the simulated models are much too simplistic and based on a narrowly conceived engineering approach. When a highway, dam, shopping center, housing development, or factory is built, only a few physical variables are analyzed and the long-term side effects—particularly on ecological diversity and the quality of life for the humans who will use the land—are ignored. However, the system dynamics computer model approach can provide planners with a dynamic and extremely useful planning tool that can be used in a sophisticated manner, as discussed in Enrichment Study 1.

In recent years some exciting new ecological approaches to land-use planning have been developed. The most renowned planner is Ian L. McHarg. His basic theme is that to use land wisely, we should work with—not against—nature. Nature performs a number of valuable functions for us free of charge. Forests help control water flow and minimize major flooding. Marshes, estuaries, and other wetlands act as spawning grounds for fish, shellfish, and wildlife and as natural waste treatment plants. Underground geological formations store drinking water for us, and topsoil can produce food over and over again if not abused. Thus, working with nature means that (1) top-quality farmland should be preserved; (2) building and farming should not occur on hillsides subject to erosion or on valuable wetlands and flood plains; (3) building near all surface waters should be regulated to keep water levels constant and to reduce pollution; (4) land above underground water aquifers should be strictly regulated; (5) mature woodlands and forests should be saved so they can act as watersheds to provide water, reduce the likelihood of floods, and absorb noise and air pollution; and (6) social needs and public participation should be a part of all planning.

In its ideal form, ecological land-use planning by McHarg and others consists of six steps:

1. *Making an environmental and social inventory.* A comprehensive geological, ecological, and social survey of the land is made. This includes an analysis of (a) geological variables, such as slopes, soil types and limitations, and aquifer and other hydrological data; (b) ecological variables, such as forest types and quality, ecological value, wildlife habitats, stream quality, estuaries, and historical or unique sites; and (c) social and economic variables, such as recreation areas, urban development, social disease (homicide, suicide, robbery, and drug addiction), physical disease (tuberculosis, diabetes, emphysema, heart disease, and syphilis), pollution, ethnic distribution, illiteracy, overcrowding, housing quality, and industrial plant quality.

2. *Determination of goals and their relative importance.* Experts, public officials, and the general public decide upon goals and establish weighting factors for the relative importance of each goal. This is one of the most important and difficult planning steps; conflicts between economic and conservationist ethics in this area must be resolved.

3. *Production of individual and composite maps.* Each variable is plotted on a single transparency map. These transparencies are then superimposed on one another or combined by computer to give three composite maps—one each for geological variables, ecological variables, and social and economic variables. Each map shows by its density (degree of blackness of different areas) or by a series of numbers how the variables interact. Computers and systems analysis models can be used to plot these composite density maps and to weight each value numerically according to the decisions made in step 2. Computer modeling can also be used to update maps and make alternative composites based on different goals and weighting factors.

4. *Development of a master plan.* The three composite maps are combined to form a master composite, which shows the suitability of various areas for different types of use. In some cases, a series of master composites are computer generated to show the effects of weighting key variables in different ways.

5. *Evaluation of the master plan.* The master plan (or series of alternative master plans) is evaluated by experts, public officials, and the general public, and a final master plan is drawn up and approved.

6. *Implementation of the master plan.* The plan is implemented and monitored by the appropriate governmental, legal, environmental, and social agencies.

The goal of ecological planning is to help planners and citizens strike a balance among unmanaged natural ecosystems, managed multiple use ecosystems, managed productive ecosystems, and urban ecosystems. This approach is still in its infancy, but it has been applied at least partially to a number of areas.

Most attempts at ecological planning have run into political difficulties because the traditional conflicts have arisen between economic and conservationist ethics and because none of the plans to date have effectively included the six steps of the ideal plan. Other difficulties with ecological land-use planning include (1) getting reliable scientific, economic, and social data; (2) weighting aesthetic and ecological factors; and (3) a lack of effective laws and other methods for implementing land-use plans. Several ecologists have attempted to assign eco-

A Suggested Plan for U.S. Land Use

1. Develop comprehensive land-use plans at the local, state, and national levels using both ecological and systems analysis methods.

2. Emphasize reducing automobile use, using solar and wind energy for heating and cooling, recycling key resources, and matter and energy conservation in the design of houses, buildings, neighborhoods, and cities.

3. Establish a national land-use planning agency in a new Department of Population, Resources, and Environment to develop national land-use plans, to help states and local areas develop coordinated land-use plans, and to integrate land-use plans with plans for food, energy, resources, population, and environmental protection.

4. Group local government units into regional planning systems based on airsheds, watersheds, and land ecosystems.

5. Instead of automatically planning for growth, consider growth as a variable that can be controlled.

6. Plan and use transportation as a major tool to limit and direct growth. The 1950s decision to develop a freeway system is responsible for the vast urban sprawl of Los Angeles.

7. Encourage carefully chosen existing cities of 5,000 to 10,000 people to grow to communities of 25,000 to 100,000.

8. Set aside 2 to 6 percent of the national GNP each year to revitalize central cities in order to attract suburbanites by establishing national standards for welfare (to stop the migration of the poor to cities where payments are high); improving schools; decreasing crime; providing low-interest loans and tax credits to firms that locate in depressed areas; giving tax credit to employers who hire the urban poor; and providing poor and middle class urban dwellers with grants, low-interest loans, tax credits, and Job Corps workers to renovate existing housing and neighborhoods.

9. Build satellite "new towns" around existing cities and revitalized "new intowns" inside existing cities, using ecological planning methods that reduce automobile use and emphasize recycling of resources.

10. Buy large open spaces with local, state, and federal funds and preserve them against urban growth to provide green space, recreation, and land and water conservation.

nomic values to ecological factors, but this important work is still in development. In spite of these problems, ecological land-use planning, especially when coupled with systems analysis and modeling, provides a bright hope for the future.

Land-Use Control Unless it can be effectively implemented, a land-use plan merely gathers dust. A number of land-use control methods have been used to implement land-use plans, including: (1) zoning so that land can be used only for certain purposes and in certain ways; (2) purchase of land by government or private foundations; (3) development easements, or purchasing the right to use land in specified ways; (4) preferential tax assessments to preserve land for agriculture, open space, or other purposes; (5) taxing profits on land sales to discourage development; (6) assigning a limited number of development rights for a land area; (7) controlling growth by limiting building permits, sewer hookups, roads, and other services; and (8) using environmental impact statements (see Section 19-2) to stop or delay harmful projects by forcing consideration of adverse impacts and alternatives to all federal projects. These methods of land-use control are discussed in more detail in Enrichment Study 14.

So far land-use control has largely been left up to local governments. This has resulted in a hodgepodge of attempts to limit or promote growth based primarily on the extrapolation and reaction-to-crisis methods of land-use planning. The artificial political boundaries of cities, towns, and counties bear little relationship to the natural airsheds, watersheds, and ecosystems in each region. As a result, land-use planning and control in one area can

11. Buy and use many small open spaces within existing urban areas (see Enrichment Study 14).

12. Instead of wiping out entire neighborhoods with monotonous urban renewal projects, keep a mixture of new and old buildings and neighborhoods, much like the mix of young and mature trees in a climax forest. Think of a city as a self-recycling system of diverse neighborhoods where buildings are thinned out and replaced continuously.

13. Plan cities, neighborhoods, and buildings to preserve and reinforce the positive elements of ethnic and cultural groups, thus preserving essential personal identity and cultural diversity.

14. Give publicly owned abandoned dwellings to or provide low-cost loans for families or co-op groups who agree to bring the buildings up to city codes within 18 months and to occupy the buildings for at least 5 years.

15. Establish more parks near and within large urban areas. In heavily used national parks, prohibit cars and development, and limit the number of users.

16. Prohibit development on prime agricultural land, valuable wetlands and estuarine systems, wilderness areas, key wildlife habitats, land above underground aquifers, large areas of mature woodlands and forests, and areas prone to fires, floods, earthquakes, and landslides.

17. Significantly increase the amount of land set aside for wilderness, parks, and wildlife refuges and the operating funds of the agencies that manage these areas.

18. Protect forests by using ecological approaches to control destructive forest fires, diseases, and pests; by improving the management of privately owned forests; by encouraging the recycling of wood wastes and paper; and by eliminating unnecessary packaging.

19. Require restoration of all strip-mined lands and ban strip mining on agricultural lands and on land that cannot be restored.

20. Enact a National Homestead Lease Act that would permit individuals to lease, at no cost, specified tracts of publicly owned lands (such as abandoned military bases), as long as the leaseholder lives on the tract and cultivates some portion of it.

be undercut by a lack of planning or by planning with opposite goals in surrounding areas. Many states have set up advisory councils of government (COGs) to coordinate planning on a regional basis, but such councils often lack expertise and the authority to implement decisions.

Hawaii, Massachusetts, Connecticut, New York, New Jersey, Washington, Vermont, Florida, California, Pennsylvania, and Oregon have attempted to develop and in some cases implement laws for land-use planning and control. This is a very encouraging trend, although many of these laws and plans have encountered political difficulties.

So far, the federal government has been unable to pass any legislation that would establish national guidelines for land-use planning or help states develop comprehensive land-use plans. Such legislation has been passed several times by the U.S. Senate, but in 1980 it had yet to be passed by the House of Representatives.

Throughout the world, Japan is the only country with comprehensive nationwide zoning. In 1968, the entire nation was divided into three major land-use zones—urban, agricultural, and other. The plan was expanded in 1974 to include areas for parks, nature reserves, and forests. During the 1960s Belgium, West Germany, France, and the Netherlands passed laws establishing guidelines for land use but left the actual planning to localities. Canada has also carried out a fairly comprehensive land-use planning program.

A comprehensive national urbanization strategy seems to be emerging in areas such as South Korea, Hong Kong, Singapore, Brazil, and Mexico. These plans consist of four elements: (1) satellite communities to be built around large cities, (2) the renewal of existing cities with an emphasis on self-help community building projects, (3) planned additions to intermediate-sized cities, and (4) efforts to reduce migration to cities by improving village and rural life.

Major Principles of a U.S. Land-Use Policy   Land use is such a complex problem that there is no single best approach. It requires a mix of approaches, including discouraging suburbanization and urbanization; designing moderate-sized new cities; rehumanizing existing cities; effectively controlling growth; revitalizing rural areas; protecting productive, multiple use, and unmanaged natural ecosystems; and coordinating all of these efforts through comprehensive land-use planning at local, state, and national levels. See the box containing suggested principles upon which a U.S. land-use plan for the next 50 years might be based (pages 230–231).

We can make our cities more livable and keep them from swelling to urban monstrosities. We can preserve a balance among agricultural fields, wilderness, and multiple use ecosystems. Exciting times are ahead, if we care.

The city is not an ecological monstrosity. It is rather the place where both the problems and the opportunities of modern technological civilization are most potent and visible.

Peter Self

Discussion Topics

1. Explain how the more developed countries can be more urbanized although less developed countries have higher rates of urban growth.

2. Discuss the positive and negative effects of the central-city-to-suburb shift and the metropolitan-to-nonmetropolitan shift in the United States on (a) the problems of central cities, (b) the problems of land use, (c) the population problem, and (d) ecosystem simplification. Should these two shifts be encouraged or discouraged?

3. List the advantages and disadvantages of living in (a) the central area of a large city, (b) suburbia, (c) a small town in a rural area, (d) a small town near a large city, and (e) a commune or farm in a rural area. Which would you prefer to live in? Why?

4. Give advantages and disadvantages of emphasizing rural rather than urban development in poor nations. Why do most poor nations emphasize urban development even though most of their population still lives in rural areas?

5. Explain why a city is really a global ecosystem. Are most city dwellers aware of this? How would you make them aware?

6. Describe how urban systems and natural ecosystems are similar and how they differ.

7. What life-support resources in your community are the most vulnerable to interruption or destruction? What alternate or backup resources, if any, exist?

8. Explain how each of the following common practices could hasten the decay of a city: (a) raising taxes, (b) building freeways and mass transit systems to the suburbs, and (c) replacing slums with new low-cost housing projects. Suggest alternative policies in each case.

9. If you live in a city, try to identify the downwind zones that receive some of the pollution that you produce. If you live in a rural area, try to determine which city or cities pollute your air. Consult your local weather bureau for information on prevailing wind patterns and airshed regions.

10. Massive traffic congestion hinders you from getting to and from work each day. Government officials say that the only way to relieve congestion is to build a highway through the middle of a beautiful urban park. As a taxpayer would you support this construction? Why or why not? What would you suggest to relieve the situation? (If you live in Memphis, Tennessee, this should be a familiar question.)

11. Examine your own dependence on the automobile. What conditions, if any, would encourage you to rely less on the automobile? Would you regularly ride to school or work in a carpool? Why or why not?

12. What types of mass transit and para transit systems are available where you live? What systems were available 20 years ago?

13. Debate the pros and cons of (a) charging commuters who drive to work alone very high commuting taxes and parking fees and (b) setting aside express lanes on freeways for buses and carpool vehicles.

14. Evaluate the following suggestions:
    a. Urban housing and buildings should be designed for a maximum life of 20 years.
    b. An optimum size should be determined and enforced for all cities.
    c. Cities should be built underground.
    d. Nuclear power plants, oil refineries, and even entire cities should be built on floating platforms in the oceans to relieve ecological and other urban stresses.

e. Cities should stop building highways between the suburbs and the central city.

15. Debate the idea that private landowners have the right to do anything they want with their land.

16. How is land use decided in your community? What roles do citizens have? Have citizens participated in this role in recent years? On the whole, has this been on behalf of economic interests or ecological interests?

17. Evaluate land use by your school or college.

Readings

See also Chapter 10 and Enrichment Studies 9, 14, and 15.

Brown, Lester R., et al. 1980. *Running on Empty: The Future of the Automobile in an Oil-Short World.* New York: Norton. Excellent analysis.

Council on Environmental Quality. 1974. *Land Use.* Washington, D.C.: Government Printing Office. Very useful summary of land-use patterns and methods of control.

Dantzig, George B., and Thomas L. Saaty. 1973. *Compact City: A Plan for a Liveable Environment.* San Francisco: Freeman. Outstanding analysis of urban design.

Darling, Frank F., and Raymond F. Dasmann. 1969. "The Ecosystem View of Human Society." *Impact of Science on Society,* vol. 19, 109–121. Excellent article showing how the urban ecosystem is a global ecosystem.

Dasmann, Raymond F. 1968. *A Different Kind of Country.* New York: Macmillan. Superb plan for using diversity as the key to land-use planning.

deBlij, Harm J. 1977. *Human Geography.* New York: Wiley. Excellent basic text.

Detwyler, Thomas R., and Melvin G. Marcus, eds. 1972. *Urbanization and Environment.* North Scituate, Mass.: Duxbury. Outstanding introduction to characteristics and problems of urban areas. See especially chap. 2.

Foin, Theodore C., Jr. 1976. *Ecological Systems and the Environment.* Boston: Houghton Mifflin. See chaps. 8 and 17

for an excellent overview of methods of land-use planning and control.

George, Carl J., and Daniel McKinley. 1971. *Urban Ecology: In Search of an Asphalt Rose.* New York: McGraw-Hill. Fine basic text.

Goodman, Percival. 1977. *The Double E.* Garden City, N.Y.: Doubleday. Exciting ideas for the design of small, self-sufficient, and ecologically sound cities.

Havlick, Spenser W. 1974. *The Urban Organism.* New York: Macmillan. Excellent basic text.

Heller, Alfred, ed. 1972. *The California Tomorrow Plan.* Los Altos, Calif.: William Kaufmann. Magnificent example of an integrated, ecological land-use plan for an entire state.

McHarg, Ian L. 1969. *Design with Nature.* Garden City, N.Y.: Natural History Press. A beautifully written and illustrated description of an ecological approach to land-use planning. Also available in paperback from Doubleday.

Mumford, Lewis. 1968. *The Urban Prospect.* New York: Harcourt Brace Jovanovich. Excellent analysis.

Odum, Eugene P. 1969. "The Strategy of Ecosystem Development." *Science,* vol. 164, 262–270. Classic article on ecological principles and land use.

Owen, Wilfred. 1976. *Transportation in Cities.* Washington, D.C.: Brookings Institution. Summary of urban transportation problems and solutions.

Reilly, William K., ed. 1973. *The Use of Land: A Citizens' Policy Guide to Urban Growth.* New York: Crowell. Useful analysis by a task force.

Richardson, Jonathan L. 1977. *Dimensions of Ecology.* Baltimore: Williams & Wilkins. See chap. 11 for an excellent discussion of the city as an ecosystem.

Sternlieb, George, and James W. Hughes. 1980. "The Changing Demography of the Central City." *Scientific American,* vol. 243, no. 2, 48–53. Very readable and useful overview.

Ward, Barbara. 1976. *The Home of Man.* New York: Norton. Superb discussion of urban problems in poor nations.

Whyte, William H. 1968. *The Last Landscape.* Garden City, N.Y.: Doubleday. Outstanding analysis of land use and discussion of open space.

12

Nonrenewable Mineral Resources

We seem to believe we can get everything we need from the supermarket and corner drugstore. We don't understand that everything has a source in the land or sea, and that we must respect these sources.

Thor Heyerdahl

We are living during an age of high consumption rates of matter and energy resources by the rich nations. Modern industrial nations depend on aluminum, chromium, iron, copper, lead, mercury, zinc, cobalt, tin, and other metals and minerals; on materials such as sand, gravel, stone, and clay; and on coal, oil, natural gas, uranium, and other energy resources (Section 1-3). This chapter will discuss nonfuel mineral resources; the following two will discuss energy resources.

12-1 Population, Technology, and Resources

J Curves Again Will the depletion of nonrenewable minerals, such as iron, copper, and zinc, limit population and economic growth (Enrichment Study 1)? Between 1980 and 2000, the world is projected to use 3 to 4 times the total quantity of materials used throughout human history.

How much longer will the supplies of these nonrenewable resources last? A major factor in determining the answer to this question is the extremely high rate of resource use in the United States. *In attaining their present standard of living, Americans have used more minerals and fossil fuels during the last 35 years than all of the peoples of the world have used throughout history.* If the entire world suddenly began using metals at the rate that the United States did in 1972, the annual world use of iron would have to increase 64 times, copper 102 times, lead 176 times, aluminum 52 times, and zinc 42 times.

With only 5 percent of the world's population, Americans use about 20 percent of the nonfuel minerals extracted each year and extracted about 26 percent of the world's supply from domestic deposits (Figure 12-1). During 1979 each American indirectly or directly used an average of 19,300 kilograms (42,500 pounds, or 21 tons) of resources—the highest per capita resource use in the world.* About half, or 1.9 trillion kilograms (2.1 billion tons), of the total resources used ended up as solid waste, with Americans throwing away at least $1 billion of recoverable metals each year (see Enrichment Study 15). Most of the remaining material will stay in circulation for several years before becoming waste or ending up as air and water pollution. In 1979 only about 8 percent of all discarded residential and commercial wastes in the United States were recycled or reclaimed. This use and waste is in sharp contrast to resource use in the poor nations. Even though the less developed countries will have 78 percent of the world's population in 2000, they will probably not be using more than 23 percent of the world's resources—little more than the 20 percent they use today.

Relationship between Resources, People, Technology, and Economics We can write a very simple equation that expresses the relationship between natural resource supplies (called resources) and people. The result gives us the average amount of useful resources potentially available per person in the world.

$$\frac{\text{average resources}}{\text{potentially available per person}} = \frac{\text{resources}}{\text{population}}$$

---

*Most of this was produced indirectly in the form of mining, agricultural, industrial, and construction wastes. Each American produces directly about 636 kilograms (1,400 pounds) of waste per year—about 1.7 kilograms (3.8 pounds) per day. For more details, see Enrichment Study 15.

Enrichment Studies 1, 3, 6, 10, and 16 are related to this chapter.

With finite resource supplies and a continually increasing population, the average decreases. If the average resources potentially available per person is to improve—or even stay at present levels—then population control (Chapter 8) is the only solution.

The situation, however, is not so simple. There are other important factors to consider—some that help the situation and some that make it worse. We are often misled by newspaper and TV statements that purport to give estimates of the total available supply of a resource. Usually these are estimates of resource reserves—not total resources or total supply. The term **resources** (or *total resources*) refers to the total amount of a particular material that exists on earth, while the term **reserves** refers to the amount of a particular material in known locations that can be extracted at a profit with present technology and prices. Much of the total supply may never be mined because it occurs in such low concentrations that it would cost more to get than it is worth. Nevertheless, reserves can increase by the discovery of new supplies, by improved technology that permits the mining of low-grade deposits at a profit, and by price rises, which make the mining of low-grade deposits economically feasible. Thus, a more widely used version of our simple equation is:

$$\frac{\text{average resources}}{\text{potentially available per person}} = \frac{\text{reserves}}{\text{population}}$$

The life of a resource supply can also be increased by recycling and reuse, by designing products that last longer, and by finding substitutes. As reserves of a particular resource drop, prices rise. As a result, recycling and reuse become economically more feasible, and consumers may demand products that last longer. Shortages and rising prices can also stimulate efforts to find substitutes for a resource. Thus, the reserves variable in the above equation is too simple. It should include several additional factors: new discoveries, price, mining technology, recycling and reuse, product life, energy supply available (for mining and processing or recycling), and resource substitution. (See V. E. McKelvey's Guest Editorial at the end of this chapter for a discussion of the role of human ingenuity in making resources available.)

The denominator of this equation is also too simple. Besides population increase, an increasing average resource use per person and an increasing population density (Section 7-5) tend to deplete resources more rapidly. In addition, some technologies accelerate depletion of a resource, and others introduce substitutes that cause more pollution and greater environmental disruption

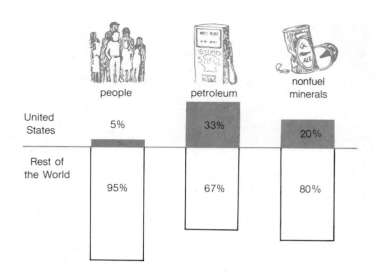

Figure 12-1 Annual use of the world's resources by the United States.

(Section 1-5). Furthermore, the average resources available are affected by the cost per unit of resource. The higher the cost, the fewer resources a person can afford to buy, even if they are available. Thus, the denominator of the original equation must include population size, population density, resource use per person, pollution per unit of resource use, and cost per unit of resource. Clearly, the two simple equations ignore many of the complexities of our resource situation. Let's look more closely at some of the factors that affect the supply of resources that will actually be available.

12-2 Are We Running Out?

An Environmental Controversy: Optimists Versus Pessimists   The future availability of metal and mineral resources is a subject of major controversy. The American experience has been one of resource abundance, not scarcity. Thus, there is a built-in tendency to believe that the nation will never run out of critical resources. As a result, experts disagree over which factors in resource availability are the most important (Section 1-5) and over how the factors will change in the future.

One group, called *cornucopians* (or "technological optimists" by their opponents), believes that we will never run out of needed metals and minerals. Their position is based on the *economic* idea that reserves of a resource will increase indefinitely: Scarcity will cause prices to rise, which will enable lower-grade deposits to be mined

Table 12-1 Views on Future Availability of Mineral Resources

Optimistic (Cornucopian)	Pessimistic (Neo-Malthusian)
Reserves can be increased indefinitely, as has been done in the past, and we are still far away from the limits to growth.	Reserves cannot be increased indefinitely on a finite earth, and there are increasing signs that we are approaching limits to growth on earth (see Enrichment Study 1).
Scarcity causes price rises that lead to an increased supply of key raw materials.	Regardless of price, we can't get a resource out of the ground if it isn't there. In addition, the cost of raw materials makes up such a small part of the total cost of consumer goods that the market prices of goods do not effectively control the supply and demand of most raw materials.
Price rises will stimulate new discoveries.	Continuing large-scale discoveries of most key resources are unlikely, and the costs of mineral exploration and environmental cleanup are increasing enormously and are expected to cost from $100 billion to $1 trillion between 1980 and 1990.
The oceans contain vast, untapped supplies of key resources.	With only a few exceptions, the resources in the ocean are so dispersed or hard to get that they will cost more to get than they are worth.
Price rises will stimulate the development of new, more efficient mining technology.	There is a limit to the efficiency of any process, and new technologies (such as nuclear explosions) needed to mine low-grade deposits can cause serious environmental disruption. Also, since technological improvements in mining generally cannot be protected by patents, individual companies have little incentive to develop them.
Human ingenuity and technology will find substitutes for scarce resources.	Substitutes for some key resources will not be found. Some substitutes will be unprofitable because getting them requires too much energy, and other substitutes will cause unacceptable environmental disruption.
Price rises will stimulate recycling and reuse.	Greatly increased recycling and reuse are very important but are limited by the availability of the necessary energy. Because some materials have been so widely dispersed, it costs more money to recycle them than to mine concentrated virgin deposits.
Price rises and inexhaustible supplies of cheap energy will make it profitable to mine lower and lower grades of key minerals.	Energy supplies are neither inexhaustible nor cheap (Chapter 13). Rising energy prices in the future will limit the mining of low-grade ores. The idea that lower grades of minerals can be mined is also based on a naive and incorrect view of how minerals are found in the earth's crust. Some, such as iron, copper, and aluminum, are widely distributed and found in deposits that range almost continuously from high grade to low grade. Most minerals, however, are found only in a few high-grade or a few low-grade deposits. Once these deposits are mined, it is not profitable or environmentally acceptable to mine massive quantities of average rock to extract very small amounts of the desired mineral.
Environmental effects from increased mining and resource use are either exaggerated or can be controlled.	Many environmental effects from resource use are very serious and can limit resource use even if supplies are available. Many effects can be controlled, but in some cases the resulting cost increase will make it unprofitable to increase use rates.
World population will level off in the next few decades and reduce demand for resources.	It is unlikely that world population will level off in time to prevent serious shortages of key resources (Chapter 8). Even if it did level off, rising affluence will increase demands for resources.

and stimulate the search for new deposits and substitutes. This group also believes that modern technology can always find ways to mine lower-grade deposits and to develop resource substitutes.

The opposing group, called *neo-Malthusians* (or "gloom-and-doom pessimists" by their opponents), believes that affordable supplies of metals and minerals are finite, that there will be shortages of some key materials in the near future, and that the environmental side effects of using key resources at high rates will limit resource use even if supplies are adequate. Theirs is primarily an *ecological* position that emphasizes recycling, reuse, resource conservation, reducing average per capita consumption, and slowing population growth. The major views of these opposing schools of thought are summarized in Table 12-1.

Economics and Resource Supply According to standard economic theory, a competitive free market controls supply and demand of all marketed items. If a resource becomes scarce, prices rise; if there is a glut, they fall.

This is a nice idea, but it often bears little resemblance to reality, especially in the case of minerals, for several reasons.

First, instead of an open, competitive market, both industry and government in the United States have gained increasing control over supply, demand, and prices of raw materials and products. Second, the costs of nonfuel mineral resources account for only a small percentage of the total costs of goods and services in the United States. Thus, increased demands for items such as cars or dishwashers have little effect on the prices of nonfuel mineral raw materials. This occurs primarily because the average per capita cost of raw materials in the United States stayed about the same or declined between 1900 and 1975 in spite of the fact that costs (in constant dollars) of products have risen sharply. Prices of these nonfuel resources have remained artificially low in the past because of market control by the more developed nations and low-cost mining leases that are beginning to expire, and because the environmental costs of mining were not included in the price of minerals. Since 1975, however, the prices of raw materials have begun to rise somewhat as the costs of mining and environmental protection have increased sharply, and low-cost mining leases have expired.

Third, the total supply of any resource on earth is limited. Regardless of what we are willing to pay, we can't get a resource out of the ground if it isn't there. Fourth, resource supplies may be limited in the future because mining and processing require too much energy and money. Between 1950 and 1980, U.S. mineral production rose 50 percent, but the energy needed to find, extract, and process these materials increased 600 percent. In 1979, nearly 16 percent of all energy used in the United States was for the mining and processing of minerals and materials. As energy prices rise, the costs for mining and processing mineral resources also rise. The U.S. metallic minerals industry is estimated to need from $100 billion to $1 trillion in capital between 1980 and 1990. It is unlikely that such large amounts of investment capital and cheap energy will be available for continual expansion of key mineral supplies.

New Discoveries   There is little doubt that new discoveries will extend present reserves of most minerals. But resource exploration, a hit-or-miss process, requires a large investment of capital for drilling or tunneling. We are now using remote sensing cameras in orbiting satellites (such as Landsat) to scan the entire globe for land, forest, mineral, energy, and water resources. Some rich new deposits will probably be found in unexplored areas in less developed nations, but in the more developed and in many less developed nations, the richest and most accessible deposits have already been discovered. Most remaining deposits are harder to find and mine and are usually less concentrated. We must spend more and more money to get fewer and fewer resources. In addition, most minerals are presently being used up faster than new deposits are being found.

Pressure from environmentalists to preserve valuable wilderness and forest areas (Sections 10-2 and 10-4) have also prevented some areas from being as fully explored as mining companies would like. By 1980, mining had been prohibited on about 65 percent of the publicly owned land in the United States. Environmental and safety regulations have also greatly increased the cost of mining and processing minerals. For example, between 1970 and 1980 eight zinc smelting plants in the United States were shut down because the owners couldn't afford the cost of stricter environmental regulations. As a result, U.S. imports of zinc rose from 25 percent to 62 percent over the same period. The question, then, is not whether we will find new deposits but whether we will be able to find enough affordable new supplies to satisfy increasing worldwide demands.

What about the oceans? Do they contain vast supplies of mineral and energy resources, as some people have suggested? As shown in Figure 12-2, the potential resources of the ocean are located in three areas: (1) seawater, (2) sediments and deposits on the shallow continental shelf and slope, and (3) sediments and nodules on the deep ocean floor.

Offshore deposits and sediments in shallow waters are already important sources of oil, natural gas, sand, gravel, and 10 other minerals. These resources may not be limited by supply or mining technology but rather by the increasing cost of energy needed to find and remove them, the possible ecological side effects of oil leaks and spills (Section 16-5), the potentially serious effects of extensive dredging and mining on the food resources of the sea (Section 9-5), and political squabbles between nations over who owns these resources.

Some of the grave political problems that have been holding up even preliminary explorations on the feasibility of seabed mining may be resolved. Since 1968, 160 nations have been trying to develop a Law of the Sea Treaty to govern exploitation of ocean resources. In 1980, the UN Conference on the Law of the Sea approved a draft treaty for ratification by the member nations. The

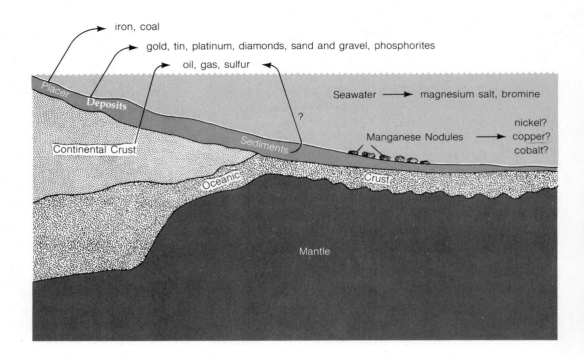

Figure 12-2 The location of oceanic mineral resources.

Continental Shelf   Continental Slope   Ocean Basin

iron, coal

gold, tin, platinum, diamonds, sand and gravel, phosphorites

oil, gas, sulfur

Placer Deposits

Continental Crust

Seawater → magnesium salt, bromine

Sediments

Oceanic

Crust

Manganese Nodules → nickel? copper? cobalt?

Mantle

draft treaty acknowledges that coastal nations have jurisdiction over mineral resources up to 320 kilometers (200 miles) beyond their coastal continental shelves. The draft treaty also provides for a $1 billion loan from industrialized nations to establish an International Seabed Authority with the responsibility for licensing and controlling production levels of ocean resources by private companies. The UN company would also do its own seabed mining and distribute any profits among less developed coastal nations. Private companies would be required to sell the latest ocean mining technology to the UN company. Private companies, however, oppose production limits and oppose being required to sell new mining technology to the UN company. As a result, by 1981 there was still dispute over the final details of the treaty.

At first glance, the huge quantity of seawater appears to be an inexhaustible source of minerals. But most of the 92 chemical elements found in seawater occur in very low concentrations. Only magnesium, bromine, and common table salt are abundant enough to be extracted profitably with present prices and technology. A few other elements may eventually be extracted profitably, but most of the key metals exist in extremely low concentrations. Because of this dispersion, it takes more energy and money to recover them than they are presently worth (the second energy law again). For example, to get a mere 0.003 percent of the annual U.S. consumption of zinc would require processing a volume of seawater equivalent to the combined annual flows of the Delaware and Hudson rivers!

The idea that mining the deep ocean bed will solve our mineral problems is a myth. The only known minerals on the deep ocean floor are manganese nodules, believed to be unevenly distributed over many world seabeds. These potato-sized lumps of rock are composed chiefly of manganese and iron, with smaller amounts of copper, nickel, cobalt, molybdenum, and vanadium. If extraction technology can be improved, these nodules may indeed be valuable, not so much for their manganese (used for making steel) but for their copper (used for wiring), nickel, and cobalt (both used for steel alloys). The United States (along with Japan, France, West Germany, and the Soviet Union) is particularly interested in these deposits because in 1980 it imported about 97 percent of its manganese, 93 percent of its cobalt, and 20 percent of its copper—largely because domestic high-grade ore deposits have been depleted. A number of environmentalists oppose seabed mining, however, because they fear that sucking the nodules off the seabed with a giant vacuum cleaner could destroy seafloor organisms, pollute the sea by stirring up ocean bottom sediments, and upset delicate ocean ecology.

Improved Mining Technology and Mining Low-Grade Deposits There is no question that advances in mining technology have allowed the mining of low-grade deposits without significant cost increases. The development of large-scale earth-moving machinery, especially for surface mining (Section 10-5), has been a very important advance. One spectacular success story involves copper. The cutoff grade for minable copper has been reduced by a factor of 10 since 1900 and by a factor of 250 over the history of mining. The question is, Can mining of ever lower grades of metals continue?

Eventually we run into geological, energy, and environmental limits. Only six metals are found in large amounts in the earth's crust—iron, aluminum, magnesium, manganese, chromium, and titanium. Other widely used metals, such as copper, tin, lead, zinc, uranium, nickel, tungsten, and mercury, are geologically scarce. They are usually found in low concentrations, and in most cases these deposits are not widely distributed over the earth. Only iron, copper, and aluminum are widely distributed and found in deposits that range almost continuously from high grade to low grade. Thus, mining lower- and lower-grade ores of most metals is too costly, not only in terms of money but also in terms of energy use, land degradation, and air and water pollution. This is because of the second law of energy (Section 3-3). Eventually, we reach such a low-grade deposit that the cost of the energy required to dig it out, transport it, crush it, process it, and haul away the waste rock becomes the primary factor in the recovery of the resource. To concentrate anything that is widely dispersed takes large amounts of energy (and money).

One of the fundamental assumptions in the cornucopian view is an inexhaustible source of cheap energy. As you will see in the next chapter, this assumption is very unlikely to hold and energy could become a limiting factor in getting resources. For example, the processing of steel, aluminum, plastics, cement, and gasoline alone account for more than 10 percent of the energy used in 1979 by the United States. All forms of energy are getting more and more expensive. Another limiting factor is water. Large amounts of water are required to extract and process most minerals, and many areas with major mineral deposits are short of water, as discussed in Chapter 15.

Substitution Cornucopians insist that if supplies of minerals should run out, technology will find substitutes for them. They argue that either plastics, high-strength fibers, or the six most abundant metals in the earth's crust (iron, aluminum, magnesium, manganese, chromium, and titanium) can be substituted for most scarce metals. For example, in today's automobiles, plastics are increasingly substituted for copper, lead, tin, and zinc. Aluminum and titanium are replacing steel for some purposes, and aluminum could replace copper in electrical wires (although there may be fire hazards). Even if a substitute can't be found, cornucopians argue that no material is so vital that its exhaustion would result in large-scale catastrophe.

Finding substitutes for scarce resources is extremely important, but there are some difficulties. First, failure to find a substitute could cause serious economic hardships during the adjustment period that would occur when a key material is no longer available. Second, finding possible substitutes and phasing them into use in complex manufacturing processes requires carefully developed research and development programs, large amounts of money, and long lead times. Third, many substitutes require more energy to make than the original materials require for processing.

Fourth, some materials have such unique properties that either they cannot be replaced or their replacements are distinctly inferior. For example, helium remains a liquid at a lower temperature than any other gas or liquid. For very low temperature cooling in electrical superconductors and for future technologies of generating and transmitting energy, helium has no known substitute. Nothing now known can replace steel in skyscrapers and dams, where strength is needed. Aluminum conducts electricity less efficiently than copper. Substitutes for chromium (in stainless steel), platinum (as an industrial catalyst), gold (for electrical contacts), cobalt (in magnets), silver (for many photographic uses), and manganese (for making bubble-free steel) will likely be inferior.

Fifth, in some cases proposed substitutes are themselves fairly scarce. Such is the case with molybdenum, the main substitute for tungsten (which has the highest melting point of all metals). Cadmium and silver, suggested substitutes for mercury in advanced batteries, are also scarce. Sixth, some of the futuristic technologies may themselves depend on scarce resources that have no known substitutes. Conventional nuclear fission energy may be limited by shortages of affordable uranium (see Section 14-3). Replacing these reactors with breeder reactors that make their own plutonium fuel is jeopardized by environmental concerns and the fact that plutonium can be made into atomic bombs fairly easily (see Section 14-3). The use of somewhat safer breeder reactors based on thorium rather than plutonium may be limited by the small supply of thorium. Nuclear fusion reactors, if they are ever developed, would put heavy demands on scarce beryllium, niobium, lead, helium, and chromium. And the development of efficient solar cells that produce electricity from sunlight may require large amounts of scarce gallium.

Recycling Both cornucopians and neo-Malthusians agree on the importance of recycling. It decreases the need for virgin resources, reduces the volume of solid wastes, and often saves energy and causes less pollution and land disruption. For example, the amount of energy saved by recycling magnesium is 98.5 percent; aluminum, 96 to 97 percent; plastics, 97 percent; copper, 88 to 95 percent; steel, 47 percent; paper and rubber, 23 to 30 percent; and glass, 8 percent.

If merely half the paper thrown away each year in the United States was recycled, about 150 million trees would be saved and enough energy would be conserved to provide residential electricity for about 10 million people annually. If returnable bottles replaced the 60 billion throwaway beer and soft drink cans now produced annually, enough energy would be saved to provide electricity for another 11 million people. Scrap iron conserves virgin iron ore and coal, requires 74 percent less energy, 40 percent less water, and 97 percent fewer raw materials, and cuts air pollution by 90 percent and water pollution by 76 percent compared with making steel from virgin ore.

"Waste is a resource out of place," "the recycling society," "urban waste is urban ore," "trash is cash," and "trash is our only growing resource" are cries now echoing throughout the land. Nevertheless, the United States presently does little recycling. Instead, it spends billions of dollars each year to dump, burn, or bury refuse that contains billions of dollars of valuable resources, as discussed in more detail in Enrichment Study 15. In 1979, only 8 percent of all U.S. residential and commercial wastes were recycled: Only 21 percent of the paper was recycled, 10 percent of the aluminum, 4.7 percent of all metals (including aluminum), 5 percent of the

rubber, 3 percent of the glass, and essentially none of the plastics.*

Yet the United States could recycle at least 35 percent of its paper (as it did in World War II) and perhaps 50 percent, as Japan now does. For some, the real answer to our solid wastes—or, more accurately, our wasted solids—is not just small-scale recycling centers, but large-scale resource recovery plants. Such plants could incinerate a city's burnable wastes for energy and recover usable materials from nonburnable refuse. By 1980, 21 municipal resource recovery plants were operating, 40 were under construction or in an advanced planning stage, and 54 other cities were looking into the feasibility of such plants, as discussed in more detail in Enrichment Study 15.

If there were a national network of such plants, the Environmental Protection Agency estimates that by 1990 about 26 percent (as opposed to the present 8 percent) of all U.S. residential and commercial wastes could be recycled. The passage of the Solid Waste Disposal Act of 1970 and the Resource Conservation and Recovery Act of 1976 are important efforts to attain this goal. The 1976 act requires regulation of hazardous wastes, bans the use of open dumps, provides funds for research and demonstration plants for resource recovery, and provides financial and technical assistance to state, regional, and local agencies for developing environmentally sound programs for waste disposal, resource recovery, and resource conservation.

Why can't we recover and recycle even more than 26 percent of U.S. wastes? Several economic, political, and scientific factors limit recycling. First, the abundance of cheap raw materials in the past has favored the development of manufacturing processes that use only virgin resources. For example, during the past 20 years American steel makers have switched from the open-hearth process, which can use scrap iron, to the basic oxygen furnace, which uses very little scrap. As a result, in 1980 less than 10 percent of all steel produced in the United States was produced from recycled scrap iron. In contrast, Japanese and West German steel plants, built after World War II, employ the electric furnace process, which can use large amounts of scrap iron.

Second, in the United States billions of tax dollars are given as subsidies in the form of tax breaks and depletion allowances to the massive primary mining and

---

*It is usually more realistic to report recycling as a percentage of the total amount of each material discarded each year rather than as a percentage of total consumption. Much of the material extracted and processed each year remains in use for long periods of time and is not available for recycling until much later.

energy resource industries to encourage them to get the world's resources out of the ground as fast as possible. For example, these subsidies amount to $375 million each year for nonfuel mineral production. So far the United States has failed to provide similar subsidies for the recycling and secondary materials industries that recover and reuse resources from wastes.

Third, in most cases the cost of recycled materials in the United States is equal to or higher than that of virgin materials. This is due to several factors, including (1) the tax advantages just mentioned; (2) railroad and trucking rates, which are often 50 to 100 percent higher for scrap materials than for virgin materials (especially glass and paper); (3) lack of large markets for recycled materials; (4) the high labor costs involved in recovering materials from mixed wastes; and (5) failure to include the cost of disposal in the price of products.

Fourth, many modern products are such complex mixtures of materials that it is too expensive and too energy consuming to separate the materials for recycling. This is a major reason why the complex metal mixtures in junked cars are rarely recycled.

Fifth, the second law of energy (Section 3-3) sets a physical limit on recycling. All matter recycling takes energy, which cannot be recycled. Eventually recycling is limited by the expense and pollution output of the energy required. Remelting scrap wastes usually requires less energy than extracting and processing most virgin materials. However, the total energy needed for the entire process of collecting, transporting, and remelting widely scattered scrap materials sometimes exceeds that used for extracting and processing virgin materials. For example, consider the ecologically sensitive citizen who drives around collecting a carload of bottles, cans, and newspapers, takes them to a recycling center, and then drives home. This process probably wastes more energy, produces more pollution, and depletes more resources than extracting and processing the equivalent quantity of virgin materials.

Reuse and Resource Conservation Resource recovery and recycling are important, but we must distinguish between the term **recycle** (to collect and remelt a resource) and the term **reuse** (to use a product over and over again). Indeed, encouraging the recycling—rather than reuse—of some objects, such as glass bottles, is an environmental sham. It takes 3 times more energy to crush and remelt a throwaway glass bottle than it does to refill returnable bottles. Thus, it makes more sense ecologically to ban nonreturnable glass bottles and use returnable bottles instead. Fortunately, by 1980, seven states—Oregon, Iowa, Delaware, Vermont, Maine, Michigan, and Connecticut—had banned or reduced the use of throwaway bottles and cans by requiring refundable deposits on beer and soft drink containers, as discussed in more detail in Enrichment Study 15.

An even more important goal of any resource and waste management plan must be resource conservation. The present one-way system in industralized nations (Figure 3-4) is based on running more and more materials through the system with little emphasis on recovering these widely scattered wasted solids. One glaring example of unnecessary resource waste is the overpackaging of products. Packaging of products in the United States consumes 65 percent of all glass, 25 percent of all plastics, 22 percent of all paper, and 15 percent of all wood used each year. This amounts to an average of 281 kilograms (618 pounds) of packaging for each American every year. How often do you find a product (such as a blouse or shirt) that has unnecessary packaging or a grocery item that has two or three levels of packaging? Cutting paper packaging in the United States in half would not only save trees but also save enough energy to provide residential electricity for 20 million people each year.

Instead of our present one-way system (Figure 3-4), we should rely on a sustainable earth, or ecological, system (Figure 3-5) that reduces the throughput of matter and energy resources by (1) designing and using products requiring less material per unit (for example, using smaller cars and eliminating excess packaging), (2) reducing the number of products used per household or individual each year (for example, fewer cars per family), and (3) developing and using products that last longer (for example, longer-lasting cars, tires, and appliances). A comparison between the present throwaway resource system used in the United States, a resource recovery and recycling system, and a sustainable earth resource system is given in Table 12-2.

Ecological Consequences of Resource Use The greatest problem we face during the next 50 years may not be the critical shortage of world resources but the ecological consequences of using them at such a high rate. Because of the second law of energy (Section 3-3), the use of any energy or mineral resource causes some form of land disturbance (Section 10-5) and air, water, and soil pollution (Figure 12-3).

Some disturbed land can be reclaimed (Section 10-5) and some forms of pollution can be controlled, but these

Table 12-2 Three Systems for Handling Matter Resources

Item	Throwaway System	Resource Recovery and Recycling System	Sustainable Earth Resource System
Glass bottles	Dump or bury	Grind and remelt; remanufacture; convert to building materials	Ban all nonreturnable bottles and reuse (not remelt and recycle) bottles
Bimetallic "tin" cans	Dump or bury	Sort, remelt	Limit or ban production; use returnable bottles
Aluminum cans	Dump or bury	Sort, remelt	Limit or ban production; use returnable bottles
Cars	Dump	Sort, remelt	Sort, remelt; tax cars lasting less than 15 years, weighing more than 818 kilograms (1,800 pounds), and getting less than 13 kilometers per liter (30 miles per gallon)
Metal objects	Dump or bury	Sort, remelt	Sort, remelt; tax items lasting less than 10 years
Tires	Dump, burn, or bury	Grind and revulcanize or use in road construction; incinerate to generate heat and electricity	Recap usable tires; tax all tires not usable for at least 64,400 kilometers (40,000 miles)
Paper	Dump, burn, or bury	Incinerate to generate heat	Compost or recycle; tax all throwaway items; eliminate overpackaging
Plastics	Dump, burn, or bury	Incinerate to generate heat or electricity	Limit production; use returnable glass bottles instead of plastic containers; tax throwaway items and packaging
Garden wastes	Dump, burn, or bury	Incinerate to generate heat or electricity	Compost; return to soil as fertilizer; use as animal feed

Figure 12-3 The environmental effects of resource use.

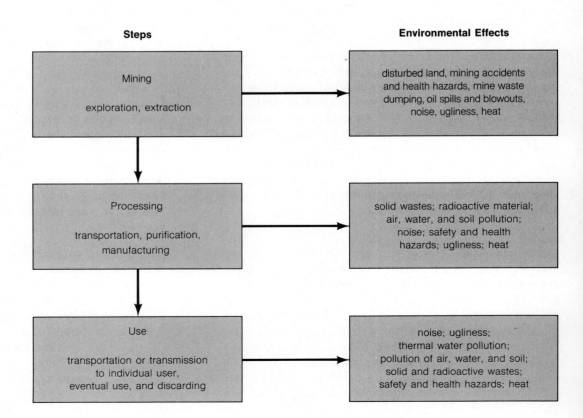

Steps

Mining

exploration, extraction

Processing

transportation, purification, manufacturing

Use

transportation or transmission to individual user, eventual use, and discarding

Environmental Effects

disturbed land, mining accidents and health hazards, mine waste dumping, oil spills and blowouts, noise, ugliness, heat

solid wastes; radioactive material; air, water, and soil pollution; noise; safety and health hazards; ugliness; heat

noise; ugliness; thermal water pollution; pollution of air, water, and soil; solid and radioactive wastes; safety and health hazards; heat

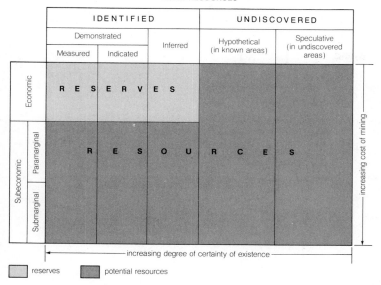

TOTAL RESOURCES

	IDENTIFIED			UNDISCOVERED	
	Demonstrated		Inferred	Hypothetical (in known areas)	Speculative (in undiscovered areas)
	Measured	Indicated			
Economic	R E S E R V E S				
Subeconomic / Paramarginal / Submarginal	R E S O U R C E S				

increasing cost of mining →

← increasing degree of certainty of existence →

☐ reserves   ☐ potential resources

Figure 12-4 U.S. Geological Survey classification of nonfuel and fuel mineral resources.

efforts require energy (which produces more pollution) and money. Even with an infinite supply of energy and money and vastly improved pollution control, we cannot continue to mine, use, and recycle resources at ever growing rates. As energy is used and transformed, it is automatically degraded to low-grade heat, in accordance with the second law of energy (Section 3-3). When this heat output from human activities becomes greater than the rate at which heat flows back into space, the earth's atmosphere will begin heating up—with serious ecological consequences (Enrichment Study 3). Thus, low-grade waste heat becomes the ultimate pollutant limiting human activities.

12-3 Key Resources: The World Situation

Estimating Resources It is very difficult to reliably estimate the available amount of a particular resource. As mentioned in Section 12-1, we must be careful to distinguish between reserves and total resources. However, the issue is even more complex. The U.S. Geological Survey classifies resources according to the relative certainty of their existence and the economic feasibility of mining and processing them, as summarized in Figure 12-4. Resources are broadly classified as either identified or undiscovered. **Identified resources** are specific bodies of mineral-bearing rock whose existence and location are known. This category is subdivided into **reserves** (or *economic resources*), identified resources that can be re-

covered profitably with present prices and technology, and *subeconomic resources,* identified resources that cannot be recovered profitably with present prices and technology. Estimates of reserves and subeconomic resources are based on analyses of rock samples and on geological projections. Since the certainty of these measurements and projections varies, these two categories are further subdivided into measured (or proven), indicated (or probable), and inferred (or possible) (Figure 12-4).

Undiscovered resources are those that are believed to exist but whose specific location, quality, and amount are unknown. They are described as either *hypothetical resources* or *speculative resources.* **Hypothetical resources** are deposits that can be reasonably expected to exist in areas where deposits have been found in the past. **Speculative resources** are deposits that are thought to be in areas that have not been examined and tested for resources. If actual discoveries are made, hypothetical and speculative resources can then be reclassified as reserves (economic resources) or subeconomic resources.

From this classification scheme we can see why there are so many conflicting estimates of the potential supply of a resource. Often estimates found in newspapers and articles do not specify which category is being used.

Depletion Curves and Depletion Rate Estimates How can we determine how long a given nonrenewable resource might last? Projection is based on two major sets of assumptions: (1) the actual or potentially available supply at existing (or future) acceptable prices and with existing (or improved) technology and (2) the annual rate at which the resource will be used. Obviously, different sets of assumptions yield different answers. It is almost certain that no resource will be completely exhausted. Rather, the cost of mining at greater depths and mining increasingly low-grade deposits ultimately becomes prohibitive. Normally, **depletion time** is defined as the time required to use up a certain fraction (usually 80 percent) of the known or estimated supply of a resource according to various assumed rates of use.

The most useful approach for estimating how long a resource will last is to project several *depletion curves* or *depletion rate estimates* based on the best available data and a clearly defined set of assumptions. A typical set of depletion curves is shown in Figure 12-5. Curve A represents our present course of mining, using, and throwing away a resource. How long a resource supply will last can be extended by efficient recycling and improved mining techniques (curve B); it can be extended still further by a combination of extensive recycling and reuse, improved mining technology, and reduced per capita consumption (curve C). Of course, finding a substitute for a resource cancels all these curves, and a new set of curves for the new resource would have to be developed.

One estimate, the **static reserve index,** is the estimated number of years until the known world reserves of a resource will be 80 percent depleted at the present rate of consumption. Usually, however, it is assumed that resource consumption rates rise by a certain percentage each year—typically 2 to 3 percent. A more realistic projection, therefore, is the **exponential reserve index**—the estimated number of years until known world reserves for a resource will be 80 percent depleted at a rate of consumption that increases by a given percentage each year.

We can get more optimistic projections by combining either the static reserve or exponential reserve assumptions with additional assumptions. For example, we can assume that recycling will extend existing reserves and that improved mining technology, price rises, and new discoveries will expand existing reserves by some factor, say, 2, or we can assume that recycling, reuse, and reduction in the use of a resource will extend existing reserves even further and that improved mining technology, rising prices, and new discoveries will expand reserves by an even larger factor, say, 5.

Figure 12-6 shows estimated times for 80 percent depletion of the world reserves for 16 important minerals based on two different sets of assumptions. One projec-

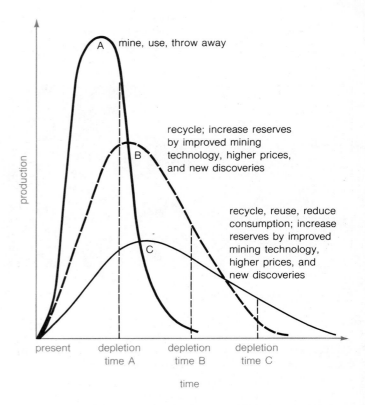

Figure 12-5 Depletion curves for a nonrenewable resource, based on different sets of assumptions, showing when 80 percent depletion occurs (dotted lines).

tion (shaded) assumes that the world usage rate of each mineral will grow by 2.5 percent each year and that we will continue our present practice of mining, using, and throwing away. The second (unshaded) is a more optimistic projection that assumes that the world use rate will grow by 2.5 percent each year and that there will be a 500 percent increase in usable reserves due to more recycling, improved mining technology, and major discoveries of new mineral deposits over the next 30 years. From Figure 12-6 we see that even if reserves are increased fivefold, we could run short of tin, tungsten, copper, lead, zinc, silver, mercury, and gold between 2000 and 2040; and of molybdenum, manganese, aluminum, platinum, and nickel between 2060 and 2090.

Figures 12-5 and 12-6 show us why there is so much controversy between cornucopians and neo-Malthusians. Cornucopians tend to believe either that any resource will probably be depleted in a pattern following curves B or C in Figure 12-5, or that if depletion should occur, we will find a substitute. In contrast, neo-Malthusians tend to believe that resource depletion will follow

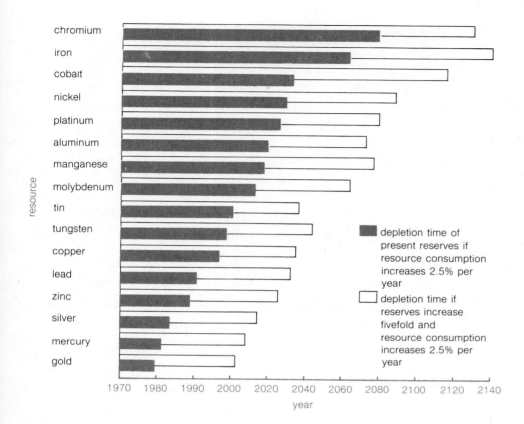

Figure 12-6 Projected times for 80 percent depletion of world reserves of 16 key metal resources based on two sets of assumptions. Note that the time scale changes after the year 2000.

the pattern represented by curve A in Figure 12-5 unless we change over to a sustainable earth approach (Table 12-2) so that curve C, rather than curve A, is followed.

Which set of curves should we use? We can use the following guidelines to help us choose: (1) Remember that all of the curves and estimated depletion times are projections based on a specific set of assumptions. They don't tell us what *will* happen but what *could* happen under different sets of circumstances; (2) Find out what specific assumptions were used to make each projection; (3) Evaluate the assumptions (and where possible the data upon which they are based) to see which seem to be the most reasonable.

Even if a resource is not in danger of rapid depletion, the second energy law shows us the need for sharply reducing the rate of resource use by reducing population growth and by increasing resource recycling, reuse, and conservation. Otherwise, the disorder buildup in the environment can overwhelm the earth's life-support systems as we use more and more energy to move more and more nonrenewable virgin or recycled mineral resources through an economic system addicted to growth at any cost.

12-4   Key Resources: The U.S. Situation

Increasing Dependence on Imports Some see the world's resource problems as an attempt by more developed nations to get raw materials from less developed nations at an unfair low price, as discussed in more detail in Enrichment Study 9. But such a view overlooks the fact that with a few important exceptions, most of the world's mineral supplies are found in more developed countries. Five more developed countries—the U.S.S.R., the United States, Canada, Australia, and South Africa— dominate in supplying the world with most of the 20 minerals that make up 98 percent of the total value of all minerals consumed in the world. The major exceptions include copper in South America and Africa, tin and tungsten in Southeast Asia, aluminum ore (bauxite) in the Caribbean, and cobalt in Zaire.

Today the United States is more self-sufficient in key metals and minerals than any other nation except the U.S.S.R. In spite of this, high consumption rates and cheaper resource supplies in other countries have prompted the United States to import more minerals

Table 12-3 U.S. Import Dependence for 12 Key Raw Materials

| Raw Material | Percentage Imported | | | | Major Exporting Countries in 2000 |
	1950	1979	1985	2000	
Chromium	**99**	**90**	**100**	**100**	U.S.S.R., South Africa, Turkey, Zimbabwe, Philippines
Tin	**77**	**81**	**100**	**100**	Malaysia, Bolivia, Thailand, Indonesia
Manganese	**85**	**98**	**100**	**100**	U.S.S.R., South Africa, Brazil, Gabon, Australia
Nickel	**94**	**77**	**88**	**89**	Canada, New Caledonia, U.S.S.R., Cuba, Norway
Aluminum (bauxite)	40	**93**	**96**	**98**	Jamaica, Surinam, Australia, Dominican Republic, Guinea
Zinc	38	**62**	**72**	**84**	Canada, Mexico, Peru, Australia, Honduras
Potassium (potash)	14	**66**	47	**81**	Canada, West Germany, Israel
Tungsten	40	**50**	**65**	**93**	China, Canada, Peru, Bolivia, Thailand
Lead	39	24	**62**	**67**	Australia, U.S.S.R., Canada, Mexico, Peru
Iron ore	8	28	**55**	**67**	Brazil, U.S.S.R., India, Canada, Venezuela, Australia
Copper	31	18	45	**75**	Chile, U.S.S.R., India, Canada, Zaire, Zambia, Peru
Sulfur	2	0	28	**52**	Canada, Mexico

Note. Boldfaced numbers indicate figures of 50 percent or more.

from resource-rich nations like the U.S.S.R., the People's Republic of China, Canada, and several countries in Africa and South America. In 1950 the United States imported more than 50 percent of only 4 of 12 key industrial nonfuel minerals. By 1979 it imported 50 percent or more of 7 of these 12 minerals. By 1985 the list is expected to grow to 9, and by the end of the century the United States is expected to import more than 50 percent of all these vital materials, as shown in Table 12-3. Other more developed nations are even more dependent on imports. In 1979, Japan and western European nations imported more than 50 percent of all these 12 minerals and were 100 percent dependent on imports for 6 of the 12.

In 1978 the United States spent about $25 billion on nonfuel mineral imports. By the year 2000 this figure could rise to more than $60 billion. The fact that the United States now imports so much of its metals and minerals can be misleading. For most minerals—except chromium, tin, platinum, gold, and palladium—the United States has enough resources (but not enough known reserves) to meet demand for the next several decades. In many cases the United States imports these minerals not because of scarcity but because they are cheaper to extract from the higher-grade ores found in other nations than from lower-grade domestic reserves. U.S. subeconomic reserves can be used later when scarc-

ity causes prices to rise. However, the U.S. Geological Survey estimates that known reserves for most key minerals will not satisfy U.S. needs for more than 100 years.

Is Import Dependence Good or Bad?   Some argue that U.S. dependence on other countries for key resources threatens economic security (if prices increase sharply) and military security (if supplies of vital resources are cut off or severely restricted). For example, in 1978 Cuban-trained troops from neighboring Angola invaded the Shaba province in Zaire. As a result, cobalt mining was interrupted and the price of available cobalt increased by more than 600 percent. The United States or any importing nation would be particularly vulnerable: (1) when most of the world's supply of a resource is held by one country, as is the case with tungsten (China), mercury (Spain), and palladium (U.S.S.R.); (2) when a group of nations holding most of the world's supply of a resource band together to form a cartel to raise prices, as is the case with the copper, tin, bauxite, and iron ore cartels (which are modeled after the Organization of Petroleum Exporting Countries [OPEC]); and (3) when substitute materials are not readily available, as for iron, chromium, and manganese. Threats to world peace could also occur because of conflicts between more developed nations competing for scarce supplies of a key resource.

But others argue (1) that countries in nonfuel resource cartels have such wide geographic and political differences that they should not be as successful as OPEC in raising prices; (2) that unlike oil, which is consumed directly, raw materials contribute such a small percentage to the price of finished products that raw material price increases have relatively small effects; and (3) that mutual dependence of nations on one another can be a stabilizing force for world peace, since conflicts are more likely to be dealt with by negotiation rather than by military action.

A Suggested Plan for Metal and Mineral Resources
Any U.S. or world plan for metal and mineral resources should involve a mixture of the following approaches: (1) a major, ongoing program to find new deposits, to improve the efficiency of mineral extraction from ores, and to find substitutes for scarce materials; (2) improved mining technology; (3) greatly increased resource recovery, recycling, reuse, and resource con-

servation (Table 12-2); (4) controlling population growth (Chapter 8); (5) creating stockpiles for vital materials; and (6) establishing world trade agreements and a UN Agency for Natural Resources to see that producer nations receive a fair price for their resources. These suggested principles should be used to develop a detailed plan for managing and conserving nonfuel metal and mineral resources over the next 50 years.

It is encouraging that there are increasing governmental efforts in the United States to treat the effluents of society as wasted solids rather than solid wastes, as discussed in more detail in Enrichment Study 15. These efforts show what can be done and remind us that we must face some crucial questions: What resources have the least environmental impact? How can we minimize the impact of resource use? And how can we decrease our waste of resources?

Solid wastes are only raw materials we're too stupid to use.
Arthur C. Clarke

Guest Editorial: Mineral Supplies as a Function of Human Ingenuity

V. E. McKelvey

V. E. McKelvey is a research geologist with the U.S. Geological Survey. One of America's most respected geologists, he served as director of the U.S. Geological Survey from 1971 to 1978. Some of his many honors include service as the senior scientific advisor to the U.S. Law of the Sea delegation and receipt of the Rockefeller

Public Service Award (1973) and two awards from the American Association of Petroleum Geologists.

Minerals and mineral fuels are the key physical resources of an industrial society. They are the materials from which are built and powered our labor-saving machines; our lighting, heating, and cooling systems; and our transportation and communication networks. Minerals, processed and utilized with the aid of energy, are the source of the bulk of our chemicals, drugs, paints, and ceramics, and they are the raw materials from which most of our homes, buildings, dams, and other engineering works are constructed. And, in the form of fertilizers, insecticides, and farm machinery, minerals constitute key elements in the high productivity of modern agriculture. It is the extensive use of mineral resources, in fact, that forms the basis for the high level of living most people in industrialized nations enjoy today.

But natural resources of all kinds, important as they are in providing the physical and biological base for human activities, are second to human ingenuity (social, political, and economic as well as scientific and technological) in determining the level of living a society enjoys—or suffers. In fact, the kinds of things we call resources (in the sense of having some known or perceived potential value) and their abundance are a function of human ingenuity, or our ability to use things to our advantage. Oil, gas, coal, and most of the minerals we use today were not resources to primitive humans. And many of the mineral deposits mined today were not considered to be resources at the end of the last century because they were too low grade, too inaccessible, or too expensive to be recovered.

Even though resources are thus literally created by human ingenuity, recoverable mineral deposits are not inexhaustible; several minerals are becoming scarce, such as silver and mercury. Fortunately, human ingenuity can be and has been directed to extending mineral supplies beyond those that can be identified and assessed now. Geological exploration—guided by better knowledge about the earth—is likely to lead to new discoveries, as it has in the past. Advances in mining and mineral technology may continue to make recoverable deposits from increasingly lower grades and at increasingly greater depths. Advances in other branches of science and technology almost surely will develop substitutes for many materials that are becoming scarce, increase the efficiency of materials in use, and thus extend supplies. For example, the credit card calculator weighing only about 28 grams (1 ounce) or so and costing around $10 will do more than the electric machine calculators of a few decades ago weighing about 13,620 grams (30 pounds) and costing $500. Nearly all of these advances take energy to accomplish, and for them to continue into the far distant future requires the continued availability of low-cost energy—a goal that the trends of recent years suggest may be difficult, if not impossible, to achieve.

One of the most important elements leading to mineral scarcity has been the exponential increase in the use of minerals and fuels—related partly to exponential population growth but also to exponential growth in per capita resource use, particularly in the industrial countries. That no mineral supply can stand up to the buzz saw of continued exponential growth may be seen from the fact that a billion-year supply of a resource used at a constant annual level of consumption would be exhausted in only 584 years if the level of consumption increased at 3 percent per year.

Among the ways to extend or conserve mineral supplies is one that is only beginning to receive attention, but it may prove to be one of the most important: increasing the efficiency of our use of minerals and fuels. This is not to be identified with zero-growth objectives or with a mandatory return to a more primitive and less comfortable way of life. Rather, the challenge is to find how to have satisfying, rewarding, and healthy lives while using less of our resource capital. Some progress is already being made in this direction. For example, growth in GNP was long a direct function of growth in energy consumption, but within the last few years energy consumption has begun to grow at a lower rate than the GNP. This indicates that we can get more resources with less energy use and suggests that we might get even more if we tried. A certain caution is required, however, for we don't want to emulate the farmer who progressively cut down on his hog's feed and complained that just after he got the amount down to zero, the hog died!

Supply-and-demand economics have evidently been at work in some materials markets—reduction in the availability of commodities has increased prices, resulting in decreased consumption and a search for new sources. Fine. But the market doesn't have much foresight, and if its scarcity responses lead to a surplus, the old patterns of excessive and wasteful consumption may return even though scarcity may be foreseeable in the longer term. Applying our ingenuity to the problem calls at least for accelerated research, exploration, and development to find and extend resources by the means previously outlined. In addition, could the consumption of raw materials and energy be reduced significantly by redesigning urban, transportation, communication, manufacturing, and agricultural systems? And do we have or can we develop the social, economic, and political ingenuity to institute such systems while still maintaining a free enterprise climate that will stimulate creativity? Positive answers to these questions can't be guaranteed, but the questions suggest another avenue of research and exploration that may help extend mineral supplies far into the future.

Guest Editorial Discussion

1. Do you agree that physical and biological natural resources are secondary to human ingenuity in determining the average level of living of a society? Why or why not?

2. What factor or factors might limit our ability to mine lower grades of ores at greater depths?

3. Suggest ways in which we could have "satisfying, rewarding, and healthy lives while using less of our resource capital." What specifically can you do in your own life-style?

Discussion Topics

1. Criticize the use of the following equations for describing the relationship between available resources, population size, and resource supplies:

$$\text{average resources potentially available per person} = \frac{\text{resources}}{\text{population}}$$

and

$$\text{average resources potentially available per person} = \frac{\text{reserves}}{\text{population}}$$

2. Debate the following resolution: The United States uses far too many of the world's resources relative to its population size and should deliberately cut back on consumption.

3. Summarize the neo-Malthusian and the cornucopian views on the availability of resources. Which, if either, of these schools of thought do you support? Why?

4. Debate each of the following propositions:
   a. The competitive free market will control the supply and demand of mineral resources.
   b. New discoveries will provide all the raw materials we need.
   c. The ocean will provide all the mineral resources we need.
   d. We will not run out of key mineral resources because we can always mine lower-grade deposits.
   e. When a mineral resource becomes scarce, we can always find a substitute.
   f. When a resource becomes scarce, all we have to do is recycle it.

5. Compare the throwaway, resource recovery and recycling, and sustainable earth approaches to handling matter resources.

6. Use the second law of energy (thermodynamics) to show why the following are not profitable:
   a. extracting most minerals that are dissolved in seawater
   b. recycling minerals that are widely dispersed
   c. mining increasingly low grade deposits of minerals
   d. using inexhaustible solar energy to mine minerals
   e. continuing to mine, use, and recycle minerals at ever increasing rates

7. Discuss each of the following as a possible limiting factor on resource use on this planet: (a) population size, (b) resource supply, (c) political tensions from competition for scarce resources, (d) environmental consequences of resource use.

8. Debate the following proposals:
   a. Eliminate all tax breaks and depletion allowances for mineral mining industries to reduce the use and waste of mineral resources.
   b. Provide tax breaks and incentives for recycling industries and for all manufacturers who use recycled materials.
   c. Ban nonreturnable bottles.
   d. Add a disposal tax to all items that last less than 10 years.
   e. Require homeowners, businesses, and industries to separate wastes so they can be more readily recycled.

9. Why is it so difficult to get accurate estimates of mineral resource supplies? In answering, be sure to distinguish among reserves, subeconomic resources, hypothetical resources, speculative resources, depletion curves, static reserve indexes, and exponential reserve indexes.

10. What is the difference between a prediction and a projection? Discuss the limitations of the projections of world resource supplies shown in Figure 12-6. Which, if either, of these projections do you believe we should use in developing a comprehensive plan for resource use and conservation? Why?

11. Study Figure 12-6 to determine which key metals might be in short supply during your lifetime. How could such shortages affect your life-style?

12. Is the increasing U.S. dependence on foreign imports for critical resources a desirable trend in relation to world peace and a sustainable earth society? Why?

13. Discuss the relationship between the use of mineral resources and the following:
   a. population growth in the less developed nations (Chapter 8)
   b. U.S. population growth (Chapter 8)
   c. increasing world food supply (Chapter 9)
   d. parks, forests, wilderness, estuaries, and wildlife (Chapter 10)
   e. increasing urbanization and urban growth (Chapter 11)

Readings

Barnet, Richard J. 1980. *The Lean Years: Politics in an Age of Scarcity.* New York: Simon & Schuster. Superb discussion of the politics and economics of resource use and increasing scarcity.

Barnett, Harold J. 1967. "The Myth of Our Vanishing Resources." *Transactions—Social Sciences & Modern Society*, June, pp. 7–10. Statement of the optimistic view of our resource situation. Compare with the article by Preston Cloud (1975).

Berry, Stephen. 1972. "Recycling, Thermodynamics and Environmental Thrift." *Bulletin of the Atomic Scientists*, May, pp. 8–15. Good discussion of the limits of recycling.

Cloud, Preston E., Jr. 1975. "Mineral Resources Today and Tomorrow." In William W. Murdoch, ed., *Environment: Resources, Pollution and Society*. 2nd ed. Sunderland, Mass.: Sinauer. Superb summary of the neo-Malthusian view. Compare with the works by Harold Barnett (1967), Herman Kahn et al. (1976), and V. Kerry Smith (1979).

Environmental Protection Agency. 1977. *Fourth Report to Congress: Resource Recovery and Waste Reduction*. Washington, D.C.: Environmental Protection Agency. Excellent summary of solid waste management, recycling, resource recovery, and resource conservation in the United States.

Gabor, D., et al. 1978. *Beyond the Age of Waste*. Elmsford, N.Y.: Pergamon. Very useful discussion of resource conservation.

Hayes, Denis. 1978. *Repairs, Reuse, Recycling—First Steps Toward a Sustainable Society*. Washington, D.C.: Worldwatch Society. Splendid summary.

Kahn, Herman, et al. 1976. *The Next 200 Years: A Scenario for America and the World*. New York: Morrow. Presentation of an optimistic view on mineral supplies.

Meadows, Donella H., et al. 1972. *The Limits to Growth*. New York: Universe Books. Very important and controversial book giving the results of a computer simulation of the world ecosystem and resource supplies. See Enrichment Study 1 for more details.

National Academy of Sciences. 1969. *Resources and Man*. San Francisco: Freeman. Authoritative reference on resources. See especially chaps. 6 and 7 on mineral resources from the land and sea and chap. 8 on energy resources.

National Academy of Sciences. 1975. *Mineral Resources and the Environment*. Washington, D.C.: National Academy of Sciences. Excellent overview of mineral resource problems and recommendations for the future.

National Commission on Materials Policy. 1973. *Toward a National Materials Policy: World Perspective—Second Annual Report*. Washington, D.C.: Government Printing Office. Excellent summary of U.S. and world use of resources.

Park, Charles F., Jr. 1975. *Earthbound: Minerals, Energy, and Man's Future*. San Francisco: Freeman, Cooper. Superb overview emphasizing the neo-Malthusian view.

Ridker, Ronald G., and William D. Watson. 1980. *To Choose a Future: Resources and Environmental Consequences of Alternative Growth Paths*. Baltimore: Johns Hopkins University Press. Excellent and fairly optimistic overview.

Skinner, Brian J. 1976. *Earth Resources*. 2nd ed. Englewood Cliffs, N.J.: Prentice-Hall. Excellent survey of the world's resources.

Smith, V. Kerry. 1979. *Scarcity and Growth Reconsidered*. Baltimore: Johns Hopkins University Press. Excellent analysis of the optimistic view of world resource supplies.

U.S. Bureau of Mines. 1976. *U.S. Imports of Strategic Materials*. Washington, D.C.: Government Printing Office. Good source of data.

13

Energy Resources: Use, Concepts, and Alternatives

Turn off the lights; in the silence of your darkened home you can hear a thousand rivers whispering their thanks.

Clear Creek

13-1 The Four Energy Crises

A Preview of the Age of Scarcity Energy is the life-blood of the ecosphere (Section 5-3) and of human society. The amounts and types of useful energy available shape not only individual life-styles but also national and world economic systems. The earth's inhabitants have always lived in a solar energy era—a fact often forgotten in national and global statistics on energy use and sources. Each year the solar energy falling on farms and commercial forests far exceeds all human energy use and the solar energy concentrated for us as chemical energy in food crops is more than all human oil use. Thus, renewable and free solar energy is the largest energy input for the earth and for national and world economies. Were it not for solar energy the temperature outside would be about −269°C (−452°F).

Humans, however, have learned to supplement direct solar energy with fossil fuels—an indirect form of solar energy stored in concentrated form for us millions of years ago. Today we live in a petroleum era with oil providing over one-third of the energy used in the world each year and about one-half of the energy used in industrialized nations. Until 1973 most nations, rich and poor, assumed that an ample and relatively cheap supply of oil would always be available to fuel economic growth and more energy-intensive life-styles. This dream was shattered by the 1973 Arab oil embargo and the over twelvefold increase in the price of crude oil between 1973 and 1980 (from about $3 per barrel in 1973 to about $38

by the end of 1980) by the Organization of Petroleum Exporting Countries (OPEC).*

For example, by 1980 Americans were shocked to find gasoline costing about 33¢ a liter ($1.25 a gallon), but this was still cheap compared with the 79¢ a liter ($3.00 a gallon) many Europeans had to pay (primarily because of high gasoline taxes imposed by governments to reduce gasoline use and waste).

To make matters worse, using conservative estimates, oil prices are expected to at least double between 1980 and 1985, triple by 1990 (to about $120 a barrel), and increase at least 10-fold by 2000 (to $400 a barrel).

Consumers throughout the world have now learned an obvious but often forgotten lesson—energy is used to manufacture, grow, or move anything. Today the industrialized world runs by supplementing free solar energy with increasingly expensive oil. Thus, when oil becomes more expensive, so do food, fertilizer, clothing, antifreeze, electricity, medicine, steel, tires, and almost everything else. In many less developed countries crop yields have dropped because poor farmers can no longer afford fuel for their irrigation pumps or fertilizer to help them sustain the green revolution (Section 9-7).

Even though the 1973 oil embargo was not a true oil shortage, it gave the oil-dependent industrialized nations a preview of the age of scarcity that lies ahead unless they begin to reduce the extravagant waste of these finite and nonrenewable energy resources. Despite the rhetoric of some politicians and oil companies, conservation does not mean freezing in the dark or not being able to get to work. Instead, it means using the energy we have more efficiently by having well-insulated buildings that have efficient heating systems (with as much reliance on direct solar heating as possible) and replacing gas-guzzling cars with more fuel-efficient models and

---

*The 13 OPEC nations, accounting for over half of the world's output of oil and about 84 percent of all oil exports, are Algeria, Ecuador, Gabon, Indonesia, Iran, Iraq, Kuwait, Libya, Nigeria, Qatar, Saudi Arabia, United Arab Emirates, and Venezuela.

Enrichment Studies 1, 3, 5, and 15 are related to this chapter.

revitalizing public transportation systems (Section 11-4). Energy conservation can also involve life-style changes such as using smaller cars, mopeds, bicycles, or walking. Such life-style changes can save consumers money but as we shall see in this chapter the United States could have all the energy it needs over the next few decades by using the energy we have more efficiently and by depending more on renewable energy resources such as the sun and wind. If the world takes the important oil embargo warning seriously and begins a massive program to use energy more efficiently and searching for alternatives to oil, natural gas, and uranium, then the temporary oil energy crisis of the mid-1970s could be a blessing in disguise. If not, we face disaster.

Types of Energy Resources Energy resources can be classified as nonrenewable, renewable, and derived, as summarized in Table 13-1. The limit on a nonrenewable resource is the *quantity* available—the total amount that can be found, converted to a useful form, and used at an affordable cost and with an acceptable environmental impact (Figure 12-4). Theoretically, the supply of a renewable resource has no limit. Here the limiting factor (besides cost) is the *rate of use.* If a renewable resource (such as wood) is used faster than it is replenished, then

it can become depleted and, for all practical purposes, nonrenewable.

Types of Energy Crises Strictly speaking, we will never run out of energy. But energy can be used to cook, to heat our dwellings, to move us from one place to another, and so on only if we can get it in a useful or concentrated form at an affordable price and without unacceptable environmental effects. Thus, the term **energy crisis** refers to either a shortage, a catastrophic price rise for one or more forms of useful energy, or a situation in which energy use is so great that the resulting pollution and environmental disruption (Sections 3-3 and 3-4) threaten human health and welfare and the diversity and sustainability of the ecosphere.

It is useful to distinguish among four closely related, present and projected energy crises (see the summary box). Three of these are *energy shortage crises;* the fourth one is an *energy policy crisis,* as described in the summary box.

Some Urgent Questions Supplies of energy from food (Chapter 9) and firewood (Section 10-4) are growing scarce in many poor nations. However, today the world faces no serious shortage of any energy resource used to

Table 13-1 Classification of Energy Resources

Nonrenewable	Renewable	Derived
Fossil fuels (indirect solar energy stored millions of years ago)	Energy conservation (improving energy efficiency)‡	Synthetic natural gas (SNG) (produced from coal)

Petroleum
  Natural gas
  Coal
	Direct solar energy (for heat and conversion to electricity in solar cells)	Synthetic oil and alcohols (produced from coal or organic wastes)

Oil shale (rock containing solid hydrocarbons that can be distilled out to yield an oil-like material called shale oil) Tar sands (sand intimately mixed with an oil-like material)	Water power (hydroelectricity) (indirect solar energy)	Biofuels (alcohols and natural gas produced from plants and organic wastes)
	Ocean thermal gradients (heat stored in ocean water) (indirect solar energy)	Hydrogen gas (produced from coal or by using electricity, heat, or perhaps sunlight to decompose water)
Nuclear fuels	Wind energy (indirect solar energy)	Urban wastes (for incineration)

Conventional nuclear fission (uranium and thorium)
  Breeder nuclear fission (uranium and thorium)
  Nuclear fusion (deuterium and lithium)
	Biomass energy (indirect solar energy) from the burning of wood, crops, food and animal wastes (if not used more rapidly than it is replenished)	

Geothermal energy (trapped pockets of heat in the earth's interior)†	Geothermal energy (continuous heat flow from earth's interior)†	
	Tidal energy (if not widely used)	

†The high-temperature geothermal energy trapped in underground pockets is a nonrenewable resource. The slow to moderate flow of heat from the interior of the earth is a renewable resource that cannot be extracted and used at a very high rate.

‡Technically, conservation is not a source of energy. Instead of providing energy, it reduces the use and waste of energy resources by using them more efficiently.

The Four Energy Crises

Today's Food and Firewood Energy Shortage Crisis

At least one-fourth and perhaps three-fourths of the people in less developed nations do not have an adequate daily intake of food or protein energy (Sections 9-1 and 9-2), and the 90 percent of the people in poor countries for whom firewood is the main fuel are having more and more trouble getting enough of it.

Today's Energy Policy Crisis

There is an urgent need to develop and carry out a carefully integrated set of short-, intermediate-, and long-term energy plans over the next 50 years. These plans will allow the world to replace dwindling supplies of petroleum, natural gas, and uranium with a new mix of environmentally acceptable energy sources and to emphasize energy conservation so that excessive energy use and waste won't overpollute the environment as a result of the second energy law (Sections 3-3 and 3-4).

The Oil Energy Shortage Crisis of 1985 to 2000

If world oil use should continue to grow at only about 2 percent a year, then sometime between 1985 and 2000 the world demand for oil will probably exceed the rate at which it can be supplied and oil prices will rise catastrophically. If this occurs, the serious economic stresses already affecting most nations in the world partially because of higher oil prices could worsen and trigger a global economic depression. In addition, international tensions could increase as industrialized nations compete for available oil.

The Energy Shortage and Environmental Disruption Crisis of 2000 to 2060

Affordable supplies of oil, natural gas, and possibly uranium (without the use of the highly controversial nuclear breeder reactor) will probably begin running out between 2000 and 2060. By this time, the world must have instituted a stringent program to improve energy efficiency and thus reduce energy waste and shifted to new, affordable, and environmentally acceptable energy sources. Otherwise the world faces massive economic disruption along with a population crash. If world energy consumption rises sharply, then even if the world somehow manages to avoid any serious energy shortages after 1980, sometime between 2000 to 2060 (if not earlier) human health and welfare could be threatened by massive water pollution (Chapter 16), air pollution (Chapter 17), land degradation (Chapter 10), and global climate change (Enrichment Study 3), caused by too many people using too much energy.

---

supplement direct solar energy, but it does face an energy policy crisis. We urgently need comprehensive and carefully integrated short-, intermediate-, and long-term plans for moving to a new sustainable earth energy era characterized by energy conservation and a mix of environmentally acceptable energy sources. *Making a relatively smooth transition to a new sustainable earth energy era is one of the most important, complex, and difficult problems the world faces.*

The critical nonrenewable resource in this transition is time. Some new oil, natural gas, and uranium deposits may buy us a few more years; we can learn how to depend more on a mix of renewable energy sources such as solar, wind, and biomass energy, and per capita energy use and waste in the more developed nations can be decreased without lowering living comfort. But all of these changes will take time. Energy shifts during the past 200 years indicate that it takes 50 to 100 years to shift to new energy sources and life-styles. Thus, we have enough time to make the shift to a new energy era, but only if we begin now. The present shift, however, will probably have to be made within 30 to 50 years.

In order to see how the world might make a successful transition to a new sustainable earth energy era, we need to look at several questions:

1. How much energy do we use and waste and how much of each kind of energy do we really need?

2. What are our present and future energy alternatives? How long will each alternative take to develop; how long will it last; and what is its net useful energy yield (Section 3-3), relative cost, and environmental impact?

3. How can energy waste (especially in more developed nations that use 80 percent of the world's energy) be reduced?

4. What are the major principles of a short-, intermediate-, and long-term plan for making the transition?

There is little doubt that these and related questions will dominate our lives over the coming decades—whether we like it or not. In this chapter and the next, we will examine these questions, emphasizing the second, third, and fourth energy crises, since the food and firewood energy crisis has been treated elsewhere (Chapter 9 and Section 10-4). The remainder of this chapter will be devoted to looking at energy use and waste, reviewing some energy concepts that can help us evaluate energy alternatives, getting an overview of the major energy alternatives, and suggesting some major principles that could be used to develop an energy transition plan for the United States. In the next chapter we will examine the major energy alternatives in greater detail. In both chapters the primary emphasis will be on the energy problems and opportunities in the United States, since it uses and wastes more energy than any other country in the world.

13-2   Energy Use and Waste

How Did We Get into This Mess?   Although the present energy predicament in the more developed nations is enormously complex, it results from the interaction of five major factors: (1) nearly complete dependence on nonrenewable fossil fuel energy resources (especially oil) because of their relatively high net energy yields (Section 3-3) and relatively low extraction costs; (2) greatly increased per capita energy use since 1950; (3) increased dependence of many industrialized nations on oil imports either because increased demand has outstripped high-quality domestic supplies or because vast and easily accessible oil deposits (especially in the Middle East) can be extracted at lower cost than most remaining deposits in importing countries; (4) little concern for reducing energy waste and for developing alternative energy sources (such as sunlight, wind, and biomass energy) because of the mistaken belief that abundant and relatively cheap supplies of fossil fuels and uranium will always be available; and (5) stimulation of high energy use and waste by keeping fossil fuel energy prices artificially low by not including environmental, health, and social costs in energy prices and by government subsidization and regulation of energy prices in some countries, including the United States.

The common thread in these factors is economics. Any useful and presumably abundant energy resource that consumers can buy at a relatively low price will be widely used with little concern either for reducing energy waste and pollution or for finding alternatives. In other words, the more developed nations got into the present predicament by using good sense: Oil was cheap, readily available, very convenient for transportation and heating, and easy to transport, so they began using it in larger and larger quantities. Now that the end of the oil energy era is in sight, these nations will hopefully have the good sense to plan for an orderly transition to a new sustainable earth energy era.

Energy Use in the World and the United States   At the primitive level of survival, energy use is limited to the food one eats, about 2,000 kilocalories a day (Figure 13-1).* Each stage of human cultural evolution (Chapter 2) has involved a dramatic increase in supplementing direct solar energy converted to food energy with energy from animals, the burning of wood and fossil fuels, and more recently nuclear fission (Figure 13-1). Today each person in most industrial nations consumes about 125,000 kilocalories a day—almost 63 times the energy use at the primitive survival level. The average American, however, consumes (or, more accurately, degrades the quality of) an average of 250,000 kilocalories of energy per day—125 times the survival level. This means that each American directly and indirectly uses an amount of energy equivalent to that in 41 kilograms (91 pounds) of coal each day or in 15,000 kilograms (16.5 tons) of coal

---

*Unfortunately, a bewildering array of units is used to express energy values. The most widely used units are kilojoules (kJ), joules (J), kilocalories (kcal), calories (cal), British thermal units (Btu), kilowatt-hours (kW·h), and quads. The following is a summary of the relationships between these units and their energy equivalents in terms of the energy content of crude oil, natural gas, and coal:

$1 \text{ kJ} = 10^3 \text{ J} = 0.239 \text{ kcal} = 239 \text{ cal} = 0.949 \text{ Btu} = 2.78 \times 10^{-4} \text{ kW·h}$

$1 \text{ kcal} = 10^3 \text{ cal} = 4.184 \text{ kJ} = 4{,}184 \text{ J} = 3.97 \text{ Btu} = 1.16 \times 10^{-3} \text{ KW·h}$

$1 \text{ kW·h} = 13.6 \times 10^3 \text{ kJ} = 860 \text{ kcal} = 3.4 \times 10^3 \text{ Btu}$

$1 \text{ quad (q)} = 1.05 \times 10^{15} \text{ kJ} = 2.52 \times 10^{14} \text{ Btu} = 2.93 \times 10^{11} \text{ kW·h}$

Approximate crude oil equivalent: 1 barrel (159 liters, or 42 U.S. gallons) $= 6 \times 10^6 \text{ kJ} = 2 \times 10^6 \text{ kcal} = 6 \times 10^6 \text{ Btu} = 2 \times 10^3 \text{ kW·h}$

Approximate natural gas equivalent: 1 cubic foot (0.0283 cubic meters) $= 1 \times 10^3 \text{ kJ} = 260 \text{ kcal} = 1 \times 10^3 \text{ Btu} = 0.3 \text{ kW·h}$

Approximate hard coal equivalent: 1 ton (909 kilograms) $= 2 \times 10^7 \text{ kJ} = 6 \times 10^6 \text{ kcal} = 2 \times 10^7 \text{ Btu} = 6 \times 10^3 \text{ kW·h}$

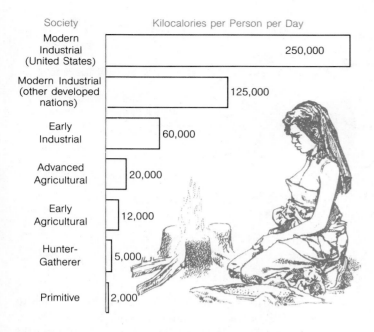

Figure 13-1 Average daily per capita energy use at various stages of human cultural evolution.

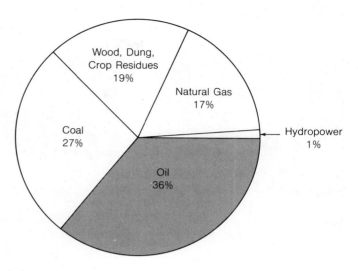

Figure 13-2 Primary world energy sources in 1979 excluding sunlight incorporated in food crops and used to warm the earth and drive its weather cycles. If the earth's solar energy input was included the supplemental energy sources shown in this figure would make up only a few percent of annual world energy use.

each year. This means that 228 million Americans use enough energy each day to provide the survival energy needs for *28 billion* people—about six times the present population of the world.

Around 1850 wood was the primary fuel used to supplement direct solar energy throughout the world, and it still is for 90 percent of the people in poor nations. But 80 percent of the energy used in the world today comes from fossil fuels (oil, coal, and natural gas), mostly oil (Figure 13-2).

The shift to new energy sources since 1850 has taken place primarily in the more developed nations and in several phases. For example, America's economic growth and increased energy use during this time has been fueled by wood, then coal, and now oil (plus moderate amounts of natural gas and coal) (Figure 13-3). However, the switch from coal to oil did not occur because of a shortage of coal, which was and is still the most abundant fossil fuel in the United States. Instead, it took place (1) because oil (and natural gas) were cleaner, easier, and safer to extract, transport, and burn, and (2) because some emerging industrial processes happened to use oil (or natural gas) instead of coal even when there wasn't an advantage of cost or convenience. In addition, oil could be converted to gasoline to power America's growing dependence on the automobile. In 1850 about 91 per-

cent of America's energy came from wood—a renewable energy source. By 1979, however, nonrenewable fossil fuels supplied 90 percent of all energy used in the United States (Figure 13-3). From Figure 13-3 we can see that the 100 years between 1850 and 1950 was an era of transition when people lived within the earth's potentially renewable energy budget by burning wood to an era of using the earth's nonrenewable energy capital by burning fossil fuels. Future historians may label the period from 1950 to the present as one of heedless waste of the world's finite and precious fossil fuel resources.

Primarily because of the increased availability of relatively inexpensive oil and natural gas, world energy consumption tripled and average annual energy consumption per person doubled between 1950 and 1975. As a result, most of the fossil fuels ever used have been consumed since 1950. Oil has been pumped out of the ground for over 100 years (since 1869), but over half of the total amount extracted was consumed between 1960 and 1978. Today the rate of energy use is so high that the world's oil and natural gas era could come to an end within 40 to 80 years, as discussed in Section 14-2.

Most of the world's increase in energy consumption per person since 1900 has taken place in the more developed nations, and the gap in average per capita energy use between rich and poor nations has been wid-

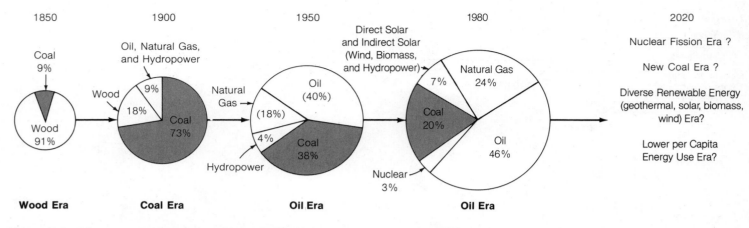

1850   1900   1950   1980   2020

Coal 9%

Wood 91%

Wood Era

Oil, Natural Gas, and Hydropower

Wood 18%

9%

Coal 73%

Coal Era

Natural Gas

Oil (40%)

(18%)

4%

Coal 38%

Hydropower

Oil Era

Direct Solar and Indirect Solar (Wind, Biomass, and Hydropower)

7%

Natural Gas 24%

Coal 20%

Oil 46%

Nuclear 3%

Oil Era

Nuclear Fission Era ?

New Coal Era ?

Diverse Renewable Energy (geothermal, solar, biomass, wind) Era?

Lower per Capita Energy Use Era?

Figure 13-3 Primary energy resources used in the United States (excluding direct sunlight). Circle size represents relative amount of total energy used.

ening (Figure 13-4). In 1975 the more developed nations, with only 25 percent of the world's people, used about 80 percent of the world's energy. Between 1975 and 2000 total world energy demand could double or triple, and average per capita energy demand could double.

But these projected demands may not be met, especially in the more developed nations. Rapidly escalating prices of oil, natural gas, and building and operating nuclear power plants and the increased pollution that automatically results from increased use of any type of energy are likely to change the J curve of increasing per capita energy use in the more developed nations to an S curve (Figure 13-4).

People who think that major oil or natural gas discoveries will solve the problem do not understand the arithmetic and conseqences of the J curve (Section 1-2). Saudi Arabia, with the world's largest known oil reserves, could supply the world's total oil needs for only 5 years at the 1980 rate of consumption if it were the world's only source of oil. Used by itself the recent petroleum find in Mexico, which some say may equal the deposit in Saudi Arabia, would merely add another 5 to 10 years' worth of oil reserves at present use rates. The estimated oil reserves under Alaska's North Slope—the largest American find ever—would meet current world demand for only about 6 months and U.S. demand for only 2 to 4 years. Even if drilling off the East coast of the United States meets the most optimistic estimates, these potential oil reserves could satisfy world oil needs for only 1 week, U.S. oil needs for less than 3 months, and U.S. natural gas needs for about 5 months. The recently developed North Sea oil reserves would satisfy current world oil demands for only about 1½ years. We need to

search the world vigorously for more oil, but according to former U.S. Secretary of Energy James R. Schlesinger, anyone who tells us that new discoveries will solve world oil supply problems is really saying that we need to dis-

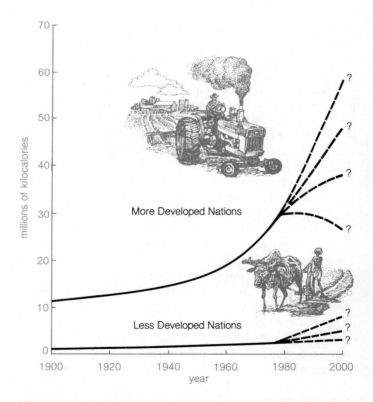

Figure 13-4 Past (solid lines) and projected (dotted lines) average per capita annual energy consumption in the world.

cover the equivalent of a new Mexico or Saudi Arabia oil deposit *every 5 years* merely to maintain our present level of oil use. Even if we could find oil equal to 4 times the present world oil reserves (which most experts consider highly unlikely), it would only provide an additional 25 years of oil at today's rate of use.

The United States is a prime example of greatly increased energy use since 1900 and especially since 1950 (Figure 13-5). Between 1900 and 1980, U.S. population increased less than threefold, while national energy consumption increased over sevenfold, and per capita energy use more than doubled. In 1980, with about 5 percent of the world's population, the United States accounted for about 25 percent of the world's energy consumption, including 49 percent of all natural gas, 25 percent of all oil, and 20 percent of all coal. In comparison, India, with about 15 percent of the world's population, consumed only about 1.5 percent of the world's commercial energy. In 1980, the average energy consumption per person in the United States was about 54 times that for the less developed nations, 8 times the world average, and 2 to 3 times that of other industrialized nations, such as Sweden, Great Britain, West Germany, and Japan. The U.S. Department of Defense alone uses enough energy to rank twenty-second in the world among nations in total energy consumed each year. In 1981, 228 million Americans used more energy for air conditioning alone than 985 million Chinese used for all purposes. Indeed, if all the barrels of oil used *each day* in the United States were laid out end to end, they would reach from New York City to Calcutta!

U.S. Dependence on Imported Oil   By the late 1960s, most low-cost, high-quality oil deposits in the United States had been depleted. For example, in the early 1960s the cost of extracting 159 liters (1 barrel) of Middle East oil was 16¢, compared with $1.73 for U.S. oil. By 1973 U.S. oil production had begun to fall (Figure 13-6). As a result, the nation began to depend more on imported oil, which was then cheap (Figure 13-6). After the sharp price rises in 1973, most industrialized nations began to reduce their oil consumption. However, in 1972 just before the oil embargo, America imported about 29 percent of its oil and by 1980 about 43 percent, with about 85 percent of it coming directly or indirectly from OPEC nations. Today, the oil the United States imports each year alone equals the annual oil consumption by all the 3 billion people living in the less developed nations. The staggering $82 billion cost of imported oil in 1980 (or an average of a quarter of a billion dollars a day), compared

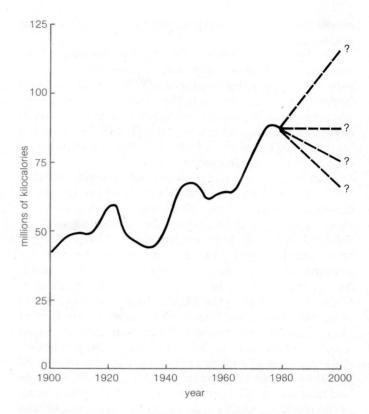

Figure 13-5   Past (solid line) and projected (dotted lines) average per capita annual primary energy consumption in the United States (excluding direct sunlight).

with $8.4 billion in 1973, created a massive trade deficit (agricultural exports only made up about half of the deficit) and undermined the strength of the American dollar throughout the world and stimulated domestic inflation. During 1980 the United States paid an average of $9.4 million each hour for imported oil, and each American paid an average of $363 to oil-exporting nations—enough money to have created 7 million new jobs or to have built 1.4 million new $60,000 homes. The annual flow of money into OPEC nations is hard to comprehend. For 1980 alone the OPEC oil income was enough to buy the entire U.S. farm crop or all the stock in the 50 biggest American industrial corporations. And this is only 1 year's income! It is encouraging, however, that between 1977 and 1980 the United States decreased its petroleum imports by 28 percent, from 8.6 million barrels per day in 1977 to 6.2 million barrels per day in 1981 (Figure 13-6). Drilling for oil and natural gas in the United States reached a 25 year high in 1980. Some forecasters believe this may increase domestic oil production slightly by 1990, while other experts project a 20 percent decline in production by 1990, despite greatly increased drilling (Figure 13-6).

If the United States does not continue to curb its wasteful use of oil and domestic oil production does not increase significantly, then by 1990 the bill for crude oil imports could easily reach $180 billion per year, with each American paying an average of $750 per year to oil-exporting nations. At this rate the United States would be paying $21 million *an hour* (or half a billion dollars a day) to foreign oil-producing nations

Actually, this oil will probably not be available. First, the OPEC nations will probably limit oil production to conserve a resource that will be worth much more if left in the ground and to discourage the extravagant and wasteful use of oil in the United States. Also, OPEC nations cannot effectively use and invest the massive amounts of money they are already receiving. Second, the oil supply could be cut off at any time because of political instability in the Middle East. The government in Saudi Arabia, the largest oil exporter to the United States, could be overthrown—like that in Iran. A crucial question that concerns the rest of the world is whether Americans are so addicted to having a large supply of oil that they would try to take over Middle East oil fields and thus risk a third world war that could destroy most of the world's population and ecosystems. A war to take over the oil fields, however, could use up or destroy more oil than would be gained. Third, even if world oil supplies were adequate, the United States probably could not afford such a large financial drain without disrupting its entire economy. Fourth, despite greatly increased drilling efforts, crude oil extraction in the United States between 1980 and 1990 is expected to decrease or increase only slightly (Figure 13-6). Fifth, major private oil companies no longer have the flexibility and power to allocate oil supplies as they did in 1973 and 1974. This is because the major oil companies' share of world oil supplies dropped from 90 percent in 1973 to only 55 percent in 1980. Sixth, the United States has not built up a national strategic stockpile to help prevent catastrophic price increases by oil-exporting nations or to help meet oil demands if oil imports drop or are cut off. By 1980, the United States had stockpiled enough oil to cover only 16 days of imports.

It is clear that over the next decade the United States must kick its dangerous addiction to its increasing and wasteful use of oil. Unfortunately, many Americans have yet to take the warning of the 1973 oil embargo seriously. In 1979 a Gallup poll indicated that only 50 percent of the American public felt that the U.S. energy situation was "fairly serious," and about 33 percent didn't even

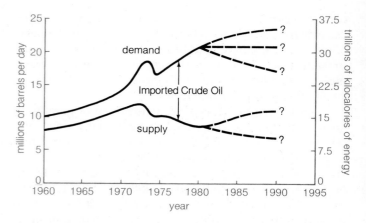

Figure 13-6 Past (solid lines) and projected (dotted lines) daily domestic crude oil supply and demand in the United States.

know that the nation imported oil, despite massive publicity between 1973 and 1979. Perhaps this is not surprising given government indecision and conflicting statements over whether the United States faces an energy crisis. After 5 years of deliberation and conflicting pressures from energy companies, environmentalists, and other special interest groups, Congress finally passed the National Energy Act of 1978 and amended it in 1980. This act, while helpful, primarily provides a short-term strategy that could lead to long-term problems. As a result, by 1981 the United States still did not have a comprehensive, long-term energy plan.

The United States is not running out of usable energy. There is plenty of it in the form of improving energy efficiency (the cheapest and easiest option), coal, sunshine, water, wind, farm and forestry wastes, uranium and geothermal heat. Only oil and probably natural gas (which make up only 1 percent of the nation's total energy resources) are running low. Yet oil and natural gas accounted for 70 percent of all U.S. energy used in 1980 (Figure 13-3). Thus, the United States has a built-in energy time bomb that will keep ticking unless the nation switches to other energy alternatives.

Energy Waste in the United States In addition to being the world's largest energy user, America is also the world's largest energy waster—about 85 to 90 percent of all the energy used in the United States each year is wasted. Each year Americans waste more fossil fuel energy than is used by two-thirds of the world population. Although Americans are slowly beginning to conserve energy, most U.S. cars are still gas guzzlers and most American homes are still underinsulated.

Japan and most industrialized European nations with standards of living (as measured by average per capita GNP and by other indicators) equal to or greater than that in the United States use only one-third to one-half as much energy per person. Because national energy use patterns vary, some types of energy savings in one nation can't always be used in other countries. Many developed nations which (unlike the United States) have little if any domestic supplies of oil are greatly affected by energy waste in the United States. For example, in 1980, Western Europe got about 55 percent of its energy from oil and Japan got 75 percent. With little or no oil of their own, they are significantly affected by U.S. competition for world oil supplies. By the mid-1980s the Soviet Union may have to start importing oil—thus increasing competition in the world oil market.

Typically about 40 to 75 percent of all energy used each year will automatically be degraded to low-temperature waste heat as a result of the second law of energy (see Section 3-3), but there is strong evidence that average per capita energy use in the United States could be cut by 25 to 50 percent without decreasing the quality of life. According to energy expert Amory Lovins (see his Guest Editorial at the end of this chapter), average per capita energy use could be cut by at least 90 percent without sacrificing the quality of life in the United States. In the words of energy expert John Holdren, the United States can no longer be "a society that uses 5,000 pound [2,300 kilogram] automobiles for half-mile [0.8 kilometer] round trips to the market to fetch a six-pack of beer, consumes the beer in buildings that are overcooled in summer and overheated in winter, and then throws the aluminum cans away at an energy loss equivalent to one-third of a gallon [1.3 liters] of gasoline per six-pack."

13-3 Energy Concepts: Energy Quality, Energy Efficiency, and Net Useful Energy

Energy Quality and Flow Rates   Since we cannot create or destroy energy (Section 3-2), we never really consume it. Instead we consume **energy quality,** the ability of a form of energy to do useful work for us. According to the second law of energy (Section 3-3), whenever we use any form of energy, we automatically degrade it to a lower-quality or less useful form of energy—usually low-temperature heat energy that flows into the environment. As shown in Table 13-2, different forms of energy vary in their energy quality. High or very high quality energy (such as electricity, oil, gasoline, sunlight, wind,

uranium, and high-temperature heat) is concentrated. By contrast, low-quality energy (such as low-temperature heat) is dispersed, or dilute. Note that a major factor determining the usefulness of a form of energy is its quality, not its quantity. A kilocalorie of dispersed heat energy at room temperature or a kilocalorie of dispersed solar energy can do little (if any) work. For example, there is more low-temperature heat in the Atlantic Ocean than in all of the oil in Saudi Arabia, but the heat stored in the ocean is so dispersed that you can't do much with it. But a kilocalorie of high-temperature heat energy released when a fossil fuel is burned or when the nuclei of uranium atoms undergo nuclear fission is a concentrated form of very useful energy.

Concentrated solar energy has such a high quality that it has the potential to provide temperatures as high as 5,500°C (9,932°F). Even normal sunlight on a cloudy day can potentially give temperatures up to 1,200°C (2,192°F). The reason that normal sunlight does not melt metals or burn our clothes off is that only a relatively small amount of this high-quality energy reaches each square meter of the earth's surface per minute or hour—even though the total amount of solar energy reaching the entire earth each minute or hour is enormous. Thus, to provide high temperatures, the solar energy reaching a fairly large area of the earth must be focused (with mirrors or other devices) to the small area of the earth where high temperatures are needed to perform useful work. Wind energy also has a high energy quality, but to perform large amounts of useful work it must flow into a given area at a fairly high rate. Thus, *the overall usefulness of a renewable energy source (such as solar energy and wind energy) is determined both by its energy quality and by the amount of high-quality energy reaching a fairly small area of the earth per minute or hour.*

Unfortunately, many of the highest-quality forms of energy (such as high-temperature heat, electricity, hydrogen gas, concentrated sunlight, synthetic oil, and synthetic natural gas) do not occur naturally. We must use other forms of high-quality energy (such as fossil or nuclear fuels) either to produce them, focus them, or to upgrade their quality. Other forms of very high- to high-quality energy (such as nuclear fission, nuclear fusion, and burning of fossil fuels) take large quantities of high-quality energy to find and extract the fuels and to build and run environmentally acceptable power plants.

It is wasteful to use high- or very high-quality energy to perform a task that only requires low- or moderate quality energy. Thus, *an important way to reduce energy waste is to supply energy only in the quality needed for the task at hand* using the cheapest possible approach as

Table 13-2 Energy Quality of Different Forms of Energy

	Energy Quality	
Form of Energy	Relative Value	Average Energy Content (kilocalories per kilogram)
Electricity	Very high	—
Very high temperature heat (greater than 2,500°C)	Very high	—
Nuclear fission (uranium)	Very high	139,000,000*
Nuclear fusion (deuterium)	Very high	24,000,000†
Concentrated sunlight	Very high	—
Concentrated wind (high-velocity flow)	Very high	—
High-temperature heat (1,000°C–2,500°C)	High	—
Hydrogen gas (as a fuel)	High	30,000
Natural gas (mostly methane)	High	13,000
SNG (synthetic natural gas made from coal)	High	13,000
Gasoline (refined crude oil)	High	10,500
Crude oil	High	10,300
LNG (liquefied natural gas)	High	10,300
Coal (bituminous and anthracite)	High	7,000
Synthetic oil (made from coal)	High	8,900
Sunlight (normal)	High	—
Concentrated geothermal	Moderate	—
Water (high-velocity flow)	Moderate	—
Moderate-temperature heat (100°C–1,000°C)	Moderate	—
Dung	Moderate	4,000
Wood and crop wastes	Moderate	3,300
Assorted garbage and trash	Moderate	2,900
Oil shale	Moderate	1,100
Tar sands	Moderate	1,100
Peat	Moderate	950
Dispersed geothermal	Low	—
Low-temperature heat (air temperature of 100°C or lower)	Low	—

*Per kilogram of uranium metal containing 0.72% fissionable uranium-235.
†Per kilogram of hydrogen containing 0.015% deuterium.

discussed in more detail by Amory Lovins in his Guest Editorial at the end of this chapter. High-quality electrical energy is really needed to perform only a few specific tasks, such as running lights, motors, and electronic equipment and for obtaining some metals (such as aluminum) from their ores. Using electricity for any other task (such as heating homes or running electric cars) is wasteful of money and the energy resources (primarily fossil fuels and uranium) used to produce electricity. For example, using very high-quality electrical energy merely to heat a home to 20°C (68°F) or to provide hot water at 60°C (140°F) is extremely wasteful. First, at a power plant, high-quality fossil fuel or nuclear energy is converted to high-quality heat energy at several thousand degrees with an automatic loss of some of the heat to the local environment, or "heat tax," as required by the second energy law. Then the remaining high-quality heat is used to convert water to steam and spin turbines to produce very high-quality electrical energy, with a further loss of heat. More degraded energy or heat is lost when the electricity is transmitted to a home. There the high-quality electrical energy is converted back to low-quality heat energy to heat the home or provide hot water. According to energy expert Amory Lovins, "This is like using a chain saw to cut butter."

As Figure 13-7 shows, the essential uses for electricity in the United States amount to only about 8 percent of annual U.S. energy needs. *It is very important to realize that the United States already has more than enough power plants to produce all the electricity the nation needs between today and the year 2005 (and perhaps to 2025) to perform the tasks where electricity is really necessary.* This is true regardless of what type of power plant we are talking about building. Thus, the intense arguments over whether the United States should provide its citizens with more electricity by building more nuclear, coal, or solar power plants is a tragic waste of time. In terms of energy quality, none are needed and some of the ones already in use could be shut down. In addition, devoting the bulk (about 66 percent) of federal energy research and development funds and an enormous amount of private investment funds to designing and building electric power plants is a waste of limited capital that is vitally needed to develop other nonelectrical energy alternatives to provide heat for homes and industry (58 percent of U.S. energy needs) and fuels for vehicles (34 percent of U.S. energy needs), as shown in Figure 13-7. Thus, the real energy policy crisis in the United States (Section 13-1) is that the government and the powerful electric power industry are insisting on providing the nation with more of a form of high-quality energy (electricity) that it really has no need for.

We can save some energy in space heating by burning fossil fuels directly in a home furnace or hot water heater rather than at a power plant to make electricity. But even this process wastes large amounts of energy by burning the fuels at about 2,000°C to 3,000°C (3,632°F to 5,432°F) to heat a house to 20°C (68°F) or water to 60°C (140°F). Instead it is less wasteful and cheaper in the long run (if fossil fuel and electrical energy prices are not kept artificially low) to heat a home or water by collecting solar energy at normal outside temperatures (typically 0°C to 19°C), allowing it to flow into and heat a well-insulated, air-tight house that uses stone, water, or other materials to store the heat for use at night.

First Law Energy Efficiency   Another way to cut energy waste and save money (at least in the long run) is to use an energy-conversion device (such as a light, home heating system, or automobile engine) of maximum energy efficiency. We can define two types of energy efficiency, one based on the first energy law (Section 3-2), and the other on the second energy law (Section 3-3).

The **first law energy efficiency** is the ratio of the useful energy (or work) output to the total energy (or work) input for an energy-conversion device or process. Normally this energy ratio is multiplied by 100 so that the efficiency can be expressed as a percentage:

$$\text{first law energy efficiency (\%)} = \frac{\text{useful energy (or work) energy output}}{\text{total energy (or work) input}} \times 100$$

Whenever we use heat to perform useful work, the first law efficiency will always be less than 100 percent, partly

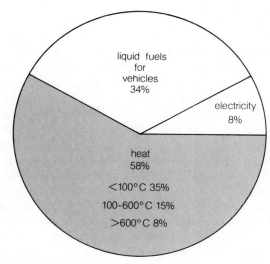

Figure 13-7   End uses of energy in the United States in 1979.

because of the automatic heat loss imposed by the second law of energy and partly because of imperfections and unnecessary waste in energy-conversion devices and systems. However, when electrical energy is used to produce heat or perform mechanical work, first law energy efficiencies can be nearly 100 percent for electric motors and as high as about 300 percent for an electric heat pump that merely moves heat from outside air to inside air without having to convert it to another energy form.

Improved technology has greatly increased the energy efficiency of many devices, but there is considerable room for improvement as discussed by Amory Lovins in his Guest Editorial at the end of this chapter. When energy was cheap, industrialized nations often found it cheaper to use inefficient devices that were less costly. For example, the incandescent light bulb is only 5 percent efficient. For every 100 kilocalories of electrical energy supplied to the bulb, 95 kilocalories are degraded to low-quality heat and only 5 percent is converted to light:

$$\text{first law efficiency of incandescent light bulb} = \frac{5 \text{ kcal of light energy}}{100 \text{ kcal of electrical energy}} \times 100 = 5\%$$

At present, the incandescent light bulb—which should really be called a heat bulb—is used for 95 percent of all home lighting in the United States. A fluorescent light bulb has a first law efficiency of about 22 percent—over 4 times that of the incandescent bulb—but its long length and bulky starting equipment have prevented it from being widely used. This could change, however, with a new type of fluorescent light bulb, which is now available, that looks like an ordinary screw-in incandescent bulb and doesn't have the bulky starting equipment of conventional fluorescents. A 75-watt bulb costs about $7.50 to $10.00, compared with about 75¢ for a conventional 75-watt incandescent bulb, but the new bulb will last 10 years or more compared with about 6 months for the incandescent. This much longer life plus its use of 70 percent less electricity than the incandescent bulb means that the fluorescent bulb will be cheaper to use over a 10-year period. Costs should fall with mass production and increased use of these new bulbs. If all homes in the United States switched to these more efficient bulbs, the resulting energy savings would be equivalent to 80 million liters (500,000 barrels) of oil *each day*. Another way to reduce energy waste is to insulate a building or home fully and heat it mainly or partially by the heat emitted from its lights (of any type).

To evaluate total energy efficiency, the first law efficiency of the energy device alone is not enough. We must also evaluate the whole system of energy-conversion steps—from finding and processing a fuel to transporting it, upgrading it to a more useful form, and finally using it. Figure 13-8 compares the net first law energy efficiencies for entire home heating systems. From this figure we see that using natural gas to drive a home heat pump is the best choice but natural gas is not available in some areas and future supplies may be limited. Heating a home with electricity from a hydroelectric plant has the next highest first law energy efficiency, but most major hydroelectric dam sites in the United States have already been developed. Next we have an oil-fired heat pump*, but oil is becoming very expensive and future supplies may be limited. Using electricity made from natural gas to drive a home heat pump is the next best choice, but natural gas is too scarce to burn in an electric power plant. This leaves us with using electricity made from coal to drive a heat pump, burning natural gas directly in a home furnace, or burning wood in an efficient stove. The best possibility not shown in Figure 13-8 is a passive solar heating system based on orienting and designing a house so that most (if not all) of its heat is obtained from the sun without the need for any fancy (and expensive) active solar collectors. In cold climates buildings should be superinsulated and air tight, but well ventilated with an air-to-air heat exchanger, requiring very little heating except on the very coldest days (see Section 14-6 for details). Another choice not shown would be a solar-assisted heat pump; in this system solar energy provides much of the heat, and an electric heat pump kicks in when there is not enough sunshine.

Note that the poorest choice for home heating systems in terms of net first law efficiency are electric heating based on oil-burning or nuclear power plants or home oil furnaces. In 1980, the average residential heating bill in the United States was $990 for oil, $840 for electricity, and $420 for natural gas (although natural gas prices will rise as it is deregulated over the next few years). Oil and electricity prices will probably rise even more. Unfortunately, about half of all new homes built in the United States are equipped with electric space-heating systems—an extremely wasteful and expensive way to provide low-temperature heat. This is due to the limited availability of natural gas in many parts of the country, consumer resistance to increasingly expensive fuel oil, special subsidies, and artificially low rates that encourage the use of electric space-heating.

Figure 13-9 shows a similar comparison for automobiles with various types of engines. Note that the overall first law efficiency for a car powered with a conventional internal combustion engine is only about 2 percent. In other words, about 98 percent of the energy in crude oil is wasted by the time it is converted to gasoline and then burned to move a car. Most other engine systems are only about 1 to 3 percent efficient except for an electric engine recharged by electricity from a hydroelectric power plant, which is 12 percent efficient. In addition, present batteries must be recharged frequently and must be replaced about every two years at a cost of about $2,000 or more. Thus, *a second way to reduce energy waste is to keep the energy transfer chain as short as possible* (Figures 13-8 and 13-9). We can also reduce energy waste within a chain by trying to capture and use the waste heat before it escapes to the environment. For example, waste heat from a coal-fired industrial boiler could be used to heat the plant or used to produce electricity for the plant (called cogeneration).

The initial costs of heat pumps, active solar heating systems, and appliances and automobile engines with high energy efficiencies are sometimes more expensive than conventional and less efficient systems. But over their lifetimes most energy-efficient devices end up saving both energy and money. A well-designed, passive solar heated house should have both a lower initial cost and operating cost than a conventionally built and heated home. *It is the lifetime (or life cycle) cost—not the initial*

---

*A heat pump is analogous to a window air conditioner turned around backwards so that the heat is pumped indoors rather than outdoors. The device extracts heat from a low-temperature reservoir (the atmosphere or body of water) and uses energy (which can be supplied by electricity, natural gas, or concentrated solar or wind energy) to inject this heat into a higher-temperature reservoir (a home or hot water heater). A refrigerator is a well-known example of a heat pump.

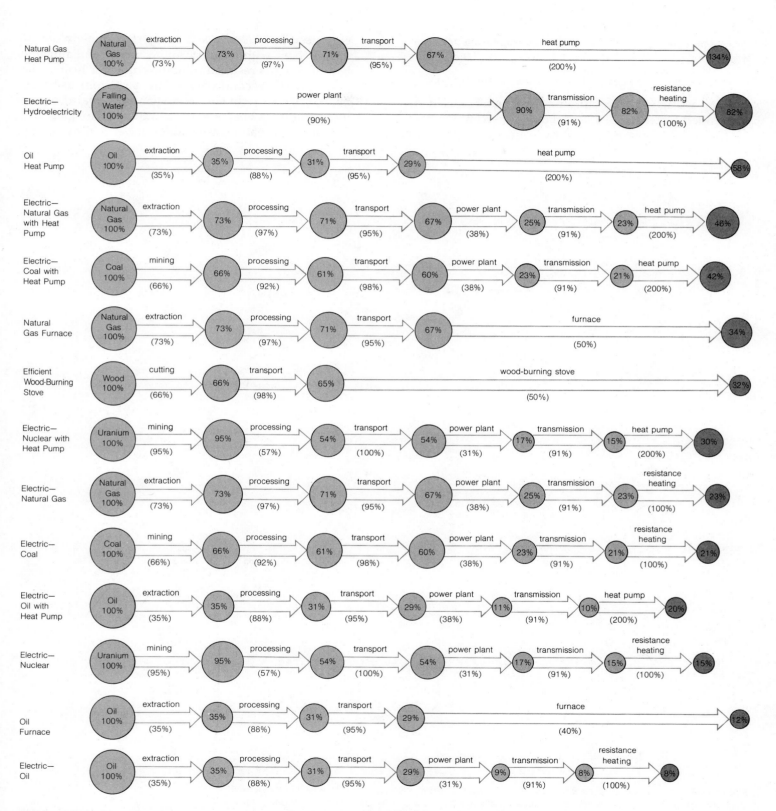

Figure 13-8 Comparison of first law energy efficiencies for home heating systems. Efficiencies between steps are shown in parentheses, and cumulative net efficiencies for the system are shown inside the circles. Each step having an efficiency less than 100% loses low-quality heat energy to the environment.

cost—that determines whether an energy-conversion device is a bargain:

$$\text{lifetime cost} = \text{initial cost} + \text{lifetime operating cost}$$

The average first law efficiency for all energy used in the United States in 1979 was about 32 percent (Figure 13-10). In other words, almost two-thirds of all the en-ergy used in 1979 was lost to the environment as low-quality heat without performing any useful function. Part of this loss resulted from the automatic heat tax imposed by the second energy law, part from using unnecessarily wasteful energy systems, and part from not using well-known energy conservation techniques, such as insulation, natural ventilation, lower and more com-

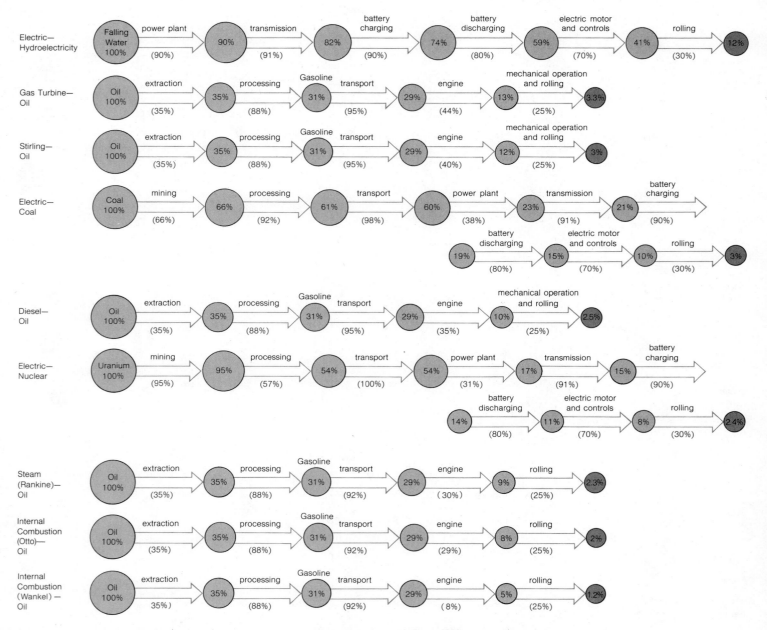

Figure 13-9 Comparison of first law energy efficiencies for automobile engine systems. Efficiencies between steps are shown in parentheses, and cumulative net efficiencies are shown inside the circles. At each step low-quality heat energy is lost to the environment.

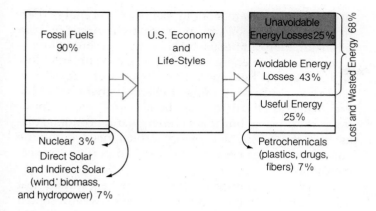

Figure 13-10 Energy flow in the United States during 1980 based on overall first law energy efficiency and excluding solar energy incorporated in food crops and used to warm the earth and drive its weather cycles.

fortable lighting levels, and buildings aligned to take advantage of sunlight and wind (as discussed in more detail in Section 14-1). The most visible symbol of energy waste, an all-glass office building lit by windows that cannot be opened, heated and cooled by blowers rather than by nature, and ablaze with light throughout the night, is now recognized as an ecological and economic disaster.

Second Law Energy Efficiency First law energy efficiency does not distinguish between the automatic losses imposed by the second energy law and those that result from using wasteful or imperfect energy systems. To get a better picture of energy loss and waste, we can use the **second law energy efficiency.** It is the ratio of the minimum amount of useful energy (or work) needed to perform a task in the most efficient way that is theoretically possible (whether we know how to do it or not) to the actual amount used to perform the task.

$$\text{second law energy efficiency (\%)} = \frac{\begin{array}{c}\text{minimum amount}\\ \text{of useful energy (or work)}\\ \text{needed to perform a task}\end{array}}{\begin{array}{c}\text{actual amount of}\\ \text{useful energy (or work)}\end{array}} \times 100$$

This ratio shows how far the performance of an energy device or system falls short of what is theoretically possible according to the second energy law.

Table 13-3 shows estimates of second law energy efficiencies for various energy systems in the United States. The overall second law efficiency for annual en-

ergy use in the United States is about 3 to 15 percent, with about 85 to 97 percent of all used energy lost or wasted (Figure 13-11). In other words, the second law efficiency of energy systems in the United States can be improved significantly. Of course, some improvements in efficiency are too expensive, even considering lifetime costs. But at least 50 percent and possibly as much as 90 percent of the present energy waste in the United States could probably be eliminated with no major changes in the standard of living.

Net Useful Energy: It Takes Energy to Get Energy The two energy laws, which can't be repealed, tell us that the only energy that really counts is *net* useful energy—not *gross* or *total* useful energy. **Net useful energy** is the total useful energy of a resource as it is found in nature *minus* the useful energy used to find, extract, process, and upgrade it in energy quality, to meet environmental and safety requirements, and to deliver the energy to the user *minus* the useful energy lost as a result of the second energy law and the use of unnecessarily inefficient and wasteful energy systems:

net useful energy =

$$\begin{array}{c}\text{total useful}\\ \text{energy}\end{array} - \begin{array}{c}\text{useful energy to}\\ \text{find, prepare,}\\ \text{upgrade, and deliver}\\ \text{the energy in a}\\ \text{useful form}\end{array} - \begin{array}{c}\text{useful energy}\\ \text{lost and wasted}\end{array}$$

Table 13-3 Estimated Second Law Energy Efficiencies for U.S. Energy Systems

Energy System	Second Law Energy Efficiency (percent)
Space heating	
Heat pump	9
Furnace	5–6
Electric resistance	2.5
Water heating	
Gas	3
Electric	1.5
Air conditioning	4.5
Refrigeration	4
Automobile	8–10
Power plants	33
Steel production	23
Aluminum production	13
Oil refining	9
All systems	10–15*

*Other estimates put this much lower at 3 to 5 percent.

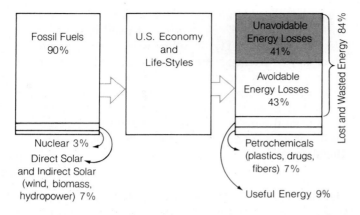

Figure 13-11 Energy flow in the United States during 1980 based on overall second law energy efficiency, and excluding solar energy incorporated in food crops and used to warm the earth and drive its weather cycles.

Net useful energy is like net profit. If you have a business with a total annual income of $100,000 but it costs you $90,000 a year to operate, then your net profit is only $10,000 a year. With operating expenses of $110,000 a year, you would have a net loss of $10,000 a year. If you had $200,000 in savings, you could use this capital to subsidize your losses. In 20 years, however, you would go bankrupt and have no capital left to keep your business afloat.

We can apply a similar analysis to energy use. The remaining fossil fuels are our useful energy capital or savings account—deposited for us free by nature over millions of years. At present rates of use, we will probably use up the world's oil and natural gas energy capital within 40 to 80 years and our coal energy capital within 200 to 400 years (Section 14-2). At present we are spending (burning up) this capital at a high rate to provide us with a daily supply of high-quality energy, but we must also invest some of this irreplaceable energy capital to subsidize the development and use of new energy sources. We must not squander it to develop energy alternatives that have a low or negative yield of net useful energy or use them to supply high-quality energy for tasks that can be performed with low-to-moderate quality energy at a lower cost. In addition, the burning of fossil fuels may be limited before supplies run out by climate changes resulting from carbon dioxide emitted into the atmosphere when these fuels are burned (see Enrichment Study 3).

For example, if we must use 9 units of useful fossil fuel (or other high-quality energy) to deliver 10 units of

useful nuclear, solar, or additional fossil fuel energy (perhaps from a deep oil well at sea or in the Arctic or from oil shale), then our net useful energy gain is only 1 unit—a poor long-term energy and financial investment of fossil fuel capital. Putting in 11 units of useful fossil fuel energy to get back 10 units of useful higher-quality energy (such as electricity) may be necessary for performing certain tasks, but it is an energy and economic disaster if the fossil fuel energy capital needed for the subsidy runs out because it is used to perform unnecessary tasks.

From a net energy standpoint, the best way to heat a home or building is to use passive or well-designed active solar heating. Similarly, the best way to provide hot water for bathing and washing is to use a relatively small array of solar collectors. The concept of net useful energy also explains why large-scale electric power plants powered by solar energy may not be feasible. Solar energy is abundant and free, but it is so widely dispersed that collecting it over a fairly large area and focusing it to a small area to create high-quality heat will be very costly and might give a low net energy yield or even a net energy loss. This analysis, however, is controversial and net energy yields for all systems appear to be decreasing so that high-temperature solar heat may be acceptable even at low yields. There is also controversy over the net energy yield of conventional nuclear fission energy. Because of the fossil fuel energy inputs used for (1) mining uranium ore; (2) processing and upgrading uranium fuels; (3) building and operating nuclear power plants; (4) meeting complex safety and environmental costs; (5) transporting, reprocessing, and storing nuclear fuels and radioactive wastes; and (6) decommissioning the highly radioactive plant after its 30-year lifetime, the net useful energy yield for the entire system (not just the plant itself) over the plant's lifetime is probably low. Some estimates, however, indicate that the net useful energy yield is moderate.*

Some additional high net energy yield deposits of fossil fuels, such as Middle Eastern oil, will be found in the future. But most of the accessible and richer deposits have already been found and are rapidly being depleted. For example, only 19 bonanza oil fields (10 million barrels or more) have been found in the United States during

---

*At present, different and often conflicting estimates of net energy yields of energy systems occur primarily because people making the estimates have not all used a recommended set of guidelines that defines what energy inputs shall be included or omitted. Also, people disagree on estimates of some of the inputs. As net useful energy analysis improves in coming years, many of these difficulties and conflicting claims will be resolved.

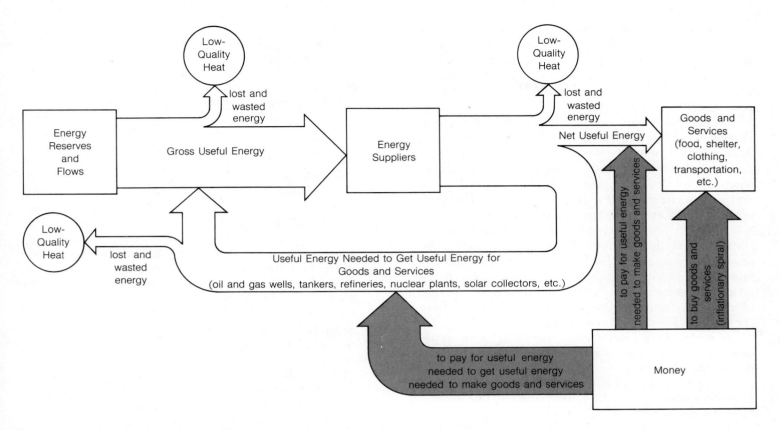

Figure 13-12 Net useful energy and money. Because we can't beat the first and second laws of energy, as energy supplies become harder to find, process, and deliver, the net useful energy yield decreases. As a result, more and more dollars are used to get the useful energy needed for basic goods and services, so that inflation increases and average per capita well-being decreases.

the last 100 years. To find the remaining oil and natural gas, we have to drill and dig deeper into the earth or into the sea bottom, tap into more dilute deposits, and extract deposits in remote and hostile areas (such as Alaska and the Arctic) that are far from where the energy is needed. As a result, while total and per capita energy use in the world (Figure 13-4) and the United States (Figure 13-5) are increasing, the total and per capita net useful energy yields are decreasing. It is estimated that the drilling for and extraction of petroleum in the United States could cease to be a net source of energy by about 2004 at low drilling rates and 2000 or sooner at high drilling rates. We are having to use more and more of the remaining high-quality fossil fuel energy (and money) to find and deliver new deposits of fossil fuel and other types of energy (Figure 13-12). For example, deepwater offshore drilling platforms with the latest technology now cost about $1 billion each, and it now costs an average of about $6 million to drill just one oil well on the land in

the United States. Thus, even as more oil is found in the United States, most of it will take more energy to find and process than the energy it will yield.

In 1978 about one-fourth of the energy consumption in the United States was used to mine, extract, concentrate, and transport fuels with much of this from electrical conversion losses. By the year 2000 this figure could rise to more than a third. As a result, more of the available money will be used to pay for lower net useful energy yields, so that inflation will increase (Figure 13-12) and average per capita well-being will decline. As more and more energy flows through the economic system to deliver useful energy, more and more money must be used to find, extract, and process the energy and to maintain environmental quality (Figure 13-12). As a result, consumers pay higher prices for the same amount of less useful or lower-quality energy, as discussed further by Howard Odum in his Guest Editorial at the end of this chapter.

At present, the estimated supplies of nonrenewable energy resources are calculated as proven or expected *total energy* supply (Figure 12-4), not as the more realistic *net useful energy* supply. Thus, reserves that are supposed to offer so many years of supply will be gone sooner than present estimates show.

Net useful energy analysis, if done under a consistent set of guidelines, is a very important tool in helping us to evaluate possible energy alternatives and to invest our limited fossil fuel and monetary capital wisely, as discussed in Howard T. Odum's Guest Editorial at the end of this chapter. But it is not a panacea. The most efficient use of energy in terms of physical laws may not always match up with what people and governments consider to be the most efficient social or economic use of an energy resource. For example, homeowners may find electric heating so convenient and maintenance free (at least at the home site) that they exert political pressure to maintain electricity at artificially low prices and have the losses made up by government subsidies.

In summary, we can use the two energy laws to develop six guidelines for wasting less energy and for evaluating energy options:

1. Supply energy only in the quality needed for the task at hand using the cheapest possible source, primarily by matching the temperature of the energy-producing process as closely as possible with the temperature needed by energy users and by using high-quality electrical energy only when it is the best way to perform a task (see Amory Lovins's Guest Editorial at the end of this chapter).

2. When economically feasible on a lifetime cost basis, switch to more energy efficient processes (and appliances or improve existing processes and appliances) so they approach the maximum energy efficiency allowed by the second energy law.

3. When economically feasible keep the energy transfer chain as short as possible and capture and use waste heat produced in energy transfer chains before allowing it to flow into the atmosphere.

4. In buying any energy conversion device (such as a car, house, or appliance), use the lifetime cost—not the initial cost—to determine whether it is a bargain.

5. Improve energy efficiency by using well-known practices such as insulation, reduced and more comfortable lighting levels, buildings that take advantage of energy from the sun and wind, and plugging up cracks and holes in homes and buildings.

6. In evaluating any energy option, consider the net useful energy it can deliver—not just the total energy available.

13-4 Energy Alternatives: An Overview

Overall Evaluation In evaluating possible energy alternatives, we have to think and plan in three time frames: the short term (1982 to 1992), the intermediate term (1992 to 2002), and the long term (2002 to 2032). The first step is to decide how much of what kinds of energy (such as heat and electricity) we need to provide desired energy services. Then we need to know what mix of energy alternatives can provide the needed amounts and kinds of energy at the lowest cost with acceptable environmental impacts. Thus, for each alternative we need to know the total estimated supply available in each time frame, the estimated net useful energy yield, projected costs for development, and potential environmental impact for the entire energy system.* Table 13-4 gives an overall evaluation of energy alternatives for the world, and Table 13-5 provides a slightly more detailed evaluation of energy alternatives for the United States.

We can draw three important conclusions from Tables 13-4 and 13-5:

1. The best short-, intermediate-, and long-term alternative for the United States (and other industrialized nations) is to reduce unnecessary energy waste by improving energy efficiency. It extends the supplies of fossil fuels, sharply cuts dependence on imported oil, greatly reduces or eliminates the need for any new coal and nuclear power plants, reduces international competition for oil and thus reduces the chances of nuclear war, buys time to develop energy alternatives, frees capital for developing energy alternatives, saves money, and reduces environmental impact by decreasing energy use and waste. Indeed, it is estimated that the United States could probably meet all of its energy needs between 1980 and 2005 (and possibly to 2025) by implementing a strong and comprehensive program to improve energy efficiency without building any new electric power plants of any type, as discussed by Amory Lovins in his Guest Editorial at the end of this chapter.

*It may not be possible to prevent or control some of the adverse environmental impacts that result from developing and using an energy resource. Those controls that are possible, however, will add to the cost and cause some decrease in net useful energy yields.

Table 13-4 Evaluation of Energy Alternatives for the World

Energy Resource	Advantages	Disadvantages
Nonrenewable Resources		
Fossil fuels Petroleum	1. Can be used in stationary (power plants) and mobile (cars) systems 2. Technology well developed 3. Historically cheap (but prices rising rapidly) 4. Fairly easy to transport within and between nations 5. High net useful energy yield 6. Moderate environmental impact	1. Supply may be depleted within 40 to 80 years 2. Net useful energy yield will decline and prices will rise as more accessible deposits are depleted 3. Production of carbon dioxide when fuel is burned could alter global climate
Natural gas	1. Technology well developed 2. Fairly easy to transport within nations 3. Historically cheap (but prices rising rapidly) 4. High net useful energy yield 5. Low environmental impact	1. Supply may be depleted within 40 to 80 years 2. Net useful energy yield will decline and prices will rise as more accessible deposits are depleted 3. Difficult and expensive to transport from one country to another as liquefied natural gas (LNG) 4. Production of carbon dioxide when fuel is burned could alter global climate
Coal	1. Technology well developed 2. Fairly easy to transport within and between nations 3. Large supplies (several hundred years) 4. High net useful energy yield 5. Historically cheap (but prices rising rapidly) 6. Economically feasible to burn in power plants fairly cleanly with existing technology 7. May be burned in the future (20 to 50 years) with lower pollution and less waste by fluidized-bed firing and magnetohydrodynamic (MHD) generators 8. Can be converted to cleaner burning synthetic natural gas (coal gasification) or synthetic oil (coal liquefaction)	1. Very harmful environmental impact (large amounts of air pollution, water pollution, and land disruption) without adequate pollution control 2. Not useful in solid form for powering cars and trucks (but conversion to electricity can be used to recharge batteries in electric cars) 3. Net useful energy yield will decline and prices will rise as rich and accessible deposits are depleted and extensive pollution controls are implemented 4. Net useful energy yield declines and prices rise sharply when coal is converted to synthetic natural gas or oil 5. Requires large amounts of water for coal processing and cooling of power plants 6. Carbon dioxide produced when fuel is burned could alter global climate
Oil shale	1. Very large supplies if developed 2. Can be used in stationary and mobile systems	1. Technology not fully developed 2. High cost 3. Low to moderate net useful energy yield 4. Harmful environmental impact (very large land disruption for above-ground processing, moderate air and water pollution) 5. Requires fairly large amounts of water for processing 6. Carbon dioxide produced when fuel is burned could alter global climate
Tar sands	1. Very large supplies 2. Can be used in stationary and mobile systems	1. Technology not fully developed 2. Very high cost 3. Low net useful energy yield 4. Moderate to high environmental impact 5. Requires large amounts of water for processing 6. Carbon dioxide produced when fuel is burned could alter global climate
Nuclear energy Conventional fission (uranium and thorium)	1. Technology well developed 2. Low environmental impact on air and water and moderate impact on land if entire system operates normally	1. Fuel supplies at an affordable cost could be depleted within 100 to 200 years 2. Costs have been rising so rapidly that in recent years very few orders for new nuclear power plants have been made and many previous orders have been cancelled 3. Low to moderate net useful energy yield, which will decline as more strict safety and environmental standards are applied

Table 13-4 Evaluation of Energy Alternatives for the World (cont.)

Energy Resource	Advantages	Disadvantages
		4. Potentially very serious and long-lasting (hundreds to thousands of years) environmental impact if an accident or sabotage should melt down the reactor core and release deadly radioactive material or if radioactive wastes are not stored safely 5. Requires very large amounts of water for cooling power plants 6. Commits future generations to storing radioactive wastes safely for hundreds to thousands of years, even if nuclear power is abandoned as an energy source 7. Cannot be used to power vehicles unless electricity it produces is used to produce hydrogen gas fuel or to recharge batteries in electric cars 8. Spreads knowledge and materials for building nuclear weapons
Breeder fission (uranium and thorium)	1. Extends uranium supplies for hundreds to thousands of years 2. Low environmental impact on air and water and moderate impact on land if entire system operates normally	1. Technology not fully developed 2. Projected costs are very high even with extensive government subsidies 3. Net useful energy yield unknown but probably moderate 4. Potentially very serious and long-lasting (hundreds to thousands of years) environmental impact if an accident or sabotage should melt down the reactor core and release deadly radioactive material, if fuel shipments are hijacked or diverted by countries to make atomic bombs, or if wastes are not stored safely 5. Requires large amounts of water for cooling power plants 6. Commits future generations to storing radioactive wastes safely for hundreds to thousands of years, even if nuclear power is abandoned as an energy source 7. Cannot be used to power vehicles unless electricity it produces is used to produce hydrogen gas fuel or to recharge batteries in electric cars
Fusion (deuterium and tritium)	1. Almost unlimited supply of energy if fusion of deuterium (extracted from water) can be developed 2. Probably moderate environmental impact 3. Less dangerous than conventional and breeder fission because reactor meltdown could not occur, and smaller quantities of radioactive wastes would be produced 4. Could be used as an almost infinite source of electricity to produce hydrogen gas for use as a fuel in vehicles when petroleum and natural gas supplies are depleted 5. One possible fuel (water) readily available	1. Technology extremely difficult and in very early stages of development 2. Would not supply large amounts of energy for 50 to 100 years and may never be developed 3. Capital costs very high 4. Operating costs unknown but probably high 5. Net useful energy yield unknown 6. Radioactive wastes that are produced must be stored safely 7. Requires very large amounts of water for cooling power plants 8. May depend on rare elements, such as helium and lithium (used to surround the reactor and transfer the heat produced) 9. One approach involves concepts that could be used to produce hydrogen or nuclear fusion bombs 10. Produces neutrons usable to breed atomic bomb materials 11. Cannot be used to power vehicles unless electricity it produces is used to produce hydrogen gas fuel or to recharge batteries in electric cars
Geothermal energy (trapped pockets)	1. Technology fairly well developed and relatively simple 2. Low overall supply but very high in some areas near deposits 3. Moderate cost and moderate net useful energy yield for easily accessible and large deposits	1. Only useful in certain areas 2. Must be converted to electricity at the site 3. Cannot be used to power vehicles unless electricity is used to produce hydrogen gas fuel or to recharge batteries in electric cars 4. High cost and low net useful energy yield for less accessible and small deposits 5. Requires large amounts of water for processing and cooling 6. Moderate to serious environmental impact

Table 13-4 Evaluation of Energy Alternatives for the World *(cont.)*

Energy Resource	Advantages	Disadvantages
Renewable Resources		
Conservation (improving energy efficiency)	1. Can be implemented fairly quickly 2. Technology fairly simple and well developed 3. Saves money 4. Reduces energy waste 5. Reduces environmental impact by requiring less use of other energy alternatives 6. Extends useful supplies of petroleum, natural gas, and other nonrenewable energy resources 7. Very high net useful energy yield 8. Does not increase heat buildup in the atmosphere from energy use 9. Requires no significant changes in life-style	1. Requires mandatory regulations or economic incentives since it is very hard to implement by preaching and voluntary action 2. Requires individuals to consider more complex lifetime energy costs of all energy systems and devices rather than just initial costs 3. Requires high initial cost for purchase and installation of conservation devices
Water power (hydroelectricity)	1. Source of energy (falling water) is free 2. Relatively low operating and maintenance costs 3. Technology well developed 4. Can be operated automatically from remote locations 5. Low overall supply but plentiful in areas near rivers that can be dammed 6. Moderate to high net useful energy yield 7. Has a long life (50 to 300 years) 8. Low environmental impact on air and moderate impact on water 9. Does not increase heat buildup in the atmosphere 10. Many now abandoned small hydropower dams and plants could be put back into use with relatively moderate costs and low environmental impact	1. Available only in selected areas on a large scale 2. Most rivers near large population centers have already been dammed 3. Dams tend to fill up with silt 4. Destroys land ecosystems behind dam and alters those below dam 5. Moderate to very high capital costs 6. Cannot be used to power vehicles unless electricity produced is used to produce hydrogen gas fuel are to recharge batteries in electric cars 7. Alters aquatic ecology
Tidal energy	1. Source of energy (tides) is free 2. Very small overall supply, but plentiful in areas with very high daily tidal flows 3. Low environmental impact on air 4. Net useful energy yield unknown but probably moderate 5. Does not increase heat buildup in the atmosphere from energy use 6. Technology fairly well developed	1. Available in only a few areas 2. Capital and operating costs unknown but probably high 3. Ecology of bays and estuaries could be drastically changed and probably damaged 4. Cannot be used to power vehicles unless electricity is used to produce hydrogen gas fuel or to recharge batteries in electric cars
Ocean thermal gradients	1. Energy supply free (heat stored in the ocean) 2. Almost infinite supply in certain areas if ever developed 3. Low environmental impact on air and land 4. Does not increase heat buildup in the atmosphere from energy use	1. Technology in early stages of development 2. Sites with sufficient temperature difference between surface and deep water may be limited 3. Net useful energy yield unknown but probably low to moderate 4. Development costs probably high 5. Could disrupt ocean ecosystems and perhaps affect regional and global climate 6. Cannot be used to power vehicles unless electricity it produces is used to produce hydrogen gas or to recharge batteries
Solar energy Low-temperature heating (for homes and water)	1. Energy supply free and readily available even on a cloudy day 2. Technology for heating individual homes and hot water heaters is fairly simple and available and can be installed quickly	1. Usefulness depends on climate and building energy efficiency (especially orientation and amount of insulation) 2. Supply not available at night so that storage systems or conventional furnaces or other backup systems must also be used 3. Production and installation costs moderate to high

Table 13-4 Evaluation of Energy Alternatives for the World *(cont.)*

Energy Resource	Advantages	Disadvantages
	3. Moderate to high net useful energy yield 4. Low environmental impact 5. Very safe energy source 6. Does not increase heat buildup in the atmosphere from energy use	4. Cannot be used effectively to power vehicles
High-temperature heating and photovoltaic production of electricity	1. Energy supply free and readily available especially on sunny days 2. Moderate environmental impact 3. Very safe energy source 4. Does not increase heat buildup in the atmosphere from energy use	1. Technology in early stages of development 2. Most useful in areas with ample sunlight (though usable elsewhere) 3. Supply not available at night so that storage systems or other backup energy systems must be used 4. Moderate to very high capital costs (but probably declining) and probably moderate operating costs 5. Moderate to low net useful energy yield 6. Photovoltaic cells made of expensive or rare elements (pure silicon, gallium, cadmium) 7. Disruption of desert ecosystems 8. Cannot be used to power vehicles unless electricity is used to produce hydrogen gas fuel or to recharge batteries in electric cars 9. Requires large amounts of water for cooling thermal-electric systems
Wind energy Home and neighborhood turbines	1. Free and readily available energy supply on a breezy day 2. Technology fairly well developed 3. Very low environmental impact 4. Moderate net useful energy yield 5. Does not increase heat buildup in the atmosphere from energy use 6. Can be connected to existing electrical grid with excess electricity being sold to utility companies	1. Insufficient wind in many places 2. Requires conventional backup electrical system or fairly expensive storage system unless connected to existing electrical grid 3. Capital costs moderate to high (but should decrease with mass production) 4. Cannot be normally used to power cars and trucks unless electricity is used to produce hydrogen gas fuel or to recharge batteries in electric cars
Large-scale power plants	1. Free and readily available energy supply on a very windy day 2. Low environmental impact 3. Does not increase heat buildup in the atmosphere from energy use	1. Adequate wind levels only available at a few sites 2. Technology in early stages of development 3. Requires backup by conventional electric power plants or a very expensive storage system unless connected to existing electrical grid 4. Capital costs high and operating costs probably moderate 5. Probably low net useful energy yield 6. Cannot be used to power vehicles unless electricity is used to produce hydrogen gas or to recharge batteries
Geothermal energy (low heat flow)	1. Moderate overall supply	1. Technology needs further development 2. Only useful in some areas and may be limited because rate of use exceeds low to moderate rate of renewal 3. Must be converted to electricity on site 4. Low net useful energy yield 5. Capital and operating costs probably high 6. Requires large amounts of water for processing and cooling 7. Cannot be used to power vehicles unless electricity is used to produce hydrogen gas fuel or recharge batteries 8. Moderate to high environmental impact
Biomass (burning of wood, crop, food, and animal wastes)	1. Technology well developed 2. Moderate net energy yield 3. Development costs are moderate (but may be high depending on location and system)	1. Large land requirements 2. May be limited because rate of use exceeds rate of renewal and sufficient land not available in some areas 3. Moderate to high environmental impact from ecosystem disruption

Table 13-4 Evaluation of Energy Alternatives for the World *(cont.)*

Energy Resource	Advantages	Disadvantages
		and simplification, erosion when land is cleared, water pollution from runoff of fertilizers and pesticides, and air pollution when fuel is burned
Derived Fuels		
Synthetic natural gas (SNG) from coal	1. Fairly easy to transport within nations 2. Low environmental impact on the air when burned 3. Technology fairly well developed	1. Accelerates reduction in coal supply 2. Low to moderate net useful energy yield 3. High capital and operating costs 4. High environmental impact on land and water because of increased coal mining and from the conversion process 5. Difficult and expensive to transport from one country to another as liquefied SNG 6. Not presently used in vehicles (but motors could be adapted) 7. Requires fairly large amounts of water for processing 8. May produce cancer-causing byproducts
Synthetic oil and alcohols from coal and organic wastes	1. Can be used in stationary and mobile energy systems 2. Fairly easy to transport within and between nations	1. Accelerates reduction in supply of coal 2. Supply of organic wastes widely dispersed and somewhat limited in supply 3. Could hinder recycling of organic wastes back to land as fertilizer 4. Some of the technology needs further development 5. Low to moderate net useful energy yield 6. High environmental impact on land and water because of increased mining of coal 7. Requires fairly large amounts of water for processing coal
Biofuels (alcohols and natural gas from plants and organic wastes)	1. Technology in late stages of development 2. Can be used in stationary and mobile energy systems 3. Alcohols fairly easy to transport within nations and between nations 4. Moderate capital costs but could be high depending on system used	1. Large land requirements 2. Use cannot exceed sustainable rate of renewal 3. Moderate to high environmental impact from ecosystem disruption and simplification, soil erosion, water pollution from runoff of fertilizers and pesticides, and air pollution if not done carefully 4. Low to moderate net useful energy yield
Urban wastes (for incineration)	1. Moderate to large supplies in heavily populated areas 2. Technology fairly well developed 3. Decreases solid waste disposal 4. Low environmental impact on the land	1. Supply could be reduced if matter recycling and reuse programs are put into effect 2. High capital and operating costs 3. Low to moderate net useful energy yield 4. Moderate environmental impact on air and water 5. Burns paper and other organic wastes rather than recycling them
Hydrogen gas (from coal or water)	1. Very low environmental impact from burning of fuel 2. Does not produce carbon dioxide when burned 3. Fairly easy to transport 4. Technology in late stages of development 5. Good alternative for heating homes (by using heat from fuel cells) and powering vehicles when oil supplies run out 6. Fairly easy to transport within countries by pipeline	1. Requires an essentially infinite source of heat or electricity (such as fusion, breeder fission, or wind and solar energy) to produce hydrogen gas from coal or water 2. Capital and operating costs will probably be high to very high depending on source of heat or electricity 3. Net useful energy yield will be low to moderate depending on source of heat or electricity 4. Environmental impact of entire system could be low to very high depending on source of heat or electricity.

Table 13-5 Evaluation of Energy Alternatives for the United States (Shading Indicates Favorable Conditions)

Energy Resource	Estimated Availability*			Estimated Net Useful Energy of Entire System†	Projected Cost of Entire System	Actual or Potential Environmental Impact of Entire System‡
	Short Term (1982–1992)	Intermediate Term (1992–2002)	Long Term (2002–2032)			
Nonrenewable Resources						
Fossil fuels						
Petroleum	High (with imports)	Moderate (with imports	Low	High but decreasing§	High for new domestic supplies	Moderate
Natural gas	High (with imports)	Moderate (with imports)	Low	High but decreasing§	High for new domestic supplies	Low
Coal	High‖	High‖	High‖	High but decreasing§	Moderate but increasing	Very high‖
Oil shale	Low	Low to moderate?	Low to moderate?	Low to moderate	High	High
Tar sands	Low	Fair? (imports only)	Poor to fair (imports only)	Low	Very high	Moderate to high
Nuclear energy						
Conventional fission (uranium and thorium)	Low to moderate	Low to moderate	Low to moderate	Low to moderate?	Very high	Very high
Breeder fission (uranium and thorium)	None	None to low	Moderate	Unknown, but probably moderate	Very high	Very high
Fusion (deuterium and tritium)	None	None	None to low (if developed)	Unknown	Very high	Unknown (probably moderate)
Geothermal energy (trapped pockets)	Poor	Poor	Poor	Low to moderate	Moderate to high	Moderate to high
Renewable Resources						
Conservation (improving energy efficiency)	High	High	High	Very high	Low	Decreases impact of other sources
Water power (hydroelectricity)						
New large scale dams and plants	Low	Low	Very low	Moderate to high	Moderate to very high	Low to moderate
Reopening abandoned small scale plants	Moderate	Moderate	Low	Moderate to high	Moderate	Low
Tidal energy	None	Very low	Very low	Unknown (moderate?)	High	Low to moderate
Ocean thermal gradients	None	Low	Low to moderate (if developed)	Unknown (probably low to moderate)	Probably high	Unknown (probably moderate)
Solar energy						
Low-temperature heating (for homes and water)	Moderate	Moderate to high	High	Moderate to high	Moderate to high	Low

Table 13-5 Evaluation of Energy Alternatives for the United States *(cont.)*

Energy Resource	Estimated Availability*			Estimated Net Useful Energy of Entire System†	Projected Cost of Entire System	Actual or Potential Environmental Impact of Entire System‡
	Short Term (1982–1992)	Intermediate Term (1992–2002)	Long Term (2002–2032)			
High-temperature heating and photovoltaic production of electricity	Low	Moderate	Moderate to high	Low to moderate	Very high initially (but probably declining fairly rapidly)	Low to moderate
Wind energy Home and neighborhood turbines	Low	Moderate	Moderate to high?	Moderate	Moderate to high	Low
Large-scale power plants	None	Very low	Probably low	Low?	High	Low to moderate?
Geothermal energy (low heat flow)	Very low	Very low	Low to moderate	Low	High	Moderate to high
Biomass (burning of wood, crop, food, and animal wastes)	Moderate	Moderate	Moderate	Moderate	Moderate	Moderate to high
Derived Fuels						
Synthetic natural gas (SNG) from coal	Low	Low to moderate	Low to moderate?	Low to moderate	High	High (increases use of coal)
Synthetic oil and alcohols from coal and organic wastes	Low	Low	Low	Low to moderate	High	High (increases use of coal)
Biofuels (alcohols and natural gas from plants and organic wastes)	Low to moderate?	Moderate	Moderate to high?	Low to moderate?	Moderate to high?	Moderate to high
Urban wastes (for incineration)	Low	Low	Low	Low to moderate	High	Moderate to high
Hydrogen gas (from coal or water)	None	None	Moderate?#	Unknown (probably low to moderate)#	Unknown (probably high)#	Variable#

*Overall availability based on supply and technological, net useful energy, economic, and environmental impact feasibility.
†Rough estimates only. Better and less conflicting estimates will be available when standard guidelines for net energy analysis are adopted by all investigators.
‡See Table 13-7 for more details.
§As accessible high-grade deposits are depleted, more and more energy and money must be used to find, develop, upgrade, and deliver remote and low-grade deposits.
‖Coal's very high environmental impact can be reduced to an acceptable level, however, by methods that are technically and economically feasible today.
#Depends on whether an essentially infinite source of heat or electrical energy (such as fusion, breeder fission, wind, or the sun) is available to produce hydrogen gas from coal or water. Net useful energy, costs, and environmental impact will depend on source of heat or electricity.

2. Total systems for future energy alternatives in the world and the United States will probably have low to moderate net useful energy yields and moderate to very high development costs. Since there may not be enough capital available to develop all alternative energy systems, they must be carefully chosen now so that capital will not be depleted on systems that will yield too little net useful energy or prove to be environmentally unacceptable. Even if there is no shortage of capital, lending institutions may be unwilling to make loans to energy companies for investment in risky long-term energy development schemes.

3. In the future, energy should be provided by a mix of alternative sources based on local availability and conditions rather than relying primarily on one resource (such as the present dependence on oil).

Hard Versus Soft Energy Paths to a New Energy Era At present there is vigorous debate over whether the intermediate- and long-term energy strategy for the United States should follow a "hard path" or a "soft path," as summarized in Table 13-6. The conventional strategy, or hard path, emphasizes building a number of huge, centralized coal-burning and conventional nuclear fission power plants between 1980 and 2000. After 2000 the use of coal-burning power plants would continue to increase, coupled with a shift from conventional fission to breeder fission nuclear power plants. After 2020 (or perhaps later) there would be a gradual shift to almost complete dependence on centralized nuclear fusion power plants, if this energy alternative should ever prove to be technologically, economically, and environmentally acceptable (see Section 14-4).

In sharp contrast to this strategy, energy expert Amory Lovins has suggested a soft path. This approach emphasizes increased energy efficiency (to reduce waste), cogeneration (using industrial waste heat to generate electricity), not using high-quality electricity for tasks where other forms of energy are cheaper and less wasteful, and greatly increased use of renewable and more environmentally benign energy flows—sunlight, wind, and biomass wastes. Cost effective increases in energy efficiency could cut energy waste at least in half, reduce the need to build additional coal-burning and nuclear power plants, decrease the environmental impact of energy use, and buy precious time to phase in a diverse and flexible array of decentralized soft-energy technologies. Oil and natural gas would continue to be used as transition fuels at a slower rate because of reductions in energy waste. Coal might be used slightly more between 1980 and 2000 as a transition fuel, but only with adequate pollution control and land reclamation and only if increases in energy efficiency are not adequate to meet essential energy demand. Conventional nuclear fission power plants would be phased out by about 1990 and breeder fission and nuclear fusion would not be developed because of their potentially serious and irreversible environmental impacts (Table 13-7) and the lack of enough capital to develop both them and soft-energy technologies.

In Lovins's view, the hard-path option is already collapsing economically, technologically, and socially because of huge capital costs, energy waste because of overreliance on inefficient use of electricity, proliferation of nuclear weapons, nuclear terrorism, unacceptable environmental damage, overdependence on vulnerable centralized energy systems, and excessive concentration of power in centralized institutions. Furthermore, the trend toward large and highly centralized power plants and other energy facilities makes the entire energy system highly vulnerable to even a limited nuclear war strike. Just two well-placed nuclear warheads detonated in the upper atmosphere could release an electromagnetic pulse (a microsecond burst of electromagnetic energy, 100 times more powerful than a lightning bolt). This pulse can incapacitate solid-state electronic equipment and could cause failure of the entire national power grid by incapacitating the electronic control facilities at modern electric power plants. In contrast, the more decentralized small-scale soft path gives people more control over how they wish to get their energy based on locally available renewable resources and greatly reduces the vulnerability of the energy system to nuclear attack.

The political and economic power concentrated in the large energy companies, however, is presently being used to persuade the United States to follow the hard path. Between 1980 and 1990, it is estimated that the oil industry alone will need $2 trillion in capital to meet the projected demand for oil. In addition, between 1980 and 2000, the U.S. nuclear industry will need at least $1 trillion to build and operate the nuclear plants it thinks the United States needs. Even if such unprecedented amounts of capital can be raised (primarily from sharp price increases in the price of oil and electricity and direct and indirect government subsidies), this drain of available capital would prevent the United States from seriously following the soft path.

While politicians, energy company executives, and environmentalists argue over which path to follow, more and more individuals are taking energy matters into their own hands. They are insulating, caulking, and making

Table 13-6 Comparison of Hard and Soft Energy Paths for the United States

Hard Energy Path	Soft Energy Path
Increase the supply of energy to meet greatly increased total and per capita energy demand with emphasis on government subsidies and tax breaks to energy companies.	Emphasize economically efficient energy use to reduce waste. Use the right amount and type of energy to do each task at the lowest possible cost. Eliminate government energy subsidies to allow a genuinely competitive marketplace to choose between reducing energy waste and increasing energy supply and between hard and soft technologies.
Greatly increase the use of electricity to provide energy for both high-quality and low-quality energy needs.	To conserve money, use electricity only for appropriate high-quality energy needs.
Depend primarily on nonrenewable energy resources (energy capital)—oil, natural gas, coal, and uranium.	Greatly increase the use of renewable energy flows (energy income)—sunlight, wind, and biomass wastes.
Continue to increase the use of oil and natural gas.	Continue to use oil and natural gas as transitional fuels but decrease their rate of use through more efficient energy use.
Greatly increase the use of large, complex, centralized coal-burning and nuclear fission power plants, followed by a shift to centralized breeder fission power plants, and then to centralized nuclear fusion power plants (if they become feasible). Use minor amounts of solar energy, chiefly in large, centralized electric furnaces (power towers), large scale wind machines, and monoculture biomass plantations (for fuel).	Do not build any more centralized electric power plants of any type since the United States already produces more electricity than is needed for the tasks where it is essential. Greatly increase the use of a diverse array of relatively simple, small-scale and dispersed energy production facilities using sunlight, wind, and biomass wastes depending on local availability to provide heat for homes and industrial processes and fuels (such as alcohol) for vehicles. Do not increase the use of coal (with effective pollution control) except to displace industrial use of oil and natural gas until a mix of renewable energy resources can be phased in. Phase out the use of conventional nuclear fission power by 1990 and do not develop breeder fission and nuclear fusion energy.
Minimize pollution by building complex safety and pollution control devices into energy production facilities and assume that global climate changes from increased production of carbon dioxide and heat (Enrichment Study 3) either won't be serious or can be dealt with by some technological breakthrough.	Minimize pollution by using energy sources that have relatively low environmental impacts and that decrease the possibility of changing global climate.

other energy efficiency improvements, building passively heated solar homes (easily the cheapest way to heat and cool any energy efficient home), adding passive solar heating (such as attached solar greenhouses) to existing homes, and growing more of their own food. The beauty of the soft path is that people don't have to wait for Washington or state capitals to act. The advantages and disadvantages of the specific energy options that make up both the hard and soft energy paths are summarized in Table 13-4 and 13-5 and are discussed in more detail in the next chapter.

Environmental Impact Options: Choosing the Least of Several Evils In accordance with the second law of energy, using any form of energy or nonrenewable metal or mineral resource has some environmental impact (Figure 12-3), and the faster the rate of energy use or flow,

the greater the impact (Figure 3-4). This is why energy use is a major factor in almost every phase of the environmental crisis and is directly or indirectly responsible for most land disruption (Chapter 10, Sections 11-4 and 15-4), water pollution (Chapter 16), and air pollution (Chapter 17; Enrichment Study 3). For example, nearly 80 percent of all U.S. air pollution is caused by fuel combustion in cars, furnaces, industries, and power plants. Electric power plants (mostly coal burning) account for more air pollution than any other source except cars; this pollution includes 55 percent of the nation's sulfur oxides, 25 percent of the soot (particulates), and 25 percent of the nitrogen oxides (see Chapter 17). Electric power plants (coal and nuclear) are the biggest thermal water polluters (Section 16-4), responsible for 80 percent of all discharges of hot water. Table 13-7 provides more details about the potential environmental effects of the different energy alternatives.

Table 13-7 Actual and Potential Environmental Impacts of Alternative Energy Systems

Energy System	Air Pollution	Water Pollution	Land Disruption	Possible Large-Scale Disasters
Nonrenewable Resources				
Fossil fuels				
Petroleum	Sulfur oxides, nitrogen oxides and hydrocarbons (Chapter 17); global climate change from carbon dioxide (Enrichment Study 3)	Oil spills from well blowouts, tanker accidents, pipeline ruptures (Section 16-5); excess heat (Section 16-4); brines	Subsidence (caving in over wells); estuary pollution (Section 10-6)	Massive spills on water from tanker accidents and offshore well blowouts; massive spills on land from pipeline breaks; refinery fires
Natural gas	Global climate change from carbon dioxide	Excess heat	Subsidence	Pipeline explosions; liquefied natural gas (LNG) tanker explosions
Coal	Sulfur oxides, particulates, nitrogen oxides, cancer-causing substances; global climate change from carbon dioxide; radioactive emissions	Acid mine drainage; acid rain; dissolved solids from washing coal; excess heat	Underground and strip mining (Section 10-5); subsidence; slag disposal; erosion	Mine accidents; landslides; sudden subsidence in urban areas; depletion and contamination of water resources in arid regions
Oil shale	Sulfur oxides, particulates, hydrogen sulfide, nitrogen oxides, hydrocarbons; global climate change from carbon dioxide; odor	Dissolved solids (salinity) and toxic trace metals (Enrichment Study 5) from processed shale rock; sediment; groundwater contamination	Disposal of processed shale rock; subsidence	Depletion and contamination of water supplies in arid regions where most shale is found; massive oil spills from pipeline breaks; depletion and contamination of water resources in arid regions
Tar sands	Sulfur oxides, hydrogen sulfide, hydrocarbons, nitrogen oxides; global climate change from carbon dioxide	Possible contamination of underground water supplies if extracted and processed underground	Surface mining (for some deposits); subsidence; loss of wildlife habitats	Massive oil spills from pipeline breaks; earthquakes if nuclear blasts used for underground extraction and processing; depletion and contamination of water resources in arid regions
Nuclear energy				
Conventional fission (uranium and thorium)	Radioactive emissions	Radioactive mine wastes; excess heat; radioactive effluents	Open pit and underground mining (Section 10-6); storage of radioactive wastes	Release of radioactive materials from meltdown of reactor core, sabotage, and shipping accidents; hijacking of fuel shipments to make nuclear bombs, spreads knowledge and materials to make nuclear weapons
Breeder fission (uranium and thorium)	Same as above	Same as above except fewer radioactive mine wastes	Same as above	Same as above
Fusion (deuterium and tritium)	Same as above	Excess heat	Little	Accidental release of radioactive materials; may spread knowledge and material to make hydrogen bombs

Table 13-7 Actual and Potential Environmental Impacts of Alternative Energy Systems *(cont.)*

Energy System	Air Pollution	Water Pollution	Land Disruption	Possible Large-Scale Disasters
Geothermal energy (trapped pockets)	Hydrogen sulfide and ammonia; radioactive materials; noise; local climate change; odor	Dissolved solids (salinity); boron runoff; excess heat	Subsidence	Depletion and contamination of water resources in arid regions
Renewable Resources				
Conservation (improving energy efficiency)	Decreased (except for indoor air pollution)	Decreased	Decreased	None
Water power (hydroelectricity)	Negligible	Disruption of aquatic ecosystems	Flooding of areas to form lake; ecosystem disruption; loss of wildlife and human habitat; disruption of estuary into which river flows. Very little impact for reopening abandoned small-scale plants	Dam breaks
Tidal energy	Negligible	Estuary disruption	Very little	None
Ocean thermal gradients	Local climate change	Ocean ecosystem disruption; marine life disruption	Estuary disruption	None
Solar energy				
Low-temperature heating (for homes and water)	Negligible	Negligible	Negligible	None
High-temperature heating and production of electricity	Negligible except for moderate amount from materials needed to make collectors (cement, steel, glass)	Negligible	May require land for large farms of solar collectors; disruption of desert ecosystems	Depletion of water resources in arid regions
Wind energy				
Home and neighborhood turbines	Negligible except for some aesthetic degradation	Negligible	Negligible	None
Large-scale power plants	Possible local climate changes	Negligible	Negligible	None
Geothermal energy (continuous heat flow)	Hydrogen sulfide and ammonia; radioactive materials; noise; local climate change; odor	Dissolved solids (salinity); runoff; excess heat	Subsidence	Depletion and contamination of water resources in arid regions
Biomass (burning of wood, crop, food, and animal wastes)	Particulates and hydrocarbons; possible cancer-causing emissions from badly designed wood stoves	Potential runoff of fertilizers and pesticides and sediment from erosion if poor farming and forestry practices used	Large use of land; soil erosion; loss of habitat for wildlife	None
Derived Fuels				
Synthetic natural gas (SNG) from coal	Similar to coal but somewhat less	Same as coal plus increased pollution from toxic trace metals, phenols, hydrocarbons	Same as coal but greater land disruption and more harmful solid wastes	Same as coal, earthquakes from blasts for underground coal gasification; pipeline explosions

Table 13-7 Actual and Potential Environmental Impacts of Alternative Energy Systems *(cont.)*

Energy System	Air Pollution	Water Pollution	Land Disruption	Possible Large-Scale Disasters
Synthetic oil and alcohols from coal and organic wastes	Similar to coal but less	Same as coal except increase in pollution from heavy metals, phenols, hydrocarbons	Same as coal	Same as coal; pipeline spills
Biofuels (alcohols and natural gas from plants and organic wastes)	Low	Runoff of fertilizers (Enrichment Study 16) and pesticides (Enrichment Study 11) and sediment from soil erosion if poor farming practices used	Large use of land; soil erosion (Section 16-6); soil salinity and waterlogging from irrigation (Section 15-4); ecosystem simplification (Section 6-3); loss of wildlife habitats (Section 10-7)	Fire or explosion in biofuel plant
Urban wastes (for incineration)	Sulfur oxides, particulates (especially heavy metals), nitrogen oxides, hydrogen chloride, hydrocarbons, hydrogen sulfide	Leaching of dissolved solids and heavy metals from ash	Decreases solid waste disposal (Enrichment Study 15)	Fire or explosion in incinerator
Hydrogen gas (from coal or water)	Depends on source of electricity or heat to make hydrogen. Large-scale disasters possible from pipeline explosions.			

In 1978, a highly controversial Canadian study, known as the Inhaber report, estimated that occupational and public health risks from solar, wind, and biomass (conversion of wood to methyl alcohol) energy were equal to or greater than those from the use of oil, coal, and nuclear energy. A team of energy experts at the University of California at Berkeley made a detailed analysis of this study (which, not surprisingly, had been widely publicized by the nuclear power industry) and found that the study was full of errors in calculation, misrepresentation of data, and faulty assumptions. Once corrections were made, coal, oil, and nuclear energy were found to have high public and occupational health impacts; solar, ocean thermal, wind, and biomass (methyl alcohol) energy were found to have moderate to low impacts—the reverse of the findings of the original study. The Inhaber study was then declared officially out of print by its sponsors, and the leader of the Berkeley group received the 1980 Public Service Award of the Federation of American Scientists.

13-5 Land, Energy, and Water Resources in the Rocky Mountain Region: A Case Study

The major storehouse of undeveloped fuel resources in the United States is found in the eight Rocky Mountain states—Arizona, Colorado, Idaho, Montana, Nevada, New Mexico, Utah, and Wyoming. As a result, this region has become a major battleground over land, energy, and water resources.

The diverse land of the Rocky Mountain region consists of rolling plains, irrigated farmland, ranchlands, Indian-owned lands, arid deserts, national forests (Section 10-4), and some of the nation's most scenic national parks (Section 10-3). Almost half of the land in this region is owned by the federal government—or, more accurately, the citizens of the United States. According to a U.S. Senate study, the region also contains (1) about 42 percent of this nation's bituminous and lignite coal; (2) 60 percent of the low-sulfur coal that can be strip mined economically; (3) almost all of the richest oil shale deposits; (4) 95 percent of U.S. uranium; (5) vast potential supplies of geothermal energy; (6) potential sources of natural gas and petroleum; (7) a large, sunny desert area that might be the site of a giant electric power plant complex run by solar energy, which could desalinate water for this water-starved region and provide about half of all the electricity needed in the United States in the year 2000; and (8) underground salt deposits that might be useful for storing the nation's deadly radioactive wastes. If fully utilized, the energy resources in these eight states could supply U.S. energy needs for the next 100 years.

As Figure 13-13 shows, the deposits of many of these energy resources either overlap or are located near one another; some also overlap with national forests and parks. In addition, some of these energy resources lie under land now used for farming and ranching, and 50 percent of the uranium and about 20 percent of the coal reserves lie on Indian lands.

The result is an extremely complex conflict over land use. Farmers and ranchers want enough irrigation water, and they don't want their land torn up or their water supplies polluted. Environmentalists and many ranchers who value their way of life want to preserve the sparsely populated land from the severe ecological disruption caused by mining and rapid population growth. Energy companies want to develop the area's rich energy resources for profit, to meet the nation's energy needs, and to reduce dependence on foreign oil. Some residents of these states welcome the money and jobs that energy development and boom towns would bring, but other residents do not want their nonurban way of life disrupted by the doubling and tripling of populations of isolated rural hamlets, which could occur in a matter of months.

The federal government, which owns much of the land, is caught in this crossfire of conflicting interests and is trying to decide which of the resources should be developed and in what order. State governments are torn between preserving the environment, encouraging economic growth, and ensuring that the federal government allows energy development in a manner that does not harm nearby nonfederal lands.

The conflict over the use of land and energy resources is made even more intense by a lack of water. Much of this arid region already has serious water shortages, and these are expected to get worse by 2000 (Figure 13-13; Section 15-3). To extract and process almost any one of the region's energy resources will require enormous amounts of water. Large quantities of water are required for cooling power plants, washing mined coal, coal gasification and liquefaction, forming a slurry that can transport coal by pipeline, converting oil shale to liquid fuel, and reclaiming mined arid lands. Water needs for coal and synthetic fuel plants could be greatly reduced by treating the effluents to remove pollutants and then recycling the water, but this would be costly.

At present, the major emphasis is on increased coal mining to reduce U.S. dependence on oil imports by 1990. Since most of the coal extracted in this region will be exported to other heavily populated areas of the United States, there is a conflict over whether the coal should be (1) mined and shipped out by rail or slurry pipeline, (2) burned in power plants near mining sites (Figure 13-13) and exported as electricity, or (3) converted to synthetic natural gas in coal gasification plants to be built near mining sites and then distributed by pipeline.

Water, then, may be the limiting factor that determines which, if any, of the energy resources in the Rocky Mountain region will ever be extracted on a large scale. With careful planning and management (Chapter 15), there may be enough water for considerable extraction of the available fuels, but only at the expense of agriculture. At present, agriculture uses 90 percent of the region's annual water supply, much of it allegedly "inefficiently applied and producing low-value crops." Some additional water could be supplied by tapping underground water aquifers (permeable layers of rock or sand formations that serve as conduits for the underground flow of water). But this would amount to mining precious water that is needed during drought years, since it takes hundreds to thousands of years to replenish underground aquifers (see Section 15-2). Depleting this supply for short-term purposes could set up an irreversible conversion of western grasslands to desert if a drought should last more than a year. Thus, the people of the United States, especially people in the Rocky Mountain region, face some difficult and important questions in this conflict between the use of land, energy, and water resources.

13-6 A Suggested Energy Plan for the United States

Suggested Principles of a U.S. Energy Plan We can use the energy concepts (Section 13-3) and the evaluation of the various energy alternatives (Section 13-4) to help us develop a possible energy plan to make the transition to a new sustainable earth energy era over the next 50 years. The intense struggle over a national energy policy in the United States is really a conflict over the future structure of American society. The issues are who will make key energy decisions, who benefits, and who sacrifices. The accompanying box lists some suggested principles for developing an integrated energy plan for the United States.

One highly controversial principle is the suggestion that the large energy companies be broken up. The purpose of this action is twofold. First, it would eliminate the possibility of *horizontal* monopolistic control of energy prices and supplies, which occurs when one company or a group of companies own large shares of normally competing energy sources (such as oil, coal, natural gas, and uranium). Second, it would prevent the possibility of *vertical* monopolistic control of the prices

Uranium

Geothermal

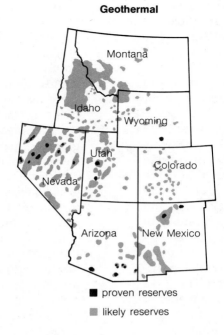

■ proven reserves

▨ likely reserves

**Electric Power Plants
(greater than 300 megawatts)**

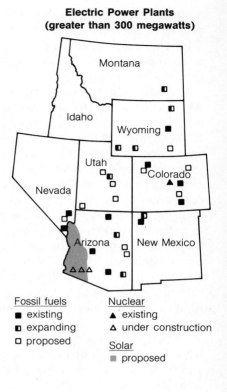

<u>Fossil fuels</u>   <u>Nuclear</u>

■ existing   ▲ existing

▨ expanding   △ under construction

□ proposed   <u>Solar</u>

             ▨ proposed

Potential Nuclear Waste Storage

▨ major underground salt deposits

National Parks and National Forests

■ national parks

▨ national forests

Water Shortages

▨ shortages today

□ shortages by 2000

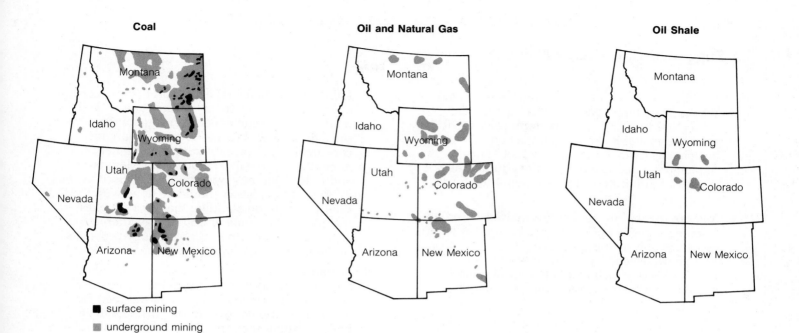

Coal

Montana
Idaho
Wyoming
Utah
Nevada
Colorado
Arizona
New Mexico

■ surface mining
▦ underground mining

Oil and Natural Gas

Montana
Idaho
Wyoming
Utah
Nevada
Colorado
Arizona
New Mexico

Oil Shale

Montana
Idaho
Wyoming
Utah
Nevada
Colorado
Arizona
New Mexico

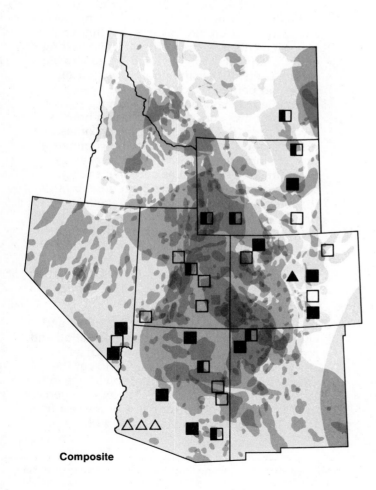

Composite

Figure 13-13 Conflicts between land use, energy resources, and water resources in the eight Rocky Mountain states. Composite map shows areas of most intense overlap and conflict (darkest regions).

A Suggested U.S. Energy Plan

1. Develop a comprehensive national energy plan for the short term (1982 to 1992), intermediate term (1992 to 2002), and long term (2002 to 2032) with the goal of making the transition to a sustainable earth energy era by 2030* and implement a massive program to educate the American public and Congress about the four energy crises (Section 13-1).

2. Require that net useful energy analysis based on a standardized set of guidelines be applied to all estimates of remaining supplies of nonrenewable energy resources and to all evaluations of which mix of energy alternatives should form the basis for a national energy strategy.**

3. Place primary emphasis on a massive program to increase energy efficiency (see Section 14-1 for details) to reduce energy waste, match energy quality with energy needs, decrease the environmental impact of energy use, reduce dependence on oil imports, save money, decrease the total and average per capita use of energy, and buy time to develop and phase in a mix of other energy alternatives before fossil fuel supplies (especially oil and natural gas) are depleted. Devote more money to developing improved methods for increasing energy efficiency and to alternatives for the internal combustion engine (see Section 17-5).

4. Deregulate domestic oil and natural gas prices and allow them to rise to world price levels, rather than keeping them artificially low. This principle (which has been or is being carried out) should stimulate energy exploration, increase domestic supplies, encourage consumers to reduce energy waste to save money, and give consumers a more realistic view of the four energy crises. Price rises, however, should be coupled with a program to ensure that poor and lower middle class citizens do not bear the brunt of price increases. This program might consist of one or more of the following methods: (a) excess profits taxes on energy companies, (b) tax rebates to low- and middle-income consumers, (c) a guaranteed low price for a basic "lifeline" energy supply for consumers, and (d) providing a guaranteed annual income to make poor people less poor* and to let them buy what they want (Section 18-2). Price deregulation should be done with the clear public understanding that new supplies will merely buy time to find energy alternatives and will not solve the nation's energy problems in the intermediate and long terms.

5. Encourage cost-effective increases in energy efficiency by (a) using positive incentives such as tax credits (up to 50 percent of the cost) for individuals and companies that insulate their homes or buildings and that install passive solar heating or other energy-saving devices; (b) changing building codes, moneylending policies and other institutional barriers that hinder improvements in energy efficiency; (c) barring utility companies from giving discounts to big energy users; (d) raising utility rates during peak-load periods; (e) requiring utility companies to make home and business energy audits and give consumers advice on how to save energy; (f) requiring utility companies to provide loans to finance home and commercial projects for increasing energy efficiency; (g) providing inspectors to be sure that energy savings improvements have been done properly; (h) using tax incentives to encourage factories to produce steam and electricity at the same facility (cogeneration); and (i) removing all government tax breaks and other subsidies for conventional fuels (oil, natural gas, coal), synthetic natural gas and oil, and nuclear power so that soft and hard energy technologies can compete openly and fairly in the marketplace.

6. Use tax breaks, low or interest free loans, and energy savings practices (such as insulating and sealing) and architectural design (such as passive solar and superinsulation) to cut the energy requirements for all new buildings in the United States by an average of at least 75 percent by 1990. Use tax breaks and low or interest free loans to retrofit existing buildings with

---

*Existing law requires the Department of Energy to develop a comprehensive national plan but most environmentalists consider that the present long-term plan is really only a short-term plan that, by overemphasizing the uneconomical and environmentally harmful hard energy path (Table 13-6), greatly reduces the chances of achieving a sustainable earth energy era.

**This is also required by law but at present is poorly and inconsistently done by the Department of Energy.

---

*One utility company reported that after a lower income customer paid her February light bill with her social security check, she had less than $30 to live on for the rest of the month.

insulation, sealing, attached solar greenhouses, solar hot water heaters, and other energy saving practices so that they use an average of at least 35 to 50 percent less energy by 1990.

7. Put a strict limit on oil imports to encourage conservation. The resulting short-term hardships will be much less severe than those from a sharp drop or cutoff of the oil supply at a later date.

8. Set aside a 2-year supply of emergency oil by 1990 to prevent an oil embargo, to keep world oil prices from rising too rapidly, and to reduce chances of international conflict over remaining world oil supplies. Also, set aside 10 percent of all undeveloped oil and natural gas reserves to supply petrochemical industries in the future.

9. Establish a Federal Energy Company that would (a) acquire and store a 2-year supply of emergency oil by 1990 from imported oil and oil from federally owned lands and (b) evaluate how and whether energy resources on federally owned lands should be mined (Section 13-5).

10. Prohibit any energy company, such as an oil company, from owning stock, reserves, or major patents in any other energy alternative. This should increase competition and reduce the possibility of horizontal monopolistic control of energy prices and supplies. The present practice of allowing oil companies to own and control oil from the well to the gas pump should also be prohibited in order to encourage competition and reduce the possibility of vertical monopolistic control of oil and gasoline prices and supplies.

11. Between 1980 and 2000 phase in of a mix of appropriate scaled soft energy alternatives based on renewable energy flows, such as sunlight, wind, small hydroelectric, and biomass wastes, that are best suited for each region of the country.

12. Since utilities already have the capacity to produce more electricity than presently needed and projected for the future, do not increase the use of coal to produce electricity (see Amory Lovins's Guest Editorial at the end of this chapter). If coal use should be increased this use must employ strict environmental controls and be applied only to take up any slack not provided by improvements in energy efficiency. Increase research and development on the more efficient burning of coal (fluidized beds) and on increased pollution control for coal-burning power plants (Chapter 17). Remove all present government subsidies for the development of coal gasification, coal liquefaction, and oil shale, and let these alternatives compete fairly and openly in the marketplace.

13. Place a moratorium on the building of any new conventional nuclear power plants, shelve plans to develop nuclear breeder reactors, and remove all government subsidies from nuclear power so it can compete openly and fairly with other energy technologies in the open marketplace. Since nuclear power is already in very serious economic difficulties even with massive government subsidies, the goal should be to phase out nuclear power in an orderly fashion by 1990. A successful energy conservation program (principle 3) should eliminate the need to construct any new nuclear (or coal) power plants between 1980 and 2000 or to put into operation those already under construction. In effect, the rapidly escalating costs of nuclear power have already produced such a moratorium (see Section 14-3), and such a moratorium will not have any catastrophic effects on energy use between 1980 and 2010.

14. Until existing nuclear power plants are phased out, require all key workers to be better trained and licensed according to much stricter government standards, with frequent recertification mandatory. Each plant should have a highly trained federal inspector on the premises at all times who has full authority to shut down the reactor in case of an emergency.

15. Stabilize the U.S. population at about 250 million by 2015 (Chapter 8). Between 1955 and 1978 more than a third (38 percent) of the increase in U.S. energy use was due to population growth. Based on the projected population increase alone, U.S. energy supply will either have to rise by 17 percent between 1980 and 2000 or average per capita energy use will have to be cut by 17 percent just to maintain the 1980 average per capita energy use.

16. Carefully integrate energy plans with those for population control, land use, agriculture, nonfuel mineral resources, water resources, and pollution control.

and supply of a single energy source (such as oil), which occurs when oil companies own everything from the well to the gasoline pump. There are four ultimate monopolies over people's lives—control of air, water, food, and energy. Regardless of whether one believes that energy companies have attempted directly or indirectly to manipulate energy supplies and prices, the potential for such control is clear and could increase. For decades the energy companies have used some of their vast financial resources to influence American and world politics in ways favorable to their interests. With even more money flowing into these companies today because of higher oil prices, the danger of undue political influence by energy companies is increasing sharply. Even if they know what is best for the nation, energy company executives are not paid to think about the long-term energy needs of the United States. They keep their jobs only as long as they show short-term profits. Energy companies also influence government energy agencies. A 1976 study by Common Cause showed that more than half of the 139 top-level employees in the Energy Research and Development Administration (ERDA), the predecessor of today's DOE, came from private energy companies—most of which had contracts with ERDA. As President Franklin D. Roosevelt once said, "The trouble with the country is that you can't win an election without the oil bloc and you can't govern with it."

Energy companies argue that they need a just profit (15 to 20 percent) as an incentive to risk their capital to find and extract new fuel supplies. But the financial profit and loss statements of oil companies can easily be distorted by accounting methods (such as tax havens, transfer pricing overseas, and the like) to the advantage of the companies so that the actual profits are hidden from the public eye.

Vertical integration of many oil companies—the control of every step of oil production and distribution— already exists. But the real danger in the long run is horizontal integration of many big oil companies, which can be more accurately described as energy companies. Government investigations have revealed that the large oil companies (1) own at least 70 percent of the U.S. natural gas reserves; (2) own 47 percent of economically recoverable U.S. uranium reserves and 41 percent of the uranium-milling capacities; (3) own 25 percent of the nation's recoverable coal reserves, 20 percent of the annual coal mining and 7 of the top 15 coal-mining companies; (4) are moving to lease much of the richest oil shale and geothermal energy reserves on federal lands and to dominate the newly emerging coal gasification industry; and

(5) are rapidly buying up solar patents and small solar energy companies.

Energy companies and other opponents of vertical and horizontal divestiture argue the following: (1) The oil industry is highly competitive and is not a monopoly, with no one company dominating more than 10 percent of the nation's petroleum supply, refining capacity, and retail sales; (2) vertical integration is commonplace in many U.S. industries and increases efficiency of service; (3) if oil companies are broken up, energy costs will rise and the amount of energy available will decrease because large, integrated companies can raise the large amounts of capital needed for energy exploration and development more readily; (4) it is in the best interests of the nation for oil companies to use their expertise and capital to develop other energy resources; and (5) there is no danger of an energy monopoly, since the four largest oil companies control only about 18 percent of the total national energy output. Thus, American citizens must weigh the risk of decreasing the efficiency at which national energy is supplied against the risk of a group of large energy companies gradually controlling more and more of the national energy supply and prices and thus gaining even greater political influence and control over individual lives.

The Present U.S. Short-Term Energy Plan After the 1973 oil embargo, Congress was prodded to pass a number of laws, including the Energy Reorganization Act of 1974, the Federal Nonnuclear Energy Research and Development Act of 1974, the Energy Policy and Conservation Act of 1976, the Energy Conservation and Production Act of 1976, and finally, after almost 2 years of delay and vigorous debate, the National Energy Act of 1978 with amendments added in 1980. The acts passed before 1978 included some important steps, such as (1) establishing a national 88-kilometer-per-hour (55-mile-per-hour) speed limit, (2) requiring new fleets of automobiles to get an average of 8.5 kilometers per liter (20 miles per gallon) by 1980 and 12 kilometers per liter (27.5 miles per gallon) by 1985, (3) providing funds to stockpile a 3-month supply of oil by 1985, (4) requiring all major appliances to have labels indicating energy efficiency or average annual operating cost, (5) significantly increasing budget allocations for energy research and development, and (6) establishing the Federal Energy Administration (FEA) to oversee national energy policy and the Energy Research and Development Administration (ERDA) to oversee research and development of energy alternatives (both of these agencies have been replaced by the Department of Energy or DOE). But despite these and other encouraging changes, none of the laws represented a comprehensive short-, intermediate-, or long-term plan.

In April 1977 President Carter presented his National Energy Plan. The proposed plan represented the first major attempt to develop a comprehensive short-term energy plan (to 1985), and it included a careful balance of some of the principles suggested in this section. The plan was built around the principles of (1) increasing energy efficiency by 1985, (2) increasing but not deregulating the prices of domestic oil and natural gas, (3) increasing the use of coal through 1985, (4) establishing a 10-month strategic oil reserve by 1985, (5) shelving indefinitely plans to reprocess spent nuclear fuel and build a nuclear breeder demonstration reactor, (6) increasing funding for development of solar, wind, and biomass energy alternatives, and (7) creating a Department of Energy (DOE) to oversee national energy policy and energy research and development, which would replace FEA and ERDA.*

The proposed National Energy Plan was subjected to intense and often conflicting lobbying pressures from the oil industry, the coal industry, labor unions, environmental groups, and consumer groups. As a result, the National Energy Act of 1978, which emerged from Congress after almost 2 years of intense debate, bore only modest relationship to the original plan. Some efforts to encourage energy efficiency remained, but many of the important measures were eliminated; one result is that the original 1985 goals for increased energy efficiency will not be completely met. Tax credits for homeowners who install insulation, solar heating, and energy-saving equipment were retained. Domestic extraction of natural gas was encouraged by allowing prices to rise more than proposed in the original plan. Taxes on gas-guzzling cars were retained, but vans, pickup trucks, and recreational vehicles were exempted from the tax.

A proposed standby tax on gasoline to encourage conservation was not passed, but the federal income tax deduction for state and local taxes on gasoline was eliminated. A proposed federal requirement that utility rates be restructured to reduce energy waste by having small users of electricity pay the lowest rather than the highest rates was not passed. Utilities, however, were required to buy excess power from industries that produce their own power from waste heat (cogeneration). The proposed wellhead tax on oil was eliminated so that wasteful use of oil and gasoline will continue and dangerous dependence on imports will probably not be reduced nearly enough by 1985. However, a tax credit was provided for equipment used to produce synthetic oil from oil shale and synthetic natural gas from coal by using an underground (in situ) conversion process (Section 14-2). The goal of increasing the use of coal from 20 percent of all energy used in 1979 to 25 percent by 1985 was undermined. If energy efficiency is improved and electricity is used only for tasks where it is necessary, there need be no increase in the use of coal except to shift existing plants that burn oil or natural gas over to coal. Industries that install energy-saving equipment and convert from oil or gas to coal will be given a tax credit (the carrot). But the proposal to impose strict penalties on industries not making such a switch (the stick) was eliminated, and burning oil and natural gas to generate electricity will not be banned until after 1990 except in special cases for environmental reasons. The controversial demonstration nuclear breeder reactor was shelved, but Congress voted funds to continue large-scale research on this project and the project may be revived because of the pro-nuclear stance of the Reagan administration and of new members of Congress elected in 1980. Increased, but still inadequate, funding for research and development of energy alternatives was approved. In separate legislation, the DOE was officially established.

In 1979, President Carter proposed a revised energy plan that included the following:

1. decontrol of the price of domestically extracted crude oil by 1981 (passed by Congress in 1980);

2. a tax on excessive oil profits with the tax revenues going to an Energy Security Fund to (a) finance a crash program to produce synthetic fuels from coal, oil shale, and other sources; (b) help low-income families with fuel bills; and (c) stimulate the development of energy-efficient mass transit systems and upgrade existing systems (modified and passed by Congress in 1980);

3. increasing the tax credits for homeowners who install insulation, solar heating, airtight wood-burning stoves, and other energy-saving equipment (passed by Congress in 1980);

4. adding tax incentives to encourage businesses to develop new energy alternatives, such as solar, wind, and geothermal energy (passed by Congress in 1980);

---

*Actually the DOE was part of a separate reorganization plan submitted to Congress, but it was an important part of the president's national energy strategy.

Table 13-8 Proposed U.S. Expenditures for Energy Research and Development for 1981

Program	Expenditure (millions of dollars)	Percentage of Total Energy Budget	Approximate Military Expenditure Equivalents
Nuclear energy	1,234	29	One missile-carrying submarine
Breeder fission	(510)	(12)	Five long-range bombers
Conventional fission and nuclear waste management	(331)	(8)	One conventional submarine
Nuclear fusion	(394)	(9)	Three destroyers
Fossil fuel energy	1,084	25	One missile-carrying submarine
General science and research	508	12	Five long-range bombers
Solar energy	341	8	Two MX missiles
Conservation	276	6	Three long-range bombers
Basic energy sciences	244	6	Two long-range bombers and two jet fighter planes
Environmental research and development	237	5.5	Two long-range bombers and two jet fighter planes
Geothermal energy	156	3	One destroyer
Wind energy	86	2	Four jet fighter planes
Biomass energy	80	2	Four jet fighter planes
Energy storage systems	72	1.5	Four jet fighter planes
Total	4,298	100	Two nuclear-powered aircraft carriers

5. setting up a $35-million fund to provide low-interest loans to homeowners and businesses to install solar energy equipment (passed by Congress in 1980);

6. creation of a cabinet-level Energy Mobilization Board to cut through federal and state "red tape" and environmental regulations to speed up the development of energy projects such as oil refineries, gas and oil pipelines, synthetic fuel plants, offshore oil rigs, strip mines, dams, and coal and nuclear power plants (disapproved by Congress in 1980).

Some of these steps strengthened the National Energy Act of 1978. Environmentalists successfully opposed the creation of an Energy Mobilization Board on the grounds that it would undercut strip mining, air pollution, and water pollution laws and lead to increased environmental damage. Although this proposal was defeated by Congress in 1980, energy companies hope to have it reintroduced in the future. Many oil and coal executives and environmentalists believe that the present

government-funded crash program to extract oil shale and to produce synthetic natural gas and oil (called synfuels) from coal is unnecessary and wasteful (since projected oil price increases may make development of these alternatives by private industry economically feasible in a few years) and could lead to serious environmental damage (as discussed in Section 14-2).

At the time of this writing (early 1981), it is too early to evaluate President Ronald Reagan's energy program. Based on campaign promises, however, he may (1) place greater emphasis on increasing energy supply, with a relaxation of environmental regulations on coal burning and reclamation of strip mined land; (2) decrease the funding and efforts to improve energy efficiency and to reduce the unnecessary waste of energy (for example, by proposing that improved fuel-efficiency requirements for new cars be relaxed or postponed);* and (3) attempt to decrease regulatory actions by the Environmental Pro-

---

*You might want to update and evaluate what has been done with respect to U.S. energy policy since early 1981.

tection Agency and the Department of Energy (which he promised to abolish). It remains to be seen whether he will be consistent with his conservative principles and propose that all government subsidies for nuclear power, oil, coal, natural gas, synfuels, and any energy alternative be removed so they can all compete openly and fairly in the marketplace.* In summary, by 1981 the United States had taken a few cautious steps toward dealing with its present energy crisis, but a comprehensive long-range program to deal with the more serious energy crises coming up (see Section 13-1) had yet to be implemented.

Federal expenditures for energy research and development increased sevenfold between 1973 and 1981. But as Table 13-8 reveals, total spending is still a drop in the bucket compared with the importance of energy to American society. *The total government energy research and development expenditure approved by Congress for 1981 was no more than the amount that was spent on building two nuclear aircraft carriers.* Table 13-8 also reveals that nuclear energy still makes up the largest fraction (29 percent) of the total energy budget, despite its serious economic difficulties even after being subsidized by tens of billions of tax dollars over decades. Almost one-half of this amount is being used to develop the nuclear breeder reactor, which is supposed to have been shelved. Environmentalists have become increasingly alarmed over this commitment to nuclear power at the expense of renewable solar, wind, and biomass alternatives. After over three decades of development and massive government subsidies of $39 billion between 1950 and 1981, nuclear power still provided only about 3 percent of the nation's energy in 1980 and was in serious economic trouble. This fear is heightened by the fact that in 1978 the DOE had 1,700 employees involved in nuclear energy

development work (1,300 field persons and 400 people at the Washington headquarters) compared with fewer than 50 people working on wind and solar energy research. In addition, President Ronald Reagan (who strongly supports the use of nuclear energy) appointed a strong proponent of nuclear energy to head the Department of Energy.

Furthermore, the energy research and development budget proposed for 1982 by the Reagan administration increased the share of funds allocated for nuclear energy from 29 percent to 43 percent of the total budget (75 percent if one looks at nuclear energy items hidden under other categories). This was done despite the fact that most financial experts and utility company executives believe that nuclear power is an uneconomic energy option even with massive government bailout funds (see Section 14-3). The Reagan administration also proposed that funds for solar energy, wind power, small hydro power, and energy conservation be cut drastically. This includes cutting research on the development of low-cost photovoltaic solar cells that would be a threat to electric power utilities by allowing people to use the sun to generate their own electricity.

Since 1918 the federal government has spent somewhere between $151 billion and $500 billion to stimulate the production of electricity with oil, natural gas, coal, hydroelectric, and nuclear power. Providing more federal funds to help develop new energy alternatives for producing heat and to fuel vehicles may be desirable. At present, however, about two-thirds of these tax dollars are being used to develop ways of generating electricity—a type of energy that the United States already has more of than it needs to perform tasks where this type of high quality energy is necessary.

It may make more economic sense to remove most, if not all, government subsidies for energy alternatives and let them compete fairly in the marketplace. Such an approach, however, is a difficult feat to accomplish politically. Instead of having open and free competition, the emerging energy alternatives (such as solar and wind) might be eliminated and those already developed (such as nuclear and coal) might remain because they were developed with massive government subsidies.

The First and Second Thermodynamic Revolutions The more developed nations have engineered what might be called the *first thermodynamic* (or energy) *revolution*. It consists of a dramatic increase in material goods, political participation, and education for a high percentage of their citizens by means of a large increase in total and per capita energy use. It has been based, however, on

*Specifically, as Amory and Hunter Lovins suggest: (1) Will he seek to repeal the government subsidies for the new synfuels industry that he so strongly opposed during his election campaign? (2) Will he allow the participating manufacturers who believe that the Clinch River Breeder Reactor (shelved by the Carter Administration) is such a good business deal, to pay for it themselves? (3) Will he refuse to bail out the nuclear waste and fuel reprocessing plant in Barnwell, South Carolina and make the nuclear industry (like the chemical industry) pay for cleaning up its own wastes? (Highly unlikely, since he appointed a former Governor of South Carolina who is also a strong supporter of nuclear power as secretary of the Department of Energy); and (4) Will he remove government subsidies from all energy alternatives and allow a genuinely competitive marketplace to choose between energy conservation and production, between hard and soft energy technologies, and between big and small businesses? Whether the Reagan Administration pursues an energy policy of free-market competition, individual choice, and local self-determination, which is consistent with its conservative political philosophies, can go far to determine America's energy future.

improving human well-being at the expense of the environment and by depleting low-cost, high net useful energy yield resources. The thermodynamic debt required by the first and second energy laws is now coming due.

But two-thirds of the world's population have yet to participate in this first thermodynamic revolution. People talk glibly about countries becoming more developed by following the present American approach to industrialization. But if the present level and pattern of American industrialization and energy use were employed throughout the world, within a short time the planet would be uninhabitable. The atmosphere would contain about 200 times more sulfur dioxide, 750 times more carbon monoxide and several times more carbon dioxide than it now does. The world's lakes, rivers, and oceans would be loaded with 175 times more chemical wastes, and thermal pollution could completely disrupt aquatic ecosystems. Two-thirds of the world's forests would be eliminated, and each year 121,000 square kilometers (30

million acres) of vital farmland would be converted to cities and highways. The earth's reserves of fossil fuels, nonfuel minerals, and uranium would be depleted within a very short time.

The real hope for all countries lies in our ability to halt population growth (Chapter 8) and to bring about a *second thermodynamic,* or *sustainable earth, revolution* over the next 30 to 50 years. It would be an ecological revolution that involves taking seriously the limits imposed by excessive population growth, resource supplies, and the laws of energy. It means a life-style based on the thrifty use of energy and matter and on accepting the responsibility to control population growth and to distribute the world's resources more equitably.

A country that runs on energy cannot afford to waste it.
Bruce Hannon

Guest Editorial: Technology Is the Answer (But What Was the Question?)

Amory B. Lovins

Amory B. Lovins is a physicist and energy consultant who is recognized as one of the world's leading experts on energy strategy. He was based in England from 1967 to 1981, and since 1981 has worked for Friends of the Earth, Inc. (FOE), a U.S. non-profit environmental conservation lobbying group. In 1979, he became vice-president of the FOE Foundation. He has served as a consultant to several

United Nations agencies: the Organization for Economic Cooperation and Development (OECD); the MIT Workshop on Alternative Energy Strategies (WAES); the Science Council of Canada; Petro-Canada; the U.S. Department of Energy (joining its Energy Research Advisory Board in 1980); the U.S. Congress's Office of Technology Assessment; the U.S. Solar Energy Research Institute; Resources for the Future; the governments of California, Montana, Alaska, and Lower Saxony; and other organizations in several countries. He is active in energy affairs at a technical and political level in about fifteen countries, and has published eight books (including the very important and widely discussed Soft Energy Paths, *New York: Harper Colophon, 1979, and the non-technical version of this work with co-author L. Hunter Lovins,* Energy Unbound: Your Invitation to Energy Abundance, *San Francisco: Friends of the Earth, 1982), and many technical papers.*

The answers you get depend on the questions you ask. But sometimes it seems so important to resolve a crisis that we forget to ask what problem we're trying to solve.

It is fashionable to suppose that we're running out of energy, and that the solution is obviously to get lots more of it. But asking how to get more energy begs the question of how much we need. That depends not on how much we used in the past but on what we want to do in the future and how much energy it will take to do those things. How much energy it takes to make steel, run a sewing machine, or keep you comfortable in your house depends on how cleverly we use energy, and the more it costs, the smarter we seem to get. It is now cheaper, for example, to double the efficiency of most industrial electric motors than to get more electricity to run the old ones. (Just this one saving can more than replace the entire U.S. nuclear power program.) We know how to make lights three times as efficient as those presently in use, and how to make household appliances that give us the same work as now using a quarter as much energy (saving money in the process). The Volkswagen Corporation has made a good-sized, safe car averaging 30–34 kilometers per liter (70–80 miles per gallon). We know today how to make new buildings, and many old ones, so heat-tight (but still well ventilated) that they need essentially no energy to maintain comfort year-round even in severe climates. These energy-saving measures are uniformly cheaper than going out and getting more energy. Detailed studies in over a dozen countries have shown that supplying energy services in the cheapest way—by wringing more work from the energy we already have—would let us increase our standard of living while using several times *less* total energy (and electricity) than we do now.

But the old view of the energy problem embodied a worse mistake than forgetting to ask how much energy we needed: it sought more energy, in any form, from any source, at any price—as if all kinds of energy were alike. This is like saying, "All kinds of food are alike; we're running short of potatoes and turnips and cheese, but that's OK, we can substitute sirloin steak and oysters Rockefeller." Some of us have to be more discriminating than that. Just as there are different kinds of food, so there are many different forms of energy whose different prices and qualities suit them to different uses. There is, after all, no *demand for energy* as such: nobody wants raw kilowatt-hours or barrels of sticky black goo. People instead want energy *services:* comfort, light, mobility, ability to bake bread, or ability to make cement. We ought therefore to start at that end of the energy problem: to ask, "What are the many different tasks we want energy *for,* and what is the amount, type, and source of energy that will do *each task in the cheapest way?"*

Electricity is a particularly special, high-quality, expensive form of energy. An average kilowatt-hour delivered in the United States in late 1980 was priced at about 5¢, equivalent to buying the heat content of oil costing $80 per barrel (50¢ per liter). A power station ordered at that time will deliver electricity costing, in 1980 dollars, at least 8¢ per kilowatt-

hour, equivalent on a heat basis to about $130 per barrel—four times the 1980 OPEC oil price.

Such costly energy might be worthwhile if it could be used for the premium tasks that require it, such as lights, motors, electronics, and smelters. But those special uses, only 8 percent of all delivered U.S. energy needs, are already met twice over by today's power stations. Two-fifths of our electricity is already spilling over into uneconomic, low-grade uses such as water heating, space heating, and air conditioning: uses where, no matter how efficiently we use electricity (even with heat pumps), we can never get our money's worth out of it. Electricity is far too expensive to be worthwhile for the 58 percent of the delivered energy that is needed in the form of heat in the United States, and for the 34 percent needed to run non-rail vehicles. But these tasks are all that additional electricity could be used for without wasting energy and money, because today's power stations already supply the real electric needs twice over.

Thus, *supplying more electricity is irrelevant to the energy problem that we have.* Even though electricity accounts for two-thirds of the federal energy research and development budget and for about three-quarters of national energy investment, it is the wrong kind of energy to meet our needs economically. Arguing about what kind of new power station to build—coal, nuclear, solar—is like shopping for the best buy in brandy to burn in your car, or for the best buy in Chippendales to burn in your stove. *It is the wrong question.*

Indeed, *any* kind of new power station is so uneconomical that if you have just built one, you will save the country money by writing it off and never operating it! Why? Because its additional electricity can only be used for low-temperature heating and cooling (the premium, "electricity-specific" uses being already filled up); but to do low-temperature heating and cooling, it is only worth paying what it costs to do it in the cheapest way. That means weatherstripping, insulation, heat exchangers, greenhouses, window shades and shutters and overhangs, trees, and so on. These measures generally cost about 0.4¢ per kilowatt-hour, whereas the running costs *alone* for a new nuclear plant will be nearly 2¢ per kilowatt-hour, so it is cheaper not to run it. In fact, under our crazy U.S. tax laws, the extra saving from not having to pay the plant's future subsidies and profits is probably so big that society can also recover the capital cost of having built the plant!

If we want more electricity, we should get it from the cheapest sources first. In approximate order of increasing price, these include:

1. Eliminating pure waste of electricity, such as lighting empty offices at headache level. Each kilowatt-hour saved can be resold to somebody else without having to generate it anew.

2. Displacing with good architecture, and with passive and some active solar techniques, the electricity now used for

water heating and space conditioning. Some U.S. utilities now give zero-interest weatherization loans, which you need not start repaying for ten years or until you sell your house—because it saves them millions of dollars to get electricity that way compared with building new power plants.

3. Making lights, motors, appliances, smelters, and the like cost-effectively efficient.

Just these three measures can quadruple U.S. electrical efficiency, making it possible to run today's economy, with no changes in lifestyles, using no thermal power plants, whether old or new, and whether fueled with oil, gas, coal, or uranium. We would need only the present hydroelectric capacity, readily available small-scale hydroelectric projects, and a modest amount of windpower. But if we still wanted more electricity, the next cheapest sources would include:

4. Industrial cogeneration, combined-heat-and-power plants, low-temperature heat engines run by industrial waste heat or by solar ponds, filling empty turbine bays in existing big dams, modern wind machines or small-scale hydroelectric turbines in good sites, and perhaps even some recent developments in solar cells with waste-heat recovery.

It is only after we had clearly exhausted all these cheaper opportunities that we would even consider:

5. Building a new central power station of any kind—the slowest and costliest known way to get more electricity (or to save oil).

To emphasize the importance of starting with energy *end-uses* rather than energy *sources,* consider a sad little story from France, involving a "spaghetti chart" (or energy flow chart)—a device energy planners often use to show how energy flows from primary sources via conversion processes to final forms and uses (a greatly simplified example is shown in Figure 13-10). In the mid-1970s, the energy conservation planners in the French government started, wisely, on the right-hand side of the spaghetti chart. They found that their biggest single need for energy was to heat buildings, and that even with good heat pumps, electricity would be the most uneconomic way to heat buildings. So they had a fight with their nationalized utility; they won; and electric heating was supposed to be discouraged or even phased out because it is so wasteful of money and fuel.

But meanwhile, down the street, the energy supply planners (who were far more numerous and influential in the French government) were starting on the left-hand side of the spaghetti chart. They said: "Look at all that nasty imported oil coming into our country! We must replace that oil. Oil is energy," they mused. "We must need some other source of energy. Voilà! Reactors give us energy; we'll build nuclear reactors all over the country." But they paid little attention to what would happen to that extra energy, and no attention to relative prices.

Thus, the two sides of the French energy establishment went on with their respective solutions to two different, indeed contradictory, French energy problems: *more energy of any kind,* versus *the right kind to do each task cheapest.* It was only in 1979 that these conflicting perceptions collided. The supply planners suddenly realized that the only way they would be able to *sell* all that nuclear electricity would be for electric heating, which they had just agreed not to do.

Every industrial nation is in this embarrassing position (especially if we include in "heating" also air conditioning, which just means heating the outdoors instead of the indoors). Which end of the spaghetti chart we start on, or *what we think the energy problem is,* is not an academic abstraction: it *determines what we buy.* It is the most fundamental source of disagreement about energy policy. People starting on the left side of the spaghetti chart think the problem boils down to whether to build coal or nuclear power stations (or both), while people starting on the right realize that *no* kind of new power station can be an economic way to meet the needs for heat and for vehicular liquid fuels that are 92% of our energy problem.

So if we want to provide our energy services at a price we can afford, let's get straight what question our technologies are supposed to provide the answer to. Before we argue about the meatballs, let's untangle the strands of spaghetti, see where they're supposed to lead, and find out what we really need the energy *for!*

Guest Editorial Discussion

1. List the energy services you would like to have and note which of these need to be furnished by electricity.

2. The author argues that building more nuclear, coal, or any type of power plants to supply more electricity for the United States is unnecessary and wasteful. Summarize the reasons for this conclusion and give your reasons for agreeing or disagreeing with this viewpoint.

3. Do you agree or disagree that increasing the supply of energy for the United States, instead of concentrating on improving energy efficiency, is the wrong answer to U.S. energy problems? Why?

Guest Editorial: Energy Analysis and the Dynamic Steady State

Howard T. Odum

Howard T. Odum is the graduate research professor of environmental engineering sciences and director of the Center for Wetlands at the University of Florida. During his distinguished career as a research scientist, lecturer, and writer, he has received the George Mercer Award of the Ecological Society, the Award of Distinction from the International Technical Writers Association, the Distinguished Service Award of the Industrial Development Research Council, and Prize of the Institute de la Vie of Paris. He is internationally known for his important pioneering work in making net useful energy analysis a part of energy planning in an increasing number of countries.

The growth in the production of net useful energy in the United States and much of the industrial world has almost stopped. Since 1973 the American economy has produced enough to maintain national assets and to exchange money and goods for energy imports but not enough for significant further economic growth. U.S. natural gas and older oil reserves were yielding about 10 units of useful energy for each unit used in processing until the gas crisis of the winter of 1977. Now most energy sources yield 6 units of useful energy for each unit put directly and indirectly into the work of acquisition (either through foreign exchange or through exploration and processing). Nuclear energy yields only 3 to 4 units of net useful energy for each unit of useful energy put into the system. The net useful energy that can be obtained by importing fuels depends on the availability of fuel reserves in the United States to keep the prices of foreign fuels down. The average standard of living may hold steady for a while as emphasis shifts to eliminating waste, but eventually it may drop as net useful energy yields decline (Figure 13-12). Here are some suggestions for adapting to these new times.

1. A 10 percent cut in salary for everyone in the United States may be needed so that unemployment can be reduced without a change in GNP, net energy use, or inflation. This action will allow each American to eliminate what is less essential or less productive. Unions might take the lead, emphasizing employment for all instead of high wages for the few.

2. If U.S. money flow can be adjusted to U.S. energy flow each year (Figures 13-10 and 13-11), the buying power of the dollar in real value will hold constant and the dollar will then be on an energy standard. This protects the individual and prevents unwise attempts to expand the economy when such attempts will fail. This is the reverse of the deficit financing that is used in growth times.

3. It is useful to use energy costs to estimate net energy value. The unit of measure is kilocalories of solar energy to develop a kilocalorie of useful energy. Good energetics suggest items should not be used for less effect than their energy cost. Because they are at the end of a chain of energy transformations, wildlife, people, and information have high energy costs and thus are valued.

4. In planning and judging what energy alternatives and uses will be economical, purchased energy should be matched with the free resources of the sun, rain, and land.

5. In all considerations of the realm of environment, economics, and energy, a basic energy analysis is needed to show the interactions of money, energy, materials, and information. Drawing and numerically evaluating energy analysis diagrams is a starting procedure that can be understood from the grammar school to the graduate school. Rather than being interdisciplinary, energy analysis is a new discipline that realigns knowledge and principles. We may need to institutionalize courses and degrees using energetic holism as a key to understanding the systems of humans and nature.

Guest Editorial Discussion

1. Explain how overall energy use continues to rise whereas the growth in net useful energy has leveled off in most industrial nations and may begin to decline.

2. What are the advantages and disadvantages of relating energy flow in a society to dollar flow?

3. Explain how unemployment could be reduced without a change in GNP, energy use, or inflation if everyone in the United States took a 10 percent cut in salary. Debate the pros and cons of this suggestion.

Discussion Topics

1. What is an energy crisis? What are the four energy crises described in this chapter? Do you agree or disagree with this classification? Defend your answer.

2. Trace your own direct and indirect energy consumption each day and see whether it might average 250,000 kilocalories per day. Contrast your total with that of a Mississippi farm laborer, an Indian peasant, and a Chicago slum dweller.

3. Why has the United States in recent years shifted from coal to natural gas and oil, even though coal is the nation's most abundant fossil fuel?

4. List the following forms of energy in order of increasing energy quality: heat from nuclear fission, normal sunlight, oil shale, air at 500°C.

5. Give three examples of the use of high-quality energy for tasks requiring low-quality energy.

6. Distinguish among first law energy efficiency, second law energy efficiency, and net useful energy, and give an example of each. Explain how net useful energy is related to dollar flow and inflation.

7. How can one estimate indicate that 63 percent of all energy used in the United States each year is wasted and a second estimate indicate 85 percent?

8. You are about to build a house. What energy supply (oil, gas, coal, or other) would you use for space heating, the stove, the refrigerator, and the hot water heater? Consider long-term economic and ecological factors.

9. List the major U.S. energy alternatives for the short term (1982 to 1992), intermediate term (1992 to 2002), and long term (2002 to 2032).

10. List the major advantages and disadvantages of each of the following energy alternatives: (a) coal, (b) petroleum, (c) natural gas, (d) conventional nuclear fission reactors, (e) nuclear breeder reactors, (f) oil shale, (g) geothermal energy, (h) wind energy, (i) solar energy, (j) coal gasification, (k) nuclear fusion, and (l) biomass.

11. Which, if any, of the major energy resources in the Rocky Mountain region of the United States should be mined first and under what restrictions? Defend your choice. Which resource, if any, should be mined second? If none of these resources were mined, what effects (if any) might this have on the United States and on your own life and life-style in 1990?

12. Explain how the use of nonfuel mineral resources (Chapter 12) and food production (Chapter 9) depends on the availability of energy resources.

13. Do you agree or disagree with the following propositions? Defend your choice.

    a. To conserve finite and dwindling supplies of oil and natural gas, the United States should shift back to coal and ease air pollution and strip mining regulations to make this possible.

    b. The energy crisis of the early 1970s was staged by the major oil companies to drive prices up, increase profits, and eliminate competition from independent gas stations.

    c. To conserve finite and dwindling supplies of oil and natural gas and to decrease reliance on imports, the United States should shift to nuclear power, especially the breeder reactor, as soon as possible.

    d. The price of electricity and domestic fossil fuels in the United States should be increased significantly in order to promote energy conservation and to reduce environmental impact of energy use.

    e. The United States should not be overly concerned about foreign oil imports because they improve international relationships and prevent the nation from depleting its own remaining oil and natural gas supplies.

    f. The United States uses far too much energy relative to its needs and should institute a program designed to cut average per capita energy use by at least 35 percent.

    g. The United States should declare a moratorium on the building and licensing of any new nuclear power plants until there is greater assurance of their safety and of the feasibility of safe transportation and long-term nuclear waste storage.

    h. A mandatory energy conservation program should form the basis of an energy policy for the United States.

    i. The vertical and horizontal structure of the major oil or energy companies should be broken up within the next 10 years.

    j. A National Energy Company, supported by taxes, should be established to develop and control about one-fourth to one-third of U.S. energy resources in competition with major energy companies in order to protect the consumer from rising prices.

    k. A National Energy Company should be created, but instead of competing directly with private energy companies, its mission should be to develop a 2-year reserve supply of oil and to evaluate how and whether energy resources on federally owned lands should be mined.

    l. All we need to do to solve the energy crisis is to find more oil and natural gas.

m. All we need to do to solve the energy crisis is to learn how to recycle energy.

n. Eliminate federal subsidies for all energy alternatives so that they can be fairly evaluated in an open, competitive marketplace.

Readings

American Physical Society. 1975. *Efficient Use of Energy*. New York: American Institute of Physics. Superb summary of energy waste and opportunities for energy conservation based on second law energy efficiencies in the United States.

Bent, Henry A. 1977. "Entropy and the Energy Crisis." *Journal of Science Teaching*, vol. 44, no. 4, 25–29. Very readable introduction to implications of the second energy law.

Carr, Donald E. 1976. *Energy & the Earth Machine*. New York: Norton. Very readable introduction to energy problems and alternatives.

Cheney, Eric S. 1974. "U.S. Energy Resources: Limits and Future Outlook." *American Scientist*, January-February, pp. 14–22. Excellent overview of options.

Clark, Wilson. 1974. *Energy for Survival: The Alternative to Extinction*. New York: Anchor. Very useful analysis of energy use and evaluation of alternative energy resources.

Cook, Earl. 1976. *Man, Energy, Society*. San Francisco: Freeman. One of the best introductions to energy concepts, problems, and alternatives.

Council on Environmental Quality. 1979. *The Good News About Energy*. Washington, D.C.: Government Printing Office. Useful summary of what has been done and what can be done to deal with the energy crisis in the United States.

Darmstadter, Joel, et al. 1979. *Energy in America's Future*. Baltimore: Johns Hopkins University Press. Very useful analysis of energy problems and alternatives.

Demand and Conservation Panel of the Committee on Nuclear and Alternative Energy Systems, National Academy of Sciences. 1978. "U.S. Energy Demand: Some Low Energy Futures." *Science*, vol. 200, 142–152. Very useful analysis showing how the United States could get along with much less energy without affecting life-styles.

Dorf, Richard C. 1978. *Energy, Resources, and Policy*. Reading, Mass.: Addison-Wesley. Excellent textbook.

Energy Policy Project. 1974. *A Time to Choose: The Final Report of the Energy Policy Project of the Ford Foundation*. Cambridge, Mass.: Ballinger. Superb overview by a high-level task force.

Environmental Protection Agency. 1974. *Control of Environmental Impacts from Advanced Energy Sources*.

Washington, D.C.: Environmental Protection Agency. Very useful information on environmental impacts of energy use.

Farhar, Barbara C., et al. 1980. "Public Opinion About Energy." In Jack M. Hollander et al., eds., *Annual Review of Energy*, vol. 5. Palo Alto, Calif.: Annual Reviews, pp. 141–172. Good source of data.

Fowler, John W. 1975. *Energy and the Environment*. New York: McGraw-Hill. Excellent summary of energy problems and alternatives at a slightly higher level than this text.

Hammond, Allen L., et al. 1973. *Energy and the Future*. Washington, D.C.: American Association for the Advancement of Science. One of the best evaluations of our energy options. At a slightly higher level than this text.

Harte, John, and Mohamed El-Gasseir. 1978. "Energy and Water." *Science*, vol. 199, 623–634. Superb analysis of the conflict over energy, land, and water resources.

Hayes, Denis. 1977. *Rays of Hope: The Transition to a Post-Petroleum World*. New York: Norton. Outstanding analysis of energy problems and alternatives.

Hayes, Earl T. 1979. "Energy Resources Available to the United States, 1985 to 2000." *Science*, vol. 203, 233–239. Superb overview.

Holdren, John P., et al. 1980. "Environmental Aspects of Renewable Energy Sources." In Jack M. Hollander et al., eds., *Annual Review of Energy*, vol. 5. Palo Alto, Calif.: Annual Reviews. The best available analysis of the environmental impacts of renewable energy alternatives.

Hollander, Jack M., et al., eds. Annual. *Annual Review of Energy*. Palo Alto, Calif.: Annual Reviews. Excellent series of articles.

Kendall, Henry, and Steven Nadis. 1980. *Energy Strategies: Toward a Solar Future*. Cambridge, Mass.: Ballinger. Splendid analysis of energy alternatives.

Knowles, R. S. 1980. *American's Energy Famine: Its Causes and Cures*. Norman, Okla.: Oklahoma University Press. Very useful analysis.

Landsberg, Hans H., et al. 1979. *Energy: The Next Twenty Years: Report of the Study Group*. Cambridge, Mass.: Ballinger. Very useful analysis of U.S. energy alternatives by a team of experts.

Lovins, Amory B. 1977. *Soft Energy Paths*. Cambridge, Mass.: Ballinger. Superb analysis of energy alternatives. See also Nash (1979).

Lovins, Amory B., and L. Hunter Lovins. 1982. *Energy Unbound: Your Invitation to Energy Abundance*. San Francisco: Friends of the Earth. Outstanding non-technical version of *Soft Energy Paths*.

Maddox, John. 1975. *Beyond the Energy Crisis: A Global*

Perspective. New York: McGraw-Hill. Attack on environmentalist approach to energy problems. Optimistic view that we can solve the problems by finding more fossil fuels and using nuclear energy. Compare with Lovins (1977).

Miles, Rufus E., Jr. 1980. "Energy Obesity." *The Futurist,* December, pp. 34–44. Superb discussion of the impact of energy waste on American society.

Nash, Hugh, ed. 1979. *The Energy Controversy: Soft Path Questions and Answers.* San Francisco: Friends of the Earth. Pros and cons of the soft energy path.

National Academy of Sciences. 1980. *Energy in Transition 1985–2010: Final Report of the Committee on Nuclear and Alternative Energy Systems.* Washington, D.C.: National Academy of Sciences. Very useful analysis.

Odum, Howard T., and Elisabeth C. Odum. 1976. *Energy Basis for Man and Nature.* New York. Superb introduction to energy concepts and alternatives with emphasis on net useful energy analyses.

Purcell, Arthur. 1980. *The Waste Watchers: A Citizen's Handbook for Conserving Energy and Resources.* New York: Anchor Press/ Doubleday. Superb guide.

Rifkin, Jeremy. 1980. *Entropy: A New World View.* New York: Viking. Very readable popular account of the sustainable earth approach to energy and society based on the two energy laws.

Rose, David J. 1974. "Energy Policy in the U.S." *Scientific American,* vol. 230, no. 1, 20–29. Fine summary of energy options.

Ross, Marc H., and Robert H. Williams. 1977. "The Potential for Fuel Conservation." *Technology Review,* February, pp. 49–56. Excellent overview of opportunities for conservation.

Schurr, Sam H., et al. 1979. *Energy in America's Future: The Choices Before Us.* Baltimore: Johns Hopkins University Press. Very useful analysis.

Stobaugh, Robert, and Daniel Yergin, eds. 1979. *Energy Future: Report of the Energy Project at the Harvard Business School.* New York: Random House. Superb analysis of U.S. energy alternatives.

U.S. Senate. 1976. *Land Use and Energy: A Study of Interrelationships.* Washington, D.C.: Committee on Interior and Insular Affairs. Analysis of land use, water, and energy resources in the Rocky Mountain region.

Wilson, Carroll L., ed. 1977. *Energy: Global Prospects 1985–2000.* New York: McGraw-Hill. Superb overview of potential energy supplies by a team of experts.

Woodwell, G. M. 1974. "Success, Succession and Adam Smith." *BioScience,* vol. 24, no. 2, 81–87. Outstanding overview of energy crisis and its ecological implications.

14

Energy Resources: A More Detailed Evaluation

14-1 Energy Conservation: Improving Energy Efficiency and Altering Life-Styles

Our Most Important Energy Alternative We have three basic approaches for dealing with the present and future energy crises (Section 13-1): (1) developing new sources of energy, (2) improving energy efficiency, and (3) adopting new life-styles using less energy. In Chapter 13 we saw that improving energy efficiency is the best and cheapest energy alternative (and also the largest potential source of energy) available to the United States.

Without a massive program to improve energy efficiency and to phase in a mix of renewable energy sources to replace much of the use of nonrenewable oil, natural gas, and coal to provide heat and to fuel vehicles, the United States has little (if any) chance of creating a sustainable earth energy society, as discussed by Denis Hayes in his Guest Editorial at the end of this chapter. If such a program is not begun vigorously now, then major and undesirable changes in life-style and a sharp drop in the average standard of living will be imposed by shortages of affordable energy. Between 1973 and 1980, the greatest single factor in reducing average per capita energy use in the United States (Figure 13-5) was using energy more efficiently. Yet many people seem reluctant to get serious about energy conservation, partly because they think energy conservation means hardship and life-style change. Not so. Conservation means doing more with the energy that is used, not doing without. The United States wastes so much energy each year (see

Enrichment studies 1, 3, 5, and 15 are related to this chapter.

Figures 13-10 and 13-11) that enormous amounts of energy can be saved without cutting off any vital services or making any major changes in life-style. For instance, energy conservation means an efficient heating system and a well-insulated house, not a cold house. For car owners energy conservation means driving a car that gets 6.6 kilometers per liter (40 miles per gallon) instead of 2.5 kilometers per liter (15 mpg), not giving up a car altogether.

Americans use energy in four basic sectors: transportation (34 percent), residential (20 percent), commercial (9 percent), and industrial (37 percent). In the rest of this section, we will look at specific ways to save energy in each of these four sectors.

Transportation Transportation accounts for about 34 percent of the energy used each year in the United States (Figure 13-7). If the gasoline consumed each year by the 140 million registered automobiles in the United States were poured into 3.8 liter (1 gallon) cans and lined up side by side, the line would stretch around the world 287 times. Ways to save energy in transportation include the following:

1. Build smaller, lighter cars, averaging 1,100 kilograms (2,500 pounds) by 1985 and 907 kilograms (2,000 pounds) by 1990 by using smaller engines, front wheel drive (eliminates the drive shaft), more plastic, aluminum, and glass, and less steel. Cutting a car's weight in half typically halves fuel consumption and with proper design need not reduce car safety.

2. Require automobiles sold in the United States to average 11.7 kilometers per liter (27.5 miles per gallon) by 1985 (compared with 14 kilometers per liter or 33 miles per gallon required in Canada by 1985). Raise American standards to 14.5 kilometers per liter (34 miles per gallon) by 1990 and 17 kilometers per liter (40 miles per gallon) by 1995.

3. Give large tax credits (30 to 50 percent of the purchase price) to individuals and businesses using cars and trucks that get over 17 kilometers per liter (40 miles per gallon)* and require fleets of government-owned cars to meet the average fuel consumption standards set by Congress. Add a heavy annual tax (at least 10 percent of value) on cars that average less than 8 kilometers per liter (20 miles per gallon).

4. Raise gasoline taxes to discourage excessive automobile use and get gas-guzzling vehicles off the road as a short-term method while mandatory fuel standards for new cars are being phased in.

5. If you need a car, buy a small, energy-efficient one and maintain it to save energy. Obey the 89 kilometer-per-hour (55 mile-per-hour) speed limit,† drive smoothly (up to 15 percent energy savings), shift into higher gears as soon as possible, don't warm up the engine more than one minute after starting, cut off the engine if the car must be idled more than one minute, don't brake excessively, don't race the engine, keep tires properly inflated (each pound per square inch of underinflation wastes 2 percent of the energy), clean the air filter regularly and replace as needed, keep the engine tuned (20 percent energy savings), and use an air conditioner only when really necessary. Save even more gas by buying a car with radial ply tires, electronic ignition, fuel injection, overdrive, cruise control, diesel engine, and a light color and tinted glass in hot climates (to keep it cooler and reduce the load on the air conditioner).

6. Consolidate car trips to accomplish as much as possible in one trip, choose the most direct and efficient route (using freeways where possible and routes with a minimum number of traffic lights and stop signs), and try to schedule trips to avoid rush hours.

7. By 1985, require that all cars be recycled at the end of their useful life and by 1985 design all new cars

so that their average life is doubled from their present 6 years to about 12 years.

8. Organize and use ride sharing systems (saves 50 percent or more energy). Provide reduced road and bridge tolls, free parking, and income tax deductions for those using carpools (Section 11-4).

9. Cut fuel consumption through measures such as making easier rolling radial tires standard equipment (up to 10 percent savings), perfecting puncture proof plastic tires that could save even more energy and eliminate the cost and weight of a spare tire and wheel, using miniprocessors to run the car at peak energy efficiency, replacing automatic transmissions with standard transmissions (up to 10 percent savings) or replacing automatic transmissions with new continuously variable transmissions, improve aerodynamic design to reduce wind resistance (up to 10 percent savings), using better electronic emission systems (about 8 percent savings), developing more efficient motor systems such as a hybrid car with an electric motor for city driving and a small combustion engine for high speed and long distance driving (see Section 17-5), and omitting air conditioning (9 to 20 percent savings).*

10. Walk or ride a bicycle or moped, especially for trips less than 8 kilometers (5 miles). Use highway trust funds (from gasoline tax revenues) to build bike paths on all major streets and highways in urban areas.

11. Use existing public transportation systems (buses, subways, and trolleys) as much as possible. Expand bus and other flexible systems rather than building expensive, high technology mass transit systems in urban areas (Section 11-4).

12. Shift more freight from fuel inefficient trucks and airplanes to less wasteful rail, water, and pipeline transport, and strictly enforce for trucks the 88 kilometer-per-hour (55 mile-per-hour) speed limit (which, despite the claims of truckers, cuts fuel consumption by about 32 percent).

---

*If the government gave a $4,000 cash grant to people who bought a car averaging 17 kilometers per liter (40 miles per gallon) provided they scrap their gas guzzler and get it off the road, this would save the nation more oil and the taxpayers more money than spending the $83 billion authorized by Congress to help private industry produce very expensive and energy inefficient oil shale and synfuels from coal (see Section 14-2).

†Gas mileage is about 21 percent better at 89 kilometers per hour 55 miles per hour) than at 113 kilometers per hour (70 miles per hour). The optimum speed for saving gas is about 56 kilometers per hour (35 miles per hour). To save gas accelerate smoothly (but fairly quickly) to 56 kilometers per hour (35 miles per hour) and then accelerate gradually to any higher speeds.

Residential and Commercial Sectors These two sectors account for about 29 percent of all the energy used each year in the United States. About half of this energy is

---

*An air conditioner typically increases fuel consumption by 9 percent and by as much as 20 percent in stop-and-go traffic on a hot day. The more efficient air conditioners found in many new cars can actually save gas at speeds of more than 64 kilometers per hour (40 miles per hour) because the wind drag from open car windows (but not open air vents) can increase fuel consumption more than using the air conditioner. The data for this conclusion, however, are controversial.

used for space heating (primarily of homes, stores, office buildings, and hotels. The remainder is used mostly for water heating, air-conditioning, refrigeration and cooking. The increase in energy use in the U.S. residential and commercial sectors dropped from about 5 percent a year in the 1960s to approximately 2 percent in the late 1970s. Most of this improvement came from adding more insulation, lowering thermostat settings in winter and raising them in summer, and cleaning and adjusting furnaces and air conditioners at least once a year. Despite these improvements, however, there is a long way to go. Most U.S. buildings and homes are still underinsulated and contain many air leaks. Low-income groups are hardest hit bcause they can't afford to weatherize their dwellings and end up paying a large fraction of their meager incomes for heating. The 1976 Energy Conservation and Production Act included a national weatherization program for low-income households. By 1979, however, only 5 percent of the 14 million eligible homes had been weatherized (most only partially) because of administrative delays and red tape, lack of enough trained workers, and insufficient funds. At the present rate it will take 30 years to weatherize the eligible low-income houses unless funding and program efficiency are greatly increased.

American buildings typically consume about 50 to 90 percent more energy each year than they would if they were oriented, designed, insulated, and lighted to use energy more efficiently. Eliminating this waste by proper design of new buildings and retrofitting existing buildings to improve their energy efficiency is the quickest, easiest, and cheapest way to save oil and other forms of energy with no loss of comfort or major changes in life-style. Today, well-designed, passively solar heated above ground and earth-sheltered (underground) homes and superinsulated homes can get all of their heat either from the sun or from the waste heat from human occupants and appliances, even in sub-Arctic climates. No conventional heating systems are needed at all, although banks and lending institutions unfamiliar with these new energy-efficient types of housing still usually require owners to install a conventional heating system as a backup before making a mortgage loan. Such energy-saving houses need not cost any more to build than conventional, energy-wasting ones and their lifetime cost (which is the only true cost to consider) is much less. In an energy-short world they should also have much higher resale prices—making them much better investments than conventional homes.

A monument to energy waste is the 110-story World Trade Center in lower Manhattan, which uses as much electricity each year as a city of 100,000 persons. Not a single window in its large towering walls of glass can be opened to take advantage of nature's warming and cooling, and its heating and cooling system must work around the clock, even when the building is empty.

This is in sharp contrast to Atlanta's new 24-story Georgia Power Company office building which uses 60 percent less energy than conventional office buildings. Energy saving features include (1) having each floor stick out over the one below to allow heating by the low winter sun while blocking out the higher summer sun to reduce air conditioning needs, (2) using a computer to shut off all lights at 6 p.m. unless instructed to leave specific ones on, (3) using efficient lights to focus on desks rather than illuminating entire rooms like hospital operating rooms, and (4) using an adjoining three-story building for work at unusual hours to save having to heat and cool the larger building.

Major ways to save energy (and money) in the residential and commercial sectors include the following:

1. Weatherproof new and old houses by (a) heavily insulating roofs, walls, and subfloors (saves 20 to 50 percent energy*); (b) using double- or triple-glazed windows with insulated window quilts or shades and storm doors or double air-lock entries (saves 10 to 30 percent energy); and (c) making the house air tight by weather stripping doors, caulking windows, and plugging all air leaks (saves 10 to 30 percent energy). Once the house is airtight install an air-to-air heat exchanger (a small unit resembling an air conditioner) that ventilates the building to prevent buildup of indoor pollutants and stagnant air and reduces the loss of heated air in cold weather and cooled air in summer.

2. Establish a national cadre of well-trained and certified "house doctors" to make complete energy audits of houses and buildings using devices such as (a) hand held infrared scanners to detect leaks (hot areas appear red and cold areas black), (b) a small exhaust fan to cause air to infiltrate through any leaks, and (c) pencil-like sticks that puff smoke

---

*One study has shown that if the federal government or utility companies provided $10 billion a year between 1980 and 1990 as interest-free loans for home insulation, this would save energy equivalent to 75 percent of all oil imported into the United States during 1980. This ten year, $100 billion loan program (which would be paid back) would eventually cost consumers nothing because of the money they would save on heating bills. This is in sharp contrast to the present 12 year, $83 billion government subsidy program for producing oil shale and synfuels from coal. This program won't save consumers any money (since they will have to purchase the very expensive fuels and part of it is to be paid for with their tax money), and it is not expected to save any more than 15 percent of the nation's imported oil by 1990.

which streams into normally invisible leaks along the floors, ceiling moldings, and electrical outlets. An aggressive house doctor program for the nation's 70 million houses carried out between 1980 and 1990 would cut home-heating demand by at least 50 percent and save energy equivalent to two-thirds of the oil imports in 1980. A house-doctor visit with a quick fix would cost about $200 to $400 (1980 prices) and lower heating bills by 15 to 20 percent. A full-fledged retrofit by a contractor would cost $1,500 to $3,000 (1980 prices) and save up to 50 percent of the yearly heating costs. Such a program is already being carried out for customers of the Tennessee Valley Authority (TVA) utility company. The TVA house doctor provides the customer with estimates of the costs and savings and pay back times for each energy saving measure, and supplies a list of approved contractors. TVA pays the contractor selected for the job, but only if the work is approved by a TVA house doctor. The customer then pays for the work—interest free—by a charge added to the monthly utility bill. A typical $1,500 job would cost about $17.85 a month for seven years. By that time the energy savings coupled with federal and state tax deductions allowed for energy saving measures should equal the energy retrofit cost so that the customer gets the job done free of charge and the utility company reduces electricity demand and the need to tie up its capital at high interest rates for 10 to 15 years to build new nuclear and coal-fired power plants. The Pacific Gas and Electric Company, California's biggest utility, is also attempting to reduce the demand for electricity and new power plants by offering many of its customers incentives to install solar water heaters, providing money to builders of energy-efficient houses, and giving grants to cities that cut energy use.

3. By 1985, require that no house—new or old—can be sold in the United States unless it has been audited by a certified house doctor, weatherproofed up to certain minimum standards, and inspected to be sure the job has been done correctly. A program similar to this goes into effect in Portland, Oregon, in 1984.

4. Raise present mandatory insulation standards for new houses (set by the Energy Conservation and Production Act of 1976) to higher standards of 30 centimeters (12 inches) in roofs or attics, 15 centimeters (6 inches) in walls, and 25 centimeters (11 inches) under bottom floors, saving homeowners so much energy (60 to 80 percent) that their initial investment would be paid back within a few years.

5. Require all new buildings and homes to take advantage of heating and cooling provided free by nature by having them oriented to take advantage of sunlight and prevailing winds and by having windows that can be opened.

6. For a new house, use passive solar heating* by (a) building a heavily insulated, airtight structure (with an air-to-air heat exchanger for ventilation), (b) using double- or triple-glazed windows and possibly an attached solar greenhouse (or sun room if vegetables or other plants are not grown in this space) on its south side in the Northern Hemisphere (or in the Southern Hemisphere on the north side) so that most if not all of its heat is supplied by the low winter sun, and (c) using few and small windows on the east, west, and north wall because they tend to lose more heat than they gain and can cause overheating during the summer. The north side can also be banked (bermed) with earth to help keep the house warm in winter and cool in summer. Heat is stored for slow radiation into the house at night by using stone, concrete, adobe, or brick walls and floors or tanks or barrels of water (painted black to absorb the heat). During hot weather passive solar cooling is provided by (a) using heavy insulation, (b) using deciduous trees and window overhangs or shades on the south side to block the high summer sun, and (c) using earth pipes (buried pipes that bring in cool air), an air-to-air heat exchanger, and a well-designed ventilation system to take advantage of breezes and to keep air moving continuously through the building. According to some experts, the use of passive solar cooling and natural ventilation should make it possible to construct all but the largest buildings without air conditioning in most parts of the world.

7. Another increasingly popular option is to build a passively heated and cooled earth-sheltered (underground) or partially earth-sheltered house or commercial building. By having the only exposed wall facing south (in the Northern Hemisphere) and using windows or an attached solar greenhouse (or sun room) to capture solar energy, these structures can provide from 50 to 100 percent of the heating and cooling needs of the building. They also eliminate exterior maintenance and painting (and interior maintenance if interior walls and floors are built of materials such as stone,

---

*Pump driven active solar heating with flat plate collectors on the roof or in the yard is a highly effective method for heating hot water (with properly designed systems) but it is usually an expensive way to heat a building's interior (compared to passive solar heating). The plumbing will also require maintenance and the collectors may have to be repaired or replaced periodically at considerable cost.

brick, or natural wood), and provide more privacy, quietness, and security (from break-ins, hurricanes, tornadoes, earthquakes, storms, and nuclear attack) than conventional above-ground buildings. Contrary to popular belief, living in an earth-sheltered building is not like living in a cave. The interior can look like that of any ordinary home, and atriums, small windows, and skylights can provide more daylight than is found in most conventional homes. By 1980, at least 3,000 earth-shelter structures had been built or were under construction in the United States. This number is expected to grow rapidly once banks and other lending institutions realize that in the 1980s and 1990s such energy-efficient structures will have far better resale values than conventional homes.

8. In very cold climates where the sun is present only a few hours a day, build superinsulated and extremely airtight homes (with an air-to-air heat exchanger). These buildings—often called low energy or zero energy homes—can be made so energy efficient that they can be heated totally (even in sub-Arctic climates) merely by using the body heat from their occupants and waste heat from appliances.

9. Greatly increase the tax credits already provided by the federal government (and by some states) for homeowners who add active solar energy devices and energy-conserving devices and materials (such as insulation). It is crucial that tax credits (of 50 to 100 percent) be allowed for individuals and businesses who get 50 to 100 percent of their heating requirements by building (a) a passively solar heated above-ground home or building, (b) a passively heated and cooled earth-sheltered home or building, or (c) a superinsulated home or building.

10. Reduce the energy needed to construct buildings by 20 percent through (a) using less energy-intensive building materials (for example, steel instead of aluminum), (b) designing buildings to minimize total lifetime cost, (c) using stress analysis to reduce concrete needs, and (d) saving energy in industries that supply building materials.

11. For new and existing houses, reduce heating requirements during cold weather by (a) planting year-round shade trees (conifers) on the north side of the house (in the Northern Hemisphere), (b) lowering the thermostat to 18°C (65°F) or lower during the day and to 13°C (55°F) or lower at night and while away for extended periods of time (each degree higher than these recommended settings can add 3 percent to the heating bill), (c) cutting off or lowering the heat in bedrooms coupled with

the use of sleeping bags or more blankets (nonelectric), (d) using humidifiers to provide comfort at lower temperatures, (e) wearing heavier clothing indoors, (f) closing off unused rooms, (g) using insulated draperies, quilts, or shades on windows and opening them by day on the sunny side of the house and closing them by night (saves 5 to 16 percent energy), (h) closing fireplace dampers (saves up to 8 percent), (i) having an expert clean and adjust the furnace at least once a year (saves 10 to 20 percent energy), (j) insulating all heating ducts and checking them closely for air leaks, (k) cleaning furnace air filters at least every 2 weeks and replacing them as necessary (usually every 4 to 6 months), (l) installing a clock thermostat to carry out night and day temperature change settings automatically, (m) carefully cleaning the thermostat once a year to remove dust, (n) not blocking heating (or cooling) outlets with furniture, drapes or other obstacles, (o) using energy efficient ceiling fans or small room fans to distribute and circulate heated air and to make lower temperature settings more comfortable, and (p) venting hot moist air from an electric (not a natural gas) clothes dryer into the house to lighten the heating load.

12. For new and existing homes, reduce cooling requirements during hot weather by (a) planting leaf-shedding (deciduous) trees on the sunny side of the house, (b) adding awnings to windows receiving sunlight, (c) using an automatic clock thermostat to raise the minimum temperature for an air conditioned house to 26°C (78°F) during the day and a few degrees higher at night, (d) using a dehumidifier to provide comfort at higher temperatures, (e) wearing lighter clothing indoors, (f) closing insulated drapes, quilts, or shades on the sunny side of the house during the day and opening them at night, (g) using energy-efficient ceiling fans and small room fans to distribute and circulate air and to make higher temperatures more comfortable, (h) installing a whole-house ventilating fan (attic fan) to pull outside air in through open doors and windows and exhaust it through the attic to eliminate or greatly reduce the need for air conditioning, (i) not cooling unused rooms, (j) opening windows and doors and using natural breezes as much as possible, (k) using light-colored roofing and outside paint to reflect incoming solar radiation, (l) placing an outdoor air conditioning unit on the shady side of the house or if it is already installed on the sunny side use plants or an awning to shade it but be sure not to block the air flow from the back of the unit, (m) closing the bathroom door before bathing or

showering and using an exhaust fan or opening the bathroom window to remove the heat and moisture so the rest of the house won't become hot and muggy, (n) scheduling moisture and heat producing activities such as bathing, mopping, ironing, and washing and drying dishes and clothes for the coolest part of the day, (o) buying an air conditioning unit with a very high energy efficiency ratio (EER) between 8 and 10, selecting the smallest and least powerful unit for the room or house you need to cool, and cleaning grills and filters monthly, (p) turning off lights and machines as much as possible to reduce the heat load, (q) venting hot moist air from a clothes dryer outside to reduce the load of moisture and heat, and (r) closing off all heating ducts not used for air conditioning to prevent escape of cool air into the ducts.

13. Don't use fireplaces for heating unless (a) the house thermostat is lowered to 10°C (50°F), (b) doors and air ducts to the fireplace room are closed, (c) an outside window closest to the fireplace is cracked about 1 centimeter (½ inch), and (d) a glass screen is installed over the fireplace opening. Otherwise, the fireplace will warm the room it is in (by radiant heat) and cool the rest of the house by expelling warm air through the chimney so that overall the house loses more heat than the fireplace provides.

14. For existing houses that are heated with an oil furnace or electric space heating and that cannot be adapted for passive solar heating (such as attaching a solar greenhouse or sun room) seriously consider changing the heating system to a solar-assisted heat pump, a natural gas heat pump, a very efficient electric heat pump, an efficient well-designed wood stove, or a natural gas furnace (see Figure 13-8) and be sure to insulate all heating system ducts.

15. Always buy the most efficient house and appliances possible (even though the initial cost may sometimes be higher). To determine the true cost of a house or appliance use only its estimated lifetime cost (initial cost plus energy operating costs)—not the initial cost. For example, a refrigerator with heavy insulation, higher motor efficiency, and an efficient cooling system, more than one door (to reduce cool air losses from the entire unit each time the door is opened) and power-saving switches which turn off the electric heater strips in the door when humidity is low, and one that does *not* have a frost-free feature (requires 36 percent more energy) and a water and

ice dispenser in the door would normally use about 85 percent less energy than a conventional refrigerator.

16. Reduce hot water use and overall water use (and thus energy use) by (a) installing low-flow showerheads, (b) repairing all leaky hot water faucets, (c) doing only full loads in clothes washers and dishwashers* (or adjusting the water level in clothes washers for small loads if possible), (d) washing dishes and clothes in warm or even cold water, (e) taking 3- to 5-minute showers rather than baths, and (f) not letting hot water run while washing, shaving, or washing dishes. (For more water-saving suggestions see Section 15-6).

17. Along with reducing hot water use, switch from electric hot water heaters to either solar water heaters (preferable) or natural gas water heaters (with electric igniters instead of pilot lights). All should be well-insulated.† Require all new hot water heaters to meet much higher energy efficiency and insulation standards. To save additional energy (a) adjust the thermostat on the water heater to heat the water no higher than 60°C (140°F), (b) use the smallest size water heater possible to meet needs (typically about 38 liters or 10 gallons per person or a 1300 liter or 40 gallon tank for a family of four), (c) locate the water heater as close as possible to where it is needed to reduce heat loss, (d) use the smallest practical diameter hot water pipes to reduce heat loss, (e) remove sediment (which reduces efficiency) from the tank once or twice a year by using the drain faucet to remove several buckets of water, (f) turn down or turn off water heaters while away from home for extended periods, and (g) recover heat from hot water heaters and used hot water, and use it to help heat living areas.

18. Save additional energy by (a) not buying or using

---

*Actually, washing and rinsing dishes by hand three times a day usually uses more hot water and energy than washing them with a full load once a day in an automatic dishwasher (if the energy saving switch on most modern dishwashers is turned so the dishes are allowed to dry in the air rather than by using an electric heater). The best way to save hot water and energy, however, is to wash all dishes in a double sink or two pans (one for washing and one for rinsing) only once a day without running any water except to fill the sinks or pans.

†For existing electric water heaters, replace the typical jacket of 5 centimeters (2 inches) of fiberglass with 10 centimeters (4 inches) of urethane foam. For natural gas water heaters, replace the typical insulation of 2.5 centimeters (1 inch) of fiberglass with 5 centimeters (2 inches) of urethane foam but be sure not to close off the air vents. These insulation jacket thicknesses should become minimum standards on all new hot water heaters. All hot water pipes should be wrapped with 2.5 centimeters (1 inch) of fiberglass insulation.

gadget appliances (hot dog cookers, electric can openers, etc.) and instant-on TVs,* (b) substituting a crock pot or a microwave oven of a safe design for a conventional oven whenever possible, (c) thawing out frozen foods before cooking, (d) not placing hot foods in a refrigerator, (e) keeping a refrigerator or freezer level so the door seals properly, (f) keeping the refrigerator temperature between 2.8°C and 4.4°C (37°F and 40°F) for best operation and a freezer at −17.8°C (0°F), (g) using up perishable foods before going on an extended vacation, turning off the refrigerator or freezer, cleaning it, inserting an open box of baking soda, and propping the door open, (h) keeping the condenser coils of refrigerators and freezers clean and unobstructed, (l) choosing the smallest refrigerator or freezer that will meet your needs and keeping it full but not overfull, and (m) using a chest freezer rather than an upright model because an upright freezer allows more air to flow down out of the door when it is opened.

19. Make all energy-using appliances more efficient and progressively enact stricter energy-efficiency standards for energy-using appliances.

20. Reduce lighting levels and the number of lights, and improve lighting efficiency. Recommended lighting levels in buildings have risen 300 percent in the past 20 years with no evidence that the higher levels are necessary or desirable. Specific suggestions include (a) reducing lighting levels by 50 percent, (b) providing strong lighting only for small work areas such as over desks and tool benches (as with the reading lights in an airplane), (c) switching from incandescent to new screw-in fluorescent bulbs (which last 10 years and use 70 percent less electricity) indoors and to more energy-efficient sodium or mercury vapor lamps where outdoor lighting is needed, (d) using low-wattage (4 and 7 watts) night light bulbs to light hallways, bathrooms and other rooms when brighter lighting is not needed, (e) using dimmer switches to provide no more light than is needed, (f) using a photo-electric cell to turn outdoor security lights off automatically at dawn and back on at dusk, (g) buying bulbs that provide the most lumens per watt†, (h) turning lights off when they are not needed (it is not true that there is a surge of power when a bulb is turned on so turning off a light for even one second saves one second's worth of electricity), and (i) using natural daylight whenever possible.

21. Prohibit the use of natural gas as a fuel to generate electricity in power plants and also in industrial plants (unless the plant uses the waste heat to generate some or all of its own electricity by cogeneration), and ban decorative outdoor natural gas lights. Gas pilot lights for natural gas stoves, furnaces, clothes dryers, water heaters, and other appliances should also be banned (as is done in California) and replaced with electric igniters (can save up to 50 percent of the natural gas used).

22. Develop district heating systems that use available local conditions (such as sun, wind, geothermal energy, small hydroelectric dams, farm and forestry wastes, and industrial waste heat). A combination of these locally available renewable energy resources and improved energy efficiency could completely eliminate the need for local dependence on any new or old large, centralized power plants.

Energy Savings in Industry Industry uses more energy—37 percent—than any other sector of the American economy. About 99 percent of that energy goes for three purposes: (1) producing process steam (45 percent); (2) providing heat for manufacturing processes and buildings (29 percent); and (3) running motors, lights, and electrolytic processes (bringing about chemical changes by passing electricity through solutions of chemicals) (25 percent). Most of the steam used is produced in the plants themselves, whereas most electricity is purchased from utilities. Over 52 percent of the energy consumed by industry is in three sectors: primary metals (especially iron, steel, and aluminum), chemicals (including synthetic fibers and plastics), and petroleum refining. The U.S. military system (including defense contractors) alone uses 6 percent of all energy used each year in the United States.

Although U.S. industry uses (and thus wastes) more energy than other sectors, it has also made the greatest efforts to cut waste since 1973. Even more energy can be saved by using the following methods:

---

*If you have any instant-on appliances, turn them on and off at the plug or deactivate this feature with the switch often found on the back of the appliance.

†The amount of light from a bulb is measured in lumens, not watts. Wattage is a measure of the amount of energy needed to light the bulb. Larger bulbs generally produce more lumens per watt than smaller bulbs. Thus, buy a single bulb with enough wattage to provide the lumens you need rather than having to use several lower wattage bulbs (it usually takes six 25-watt bulbs to give the same amount of light as one 100-watt bulb). "Long-life" incandescent bulbs give less lumens than a standard one of the same wattage.

1. Save 10 percent by (a) putting automatic shutoff timers on all electrical devices, (b) insulating factories and buildings, (c) maintaining boilers, (d) turning off lights, (e) reducing or eliminating unnecessary lighting, heating, and cooling, (f) cleaning heating and cooling equipment more frequently, and (g) doubling motor efficiency by proper sizing, coupling, and controls (this last saving alone would save enough electricity each year to more than eliminate the need for all the present and proposed nuclear power plants in the United States).

2. Save 20 to 30 percent within existing industrial processes by collecting and reusing waste heat, using computerized monitors and controls, and using industrial waste heat to cogenerate electricity for use at the plant instead of buying it from utilities. Cogeneration in the United States could supply as much electricity as 208 large nuclear power plants—about 4 times as many as were operating in 1980. In almost all cases cogeneration is cheaper than building new electric power plants. Since cogeneration uses about half as much fossil fuel as a conventional coal-burning power plant, its use can reduce air pollution, strip mining of coal, and thermal water pollution. In West Germany cogeneration provided nearly one-third of the electricity used by industry and about 12 percent of the nation's electricity in 1978.

3. Develop and convert to more efficient equipment and processes. Here the savings will vary from industry to industry. Steel, for example, has the biggest energy appetite of any U.S. industry. Half of all American steel is still being made in open-hearth furnaces using 4 times as much energy as the basic oxygen process.

4. Greatly increase matter recycling (Section 12-1; Enrichment Study 15). For example, steel made from scrap in an electric furnace uses only about one-fourth the energy of steel made from virgin ore. Recycling aluminum cans uses 95 percent less energy than producing new aluminum, but banning aluminum cans altogether and using returnable bottles saves much more energy (Section E15-4). Provide economic incentives and favorable transportation rates for secondary (recycled) materials industries and users, require that where possible materials bought by government agencies use a specified percentage of recycled material (depending on the item), impose a tax on all energy-intensive products, and require that an energy price index or lifetime energy cost be listed on all products. Virgin materials may have to be taxed to slow down their use and favor recycled materials.

5. Greatly increase the useful life of all products (to reduce the use of matter and energy resources) and add a disposal or resource recovery tax to all products that last less than a specified number of years.

6. Give smaller users of electricity, rather than larger users, the lowest rates.

7. Increase electrical rates during peak load times to shift some of the electrical load and to reduce waste. The size and number of electrical power plants are usually determined by peak loads, not by average daily or annual use.

8. Encourage industrial energy conservation by buying only the most energy-efficient products and appliances, buying goods made of recycled materials, avoiding products packaged in throwaway containers or excessive packaging, and buying products that are designed to last.

The energy-saving steps discussed in this section are crucial for making the transition to a new sustainable earth era. Despite much talk and preaching about the need for reducing energy waste, proposed government expenditures for improving energy efficiency in 1981 amounted to only 6 percent of the total federal energy budget (Table 13-8) and the Reagan administration proposed a cut in funding for energy conservation research and development in 1982.

14-2 Fossil Fuels

Formation and Recovery of Fossil Fuels We are nearing the end of the so-called fossil fuel era, in which natural gas, petroleum, and coal are the major sources of energy for industrial societies. The original source of the chemical energy stored in fossil fuels is the sun. Over eons, green plants have used photosynthesis (Section 5-4) to change solar energy to chemical energy stored in glucose and other chemicals. As plants and animals died and decayed, they were converted over millions of years to rich deposits of natural gas, petroleum, and coal.

Natural gas consists of 50 to 90 percent methane (a hydrocarbon compound made of hydrogen and carbon, CH_4) and small amounts of more complex hydrocarbon compounds such as propane (C_3H_8) and butane (C_4H_{10}). It is a clean-burning fuel, producing only water and carbon dioxide. **Petroleum,** or **crude oil,** is a dark, greenish-brown, foul-smelling liquid containing a complex mixture of hydrocarbon compounds plus small amounts of oxygen, sulfur, and nitrogen compounds. Low-sulfur petroleum is the most valuable, because one of the most dangerous air pollutants, sulfur dioxide, forms when sulfur impurities in petroleum combine with oxygen as oil burns (see Section 17-2).

Typically, deposits of natural gas and petroleum accumulate together under a dome-shaped layer of rock several thousand meters under the earth's surface. If a hole is drilled through the rock layer, the pressure under the dome forces the gas and oil to the surface. Once this pressure is gone, oil must be pumped to the surface and eventually extracted by pumping water or gas in to repressurize the reservoir (secondary recovery). At today's prices, drillers usually recover about 32 percent of the oil. But as oil prices rise, they may go after the remaining oil by tertiary recovery. One common tertiary recovery method is to pump steam or hot air into the well to make the oil flow more freely and help push it to the surface. Today fossil fuel energy is used to produce the steam. This makes tertiary recovery a poor net useful energy investment (Section 13-3) unless the steam can be produced by using solar energy. Other less used and usually more expensive tertiary recovery processes are (a) "in-situ" combustion—burning the remaining oil underground and collecting the resulting gases for use as a fuel, (b) using chemicals called surfactants (surface-acting agents) to dissolve the oil and make it easier to pump out, and (c) pumping gases such as carbon dioxide into the reservoir to reduce the surface tension that makes the oil cling stubbornly to rock.

When a natural gas deposit is tapped, the propane and butane are liquefied and taken off as LPG (liquefied petroleum gas) before the remaining gas (mostly methane) is pumped into pipelines for distribution. The liquid propane and butane are stored in pressurized containers for use in areas (often rural) not served by natural gas pipelines. Of all the fossil fuels, natural gas is the easiest to process and transport in pipelines, and it burns the hottest with the least pollution—which explains why it is so widely used. Natural gas serves over 55 percent of all American homes and provides about 40 percent of the energy for industry.

In many countries with oil and natural gas deposits, the natural gas released when an oil well is tapped is simply burned off (flared) because there is no local market. Only 1 percent of the gas extracted in the United States is flared, but elsewhere the figure is over 20 per-

cent. One way to reduce this waste is to liquefy the gas at $-161°C$, transport it to markets, and regasify the liquid at receiving terminals. Unfortunately, there are three problems with this approach: (1) it is expensive; (2) about 25 percent of the gas's original energy content is lost in the process; and (3) an LNG (liquefied natural gas) explosion or accident in a port could create a massive and deadly fireball.

Once out of the ground, crude oil goes to a refinery. There its various components, such as gasoline, kerosene, heating oil, diesel fuel, lubricating oils, and greases, are separated from one another by means of their different boiling points (temperatures at which liquids change to gases). All of the separated components are used commercially, but the greatest demand is for *gasoline*, which makes up 25 to 45 percent of refined petroleum. The gasoline that originally boils off is not good enough for today's high-compression car engines, so refineries upgrade it and also convert other petroleum components into high-quality gasoline. Of course, some of the useful chemical energy in the petroleum is lost in this processing. However, in 1980 Ashland Oil developed a new refining process that gets about 25 percent more gasoline from a barrel of oil.

Petroleum and natural gas are valuable not only as sources of high-quality energy but also as raw materials in manufacturing most of the industrial chemicals, fertilizers, pesticides, plastics, synthetic fibers, medicines and other products used in modern society (Figure 14-1). About 7 percent (Figure 13-10) of all fossil fuels used in the United States each year and 3 percent of all used in the world go to produce these petrochemicals. From Figure 14-1 we can see why most prices go up when oil and natural gas prices go up. Some of these chemicals can be produced from coal and from the fermentation of biomass, but such a major transformation of the entire chemical industry in an industrialized nation would take decades and be complex and expensive. Recently the large energy companies have begun to take over a larger share of the petrochemicals industry—giving these companies even greater power to control most of the products used by other businesses and individual consumers.

The use of some synthetic materials can save energy. For example, substituting plastics for metals in automobiles reduces weight and increases gas mileage. A cotton shirt requires up to 90 percent more energy over its life cycle than a shirt made from a blend of polyester and cotton. A polyester-cotton shirt requires 25 percent more energy to make, but because of the more frequent

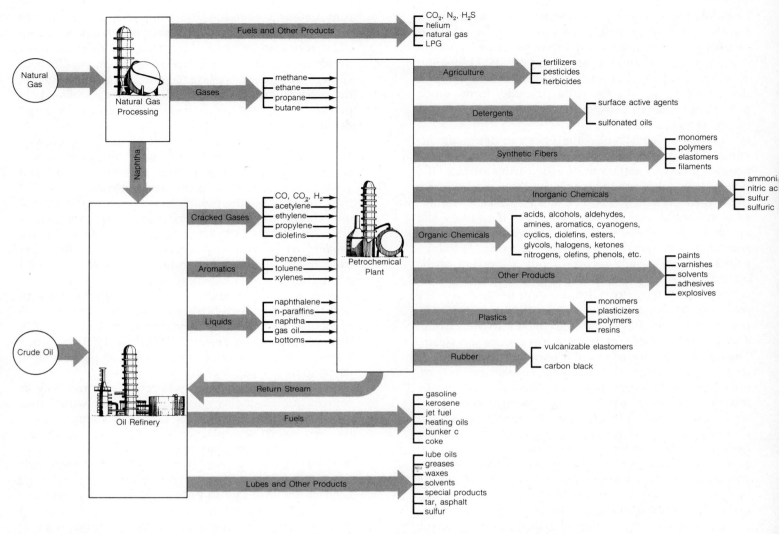

Figure 14-1 The petrochemical industries. Crude oil and natural gas are used as raw materials to produce most of the products in modern society.

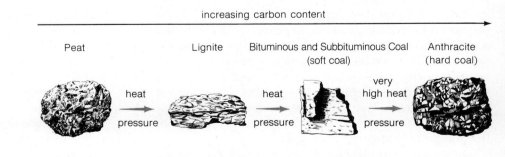

increasing carbon content

| Peat | Lignite | Bituminous and Subbituminous Coal (soft coal) | Anthracite (hard coal) |

heat → pressure → heat → pressure → very high heat → pressure

partially decayed plant and animal matter in swamps and bogs; not a true coal

limited use as a fuel because of low energy content and limited supplies

extensively used as a fuel because of its high heat content and large supplies; normally has a high sulfur content

highly desirable fuel because of its high heat content and low sulfur content; supplies are limited in most areas

Figure 14-2 Stages in coal formation over many millions of years.

washing and ironing needed, a cotton shirt uses more energy over the life of the shirt. Synthetic materials also play an important role in energy conservation. Fiberglass insulation is held together with a plastic epoxy resin and the foam insulation blown into house walls and ceilings is made from plastic. Delicate photovoltaic solar cells will probably be wrapped in plastic for protection.

Thus, natural gas and petroleum can be considered almost too valuable to burn up as a fuel. Thus, the world's oil and natural gas extracting nations should have enough wisdom to set aside at least a third of the world's known petroleum and natural gas reserves as raw materials for producing petrochemicals in the future. However, Barry Commoner has argued that we should use fewer harmful petrochemical products and more natural products (Table 1-4).

Coal, the other major fossil fuel, is a solid containing from 55 to 90 percent carbon and small amounts of hydrogen, oxygen, nitrogen, and sulfur compounds. As with petroleum, the low-sulfur type is more desirable because it produces less sulfur dioxide when burned. Coal is formed over millions of years in several stages, each representing an increase in carbon content and fuel quality (Figure 14-2). Depending on its location, coal is mined from deep underground deposits or by strip mining (Section 10-5) shallow deposits near the earth's surface.

About 70 percent of the coal mined each year in the world is burned to provide heat, to supply steam for industry and transportation, and to produce electricity at power plants. Most of the remaining 30 percent is converted to coke, liquid coal tar, or a mixture of gases known as coal gas. Coke is often used to make iron and steel. Coal tar, is used in making dyes, plastics, explosives, some drugs and medicines, and many other products.

Estimates of Petroleum and Natural Gas How much longer can nonrenewable fossil fuels last if the world's appetite for energy continues to grow (Figure 13-4)? As with nonrenewable mineral resources (Chapter 12), estimates of recoverable amounts of fossil fuels depend on how well geologists can determine identified and undiscovered supplies (see Figure 12-4) and on the rate of use. However, there is an important difference. The supplies of some nonfuel minerals can be extended by recycling and reuse (Section 12-2, Figure 12-5), but the useful energy from fossil fuels (or any energy source) cannot. Once burned, they are gone forever.

Geophysicist M. King Hubbert has projected depletion curves for world and U.S. supplies of petroleum

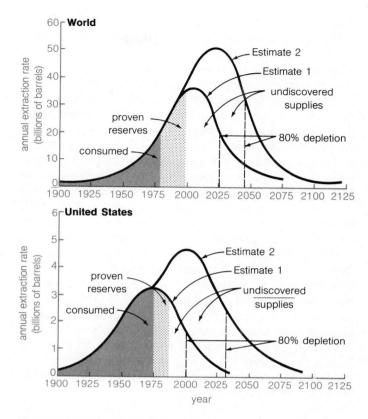

Figure 14-3 Estimated depletion curves for world and U.S. supplies of petroleum. Estimate 1 is based on what most experts believe to be the ultimately recoverable supplies assuming usage increases at 5 percent annually. Estimate 2 assumes either twice the petroleum supply of that in estimate 1 or that the annual rate is cut in half to 2.5 percent.

(Figure 14-3). Some observers are more optimistic, but recent estimates generally agree with Hubbert's.

If current trends in exploration and usage continue, world supplies of oil could fall short of demand somewhere between 1985 and 2000 and become 80 percent depleted between 2015 to 2030 (Figure 14-3). Oil production in the Soviet Union, the world's largest producer of oil, is expected to peak before 1985 so that it may have to start importing oil to meet demands. And the rich North-sea fields may begin to decline by 1984 and the vast deposits in Saudi Arabia may be gone within a few decades. Figure 14-3 also shows that petroleum production in the United States peaked around 1970 (just as Hubbert predicted many years ago), with 80 percent depletion predicted for 1990 to 2105. Estimate 2 in Figure 14-3 assumes either that we will find twice as much oil as the experts expect or that conservation and high prices will cut usage rates in half (from 5 percent to 2.5

percent). Even if estimate 2 proves to be correct, 80 percent depletion would be postponed only a few decades.

Even though the United States imports about 43 percent of the oil it uses, it is still the world's third largest extractor of petroleum after the Soviet Union and Saudi Arabia. Usage rates are so high, however, that domestic reserves of oil are being depleted much faster than new supplies are being found. This is happening despite the fact that in 1980 U.S. oil companies spent $20 billion sinking a record 60,000 domestic oil and gas wells. Most experts believe that at best the depletion of U.S. proven oil reserves can only be slowed somewhat—not halted. According to Gulf Oil executive, Robert N. Baldwin, "There is no way, over the long run, that you can reverse the present decline of crude oil reserves in the United States." For example, the Prudhoe Bay oil deposit in Alaska, the largest find in U.S. history, could be exhausted in about 10 years at present rates of depletion. One study concluded that if U.S. oil firms continue to search for oil at the 1980 rate or higher with the same relatively low rate of success, then somewhere between 1985 and 1995 more energy will be used to find and extract the oil than the energy in that oil.

Supplies of natural gas are harder to predict, but at best they are expected to last only several decades longer than those of petroleum. Thus, world supplies of natural gas could be 80 percent depleted somewhere between 2025 and 2060 (in the United States between 2015 to 2040). Today, the natural gas that flows from about 165,000 wells throughout the United States supplies about 24 percent of the nation's annual energy needs. As with oil, the rate of depletion of proven domestic natural gas reserves has exceeded the rate at which new reserves have been found. Since 1978, when gradual decontrol of natural gas prices began, increased exploration has uncovered large new gas fields in the Gulf Coast of Louisiana and the Rocky Mountain region. Their potential, however, is unknown and the rate at which natural gas is used is so high that doubling the known domestic reserves only adds a few years to the supply.

As prices rise, companies may begin trying to tap unconventional sources of natural gas that so far have been considered uneconomic to extract. One promising unconventional source is found in concrete-hard geologic formations called *tight sands*. To tap these deposits, drillers must fracture the rock by injecting high pressure fluids so the natural gas can be released. Another potential unconventional source may be *geopressured zones* buried deep in the rocks off the coast of Louisiana and Texas. These zones are deposits of hot water under such high pressure that large quantities of natural gas are dissolved in the water. After drilling strikes one of these zones the water would be brought to the surface, and both the heat it contains and the natural gas dissolved in it would be extracted. Unfortunately, the idea that larger domestic supplies of natural gas can be obtained from tight sands and geopressurized zones may be a dream because they may take more money and energy to drill and extract than the resulting gas is worth.

Even the estimates in Figure 14-3 may be too optimistic because they are based on total energy resource supplies, not net useful energy supplies (Section 13-3). For example, between 1870 and 1970 the average depth of an oil well in the United States increased 20-fold. Most of the undiscovered and potential natural gas reserves in the United States are believed to lie deeper than 6,100 meters (20,000 feet), and most of the remaining oil reserves are either in remote and hostile areas (such as Alaska) or in deep offshore deposits. To remove and transport the oil in these deeper and more remote oil fields requires a larger energy input than that required by Middle Eastern and other, more accessible oil deposits.

The world still has lots of natural gas and oil. As a result countries may in some years extract more oil and natural gas than the world can consume. Such short-term gluts, however, should in no way be interpreted as indications that the long-term energy crisis is a hoax. Indeed, if oil-extracting nations raise the price of oil so high that nations can't afford to buy it, it makes little difference how much oil is still left in the ground.

The message of Figure 14-3, even estimate 2, is very clear. Don't waste oil and natural gas; use them only for essential purposes; look for more oil and natural gas to buy a little time; and start an urgent program to improve energy efficiency and to shift to other renewable energy alternatives over the next few decades.

Oil Shale Some have raised the possibility of getting oil from shale. Actually, **oil shale** is not shale rock and contains no oil. Instead, it is an underground formation of marlstone sedimentary rock containing varying amounts of a rubbery, solid mixture of hydrocarbons known as **kerogen.** The conventional way to extract the kerogen is to strip mine or deep mine the oil shale rock (much like coal). The rock is then sent to a nearby processing plant, where it is crushed and then heated to about 462°C (900°F) in a large vessel called a *retort.* This process vaporizes the solid kerogen; the vapor is then condensed to yield an extremely viscous (slow-flowing) dark brown fluid called **shale oil.** Part of the decomposed kerogen stays a gas and can be burned to furnish power at the processing plant or upgraded to pipeline-quality synthetic natural gas. After its flow rate is increased, the shale oil is upgraded and then sent through a pipeline to a refinery, where it can be converted to some petroleum products (see Figure 14-1)—although at present it is not known how to convert shale oil into gasoline. Shale oil is fairly low in sulfur, but it is high in nitrogen (about 10 times the amount in petroleum) and paraffinic waxes. Since nitrogen compounds make car engines knock and the waxes foul engines, these substances must be removed before refining—adding to its cost and cutting the net useful energy yield. As a result shale oil is better used as a source of jet fuel, diesel fuel, and other heavier petroleum distillates than as gasoline.

The world's largest known deposits of oil shale lie in the United States, with significant amounts also in Canada, China, and the U.S.S.R. At least 80 percent of the rich oil shale deposits in the United States are on federally owned land in Colorado, Utah, and Wyoming, which also contain other energy resources. At present, several oil companies have leased small amounts of these federal lands to build pilot plants to explore the economic and environmental feasibility for producing shale oil. The total amount of shale oil locked in this deposit may equal the world's proven and estimated petroleum deposits. Even the 0.004 to 0.03 percent of it that seems economically feasible to extract and upgrade could equal the world's proven reserves of crude oil and could supply all U.S. oil needs at 1980 levels for 90 years.

Before painting a rosy future rich in shale oil, however, let us face the problems involved. The main one is economic. The economically feasible price per barrel for shale oil rises each time the price of conventional oil rises because of inflation; environmental controls; and, more important, because it takes almost the energy equivalent of one barrel of conventional oil to produce one barrel of shale oil. Thus, shale oil may always be 1.5 to 2 times more costly than conventional oil unless its price is heavily subsidized by the government (or more accurately taxpayers). Moreover, the 40 large-scale shale oil plants needed to produce just 10 percent of U.S. needs by the year 2000 would cost at least $40 billion.

In addition, shale oil has a low net useful energy yield. Taking into account the entire mining, processing, and transport system for shale oil, the net useful energy yield has been estimated to be only about one-eighth that for crude oil.

Producing shale oil also creates serious environmental problems. The basic problems are (1) land disruption from surface mining (Section 10-5) and disposal of the waste or spent shale rock, (2) air and water pollution from the mining and retorting operations, and (3) the possible impact of shale oil boom towns on fragile semiarid ecosystems.

The 40 proposed shale oil processing plants would produce waste rock per year equal to almost 8 times the total solid waste produced by all homes and businesses in the United States during 1980 (Enrichment Study 15). Because the rock breaks up and expands when heated (somewhat like popcorn), the waste takes about 12 percent more space than the original—so it can't be stuffed back into the ground. If dumped into canyons and ravines, the rock could scar the land, upset drainage patterns, and threaten surface and groundwater supplies as sediment, soluble salts, and toxic metal compounds (Enrichment Study 5) leach or erode out of it.

Air pollution from emissions of sulfur oxides, nitrogen oxides, hydrocarbons, and particulates would also be a serious problem without a large investment in air pollution control equipment. In addition, cooking (retorting) oil shale may release from 1.5 to 5 times more carbon dioxide into the atmosphere than burning conventional oil to get the same amount of energy. This additional carbon dioxide in the atmosphere could affect world climate and food-growing patterns, as discussed in Enrichment Study 3.

Even if all the other problems could somehow be solved, the production of shale oil may be limited by a lack of water. Water is needed for cooling and washing out impurities. The 40 projected oil shale processing plants would use as much water each year as all the households in New York City. Already short of water, the oil shale region has competing plans to irrigate crops, supply cities, strip mine coal, and develop geothermal energy deposits (Section 13-5). In addition, water used to process oil shale could return to the Colorado River basin so full of dissolved minerals that downstream users in the rich agricultural valleys of Arizona, California, and Mexico could not use the water for irrigation.

One possible solution to many of these problems is to retort the kerogen out of the rock in place (in situ)—underground. After conventional explosives loosen the rock, natural gas can be pumped in and ignited in a controlled manner at the top of the formation. As steam and air force the flames downward, the kerogen would flow out through pipes at the bottom. A by-product gas, recovered separately, could power electric generators and sustain the flame front. Other exhaust gases could be passed through a scrubber to remove air pollutants. Since this approach is in the pilot-plant stage, it is far too early to determine its financial, net useful energy, and environmental feasibility, but so far the yield of shale oil produced by this method is not as high as expected.

Scientists have also suggested detonating small atomic bombs underground to break up the shale rock and retort the kerogen, but this approach could contaminate both groundwater and kerogen with radioactivity and trigger small earthquakes. Just to supply 18 percent of projected U.S. oil by 1985 would require about six underground nuclear blasts a day.

A 1980 study by the Office of Technology Assessment (OTA) indicated that because of water, environmental, social, and economic impacts, the largest feasible output of a shale oil industry in Utah, Wyoming, and Colorado (see Figure 13-13) by 1990 could provide only about 1 percent of the projected oil needs of the United States in 1990. To develop this risky financial venture would require a large government subsidy ($3 to $7 per barrel) and a capital investment of $35 to $45 billion. Despite the many serious environmental problems, a low net useful energy yield, and economic drawbacks, in 1980 the U.S. Congress passed an $83 billion subsidy and loan program to help private industry (mostly oil companies) develop a shale oil and synfuel industry between 1980 and 1992. President Ronald Reagan and a more conservative Congress, however, may sharply reduce this program so these energy alternatives can compete more openly in the marketplace.

Tar Sands Tar sands (or oil sands) are enormous swamps of fine clay and sand mixed with water and variable amounts of a black, gooey, high-sulfur, tarlike oil known as **heavy oil** (or bitumen). Shallow deposits can be dug up by strip mining and then superheated with steam at high pressures to make the thick tar flow and float to the top. Just to heat enough steam to liquefy and force 3 barrels of heavy oil up can take the energy equivalent of one barrel of petroleum. The extracted heavy oil (which can contain large amounts of sulfur) has a low energy content, and must be upgraded to synthetic crude oil and purified by removing the sulfur impurities. About 25 percent of the available energy is wasted in this process. Deeper underground deposits must be processed in place (in situ) by a process yet to be developed.

Canada has the world's largest known deposits, located in a cold, desolate area of north central Alberta. The fraction of deposits that could be recovered economically almost equal the Middle East's remaining known oil reserves. Only about 10 percent of the extractable Canadian deposits can be processed by strip mining. The remaining 90 percent is too deeply buried and must somehow be processed in place.

Venezuela's tar sands may be almost as rich as Canada's. The U.S.S.R. also probably has a large deposit, with smaller deposits in Albania, Rumania, Colombia, and Utah. Estimates of total worldwide deposits vary from 1 to 4 times the world's known oil reserves, with 98 percent of the world's tar sands reserves in North America.

But large-scale production of synthetic crude oil from tar sands is costly and beset with problems. Tar sands are more difficult to handle than any other substance ever mined on a large scale. They are so abrasive that they wear out the teeth of gigantic bucket scrapers every 4 to 8 hours. In addition, they stick to everything, clog up extraction equipment and vehicles, and slowly dissolve natural rubber in tires, conveyor belts, and machinery parts.

Since large amounts of steam and electricity must be used to mine and process tar sands, the estimated net useful energy yield will probably be low. There are also potentially serious environmental problems. Strip mining tar sands produces more waste per unit of heavy oil than is produced in mining oil shale. In addition, the steam extraction and processing of the heavy oil requires large quantities of water. Thus, as with oil shale, large-scale production may be limited by water supplies (Section 13-5). Researchers, however, are trying to find ways for reusing the processing water. Now, though, much of the water ends up as an oily mess in ever growing ponds, which mar the landscape and could contaminate nearby rivers. Underground water supplies could also be polluted if an in situ process is eventually developed. Also, the refining process spews sulfur dioxide, hydrogen sulfide, hydrocarbons, and nitrogen oxides into the air unless they are removed, at considerable expense, from stack emissions.

Canada hopes to eventually get about 6 percent of its annual oil needs by extracting and processing heavy oil from its vast deposits. Even if the Canadian tar sands should succeed, little or none of the synthetic crude oil produced in Canada will reach the United States. The experience gained, however, will be useful in determining the feasibility of developing large tar sand deposits in Venezuela and the U.S.S.R. and perhaps the smaller (but still substantial) deposits in Utah, California, New Mexico, and Louisiana.

Coal: A Possible Transition Fuel Based on known reserves, coal is the most abundant fossil fuel in the world

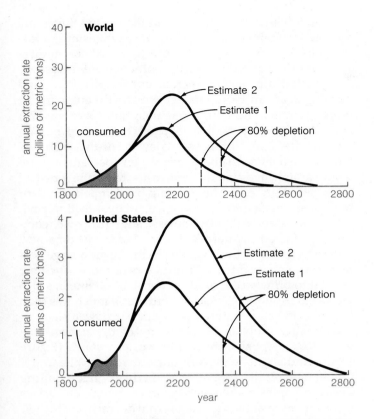

Figure 14-4 Estimated depletion curves for world and U.S. supplies of coal assuming the use of coal increases by 3.6 percent annually. Estimate 2 assumes that the ultimately recoverable supplies of coal are roughly twice as large as those assumed in estimate 1.

and in the United States, as shown in Figure 14-4. At present rates of consumption and according to conservative estimates, the world's coal reserves would last for at least 200 years. Furthermore, geologists think the world reserves can be increased severalfold by further exploration, but much of this additional coal may be buried so deep that it may be uneconomical to extract. Today's coal reserves, however, would only last about 81 years if world demand for coal increased by 5 percent each year.

According to a major 1980 study, coal could provide from one-half to two-thirds of all the new energy that the world may need between 1980 and 2000. Coal is seen as the only viable energy source to help the world make the transition from oil and natural gas to renewable energy sources (sun, wind, water, and biomass) between 1980 and 2030, because according to this study renewable energy sources will require at least 50 years to make a major impact and because nuclear energy (Section 14-3)

appears to be increasingly unacceptable both politically and economically. Energy expert Amory B. Lovins, however, disputes some of the assumptions of this study. Specifically, he believes that (1) the projected future energy demands in this study are too high, (2) that the potential savings from improved energy efficiency and increased use of renewable energy sources are greatly underestimated, and (3) that the only major use for coal is to make electricity, which is already being made in larger quantities than needed in many nations.

Known world coal reserves are very unevenly distributed. The U.S.S.R. has an estimated 56 percent of the world's coal resources—a higher percentage of the world's coal than the Middle East has of the world's oil. The United States has about 19 percent of the world's estimated coal resources (31 percent of the known reserves), and China has about 8 percent.

In 1980, coal provided about 20 percent of the primary energy used in the United States (Figure 13-3), with 77 percent of this being burned at power plants to produce electricity. Known U.S. coal resources are geographically widespread (Figure 10-10) and could support American coal needs at present levels for about 300 years. If coal became America's sole source of fossil fuel energy, however, proven reserves would last only about 47 years, and proven plus estimated reserves would last only about 80 years, assuming a 5 percent rise in the demand for coal each year. Unfortunately, about 90 percent of the recoverable coal reserves in the United States are bituminous (52 percent) and subbituminous (38 percent) with a high sulfur content (Figure 14-2). The more desirable anthracite coal, with a low sulfur content, makes up only 8 percent of U.S. recoverable reserves. Coal is not only more plentiful, but at present cheaper than oil, natural gas, and nuclear energy. Coal prices, however, will undoubtedly rise as environmental controls become more strict. Coal is expected to remain cheaper than oil, natural gas, and nuclear energy for the remainder of this century and well into the next.

Coal also has a high net useful energy yield that is decreasing at a slower rate than the yields of oil and natural gas. The net useful energy yield for coal is much higher than the low to moderate net useful energy yield for conventional nuclear fission energy (Table 13-5).

With these important advantages, why isn't coal used to supply a much larger percentage of the energy used in the world and the United States? The key reasons are that, compared with oil and natural gas, coal is dirty to mine and burn and awkward to distribute and use. Another problem is that coal cannot be burned in cars. Thus, it is used primarily to produce electric power. In

1980, coal was used to produce more than half of the electricity in the United States. U.S. coal extraction could be tripled between 1975 and 2000 to produce 35 percent of the nation's energy.

Before the United States (and other coal-producing nations) can make greater use of coal (assuming it is necessary—which may not be the case), however, they must solve many formidable environmental, logistic, water supply, and social problems. Coal is the most polluting fossil fuel, emitting dangerous toxic metal compounds (Enrichment Study 5), cancer-causing organic compounds, radioactive substances, sulfur dioxide, and particulates when it burns (Section 17-4). These air pollutants, especially particulates and sulfur oxides, have been shown to contribute to illness and premature death from respiratory ailments such as asthma, bronchitis, emphysema, and lung cancer (Section 17-3). The sulfur dioxide in coal smoke can attack plants directly and also create an acid rain that can leach nutrients from the soil, stunt trees and food crops, and kill fish in lakes and ponds (Section 17-3). If uncontrolled, the sulfur dioxide emissions from one typical coal-fired plant can cause an estimated 25 deaths, 60,000 cases of respiratory disease, and $12 million in property damage each year. However, sulfur dioxide and most pollutants from coal burning can be controlled with existing technology at a cost that still makes coal the cheapest major energy source for producing electricity.

One potentially dangerous pollutant that cannot be controlled with present technology is carbon dioxide (CO_2). Per unit of energy produced, coal releases about 25 percent more carbon dioxide into the atmosphere than oil, and 75 percent more than natural gas. There is growing concern that increasing carbon dioxide concentrations in the atmosphere could change global climate (Enrichment Study 3). This threat, rather than the supply, may be the fact that limits the use of coal—and all fossil fuels—in the long run. Coal-burning plants also produce large amounts of fly ash and solid waste which must be disposed of safely (Enrichment Study 15).

Underground mines can cause surface lands to cave in, and their drainage has seriously polluted about 18,000 kilometers (11,000 miles) of American streams. The strip mining of coal can disrupt land, water supplies, wildlife, and humans (Section 10-5). In addition, since 1900 more than 100,000 miners have been killed and more than a million permanently disabled in mine accidents. About 75 percent of all retired miners suffer from black lung disease and spend their last few years gasping for breath. More strict laws have improved mine safety since 1969, but coal mining is still the nation's most dan-

gerous industrial occupation, and the United States still has the worst mine safety record among Western industrial nations. In 1979 alone more than 100 coal miners lost their lives and thousands of others were injured.

The harmful environmental impact of mining and burning coal can be minimized by strictly enforcing or even strengthening current air pollution (Sections 17-4 and 17-5), water pollution (Section 16-6), strip mining (Section 10-5), and mine safety laws. But this plan will reduce the net useful energy yield a few percent, require large capital investments, and thus raise the price of coal—although coal should still be competitive with other fossil fuels for producing electricity. Meeting environmental standards also slows things down. A company may need 100 permits before it can start on a new mine. As a result, the time needed to open a large coal mine has increased from 5 to 10 years or more. The time needed to bring a coal-fired power plant on line has also increased to about 5 to 6 years, but is still much less than the 10 to 15 years required for a nuclear power plant.

Another problem is that many of the richest low-sulfur coal deposits are in the western states (Figure 13-13), and about 16 percent of these reserves lie under Indian land. Indian tribes have filed lawsuits requiring coal companies to renegotiate low-paying coal leases signed many years ago and to prevent degradation of their land, air, and water resources. Even if water shortages don't limit coal mining (Section 13-5), shipping most of the coal to the East where it is needed will raise its price and decrease its net useful energy yield. Contrary to popular belief, Western coal also has no air pollution advantage. It has a lower sulfur content by weight, but most of it also has a lower heat value per unit of weight than eastern coal. As a result, most western coal will actually produce more sulfur dioxide pollution per unit of *heat* (which is the measure that really counts) than much eastern coal.

Other factors that could slow the increased use of coal include (1) a much lower demand for electricity because of improvements in energy efficiency (many new projected coal burning power plants have already been cancelled or postponed), (2) the threat of strikes, and (3) shortages of capital, miners, geologists, mining engineers, housing near mining areas, and railroad coal cars. For example, the U.S. Bureau of Mines says that to increase U.S. coal mining by 50 percent between 1978 and 1985, the coal industry will have to open 254 new large mines (an average of 41 per year), recruit and train 157,000 new miners for the nation's most hazardous occupation, and raise $15.7 billion in capital (more than twice the capital raised between 1965 and 1974). Between 1980 and 2000, almost $1 trillion will have to be raised to make coal a major fuel. Worldwide, shipbuilders will have to raise about $1 trillion to build 50 new coal-carrying ships a year at a cost of $25 to $45 million each.

Burning Coal More Cleanly and Efficiently Two potential ways to burn coal more efficiently, use less water, and reduce harmful sulfur dioxide emissions without expensive scrubbers are *fluidized-bed combustion* and *magnetohydrodynamic generation*.

In **fluidized-bed combustion,** a stream of hot air flows up through the boiler and suspends a mixture of sand and powdered coal and limestone. The heat transfer thus provided lets the coal burn more efficiently. In addition, the limestone removes 90 to 98 percent of the sulfur in the coal, and the process reduces nitrogen oxides emissions, possibly making costly stack gas scrubbers unnecessary. However, the resulting solid calcium sulfate and sludge must be disposed of safely, and emissions of particulates and nitrogen oxides will also have to be controlled.

Fluidized-bed combustion should also be cheaper than conventional coal-burning boilers and could easily be used in both large-scale and smaller district power plants. Successful pilot plants have been built, and commercial-scale boilers were available by 1981.

In a **magnetohydrodynamic,** or MHD, **generator,** crushed coal (or any fossil fuel) is mixed with a chemical (such as potassium carbonate); it then flows into a combustion chamber and burns at a very high temperature. The chemicals in the rapidly expanding hot gas produced during combustion are then converted to ions (charged chemical species). This hot stream of ionized gases (or plasma) is then forced at the speed of a bullet down a pipe and through a magnetic field, producing electricity. This is a much more efficient method for producing electricity than the conventional coal or nuclear power plant. The process also removes at least 95 percent of the sulfur impurities in coal. Total particulate emissions are less than those from conventional coal-fired plants, but contain more fine particles that are more harmful to the human respiratory system (see Sections 17-3 and 17-4). Nitrogen oxides emissions are much higher than for conventional coal plants because of the higher combustion temperatures.

Unfortunately, many technical difficulties remain and the process is considered by many as an engineer's nightmare. After over 20 years of research in the United States, the U.S.S.R., and Japan, only a few pilot plants are operating.

Synfuels: Coal Gasification and Coal Liquefaction Two ways that are supposed to reduce some of the serious air pollution from coal burning are **coal gasification** and **liquefaction.** In these processes solid coal is converted to synthetic natural gas (SNG) or synthetic crude oil, called **synfuels.**

Coal has more carbon and less hydrogen than oil or natural gas. Thus, in simplest terms, converting coal to synfuels involves getting some of the carbon in coal to react with hydrogen gas at high pressures and temperatures. The resulting gases or liquids are then purified to remove sulfur or other impurities. Thus a bulky, inconvenient, dirty solid fuel becomes a relatively clean gaseous or liquid fuel that can be easily transported in existing pipelines.

Processes for producing low-energy fuel gas, called industrial gas, have been used for hundreds of years. This gas can be burned in industrial boilers and electric power plants, but it has too little heat content per unit of fuel to transmit for long distances by pipeline, for use in home heating. In recent years a number of different methods for producing high-grade or pipeline-quality synthetic natural gas have been developed. Coal-rich South America already produces 10 percent of its oil and gas from coal. Several of the processes have been conducted in small pilot plants in the United States, the U.S.S.R., and some European nations. Several liquefaction processes have also been developed. Full-scale coal gasification plants could be built in the United States by the late 1980s. By 2000, some 20 coal gasification and liquefaction plants could supply energy equal to 6 percent of all energy used in the United States in 1976.

There are some problems, however. One of these is high cost. The capital cost of building a synfuel plant is $1.3 to $2 billion, much higher than an equivalent coal-fired power plant equipped with stack gas scrubbers. The total cost of building 20 large synfuel plants may be $100 billion to $300 billion if the pipeline and transportation is included.

Since it takes about 2 to 13 barrels of water to produce each barrel of synfuel, a second serious problem is water availability (Section 13-5). Coal gasification and liquefaction plants will probably be built near coal-mining sites to cut shipping costs. An alternative would be to transport the coal to distant synfuel plants through pipelines as slurry containing 50 percent coal particles. Either alternative will require large amounts of water. In the Rocky Mountain states, for example, synfuel plants could seriously deplete water supplies. Thus, water availability may be the limiting factor in the production of synfuels in the United States. The Department of Energy found only 41 counties in the United States that have both the coal reserves and enough water to supply a synfuel plant, and many of these counties use Missouri River water which the Sioux Indians claim to own.

A third problem is where to put these gigantic plants. Everyone wants fuel, but few people want a large plant in their community. Between 1970 and 1980, oil companies were able to locate just one construction site for a major oil refinery—which is similar to the problem of locating synfuel plants.

A fourth difficulty is the lower net useful energy yield compared with the direct burning of coal. When coal is converted to synfuels, about 30 to 40 percent of its energy content is lost as waste heat. Taking into account the energy needed to mine the coal, build giant synfuel plants, and construct pipelines and transport systems, synfuels have only one-third the net useful energy yield of oil.

Since synfuel production requires much more coal, it also requires much more strip mining (Section 10-5), (actually about one and one half times more), and a much more rapid depletion of U.S. coal reserves. A single large synfuel plant would normally require the development of a nearby coal mine larger than any in operation in the U.S. today. Sulfur dioxide and particulates air pollution from coal gasification plants is about half that from scrubber-equipped coal-burning power plants but higher than that from oil- or natural-gas-burning power plants. In addition, toxic metal compounds and cancer-causing organic compounds may be released during the coal gasification process. A commercial plant would also produce large quantities of ash, containing trace amounts of toxic metal compounds. This ash would have to be disposed of to avoid contamination of nearby water supplies. The use of synfuels will also increase the possibility of global climate change from the greenhouse effect that occurs when carbon dioxide builds up in the atmosphere (Enrichment Study 3). For the production of the same amount of energy, synfuels emit 1.4 times as much carbon dioxide as coal, 1.7 times as much as oil, and 2.3 times as much as natural gas.

At present, the best way to avoid some of these problems (but not the carbon dioxide problem) is the underground gasification of coal. In this process, superheated air and steam or air and lighted charcoal are forced into an underground coal seam already loosened by explosives. As the coal burns, it is converted to industrial gas (carbon monoxide and hydrogen), which can either be burned in power plants and industrial boilers or possibly upgraded to synthetic natural gas or alcohol. The U.S.S.R. has used this process for more than 50 years and has several underground gasification plants that fuel electric power plants. Underground gasification is the cheapest way to produce industrial gas, and several pilot plants in the United States show promise. Widespread use of this process could triple or even quadruple the usable coal supplies in the United States, since it allows gasification of deep underground coal deposits that are too expensive to mine by conventional methods. Underground gasification might contaminate underground water supplies, though choosing sites carefully could reduce this problem.

Despite the serious problems of high costs, inadequate water supply, siting difficulties, low net useful energy yield, increased strip mining of coal, more rapid depletion of coal reserves, and higher carbon dioxide emissions, the U.S. Congress in 1980 authorized $83 billion in government price subsidies and loan guarantees to help private companies (mostly oil companies) develop a synfuel and shale oil industry between 1980 and 1992.

14-3 Nuclear Fission

A Fading Dream One of the most complex and hotly debated decisions facing the more developed nations is whether to use nuclear fission as a major source of electrical power in coming decades. Nuclear power has been heralded as a clean, cheap, and already developed source of energy that with 1,800 projected plants could provide as much as 21 percent of the world's energy by the year 2000. By 1980, however, this projection had proved much too optimistic with only 480 nuclear plants projected to be in operation by the end of this century.

In 1973, the now defunct U.S. Atomic Energy Commission predicted that by 2000, the United States would have 1,500 nuclear plants producing more than half of the nation's electricity and 25 percent of its primary energy. By 1980, however, there were only 72 nuclear plants operating in the United States, mostly in the Northeast and Midwest. In 1980, these plants produced only about 12 percent of the nation's electricity and about 3 percent of all U.S. primary energy, despite the fact that the nuclear industry received more than $39 billion in government subsidies between 1950 and 1980. Another 85 plants were under construction and 19 new plants were on order by the end of 1980. However, some of these new orders may be cancelled and some of the plants under construction may either be abandoned or converted to coal.

Today, nuclear power, once the shining hope of

America's energy future, is on the ropes, struggling for survival and credibility. Utilities are now faced with (1) a lower demand for electricity than they projected, (2) soaring costs for nuclear plants, (3) a reluctance of lending institutions to provide large amounts of capital for an uneconomic energy alternative, (4) tighter government standards for nuclear plants, (5) no official policy for storing spent radioactive nuclear fuel and other nuclear wastes, and (6) increased public opposition to nuclear power (especially after the Three Mile Island accident in 1979). As a result utilities are turning to a combination of encouraging improvements in energy efficiency, using coal to produce electricity, and relying more on renewable energy alternatives. Between 1975 and 1977, only 5 new nuclear plants were ordered in the United States, and no new orders were placed between 1978 and early 1981. Furthermore, between 1974 and early 1981, at least 32 previous orders were cancelled, and at least 75 others were delayed indefinitely. As a result, some of the companies making nuclear reactors may soon have to drop out of the business.

Since it can't be used to run conventional vehicles, nuclear power will do little to reduce U.S. dependence on oil imports—despite the nuclear industry's highly publicized claims to the contrary. In addition, most fossil fuel power plants no longer burn oil because it is too expensive. By late 1980, less than 7 percent of all U.S. oil consumption was used to produce electricity, and this figure was falling rapidly as most of the remaining oil-burning power plants were being converted to coal. Actually, most of the operating nuclear plants in the United States have saved little oil, since they merely replaced plants powered by coal—an energy resource the United States has in abundance. In 1979, the entire U.S. nuclear energy output could have been replaced simply by raising the output of partially idle coal-burning plants to practical operating levels.

The United States already produces more electricity than is needed to perform the energy tasks for which it is best suited. All electricity needs in the United States between 1980 and 2000 could easily be met by a combination of improvements in energy efficiency and more reliance on renewable energy resources. Additional coal-burning plants could also be used to provide more electricity, but according to some experts even this alternative is unnecessary. Any increase in coal use should be done only with strict air pollution control, and there still would be an increased risk of global climate change from the carbon dioxide released (Enrichment Study 3). One study showed that 64 of the 72 nuclear power plants operating in the United States in 1980 could be shut down with no loss of national electricity output by a combination of improved energy efficiency, increased use of hydroelectric power (especially from unused, existing small dams), cogeneration of both heat and electricity by industrial plants, and an 11 percent increase in the use of coal. The remaining 8 plants, in areas heavily dependent on nuclear power (such as New England, the Southeast, and the Chicago area), could be phased out over a 5 to 10 year period, and all nuclear plants presently under construction could be cancelled (with large savings to utilities and consumers) with no shortages of electricity.

In other words, by 1980, after 30 years of development and a $150 billion investment (with $39 billion in government subsidies), it appeared that nuclear power was both uneconomical and unnecessary to meet the future energy needs of the United States. Energy expert Amory B. Lovins said, "It is my considered judgment that nuclear power is dead—in the sense of a brontosaurus that has had its spinal cord cut, but because it's so big, and has all those ganglia near the tail someplace, can keep thrashing around for years not knowing it is dead. . . . Keeping the nuclear industry alive demands heroic measures to resuscitate and artificially sustain the victim of an incurable attack of market forces."

Nuclear power is also in economic and political trouble in Japan, Great Britain, Austria, West Germany, and many other countries. Sweden's citizens voted to phase out nuclear power within 25 years or less and replace its output with improved energy efficiency and use of renewable energy resources. In sharp contrast, the Soviet Union with 32 nuclear plants producing 5 percent of its electricity in 1980 and with virtually no public discussion of the risks and benefits of nuclear power, hopes to get 25 percent of its electricity from nuclear power by 1990. France, which has Europe's most ambitious nuclear program, hopes to get 20 percent of its electricity from nuclear power by 1985 and a possible 50 percent by 2000, compared with 17 percent in 1979. However, political opposition to nuclear power in France is growing.

There are seven obstacles hindering the development of nuclear power as a major energy source: (1) controversy over whether there are sufficient supplies of uranium fuel; (2) concern over the possibility of a serious nuclear plant accident (meltdown) or plant sabotage that could expose humans to deadly, long-lived radioactive materials; (3) possible theft of nuclear fuel to make atomic bombs; (4) the waste storage problem; (5) proliferation of nuclear weapons; (6) soaring costs; and (7) controversy over the net useful energy yield for the entire system (Section 13-3). Before examining these major obstacles to the development of nuclear power, let's look briefly at how a nuclear power plant works.

How a Nuclear Power Plant Works In a nuclear power plant, a nuclear fission reactor is substituted for the firebox in a fossil fuel power plant. Figure 14-5 shows one type of reactor called a pressurized water reactor (PWR).* Inside the reactor, energy is released by the process of **nuclear fission,** in which the nucleus of a heavy atom such as uranium-235 is split apart by a slow- or fast-moving neutron into two lighter fission fragments and ejects two or three neutrons (see Figure 14-6).† In most reactors these fast-moving, ejected neutrons are slowed as they pass through a *moderator* (Figure 14-5), such as graphite or water. These neutrons can then split other uranium-235 nuclei, releasing more energy and more neutrons. If controlled, the result is a *self-sustaining nuclear chain reaction* that steadily releases enormous amounts of energy. The fission rate is controlled by moving neutron-absorbing *control rods* (usually made of cadmium) in or out of the fuel core. A coolant—water, heavy water (where the hydrogen is hydrogen-2, or deuterium), gas, or a liquid metal such as sodium—is then passed through the reactor to absorb heat. The heat is used directly or indirectly to convert water into superheated steam. This steam drives the blades of a turbine, which in turn runs an electrical generator, as with fossil fuel plants. As the fission process proceeds, high concentrations of the radioactive isotopes produced build up inside the reactor. These dangerous nuclear waste materials must be periodically removed and safely stored for hundreds to thousands of years.

In contrast to the continuous refueling of fossil fuel plants, a typical nuclear reactor is loaded only with about 100,000 kilograms (110 tons) of thimble-sized uranium oxide pellets encapsulated in an expensive zirconium alloy—with about one-third of the fuel being replaced each year. About 10 million of these tiny pellets are inserted into long tubes, or *fuel rods*. The uranium-235 in each fuel rod can produce energy equal to that from about three railroad cars of coal. Precisely arranged bundles of these rods are lowered into the huge steel reactor vessel having walls 18 centimeters (8 inches) thick. The reactor vessel is surrounded by a massive shield, and the entire system is then surrounded by a 1.2-meter-thick (4-foot-thick) reinforced concrete containment shell for added safety should the reactor core vessel or pipes leak (Figure 14-5).

Normally operating nuclear plants emit no air pollutants. Under normal conditions nuclear plants with pressurized water reactors (but not boiling water reactors) emit less radiation than coal-burning plants. Nuclear plants, however, produce considerable amounts of high- and low-level radioactive materials as wastes and as spent fuel. These wastes must not escape to the environment, and so they must be taken periodically to reprocessing or waste disposal sites. Because they are only about 25 to 30 percent thermally efficient, present light-water reactor nuclear power plants are less heat efficient than fossil-fuel-burning plants. As a result, they emit more heat to the surrounding air or body of water per unit of electricity generated than fossil fuel plants, thus increasing the potential for thermal water pollution (Section 16-4).

---

*There are three major types of fission reactors: (1) In the *boiling-water reactor,* water is used as both the coolant and moderator and is converted directly to steam inside the reactor core. (2) In the *pressurized-water reactor* (Figure 14-5), water is used as both the coolant and moderator but is kept under pressure to keep it from changing directly to steam. Water in a second circuit and under less pressure is then converted to steam to drive the turbine. Canada uses pressurized heavy-water reactors called CANDUs, which are fueled with natural uranium and use heavy water as a moderator. Finally, (3) the *high-temperature-gas-cooled reactor* uses a gas, such as helium, as a coolant. The superheated gas is passed through a heat exchanger and used to convert water to steam in a second heat-transfer loop. Most reactors in the United States are either boiling-water or pressurized-water reactors, which are known collectively as *light-water reactors.*

†An atom consists of an extremely small center, called the **nucleus,** and one or more **electrons** whizzing around the nucleus. According to a crude model, the nucleus of an atom contains *neutrons* (uncharged particles) and *protons* (positively charged particles), each with a relative mass of 1. The number of protons plus the number of neutrons in a nucleus gives the **mass number,** which is a measure of the atom's mass since the electrons outside the nucleus have essentially no mass. Atoms of the same element can have different numbers of neutrons in their nucleus, and these different forms are called **isotopes.** The table below shows the three isotopes of hydrogen and the three major isotopes of uranium:

Isotope	Mass Number	No. of Protons	No. of Neutrons
Hydrogen-1	1	1	0
Hydrogen-2 (deuterium)	2	1	1
Hydrogen-3 (tritium)	3	1	2
Uranium-233	233	92	141
Uranium-235	235	92	143
Uranium-238	238	92	146

A sample of uranium ore contains only about 0.7 percent of fissionable uranium-235. The remaining 99.3 percent is nonfissionable uranium-238, which has three more neutrons in its nucleus. Some isotopes of an element are stable, while others are unstable (radioactive) and emit radiation in the form of **alpha particles** (a helium nucleus with two protons and two neutrons), **beta particles** (an electron), or **gamma rays** (high-energy electromagnetic radiation). Fission of uranium-235 nuclei can produce any of over 450 different fission fragments and isotopes—most of which are radioactive. The length of time that a particular radioactive isotope remains radioactive is often expressed in terms of **half life.** It is the length of time it takes for one half of the atoms in a given radioactive substance to decay and in the process change into another nonradioactive or radioactive isotope. Normally, a radioactive isotope does not decay to what is considered a fairly harmless level until a time equal to 10 to 20 times its half life.

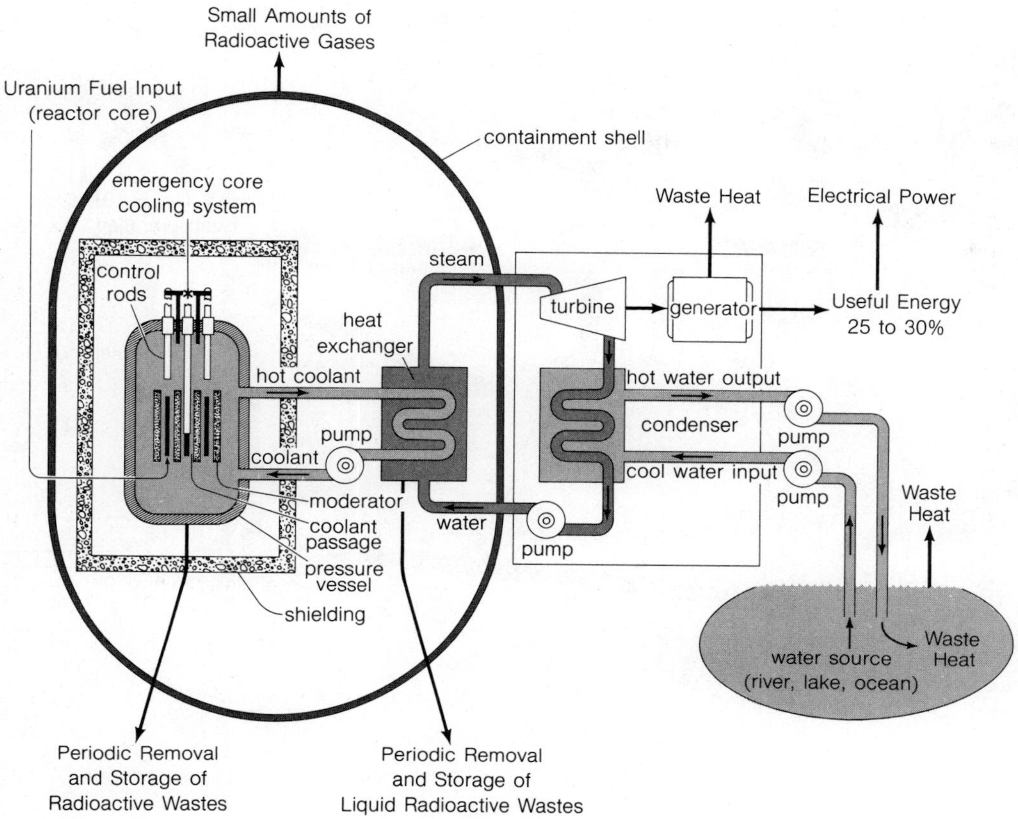

Small Amounts of
Radioactive Gases

Uranium Fuel Input
(reactor core)

containment shell

emergency core
cooling system

Waste Heat   Electrical Power

control
rods

steam

heat
exchanger

turbine → generator → Useful Energy
25 to 30%

hot coolant

coolant

pump

hot water output

condenser   pump

moderator

water

cool water input
pump

coolant
passage

pump

Waste
Heat

pressure
vessel

shielding

Waste
Heat
water source
(river, lake, ocean)

Periodic Removal
and Storage of
Radioactive Wastes

Periodic Removal
and Storage of
Liquid Radioactive Wastes

Figure 14-5 A nuclear power
plant with a pressurized water
reactor.

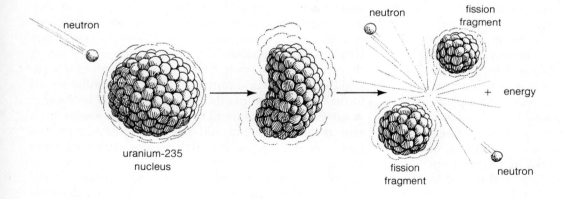

neutron

uranium-235
nucleus

neutron

fission
fragment

+ energy

fission
fragment

neutron

Figure 14-6 Nuclear fission of a
uranium-235 nucleus.

The Nuclear Fuel Cycle When we evaluate the nuclear
energy alternative, we must look at the whole nuclear
fuel cycle, of which the nuclear plant is only one part, as
shown in Figure 14-7. Because of the deadly chemicals
involved (especially highly toxic plutonium-239), this
cycle must operate in essentially absolute safety, with no
leaks or disruptions at any point. As the rate and volume

of materials moving through it increase, the difficulty in
maintaining this safety increases significantly.

The fuel cycle for a light-water reactor begins with
uranium ore, which is mined and processed to form a
concentrate of uranium oxide (U_3O_8) or yellowcake containing a mixture of uranium-238 and a little uranium-
235. Already, at least 91 billion kilograms (100 million

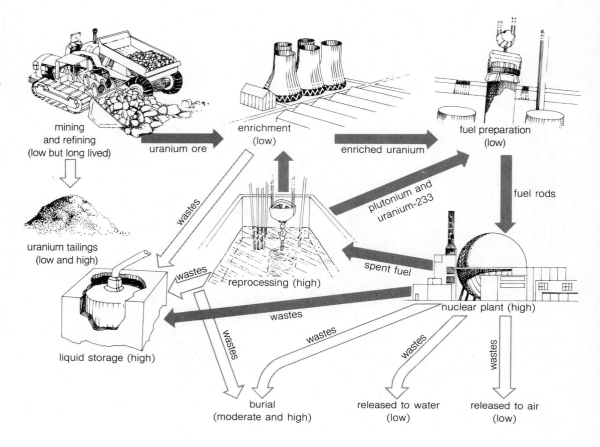

Figure 14-7 The nuclear fuel cycle (shown with solid arrows). Radioactive nuclear wastes that are produced by the cycle are shown with unshaded arrows. The relative radioactivity level of the nuclear materials at each step is shown.

mining
and refining
(low but long lived)

uranium ore

enrichment
(low)

enriched uranium

fuel preparation
(low)

fuel rods

wastes

plutonium and
uranium-233

uranium tailings
(low and high)

wastes

reprocessing (high)

spent fuel

liquid storage (high)

wastes

nuclear plant (high)

wastes

wastes

wastes

wastes

burial
(moderate and high)

released to water
(low)

released to air
(low)

tons) of uranium tailings (waste from uranium mining) have accumulated in the southwestern states. In Colorado, congenital birth defects have increased among children whose parents live or work in homes or buildings constructed either above the tailings or in part from rock taken from radioactive uranium tailings. After processing, the uranium oxide is converted to a gas (uranium hexafluoride, UF_6), which goes to an enrichment plant. There the concentration of uranium-235 is increased from the naturally occurring 0.7 percent to about 3 percent for light-water reactor fuel. At a fuel preparation plant, the uranium hexafluoride is converted to uranium dioxide (UO_2), encapsulated into pellets, and placed in fuel tubes, and then put together in bundles or fuel assemblies for shipping to the power plants.

About one-third of the radioactive fuel elements in a reactor are replaced each year. These spent elements and other contaminated radioactive reactor materials are removed and allowed to cool for several months. Presently, spent fuel is being stored at nuclear plants and other sites indefinitely, since the United States has delayed the development of commercial nuclear fuel reprocessing plants because they could handle and ship ura-

nium in a form that could be used to make nuclear weapons and because of technical difficulties and very high cost.* If processing plants are ever developed, spent fuel would be sealed in heavily shielded casks. They would then be transported to reprocessing plants, where they would be cut open, their contents dissolved in acid, and the uranium and plutonium recovered and shipped to fuel preparation plants for reuse (Figure 14-7). Large volumes of gaseous and liquid radioactive wastes from reprocessing plants would have to be stored permanently or released to the environment after temporary storage.

With this background on how a nuclear plant works let us return to the seven obstacles to nuclear development listed earlier.

---

*A commercial fuel reprocessing plant near Barnwell, South Carolina, has been completed, but as of early 1981 the government had indefinitely delayed giving it a license to operate. Another private nuclear fuel processing plant built near Buffalo, New York, in 1966 was shut down permanently because of serious engineering difficulties. In 1980, New York State and federal government officials were still arguing about who should be responsible for the messy cleanup job, estimated to cost as much as $1.1 billion—about 31 times the cost of building the plant in 1966.

Uranium Supplies, Breeder Reactors, and Nuclear Proliferation Estimates of how long world supplies of uranium-235 will last vary from less than a decade to 1,500 years. This latter estimate assumes that since price rises in uranium fuel add relatively little to the overall cost of nuclear-generated electricity, even a price of $440 per kilogram ($200 per pound) will not price the fuel out of the market. Instead, they will stimulate the discovery and mining of low-grade deposits. Another way to extend uranium supplies is to switch from light-water reactors to the more efficient heavy-water, or CANDU-type, reactors used successfully in Canada since 1972. These plants use natural uranium as fuel (thus eliminating the expensive and energy-consuming enrichment step).

Uranium supplies in the United States may last for a long time because of an increase in the estimated uranium resources and the drastic cutback in the projected use of nuclear power in the United States and abroad. In 1980, the Department of Energy estimated that there would be enough uranium to supply conventional nuclear reactors through the year 2040, even if the U.S. nuclear capacity should somehow increase eight-fold by the year 2000. Other investigators, however, project that the United States will run out of sufficient reserves of uranium within a decade if new large deposits are not found.

Proponents of nuclear power argue that if uranium should become scarce, the problem could be solved for the foreseeable future by a crash program to develop the **nuclear fission breeder reactor.** The liquid-metal fast breeder reactor (LMFBR), for example, uses a mixture of uranium-238 and plutonium-239 as a fuel and liquid sodium as a coolant. Uranium-238 is relatively abundant, and plutonium-239 can be purified from conventional reactor wastes. In the LMFBR, fast neutrons fission plutonium-239 and at the same time convert nonfissionable uranium-238 into fissionable plutonium-239, thus "breeding" its own fuel. If successful, LMFBR's would extend U.S. uranium supplies at least 50-fold and perhaps indefinitely. But even a 50-fold increase in the use of uranium would not be possible for at least 100 years because of the many decades it takes for breeder reactors to breed a significant supply of plutonium-239 fuel.

In recent years a growing number of experts favor delaying the implementation of breeder reactors until well into the twenty-first century or scrapping them altogether. The major arguments against the development of breeder reactors are as follows: (1) They are unnecessary either because uranium supplies will not run out or because a mix of safer and cheaper energy alternatives can be developed faster; (2) the costs would be too high;

(3) if a cooling system failed and the breeder's plutonium fuel fused together in a critical configuration, the resulting explosion could shatter the reactor containment building and release large quantities of highly radioactive materials; (4) the plutonium-239 could be hijacked and converted to atomic bombs; (5) nuclear weapons could proliferate because of the spread of breeder technology, fuel reprocessing, and plutonium fuel elements to other countries; and (6) the United States and many other industrialized nations already produce more electricity than is needed (see the Guest Editorial by Amory Lovins at the end of Chapter 13).

Plutonium-239 is not the most toxic substance on earth, as is often claimed. Moreover, the alpha particles it emits cannot penetrate the skin. But it is highly toxic, and it can cause cancer (especially lung cancer) in humans. In fact, according to the highly controversial hypothesis, a single tiny particle of plutonium-239 (in the form of plutonium oxide, or PuO_2) inhaled into the lungs can cause lung cancer 15 to 45 years later. A breeder reactor that suffered a meltdown and small nuclear explosion could release up to 3,000 kilograms (3.3 tons) into the environment. Plutonium could also be released if crude atomic bombs made from hijacked plutonium fuel were set off in populated areas by terrorist groups.

Despite these problems, prototype LMFBR reactors have been built in the U.S.S.R., Great Britain, and France. So far, however, these reactors have bred little plutonium fuel and are better described as "fast reactors," not as breeders. West Germany and Japan also have active breeder development programs. So far, only the French Phoenix reactor has performed very well. In the United States a prototype breeder reactor, scheduled for completion in Clinch River, Tennessee, by 1985, was delayed indefinitely in 1978 because of engineering design problems, an astronomical rise in cost estimates from $700 million to $2.7 billion, and concern about proliferation of nuclear weapons.

Suggestions for avoiding the dangers of nuclear proliferation (and hijacking) include the following: (1) greatly increasing security measures, (2) doctoring the fuel elements to make them difficult and dangerous to hijack and convert to bombs (a proposal the U.S. Office of Technology Assessment says won't work), and (3) shifting to proliferation-resistant breeder reactors—called "advanced converters" or "thermal breeders"—that use a mixture of thorium-232 and fissionable uranium-233 instead of uranium-238 and plutonium-239. In these reactors, nonfissionable thorium-232, which is abundant and cheap compared with uranium, is converted by slow neutrons to fissionable uranium-233. But as Amory Lovins has pointed out, uranium-233 is similar and in some respects superior to plutonium-239 as a material for making atomic bombs.

Thus, there appears to be no urgent need—now, or perhaps ever—for the United States to develop the breeder reactor. Nevertheless, the proposed federal expenditures for developing the breeder reactor in 1981 amounted to $510 million—considerably more than expenditures proposed for energy conservation, solar, wind, biomass, and geothermal energy (Table 13-8).

Radiation Effects and Levels When people shudder about nuclear accidents, what they fear, of course, is radiation. Radiation damage to humans varies with the type of radioactivity and the parts of the body exposed. In general, however, exposure to radiation has two major effects: genetic damage (mutations that can be passed on to future generations) and damage to nonreproductive tissues, which can cause leukemia, various forms of cancer, miscarriages, cataracts, and death.

Most experts agree that *any* exposure to radiation can have genetic effects. In other words, from a genetic standpoint, any dose of radiation is an overdose. But experts don't agree on whether exposure to very low radiation levels causes nongenetic damage, such as cancer. Some say that any dose of radiation is harmful; others hold that doses are not necessarily harmful if they are below a certain *threshold level* (Figure 1-4). Unfortunately, the evidence is highly controversial. Until this controversy is resolved, human radiation-exposure standards must be set as low as possible while still allowing for some beneficial exposures (such as medical X rays). Each of us is also exposed to natural or **background radiation** from naturally radioactive materials and from cosmic rays entering the atmosphere, which averages between 38 and 150 millirems per year in the United States. (A millirem is equivalent to the radiation dose that delivers 10^{-10} joules of energy to 1 gram of matter.) In addition, human activities expose each person to an additional average radiation dose of about 80 to 125 millirems per year. This brings the total annual average exposure for U.S. residents to between 118 and 275 millirems.

The major sources of artificial radiation in the United States are medical X rays (72 millirems per person per year); nuclear weapons fallout (4 millirems); TV, consumer products, and air travel (2.7 millirems); radioactive isotopes used to diagnose and treat disease (2 millirems); job exposure (0.8 millirem); and nuclear power plants, fuel-processing plants, and nuclear research facilities (0.3 millirem). Despite this low exposure rate, the Union of Concerned Scientists estimates that by the year 2000, about 15,000 Americans will have died because of minor leaks of radiation from nuclear power plants.

From this information we see that the largest average exposure to artificial radiation each year is from X rays, and our smallest exposure is from nuclear power plants and related facilities (assuming, of course, that they are operating normally). Such comparisons, however, don't tell the whole story. X-ray radiation comes from brief exposure to an energy source that does not stay in the environment and requires no long-term protection. In contrast, radioactive wastes from nuclear plants must be isolated from the environment for hundreds to thousands of years. Because of its half-life of 24,000 years, for example, plutonium-239 can remain active for up to 250,000 years (based on the crude rule of thumb that an isotope normally decays to a safe level after about 10 times its half-life). Furthermore, the radiation that is released by nuclear power is imposed upon the entire population without their individual consent. An X ray, however, is done only with an individual's approval.

Present federal and international standards set the maximum allowable occupational exposure to radiation at 5,000 millirems per year. Standards for the maximum allowable exposure of the general population to artificial sources of radiation (except X rays) have been set at a much lower figure of 25 millirems per year by the Environmental Protection Agency. There is, however, considerable pressure to lower both of these standards—a proposal that is not supported by a recent study by the National Academy of Sciences. Proponents of lowering the standards argue that since a normally operating nuclear power plant emits no more than 0.3 millirem per year, then the nuclear industry should not fear lowering the present standard of 25 millirems to 0.3 millirem per year. Indeed, such a move could help establish more public confidence in nuclear power.

Nuclear Reactor Safety Although a thermal nuclear fission reactor cannot blow up like an atomic bomb, it can blow up like a steam boiler or split open and release its deadly radioactive contents to the environment.* Because of this very remote but real possibility, nuclear fission is potentially the most hazardous of all known energy alternatives. A serious accident could release large quantities of radiation that could kill and injure many thousands of people and contaminate large areas for hundreds to thousands of years. One of the most feared

---

*A fast neutron breeder reactor, however, could probably blow up like a small atomic bomb.

accidents could begin with a break in one of the pipes that conduct cooling water and steam to and from the reactor core (Figure 14-5). This would result in a "blow-down," in which a mixture of steam and water would be expelled from the reactor core. In the presence of the core's intense radioactivity, steam could react with the zirconium alloy used to encapsulate the uranium fuel pellets and be converted into hydrogen and oxygen, which could then explode violently and rupture the reactor core. Radioactive materials and gases would be released, but if the strong containment shell did not rupture, they would not enter the atmosphere. Meanwhile, the residual heat from the radioactive materials in the core would melt the fuel rods within a few hours and cause a complete meltdown of the reactor core. Within 13 hours to 14 days the molten core might drop to the bottom of the reactor containment vessel, melt through its thick concrete slab, and melt itself into the earth. Depending on the geological characteristics of the underlying strata, it might sink to a depth of 6 to 30 meters (20 to 100 feet) and gradually dissipate its heat, or it might burn itself deeply into the earth's crust. A melt-through accident is sometimes called the "China syndrome" because the molten reactor core would melt itself into the earth, presumably heading in the general direction of China. (Instead of melting through, the molten core might interact with the water in the system to cause a massive steam explosion that could rupture the containment building and release large amounts of radioactive materials into the atmosphere.)

A melt-through is a nightmare for reactor engineers, but the most serious hazard would be the release of highly radioactive gases and particulates into the atmosphere, which could occur from blowholes in the ground or failure of the containment shell during the first hour or two. This cloud of radioactive materials would be at the mercy of the winds and weather.

Advocates of nuclear power, however, argue that a nuclear power plant (when operating properly) causes less health and environmental damage than the use of coal, and that a catastrophic nuclear accident is so unlikely that nuclear power is worth the risk. They also state that a meltdown and radioactive spill would demand the simultaneous failure of a series of safeguards. First, fuel pellets are clad in metal to confine most of the fission products. Next, the primary reactor pressure vessel (Figure 14-5) provides very strong containment for the radioactive materials in the reactor core. Third, a sophisticated backup system automatically inserts control rods into the core to stop fission if certain emergencies occur. Finally, if the coolant water pipeline breaks, the

system has an emergency core cooling system (ECCS) that should flood the reactor core with emergency cooling water within one minute. But equipment failure, human error, or both could keep the emergency cooling water out, and no full-scale test of the ECCS has ever been made.

Since the 1950s, the Atomic Energy Commission (AEC) has commissioned several studies to assess the probability of a serious nuclear accident and to project the resulting deaths, injuries, and property losses. The first of these studies, published in 1957 (and known by its document number, WASH-740), projected that a "maximum credible accident," releasing 50 percent of all fission products 48 kilometers (30 miles) from a city of 1 million people with no evacuation, might at worst kill 3,400 persons, injure 43,000, and cause property damages valued between $500,000 to $7 billion. In the early 1960s a second, updated version of the 1957 safety study was commissioned by the AEC but not made available to the public. Documents obtained under the Freedom of Information Act revealed that between 1955 and 1975, the AEC suppressed this study and a number of other documents and studies concerning the risks of nuclear power. This is not surprising, since the AEC had the dual and often conflicting roles of promoting and regulating nuclear power. The AEC contended, however, that the second, updated safety study was not released because it was never completed. In 1975, the AEC was dissolved and its two roles were split, with its research role assigned to the Energy Research and Development Administration (ERDA) (now a part of the Department of Energy) and its regulatory role assigned to the Nuclear Regulatory Commission (NRC).

The most recent and extensive reactor safety study was published in 1975. It is known by various names, including WASH-1400, the Rasmussen report (after its director, Dr. Norman Rasmussen) and RSS. This report attempted to evaluate the probability and consequences of serious nuclear accidents involving 100 light-water reactor power plants either in operation or planned, but it did not cover sabotage, hijacking, and dangers associated with other parts of the nuclear fuel cycle. According to this study, for 100 plants, a core meltdown accident might occur once in a million years—about the same likelihood that a meteor would strike a major population center and cause 1,000 immediate fatalities.* Under the

---

*Equating the immediate fatalities from a nuclear accident to those from a single nonnuclear accident, such as a meteor falling, is misleading. The meteor would kill only 1,000 people immediately. The nuclear accident would kill 1,000 people immediately and perhaps 7,500 to 180,000 additional persons from cancer over the next few decades.

worst-case accident, there might be 825 to 13,200 immediate deaths, 7,500 to 180,000 deaths from cancer a number of years later, 12,375 to 198,000 illnesses, 4,750 to 171,000 delayed genetic effects, and property damage ranging from $2.8 billion to $28 billion.

The Rasmussen report, however, has been criticized by a number of prominent scientists and nuclear safety experts for (1) systematically underestimating the chances and consequences of serious reactor accidents, (2) covering only part of the risks from the entire nuclear fuel cycle, (3) covering only 100 plants rather than the at least 480 presently projected worldwide by 2000, (4) using some questionable assumptions and statistical procedures that make many of its fatality and risk projections almost meaningless, and (5) inadequately treating the probability and effects of human error. In January 1979, after reviewing these criticisms, the NRC withdrew its endorsement of the Rasmussen report and said it no longer considered the report's risk estimates reliable.*

We can do a lot to make mechanical systems safer, but what can we do to reduce human error? In evaluating something as risky and complex as nuclear power, perhaps we should assume that both Murphy's law—if anything can go wrong, it will—and its corollary—Murphy was an optimist—will apply. To these two laws perhaps we should add Gib's law of unreliability: "Any system that depends on human reliability is an unreliable system." This became evident in 1979 when a highly improbable series of mechanical failures and human operator errors caused a near core meltdown and the release of small amounts of radiation from the Three Mile Island nuclear plant in Pennsylvania. In this accident, described as the worst in the history of commercial nuclear power, no lives were lost. Furthermore, according to the official presidential commission that investigated the accident, there will be little if any, long-term health effects from the accident. However, some doubts persist about the basis for this conclusion since actual measurements of radiation exposure levels were spotty and sometimes unreliable. In addition, nearby residents have to live with increased anxiety about their health and the long-term health of their children and about the devaluation of their property because most people don't want to live near the plant (which still has another reactor operating). In addition, the cleanup alone will cost at least $1.5 billion

(more than building the reactor) and may not be complete until 1986 or later.

In addition, confusing and conflicting statements about the seriousness of the accident by Metropolitan Edison power plant officials and NRC officials eroded public confidence in the safety of nuclear power and the ability of nuclear officials to provide the public with accurate information about the potential or actual dangers of nuclear power. In 1979, the National Council of Teachers of English awarded the nuclear industry their annual Doublespeak Award for the jargon used to understate the dangers of the Three Mile Island accident to the public. For example, Metropolitan Edison used the term "energetic disassembly" for a possible explosion; a fire was called "rapid oxidation"; and the reactor accident was described as a "normal aberration."

The President's Commission on the Accident at Three Mile Island criticized both Metropolitan Edison and the NRC. The commission found that Metropolitan Edison did not follow established safety procedures, had deficiencies in maintenance and operator training for emergencies, and had control room equipment that was unnecessarily out-of-date. Also, they concluded that the utility company and the state of Pennsylvania had inadequate plans for evacuating the public. According to the commission, the NRC, which is supposed to insure the safe operation of nuclear plants, failed to establish adequate standards for operator training, had weak inspection and enforcement of reactor safety, and was organized in such a way (a five-member committee) that it could not respond promptly and effectively to an emergency.

The president's commission made 44 recommendations. Among them were the following: (1) The education and training of nuclear plant operators should be significantly upgraded; (2) all new nuclear plants should be constructed in remote areas; (3) the NRC should not license the operation of any new plants until the safety improvements recommended by the commission are implemented, operators are better trained, emergency planning is improved, and each state has an evacuation plan approved by the NRC; (4) control room equipment should be upgraded with modern computer technology; (5) research on the effects of radiation should be expanded and better coordinated; and (6) the five-member NRC should be abolished and replaced by a new executive agency with a single chief executive.

These recommendations (except abolishment of the NRC) are gradually being instituted in some form, although environmentalists have accused the NRC of making only cosmetic changes rather than dealing with the

---

*Another study (known as the Inhaber report) made for the Atomic Energy Control Board of Canada rated nuclear power safer than renewable solar, wind, and biomass energy. This report, however, was found to be so full of errors, and erroneous assumptions and conclusions, that the Atomic Energy Control Board of Canada declared it officially out of print in 1980.

serious safety problems raised by the Three Mile Island accident. The nuclear industry moved to upgrade reactor safety by (1) establishing a Nuclear Safety Analysis Center to study any new small or large accidents that may occur; (2) setting up the Institute of Nuclear Power Operations, which is attempting to develop better operator training and standards; (3) installing two telephone hotlines to link each reactor in the country to the NRC's emergency response center; and (4) mounting a well-funded public relations program to convince the public that the Three Mile Island accident proves how safe nuclear power is—pointing out that there was no meltdown, asserting that there was no damage to human health, and arguing that nuclear power has fewer risks than the increased use of coal. Critics, however, attribute the absence of catastrophe at Three Mile Island partially to luck, and further argue that coal (except for the potential danger of climate change from carbon dioxide emissions) can be made acceptably safe. According to NRC commissioner Victor Gilinsky, the accident at Three Mile Island has shifted the burden of proof for the safety of nuclear power from its critics, who have long claimed that it was not safe, to its proponents, who claim that it is.

Thus, after over 25 years of studies on nuclear reactor safety, we are back at square one. By 1980 no identifiable loss of life has resulted from radiation releases in any commercial reactors in the United States or in other nations (no statistics are available for the U.S.S.R. and its satellites). However, this excludes deaths from experimental and military reactors, fuel-cycle facilities, and uranium mining. Although the record of commercial reactors is reassuring, it does not really tell us much about the probability of future accidents, when there may be 400 to 1,000 nuclear power plants throughout the world and thousands of shipments of nuclear materials each year. Nor does it tell us about the long-term effects of low levels of radiation released accidentally from nuclear plants and other parts of the nuclear fuel cycle. We still have no authoritative evaluation of nuclear reactor safety and of the safety of the entire nuclear fuel cycle (Figure 14-7). Nuclear power could be as safe—or even safer—than the Rasmussen report says. But it could also be much less safe. We don't know!

Insurance companies have refused since the 1950s to insure nuclear reactors. Because this would have prevented the fledgling nuclear industry from ever getting off the ground, Congress in 1957 passed the Price-Anderson Act, which makes the public primarily responsible for nuclear liability payments. This law relieves the nuclear power industry of any liability claims greater than $560 million (a very small sum in the event of a major nuclear accident). Congress has also decreed that of the $560 million (plus $5 million that must be kicked in by each operating nuclear plant in the United States) at most only $250 million would be paid out by private insurance companies, with the government (you and me) accounting for the remaining $310 million. Additional government funds could be made available if the accident area is declared a major disaster area. In the event of a major accident, however, the damage to some injured parties in the form of cancer may not show up for 10 to 20 years, and these individuals would have great legal difficulty in establishing that their cancers resulted from the accident.

Nuclear proponent Alvin M. Weinberg (see his Guest Editorial at the end of this chapter) has called for utilities to show that they really believe in the low-risk figures they keep quoting to the public by insuring each reactor for damage up to $1 billion with their own funds, with the government assuming responsibility for losses greater than $1 billion, as it now does in the case of floods and natural disasters. Although he believes that nuclear power can be safe, he has been one of the few strong proponents of nuclear power who emphasize that the widespread use of nuclear power is the greatest single long-term risk ever taken by humankind, one that should be accepted only after intensive public education and debate. He advocates that, if we are to live with nuclear power, the present risk estimates must be reduced by at least a factor of 100. In his words, "We nuclear people have made a Faustian compact [a compact with the devil] with society; we offer . . . an inexhaustible energy source . . . tainted with potential side effects that if not controlled, could spell disaster." Weinberg envisions a permanent, elite nuclear priesthood of responsible technologists who will guard and protect all nuclear plants, shipments, and waste deposits for hundreds of thousands of years.

Terrorism and Hijacking of Nuclear Fuel Shipments
Like any centralized industrial facility, a nuclear power plant could be sabotaged by one person or a team of people. By 1980 no nuclear plant had been severely sabotaged, but between 1969 and 1975 alone there were 11 bombs set off, hundreds of threats and hoaxes, 15 acts of vandalism and sabotage, and numerous breaches of security in or near nuclear test laboratories and nuclear plants throughout the world, but mostly in the United States. A nuclear plant is a central-

ized facility that can be made very secure, and since 1975 the often lax security around nuclear plants has been tightened. But absolute protection cannot be guaranteed.

A much more dangerous problem is the hijacking of nuclear fuel shipments. Protecting hundreds to thousands of nuclear material shipments is much harder than protecting a few centralized nuclear power plants. The hijacking of spent fuel being sent to reprocessing plants (Figure 14-7) is not a serious problem, since the materials are intensely radioactive and must be shipped in radiation-shielding casks weighing up to 91,000 kilograms (100 tons). Spent fuel shipments, however, could be sabotaged (for example, by a bazooka). Shipments of uranium from enrichment plants to fuel preparation plants and of uranium fuel elements from fuel preparation plants to light-water nuclear plants (Figure 14-7) are much more vulnerable. By 1980, more than 20 states had passed laws either banning or restricting transportation of nuclear wastes within their borders, and many other states were considering such actions.

If commercial breeder reactors are ever developed, the prime target of hijackers will be shipments of plutonium-239 from fuel preparation plants to breeder power plants. Plutonium-239 can be used directly to make crude nuclear bombs that could easily blow up a large building or a city block and contaminate much larger areas with deadly radioactive materials. Less than 4.5 kilograms (10 pounds) of plutonium-239 metal—about the size of an orange—or about 10 kilograms (22 pounds) of plutonium oxide are needed to make an atomic bomb. To get this amount of plutonium would require at most from 227 to 682 kilograms (500 to 1,500 pounds) of plutonium reactor fuel. Plutonium-239 is deadly, but only when inhaled or, to a lesser extent, ingested in soluble form. Thus, in its solid form it poses little danger to thieves. By 1978, at least 318 kilograms (700 pounds) of plutonium-239 were missing from commercial and government-operated reactors and storage sites in the United States—enough to make 32 to 70 atomic bombs (each capable of blowing up a city block). No one knows whether this missing plutonium was stolen or whether it represents sloppy measurements and bookkeeping. In 1980, a report prepared by the safeguards division of the Nuclear Regulatory Commission indicated that the NRC's statistical accounting checks on nuclear fuel shipments in recent years have become so muddled that they probably would not detect losses by a skillful thief.

How easy would it be to convert stolen plutonium to a "blockbuster" atomic bomb? Experts disagree. But since a Princeton undergraduate and several other col-

lege students used easily available library resources to develop plans for building a crude (but probably workable) nuclear bomb from plutonium, a small group of trained people could probably make such a bomb.

However, hijackers need not bother to make atomic bombs. They could simply use a conventional explosive charge to blow the stolen plutonium into the atmosphere from atop any tall building. Dispersed in this manner, only 2.2 kilograms (1 pound) of plutonium could theoretically contaminate 7.7 square kilometers (3 square miles) with lethal radioactivity for 100,000 years.

In recent years the NRC has tightened the NRC security measures for nuclear plants and fuel shipments. Plutonium fuel is carried in armored trucks with expert marksmen as guards, who have orders to shoot to kill. Elaborate communications facilities should bring help rapidly. A new $100,000 shipment vehicle is being considered that permanently locks its wheels when signaled. Its sides are made of a material that resists attack, but in case of attack, a rapidly hardening plastic foam is automatically injected into the interior to cover the nuclear fuel. With such security measures, it is estimated that a nuclear security force of a few thousand persons could guard plutonium in the United States—less than the number of guards used to guard and transport money in the U.S. banking system. If adequate security measures are established and rigidly monitored and enforced, it would be much harder—but still by no means impossible—for a shipment of plutonium fuel to be stolen or for small amounts of fuel to be stolen from a fuel preparation plant or from a reprocessing plant (Figure 14-7).

Even Alvin M. Weinberg, one of the most thoughtful and optimistic advocates of nuclear energy (see his Guest Editorial at the end of this chapter), believes that the problem of shipping dangerous breeder fuel will be "difficult" and suggests that we develop nuclear parks to minimize this risk. In this concept, a cluster of 8 to perhaps 40 nuclear plants, along with fuel preparation, fuel-reprocessing, and waste storage plants, would be grouped in one complex to reduce the need for shipping. But building such large complexes would be very expensive and might affect local climate, and opposition from nearby residents could be strong. Another suggestion for reducing hijacking risks is to deliberately contaminate the plutonium fuel with hot radioactive wastes, which would make the fuel very dangerous to steal and hard to purify. But so far there is no acceptable spiking agent. Some possible isotopes would require a major overhaul of the fuel cycle processing steps, and others are too scarce.

Nuclear Wastes One thousand grams of uranium-235 undergoing fission produce some 999 grams of radioactive waste—a mixture of solids, liquids, and gases that must be stored until their radioactivity is no longer harmful. For example, a typical 1,000-megawatt reactor produces about 125 kilograms (275 pounds) of deadly plutonium-239 each year. Table 14-1 shows some of the isotopes produced in nuclear fission reactors. Iodine-131, cesium-137, and strontium-90 are particularly dangerous because, unlike many radioisotopes, they can become concentrated in food chains.

Three methods are used to dispose of radioactive wastes: (1) dilution and dispersion, (2) delay and decay, and (3) concentration and containment. In *dilution and dispersion*, low-level wastes are released into the air, water, or ground to be diluted to presumably safe levels. As wastes proliferate, this already dangerous practice will begin to add significantly to artificial radiation levels in the environment, particularly from hydrogen-3 (tritium) and krypton-85, which are difficult and fairly expensive to contain and remove. *Delay and decay* can be used for radioactive wastes with relatively short half-lives, which are stored as liquids or slurries in tanks. After 10 to 20 times their half-lives, they normally decay to relatively harmless levels, at which time they can be diluted and dispersed to the environment. Unfortunately, between 1946 and 1970, tens of thousands of steel drums containing low-level radioactive wastes from Europe and the United States were dumped into the ocean and this practice is still being carried out by some European nations.

The third method, *concentration and containment*, is used for highly radioactive wastes with long half-lives.

Table 14-1 Dangerous Isotopes Produced in Nuclear Fission Reactors

Isotope	Half-life*	Organ Affected
Iodine-129	17,000,000 years	Thyroid
Plutonium-239	24,000 years	Entire body, especially lungs and bone
Strontium-90	28 years	Bone
Cesium-137	27 years	Entire body
Hydrogen-3 (tritium)	12 years	Entire body
Krypton-85	11 years	Lungs, skin
Iodine-131	8 days	Thyroid

*Isotopes must be stored for periods of 10 to 20 times their half-life before they decay to levels that are normally considered safe.

These wastes must be stored for tens, hundreds, thousands, or even millions of years, depending on their composition. They are not only extremely radioactive but also thermally hot. Nuclear scientists, the NRC, and the Department of Energy assure the public that the problem of long-term waste storage can be solved, but after more than 5,700 studies and 20 years of effort, no method has been officially accepted in the United States. These assurances have not satisfied many environmentalists, scientists, and citizens who think that nuclear power should not become widespread until the waste storage problem has been solved. To such nuclear critics, this proceeding with nuclear power without an acceptable solution to the waste problem is like jumping out of an airplane without a parachute while the pilot reassures you, "Don't worry, we'll find a way to save you before you hit the ground." By 1980, seven states had banned the construction of new nuclear power plants until the government demonstrated a safe method for long-term nuclear waste disposal. In one sense, it is impossible to demonstrate that a particular method of nuclear waste disposal is safe, since such a test would take many thousands of years. Instead, scientists must rely on judgment and computer models—techniques not always acceptable to government officials who must decide which method to use and to citizens who may live near national nuclear waste disposal sites or along shipping routes to such disposal sites.

By 1980 most of the wastes produced by U.S. nuclear power plants were temporarily being stored underwater in huge, specially constructed pools at nuclear plants until a method for long-term disposal was found. There is concern over whether such a large quantity of spent fuel can continue to be safely stored for extended periods at nuclear plants. Thus, unless one or more permanent storage sites are developed by 1990, some nuclear plants may be forced to close. In 1980, President Carter proposed that the federal government construct or acquire one or more temporary, "away from reactor" storage pools to store the overflow of spent nuclear fuel. One proposal would use the unlicensed nuclear fuel processing plant at Barnwell, South Carolina, for such storage.

Liquid wastes from nuclear weapons production (equal in volume to about 200 Olympic-sized swimming pools) are also awaiting some form of permanent storage in underground tanks in government facilities in Idaho, South Carolina, and Washington state. These tanks must be carefully guarded and continuously maintained and checked to prevent corrosion and leaks. More than 1.7 million liters (450,000 gallons) of highly radioactive wastes have already leaked from 20 underground tanks

Table 14-2 Proposed Methods for Long-Term Storage or Disposal of Nuclear Wastes

Proposal	Possible Problems
Surround wastes with concrete or several layers of metal and store in surface warehouses or underground tunnels with careful monitoring until a better solution is found.	Concrete or metal liners might deteriorate; above ground warehouses may be difficult to guard against sabotage; states may not want the storage sites or the wastes to be shipped through their area; the government might not provide enough funds to investigate more permanent storage methods.
Solidify wastes, encapsulate them in glass or ceramic, place in metal containers, and bury the containers deep underground in earthquake- and flood-free geological formations, such as dug-out salt or granite deposits.	Occurrence of natural disasters cannot be predicted; heat from radioactive decay might crack glass containers, fracture salt or granite formations so that groundwater could enter the depository, or release water from water-containing minerals that could leach radioactive materials into groundwater supplies; transportation of deadly radioactive wastes to depository sites could be dangerous; wastes might be difficult to retrieve if project fails.
Use rockets or a space shuttle to shoot the wastes into the sun or into space.	Costs would be very high and a launch accident could disperse deadly radioactive wastes over a wide area. The project may also not be technically feasible.
Bury wastes in an underground hole created by a nuclear bomb so that the wastes eventually melt and fuse with surrounding rock into a glassy ball.	Effects unknown and unpredictable; if project fails, wastes cannot be retrieved and could contaminate groundwater supplies.
Bury wastes under Antarctic ice sheets or Greenland ice caps.	Long-term stability of ice sheets is unknown; knowledge about thermal, chemical, and physical properties of large ice sheets is lacking; retrieval could be difficult or impossible if project fails.
Encase wastes in well-designed containers and drop them into the ocean in isolated areas.	No one knows how to design a container that will last long enough; oceans and marine life could become seriously contaminated if containers leak; small currents near the ocean bottom could move the wastes to less isolated sites over hundreds to thousands of years.
Enclose wastes in well-designed containers and drop them into deep ocean bottom sediments that are descending deeper into the earth.	Long-term stability and motion of these sediments are unknown; containers might leak and contaminate the ocean before they are carried downward; containers might migrate back to the ocean or be spewed out somewhere else by volcanic activity; wastes probably cannot be retrieved if project fails.
Change harmful isotopes into harmless ones by using high-level neutron bombardment, lasers, or nuclear fusion.	Technological feasibility has not been established; the costs would be extremely high, and this process would also create new toxic materials also needing disposal; its main effect would be to spread the long-lived radioactive isotopes into more dilute radioactive wastes, not to eliminate them.

at the Richland, Washington, site. However, a study by the National Research Council concluded that because of the isolation of the site, the leaks have not caused any significant radiation hazard to public health. In 1980, Washington state voters banned the use of the Richland nuclear facility for storage of any nuclear wastes produced outside their state. Leaks from the wastes stored at the Savannah River plant in South Carolina could be extremely dangerous, however, because the plant is perched atop the Tuscaloosa water aquifer.

Table 14-2 summarizes the methods proposed for long-term storage or disposal of nuclear wastes. For over 20 years most scientists have considered underground salt or granite deposits the best sites for long-term disposal of dangerous nuclear wastes. West Germany has been storing limited amounts of its low-level nuclear wastes in a deep underground salt mine for several years—but not its high-level wastes. Several reports by geologists, however, have raised doubts about the long-term stability of salt deposits exposed to high-temperature nuclear wastes. In addition, by 1980, at least 15 states had enacted laws that either forbade or strictly regulated storage of wastes within their borders. At least 12 more states were thinking of following suit.

Salt deposits or one of the other schemes shown in Table 14-2 may work, but one is justified in doubting whether a nation that is only 200 years old can design a foolproof method for storing lethal radioactive wastes through wars, natural disasters, and other upheavals for many thousands of years longer than all recorded human history. A more realistic appraisal is that there is no assurance that this problem can be solved and that by using nuclear power today we pass this risk on to future generations.

Soaring Costs Concern over safety, hijacking, long-term storage, and nuclear proliferation are important issues, but the present depression in the U.S. nuclear industry has occurred primarily for economic reasons and because the use of electricity has not risen as rapidly as originally projected since the 1973 oil embargo—thus decreasing the need for new power plants. Utilities are finding it harder and harder to get stockholders' approval for borrowing and tying up billions of dollars for the 12 to 15 years required to bring a nuclear plant into operation. Coal-fired power plants can be on-line in about 5 years, saving as much as $100 million a year on interest payments alone.* Increasingly, lending institutions are urging utilities to sharply cut back on the building of both nuclear and coal large-scale power plants. Instead, they recommend that the utilities invest in (1) promoting improved efficiency as the lowest-cost source of new energy, (2) installing equipment and using techniques to cut demand for electricity, and (3) when needed, investing in small-scale generating stations.

As with most aspects of nuclear power, there is a heated and complex debate over the economics of nuclear power. Between 1971 and 1978 nuclear plants completed in the United States cost an average of 50 percent more to build than comparable coal plants completed during the same period; for nuclear plants started since 1978, the figure is 75 percent. The controversial nuclear plant at Seabrook, N.H., for instance, originally estimated to cost $900 million, is now expected to cost more than $3 billion. One expert has claimed it is cheaper to scrap a nuclear plant less than 40 percent complete than to build a new coal-fired plant. These estimates do not even include the higher costs of nuclear plant construction and operation due to tighter safety standards prompted by the Three Mile Island accident.

Nuclear power plants, however, have lower operating costs than coal-fired plants. One of the reasons that utility companies built nuclear plants was because the nuclear industry projected that the plants would have an 80 percent *capacity factor*—the electricity it actually produces expressed as a percentage of how much it would produce if it operated full-time at its full rated power. Actually, commercial nuclear power plants in the United States have operated far below this 80 percent capacity factor level because of frequent breakdowns, lengthy maintenance operations, and the need to comply with federal safety standards. Between January 1979 and June 1980, U.S. nuclear plants had a capacity factor of only 57 percent, and larger plants (over 800 megawatts) of only 51 percent. Coal-fired plants performed only slightly better, but with their lower construction costs today they can produce electricity more cheaply where coal is available. These plant capacity figures vary with plant size and age, and are highly controversial.

The real question is whether nuclear power will be cheaper than coal in the future. The stiffer safety standards imposed after the Three Mile Island accident are estimated to cost from $25 million to $204 million per plant, and may be the last blow in the battle between coal and nuclear power. Furthermore, the projected costs of electricity from nuclear power do not include the costs of (1) waste disposal (since no official method has been established), (2) decommissioning (dismantling, entombing, or mothballing) a highly radioactive plant when it simply wears out after 30 to 40 years of use (estimated to be at least $50 million per plant, although the cost will probably be at least twice as high),* and (3) burying large amounts of hazardous tailings left over from uranium mining. A 1978 congressional report stated: "When the still unknown costs of radioactive waste and spent fuel management, decommissioning, and perpetual care are finally included, nuclear power

---

*For example, in 1968 Pacific Gas and Electric company began building the Diablo Canyon nuclear power plant near San Luis Obispo, California. Utility officials predicted that the plant could be built and put into operation within 2 years at a cost of $450 million. By 1981, after more than 12 years and an expenditure of $2 billion (almost 5 times the original estimate) the plant was still not in operation and the utility company was paying $14 million a month in interest on the money it had borrowed to build the plant.

*After 30 to 40 years of neutron bombardment, the carbon-steel reactor vessel becomes too brittle to use and the miles of cooling water pipes become too corroded for safe use. Since the high levels of radiation in the reactor vessel make repairs unthinkable, the plant must be shut down in a safe condition. Although no plant of commercial size has ever been decommissioned, scientists say it can be done in one of three ways: (1) mothballing by removing spent uranium fuel rods, draining all slightly radioactive water from its cooling pipes, and setting up a 24-hour security system to guard against sabotage; (2) entombment, another mothballing system where the entire facility is sealed in reinforced concrete after radioactive fuel rods and radioactive water and other materials have been removed; and (3) dismantlement by tearing down the entire plant, removing and safely storing the radioactive materials, and restoring the surrounding land to its original state.

may prove to be much more expensive than conventional energy alternatives such as coal."

A Complex Decision   From the discussion in this section, we have seen that reliance on nuclear energy as a major source of energy is by no means a simple issue. Proponents of nuclear power argue that it is safe and economical and that it is the only energy technology sufficiently developed to reduce dependence on fossil fuels over the next 30 to 50 years. In contrast, opponents argue that nuclear power is unsafe, uneconomical, unethical (since it commits future generations to storing our radioactive wastes in absolute safety), and unnecessary since a mix of improving energy efficiency, and other energy sources (such as the sun, wind, and biomass, and possibly coal, with adequate pollution control) can reduce dependence on oil and natural gas over the next 30 to 50 years. To these critics, pouring money into nuclear power is equivalent to Santayana's description of fanaticism as "redoubling your efforts when you have forgotten your aim." In the words of Nobel Prize-winning physicist Hannes Alfvén, "Nuclear fission energy is safe only if a number of critical devices work as they should, if a number of people in key positions follow all their instructions, if there is no sabotage, no hijacking of the transport, if no reactor fuel processing plant or repository anywhere in the world is situated in a region of riots or guerrilla activity, and no revolution or war—even a 'conventional one'—takes place in these regions. . . . No acts of God can be permitted."

14-4   Nuclear Fusion

Nuclear Fusion Reactions   In laboratories in the United States, the U.S.S.R., Japan, and western Europe, scientists are competing to harness nuclear fusion as a source of energy. The potential energy locked in atomic nuclei can be released by two processes, *nuclear fission* and *nuclear fusion*. In nuclear fission a slow or fast moving neutron splits the nucleus of a heavy atom, such as uranium-235, into two lighter fragments, releasing more neutrons, and extra energy (see Figure 14.6). In **nuclear fusion**—which takes place in the sun, stars, and hydrogen bombs—two nuclei of light atoms (such as hydrogen) are forced together at ultrahigh temperatures to form a heavier nucleus (such as helium), and releasing large amounts of energy. Fusion releases 4 times as much energy per gram as fission (uranium) and about 10 million times as much per gram as the combustion of fossil fuel. At present, the two most attractive fusion reactions are the D-D reaction, in which two deuterium (or hydrogen-2) nuclei fuse to form a helium-3 nucleus, and the D-T reaction, in which a deuterium nucleus and a tritium (hydrogen-3) nucleus fuse to form helium-4 (Figure 14-8).

Since atomic nuclei have positive electrical charges, they repel one another and stubbornly resist fusing. Forcing the nuclei together requires an enormous input of energy. The D-D reaction, for example, requires an ignition temperature of about 1 billion degrees Celsius. Because of its much lower ignition temperature (100 million degrees Celsius), the D-T reaction is the only one being studied seriously at this time.

Even though deuterium is a rare form of hydrogen, seawater provides an almost inexhaustible supply. If nuclear fusion is ever developed, the deuterium in the ocean could supply humankind with energy at many times present consumption rates for 100 billion years—about 10 times the estimated age of the universe. But such rosy projections are based on the deuterium-deuterium fusion reaction, which will probably not be a significant energy source for at least 100 years, if ever. The long-term supply for the deuterium-tritium fusion reaction does not appear so optimistic, since there is no significant natural source of tritium. As a result, the tritium supply must be continuously bred in a nuclear fusion reactor by using neutrons to bombard a surrounding blanket of the isotope lithium-6. Natural lithium—an element not much more abundant than uranium—consists mostly of the isotope lithium-7, mixed with fairly small amounts of lithium-6. Thus, the scarcity of lithium-6 will probably limit the use of D-T fusion.

Problems to Overcome   Controlled nuclear fusion has important advantages, including no chance of a meltdown or atomic explosion (see Table 13-4), but it also has many incredibly difficult and complex problems. After 30 years and $3 billion spent in research, by 1980 no sustained fusion reaction yielding any net useful energy has yet been achieved.

There are three difficult requirements for a sustained nuclear fusion reaction, and they must all be met simultaneously. Scientists must (1) heat a small quantity of fusion fuel to about 100 million degrees Celsius to create a plasma,* (2) contain and squeeze the resulting plasma

---

*At ultrahigh temperatures, the nuclei are stripped of their surrounding negatively charged electrons, leaving an intensely hot mixture of positively charged nuclei and negatively charged electrons known as **plasma.**

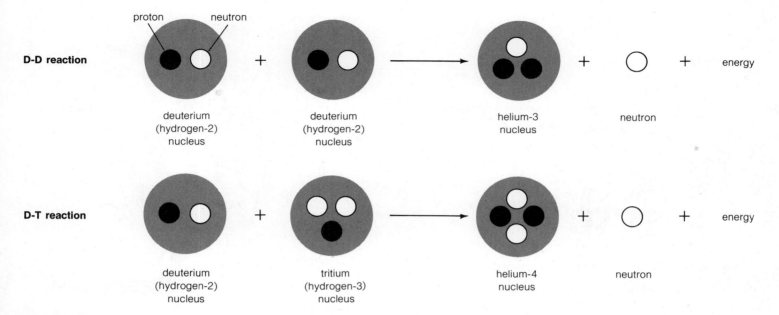

proton   neutron

D-D reaction

deuterium
(hydrogen-2)
nucleus
+
deuterium
(hydrogen-2)
nucleus
→
helium-3
nucleus
+
neutron
+
energy

D-T reaction

deuterium
(hydrogen-2)
nucleus
+
tritium
(hydrogen-3)
nucleus
→
helium-4
nucleus
+
neutron
+
energy

Figure 14-8 Two potentially useful nuclear fusion reactions.

together long enough and at a high enough density for the positively charged nuclei of the fuel atoms to overcome their electrical repulsion, collide, fuse, and then release energy, and (3) recover enough net useful energy to make fusion profitable. The first two requirements have been met separately, but by 1980 no single experiment had achieved both at once, and the third requirement had yet to be achieved.

Most of the past research has sought a nonmaterial means or "magic bottle" that could contain the plasma safely and press it together long enough for self-sustaining fusion to occur. The temperature is so high (100 million degrees Celsius) that it would vaporize any container. The two major approaches to this problem are *magnetic confinement* and *inertial containment* (Figure 14-9). Since the particles of plasma are charged, they can be guided—attracted or repelled—by magnetic fields. In magnetic confinement, very powerful magnetic fields are used to force the atomic nuclei together. The most promising magnetic approach is the Russian *tokamak*, in which the plasma is confined in a doughnut shape by two magnetic fields (Figure 14-9). The giant $300 million tokamak fusion test reactor (TFTR) at the Princeton University Plasma Physics Laboratory should be completed by 1983 and may be the first to reach the net energy break-even point (producing as much energy as it uses)—hopefully by 1985. Even if the break-even point is reached in the laboratory, the next and even more

difficult step will be to reach the burning point, or true ignition, where the nuclear fusion reaction produces enough energy to take over the job of heating the plasma and become self-burning. But some researchers still consider the tokamak noncommercial because of the engineering problems and high costs—probably 2 to 4 times more costly than breeder fission.

A second approach to nuclear fusion is *inertial containment*. High-powered laser beams, electron beams, or beams of light atoms (such as carbon or oxygen) bombard and implode a tiny pellet crammed with deuterium and tritium fuel (Figure 14-9). The impact should drive the contents of the pellet inward, creating an intensely hot, dense core where fusion can take place. In effect, the beams set off miniature hydrogen bombs whose released energy produces heat. Major problems are developing lasers with enough power to get a net useful energy yield. At present, there is apparently no laser or beam source that meets the criteria for a commercial fusion reactor. Advocates of inertial containment, however, believe that they can be developed and that in the long run this method will be cheaper than the magnetic approach.

Both the magnetic and inertial confinement approaches to nuclear fusion could increase the threat of nuclear weapons proliferation. The magnetic approach produces a copious supply of fast neutrons that could be used to breed bomb materials. The inertial containment

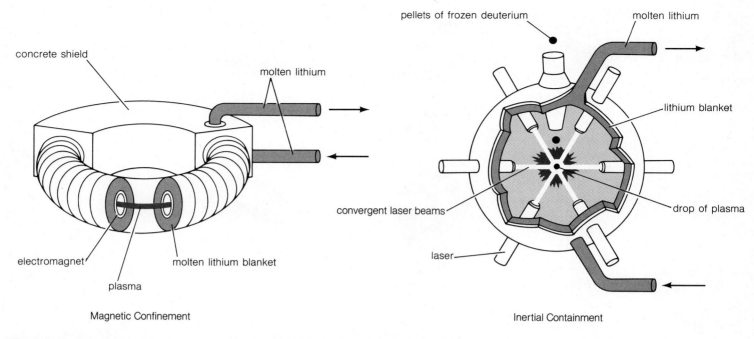

Figure 14-9 Comparison of magnetic confinement and inertial containment methods for initiating a nuclear fusion reaction.

approach could give other nations technological insights enabling them to develop hydrogen or nuclear fusion bombs. As a result, much of the research on inertial containment is highly classified. Another fear is that in the rush to show the feasibility of nuclear fusion, scientists might be tempted to use a hybrid fusion-fission reactor. In this case, the fast neutrons from a fusion (or near-fusion) reactor are used to breed fission fuel (in a blanket) for external use in a separate fission reactor. Such an approach would combine the worst and most potentially dangerous aspects of nuclear fusion and fission.

Even if the ignition and confinement problems are solved, scientists still face formidable engineering problems in developing a workable nuclear fusion reactor and plant, which may be the most complicated engineering feat attempted in human history.

One such problem is a little like trying to preserve an ice cube next to a blazing fire—only harder. At the center of the reactor the plasma may be 100 million degrees Celsius, but only 2 meters away, around the magnets, the temperature must be near absolute zero (−273°C). This feat requires liquid helium—a substance that may soon be scarce unless the United States quickly establishes a helium conservation program. The entire massive chamber must also be maintained at a near per-

fect vacuum. More mind-boggling still, the inner wall of the reactor must resist constant baths of highly reactive liquid lithium (at 1,000°C) and steady bombardment by fast neutrons (which destroy or alter the composition of most known materials) for 10 to 20 years. A wall of any known metal or metal alloy would have to be replaced every 2 to 10 years at such an enormous cost that fusion may never be economically feasible. Many of these wall materials might also be scarce. Another problem is that the bombardment of the walls and other structural materials by the neutrons produced by fusion makes many of these materials radioactive. As a result, repairs would have to be made by automatic devices, since no human worker could withstand the radiation. Scientists hope to overcome some of these problems by developing special new alloys. Another concern is whether the high-level magnetic and electrical fields near the reactor might be a health hazard to power plant employees.

Fusion reactors, though much less dangerous than conventional or breeder reactors, do have some potential radioactivity hazards. Worst would be the release of radioactive tritium (hydrogen-3), either as a gas or as tritiated water, which in turn could enter the human body through the skin, mouth, or nostrils. Tritium is extremely difficult to contain, because at high temperatures and high neutron densities it can diffuse through metals. It is also produced in fission reactors, and scientists are already testing methods for controlling it. The long-term disposal of worn-out, intensely radioactive metal parts from fusion reactors could also create a problem. Another concern is that the vessel containing the lithium blanket could be ruptured as the container metals weaken from the intense neutron bombardment. The very reactive lithium could then escape and catch fire on contact with air, water, concrete, or other materials. The burning lithium would then be hot enough to decompose concrete and melt stainless steel. Such a rupture would also release large amounts of tritium and other radioactive materials—equal to about one-fourth the amount that could be released from the rupture of an equivalent nuclear fission plant.

Future Prospects The scientific, engineering, and economic problems associated with nuclear fusion stagger the imagination. However, many fusion scientists feel that these difficulties can eventually be overcome with enough government funding. The research and development costs worldwide for a fusion program may cost at least $50 billion. If everything goes right—which may be one of the biggests ifs in scientific and engineering history—laboratory feasibility might be established by 1985, engineering feasibility by the early 1990s and commercial feasibility sometime between 2000 and 2020. Then, between 2050 and 2100, nuclear fusion might produce as much as 18 percent of U.S. annual energy needs. At best, nuclear fusion is a very long-term energy possibility that offers no help at all in the severe energy crisis we face between now and 2020. Furthermore, using very expensive nuclear fusion to produce high quality electrical energy (which is not needed to perform most of our energy tasks) is unnecessary (see Section 13-3) and may be wasteful of capital needed to develop more useful energy alternatives. Despite the fact that the chances of ever developing commercial nuclear fusion are very slim and that the electricity it might produce may not be really needed, the U.S. Congress passed the Magnetic Fusion Energy Engineering Act of 1980. It establishes as a national goal the demonstration of the engineering feasibility of magnetic fusion in the early 1990s and the building of a workable fusion demonstration by 2000 and authorizes the Department of Energy to spend up to $20 billion between 1980 and 2000 to try to meet this goal. As a result, more of the proposed federal energy budget for 1981 was to be allocated for fusion than for other

more promising energy alternatives such as solar, wind, biomass, and improving energy efficiency (Table 13-8).

14-5 Energy from Rivers and Oceans

Hydroelectric Power: An Indirect Form of Solar Energy Humans have used falling water as a source of energy for centuries. As water flows from high to low land, its gravitational potential energy is converted into the kinetic energy of streams and rivers. This kinetic energy can turn waterwheels, which can do useful work (such as milling or driving machinery), or spin turbines, which can produce electricity. Dams have stored water in reservoirs, where it can be released to produce electricity at any time. Although water power is theoretically a renewable resource (Table 13-1), all hydroelectric power dams have finite lives, ranging from 50 to 300 years, because their reservoirs eventually fill up with silt.

Hydroelectric power plants have several important advantages: high efficiency, high net useful energy yield (Figure 13-8), low to moderate environmental impact on air and water, a long life, and relatively low operating costs (Table 13-4). In addition, they are run by a free source of energy (falling water). The large-scale development of hydroelectric power, however, is limited by the availability of suitable sites. A good site has a high head (a steep drop), a high rate of flow, a large storage capacity (reservoir), and nearness to a large population center. As a result, the best hydroelectric sites are in areas that have heavy rainfall and large variations in elevation. In the United States, most hydroelectric projects are concentrated in two areas, the Southeast and the Northwest, as shown in Figure 14-10. Not only are good sites limited, but they are also unevenly distributed throughout the world and are often far from major population centers.

Most of the best major hydroelectric sites in the United States (except Alaska) and other industrial nations have already been used. Canada, Africa, South America, Southeast Asia, and Siberia, however, have major sites that can still be used. In the 1920s water power provided about one-third of all electricity used in the United States. Between 1950 and 1980 hydroelectric capacity in the United States more than doubled, but it provided only about 13 percent of the electricity and only about 4 percent of the total energy used in 1980.

Although operating costs are low for a hydroelectric plant, construction costs can be very high, depending on size, land costs, and the expense of relocating people and facilities flooded by the reservoir. Large-scale hydroelectric installations also harm the surrounding land, lowering water levels below the dam and submerging farmland, wildlife habitats, mineral deposits, timber areas, and historical and archaeological sites above it (Sections 6-3 and 15-4). As a result, the Wild and Scenic Rivers Act (Section 10-2) and pressure from environmentalists will kill some remaining major dam proposals in the United States.

One possibility is to revitalize some of the abandoned or underused small hydroelectric sites. Throughout the United States many of the nearly 50,000 existing small dams might be put back to work, providing as much electricity as 85 nuclear or coal-burning power plants at only a fraction of the cost. According to a U.S. Army Corps of Engineers study, at least 5,162 of these small dams could easily be put into use and supply electricity equal to that from six nuclear or coal-fired power plants. The environmental impact from rehabilitating these existing dams is often small and does not require any new technology. As always, there are some problems: (1) Silting may have cut reservoir capacity; (2) about 60 percent of these dams are on streams that usually dry up for part of the year; (3) American industries are geared to produce only large-scale hydroelectric machinery; and (4) the owners may block their use. Another promising potential for increasing the use of hydropower in the United States is to fill the empty turbine bays in existing large dams that are not being used to full capacity.

Despite the problems, developing these sources, along with improving energy efficiency, would be much simpler, cheaper, and more environmentally favorable than developing other major energy alternatives for producing electricity (such as nuclear and coal) (Tables 13-4, 13-5, and 13-7).

Tidal and Wave Power   Two potential sources of energy from the sea are *tidal power* (or moon power) and *wave power*. As the tide rises and falls, water flows into and out of bays and estuaries. If the bay or estuary can be closed by a dam, the energy in the tidal flow can be extracted 4 times a day and used to spin a turbine to produce electricity. But only about two dozen places in the world have enough change in water height between tides to provide economically feasible energy. Other problems are intermittent delivery of power, seawater corrosion, storm damage, and disruption of estuarine ecosystems. Today only two commercial tidal electric

installations are in use, one in France and one in the U.S.S.R. The only two feasible locations in the United States are the Cook Inlet in Alaska and Passamaquoddy Bay in Maine. Canada has the largest tidal fluctuation in the world—17 meters (55 feet)—in the areas along the Bay of Fundy. If this area and all other well-suited locations in the world were developed, they would produce electricity equivalent to only 13 nuclear or coal-burning power plants. Extracting this much tidal energy, however, could gradually slow down the revolution of the earth on its axis!

Wave energy is derived from wind energy, which in turn is derived from solar energy. Capturing this energy has been a dream since at least 1799, when two Frenchmen patented a wave-power device, and serious research is under way, especially in Japan, France and Great Britain, to develop devices for harnessing it. Despite such serious problems as high cost, interference with shipping, seawater corrosion, storm damage, variability in wave height, transmission of the energy to shore, and low net useful energy yields, some scientists believe that wave power machines could supply all of Great Britain's electricity needs cleanly, safely, and eternally. They also believe that energy from wave power may become economically feasible by 1990.

14-6   Solar Energy

Types of Solar Energy   Breeder reactors, nuclear fusion, and solar energy are the only energy alternatives that could support a high-energy civilization indefinitely and at the same time minimize the potential danger of climate change from emissions of carbon dioxide (Enrichment Study 3). But breeders have potentially serious environmental and economic problems (Section 14-3) and nuclear fusion is so complex it may never be economically and technically feasible (Section 14-4). In contrast, solar energy is an abundant, fairly clean and safe, virtually inexhaustible, and free fuel (Table 13-7). Thus, it is not surprising that more and more energy specialists see a mix of various forms of solar energy as an important energy alternative, as discussed by Denis Hayes in his Guest Editorial at the end of this chapter.

We usually think of solar energy simply as sunlight, but the term includes many other energy resources. Broadly defined, **solar energy** includes not only direct radiation from the sun but also indirect forms of solar energy produced when the sun heats the earth's surface and its atmosphere and when some of it is converted to stored chemical energy in trees and other plants. These

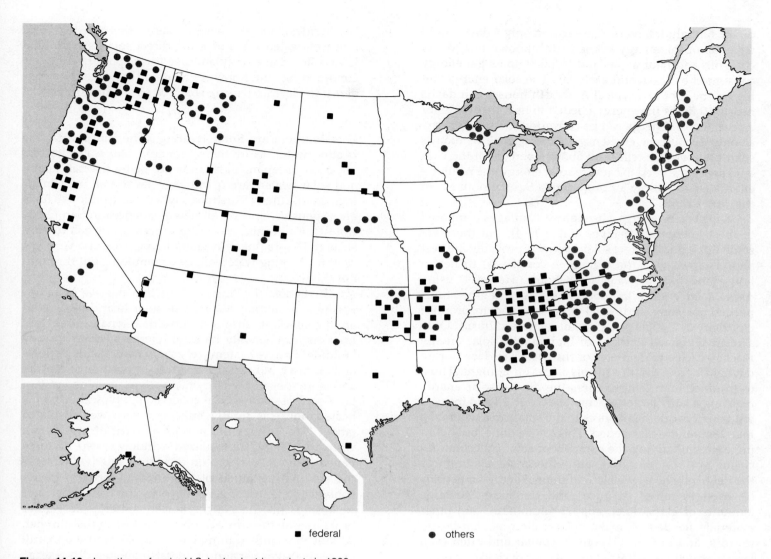

■ federal   ● others

Figure 14-10 Locations of major U.S. hydroelectric projects in 1980.

indirect forms of solar energy include wind power (Section 14-7), water power (Section 14-5), ocean power (stored in ocean temperature differences; Section 14-6), and biomass power (stored in plants) (Section 14-8). In 1980, direct and indirect solar energy, including wind, wood, and water provided about 7 percent of all energy used in the United States—more than twice that from nuclear power (see Figure 13-3). The Department of Energy and the Council on Environmental Quality estimated that these direct and indirect sources of solar energy could supply 20 to 25 percent of all U.S. energy needs by 2000 and more than half by 2020 with a $113 billion program. One observer went even further: solar energy

could provide 40 percent of the world's energy by 2000 and 75 percent by 2025. Others, however, estimate that solar energy might not provide any more than about 7 to 10 percent of U.S. energy needs by the end of the century. Whether we achieve a high or low use level of direct or indirect solar energy is in our own hands. These forms of renewable energy flows are already here, just waiting for us to tap them in an appropriate way.

Direct Solar Energy   Without solar energy our planet's temperature would be about $-268°C$ ($-450°F$). If concentrated and converted to usable forms of energy, the direct sunlight falling on the earth in only 3 days would equal all of the energy in the earth's known reserves of coal, oil, and natural gas and is 9,000 times the energy consumed by the world each day. The solar energy falling on the roof of a typical American house each day is nearly 10 times the energy needed to heat the house for a year. If solar energy can be converted to useful energy at only 10 percent efficiency (the efficiency of today's solar photovoltaic cells) and about 4 percent of the U.S. land area were used to capture solar energy, the resulting energy could supply all projected U.S. energy needs in the year 2000.

Direct solar energy has many advantages compared to most energy alternatives (Table 13-4), but there are some difficulties. Direct solar energy is probably the best and cheapest way (on a lifetime cost basis) to heat a house and to heat water for a home. However, using direct solar energy to produce the high temperatures needed for some industrial processes and to produce electricity at a solar power plant is more difficult. Only a relatively small amount of high-quality solar energy reaches each square meter of the earth's surface during daylight hours and the supply is cut off at night. Thus, to produce high temperatures the diffuse solar energy reaching a fairly large area must be collected and focused with mirrors or other devices to the small area where the high temperature is needed. This can be done, but building and maintaining the complex of solar collectors, focusing mirrors, plumbing, and other materials, reduces the net useful energy yield. Additional energy must also be used to mine, produce, and transport the large amounts of glass, steel, copper, aluminum, and other materials needed to make solar collectors, hardware, mirrors, and piping. Of course, similar and often even larger reductions in the net useful energy yield also occur with the building, maintaining, and supplying of fossil fuel fired industrial boilers and fossil fuel and nuclear plants.

A second difficulty is that some locations have more hours of sunlight on an average than others throughout the cold weather period. Despite this drawback, an efficient and airtight home with a properly designed passive solar heating system can get essentially all of its heating needs by using direct solar energy. Furthermore, with proper design for each type of climate such a home can be built practically anywhere in the United States. Such a passive solar energy home is also the cheapest way to heat a house on a lifetime cost basis. This already favorable economic advantage will increase as fossil fuel and electricity prices rise.

Besides photosynthesis in plants, there are two basic and well-tested ways of using direct solar energy. One is to collect the energy and use it for space heating, air conditioning, and hot water heating. The other is to convert it to electricity using solar, or photovoltaic, cells.

Low-Temperature Solar Heating The simplest task is heating water. More than 2 million solar water heaters are used in Japan, thousands are being used in Israel, and solar heaters are required by law on all new buildings in northern Australia, where conventional fuels are expensive, and on all new residences in San Diego County, California. As energy prices rise, small rooftop solar collectors (many of them homemade at a very low cost) for heating water will be a common sight throughout the world.

Direct solar heating can be either passive or active. *Passive solar heating systems* use solar heat directly, and are the simplest, cheapest, most maintenance-free, and least environmentally harmful energy systems for any building. Passive systems rely upon natural energy flows and upon a building's design and composition to capture and store the sun's energy rather than upon an array of fans, pumps, and special collectors. A typical passively heated house is tightly built and very well insulated (about 2 to 3 times the normal amount of insulation), with double- or triple-glazed windows (two or three panes with air between) on the south side (which faces the sun during much of day in the Northern Hemisphere) and few (if any) windows on the north, east, and west sides (in the Northern Hemisphere)—to reduce heat losses in the winter and overheating in the summer. All but the south wall may even be covered with earth (a passive solar version of an earth-sheltered house) to reduce heat losses and protect the house from the wind and outside temperature fluctuations. The south-facing windows also have an overhang or movable awnings to allow the sun to enter in winter (the low sun season) but not in the summer when the sun is higher. A large thermal mass (such as stone, concrete, adobe, brick, glass columns filled with water, or oil barrels filled with water) is built into the house to store the heat and slowly radiate it into the house at night or on a cloudy day, and help reduce temperature fluctuations year round. Easily movable or detachable (by means of simple magnetic clips) insulating panels may cover the windows at night to retard loss of heat stored in the building's walls and floors during the day. During hot weather the panels can be closed during the day and opened at night.

Other approaches include the following: (1) attaching a solar-heated greenhouse or solar room (if not used to grow food or plants) to the south-facing wall of the building (in the Northern Hemisphere) to serve as a solar collector and to grow food and ornamental plants, (2) putting a simple solar water heater inside the upper part of the solar greenhouse where it can never freeze, thus greatly reducing its complexity and cost; (3) reducing temperature variations by storing the solar energy in special south-facing, heat-storage walls (Trombe walls)*, water-filled metal drums, or several thousand water-filled bottles; and (4) storing the heat in a roof pond that is exposed to the sun during the day and covered with an insulated panel at night (and vice versa during the summer). A fairly low-cost air-to-air heat exchanger is used to provide ventilation and minimize the indoor air pollution that can build up in an airtight house. A well-designed passive solar heating system in a highly energy efficient house can provide all of its heat at almost any location. By 1980, there were at least 20,000 passive solar buildings in the United States (about half of them retrofits of older buildings) and by 1985 there could be at least a million such buildings. Davis, California, is one of the passive solar energy capitals of the United States. In 1977, the Davis city council adopted a building code that requires all buildings to have south-facing windows, shading from the summer sun, good ventilation, heavy insulation, and light-colored roofs and walls. A very successful 240-unit solar subdivision was built in Davis in the late 1970s. Several other solar subdivisions are being built in various parts of the United States, as well as in West Germany and England.

Passive solar heating coupled with improving energy efficiency is also the best and cheapest way to retrofit existing buildings. This is very important, since even if all the new homes and commercial structures built between 1980 and 2000 were solar buildings, they would make up only about one-third of the homes and buildings in the United States by the year 2000. Once an existing building has been made energy efficient (see Section 14-1), a passive solar greenhouse can easily be attached to the south side of the building without replacing the existing wall. Vents can be cut in the existing

wall and a fan can be used to circulate the captured heat into the house. Such a greenhouse can be built at a very low cost by a homeowner or can be bought in prefabricated form for about $2,000 to $3,000. Other possibilities include creating a Trombe wall by adding glazing (glass or plastic) a few centimeters outside of an existing masonry wall. Clerestory windows can also be added to the roof on many homes to admit more sunlight.

In a typical *active solar heating system*, either flat-plate solar collectors, evacuated tubes, or other even more efficient concentrators are mounted in the roof facing south and angled to capture the sun's rays. Flat-plate collectors are coated with a dark heat-absorbing substance covered by one or more glass or plastic transparent covers that trap the absorbed heat. Sunlight travels through the glass or plastic and is absorbed by the dark surface. Plastic, trickle collectors, paper, coils of copper, or other metal pipes are then attached to the collector to pick up and transfer the trapped heat to air or to a liquid (such as a water-antifreeze solution) circulating in the pipes behind the collector. This heat can then be pumped or blown into the heating system's radiators and ducts or stored in a large bed of rocks or an insulated hot water tank for release at night or in bad weather. Evacuated tube collectors can be twice as efficient and half as costly as flat-plate collectors. In 1980, a typical active solar heating system for a moderate-sized American home cost $5,000 to $12,000. These costs, however, can be cut considerably by building a highly energy efficient house (which cuts the solar system size 5- to 10-fold) and by having the collectors assembled at the building site instead of buying packaged collectors (cuts collector cost by a factor of 2 to 3). Even with such high initial cost, active solar heating systems are already economically feasible in much of the United States when both lifetime costs and federal, and often state, tax credits for installation (up to 60 percent of the cost) are considered. Active solar heating systems, however, require more materials (to build the collectors, pipes, and storage systems) than passive solar heating systems and thus have a lower net useful energy yield, are more expensive (initially and on a lifetime basis because of more maintenance and eventual replacement of deteriorated solar collectors), and have a greater environmental impact.

Solar energy can also cool buildings by evaporation, by other passive techniques (such as earth pipes buried underground that bring in cool and partially dehumidified air), and by driving absorption air conditioners. At present, absorption air conditioners are still too expensive for widespread use. The best solution, however, is

---

*A Trombe wall (named after its designer Felix Trombe) is a thermal-storage wall placed several centimeters inside a large expanse of glass (or plastic) on a building's south side (in the Northern Hemisphere). To provide thermal mass, the wall is either constructed of masonry or filled with water (usually in tall cylindrical columns) and is painted a dark color to absorb heat from the sun. Heat collected during the day is then slowly radiated to the rest of the house during the night.

to build a very energy-efficient home or to build an earth-sheltered house with only the south-facing wall exposed, so the house does not overheat in the first place. Before solar energy is used widely, people will have to establish solar rights to prevent a neighbor from putting up trees or buildings that block out the sun. In addition, home-owners should get adequate warranties for solar devices, and they must become aware of solar energy con artists. Solar energy is expected to be one of the biggest growth businesses in the United States over the coming decades. By 1980, Americans were already spending $280 million a year on solar heating units, and are projected to spend as much as $375 billion on such units between 1980 and 2000. This also means more jobs since the manufacture and installation of solar equipment (unlike building oil refineries and nuclear plants) is a labor-intensive industry.

High Temperature Solar Heating and Conversion to Electricity Researchers are looking for economically feasible technologies to concentrate solar energy to make high-temperature heat (solar-thermal approach) and convert solar energy directly to electricity with photo-voltaic cells (solar-electric approach).

One solar-thermal approach that is undergoing extensive evaluation is the power tower, or solar furnace. A 10- to 20-story-high tower containing a boiler is located near the center of a field containing hundreds of computer-controlled mirrors called *heliostats*. These mirrors track the sun and focus its rays on the boiler to produce steam, which can be used to produce electricity. A prototype, 1-megawatt power plant in southern France has been producing electricity since 1977. In the United States two prototype pilot power projects (one in Barstow, California, and the other in Sandia, New Mexico) were completed by 1981 and were being evaluated to see if such an approach is economically feasible. If these projects are successful, the next step will involve building a large (100-megawatt) power tower plant. Obviously, this approach needs a number of engineering break-throughs to become competitive for widespread use.

In the solar-electric approach, photovoltaic cells transform sunlight directly into electricity. The cell consists mainly of two layers of material, one a semiconductor (such as silicon, germanium, or cadmium sulfide) and the other a metal (such as aluminum or silver). When light strikes the cell, it causes electrons to flow between the two layers—the so-called photovoltaic effect—and generates electricity.

Solar cells have many advantages. Panels of them can be installed virtually anywhere—thus eliminating the need for long transmission lines. The cells are also safe (since they don't get hot), emit no pollution, and appear to have a long life. Photovoltaic cells are already used to power all U.S. space satellites, and some people envision solar cells being delivered to houses like rolls of roofing paper, tacked on south-facing roofs, and plugged in to provide more electricity than the average home needs. The solar power can also be used to charge the batteries in an electric car. The surplus electricity can be sold for a profit to the utility company. General Electric is already designing nail-on shingles of photovoltaic cells. But today's solar cells have such low-energy conversion efficiencies (10 to 15 percent) that they are much too costly for everyday use. For example, in 1980, the cells needed to provide all the electricity for an average (energy-inefficient) home would be about $20,000 a year. Researchers are trying to bring down the costs of the cells, and the U.S. Department of Energy believes that the cost per watt for electricity from solar cells can be made competitive with conventional sources of electricity by at least 1990 and perhaps by 1985.

However, some scientists doubt that solar cells will ever become cheap enough to make a significant contribution to energy needs. In addition to high costs, their use could eventually be limited by scarce supplies of arsenic, gallium, germanium, selenium, and cadmium used to make some promising types of solar cells. For this reason, the best hopes for making efficient, afford-able solar cells involve silicon—the second most abundant element in the earth's crust.

Other scientists expect affordable photovoltaic cells to become available very rapidly and to bankrupt utilities with billions of dollars tied up in coal, nuclear, and large hydroelectric power plants that will no longer be needed.

A futuristic—and extremely expensive—scheme is to build at least 60 solar-power satellites. The crew and materials to build each satellite—roughly the size of a small city—would be shuttled into space by a still to be designed freighter spacecraft, much larger than the U.S. space shuttle vehicle. After assembly in space, each satellite would be in a geosynchronous orbit 36,000 kilometers (23,300 miles) above the earth; there each satellite's orbital speed would match the earth's rotation, thus holding the satellite over the same spot on earth for continuous transmission of energy to a receiver on earth. Each satellite would be covered with some 10 billion solar cells. These cells would be bathed in solar energy (which is more intense in space than on the earth's surface) almost continuously, interrupted only twice a year at the equinoxes when the satellite would pass through the earth's shadow for periods up to 72 minutes. The solar energy hitting the cells would be converted to electricity, which would then be beamed back as microwaves to a fixed position on earth. On the earth, giant 225-square kilometer (55,000-acre) microwave antenna farms, called *rectennas,* would receive the microwaves, convert them to electricity, and feed it out over the nation through high-voltage power lines.

The estimated cost for the first satellite—to be in operation by 2010—is at least $100 billion. The entire system of 60 satellites, which would be in place by 2025, would cost at least $1 trillion—29 times the cost of the lunar space program. This costly system would supply only 20 percent of the projected U.S. electricity demand by the year 2025 and only a few percent of the nation's total energy. Even if the formidible technical problems could be solved, the program would drain virtually all available funds for other energy alternatives. To make matters worse, preliminary estimates indicate that the system will not produce much net useful energy.

This proposal also has other potentially serious problems. Of the renewable energy alternatives, satellite power stations (along with new large-scale hydroelectric dams and large biomass plantations) have the worst environmental impact. The hydrochloric acid and other pollutants emitted into the atmosphere by the large number of space shuttle flights (200 per satellite) could affect global climate and deplete the vital ozone layer. To build the entire system, these flights would have to take place every day for 30 years. The microwave beams would probably interfere with military and commercial radar systems, disrupt flight patterns for airplanes, and destroy many migratory birds (birds flying through the beams could be cooked to death, similar to putting them in a microwave oven). The 60-satellite scheme would require about 1.5 percent of all U.S. land area for the rectennas and massive amounts of materials (such as aluminum, steel, and cement), whose production would consume large amounts of energy, thus reducing the net useful energy yield. In addition, the microwaves beamed to earth might harm humans by causing cataracts, genetic damage, and injury to the central nervous system. To make matters worse, the solar satellites could easily be destroyed (for example, by inexpensive weather rockets loaded with buckshot).

Actually, the only significant advantage of the space satellite system is that it would provide electricity 24 hours a day, but the demand for electricity between 1 A.M. and 6 A.M. is not large enough to offset the disadvantages. Furthermore, this is another high-technology project to provide the United States with electricity—a form of energy not really needed in large quantities to perform the tasks for which it is best suited (see Section 13-3). Even if the electricity were needed, the success of the project depends (among other things) on being able to produce affordable solar cells. If this becomes feasible, it will be much easier and cheaper for people to lay the cells on their roofs and sell their excess power to the utility company than to buy expensive satellite-produced electricity from the utility company. Nevertheless, the space and military industry, NASA, and the Department of Defense (because of the military potential of using microwave satellites as mechanisms to disrupt enemy communications and as space stations for high-powered antiballistic missile systems) are pressuring Congress to fund this project, and the project is under serious consideration by the Department of Energy.

Energy from Ocean Thermal Gradients Another potential indirect source of solar energy is **ocean thermal gradients**—the temperature differences between sun-warmed surface waters and the cold ocean depths. Like a vast storage tank, the world's oceans collect and store nearly 75 percent of the solar energy striking the earth for us free of charge.

One way to tap this energy would be to build a floating *Ocean Thermal Energy Conversion* (OTEC) plant in a deep tropical ocean where there is a large temperature difference between the warm surface water and the cold bottom water. For the United States, such sites might be in the Gulf of Mexico (which is also subject to hurricanes and strong currents) and off the coasts of Puerto Rico, Hawaii, and Guam. Each OTEC plant would be a gigantic floating platform with massive pipes reaching down as far as 905 meters (3,000 feet) to the ocean bottom. Each pipe would be large enough to enclose 5 stacked Washington Monuments. The system would use warm ocean water to vaporize a low-boiling liquid such as ammonia. The resulting vapor would then expand and drive a turbine to generate electricity. Cold water pumped up from the ocean bottom by pumps larger than any ever devised would be used to condense the vapor back to the liquid state for reuse. A large cable might transmit the electricity to shore, or the plant could use its electricity to desalinate ocean water and extract minerals and chemicals from the sea. Another alternative would be to use the electricity to electrolyze water to produce hydrogen gas which could be piped or transported to shore for use as a fuel (Section 14-8). In addition, the nutrients brought up from the ocean bottom by the plant might nourish schools of fish and shellfish (Section 9-5).

The technology for developing such plants on a small scale is fairly well developed, but an economic and satisfactory method for transmitting electricity to land has yet to be worked out. The Department of Energy estimates that large commercial OTEC plants would cost 2 to 3 times more to build than a comparable coal-fired power plant. The fuel for the OTEC plant, however, would be free. The costs of operating and maintaining the plant and transmitting the electricity it produces to shore are still unknown. In 1979, a U.S. Navy scow, converted to a small-scale OTEC plant and moored off the coast of Hawaii, produced more energy (as electricity) than it consumed. Advocates of this approach believe that with enough research and development funding, large-scale OTEC plants could be built within 5 to 10 years and could meet 1 to 5 percent of all U.S. energy needs by 2000. Encouraged by the success of the pilot OTEC plant off the coast of Hawaii, Congress passed legislation in 1980 setting up $2 billion in loan-guarantees to underwrite the development of commercial OTEC plants by 2000.

But these rosy projections are clouded by problems: (1) seawater corrosion, (2) damage from severe storms, (3) few good sites—usually they are far offshore in tropical oceans and often far from population centers, (4) transmission of the electricity (or hydrogen gas produced by the electricity) long distances to shore, (5) unknown and potentially harmful changes in the ecology of large ocean areas, (6) an energy-conversion efficiency of only 2 to 3 percent, and (7) fouling of the plant by biological organisms. In addition, this is another scheme for producing large amounts of electricity that may not be needed (Section 13-3).

Because of this low energy efficiency, the net useful energy yield will probably be low. Moreover, a third of the energy produced would have to be used to pump the enormous amounts of water through the plant, with a moderate-sized (100-megawatt) plant having to pump water *each second* greater than the average flow rate of the Potomac River near Washington, D.C. Withdrawing very large amounts of heat from the Gulf Stream might affect the climate of western Europe. Although nutrients brought up from the ocean depths by OTEC plants could increase fish catches, more carbon dioxide might be released from the ocean to the atmosphere, possibly affecting global climate (Enrichment Study 3). Despite the enthusiasm of OTEC advocates, this energy source may never compete economically with other alternatives.

Summary of Solar Energy Development   Before we get carried away with the use of high technology, centralized solar energy systems to provide high temperatures and electricity, we need to remember the second law of energy (Section 3-3). Since solar energy itself is decentralized or spread out, it makes more thermodynamic and economic sense to capture and use it for low-temperature heating for individual homes and small buildings and moderate temperature process heat for industry. For space heating the emphasis should be on passive rather than active solar heating systems (except for hot water heaters), since they are cheaper and involve no expensive collectors and plumbing that have to be maintained and occasionally replaced. Decentralized, intermediate, solar energy technology can be a major tool in helping us make the transition to a low-entropy producing, sustainable earth society.

Large corporations (especially oil companies) are nevertheless encouraging the high technology, centralized approach to solar energy. This allows them control over the use and cost of solar energy. By 1980, eight of the nine largest photovoltaic firms in the United States had been bought up in whole or in part by large corporations, five of them major oil companies. Major oil companies are also buying up major photovoltaic patents. In addition, by 1979 big corporations had bought up 12 of the 25 largest companies making active solar collectors. To counteract this potential control of solar energy by large energy companies, the government should (1) give large tax credits (up to 50 percent) to people who build passive solar homes and commercial buildings or retrofit existing ones; (2) require that all new federal, state, and privately owned buildings incorporate passive solar design features by 1985; (3) increase tax credits (up to 50 percent) to homeowners and businesses who use active solar devices; (4) greatly increase federal support for the development of low-temperature solar energy as a major energy alternative; and (5) prohibit any energy company (such as an oil company) from owning enough stock, reserves, or major patents to control the use and price of another energy alternative (Section 13-6).

The federal budget for research and development of direct solar energy increased more than fourfold between 1975 and 1981. But in 1981 the proposed government expenditures for direct solar energy amounted to

8 percent of its total energy budget, and most of this was for the high technology approach (Table 13-8)—a trifling amount compared to the importance of low-temperature solar energy. Fortunately, we don't have to wait for the government to act. Solar heating requires such simple and readily available technology—compared to building large, centralized power plants to produce electricity that is wastefully used for space heating—that people can take matters into their own hands.

14-7 Wind and Geothermal Energy

Wind Power: An Indirect Form of Solar Energy Wind is an indirect form of solar energy that can be used to produce electricity, perform mechanical work (such as grinding grain), pump heat or water, and compress air. Wind energy is produced by the unequal heating of the earth and its atmosphere by the sun. It is then given characteristic flow patterns by the earth's rotation. In the early 1900s more than 6 million windmills pumped water and generated electricity in rural areas throughout the United States. By the 1940s cheap hydropower, fossil fuels, and rural electrification replaced most of these windmills. In 1941 the world's largest wind turbine was built on a mountaintop in central Vermont, but one of its massive rotors (built with scrap materials) broke off during a storm. Because of a wartime shortage of materials and a lack of funds by the investor, the project was abandoned. The still unfulfilled promise of cheap nuclear power caused the United States to abandon the development of wind turbines to produce electricity—a trend that may be reversed in the next few decades.

Wind is an almost unlimited, free, renewable, clean, and safe source of energy that has a moderate net useful energy yield and is based on a fairly well developed technology (Tables 13-4, 13-5, and 13-7). Wind energy in a windy site can be tapped 24 hours a day. The World Meterological Organization estimates that tapping the choicest wind sites around the world (not even including large clusters of wind turbines at sea) could produce about 13 times the electricity now produced in the world each year. The total amount of wind energy available in the United States is enormous—amounting to about 20 times today's yearly consumption of energy. Experts estimate that, with a vigorous development program, wind energy could provide 13 to 19 percent of the projected demand for electricity in the United States by 2000.

Wind power expert William E. Heronemus suggests that a band of about 300,000 to 1 million giant 260 meter-high (850-feet high) wind turbines in the high-wind belt from Texas to the Dakotas could provide half of the annual electrical needs of the United States. For the heavily populated eastern seaboard, these huge wind turbines could float on offshore platforms. In this case electricity produced from the wind would probably be used to produce hydrogen gas from the electrolysis of sea water. The hydrogen gas could then be piped or shipped to land as fuel for homes, factories, and cars. Heronemus believes that enough hydrogen could be produced to supply all of the heating needs of the industrial Northeast. A 1980 study by the National Swedish Board for Energy Source Development concluded that offshore wind turbines are both technically and economically feasible.

There is no doubt that wind turbines work. In Hawaii, Puerto Rico, Rhode Island, Ohio, and North Carolina, large wind generators are being operated under government-sponsored test programs. A government-sponsored wind turbine in Clayton, New Mexico, already provides electricity for more than half of the town's 3,000 residents. The State of California is moving ahead rapidly with wind power development on its own, with a goal of using wind to generate at least 10 percent of the state's electricity needs by 2000. In fact, the largest wind energy system on earth is planned for Pacheco Pass, California. There a private windpower company from Massachusetts plans to install, operate, and maintain 2,000 windmills to provide power at a very low price to the California Department of Water Resources, the state's largest user of electricity. Large experimental wind turbines are also being constructed in Sweden, Denmark, Great Britain, and West Germany. Research by Boeing, General Electric, and Rockwell International indicates that large-scale wind generators could be built within a few years at about half of what it would cost for a nuclear power plant to produce an equivalent amount of energy. Building large wind systems will also generate about 2 to 4 times as many jobs as building coal or nuclear power plants. These companies argue that all that is needed for mass production is a guarantee of enough government orders to reduce the financial risks involved to establish a wind power industry.

Other observers believe that building large-scale wind systems to produce large quantities of electricity is not the way to go, since more electricity is already being produced than is needed to perform the tasks where it is really needed. Some of these observers think developing sophisticated moderate-size wind turbines to be shared by a small community or group of homeowners makes more economic sense. Smaller wind turbines are easier to mass-produce, and their small rotors are less vulnerable to the stress and metal fatigue that makes large wind turbines so expensive to build and maintain. In addition, small windmills can produce more power in light winds than large ones and can thus operate a greater percentage of the time. They are also easier to locate close to the ultimate users (thus reducing electricity transmission costs). Finally, small-scale turbines allow greater decentralization of ownership and control and reduce the impact from equipment failure.

Local wind conditions determine whether a specific site is suitable for wind power. Its use is limited to areas having fairly steady and moderate winds—neither too weak nor too strong (which could damage the rotors). The minimum average annual wind speed normally practical for a home or small community wind system is about 16 to 19 kilometers per hour (10 to 12 miles per hour). Figure 14-11 shows the general feasibility for using wind energy in the United States (excluding Alaska and Hawaii, which contain some of the world's best wind areas). There are many locally favorable exceptions to this generalized map. Local exceptions often include hilltops (except those having air turbulence), some coastal areas, lakeside sites, and unobstructed areas on flat, windy plains.

In 1980, the price for a wind system that could provide most (if not all) of the electricity needs of a typical home in a suitable location ranged from $5,000 to $20,000 completely installed, but with no power storage system. This fairly high cost can be greatly reduced by the 40 to 60 percent tax credits now available from the federal government and in some states. Further savings can be obtained by using reconditioned wind turbines. Do-it-yourself projects can be built for little or nothing. One system using wood propellers and a car alternator salvaged from a junkyard cost only $75 to build (excluding the homeowner's labor). In 1980, any home in a suitable wind area and with monthly electric bills of $200, could save money on a lifetime-cost basis by installing a home wind generator and using the local utility company for backup when the wind isn't blowing. This economic break-even point will drop sharply when wind system costs can be reduced through mass production and with the average cost of electricity projected to double between 1979 and 1984, and to double again by 1990. Owners of home wind systems can also save money on gasoline by using the electricity produced at night (when

home needs are low) to recharge the batteries in an electric car.

Additional savings can be made by selling surplus electricity to the local power company. In 1978, Congress passed the Public Utilities Regulatory Policies Act (PURPA). It requires electric utilities to buy excess electricity from customers who develop wind, small hydro, geothermal, solar, biomass, cogeneration, and other small-scale power producing systems. Utilities must buy the power from a customer at the same average price it costs them to generate electricity. This act also requires utilities to sell back-up power to small power producers at reasonable rates. This should prevent utility companies from discouraging small power producers by charging them very high rates for serving as a back-up supply of electricity. Thus, for the first time people who invest in renewable energy alternatives to produce electricity have a guaranteed market for selling any surplus power they produce.

Wind energy does have its problems, however. As shown in Figure 14-11, its use is limited to certain favorable areas. Another problem is the need to store the energy for use when the wind isn't blowing, unless the local electric utility company supplies back-up power. Today, wind energy can be stored for use in homes and small buildings by charging batteries, producing hydrogen gas to be used as a fuel, or using a flywheel. While spinning, the flywheel stores energy, which can be tapped as it runs down after the wind stops. A good home flywheel system can provide electrical power for a week of windless days. If the electricity were fed into the lines of an electric utility, energy from the wind could be stored by using it to pump water into a huge reservoir or to compress air in an underground deposit. Released on windless days, the water or air could operate an electric generator.

Other proposals bypass the need for storage. For example, a series of windmills (probably on top of existing electric transmission towers) could be coupled directly to the regional utility power grid to provide a base of power with no fuel costs. On windless days the system could be boosted by other fuel sources. In addition, homeowners or small communities with wind generators could sell excess electricity to utilities when the wind was blowing and then buy electricity from the utilities when the wind died down.

One environmental objection to wind power is the visual pollution created by large turbines dotting the landscape, especially in areas of high prevailing winds, where turbines would be concentrated. This would be

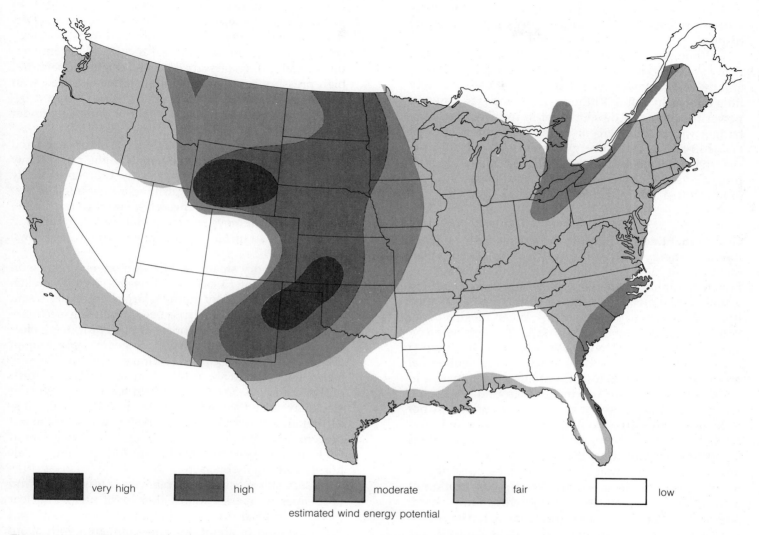

| very high | high | moderate | fair | low |

estimated wind energy potential

Figure 14-11 General areas of greatest wind energy potential in the United States (excluding Alaska and Hawaii, which contain some of the world's best wind areas). There are numerous local exceptions to the general trends shown on this map.

similar to the visual pollution created by today's large electrical transmission lines. Low-frequency noise pollution may also be a problem, but can be eliminated by proper design. The giant federally-sponsored wind turbine atop a mountain in Boone, North Carolina, is being altered to reduce noise levels because of residents' complaints.

We also need to determine whether several wind turbines in one area could affect the local weather or migratory-bird flight patterns. Large wind turbines can also interfere with TV reception and microwave communications, depending on the site. However, the use of fiberglass blades (also much cheaper than metal blades) would cut TV interference in half. Also, although their environmental impact will be small compared with that of most other energy alternatives (Table 13-7), wind systems will require moderate amounts of materials whose mining, manufacturing, processing, and waste disposal will affect the environment.

Although the potential for wind power is great in many areas and its technology well developed, industry and the federal government have so far shown relatively little interest in it. In 1981 the amount proposed for wind power research and development in the federal energy budget was only 2 percent of the total energy budget (Table 13-8). The Wind Energy Systems Act of 1980, however, has initiated a fairly modest, $900 million federal program to develop cost-effective wind-power systems in the United States by 1988.

Geothermal Energy: Tapping the Earth's Heat—or geothermal energy—or earth heat—is produced when rocks lying deep below the earth's surface are heated to high temperatures by energy from the decay of radioactive elements in the earth and from magma (the molten rock within the earth). When magma penetrates through to the earth's surface, it erupts as a volcano. But when it does not reach the surface, the trapped magma heats rocks near the surface to form geothermal reservoirs—analogous to concentrations of minerals in ore deposits or petroleum in underground reservoirs. The resulting heat energy may remain trapped in hot rocks or be transferred to underground water and form hot water or steam. Natural crevices, such as hot springs or geysers, or drilled geothermal wells can then bring this steam or hot water to the surface. Geothermal resources can be used for the direct space heating of homes and greenhouses, drying crops and wood, processing food and various industrial materials requiring low to moderate temperatures, and distilling ethanol for use as a fuel.

Geothermal reservoirs must be used in the region where they are found, which is usually the site of volcanic and mountain-building activity. Geothermal energy can be considered a renewable energy source if deep underground, continuous heat flows can be tapped. Outside these zones geothermal energy is not a renewable resource. In this case, geothermal reservoirs could be depleted. At least 80 nations have geological conditions favorable for geothermal energy. Because geothermal energy is cheap, almost inexhaustible, and in some cases has a moderate environmental impact (Tables 13-4, 13-5, and 13-7), it is already being developed in 25 countries.

There are three major types of geothermal resources: (1) *hydrothermal reservoirs* consist either of dry steam, hot water, or a mixture of the two trapped in fractured rocks below impermeable layers of the earth's crust; (2) *hot dry rock zones* where magma has penetrated into the earth's crust and is heating subsurface rock to high temperatures; and (3) *geopressurized zones*, high-temperature, high-pressure reservoirs of water (often saturated with natural gas because of the high pressure) trapped beneath impermeable beds of shale or clay, usually under ocean beds.

Dry steam hydrothermal deposits are the preferred geothermal resource, but they are also the rarest. Only dry steam wells can be tapped easily and economically at present. This is done by drilling a hole into the reservoir, releasing the superheated steam through a pipe, filtering out to remove solid material, and then piping it out directly to a turbine to generate electricity, as shown in Figure 14-12.

A typical dry steam well has a moderate net useful energy output of 13 calories of useful energy for each calorie of useful energy input. A large natural dry steam well near Larderello, Italy, has been producing electricity since 1904 and is a major source of power for Italy's electric railroads. Three other major dry steam sites are Japan (Matsukawa), New Zealand (Wairakei), and the Geysers steam field, located about 145 kilometers (90 miles) north of San Francisco. The Geysers field has been producing electricity since 1960 more cheaply than comparable fossil fuel and nuclear plants. By 1980 it was supplying 2 percent of California's electricity, and its owner, Union Oil Company, believes it could supply 25 percent of California's electricity by 1990.

A dry steam geothermal plant costs less to build and is cheaper to operate than either fossil fuel or nuclear plants. A typical dry geothermal plant can also be put into operation in about 3 years—compared with about 5 to 10 years for a fossil fuel plant and 12 to 15 for a nuclear plant—and should have a useful life of 30 to 50 years before the geothermal deposit is depleted.

Wet or hot water hydrothermal reservoirs, with a net useful energy ratio of 11 calories output per calorie input, are much more common, and are already generating electricity in New Zealand (Wairakei), Mexico, Japan, the Soviet Union, and Iceland. Reykjavik, the capital of Iceland, has been 99 percent heated by geothermal energy for years. In the United States, most accessible and fairly hot geothermal sites lie in the West (Figure 14-13). By 1980, low-to-moderate temperature wet hydrothermal reservoirs were being used in over 180 locations in the United States. In South Dakota, they dry crops and heat

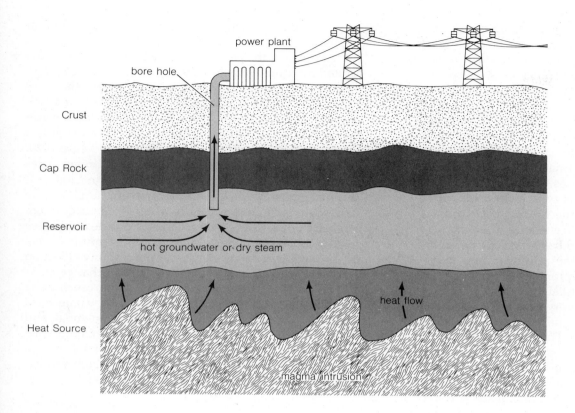

Figure 14-12 Dry (steam) or wet (hot water or brine plus steam) geothermal well and power plant.

power plant

bore hole

Crust

Cap Rock

Reservoir

hot groundwater or dry steam

Heat Source

heat flow

magma/intrusion

farm buildings; in Idaho they heat homes and fish ponds; and in Oregon they are used to heat homes, hospitals, and school buildings and to grow mushrooms and trees. Some cities in California, Colorado, Idaho, and Oregon, will soon have district heating systems powered by wet hydrothermal reservoirs.

One expert estimated that just the hot water geothermal resources below southern California's Imperial Valley could produce enough electrical energy to meet the needs of the entire American Southwest for at least 200 years. As energy prices rise, there is also increasing interest in exploiting low-to-moderate temperature (below 125°C) wet geothermal deposits found in other parts of the United States, especially along the East Coast between New Jersey and Florida, where exploratory wells are being drilled. These deposits are too cool for generating electricity, but if they can be tapped at an acceptable cost, they could be used for residential space heating, drying crops and wood, district heating, and industrial processing.

In wet fields, the steam is mixed with hot water or mineral-laden brine. Such fields can provide energy in three ways: the existing steam separated from the hot water, hot water converted to steam, or hot water used to vaporize another low-boiling-point liquid that can then be used to drive a turbine. The main problem is brine, which corrodes metal parts, clogs pipes, and could pollute nearby water sources.

Another method now being tested avoids these problems completely. A heat exchanger containing a low-boiling-point liquid (such as isobutane or Freon) is immersed in the underground well. The heat from the hot water is used to vaporize the liquid, which is then brought to the surface to spin the turbine. Not only does this avoid corrosion and wastewater problems, but it leaves the water and steam in the well for continual reheating rather than depleting the resource.

Hot dry rock deposits lying deep underground are potentially the largest and most widely distributed geothermal resource in the United States. This resource is tapped by drilling a well in the hot rock, fracturing the rock (by injecting water at high pressure or by using conventional or nuclear explosives), injecting a fluid (such as water) to absorb the heat, and removing the heated fluid through a second well. After the heat is extracted, the cooled water could be sent down the first well again—thus reducing water use and pollution. This approach also eliminates most air pollution. Several experimental projects are already operating in the United States. However, before this approach can be developed on a commercial scale, several technical problems associated with the rock fracturing process must be solved and the economics of the process must be evaluated.

So far little is known about the *geopressurized zones* that lie far beneath ocean beds in the Gulf of Mexico. These high temperature, high pressure reservoirs contain large quantities of hot water, and are also often saturated with large quantities of natural gas that would significantly expand U.S. reserves. Thus, if tapped they could yield three types of energy: (1) electrical (from high-temperature water); (2) mechanical or hydraulic (from the high pressure); and (3) chemical (from the natural gas). These resources could be tapped by very deep (and expensive) drilling, but the extremely high pressures create some technical problems that must be solved. At present, this potential type of geothermal resource is at the early, exploratory phase.

There are some potentially harmful environmental effects from geothermal energy. These vary widely from each site and with the type of geothermal resources being used, but most experts consider them to be less than or at worst about equal to those from fossil fuel and nuclear power plants (Table 13-7). Mineral-laden water wastes are produced from most geothermal reservoirs, but they could be injected back into the deep wells or desalinated to produce fresh water and salable minerals. Reinjection, however, would not be feasible for geopressurized sites, because of the great depths and high pressures. Large-scale withdrawal of geothermal fluids (especially from wet hydrothermal reservoirs and geopressurized zones) could lead to sinking of the land (subsidence) and earthquakes, but reinjecting the fluids into the wells could minimize this danger. Air pollution occurs in most wells from the trace of highly toxic hydrogen sulfide (which smells like rotten eggs) in the steam. This could be controlled by emission devices (Section 17-4) or eliminated by using an underground heat-transfer system. At present, there are no federal standards regulating such emissions, although some states (such as California) have established standards. There is also concern over emissions of radioactive radium-226 and radon-222, toxic mercury compounds (and other toxic heavy metal compounds), and boron (which can cause leaf burn on sensitive nearby trees). Noise pollution (Enrichment Study 13) also occurs because of the earsplitting hiss of escaping steam, but can be reduced by appropriate muffling systems. As with most energy sources, waste heat injected into the atmosphere or bodies of cooling water is a problem (Section 16-4), but no

more so for geothermal than for fossil fuel and nuclear plants.

At present, the potential of geothermal energy in the United States remains largely unknown. Estimates vary widely. The Department of Energy estimates that geothermal resources could meet 6 to 7 percent of total U.S. energy needs by 2080. Others believe that with a vigorous development program this resource could supply a much larger fraction of U.S. energy needs before 2020.

So far, most geothermal deposits in the United States remain undeveloped for several reasons. First, most of the rich ones are on government-owned lands in the Rocky Mountain states (Figure 13-13). The government has been slow in leasing these lands to private companies for exploratory drilling and development primarily because of concern over water rights and resources (Section 13-5). Second, there are legal problems in that geothermal deposits are classified as mineral resources in some states, water resources in others, and as a vague third category in still others. Finally, despite its potential, and despite increased funding as a result of the Geothermal Act of 1974, geothermal energy received only about 3 percent of the proposed U.S. energy research and development expenditures for 1981 (Table 13-8).

14-8 Biomass, Biofuels, Urban Wastes, and Hydrogen Gas

Plant Power: Indirect Solar Energy from Biomass Another indirect source of solar energy is plant biomass—the earth's plant life produced by photosynthesis. Biomass is a catchall category that includes trees and wood wastes, agricultural crops and wastes, and aquatic plants such as algae and kelp. It can also include animal wastes and municipal sewage and wastes that are derived from plants. The biomass produced in the world each year contains energy equal to about 6 times the energy used in the world each year. In 1980, biomass supplied 19 percent of the world's primary energy (Figure 13-2) and 3 percent of all primary energy used in the United States (mostly from wood wastes burned for fuel by the pulp paper and forest industries). Thus, in the United States biomass energy (without billions of dollars for government subsidies and the need to build expensive power plants) equalled nuclear power as an energy source in 1980. The U.S. Office of Technology Assessment projects that biomass energy could supply 15 to 18 percent of the total energy needs of the United States by the year 2000, with a much more vigorous program of

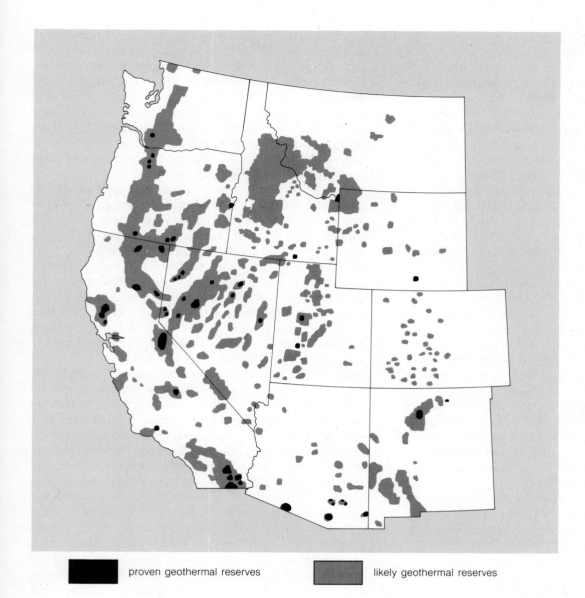

Figure 14-13 Most of the proven and potential geothermal fields in the United States are located in the West.

proven geothermal reserves   likely geothermal reserves

research and development, with tax incentives, and with a drop in energy demand due to increased energy efficiency. One study suggests that waste wood (such as trimmings, scraps, sawdust) alone could supply 12 percent of all U.S. energy needs by the year 2000.

Biomass energy has several appealing advantages (Tables 13-4 and 13-5). Like other types of solar energy, it is renewable; unlike direct solar energy, it has no storage problem. The solar energy is naturally stored in the leaves, stems, and trunks of plants and trees, and can be tapped as needed either by direct burning or by conversion to gas or liquid **biofuels** (fuels derived from biomass), such as synthetic natural gas (methane) and

alcohols. When collected and burned directly near its source, biomass has a moderate to high (if efficiently burned) net useful energy yield, but yields are low when the biomass must be collected in areas of sparse plant growth and then transported long distances for use. This efficiency is about equal to that for a conventional nuclear power plant and lower than that for a coal-fired plant. Because biomass and biofuels are low in sulfur, they cause less air pollution from sulfur dioxide than the burning of coal and oil. They also yield smaller amounts of both large particulates, which are easier to filter out, and nitrogen oxides. Emission of fine particles (which are most hazardous to human health), however, are larger with some types of biomass. As long as trees and plants are not cut faster than they grow back, burning biomass and biofuels will not add to the net amount of carbon dioxide in the atmosphere (since plants use carbon dioxide in photosynthesis).

Wood and wood wastes are the most commonly used forms of biomass. In less developed nations, wood is a major source of energy. As energy prices have risen, Americans have rediscovered the wood-burning stove. Fireplaces, which are only 10 percent efficient, can remove more heat from a home than they add (because as the heat goes up the chimney it drains heated air out of the house unless the room with the fireplace is carefully sealed off from the rest of the house). Good wood stoves, costing about $200 to $1,000 ($400 to $2,000 installed) are about 30 to 90 percent efficient (compared with 60 to 75 percent for oil or gas furnaces)* and throw their heat into the room instead of up the chimney. Many stoves also have automatic thermostats (dampers), enabling two or three hardwood logs to last for 8 to 12 hours. Between 1970 and 1980 the private use of wood as a source of energy in the United States grew more than sixfold. By 1980, about 7 percent of the homes in the United States were totally or partially heated with wood stoves or furnaces, and the proportion is steadily increasing. Sales of wood stoves in the United States soared from about 150,000 in 1973 (before the Arab oil embargo) to about 1.5 million in 1979. Many homeowners are holding off buying a wood stove in the hope that Congress will pass a tax credit for their purchase.

In 1980, a homeowner with an oil-burning furnace could save money by switching to an efficient wood stove (at least 50 percent efficiency) if a cord of wood† could be purchased for less than $150; with electric heating the switch would save money with a cord of wood costing less than $190 and higher in areas with high electricity rates; and for natural gas heating if a cord costs less than $70 (although this latter figure will rise as natural gas prices are gradually deregulated). The Tennessee Valley Authority provides interest-free loans up to $800 for customers wishing to switch from electrical heating to wood stoves.

---

*A well designed airtight wood stove should have an efficiency of 50 to 65 percent. Massive "Finnish" or "Russian" brick wood stoves reportedly are 90 percent efficient. They are built with a convoluted series of baffles that delay the exhaust of the hot gases and allow the brick to absorb the heat and radiate most of the heat into the house.

†A cord of wood is a stack of wood 1.2 meters (4 feet) high, 1.2 meters (4 feet) deep, and 2.4 meters (8 feet) high. A cord of well-seasoned hardwood contains roughly as much as 568 liters (150 gallons) of heating oil. It takes from 3 to 8 cords of wood to heat a house, depending on its size and energy efficiency and the efficiency of the wood stove.

Wood-fired boilers are also making a comeback in industry. The U.S. pulp and paper industry provides 50 percent of its energy needs by burning wood wastes. Wood products industries or other industries located close to sources of sawdust, wood chips and pellets, and other forms of wood wastes have installed wood-fueled boilers that can pay for themselves in only a few years by the oil, electricity, or natural gas saved. In 1980, Congress allocated $437 million to encourage the use of wood wastes generated by logging operations.

Using wood as a major energy source does have its problems. Wood has a much lower energy content per unit of weight than coal, oil, or natural gas, and it also contains a lot of water that must be removed by drying. Thus, large quantities of wood must be cut to get the amount of energy provided by a much smaller quantity of fossil fuel, and fossil fuel energy is often used to dry the wood out. Intensive tree farming (unless done with great care) could cause extensive deforestation (Section 10-4), erosion, siltation, flooding, and loss of wildlife habitat (Section 10-7), deplete soil nutrients; and pollute water with erosion and runoff of fertilizers and pesticides. Wood-burning stoves also greatly increase the chances of home fires, can create an atmospheric haze, and could create serious public health problems from the soot, small particles and cancer-causing substances they emit into the air. They can also cause indoor air-pollution in well-insulated, tightly sealed, energy-efficient homes, unless air-to-air heat exchangers are installed (especially from the more efficient wood stoves—except the "Finnish" or "Russian" brick stove). Some areas may soon have to enact emission standards for wood stoves that will require installation of air pollution control devices on chimneys—making wood a more costly fuel to burn. In London and in South Korean cities wood fires have already been banned to reduce air pollution. There is also concern that new wood-harvesting machines that can swallow and grind up an entire tree in 30 seconds will deplete soil fertility by leaving no small limbs, leaves, and debris to rot and replenish the earth. From an environmental standpoint, intensively managed biomass plantations (along with satellite solar power stations and new large hydroelectric dams) are the worst renewable energy options.

In agricultural areas, crop residues (the inedible, unharvested portions of food crops) and animal manure can be collected and burned or converted to biofuels. But most plant residues are widely dispersed and require large amounts of energy to collect, dry, and transport—unless collected along with harvested crops. In addition, it makes more sense ecologically to use these valuable nutrients to feed livestock, retard erosion, and fertilize the soil (Enrichment Study 16). There is also greatly increased interest in burning urban wastes as a source of energy, as discussed in more detail in Enrichment Study 15. But it may be more sound ecologically to compost or recycle these organic wastes rather than burn them (Table 12-2; Enrichment Study 15).

Another approach is to establish large *energy plantations*, where specific trees, grasses, or other crops would be grown for biomass. This biomass would be directly burned, converted to biofuels, or converted to plastics, rubber, and other products produced from petroleum and natural gas (Figure 14-1). Ideal energy crops would be fast-growing, high-yield perennials that reproduce themselves from cuttings (since seed requires costly collection and sowing). Possible crops include warm-season grasses (such as Sudan grass, Bermuda grass, sugarcane, sorghum, and cassava) and certain deciduous trees (such as alder, poplar, eucalyptus, cottonwood, and sycamore). Grasses would be harvested every few weeks. Trees, planted close together like crops, would be harvested by clear-cutting every 3 to 4 years on a rotating schedule. This approach, however, can be environmentally destructive (Section 10-4) and can strip the soil of certain nutrients.

The Department of Energy is presently funding an experimental "energy plantation" in South Carolina that will grow fuel trees like agricultural crops. Sweden (with no coal, oil, or natural gas of its own) is considering switching to wood as its prime energy source by using plantations of fast-growing trees. Tree plantations, however, could compete with food crops for prime farmland unless abandoned farms and areas that now have only scrub brush are converted into tree plantations and soil erosion is carefully controlled.

Another suggestion is to plant "petroleum plantations" of plants (such as some of the 2,000 varieties of plants of the genus *Euphorbia*) that store energy in hydrocarbon compounds (like those found in oil) rather than carbohydrates. After harvesting, the oil-like material would be extracted (much like crushing grapes to make wine) and refined to produce gasoline, and the unused woody plant residues could be converted to alcohol fuel. Such plants could be grown on semiarid, currently unproductive land. The recent discovery of another tree, the copaiba (*Copaifera langdorfii*) might eliminate the refining step since each 6 months the copaiba plant produces oil that can be used directly to power a diesel engine. Planting a land area the size of Arizona with *Euphorbia* or copaiba plants could produce all of the gasoline needed by the United States. The economic feasi-

bility and net useful energy yield of this approach, however, have not yet been determined, and such plantations may not be applicable on a large scale because of insufficient water.

Another category of potential biomass resources is the large-scale growth and harvesting of aquatic plants such as algae, water hyacinths, and kelp seaweed. Collecting, drying, and processing these plants, however, might require so much energy (and money) that net useful energy yields would be too low and costs would be too high. In addition, large-scale harvesting could disrupt ocean and freshwater ecosystems.

Biofuels There is increasing interest in converting biomass into biofuels such as biogas or methane (the major component of natural gas), methanol (methyl alcohol or wood alcohol), and ethanol (ethyl alcohol or grain alcohol) and into raw material chemicals that would replace petrochemicals. The processes for such bioconversions have been known and used for centuries, but their products have been too expensive compared with fossil fuels. As gasoline, natural gas, and coal prices continue to rise, however, this picture could change.

All biomass except woody substances can be converted to a **biogas** mixture of methane and carbon dioxide by *anaerobic digestion*—fermentation by microorganisms in the absence of oxygen. After the biogas is removed, an improved fertilizer is left behind that can normally be used on food crops or, if contaminated, on nonedible crops such as trees. Many less developed and some more developed nations are returning to this ancient technology. For example, the People's Republic of China has about 7 million biogas digesters. When they work, anaerobic or biogas digesters are highly efficient, but they are somewhat slow and unpredictable, and vulnerable to low temperatures, acidity imbalances, and contamination by heavy metals, synthetic detergents, and other industrial effluents. These same contaminants can cause serious problems if the digested residues are used to fertilize food crops. As a result, few more developed nations so far use anaerobic digestion on a large scale. The economics of biogas production varies widely depending on the type of biomass fuel and the predictability of the process.

Anaerobic digestion occurs spontaneously, of course, in the estimated 20,000 landfill sites around the United States. Los Angeles has tapped into this source to heat some 3,500 homes. In 1976, an Oklahoma company, Calorific Recovery Anaerobic Process, Inc.—CRAP for short—began providing Chicagoans with methane made from cattle manure collected from animal feedlots. Converting all the manure that U.S. livestock produce each year to methane could provide nearly 5 percent of the nation's total natural gas consumption at 1980 levels. But collecting and transporting this manure for long distances would require a large energy input. Recycling this manure to the land to replace artificial fertilizer, which requires large quantities of natural gas to produce, would probably save more natural gas.

A second promising source of biofuels is the conversion of biomass to alcohols, primarily methanol (wood alcohol) or ethanol (grain alcohol). One of the major and most urgent energy problems facing the world today is not to produce large amounts of electricity (by any means) but to find a liquid fuel substitute for gasoline and diesel fuel. Some see ethanol and methanol as the answer to this problem, since both alcohols can be burned directly as a fuel or mixed with gasoline to produce *gasohol*—which is gasoline mixed with 10 to 20 percent by volume ethanol or methanol. A mixture of diesel fuel with 15 to 20 percent by volume methanol, called "diesohol," is also being tested and will probably lower the emissions of nitrogen oxides that are an air pollution drawback of regular diesel fuel. Another possibility being tested is a mixture of diesel fuel with up to 30 percent by volume soybean oil. Wood, wood wastes, other woody crop residues, sewage sludge, garbage, and coal can be gasified and converted to methanol, a liquid fuel that has long been used to power racing cars. Almost any form of biomass that contains starch and cellulose—anything from urban wastes to cornstalks and manure—can be converted by fermentation and distillation (or other processes) to ethanol or grain alcohol.

In the long run, some methanol or ethanol might be burned directly in cars when petroleum supplies are depleted. Neither fuel requires lead compounds or other additives to boost octane ratings, and today's engines can burn these fuels with relatively minor modifications.

At present, the main interest is in "gasohol." Alcohol-water blends supplied 18 percent of Europe's motor fuel in the late 1930s, but is not used widely today. By 1980, Brazil, the United States, South Africa, New Zealand, and Australia were producing gasohol (primarily with ethanol). Brazil is leading the way with an ambitious program to convert surplus sugarcane and cassava (manioc) into ethanol and to completely replace gasoline with 20 percent gasohol. In 1980 ethanol (mostly as gasohol) made up 20 percent of Brazil's automotive fuel consumption. The Brazilian chemical industry is also building plants to produce some of the same petrochemicals

from ethanol that are normally made from oil and natural gas (see Figure 14-1). By 1980 gasohol (made from ethanol produced from grain) was available in many areas of the United States. Hawaii and Puerto Rico plan to make ethanol gasohol from sugarcane distilled in now idle rum plants. Today's cars can run on gasohol with only minor carburetor adjustments as long as the alcohol content does not get too high. Gasohol should improve fuel economy and reduce emissions on older cars (pre-1973) but has a lower fuel economy than gasoline in newer, low compression cars with emission controls.

Oil companies with large coal holdings are more interested in using methanol for gasohol, since methanol can be produced from coal as well as biomass—thus giving these diversified companies an added share of the total energy market. So far, however, most of the emphasis has been on ethanol, since it can be made so easily from so many forms of biomass and has a higher heat content per unit of volume than methanol. In 1980, Congress set a national production target of using ethanol for 10 percent of U.S. gasoline consumption by 1990. Methanol, however, will most likely be used first to fuel buses and trucks, since diesel engines run well on it provided it is mixed with about 5 percent oil to aid in starting.

Unfortunately, there are some problems with a future built around gasohol or the direct burning of alcohols. The burning of pure methanol and ethanol produces acetaldehyde, which smells bad, harms vegetation, and at high concentrations can irritate the skin and eyes and damage the lungs. These harmful emissions, however, could be eliminated by better design or by equipping cars with catalytic filters. Another problem is that each liter of alcohol produced also creates about 12 liters of waste material, which if allowed to flow into waterways could kill algae, fish, and plants. This could be minimized by using the valuable, protein-rich liquid waste as livestock feed. Methanol can cause vapor lock during hot weather and engine failure if the methanol separates from the gasoline due to contact with water drops. Engine corrosion from both ethanol and methanol is another possible problem. Both problems, however, can probably be solved. High costs may be another drawback, but this could change when gasoline costs about 53¢ a liter ($2.00 a gallon) in the United States—a price already exceeded in most of the world. Until gasoline prices reach this level (which could happen soon) gasohol competes with gasoline in the United States only because of a government subsidy that reduces motor fuel taxes on gasohol. By 1980 at least 16 states had also exempted gasohol from state gasoline taxes. New, energy efficient distilleries, however, could reduce the costs of producing ethanol. Unless more efficient production methods are developed, the use of pure methanol as a fuel will not be economically feasible until gasoline prices reach about 79¢ a liter ($3.00 to $4.00 a gallon)—already a reality in many European nations.

Another problem is that if U.S. cropland is used to produce grain for conversion to ethanol, the United States may not have an exportable surplus of grain to help feed the world's growing population and to help counter American trade deficits from importing oil. This could lead to a tragic situation where affluent nations use much of the world's annual grain production to make fuel for their cars, while more and more of the world's poor starve because of higher grain prices (due to greater demand) and too few grain exports. This problem can be greatly reduced (and perhaps eliminated) if grain producing nations stopped or greatly reduced the amount of grain used to feed livestock (Section 9-4). Instead, more livestock could feed on rangeland or perhaps on the grain residues produced in alcohol distilleries (if these residues are enriched by yeast proteins). Using methanol as a fuel greatly reduces these problems since trees and woody plants can be more easily grown on marginal land with fairly poor soils and drier climates, and are not used as food for humans. Some potential for conflict does exist, however, if in the future food production may have to expand onto some of these lands.

Land degradation could become serious if the United States converted all or most of its gasoline use to gasohol. Some 81,000 to 324,000 square kilometers (20 to 80 million acres) of land would have to be used to produce grain. Most of this would probably have to be marginal land to avoid competition for prime farmland. This would increase the already serious problems of soil erosion (Section 16-6) and the resulting runoff of fertilizers, pesticides, and sediments into nearby bodies of water. The U.S. Department of Agriculture indicates that these marginal lands would, on the average, undergo about 20 percent by weight more soil erosion than present cropland. Similarly, a massive increase in the use of methanol as a fuel could degrade the quality of U.S. forestland (Section 10-4).

Another problem is that the net useful energy yield for gasohol is moderate to low and may be negative—depending on how it is produced. In most of today's energy-inefficient distilleries it takes about 1.5 units of energy (mostly natural gas or oil) to produce 1 unit of energy obtainable from ethanol. This net energy loss

might be converted to a low to moderate net energy gain by (1) replacing older distilleries with more energy-efficient ones (or with other more energy-efficient separator processes); (2) fueling them with coal, biomass, or solar energy rather than natural gas or oil; and (3) using the distillery byproduct as cattlefeed. Gasohol proponents, however, dispute the unfavorable net energy estimates, pointing out that replacing all gasoline with gasohol would cut annual U.S. consumption of gasoline by 10 percent and reduce dependence on foreign oil by 20 percent. Critics of the gasohol approach suggest that much simpler and cheaper methods, such as banning automatic transmissions in cars, would save the same amount of gasoline. Some observers also suggest that biomass would be more valuable as feedstock for the petrochemical industry (Figure 14-2) than as a fuel.

Hydrogen Gas as a Fuel How will cars and other vehicles be powered when petroleum gets too expensive? Solar energy, nuclear fission, and most of the alternatives discussed in this chapter—except alcohol biofuels—are schemes for producing electricity at power plants. They do not apply to automobiles and other forms of everyday transportation. Electric cars are extremely energy wasteful (Figure 13-9), and a number of technological problems must be solved to develop batteries with sufficient life and power density.

Hydrogen gas has been suggested as the transportation fuel of the future (Figure 14-14). Lightweight, easily transportable, colorless, odorless, and rapidly renewed in the water cycle, it can be burned cleanly in a fuel cell (a device that can convert the energy in chemical fuels directly into low-voltage, direct-current electricity), a power plant, or an automobile to produce water. By producing water or fog—not smog—it eliminates most of the serious air pollution problems associated with the gasoline-burning internal combustion engine. If air is used as the source of oxygen for combustion, however, small amounts of nitrogen oxides will be formed as byproducts. In addition, some of the water electrolysis cells presently used to produce hydrogen can release small cancer-causing asbestos particles into the air.

Because seawater could be used as the basic resource for hydrogen, we have an affordable, readily available, and almost infinite energy supply, in sharp contrast to fossil fuels. The hydrogen could be stored in tanks (like compressed air) and shipped or transported by pipeline to households, industries, or fueling stations (once gas

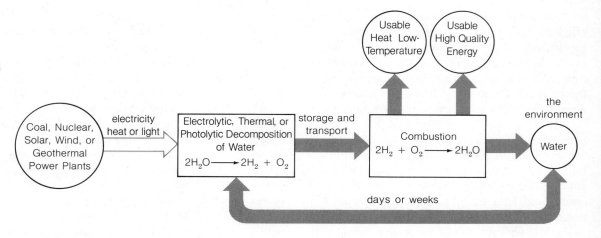

Figure 14-14 The hydrogen energy cycle has a number of advantages over the present fossil fuel energy system. But its widespread use requires the availability of an almost infinite and economically feasible, high-quality energy source for decomposing water to produce hydrogen gas.

stations). It could also be reacted with metals such as magnesium or nickel and stored, transported, and used in cars as metal hydrides, which would release hydrogen gas when heated. Large-scale use of this approach, however, might be limited by available supplies of nickel and magnesium. Also, hydrogen is highly explosive and dangerous. Gasoline is also dangerous, but hydrogen is stored as a gas under high pressure and would explode even more readily if exposed to a spark. Society, however, could learn how to deal with hydrogen safely, as it has with other explosive fuels such as gasoline and natural gas.

Besides being used for vehicle fuel, hydrogen can be used, as mentioned above, to store energy from other sources. For example, the electrical energy from a wind turbine or from a solar, hydroelectric, nuclear, or geothermal power plant could be stored by using it to produce hydrogen by the electrolysis or high-temperature decomposition of water or by the high-temperature decomposition of solid hydrogen-containing compounds.

But there are some major catches to this glowing hydrogen energy future. The basic problem is that pure hydrogen gas is not found in nature. It is a secondary fuel that must be produced by using electricity, high temperatures, or perhaps light (photolysis) to decompose water or other hydrogen-containing compounds. Thus, it takes so much energy (and money) to produce hydrogen that its net useful energy yield will be negative, unless scientists can learn how to break down water efficiently and rapidly enough by direct photolysis, in which sunlight and a catalyst (a special chemical that will speed up the decomposition reaction) decompose water without using electricity or high-temperature heat. This approach is still in the early experimental stages. The

problem is to find a chemical catalyst, that will speed up the chemical reaction by which light or solar energy can split water molecules into hydrogen and oxygen. Researchers are actively evaluating possible catalysts (mostly metals or metallic compounds); but the metals that make the best catalysts may not be available in large enough quantities. If cheap and fairly efficient photovoltaic solar cells (Section 14-6) are developed, they might be used to produce the electricity needed to decompose water and produce hydrogen gas. Thus, an affordable large-scale hydrogen fuel system is feasible only if an essentially limitless and affordable, high-quality energy source, such as nuclear fission (from breeder reactors), nuclear fusion, solar energy, geothermal energy, or wind energy can be used to produce the hydrogen fuel.

In this chapter we have seen that each energy alternative has a mixture of advantages and disadvantages. With the exception of improving energy efficiency (Section 14-1)—which must form the backbone of any energy plan—our energy supplies in the future must be based on a mix of energy sources. Deciding upon and developing the appropriate mix is one of the most urgent tasks facing the world today.

Through most of human history, people have relied on renewable resources—sun, wind, water, and land. They got by well enough, and so could we.

Warren Johnson

Guest Editorial: A Faustian Bargain We Should Accept

Alvin M. Weinberg

Alvin M. Weinberg is former director of the Oak Ridge National Laboratory and former director of energy research and development for the Federal Energy Administration. He now serves as director of the Institute for Energy Analysis at Oak Ridge, Tennessee. He has been one of the leading and most thoughtful advocates of nuclear energy and has written extensively on some of the difficult public policy problems posed by modern science. In 1960 he received both the Atoms for Peace Award and the Atomic Energy Commission's E. O. Lawrence Memorial Award for his contributions to the theory and development of nuclear fission reactors for electric power plants. In 1980, he shared the Enrico Fermi Award.

There are basically two different views of the world's future. The one most popular these days is attributed to Malthus and holds that the resources of Spaceship Earth are limited. Nothing except a drastic reduction in population, affluence, or technology can avoid the ultimate disaster predicted by Thomas Malthus in 1803 and more recently by a team of scientists (Enrichment Study 1). The other view, attributed sometimes to the economist David Ricardo, holds that as scarce materials are exhausted there will always be new, more expensive ones to take their place: Spaceship Earth has practically infinite supplies of resources, but it will cost more and more to stay where we are as we use up those that are readily available.

The Ricardian view seems to me to be the more reasonable, especially since all of our past experience has shown that as one resource becomes scarce, another takes its place. We do not use whale oil any longer, yet we have far better artificial lighting than did our lamp-lighting ancestors. And, in the very long run, humankind will have to depend on the most common and almost infinitely abundant elements: iron, sodium, carbon, nitrogen, aluminum, oxygen, silicon, and a few others. Glass, cement, and plastics will perform many more functions than they now do. Our standard of living will be diminished, but I cannot see this reduction as being by a factor of 10: More likely it would be, say, a factor of 2.

Thus, in contrast to what seems to be the prevailing mood, I retain a basic optimism about the future. My optimism, however, is predicated on certain assumptions.

1. Technology can indeed deal with the effluents of this future society. Here I think I am on firm ground, for, on the whole, where technology has been given the task and given the time, it has come through with very important improvements. For example, many experts believe that the stringent emission standards imposed on cars by the Clean Air Act will indeed be met by 1985, if not before.

2. Phosphorus, though essentially infinite in supply (1,000 ppm in the earth's crust), has no substitute. Will we be able to so revolutionize agriculture that we can eventually use this "infinite" supply of residual phosphorus, at acceptable cost, for growing our food? This technological question is presently unresolved, though I cannot believe it to be unresolvable.

3. All of this presupposes that we have at our disposal an inexhaustible, relatively cheap source of energy. As we now see the technological possibilities, there is only one that we can count on—and this is nuclear fission, based on fission breeder reactors. This is not to say that nuclear fusion or geothermal or solar energy will never be economically available. In my opinion, we simply do not know now that any of these will ever be successful, whereas we know that conventional fission reactors are feasible and that fission breeder reactors could become feasible with a vigorous development.

In opting for nuclear fission breeders—and I believe that we hardly have a choice in the matter—we assume a moral and technological burden of serious proportion. A properly operating nuclear reactor and its subsystems are environmentally a very benign energy source. The issue hangs around the words "properly operating." Can we ensure that henceforth we shall be able to maintain the degree of intellectual responsibility, social commitment, and stability necessary to manage this energy form so as not to cause serious harm? This is basically a moral and social question, though it does have strong technological components.

It is a Faustian bargain that we strike: In return for this inexhaustible energy source, which we must have if we are to maintain ourselves at anything like our present numbers and our present state of affluence, we must commit ourselves—essentially forever—to exercise the vigilance and discipline necessary to keep our nuclear fires well behaved. As a nuclear technologist who has devoted his career to this quest for an infinite energy source, I believe the bargain is a good one, and that it may even be an inevitable one. It is well that the full dimension and implication of the Faustian bargain be recognized, especially by the young people who will have to live with the choices that are being made on this vital issue.

Guest Editorial Discussion

1. Do you agree that the resources of Spaceship Earth are practically infinite?

2. The author bases his optimism on three assumptions. What evidence can you provide to support or question the reasonableness of these assumptions? Are there any other assumptions that should be added?

3. Who was Faust and what is a Faustian bargain?

4. Do you agree that we should accept the Faustian bargain of nuclear fission with either conventional or breeder reactors? Why or why not? What are the consequences of not having this service and depleting our fossil fuels over the next few decades? How will your life be affected?

Guest Editorial: The Solar Transition

Denis Hayes

Denis Hayes has served as director of the Department of Energy's Solar Energy Research Institute (SERI) in Golden, Colorado, since 1979. He is a long-time solar energy and environmental activist, as well as a scholar and highly-capable administrator. He served as national coordinator for the first Earth Day in 1970, director of Environmental Action (a politically-active environmental organization) in the early 1970s, organizer of Sun Day in 1978, and founder of the Solar Lobby in Washington, D.C., in 1978. He was also a senior researcher at the Worldwatch Institute, where he authored the highly regarded book on solar energy, Rays of Hope: The Transition to a Post-Petroleum World *(New York: Norton, 1977). In addition, he has served as a scholar at the Woodrow Wilson Center of the Smithsonian Institution, director of the Illinois State Energy Office, member of the Department of Energy's Research Advisory Board, and as a trustee of Stanford University, where he received his undergraduate degree in history. In 1978 he received the DOE's Outstanding Public Service Award, and in 1979 the Thomas Jefferson Award for Outstanding Public Service by an individual younger than 35.*

A major energy transition of some kind is inevitable. For rich lands and poor alike, the energy patterns of the past are not prologue to the future. The oil-based societies of the industrial world cannot be sustained and cannot be replicated; their spindly foundations, anchored in the shifting sands of the Middle East, have begun to erode. Until recently most poor countries eagerly looked forward to entry into the oil era with its airplanes, diesel tractors, and automobiles. However, the more than ninefold increase in oil prices between 1973 and 1980 virtually guarantees that the Third World will never derive most of its energy from petroleum. Both worlds thus face an awesome discontinuity in the production and use of energy.

In the fossil fuel era, the sun has been largely ignored. No nation includes the sun in its official energy budget, even though all the other energy sources would be reduced to comparative insignificance if the huge amounts of energy powering the carbon cycle, the nitrogen cycle, and the hydrological cycle were tabulated. We think we heat our homes with fossil fuels, forgetting that without the sun the temperature inside those homes would be minus 240°C, when we turned on the furnace. Ninety-nine percent of the heat in our homes comes from the sun already; solar houses merely tap the sun for the last one percent as well.

The amount of solar energy arriving at the earth's outer atmosphere each year is 28,000 times greater than all the commercial energy used by humankind. Roughly 34 percent of this energy is reflected back into space; another 23 percent is used to evaporate water; 1 percent to drive the wind and waves; and about 42 percent reaches the earth to heat the atmosphere and the earth's surface and to carry out photosynthesis (Figure 5-4). No country uses as much energy as is contained in the sunlight that strikes just its buildings. Indeed, the sunshine that falls each year on U.S. roads alone contains twice as much energy as does the fossil fuel used annually by the entire world. In addition, we can tap several indirect forms of solar energy to meet the world's energy needs. The wind power available at prime sites could produce several times more electricity than is currently generated from all sources. Only a fraction of the world's hydropower capacity has been tapped. As much energy could be obtained from biomass each year as fossil fuels currently provide.

Solar energy sources—wind, water, biomass, and direct sunlight—hold formidable advantages over conventional alternatives. They add no heat to the global environment and produce no radioactive or weapons grade materials. The carbon dioxide emitted by biomass systems, if not harvested faster than it is renewed, will make no net contributions to atmospheric concentrations, since green plants will capture carbon dioxide at the same rate it is being produced. Renewable energy resources can provide energy as heat, liquid or gaseous fuels, or electricity. And they lend themselves well to production in decentralized facilities.

About one-fifth of all commercial energy used around the world now comes from solar resources—mostly biomass and hydropower. It is my judgment that by the year 2000, renewable energy sources could provide more than one-third of the world's commercial energy budget.

Such a transition would not be cheap or easy, but its benefits would far outweigh the costs and difficulties. The proposed timetable would require an unprecedented worldwide commitment of resources and talent, but the consequences of failure would be similarly unprecedented. Every essential feature of the proposed solar transition has already proven technically viable; if the timetable is not met, the roadblocks will have been political—not technical.

Different solar sources will see their fullest development in different regions. Wind power potential is greatest in the temperate zones, while biomass flourishes in the tropics. Direct sunlight is most intense in the cloudless desert, while water power depends upon mountain rains. However, most countries have some potential to harness all these renewable resources, and many lands have begun to explore the feasibility of doing so.

Guest Editorial Discussion

1. What are some of the political roadblocks to making the transition to a world depending on direct and indirect solar energy for much of its energy needs?

2. What might be some of the consequences for your life and life-style if such a solar energy transition is not made?

3. Can you think of any disadvantages of making the transition to a world heavily dependent on renewable, solar-derived energy resources?

Discussion Topics

1. Explain why improving energy efficiency should form the basis of any individual, corporate, or national energy plan. Does it form a significant portion of your personal energy plan or life-style? Why or why not? Is it a significant factor in the national energy policy? Why?

2. List 20 ways in which you unnecessarily waste energy each day, and try to order them according to the amount of energy wasted. Draw up a plan showing how you could eliminate or reduce each type of waste. Which ones are the most difficult to reduce? Why?

3. Make an energy use study of your campus or school, and use the findings to develop an energy conservation program.

4. Contrast large-scale fossil fuel, conventional fission, breeder fission, geothermal, and solar power plants in terms of (a) how they work, (b) their environmental impact, and (c) their technological and economic problems.

5. Criticize the following statements:
   a. A nuclear fusion plant can blow up like a hydrogen bomb.
   b. A conventional nuclear fission plant can blow up like an atomic bomb.
   c. Nuclear fusion plants could release large amounts of radioactive materials.
   d. Solar power plants shouldn't be developed because they will take up 10 percent of the desert area in the United States.

e. Development of solar and wind energy should be left up to private enterprise rather than the federal government.

f. Wind power is not feasible at present.

g. Natural dry geothermal fields offer a clean and abundant source of energy.

h. Electric toothbrushes and carving knives waste large amounts of energy and should be abolished.

i. A requirement of 17 kilometers per liter (40 miles per gallon) by 1995 for all cars is unreasonable and should not be required by law.

j. To save energy, emphasis should be placed on building a network of sophisticated mass transit systems in all major urban areas.

k. Requiring all homes to be heavily insulated and to be oriented to take advantage of sunlight and prevailing winds violates the rights of homeowners to do as they please with their homes.

l. Talk of an energy crisis is a hoax. All we must do is to find and use the vast supplies of oil and natural gas that the earth contains (the basic energy program proposed by President Ronald Reagan in 1980).

m. Since shale oil deposits in the United States equal the entire world's proven and estimated petroleum deposits, shale oil is the key to America's energy future.

n. Coal gasification and liquefaction can solve America's energy problems.

o. Hydroelectric power can solve America's energy problems.

p. Tidal energy is a clean, untapped source that can solve our problems.

q. Using hydrogen as a fuel will save us.

r. We can solve the energy crisis by converting agricultural, forest, animal, and urban wastes to biofuels.

s. Large-scale solar electric power plants can solve our energy problems.

6. In May of 2020, the director of the National Nuclear Security Guard announces that one of the several thousand heavily guarded shipments of deadly plutonium made each year to nuclear breeder reactors has been hijacked by a small but well-organized terrorist group calling itself the Nuclear Liberation Army (NLA). About 23 kilograms (50 pounds) of plutonium were taken. Because plutonium is a weak emitter of alpha radiation, its presence is almost impossible to detect. The hijackers could break up the material into smaller pieces and carry it in their pockets, briefcases, or suitcases with only newspaper, aluminum foil, or any thin covering to protect themselves from the radiation. The primary danger is lung cancer if plutonium dust particles are inhaled. One week after the hijacking, the president of the United States receives an ultimatum from the NLA that within 6 weeks he must shut down and dismantle all nuclear power plants and have the U.S. Treasury send checks for $15,000 to every person below the poverty level. Otherwise the NLA threatens to use conventional plastic explosives to blow up the plutonium, injecting particles into the air above 10 major U.S. cities, and pour dissolved plutonium compounds into the water systems of these cities. If this occurs, thousands and probably millions could contract lung or other cancers within 15 to 45 years, and large urban areas of the United States would be uninhabitable for centuries. As president of the United States, how would you respond? Check the feasibility of this scenario with a chemist, a physicist, and a security expert and see if you can conceive of a way to prevent such a possibility. Do you favor a U.S. energy plan based on the widespread phasing in of breeder reactors between 2000 and 2040? Why or why not? What are the alternatives?

7. In what respects does tidal power differ from hydroelectric power?

8. Nuclear fusion, solar, geothermal, wind, and biomass energy and conservation are all proposed as significant and less harmful energy sources than fossil fuel and nuclear fission energy. Assuming this is valid, explain in each case why they haven't been developed. Outline a plan for their development.

9. Outline the major advantages and disadvantages of the following types of energy: nuclear fusion, solar, wind, biomass, hydroelectric, tidal, and geothermal. In each case explain how they are limited by the first and second laws of thermodynamics. How do these limitations compare with those on fossil fuel and nuclear fission energy?

10. Distinguish between direct use of solar energy as heat, its conversion into electricity, and solar power from ocean thermal gradients. Which is the most promising and has the least environmental impact?

11. How is the sun's energy responsible for (a) wind energy, (b) biomass energy, and (c) hydroelectric energy?

Readings

See also the references for Chapter 13.

Alfvén, Hannes. 1974. "Fission Energy and Other Sources of Energy." *Bulletin of the Atomic Scientists*, January, pp. 4–8. Superb analysis of the dangers of nuclear energy that includes a proposed alternative plan.

American Nuclear Society. 1976. *Nuclear Power and the Environment.* Hinsdale, Ill.: American Nuclear Society. Excellent defense of nuclear power.

Beckmann, Peter. 1976. *The Health Hazards of Not Going Nuclear.* Boulder, Colo.: Golem Press. Readable, hardhitting defense of nuclear power.

Berger, John J. 1977. *Nuclear Power: The Unviable Option.* New York: Dell. Discussion of the case against nuclear power.

Bockris, J. O. 1980. *Energy Options: Real Economics and the Solar-Hydrogen System.* London: Taylor & Francis. Excellent analysis.

Brown, Lester R., et al. 1980. *Running on Empty: The Future of the Automobile in an Oil-Short World.* New York: Viking. Try to read this important book.

Bupp, Irvin C., and Jean-Claude Derian. 1978. *Light Water: How the Nuclear Dream Dissolved.* New York: Basic Books. Outstanding discussion of why nuclear power is an economic disaster.

Calvin, Melvin. 1979. "Petroleum Plantations for Fuels and Materials." *BioScience,* vol. 29, no. 9, 533–538. Nobel Prize-winning chemist discusses his proposal to grow plants that yield petroleum.

Center for Science in the Public Interest. 1977. *99 Ways to a Simple Lifestyle.* New York: Doubleday. Superb summary of how you can conserve matter and energy.

Clarke, Robin. 1977. *Building for Self-Sufficiency.* New York: Universe Books. Use this to see how to prepare for the energy and economic crunch that may come between 1985 and 1995.

Cohen, Bernard L. 1974. *Nuclear Science and Society.* New York: Anchor Books. Excellent defense of nuclear power.

Cummings, Ronald G., et al. 1979. "Mining Earth's Heat: Hot Dry Rock Geothermal Energy." *Technology Review,* February, pp. 58–78. Very good summary.

Department of Energy. 1980. *Geothermal Energy and Our Environment.* Washington, D.C.: Department of Energy. Superb summary.

Dingee, David A. 1979. "Fusion Power." *Chemical and Engineering News,* April 2, pp. 32–47. Fine overview. See also Kulcinski et al. (1979).

Energy Conservation Research. 1979. *Energy for Today and Tomorrow.* Malvern, Pa.: Energy Conservation Research. One of the best lists of how to avoid energy waste.

Farallones Institute. 1979. *The Integral Urban House: Self-Reliant Living in the City.* San Francisco: Sierra Club Books. Excellent discussion of how to survive in the city.

Flavin, Christopher. 1980. *Energy and Architecture: The Solar and Conservation Potential.* Washington, D.C.: Worldwatch Institute. Excellent summary. See also Stein (1977).

Flavin, Christopher. 1980. *The Future of Synthetic Materials: The Petroleum Connection.* Washington, D.C.: Worldwatch Institute. Explains the importance of using oil to produce petrochemicals and evaluates alternatives.

Gofman, John W., and Arthur R. Tamplin. 1979. *Poisoned Power: The Case Against Nuclear Power.* 2nd ed. Emmaus, Pa.: Rodale. Attack on nuclear power by two prominent nuclear scientists.

Gyorgy, Anna, and Friends. 1979. *No Nukes: Everyone's Guide to Nuclear Power.* Boston: South End Press. Attack on nuclear power.

Hayes, Dennis. 1976. *Nuclear Power: The Fifth Horseman.* Washington, D.C.: Worldwatch Institute. Superb presentation of the case against nuclear power. See also Hayes (1977) in Chapter 13.

Hill, Ray. 1980. "Alcohol Fuels—Can They Replace Gasoline?" *Popular Science,* March, pp. 25–34. Very good summary.

Inglis, David R. 1973. *Nuclear Energy: Its Physics and Social Challenge.* Reading, Mass.: Addison-Wesley. Excellent introduction to nuclear energy.

Inglis, David R. 1978. *Windpower and Other Energy Options.* Ann Arbor: University of Michigan Press. Outstanding evaluation of potential for wind, solar, biomass, and other energy alternatives.

Jakimo, Alan, and Irvin C. Bupp. 1978. "Nuclear Waste Disposal: Not in My Backyard." *Technology Review,* March–April, pp. 64–72. Excellent summary. See also Lipschultz (1980).

Kemeny, John G. 1980. "Saving American Democracy: The Lessons of Three Mile Island." *Technology Review,* June-July, pp. 65–75. Excellent analysis by the chairperson of the presidential panel investigating the Three Mile Island nuclear accident.

Kendall, H. W., ed. 1977. *The Risks of Nuclear Power Reactors.* Washington, D.C.: Union of Concerned Scientists. Excellent discussion of problems with nuclear power.

Kulcinski, G. L., et al. 1979. "Energy for the Long Run: Fission or Fusion." *American Scientist,* vol. 67, 78–89. Superb evaluation of nuclear fusion. See also Dingee (1979).

Lapp, Ralph E. 1974. *The Nuclear Controversy.* Greenwich, Conn.: Fact Systems. One of the best presentations of the case for nuclear power.

Lipschultz, Ronnie. 1980. *Radioactive Waste: Politics, Technology, and Risk.* Cambridge, Mass.: Ballinger. Very useful analysis of this serious problem.

Lovins, Amory B. 1973. "The Case Against the Fast Breeder Reactor." *Bulletin of the Atomic Scientists,* March, pp. 29–35. A physicist presents a strong case against the breeder. See also Lovins (1977) in Chapter 13.

Lovins, Amory B., et al. 1980. "Nuclear Power and Nuclear Bombs." *Not Man Apart*, March, pp. 3–8. Try to read this very important article on nuclear proliferation.

Martin, Daniel W. 1980. *Three Mile Island: Prologue or Epilogue?* Cambridge, Mass.: Ballinger. Excellent analysis.

Mazria, Edward. 1979. *The Passive Solar Energy Book: A Complete Guide to Passive Solar Home, Greenhouse, and Building Design.* Emmaus, Pa.: Rodale. One of the best available books on passive solar energy.

Metz, William D., and Allen M. Hammond. 1978. *Solar Energy in America.* Washington, D.C.: American Association for the Advancement of Science. Superb summary of solar energy.

Morris, James W. 1980. *The Complete Energy Saving Handbook for Homeowners.* New York: Harper & Row. Very useful guide.

Najarian, Thomas. 1978. "The Controversy over the Health Effects of Radiation." *Technology Review,* November, pp. 78–82. Excellent summary.

Nero, Anthony V., Jr. 1980. *No Nukes? Know Nukes.* Berkeley, Calif.: University of California Press. Very useful evaluation of nuclear energy.

Office of Emergency Preparedness. 1972. *The Potential for Energy Conservation.* Washington, D.C.: Government Printing Office. Stock no. 4102–00009. Superb evaluation. Includes extensive bibliography.

Pimentel, David, et al. 1978. "Biological Solar Energy Conversion and U.S. Energy Policy." *BioScience,* vol. 28, no. 6, 376–381. Excellent evaluation of potential of biomass energy.

Plotkin, Steven E. 1980. "Energy From Biomass: The Environmental Effects." *Environment,* vol. 22, no. 9, 6–37. Superb summary.

President's Commission on the Accident at Three Mile Island. 1979. *Report of the President's Commission on the Accident at Three Mile Island.* Washington, D.C.: Government Printing Office. Very useful analysis of nuclear safety.

Pringle, Laurence. 1979. *Nuclear Power: From Physics to Politics.* New York: Macmillan. Very useful evaluation of this controversial option.

Purcell, Arthur H. 1980. *The Waste Watchers: A Citizen's Handbook for Conserving Energy.* New York: Anchor/ Doubleday. Excellent guide.

Rasmussen, Norman C., et al. 1979. "Nuclear Power: Can We Live With It?" *Technology Review,* June-July, pp. 32–47. Very useful evaluation.

Rattien, Stephen. 1976. "Oil Shale: The Prospects and Problems of an Emerging Energy Industry." In Jack M. Hollander and Melvin R. Simmons, eds., *Annual Review of Energy,* vol. 1. Palo Alto, Calif.: Annual Reviews. Authoritative summary.

Smith, Nigel. 1981. *Wood: An Ancient Fuel With a New Future.* Washington, D.C.: Worldwatch Institute. Outstanding overview.

Stein, Richard G. 1977. *Architecture and Energy.* Garden City, N.Y.: Anchor Books. Outstanding analysis of energy conservation in buildings. See also Flavin *(Energy and Architecture).*

Stephens, Mark. 1980. *Three Mile Island.* New York: Random House. Useful description of this accident.

Underground Space Center, University of Minnesota. 1979. *Earth-Sheltered Housing Design.* Princeton, N.J.: Van Nostrand Reinhold. The best available source.

Weinberg, Alvin M. 1972. "Social Institutions and Nuclear Energy." *Science,* vol. 177, 27–34. Highly optimistic view based on widespread and safe use of nuclear energy.

Weinberg, Alvin M. 1980. "Is Nuclear Energy Necessary?" *The Bulletin of Atomic Scientists,* March, pp. 31–35. Excellent case for nuclear power.

Weinberg, Alvin M., et al. 1979. *Economic and Environmental Impacts of a U.S. Nuclear Moratorium, 1985–2010.* Cambridge, Mass.: M.I.T. Press. Excellent analysis.

Wells, Malcolm. 1977. *Underground Designs.* Available from the author, Box 1149, Brewster, Maine 02631. Superb discussion of earth-sheltered homes and buildings.

Wells, Malcolm, and Irwin Spetgang. 1978. *How to Buy Solar Heating and Cooling . . . Without Getting Burnt.* Emmaus, Pa.: Rodale. Before you install solar energy, be sure to read this important book.

15

Water Resources

If there is magic on this planet, it is in water.

Loren Eisley

15-1 Importance and Properties of Water

A Vital Resource Water is one of our most vital resources. It dissolves and transports nutrients from the soil into the bodies of plants and animals, dissolves and dilutes many of our wastes, serves as a raw material for photosynthesis (Section 5-4) (which provides food for all living organisms), and is a major factor in world climate and weather patterns. Thus, all life on earth depends on water. We might survive a month without food, but only a few days without water.

Unusual Physical Properties Water is not only vital, it's unusual. Much of water's usefulness results from its remarkable physical properties:

1. *Water has a high boiling point.* Without this property water would be a gas rather than a liquid at normal temperatures, and there would be no oceans, lakes, rivers, plants, or animals on earth.

2. *Water has the highest heat of vaporization of all liquids.* This means that it takes a lot of energy to evaporate a given amount of liquid water. This is a major factor in distributing the sun's heat over the world. The huge amount of solar energy stored as heat in evaporated ocean water is released over land and bodies of water when this water vapor condenses and falls back to the earth as precipitation. Water's high heat of vaporization also helps to regulate human body temperature by allowing the body to eliminate large amounts of heat by evaporating relatively small quantities of water.

3. *Water has one of the highest capacities to store heat (heat capacity) of any known substance.* This means that a given amount of water (by weight) has a very small increase in temperature when a specific amount of heat is added to it. As a result, water heats and cools more slowly than most other substances. This property of water prevents extreme climatic temperature changes, helps protect living organisms from the shock of abrupt temperature changes, and removes heat from electrical power plants and industrial processes.

4. *Water is less dense as a solid than as a liquid.* When most substances freeze, their volume decreases; thus, the density (mass per unit volume) of the solid is higher than that of the liquid. In contrast, when water is cooled below 4°C, it expands and its density decreases. Without this property, ice would not float on water, bodies of water would freeze from the bottom up, most aquatic life would not exist, and the earth would be locked in a permanent ice age. However, because water expands on freezing, it can also break pipes, crack engine blocks in cars (which is why we add antifreeze), and cause cracks in streets, soil, and rocks.

5. *Water is unsurpassed as a solvent.* Water dissolves an incredible variety of substances. This enables it to carry nutrients throughout the bodies of plants and animals, to be one of the best cleansers, and to remove and dilute water-soluble wastes. However, because water dissolves so many things, it is also easily polluted.

Some Important Questions Because of its importance, the availability of usable water—not the availability of food, forests, metals, minerals, or energy resources—is the factor that limits human population growth and determines life quality in much of the world. But the problems of population size, population density, technology, pollution, and natural resources (including water) are all related. Water is necessary to grow food and trees; to

Enrichment Study 6 is related to this chapter.

keep plants and animals alive; to process metal, mineral, and energy resources; to manufacture almost anything; and to help dilute the wastes of the increasingly urbanized, industrialized, and growing world population. At the same time, forests and estuaries (Chapter 10) help hold water and release it slowly, which aids in growing crops and preventing floods; energy (Chapters 13 and 14) is needed to purify and transport water; and metals and minerals are needed to build the dams, canals, troughs, pipes, and waste treatment plants necessary to hold, transport, and purify water.

Thus, we must consider some important questions. With increasing demands for water and with world population increasing by 205,000 each day, is the world in danger of running out of usable water? What is the present and future water situation in the United States? How can we manage the world's fixed supply of water to get enough of it in the right place, at the right time, and with the right quality? This chapter will deal with these problems of water supply, while the next chapter will discuss water pollution.

15-2 Worldwide Supply, Renewal, and Distribution

World Water Resources The world supply of water in all forms (vapor, liquid, and ice) is fixed. However, this supply is enormous, as spacecraft pictures of the blue-green earth so dramatically show. The total amount of water on earth is about 1.5 billion cubic kilometers (396 billion billion gallons). If this water could be distributed equally, every person would have 0.34 cubic kilometers (90 billion gallons)—more water than a person could ever use. But there are two major problems with this optimistic calculation. The world's water is unevenly distributed, and about 99.997 percent of it is not readily available for human use. In other words, *only about 0.003 percent of the world's water supply is uncontaminated fresh (or sweet) water—which is found in rivers, lakes, swamps, and shallow underground wells.*

From Table 15-1 we see that about 97.1 percent of the world's water is in the oceans and saline lakes; this water is unfit for drinking and agriculture. Most of the remaining 2.9 percent that is fresh is also not available for use. It is tied up in ice caps, glaciers, the atmosphere, and the soil, or it lies too far under the surface of the earth. This leaves only 0.32 percent of the world's water easily accessible to us as fresh water in rivers, lakes, and relatively shallow underground deposits. But over 99 percent of

this fresh water* is either too expensive to get, not readily available because of remote locations (Amazon and Siberian rivers), or polluted. So we have only 0.003 percent of the earth's total water supply to draw from.

To understand the relative amounts involved, imagine that the total water supply on the planet is 38 liters (10 gallons). After we take out the salt water, about 1.1 liters (4½ cups) remain. Of this, about 0.83 liter (3½ cups) is located in glaciers, ice caps, the soil, and the atmosphere, leaving only about 0.27 liter (1 cup). When we take out the water that is polluted, relatively inaccessible, and too expensive to get, then the remaining usable fresh water supply is only about 0.001 liter, or 1 milliliter (10 drops).

Even this tiny fraction of usable fresh water amounts to about 45,000 cubic kilometers (12,000 trillion gallons)—an average of 0.00001 cubic kilometer (2.7 million gallons) for each person, or an average of about 0.000005 cubic kilometer (1.35 million gallons) per person if the world population should increase from the present 4.6 billion to 8 billion. Thus, we seem to have plenty of water. An even more optimistic picture emerges when we realize that this freshwater supply is continually purified and replenished by the natural hydrological (water) cycle.

The Hydrological Cycle *In contrast to fossil fuels (Chapter 13) and most nonfuel minerals (Chapter 12), usable water is a renewable resource. It cannot be depleted unless we use and degrade it faster than it is cleaned up by human processes and replenished by natural chemical cycling.*

Water, like carbon, oxygen, nitrogen, phosphorus, and other vital chemicals (Section 5-4), is continually cycled through the ecosphere. The **hydrological cycle,** or *water cycle* (Figure 15-1), is a gigantic water distillation and distribution system. Water evaporates into the atmosphere from the oceans, lakes, rivers, soil, and plants (transpiration)[†] by solar energy and eventually cools and precipitates as fresh water, falling either onto land or back into the oceans, rivers, and lakes. Thus, as shown in Figure 15-1, solar energy and gravity continuously

---

*Fresh water contains lower concentrations of dissolved substances than seawater, but it is definitely not pure. The concentrations of dissolved substances in fresh water are normally low enough so that it can be used without harm for various human purposes (see Section 16-1 for the definition of water pollution).

†**Transpiration** is the direct transfer of water from living plants to the atmosphere. Water also evaporates from the leaves of plants and from the soil. The combination of evaporation and transpiration is called **evapotranspiration.**

Table 15-1 World's Water Resources and Their Average Rates of Renewal

Location	Percentage of World Supply	Average Rate of Renewal
Oceans	97.134	3,100 years (37,000 years for deep ocean water)
Atmosphere	0.001	9 to 12 days
On land		
Ice caps	2.225	16,000 years
Glaciers	0.015	16,000 years
Saline lakes	0.007	10 to 100 years (depending on depth)
Freshwater lakes	0.009	10 to 100 years (depending on depth)
Rivers	0.0001	12 to 20 days
In land		
Soil moisture	0.003	280 days
Groundwater		
To a depth of 1,000 meters (1.6 miles)	0.303	300 years
1,000 to 2,000 meters (1.6 to 3.2 miles)	0.303	4,600 years
Total	100.000	

move water from the oceans to the atmosphere, from the atmosphere to the land and oceans, and from the land back to the oceans.

It is important to realize that only about 0.029 percent of the world's water is cycled through the ecosphere annually. All of the world's water cycles eventually, but different parts of the supply are renewed at different average rates, as shown in Table 15-1. Note from Table 15-1 that most of the world's water resources take from 10 to 37,000 years to be renewed. Only the water in the atmosphere, rivers, and the soil is recycled at relatively rapid rates. Water also cycles through living organisms. The water in a tree is replenished thousands of times as the tree grows. The water that makes up about 65 percent of the weight of your body is replaced several times each year.

Our two main sources of fresh water are the fairly rapid (12 to 20 days) runoff of rivers and the very slowly replenished (300 years) groundwater deposits found less than 1,000 meters (1.6 miles) below the earth's surface. The average amount of water falling onto land each year is 10 percent more than the amount that evaporates from land. This difference comprises the maximum flow of fresh water—through rivers and groundwater movement—that is available for human use each year. This flow amounts to about 38,000 cubic kilometers (10 quadrillion gallons) per year, or an average of 104 cubic kilometers (274 billion gallons) a day. Of course, much of this flow is far from where we need it and remains unused.

Let's look more closely at the groundwater portion of the water cycle. Most rainwater that falls onto land runs off into streams and lakes and eventually returns to the sea. Some of this water, however, slowly percolates down through the soil until it reaches a layer, or stratum, of rock that the water cannot penetrate (Figure 15-2). Water builds up in the overlying sand and rock above this impervious rock layer and fills all the openings and cracks. The soil and rock become saturated up to a certain level, called the **water table** (Figure 15-2); above the water table line, the soil is relatively dry. In swamps and areas with high rainfall, the water table may lie at or near the land surface, while in dry areas it may be hundreds to thousands of meters below the surface or even not exist at all.

Water below the water table slowly flows toward the sea at a rate determined by the difference in its elevation

Figure 15-1 The hydrological cycle, showing the chemical cycling of water (solid arrows) and the one-way flow of energy (open arrows).

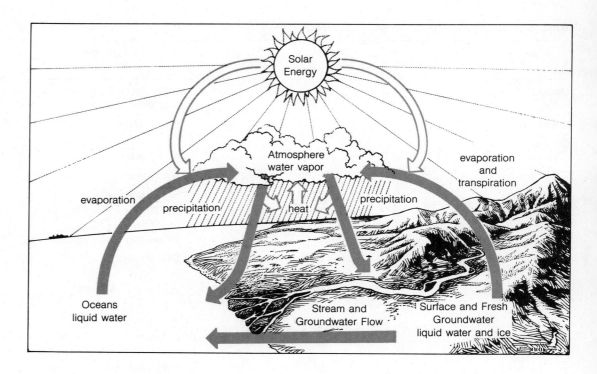

and that at sea level and by the permeability of the intervening sediment or rock. Permeable layers of gravel or sand that serve as conduits for the normally slow flow of groundwater are called **aquifers.** *Unconfined aquifers* are found above the first impervious rock layer; *confined aquifers* are between two impervious rock layers (Figure 15-2). The difference in water height from one place to another in an aquifer generates hydraulic pressure at the lower point. To get fresh water, a well is drilled below the water table. If a well reaches into a confined aquifer, the hydraulic pressure may be so great that the water flows freely out of the well without pumping. Such wells are called **artesian wells** (Figure 15-2).

The world supply of groundwater is enormous—comprising about 95 percent of the world's fresh water. Groundwater is a primary source of water in many places, especially rural areas and small towns. The volume of groundwater found up to a depth of 1,000 meters (1.6 miles) is more than 3,000 times the volume of fresh water found in all the world's rivers at any given time and 33 times the volume found in all the world's rivers and freshwater lakes (Table 15-1). However, there are some problems in using groundwater as a source of fresh water: (1) When soil and rock are not very permeable, water flows into aquifers so slowly that it cannot be removed at a worthwhile rate. (2) If groundwater is withdrawn faster than it is recharged by rainfall, the water

table drops and wells must be drilled deeper. Since groundwater takes hundreds of years to recharge (Table 15-1), rapid depletion resembles mining a nonrenewable resource—like taking money out of a checking account faster than you put it in. (3) Groundwater can dissolve salts as it flows through some types of rock and become too contaminated or saline (salty) for human use. (4) Groundwater aquifers are being polluted by industrial and other wastes at an alarming rate. Contrary to popular belief, an aquifer is not a swift-running underground stream that can cleanse itself like a river if not overloaded with pollutants. The contamination of vital groundwater is essentially irreversible—once contaminated, there's very little we can do about it.

Distribution of the World's Fresh Water *A major problem is that the world's supply of usable fresh water is unevenly distributed.* The rivers, lakes, and shallow underground water from which we get our fresh water are replenished by rainfall. Average annual rainfall varies widely throughout the world, and these averages often represent a combination of periods with too much rain and periods with too little rain. In addition, natural processes (erosion and dissolving of chemicals in the soil) and human activities contaminate much of this rainwater.

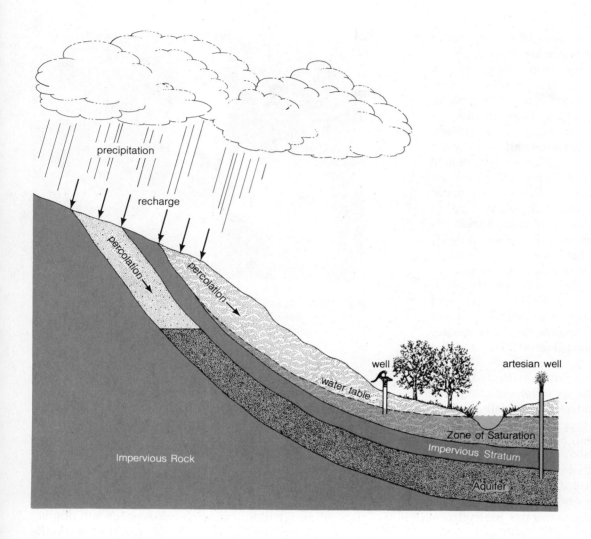

Figure 15-2 The groundwater system.

precipitation

recharge

percolation

percolation

well

artesian well

water table

Zone of Saturation

Impervious Stratum

Impervious Rock

Aquifer

The distribution of fresh water also varies because climate differences cause different evaporation rates in different parts of the world. This varies the amounts of annual runoff for different continents. For most of the world the usable rainfall, or average annual runoff of rivers and groundwater flow, is between 33 and 42 percent of the total rainfall. But in Africa, where evaporation rates are high, the average annual runoff is only about 16 percent of the average annual rainfall.

15-3 Human Water Use in the World and the United States

Present and Future World Water Use Humans use water for three major purposes: (1) irrigation to grow food, (2) industrial uses, and (3) domestic and commercial uses. During 1981 the 4.6 billion people in the world withdrew only about 9 percent of the potentially available annual freshwater runoff. About 85 percent of this was used for irrigation, 7 percent for industry (mining, manufacturing, and cooling), and 5 percent for domestic and commercial purposes.

The world seems to have an ample supply of fresh water for human use. Only about 9 percent of the annual runoff is withdrawn, and according to estimates, it is economically feasible for most areas to tap 20 percent of the annual runoff. The remaining 80 percent is in rivers and groundwater flows that are too far away from human population or is too expensive or contaminated to use.

Although the average world water supply seems sufficient, many parts of the world face continuous or periodic water problems, which are expected to get worse in the future. This situation is caused by three major factors: (1) rising demands for water for all uses, (2) the very unequal distribution of the world's water, and (3) increasing pollution of water supplies. In other words, much of the world's water is located in the wrong place, available at the wrong time, or of the wrong quality.

Consequently, many areas in the world are already withdrawing or soon will be withdrawing more water than is being replenished by annual runoff. Between 30 and 40 percent of the world's food production now depends on irrigation. Between 1975 and 2000, the amount of irrigated land will have to at least double in order to provide enough food for the world's growing population (Chapter 9). Industrial use is growing even more rapidly. Already the following areas have shortages of usable water: Spain, southern Italy, the Dalmatian coast, Greece, Turkey, all Arab states except Syria, most of Iran, Pakistan, western India, Taiwan, Japan, Korea, western and southern Australia, New Zealand, the northwestern and southwestern African coasts, Panama, northern Mexico, central Chile, the Peruvian coast (Figure 15-3), and the southwestern United States.

Scarcely any part of the world is unaffected by the problems of flooding, drought, or water pollution. The struggling economy of Bangladesh rises or falls with the periodic flooding of the Ganges River. California and much of the western United States suffered severe drought during 1976 and 1977 and then were overwhelmed in 1978 with rains that caused flooding, mudslides, and crop damage. In 1981, much of the United States suffered water shortages because of an unusually dry winter coupled with below-average precipitation during the spring and summer of 1980. In the early 1970s severe drought in mid-Africa practically wiped out food supplies and resulted in the deaths of thousands of cattle and humans. Oil has made Kuwait rich, but a barrel of water in this water-starved country is more precious than a barrel of oil.

By the year 2000 the situation will probably be much worse, with at least 30 countries having a demand for water that exceeds their maximum sustainable supply. The United Nations projects that most of the Soviet Union except Siberia, most of Europe, almost half of the United States, most of India, the central Thailand plains, Tasmania, the islands east of Java, the larger Caribbean islands, Mexico, and parts of Brazil and Argentina will be short of water by the year 2000.

It is estimated that by the year 2000 world withdrawal will amount to 16 to 25 percent of the annual runoff—near or above the 20 percent limit of runoff economic feasibility. The actual figure varies considerably among

United Nations

Figure 15-3 Three out of four of the world's rural people and one out of five city dwellers don't have ready access to uncontaminated water. This fact is already obvious to these two children in Lima, Peru, who are forced to bail their drinking water from a puddle near an inadequate public pump.

the continents, and water shortages could be particularly acute in much of Europe, Africa, and Asia. Of course, such projections are based on various assumptions about increases in population and water use. As with estimates of nonfuel and mineral resources (Chapter 12) and energy resources (Section 14-2), we get different projections by using different assumptions. These particular projections assume that by the year 2000 world population will be 7 billion, irrigation water needs will double, industrial needs will increase 20-fold (mostly for cooling industrial and electric power plants), and domestic and commercial uses will increase 5-fold.

In projecting the future availability of freshwater, we need to distinguish among four types of uses: (1) withdrawal (or total use), (2) consumptive (or displaced) use, (3) net use, and (4) degrading use. **Withdrawal use** is simply the total amount of water taken out of a lake or river or pumped out of an underground or surface reservoir; it is the figure usually compared with the available supply in determining water shortages. Some of this water, typically about 50 percent, is returned to the environment in usable condition. **Consumptive use** consists of the water lost to the air by evaporation and transpiration. It is not really consumed but is lost by natural processes to be precipitated elsewhere. **Net use** is the total use minus consumptive use. **Degrading use** is the amount of water contaminated by dissolved salts, other chemicals, or heat before the water returns to the hydrological cycle. As world population and industrialization continue to grow, the world's freshwater supply is being polluted at a rate of about 2 percent per year. Consumptive and degrading uses make about half of the amount withdrawn unavailable or unsuitable for human use. Thus, about half of all withdrawn water is returned in satisfactory condition to the lakes, rivers, and underground flows, and eventually to the world's oceans.

Although water scarcity, droughts, and flooding are serious problems in some regions, the major human hazard at present is impure water. In its latest 1975 survey the World Health Organization (WHO) found that *1 out of 2 of the 2 billion human beings living in the less developed nations do not have safe water to drink and 3 out of 4 are without adequate sanitation facilities.* The situation is worst in South and Southeast Asia—where two-thirds of the people are without a safe supply of drinking water. It is not surprising that the World Health Organization estimates that some 25 million people die every year from waterborne diseases caused by unclean or inadequate water and from a lack of adequate sanitation—an average of 68,500 deaths each day. Most of the difference in average life expectancy between 73 years for the more developed nations and 57 years for the less developed nations is due to the much higher infant and child mortality rates in the poorer nations. This in turn is due largely to widespread incidence of infectious (and often waterborne) diseases such as cholera, dysentery, and diarrhea in these nations (see Enrichment Study 6).

The lack of pure drinking water in many less developed nations also means tens of millions of women and children have to spend much of their day carrying heavy cans or jugs long distances to collect their precious, but often polluted, daily supply of drinking water—often walking up to 24 kilometers (15 miles) a day to get untreated water from the nearest river or community pump (Figure 15-3). When a young girl in Sudan was asked what it would mean if her village got a well, she replied: "Then maybe I can go to school again." Thus, the often inadequate and unsafe water supply in the poorer nations determines who lives, who dies, who eats, and how people—especially women and children—spend most of their day.

To help correct this tragic situation, the U.N. General Assembly has declared the 1980s the International Drinking Water Supply and Sanitation Decade with the goal of bringing clean water and adequate sanitation to all by 1990. To achieve this goal will require at least $300 billion (1978 dollars), assuming the widespread use of cheaper, appropriate technology (such as, using public standpipes in cities instead of individual home hook-

ups). This amounts to an average expenditure of $80 million per day between 1980 and 1990. This may seem like a lot of money, but a world that spends an average of $240 million dollars a day on cigarettes should be able to spend one-third this amount on providing the needy with safe drinking water and adequate sanitation.

Water problems often differ between more developed and less developed nations. Less developed nations may or may not have enough water, but they rarely have the money needed to develop water storage and distribution systems. Their people must settle where the water is. In more developed nations people tend to live where the climate is favorable and then bring in water through sophisticated systems. As Raymond Dasmann put it, "Today people in affluent nations often settle in a desert and demand that water be brought to them, or they settle on a flood plain and demand that water be kept away." More developed nations in warm, arid areas face shortages, but their biggest problems result from using and polluting water at extremely high rates, especially in urban centers, as discussed in Chapter 16.

The U.S. Situation The United States is blessed with a bountiful supply of fresh water. Its average annual runoff could theoretically supply each American with an average of about 23,000 liters (6,000 gallons) per day. But all of this runoff cannot be withdrawn for human use. In 1980, the United States withdrew about 29 percent of its annual runoff. As in most of the world, much of the annual runoff is not always in the right place, at the right time, or of the right quality.

Only about 9 percent of the water withdrawn each year in the United States is used for domestic and commercial purposes. About 40 percent of the water withdrawn is used for irrigation—compared with 88 percent for the world as a whole. Only about 10 percent of the U.S. cropland is irrigated, but this land produces more than 25 percent of the cash value of crops grown each year. Another major difference between the United States and the world is in the use of water for industrial purposes (mining, manufacturing, and cooling). In the world only about 7 percent of water withdrawn each year is used for industrial purposes, compared with 43 percent in the United States. About 60 percent of the annual U.S. industrial use—or about 26 percent of the total use—is for cooling electric power plants. Thus, water use in the United States is closely tied to energy use. In turn, cleaning up and pumping this water requires large amounts of energy, creating a vicious circle that increases the use of both vital resources. For example, the limiting

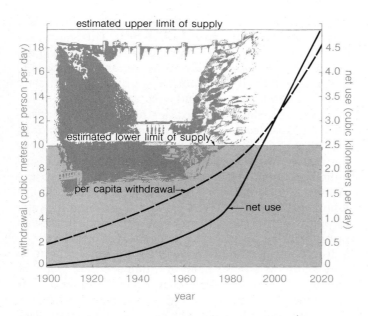

Figure 15-4 The J curves of average per capita withdrawal and net water use in the United States.

factor in irrigation in many areas tends to be the high cost of electricity used to run the pumps as the water table recedes. The vast state water project in California uses almost as much electricity to pump water around the state as is used by Los Angeles. Massive amounts of water will be needed to surface mine coal and reclaim the land (Section 10-5), to convert coal to synthetic liquid and gaseous fuels, and to recover and process oil shale (Section 13-5).

Water use in the United States has been increasing rapidly (Figure 15-4). Between 1900 and 1980, the average net use withdrawn each day increased eightfold, and average daily use per person tripled (Figure 15-4).

The United States has an almost insatiable thirst for water; Table 15-2 gives some of the uses. Of the 6.2 cubic meters (1,662 gallons) used each day by each person in 1980, about 0.23 cubic meter (60 gallons) was used for direct personal use. Indirect use, which provides each American with jobs, food, energy, and manufactured goods, amounted to another 6 cubic meters (1,596 gallons) per day, including 0.34 cubic meter (89 gallons) for commercial purposes (various businesses and service agencies that provide jobs), 2.6 cubic meters (693 gallons) to irrigate and grow food, 2.4 cubic meters (632 gallons) to cool electric power plants, and 0.7 cubic meter (183 gallons) to mine and manufacture various products. An average of 1.6 cubic meters (417 gallons) per person of water are used in the United States each day to produce energy.

As Figure 15-4 shows, per capita water withdrawal and net use are projected to rise rapidly in the future. By the year 2000, net use is projected to be slightly below the minimum estimate of the usable supply, and by 2020 it could be very near the maximum estimate. But this is only one projection. Actual water withdrawal by 2020 could be much less with greatly increased recycling by industry, more efficient use in irrigation, and a national water conservation program.

Many areas in the United States are already short of water either chronically or periodically because of recurring droughts. The problem is that U.S. water resources are not distributed evenly, as shown in Figure 15-5. It is estimated that by the year 2000 only 3 of the 21 federally designated water regions—New England, the Ohio Basin, and the South Atlantic–Gulf area—will have ample water supplies (Figure 15-5). The 1976 and 1977 drought in the western states, the 1980 drought in some southeastern states, and the 1981 water shortages over much of the United States (including the usually water-rich eastern states) were only test runs of what those areas and most others will probably experience continuously by 2000.

The water problems of the eastern half and the western half of the United States tend to be different. As seen from Figure 15-5, the eastern United States has the largest concentration of industry and people in metropolitan areas. Here the main problem is not a shortage of water but increasing water pollution by industries and large cities. In the western half of the United States, the main use of water is irrigation. The arid western states account for about 85 percent of U.S. water consumption, although they contain only 25 percent of the population.* The major problem in many of these areas is a shortage of water. These shortages could get much worse if more industries and people move in and if more of this region's precious water is used to mine the coal and oil shale and to tap geothermal energy resources found there (Section 13-5). You might find Figure 15-5 useful in helping you decide where to live in the coming decades.

Methods for Managing Water Resources Although we can't increase the earth's supply of water, we can manage what we have more effectively. The three basic methods

---

*Arid lands are those that receive an average of 51 centimeters (20 inches) or less rain per year.

of water management are: (1) the *input approach* to increase the supply of usable water by building dams and restructuring rivers; by using groundwater, desalting seawater, and towing icebergs; (2) the *output approach* to decrease loss by evaporation and to remove pollutants from existing supplies; and (3) the *throughput approach* to conserve water by reducing waste and average per capita use. The major methods of these approaches are summarized in Table 15-3.

Obviously, any effective plan for water management must use a combination of input, output, and throughput approaches. In the United States, much greater emphasis must be placed on this last approach.

15-4 Input Water Management: Dams and Water Diversion

Should We Build More Dams? Ever since people began to irrigate cropland and to live in cities, they have built dams, reservoirs, aqueducts, and pipes to store and carry water. When a river is dammed, a reservoir or lake forms behind the dam, which represents a temporary storage of water. A dam can capture high spring water flows resulting from heavy rainfall and melting snow in mountains above the dam. This water can then be released as needed. A dam and its reservoir offer several major benefits: (1) They reduce the danger of flooding in areas below the dam; (2) they provide a controllable and reliable flow of water for agricultural, industrial, and domestic uses in the areas below the dam; (3) they create a large water reservoir that can be used for water recreation; and (4) they can produce cheap hydroelectric power (Chapter 13 and Section 14-5).

Dams and reservoirs also have some serious disadvantages. First, they help prevent and control small floods, but they cannot prevent very large floods when abnormally high rains cause even the largest dams to overflow. Because most people mistakenly believe that dams protect them from all floods, they build cities and grow crops on flood plains (land vulnerable to flooding)* below the dam. Then when a large flood occurs, the damage is much greater than if the dam had not been built.

---

*Flood plains are normally classified as 18-year, 25-year, 50-year, or 100-year flood plains, according to the average frequency of a major flood. As a result, people mistakenly believe that floods will only occur every 18, 25, 50, or 100 years. But this is merely a statistical average; major floods could occur 3 times in 1 month or annually for 5 consecutive years.

Table 15-2 Average U.S. Water Requirements

Use or Product	Average Amount Used	
	Cubic Meters	Gallons
Home Use		
Direct use per person (per day)	0.23	60
Drinking water (per day)	0.001	0.26
Toilet (per flush)	0.02	6
Bath	0.14	36
Shower (per minute)	0.01	5
Shaving, water running (per minute)	0.008	2
Cooking (per day)	0.03	8
Washing dishes, water running (per meal)	0.04	10
Automatic dishwasher (per load)	0.06	16
Washing machine (per load)	0.23	60
Watering lawn (per minute)	0.04	10
Leaky faucet (per hour)	0.008–0.04	2–10
Leaky toilet (per hour)	0.004–0.02	1–5
Commercial Use		
Indirect use per person (per day)	0.34	89
Agricultural Use (Irrigation)		
Indirect use per person (per day)	2.60	693
One egg	0.15	40
454 grams (1 pound) of flour	0.28	75
Ear of corn	0.30	80
Orange	0.38	100
Glass of milk	0.38	100
454 grams (1 pound) of sugar	0.47	125
Loaf of bread	0.57	150
454 grams (1 pound) of rice	1.89	500
454 grams (1 pound) of beef	9.47	2,500
Industrial Use		
Indirect use per person (per day)	2.97	784
Cooling water for electric power plants per person (per day)	2.40	632
Industrial mining and manufacturing per person (per day)	0.70	183
Refine 0.004 cubic meter (1 gallon) of gasoline from crude oil	0.04	10
454 grams (1 pound) of steel	0.13	35
Refine 0.004 cubic meter (1 gallon) of synthetic fuel from coal	1.00	265
Sunday newspaper	1.06	280
454 grams (1 pound) of synthetic rubber	1.14	300
454 grams (1 pound) of aluminum	3.79	1,000
Automobile	379	100,000

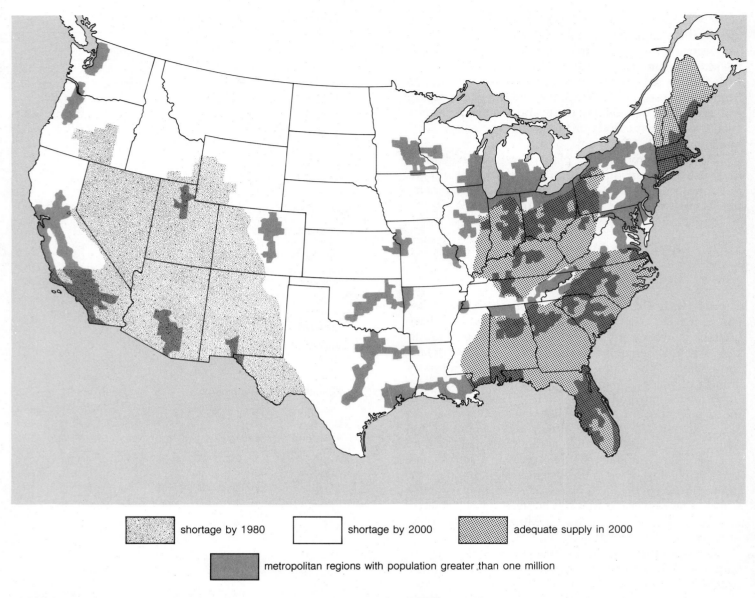

Figure 15-5 Present and projected water-deficit regions compared with present metropolitan regions with populations greater than 1 million. By the year 2000, only 3 of the 21 U.S. water regions are expected to have ample water supplies.

shortage by 1980   shortage by 2000   adequate supply in 2000

metropolitan regions with population greater than one million

Over the past 30 years the U.S. Bureau of Reclamation, Soil Conservation Service, and the Army Corps of Engineers have spent over $8 billion on flood-control projects to reduce losses from floods. Yet the total loss from floods continues to grow, and annual U.S. flood damage averages $3 billion. Flood control and reduction of flood losses are better accomplished by reforestation, erosion control, upstream watershed management, and land-use zoning that prohibits or severely limits human settlements and farming on flood plains.

A second disadvantage is that although dams control water flow, they do not increase the supply of water, contrary to popular belief. Indeed, a dam often decreases the available water supply because water that would normally flow in the river evaporates from the larger reservoir surface and seeps into the ground under the enormous pressure created by the reservoir. Third, reservoirs may offer some flood protection below the dam, but they permanently flood a large amount of land. This displaces people, destroys scenic natural areas and wildlife habitats, and, in the opinion of some outdoor enthusiasts, replaces a more desirable form of water recreation (white water canoeing and stream fishing) with a less desirable form (motor and sail boating and lake fishing). Finally, dams and reservoirs can have a number of unpredictable and undesirable ecological, economic, and health effects in surrounding areas.

The decision to build a dam should involve a careful analysis of potential benefits and drawbacks. Dams are favorite "pork barrel" projects for senators and representatives, who use them as visible evidence of federal money that they funneled into their state or district. Thus, many dams are built for political reasons, even though analysis shows that cheaper, less harmful, and better alternatives are available.

Water Diversion Projects People continue to dream up large-scale engineering schemes for diverting water from one area to another, usually for irrigation. Unfortunately, such multibillion-dollar projects sometimes generate even more expensive schemes to correct the problems that they create. Two of the largest irrigation projects in the United States serve California. Over 2,000 square kilometers (500,000 acres) have been brought under cultivation in the Imperial Valley of southern California by building a canal to divert water from the Colorado River.

The San Joaquin Valley in central California, which contains 32,400 square kilometers (8 million acres) of the most fertile land in the United States, is irrigated by water diverted from rivers in northern California.

These projects successfully supply water to fertile, dry land. But we are learning, as have past civilizations, that surface irrigation without adequate drainage is disastrous in the long run and destroys the cropland. As water flows over and through the ground, it dissolves various salts, a condition that is commonly referred to as **salinity.** As this saline water is spread over the soil for irrigation, much of the water is lost by evaporation and transpiration—processes that leave the salts behind. If these salts are not flushed or drained out, they can build up in the soil and make it infertile.

A problem that often accompanies soil salinity is **waterlogging.** Irrigation water percolating downward and accumulating underground can gradually raise the water table close to the surface. Too much water around plant roots inhibits growth.

Salinity and waterlogging are decreasing the productivity of at least one-third and perhaps as much as 80 percent of all irrigated lands throughout the world, especially in hot, dry climates where evaporation is rapid. Once fertile areas of southern Iraq and Pakistan now glisten with salt—looking like fields of freshly fallen snow. Salt-whitened soil is also found in California, Colorado, Wyoming, and other heavily irrigated areas in the United States. Salt buildup is a potential hazard on half of all irrigated land in the 17 western U.S. states and has already reduced crop production in a number of areas.

Table 15-3 Major Methods for Managing Water Resources

Input (increase supply in selected areas)	Output (reduce degradation and loss of existing supplies)	Throughput (reduce waste and per capita use)
Build dams to create lake reservoirs	Decrease evaporation losses in irrigation	Reduce overall population growth and growth in areas with water problems (arid regions and flood plains)
Divert water from one region to another	Use better drainage for irrigated agriculture to minimize salt buildup in soils	
Tap and artificially recharge more groundwater		
Desalt seawater and brackish water	Purify polluted water for reuse (Chapter 16)	Redesign mining, industrial, and other processes to use less water
Tow freshwater icebergs from the Antarctic to water-short regions		Reduce water waste
Control the weather to provide more desirable precipitation patterns		Decrease the average per capita use of water
Control pollution by preventing or limiting the addition of harmful chemicals (Chapter 16)		
Encourage people to move to areas with adequate water		

By 1990, up to one-fourth of the very productive San Joaquin Valley in California could be made infertile from salt buildup. The situation can be reversed, but only at great cost. One solution is to take the land out of production for 2 to 5 years, use large quantities of water to flush the salts out, and then install perforated drainage pipes underground. The U.S. Department of Interior has begun work on a $300 million "master drain" system for California's San Joaquin Valley. Drainage, however, can only slow down—not stop—the destruction of fertile soil by salinity.

Large-scale water diversion projects can have unknown, potentially serious ecological effects and can cost astronomical sums. One such project is now under way in the Soviet Union. On paper, the Soviet Union has plenty of fresh water—about 12 percent of the world's total. The trouble is that most of it is in the sparsely populated northern and eastern regions. To correct this situation, the U.S.S.R. has begun a long-range program to make several rivers in Siberia flow southward toward populated areas rather than northward toward uninhabited tundra as they do now. This project will take 20 years or more and cost at least $100 billion—possibly more than its estimated economic benefits. It could also have serious ecological and climatic effects. Since these rivers now flow into the Arctic Ocean, reversing their flow could change ocean currents. This in turn could cause serious shifts in world and regional climates and change ecological patterns of plant and animal life in the oceans.

An even more grandiose—but now defunct—water diversion scheme was the North American Water and Power Alliance (NAWAPA) proposal to divert huge amounts of water from Alaskan and northwest Canadian rivers and to pump the water uphill 300 meters (984 feet) through gigantic pipelines to 7 provinces in Canada, 33 U.S. states, and 3 states in Mexico. Thousands of kilometers of the world's most beautiful valleys would have been permanently flooded to create gigantic reservoirs, 15 of them much larger than Lake Mead, North America's largest artificial lake. The economic, hydrological, ecological, and political problems—to say nothing of possible climatic effects—of a project this size would be profound throughout the 20- to 30-year construction period and thereafter. The estimated cost in 1969 (before energy prices took off) was $200 billion. Another scheme—called the Grand Canal Concept—has been proposed in recent years to resolve many of the water supply problems for Canada and the United States. Much of the freshwater runoff now flowing into the Arctic Ocean from the James River Bay in eastern Canada would be recycled (not diverted) to form a new, dike-enclosed freshwater lake within the James Bay. From here it would be allowed to flow by various rivers into the Great Lakes to reduce the need to flood land areas. Then, open channels and pumping stations would be used to distribute the water to the major rivers that flow into the Canadian prairies and most of the United States. Economists have generally concluded that such massive projects are much too costly compared with their benefits and with other options. In addition, new federal laws requiring a thorough environmental impact analysis (Section 19-2) make it unlikely that projects such as NAWAPA, and the proposed diversion of part of the Mississippi River into western Texas and New Mexico, will ever be built.

15-5 Input Water Management: Groundwater Use, Desalination, Towing Icebergs, and Controlling the Weather

Use of Groundwater Groundwater makes up over 95 percent of all fresh water in the United States and can be found almost anywhere. This water is taken from a network of underground aquifers, which store water deposited thousands of years ago (Figure 15-6). These underground aquifers already supply about 20 percent of the fresh water and 40 percent of the water used for irrigation in the United States. More than 95 percent of rural Americans and 50 percent of all Americans use groundwater for drinking and other domestic uses. Twenty large cities depend solely on groundwater for their public water supply, and 12 states use groundwater for more than half of their public supplies. One solution to water supply problems is heavier reliance on groundwater. While more groundwater can be used, there are several problems: (1) depletion; (2) sinking, or subsidence, of the ground as groundwater is withdrawn; (3) salinization of fresh groundwater in coastal areas; and (4) groundwater contamination from human activities.

Groundwater depletion is a serious problem in some areas, as shown in Figure 15-6. Upper-level groundwater aquifers are refilled or recharged naturally where rainfall is abundant, but this renewal time is slow. For shallow groundwater (less than 1,000 meters deep) the average renewal time is 300 years, and for deep groundwater, 4,600 years (Table 15-1). Thus, removing groundwater faster than it is naturally recharged amounts to mining this valuable resource. This is occurring in Texas, New Mexico, Kansas, Colorado, Arizona, Hawaii, and California, where water tables have been dropping sharply

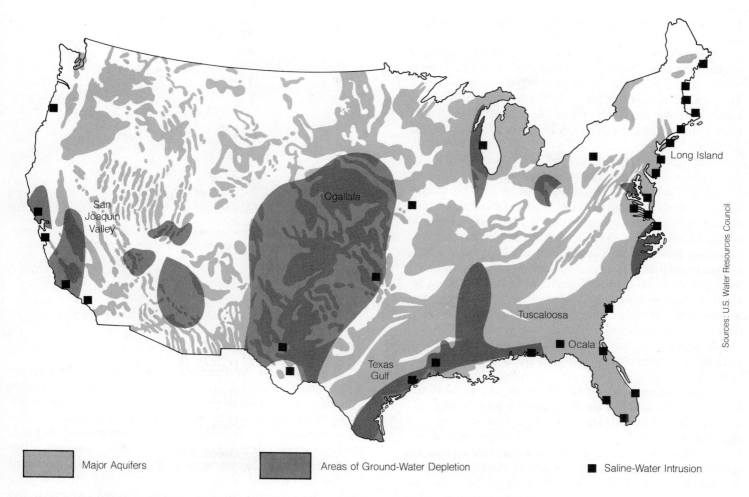

San Joaquin Valley

Ogallala

Long Island

Tuscaloosa

Ocala

Texas Gulf

Sources: U.S. Water Resources Council

| Major Aquifers | Areas of Ground-Water Depletion | ■ Saline-Water Intrusion |

Figure 15-6 The major underground aquifers that contain 95 percent of all the fresh water in the United States are being depleted in many areas and contaminated in other areas as salt (saline) water seeps in from the oceans or underground salt deposits to replace depleted groundwater.

(Figure 15-6). By 1980, the United States was removing an average of 29 cubic kilometers (7.7 trillion gallons) per year more from these underground deposits than was being put back in by natural processes.

For example, water from the great Ogallala Aquifer—stretching across the important farming belt from West Texas to northern Nebraska—is being depleted (Figure 15-6). This aquifer, which was formed thousands of years ago, is probably the largest underground reserve of fresh water in the world. Today, farmers withdraw more water each year from this aquifer than the entire annual flow of the Colorado River. The low rainfall in much of this area replenishes the aquifer at a lower rate than it is being used. As a result, the water tables in much of this region are falling at an average of 15 centimeters (6 inches) to

91 centimeters (3 feet) a year. At this rate, most of the Ogallala Aquifer could be depleted within 40 years. Already the amount of irrigated land is declining in 5 of the 6 states drawing water from the Ogallala, and farmers in some areas are having to shift from corn to crops such as cotton and sorghum that require less water.

One partial solution is to recharge groundwater artificially. Deep groundwater is pumped up and spread out over the ground to recharge shallow groundwater aquifers. But this can deplete deep groundwater deposits; also, because deep groundwater is often very salty, it can contaminate shallow deposits. Another approach is to use irrigation water, wastewater, and cooling water from industries and power plants to recharge aquifers. But much of this water is lost by evaporation, and in many cases it is better and cheaper to reuse cooling water.

Another problem is *subsidence*. When groundwater is removed from porous underground rocks and sediments, these materials tend to compact, which causes the ground to settle. The U.S. Geological Survey estimates that the city of San Jose, California, sank more than 3 meters (10 feet) between 1912 and 1962 due to this process.

When groundwater in coastal areas is removed faster than it is replaced, it can cause *saltwater intrusion*. As Figure 15-7 shows, in such areas there is a boundary between fresh and saline groundwater below the ocean bottom. When fresh groundwater is pumped from wells along the coast, the saline groundwater moves inward, replacing fresh groundwater with unusable salt water. Saltwater intrusion is already a serious problem in heavily populated coastal areas, such as New York (Long Island), New Jersey, Florida, and southern California. One remedy for both subsidence and saltwater intrusion is to recharge local groundwater with wastewater.

Another problem is *groundwater contamination*, especially near urban areas and large animal feedlots (Enrichment Study 16). Once contaminated, groundwater may remain unusable for hundreds of years. Bedford, Massachusetts, had to close its wells when its groundwater became contaminated from an industrial park built right above the aquifer that supplied 80 percent of the town's drinking water. In dozens of other Massachusetts communities citizens on low-sodium diets have been warned to drink expensive bottled water because salt spread on icy roads has reached into aquifers. The United States needs enforceable laws to protect underground water supplies from surface disposal of wastes, seepage from improperly operating septic tanks, mine drainage, sanitary landfills, animal feedlot wastes, agricultural pesticides and herbicides, and the rapidly growing practice of injecting wastes into deep underground wells (see Section 16-3). So far most U.S. water pollution laws (Section 16-6) have concentrated on rivers and lakes.

In 1980, a report by the Environmental Protection Agency indicated that groundwater depletion and contamination will be one of the most serious environmental problems of the 1980s in the United States. According to this report, 70 percent of 26,000 industrial liquid waste treatment or disposal sites (almost a third of which may contain potentially hazardous chemicals) are located above such porous ground that contamination can seep into the groundwater. Furthermore, over 90 percent of

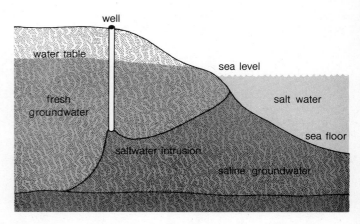

Figure 15-7 Saltwater intrusion along a coastal region. As the water table is lowered, the interface between fresh and saline groundwater moves inland.

these potential threats to groundwater purity are virtually unmonitored.

Desalination *Desalination*, or desalting, involves the removal of dissolved salts from water that is too salty for irrigation or human use. The two major methods of desalting are *distillation*, in which energy is used to evaporate fresh water from salt water to leave the salts behind, and *osmosis*, in which energy is used to force salt water through membranes with very tiny pores that prevent the salts from passing through.

Most people think of desalination with regard to the oceans, which make up 97 percent of our total water supply. Actually, **saline water** is any water containing more than 1,000 parts per million (ppm) of dissolved solids of any type. Saline water includes **brackish water** (having 1,000 to 4,000 ppm of dissolved solids), **salted water** (having 4,000 to 18,000 ppm), and **seawater** (having 18,000 to 35,000 ppm). Thus, desalination can be used on the coasts for purifying seawater and inland for purifying brackish water.

In 1979 the desalting plants produced only about 0.002 percent of the world's daily water use and only 0.017 percent of the daily use in the United States. Most of these plants are small and serve coastal cities in arid, water-short regions.

Some people see desalination as a major solution to freshwater shortages, but widespread use of desalination has two major problems. One is *economic*: Desalted water is very expensive, even though the price has come down considerably in recent years. Optimists have faith that new technology can lower the cost of desalination, but this seems very unlikely. Desalination requires large amounts of energy; as energy becomes more and more expensive, this technological dream fades away. Furthermore, it would take even more energy and money to pump desalted water uphill and inland from coastal desalting plants. Desalted water can be very useful in coastal areas where water shortages make the price of water by any method fairly high. But the main use of water throughout the world is for irrigation, and the price of desalted water will probably never be low enough for widespread use in irrigation.

The other problem with desalination is *ecological*. Building and using a vast network of desalination plants would release significant amounts of heat and other air pollutants (depending on the energy source). There would also be the problem of disposing of vast mountains of salt. If the salt is returned to the ocean, it would increase the salt concentration near the coasts and threaten food sources located in estuaries and the continental shelf.

Towing Icebergs   A 1990s travel ad for California might begin, "As the sun slowly sinks behind the icebergs off the golden California shore, tourists return to their hotels after a day of swimming and ice skating."

Some scientists feel it may be economically feasible to tow huge Antarctic icebergs to southern California, Australia, Saudi Arabia, Chile, and other dry coastal places. Icebergs are composed of fresh water, not seawater. Antarctic icebergs are broad and flat, resembling giant floating table tops, and they represent a potential freshwater source equal to 5 times the world's current domestic use of water, and one-third of the world's consumption for all purposes. They are better suited for towing than Arctic ones, which have mountainlike, irregular shapes and frequently roll over. Small icebergs were towed as early as 1890, but present proposals dwarf these early efforts.

It is now proposed that satellites and aircraft locate suitable flat icebergs. The total volume of such an iceberg could easily enclose 40 buildings the size of the Pentagon. Such an iceberg would contain enough to supply Los Angeles with 10 percent of its annual consumption of fresh water. Once located, helicopters and ships would be used to lasso the berg (a procedure still to be worked out) and to wrap it in an insulating covering (an object still to be designed) that would reduce melting while the iceberg was towed. Torpedoes and electrically heated cables would be used to cut a primitive prow, and then a fleet of tugboats (possibly nuclear powered) would tow the berg to its destination. It would probably take about a year to tow such a berg to California.

This technological feat, however, has a number of problems. First, the technology has not been worked out. No one really knows how to lasso, wrap, and tow such a huge object or how to prevent most of it from melting on its long journey through warm waters. One scientist believes that after spending $100 million, all you would have is an empty towline. It is apparently not feasible to tow an iceberg north of the equator (such as to Saudi Arabia or California) without somehow protecting it from melting. In addition, the system for getting the fresh water to shore has not been worked out. Second, no one knows whether the project is economically feasible. Towing and mining or melting the ice and then pumping it ashore and then uphill to inland areas will require enormous amounts of expensive energy and may make the project far too costly. However, because of increased water demand and dwindling supplies, such a project might be economically attractive by 2000. Third, towing and anchoring such a large, cold mass in semitropical areas could cause weather disturbances (possibly creating considerable fog and rain) and have harmful effects on marine life. Fourth, the scheme is a source of political conflict between nations over who owns the icebergs in the Antarctic. Fifth, there could be hazards to other ships, if chunks of the icebergs under tow should break off and be abandoned in international shipping lanes.

Controlling the Weather   Several countries, particularly the United States, have been experimenting for years with seeding clouds with chemicals to produce rain over dry regions and snow over mountains for subsequent river runoff. In principle, cloud seeding involves several steps: (1) Find a rain cloud; (2) fly a plane under or over the cloud or use ground mounted burners to inject it with a powdered chemical (the particles serve as nuclei that cause the small water droplets in the cloud to condense and form raindrops or ice particles); and (3) open up your umbrella. The most effective cloud seeding chemical is silver iodide in crystal form, but salt crystals, dry ice, and clay particles have also been used.

We know that cloud seeding works. In 1977, clouds were successfully seeded in 23 states covering 7 percent of the land area of the United States. But we do not know whether we are increasing total rainfall in an area or merely shifting rain from one area to another. There are also some problems. First, cloud seeding doesn't work in very dry areas, where it is most needed, because there are rarely any rain clouds available. Second, large-scale seeding could change regional or even global weather patterns in undesirable ways. Third, there could be serious ecological side effects, including (1) the unknown effects of silver iodide on humans and wildlife, (2) changes in snowfall and rainfall, and (3) additional flooding that could destroy or alter wildlife populations, upset food webs, and modify the soil. Fourth, there are legal disputes over who has the rights to water in a cloud. If one area removes water from clouds, it could deprive another area of water. During the 1977 drought in the western United States, the attorney general of Idaho accused neighboring Washington state of "cloud rustling" and threatened to file suit in federal court. Before deliberate attempts are made to change local and regional weather on a large scale, we need to know much more about the factors that determine local, regional, and global climate (Enrichment Study 3).

15-6   Output and Throughput Management

Output Approaches   In addition to finding new water sources, we can reduce water loss. Evaporation from lakes, reservoirs, and irrigated fields and transpiration from plants constitute a major problem. To reduce evaporation losses, the United States, Israel, Chile, Australia, and Italy have experimented with covering lakes and reservoirs with thin films of chemicals or plastic and with polystyrene spheres. But there are some major problems: (1) These coverings are disrupted by waves, winds, and boats (thus lakes having such coverings can't be used for recreation); (2) there is evidence that such coverings disrupt aquatic life by increasing the water temperature and by preventing essential oxygen in the air from reaching the water; (3) the resulting increase in water temperature can promote rather than diminish evaporation; and (4) this approach is very expensive. Much more research is needed before such films can be widely used.

Another method for decreasing evaporation is to use a network of underground plastic tubes to drip irrigation water directly onto the roots of plants. The approach, called *trickle irrigation,* uses only about one-fourth as much water as conventional ditch irrigation. Also, scientists may be able to breed new varieties of crops that require less water or that lose less water by transpiration. Also, see Section 16-6 for approaches involving the reclamation of polluted water.

Throughput Approaches   During the next three decades water management will be a major part of a total approach to our environmental crisis. Such water management will involve transporting vast amounts of water to increase inputs, bringing population growth and distribution into line with water supplies, strengthening pollution control, and above all, water conservation. *At least 30 percent and perhaps 50 percent of the water used in the United States is unnecessarily wasted.* This occurs primarily because water, like air, is treated as if it was free and to be used as one sees fit. Water, as vital as it is, makes up only 0.5 percent of industrial costs. It is not surprising, then, that industry uses vast amounts of water with little effort to design manufacturing processes that conserve rather than waste water. The United States (and other nations) can learn a lot about water conservation from Israel. Between 1950 and 1980, Israel has increased the utilization of the water it receives from 17 percent to 95 percent by a combination of output and throughput approaches.

As stated earlier, most of the world's water is used for irrigation. Since less than half of this water is actually used by the crops, even a small savings of 5 to 10 percent saves an enormous amount of water. Techniques for using irrigation water more efficiently include: (1) lining irrigation ditches to reduce seepage losses (although this could decrease the rate of groundwater recharge), (2) applying water less often and in smaller quantities (most farmers use too much),* (3) using trickle irrigation, (4) shifting to or developing crop varieties that require less water or that have a high enough salt tolerance so they can be irrigated with saline water, (5) growing more crops in areas with ample water rather than in arid regions that need expensive irrigation, (6) making farmers pay for water on the basis of the amount of water used (in some areas farmers pay on the basis of the number of acres farmed and thus have no incentive to cut consumption), (7) allocating more water to those who use conservation measures, and (8) raising water prices to promote conservation.

The wastage of industrial and municipal water could also be cut. Leaky pipes, toilets, and faucets alone may waste as much as 35 percent of the total water supply. Faucet and toilet leaks waste an estimated 757,000 cubic meters (200 million gallons) of water each day in New

---

*In Israel computers are used to monitor humidity, air temperature, and wind speed and adjust the amount of water delivered to plant roots in underground drip irrigation systems (sometimes doubling crop yields while cutting irrigation water use in half).

York City. There is little incentive to reduce leaks and waste in New York City because it does not have individual water meters. Instead, users are charged flat rates. Charging for water according to the amount used (as is done with natural gas and electricity) should encourage conservation. The biggest savings in industry result from cleaning up and recycling wastewater and reusing water again and again where it is used for cooling or other purposes that do not degrade the water. About 48 percent of all water used in the United States is for cooling, so reusing this water would substantially reduce per capita water withdrawal.

Partially degraded water could also be used for other purposes. For example, waste treatment plant effluent could be used to water golf courses and parks and to recharge groundwater aquifers; "gray" water produced in homes (water not used in toilets) could be used on lawns and gardens; and bath and shower water could be used in toilets. Water conservation could also be encouraged by reducing water rates during nonpeak hours (night) and seasons (winter). During the 1977 drought, residents of Marin County in California were able to reduce their water consumption by 65 percent by use of conservation measures. A year after the drought ended,

water consumption was running 45 percent below predrought levels.

Another approach is to change the entire water distribution system. Only 2 percent of U.S. municipal and industrial effluents are polluted by direct use. The other 98 percent is potable (drinkable) water that gets contaminated when it is mixed with the directly polluted water. Much money is spent to make all water coming into homes, buildings, and factories of drinkable quality. The water is then quickly contaminated so that it must be cleaned up again. Why not make the 98 percent pure water (most of which is used for cooling) part of a separate system that is continually recycled with minor purification? A national goal should be to establish two water systems—one for cooling and domestic consumption and one for carrying off wastes.

Finally, we get down to what you and I can do to waste less water. We don't have to go as far as the Californian who, in the middle of the 1977 drought, stapled a stamp to an envelope to save saliva, or the California couple who jokingly said they were going to get a divorce because of "shower temperature incompatibility." But there is a lot we can do, as the following suggestions and Table 15-4 show.

Table 15-4 How to Save Water

Item	Normal Use		Conservation Use	
	Cubic Meters	Gallons	Cubic Meters	Gallons
Shower	0.09	25	0.015	4
	Water running		Wet down, soap up, rinse off	
Brushing teeth	0.04	10	0.002	½
	Tap running		Wet brush, rinse briefly	
Tub bath	0.13	35	0.040 to 0.045	10 to 12
	Full		Minimal water level	
Shaving	0.08	20	0.04	1
	Tap running		Fill basin	
Dishwashing	0.11	30	0.02	5
	Tap running		Wash and rinse in dishpans or sink	
Automatic dishwasher	0.06	16	0.03	7
	Full cycle		Short cycle	
Washing hands	0.008	2	0.004	1
	Tap running		Fill basin	
Toilet flushing	0.02 to 0.03	5 to 7	0.015 to 0.023	4 to 6
	Depending on tank size		Using tank displacement bottles	
Washing machine	0.23	60	0.10	27
	Full cycle, top water level		Short cycle, minimal water level	
Outdoor watering	0.04	10	—	—
	Per minute		Lowest priority—eliminate	

Turn off the faucet when brushing your teeth, shaving, and washing dishes. Don't use the dishwasher or clothes washer until you have a full load. Repair all leaks quickly. Put a plastic container weighted with gravel into toilet tanks; bricks also work but tend to deteriorate and gum up the water. If every toilet in the United States had such a container, about 227,000 cubic meters (60 million gallons) of water would be saved each day. For new houses, install water-saving toilets or waterless toilets (where health codes permit). Shower quickly, and install reduced-flow faucets and shower heads, rather than taking a bath (which uses more water than a typical 5-minute shower).

Don't use a garbage disposal or water-softening system (both are major water users). Wash your car less and wash it from a bucket, using a hose to wet the car down and rinse it off afterward. Sweep walks and driveways instead of hosing them off. Water your lawn and garden in the early morning or in the evening, not in the heat of midday. Better yet, landscape with native plants instead of grass or plants that need watering. While waiting for faucet water to get hot, catch the cool water in a pan and use it to water plants. Do your utmost to conserve water in summer and during hot periods, when stream flows are low and demands are great.

The water you save by these and other practices is only a small portion of the total water wasted, but if 100 or 200 million individuals do the same thing, the impact is significant. You will be more sensitive to the problem and will have a constant reminder to tackle the big picture by becoming politically involved. If you and I don't begin, who will?

When the well is dry, we learn the worth of water.
Benjamin Franklin, 1746

Discussion Topics

1. What physical property (or properties) of water:
   a. accounts for the fact that you exist?
   b. allows lakes to freeze from the top down?
   c. helps protect you from the shock of sudden temperature changes?
   d. helps regulate the climate?

2. Explain how the use of water resources is related to:
   a. population growth (Chapter 8).
   b. forests and wilderness (Chapter 10).
   c. urbanization and urban growth (Chapter 11).
   d. land-use planning (Chapter 11).
   e. use of metals and minerals (Chapter 12).
   f. energy use (Chapters 13 and 14).

3. Criticize the following statement: We will run out of water by the year 2000.

4. Use the hydrological cycle to trace a possible route that the water you drink may take from the ocean to your faucet.

5. Explain why average annual precipitation is not a measure of the water available for human use.

6. If groundwater is a renewable resource, how can it be "mined" and depleted like a nonrenewable resource?

7. Criticize the following statement: Since each person in the world has an average of 12.7 million gallons of usable water, there are no serious water problems.

8. In your community:
   a. What are the major sources of the water supply?
   b How is water use divided among agricultural, industrial, and domestic and commercial uses? Who are the biggest users of water?
   c. What future water problems are projected for your community?
   d. How is water being wasted in your community and school?

9. Distinguish between withdrawal use and consumptive use of water, and give examples of each. Criticize the use of the word *consumptive* in this context.

10. Explain how you and I each can use, directly and indirectly, an average of 6.2 cubic meters (1,662 gallons) of water per day. How much of this is wasted or unnecessary?

11. What are the main functions of dams? What are some of the problems that they create? Should all proposed dam projects be scrapped? What criteria would you use in determining desirable dam projects?

12. Explain why dams, despite providing flood control, may lead to more flood damage than if they had not been built.

13. How could we prevent or minimize:
    a. soil salinity from irrigation?
    b. saltwater intrusion in coastal areas?

14. Explain why desalting, although useful and important, will not solve our water problems in the next 30 years. Using the scond law of energy (Section 3-3), explain why desalted water will not be available for widespread use in irrigation.

15. Explain some of the ecological problems in building a vast array of desalting plants in the United States. Should we build them? Why or why not? What are the alternatives?

16. Debate the proposition that we should raise the price of water for all users because its price is too low compared with the increasing costs of providing adequate, usable supplies for our growing population and water consumption. What political effects might this have? What effects on the economy? On you? On the poor? On the environment?

Readings

Clawson, Marion, et al. 1969. "Desalted Seawater for Agriculture: Is It Economic?" *Science*, vol. 164, 1141–1148. Shows why desalted water will be too expensive for widespread agricultural use.

Falkenmark, Malin, and Gunnar Lindh. 1974. "The Global Freshwater Circulation—The Most Spectacular of All Desalination Systems." *Ambio*, vol. 3, no. 3–4, 115–122. Superb discussion of water cycles and present and projected world supplies of fresh water.

Gelhar, Lynn W. 1972. "The Aqueous Underground." *Technology Review*, March-April, pp. 45–53. Excellent discussion of groundwater.

Hunt, Cynthia A., and Robert M. Garrells. 1972. *Water: The Web of Life*. New York: Norton. Outstanding overview of water as our most valuable resource.

Leopold, L. B. 1974. *Water: A Primer*. San Francisco: Freeman. Outstanding and easy-to-read introduction to the fundamentals of water resources.

Marx, Wesley. 1977. *Acts of God, Acts of Man*. New York: McCann & Gohegan. Excellent discussion of adverse impacts of building dams for flood control.

Murray, C. R., and E. B. Reeves. 1977. *Estimated Use of Water in the United States in 1975*. U.S. Geological Survey Circular 765. Washington, D.C.: Government Printing Office. Excellent source of data on present and future water use.

National Water Commission. 1973. *Water Policies for the Future*. Washington, D.C.: Government Printing Office. Detailed analysis of U.S. water resources, problems, and management policies.

Schanke, John C., Jr. 1972. "Water and the City." In Thomas R. Detwyler and Melvin G. Marcus, eds., *Urbanization and Environment*. North Scituate, Mass.: Duxbury. Excellent summary of urban water problems.

Stead, Frank M. 1969. "Desalting California." *Environment*, June, pp. 2–7. Discusses salt buildup in the soil resulting from improper irrigation practices.

van Hylckama, Tinco E. A. 1975. "Water Resources." In W. W. Murdoch, ed., *Environment: Resources, Pollution and Society*, 2nd ed. Sunderland, Mass.: Sinauer. Excellent summary.

White, Gilbert F. 1971. *Strategies of American Water Management*. Ann Arbor, Mich.: Ann Arbor Paperbacks. Basic reference for water management.

16

Water Pollution

Brush your teeth with the best toothpaste,
Then rinse your mouth with industrial waste.

Tom Lehrer

16-1 Types and Sources

What Is Water Pollution?   Water pollution is found in many forms. It is contamination of water with city sewage and factory wastes; the runoff of fertilizer and manure from farms and feedlots; kepone pollution of the James River; the Santa Barbara oil spill; sudsy streams; sediment washed from the land as a result of storms, farming, construction, road building, and mining; radioactive discharge from nuclear power plants; heated water from power and industrial plants; wastes from mining operations; sludge dumped into the ocean; asbestos fibers in the water supply of Duluth, Minnesota; some possible cancer-causing chemicals in New Orleans drinking water; plastic globules floating in the world's oceans; and female sex hormones entering water supplies through the urine of women taking birth control pills. Some of the effects of water pollution are foul-tasting drinking water; smelly lakes and rivers; beaches closed to swimmers in Italy and Israel; the burning Cuyahoga River; a Rhine River fish kill; the U.S. Food and Drug Administration seizing fish because of high levels of DDT or mercury; a hepatitis outbreak in New York City; a cholera outbreak in Naples, Italy, that kills 19 people who ate contaminated mussels; and dead rivers in São Paulo, Brazil.

Water pollution occurs when some substance or condition (such as heat) degrades a body of water to such a degree that the water doesn't meet specified standards or cannot be used for a specific purpose. Thus, water pollution depends not only on the nature of the pollutants but also on the intended uses of the water. Water

that is too polluted to drink may be satisfactory for industrial use. Water too polluted for swimming may not be too polluted for fishing. Water too polluted for fishing may still be suitable for sailing or for generating electrical power. In deciding what constitutes water pollution, we encounter the controversial problem of human value judgments.

Even though scientists have developed highly sensitive measuring instruments, determining water quality is very difficult. There are a large number of interacting chemicals in water, many of them only in trace amounts. About 30,000 chemicals are now in commercial production, and each year about 1,000 new chemicals are introduced. Sooner or later most chemicals end up in rivers, lakes, and oceans. In addition, different organisms have different ranges of tolerance and threshold levels for various pollutants (Section 6-2). To complicate matters even further, while some pollutants are either diluted to harmless levels in water or broken down to harmless forms by decomposers and natural processes, others (such as DDT, some radioactive materials, and some mercury compounds) are biologically concentrated in various organisms (Section 6-2).

Major Water Pollutants   Following are the eight major types of water pollutants:

1. *oxygen-demanding wastes** (domestic sewage, animal manure, and some industrial wastes)

2. *disease-causing agents* (bacteria, parasites, and viruses)

3. *inorganic chemicals and minerals* (acids, salts, and toxic metals)

Enrichment Studies 5, 6, 11, and 16 are related to this chapter.

*These wastes don't use up the oxygen that is dissolved in water, but the bacteria and other microorganisms that decompose them do. If water systems are overloaded with these wastes, the resulting population explosion of decomposer organisms can use up much of the dissolved oxygen supply so that most fish and many other forms of aquatic life cannot survive (see Enrichment Study 16 for more details).

4. *organic chemicals* (pesticides, plastics, detergents, industrial wastes, and oil)

5. *plant nutrients* (nitrates and phosphates)

6. *sediments* (soils, silt, and other solids from land erosion)

7. *radioactive substances*

8. *heat* (from industrial and power plant cooling water)

Table 16-1 summarizes the sources, effects, and methods for controlling these water pollutants.

All but a very few of the 246 water basins in the United States are affected, in whole or in part, by some kind of water pollution (Figure 16-1). In terms of quantity, sediments or water-suspended solids from land erosion are the largest source of water pollution each year in the United States (Figure 16-2) and throughout most of the world. Rates of natural land erosion, already high in many areas, may be increased 4 to 9 times by agricultural development, 10 to 100 times by careless construction, and 50 to 500 times by uncontrolled strip mining. About three-fourths of this sediment erodes from agricultural lands, especially in heavily farmed midwestern, western, and southern areas. The remaining fourth comes from other activities such as logging, mining, and construction. Enough topsoil erodes away each year in the United States to fill 18 freight trains, each long enough to reach around the world. During the past 200 years, a third of the topsoil on U.S. croplands has eroded away. The soil erosion problem in less developed countries is estimated to be nearly twice as bad as more land is stripped of trees for firewood (Section 10-4) and more marginal land is overcropped and overgrazed.

Although sedimentation is the major water pollutant in terms of quantity, other water pollutants can pose serious threats to plants and animals (including humans) when present in minute quantities. Some organisms have low tolerance levels (Section 6-2) to chemicals such as oil, some pesticides, and lead and mercury compounds. Other organisms with higher tolerance levels can be affected when the levels of some pollutants are biologically concentrated in food chains (Section 6-2).

Water pollutants can be classified as degradable (either rapidly or slowly) or nondegradable (Section 1-4). *Rapidly degradable* (nonpersistent) *pollutants* can be broken down fairly quickly by natural chemical cycling processes (Section 5-4) as long as the pollutants do not overload the system. They include domestic sewage, other oxygen-demanding wastes, plant nutrients, and some synthetic organic chemicals. To control these pollutants we need to prevent overload. Normally these pollutants are degraded into harmless or less harmful forms, but sometimes they are converted into more harmful forms. For example, microorganisms in acidic waters can convert moderately harmful mercury metal and inorganic mercury compounds into very toxic organic methyl mercury, as discussed in Enrichment Study 5. *Slowly degradable* (persistent) *pollutants* remain for long periods of time but are eventually broken down or reduced to harmless levels by natural processes. Examples include some radioisotopes and many synthetic organic chemicals, such as DDT, PCBs, phenols, and older-type detergents. Some of these substances, such as DDT, may be magnified up the food chain to levels that are harmful for wildlife and possibly for humans (Section 6-2). Because most of these pollutants are extremely difficult to

Table 16-1   Major Water Pollutants

Pollutant	Sources	Effects	Control Methods
Oxygen-demanding wastes	Natural runoff from land; human sewage; animal wastes; decaying plant life; industrial wastes (from oil refineries, paper mills, food processing, etc.); urban storm runoff	Decomposition by oxygen-consuming bacteria depletes dissolved oxygen in water; fish killed or migrate away; plant life destroyed; foul odors; poisoned livestock	Treat wastewater; minimize agricultural runoff
Disease-causing agents	Domestic sewage; animal wastes	Outbreaks of waterborne diseases, such as typhoid, infectious hepatitis, cholera, and dysentery (Enrichment Study 6); infected livestock	Treat wastewater; minimize agricultural runoff
Inorganic chemicals and minerals			
Acids	Mining (especially coal); industrial wastes	Kills some organisms; increases solubility of some harmful minerals	Seal mines; treat wastewater

Table 16-1 Major Water Pollutants *(cont.)*

Pollutant	Sources	Effects	Control Methods
Salts	Natural runoff from land; irrigation; mining; industrial wastes; oil fields; urban storm runoff; deicing of roads with salts	Kills freshwater organisms; salinity buildup in soil; makes water unfit for domestic use, irrigation, and many industrial uses	Treat wastewater; reclaim mined land; use drip irrigation; ban brine effluents from oil fields
Lead	Leaded gasoline; pesticides; smelting of lead (see Enrichment Study 5)	Toxic to plankton and humans	Ban leaded gasoline and pesticides; treat wastewater
Mercury	Natural evaporation and dissolving; industrial wastes; fungicides	Highly toxic to humans (especially methyl mercury)	Treat wastewater; ban unessential uses
Plant nutrients	Natural runoff from land; agricultural runoff; mining, domestic sewage; industrial wastes; inadequate wastewater treatment; food-processing industries	Algal blooms and excessive aquatic growth; kills fish and upsets aquatic ecosystems; eutrophication; possibly toxic to infants and livestock (see Enrichment Study 16); foul odors	Advanced treatment of industrial, domestic, and food-processing wastes; recycle sewage and animal wastes to land; minimize soil erosion
Sediments	Natural erosion; poor soil conservation; runoff from agricultural, mining, forestry, and construction activities	Major source of pollution (700 times solid sewage discharge); fills in waterways, harbors, and reservoirs; reduces shellfish and fish populations; reduces ability of water to assimilate oxygen-demanding wastes	More extensive soil conservation practices
Radioactive substances	Natural sources (rocks and soils); uranium mining and processing; nuclear power generation; nuclear weapons testing	Cancer; genetic defects (see Section 14-3)	Ban or reduce use of nuclear power plants and weapons testing; more strict control over processing, shipping, and use of nuclear fuels and wastes (see Section 14-3)
Heat	Cooling water from industrial and electric power plants	Decreases solubility of oxygen in water; can kill some fish; increases susceptibility of some aquatic organisms to parasites, disease, and chemical toxins; changes composition of and disrupts aquatic ecosystems	Decrease energy use and waste; return heated water to ponds or canals or transfer waste heat to the air; use to heat homes and buildings
Organic chemicals			
Oil	Machine and automobile wastes; pipeline breaks; offshore oil well blowouts; natural ocean seepages; tanker accidents	Potential disruption of ecosystems; economic, recreational, and aesthetic damage to coasts; taste and odor problems	Strictly regulate oil drilling, transportation, and storage; collect and reprocess oil and grease from service stations and industry; develop means to contain spills
Pesticides and herbicides	Agriculture; forestry; mosquito control	Toxic or harmful to some fish, shellfish, predatory birds, and mammals; concentrates in human fat; some compounds toxic to humans; possible birth and genetic defects and cancer (see Enrichment Study 6)	Reduce use; ban harmful chemicals; switch to biological and ecological control of insects (see Enrichment Study 11)
Plastics	Homes and industries	Kills fish; effects mostly unknown	Ban dumping, encourage recycling of plastics; reduce use in packaging
Detergents (phosphates)	Homes and industries	Encourages growth of algae and aquatic weeds; kills fish and causes foul odors as dissolved oxygen is depleted	Ban use of phosphate detergents in crucial areas; treat wastewater (see Enrichment Study 16)
Chlorine compounds	Water disinfection with chlorine; paper and other industries (bleaching)	Sometimes fatal to plankton and fish; foul tastes and odors; possible cancer in humans	Treat wastewater; find substitute disinfectant for chlorine

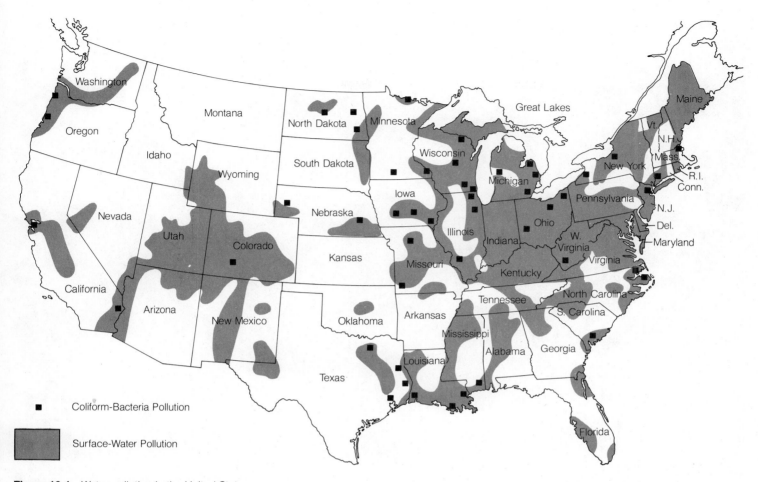

Figure 16-1 Water pollution in the United States.

remove by waste treatment methods, control measures must emphasize (1) preventing or minimizing their entry into the environment, (2) long-term storage until levels are safe, and (3) research to determine which of these pollutants are dangerous and capable of being magnified up the food chain. *Nondegradable pollutants* are not broken down by natural purifying processes. They include some metals (such as mercury, lead, and arsenic), some salts of metals, sediments, some synthetic organic componds (such as plastics), and some bacteria and viruses. These pollutants must be controlled either by removing them through waste treatment or by preventing them from entering the environment.

Sources of Water Pollution   As seen from Table 16-1, water pollution can result from natural runoff; dissolved

chemicals in water that percolates through the soil; and human sources, such as agriculture, mining, construction, industry, homes, and businesses. It is useful to classify pollution sources as either point sources or nonpoint sources. **Point sources** involve discharge of wastes from identifiable points. They include (1) sewage treatment plants (which remove some but not all pollutants, as discussed in Section 16-6); (2) storm water runoff from combined storm and sanitary sewer lines in urban areas; (3) industrial plants; and (4) animal feedlots where large numbers (sometimes 10,000 or more) of animals are scientifically fed in tightly restricted quarters before slaughter. **Nonpoint sources** involve the diffuse discharge of wastes from land runoff, atmospheric washout, and sources that are difficult to identify and control. They include (1) runoff of sediment from natural and human-caused forest fires, construction, logging, and farming;

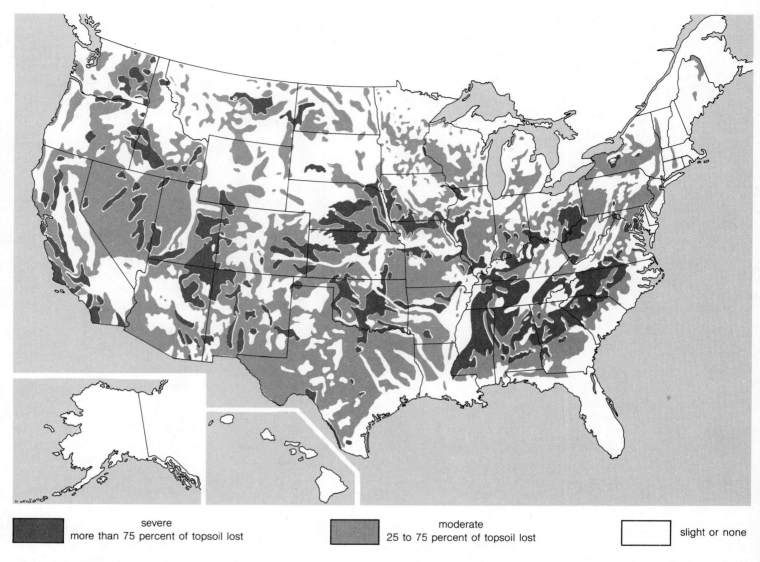

| severe
more than 75 percent of topsoil lost | moderate
25 to 75 percent of topsoil lost | slight or none |

Figure 16-2 Soil erosion in the United States.

(2) runoff of chemical fertilizers, pesticides, and saline irrigation water from croplands; (3) urban storm water runoff; (4) drainage of acids, minerals, and sediments from active and abandoned mines; and (5) spills of oil and other hazardous materials. Nonpoint source pollution is now recognized as a major problem, since the sources are widely spread out, difficult to identify, and hard to control. For example, nonpoint pollution from agriculture affects approximately 68 percent of the 246 river basins in the United States. About 98.7 percent of the sediments and oxygen-demanding wastes polluting U.S. waters came from nonpoint sources, 1.2 percent

from point source industrial discharges, and 0.1 percent from point source municipal discharges.

16-2   Effects of Water Pollution

Classification   Water pollution and other forms of environmental stress can have a number of harmful effects on individual organisms, populations, and biological communities and ecosystems, as summarized earlier in Table 6-2. We can rank water and air pollution effects in order of increasing danger to humans:

class 1: nuisance and aesthetic insult (odor, taste, and ugliness)

class 2: property damage

class 3: damage to plant and animal life

class 4: damage to human health

class 5: human genetic and reproductive damage

class 6: major ecosystem disruption

Table 16-2 summarizes the estimated effects of different types of water pollutants according to these six categories.

Is the Water Safe to Drink? For most of the world's population, especially in less developed nations, the major water pollution problem is drinking water contaminated with bacteria and viruses that cause sickness and death (Enrichment Study 6). In the United States, purification of drinking water led to a sharp drop in the incidence of waterborne diseases until the mid-1960s, when it started to rise again as discussed in Barbara Blum's Guest Editorial at the end of this chapter.

In 1974 and 1975 scientists found at least 253 synthetic organic chemicals in the drinking water supplies of 80 major U.S. cities, including at least 20 organic chemicals known or suspected to cause cancer in humans and test animals. Some of these chemicals are discharged into water supplies by industries. There is strong evidence, however, that some chlorine-containing organic chemicals (chlorinated hydrocarbons) which could cause cancer are formed when the chlorine—used to kill bacteria in drinking water consumed by about 75 percent of the U.S. population—combines with organic matter in raw water. It is difficult to relate chemicals in drinking water directly to various types of cancer, but there are a number of suspicious correlations. In 1980, the Council on Environmental Quality warned that several studies indicated that drinkers of chlorinated water have a 13 to 93 percent greater risk of getting rectal cancer, and about a 53 percent greater risk for colon and bladder cancer.

The Safe Drinking Water Act of 1974, as amended in 1977, requires the Environmental Protection Agency (EPA) to set standards for chemicals found in drinking water, protect underground sources of drinking water, and establish a joint federal-state program for assuring compliance with federal regulations. However, because of a lack of reliable scientific data, it is difficult to set safe-level standards for many of these inorganic and organic chemicals and the EPA has fallen behind in setting the standards for many chemicals found in drinking water. In addition, only a fraction of the chemicals in drinking water have ever been tested to determine whether they cause cancer. In 1978 the EPA issued regulations requiring additional treatment to reduce the amount of organic chemical contaminants in U.S. drinking water supplies at an estimated cost of $616 to $821 million.

16-3 Chemical Pollution of Rivers, Lakes, and Underground Water

River Characteristics and Pollution Freshwater ecosystems can be classified as **lotic** (flowing) **systems** (such as rivers and streams) and **lentic** (standing) **systems** (such as lakes and ponds). Because of differences in water movement, rivers and lakes differ considerably in their ecosystem structure and functions (Chapters 4 and 5) and in their water pollution problems.

Because they flow, most rivers can recover fairly fast from some forms of pollution, especially oxygen-demanding wastes and heat (Figure 16-3). Just below the area where large quantities of oxygen-demanding wastes are added, the concentration of dissolved oxygen in the water drops sharply (Figure 16-3). Further downstream, however, the concentration can return to its normal level. The depth and width of the *oxygen sag curve,* shown in Figure 16-3, and the time and distance a river takes to recover depend on a river's volume and flow rate and the volume of incoming oxygen-demanding wastes. Thus, rivers differ in their self-cleansing capacity. They can easily be overloaded if flow is naturally sluggish, as in the Potomac, or slowed by dams or drought, or if they are contaminated at many different point sources. A typical pattern, repeated hundreds to thousands of times along many rivers, is this: Water for drinking is removed *upstream* from a town, and industrial and sewage wastes are discharged *downstream* from the town. Because the river often does not have enough time to recover before receiving the next load of wastes, pollution tends to intensify closer to the ocean. If each town had to withdraw its drinking water from downstream rather than upstream, the quality of rivers would improve dramatically.

Another problem occurs when large quantities of toxic, nondegradable pollutants from agricultural runoff and industrial discharges enter a river. Both bottom life and fish may be killed, which can impair the river's abil-

Table 16-2 Effects of Water Pollution

Pollutant	Residence Time	Area Affected	When Threshold Levels Reached
Class 1: Nuisance and aesthetic insult			
Color (sediments, acid mine drainage)	Variable, usually short	Local, regional	Now in many places
Odor (phenols, eutrophication)	Weeks to decades	Local, regional	Now, especially in slow-moving rivers and shallow lakes near industrial centers
Taste (organic chemicals, sediment)	Days	Local	Now in some places
Class 2: Property damage			
Dissolved salts (corrosion)	Variable	Local	Now in some places
Muddy water (sedimentation)	Variable	Local, regional	Now in many places
Loss of real estate and recreation values (odor, eutrophication)	Variable	Local, regional	Now in many places
Class 3: Damage to plant and animal life			
Nutrients—nitrogen and phosphorus (eutrophication, excessive plant growth)	Decades	Local, regional	Now in shallow lakes and slow-moving rivers near industrial and agricultural centers
Heat (fish kills)	Days (but variable)	Local	Rarely, but has increased significantly within last 30 years
Some pesticides and other chemicals (fish kills)	Weeks to years	Local, regional	Infrequently, but could increase soon
Class 4: Damage to human health			
Bacteria	Days	Local, regional, global	Common in less developed nations; rarely in more developed nations, but could occur without careful supervision
Viruses	Days to months	Local, regional, global	Frequently
Nitrates	Continuous	Local, regional, global	Rarely, but may increase over next 30 years in heavily fertilized areas
Some industrial chemicals	Weeks to years	Local, regional	Now in some areas and increasingly over next 30 years
Some pesticides (in food chain)	Days to years	Local, regional, global	Unknown, but levels may increase over next 30 years
Metals (mercury, lead, cadmium)	Months to years	Local, regional	Now and increasing
Class 5: Human genetic and reproductive damage			
Pesticides	Days to years	Local, regional	Unknown, but probably not serious in water supplies
Some industrial chemicals	Weeks to years	Local, regional	Now and increasing
Radioactivity	Days to years	Local, regional, global	Rarely, but may increase over next 30 years as quantity of radioactive wastes from nuclear power plants rises
Class 6: Major ecosystem disruption			
Oil (especially refined)	Months to years	Local, regional, global	Rarely, but increasing over next 30 years
Some organic chemicals	Months to years	Local, regional	Rarely, but increasing over next 30 years
Some pesticides	Months to years	Local, regional, global	Rarely, but increasing over next 30 years
Erosion	Continuous	Local, regional, global	Now and increasing
Nutrients—nitrogen and phosphorus	Decades	Local, regional, global	Occasionally, but increasing over next 30 years
Heat	Variable	Local	Rarely, but increasing significantly over next 30 years

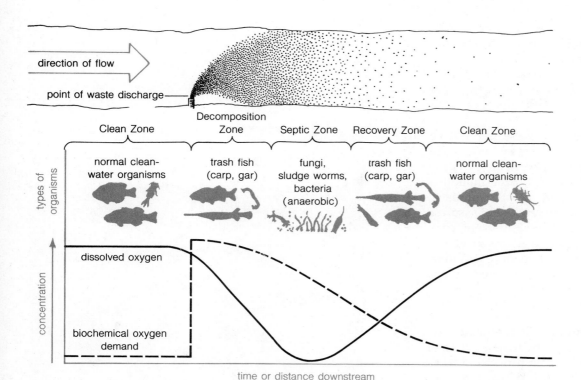

Figure 16-3 Depending on their flow rates and the amount of pollution, rivers can recover from oxygen-demanding wastes and heat if given enough time.

ity to handle oxygen-demanding biodegradable wastes. Of the 400 to 500 fish kills reported each year in the United States, industrial and municipal discharges account for 50 to 75 percent, and insecticide runoff for about 10 percent.

Dilution by the river can effectively treat heat, oxygen-demanding wastes, and short-lived toxic chemicals but only if the flow is adequate and the river is not overloaded with these pollutants. But for radioisotopes, heavy metals, slowly degradable organic chemicals (such as DDT and PCBs, which can be biologically magnified), oil, sludges, and other bottom-destroying chemicals, dilution and natural breakdown is ineffective. We must prevent these pollutants from entering rivers and lakes in large amounts.

Pollution of U.S. rivers and streams varies from region to region. A good indicator of water of drinking and swimming quality is a count of *fecal coliform bacteria.* These intestinal microorganisms are found in human and animal wastes. Although coliform bacteria themselves do not cause disease, their presence can indicate the presence of bacteria that cause typhoid, cholera, dysentery, and other wasteborne bacterial diseases.

A count of fecal coliform bacteria gives the number of bacterial colonies per 100 milliliters of water. A sample with a count of less than 100 is considered safe to drink. The EPA criterion for safe swimming is that the water should not have a count over 200, although some cities and states allow swimming at much higher levels. High coliform levels (over 200) are found in heavily populated areas of the Midwest, Northeast, and southern California (see Figure 16-1). The Great Plains and Southwest also show high coliform counts, often caused by low summer stream flow and runoff of livestock wastes (Figure 16-1).

Rivers are complex, varying, and poorly understood systems. Decreasing or preventing river pollution must be done throughout a river's entire length—not just at a few industrial plants or towns. Between 1963 and 1979, water pollution control efforts lowered average levels of coliform bacteria and oxygen-demanding wastes in most rivers, but not for heavily used major rivers such as the Mississippi, Missouri, Delaware, Hudson, Potomac, and Susquehanna. During this same period, however, average sediment and dissolved-solid levels rose in most rivers and streams. Because sediments and dissolved solids come from a large number of spread-out nonpoint sources, they are difficult to control.

Some heavily used rivers may never be clean. Yet there are fishable and swimmable rivers and streams that just 10 years ago were filthy. Fish have returned to a number of rivers, including the Connecticut, Mohawk, Detroit, Savannah, Tombigbee, and Arkansas. The Willamette River is a classic example of how integrated pollution control efforts can dramatically improve water quality.

Perhaps the most spectacular river cleanup has occurred in the river Thames, which flows by London. By the 1950s the Thames was little more than a lifeless, flowing sewer. But after 25 years of effort, $200 million of taxpayers' money, and millions more spent by industry, the Thames has made a remarkable recovery. Dissolved oxygen levels have risen between 21 and 30 percent, commercial fishing is thriving again, and many species of birds have returned to their former feeding grounds. Continuing cleanup efforts are being directed by the Thames River Authority, created in 1974.

Lake Characteristics and Pollution In contrast to rivers, lakes have relatively little flow. The flushing time of a river can be measured in weeks, but renewal in lakes may take 10 to 100 years (Table 15-1). As many as two-thirds of all lakes and 80 percent of the urban lakes in the United States may have serious pollution problems.

Lakes consist of three distinct zones (Figure 16-4): (1) the **littoral zone** near the shore, in which rooted aquatic plants are found; (2) the **limnetic zone** (or open-water surface layer) through which sunlight can penetrate, which is dominated by tiny floating plankton that use sunlight to carry out photosynthesis; and (3) the **profundal zone** of deep water, which is not penetrated by sunlight.

Lakes in temperate-climate regions tend to have layers of water with different temperatures during the summer and winter. During the summer, the surface water is heated by the sun so that an upper warm layer, called the **epilimnion** (Greek for "over lake"), floats over a denser bottom layer of cold water, called the **hypolimnion** (Greek for "under lake"), as shown in Figure 16-5. These two layers are separated by a fairly thin layer called the **thermocline** (or *metalimnion*), in which the temperature drops sharply. During autumn, winds cool and blow the upper layer so that the entire lake turns over. Thus, in winter the cold layer is on top and the warm layer on the bottom. This turnover normally occurs again in the spring. This movement allows the bottom layer of a lake to be exposed to air, enabling it to store dissolved oxygen that can be used by living organisms.

Like rivers, lakes have the pollution problems of fish kills from toxic chemicals and destruction of bottom life

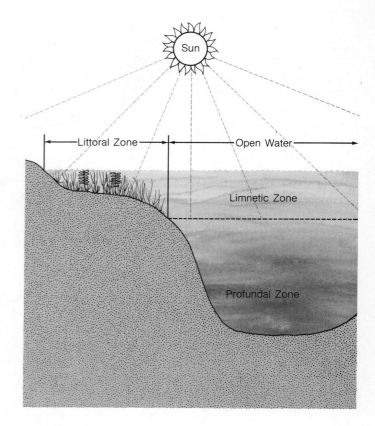

Figure 16-4 The major zones of a lake.

from oil and sludges. Lakes, with their low flow-rates, are even more susceptible than rivers to biological magnification of persistent and nondegradable chemicals (Section 6-2). The major pollution problem of lakes is accelerated **eutrophication** by plant nutrients (nitrates and phosphates) from wastes and runoff due to natural, agricultural, urban, and industrial activities. A lake with a large or excessive supply of plant nutrients is called a **eutrophic lake** (from the Greek "well nourished"). A lake with a low supply of plant nutrients is called an **oligotrophic lake** (from the Greek "poorly nourished"). All lakes undergo **natural eutrophication** as nutrients naturally flow in from surrounding land. Many lakes, particularly shallow ones near urban or agricultural centers, are choked by **cultural eutrophication,** which is the acceleration of natural nutrient enrichment by added nitrates and phosphates from runoff and wastes from farming (fertilizers and erosion), sewage treatment plants, animal feedlots, synthetic detergents, construction, mining, and poor land use, as summarized earlier in Figure 6-10.

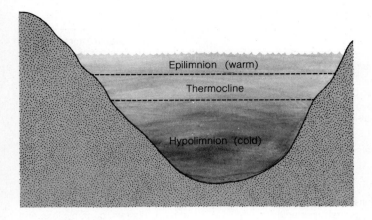

Figure 16-5 Temperature layers in a temperate-zone lake during the summer. A warm layer (epilimnion) floats over a cold layer (hypolimnion), with the two layers separated by a layer of rapid temperature change (thermocline).

During the summer months, excess nutrient enrichment can deplete the dissolved oxygen in the lake's bottom layer (hypolimnion) (Figure 16-5). This in turn can kill fish and other bottom species that must have a supply of dissolved oxygen to stay alive. Let's see how this process occurs. When a lake is overloaded with nitrate and phosphate plant nutrients, rooted plants (water chestnuts and water hyacinths, Enrichment Study 12) in the littoral zone and the floating phytoplankton plants (especially green and blue-green algae) in the limnetic zone may undergo a population explosion, or *bloom*, until they cover much of the lake's surface. The water then begins to look like pea soup or green paint. Some algal blooms, particularly those of blue-green algae, make the water taste and smell bad. Blooms of some species of blue-green algae and of dinoflagellates (red tides) in southern coastal regions can kill fish.

These blooms contribute oxygen to the water during daylight hours through photosynthesis. But as they die and fall to the bottom, they rob the lake's bottom layer of dissolved oxygen as they are decomposed by oxygen-consuming bacteria. Trout, whitefish, and many other species of fish die of oxygen starvation, while perch and carp, which need less oxen, thrive. The actual number of fish may even increase, but there will be *fewer kinds* of fish. Also, though this is irrelevant from nature's point of view, there may be fewer of the kinds of fish that most humans prefer to catch and eat. In shallow lakes or in the shore zone in deep lakes, the dead algae can also use up oxygen and kill fish in the surface layer of water. If nutrients continue to flood in, a lake's entire chemical

cycling system may fail. Then the water becomes foul and almost devoid of animals as anaerobic (non-oxygen-requiring) bacteria take over and produce foul-smelling hydrogen sulfide and other chemicals.

An estimated one-third of the 100,000 medium to large lakes in the United States are endangered by accelerated eutrophication. A National Eutrophication Survey of several hundred major U.S. lakes showed that 75 percent were eutrophic, and 6 percent very eutrophic. One of the most famous eutrophic lakes is Lake Erie. In the 1960s there were persistent rumors that it was dying, but its main problem is that much of it is overnourished and much too alive with plant life. This problem is intensified because Lake Erie is fairly shallow and is located near major population centers in the United States and Canada. As a result it receives massive doses of nitrates, phosphates, and various toxic chemicals (Figure 6-10).

Excessive eutrophication can be controlled either by decreasing nutrient flow into lakes (input approaches) or by cleaning up lakes that are already eutrophic (output approaches), as discussed in more detail in Enrichment Study 16. Fortunately, because of intensive pollution control efforts by the United States and Canada, conditions in Lake Erie and the other Great Lakes are slowly improving. Today most swimming beaches that had been shut down for 30 years have been reopened. Highly prized sport fish, such as lake trout and walleye, have made a comeback.

Contamination of Groundwater We have seen that groundwater is an extremely important source of fresh water (Section 15-5). Almost half of the U.S. population depends on underground sources for drinking water. As water percolates down through the ground to underground aquifers, it is naturally filtered and purified of most harmful chemicals. However, this water source, along with rivers and lakes, is threatened by pollution. Some groundwater can be contaminated by mercury, lead, arsenic, various nondegradable and very persistent wastes, and viruses from human wastes. In 1975 groundwater in Oregon and Washington was found to be contaminated with viruses that were present in water that leached out of "sanitary" landfills where disposable diapers containing fecal matter had been buried. Symptoms of arsenic poisoning that showed up in 1972 in a small Minnesota farming community were traced to an arsenic-based pesticide that had been massively applied in 1934 to deal with a grasshopper infestation. It took 38 years for the nondegradable arsenic compound to per-

Table 16-3 Undesirable and Desirable Effects of Thermal Water Pollution

Undesirable Effects	Desirable Effects
Thermal shock (the sudden death of thermally sensitive aquatic life due to sharp changes in temperature). When a power plant first opens, the sudden injection of hot water can kill some existing species. Then when the plant shuts down for repairs, the sudden temperature drop could kill the new heat-resistant species that have moved in.	Longer commercial fishing season and increased catches when desirable warm-water species are attracted to heated water areas
Increased susceptibility of aquatic organisms to parasites, disease, and toxic chemicals	Reduction in winter ice cover
Disruption of fish migration patterns	Increased recreational use because of the warming of very cold bodies of water
Lowered dissolved oxygen concentrations at a time when the higher water temperature raises organisms' oxygen requirements	Use of warm water for aquaculture (Section 9-5) to cultivate catfish, shrimp, lobsters, carp, oysters, and other species eaten by humans
Fewer eggs and fewer surviving young for thermally sensitive species (Figure 6-7)	Use of heated water to heat buildings, provide hot water, remove snow, desalt ocean and brackish water, and provide low-temperature heat for some industrial processes. These uses, however, require that fossil fuel and nuclear power plants be built near urban areas, increasing the risks from air pollution and accidental releases of radioactivity.
Reduction of diversity of species by elimination of thermally sensitive organisms	
Shifts in species composition (This may be beneficial or harmful, depending on the new species that thrive in heated water. Undesirable slime and blue-green algae thrive in heated water.)	
Disruption of food webs by loss of one or several key species, especially plankton, at lower levels of the food webs	
Delay of spring and fall lake turnover	
Mutilation or killing of small organisms and fish sucked through power plant intake pumps, pipes, and heat exchange condensers	
Fish kills and other ecological damages caused by the chlorine, copper sulfate, or other chemicals used to keep bacteria and other microbes from fouling the water-cooling pipes in power plants.	

colate down to the groundwater that served as a source of drinking water for the community.

Fortunately, such cases are rare, but a new and more serious threat has arisen. Faced with tougher water pollution laws, U.S. industries have begun injecting their liquid wastes directly into deep underground disposal wells. By 1979 there were 500,000 wells injecting fluids under the ground, with at least 5,000 new wells being added each year.

In theory, deep-well injection seems safe and has worked reasonably well in many cases. Such wells are usually drilled below freshwater zones (Figure 15-2) into a layer of porous rock. This layer must be bound between thick impermeable rock layers that have no cracks so that wastes cannot escape into groundwater supplies.

But there are several problems that may limit the use of this disposal method. First, the number of disposal sites with the desired geological conditions are limited. Second, wastes in some "safe" sites have migrated to other underground areas, to groundwater used to supply drinking water, or even back to the surface through nearby abandoned gas, oil, or water wells. If well sites are overloaded, pressure builds up and escape routes can multiply. Some wastes, such as acids, can cause clay minerals and iron oxides from the supposedly impermeable rock layers to dissolve, allowing the pollutants to migrate into fresh groundwater supplies. For example, industrial wastes injected underground in Canada came out of the ground in Michigan. Deep brine injection wells in Texas often leak, and some have spouted forth like geysers. Acidic wastes from a Wilmington, North Carolina, chemical company leaked from a deep disposal well into an overlying freshwater aquifer. These extreme cases warn of real danger and expose our ignorance about this growing practice for waste disposal. They also demonstrate the fallacy of the idea "out of sight, out of mind."

Third, the metal casing of the well injection pipes

can burst under pressure or be corroded by the wastes, allowing the pollutants to flow into fresh groundwater aquifiers. Fourth, deep-well injection in some areas can cause earthquakes. Between 1962 and 1965, the U.S. Army injected large amounts of poisonous war gases and insecticides in deep wells near Denver. During this same period the Denver area experienced a series of 28 earthquakes—the first earthquakes ever recorded there. Once fluid injection stopped, the earthquakes did too. Investigators believe that the injected fluid allowed underground rock layers to slip past one another, thus triggering the earthquakes.

Fortunately, the Safe Drinking Water Act of 1974 may lead to better control over deep-well disposal. It requires the states to establish programs to protect underground drinking water sources from underground waste injection and other means of introducing contaminants. It also requires the EPA to monitor groundwater quality and conduct a survey to find safe disposal sites. Since 1978 all existing and new deep disposal wells must have permits issued by the respective state or the EPA.

16-4   Thermal Pollution of Rivers and Lakes

Huge quantities of heated water are being dumped into streams, lakes, and oceans by power and industrial plants. About 26 percent of all water used in the United States each year is for cooling electric power plants and it is estimated that the use could increase by 650 percent between 1975 and 2000. It has also been projected that by 2000 one-fourth to one-third of all the freshwater runoff in the United States will be used to cool power plants. This percentage could double during the summer when water flow is low. However, these figures mask the fact that streams near urban areas will be intensely heated while isolated ones may not. Although average temperature increases may not be too large, most of the hot water will be discharged near the ecologically vulnerable shoreline where fish spawn and young fish spend their first few weeks.

We also have the problem of the threshold effect (Section 6-2). One or several power plants may use a given body of water without serious damage, thus giving the misleading impression that others can be built. Then just one more plant can completely disrupt the system by causing the system's threshold level to be exceeded.

You can see why environmentalists are concerned about aquatic ecosystems receiving large amounts of heated water. But again we run into a controversy. Some

Table 16-4 Methods for Minimizing Thermal Water Pollution

Input Approach	Output Approach
Use less energy (Section 14-1).	Return heated water in a way that minimizes damage (for instance, away from the fragile shore zone).
Waste less energy (Section 14-1).	Dissipate some of the heat in cooling ponds or canals (in places where land is cheap enough).
Limit the number of power and industrial plants allowed to use a given body of water.	Transfer heat to the air either by evaporation (wet cooling towers) or by conduction and convection (dry cooling towers). However, cooling towers may rise as high as a 30-story building and measure more than a block in diameter at the base (Figure 16-6). Wet cooling towers can cause mist, fog, and ice around them. Both kinds are expensive, but the dry kind costs 2 to 4 times as much as the wet.

view waste heat as a potential water pollutant that can damage and disrupt aquatic ecosystems while others talk about using heated water for beneficial purposes and speak of *thermal enrichment* rather than *thermal pollution*, as summarized in Table 16-3.

Possible Solutions   The sites of most existing and possible future fossil fuel and nuclear power plants prevent the beneficial use of their enormous outputs of hot water. Pumping water for long distances to croplands, aquaculture ponds, and buildings requires energy (and money), and most of the heat is lost in the transport. Thus, the best course is to reduce thermal water pollution as much as possible. This leaves us with several alternatives, which are summarized in Table 16-4).

Because of strict federal water pollution laws, more power plants are using cooling ponds, canals, or cooling towers (Figure 16-6) to prevent thermal overload of rivers and lakes. Perhaps the real question we should ask ourselves is whether we really need all of this electricity.

16-5   Ocean Pollution

The Ultimate Sink   The oceans are the ultimate sink for both natural and human wastes. Everything flushed from the land, whether by humans or by natural erosion, eventually reaches the sea (Figure 16-7). Water used and

Figure 16-6 Cooling towers for the Rancho Seco nuclear power plant near Sacramento, California. Compare the size of the towers with the power plant and automobiles. Each tower is over 122 meters (400 feet) high and could hold a football field in its base.

Sacramento Municipal Utility District

contaminated in homes, factories, and farms flows into rivers, which eventually empty into the ocean. In addition, wastes are loaded on barges and dumped directly into the ocean. As a result, about 85 percent of all ocean pollution comes from sources on the land.

Fortunately, the vastness of ocean waters and their constant mixing dilute many of these wastes to harmless levels. Other wastes are broken down and recycled by natural chemical cycles (Section 5-4) in ocean ecosystems. But the vastness of the oceans as a resource can be deceiving. Although the oceans can purify and recycle large amounts of some pollutants, their capacity to do so has limits. The sheer magnitude of discharges, especially near the coasts, can overload these natural purifying systems. In addition, these natural processes cannot readily degrade many of the plastics, pesticides, and other synthetic chemicals created by human ingenuity.

Slowly we are learning that even this magnificent resource can be degraded by human activities. We are abusing the ocean in three major ways: (1) overexploiting its marine resources (as discussed in Section 9-5 and Enrichment Study 12), (2) using it as a dumping ground for wastes, and (3) polluting it with oil. Before discussing ocean dumping and oil pollution, let's look at the ocean as an ecosystem.

The Marine Ecosystem The ocean can be divided into several zones (Figure 16-8). The **neritic zone** includes the *estuarine zone* (Section 10-6), where the sea and land meet, and extends out to the edge of the continental shelf. This zone—representing less than 10 percent of the total ocean area—contains 90 percent of all sea life. Sunlight can penetrate the waters in this shallow zone, allowing photosynthesis to occur among its vast population of phytoplankton, the floating plants that are the

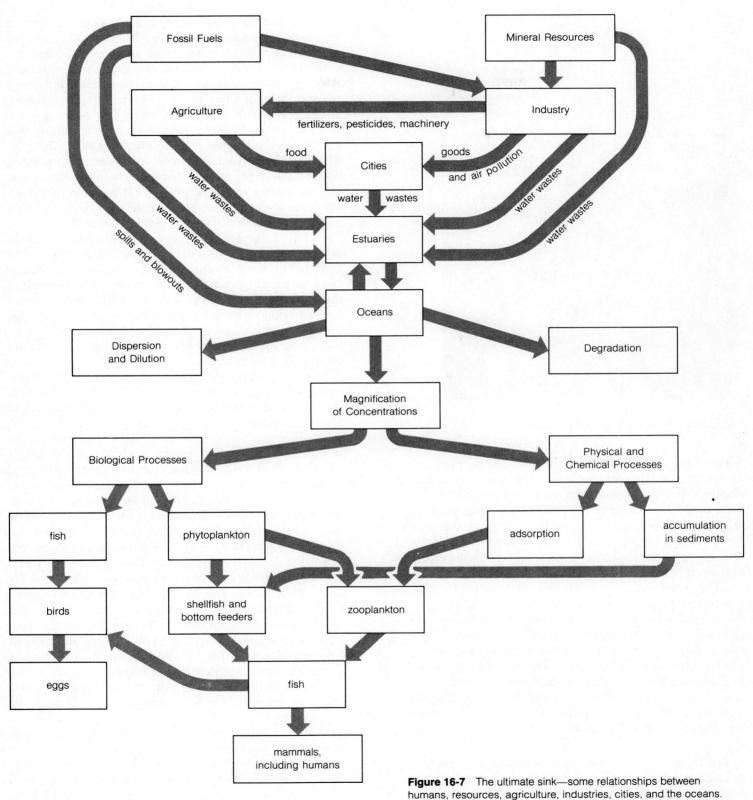

Figure 16-7 The ultimate sink—some relationships between humans, resources, agriculture, industries, cities, and the oceans.

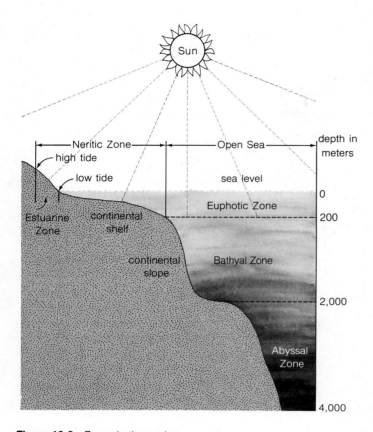

Figure 16-8 Zones in the marine ecosystem.

grass of the sea. These plants support the zooplankton and bottom-feeding (or benthonic) invertebrates, such as shellfish, that in turn support larger fish and add to our food supply. As we move out from the continental shelf, we enter the **open sea** (or *oceanic zone*). Because there are few nutrients in the open sea, it can support relatively little life compared with the neritic zone. Thus 90 percent of the sea can be considered a biological desert.

The open sea is divided into three vertical zones. The layer through which light can penetrate is known as the **euphotic zone**—the zone in which photosynthesis can occur. Below the euphotic zone is the **bathyal** (*dark open-water*) **zone,** in which many of the larger organisms, such as tuna and whales, cruise. But most ocean species important to people are found either on the continental shelves or where upwelling currents sweep up nutrients from the ocean bottom. Finally, we encounter the **abyssal** (*bottom*) **zone** of the ocean.

Ocean Dumping Obviously the waters most important to us for food, habitation, and recreation are the estuarine zone and the shallow continental shelf waters (Sec-

tions 9-5 and 10-6). Yet these very waters take the brunt of our pollution assault. Wastes dumped at sea can kill marine life, stimulate excessive algae growth, and deplete the water's dissolved oxygen. Some persistent and nondegradable pesticides and metals can kill or damage marine life even when present in trace amounts. For example, copper in concentrations as low as 0.1 ppm is lethal to softshell clams. Toxic chemicals and those that can undergo biological magnification can also reduce the diversity (Section 6-2) of marine ecosystems. Simplifying ocean ecosystems can shorten food chains and eliminate top carnivores (most larger fish). These simpler communities are also more susceptible to such threats as a sudden massive oil spill or a pesticide runoff.

In the United States, barges and ships dump wastes at designated sites near the Atlantic, Gulf, and Pacific coasts. The most intensely used dumping area is the New York bight, a portion of the ocean off the mouth of the Hudson River. Each year the New York bight receives over 8.6 billion kilograms (9.5 million tons) of waste. This dumping has covered a 104-square-kilometer (40-square-mile) area on the ocean bottom east of New York City with a black toxic sludge.

In 1972 a small gleam of hope for the world's oceans appeared when representatives of 91 countries, including all major maritime powers, met in London and signed an ocean dumping agreement. The signing nations agreed to stop dumping high-level radioactive wastes, biological and chemical warfare agents, various kinds of oil, some pesticides, durable plastics, mercury, and cadmium. Arsenic, lead, fluorides, cyanides, zinc, and several other metals can still be dumped, but only with special permits. The agreement does not include wastes related to offshore mineral exploration and development of seabed mineral resources, nor does it apply to wastes dumped into rivers and lakes that empty into the oceans. In spite of these weaknesses, it was a historic international step, and by 1975, 54 nations had signed the final agreement. In 1980, after 12 years of debate, the UN Conference on the Law of the Sea approved a draft treaty with standards to prevent overfishing and rules to control ocean pollution. In 1981, however, the Reagan administration indicated that it wanted to reopen the entire text of the treaty—a move that could destroy the tentative agreement among nations after 12 years of negotiation.

In the United States, the 1972 international ocean dumping agreement and the U.S. Ocean Dumping Act of 1972 have led to a sharp decrease in ocean dumping off U.S. shores since 1972. The 1972 act bans ocean dumping of wastes (except dredged materials) by U.S.

vessels unless they have a permit approved by the EPA. Since 1981 all ocean dumping judged to be harmful by the EPA has been banned (including municipal sewage sludge). But everything must go somewhere (Section 3-1). As cities increase waste treatment to meet more strict water pollution standards, more sewage sludge is produced. It must then be burned (air pollution), dumped onto the land (water and soil pollution), or dumped into the ocean. Since the ocean can recycle much of this waste if not overloaded (except for various pesticides and toxic metals), some argue that the ocean may be the best place for sewage sludge. However, if bacteria, pesticides, and toxic metals can be removed, this sludge can be returned to the land as fertilizer, as discussed in Section 16-6.

Progress is being made in controlling ocean dumping, but there is a long way to go. Some wastes can be safely dumped and absorbed or broken down by the ocean, but not radioactive wastes, persistent and nondegradable synthetic organic compounds, metals that

are toxic to marine organisms, and toxic chemicals that can be biologically magnified. Since we must protect the oceans, the wisest course may be to ban or limit the dumping of many potentially toxic materials until we know that they have no or little effect. We can get some idea of these problems by looking at one major ocean pollutant in more detail.

Ocean Oil Pollution Each year over 6 billion kilograms (7 million tons) of oil and petroleum are added to the oceans. This oil comes from a number of sources, as shown in Figure 16-9. About 10 percent of the annual input is due to natural seepage of crude petroleum from deposits below the ocean bottom. Human activities account for the remaining 90 percent, which is added in the forms of *crude petroleum* (oil as it comes out of the ground) and *refined petroleum* (obtained by distillation and chemical processing of crude petroleum). Despite

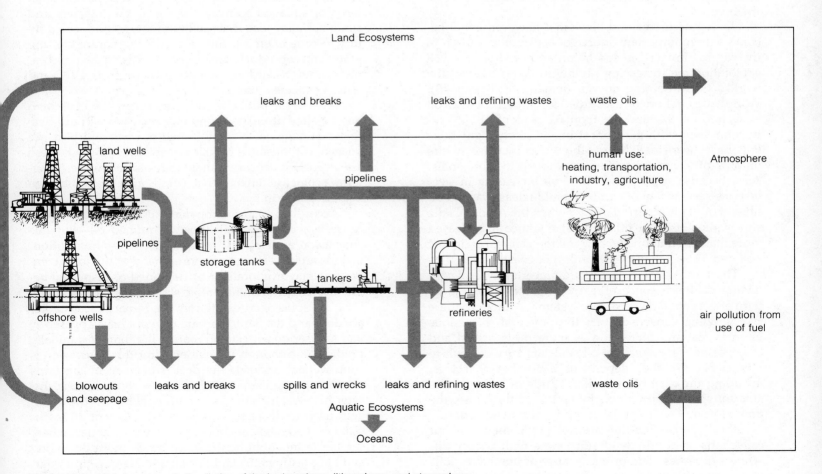

Figure 16-9 Major sources of oil pollution of the hydrosphere, lithosphere, and atmosphere.

widespread publicity, spills from oil tanker accidents (such as the *Torrey Canyon*, which broke up off the coast of England in 1967) account for only about 5 percent of the annual input. The accidental rupture of offshore oil wells, such as the Santa Barbara, California, oil blowout in 1969 and the much larger blowout of the Pemex oil well off the coast of Mexico in 1979, make up only about 1 to 5 percent of the annual input. About 61 percent of the annual input comes from two sources: (1) river and urban runoff, mostly from the disposal of lubricating oil from machines and automobile crankcases (31 percent), and (2) intentional discharges from tankers during routine shipping operations, including loading, unloading, cleaning oil tanks, and discharging oil-contaminated ballast water (30 percent). The discharge of ballast and cleaning water is the major problem. After a tanker unloads its oil cargo, it takes on seawater to help stabilize the large and unwieldy craft and also to clean the emptied oil tanks. Then at sea or just before the tanker reaches its home port, this water-oil mixture is discharged into the ocean.

Tanker accidents and blowouts, however, could become a more important source of ocean oil pollution in the future. Tanker transportation and offshore oil well exploration are increasing rapidly in order to meet the world's mushrooming energy demands (Chapter 13). Worldwide offshore oil accounted for 20 percent of all oil extraction in 1979 and for about 12 percent of U.S. extraction. Even with the more stringent safety regulations that have been introduced, the sheer increase in the number of wells and tankers could lead to more spills. Also, because supertankers are still increasing in size, just one serious tanker accident could release vast quantities of oil. This occurred in 1978 when the Amoco Cadiz supertanker broke up off the coast of France and released more than 254 million liters (67 million gallons) of oil that polluted 322 kilometers (200 miles) of coastline.

There is considerable dispute, uncertainty, and conflicting evidence concerning the short-term and long-term effects of oil on ocean ecosystems. Although, there is a growing consensus that the potential for serious harm is real and increasing as more oil is drilled and transported. The effects of oil spills are very difficult to predict because they depend on a number of factors, including the type of oil spilled (crude or refined), the amount spilled, how close the spill is to the shore, the time of year, weather, tidal currents, and wave action.

Crude and refined oil are not single chemicals but collections of hundreds of substances with widely different properties. The primary cause of immediate kills of a number of aquatic organisms, especially in their lar-

val forms, are low-boiling, aromatic hydrocarbons. Fortunately, most of these highly toxic chemicals evaporate into the atmosphere within a day or two. Some other chemicals remain on the water surface and form floating, tarlike globs, which can be as big as tennis balls, while other chemicals sink to the ocean bottom. A number of these chemicals are degraded by marine microorganisms, but this natural process is slow (especially in cold Arctic and Antarctic waters), requires a large amount of dissolved oxygen, and tends to be least effective on some of the most toxic petroleum chemicals.

Some marine birds, especially diving birds, die when oil interferes with their normal body processes or destroys the natural insulating properties of their feathers. Some oil components find their way into the fatty tissues of some fish and shellfish, making the fish unfit for human consumption because of their oily taste. Among these compounds may be such well-known carcinogenic chemicals as 3,4-benzopyrene. Some petroleum chemicals can also cause subtle changes in the behavioral patterns of aquatic organisms. For example, lobsters and some fish may lose their ability to locate food, avoid injury, escape enemies, find a habitat, communicate, migrate, and reproduce. Floating oil slicks can also concentrate other hazardous compounds, such as DDT and other pesticides, that are soluble in oil.

Most of the publicity and outcry against oil pollution has resulted from its economic, recreational, and aesthetic damage, such as oil-coated beaches and pleasure boats and thousands of killed seabirds. Although these are important concerns, there may also be hidden long-term ecological effects that could upset and damage aquatic communities.

According to oil companies, crude oil spills may cause less damage than those of refined oil—but this conclusion is disputed by some scientists. In addition, if spills are far enough offshore, many of the toxic compounds may evaporate or be degraded or dispersed before they reach the vulnerable shore zone. For example, the large spills of crude oil from the *Torrey Canyon* tanker accident and the Santa Barbara blowout have apparently had less serious effects on marine life than was initially predicted—although the evidence for this conclusion is controversial. Indeed, the deaths of most of the birds and other organisms killed after the *Torrey Canyon* disaster have been blamed not on the oil but on the detergent used to disperse it. In contrast, spills of oil (especially refined oil) near shore or in estuarine zones, where sea life is most abundant, have much more damaging and long-lasting effects. For example, damage to estuarine zone species from the spill of refined oil at West Fal-

Table 16-5 Approaches to Oil Pollution Control

Input Approaches	Output Approaches
Use and waste less oil (Section 14-1) and reduce population growth (Chapter 8).	Use mechanical barriers to prevent oil from reaching the shore, then vacuum oil up or soak it up with straw. This works well only on calm seas and is like trying to get smoke back into a smokestack (the second energy law again).
Collect used oils and greases from service stations and other sources (possibly by a payment-incentive plan) and reprocess them for reuse.	
Strictly regulate the building of supertankers and superports.	Treat spilled oil chemically (usually with detergents) so that it will disperse, dissolve, or sink. Since this method can kill more marine life than does the oil, it is not favored by ecologists.
Use load-on-top (LOT) procedures for loading and emptying all oil tankers (already done on 80 percent of all tankers).	
Build supertankers with double bottoms, or hulls, to reduce chances of a spill and to separate oil cargo from ballast water.	Ship oil in a solid state, much like a gel, so that it can be picked up quickly and easily if an accident occurs.
Reduce the potential for tanker accidents by better training for tanker crews and better navigation aids.	Develop bacterial strains (by genetic recombination) that can degrade compounds in oil faster and more efficiently than natural bacterial strains. Possible ecological side effects of these "superbugs" should be investigated before widespread use.
Strictly enforce safety and disposal regulations for offshore wells and international agreements prohibiting discharge of oily ballast and cleaning water from tanks.	
Strictly enforce safety and disposal regulations for refineries and industrial plants.	Add oil-soluble ferrofluids (iron-containing material) to the spill, which will enable electromagnets to remove the oil.
Strengthen existing international agreements on oil spills and establish a strong international control authority for the oceans.	

mouth, Massachusetts, in 1969 was still being detected 10 years later.

Oil spills damage the environment. They are also a waste of valuable energy resources and are expensive to clean up—at least $28,000 for each 3.8 cubic meters (1,000 gallons) of oil spilled. Since the *Torrey Canyon* and Santa Barbara incidents, a great deal of effort has gone into trying to reduce the amount of oil reaching the ocean (input approaches) and to remove or minimize its effects once it does (output approaches). The major input and output methods for controlling oil pollution are summarized in Table 16-5. Emphasis should be placed on input approaches to reduce environmental effects, oil wastes, and costs.

16-6 Water Pollution Control

Principles and Methods of Pollution Control Controlling a particular water, air, or land pollutant is not a simple process. It involves a number of scientific, technological, economic, and political factors. An *idealized*

scheme for pollution control would consist of the following steps:

1. Set up local, regional, national, and global measurement systems to identify pollutants and their sources. Emphasize ecological and biological measurements of ecosystems and organisms in addition to the physical and chemical measurements presently being used.

2. Trace the movement, change in form, concentration, biological magnification (Section 6-2), and residence time of each pollutant in the land, air, water, and plant and animal life, including people.

3. Determine any synergistic interactions (Section 6-2) between each pollutant and other chemicals.

4. Find the level of a pollutant that can be tolerated by an organism and ecosystem before short-term or long-term harmful effects occur.

5. Determine whether each pollutant can be a nuisance, cause property damage, endanger plants and animals, endanger human health, cause human genetic damage, and disrupt ecosystems by

interfering with chemical cycling or energy flow on a local, regional, or global basis.

6. Carry out a cost-benefit analysis that compares the benefits of using a pollution source (such as an automobile or paper factory) with its harmful effects, and determine how much money is required to reduce the pollutant concentration to a desirable level (see Chapter 18 for details).

7. Set short- and long-range qualitative goals for a pollution control program (for example, making water suitable for swimming, cleaning the air so that it will not produce disease in healthy humans, and preserving ecosystem stability). Establishing these goals involves tradeoffs between what is desirable and what is politically and economically feasible.

8. Set short- and long-range *ambient air and water quality standards* that translate qualitative goals into quantitative maximum levels allowed in the air, water, soil, and food. These standards may vary from region to region and are only enforceable if emission and effluent standards are used.

9. Set short- and long-range *emission (or effluent) standards* that prescribe how much of each kind of pollution is allowed from each source. These standards may also vary among areas, depending on population density, weather and climate, types of industry, and other factors.

10. Pass the necessary laws and enforce each standard, balancing out the conflicting political and economic interests. These laws must be directed at polluters, not pollution, and penalties must be sufficient to deter polluting but not cause widespread economic and personal injustice by being either too lenient or too severe.

11. Once ambient and emission standards have been legally established, set up a local, regional, national, and global monitoring system that can quickly and accurately measure pollutant levels in the air, land, water, and living organisms.

12. Develop an integrated short-term, intermediate-term, and long-term plan of pollution control that uses the technology, laws, taxes, and economic incentives (Chapter 18) needed to reduce or keep pollutants below harmful levels.

13. Wherever possible, try to use input, throughput, operation, and substitution pollution control methods rather than output control methods, which are normally more expensive and difficult (see Table 16-6 and Kenneth E. F. Watt's Guest Editorial at the end of Chapter 17). Also, recycle chemicals, such as sewage treatment plant effluents, to places on the land where they can be useful rather than dumping them into the water or air, where they can cause overloads.

14. Institute an effective citizen education and awareness program to develop the funds and public support necessary to carry out the pollution control program.

The general approaches used to control a particular type of pollutant are summarized in Table 16-6.

The fourteen principles just described and the pollution control methods given in Table 16-6 can be used to control almost any type of pollution. Although we often separate air, water, and land pollution, they are related and must be controlled in an integrated program. Otherwise, we may merely transfer a pollutant from one part of the ecosphere to another and thus trade one pollution problem for another. Pollution control programs must also be carefully integrated with population, resource use, and land-use control programs.

The idealized program just described, of course, cannot be instituted without considerable difficulty and uncertainty. For example, because of the complex and mostly unknown effects and interactions of pollutants, we will probably never be able to set exact standards or determine specific pollutant levels that cause specific diseases or ecological effects. However, just because we can't determine allowable pollutant levels perfectly does not mean that we shouldn't establish tentative levels that can be adjusted as we get better information, as discussed by Barbara Blum in her Guest Editorial at the end of this chapter.

Although there are many significant gaps in our scientific and technological knowledge of pollution, we can control over the short range most of the air and water pollutants now considered dangerous. Often the major problems are political and economic, involving balancing the ecological and health risks and cleanup costs of a pollutant with its economic and social benefits (see Chapters 18 and 19). Further, what constitutes a cost, a risk, or a benefit must also be established.

One dangerous aspect of pollution control is that public political pressure will diminish as the most obvious and annoying forms of pollution, such as smoke and bad tasting and smelling air and water, are eliminated. We could be lulled into a false sense of security. We might delay the development of improved technology or the control of population size and wasteful consumption that is necessary to prevent the invisible and

Table 16-6 Approaches to Pollution Control

Input Control	Operation and Substitution Control	Throughput Control	Output Control
Prevent or reduce the amount of pollutant from reaching the atmosphere or a body of water (for example, use soil conservation techniques to reduce dust blown into the air and sediment washed into aquatic systems).	Alter or replace a process to generate less or none of the pollutant (for example, develop a car engine or a paper-making process that produces less pollution).	Reduce the rate of throughput; that is, slow down production and consumption (for example, reduce consumption by price increases, pollution taxes, economic incentives, or, as a last resort, rationing).	Remove the pollutant or dilute it at the emission source (exhaust pipe, smokestack, or sewage line).
Select inputs that contain or produce little if any of the pollutant (for example, use natural gas, coal gasification, or low-sulfur oil for electric power plants).	Make the process more efficient so that less energy and matter are wasted and less pollution is produced (for example, convert aluminum ore to aluminum metal with a process requiring less electricity).	Find and promote shifts to substitute products or services that are less harmful (for example, emphasize mass and para transit rather than cars in cities and use reusable soft drink bottles instead of cans).	Remove the pollutant or lower its concentration (usually harder and more expensive because the pollutant is dispersed—the second energy law again).
Remove the pollutant before using the input (for example, remove the sulfur from coal and oil).		Stabilize and redistribute population to help reduce total consumption and to prevent pollution buildup.	Convert the pollutant to a less harmful form (for example, convert very toxic methyl mercury to less harmful inorganic forms of mercury, as discussed in Enrichment Study 5).
Improve the natural ability of an ecosystem to dilute or degrade a pollutant (for example, add oxygen to a river or lake to increase its ability to degrade oxygen-demanding wastes).			Choose the time and place of discharge to minimize damage (for example, use tall smokestacks to disperse air pollutants at high levels where they may be dispersed more effectively, or stagger work hours to reduce air pollution by motor vehicles). This approach does not reduce the total pollution load, but it can spread it out so that harmful levels may not be exceeded.

often more dangerous forms of pollution from eventually rising beyond acceptable levels. Thus, a crucial part of any pollution control program involves educating people to realize that the most dangerous pollution threats to human health and ecosystems are often unseen. Let's look more closely at some of the technological, ecological, economic, and political aspects of water pollution control.

Soil Conservation Since soil erosion is the single largest source of water pollution, soil conservation is the most important approach for reducing sedimentation in streams. Reducing this loss of soil is also a major factor in maintaining the fertility of the land. Although soil is technically a renewable resource, the average rate of erosion per unit of cropland in the United States is about 3 times the rate at which soil is reformed. A number of

practices, summarized in Table 16-7, can be used to reduce soil erosion.

In 1935, after the disastrous dust bowl years, the United States became the first nation in the world to establish a Soil Conservation Service to provide farmers and ranchers with technical assistance to reduce soil erosion. With the cooperation of state and county agencies, the U.S. Soil Conservation Service has divided land into eight major classes. Four classes can be cultivated to varying degrees, three others are best suited for grazing or forestry, and the last class is suited primarily for wildlife or recreation.

Although nearly $15 billion has been spent on soil conservation since 1935, soil erosion is still one of the most severe environmental problems in the United States. Indeed, topsoil losses today are 2.5 percent worse than in the dust-bowl years of the 1930s. One reason is that many farmers are more interested in maximizing

Table 16-7 Soil Conservation Methods

Method	Description
No-tillage farming	Planting without first removing the existing plant cover and previous crop residues (can reduce soil erosion by 95 percent)
Minimum tillage farming	Plowing only to the depth needed to ensure quick seed germination and leaving crop residues and ground litter to protect the soil
Contour cropping	Plowing and planting along the contours of the land so that water cannot run off of the soil as easily (can reduce soil erosion by 50 percent)
Strip cropping	Alternating strips of close-growing plants (such as grass and clover) and regular crops (such as corn, cotton, and potatoes). The strips of close-growing plants slow water runoff and when combined with contour cropping can reduce soil erosion by 75 percent.
Terracing	Developing flat, steplike terraces to reduce water runoff on very steep slopes
Crop rotation and cover crops	Planting fields periodically with close-growing secondary crops that allow less soil erosion and planting dense-growing cover plants when no crop is being grown
Gully reclamation	Seeding gullies with quick-growing plants and using check dams of manure and straw to reduce erosion
Windbreaks (shelterbelts)	Planting rows of shrubs and trees as wind-breaking barriers along the windward edges of croplands to reduce soil loss from wind; replanting trees on land no longer used to grow crops (Section 10-4)
Not planting marginal land	Raising crop yields on good land (Section 9-7) to reduce pressures to farm marginal land
Land classification and zoning	Classifying land according to its suitability for cultivation and using land-use zoning and controls to prevent the loss of good cropland and the planting of marginal land (Section 11-5)

short-term crop yields than in conserving the soil. Heavy and increasingly expensive applications of fertilizer and pesticides to maintain high yields merely hide the fact that the natural fertility and productivity of U.S. soils are being depleted at an alarming rate. Until soil erosion can be sharply reduced, sediments will be the major source of water pollution from nonpoint sources.

Sewage Treatment Two major approaches for dealing with the liquid wastes of civilization are dumping them into the nearest waterway and cleaning them up to vary-ing degrees by means of septic tanks, lagoons, or sewage treatment. In many less developed countries the first approach is widely used, causing widespread infection from waterborne disease (Enrichment Study 6). More developed nations emphasize municipal sewage treatment. Waterborne wastes from homes, businesses, and factories and storm runoff flow through a network of sewer pipes to a sewage treatment plant. Some areas have separate sewer lines for sewage and storm water runoff, whereas in other areas lines for these two sources are combined. The combined system is cheaper, but during a large storm the total volume of wastes may be larger than the treatment plant can handle. When this occurs, some of the wastes are allowed to overflow and go untreated into the nearest river or stream.

When sewage reaches a treatment plant, it can undergo various levels of treatment, or purification, depending on the sophistication of the plant and the degree of purity desired. Figure 16-10 and the accompanying box summarize primary, secondary, and tertiary sewage treatment. A sewage or wastewater treatment plant is essentially a factory where very clean or relatively clean water is produced by using a combination of physical, chemical, and biological purification processes. In 1977 the liquid wastes of approximately 58 percent of the U.S. sewage received primary and secondary treatment, 25 percent received primary treatment, and about 17 percent was either degraded in cesspools and septic tanks or discharged directly into waterways. By contrast, nearly 90 percent of the sewage that pours into the Mediterranean Sea is untreated.

Building secondary sewage treatment plants throughout the United States is an important step in water pollution control, especially in reducing oxygen-demanding wastes, suspended solids, and bacterial contamination. But there are some problems with this engineering approach. Two major products of the bacterial degradation of oxygen-demanding wastes are nitrates and phosphates, which can act as plant nutrients. Allowing these sewage effluents from sewage treatment plants to flow back into lakes and slow-moving rivers can overload these systems, triggering algae blooms and oxygen depletion (Enrichment Study 16). In addition, solid sludge from sewage treatment plants can pollute the ocean whenever it is dumped there, pollute the air whenever it is burned, and pollute groundwater whenever it leaches out of landfills or deep disposal wells.

Ecological Waste Management and Recycling Instead of overloading aquatic systems with nitrate- and phos-

Waste Treatment Methods

Primary treatment is a mechanical process that uses screens to filter out large debris (such as stones, sticks, and rags) and a sedimentation tank, where suspended solids settle out as **sludge.** These two operations remove about 60 percent of the solid material but only one-third of the oxygen-demanding wastes. Chemicals are sometimes added to speed up the settling of suspended solids, a process called *flocculation,* which brings down most bacteria and suspended matter.

Secondary treatment is a biological process that uses bacteria to break down wastes. This removes up to 90 percent of the oxygen-demanding wastes by using either *trickling filters* (sewage is degraded by bacteria as it trickles through a bed of stones) or an *activated sludge process* (sewage is aerated with either air or pure oxygen to aid bacterial degradation). The water from the trickling filter or aeration basin is then sent to a sedimentation tank, where more suspended solids settle out as sludge. Primary plus secondary treatment still leaves 10 to 15 percent of the oxygen-demanding wastes, 10 percent of the suspended solids, 50 percent of the nitrogen (mostly as nitrates), 70 percent of the phosphorus (mostly as phosphates), 95 percent of the dissolved salts (including toxic metals, such as lead and mercury), and essentially all of the long-lived radioactive isotopes (Section 14-3) and dissolved and persistent organic substances, such as pesticides.

Tertiary treatment refers to a whole series of specialized chemical and physical processes used to reduce the quantity of one or more of the pollutants remaining after primary and secondary treatment. At present, tertiary treatment is rarely used because it is expensive (twice as costly to build the plant and up to 4 times the operating costs of primary plus secondary treatment), because it normally requires large amounts of energy, and because many methods are still in the experimental stage. Following are three tertiary treatment processes:

1. *Precipitation* (coagulation-sedimentation): removal of suspended solids and phosphorus compounds
2. *Adsorption* (using activated carbon): removal of dissolved organic compounds
3. *Electrodialysis or reverse osmosis:* reduction of dissolved organic and inorganic substances to their original levels

Disinfection is carried on as part of all three forms of sewage treatment to remove water coloration and to kill disease-carrying bacteria and some (but not all) viruses. Chlorine is the most widely used disinfectant, but its use may form cancer-causing chlorine compounds in drinking water. A new disinfection method that may be more effective and less harmful uses ultrasonic energy to break down wastes mechanically and other disinfectants, such as ozone or chlorine dioxide, to kill bacteria. This approach, however, is more expensive than chlorination. A less-costly approach is to wait until the water is filtered, or organic materials have settled, before adding chlorine and filtering the water with activated charcoal (which removes organic material) where local supplies are heavily contaminated with organics.*

---

*Concern over drinking water contamination has led many homeowners to begin drinking bottled water. However, the standards for bottled water are based on removing bacterial contamination, not toxic chemicals. Home units that attach under the sink and that filter water through activated charcoal offer the most protection against toxic and possibly cancer-causing organic contaminants, until water-treatment plants install safer purification systems, as required by the EPA by 1985 for most public water systems.

phate-rich sewage effluents, these plant nutrients should be returned to the land (forests, parks, and croplands) or to aquaculture ponds (Section 9-5) as fertilizer. We need to use a sustainable-earth approach to waste management that mimics nature by recycling plant nutrient wastes to the land, as shown in the shaded areas of Figure 16-10 and in Figure 16-11.

Five major methods have been suggested for using sewage wastes as resources: (1) using the liquid effluent from secondary sewage treatment plants to irrigate and fertilize croplands, forests, parks, and strip-mined land and to grow fish and shellfish in aquaculture ponds and estuaries (Section 9-5); (2) using the solid sludge from sewage treatment plants to fertilize croplands, forests, parks, and strip-mined land; (3) fertilizing land and allowing natural systems to treat our sewage by directly applying untreated wastewater to land and aquaculture systems; (4) collecting and transporting sewage wastes to biogas plants, which produce natural gas that can be burned as a fuel and a residue that can be used as fertilizer; and (5) reducing the amount of sewage, conserving water (Section 15-6), and fertilizing land by switching to waterless toilets. For example, the Clivus Multrum waterless toilet, now widely used in Sweden (Figure

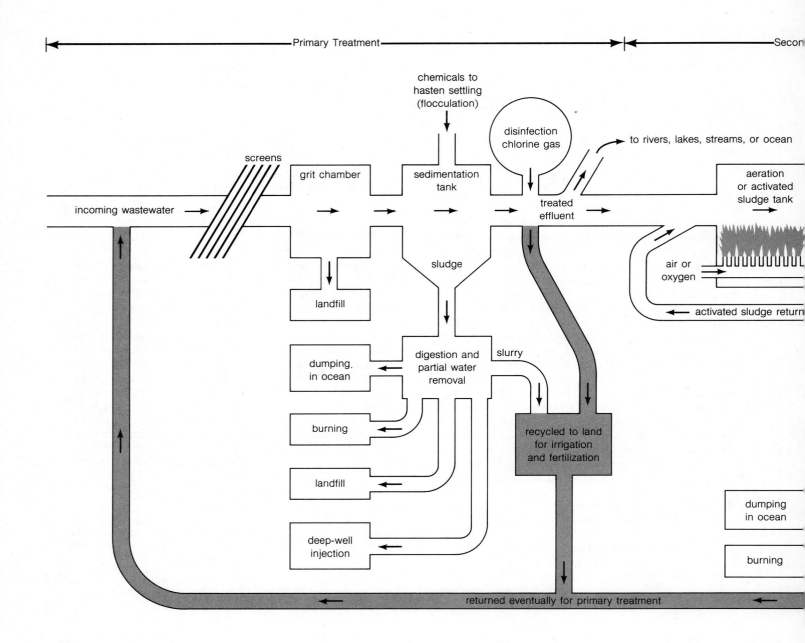

chemicals to
hasten settling
(flocculation)

disinfection
chlorine gas

to rivers, lakes, streams, or ocean

screens

grit chamber

sedimentation
tank

aeration
or activated
sludge tank

incoming wastewater →

treated
effluent

landfill

sludge

air or
oxygen

activated sludge return

dumping
in ocean

digestion and
partial water
removal

slurry

burning

recycled to land
for irrigation
and fertilization

landfill

dumping
in ocean

deep-well
injection

burning

returned eventually for primary treatment

16-12), uses bacteria to break down human and food wastes and forms a dry, odorless, solid fertilizer.*

*The Clivus Multrum is expensive ($1,500 to $2,000) and takes up a lot of space, but in the long run it should be cheaper than the combined costs of water toilets, septic tanks, water, and monthly sewage treatment fees. Mass use will also bring its costs down. Unfortunately, outdated health codes in some parts of the United States still prohibit this safe alternative, which has been used in Sweden since the 1930s. For further information, write Clivus Multrum USA, 14a Eliot St., Cambridge, Mass. 02138. A new and supposedly improved composting toilet has been developed by Bio Recycler Company of Sykesville, Maryland, and is presently being tested in some homes in the United States.

Waterless toilets not only save water but also reduce the need for more and more expensive sewage treatment plants. If use of these toilets was coupled with a system that required industries to treat and recycle their own wastewater, sewers and municipal waste treatment plants could gradually be phased out. There is concern that methods 2, 3, and 4 above could allow bacteria, viruses, and toxic metal compounds to build up in the soil, food crops, and fish and shellfish grown by aquaculture. But others argue that these problems could be controlled by removing certain pollutants, banning the use of highly

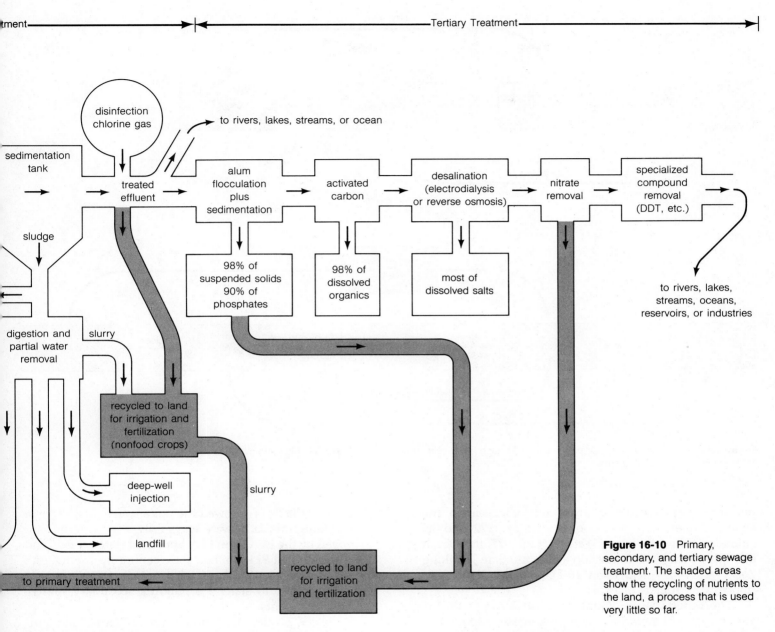

Figure 16-10 Primary, secondary, and tertiary sewage treatment. The shaded areas show the recycling of nutrients to the land, a process that is used very little so far.

contaminated liquid wastewater and sewage sludge, and using wastewater and sludge for noncrop purposes on forest lands and strip-mined lands.

Liquid effluent from sewage treatment plants is already being successfully used as fertilizer in some cities near farming ares, forest lands, and estuaries. Since this effluent has already been treated, contamination from bacteria, viruses, and toxic metals (which mostly remain in the solid sludge) is not a major problem. However, the use of liquid effluent and solid sludge for fertilizer does not reduce the need for expensive sewage treatment

plants. If health problems can be controlled, the best ecological approach appears to be a combination of waterless toilets (method 5), the use of natural systems to purify municipal and agricultural wastes (method 3), and the treatment of toxic industrial wastes at each plant or cluster of plants. Methods 1, 2, and 4 would also be used but be phased out gradually as the need for municipal sewage treatment plants decreased.

Politics and Economics of Water Pollution in the United States During the 1970s Congress passed several im-

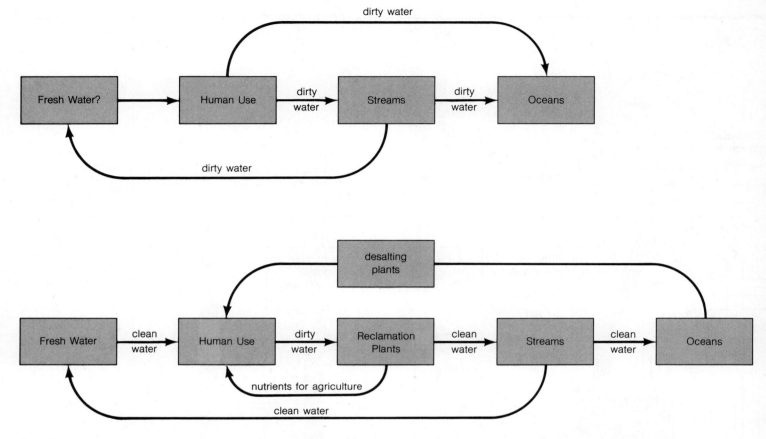

Figure 16-11 A comparison of our present self-defeating linear system with a cyclical sustainable earth system of water use and pollution control.

portant pieces of water pollution control legislation: the Federal Water Pollution Control Act of 1972 and its amended form, the Clean Water Act of 1977; the Ocean Dumping Act of 1972 (Section 16-5); the Safe Drinking Water Act of 1974 (Section 16-2); and the Toxic Substances Control Act of 1976.

The Federal Water Pollution Control Act of 1972 is one of the most ambitious, comprehensive, and controversial pieces of environmental legislation ever passed by Congress. This act (1) required the EPA to establish a system of national effluent standards; (2) required all municipalities to use secondary sewage treatment by 1977 and all industries to use the best *practicable* technology (BPT) for treating any discharges into U.S. waters by 1977 and the best *available* technology (BAT) economically achievable in 1983; (3) set an interim goal of making all U.S. waters safe for fish, shellfish, wildlife, and people by mid-1983 and a national goal of eliminating the discharge of all pollutants (zero discharge) into U.S.

waters by 1985; (4) allowed the point source discharge of pollutants into U.S. waterways only with a permit approved by the EPA or an EPA-approved state agency; and (5) authorized $24.6 billion for cleaning up the nation's waters between 1972 and 1977, including $18 billion in federal grants to states for building secondary sewage treatment plants.

By 1977 water pollution from industrial and municipal point discharges had decreased, over 5,000 new wastewater treatment plants had either been built or were under construction, and about 97 percent of all point source water dischargers were either in compliance with pollution control standards or were on definite water cleanup schedules.

Since its passage, the controversial 1972 act has been under attack from industries, some scientists and environmentalists, and the National Commission on Water Quality, which was set up by the act to investigate the problems of achieving the 1983 goals and to make recommendations for changes. The goal of zero discharge by 1985 has been attacked as (1) being unrealistic, because it does not recognize that some wastes are toxic and require zero discharge, while others are not; (2) being unecological, because it does not take into account that some wastes can be tolerated and broken down by natural systems; (3) being uneconomic, because the enormous costs of achieving this goal would outweigh the benefits; (4) being ineffective, because it deals primarily with point sources and ignores nonpoint sources, which are much more difficult and expensive to control (see Enrichment Study 16); and (5) possibly leading to increased air and land pollution, since the wastes not discharged into water must go somewhere. Industries have also wanted to eliminate the goal of using the best available technology by 1983.

After intense debate and pressure from industry and environmentalists, Congress amended the 1972 act with the Clean Water Act of 1977, which weakens some aspects of the 1972 act but strengthens others. It keeps the controversial goal of zero discharge by 1985 but applies the goal primarily to toxic pollutants. The bill divides water pollutants into three categories: (1) toxic (with the list of such chemicals and standards for their control to be set by the EPA); (2) nonconventional (a new category that includes some pesticides and metal compounds whose toxicity has yet to be determined); and (3) conventional (dirt, organic wastes, and sewage). The deadline for industrial installation of best available technology (BAT) for control of conventional pollutants has been postponed from 1983 to 1984, and the EPA can grant waivers in cases where costs outweigh benefits. For nonconventional pollutants the deadline for best available control technology was postponed to mid-1987 with waivers possible but more difficult to get. For toxic pollutants the deadline is 1984 with no waivers allowed. The 1977 act also: (1) allows the EPA to postpone the deadline for a municipality to have secondary sewage treatment plants to as late as mid-1983 if the project has had construction or funding delays; (2) authorizes $24.5 billion for the construction of sewage treatment plants between 1978 and 1983 and provides more matching funds (85 percent instead of 75 percent) to states and localities using treatment methods that save energy, reclaim and reuse water, and spray effluents on land for fertilizer; (3) exempts congressionally approved federal projects such as dams, bridges, and dredging from the provisions of the National Environmental Policy Act; and (4) extends industry liability for oil spill cleanup from 19 kilometers (12 miles) to 322 kilometers (200 miles) offshore.

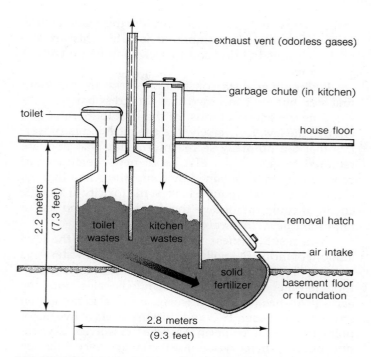

Figure 16-12 The Clivus Multrum waterless toilet uses bacteria to break down human and kitchen wastes (food and paper) and form a dry, odorless, solid fertilizer that can be removed every 1 or 2 years and returned to the soil.

After a 5-year fight, Congress passed another landmark piece of environmental legislation, the Toxic Substances Control Act of 1976, which is designed to control the approximately 1,000 new chemicals that are used in commercial production each year. Under this law in 1977 the EPA drew up a list of approximately 45,000 chemicals being manufactured in the United States. Any substance not on this list is considered a new chemical (except for pesticides, drugs, cosmetics, food additives, and radioactive materials, which are covered by other regulations). A chemical manufacturer must notify the EPA at least 90 days before beginning manufacture of a new chemical or of an old chemical used in a new way. If the EPA believes that testing is required to assure a chemical's safeness, it can block the manufacture for up to 180 days. If the industry objects to a continued ban beyond the 180 days, the EPA can seek a court injunction. The court is required by law to issue the injunction if the EPA shows that there is insufficient data to make a valid judgment, that the compound may present an unreasonable risk of injury to health or the environment, or that the compound may be expected to enter the environment in large quantities. The EPA must provide proof to substantiate any of these three claims, but after an injunction the manufacturer must prove that the compound is safe. This act also allows citizens to bring suit to seek compliance with its provisions.

Environmentalists consider this law an important first step but are concerned that Congress has not provided nearly enough funds for the EPA to monitor and enforce the law. Conversely, the chemical industry worries that the normally secret information that they are required to give to the EPA about new chemicals and products could be obtained by competitors and that the estimated $500,000 required to test the toxicity of a single chemical could discourage the development and use of important new chemicals.

As a result of these water pollution laws, the total amount of industrial pollutants entering U.S. waterways was cut in half between 1972 and 1980. However, although water pollution in the United States since the early 1970s has not gotten worse, it has also not gotten any better. Between 1975 and 1978 the levels of five major pollutants (fecal coliform bacteria, dissolved oxygen, phosphorus, mercury, and lead) changed very little. Existing laws, if funded and enforced, should lead to greater improvement in the future and could, by 1985, save about $12.3 billion annually in estimated damages from water pollution in the United States.

Despite such progress, water pollution is increasing in several major categories where control is more difficult. These include ocean pollution (Section 16-5) and estuarine zone pollution (Section 10-6), viruses that are hard to destroy by conventional waste treatment, some pesticides, metal compounds and other persistent or nondegradable chemicals that are toxic in very small amounts or that can be biologically magnified in food chains (Enrichment Studies 5 and 11), and nonpoint source pollution and accelerated eutrophication from land erosion and the runoff of fertilizers and animal wastes (Enrichment Study 16).

The reason we have water pollution is not basically the paper or pulp mills. It is, rather, the social side of humans—our unwillingness to support reform government, to place into office the best qualified candidates, to keep in office the best talent, and to see to it that legislation both evolves from and inspires wise social planning with a human orientation.

Stewart L. Udall

Guest Editorial: Economic Progress and Human Health

Barbara Blum

Barbara Blum served as deputy administrator of the U.S. Environmental Protection Agency during the Carter administration. As deputy administrator, she concentrated on energy issues, management and regulatory reform, and development of EPA's first intensive focus on the urban environment. She directed efforts to encourage energy conservation within the Federal government and to make sure that the government lives up to the same laws that companies are required to obey. Under her leadership, the number of women in top policymaking positions at EPA more than tripled. Her work also led to the creation of President Carter's Regulatory Council, a group of top Federal officials organized to streamline the federal regulatory process and to eliminate unnecessary costs and burdens imposed on business. Internationally, she served as head of the U.S. delegation to important environmental meetings of the Organization for Economic Cooperation and Development (OECD) and as principal adviser to the U.S. delegation to the governing council of the United Nations' Environmental Program. In 1978, she received a distinguished service award from Americans for Indian Opportunity. In 1980, the Federal Republic of Germany awarded her the Commander's Cross of the Order of Merit in recognition of her international environmental leadership.

Is "progress" a menace to public health? That question isn't totally farfetched.

Certainly, in many ways and in many places, the world is a healthier place than it was 100 or 200 years ago. We have conquered many of the infectious diseases so deadly to past generations. But we have also created new hazards.

In the more developed nations of the world, people are no longer dying of malaria, cholera, or tuberculosis. But they *are* dying of cancer and heart disease, are handicapped by birth defects, or are chronically ill with respiratory or other degenerative ailments. Drinking water no longer triggers epidemics of typhoid fever, but water sources are increasingly threatened by contamination with toxic chemicals. We can immunize our children today against measles, diphtheria, and whooping cough, but in their daily activity—playing, eating, simply breathing—they may be exposed to hundreds of alien substances that are byproducts of modern technology.

I am not trying to make the point that progress is bad, or that living is hazardous to human health. No, these comparisons simply show that while we have learned to cure or prevent many forms of disease, we still have a great deal to learn about managing our environment to control natural or manufactured hazards.

Common sense taught us that most infectious diseases were, in the broadest sense, environmentally induced. Though people knew little about viruses or bacteria, they learned to prevent, through environmental controls, the diseases these microorganisms caused. Cholera was virtually halted in the nineteenth century not because people suddenly understood the connection between bacteria and disease, but because public authorities cleaned up sewage-contaminated water supplies. In like manner, malaria was curbed effectively by community measures to control mosquitoes rather than by treating patients.

It is only in recent years, however, that we have begun to suspect that the diseases of industrialized societies may also have environmental origins. These causes are highly complex and interdependent, and we have scarcely begun to unravel them. There is no simple, single step public authorities can take to prevent cancer, diabetes, or heart disease. Instead, we face a mind-boggling snarl of latency (or time-delay) factors, multiple and synergistic causes and effects, cost-benefit ratios, and the like, all the while being inundated by confusing and often conflicting data.

For these and other reasons, it is extremely difficult to establish a direct chain of cause and effect that can be broken by preventive measures to decrease the incidence of cancer. Nevertheless, it would be foolhardy to simply ignore the environmental effects we do understand.

The U.S. Environmental Protection Agency recognizes that its primary responsibility is the protection of the public health. We cannot always delay regulatory action until a suspected hazard becomes a scientific certainty. At times, we must base our decisions upon the scientific equivalent of circumstantial evidence. This evidence may take the form of tests that show how a pollutant affects laboratory animals, or studies of its impact on human beings exposed to it in the workplace or in food products. In short, EPA must act with caution, but it must *act*.

An estimated five million chemicals are now known to exist, and 45,000 of these are in commercial use. Hundreds more are introduced each year. Until recently, most of these were never tested to ascertain their long-term effects upon human health or the environment. Yet, we know that even low-level chronic exposure to some of these compounds may lead to behavior modifications, cellular damage, loss of reproductive capability, genetic changes, or damage to any or all of the body's organs and systems.

Today, almost 40 percent of the U.S. population carries toxic PCBs in their tissues at levels exceeding one part per million; levels of the heavy metal cadmium are increasing in the human body; mothers' milk routinely contains significant residues of DDE, DDT, and other pesticides.

It is only too clear, then, that the environment is not something "out there." It is literally part of us. Obviously, no one would say that we must immediately stop producing and using all synthetic substances. With prudent use, in fact, most of them are safe, while many naturally-occurring materials can be toxic or carcinogenic.

The real message is that we must undertake a continuing, comprehensive, and sophisticated effort to truly understand our environment and its hazards. And we must be willing to act on what we learn if we are to safeguard the health of our own generation and those still to come.

Guest Editorial Discussion

1. Should the Environmental Protection Agency regulate the level of a pollutant that statistically appears to be a cause of cancer (or other health disorder) even when no direct cause and effect between the pollutant and the disease can be established in humans? Why or why not? What are the possible benefits from such regulation? What are some of the possible harmful effects?

2. The U.S. EPA has been criticized by some business leaders and politicians for overregulating American business and thus stifling economic productivity and growth. Do you agree or disagree with this criticism? Explain your position. What are the workable alternatives to Federal regulation of air and water pollution?

Discussion Topics

1. Why is it so difficult to define water pollution and to set water quality standards?

2. What is the largest category of U.S. water pollution in terms of quantity? Explain why looking at water pollutants in terms of the annual quantity discharged can be misleading.

3. How would you control (a) nondegradable pollutants, (b) slowly degradable (persistent) pollutants, and (3) rapidly degradable (nonpersistent) pollutants?

4. Give an example of a point pollution source and of a nonpoint pollution source, and explain how you would control pollutants from these two sources.

5. What is the source of drinking water in your community? How is it treated? What chemicals (if any) have been found in this water after treatment? Is chlorination still used for disinfection? Are there plans to use activated charcoal or other methods to remove organic contaminants?

6. Explain why "dilution is not always the solution to water pollution," and relate your explanation to the second law of energy. Cite examples and conditions when it is the solution and when it is not.

7. Explain how a river can cleanse itself of oxygen-demanding wastes. Under what conditions can this natural cleansing system fail?

8. Why is water usually tested for coliform bacteria? What is the average annual coliform bacterial count for drinking water in your community? During the past 10 years have any swimming areas in your community been closed because of high coliform counts?

9. Distinguish between natural eutrophication and cultural eutrophication, and explain how eutrophication can deplete dissolved oxygen in the hypolimnion of a lake.

10. Should we ban injection of wastes into deep underground disposal wells? Under what conditions, if any, should such wells be allowed?

11. Some studies have shown that thermal outputs from nuclear and fossil fuel plants have had no harmful ecological consequences so far. Why should we be concerned?

12. Explain the fallacies in these statements about water pollution:
   a. Rivers and lakes have similar water pollution problems.
   b. Thermal pollution is a problem only for lakes, not rivers or estuaries.

13. Explain why the ocean is called the ultimate sink. Discuss this phrase in terms of the second law of energy.

14. Debate the following resolution: We should deliberately dump most of our wastes in the ocean. It is a vast sink for dilution and mixing, and if it is polluted, we can get food from other sources. Let the ocean go as a living system so that we can live.

15. Should the world ban all dumping of wastes in the ocean? If so, where would you put these wastes? What exceptions, if any, would you permit? Under what circumstances? What types of wastes are allowed now? Which of these should be banned? Explain why banning ocean dumping only will not stop ocean pollution.

16. Explain why aesthetic and economic damage to recreational areas and the killing of seabirds are not necessarily the most serious consequences of oil pollution.

17. Should the United States (or any other coastal nation) ban all offshore oil wells? Why or why not? What might be the consequences of this restriction for the nation? For foreign policy? For security? For your town? For you? What might be the consequences of not doing this?

18. Why are soil conservation and land-use planning key methods for controlling some types of water pollution?

19. Discuss the pros and cons of the pollution control methods given in Table 16-6.

20. Should we switch from our present engineering approach of sewage treatment to a sustainable earth approach? What are some of the political and economic implications of such a change? What problems does it solve? What problems does it create? What effects might it have on the poor? On you? On the next generation?

21. What has happened to water quality as a result of the Clean Water Act of 1977, the Safe Drinking Water Act of 1974, the Ocean Dumping Act of 1972, and the Toxic Substances Control Act of 1976 since 1980? Have these acts been amended or have any new acts been passed?

Readings

Bascom, Willard. 1974. "The Disposal of Waste in the Ocean." *Scientific American*, vol. 231, no. 2, 16–25. Argues that with careful control we can safely dispose of many types of wastes in the ocean.

Brubaker, Sterling. 1972. *To Live on Earth*. Baltimore: Johns Hopkins University Press. (Also available in paperback; New York: New American Library, 1972.) One of the most authoritative and balanced views of all types of pollution and their causes.

Cairns, John, Jr. 1971. "Thermal Pollution—A Cause for Concern." *Journal of the Water Pollution Control Federation*, vol. 43, no. 1, 55–66. Outstanding summary of problems and solutions.

Claus, George, and Karen Bolander. 1977. *Ecological Sanity*. New York: David McKay. Excellent discussion of pollution control.

Culliney, John L. 1979. *The Forest of the Sea: Life and Death on the Continental Shelf*. Garden City, N.Y.: Anchor/Doubleday. Superb description.

Davies, J. Clarence, III, and Barbara S. Davies. 1975. *The Politics of Pollution*. 2nd ed. Indianapolis: Pegasus. Account of the political realities (as opposed to the political theory) of pollution control.

Forrestal, Liz. 1975. "Deep Mystery." *Environment*, vol. 17, no. 8, 25–35. Very good overview of the problems of injecting wastes into deep underground wells.

Goldberg, Edward D. 1976. *The Health of the Oceans*. Paris: UNESCO Press. Very useful overview of ocean pollution problems and possible solutions.

Grundlach, Erich R. 1977. "Oil Tanker Disasters." *Environment*, vol. 19, no. 9, 16–28. Superb summary.

Hodges, Laurent. 1977. *Environmental Pollution*. 2nd ed. New York: Holt, Rinehart and Winston. See chaps. 8, 9, 10, 11, and 14 for a discussion of water pollution and water pollution control at a slightly higher level than that found in this book.

Leich, Harold H. 1975. "The Sewerless Society." *Bulletin of the Atomic Scientists*, November, pp. 38–44. How waterless toilets can save money, water, and energy and reduce our need for sewage treatment plants.

Lieber, Harvey. 1975. *Federalism and Clean Waters*. Lexington, Mass.: Heath. Good case study of how the Federal Water Pollution Control Act of 1972 came to be and an analysis of its strengths and weaknesses.

Marx, Wesley. 1967. *The Frail Ocean*. New York: Ballantine.

McCaull, Julian, and Janice Crossland. 1974. *Water Pollution*. New York: Harcourt Brace Jovanovich. Excellent overview of water pollution and its control.

Pimental et al. 1976. "Land Degradation: Effects on Food and Energy Resources," *Science*, vol. 194, 149–155. Excellent summary of soil erosion in the United States.

Steinhart, Carol E., and John S. Steinhart. 1972. *Blowout: A Case Study of the Santa Barbara Oil Spill*. North Scituate, Mass.: Duxbury. Superb case study.

Stoker, H. S., and Spencer L. Seager. 1976. *Environmental Chemistry: Air and Water Pollution*. 2nd ed. Glenview, Ill.: Scott, Foresman. Probably the best summary of air and water pollution at a slightly higher level than that found in this book.

Stokinger, H. E. 1971. "Sanity in Research and Evaluation of Environmental Health." *Science*, vol. 174, 662–665. Interesting and perhaps provocative look by a toxicology expert at how pollution standards should be set. He claims that many standards are far too strict and that outright banning should rarely be imposed.

U.S. Department of the Interior. 1969. *A Primer on Waste Treatment*. Washington, D.C.: Government Printing Office. Simple and excellent survey.

Warren, C. E. 1971. *Biology and Water Pollution Control*. Philadelphia: Saunders. Good introduction at a slightly higher level.

Westman, Walter E. 1972. "Some Basic Issues in Water Pollution Control Legislation." *American Scientist*, November-December, pp. 767–773. Probably the best summary of the ecological versus the technological-economic approach to water pollution control.

Wilber, C. G. 1969. *The Biological Aspects of Water Pollution*. Springfield, Ill.: Thomas. Fine basic text.

Woodwell, George M. 1977. "Recycling Sewage Through Plant Communities." *American Scientist*, vol. 65, 556–562. Excellent overview of this natural alternative to expensive waste treatment plants.

17

Air Pollution

Tomorrow morning when you get up take a nice deep breath.
It will make you feel rotten.

Citizens for Clean Air, Inc. (New York)

17-1 Types and Sources

Our Polluted Air Take a deep breath. If the air you just took in was not polluted, you are in a small and fast-shrinking minority. It makes little difference whether you are in Los Angeles, Denver, Washington, D.C., Tokyo, or Mexico City, inside a home, or in a rural area. Most Americans breathe air that is considered harmful to their health despite the fact that between 1970 and 1980 air pollution control efforts improved the overall air quality.

Los Angeles gets all the publicity, but an EPA study of 42 major U.S. cities ranked Denver as the city with the unhealthiest air between 1974 and 1977. Denver, the "mile-high" (1.6-kilometer-high) city, once had air so clean that doctors sent asthma patients there for relief. Following Denver, in order, were Cleveland, Los Angeles, Louisville, New York City, and Riverside, California.

The problem is not confined to the United States. Air pollution alerts in heavily populated and industrialized Tokyo have become a way of life, and in Mexico City on an average day air pollution levels are 5 to 6 times greater than the maximum safety level set for U.S. citizens by the EPA. The air pollution capital of the world may be Cubato, Brazil, a petrochemical center where essentially no birds or insects remain, most trees are merely blackened stumps, 40 of every 1,000 babies are stillborn, air pollution monitoring machines break down from contamination, and the city's mayor refuses to live there.

Normally, air pollution levels in rural areas are lower than those in cities, but cities do spread their pollutants to nearby rural areas. As more and more people and industries move to rural areas, they create the air pollution that they are hoping to escape. Indeed, air pollutants respect no local, regional, or national boundaries. Smokestacks in Great Britain and western Europe produce acid rains over Sweden and Norway, and a lead smelter in El Paso, Texas, is apparently responsible for dangerously high levels of lead in the blood of thousands of children in Ciudad Jaurez, Mexico.

Indoor Air Pollution To escape the smog you might go home, close the doors and windows, and breathe in clean air. But a number of scientists have found that the air inside homes and offices is often more polluted and dangerous than outdoor air on a smoggy day. The indoor pollutants include (1) nitrogen dioxide and carbon monoxide from gas and wood-burning stoves without adequate ventilation; (2) carbon monoxide, soot, and cancer-causing benzopyrene (from cigarette smoke); (3) various organic compounds from aerosol spray cans and cleaning products; (4) formaldehyde (which causes cancer in rats) from urea-formaldehyde foam insulation, plywood, carpet adhesives, and particle board; (5) radioactive radon and some of its decay products from stone, soil, cement, and bricks; and (6) ozone from the use of electrostatic air cleaners. Energy conservation efforts to make houses even more airtight (Section 14-1) could lead to even higher indoor pollution levels. Indeed, measurements in one airtight, extremely energy-efficient home revealed high levels of formaldehyde throughout the house and indoor radioactivity levels more than 100 times the natural outdoor background level. Formaldehyde levels in newly insulated homes have been high enough to cause dizziness, rashes, chest pains, nosebleeds, and vomiting. It is also estimated that radioactive

---

Enrichment Studies 1, 3, 5, 6, and 13 are related to this chapter.

levels in U.S. homes could be causing thousands of cases of lung cancer each year.

Solutions to the serious problem of indoor air pollution include (1) restricting public smoking indoors (Enrichment Study 6); (2) banning the use of formaldehyde-containing insulation and plywood (found especially in mobile homes); (3) venting natural gas ovens and furnaces to the outdoors; (4) painting radon-containing concrete, stone, and brick or formaldehyde-containing products with a sealant; and (5) using an air-to-air heat exchanger to change the air in energy-efficient buildings without a significant loss of heat or cool air.

What Is Air Pollution? **Air pollution** is normally defined as air that contains one or more chemicals in high enough concentrations to harm humans, other animals, vegetation, or materials. There are two major types of air pollutants. A **primary air pollutant** is a chemical added directly to the air that occurs in a harmful concentration. It can be a natural air component, such as carbon dioxide, that rises above its normal concentration (Enrichment Study 3), or something not usually found in the air, such as a lead compound emitted by cars burning leaded gasoline. A **secondary air pollutant** is a harmful chemical formed in the atmosphere through a chemical reaction among air components. Serious air pollution usually results over a city or other area that is emitting high levels of pollutants during a period of air stagnation. The geographic location of some heavily populated cities, such as Los Angeles and Mexico City, makes them particularly susceptible to frequent air stagnation and pollution buildup.

We must be careful about depending solely on concentration values in determining the severity of air pollutants. By themselves, measured concentrations tell us nothing about the danger caused by pollutants, because threshold levels, synergy, and biological magnification (Section 6-2) are also determining factors. In addition, we run into the issue of conflicting views of what constitutes harm.

However, it cannot be disputed that air pollution can corrode paint, buildings, and statues, rot nylon stockings, and damage crops and trees. It can also cause humans to suffer everything from burning eyes and headaches to bronchitis, emphysema, and lung cancer. However, as with most forms of pollution, it is difficult to establish a direct cause-and-effect relationship between a particular air pollutant and a particular disease.

We normally associate air pollution with smokestacks and cars, but volcanoes, forest fires, dust storms, marshes, oceans, and plants also add to the air chemicals we consider pollutants (Table 1-3). Since these natural inputs are usually widely dispersed throughout the world, they normally don't build up to harmful levels. And when they do, as in the case of volcanic eruptions, they are usually taken care of by natural weather and chemical cycles (Section 5-4).

Air Pollution in the Past Air pollution from human activities, of course, is not new. Our ancestors had it in their smoke-filled caves and later in their cities. Over 2,000 years ago Seneca complained of bad air in Rome. In 1273 King Edward I of England passed the first known air quality laws, which forbade the use of a particular type of coal. One man was even hanged for burning coal. In 1300 King Richard III put a heavy tax on coal to discourage its use. In the early 1800s Shelley wrote, "Hell is a city much like London, a populous and smoky city." In 1911, 1,150 Londoners died from the effects of coal smoke. In his report on the disaster, Dr. Harold Antoine Des Voeux coined the word *smog* for the mixture of smoke and fog that often hung over London. An even more deadly London air pollution incident killed 4,000 people in 1952. This triggered a massive air pollution control effort that has made London's air cleaner today than it has been in over 100 years.

In America the industrial revolution brought air pollution as coal-burning industries and homes filled the air with soot and fumes. In the 1940s the air in industrial centers, such as Pittsburgh, became so thick with dust that automobile drivers sometimes had to use their headlights at midday. The rapid rise in the use of the automobile, especially since 1940, brought new forms of pollution such as photochemical smog and lead from the burning of leaded gasoline. The first known air pollution disaster occurred in 1948, when fumes and dust from steel mills and zinc smelters became trapped in a stagnated air mass over Donora, Pennsylvania. Twenty people died and over 6,000 became ill. In the 1950s and 1960s recurrent air pollution disasters in New York, Los Angeles, and other large cities eventually led to efforts to reduce U.S. air pollution levels.

Our Finite Air Supply The J curves of increasing urbanization, population growth, industrialization, and automobile use have forced us to realize that we can no longer take for granted the 14 kilograms (30 pounds) of relatively pure air that every person must breathe each day. We can control or reject contaminated water and food, but we cannot stop breathing. Thus, there is a sig-

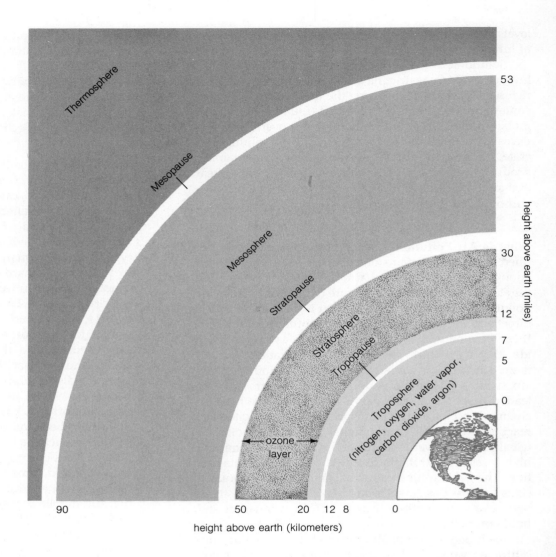

Figure 17-1 Structure of the earth's atmosphere. About 95 percent of the earth's air is found in the troposphere.

Thermosphere

Mesopause

Mesosphere

Stratopause

Stratosphere

Tropopause

Troposphere (nitrogen, oxygen, water vapor, carbon dioxide, argon)

ozone layer

height above earth (miles)

53

30

12

7

5

0

height above earth (kilometers)

90   50   20 12 8   0

nificant difference between the problems of air and water pollution. Unlike water, we can't get our supply of clean air through pipes. We normally use an output approach for water, cleaning up polluted water by passing it through water treatment plants. This is not physically or economically feasible for polluted air. Air pollution control must rely primarily on input approaches, as discussed in more detail in Kenneth E. F. Watt's Guest Editorial at the end of this chapter and in Table 16-6.

Contrary to popular belief, we do not live at the bottom of an infinite sea of air. The *atmosphere* is the gaseous envelope that surrounds the earth. As shown in Figure 17-1, the atmosphere consists of several distinct layers. About 95 percent of the air is found in the **troposphere,**

which extends only 8 to 12 kilometers (5 to 7 miles) above the earth's surface. In fact, if we were to compare the earth with a waxed apple, our vital air supply would be no thicker than the layer of wax. Ozone gas in the *ozone layer* (found in the upper two-thirds of the stratosphere) filters out harmful ultraviolet radiation from the sun and allows life to exist on earth. Most air pollutants are added to the troposphere, where they mix vertically and horizontally and often react chemically with each other or with the natural components of the atmosphere. Eventually, most of these pollutants and the chemicals that they form are returned to the land or water by precipitation or fallout. Some water-insoluble and unreactive chemicals, such as the fluorocarbons, may diffuse upward into the ozone layer. Under the influence of intense solar radiation, they may break down and possibly deplete ozone levels (Section 6-3).

The composition of the earth's atmosphere is not fixed. Billions of years ago it consisted mostly of gaseous hydrogen (H_2), methane (CH_4), and ammonia (NH_3). Gradually photosynthesis and aerobic respiration by living organisms changed the composition so that today the atmosphere is about 78 percent nitrogen (N_2) and 21 percent oxygen (O_2) by volume, with small amounts of argon (Ar), carbon dioxide (CO_2), water vapor (H_2O), and other gases. The percentages of carbon dioxide and water in the atmosphere vary, but the other percentages remain relatively constant.

Changes in the composition of the atmosphere, then, are normal. Nevertheless, chemicals added to the atmosphere as a result of human activities could increase to such a degree that changes in atmospheric composition could alter world climate (Enrichment Study 3) and threaten all forms of life. The troposphere receives about 498 million kilograms (548,000 tons) of air pollutants *each day* from the United States—an average of about 2.3 kilograms (4.8 pounds) per day for each American.

Major Air Pollutants   Following are the 11 major types of air pollutants:

1. *carbon oxides:* carbon monoxide (CO), carbon dioxide (CO_2)

2. *sulfur oxides:* sulfur dioxide (SO_2), sulfur trioxide (SO_3)

3. *nitrogen oxides:* nitrous oxide (N_2O), nitric oxide (NO), nitrogen dioxide (NO_2)

4. *hydrocarbons* (organic compounds containing carbon and hydrogen): methane (CH_4), butane (C_4H_{10}), benzene (C_6H_6)

5. *photochemical oxidants:* ozone (O_3), PAN (a group of peroxyacylnitrates), and various aldehydes

6. *particulates* (solid particles or liquid droplets suspended in air): smoke, dust, soot, asbestos, metallic particles (such as lead, beryllium, cadmium), oil, salt spray, sulfate salts

7. *other inorganic compounds:* asbestos, hydrogen fluoride (HF), hydrogen sulfide (H_2S), ammonia (NH_3), sulfuric acid (H_2SO_4), nitric acid (HNO_3)

8. *other organic (carbon-containing) compounds:* pesticides, herbicides, various alcohols, acids, and other chemicals

9. *radioactive substances:* tritium, radon, emissions from fossil fuel and nuclear power plants (Sections 14-2 and 14-3)

10. *heat* (see Enrichment Study 3)

11. *noise* (see Enrichment Study 13)

Table 17-1 summarizes the major sources and effects of these pollutants and possible methods for controlling them.

Sources of Air Pollution   If we look at the total amount of each major pollutant emitted each year in the United States, carbon monoxide is the number one air pollutant and the automobile is by far the major source of air pollution, as shown in Table 17-2. But we should not judge either the importance of an air pollutant or its source solely on the basis of the total amount emitted each year. We must also consider how harmful a pollutant is—especially to human health. When considering harmful health effects, we get a very different picture of the relative importance of various air pollutants and their sources, as shown in Table 17-2. On this basis sulfur oxides and particulates rank as the top two pollutants, and carbon monoxide drops to last place. In terms of air pollution sources, stationary fuel combustion (primarily at fossil fuel power plants) is the most dangerous, with industry (especially pulp and paper mills, iron and steel mills, smelters, petroleum refineries, and chemical plants) and transportation in second and third places, respectively.

The health rankings of air pollutants provide a more realistic basis for designing programs to reduce air pollution. Of course, controlling automobile emissions is very important, but controlling emissions of sulfur oxides and particulates from fossil-fuel-burning electric power and industrial plants is even more so, as seen from Table 17-2. This is particularly important in the United States, which is increasing its reliance on coal-burning electric power plants as part of its national energy strategy (Sections 13-6 and 14-2).

On the basis of a pollutant's effects on human health and the average time that the pollutant remains in the air, the EPA has established *national ambient air quality standards*. These standards specify maximum allowable levels for each major air pollutant, beyond which harmful health effects can occur (Table 17-3). These standards are normally expressed as the number of micrograms (millionths of a gram) of a pollutant allowed in a cubic meter of air for a given time period. The ambient stan-

Table 17-1 Major Air Pollutants

Pollutant	Sources	Effects	Control Methods
Carbon oxides Carbon monoxide (CO)	Forest fires and decaying organic matter; incomplete combustion of fossil fuels (about two-thirds of total emissions) and other organic matter in cars and furnaces; cigarette smoke	Reduces oxygen-carrying capacity of blood; impairs judgment; aggravates heart and respiratory diseases; can cause headaches and fatigue at moderate concentrations (50 to 100 ppm); can cause death at prolonged high concentrations (750 ppm or more); can be a traffic hazard at 30 ppm for 9 hours or 120 ppm for 1 hour	Modify furnaces and automobile engines for more complete combustion; remove from automobile, home, and factory exhaust gases; stop smoking
Carbon dioxide (CO_2)	Natural aerobic respiration of living organisms; burning of fossil fuels	Could affect world climate through the greenhouse effect at excessive concentrations (see Enrichment Study 3)	Switch away from use of fossil fuels; remove from automobile, home, and factory exhaust gases
Sulfur oxides (SO_2 and SO_3)	Combustion of sulfur-containing coal and oil in homes, industries, and power plants; smelting of sulfur-containing ores; volcanic eruptions	Aggravates respiratory diseases; impairs breathing; irritates eyes and respiratory tract; increases mortality; damages plants and reduces growth; causes acid rain; corrodes metals; deteriorates building stone, paper, nylon, and leather	Use low-sulfur fossil fuels; coal gasification; remove from fuels before use; remove from smokestack exhaust gases; shift to non-fossil-fuel energy sources
Nitrogen oxides (NO and NO_2)	High-temperature fuel combustion in motor vehicles and industrial and fossil fuel power plants; lightning	Aggravates respiratory disease; increases susceptibility to chronic respiratory infections; can cause acute bronchitis; contributes to heart, lung, liver, and kidney damage; irritates lungs, eyes, and skin; reduces ability of lungs to cleanse themselves of particulates; causes acid rain; inhibits plant growth; decreases atmospheric visibility; fades paints and dyes; takes part in formation of photochemical smog; injures respiratory system	Discourage automobile use; shift to mass transit, electric cars, and fuel cells; modify automobiles to reduce combustion temperature; remove from automobile and smokestack exhausts
Hydrocarbons	Incomplete combustion of fossil fuels in automobiles and furnaces; evaporation of industrial solvents and oil spills; tobacco smoke; forest fires; plant decay (about 85 percent of emissions)	Injures respiratory system; some cause cancer; takes part in formation of photochemical smog; irritates eyes	Modify furnaces and automobile engines for more complete combustion and less evaporation; remove from automobile exhaust; improve handling of solvents and petroleum to reduce spills (Section 16-5) and loss by evaporation
Photochemical oxidants	Sunlight acting on hydrocarbons and nitrogen oxides	Aggravates respiratory and heart diseases; irritates eyes, throat, and respiratory tract; injures leaves and inhibits plant growth; decreases atmospheric visibility; deteriorates rubber, textiles, and paints	Reduce emissions of nitrogen oxides and hydrocarbons
Particulates Dust, soot, and oil	Forest fires, wind erosion, and volcanic eruptions; coal burning; farming, mining, construction, road building, and other land-clearing activities; chemical reactions in the	Can cause cancer; aggravates respiratory and heart diseases; is toxic at high levels; causes coughing, irritates throat, and causes chest discomfort; interferes with plant	Decrease use of coal; improve land use and soil erosion control; remove from smokestack exhausts

Table 17-1 Major Air Pollutants *(cont.)*

Pollutant	Sources	Effects	Control Methods
	atmosphere; dust stirred up by automobiles; automobile exhaust; coal-burning electric power and industrial plants	photosynthesis; harms animals; reduces atmospheric visibility; soils and deteriorates buildings and painted surfaces; may affect weather and climate (Enrichment Study 3)	
Asbestos	Asbestos mining; spraying of fireproofing insulation in buildings; deterioration of brake linings	Can cause cancer; hinders breathing; aggravates respiratory and heart diseases; causes fibrosis of lungs	Reduce use; prevent escape into the atmosphere; protect construction workers and miners from inhaling dust
Metals and metal compounds (Enrichment Study 5)	Mining; industrial processes; coal burning; automobile exhaust	Can cause respiratory diseases, cancer, nervous disorders, and death; is toxic to some animals; damages plants	Remove from exhaust gases; ban highly toxic chemicals
Other inorganic compounds Hydrogen fluoride (HF)	Petroleum refining; glass etching; aluminum and fertilizer production	Burns skin and eyes; irritates mucous membranes; damages plants and animals	Control industrial processes more carefully; remove from smokestack exhausts
Hydrogen sulfide (H_2S)	Chemical industry; petroleum refining	Has unpleasant odor; causes nausea; irritates eyes and throat; is toxic at high levels	Control industrial processes more carefully; remove from smokestack exhausts
Ammonia (NH_3)	Chemical industry; fertilizers	Irritates upper respiratory passages; forms particulates in atmosphere; corrodes metals	Control industrial processes more carefully; remove from smokestack exhausts
Sulfuric acid (H_2SO_4)	Reaction of sulfur trioxide and water vapor in atmosphere; chemical industry	(Same as sulfur oxides)	(Same as sulfur oxides)
Nitric acid (HNO_3)	Reaction of nitrogen dioxide and water vapor in atmosphere; chemical industry	(Same as nitrogen oxides)	(Same as nitrogen oxides)
Pesticides and herbicides	Agriculture; forestry; mosquito control	Is toxic or harmful to some fish, shellfish, predatory birds, and mammals; concentrates in human fat; may cause birth and genetic defects and cancer (see Enrichment Study 11)	Reduce use; switch to biological and ecological control of insects (see Enrichment Study 11)
Radioactive substances	Natural sources (rocks, soils, cosmic rays); uranium mining; nuclear processing; power generation; nuclear weapons testing; coal burning	Causes cancer and genetic defects (Section 14-3); injures leaves; reduces plant growth	Ban or reduce use of nuclear power plants and weapons testing; strictly control processing, shipping, and use of nuclear fuels and wastes; remove from exhausts; reduce burning of coal; use coal gasification
Heat	Use of fossil and nuclear fuels	May affect world climate (see Enrichment Study 3)	Reduce population; reduce energy use
Noise	Automobiles, airplanes, and trains; industry; construction	Causes annoyance; disrupts activities; causes nervous disorders; impairs hearing	Reduce noise levels of automobiles, airplanes, trains, machines, and factories; protect workers and residents from noise by ear cover and better building construction (see Enrichment Study 13)

Table 17-2 Relative Importance of Major Pollutants and Their Sources in the United States in 1977

	Annual Emissions		Estimated Relative Health Effect	
	Percentage of Total	Rank	Percentage of Total	Rank
Pollutant				
Sulfur oxides	14	3	34	1
Particulates	6	5	28	2
Nitrogen oxides	12	4	19	3
Hydrocarbons	15	2	18	4
Carbon monoxide	53	1	1	5
Total	100		100	
Source				
Stationary fuel combustion	17	2	43	1
Industry	15	3	26	2
Transportation	55	1	22	3
Agricultural burning	7	4	4	4
Solid waste disposal	4	5	3	5
Miscellaneous	2	6	2	6
Total	100		100	

dards have been used to develop a relative air pollution warning index (see Table 17.3), which can be used by the news media to give the public a daily air pollution report. Note that when the index rises above 100, the air exceeds the national ambient air quality standards and can be harmful.

17-2 Industrial and Photochemical Smogs

Types of Smog Serious air pollution occurs mostly in cities, with each city facing unique problems. However, big cities generally fall into one of two basic classes—the *gray air cities* and the *brown air cities*. These correspond to two major types of smog, *industrial smog* and *photochemical smog*, respectively. The characteristics of these two types of smog are summarized in Table 17-4.

Formation of Industrial Smog Gray air, or industrial smog, cities* usually have cold, wet, winter climates; such cities include London, Chicago, Baltimore, Philadelphia, and Pittsburgh. These cities also depend heavily on the burning of coal and oil for heating, manufacturing, and producing electric power. These fuels release two major classes of pollutants—**particulates** (solid particles or liquid droplets suspended in the air), which give the air over such cities its gray cast, and **sulfur oxides** (sulfur dioxide and sulfur trioxide), which are the major ingredients of **industrial smog.**

Coal and oil contain small amounts (0.5 to 5 percent by mass) of sulfur as an impurity. When the fuel is burned, the sulfir impurities react with oxygen to produce sulfur dioxide (SO_2). This gas spews out of chimneys and smokestacks and enters the atmosphere. Within several days most of the sulfur dioxide in the atmosphere is converted to sulfur trioxide (SO_3), which reacts almost at once with water in the air to form droplets of sulfuric acid (H_2SO_4). This atmospheric mist of sulfuric acid eats away metals and other materials and can irritate and damage the lungs.

Some of the sulfuric acid droplets can react with ammonia (NH_3) in the atmosphere to form solid particles of ammonium sulfate. Droplets of sulfuric acid and other chemicals that are inhaled can then become attached to these particles once they are also inhaled. The combined effect of sulfuric acid droplets and ammonium sulfate particles is considered the most serious air pollution threat to human health.

Fortunately, in many areas this mist of sulfuric acid droplets and ammonium sulfate particles is washed out of the atmosphere by rain within a few days or weeks. However, if it does not rain and if winds do not disperse them, these pollutants can build up to deadly levels. Such events are associated with the air pollution disasters in London in 1952 (3,500 to 4,000 deaths) and 1956 (900 deaths), in Donora, Pennsylvania, in 1948 (20 deaths, 6,000 sick), and in New York City in 1965 (400 deaths).

Formation of Photochemical Smog Brown air cities, like Los Angeles, Denver, Salt Lake City (Figure 17-2), Sydney, Mexico City, and Buenos Aires, usually have

---

*A well-matured photochemical smog can also look gray. Southern California often has a gray haze caused by the particulates produced in photochemical smog, because the nitrogen dioxide level has been diluted until its brownish color can't be seen.

Table 17-3 U.S. Pollutant Standards Index

Air Quality Index Value	Air Quality Level	Health Effect Description	Suggested Actions	Air Pollutant Levels (micrograms per cubic meter)				
				Total Suspended Particulates (24 hours)	Sulfur Dioxide (24 hours)	Ozone (1 hour)	Nitrogen Dioxide (1 hour)	Carbon Monoxide (8 hours)
500	Significant harm	Very hazardous	All people should remain indoors, keep windows and doors closed, minimize physical exertion, and avoid traffic.	1,000	2,620	1,200	3,750	57,500
400	Emergency	Hazardous	Elderly people and persons with heart or lung diseases should stay indoors and avoid physical exertion. General population should avoid outdoor activity.	875	2,100	1,000	3,000	46,000
300	Warning	Very unhealthful	Elderly people and persons with heart or lung diseases should stay indoors and reduce physical activity.	625	1,600	800	2,260	34,000
200	Alert	Unhealthful	Persons with heart or lung diseases should reduce physical exertion and outdoor activity.	375	800	400	1,130	17,000
100	National Ambient Air Quality Standard	Moderate	—	260	365 (0.14 ppm)	235 (0.12 ppm)	100 (0.05 ppm)	10,000 (9 ppm)
50	50 percent of National Ambient Air Quality Standard	Good	—	75	80	80	Not reported	5,000
0	—		—	0	0	0	0	0

Table 17-4 Basic Types of Smog

Characteristic	Industrial Smog	Photochemical Smog
Typical city	London, Chicago	Mexico City, Los Angeles
Climate	Cool, humid air	Warm, dry air
Chief pollutants	Sulfur oxides, particulates	Ozone, PAN, aldehydes, nitrogen oxides, carbon monoxide
Main sources	Industrial and household burning of oil and coal	Motor vehicle gasoline combustion
Time of worst episodes	Winter months (especially in the early morning)	Summer months (especially around noontime)

Figure 17-2 A heavy band of photochemical smog chokes the heart of Salt Lake City.

warm, dry climates, and their main source of air pollution is the internal combustion engine. At normal temperatures the nitrogen gas (N_2) and oxygen gas (O_2), which make up most of the atmosphere, do not react with each other. At the high temperatures inside an internal combustion engine, however, they react to produce nitric oxide (NO), which then passes out of the exhaust and into the atmosphere. Once in the atmosphere, nitric oxide reacts with the oxygen to form nitrogen dioxide (NO_2), a yellowish-brown gas with a pungent, choking odor. It is mostly responsible for the brownish haze over brown air cities.

Typically nitrogen dioxide remains in the atmosphere for about 3 days. Just as sulfur dioxide can be converted into sulfuric acid, small amounts of nitrogen dioxide can react in the atmosphere to form nitric acid (HNO_3), which can then be precipitated out of the atmosphere (another contribution to acid rainfall). Atmospheric nitric acid can also react with ammonia in the air to form particles of ammonium nitrate, which eventually fall to the earth's surface or are washed out of the atmosphere by rainfall.

Most of the air pollution problems with nitric oxide and nitrogen dioxide arise when ultraviolet radiation from sunlight causes them to react with gaseous hydrocarbons, which mostly come from spilled or partially burned gasoline. This reaction forms a complex mixture of new pollutants called *photochemical oxidants*. These oxidants and other compounds form what is called **photochemical smog** (Figure 17-3). This mixture in-

cludes ozone and a number of compounds similar to tear gas, which are known collectively as PANs (for *peroxyacylnitrates*). Mere traces of these compounds in the air can cause the eyes to smart and can damage crops.

Although the distinction between photochemical smog cities and industrial smog cities is convenient, most cities suffer from both types of air pollution (Figure 17-4).

Acid Deposition: A Growing Problem As we have seen, emissions of sulfur dioxide (primarily from coal-burning power plants, factories, and metal smelters) and nitrogen dioxide (from cars and fossil fuel power plants) can be converted in the atmosphere to sulfuric acid and nitric acid. These acids can then be carried long distances by the winds before falling back to the earth's surface in rain and snow as acidic as lemon juice. There is growing concern and numerous political squabbles over the damage that this **acid rain** can do to food crops, trees, materials, buildings, and aquatic life in the United States, Canada, western Europe, Scandinavia, and Japan. This

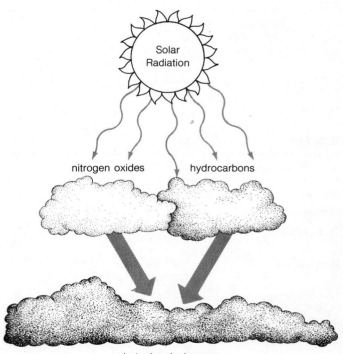

Figure 17-3 Photochemical smog occurs when nitrogen oxides and hydrocarbons react chemically under the influence of sunlight.

problem can be aggravated when acidic snow melts quickly and dumps large quantities of acid (as runoff and melt) in nearby bodies of water. Although acid rain is the catchword for this problem, from 10 to 30 percent of the acid problem is not from the deposition of acids in rain and snow. Instead, it results from *dry acid deposition* when very small acidic particles slowly fall to the earth or when gases in the atmosphere (such as SO_2 and SO_3) dissolve in water to produce acids. This dry and wet acid deposition can (1) destroy forms of aquatic life (especially trout and salmon); (2) reduce species diversity in aquatic ecosystems; (3) damage trees and food crops (such as soybeans); (4) leach plant nutrients from the soil, and (5) convert fairly harmless mercury deposits in lake bottom sediments to highly toxic methyl mercury (see Enrichment Study 5). In Scandinavia, forests are being stunted by acid rain, most of which apparently comes from the industrial regions of England and West Germany.

The United States plans to build 350 coal-burning power plants between 1979 and 1995. Under existing government air pollution standards, this could lead to a 10 to 15 percent increase in acid deposition. Indeed, in 1979, President Carter authorized a $10 million per year research program on acid deposition and stated that he considered acid deposition and increasing levels of carbon dioxide in the atmosphere (see Enrichment Study 3) the two gravest environmental threats of the 1980s.

More than 300 lakes in the Adirondack Mountains of New York are so acidified that they no longer contain fish. The problem has spread from the northeastern United States to Canada and much of the eastern and western United States, as shown in Figure 17-5. On the East Coast, sulfuric acid from coal burning is the major component of acid rain. On some parts of the West Coast, where nitrogen oxides from cars are the major problem, the major component of acid rain is nitric acid. In Canada, scientists project that some 48,000 Ontario lakes will be devoid of life within 18 to 20 years if acid rain continues.

The coal and automobile industries question the seriousness of the acid deposition problems in the United States. They contend that (1) the evidence used to show that acidity levels are increasing in intensity and geographic scope is highly suspect and not based on adequate measurements (no monitoring network has been maintained from 1950 to 1980); (2) the extent of damage from acid deposition is a matter of considerable scientific dispute (some lakes in the Adirondack mountains that were close to one another varied widely in acidity levels, indicating that run off from forestry and

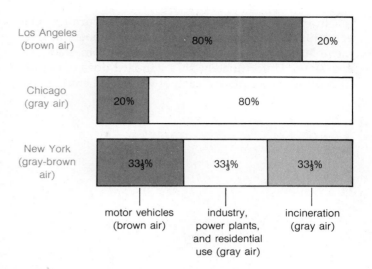

Figure 17-4 The types of air pollution in three cities. (The percentage values are crude estimates.)

agriculture may be a major factor); and (3) there is no reliable evidence linking emissions from power plants and vehicles to the alleged increases in the acidity of rainfall in the Eastern United States. A number of environmentalists and the EPA, however, dispute these industry claims. These questions should be resolved within a few years if government funding authorized for acid deposition research is not cut by the Reagan administration.

Ironically, the trend toward building taller smokestacks to relieve local air pollution problems increases acid deposition in areas downwind from the stacks. The world's tallest smokestack (about as high as the Empire State Building), located on a copper-nickel smelting plant in Sudbury, Ontario, by itself accounts for about 1 percent of the world's annual emissions of sulfur dioxide. Canada, however, receives more acid deposition from the United States (mostly from the industrial Ohio River valley) than it sends across American borders.

Some possible solutions for controlling acid rain include (1) banning tall smokestacks; (2) setting tighter emission standards for tall smokestacks; (3) reducing sulfur dioxide emissions by 20 to 40 percent by requiring coal to be washed before burning to remove some of the sulfur impurities; (4) taxing each unit of sulfur dioxide and nitrogen oxides emitted; (5) requiring emission controls on smokestacks and automobiles to remove nitrogen oxides; and (6) requiring all coal-burning power plants, factories, and smelters to use scrubbers (or other devices) to remove sulfur dioxide.

In 1980, the EPA required all new coal-burning power plants in the United States to use scrubbers that remove 70 percent of the sulfur dioxide from stack gas emissions. Unfortunately, this standard does not apply to existing power plants, each of which will emit almost 7 times as much sulfur dioxide each year as a new plant. In 1979, some 33 nations met to discuss the global acid deposition problem, and in 1980 the United States and Canada agreed to start negotiations to limit acid deposition.

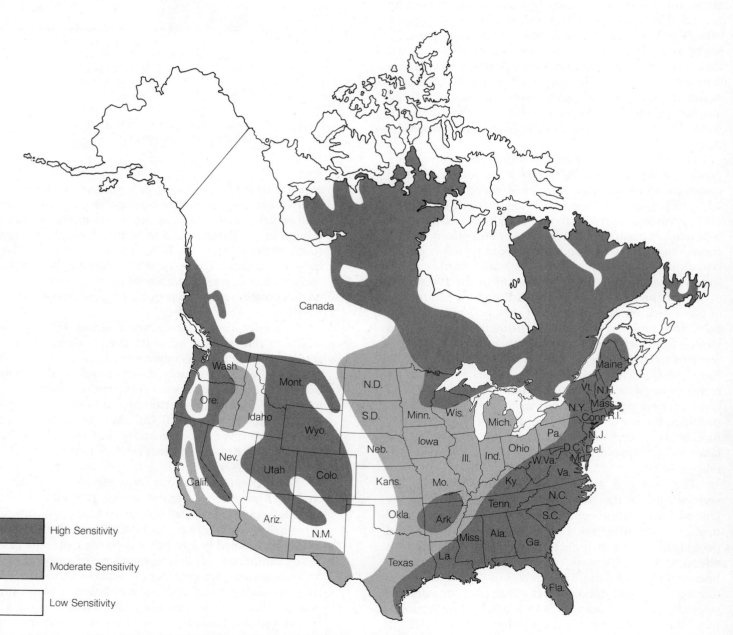

Figure 17-5 Areas of the continental United States and Canada that are sensitive to acid deposition.

Climate, Topography, and Air Pollution The frequency and severity of both photochemical smog and industrial smog in a given area depend on climate, topography, heating practices, traffic, and the density of population and industry. Some effects of climate and topography on air pollution are summarized in Table 17-5.

One climate effect that can greatly intensify the effects of air pollutants is a **thermal inversion** (Figures 17-6 and 17-7). Warm air cools as it rises and expands, just as air escaping from an automobile tire does. But under some climatic conditions, which are often related to topography, a layer of dense cool air can be trapped beneath a layer of light warm air, as shown on the right in Figure 17-6. In effect, a thermal lid is clamped over the region, and pollutants can slowly accumulate to dangerous and even lethal levels. Most air pollution disasters have been caused by prolonged thermal inversions. Such disasters usually happen in fall or winter for two reasons: (1) The sun's rays cannot penetrate to create a warm air layer that would rise from the ground and push away the trapped cold air; and (2) the cold weather increases the fuel-combustion emissions from space heating. In the United States, Atlantic coast cities have inversions 10 to 35 percent of the time, and Pacific coast

Table 17-5 Effects of Climate and Topography on Air Pollution

Characteristic	Effect
Precipitation	Cleanses the air
Humidity	Dissolves many air pollutants
Sunshine	Initiates formation of photochemical smog, but can reduce industrial smog by decreasing fuel burning for space heating
Wind	Decreases pollution near the source but can carry it to other areas
Atmospheric pressure	High-pressure systems hold pollution in local area
Mountains and hills	Hinders dispersion of pollution by reducing winds
Valleys	Traps pollutants

cities 35 to 40 percent of the time. Usually, these inversions last for only a few hours, but occasionally a high-pressure system stalls over an area for several days. Such a high-pressure system over Donora, Pennsylvania, in 1948 allowed pollution to build up to serious levels.

Actually there are several types of thermal inversions. *Subsidence inversions* can occur whenever a mass

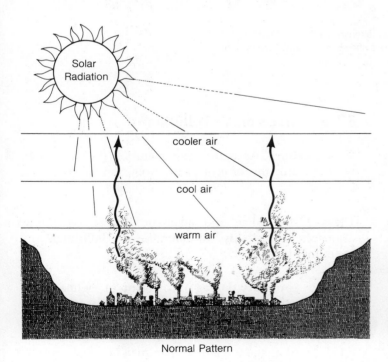

Normal Pattern · Thermal Inversion

Figure 17-6 Thermal inversion traps pollutants in a layer of cool air that cannot rise to carry the pollutants away.

New York Daily News, courtesy Environmental Protection Agency

Figure 17-7 Two faces of New York City. The almost clear view on the left was taken on Saturday afternoon, November 26, 1966. The effect of more cars in the city and a thermal inversion is shown in the right photograph, which was taken the previous day.

of high pressure stalls over a region and forces a warm layer of air down over that region. These happen over both U.S. coasts but are especially common on the West Coast during much of the year. *Radiation inversions* are a normal nighttime phenomenon. After sundown the ground radiates heat into the atmosphere. On a clear night the ground air layer cools quickly and is trapped by the overlying warmer air. Such inversions usually break up when the morning sun heats the ground. Both types of inversion can happen more often and last longer when they occur over a town or city that lies in a valley surrounded by mountains or that is near the coast (Los Angeles has both characteristics). After sunset the cool air from the ocean or from the mountains flows into the valley, creating almost daily inversions, and because the sun penetrates the valley less readily than it does the hills, the inversion stays longer.

17-3 Effects of Air Pollution

Classification As with water pollution (Section 16-2), we can rank the effects of air pollution in six major classes:

Class 1 (nuisance and aesthetic insult): odor; low atmospheric visibility; discoloration of buildings and monuments

Class 2 (property damage): corrosion of metals; accelerated weathering (dissolution) of buildings and monuments; soiling of clothes, buildings, and monuments

Class 3 (damage to plant and animal life): leaf spotting and decay; decreased food crop yields; decreased rate of photosynthesis; harmful effects on the respiratory and central nervous systems of animals

Class 4 (damage to human health): oxygen deficiency in the blood; eye irritation; respiratory system irritation and damage; cancer

Class 5 (human genetic and reproductive damage): largely unknown at present, but possible

Class 6 (major ecosystem disruption): alteration of local and regional climate and perhaps global climate (see Enrichment Study 3)

Let's look more closely at damages from classes 2, 3, and 4 (for a discussion of class 6 effects, see Enrichment Study 3).

Damage to Property, Plants, and Animals Most air pollution damage to materials and property is caused by photochemical oxidants (such as ozone), particulates, and sulfur oxides. Much of this damage occurs when sulfur oxides are converted to highly destructive droplets of sulfuric acid. For example, marble statues and building materials such as limestone, marble, mortar, and slate are discolored and attacked by sulfuric acid (and nitric acid formed from nitrogen oxides). As a result, some of the world's finest historical monuments—cathedrals, sculptures, and public buildings—have deteriorated rapidly in recent years. Famous Greek ruins in Athens have deteriorated more during the past 40 years than during the previous 2,000 years. Atmospheric fallout of soot and grit also soils statues, buildings, cars, and clothing—causing greatly increased costs for cleaning.

Sulfuric acid, sulfur dioxide, nitrogen oxides, nitric acid, and some particulates also greatly accelerate the corrosion of metals, especially steel, iron, and zinc. Metal corrosion rates are often 2 to 5 times higher in polluted urban areas than in rural areas. Sulfuric acid and ozone also attack and fade rubber, leather, paper, some fabrics (such as cotton, rayon, and nylon), and paint. Women walking down the street have had their nylon stockings and blouses disintegrate. Extra lighting needed because of skies darkened by particulates costs Americans at least $16 million a year and uses large amounts of energy that produce more pollution—thus creating a vicious circle.

Air pollution can also stunt plant growth and damage food crops and trees. Many plants are sensitive to high and very low concentrations of sulfur dioxide, ozone, and PAN. Fruits and vegetables grown near big cities are particularly vulnerable. In southern California, citrus crops are damaged mainly by ozone and PAN in photochemical smog. In the Middle Atlantic states potatoes, tomatoes, green peas, corn, apples, peaches, and leafy vegetables are damaged primarily by sulfur dioxide and sulfuric acid, which discolor leaves and sometimes stunt growth.

In Ontario, Canada, sulfur dioxide pollution from an iron-sintering plant essentially destroyed a forest ecosystem for 8 kilometers (5 miles) downwind and caused tree and plant damage as far as 30 kilometers (19 miles) away. Ozone in photochemical smog produced in Los Angeles has moderately or severely damaged trees in two-thirds of the San Bernardino National Forest.

In addition to humans, other animals are affected by air pollution. Many industrial emissions, such as fluorides, lead (which also comes from cars using leaded gasoline), arsenic, and zinc, can be retained in the soil after being washed out of the atmosphere. These poisonous substances can then be taken up by vegetation, which is then eaten by grazing animals. One of the best-known pollutants affecting livestock (especially cattle, sheep, and swine) is fluoride, which causes mottled teeth, lameness, and ultimately death.

Damage to Human Health Air pollution can affect humans in a number of ways (Figure 17-8). After decades of research there is overwhelming statistical evidence that air pollution can kill, induce and aggravate a number of diseases, and increase human suffering. Air pollution is particularly harmful to the very young, the old, the poor (who are usually forced to live in highly polluted areas; see Enrichment Study 9), and those already weakened by heart and lung diseases. In spite of the massive statistical evidence, establishing that a particular pollutant causes a particular disease or death is extremely difficult. Officially almost no one dies of air pollution. Instead the death certificate reads chronic bronchitis, emphysema, lung cancer, stomach cancer, or heart disease, even though air pollution may have been a major contributing factor.

Correlating air pollution with specific health effects is difficult because of (1) the number and variety of air pollutants; (2) the difficulty in detecting pollutants that cause harm at extremely low concentrations; (3) the synergistic interaction of pollutants (Section 6-2); (4) the difficulty in isolating single harmful factors when people are exposed to so many potentially harmful chemicals over many years; (5) the unreliability of records of disease and death; (6) the multiple causes and lengthy incubation times of diseases such as emphysema, chronic bronchitis, cancer, and heart disease (Enrichment Study 6); and (7) the problem of extrapolating test data on laboratory animals to humans. Because of these difficulties and public misunderstanding of the nature of science, many people are misled when they hear such statements as "science has not proven absolutely that air pollution or smoking has killed anyone." Like the statement "cats are not elephants," such a statement is true but meaningless. Science never has proven anything absolutely and never will. Science does not establish absolute truths but only a degree of probability or confidence in the validity of an idea.

Air pollution has been connected with suffering and death from heart disease, chronic respiratory diseases (such as bronchial asthma, chronic bronchitis, and pulmonary emphysema), and lung cancer. Diseases of the heart and blood vessels caused only 20 percent of U.S. deaths in the early 1900s but now account for more than half. Heart disease has many causes but has been linked to carbon monoxide, even at low levels, and to inhaled sulfate particles.

The major sources of carbon monoxide in the air and lungs are automobile exhausts and cigarette smoking. Carbon monoxide reacts with oxygen-carrying hemoglobin in blood over 200 times more rapidly than the oxygen gas we inhale. Thus, high concentrations of carbon monoxide tie up hemoglobin in the blood and deprive the body of oxygen. This can lead to headaches, fatigue, impaired judgment, and a greater workload on the heart. In addition to heart disease, carbon monoxide may cause some automobile accidents by causing driver fatigue and poor judgment. Carbon monoxide inhaled during smoking ties up about 5 to 20 percent of the smoker's hemoglobin. This form of personal air pollution is the primary source of carbon monoxide and a number of other pollutants for both smokers and nonsmokers who are exposed to cigarette smoke (Enrichment Study 6).

As you might expect, there are strong correlations between air pollution and chronic respiratory diseases. Although cigarette smoking almost certainly ranks as the major cause of chronic respiratory disease, sulfur oxides, sulfuric acid, particulates, and nitrogen dioxide have been shown to aggravate bronchial asthma and cause and aggravate chronic bronchitis and pulmonary emphysema. *Chronic bronchitis* now affects one out of five American men between 40 and 60 and has been related to smoking and to living in polluted urban areas.

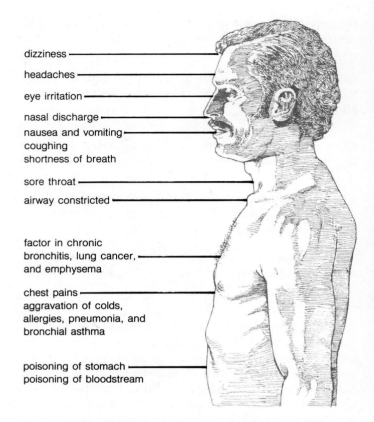

dizziness

headaches

eye irritation

nasal discharge

nausea and vomiting
coughing
shortness of breath

sore throat

airway constricted

factor in chronic
bronchitis, lung cancer,
and emphysema

chest pains
aggravation of colds,
allergies, pneumonia, and
bronchial asthma

poisoning of stomach
poisoning of bloodstream

Figure 17-8 Some possible effects of air pollution on the human body.

Emphysema is the fastest-growing cause of death in the United States, killing almost more Americans each year than lung cancer and tuberculosis put together. This disorder is usually accompanied by chronic bronchitis. In addition, an estimated 1.5 million emphysema sufferers in the United States (over half of them under 65) cannot work or live normal lives because even the slightest exertion causes them to gasp for breath. At present, emphysema is incurable and basically untreatable. It is caused and aggravated by a number of factors, including smoking, air pollution, and heredity. About 25 percent of emphysema cases seem due to a hereditary condition in which a protein is lacking that is vital in keeping the lungs elastic. Such persons have a very good chance of getting emphysema, especially if they smoke or if they live or work in a polluted area. Recently a test has been devised to detect this genetic defect. Anyone who smokes or lives in a polluted atmosphere should have this test made.

Lung cancer is caused by a number of factors (see Enrichment Study 6). Smoking is considered the number

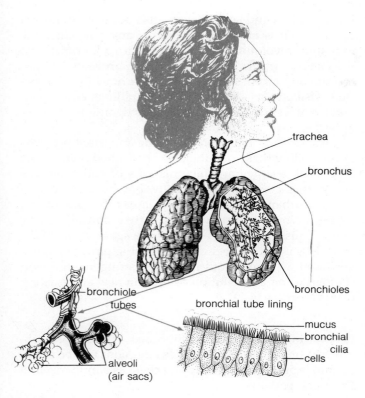

Figure 17-9 The respiratory system.

one cause, but lung cancer has also been linked to air pollution from (1) some radioactive isotopes, such as inhaled particles of plutonium-239; (2) polynuclear aromatic hydrocarbons (PAH), such as 3,4-benzopyrene, found in cigarette smoke; (3) automobile exhaust; (4) particulates (especially of asbestos, beryllium, arsenic, chromium, and nickel); and (5) fine particles that may pick up cancer-causing agents. Urban nonsmokers are 3 to 4 times more likely than rural nonsmokers to develop lung cancer.

To understand how air pollutants can cause or aggravate respiratory diseases, let's look briefly at what happens to the air that we inhale each day into our respiratory system (Figure 17-9). Each breath swirls down the trachea, which divides into two big bronchial tubes that enter the lungs. These tubes divide and subdivide into many small ducts, or bronchiole tubes. At the end of these many bronchiole tubes are around 500 million tiny, bubblelike air sacs, called **alveoli,** which lie like clusters of tiny grapes within the lungs. Oxygen in the air passes through the walls of the alveoli and combines with hemoglobin in the blood. At the same time carbon

dioxide passes from the blood back through the alveoli walls into the lungs for exhaling. If carbon monoxide ties up too much of the blood hemoglobin, the heart must work harder to supply enough oxygen.

Humans have several defenses against dirty air: Hairs in the nose filter out large particles, and the upper respiratory tract is lined with hundreds of thousands of tiny mucus-coated hairs, called **cilia,** which continually wave back and forth to sweep out any foreign matter. Smoking and some air pollutants apparently destroy, stiffen, or slow the cilia and thus make them less effective. As a result, bacteria and particulates can penetrate the alveoli, increasing the chance of respiratory infection and lung cancer. If you smoke or have lived long in an urban area, you can assume that your lung tissue is black from particulate deposits, unlike the pink lung tissue of a young child.

Another lung protector is mucus, which is constantly secreted in small amounts. If the lungs become irritated, mucus flows more freely to wash out or dissolve the irritants. A coughing mechanism then expels the dirty air and some of the mucus. Cigarette smoking and pollutants such as sulfur dioxide and sulfuric acid can trigger so much mucus flow that air passages become blocked. The stoppage then causes coughing. As muscles surrounding the bronchial tubes weaken, more mucus accumulates, and breathing becomes progressively more difficult. If this cycle persists, it indicates **chronic bronchitis**—a persistent inflammation of the mucous membranes of the trachea and bronchi.

Lung cancer is the abnormal, runaway growth of cells in the mucous membrane of the bronchial passages. Some air pollutants can cause lung cancer directly, and others can disrupt the action of the mucus-carrying cilia. If the cilia and mucus do not remove carcinogenic pollutants, lung cancer is more likely (see Enrichment Study 6).

A person suffering from **bronchial asthma** has recurrent episodes of shortness of breath, prolonged coughing, and difficulty in breathing. These symptoms result from the narrowing of the bronchial passages and excessive mucus secretion that obstructs the flow of air to the lungs. Most asthma is not caused by air pollution, but pollutants can trigger attacks in people suffering from this disease.

Pollutants can also irritate the bronchial tubes so that they close up. The trapped air may expand and fuse clusters of alveoli together. The air sacs then lose their ability to expand and contract and can even tear (Figure 17-10). As a result, the lungs become enlarged and less efficient. As more and more alveoli become damaged,

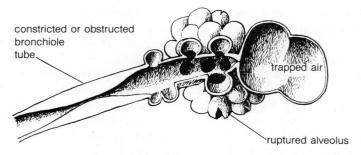

constricted or obstructed
bronchiole
tube

trapped air

ruptured alveolus

Figure 17-10 Pulmonary emphysema. Constricted or blocked bronchial tubes cause trapped air to enlarge the alveoli so that they lose resilience and sometimes disintegrate. This causes excessive shortness of breath, susceptibility to respiratory infection, and possible heart strain.

the bronchial tubes tend to collapse and breathing gets harder. Walking becomes painful and running impossible. After a period of years breathing efficiency can become so low that the victim can die of suffocation or heart failure. People suffering from these problems have **pulmonary emphysema.**

17-4 Control of Industrial Smog

Importance of Controlling Emissions Control of sulfur oxides and particulates is closely related to the energy crisis (Chapter 13), because the burning of fossil fuels (especially coal) in electric power plants and industrial plants is the major source of these pollutants. Each year U.S. power plants and industrial plants produce 91 percent of the total weight of sulfur oxide emissions, 82 percent of the particulates, 59 percent of the nitrogen oxides, 25 percent of the hydrocarbons, and 17 percent of the carbon monoxide. If the United States shifts back to greater use of coal for electric power production (Sections 13-6 and 14-2), then improved control of sulfur oxides and particulates emissions will be essential to protect human health, food crops, livestock, buildings, materials, and natural ecosystems. Some argue that the costs of such control are too great, but studies reveal that the resulting health benefits exceed the costs of controlling stationary sources of air pollution by 70 percent.

Fortunately, at least one city has succeeded in sharply reducing air pollution from sulfur oxides and particulates. After several air pollution disasters in the 1950s, the city of London enacted and enforced strong air pollution control measures on industrial and residential

burning of oil and coal. The results have been dramatic. London's air is now cleaner than at any time since the industrial revolution. Severe smogs are a bad memory, respiratory attacks have dropped, sunshine has increased 50 percent during the winter home-heating period, visibility has tripled, public buildings and monuments are less corroded and blackened, and the number of bird species has doubled.

The United States has also made important progress in controlling these pollutants in the United States since 1970, with average annual emissions of sulfur dioxide and particulates dropping slowly, but steadily—except in some urban and industrialized areas. In spite of this significant overall improvement, there is still a long way to go. Emissions could begin to rise again in the 1980s and 1990s if the number of coal-burning power plants is increased without requiring more stringent emission standards and air pollution control on new and existing plants (Section 14-2).

Controlling Sulfur Oxides Emissions The major methods for controlling sulfur oxides emissions can be divided into input and output approaches, as summarized in the accompanying box.

Particulates Control Unlike most air pollutants, particulates consist of a large number of different chemicals that form particles and droplets of widely varying sizes (Figure 17-11) and with diverse chemical and health effects. *Large particles,* which have diameters greater than 10 micrometers (1 micrometer is equal to one-millionth of a meter, or about 0.000039 inch), tend to fall out of the atmosphere in a short time. Most natural emissions (dust and material from volcanoes) consist of large particles. *Medium-sized particles,* which have diameters between 1 and 10 micrometers, tend to remain suspended in the air for longer periods, but most can be removed by several methods discussed in the box on controlling particulates emissions. The largest human sources of these particles are fly ash and coal dust from coal-burning electric power and industrial plants.

The most serious threats to human health are posed by *fine particles,* which have diameters less than 1 micrometer (Figure 17-11). Fine particles are found in cigarette smoke, oil smoke, photochemical smog formed from car exhausts, toxic metal dusts (some of which can cause cancer), and tiny particles of sulfate and nitrate salts formed in the atmosphere by the reaction of power plant and automobile exhaust gases with other chemi-

Methods for Controlling Sulfur Oxides Emissions

Input Approaches

1. *Reduce population growth and the wasteful use of energy.* This is the single most important approach. From 50 to 90 percent of the energy used each year in the United States is wasted (Sections 13-2 and 13-3).

2. *Shift from fossil fuels to other energy sources such as solar, wind, or geothermal energy* (Chapters 13 and 14). Even if half the electrical power used in the United States is produced by alternative energy sources by the year 2000, sulfur oxides produced from existing and projected coal-burning plants are expected to be a massive problem—3 or 4 times higher than today's levels. Conversion to other energy sources must be coupled with other strategies for controlling sulfur oxides emissions.

3. *Use coal gasification and liquefaction instead of solid coal* (Section 14-2). Converting coal to a gaseous or liquid fuel would remove most of its sulfur impurities and reduce air pollution from burning coal. But economic feasibility is still unknown and the net useful energy yield is low (Table 13-4 and Section 14-2).

4. *Shift to low-sulfur fossil fuels* (less than 1 percent sulfur). The projected reserves of natural gas, which contains essentially no sulfur, is too low for it to be used as a fuel to produce electricity (Section 14-2). Substantial use of low-sulfur oil would force the United States and most industrial nations to depend even more on foreign imports. Major U.S. supplies of relatively low-sulfur coal are located west of the Mississippi, far from major population centers to which the coal would have to be transported at high economic and energy costs. In addition, western coal tends to have a lower energy value per unit weight than high-sulfur eastern coal, and boilers in a number of older power plants cannot burn low-sulfur coal without expensive modifications.

5. *Remove sulfur from the fuel before burning.* This method is technologically feasible but could increase fuel costs by 25 to 50 percent.

Output Approaches

1. *Remove sulfur oxides during combustion or from stack exhaust gases* (known as flue gas desulfurization, or FGD). A number of chemical processes are now technologically feasible. Usually sulfur dioxide is removed by a high-temperature reaction with a chemical such as limestone (calcium carbonate) or by bubbling exhaust gases through wet scrubbers that remove 80 to 95 percent of the sulfur dioxide, which dissolves in or reacts with a liquid such as water (see Figure 17-13d). Scrubbers are now required by the EPA for all new coal-burning plants in the United States. Electric utilities argue that scrubbers are unreliable, too expensive, and produce large amounts of toxic sludge that must be disposed of at considerable cost. The EPA insists: (a) Scrubbers can be made reliable; (b) they are the only proven technology available; (c) their use will increase the cost of electricity to the consumer by only 15 to 20 percent—far less than the health and materials costs to consumers that would result if these emissions were not controlled; and (d) the sludge and fly ash produced each year can be safely disposed of and represent far less of a health hazard than sulfur oxides emissions.

2. *Discharge emissions from smokestacks tall enough to pierce the thermal inversion layer* (Figure 17-6). This widely used approach is strongly favored by industry because it is cheaper than scrubbing stack gases. It is strongly opposed, however, by the EPA and most environmentalists. It is at best only a short-term measure and at worst a long-range threat to human health and global climate patterns. This method merely ensures wider dispersion of deadly pollutants; thus, although pollution may be decreased in areas near the power plant, it can be increased in more distant areas. Part of Scandinavia's acid rains have been blamed on wind-borne emissions from tall stacks in Great Britain and western Europe. In addition, tall stacks may not disperse the pollutants as effectively as is commonly thought.

3. *Use intermittent emission control.* This method involves shutting down a plant or switching to low-sulfur fuels during adverse meteorological conditions. At other times emissions through tall smokestacks are allowed. This method is favored by industry but opposed by the EPA and most environmentalists for the same reasons discussed for output method 2.

4. Add a pollution charge (see Section 18-3) on sulfur emissions to reduce emissions and to encourage development of more efficient, cost-effective methods of sulfur emissions control.

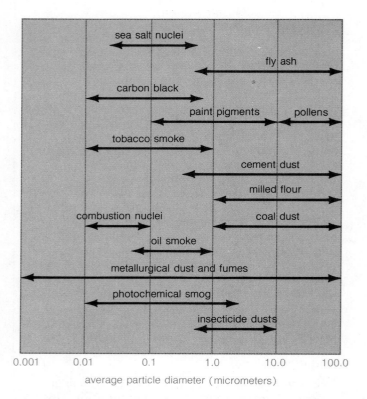

Figure 17-11 Suspended particulates are found in a wide variety of types and sizes.

Particulates control can be divided into input and output approaches (see the accompanying box). These methods are similar to those for the control of sulfur oxides; in addition, particulates from automobile exhausts must also be controlled.

17-5 Control of Photochemical Smog: The Automobile Problem

Methods for Controlling Automobile Pollution In 1979 the 140 million cars, trucks, and buses in the United States produced about 71 percent of the total weight of carbon monoxide emissions, 53 percent of the hydrocarbons, 50 percent of the nitrogen oxides, 3 percent of the particulates, and 12 percent of the sulfur oxides. In many areas cars produce about 85 percent by weight of all urban air pollution. However, automobile emissions are not considered to be as serious a threat to human health as sulfur oxides and particulates from stationary sources (Table 17-2). Controlling automobile pollution is important, but the resulting economic and health benefits are not as great as those from controlling sulfur oxides and

cals. Fine particles are dangerous because they remain suspended in the air long enough to be carried throughout the world and because they are small enough to penetrate the natural defenses set up by our lungs. They are also a major factor in reducing visibility and in altering global weather and climate (Enrichment Study 3). Although automobiles account for only about 1 percent of the total mass of atmospheric particulates, their impact is more severe because approximately 60 to 80 percent of these particulates have diameters less than 2 micrometers. Another major problem is that most fine particles are secondary pollutants formed in the atmosphere by the reaction of various chemicals. Thus, even if methods could be developed to remove fine particles from stack and automobile exhausts, it would not significantly improve the situation. Although U.S. control programs reduced average levels of particulates by 10 percent between 1972 and 1978, emissions of more dangerous fine particles increased; these emissions are expected to increase even more in the future with or without control (Figure 17-12).

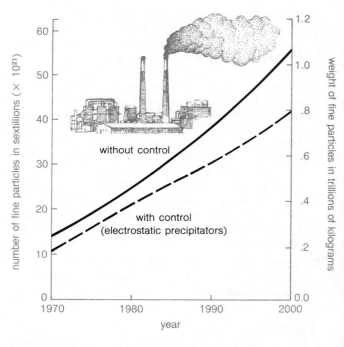

Figure 17-12 Atmospheric concentrations of suspended fine particles from coal-burning sources are expected to rise with or without pollution control.

Methods for Controlling Particulates Emissions

Input Approaches

1. *Reduce population growth, energy waste, and energy use by power plants and automobiles.* This is the single most important approach and is the most effective way to reduce the number of dangerous fine particles that are formed in the atmosphere.

2. *Shift from fossil fuels to other energy sources such as nuclear, solar, wind, and geothermal energy to produce electricity* (Chapter 13).

3. *Use coal gasification and liquefaction instead of solid coal* (Section 14-2).

4. *Discourage automobile use and shift to mass and para transit* (Section 11-4).

5. *Shift to less polluting automobile engines and fuels* (as discussed in Section 17-5).

Output Approaches

1. *Remove particulates from stack exhaust gases.* This is the most widely used method in electric power and industrial plants. Several methods are in use (Figure 17-13), including (a) *electrostatic precipitators* (Figures 17-13 and 17-14) which remove up to 99.5 percent of the total mass of particulates (but not most fine particles) by means of an electrostatic field that charges the particles so that they can be attracted to a series of electrodes and removed from exhaust gas; (b) *baghouse filters* (Figure 17-13b), which can filter out up to 99.9 percent of the particulates (including most fine particles) as exhaust gas is passed through fiber bags in a large housing; (c) *cyclone separators* (Figure 17-13c), which remove from 50 to 90 percent of the large particles (but very few of the medium-sized and fine particles) by swirling exhaust gas through a funnel-shaped chamber in which particles collect through centrifugal force; and (d) *wet scrubbers* (Figure 17-13d), which remove up to 99.5 percent of the particulates and 80 to 95 percent of the sulfur dioxide by passing exhaust gas through a liquid such as water. Except for baghouse filters, none of these methods remove many fine particles, and all of these methods produce highly toxic solid wastes, or sludge, that must be disposed of safely. Except for cyclone separators, all methods are expensive and require an initial investment of up to several million dollars. Of course, none of these methods are effective when particulates are formed as secondary pollutants.

2. *Discharge emissions from smokestacks tall enough to pierce the thermal inversion layer* (see comments in the box for sulfur oxides control methods).

3. *Intermittent emission control* (see comments in the box for sulfur oxides control methods).

4. *Use emission control devices on automobiles to remove particles from exhausts or to reduce particle formation through more complete combustion* (see next section for details). This method reduces pollution by primary particulates but has little effect on secondary particulates, which make up most fine-particle pollution from automobiles.

---

particulates pollution from stationary sources. It is estimated that the approximately $10 billion annual investment needed to control mobile source emissions would probably produce at best only $5 billion per year in work and health benefits. In addition, controlling emissions from 140 million mobile sources is more difficult politically and economically than controlling emissions from several thousand stationary sources.

The major methods for controlling emissions from mobile sources can be divided into input and output approaches, as summarized in the accompanying box.

Table 17-6 compares various methods for controlling emissions from automobiles.

Smog Control in the United States The overall strategy for controlling photochemical smog and conserving finite oil supplies (Chapter 13) must employ all of the approaches given in the box on controlling mobile source emissions, especially input methods 1 through 4. Possible new engines and fuels are given in Figure 17-15. We are not going to do away with cars, but there is no

Figure 17-13 Four commonly used methods for removing particulates from the exhaust gases of electric power and industrial plants.

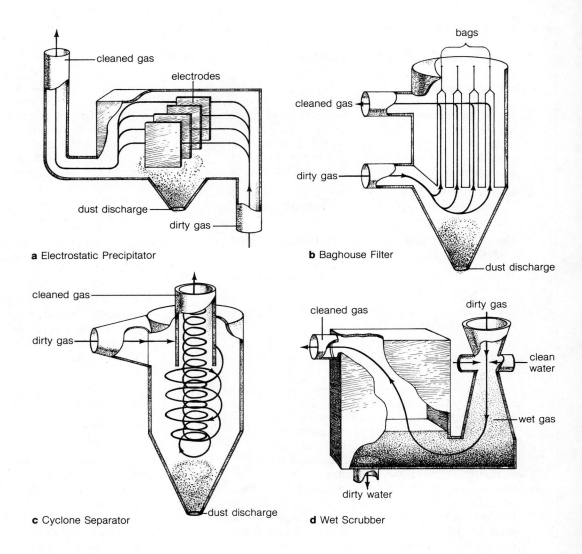

a Electrostatic Precipitator

b Baghouse Filter

c Cyclone Separator

d Wet Scrubber

reason why new fuels and new engines can't be developed that waste less fuel and produce less pollution. In the April 1963 issue of *American Engineer*, an engineer said, "It would be hard to imagine anything on such a large scale that seems quite as badly engineered as the American automobile. It is . . . a classic example of what engineering should not be."

17-6 Politics of Pollution Control in the United States

Misplaced Priorities With all the advantages of alternate fuels and the improved types of engines (Table 17-6), why don't we have these technological improve-

ments now? For the most part the reasons are political rather than technological. Part of the problem has been that until 1973, gasoline was so cheap that fuel economy was not a major problem of either consumers or auto manufacturers. Another factor is that of misplaced corporate and individual priorities. Large corporations with capital and outstanding research staffs often refuse to do serious research and development on new, cleaner engines and must be forced step by step to meet safety and emission standards.

At the individual level, many of us insist on large cars with hundreds of horsepower on streets so crowded that we can only drive 19 kilometers per hour (12 miles per hour). We fail to ride on or support the development of mass and para transit systems (Section 11-4). To get a better perspective on the politics of air pollution control

Eastman Kodak Company

Figure 17-14 The effectiveness of an electrostatic precipitator in reducing particulates emissions. A stack with the precipitator turned off (left) and with the precipitator operating (right). Although this method can remove up to 99.5 percent of the total mass of particulates in exhaust gases, it does not remove very many of the invisible and more harmful fine particles.

in the United States, let's look at the history of emission control in Los Angeles and the state of California.

Photochemical Smog: The Los Angeles Saga Put several million people with an almost equal number of automobiles together in a subtropical climate with light winds. Then put mountains on one side and the sea on the other and you have Los Angeles—and the ideal recipe for photochemical smog. The world owes a great debt to Los Angeles for teaching us much of what we know about air pollution and air pollution control.

Los Angeles has been working hard at controlling air pollution for a long time. Its topography and climate make it particularly susceptible to thermal inversions (Figure 17-6), which occur about 160 days a year. Four

centuries ago Spanish explorer Juan Cabrillo gave the name "Bay of Smokes" to what is today called the San Pedro Bay because of the smoke from Indian fires that hung over the Los Angeles basin.

Air pollution first became serious in Los Angeles between 1942 and 1946, when average daily particulates emissions quadrupled. By 1947 strict laws banned all outdoor burning, and industrial plants and incinerators were forced to install particulate precipitators (Figure 17-14) for smoke emission. By 1949 particulates emissions had been cut in half, but the air still had a yellow-brown haze and irritated the eyes. Officials and scientists blamed sulfur dioxide for the discomfort. In 1949, strict controls were placed on sulfur dioxide emissions and coal burning became illegal, but the air pollution remained.

Table 17-6 Methods for Controlling Air Pollution from Automobiles

Method	Advantages	Disadvantages
Input Approaches		
Reduced automobile use	Reduces air pollution and use of fossil fuels and other resources (see Table 11-3)	Is inconvenient to car-oriented society unless mass and para transit available; could cause economic disruption and unemployment (see Table 11-3)
Mass and para transit	Reduces air pollution and use of fossil fuels and other resources (see Table 11-3)	Is inconvenient; has high initial cost (see Table 11-3)
New engine designs (Figure 17-15) Electric	Eliminates exhaust emissions; eliminates direct burning of fossil fuels; decreases photochemical smog in urban areas; is quiet; requires little maintenance; is ideal for short trips; has lower fuel costs than gasoline engine; may be used in a hybrid system with electric power for low speeds and short distances and a small combustion engine or fuel cell for highway cruising; new batteries may increase range and cruising speed with less recharging	Could trade one form of pollution for another more harmful one (if daily charging of batteries increases electricity use, thus increasing SO_2 and particulates emissions and radioactive wastes from nuclear power plants); could cause economic depression in oil industry; net energy yield not much higher than that of internal combustion engine (see Figure 13-9); present vehicles are slow, expensive, and inefficient and must be recharged every 80 to 160 kilometers (50 to 100 miles); present batteries must be replaced periodically at costs up to $3,000
Gas turbine	Has low CO and hydrocarbon emissions; runs on most liquid fossil fuels; requires little maintenance; may last longer; vibration-free power; has potentially higher fuel economy per unit of engine weight than conventional engines	Gets poor fuel economy with present designs; operates best at a constant speed; is expensive; depletes fossil fuels; has high nitrogen oxides emissions; breakthrough in ceramic technology needed to permit use of higher combustion temperatures to improve fuel economy
Stirling (external combustion)	Has low emissions; makes few vibrations and little noise; runs on most liquid fossil fuels; has potentially very good fuel economy	Has high cost; is heavy; gets moderate fuel economy with present designs (but should improve); power control is difficult and expensive
Rankine, or "steam" (external combustion)	Reduces air pollution; runs on most liquid fossil fuels; should require less service and last longer than conventional engines; has potentially fairly good fuel economy	Is expensive; more research needed before it can be mass produced; has poor fuel economy (but may improve with new designs)
New fuels for internal combustion engines Natural gas	Burns cleanly with very little pollution (except CO_2)	Supplies are insufficient; range is limited; distribution systems are not in place and each station pump could cost $30,000; could cause economic disruption of oil industry
Alcohol	Could substitute for or be added to gasoline	Supplies are limited (Section 14-8); large land requirements; moderate to high environmental impact from soil erosion; water pollution from runoff of fertilizer and pesticides; competition for cropland to grow grain for fuel may raise prices and reduce food available for the world's poor; net useful energy yield may be low (see Table 13-4 and Section 14-8)
Fuel cells and hydrogen	Causes no pollution (except heat)	Still being developed; storage and distribution of hydrogen are difficult; requires an economic and environmentally acceptable energy source to produce hydrogen (see Table 13-4 and Section 14-8)
Improved fuel efficiency	Reduces emissions by burning less gasoline; can be done quickly	Is somewhat costly; is inconvenient for some; is only a short-term measure

Table 17-6 Methods for Controlling Air Pollution from Automobiles *(cont.)*

Method	Advantages	Disadvantages
Modified internal combustion engine		
Carburetor adjustment	Is easy and quick	Is only a short-term measure; increases emission of other pollutants (see Figure 17-16)
Wankel engine	Has low nitrogen oxides emissions; reduces fuel consumption by 10% to 15% because of light weight; should require less service and last longer than conventional engines	Consumes fossil fuels; rotary seals fail periodically (being improved); without emission controls emits more hydrocarbons and CO than conventional engine; increases fuel consumption by 10% to 30% in present models; is inefficient
Stratified-charge engine	Has low emissions without emission control devices; gets better gas mileage than most conventional engines	Consumes fossil fuels
Diesel engine	Gets 25% better gas mileage than conventional engine; requires little maintenance; has low CO and hydrocarbon emissions; new turbocharged type may sharply reduce emissions; lasts longer and is more efficient than conventional engine; new direct injection diesel engines may improve gas mileage over standard diesels (but increase nitrogen oxides emissions)	Consumes fossil fuel; has higher nitrogen oxides and particulates emissions and is more expensive and noisier than conventional engine; emissions can cause eye irritation and possibly genetic damage; has sluggish performance unless turbocharged; one barrel of crude oil yields 2.3 more times gasoline than diesel fuel so overall fuel economy per barrel of oil (not per car) is lower than for conventional engines
Output Approaches		
Emission control	Reduces pollution without major changes in engine design; causes no economic disruption of automobile industry	Consumes fossil fuels; doesn't reduce pollution enough in long run; devices become less effective with use; devices must be adjusted or replaced frequently; catalytic converters may emit toxic metal particles
Treatment of urban air to reduce formation of photochemical smog	Is much cheaper than controlling each automobile; controls stationary as well as moving sources; involves no government regulation of individual cars; preliminary (but incomplete) tests indicate no adverse health effects	Has not been thoroughly tested; could have harmful health and ecological side effects; could transfer smog formation to suburban and rural areas near a city; does not reduce CO levels; bacterial infection could increase as ozone levels are reduced

In the early 1950s, A. J. Haagen-Smit of the California Institute of Technology accidentally solved the mystery. He was trying to isolate the main ingredient that causes pineapple odor by condensing it in a trap cooled by liquid nitrogen. After removing the trap he smelled highly toxic and reactive ozone (O_3), which would certainly not be expected from a pineapple. Noticing that the smog was bad that day, he pulled an air sample through the trap and got a dark, smelly liquid that smelled like ozone and contained a complex mixture of hydrocarbons, aldehydes, and other organic compounds. This chance experiment turned out to be very important in the history of air pollution. He concluded that automobiles, along with oil refineries, were causing the smog.

Los Angeles authorities moved quickly and firmly to reduce hydrocarbon emissions from oil refineries—an obvious suspect—but they failed to recognize the importance of the automobile and the smog got still worse. Finally, in 1953, the culprit was confirmed when a survey showed that most of the hydrocarbons were coming from motor vehicles.

Los Angeles officials now faced powerful adversaries—the automobile and petroleum industries, which directly and indirectly account for about $1 out of every $6 spent in the United States. Through the persistent efforts of Los Angeles County Supervisor Kenneth Hahn, the automobile manufacturers agreed to begin studying the problem. However, this research was given a very low priority. In 1959, "blow-by" emissions escap-

Methods for Controlling Emissions from Automobiles and Other Mobile Sources

Input Approaches

1. *Reduce automobile use.* Discourage automobile use by (a) placing taxes on gasoline, horsepower, and car weight, (b) banning cars in downtown areas (see Section 11-4), and (c) modifying life-styles and the design of cities to require less automobile use (see Section 11-5).
2. *Develop mass and para transit systems* (see Section 11-4).
3. *Develop less polluting and more energy-efficient engines.* Possibilities include electric, gas turbine, Stirling, and Rankine engines (Table 17-6).
4. *Use a cleaner fuel for the internal combustion engine.* Examples include natural gas, fuel cells (batteries), and liquid hydrogen (Table 17-6).
5. *Improve fuel efficiency.* This can be accomplished by reducing the size, weight, wind resistance, and power of cars and by improving the energy efficiency of transmissions, air conditioning, and other accessories.
6. *Modify the internal combustion engine to lower emissions and improve gas mileage.* Such modifications include carburetor adjustments, fuel injection, and diesel and stratified-charge engines (Table 17-6).

Output Approaches

1. *Control emissions from the internal combustion engine more strictly.* Examples include afterburners and catalytic converters (Table 17-6).
2. *Treat urban air with chemicals to reduce formation of photochemical smog.*

ing from car pistons and vented out of the crankcase were found to account for about 20 to 25 percent of the hydrocarbon emissions of a typical car. General Motors finally installed a crankcase ventilation device on all new cars sold in California in 1961 and on all new cars sold nationwide in 1963. General Motors said that this device, which had been known to them since the 1930s, "would bring about a major reduction in air pollution." But this device had nothing to do with automobile exhaust, and smog levels got worse.

By 1963 the California legislature had become tired of the automobile industry's slow progress in controlling emissions. It passed legislation that required the installation of exhaust control systems on all new cars sold in California. The automobile companies said that the earliest they could possibly develop and install such systems would be 1967—a 4-year delay. But in 1964 several parts manufacturers not connected with the automobile companies had developed four different exhaust control systems that met the state's requirements. In the same year the automobile companies said they could provide exhaust control after all for all 1966 cars sold in California. By 1968 total hydrocarbon and carbon monoxide levels in California, along with eye irritation, were slowly dropping.

So 1968 should have been a victory year for Los Angeles officials and residents. But a new twist appeared that shows how everything is indeed connected to everything else. Although the hydrocarbon levels dropped 12 percent between 1965 and 1968, the concentration of nitrogen oxides (NO and NO_2) increased by 28 percent, exceeding harmful levels on 132 days in 1968.

Automobile manufacturers had reduced carbon monoxide and hydrocarbon emissions by increasing air intake. This leaner fuel mixture (less fuel, more air) made engine combustion more complete, produced less carbon monoxide (and more carbon dioxide), and left fewer unburned hydrocarbons to be exhausted. But as shown in Figure 17-16, this mixture increases fuel consumption and causes nitrogen and oxygen gases in the air intake to react more rapidly at the high engine temperatures, producing increased nitrogen oxides emissions. An improvement in one problem had aggravated another.

Figure 17-16 also shows that burning a richer fuel mixture decreases fuel economy and nitrogen oxides emissions and increases carbon monoxide and hydrocarbon emissions. Engineers also tried to reduce emission by tinkering with spark timing. By advancing spark timing they got better fuel economy but higher emissions of hydrocarbons and nitrogen oxides (Figure 17-

Now to 1985

electronic fuel injection
three-way catalytic converters
stratified-charge engines (Honda CVCC)
conventional diesel engines
turbocharged diesel engines
gasohol in moderate quantities

1986 to 2000

direct injection diesel engines
gas turbine engines
Stirling engines
Rankine engines
electric cars (limited use in urban areas)
hybrid cars (electric and small combustion engines)
alcohol fuels in moderate quantities

After 2000

fuel-cell-powered cars
hybrid electric and fuel-cell cars
hydrogen-fueled cars
solar electric cars (?)
alcohol fuels in substantial quantities (?)

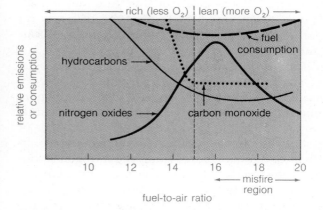

Figure 17-15 Possible automobile engines and fuels of the future.

16). Retarding the timing gave the reverse, lower emissions of hydrocarbons and nitrogen oxides but poorer fuel economy. Because of these fundamental properties of the standard internal combustion engine, merely modifying the fuel-to-air ratio and spark timing cannot simultaneously reduce all major pollutants and improve fuel economy.

When the automobile companies finally admitted to California officials in 1964 that exhaust control systems were feasible, they could no longer avoid installing such devices on all cars throughout the United States. As a result, Congress passed the Clean Air Act of 1965. In this act the standards adopted by California in 1966 were made national standards, to be effective in 1968. By 1970 the automobile industry had made little progress in developing either a clean conventional engine or an alternative engine. Also, emission control systems installed by Detroit usually performed below the level for which they were certified. This dissatisfaction with the automobile industry's progress and rising pressure from the public and scientists concerned about the health effects of air pollution led to the passage of the Clean Air Act of 1970—one of the strongest pieces of environmental legislation yet passed in the United States. If it had not been for the persistent earlier efforts of California, this law may not have been enacted.

Clean Air Acts of 1970 and 1977 The stated goal of the Clean Air Act of 1970 was to have air "safe enough to protect the public's health" by May 31, 1975. To accomplish this goal, the EPA was required to set national ambient air quality standards for the major air pollutants (Table 17-3); enforcement of the standards was left to the states. The 247 air quality regions of the country were required to submit plans for achieving the standards by May 31, 1975. For automobiles Congress went even further and set standards itself, hoping to force the automobile companies to speed up their research on emis-

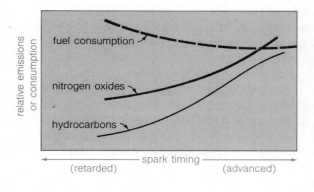

Figure 17-16 Effects of fuel-to-air ratio (left) and spark timing (right) on pollutant emissions (solid lines) and fuel consumption (dashed lines) in the conventional internal combustion engine.

sion reduction and alternative engines. The act required a 90 percent reduction in hydrocarbon and nitrogen oxides emissions from 1970 levels for all 1975 automobiles and a 90 percent reduction in nitrogen oxides emissions from 1971 levels for 1976 models. The EPA, however, was given the power to grant 1-year extensions if it found that the technology was not available after the companies had made good-faith efforts to develop it. At the same time California maintained its leadership role by setting emission standards lower than national standards.

Almost immediately the automobile companies requested an extension. They claimed that the 90 percent reductions were impossible or so costly that the companies would have to shut down. In 1973 the EPA granted Detroit a 1-year delay in meeting the 1975 standards for hydrocarbons and carbon monoxide and the 1976 nitrogen oxides standard. Although Detroit claimed it couldn't develop the technology to meet the 1975 national standards, they met them in California. In addition, during this same year the Honda Motor Company of Japan introduced its stratified-charge internal combustion engine (CVCC), which met the 1975 standards without using any add-on emission control devices. In 1973 Peugeot of France and Mercedes-Benz of West Germany also had diesel engine cars that met the 1975 standards.

In 1974, 1975, and 1976 Detroit was granted three additional 1-year extensions, claiming that it couldn't reduce emissions and at the same time improve fuel economy, which was necessary because of the energy crisis. During this same period the Honda CVCC was meeting the standards and getting about 17 kilometers per liter (40 miles per gallon) of gasoline. In 1976 Volkswagen introduced in the United States a lightweight diesel engine, which Detroit said couldn't be built. Automobiles with this engine met the 1975 standards and got about 21 kilometers per liter (50 miles per gallon). In 1977, with great fanfare, General Motors announced that it would offer a conventional diesel engine option for some of its models—something Peugeot and Mercedes-Benz had already been doing for decades. By 1980 Detroit finally got excited about conventional diesels and predicted they would represent 20 percent of the market by 1985. But Volkswagen had already been testing a turbocharged diesel car that gets almost 30 kilometers per liter (70 miles per gallon).

There is still another chapter in this story of delaying tactics by Detroit. To meet the federal emission standards, automobile manufacturers began adding afterburners and catalytic converters to car engines to control emissions. Afterburners, or thermal exhaust reactors, recirculate exhaust gas into high-temperature chambers to convert carbon monoxide to carbon dioxide and to get more complete combustion of unburned hydrocarbons. Unfortunately, at these high temperatures the nitrogen and oxygen gases used to burn gasoline react at a faster rate; thus nitrogen oxides emissions tend to rise. In a catalytic converter, engine exhaust is mixed with outside air and passed through a chamber containing two types of catalysts (one for carbon dioxide and one for hydrocarbons). These catalysts speed up the combustion reaction of carbon monoxide and hydrocarbons with oxygen gas. Detroit claimed that catalytic converters couldn't be developed to remove nitrogen oxides. In 1977, however, Volvo of Sweden introduced a three-way catalyst that reduced nitrogen oxides as well as carbon monoxide and hydrocarbons. Their engine with catalytic converter met the stricter 1978 California standards for carbon monoxide and produced less than half the hydrocarbons and nitrogen oxides emissions that these "impossible" standards allowed. In addition, by removing nitrogen oxides from the exhaust, Volvo could adjust the spark timing and fuel-to-air ratio to improve gas mileage. Meanwhile, California's stricter automobile standards led to a 37 percent decrease in carbon monoxide levels. The number of heavy smog days annually in the Los Angeles basin dropped from 176 in 1965 to 120 in 1977.

In 1977, after 7 years of pressure from automobile companies, industries, and environmentalists, Congress amended its 1970 act by passing the Clean Air Act of 1977. Despite vigorous industry pressure, the principles of the 1970 act were reaffirmed. But in recognition of past delays, the dates set for compliance with standards in the 1970 act were postponed. The nation's 247 air quality regions were given until 1982 to comply with national ambient air quality standards for major pollutants and until 1987 for photochemical oxidants. Automobile companies were given until 1981 to meet the 1975 new car emission standards for carbon monoxide and hydrocarbons and a less severe nitrogen oxides standard.

In 1980, the EPA decided to waive the 1981 nitrogen oxides standards for diesel-powered vehicles until 1983. The automobile companies wanted to produce more fuel-efficient diesels so they could meet more strict fuel economy standards for all cars in 1985 without major changes in automobile design. The companies also argued that they could control either the nitrogen oxides or particulates emissions from diesel engines, but not both, with present technology. By 1980, however, Volkswagen's Rabbit diesel cars were already meeting the proposed 1983 standards for both nitrogen oxides and particulates. There is, however, considerable debate and confusion over the potential health effects of a large-scale switch to diesel-powered cars.

Whether further delays will be granted to cities and automobile companies remains to be seen; past history, however, suggests that the original standards may never be enforced without considerable public pressure to counter lobbying from powerful industrial interests. Hopefully, the United States will follow the examples set by California and Japan, where tougher emission standards have been set and enforced without annual delays.

The 1977 amendments also failed to deal with what environmentalists feel to be a serious deficiency of the Clean Air Act of 1970. Even though new cars meet federal emission standards, spot checks reveal that after a short time, emission control systems become less effective or are tampered with or removed. To control this problem, environmentalists agree that tampering with emissions should be banned by law and that states should require every vehicle to have a simple pollution emission inspection (cost about $5) at annual license renewal time. New Jersey, for instance, already has such an annual inspection system and has found that the emission control system is tampered with in 1 out of every 10 cars.

It is also clear that important improvements such as the stratified-charge and diesel engines, lighter cars, and three-way catalytic converters are only temporary solutions. In the late 1980s and 1990s the United States must develop and begin phasing in a new generation of fuels and engines that produce less pollution, waste less fuel, and depend less and less on dwindling supplies of petroleum, as summarized earlier in Figure 17-15. U.S. automobile makers have the talent and money needed to become leaders rather than followers in making this important transition.

In recent years, the EPA has attempted to adopt more flexible policies for air pollution control by industry. In 1979, the EPA announced a new policy for the control of air pollution from stationary industrial plants. The EPA now permits state authorities to set maximum limits for total air pollution from all types emitted by the plant instead of for each type of pollutant. This policy—known as the bubble concept—treats the entire plant as if it were contained inside a bubble. Using this approach, a company can meet total emission standards by reducing pollution sharply from sources that are cheap and easy to control, while still having high emissions from sources that are difficult and expensive to control. This change is in response to industry's claim that it can control pollution more effectively and cheaply if regulators simply set overall standards and let the companies decide the best way to meet them. By 1980, some 100 companies were using the bubble concept with big savings on the costs of air-pollution control. In another new approach, known as an *offset policy*, the EPA is allowing companies to offset emissions from one plant in an area by cleaning up a neighboring plant's emissions. By 1980, at least 650 offset transactions had been approved by EPA. Another approach is EPA's banking policy. When a company makes extra reductions in air pollution in an area, these savings can be transferred to allow new plants to be built in the same area. Environmentalists warn, however, that some offset and bank transactions do not result in lower emissions because they represent "paper" transactions that would have taken place without the offset or banking requirement. For example, a company may claim a banking credit for shutting down an old plant that is already planned to close because it was outdated and uneconomical to operate.

Many industrial leaders in the United States complain that (1) unnecessarily strict air pollution standards and bureaucratic redtape in getting environmental permits make it easier and cheaper to build new plants in other countries—thus inhibiting economic growth in the United States; (2) it is so expensive to retrofit some existing plants to meet air pollution standards that they must be shut down; (3) it is almost impossible to find locations for new plants because in some areas federal law does not allow existing good quality air to be degraded significantly and they can't be put into other areas because the air is too dirty; (4) the costs of pollution control have been an important factor in raising consumer prices and the annual rate of inflation; (5) unnecessarily strict air pollution standards prevent the United States from relying more on coal to produce electricity; and (6) the EPA is constantly changing its rules, making long-range planning very difficult.

Several studies, however, including a 1981 study by the National Commission on Air Quality, have shown that (1) the benefits (such as improved health) from air pollution control far outweigh the costs—amounting to an estimated $21.4 billion in benefits between 1970 and 1978 alone (see Section 18-4 for more details); (2) the funds spent nationally on air pollution control since 1965 have not impeded overall economic growth and in fact have stimulated innovation and economic growth and created more new jobs than have been lost by stimulating the very rapid growth of the new pollution control industry—which employs about 2 million people and has annual sales growth about twice that for all manufacturing firms in the United States; (3) environmental regulation increases consumer prices by such a small amount that relaxing the controls would hardly dent the annual rate of inflation; (4) despite dire warnings from industry of massive shutdowns and layoffs since the 1960s, plant closings attributable to air pollution standards have been few, and are expected to be insubstantial in the future because of present standards; (5) present air pollution standards should not inhibit significantly the development of any U.S. energy resource; and (6) the EPA has in recent years used a much more flexible approach, as evidenced by its bubble concept, offset policy, and banking policy.

In 1981, the Clean Air Acts of 1970 and 1976 were up for renewal by Congress. With intense pressure from industry, the Reagan administration and a more conservative Congress may amend the Clean Air Act by (1) extending or eliminating deadlines and perhaps relaxing some standards for automobile emissions; (2) requiring the use of cost-benefit analysis in setting any standard (see Section 18-3); (3) using cost-effectiveness analysis to set air pollution standards so that the cheapest effective approach is used; (4) relaxing air pollution standards that restrict industrial growth or the development of any U.S.

Table 17-7 Effects of Air Pollution and Technological Control Feasibility

Pollutant	Residence Time	Area Affected	Control Feasibility	Economic Cost	Political Feasibility
Class 1: Nuisance and aesthetic insult					
Noise	Short	Local	Good	Moderately low	Good
Odor	Usually short	Local, regional	Good	Moderate	Good
Smoke, obscured visibility	Hours to days	Local	Good	Moderate	Good
Class 2: Property damage					
Particulates	Hours to days	Local, regional	Fair	Moderate	Fair
Sulfur dioxide	4 to 8 days	Local, regional	Fair	High	Fair to poor
Class 3: Damage to plant and animal life					
Photochemical oxidants	Hours to days	Local, regional	Fair	High	Poor
Particulates	Hours to days	Local, regional	Fair	Moderate	Fair
Sulfur dioxide	4 to 8 days	Local, regional	Fair	High	Fair to poor
Class 4: Damage to human health					
Nitrogen oxides	3 to 4 days	Local, regional	Poor	High	Poor
Photochemical oxidants	Hours to days	Local, regional	Fair	High	Poor
Carbon monoxide	2 to 3 months	Local, regional	Poor	High	Poor
Sulfur dioxide	4 to 8 days	Local, regional	Fair	High	Fair to poor
Particulates	Hours to days	Local, regional	Fair	Moderate	Fair
Class 5: Human genetic and reproductive damage					
(None known at present)					
Class 6: Major ecosystem disruption					
Water vapor in stratosphere	1 to 2 years	Regional, global	Good with no SSTs	Low	Good to fair
Nitrogen oxides in stratosphere	1 to 2 years	Regional, global	Good with no SSTs	Low	Good to fair
Particulates in stratosphere	1 to 2 years	Regional, global	Poor	High	Poor
Fluorocarbons in stratosphere (Section 6-3)	Unknown	Regional, global	Good with ban of fluorocarbon aerosols	Moderate	Good
Carbon dioxide	2 to 4 years	Regional, global	Very poor	Very high	Very poor
Heat	Variable	Local, regional, global	Very poor	Very high	Very poor

energy resource; (5) cutting down the redtape needed to get environmental permits for power and industrial plants; and (6) eliminating the EPA's present authority to impose fines on businesses not complying with federal pollution standards. At the time of this writing, the intense debate over amendments to the Clean Air Act was just beginning.

Overview of Air Pollution Problems and Feasibility of Control In this chapter we have seen that there are many air pollutants, which come from different sources and have different effects. In some cases adequate control technologies are available, but in others new or improved technologies are needed. Table 17-7 gives an overview of the relative severity of the major air pollutants and the feasibility of their control.

Air pollution problems in classes 1 through 4 are serious now on a local and occasionally a regional level. In most cases technology for short-range control is available and can be put into effect with moderate to high costs. For instance, short-range political feasibility for controlling sulfur oxides and particulates from power plants and other stationary sources is fair. If the major U.S. response to the energy crisis is to shift back to coal, levels of sulfur dioxide and particulates, the two most dangerous air pollutants, will rise unless stringent and expensive controls are used. For the nitrogen oxides, photochemical oxidants, fine particulates, and carbon monoxide from automobiles control feasibility is fair to poor, primarily because of the multiple sources, the political and economic power of the automobile and oil industries, and the lack of individual concern or willingness to change driving habits or to support mass and para transit. Unfortunately, very little is known about the probability of serious global ecosystem disruption (class 6), especially effects on climate, as discussed in Enrichment Study 3.

Despite the problems discussed in this chapter, the United States has one of the most aggressive air pollution control programs in the world. By 1980, over 80 percent of major U.S. stationary air pollution sources had complied with the 1970 Clean Air Act. Between 1965 and 1979, sulfur dioxide levels in the United States decreased 62 percent, carbon monoxide 40 percent, particulates levels 31 percent, and lead levels 35 percent. Ozone levels, however, showed little change during the same period, and levels of nitrogen oxides (which were not as well monitored) probably increased. By 1978, an estimated 14,000 lives and $21.4 billion were saved by improvements in air quality since the 1970 Clean Air Act was passed. Progress has also been made in other parts of the world. Sulfur dioxide levels were cut by 30 percent in London, 50 percent in Tokyo, and 75 percent in Toronto between 1970 and 1976.

Air pollution consists of a complex set of interlocking problems. But it can be controlled if we are willing to pay the moderate costs needed to protect our own health, to exert political pressure to see that deadlines for meeting air pollution standards are met, and to shift to less wasteful and environmentally harmful consumption and life-style patterns.

Daddy and Mommy, why did you let the air get so bad?

A 6-year-old girl talking in 1993 to her parents
who were college students in 1982

or

Sally, come outside. We can see the mountains
for the fifteenth day in a row. Maybe all those strict air
pollution meausures and electric cars are beginning to pay off
after all. When Daddy and I rode our bicycles home from
work, the air smelled cleaner than it has for a long time.

Anonymous but hopefully not a fictional parent of one child
in 1993

Guest Editorial: Pollution Control: An Input or an Output Approach?

Kenneth E. F. Watt

Kenneth E. F. Watt is a professor of zoology at the University of California at Davis and one of the foremost scholars applying systems analysis to ecological problems. He is the principal investigator in a 30-person team engaged in building computer simulation models of human society. He has done research in 24 countries and has been awarded the Fisheries Ecology and Management Award of the Wildlife Society and the Gold Medal of the Entomological Society of Canada. He combines research talents with the ability to communicate complex ideas to others. Among his numerous important articles and books are Principles of Environmental Science *(1973, New York: McGraw-Hill) and* The Titanic Effect *(1974, Sunderland, Mass.: Sinauer).*

There are two possible approaches to solving the pollution problem, an input approach and an output approach. Remarkably, almost all the attention has been focused on the latter, though it is far less useful and effective. We can think of all industrial and transportation activity as the systems analyst's black box, into which useful energy and matter flow and out of which pollutant solid, liquid, and gaseous products emerge. The current philosophy of pollution control is to ask, "Given the amount of matter and energy flowing into the black box, what can we do to get rid of the output?" Even recycling is an output approach to this problem, albeit a sophisticated one.

A more useful approach is to question why so much matter and energy flow into the system in the first place. If, for example, all the goods, services, and transportation now available in our society could be available with 5 percent of the present expenditure of matter and energy, then we would have 5 percent of the present pollution without even trying to control it.

When we inspect the relevant figures, it appears that the central reason we use so much matter and energy is not our demand for goods, services, and transportation but rather the fantastically inefficient way in which we now use matter and energy. For example, consider transportation. Cars, with the typical load of 1.3 passengers, deliver only 7.8 passenger-kilometers of transportation per liter of fuel (18.3 passenger-miles per gallon). Jet aircraft average 54 passengers (most flights are not full) and deliver only 5.5 passenger-kilometers of transportation per liter of fuel (13 passenger-miles per gallon). These form the backbone of the current U.S. transportation system. Buses, amazingly, can deliver about 115 passenger-kilometers of transportation per liter of fuel (270 miles per gallon), and electric trains can deliver about 481 passenger-kilometers per liter (1,130 miles per gallon) in terms of fuel equivalents. Thus, we have drifted into a social system that makes shockingly wasteful use of matter and energy and develops a totally unnecessary amount of pollution per passenger-kilometer.

But this is only the beginning. Cars and aircraft also make fantastically inefficient use of the space around cities. Trains and buses use a small fraction of the right-of-way to move a given number of passengers per hour: A train can move about 100 times the number of people per meter-width of right-of-way per hour as a car-freeway system.

Some readers will argue that the reason for traveling by car and aircraft is to save time. An analysis of the portal-to-portal times on a series of sample trips between various pairs of points will show how faulty this argument is. On some short jet trips, mean velocity, portal to portal, can be as little as 30 kilometers per hour (24 miles per hour). We in North America forget about the Tokkaido High Speed Express train in Japan, which runs at 282 kilometers per hour (175 miles per hour), and much faster trains are already in use.

Personal experience makes these numbers very real. I grew up in Toronto and remember vividly the unimaginable traffic jams before the advent of the rail subway system. The Toronto rail system has made travel so much more rapid and pleasant that masses of people now return downtown at night for entertainment. The result has been a rebirth of the urban core. Recently, I was traveling by rail in Switzerland. I noticed that between Geneva and Lausanne, where the highway parallels the railway, the train passed every car I could see on the highway, even though European drivers are known for their high speeds. The North American traveler is always amazed at the ease with which one can move around in much of Europe because of the integrated transportation system.

This same type of analysis can be applied to most areas of our lives. We have unwittingly drifted into a life-style in which we pay a tremendous price in matter, energy, pollution, and pollution-related sickness for goods, services, and transportation that are less useful or of poorer quality than those we could buy with less pollution and resource depletion if we reconsidered the aims of our society. If the true purpose of society is to provide a high-quality existence for people, we somehow seem to have lost sight of this. We should now use our best scientific and engineering know-how to get back on a rational track.

Guest Editorial Discussion

1. Why has the input approach to pollution control been so neglected in the United States?

2. Why are output approaches used more often for water pollution control and input approaches more frequently for air pollution control? Relate this to the second law of energy (Section 3-3).

3. What are the economic, political, and ecological consequences of shifting to an input approach for pollution control? How would it affect your life-style?

Discussion Topics

1. Criticize the statement "We shouldn't get so worked up about air pollution because we have always had it, and the atmosphere is always evolving and changing anyway."

2. Criticize the following definition of air pollution: Air pollution involves the addition of any chemical that changes the fixed composition of the air.

3. Why is it so difficult to establish an air quality standard for a specific air pollutant? Does this mean that such standards shouldn't be established?

4. Trace your own direct and indirect contribution to air pollution for one day. Try to list pollutants and relative amounts. Don't forget electricity (from all kinds of devices, including hall lights), heating and air conditioning, and don't forget to trace the air pollution produced back to the power plant, fuel transportation to the power plant, and the strip mine or oil well.

5. Distinguish between photochemical smog and industrial smog in terms of major pollutants and sources, major human health effects, time when worst episodes occur, and methods of control.

6. Discuss the favorable and unfavorable effects of the automobile on the ecosphere, the social environment, and your personal life-style. Consider the following: (a) building of roads and superhighways, (b) access to national parks and other areas hitherto rarely visited, (c) billboard advertising, (d) solid wastes, (e) the spread of suburbs, (f) the use of petroleum, (g) the use of iron ore and rubber, (h) international tension related to petroleum supplies, (i) air pollution, and (j) mass transit systems.

7. Evaluate the pros and cons of the statement "Since we have not proven absolutely that anyone has died or suffered serious disease from nitrogen oxides, automobile manufacturers should not be required to meet the federal air pollution standards."

8. Explain why cleaning up smoke emissions from smokestacks (Figure 17-14) is important and at the same time dangerous and misleading to the public.

9. Rising oil and natural gas prices and environmental concerns over nuclear power plants could force the United States to depend more on coal, its most plentiful fossil fuel, for electric power. Comment on this in terms of air pollution. Would you favor a return to coal instead of increased use of nuclear power? Why?

10. How should we deal with the problem of air pollution from fine particulate matter? Why is it one of our more serious pollution problems?

11. Discuss the relative advantages and disadvantages of banning the internal combustion engine (not cars, just this type of engine) by 1990.

12. Discuss the short- and long-term advantages and disadvantages of replacing the standard internal combustion engine with (a) an electric engine, (b) a Rankine engine, (c) a gas turbine, (d) a Wankel engine, (e) a stratified-charge engine, (f) a diesel engine, and (g) a Stirling engine. Which type of engine, if any, would you like to see used? Why?

13. One way to improve the pollution control efforts of major automobile manufacturers might be to organize a nationwide grass roots campaign in which individuals write letters stating that they will not buy a new car unless certain standards or conditions are met. If only 5

percent of potential purchasers agreed, this would represent an annual loss of over $1.2 billion to General Motors alone. Individuals could still buy used cars if needed. Discuss the pros and cons of such a plan.

14. Give several reasons why controlling air pollution is generally a more difficult political problem than controlling water pollution.

15. Simulate an air pollution hearing at which the automobile manufacturers request a delay in meeting the 1983 air pollution standards until 1987. Assign three members of the class as members of a decision-making board and other members as the president of an automobile manufacturing company, two lawyers for that company, two government attorneys representing the EPA, the chief engineer for an automobile manufacturer, a public health official, and two citizens (with one opposing and one favoring the proposal). Have a class discussion of the final ruling of the board.

16. Use the literature to determine what changes have been made since 1981 in the Clean Air Acts of 1970 and 1976. Which changes do you believe strengthened the act? Which ones weakened the act? Explain your position.

Readings

Berry, James W., et al. 1974. *Chemical Villains: A Biology of Pollution*. St. Louis: Mosby. Readable summary of the effects of pollutants on living systems.

Brodine, Virginia. 1973. *Air Pollution*. New York: Harcourt Brace Jovanovich. Very good nontechnical survey.

Davies, J. Clarence, III, and Barbara S. Davies. 1975. *The Politics of Pollution*. 2nd ed. Indianapolis: Pegasus. Superb discussion of the politics of air pollution control.

Elipper, Alfred W. 1970. "Pollution Problems, Resource Policy, and the Scientist." *Science*, vol. 169, 11–15. Good discussion of pollution management policies.

Epstein, S. S., and D. Hattis. 1975. "Pollution and Human Health." In William W. Murdoch, ed., *Environment: Resources, Pollution and Society*, 2nd ed. Sunderland, Mass.: Sinauer. Excellent overview.

Fennelly, Paul F. 1976. "The Origin and Influence of Airborne Particulates." *American Scientist*, vol. 64, 46–56. Superb overview.

Gold, Michael. 1980. "Indoor Air Pollution." *Science 80*, March-April, pp. 30–33. Excellent discussion of this increasingly serious problem.

Hesketh, H. E. 1974. *Understanding and Controlling Air Pollution*. Ann Arbor, Mich.: Ann Arbor Science Publishers. Excellent overview.

Heywood, John, and John Wilkes. 1980. "Is There a Better Automobile Engine?" *Technology Review*, November/December, pp. 19–29. Superb overview of advantages and disadvantages of possible new engines.

Lave, Lester B., and Eugene B. Seskin. 1977. *Air Pollution and Human Health*. Baltimore: Johns Hopkins University Press.

Likens, Gene. 1976. "Acid Precipitation." *Chemical and Engineering News*, November 22, pp. 29–44. Excellent summary of this serious problem.

Lundquist, Lennart J. 1980. *The Hare and the Tortoise: Clean Air Policy in the United States*. Ann Arbor: University of Michigan Press. Superb analysis.

Lynn, David A. 1976. *Air Pollution—Threat and Response*. Reading, Mass.: Addison-Wesley. One of the best available treatments at a slightly higher level.

Mills, Edwin S., and L. J. White. 1978. "Auto Emissions: Why Regulation Hasn't Worked." *Technology Review*, March-April, pp. 55–63. Very good analysis of problems with the Clean Air Acts of 1970 and 1977.

National Academy of Sciences. 1975. *Air Quality and Stationary-Source Emission Control*. Washington, D.C.: National Academy of Sciences. Authoritative summary of control of sulfur oxides and particulates emissions.

Stoker, H. S., and Spencer L. Seager. 1976. *Environmental Chemistry: Air and Water Pollution*. 2nd ed. Glenview, Ill.: Scott, Foresman. Outstanding summary of air pollution.

Waldbott, George L. 1978. *Health Effects of Environmental Pollutants*. 2nd ed. St. Louis: Mosby. Superb overview at a slightly higher level. Detailed bibliography.

Williamson, Samuel J. 1973. *Fundamentals of Air Pollution*. Reading, Mass.: Addison-Wesley. Magnificent discussion at a slightly higher level.

PART FOUR

Environment and Society

We cannot hope for world peace when 20 percent of the people in the world have 80 percent of the goods.
Father Theodore Hesburgh

There is a need for a revolution in our thinking as basic as the one introduced by Copernicus, who first pointed out that the earth was not the center of the universe.
Lester Pearson

18

Economics and Environment

18-1 Economic Growth, GNP, and the Quality of Life

The words *economics* and *ecology* come from the same Greek root, *oikos*, meaning "house" or "home." Ecology is the study of our earthly home—an analysis of interactions among species and between species and their environment. **Economics** literally means "household management"; today the term refers to the study of principles and customs that affect the production, consumption, growth, and distribution of material wealth for human needs. In spite of their common etymological origin, ecology and economics have scarcely interacted until recently, as discussed further by Kenneth E. Boulding in his Guest Editorial at the end of this chapter. This interaction has centered on four major questions: (1) What types of economic growth are good and what types are harmful? (2) What types of economic systems are compatible with preserving the environment and the earth's finite resources? (3) How can economics be used to protect and improve environmental quality? (4) Will the economic costs of environmental protection and im-

provement be too high? This chapter is devoted to a brief discussion of these four questions.

The Economic Growth Debate One basic difference between the economic and environmental viewpoints is in the perception of the benefits and drawbacks of economic growth. To most economists, chambers of commerce, and industrialists, growth is equated with progress. Only a vigorously growing economy coupled with maximum production and maximum consumption is considered healthy and sound. Poor nations are encouraged to develop and grow like the rich nations. More and more rapid economic growth is supposed to increase human well-being, help provide full employment, control inflation, help cure poverty, and provide enough funds to clean up the environment, as summarized in Table 18-1.

In the last decade the goal of ever increasing economic growth has come under attack by a growing chorus of environmentalists, economists, and some industrialists (see Enrichment Study 1). These critics argue that continued economic growth is neither possible nor desirable because of finite resource supplies and the limited ability of the environment to absorb heat and matter wastes. As summarized in Table 18-1, these critics argue that the harmful consequences of economic growth often outweigh the benefits. Economic growth can promote planned waste, obsolescence, and the production of totally worthless goods, and it doesn't necessarily increase human well-being, provide full employment, or help cure poverty (Enrichment Study 9). As environmental economist Ken Penny puts it, "It seems to be financially efficient to adopt technologies that put people out of work; to produce commodities that fall apart more and more rapidly; and to use resources that have a greater and greater energy cost. All this is seemingly done to provide more people *(many of whom have lost their jobs because of technology)* with work, in order for them to earn

Enrichment Studies 1, 9, and 14 are related to this chapter.

Table 18-1 Views on Economic Growth

Pro	Con
Economic growth increases human well-being.	Some types of economic growth increase well-being for some, but other types worsen the well-being of others. In spite of decades of worldwide economic growth, the gap between the rich and the poor is growing.
Economic growth promotes full employment and controls inflation.	Recent runaway inflation and growing unemployment in most rich nations despite economic growth cast serious doubt on this idea.
Economic growth is the cure for poverty and makes it easier for the rich nations to help the poor nations. As long as the economic pie is growing, more wealth can "trickle down" to the world's poor.	Even if this hypothesis is valid, most economic growth in the rich countries has not been used to help the world's poor. The gap between the rich and poor is growing, and most rich nations are giving less and less aid to poor countries. In most cases, this argument is merely a smokescreen to direct attention from the important ethical and political issue of a more just distribution of the world's wealth (Enrichment Study 9).
The benefits of economic growth outweigh its harmful effects.	As we approach environmental thresholds, the harmful effects of air, water, heat, and noise pollution; land disruption; traffic jams; and other environmental and social disruptions that result from growing production and consumption begin to outweigh the benefits of economic growth.
Economic growth is necessary to provide the money for cleaning up the environment and to pay for higher-priced energy.	It is economically and ecologically unsound to use and waste more and more matter and energy at higher and higher costs. Decreasing the rate of harmful, wasteful growth is a cheaper approach and is the only way to avoid the limits to growth imposed by finite resources and the second law of energy.
Economic growth promotes the growth of technology, which can solve the problems of resource depletion and pollution.	Substitutes for some resources will not be found; other approaches, such as mining lower-grade resources, are too expensive (see Table 12-1). Technology often creates as many (if not more) problems as it solves. No technological development will overcome the unalterable limits imposed by the second law of energy.

incomes to buy the things that fall apart more quickly" (emphasis added). Modern advertising and marketing are then used to create artificial wants—as opposed to real needs—to help keep the economic machine running at full tilt.

But things don't have to be this way! Economics and technology can be redirected toward improving rather than destroying the quality of the air, water, and land. In the words of economist Herman E. Daly, "What we need is growth in things that really count, rather than in things that are merely countable." (See his Guest Editorial at the end of this chapter.)

The issue is much more complicated than growth at-any-cost versus no growth. Such a misleading and simplistic view merely polarizes the issue by attempting to fix blame. Fortunately, more and more economists and environmentalists have moved beyond this counterproductive stage in the debate. Both groups generally agree on the following:

1. Some forms of economic growth are neither desirable, necessary, or inevitable.

2. The major problem is to redirect growth. Some things need to grow and some need to decline, because the earth's resources are finite.

3. We still know relatively little about which types of growth have good effects and which have bad or about how to measure these effects.

4. If we can place monetary values on these bad effects, then the price of any growth can be made to reflect the bad effects so that desirable growth is encouraged and undesirable growth is discouraged. Putting a price on long-term effects (such as the storage of nuclear wastes), however, is difficult and is usually passed on as a cost to future generations.

The U.S. public is also getting more sophisticated about growth:

1. A few years ago Colorado voters defeated a proposal to provide funds for hosting the 1976 Winter Olympic Games.

2. Oregon is deliberately discouraging growth, saying "visit us but don't come here to live."

3. The governor of Delaware turned down a proposed $360 million oil-steel complex on Delaware Bay, and the state now has a coastal zoning law that prohibits all heavy industry within 3.2 kilometers (2 miles) of the shore.

4. Petaluma, California, as well as a growing number of towns and cities, is trying to limit its growth (Enrichment Study 14).

5. In San Jose, California, voters turned out council members favoring rapid growth and replaced them with candidates favoring slower development.

6. California voters passed Proposition 20, which set tight restrictions on coastal development, despite strong opposition from real estate people and oil companies.

7. Laws banning or restricting throwaway beverage containers have been passed in several states (Enrichment Study 15).

There is also increasing interest in and use of inter-mediate technology (Section 1-5), especially in poor countries, to avoid the traps of Western-style economic growth. In addition, a growing number of people in the United States are voluntarily adopting life-styles built around simplicity.

The problem is that modern economic theory does not recognize that economics is totally dependent on the ecosphere to supply all of our food and most of our raw materials, and to handle the waste products automatically produced when anything is made, used, and eventually discarded. Modern economists are proving less and less capable of predicting and controlling the economy. This strongly suggests that the problem is economic theory itself. This has been expressed by the editors of *Business Week*: "When all forecasts miss the mark, it suggests that the entire body of economic thinking accumulated during the past 200 years is inadequate to describe and analyze the problems of our times." Instead of tampering with dangerously out-of-date economic models, economists should work on developing a more comprehensive and realistic body of economic theory that is based on preserving the health of the earth's basic biological systems (fisheries, forests, grasslands, and croplands), which form the foundation of the entire global economic system.

Gross National Product and Gross National Quality The gross national product (GNP) is a source of confusion and controversy. The **gross national product** is the market value of all goods and services produced by the econ-omy of a given area (usually a nation) in a given year. The simplistic notion is that a rising GNP indicates improved well-being of the nation's citizens.

Most environmentalists and some economists argue that GNP is a misleading indicator of the quality of life. It does not reveal how well goods and services are meeting human needs or how they are distributed among the people. In addition, the concept does not distinguish between products that have positive effects and those that have negative effects and make society as a whole poorer—although they put money in some people's pockets. For instance, the GNP includes the production, consumption, and disposal of all environmentally harmful goods, the costs of crime and welfare, the costs of providing equipment and services to clean up the air and purify streams, and the cleaning and health bills that result from pollution. Producing more cigarettes raises the GNP, but it also causes more cancer (Enrichment Study 6). This increases medical expenditures, which increases the GNP, but in a negative way. More automobiles cause more accidents, congestion, and pollution, causing the GNP to grow, but again by including the costs of a harmful activity. Some economists have pointed out that the GNP was not meant to be a measure of human well-being, but many of them still use it that way.

What we really need is a better indicator. In theory, we could list and put a price tag on all of the "negative" products and services included in the GNP. The total value of these negatives could be subtracted from the GNP to obtain the **gross national quality,** or GNQ.

A number of scholars are attempting to develop definitions and measures of the quality of life based on such a concept as the GNQ, but this task is very difficult if not impossible. For example, what are negatives, and how do we put a value on them? How do we put a value on positives such as clean air, clean water, and redwood trees (see the Guest Editorial by Garrett Hardin in Chapter 10)? Should the value be based on the present or the future? Even when we agree on values, it is often hard to put numbers on them. However, the inability to find perfect social indicators should not prevent us from improving the very imperfect ones we now use.

18-2 Dynamic Steady State and Sustainable Earth Economic Systems

A Dynamic Steady State Economy Since we live in a finite system with limited supplies and a limited capacity to absorb matter and energy outputs, harmful forms of growth must eventually stop (Enrichment Study 1). We have two choices. We can run full blast until we rupture our life-support system (Figure 3-4), or we can rationally and ethically decide to conserve matter and energy resources, recycle matter resources, and reduce the rates of matter and energy flow (throughput), thus averting catastrophe (Figure 3-5). Since the human dieback if we should rupture the system would be unthinkable, the major argument among scholars is how close we are to the limits of growth (Enrichment Study 1). Evidence is piling up that we must make the transition to a sustainable earth society within the next 50 years to avoid nature's harsher dieback route. A sustainable earth society involves more than economics, but economics is an important component.

It appears that all existing economic systems—including capitalism, socialism, and communism—have the same fatal flaw: the need to continually increase input. Rising pollution is a problem in all industrialized countries, regardless of their economic system. Fortunately, a major shift in thinking has occurred in the United States since 1970. Instead of being ridiculed, the question of limiting some forms of growth has become a central question. Over the next few decades, the major problem for the United States and other more developed nations will be to move from the present frontier economy to a dynamic steady state economy. Recall from Section 6-2 that a *dynamic steady state* occurs in an open system (such as a country or a living organism) when the system's input of matter and energy is balanced by its output of matter and energy; in this way the system maintains its stability. Since money is used to regulate the flow of matter (goods) and energy through a society, a dynamic steady state economy uses monetary rewards and penalties to maintain a dynamic steady state.

Each time we exchange money for a product or service, we are merely paying (directly or indirectly) either for energy and matter to make and distribute the product or for people and machines to use energy and matter to provide us with a service. Salaries and wages then represent payment for energy and matter expended in one way or another. In our present growth-oriented, high-waste society, money is used to stimulate a more rapid flow of matter and energy resources (Figure 3-4). In a dynamic steady state or low-waste economy, based on the first and second energy laws and the law of conservation of matter (Chapter 3), money would be used to reward those who produce products and services that last the longest and that use the least amount of matter and energy resources. In other words, money would be used to slow down—not speed up—the rate at which we convert the world's matter and energy resources to trash and low-quality heat (Figure 3-5). *It means that we would turn the present role of money in society upside-down.* Ideally, the throwaway product would become extinct. Instead, consumers will expect the products they buy to be durable, recyclable, revisable, easily repaired, have multiple uses, and produced in standardized shapes and sizes. In such a society waste and scrap matter—what we now call secondary materials—would become the primary matter resources and our natural, untapped matter resources would become our backup supplies.

Most modern economists refuse to accept the fact that the entire economic system is governed by the first and second laws of energy and the law of conservation of matter. These narrowly trained economists won't realize that people can't create anything material. All we can do is put together existing matter in different forms and in the process automatically degrade some of the earth's finite supply of high-quality energy to low-quality energy (Section 13-3). This means that, like the automatic energy waste in food chains (Figure 9-6), the more stages or steps there are in a manufacturing and distribution process, normally the greater the waste of energy and matter.

In a dynamic steady state economic system, emphasis is on reducing the number of steps used in finding, making, transporting, using, and throwing away or recycling anything we use. This means that, when possible, manufacturing should be done on a decentralized, small-scale basis near where the products are used (see Section 1-5). This is the opposite of the present system, which uses money and energy to bring raw materials from all over the world to a few, large, centralized, energy-guzzling plants. Then more energy and money are used to ship the resulting products all over the world. When energy and matter resources are cheap, this makes economic (but not ecological) sense. But in the age of resource scarcity that we are entering, these large, centralized national and international companies may be the first to fall, unless they can rely on government bailouts (as happened with the Chrysler Corporation).

As we make the necessary transition to a dynamic steady state economy, there are four important things to remember about such a system:

1. *It is a very dynamic system.* It is not dull and static.

2. *It is not a "no-growth" system* (a false label used by opponents). The dynamics of the system require that some things must grow, some must decline, and some must remain fairly constant. These dynamic ups and downs help keep the system from

being destroyed or harmed by exceeding its limits of tolerance. Some of the things that could grow are art, music, education, athletics, philosophy, aesthetics, religion, cultural and ecological diversity, scientific research, and cooperative rather than competitive human interactions. Some types of business and technology would be encouraged to grow—pollution control; recycling; intermediate technology; design and production of long-lasting products; medical research; more efficient use of energy; resource recovery; solar, wind, and biomass energy; resource self-sufficiency; and the psychology and sociology of human behavior and interactions. Industries that couldn't conserve resources and decrease harmful outputs would have to decline—as they should.

3. *It is not an unnatural, undesirable system.* Since all life represents a dynamic steady state, any linear growth or non-steady-state system is merely temporary and must eventually reach a steady state level either by slowly leveling off or by a sharp dieback or fallback (Figures 8-1 and 8-2).

4. *It does not necessarily require a fixed level of population or resource use.* There are many possible combinations of population size and resource use that allow a system to exist without exceeding harmful limits. A dynamic steady state system can adapt to changes in population size, resource use, and technology within certain basic limits.

5. *It is based on greatly increased use of renewable energy resources (sun, wind, water, and biomass) and decreasing the rate at which matter and energy resources are used and wasted to avoid overloading the ecosphere.*

There are numerous examples of dynamic steady state societies within modern societies that haven't changed their life-styles significantly since 1700 and still exist quite happily, including the Amish and Mennonites in the United States and the Hutterites in Canada. For further discussion of steady state economics, see Herman E. Daly's Guest Editorial at the end of this chapter.

A Sustainable Earth Economy The fourth characteristic of a dynamic steady state economy is one of its major weaknesses. Since a dynamic steady state could exist in many forms, rich nations could continue to use and waste resources at a fairly high rate and still not aid the poor nations. Another problem with the dynamic steady state economy is that it can't exist technically at a world level. A nation is an open system through which matter and energy flow, but the world as a whole is a closed system sustained by energy flow and matter cycling (Fig-

ure 5-1). Instead of reaching a dynamic steady state, a closed system reaches a *dynamic equilibrium state* based on optimal energy flow and matter cycling, which keep the system from breaking down or becoming seriously disrupted.*

Like the steady state, the equilibrium state is dynamic and not static, is not a no-growth state (some things must grow and some must decline), and is not unnatural or undesirable. To help us focus on the earth's life-support system and to shorten the name, I use the term *sustainable earth economy* to signify a dynamic equilibrium economy for the world. Table 18-2 summarizes some of the important differences between our present frontier, throwaway, and immature economic system and a sustainable earth or mature economic system, analogous in some ways to immature and mature ecosystems.

Achieving a sustainable earth economic system within the next 50 years is crucial but not enough. We must move beyond economics to politics (Chapter 19) and ethics (Chapter 20) to achieve a *sustainable earth society*. We must choose as guidelines such ethical goals as (1) population stabilization, (2) a philosophy of enoughness (using a minimum amount of resources in the least wasteful manner in order to satisfy our real needs), and (3) a more just distribution of the world's wealth. In such a society we might be guided by Malkin's rule ("The more things you own, the more you are owned by things") and Raven's raving ("The best things in life aren't things").

In a sustainable earth economy, the gross national product will be recognized for what it really is—the gross national cost. Because of the second energy law, the GNP is actually a measure of how rapidly we are depleting high-quality matter and energy resources. A sustainable earth or low-waste economy that produces low entropy (or environmental disorder) will also recognize and reward the value of meaningful human labor—in sharp contrast to our present growth economy, where a major goal is to replace people with automated machines. Even those humans who are not replaced by machines often have such specialized tasks that they have no sense of pride, accomplishment, or creativity in their work. In a decentralized sustainable earth economy, workers would gain a sense of dignity and purpose by working with more understandable and satisfying intermediate technology (Section 1-5). The transition to a sustainable earth economy will by no means be painless, but the alterna-

---

*Most writers falsely consider the dynamic equilibrium state and the dynamic steady state to be identical. A nation or group of nations can have a steady state economy, but at the world level in the long run we can only have a dynamic equilibrium, or sustainable earth economy.

Table 18-2 Characteristics of Frontier and Sustainable Earth Economic Systems*

Frontier or Immature Economic System	Sustainable Earth or Mature Economic System
Assumes essentially infinite matter and energy resources	Assumes finite matter and energy resources (unless solar, wind, or some form of almost unlimited energy can be developed at an affordable economic and environmental cost)
One-way flow of both matter and energy (Figure 3-4)	One-way flow of energy but recycling of matter (Figure 3-5)
Continually increases flow rates of matter and energy through the system (maximizes throughput)	Reduces the flow rate of energy and the flow and cycling rate of matter; throughput is deliberately reduced to reduce waste of matter and energy resources and keep from exceeding the ecosphere's capacity to handle waste heat and matter
Emphasis on efficiency, quantity of goods, simplification, and cultural and physical homogeneity to maintain short-term stability	Emphasis on quality of goods and preservation of cultural and physical diversity to attain long-term stability at the expense of some efficiency
Output control of pollution (Section 16-6) (consequences of second energy law can be avoided or minimized by cleaning up pollution output)	Input, throughput, and output control (Section 16-6) (consequences of second energy law can be decreased in the long run by decreasing throughputs of matter and energy and cleaning up pollution output)
Continued growth provides capital for output pollution control and technological breakthroughs	If growth continues, capital must be increasingly devoted to maintenance and repair (because of the second law) instead of being available for technological innovations
Emphasis on initial cost of goods—buy now, pay more later	Emphasis on the life cycle costing (LCC) of goods— buy now, pay now
Assumes that a competitive market system or a centralized controlled economy will respond to undesirable side effects	Market responds only if quality-of-life indicators help determine the prices of goods and services
Local or national outlook	Global outlook

*Compare this table with Table 6-1.

tive of running our present high-waste economy at full speed until environmental disorder and resource depletion overwhelms us is much worse.

No one can prescribe exactly how we can make the transition to a sustainable earth economy and society, but the principles presented throughout this book are specific suggestions that can be analyzed, debated, and improved. Economist Herman E. Daly (see his Guest Editorial at the end of this chapter) has offered an economic plan for achieving the major goals of a sustainable earth society (which he calls a steady state society). He suggests the following: (1) We should stabilize population by giving every woman (or couple) a license to have a certain number of children and allowing each woman (or couple) to give away or sell their licenses, an idea originally suggested by economist Kenneth Boulding; (2) we should reduce the throughput of resources by

having the government set and auction off depletion quotas for each resource, thus limiting the amount of each resource used each year; and (3) we should set up a world institution to determine a more just distribution of the world's wealth so that everyone would be guaranteed a minimum share (a *sustainable earth share*) needed for survival and a life of dignity, and as an aid in promoting world peace. In addition, no one would be allowed to accumulate more than a certain amount of the world's wealth (probably equivalent to a maximum annual income of around $100,000, with all additional income taxed at 100 percent).* This third goal would allow a fairly broad range of wealth, from a guaranteed mini-

*Such an idea was proposed thousands of years ago by the Greek philosopher Plato. In his book, *The Laws*, no person should be permitted to be four times richer than the poorest person. Herman Daly proposes that the rich be allowed to be 10 times richer than the poor.

mum to a maximum that should easily satisfy anyone's needs, as opposed to wants that are often artificially created by advertising. Because each of the three elements of this plan complement one another and interact, all three are necessary to make the plan work.

The guaranteed annual minimum income, or sustainable earth share, could be distributed by using a **negative income tax** scheme to replace present welfare systems. Each household or individual would report its total earnings on a tax form, just as now. If the amount is over the established minimum, the household or individual pays an income tax. Otherwise the family (or individual) receives enough money to bring it up to that level. The costly, cumbersome, and often humiliating welfare bureaucracy could be scrapped, and the new program could be handled much more simply and efficiently by the existing tax collection bureau of the country. Foreign aid from more developed to less developed countries would flow through an international distribution agency, which would provide tax bureaus of poor countries with funds to distribute to their poor. The annual amount that each country received would be based on how effectively the country distributed the funds to its poor. In a test conducted with 8,500 low-income U.S. families, only a small percentage of those receiving guaranteed annual minimum incomes quit their jobs or worked less. Indeed, many used the financial support to seek training or find a better job. Eventually about 25 percent of the participants earned so much that they were no longer eligible for the program. The families receiving income support, however, did have a 60 percent higher rate of separation and divorce than families in the control group. Apparently, because the guaranteed income was given to both husbands and wives separately, it had a liberating effect on some women (or men) who might have otherwise remained in unsatisfactory marriages for financial reasons.

The real problems facing the transition from the present high-entropy-producing American economy to a low-entropy-producing sustainable earth economy will be political and ethical. For the first time, the United States will have to face up to the question of a more just redistribution of wealth—if not for humanitarian reasons, then to enhance personal and national security by promoting world security. The question will no longer be "How can I get a share of a pie that is growing larger and larger?" Instead, it will be "How can I get my share of a pie that is no longer growing in size?" As Herman Daly put it, "Our choice is not so much economic as a moral and ethical decision . . . and one that will determine the fate of the planet."

18-3 Economics and Pollution Control

Internal and External Costs We can use a number of methods to control pollution and improve the environment. In order to understand these methods, we need to distinguish between what economists call *internal costs* and *external costs.*

In making or using anything there are **internal costs** and benefits (sometimes called *internalities*). For example, if you buy a new car, the price you pay includes the construction and operation of the factory, raw material and labor, marketing expenses, shipping costs, and automobile company and dealer profits. There are also side effects that are external to the act of production. These **external costs** and benefits (often called *externalities*) are passed on to someone else. For instance, mining and processing the matter and energy used to make a car cause land disruption and air and water pollution. This air pollution may eventually harm you or someone else, but these health side effects are not included in the price of the car. In addition, you have to pay more for water purification because of the additional water pollution— again a cost not included in the car's price. These hidden external costs are always present with any product and must always be paid somewhere, sometime, by someone—usually by everyone, not just the ones wealthy enough to consume all of the pollution producing goods. In fact, the poor probably pay a disproportionate share of pollution clean-up cost compared to the amount their meager incomes allow them to produce and end up having to live or work in high-pollution environments (see Enrichment Study 9). There is no free lunch. The environmental crisis consists largely of external costs that degrade the environment, which is a common property resource to all. Thus, the true cost of any item or service is its internal cost plus the hidden external costs, such as poorer health, increased cleaning bills, or pollution control.

Our present economic system makes it profitable to pollute. Many of the undesirable environmental resource depletion and social costs are passed on to present or future consumers—who must eventually pay for all costs, direct or hidden. In some cases these costs are passed on to future generations who might inherit a polluted and resource-depleted earth. But what if the external costs were added onto the price of every item or service so that we knew its true long-term cost? In this way we as consumers would get a more accurate picture of the effects of using a particular good or service. The resulting higher prices of environmentally harmful products would discourage their use and stimulate the technological development of products that use fewer resources and produce less pollution. This honest listing of all costs is the opposite of our present linear growth system, with its hidden external costs, that is fueled by polluting wastes and planned obsolescence. In addition, the emphasis would also be on life cycle costs—the total cost of an item over its useful life—rather than on the initial cost. Consumers would use a buy now, pay now approach so they would know the full cost of an item, rather than the present buy now, pay more later approach. In other words, *the economists' solution to pollution is to internalize the external costs of an item or service so that each purchaser knows its full cost over its lifetime.*

Throughout human history there have been important examples of internalizing external costs, as shown in Table 18-3. Minerals and raw materials were once so plentiful that they were considered free and were either not included or minimally included in the cost of manufactured goods. Until the abolition of slavery, labor was free (except for minimal subsistence costs) and thus not included in the prices of items. The history of the labor movement has been a process of internalizing the costs of keeping the labor force in reasonably good health. Accident and medical benefits for workers are no longer passed on to society indirectly but are included in the cost of production.

Table 18-3 Historical Sequence of Internalizing External Costs

Type of External Cost	Factor Enabling Abuse	Time of Internalization
Raw materials	Abundance	Before Christ
Labor	Slavery	A.D. 1000 to 1862
Industrial working conditions (accidents, diseases, lack of old-age security)	High profits of owners	1875 to date
Cleaning up pollution (output approach)	Assuming natural resources are infinitely abundant and the environment is infinitely resilient	Future
Preventing or minimizing pollution and preserving ecological stability and diversity (input approach)	Assuming natural resources are infinitely abundant and the environment is infinitely resilient	Future

We must now internalize the costs of pollution and ecological disruption. We can no longer treat the air, land, and water as free goods. The first phase should be an output approach that adds the cost of cleaning up pollution to taxes and the prices of harmful items. This short-range internalization will buy us time to accomplish the second phase, the gradual shift to a sustainable earth economy and society.

Some businesses will flourish, others will level off, and some with high, uncontrollable levels of adverse environmental impact may have to shut down—as they should. Prices of environmentally harmful products will go up to reflect their real cost, but the advantages of internalizing costs will soon become apparent.

Opponents of adding pollution control costs to prices point out that such an approach would especially burden the poor. However, by paying a higher initial price to avoid the cost of pollution, we are reducing the later health costs, as well as other costs created by pollution. And as mentioned before, the higher, true prices would discourage harmful forms of growth, production, and consumption. In addition, because the poor now bear the brunt of environmental pollution (Enrichment Study 9), any scheme that reduces pollution will benefit them more than any other group. To avoid a financial strain on the poor, however, we need to minimize poverty by providing everyone with a guaranteed minimum income, a sustainable earth share of the world's wealth, as discussed in the previous section.

Approaches to Environmental Improvement   It is easy to suggest that we improve the environment and internalize external costs, but how do we accomplish these ends? We can use a number of methods, including the following:

1. *Moral persuasion or preaching:* Persuade polluters to refrain voluntarily from polluting as an obligation to society.

2. *Suing for damages:* Use the legal system to sue polluters for damages from pollution (see Section 19-2 for more details).

3. *Prohibition:* Establish and enforce discharge standards for each pollutant.

4. *Direct regulation:* Issue licenses and permits, and set up and enforce compulsory pollution standards.

5. *Payments and incentives:* Control pollution by paying polluters not to pollute, giving subsidies to build pollution control devices (for example, sewage treatment plants), eliminating or reducing taxes on

Table 18-4 Evaluation of Major Methods for Environmental Improvement

Method	Advantages	Disadvantages
Moral persuasion	1. Educates and sensitizes people. 2. Prepares people for action through other methods.	1. Often produces more guilt and discontent than action. 2. Rewards the socially irresponsible (those who refuse to buy pollution control equipment can make a bigger profit).
Suing for damages (torts)	1. Allows the individual or group to be compensated for damages.	1. Difficult to establish who damaged whom and to what degree. 2. Time consuming and expensive for both parties. 3. Output approach that does little to prevent damage.
Prohibition	1. Eliminates the damage. 2. May be required for some pollutants, such as toxic metals (Enrichment Study 5) and radioactive materials (Section 14-3). 3. Protects the individual from irresponsible acts by others.	1. Often not economically feasible; due to second energy law, removal of all pollution is prohibitively expensive (Figure 18-1). 2. May not be politically feasible (excessive control may lead to a political backlash that threatens even moderate control). 3. Zero or very low pollution levels are not always necessary (if not overloaded, natural chemical cycles can absorb, degrade, or recycle some types of wastes).
Direct regulation	1. Can be used to keep pollution below a threshold level (Section 6-2). 2. Protects the individual from irresponsible acts by others. 3. May be more just than prohibition.	1. Hard to enforce, especially when there are many pollution sources, such as 140 million automobiles. 2. Standards tend to be ones that are enforceable rather than optimal. 3. No incentive for polluter to reduce pollution below the standard. 4. Airsheds and watersheds cross political boundaries, so effective regulation by one governmental unit may be nullified by inaction of another. 5. Polluters can use courts and administrative procedures to delay compliance. 6. Often treats all polluters alike, regardless of the amount of pollution they contribute. This can discriminate against the small polluter and make the cost of effective pollution control higher than need be.
Payments and incentives	1. Makes it profitable not to pollute and encourages polluter to reduce pollution to lowest possible value. 2. A positive rather than negative approach. 3. Requires fewer enforcement procedures and expenses.	1. May encourage people or industries to pollute so they can qualify for payment.* 2. Pollution costs are still hidden and not internalized in the direct prices of items and services. 3. Drains limited public funds. 4. Taxpayers' money is used to pay individuals and corporations not to do something wrong.
Pollution rights and pollution charges	1. Makes it profitable not to pollute and encourages polluter to reduce pollution to lowest possible value. 2. Generates public revenue instead of draining limited public funds. 3. May reduce political maneuvering to influence or take over regulatory agencies. 4. Biggest polluters will have the greatest incentive to reduce pollution. 5. Administrative and enforcement machinery should be simpler and cheaper.	1. Hard to estimate what to charge for each pollutant. 2. The idea of being able to buy a license to pollute could encourage people to pollute up to a certain level. 3. Increases prices of a country's products, putting it at a disadvantage in international trade.

*The old joke that farm subsidies cause people to go into the "no-growing business" could apply again if people rush into the "no-polluting business" at taxpayers' expense.

pollution control equipment, and giving tax credits for investment in control equipment.

6. *Pollution rights:* Sell on the open market a limited number of rights to pollute up to a specified amount in a given place during a particular period of time.

7. *Pollution charges:* Tax each unit of effluent or emission released during a particular time period.

These various methods for environmental control are evaluated in Table 18-4.

Cost-Benefit Analysis   As with any complex problem, there is no single best approach. We must combine different approaches for reducing pollution to maximize the chance of success at the lowest possible cost. Economists call this **cost-benefit analysis**—an attempt to compare the costs of pollution control or some other project with the costs of pollution damage (dollar and otherwise). These two types of values are then plotted separately on a graph, and their intersection represents the lowest cost for reducing pollution to a certain level (Figure 18-1). As shown in Figure 18-1, the goal is to minimize the total costs and still reduce harmful environmental effects (such as pollution) to a reasonable level. Trying to reduce the level of pollution below this level can be so expensive that the costs far outweigh the economic benefits.* By the same token, not reducing the pollutant to the optimum level means that the manufacturer is passing on hidden costs to the consumer.

This approach sounds simple, but in practice it is very difficult. One major problem is that it is very difficult to put a price tag on some environmental effects. Some costs, such as extra laundry bills, house painting, and ruined crops resulting from air pollution, are fairly easy to estimate. But estimating health effects is more difficult. In addition, how do you put a price tag on a clear sky, beautiful scenery, the irreversible damage of building houses and highways on farmland, the ability of natural ecosystems to degrade and recycle wastes, or short- and long-term risks of a serious nuclear accident (Section 14-3)? Economic analysis alone cannot always answer such questions, because they involve political, social, and ethical issues as well. For example, the benefit

---

*As the pollution level is reduced, the remaining pollutants are more widely dispersed through the polluted medium (that is, they have higher entropy). Thus, rounding them up costs more and more, as expected because of the second law of energy. For example, picking up 90 percent of the bottles and cans thrown away in a large park might be economically feasible, but finding the last 10 percent could take so long that the labor and energy costs would be prohibitive.

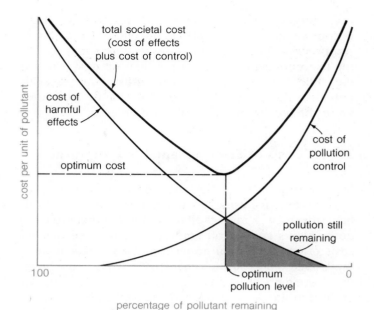

Figure 18-1   Cost-benefit-analysis involves balancing the cost of harmful effects of pollution and the cost of pollution control. The shaded area shows that some harmful effects remain, but removing these residual damages would make pollution control costs too expensive.

of electricity from a nuclear power plant over its 30- to 40-year lifetime is fairly easy to calculate. But how do you put a price tag on the long-term environmental and social costs of protecting future generations for thousands of years from the radioactive wastes that the plant produces? The marketplace operates very effectively for short-term control but is very ineffective in dealing with long-term costs and benefits.

In spite of these difficulties, some important progress is being made in estimating environmental benefits and damages. Sometimes, however, all we can do is make an educated guess and then revise the estimate as new information becomes available.

No method of pollution control will be fair to everyone. The only question is whether the method will be better than our present system. We must discover which strategy will make it unprofitable instead of profitable to pollute. Industries usually favor the subsidy approach (Table 18-4) by which some taxpayer dollars are used to pay industries not to pollute—something the industries shouldn't be doing in the first place. Because this approach is unfair to most people, politicians and environmentalists are beginning to accept the economists' view that the best way to reduce pollution through economic factors is to combine direct regulation and pollution charges (Table 18-4). This approach, however, is an output method that operates at the end of the throughput process. As a result, it wastes resources and according to economist Herman Daly is "like letting a two-year old child loose in a living room full of irreplaceable antiques, and then slapping the tot's hands every time he or she breaks an invaluable vase or lamp."

18-4 Costs of Environmental Improvement

Industries often argue that the costs of reducing pollution make their businesses unprofitable, making it difficult for them to raise capital and forcing them to close down plants and lay off employees. Are the estimated costs of environmental protection and improvement in the United States so high that they outweigh the benefits? Have more strict pollution and other environmental protection standards in the United States caused massive unemployment? The answer to both of these questions is a resounding no!

In its annual reports, the Council on Environmental Quality (CEQ) analyzes the costs (including capital, operating, and maintenance costs) of environmental protection and their economic impact in the United States for the next decade. The CEQ estimated that in 1979 the United States spent about $36.9 billion for pollution control—an average of about $164 per person. This amounted to only about 1.5 percent of the GNP for that year. By the year 2000 pollution control costs could rise to about 3 percent of the annual GNP—a very small price to pay for a vastly improved environment that benefits every U.S. citizen. The CEQ has also estimated that between 1979 and 1988 $735 billion from government and industry will be required for pollution control to meet present federal, state, and local environmental standards in the United States. According to EPA figures, industry pays 51 percent of pollution control costs, the government about 13 percent, and consumers 36 percent (mostly as antipollution controls for automobiles).

Of course, the costs of protecting the environment are ultimately paid for by consumers through increased taxes and prices. But failure to control pollution will cost us even more in the form of declining health, skyrocketing medical costs, and loss of time on the job. The cost of air pollution damage in the United States is estimated to be $20 billion each year and that of water pollution to be about $10 billion. Damages would be much higher if pollution control laws had not been enacted. Environmental protection costs are a form of preventive medi-

cine. For example, the well-known Love Canal disaster near Niagara Falls, N.Y. (Section 6-3), will end up costing billions of dollars—not to mention the possible health and psychological effects suffered by Love Canal residents. Yet, if proper environmental laws had existed, this toxic waste site could have been made safe at a cost of about $2 million. Similarly, the pesticide disaster involving kepone that polluted the James River at Hopewell, Virginia (Enrichment Study 11), which will cost billions to clean up, could have been prevented by an investment of only $200,000 by the manufacturer of this pesticide. These two examples illustrate the second law of energy in action. It is much easier and cheaper for society as a whole to use an input approach to prevent or minimize pollution than to have to use large amounts of money, time, and energy and matter resources to clean up a pollutant that has become dispersed in the environment.

Environmental cleanup *costs* should be conceived of as *benefits* that help protect air, land, water, and our health. For example, between 1970 and 1978 improvements in air pollution in the United States provided an estimated $21.4 billion in benefits—mostly from reductions in pollution-related deaths and illness, savings in cleaning costs, and increases in agricultural production. It is also estimated that enforcement of existing water pollution laws would provide an estimated $12.5 billion in benefits each year by 1985—mostly from increased water recreation, reduced waterborne disease, and lowered municipal waste treatment costs. In addition, pollution control is a major growth industry—one type of growth that we want to encourage. The pollution control market is growing at about 18 percent per year—twice the annual growth rate for all U.S. manufacturing. Pollution control creates many more jobs than it eliminates and by 1980 it provided employment for 2 million people. Between 1971 and 1977, 107 plants in the United States closed because of pollution control costs, putting 20,318 employees out of work. But pollution control enterprises during this same period created over 1 million new jobs—a net gain of about 980,000 jobs. Even more jobs will be created as pollution control expenditures rise in the next decade. Each $1 billion spent for pollution control creates from 67,000 to 85,000 new jobs.

By contrast, $1 billion in military spending results in a net loss of 11,600 jobs. Any rise in defense spending simultaneously fuels inflation and increases unemployment. Greater unemployment occurs because military spending is mostly capital and energy intensive, with machines replacing human labor. If fuels inflation because more money is put into the hands of workers without expanding the supply of goods that they can buy (since individual consumers do not purchase military weapons).

Pollution control can also save industry money in the long run—as many industries who once fought pollution control are finding out. For example, an $8 million pollution control system installed by Great Lakes Paper Company reduced the plant's operating cost by $4 million a year—paying for itself in only 2 years. The Ciba-Geigy chemical complex in Basel, Switzerland, has eliminated 50 percent of its pollution and saved about $400,000 a year. The Elf Oil Refinery in France has turned its hydrocarbon pollution into usable products with an annual profit of $1.3 million. The Minnesota Mining and Manufacturing Company (known as 3M), a multinational firm based in the United States, has initiated a pollution cleanup program (under the slogan "Pollution Prevention Pays") that has saved the company over $20 million between 1976 and 1979.

Clearly, between 1977 and 1987, the benefits from environmental protection in the United States will far outweigh the costs. A major priority of the next decade will be to use economic tools to internalize the costs of pollution (Table 18-4). This can buy the United States (and other nations) enough time to make the transition from its present frontier economy to a sustainable earth or low-waste economy over the next 50 years. Fortunately, the United States has never been in a better position to make such a transition, as long as more of its citizens are willing to become environmentally aware and politically involved, as discussed in the next chapter.

The first step is to stop the waste. Perhaps the next might be a greater willingness to share the wealth that has made the waste possible.

Barbara Ward

Guest Editorial: Economics and the Ecosystem

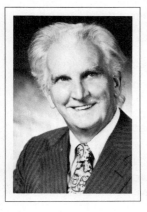

Kenneth E. Boulding

Kenneth E. Boulding is Distinguished Professor of Economics Emeritus and director of the Program of Research on General Social and Economic Dynamics, Institute of Behavioral Science, University of Colorado. He has served as president of the Society for General Systems Research, the American Economic Association, the International Studies Association, and the American Association for the Advancement of Science. He has been active in research in general systems analysis, peace,

economic theory, economics and ethics, and economics and the environment. In publishing his now classic article "The Economics of the Coming Spaceship Earth," he became one of the first economists to propose that our goal must be to move from our present frontier economy to a "spaceship earth" economy.

The history of this planet seems to have been punctuated by ecological catastrophes, which usually mark the boundaries between one geological era and another. It is not easy to assess the significance of these catastrophes in the general evolutionary process—whether, for instance, they are necessary for continued evolutionary development—but they do represent the destruction of some previously established equilibrium out of which more complex forms of life have emerged. *Homo sapiens* is perhaps the latest in this long series of catastrophes. Our species has certainly eliminated a large number of other species, though I have seen no estimate of how much it has diminished the genetic pool of the ecosphere. The fates of the dodo, the passenger pigeon, and perhaps now the whale testifies to our skill as a predator. Perhaps because of our unprecedented ability for surviving in a variety of environments—including even the moon—and our consequent propensity for introducing old species into new environments, the earth is no longer a collection of relatively isolated and unrelated ecosystems but has become a single ecosystem with people, their artifacts, and their domesticated plants and animals as the dominant complex.

Besides our influence on the biosphere, we have had some impact on the lithosphere through mining and damming, on the hydrosphere by creating artificial lakes and polluting rivers, lakes, and oceans, and on the atmosphere by burning fossil fuels and to a very small degree by weather modification. Our most significant impact may be the development of new substances, especially organic compounds like DDT and PCB's, to which the biosphere has not adapted and which therefore may produce far-reaching changes (see Enrichment Study 11).

We must not live with delusions of grandeur. We did not cause any previous ecological catastrophes. We certainly did not cause the ice ages. Nevertheless, we have some cause for worry about our cumulative impact on the earth, especially as this impact seems to be growing at a fairly constant rate.

Economic activities cause much of our harmful impact on the earth. If we do harm to ourselves and the planet, it is because of the complex interaction of isolated economic decisions, each of which seems best at the time. The great problem of economic organization is how to make the payoffs foreseen in the mind of the individual decision maker correspond to some ideal system of payoffs from the viewpoint of planetary welfare. The welfare of the planet, of course, is a human value, for no other species would have the audacity to evaluate a system so far beyond that species' personal experience. Thus, we have pollution—that is, too much production of products that we recognize as "bads" rather than "goods"—not so much because there are wicked people who like to pollute things but because we produce bads and goods in the process of producing, and if we want the goods we put up with the bads. If the bads do not have to be paid for, however—that is, if negative commodities do not have negative prices—we produce too many of them. This is why economists who are concerned about the environment tend to favor effluent taxes, marketable licenses to pollute or to extract, and other devices that make private and social costs coincide. Corresponding devices must also be worked out

in centrally planned economies, where the plan that each manager is supposed to implement should take into account the production of bads as well as goods, as it seldom does.

We can be fairly optimistic about improving local environments and the short-run impact of our activities. Social devices for dealing with these problems are largely known, and it is a matter of mobilizing public awareness into forms of political action. The longer-run problems are much more difficult, especially those involved in the long-term movement toward a "spaceship earth."

No solution of these problems is possible, either in the short run or the long run, without appropriate economic institutions. Unless the payoffs of a society are right, so that virtue is rewarded and vice is penalized, exhortations and persuasions get us nowhere. If virtue is penalized and vice is rewarded, as is too often the case in any economy, all the exhortation in the world will not prevent the flourishing of vice and the decay of virtue, even when vice and virtue are defined in terms of our long-run ecological survival. Ecology is blind and value-free. (Was the dinosaur "bad"?) Economics mirrors human values for us but does not necessarily give us the will and the power to realize what we see.

Guest Editorial Discussion

1. The author suggests that "the great problem of economic organization is how to make the payoffs foreseen in the mind of the individual decision maker correspond to some ideal system of payoffs from the viewpoint of planetary welfare." What would you include in this "ideal system of payoffs"? How?

2. Do we owe anything to future generations? Why? What?

3. Take a product such as the automobile and list all of the goods and bads associated with its production, use, and eventual discard. Do the goods outweigh the bads? How would you decrease the bads? What effects will this have on your life-style?

4. Is ecology blind and value-free? Is science blind and value-free? What about economics? If any are not value-free, list the values we can derive from them.

Guest Editorial: The Steady-State Economy in Outline

Herman E. Daly

Herman E. Daly is a professor of economics at Louisiana State University. He has been a member of the faculty at Vanderbilt University and at Louisiana State University, a Ford Foundation visiting professor at the University of Ceara (Brazil), and a research associate at the Economic Growth Center, Yale University. Currently his research interests center on the economics of ecology, problems of a steady state economy and society, and population issues in Latin America. He has written a number of articles and two key books on the steady state economy, Toward a Steady-State Economy *(1973, San Francisco: W. H. Freeman) and* Steady-State Economics *(1977, San Francisco: W. H. Freeman). He is one of a small number of economists seriously thinking about steady state and sustainable earth economics.*

The steady-state economy is basically a physical concept but with important social and moral implications. It is defined as a constant stock of physical wealth and people, each maintained at some desirable, chosen level by a low rate of throughput so that longevity of people and artifacts is high. Throughput is roughly equivalent to GNP, the annual flow of new production. It is the cost of maintaining the stocks by continually importing low-entropy matter-energy from the environment and exporting high-entropy matter-energy back to the environment (Figure 3-4). Currently we attempt to maximize the growth of GNP, whereas the reasoning just given suggests that we should follow Kenneth Boulding's advice, to relabel it *GNC (C* for *cost),* and minimize it, subject to the maintenance of a chosen level of stocks. For example, if we can maintain a desired, sufficient stock of items such as cars with a lower throughput of iron, coal, petroleum, and other resources, we are better off, not worse off.

To maximize GNP throughput (Figure 3-4) for its own sake is absurd. To maximize input to build up a larger stock is a limited process. Physical and ecological limits to the volume of throughput imply the eventual necessity of a steady state economy. Less recognizable but probably more stringent social and moral limits imply the desirability of a steady state long before it becomes a necessity. For example, the effective limit to the use of nuclear breeder reactors, as long as its development is heavily subsidized by the government, will more likely be the social problem of safeguarding plutonium from theft and immoral uses than, say, thermal pollution or low-level radiation (Section 14-3). If breeder reactors and conventional nuclear power were forced to operate in an open market without government subsidies, neither would probably be developed because of too low an economic return on the investment.

Once we have attained a steady state at some level of stocks, we are not forever frozen at that level. Moral and technological evolution may make it both possible and desirable to grow (or decline) to a different level. But growth will then be seen as a temporary process necessary to move from one steady state level to another, not as an economic norm. Moreover, technical and moral evolution will no longer be pushed by growth along the dangerous path of least short-run resistance. This requires a substantial shift in eco-

nomic thought. Ecological conservatism breeds economic radicalism.

The major challenges facing us today are: (1) for physical scientists to define more clearly the limits and interactions of the ecosystem (which determine the feasible levels of the steady state) and to develop technologies more in conformity with those limits, (2) for social scientists to design the institutions that will bring about the transition to the steady state and permit its continuance, and (3) for philosophers and theologians to stress the neglected traditions of stewardship and distributive justice that exist in our cultural and religious heritage (Chapter 20). The latter is of paramount importance, since the problem of sharing a fixed amount is much greater than that of sharing a growing amount. Indeed, this has been the major reason for giving top priority to growth—we can economize on scarce moral resources. But as physical growth reaches limits, it can no longer serve as a substitute for moral growth—if it ever was.

The kinds of economic institutions required follow directly from the definition of a steady state economy. We need an institution for maintaining a constant population (such as Kenneth Boulding's marketable license to have children), an institution for maintaining a constant stock of physical wealth and limiting throughput (such as transferable depletion quotas auctioned periodically by government to resource users), and an institution for limiting inequalities in the distribution of constant physical wealth among the constant population (such as minimum and maximum limits on personal income and maximum limits on personal wealth).

Many such institutions could be imagined. The problem is to achieve the necessary global and societal (macro) control with the least sacrifice of freedom at the individual (micro) level—to combine global stability with individual and cultural variability. Elsewhere I have outlined the three institutions mentioned above and shown how they meet this criterion to a high degree.

Guest Editorial Discussion

1. Why is a steady state economy desirable? Compare its advantages and disadvantages.

2. Discuss the steady state economy in terms of the first and second laws of thermodynamics (Chapter 3).

3. Does a steady state imply the end of technological growth? Explain.

4. Why does the concept of a steady state—or, more accurately, a sustainable earth—economy force us to face up to the moral issue of the distribution of wealth?

5. Debate the issue that we should establish minimum and maximum limits on personal wealth and income.

Discussion Topics

1. Debate the proposition that we should maximize growth as the only way of providing enough money to eliminate poverty and control pollution.

2. Do you believe the U.S. economic system is working? What is wrong with it? How would you change it?

3. If you wanted to develop an index of gross national quality (GNQ), what specific items would you include?

4. Distinguish between a dynamic steady state economy and a sustainable earth economy, and explain why a dynamic steady state is possible at the national but not the global level.

5. Criticize the statement that the United States should not establish a steady state economy because it would be a dull, stagnant system based on no growth.

6. What are the social and environmental costs associated with (a) smoking cigarettes, (b) driving a car, and (c) living or working in an air conditioned building?

7. What good and bad effects would internalizing the external costs of pollution have on the U.S. economy? Do you favor doing this? How might it affect your life-style? The life-style of the poor? If possible, have an economist discuss these problems with your class.

8. What are some problems with using moral persuasion as an approach to pollution control? Does this mean it shouldn't be used?

9. Explain how the present U.S. economic system makes it profitable to pollute.

10. Should the costs of environmental cleanup be borne partly by the public? Through tax incentives to industry? Through increased prices to consumers? Through special taxes on industry? By direct federal regulation? Give reasons for your answers.

11. Debate the following resolutions: (a) Every American citizen should have a guaranteed annual minimum income. (b) No American should be allowed to have an income exceeding a certain level.

Readings

Beckerman, Wilfred. 1974. *Two Cheers for the Affluent Society.* New York: St. Martin's. A vigorous defense of the need for an economy based on continued growth. Compare with Daly (1977) and Georgescu-Roegen (1977).

Boulding, Kenneth E. 1974. "What Went Wrong, If Anything, Since Copernicus?" *Bulletin of Atomic Scientists,* January, pp. 17–23. Penetrating analysis of the possible types of equilibrium societies.

Brown, Lester R. 1978. *The Global Economic Prospect: New Sources of Economic Stress.* Washington, D.C.: Worldwatch Institute. Excellent overview of how interlocking pollution, energy, and resource problems are creating global economic problems.

Canterberry, E. Ray. 1976. *The Making of Economics.* Belmont, Calif.: Wadsworth. A readable critique of contemporary economic theory that explains why economics so long ignored issues such as ecology and points the way to a reconstruction of economics on a humanistic base.

Cottrell, Alan. 1978. *Environmental Economics.* New York: Halsted. Good introduction.

Dales, J. H. 1968. *Pollution, Property and Prices.* Toronto: University of Toronto Press. Presents a strong case for selling pollution rights.

Daly, Herman E. 1977. *Steady-State Economics.* San Francisco: Freeman. Superb discussion of a sustainable earth economy and how we can make the transition to such a system.

Georgescu-Roegen, Nicholas. 1977. "The Steady State and Ecological Salvation: A Thermodynamic Analysis." *BioScience,* vol. 27, no. 4, 266–270. Superb analysis of steady state and sustainable earth economic systems by one of the world's most outstanding economic thinkers.

Goldsmith, Edward. 1978. *The Stable Society.* Cornwall, England: Wadebridge Press. Very useful description of a sustainable earth economy and society.

Hamer, John. 1976. "Pollution Control: Costs and Benefits." *Editorial Research Reports,* vol. 1, no. 8, 147–164. Excellent overview of approaches to pollution control.

Hardin, Garrett. 1968. "The Tragedy of the Commons." *Science,* vol. 162, 1243–1248. Superb description of how common property is ruined by our own actions.

Hines, Lawrence G. 1973. *Environmental Issues: Population, Pollution, and Economics.* New York: Norton. Excellent introduction.

Hueting, R. 1980. *New Scarcity and Economic Growth.* New York: Oxford. Superb analysis of the interaction of ecology and economics.

Johnson, Warren. 1978. *Muddling Toward Frugality.* San Francisco: Sierra Club Books. Try to read this very important economic and political analysis of how we might make it to the end of this century.

Kahn, Herman. 1979. *World Economic Development: 1979 and Beyond.* New York: Morrow. Very useful projections by a pro-growth, technological optimist.

Kneese, Allen V. 1977. *Economics and Environment.* New York: Penguin. Excellent discussion at a more advanced level.

League of Women Voters. 1977. "Growth: An Invitation to

the Debate." *Current Focus*, no. 146, pp. 1–5. Superb summary of the debate over economic growth.

Mishan, E. J. 1977. *The Economic Growth Debate: An Assessment*. London: Allen & Unwin. Superb analysis.

Pirages, Dennis C., ed. 1977. *Sustainable Society: Implications for Limited Growth*. New York: Praeger. Very useful analysis.

Ridker, Ronald G. 1973. "To Grow or Not to Grow: That's Not the Relevant Question." *Science*, vol. 182, 1315–1318. The question is what types of growth should be controlled.

Rifkin, Jeremy. 1980. *Entropy: A New World View*. New York: Viking. Very important book with a discussion of sustainable earth economics based on the second law of energy.

Ruff, Larry E. 1970. "The Economic Common Sense of Pollution." *The Public Interest*, Spring, pp. 69–85. Very readable introduction to the various economic approaches to pollution control.

Savage, Donald T., et al. 1975. *The Economics of Environmental Improvement*. Boston: Houghton Mifflin. Broad and comprehensive coverage of the economic problems involved in improving the quality of the environment.

Schumacher, E. F. 1973. *Small Is Beautiful: Economics as if People Mattered*. New York: Harper & Row. This very important environmental classic describes the need for and the nature of appropriate technology.

Socolow, Robert H. 1971. "The Economist's Approach to Pollution and Its Control." *Science*, vol. 173, 498–503. Superb evaluation of the various economic approaches with a strong case for the tax method.

Smith, Adam. 1980. *Paper Money*. New York: Summit. Very understandable explanation of economic theory and inflation.

Spencer, Milton H. 1978. *Contemporary Economics*. 3rd ed. New York: Worth. Very understandable basic text in economics with a discussion of ecology and economics.

Stivers, Robert L. 1976. *The Sustainable Society*. Philadelphia: Westminster. A superb discussion of a sustainable earth society.

Theobald, Robert. 1970. *The Economics of Abundance*. New York: Pitman. Detailed plan for the transition to a sustainable earth economy and more just redistribution of wealth.

Thompson, Donald N. 1973. *The Economics of Environmental Protection*. Cambridge, Mass.: Winthrop. A very useful discussion of air and water pollution and economic approaches to pollution control.

Thurow, Lester C. 1980. *The Zero-Sum Society*. New York: Basic Books. Outstanding analysis of a sustainable earth society.

Woodward, Herbert N. 1977. *Capitalism Can Survive in a No-Growth Economy*. New York: Brookdale. Very useful analysis.

19

Politics and Environment

Mourn not the dead . . .
But rather mourn the apathetic throng—
The cowed and meek
Who see the world's great anguish and its wrong,
And dare not speak.

Ralph Chaplin

19-1 Politics and Social Change

Politics is concerned with the distribution of resources in an orderly fashion—with *who* gets *what, when, how,* and *why.* Since resources such as food, water, and air are provided by natural systems, politics—like economics—rests on an ecological foundation. As resources become scarce, this dependence of politics on ecology becomes more and more apparent, as discussed more fully by Harvey Wheeler in his Guest Editorial at the end of this chapter.

Since there is always competition for resources, politicians must always deal with conflicting groups, each asking for resources or for money that will enable them to purchase or control the resources. Because of these conflicts, politics has been called "the art of the possible." For most politicians the art of the possible is focused primarily on making their own reelection possible. This art involves not taking a stand on controversial or long-range issues, avoiding change as long as possible, and, when backed into a corner, making as little change as possible. A favorite strategy of traditional politicians is to say, "I agree with you, but what you are suggesting is not feasible." This statement is often a smokescreen used to avoid hard thinking, risk taking, and leadership. *Throughout human history, however, the really important pol-*

itics has been that of making the seemingly impossible (or the highly improbable) possible. True politics, then, is the art of creating new possibilities for human progress. By almost any standards, for example, the founding of the United States and the drafting of the Constitution were not politically feasible. President Franklin Roosevelt's dramatic and controversial steps to pull the United States out of the devastating economic depression of the 1930s were not politically feasible either. The key to averting the "not politically feasible" trap on ecological as well as other issues is to focus on the future with a vision of converting the seemingly impossible to the possible. As George Bernard Shaw put it, "Some see things as they are and say why? I dream of things that never were and say why not?"

But how do we get from the seemingly impossible to the possible? This involves using one or more methods of *social change.* The traditional methods are (1) education and persuasion, (2) legal action (lawsuits), (3) political action to institute new laws or change (mutual coercion mutually agreed on), and (4) revolution.

Education and persuasion are always important in bringing about change, especially in the young. But by themselves these methods do not always work very well. Education can prepare people for change, but it must be coupled with other methods. Similarly, using legal action to bring about change is an important technique, but it is not enough. Revolution is a drastic and often highly destructive approach that should be used only as a last resort. Using political action to bring about change is a very useful approach, but present traditional, or linear, politics focuses primarily on short-range planning and action. We must go beyond traditional methods to sustainable earth, or cybernetic, methods, which couple long-range planning and action with short-term planning and action. The remainder of this chapter will discuss environment and law and then methods of sustainable earth politics.

Enrichment Studies, 1, 7, 9, and 17 are related to this chapter.

19-2 Environmental Law

A Primer on Law   In ecopolitics, environmental law plays an important role, particularly as a tool for delaying or preventing abuse of the ecosphere. In the traditional approach, an individual, group of individuals, or a corporation (the plaintiff) brings a civil lawsuit against a party or parties (the defendant), alleging some environmental injustice. To use the courts for a civil action the plaintiff must (1) allege that a wrongful act forbidden by a specific law has been committed, (2) be sure that the court being used has jurisdiction over the suit, and (3) have standing (that is, the legal right to sue). Then, of course, the plaintiff must prove that the actions of the accused, for example, a water polluter, are causing the alleged damage. As in a criminal case, the accused is presumed innocent until proven guilty.

Unfortunately, there are some problems with this procedure. First, bringing any suit is expensive, and the plaintiff may not have the necessary funds. Often the defendant is a large corporation or government agency with ample funds for legal and scientific advice. By contrast, the plaintiffs in environmental cases usually must use volunteer legal and scientific talent and rely on donations. Second, the court (or series of courts if the case is appealed) may take many years to reach a decision. During this time the defendant may continue its alleged damage unless the court can be persuaded to issue a temporary injunction requiring the defendant to stop allegedly harmful actions until the case is decided (adjudicated). Third, it is often very difficult for the plaintiff to prove that the accused is guilty. For example, suppose that a particular company is being charged with bringing harm to certain individuals by polluting a river. There are probably hundreds of other industries and cities dumping wastes into that river. Establishing that the one company is the culprit is extremely difficult, requiring extensive, costly scientific testing and research.

Achievements of Environmental Law   Despite these handicaps, environmental law has been able to accomplish a great deal in only a short time. One way to avoid some of the difficulties mentioned is to form an organization of public interest lawyers and experts who can raise money and pool talents. In 1965 the handful of lawyers and environmentalists in the field had no victories or proven legal strategies. Conservationist or environmental groups and individuals were not recognized

as having standing to sue. Now there are more than 100 public interest law firms and groups specializing partly or totally in environmental and consumer law, supplemented by hundreds of lawyers and scientific experts who participate in environmental and consumer law cases as needed.

In a 1965 landmark case, a citizens' group, the Scenic Hudson Preservation Conference, was given standing to sue the Federal Power Commission. The commission would have been obliged to prevent New York City's Consolidated Edison Company from building a hydroelectric power plant at Storm King Mountain. Although the group lost its suit, it won a vital precedent on standing.

The next breakthrough came in 1967, when Victor J. Yannacone, Jr., a Long Island attorney, filed a suit in state court to stop a county agency from spraying local marshes with DDT. In looking for expert testimony on the effects of DDT, he became acquainted with Charles F. Wurster, a professor of biology at the State University of New York at Stony Brook. Together they helped organize the Environmental Defense Fund (EDF), a group of lawyers and scientists organized to bring environmental lawsuits and supported by contributions from citizens. Since that time EDF membership has grown. This organization has brought a number of successful suits on behalf of the general public, including a 1970 suit that resulted in the banning of DDT in the United States. However, the EDF must decline many important cases because of a lack of funds.* (Why don't you join? See the Appendix for the address.)

Problems to Overcome   Although individuals and groups have apparently won the right of standing (but only on a case-by-case basis) and have won a number of cases, there are still many problems to overcome. Public interest groups have utilized laws that allow class action suits. A class action suit is brought by one group on behalf of a larger number of citizens who have allegedly been similarly damaged but who don't have to be listed and rep-

---

*Other important public interest law groups include the Sierra Club's Legal Defense Fund; the Center for Law and Social Policy; the Natural Resources Defense Council; the Center for Science in the Public Interest; the Center for Law in the Public Interest; Public Interest Advocates, Inc.; Businessmen and Professional People for the Public Interest; and Ralph Nader's Center for Study of Responsive Law. Other important organizations that do not sue but help develop environmental legal concepts are the Environmental Law Institute and the Council for Public Interest Law.

resented individually.* For example, a large number of people living near an airport may be subjected to harmful, disruptive noise, or a number of people may become sick or suffer economic loss because of some form of pollution.

In 1973, however, the U.S. Supreme Court restricted class action suits by environmentalists and other citizen groups. Their ruling requires that each individual claim at least $10,000 in damages to qualify as a member of a class. Although this ruling will deny a number of damaged individuals their day in court, it is probably not a disastrous decision for environmentalists. Class action suits are used mainly to recover damages and have rarely been used in environmental issues. The real success and importance of environmental and other types of citizen-protecting legal action is in preventing damage—stopping the construction of a jetport, a nuclear power plant, or a superhighway that would be routed through an urban park, a conservation area, or a poor neighborhood.

Environmental and public interest law is also threatened by a lack of money. In 1976 environmental lawyers received a serious setback when the Supreme Court ruled that public interest law groups cannot recover attorney's fees when they sue to enforce laws unless Congress specifically authorizes such a recovery in the law. This could have a disastrous effect on the already financially struggling public interest lawyers working on our behalf. The costs of research and expert witnesses are high, and these public service organizations exist only because of individual and foundation grants. Try to donate as much as you can to one or several of these organizations each year (see the Appendix). Never will we get such dedicated legal talent working to protect our indispensable air, water, and land for such a small investment. It would be tragic if these groups did not get more members and more financial support, and disastrous if they disappeared altogether.

Environmental law is a vital and growing field for lawyers and scientists interested in public service. The pay is low and the hours are long, but the satisfaction is high. Lawyers and scientists who defend our interests, as well as ordinary citizens who provide financial support for their efforts, are performing a crucial role in protecting the environment for everyone.

Environmental Legislation and Environmental Impact Statements In recent years a number of important fed-

*Class action suits should not be confused with suits that have many plaintiffs. Groups of people can still bring a joint suit and share legal costs, so long as all of them or their organizations are represented in court.

eral laws have been enacted in the United States, as summarized in Table 19-1. Similar laws, and in some cases even stronger laws, have been passed by most states. The EPA, created by administrative reorganization in 1970, has the responsibility for seeing that these federal environmental laws are enforced.

These laws attempt to provide environmental protection using five major approaches: (1) setting pollution level standards or limiting emissions or effluents for various classes of pollutants (such as the Federal Water Pollution Control Act of 1972 and Clean Air Acts of 1965, 1970, and 1977); (2) screening new substances before they are widely used in order to determine their safety (such as the Toxic Substances Control Act of 1976); (3) requiring a comprehensive environmental impact evaluation of an activity before it is undertaken (such as the National Environmental Policy Act of 1969); (4) setting aside or protecting various ecosystems, resources, or species from harmful use (such as the Wilderness Act of 1964 and the Endangered Species Act of 1973); and (5) encouraging resource conservation (such as the Resource Conservation and Recovery Act of 1976 and to some extent the National Energy Act of 1978). In 1980, former Sen. Edmund Muskie, a leading fighter for tough environmental laws, stated, "Our environmental laws are not ordinary laws, they are laws of survival."

One very important environmental law is the National Environmental Policy Act of 1969 (NEPA). This landmark legislation declared that the federal government has a responsibility to restore and maintain environmental quality and established in the Executive Office of the President a three-member Council on Environmental Quality (CEQ). The CEQ is charged with determining the condition of the national environment, preparing an annual *Environmental Quality Report*, developing and recommending new environmental policies and programs to the president, appraising and coordinating federal environmental programs and activities, advising the president on environmental problems and solutions, and establishing guidelines for the preparation of environmental impact statements (EIS's).

The key provision of NEPA, however, is the requirement that any federal agency (except the EPA) file an *environmental impact statement* for any proposed legislation or projects having a significant effect on environmental quality. In other words, the act requires a full public accounting of the costs and benefits (Section 18-3) of any federal action that could have harmful environmental effects. Each EIS must (1) describe the purpose and need for the proposed action; (2) describe the probable environmental impact (positive, negative, direct,

Table 19-1 Major U.S. Environmental Legislation

Legislation	Text Discussion
General	
National Environmental Policy Act of 1969 (NEPA)	Section 19-2
Energy	
National Energy Acts of 1978 and 1980	Section 13-6
Water Quality	
Federal Water Pollution Control Act of 1972	Section 16-6
Ocean Dumping Act of 1972	Section 16-5
Safe Drinking Water Act of 1974	Section 16-2
Toxic Substances Control Act of 1976	Section 16-6
Clean Water Act of 1977	Section 16-6
Air Quality	
Clean Air Act of 1965	Section 17-6
Clean Air Act of 1970	Section 17-6
Clean Air Act of 1977	Section 17-6
Noise Control	
Noise Control Act of 1972	Enrichment Study 13
Quiet Communities Act of 1978	Enrichment Study 13
Resources and Solid Waste Management	
Solid Waste Disposal Act of 1965	Enrichment Study 15
Resource Recovery Act of 1970	Enrichment Study 15
Resource Conservation and Recovery Act of 1976	Enrichment Study 15
Wildlife	
Species Conservation Act of 1966	Section 10-7
Federal Insecticide, Fungicide, and Rodenticide Control Act of 1972	Enrichment Study 11
Marine Protection, Research, and Sanctuaries Act of 1972	Section 10-7
Endangered Species Act of 1973	Section 10-7
Land Use	
Multiple Use Sustained Yield Act of 1960	Section 10-2
Wilderness Act of 1964	Section 10-2
Wild and Scenic River Act of 1968	Section 10-2
National Coastal Zone Management Acts of 1972 and 1980	Section 10-6
Forest Reserves Management Act of 1974	Section 10-4
Forest Reserves Management Act of 1976	Section 10-4
National Forest Management Act of 1976	Section 10-4
Surface Mining Control and Reclamation Act of 1977	Section 10-5
Endangered American Wilderness Act of 1978	Section 10-2
Alaskan Land-Use Bill of 1980	Section 10-3

and indirect) of the proposed action and of possible alternatives; (3) identify any adverse environmental effects that cannot be avoided should the proposal be implemented; (4) discuss possible alternatives to the proposed action (including taking no action); (5) describe relationships between the probable short-term and long-term impacts of the proposal on environmental quality; (6) discuss any irreversible and irretrievable commitments of resources involved should the proposal be implemented; (7) discuss the problems and objections raised by reviewers of the preliminary draft of the statement; and (8) provide a list of the names and qualifications of the people primarily responsible for preparing the EIS. A draft EIS must be made public for review by the EPA, other appropriate federal, state, and local agencies, and the general public at least 90 days before the proposed action. A final statement, incorporating all comments and objections to the draft statement, must be made public at least 30 days before the proposed action is undertaken.

Between 1970 and 1978, almost 19,000 EIS's were filed at the federal level. Individuals and environmental groups filed 4,291 law suits between 1970 and 1979 designed to force a federal agency to file an EIS or to prepare a more thorough EIS. The EIS process has also forced agencies to think more deeply about short- and long-range side effects of projects and in many cases to analyze alternatives more carefully. As a result of the EIS process scores of dams, highways, and airports have been modified or canceled and the Trans-Alaska pipeline was redesigned to avoid some of its adverse environmental impacts. In addition, by 1979, 29 states had laws or executive orders requiring EIS's for state projects. The 1970 Environmental Quality Act of California goes further than the NEPA, requiring an EIS for any government or private project that can significantly affect environmental quality. The EIS process is also spreading to other nations. By 1980, EIS's were required for a variety of projects in Australia, Canada, France, Ireland, New Zealand, and Sweden.

Despite its successes the EIS process in the United States has been criticized. Critics argue that (1) many EIS's have become voluminous documents containing excessive detail on insignificant points so that agencies can avoid court challenges; (2) EIS's are often prepared to justify a decision that has already been made rather than to evaluate alternatives; (3) many EIS's make projections on the basis of inadequate scientific data and focus on the proposal's impact on particular species when the questions and decisions clearly involve entire ecosystems; (4) an agency can sometimes avoid preparing an

EIS on an environmentally significant project by declaring that it will have no significant environmental impact; (5) an unfavorable EIS does not necessarily mean either that the project will be canceled, that a less harmful option will be selected (as upheld by a 1980 Supreme Court decision), or that the federal agency has to follow the terms of its EIS (as upheld by two federal court decisions); (6) the EIS process has diverted the efforts and limited funds of environmentalists away from questioning and redefining agency powers and responsibilities and has focused them on analyzing mountainous and often irrelevant documents; and (7) most EIS's do not receive careful scrutiny, since only a few highly controversial projects are important enough to be evaluated by underfinanced and overworked public interest groups.

To improve the quality of EIS's, the CEQ issued new regulations for their preparation in 1979. Among the new provisions are: (1) a limit of 150 pages in length except for projects of unusual scope and complexity; (2) the requirement that the statements be clear, to the point, and written in plain language; (3) the requirement of a 15-page summary pointing out major conclusions and areas of controversy; and (4) a requirement that references be given to back up all statements and conclusions. On balance the EIS process is a very important step in the right direction. Hopefully, in future years public pressure will result in amendments to the NEPA that will correct the major weaknesses in this significant environmental legislation. Specifically, federal agencies should be required by law to pick the least harmful option and follow the terms of this option. Congress should also allow public interest law groups to recover attorney's fees when they sue to enforce NEPA or any other environmental laws—thus putting public interest law groups on a more equal footing with federal agencies and large corporations.

Environmentalists, with backing from large numbers of U.S. citizens, have pressured and helped Congress to pass an impressive array of environmental legislation, but they are now recognizing that having a law is only the first step. A law is no better than its enforcement. In the 1980s, environmentalists are increasingly turning their attention to seeing that existing laws and regulations be carried out. Unfortunately, the review of environmental impact statements and the effectiveness of the Council on Environmental Quality in advising the president on environmental matters was seriously undermined in 1981. President Ronald Reagan (who had planned to abolish the council) cut its budget by 70 percent and slashed its staff from 50 to 16— making it essentially impossible for the CEQ to carry out its responsibilities effectively.

19-3 Long-Range Planning

An important technique for converting the seemingly impossible to the possible is to move beyond short-range planning to long-range planning. Only recently have we begun to make this change, which is so necessary to create a sustainable earth society. Such thinking involves three major phases: (1) projecting possible futures, (2) defining long-range social goals to help us choose among these futures, and (3) bringing about the necessary changes.

How can we project alternative futures? Four major approaches are (1) linear extrapolation, (2) the Delphi technique, (3) cybernetic (or computer simulation) modeling, and (4) holistic-imaginative projection.

Linear extrapolation consists of identifying major existing trends and extrapolating them into the future. This method is useful for analyzing the very near future but of little value in medium- and long-range studies. A variation of this approach is the construction of scenarios. Key variables are identified and extrapolated and used to develop plausible descriptions of future situations. The fallacies of linear extrapolation are illustrated by Herman Kahn and Anthony Weiner's book *The Year 2000* (1967, New York: Macmillan), in which "surprise-free" projections of existing trends were made to the year 2000. The issues of environment and population were never mentioned.

The *Delphi technique* (named after the oracle at Delphi) tries to predict technological or social breakthroughs. Experts working at the frontiers of a field are interviewed separately and asked to project when or whether certain breakthroughs might happen. If replies differ, the experts are sent the predictions of other experts and then asked to support their own positions or possibly change their predictions. This process is repeated until some convergence appears. This method is useful for predicting likely new events and discoveries, but it tells us nothing about the impact and side effects of breakthroughs and how the breakthroughs might interact with other variables.

Cybernetic (or computer simulation) *modeling* is the most promising approach for medium- and long-range projections. It is a dynamic model that tries to simulate the interaction between several major variables in a system, as discussed in more detail in Enrichment Study 1. It can be used to project future situations and to test the effects of various policy changes on achieving or preventing a particular situation. New assumptions, data, and the results from the Delphi technique can easily be introduced to update the model. It is, of course, no

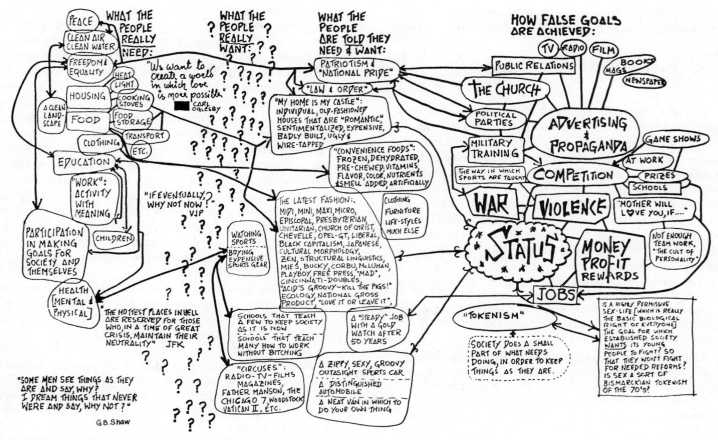

WHAT THE PEOPLE REALLY NEED:
PEACE
CLEAN AIR CLEAN WATER
FREEDOM & EQUALITY
HOUSING
HEAT LIGHT COOKING STOVES
A CLEAN LANDSCAPE
FOOD
FOOD STORAGE
CLOTHING
TRANSPORT ETC.
EDUCATION
"WORK": ACTIVITY WITH MEANING
PARTICIPATION IN MAKING GOALS FOR SOCIETY AND THEMSELVES
CHILDREN
HEALTH [MENTAL & PHYSICAL]

WHAT THE ? PEOPLE ? REALLY ? WANT: ? ?
"We want to create a world in which love is more possible" CARL OGLESBY
"IF EVENTUALLY, WHY NOT NOW!" VJP

"SOME MEN SEE THINGS AS THEY ARE AND SAY, WHY? I DREAM THINGS THAT NEVER WERE AND SAY, WHY NOT?"
G.B. SHAW

WHAT THE PEOPLE ARE TOLD THEY NEED & WANT:
PATRIOTISM & "NATIONAL PRIDE"
"LAW & ORDER"
"MY HOME IS MY CASTLE": INDIVIDUAL, OLD-FASHIONED HOUSES THAT ARE "ROMANTIC", SENTIMENTALIZED, EXPENSIVE, BADLY BUILT, UGLY & WIRE-TAPPED
"CONVENIENCE FOODS": FROZEN, DEHYDRATED, PRE-CHEWED, VITAMINS, FLAVOR, COLOR, NUTRIENTS & SMELL ADDED ARTIFICIALLY
THE LATEST FASHION: MIDI, MINI, MAXI, MICRO, EPISCOPAL, PRESBYTERIAN, UNITARIAN, CHURCH OF CHRIST, CHEVELLE, OPEL-GT, LIBERAL, BLACK CAPITALISM, JAPANESE, CULTURAL MORPHOLOGY, ZEN, STRUCTURAL LINGUISTICS, MIES, BUCKY, CORBU, McLUHAN, PLAYBOY, FREE PRESS, "MAD", CINCINNATI-DOUBLES, "ACID'S GROOVY~KILL THE PIGS!" ECOLOGY, NATIONAL GROSS PRODUCT, "LOVE IT OR LEAVE IT",
CLOTHING FURNITURE LIFE-STYLES MUCH ELSE
WATCHING SPORTS
BUYING EXPENSIVE SPORTS GEAR
"THE HOTTEST PLACES IN HELL ARE RESERVED FOR THOSE WHO, IN A TIME OF GREAT CRISIS, MAINTAIN THEIR NEUTRALITY" JFK
SCHOOLS THAT TEACH A FEW TO KEEP SOCIETY AS IT IS NOW SCHOOLS THAT TEACH MANY HOW TO WORK WITHOUT BITCHING
A "STEADY" JOB WITH A GOLD WATCH AFTER 50 YEARS
"CIRCUSES": RADIO-TV-FILMS MAGAZINES, FATHER MANSON, THE CHICAGO 7, WOODSTOCK, VATICAN II, ETC.
A ZIPPY, SEXY, GROOVY OUTASIGHT SPORTS CAR
A DISTINGUISHED AUTOMOBILE
A NEAT VAN IN WHICH TO DO YOUR OWN THING

HOW FALSE GOALS ARE ACHIEVED:
TV RADIO FILM
BOOK MAGS NEWSPAPER
PUBLIC RELATIONS
THE CHURCH
POLITICAL PARTIES
ADVERTISING & PROPAGANDA
MILITARY TRAINING
THE WAY IN WHICH SPORTS ARE TAUGHT
GAME SHOWS
AT WORK
PRIZES
SCHOOLS
COMPETITION
WAR VIOLENCE
"MOTHER WILL LOVE YOU, IF...."
STATUS
MONEY PROFIT REWARDS
NOT ENOUGH TEAM WORK, "THE CULT OF PERSONALITY".
JOBS
"TOKENISM"
SOCIETY DOES A SMALL PART OF WHAT NEEDS DOING, IN ORDER TO KEEP THINGS AS THEY ARE.
IS A HIGHLY PERMISSIVE SEX-LIFE [WHICH IS REALLY THE BASIC BIOLOGICAL RIGHT OF EVERYONE] THE GOAL FOR WHICH ESTABLISHED SOCIETY WANTS ITS YOUNG PEOPLE TO FIGHT? SO THAT THEY WON'T FIGHT FOR NEEDED REFORMS? IS SEX A SORT OF BISMARCKIAN TOKENISM OF THE 70's?

Figure 19-1 How individual and societal goals are chosen and achieved. (From *Design for the Real World* by Victor Papanek. Copyright © 1971 by Victor Papanek. Reprinted by permission of Pantheon Books, a division of Random House, Inc.)

better than its assumptions, but this is a limitation of any model.

These first three methods of projecting future situations usually involve extrapolation of present trends. The fourth method, *holistic-imaginative projection*, develops future situations by introducing imaginative and unpredictable factors and events that cannot be completely derived by extrapolating present trends. Intuitive reasoning puts together a holistic vision of a possible future, using not only present trends but also the imagination, which searches out subtle, unpredictable variables that may have more influence in the future than do existing major trends. This is what the best science fiction authors do.

It is important to realize that, at best, all of these methods are projections—not predictions—of what might happen based on certain assumptions. The future will always be full of surprises. Long-range projections, however, can help us (1) influence the future in many cases,

(2) think through the possible implications of various proposals, and (3) develop social goals.

Once plausible alternative models of the future are projected, we must begin the planning process by deciding on goals. There are three levels of planning: (1) *normative planning* (deciding our goals or what we ought to do), (2) *strategic planning* (deciding what can be done and learning the possible consequences of each alternative), and (3) *operational planning* (a detailed scheme showing how to use a particular strategy to reach a particular goal). The most difficult phase of sustainable earth thinking and planning is deciding what we ought to do, which is discussed in the next chapter on environmental ethics. Victor Papanek has done a marvelous job of illustrating the complex and diverse interactions that occur in defining goals and distinguishing between what people really need, what they really want, what they are told they need and want, and the social mechanisms for achieving and reinforcing many of our false goals (Figure 19-1). For a further discussion of long-range planning, see J. Clarence Davies's Guest Editorial at the end of this chapter.

19-4 Cybernetic Politics

Tactics of Cybernetic Politics Once goals and a strategy have been set, the next step is to implement the strategy. In linear politics, goals are usually implemented by means of laws, education, and persuasion. But this process usually leads to politics as the art of the possible, rather than the art of converting the seemingly impossible to the possible. Traditional politics is useful, but since environmental systems are dynamic, complex, interdependent, cybernetic systems (Section 6-2), we have a better chance of bringing about change by using cybernetic, or sustainable earth, politics.

The basic tactics of cybernetic politics are as follows:

1. Use positive synergy (Section 6-2) either to amplify desirable trends or to counteract or delay undesirable trends.

2. Apply political pressure at the right time and place and for enough time so that built-in time delays will amplify efforts until threshold levels are reached (Section 6-2). True success is not in immediate effects but in the second-, third-, and higher-order effects.

3. If possible, never fight linear battles, where somebody wins and somebody else loses (win-lose games).

4. Try to find social, scientific, and technological innovations that tunnel through the problem so that everyone wins (win-win games).

Let's look more closely at these tactics.

Positive Synergy and Threshold Effects An important tactic of cybernetic politics is to use *positive synergy* to amplify desirable trends. In linear tactics, 2 plus 2 always equals 4. In cybernetic tactics, 2 plus 2 may be greater than 4 because of positive synergistic interactions, in which the final effect is greater than the sum of the individual efforts (Section 6-2). This requires cooperation, not competition. For example, if you can lift 50 kilograms (110 pounds) and I can lift 50 kilograms (110 pounds), then by working together using positive synergy we can lift 200 or 300 kilograms (440 to 660 pounds).

We can use positive synergy in two major ways. One uses it to amplify a desirable trend. The other uses it to counteract, or at least slow down, an undesirable trend. In other words, we can fight J curves of undesirable trends with opposing J curves that counteract the undesirable trends. In this way a small group of people can bring about major changes, as discussed in more detail in Enrichment Study 17. For example, in 1970 a very small organization called Environmental Action initiated the "Dirty Dozen Campaign"—a program that attempts to defeat in every election year 12 U.S. congressional representatives who have consistently opposed sound environmental legislation. Of the 41 men named to the list between 1970 and 1977 (some were named more than once), 31, or 76 percent, are no longer in Congress. Twenty-five were defeated at the polls and the rest decided to retire early. A handful of workers, using the little funding provided by private contributions, carried out this important change—a remarkable example of cybernetic politics in action.

In 1980, Environmental Action launched a new campaign to clean up Congress by designating the nation's five biggest polluters—companies known as the "filthy five."* The companies are selected on the basis of the amount of campaign contributions made to congressional candidates through company political action committees and on how many times the companies have been fined or cited for environmental violations by federal and state agencies. The voting records of elected members of Congress who received contributions from these companies are then analyzed and publicized if there is evidence of influence on issues favorable to the companies.

Cybernetic tactics also make use of *lag times* and *threshold effects* (Section 6-2). Exerting pressure on a slow-moving, complex political or social system may not seem to have any effect, but if maintained long enough, a threshold level may eventually be reached, thus prompting a major change. Many people push in the right places but give up before built-in delay times have passed.

Traditional attempts to change the social system tend to be frontal and single purpose—marches, demonstrations, sit-ins, legislation, and the like. These tactics are very useful for getting media attention, informing others about the need for change, building and maintaining morale, and countering undesirable trends. But they stop too soon. When the massive inertia of the system makes change appear more superficial than substantial,

---

*In 1980, the first list of the "filthy five" included Dow Chemical Company, International Paper Company, Republic Steel Corporation, Occidental Petroleum Company, and Standard Oil Company of Indiana (Amoco). In 1978, these companies and their top officials gave a total of $714,131 to congressional campaigns and candidates.

The Hard Way   The Easy Way   **Figure 19-2** The tunnel effect.
                                                      Once an easier path becomes
                                                      available, change occurs
                                                      automatically.

mountain of
resistance

mountain of
resistance

tunnel

existing situation

existing
situation

desired situation

desired
situation

many political activists decide that it is useless to buck the system.

Such traditional approaches must be coupled with tactics that make use of positive synergy and threshold effects. To use these tactics, we must understand that the system we want to change is dynamic and complex. In such cybernetic systems, the long-term effect of an action or trend is often the opposite of what would be predicted by short-term linear thinking, as discussed in more detail in Enrichment Study 1.

Win-Win Games and the Tunnel Effect   In linear politics, if someone wins, someone else must lose (a *win-lose game*). The hostile or unresponsive majority holds the top of the mountain, and the dissenting minority must try to take over the mountaintop so that they can impose their own views. Then another minority tries to topple them, and the win-lose cycle is repeated again and again until everyone loses (a *lose-lose game*). By contrast, a major goal of cybernetic politics is to seek ways in which everyone wins (*win-win games*). This requires a sustainable earth value system emphasizing cooperation rather than competition, as discussed in more detail in the next chapter.

One important method for achieving win-win games employs the *tunnel effect*. Think of the problem of bringing about change as getting over a mountain. We can pass laws that force everyone to go over (linear thinking),

or, using positive synergy, we can all vault over the mountain. But usually the best way is to cut a tunnel through the mountain—to find a social, technological, or scientific innovation that cuts through old attitudes and resistance (Figure 19-2); then no one has to go over the mountain (a win-win solution).

The tunnel effect can be described as a *social catalyst* that lowers the resistance barrier. It is a seed crystal—a social chain reaction that is so obvious and effective that resistance disappears, and it reorders everything around it. The social catalyst may be a charismatic leader like India's Gandhi or persuasive rhetoric like Thoreau's essay on civil disobedience. Gandhi skillfully used Thoreau's ideas to develop a nonviolent strategy to win India's independence from Great Britain. Thoreau's catalytic ideas were also used later by Martin Luther King, Jr., in the civil rights movement in the United States. A social catalyst may also be a scientific or technological innovation, such as oral contraceptives and IUD's, which have revolutionized birth control and made effective population control possible. Or it could be a social innovation, such as the Constitution, compulsory school attendance, the postage stamp, the credit card, or old-age pensions. Benjamin Franklin reorganized the postal service for faster delivery of newspapers and in one stroke greatly increased the number of informed citizens ripe for independence. We have established industrial and government task forces and laboratories to discover scientific and technological innovations. Why not do the same for social innovations? A sustainable earth society, however, requires that the people be involved in deciding what social innovations are needed instead of having an elitist group of "experts" decide what the people want. For more information on public involvement, see Enrichment Study 17 and Carol A. Jolly's Guest Editorial at the end of this chapter.

Think how many of our problems would disappear if we had any of the following innovations:

1. widespread use of relatively nonpolluting sources of energy, such as the wind and sun (Sections 14-6 and 14-7)

2. a reliable index or set of indices for measuring gross national quality and gross world quality (Section 18-1)

3. workable theoretical models for dynamic steady state and sustainable earth economic systems (Section 18-2)

4. a tax scheme to finance all elections, thus eliminating all contributions by vested interests

5. a safe, readily available abortion pill that would leave the decision completely up to the individual

6. improved cybernetic models for projecting and analyzing alternative futures (Enrichment Study 1)

7. a means of deactivating radioactive nuclear wastes (Section 14-3)

8. sustainable earth leaders throughout the world (see Table 19-2)

9. a successful plan for streamlining Congress, state legislatures, and federal and state bureaucracies to make them more responsive and more efficient

10. an acceptable world disarmament plan

11. a requirement that the federal budget be balanced (30 of the necessary 34 states have petitioned for a constitutional convention to require balanced budgets)

With any of these or hundreds of other innovations that you might list, we would suddenly tunnel through "impossible" problems. For example, we could significantly reduce waste and inefficiency in government if an individual or group set up annual prizes of $100,000 to $200,000 (like the Nobel Prize) to reward and honor government employees who publicly reveal wasteful or corrupt practices in government.

How do we develop these innovations? Cybernetic politics is so new that we have hardly begun to work out detailed tactics, which would vary considerably with the

problem. But a whole range of completely new possibilities has opened up. Remember that every great human change began with only one person. As Ralph Waldo Emerson reminded us, "Every reform was once a private opinion."

19-5 Toward a Sustainable Earth U.S. Government

The U.S. Government as a Cybernetic System The founders of the United States faced an immense problem. What form of government would maximize individual freedom without intruding on the rights of others? They also had to guard against authoritarian takeovers from the outside or the inside and still encourage the development of the land and its resources in the frontier nation. In other words, the founders wanted to preserve national stability but still allow a range of human choices.

Their solution was a cybernetic marvel. In fact, the makers of the U.S. Constitution can be considered the first American cyberneticists. In effect, they preserved stability by creating a diversity of structures all connected by negative feedback loops (Figure 19-3). The Constitution calls for three major loops and control subsystems—the legislative, executive, and judicial branches—all connected by multiple checks and balances, or negative feedbacks. For the entire system to work, all three branches and the people must cooperate and interact, but checks and balances (corrective feedback mechanisms) are built in to keep one branch from taking over (see Section 6-2). The result of this system is that problems are dealt with so cautiously and inefficiently and with so much compromise that revolutionary changes are discouraged. The government established by the Constitution was not designed for efficiency. Instead it was designed for consensus and accommodation as a key to survival. Thus, by staying as close to the middle of the road as possible, the government muddles through crises. Ralph Waldo Emerson once said, "Democracy is a raft which will never sink, but then your feet are always in the water."

The muddling through approach of the U.S. government is often criticized (as discussed later in this section). Despite some possible flaws for dealing with today's complex world, the American Constitution is an outstanding social innovation—a superb example of cybernetic politics, using stability, diversity, feedback, synergy, and the tunnel effect. Yet it was drafted and agreed upon by fewer than 40 people in only 4 months. Another

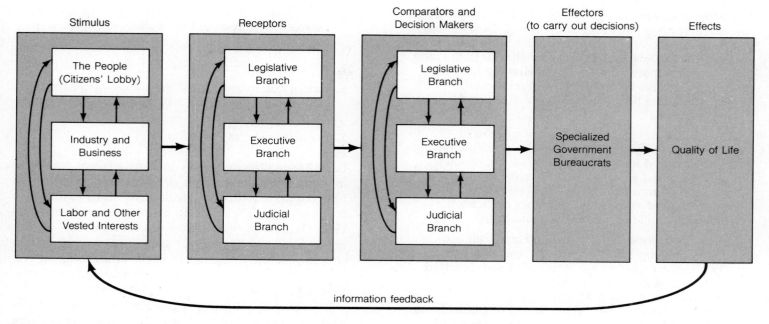

Figure 19-3 A crude cybernetic model of the U.S. political system.

social innovation, the *Federalist Papers* (written by 3 persons in 7 months), explained the workings of this new form of government to the people.

The grand design of the Constitution is like a finely balanced watch with gears and springs moving and responding at different lag times. For immediate response there is the executive branch. But to avoid too hasty a change and to be more responsive to the diversity of national interests, the Congress was created. It, in turn, contains two cybernetic loops: The House of Representatives has the faster response time, because its members are elected every 2 years; the Senate, whose members have 6-year terms, can take a longer view and guard against abuse of power by the executive branch. The counterbalance to the entire system is the Supreme Court. Its function is to protect the Constitution, to interpret it, and to settle disputes of power between the executive and legislative branches. It tends to move slowly, but in times of crisis it can move faster than either Congress or the executive branch, especially to block or delay unfavorable action or trends. Plato may have been right when he described democracy as "a charming form of government, full of variety and disorder, and dispensing a sort of equality to equals and unequals alike."

In its broad outline, the system takes into account the human potential for both good and evil. But the founders were not seriously concerned with the fact that

we live on a planet with finite resources. Indeed, they necessarily were more concerned about growth and expanding the frontier. But a good cybernetic system should be capable of growth or of approximating a dynamic, adaptable steady state (Section 6-2) as needed. The challenge over the next 50 years is to adapt the present U.S. economic system and form of government to the requirements of a dynamic steady state or sustainable earth world (Section 18-2). To decide how the U.S. political system might be adapted to meet the needs of a sustainable earth society, we must look at the major characteristics of a cybernetic political system.

Characteristics of a Cybernetic Political System The major characteristics of an effective cybernetic political system are as follows:

1. *Multiple feedback loops:* Checks and balances with different time lags ensure long-term stability, prevent takeover by one part of the system, and provide a mechanism for continuing self-renewal and adaptation to change.

2. *Minimum number of feedbuck loops necessary for stability:* Too many loops block, distort, or overload information flow; they cause chaos, overcorrection, undercorrection, and even breakdown rather than gentle and steady oscillation.

3. *Sophisticated methods for short-range, intermediate-range and long-range forecasting and planning:* Dealing only with the present or the near future often leads to counterintuitive and disastrous behavior in the long term (Enrichment Study 1). Short-range goals should always be developed and related by feedback and time lags to intermediate- and long-term goals.

4. *An array of niches (roles) with a balance between specialists and generalists:* Excessive specialization (bureaucracy) leads to self-preservation, obsolete governmental agencies, and an inability to develop or act on long-range goals. A government overbalanced with generalists does not have the necessary detailed information and facts.

5. *Accurate information flow (feedback) among all levels of government and between the government and the people:* Two major problems are (1) blocked and distorted information flows to decision makers, or an information overload when more information is received than can be evaluated; and (2) blocked and distorted information flows from government to the people because of excessive government secrecy and media manipulation.

6. *Responsive and responsible decision makers and controllers:* The persons and organizations responsible for making decisions must be willing to bring about change when it is needed. This willingness will depend on their ability as generalists to evaluate conflicting information sources, to get accurate information, and to relate decisions to short-, intermediate-, and long-term goals.

7. *Flexibility:* Parts of the system should be able to change as conditions change. If not, the people should have an orderly mechanism for removing and changing leaders and parts.

8. *Existence in a dynamic steady state* (Section 6-2).

Cybernetic Flaws of the U.S. Government An analysis of the U.S. political system reveals two things: (1) Its founders anticipated most of the major cybernetic principles, but (2) a number of bottlenecks, or cybernetic weaknesses, in the present system are seriously hindering the transition to a sustainable earth society. Following are the major cybernetic weaknesses in the U.S. government system:

1. no mechanism for developing and instituting long-range forecasts and plans (the most serious flaw)

2. excessive influence in government by large corporations and wealthy individuals

3. inadequate information flow within Congress and between Congress and the public

4. the bureaucracy bottleneck

5. failure to elect sustainable earth leaders (Table 19-2)

6. lack of quantitative social indicators—a cybernetic system can only correct what it can measure or monitor accurately

7. the arms race trap (Section 19-6)

Long-Range Planning The dangerous failure to develop long-range plans may have several causes: (1) the short terms of the executive and legislative branches (between 2 and 6 years); (2) failure to adopt an ecosphere world view; (3) failure to make effective use of the tools of long-range planning (Section 19-3); and (4) a poor understanding of the dynamics of social and ecological systems, in which some policies (such as population stabilization) require 30 to 70 years to take effect.

A national long-range planning board might be created at the executive level or as a separate bureaucratic agency, the Department of Long-Range Planning and Coordination. Congress and the citizenry would need similar boards as checks and balances. A better approach might be amending the Constitution to add a fourth branch of government, the planning branch, with its members appointed for staggered terms of 15 to 25 years. (The optimum term length and number of persons for such a government branch are unknown and would require further analysis.) The lag time for this fourth cybernetic loop would thus be shorter than the Supreme Court's, but long enough to minimize undue political influences.

To this group would be appointed the generalists and sustainable earth thinkers. This planning branch could form and direct task forces or Councils of Urgent Studies. Such councils would study and make projections of all major national and global problems for the planning branch and direct efforts to find social and technological innovations and tunnel effects for solving short- and long-range problems. The members of the planning branch would have to integrate and evaluate what ordinary people think needs to be done with what specialized experts think are the needs of the people. A sustainable earth government should make use of experts and planners, but it should not become top-heavy with them.

Perhaps a new constitutional convention should be convened to revise the Constitution and to draft an environmental bill of rights. Cybernetic analysis may also reveal that the lag times between election terms should be changed: perhaps from 2 to 4 years for representatives, from 4 to 6 years for the president, and from 6 to 10 years for senators.* The new Constitution might also simplify government structure—perhaps reorganizing the 50 states, 3,500 counties, and 76,000 local governmental units into regional areas based on airsheds, water basins, and urban heat islands.

Effective long-range planning must be based on the fact that we are entering an age of scarcity. As critical resources become scarce and more expensive, the United States (and other nations) will have to give up the idea that the economy must be kept growing at all costs and begin making the necessary transition from a high-waste to a low-waste society. Then the main political task will be to replace laws and government programs built up over the years that encourage economic growth and a high rate of resource use and waste with ones that encourage and reward the efficient use of energy and matter resources.

As the economic pie grows smaller, industries, unions, government employees, and other special interest groups will try to keep or enlarge their piece of the pie at the expense of others. This will cause intense political conflict, and politicians may be tempted not to act decisively until matters get out of hand. In a state of chaos because of failure to deal with urgent long-range problems that have suddenly become an immediate crisis, the United States may be ripe for a leader who has simple answers to complex problems, and people might be tempted to give up their freedoms for some form of stability.

Executive Branch and Election Reform President Lyndon Johnson once complained, "The only power I've got is nuclear and I can't use that!" As part of the checks-and-balances system, the U.S. Constitution provides the president with powers that are largely persuasive rather than coercive. Presidents have complained that their programs for change and improvement are talked to death or gutted by Congress, or, if approved by Congress, either ignored or altered by the federal bureaucracy or overturned by the judicial branch of government. As a result, it is not surprising that U.S. presidents have tried to get Congress to give them more power. In the 1970s the Watergate scandals, the falsified Cambodian bombing reports, and other events revealed the dangers of too much power in the executive branch of government. This

situation can only be prevented, as the founders foresaw, by a strong and vigorous Congress and by watchdog activities of citizens, citizen groups, and the press.

A second problem is that the White House staff and the cabinet have become so large that they hinder a president's effectiveness. The basic roles of the White House staff should be to provide the president with impartial information on the alternative solutions to various problems and to see that the president's decisions are clearly communicated to the necessary agencies and individuals. George Washington's staff of 14 would be too small for today's complex problems, but the staff of over 400 that recent presidents have had is much too large. Instead of providing unbiased information from Congress and the public, the large White House staff tends to insulate the president from the outside world, take up too much of the president's time with personal meetings or memos, and often attempt to make policy (as occurred in the Nixon administration). In addition to being drastically reduced in size, the White House staff might be reorganized into four major policy groups: international affairs, domestic affairs, economic affairs, and long-range planning.

The cabinet, which originally consisted of only 5 persons, should also be reduced in size. It could also be given more authority, since the larger the size of a committee, the less its effectiveness. The present cabinet of 13 might be reduced to 7 by retaining the Departments of Justice, State, Defense, and Treasury and merging the Departments of Interior, Agriculture, Commerce, Labor, Health and Human Services, Housing and Urban Development, Transportation, Energy, and Education into three major departments: Natural Resources, Human Resources, and Economic and Community Development.*

Another major problem in the executive branch (and the legislative branch) is undue influence on elections by wealthy, vested interests. This problem may never be eliminated since it plagues all governments. But a powerful and active citizens' lobby can help to counterbalance the excessive influence of business, industry, and labor by providing additional checks and balances. Public financing of all federal election campaigns by a general assessment of all taxpayers, with no other contributions allowed, would also help.

Both of these remedies have already been partially effected. In 1973 a revolutionary tunnel was dug under

---

*It has been suggested that presidents be limited to only one term and that members of Congress be allowed to serve for only so many years—say 12. However, if a president or member of Congress is doing well, why force them out after a fixed number of years?

---

*This is an updated version of recommendations made in 1971 to President Richard Nixon by a presidential commission on government reorganization.

the mountain of financing elections. (Actually, the public financing of elections was proposed 65 years ago by Theodore Roosevelt and has been used with considerable success in Ottawa, Canada, and Puerto Rico.) On their income tax returns, taxpayers can now earmark $1 of their taxes to finance presidential election campaigns. But to be effective, this financing must be the only allowed contributions for presidential campaigns. Furthermore, it should be applied to congressional elections (and perhaps to state and local elections).

To hold down election costs, the campaigns (including primaries) for presidential and congressional races should be shortened to no more than 6 months. In addition, each candidate meeting certain specific qualifications (not all candidates) should be given a fixed number of hours of free TV and radio time and a certain amount of free advertising space in the print media (as part of the public service requirements that the media are expected to meet).* There would also be a limit on the air time and amount of printed advertising space any candidate could purchase beyond the free time and space. Since officials running for reelection can more easily command or manipulate media attention, new candidates might be given longer hours or more pages of free media time and space. In addition, all major candidates for president should be expected to participate in a series of free, in-depth, TV debates, with each debate focused on a single topic (such as domestic policy, foreign policy, economic policy, and governmental reform and policy). A single moderator would be used to make the candidates stick to the topic and actually deal with the questions each candidate raises.

Congressional Reform There are several cybernetic problems with Congress: (1) undue influence by special interests, (2) outdated information storage and retrieval systems, and (3) a bloated committee and subcommittee structure that often does not reflect the needs of society.

The undue influence by wealthy, vested interests can be diluted by an active citizens' lobby and the public financing of elections. Congress is also hindered by inaccurate and inadequate information flow. Congressional representatives and senators must deal with over 25,000 bills per year, many requiring sophisticated

knowledge and the ability to confirm or refute information used to support their passage.

Tragically, the group that must evaluate more conflicting information than any other group in the United States is still handling information in a nineteenth-century fashion. Far too often Congress must depend on the president, the bureaucracies, and the industries that it is supposed to monitor and regulate for the "facts," because it has failed to develop an efficient, scientific, and professional advisory system. Much of the information that Congress needs is classified as secret by pertinent sources, and the executive branch and industry often hire most of the available experts as employees or consultants. Congress has attempted to improve this situation somewhat by using the Legislative Reference Service of the Library of Congress, passing the Freedom of Information Act and amendments that help Congress and the public gain access to executive advisory committee reports, and establishing a Congressional Clearinghouse on the Future, the Congressional Office of Technology Assessment, and the Congressional Budget Office. But efforts by Congress to make better use of computers and experts still lag behind efforts of other elements of government and industry.

There should be laws requiring that (1) the report of any governmental advisory commission automatically be made public when it is completed (except in clear cases of national security); (2) no government official be allowed to delay the release of such a report; and (3) the positions, reasoning, and votes of individual members of the commission be made part of the document. The executive advisory system has often been abused in recent years; for example, President Richard Nixon deliberately withheld a scientific and economic study advising against the development of the supersonic transport (SST) and thus deprived Congress and the public of vital information.

Until a few years ago seniority determined who would chair the powerful congressional committees. This practice was abolished because some chairpersons abused their power and ruled committees like kings for long periods of time. Today such potential abuses of power have been reduced by having committee chairpersons named by a caucus of the majority party. Congress has also slightly reduced the number of committees. Unfortunately, it also decreed that each committee should have at least 4 subcommittees, each with its own chairperson and staff—greatly increasing the complexity of getting any piece of important legislation passed. For example, any energy bill must now be dealt with by 83

---

*The main obstacle to free air time at present is not the TV networks, but the section in the Federal Communications Act that requires that equal time be given to every single candidate, regardless of how obscure they may be.

different committees and subcommittees. The number of subcommittees and the number of congressional staff members (which tripled between 1960 and 1980 from 6,650 to 17,700) should be sharply reduced.

The Bureaucratic Bottleneck A bureau is created as a response to a specific problem. In its early pioneer stages a vigorous, small agency with dynamic leadership makes progress. But as it grows its effectiveness and sense of mission decline. Some complexity allows it to accommodate the diverse and often conflicting wishes of the electorate, industrial and minority lobbies, the president, and Congress. But eventually the agency can become so large, complex, and rigid that because of the second law of energy, it begins to choke on the vast amounts of disorder, or entropy, it produces in the form of highly specialized rules and regulations. More and more energy and money are used to keep the agency operating while it puts out less and less useful work. It then becomes an energy and money parasite that creates more problems than it solves.

Because of bureaucratic overspecialization, government has become an enormous organism composed of separate cells of experts, who are often remote from the people, incapable of seeing the overall picture, competing rather than cooperating with one another, and incapable of dealing with the multiplicity of interlocking problems that characterizes society today. According to Lyndon's observation, "If the first person who answers the phone cannot answer your question, it's a bureaucracy."

By 1980, the federal bureaucracy numbered about 2.8 million people, or about 12 bureaucrats for each 1,000 citizens.* Almost all of these employees of the executive branch of government are protected from being fired (except under extreme circumstances) by their civil service status. Thus, the president, as chief executive, oversees 2.8 million employees, most of whom are extremely difficult to fire if they fail to carry out the orders of the president, Congress, or top-level cabinet executives. Indeed, the federal employee most likely to be fired or moved to a less desirable job or location is the one who blows the whistle on government waste and inefficiency.

---

*During the Carter administration the number of full-time bureaucrats was reduced by about 40,000. This was mostly offset, however, by the hiring of 30,000 part-time employees and the increased use of outside consultants (who received $1 billion in 1980 for various studies, including why consultants are needed).

To make matters worse, the system for evaluating civil servants has broken down, with 99 percent of all federal bureaucrats receiving "merit" raises in 1980 for doing an excellent job. The vast majority of bureaucrats are hard-working public servants. Every agency, however, is overstaffed with incompetent and inefficient workers whose numbers far exceed the 1 percent indicated by the level of merit raises.

Another problem is that each overspecialized bureau can become more concerned with its own survival than with its mission or even be taken over by the groups that it is supposed to regulate. For example, a 1976 study by the General Accounting Office and Common Cause revealed that more than half of the 42 commissioners appointed to governmental regulatory agencies between 1971 and 1975 came from a company regulated by their agency or from the law firms of the company, and half of the commissioners who left during this same period went to work for these companies or law firms. President Harry S Truman recognized this serious problem when he said, "You don't set foxes to watching the chickens just because they have a lot of experience in the hen house."

Often by the time a new agency is fully functioning, events have shifted to another problem. To justify its existence and its budget, each agency wants a share of any new problem. As a result, a new problem can be spread out over 20 agencies. Only when the problem grows into a crisis are all the fragments gathered together. Then a new agency, such as the EPA, is created to launch an all-out attack that may be a decade or more overdue. Soon institutional rigidity sets in and the cycle repeats. A study of EPA, made 6 years after its creation, ranked it near the top of all agencies in terms of openness, independence from the regulated industries, consumer responsiveness, and commitment to public interest. But the study criticized the EPA for being too timid in developing and enforcing controversial regulations. By 1981, industry and members of the Reagan administration had mounted an all-out attack to weaken EPA powers because they believed it was being too bold in developing and enforcing controversial regulations.

A number of government regulations are necessary to protect the environment and consumers from abuse by private industry. However, the number and complexity of various government regulations can be reduced—thus reducing the need for as large a bureaucracy. In 1980, Americans spent an estimated 1.2 billion hours filling out over 6,000 different kinds of federal forms—producing enough paper each year to lay a 0.8 kilometer (half-mile) wide strip of paper from New York to Los Angeles. Some regulations are unnecessarily complex. Many, however, must be complex and detailed. Government officials know that most industries they are required to regulate have teams of lawyers that will go through laws and regulations to find even the tiniest loophole that will allow those industries to circumvent the intent of the law.

Furthermore, much of the blame for overregulation lies with Congress—not federal regulatory agencies. In most cases these agencies are merely seeing that laws passed by Congress are carried out. In a number of cases, Congress writes vague laws and leaves it up to federal agencies and the courts to fill in the details. This allows Congress to avoid taking specific stands on controversial issues, shifting the blame to bureaucracies and the courts. For example, Title VII of the Civil Rights Act simply reads that it is illegal for anyone to discriminate on the basis of sex, without specifying what constitutes such discrimination. Federal agencies were then expected to come up with specific regulations to interpret this vague mandate. These regulations were then challenged in the courts, so that eventually the Supreme Court had to determine what constitutes sex discrimination. The federal agencies and the Supreme Court are then blamed for making law (often by members of Congress running for reelection), when the real problem was caused by a Congress unwilling to deal specifically with a controversial issue that could cost them votes back home.

Most present reforms are cosmetic or temporary. They include the following: (1) bringing in new chiefs (because a bureau chief rarely lasts longer than 4 years, the agency pretends to change but really continues business as usual); (2) establishing interagency committees or task forces to manage conflicts of interest; (3) reorganization and consolidation; (4) creating new organizations (good during the first phase if adequately funded); (5) administrative feudalism, that is, avoiding bureaucracies by creating White House "czars" who make policy not subject to public and congressional scrutiny. (This solves some of the president's headaches but clearly threatens the democratic process and the cybernetic checks and balances on executive power, as Watergate clearly showed); and (6) providing special protection and rewards for "whistle blowers" who expose fraud and waste in government.

Instead of temporary and also ineffective changes, major changes will be necessary to tame the bureaucratic monster. The number of bureaucrats needs to be reduced. Hardly anyone wants to return to the political patronage system used up to the mid-1800s, when all bureaucrats were subject to being fired after each presidential election. A number of reforms, however, can be instituted to reduce the size of the bureaucracy and increase its efficiency including: (1) exempting one-half of all annual replacements from turnover (amounting to about 300,000 per year) from civil service protection; (2) streamlining the procedures for dismissal;* (3) overhauling the evaluation and merit raise system; (4) empowering the president to appoint more high-level departmental officials (extending this down to level GS-13 civil service employees would allow the president to appoint over 93,000 high-level officials, compared to only 3,000 under the present system); (5) giving state and local officials more authority over how to spend federal grants; (6) turning more of the federal tax revenues directly back to the states; (7) having the states assume full responsibility for some areas, such as education; (8) enacting and strictly enforcing sunset laws that require each government agency and program to be evaluated every few years and eliminated unless it can show that its function is still needed and that it is doing its job effectively and efficiently with the least amount of money and personnel. For example, the Rural Electrification Administration—created in 1935 to bring electricity to American farms—still employed 740 people in 1980, and had a budget of $29 million even though 99 percent of all U.S. farms have electricity. Such reforms must be enacted by the Congress, but this may be difficult. The more errors and problems that bureaucrats create for individual citizens and businesses, the more opportunities members of Congress have to correct the errors—thus doing favors for their constituents to make their own reelection more likely.

Electing Sustainable Earth Leaders Criticizing elected leaders is easy. Instead of merely criticizing leaders, we must elect a new breed of sustainable earth leaders, whose primary loyalty is to the ecosphere and to the future of humanity rather than to nationalistic, state, or local short-term goals. Table 19-2 compares characteristics of international frontier leaders and those of sustainable earth leaders. However, if we elect such leaders, we must still recognize their limitations. The world and its problems are complex, and leaders are under tremendous conflicting pressures that will affect our lives for many decades. In criticizing and evaluating leaders we should keep in mind the Spanish verse "Advice pours

*Dismissal was made slightly easier during the Carter administration with the number of dismissals rising from 119 in 1978 to almost 2,000 in 1980. There is still, however, a long way to go.

down from the stadium full, / But only the matador faces the bull."

Politicians are caught in a predicament. They are asked to do several contradictory things simultaneous-ly—keep prices down, increase the supply of energy and matter resources, conserve matter and energy resources, maintain full employment, and keep the economy grow-ing. It is impossible to satisfy all of these goals at the

Table 19-2 Comparisons of International Frontier Leaders and Sustainable Earth Leaders

International Frontier Leader	Sustainable Earth Leader
International view. Thinks and acts internationally but in terms of national prestige, honor, and power.	Ecosphere view. Thinks in terms of preserving the ecosphere and the world's resources for everyone now and in the future.
Thinks national loyalty is the primary driving force.	Thinks ecosphere loyalty is the only viable approach in the long run.
Thinks and acts in terms of win-lose games and uses sports and battle analogies ("we won," "honor is in winning," "this play will win," "might is right," "frontiers to conquer," "God is on our side").	Sees the goal as having everyone in the world win now as well as in the future (win-win games).
Politics of the possible. Avoids really difficult problems or declares them solved. People who talk of the impossible are "naive idealists."	Politics of the seemingly impossible or improbable made possible by use of vision, cybernetic politics, and outstanding leadership. Willing to pro-pose solutions for complex and controversial problems.
Simplistic view. Problems are due to a single variable or culprit, and can be solved by enacting a short-term simple cure.	Holistic, cybernetic view. Everything interacts with everything. Problems are complex and ever changing, and require multivariable approaches over long periods of time.
Primarily concerned with his or her role in history.	Primarily concerned with ensuring future survival and human dignity for all.
Emphasizes short-term planning. Defends or talks mostly of past accom-plishments rather than future goals.	Emphasizes long-term planning with all short-term planning done in rela-tion to intermediate and long-term goals. Talks of where we must go instead of where he or she has taken us.
Thinks a nation should do whatever we can do technologically in order to maintain or "win" national prestige, honor, and supremacy.	Thinks a nation should assess all technological solutions to determine possible long-range side effects on the ecosphere and to determine whether the solutions improve human dignity and life quality.
Chooses advisers who say only what he or she wants to hear (information blockage and distortion).	Insists on having the best minds project and evaluate all major alterna-tives.
Tries to control the press, which is portrayed as a threat to national security and individual freedom.	Realizes that a free but accountable press is essential to uncover and prevent information blockage and distortion. Recognizes that there are many countries where politicians have seized or controlled the press but no country where the press has seized power from the government.
Uses secrecy to block information flow to the people.	Operates openly to ensure maximum and accurate information flow to the people.
Believes economic growth is the only way a nation can win or dominate. Sees a steady state economy as stagnant.	Evaluates growth on the basis of long-term ecosphere goals. A dynamic sustainable earth economy (Section 18-2) is the only viable long-term goal.
Thinks the problem of social justice will be solved only by economic growth—the "trickle down" approach.	Believes that in a finite world nearing its limits, the problem of social justice must be solved by a more equitable distribution of wealth.
Believes the greatest threat to peace and individual freedom is some outside -ism that a nation must overcome.	Thinks the greatest threats to peace and individual freedom are the arms race, overpopulation, overexploitation of finite resources by rich nations, and a world economic system that tends to make the rich richer and the poor poorer.
Talks about peace, poverty, population, and pollution but spends most of the money on armaments so that a nation can act from a position of strength.	Acts to promote peace, eliminate poverty, stabilize population, control pollution, and drastically reduce military expenditures and arms buildup throughout the world.
Thinks the solution to most problems is to buy or build things (more mis-siles, guns, computers, and highways).	Thinks the solution to most problems is to deliberately slow down the flow rate of matter and energy in the industrialized nations and to encourage appropriate technologies in the poor countries in order to meet the peo-ple's needs and encourage them to be more self-reliant.

same time in an age of resource scarcity. For instance, keeping resource prices artificially low by government control merely encourages a more rapid use of resources and gives the public a false message about the real world, where there is no free lunch.

Politicians in an age of scarcity will have to be true leaders rather than spending most of their time searching for the perfect compromise in which all conflicting interest groups are equally dissatisfied. They will have the thankless and unpopular task of saying no to many groups by cutting many existing government-supported programs. Unfortunately, some sustainable earth leaders who take firm stands on crucial and highly controversial issues will be rewarded for their honesty and leadership by not being reelected. On the other hand, the average citizen strongly supports reducing the unnecessary waste of energy and matter resources and has been far ahead of most politicians in being willing to accept sacrifices—provided that they are distributed fairly. The courageous sustainable earth leader who tells us the truth about our situation and the sacrifices that it will require may well be rewarded by being reelected.

Sustainable earth leaders can only be effective if they are backed up by concerned and politically involved sustainable earth citizens. Fortunately, more and more people are beginning to adopt a sustainable earth world view. Converting this new awareness into effective political action and making sure that future leaders practice sustainable earth politics (see Enrichment Study 17 and Carol A. Jolly's Guest Editorial at the end of this chapter) will be key factors in making the difficult but exciting transition to a sustainable earth government and society.

19-6 Toward a Sustainable Earth World Order

Paths to Peace In spite of concern about pollution, population growth, and resource depletion, the most shocking and dangerous J curve is that of world military expenditures. Between 1950 and 1978, world military expenditures almost quadrupled. In 1978 the world military expenditures amounted to $1 billion a day, or about $1 million a minute, on military armaments, with the United States and the Soviet Union accounting for more than half of this expenditure. The United States alone is expected to spend over $1 trillion for military purposes between 1980 and 1985. Military spending is also increasing rapidly in the poorer nations, with the United States and the Soviet Union selling them 74 percent of their arms.

This tragic situation drains financial, natural, and human resources that could be used for peaceful, constructive purposes. World military spending is about 20 times the amount of nonmilitary aid that rich countries give to poor countries. In addition, *half* of the world's physical scientists and engineers and one-fourth of all the world's scientists devote their talents and skills to military research and development—a tragic waste of human talent. By comparison, only 8 percent of the world's scientists are working on energy research and development (with most of these working on nuclear power), 7 percent on health, 5 percent on transportation, and 3 percent on agriculture. Furthermore, in the United States about 50 percent of all annual government research and development expenditures are devoted to military purposes.

Clearly, no one wins with such insane priorities. Even if we avoid nuclear catastrophe, we face the threat of ecological catastrophe because our resources are being squandered as if they were infinite. Some implications of these misplaced human priorities are shown in Table 19-3.

How do we justify the J curve of military expenditures? We say it is necessary for peace. Of the three major approaches to maintaining world peace—deterrence, pacification, and cooperation and sharing—we have so far chosen *mutual deterrence*, or maintaining a balance of terror by continuing the arms race. Treaties are designed primarily to prevent bankruptcy and don't really disarm us, since we already have enough atomic bombs to kill everyone in the world 12 times. To get off this J curve, we must begin with pacification and move to cooperation and sharing. *Pacification* involves rectifying wrongs, calming fears of open information flow and mutual inspection, and minimizing hunger, poverty, overcrowding, and drives for domination. Under these conditions we can develop *cooperation and sharing*—working together for trade and business to protect the ecosphere and to bring about a more just distribution of the world's resources.

Approaches to a Sustainable Earth World Order People have dreamed of global cooperation for years, but now it is absolutely necessary for our survival. We are finally beginning to understand the profound paradox that true independence can exist only in an atmosphere of interdependence. The arms race leads to mutual insecurity—not mutual security.

Can we make the transition to a sustainable earth global society over the next few decades? The answer is yes, as discussed further in the next chapter and in the

Table 19-3 Implications of Military Spending

Military Expenditure	Equivalent Expenditure
1 Huey helicopter	66 low-cost houses
1 prototype bomber	75 fully equipped, 100-bed hospitals
1 atomic submarine	Schooling for 16 million children in less developed countries
1 nuclear-powered aircraft carrier	Transit systems for 2 major cities
Development of 1 prototype F-14 fighter	Elimination of all hunger in the United States this year
Development of 1 prototype B-1 bomber	Lifting all poor American families (25.5 million people) above the poverty line

principles for developing integrated plans for major environmental problems presented throughout this book. Many people have already made the leap from national to global loyalty and others are coming closer, as F. M. Esfandiary has pointed out:

> The quandary of many liberals in America and elsewhere is that they have largely outgrown patriotism but are afraid to face this fact. They are afraid to be called unpatriotic. They are even more afraid to come out openly and say, "I am not patriotic, I am not a nationalist, I don't give a damn about my country or any country. For me there are no countries, no sides—only the side of humankind."

Most plans for achieving world order can be classified as multinational, imperial, or federalist. The *multinational approach* is based on maintaining peace and cooperation through mutual deterrence, balance-of-power diplomacy, and growing international economic interdependence that will lead to increased cooperation. In effect, it merely sustains the existing situation.

The *imperial approach* means domination of the world by one nation-state. Even if this were possible, much of the world would not survive the nuclear war that would probably be required.

The *federalist approach* would establish world order through nations voluntarily cooperating to create common institutions. There are two major strategies here. Federal unionists* seek world union by first uniting a

*Organizations promoting this design are Association for a Federal Union of Democratic Nations (P.O. Box 4896, Washington, D.C., 20008) and Federal Union, Inc. (1736 Columbia Road, N.W., Washington, D.C., 20009).

few nations into a new sovereign power and then getting others to join. The powers of several nations would gradually be transferred to a common governing institution. This body would then call for a constitutional convention, similar to the 1787 Philadelphia Convention, to draft a constitution for ratification by the peoples of the participating nations. (A preliminary draft of a world constitution has been drawn up and is published in *A Constitution for the World*, Santa Barbara, Calif.: Center for the Study of Democratic Institutions, 1965.)

World federalists seek world order through international institutions, in which all or most nations would participate in solving common technical problems.* With increasing cooperation and ecological and economic interdependence, the influence of such institutions would grow. Federalists hope that such institutions would become strong enough to prevent world wars and eventually lead to federal unions of cooperating states— or even to a global federation. In effect, this approach involves strengthening the United Nations as a peace-keeping and disarmament agency and as a protector and promoter of ecosphere stability.

Although its progress has been slow, the United Nations represents a crucial step toward world order. Through the United Nations, governments have begun to discuss the "new international economic order," built on the concept of decreasing the gap between rich and poor nations. In addition, the United Nations has organized a number of important global conferences to examine the problems of food, population, water, human settlements, the status of women, and the environment that affect all nations. So far, the primary result of these conferences has been talk, but talk is a necessary and important prelude to action.

Preserving Cultural Diversity Does world federation mean monolithic world government? Absolutely not! Preserving global biological and cultural diversity must be a primary goal. For long-term stability, survival, and adaptability, we need cultural diversity. This is probably best achieved by a loose federation of politically autonomous states that cooperate to prevent nuclear and ecological destruction and to improve the quality of life for all world citizens.

A political monoculture, like our vast agricultural monocultures, could easily topple whenever conditions changed. In effect, we must live and act simultaneously

*Organizations include the World Association of Federalists (46 Elgin St., Ottawa 4, Canada) and World Federalists, U.S.A. (2029 K St. N.W., Washington, D.C., 20006).

on three cultural levels: a *microculture* of families and local communities based on personal relationships; a *macroculture* of national interests based on common economic and political arrangements, laws, and customs; and a *superculture* based on economic, political, and ethical arrangements that see global loyalty and cooperation as the only viable forms of patriotism. The diversity and constantly changing patterns of this three-level world would maintain it in a dynamic steady state that can adapt to changing conditions and still not exceed regional and global environmental and resource supply limits.

We have developed the first two cultural levels, and our collective survival now depends on adding the third. Such a sustainable earth revolution involves questioning and altering almost all of our ethical, political, economic, sociological, psychological, and technological rules and systems. No one could ask for a more challenging and meaningful task. It will involve day-to-day hard work, many setbacks, bitter disputes, frustration, and anguish, but more importantly it will involve the joy that comes from caring for the earth and our fellow passengers.

Human despair or default can reach a point where even the most stirring visions lose their regenerating powers. This point, some will say, has already been reached. Not true. It will be reached only when human beings are no longer capable of calling out to one another, when the words in their poetry break up before their eyes, when their faces are frozen toward their young, and when they fail to make pictures in the mind out of clouds racing across the sky. So long as we can do these things, we are capable of indignation about the things we should be indignant about and we can shape our society in a way that does justice to our hopes.

Norman Cousins

Guest Editorial: Ecology as a New Challenge to Politics

Harvey Wheeler

In 1975 Harvey Wheeler founded the Institute for Higher Studies in Santa Barbara and the Journal of Social and Biological Structures. *He was previously a senior fellow at the Center for the Study of Democratic Institutions, and before that he taught political science at Washington and Lee University, Johns Hopkins University, and Harvard University. Besides numerous professional articles, he has been the author, editor, or coauthor of several books, including* The Politics of Revolution *(1971, Santa Barbara, Calif.: Center for the Study of Democratic Institutions). His new novel,* The Rise of the Elders, *was published in 1981.*

He is one of the most respected and creative political analysts writing in America today.

What is ecology? We know it refers to smog and pollution and the population explosion. We know it counsels conservation rather than resource depletion, recycling rather than dumping our garbage and waste. We know it teaches us to enhance the quality of our environment rather than to continue multiplying the quantity of our gadgets. Beyond this most of us have only a very hazy idea about what ecology really is.

The separate scientific branches of ecology have been quite well established for a long time. Plant ecology deals with the harmonious balances between vegetation and the rest of the environment. Marine ecology deals with the life and matter balances within various bodies of water. Each separate natural resource—our forests, our birds, even our swamps—has its own separate group of ecologists working in special institutes devoted to its study.

There are demographic ecologists, energy ecologists, epidemiological ecologists, archeological ecologists, insect ecologists, mathematical ecologists, ecological economists, and ecological political scientists: Nearly every field of inquiry can be studied in the light of its ecological implications. Does this mean that ecology is merely the sum of all these—that there is no such thing as ecology, pure and simple, considered as a separate science with its own intrinsic characteristics? I am inclined to think this is indeed the case, or rather that ecology is a new kind of synthetic applied science in which ingredients from the physical and social sciences must be blended together and then explored in terms of their ethical and political implications. This latter aspect is the novel element.

The very notion of ecology implies both a moral obligation and a political imperative. Once we discover an ecological truth, concerning, for example, the threatened extinction of the blue whale, we have an obligation to rectify the situation through collective action (politics). For 200 years we have been accustomed to thinking of science as being ethically and politically neutral. Ecology, having an ethical and political element at its core, is disturbing for scientists and difficult for them to assimilate. It is equally perplexing for politicians. They have been accustomed to dealing with science as if it truly were the neutral tool that it always claimed to be: If you wanted to explore Mars, inaugurate supersonic air travel, or introduce new sources of power, you merely called in the appropriate scientists and told them what you wanted to do and gave them money and labs; they used their science to produce what politics demanded. Scientists are not supposed to talk back, as some nuclear physicists did concerning the H-bomb. If they try that tack, you lecture them to mind their own business—this business being science, which is ethically neutral—and insist that they do as they are told. The recalcitrant ones can be fired and replaced with their more professionally scientific (amoral) colleagues. If politicians can't do this—if they can't treat science and engineering as compliant and ethically neutral tools—politics loses its autonomy. It is confronted with scientific limits and imperatives, boundaries it cannot violate and thresholds it cannot cross. Yet this is what ecology says to politics and that is why many politicians disparage, resent, and even fear ecology. Their antipathy to ecology is of a piece with that of the more tradition-minded scientists. Both wish to hold fast to the traditional dividing line between science and ethics. This explains much of the bitterness, stemming from both scientific and political quarters, that has accompanied the ecological movement: The foundation of ecology is scientific, yet its findings bring ethical and political obligations.

Ecology deals with all the interrelationships, or "transactions," that occur within the environment. But if this is so, how do we get a grasp on any single ecological problem? For this seems to mean that no matter what we decide to study, the fruit fly or the soybean, we can't understand it until we have understood the universe as a whole. There is a sense in which this is true. At least it is true that most serious ecological problems, such as pollution of the air from radioactive particles and the threatened extinction of the salmon or the whale, can be solved only on a worldwide basis. This is not only because the resource itself is found throughout the world but also because the human organizations and technologies that threaten it require worldwide controls. Human behavior inexorably forges limitless interconnections between problems—universalizing ecology, so to speak.

Human technologies and institutions form an intrinsic part of every ecological problem. Hence, the solutions to ecological problems require alterations in the application of human technologies and institutions: Controlling radioactive air pollution and preserving the ocean fisheries require concerted and cooperative behavior by people and nations. This means that ecology cannot be divorced from politics. Moreover, ecology places a stern imperative on politics. It forces politics to acquire a scope of action comparable to the scope of the problem. If nation-states are too restrictive in scope to preserve the world's ocean fisheries, then something more than the nation-state will be required to resolve the problem. In sum, politics—in the larger sense—is an intrinsic part of ecology. In fact, some who take a classical view of politics argue that ecology is part of politics: Applied ecology is but politics devoted to a special range of environmental problems, approaching their solution through a special group of ecological sciences.

Contemporary ecologists would not completely disagree, even though their own immediate concern is with the special methods and sciences that tell us the dimensions of the problems facing us. Ecology must resolve two very difficult problems that politics alone cannot answer: (1) What are the practical limits of an ecological problem, and (2) how can we reveal the crucial interrelationships of an ecological problem? Both problems involve the use of quite sophisticated mathematical methods.

So although ecology is intimately connected with politics, and although its solution ultimately will require political implementation, it nonetheless represents a new challenge to politics. Its scientific aspects require that we create a new kind of science-politics, in which science and politics are intimately intertwined. This, of necessity, will require new kinds of policy-forming, or legislative, institutions.

Guest Editorial Discussion

1. Is science ethically and politically neutral? What about ecology?

2. Give examples of some of the ethical and political imperatives (sustainable earth rules) that could be derived from the laws of thermodynamics (Chapter 3).

3. Is politics a part of ecology or is ecology a part of politics? Defend your viewpoint. Does it make any difference? Why?

4. If ecological problems tend to transcend national boundaries, is there an ecological imperative requiring the formation of regional and world governments?

Guest Editorial: Long-Range Planning

J. Clarence Davies III

J. Clarence Davies III is executive vice-president of the Conservation Foundation. Prior to this appointment he was a fellow with Resources for the Future, a senior staff member of the Council on Environmental Quality, taught politics at Princeton University, and worked in the Bureau of the Budget. He has published many articles and books, including The Politics of Pollution *(with Barbara S. Davies) (1975, Indianapolis: Pegasus).*

Everyone is in favor of long-range planning, but nobody does it. At least that is the situation within the federal government. A cynic might argue that everyone is in favor of it because nobody does it.

There are, of course, bits of long-range planning going on in various government departments. The Census Bureau knows about how many senior citizens there will be in the United States in 2030, because all of them have already been born and the death rate is not likely to change drastically. Thus, the Social Security Agency is able to plan how many clients it will have in 60 years. The Forest Service makes long-range predictions of timber supply and demand, because it is impossible to plant, grow, and harvest a tree within one fiscal year. But despite these bits and pieces, long-range planning is not an integral part of any of the government's programs.

There is so little long-range planning because there is no incentive to do it; even if there were, we would not know how to do it very well.

The time horizon of almost all governmental actors is marked by the next election, the next budget, or the next set of congressional hearings. Anything more than two or three years away either will not happen as predicted or will be someone else's responsibility. It is true that presidents, members of Congress, and many civil servants have a desire to leave their imprint on history. But the imprint must be shaped by the action-forcing processes within the government, and these processes have a very short time fuse.

The unreliability of long-range plans and predictions has been commented on by so many others that it is not necessary for me to review the many horror stories of false pictures of the future. But it should be noted that even the piecemeal predictions are simply extrapolations of whatever is the current situation. It is not known why the U.S. birth rate has declined so sharply or whether it will increase or decrease in the future. The timber supply and demand projections are not joined by any model of the timber market, and the projections do not deal adequately with pricing, new products, or innovations in silviculture. Many projections founder on what seem to be inherently unpredictable factors. We are uncertain about the food supply three years from now because we do not know what the weather will be like. We can project air and water pollution loads for the year 2000 on the basis of GNP growth and changes in industrial processes, but when we do so we find that the key variable is the government's regulatory policies.

If the key variable in a policy area is the government's own actions, predictions will be uncertain because of the difficulty of knowing what the government will do 10 or 20 years hence. But if the government's actions are the determining factor, a more comprehensive type of planning is also called for. The implicit laissez-faire assumption that the government's actions affect society only marginally must be abandoned, and the federal agencies must take responsibility for the effects of their actions in areas outside the limited scope of particular programs. The social sciences have an obligation to ascertain just how much influence government actions have and then, insofar as such actions are found to determine the future shape of important aspects of the society, to provide an intellectual and organizational framework capable of incorporating such broad societal impacts into the factors that contribute to official decisions.

When the Club of Rome's book *The Limits to Growth* (see Enrichment Study 1) was unveiled in Washington, numerous critics dissected the flaws in the study. This was not difficult to do. But no one was able to address the study's conclusions on any basis other than faith. Whether humankind is doomed, whether the economy can continue to grow, whether resources will be exhausted would seem to be questions of more than passing interest. However, no one in the government was asking them; when some members of Congress and some administrators who were stimulated by the club's efforts began to ask them, they found no government agency that considered the future of humankind to be within its jurisdiction. The interrelationships among policy areas were not analyzed by a government based on single-purpose, narrowly focused programs.

Given an accelerating pace of change and the almost unlimited scope of the changes taking place, the government's lack of interest in long-range planning is an invitation to disaster. With respect to the physical environment, the chances are just too good that the accumulated impact of past actions or some new innovation will tilt the delicate balance of the earth's ecosystem. Even if we forget disaster, policies that are not based on a reasonably accurate picture of the next 5, 10, or 20 years are likely to be unsatisfactory (see Enrichment Study 1).

Government agencies cannot be severely blamed for the absence of long-range thinking, because there is so little knowledge of how to do such thinking. The social sciences have a major obligation to improve our ability to plan, predict, and prepare for the uncertainty of an ever changing world.

Guest Editorial Discussion

1. If the time horizon of elected officials is so short, is it possible for them to do and use long-range planning? How?

2. Since long-range thinking and planning is often wrong, does this mean that it shouldn't be done? Why or why not?

Guest Editorial: Public Participation in Environmental Policy Making

Carol A. Jolly

Carol A. Jolly serves on the staff of the assistant secretary for the environment at the U.S. Department of Energy. After working for four years in the Environmental Quality Department of the League of Women Voters Education Fund, she took a position within the government where she could implement the public participation programs the league espoused. At the Department of Energy, she works with the staff to promote public involvement in program and policy development and manages the Environmental Advisory Committee.

A new phrase has entered the lexicon of environmental legislation. A number of recent pollution control laws have

specified that as federal and state agencies develop and enforce their plans, programs, and standards, they must provide for, encourage, and assist *public participation*. In addition, several executive agencies have announced that even when it is not legally mandated, they want us—the public—to help them shape decisions and determine policy directions.

At the federal level, this opportunity has been strengthened by the issuance of Executive Order 12160, which requires agencies to "establish procedures for the early and meaningful participation by consumers in the development and review of all agency rules, policies and programs." Since all of us are "consumers" of the environment, this order should expand our access to federal officials and the decision-making process.

This sounds most reassuring to those citizens and organizations that have been working for years or even decades to promote environmental protection or resource conservation. It would seem to offer great possibilities for those of you whose environmental awareness has been awakened or sharpened by this book or the course it accompanies. The natural implication of such declarations is that the government has recognized a need to incorporate the public's ideas in making major decisions on such issues as how clean water should be or whether the resources in solid waste should be recovered or tossed away.

But just what is public participation? And even after it has been defined—if it can be—how can the public effectively take advantage of the opportunities created by the mandate that it be provided for, encouraged, and assisted?

Unfortunately, many government agencies confuse public participation with public information. They believe that they have met a law's requirements by developing a lengthy mailing list and sending piles of paper to anyone who expresses an interest in their program. While the public *does* need information for meaningful participation, the former is neither a substitute for nor the same as the latter.

As environmental issues become more technical, gathering enough facts on which to base a decision becomes more of a challenge. Government agencies can help. They can guarantee direct and informative answers from agency personnel, assure citizen access to key documents, and maintain mailing lists which insure that useful materials reach all those requesting to be kept informed. Agencies can see that documents reach the public with enough lead time to be read and assimilated before a reaction is called for.

Increasing complexity may also mean that the public must rely on experts. Technical jargon often has to be translated into language that the average citizen can understand. Costs and benefits—to health, the environment, the economy—must be clearly displayed and determined through understandable processes. To have access to unbiased experts, the public may need financial assistance; by making funds available for such purposes, government agencies can directly demonstrate their willingness to encourage and assist public participation.

Once citizens have learned the facts, effective participation generally involves educating others. Those who want a policy decision made or an existing policy changed must create a demand—a demand visible, sizable, and compelling enough to persuade those with the authority to take such a course. Sometimes this is a relatively easy task—an environmental group may already exist in the area and can focus its members' attention on the issue at hand. In other cases, a group of like-minded individuals will have to form their own organization to address a specific problem or topic.

It may be that the government officials responsible for working with citizens have the most to learn about promoting public participation. As informed citizens, you may have to push or prod your local or state government, or even federal agencies with which you deal, to create a workable public participation system (see Enrichment Study 17).

Officials sometimes believe that they have encouraged public participation by holding a public hearing to learn citizens' views about a plan that the agency has developed. This opportunity to react to decisions already made is another example of what public participation is not.

Public participation is meaningful involvement in the decision-making process. To facilitate this process, government agencies must establish mechanisms that provide for continuing, systematic exchanges of views with informed citizens from the earliest stages of program or project planning.

The public's role in environmental decision making should be that of choice maker—that is, people deciding what kind of community (or country) they want to live in, making judgments about which values they wish to create or protect. Not many of us draw up lists of priorities, but consciously or unconsciously we perform this role in expressing support or opposition to specific choices through our lifestyles and through the political process. To serve such a role in affecting government policy, the public must be included in formulating plans from the beginning.

The public is increasingly insisting on the right to participate as directly as possible in expressing its value judgments, insisting on a right to explain its needs and desires throughout the planning and implementation processes, and insisting on the right to have its views taken into account by those charged with reaching decisions that will affect the general health and welfare.

And if members of the public—if you as environmentally concerned citizens—wish to play this role, responsibilities accompany the opportunities. Effective participation requires *informed* citizens—people who know the facts and understand the implications of alternative courses of action—or inaction. Often, becoming informed means learning the pros and cons of several alternatives before a judgment can be formed on the best approach to solving a problem.

The most persuasive public participation is that which reflects a broad spectrum of key interests. So the concerned citizen must often reach out to different groups, convince them that environmental decisions affect them, and mobilize them for action. A diverse coalition, clearly and thoughtfully expressing its ideas to public officials, stands the best chance of affecting key decisions (see Enrichment Study 17).

You are the public. Your studies and reading may have developed deeply felt convictions about the kind of environment you want, the costs you are willing to pay, the benefits you are willing to forgo, and the risks you are willing to accept. If public policies are to reflect these ideas, it's up to you to express them to the officials charged with shaping those policies. It may not be easy, but public participation is your best means of shaping the nation you want.

Guest Editorial Discussion

1. What specific mechanisms should government agencies establish to provide for meaningful public participation? Do you know of any examples where this has been done?

2. Make a list of basic rules or tactics that one should follow in order to be an effective public participant.

Discussion Topics

1. Evaluate the following statements:
   a. Economists have the answers to our environmental ills.
   b. Scientists have the answers to our environmental ills.
   c. Political scientists and politicians have the answers to our environmental ills.
   d. None of these groups have the answers.

2. Do you agree that real politics is the art of making the seemingly impossible possible? Why or why not? On this basis what have been the major political events of this century, and who was mainly responsible for each?

3. Although education and persuasion are important methods of social change, explain why they are not enough. Try to give examples in your own life to back up your answer.

4. What are the major trends that you see in society today? Which ones are desirable and which are undesirable? Use various combinations of these trends to construct three different scenarios of what the world might be like in 2000. Identify the scenario you favor and outline a program for achieving this alternative future.

5. Debate the following resolution: Cybernetic politics is a lot of baloney.

6. How can 2 plus 2 be greater than 4? What are the implications of this for the ecosphere? For your life?

7. Analyze the civil rights movement and the peace movement in terms of using or failing to use cybernetic politics.

8. Get a copy of the Constitution and analyze it as a class in terms of cybernetics. Use cybernetics to revise or write a new constitution for the transition to a sustainable earth society.

9. As a class, design a cybernetic constitution for your student government. Why not try to have it passed? Design a strategy for passage based on cybernetic politics.

10. Debate the following resolution: We should create a long-range planning board as a fourth branch of government.

11. Discuss the major approaches to bureaucratic reform. Which ones do you favor? Why?

12. Evaluate the last five U.S. presidents in terms of frontier and sustainable earth characteristics. Can you identify any existing sustainable earth leaders or people who should be elected because of such potential?

13. Debate the following resolution: The U.S. military budget should be cut in half.

14. Debate the following resolution: The only real path to peace is for the United States to destroy its nuclear weapons.

15. Debate the following resolution: We need to establish a world government.

16. Debate the following resolution: National patriotism is both irrelevant and dangerous. The only viable patriotism is global loyalty.

Readings

Alderson, George, and Everett Sentman. 1979. *How You Can Influence Congress: The Complete Handbook for the Citizen Lobbyist.* New York: Dutton. Superb guide.

Anderson, Walt, ed. 1975. *Politics and Environment.* 2nd ed. Santa Monica, Calif.: Goodyear. Very useful collection of articles.

Barnet, Richard J. 1980. *The Lean Years: Politics in an Age of Scarcity.* New York: Simon & Schuster. One of the best discussions of politics and the environment.

Brown, Lester R. 1972. *World Without Borders.* New York: Random House. Excellent overview of our problems and possibilities. See Chap. 11 on multinational corporations.

Caldwell, Lynton K. 1972. *In Defense of Earth: International Protection of the Biosphere.* Bloomington: Indiana University Press. Magnificent book that outlines what we must do at the international level. Excellent bibliography.

Caldwell, Lynton K., et al. 1976. *Citizens and the Environment: Case Studies in Popular Action.* Bloomington: Indiana University Press. Outstanding collection of case studies showing what informed and concerned citizens can do.

Cellarius, Richard A., and John Platt. 1972. "Councils of Urgent Studies." *Science,* vol. 177, 670–676. Very important article that outlines the task forces needed to deal with our major problems.

Cooley, Richard A., and Geoffrey Wandesforde-Smith, eds. 1970. *Congress and the Environment.* Seattle: University of Washington Press. Excellent collection of case studies.

Davies, J. Clarence, III, and Barbara S. Davies. 1975. *The Politics of Pollution.* 2nd ed. Indianapolis: Pegasus. Probably the best introduction to pollution control by government regulation.

Elgin, Duane S., and Robert A. Bushnell. 1977. "The Limits to Complexity: Are Bureaucracies Becoming Unmanageable?" *The Futurist,* December, pp. 337–349. Excellent analysis.

Falk, Richard A. 1971. *This Endangered Planet: Prospects and Proposals for Human Survival.* New York: Random House.

Overview of our ecological problems with a superb discussion of world order as a solution.

Falk, Richard A. 1975. *A Study of Future Worlds*. New York: Free Press. Superb detailed plan for achieving world order.

Gardner, John W. 1970. *The Recovery of Confidence*. New York: Norton. Brilliant and moving analysis of how to accomplish change.

Gardner, John W. 1972. *In Common Cause*. New York: Norton. Explains how to bring about political change.

Johnson, Warren. 1978. *Muddling Toward Frugality*. San Francisco: Sierra Club Books. Superb analysis of economics, politics, and environment.

Jolly, Carol A., and Gail Allison. 1976. *Federal Environmental Laws and You*. Washington, D.C.: League of Women Voters. Excellent review of major federal laws for protecting the environment.

Krier, James E. 1975. "Environmental Law and Its Administration." In William W. Murdoch, ed., *Environment: Resources, Pollution and Society*, 2nd ed. Sunderland, Mass.: Sinauer. Excellent introduction.

Nader, Ralph, and Donald Ross. 1971. *Action for a Change: A Student's Manual for Public Interest Organizing*. New York: Grossman. Important tunnel effect idea. Tells how college students can form public interest research groups.

Ophuls, William. 1977. *Ecology and the Politics of Scarcity*. San Francisco: Freeman. One of the best books on environment and politics.

Papageorgiou, J. C. 1980. *Management Science and Environmental Problems*. Springfield, Ill.: Thomas. Very useful overview.

Pirages, Dennis. 1978. *Global Ecopolitics*. North Scituate, Mass.: Duxbury. Excellent overview.

Platt, John R. 1966. *The Step to Man*. New York: Wiley. Excellent collection of essays on human nature and how to bring about change. See pp. 108–113 on the U.S. founding fathers as the first cyberneticists.

Rodgers, William H. 1977. *Environmental Law*. St. Paul, Minn.: West Publishing. Useful, more advanced treatment.

Staff report. 1981. "American Renewal." *Time*, Feb. 23, pp. 34–49. Superb in-depth report on governmental reform that includes some of the suggestions given in this chapter.

Tarlock, Anthony Dan. 1979. "Environmental Law: What It Is, What It Should Be." *Environmental Science and Technology*, vol. 13, no. 11, 1344–1348. Good summary.

Taylor, Gordon R. 1973. *Rethink: A Paraprimitive Solution*. New York: Dutton. Superb, thought-provoking analysis of society and social change.

Tinbergen, Jan, ed. 1976. *Reshaping the International Order*. New York: Dutton. Detailed analysis of the strategies for achieving world order.

Wagar, Warren. 1971. *Building the City of Man: Outlines of a World Civilization*. San Francisco: Freeman. Magnificent analysis of how we can achieve a world state.

Ward, Barbara. 1976. *The Home of Man*. New York: Norton. Superb discussion of how basic needs can be met in all countries within a framework of world order.

Wheeler, Harvey. 1971. *The Politics of Revolution*. Santa Barbara, Calif.: Center for the Study of Democratic Institutions. Blueprint for an international society with a strong emphasis on ecology and politics.

20

Environmental Ethics and Hope

The human intelligence does best when it concentrates on loving the human race more and the rat race less.

David A. Brower
President, Friends of the Earth

Through our scientific and technological genius we have made this world a neighborhood. Now through our moral and spiritual genius we must make it a brotherhood.

Martin Luther King, Jr.

20-1 Hope: The People Are Stirring

How are we to deal with the increasing pollution of water, air, and food, the dangers of nuclear power, energy crises, pesticides, food additives, land misuse, solid wastes, and potential resource shortages that have been discussed in this book?

Psychologist Rollo May says that many of us can no longer care about anyone or anything because we feel overwhelmed and powerless. After a long history of technological innovation and confident expansion in resource use, we seem to be coming up against limits. Nothing seems to work anymore. Our lives seem to be managed by impersonal and uncontrollable forces. The goals we seek are often without meaning, and many of our finest minds and most precious resources are devoted to killing, devastation, and waste. Add to this our power to destroy ourselves by nuclear and ecological disaster, and no wonder many people ask whether there is any hope. The answer to this question is a resounding *yes* (see Section 1-6)!

We can make the transition to a sustainable earth society within the next 50 years only if we avoid three

traps: (1) the *blind technological optimism* of those who believe that science and technology will always save us, (2) the *gloom-and-doom pessimism* of those who have given up hope, and (3) *apathy* resulting from a fatalistic outlook or a naive view of reality.*

Apparently a shift in American attitudes toward technology is taking place. In 1980, the majority of Americans in their twenties and thirties polled in a national survey did not believe that technology would be able to solve the problems of shortages and rising prices of natural resources. We are slowly learning that (1) some technological problems (such as nuclear fusion power, Section 14-4) are incredibly difficult if not impossible to solve; (2) many complex, centralized technologies (such as nuclear fission power plants and the related problem of nuclear waste storage) require large quantities of increasingly expensive matter and energy resources, huge investments of limited capital, and long lead times to develop and put into full-scale operation; and (3) each new technological advance creates harmful side effects that are often unpredictable (Sections 1-5 and 6-3). This does not mean that we should abandon technology. Instead, we should redirect it into channels that do not waste resources and that work with nature rather than attempting to dominate nature.

Preoccupation with gloom and doom is also not a solution to our problems. In recent years we have been subjected to many shocking facts and gloomy forecasts. But apocalyptic predictions do little to change people's basic behavior, even if the danger is acknowledged. The number of Americans smoking cigarettes, for instance, has not declined significantly in spite of the fact that it greatly increases the risk of an earlier death from cancer and heart disease. Too much gloom and doom simply

---

Enrichment Study 17 is related to this chapter.

*McLandburgh Wilson said, "The optimist sees the doughnut, but the pessimist sees the hole." Perhaps we should add that the naive realist sees the doughnut and the hole, while the ecological realist tries to see the doughnut and the hole and their relationship to the ecosphere.

paralyze. Instead of leading to action, they can lead to disbelief, apathy, withdrawal, and despair.

In contrast, hope is one of the greatest driving forces in life. Hopes goes beyond optimism and pessimism. It energizes the human spirit so that humanity can convert the impossible or highly improbable into the possible. John W. Gardner has pointed the way:

> No doubt the world is, among other things, a vale of tears. It is full of absurdities that cannot be explained, evils that cannot be countenanced, injustices that cannot be excused. Our conscious processes—the part of us that is saturated with words and ideas—may arrive at exceedingly gloomy appraisals, but an older, more deeply rooted, biologically and spiritually stubborn part of us continues to say yes to hoping, yes to striving, yes to life. All effective action is fueled by hope.

A New Dream Present undesirable trends do not necessarily indicate where we are heading. As René Dubos reminds us, "Trend is not destiny." *We can say no!* We can alter catastrophic trends if we choose to accept the sacrifices that all important transitions require and the joy that they produce. Nobel Prize-winning chemist Glenn T. Seaborg urges us to look at the present and future with new eyes: "What we are seeing today in all our social upheavals, in all our alarm and anguish over an environmental feedback and, in general, the apparent piling of crisis upon crisis to an almost intolerable degree, is not a forecast of doom. It is the birthpangs of a new world view." Or as Samuel Beckett put it, "We are between a death and a difficult birth."

If human behavior and institutions change in the next 50 years half as significantly as they did during the past 50 years, we can make the transition to a sustainable earth society. Adopting a sustainable earth consciousness means that we can no longer expect clean air and still drive big cars with internal combustion engines; instead, we must develop efficient mass and para transportation. We can no longer justify using and wasting the world's mineral, energy, and food resources at a rate that literally means misery and death for other human beings. We cannot continue to talk about peace, honor, brotherhood and sisterhood, justice, freedom, and wars on poverty while wasting enormous amounts of money and scarce resources on armaments.

The Good News There are signs that a value revolution is under way in the United States. People are stirring,

questioning, listening, and organizing. They are asking, "What is true wealth? Does economic growth always yield progress? What should be the true aims of an affluent nation?" There is a growing awareness that we must elect sustainable earth leaders (Section 19-5) who will tell the people the truth—that we can't have everything, that we are in deep trouble, that we must make some significant and difficult changes, that for everything we want to preserve we will have to give up something.* U.S. Sen. Patrick Moynihan reminds us that "the essence of tyranny is the denial of complexity." Indeed, an important part of the case for hope rests on the fact that ordinary citizens are often able to take a wider and more humanistic view than experts and leaders. Despite the simplistic solutions often proposed by politicians, the public often recognizes that, as H. L. Mencken put it, "For every problem there is a solution—simple, neat, and wrong."

J. M. Stycos has observed that major social changes go through four stages:

Phase 1: no talk, no do

Phase 2: talk, no do

Phase 3: talk, do

Phase 4: no talk, do

During the short period between 1965 and today, most U.S. citizens became aware of and concerned about the environment. On April 22, 1970, the first Earth Day took place in the United States, and 20 million people took to the streets to demand better environmental quality. At that time, polls showed that Americans considered reducing pollution to be the second most important problem. Today it is still an important concern, with nearly half (42%) of the people surveyed feeling that environmental protection is so important that continuing improvement must be made regardless of cost. Today there are environmental agencies at the national and state levels; most colleges and universities have environmental courses; and a number of the early environmental activists now hold important government and industrial

---

*Ralph Lewin exaggerated when he said, "Everything I like is either illegal, immoral, fattening, pollutes the environment, or increases the population."

positions where they can continue to influence environmental progress.*

On the pollution front the United States has already moved onto phase 3, with real progress on several environmental problems and more progress expected during the next decade. Since 1970, over 80 federal laws have been passed to protect the air, water, land, and public health, and billions have been spent on pollution control. Since 1968 levels of many air pollutants have decreased in most U.S. metropolitan areas, and they could be reduced to acceptable levels in all but a few urban areas by 1990 (see Section 17-6). California has set an example for the rest of the United States and the world by establishing stricter air pollution standards than the federal government.

The United States is behind schedule in achieving the congressional goal of fishable and swimmable waters by 1983, but significant progress has been made since 1970 in reducing water pollution. Nationwide analyses show significant improvement in water quality in most areas, and already over 70 U.S. lakes, rivers, and streams have been cleaned up through public and private efforts. Oregon has set an example by its massive cleanup of the Willamette River, as well as by being the first state to pass a law encouraging the use of returnable bottles instead of throwaway cans (Enrichment Study 15) and by discouraging growth. Also, Americans have cut down water pollution by phosphates. Between 1972 and 1977, high-phosphate detergents had essentially disappeared, and the phosphate-free detergent business had grown from a $45 million to a $500 million business between 1977 and 1980.

---

*Many strong environmentalists appointed to government positions during the Carter administration were replaced in 1981 by the Reagan administration. For example, James Watt, Secretary of the Interior, has indicated that he favors returning much government owned land to the states, relaxing strip mining regulations, and opening up government lands to more mining and forest cutting by industry. Ray Arnett, who was appointed head of the U.S. Fish and Wildlife Service, opposed enactment of a strong bill to devote some Alaskan lands to wilderness, national forests, and wildlife refuges. James Harris, now in charge of the Office of Surface Mining, filed a suit challenging the constitutionality of the 1977 Coal Strip Mining Act. John Crowell, the choice to oversee the U.S. Forest Service, had fought that agency as general counsel of a timber company seeking to cut more forests on federal land. The new head of the Bureau of Land Management seeks to turn much of the federally owned land he oversees back to the states. Anne Gorsuch, the new head of the EPA, as a state legislator in Colorado, opposed a bill to control toxic wastes as well as rules for a state auto emissions law. James Edward, Secretary of Energy, is a strong supporter of nuclear energy (at the expense of energy conservation, solar, wind, and biomass energy) and took the job with the mandate to dismantle the Department of Energy.

Pesticides such as DDT, aldrin, and dieldrin have been banned from use in the United States. As a result, brown pelicans, peregrine falcons, ospreys, and bald eagles have made a comeback from the endangered species list, and the mean level of DDT in human fatty tissue in the United States has dropped from about 8 ppm in 1971 to about 3 ppm in 1977. Despite the ban on DDT and some other harmful chemicals, the United States still makes DDT and ships it to other nations, where some of it is returned to the United States on imported fruit and other foods. There is much talk about integrated pest management (Enrichment Study 11), but it has yet to be widely used in the American agricultural system.

On the energy front, America is still mostly in the "talk, no do" phase. The United States continues to waste enormous amounts of energy, although efforts at improving energy efficiency are taking place. Some people are driving less; most thermostats have been turned down; more homes have been insulated; and a small but growing number of people are using solar energy to heat their homes. In polls the favored energy source is solar energy (61%) and the least favored is nuclear energy. But many people still only conserve energy when it is required by law or when they clearly see that it saves them money. Despite higher gasoline prices, carpools are not widely used and the nation still lacks the railroad, mass and para transit systems, and bicycle paths to help reduce dependence on automobiles.

With regard to population, the United States has made some hopeful movements into phase 3. Zero population growth is probably at least 50 years away because of the momentum from the youthful age structure (Section 7-4), but the birth rate and total fertility rate fell dramatically between 1968 and 1976 and then rose slightly between 1977 and 1980 (Figures 7-5, 7-6, and 7-7). If these low rates can be maintained, especially through 1987, the United States could have a stable population by 2020, and perhaps as early as 2010.

Of course, many far tougher problems remain, such as the energy crisis (Chapters 13 and 14), depletion of nonrenewable resources (Chapter 12), agricultural pollution (Chapter 9; Enrichment Studies 11 and 16), ecosystem simplification (Sections 6-3 and 6-4), the handling and recycling of our wasted solids (Enrichment Study 15), long-term handling and storage of radioactive materials (Section 14-3), our usable water supply (Chapter 15), land use (Chapters 10 and 11; Enrichment Study 14), deforestation (Section 10-4), urban problems (Chapter 11), the automobile (Sections 11-4 and 17-5), toxic metals (Enrichment Study 5), and possible long-term changes in global climate (Enrichment Study 3). We have awareness, research, and some action on all of these fronts, but solving or at least controlling most of these problems will require that we change to a sustainable earth society within the next 50 years as discussed by William Ophuls in his Guest Editorial at the end of this chapter.

Since 1966 American environmentalists have become much better organized and informed. In the United States they have learned how to use legal and political machinery to prevent environmental abuse and how to lobby for passage of tough environmental protection laws (Section 19-2). Indirectly and directly, environmentalists have halted, delayed, or modified a number of potentially environmentally harmful projects such as dams, power plants, highways, offshore oil leases, jetports, and SSTs.

Some industrialists are shifting from their earlier defensive positions; many industrialists are beginning to see that the public is serious, that in the long run pollution is bad for business, that the longer they wait the greater the costs of cleaning up, that technology for cleaning up the environment is a major growth market in itself (Section 18-3), and that they have a major responsibility for preserving the environment.

Citizens' groups are forming to protect the environment, to challenge the priorities and assumptions of elected leaders, to insist on equal rights for all, to protect the consumer, to form lobbies for the common people as a counterbalance to the powerful lobbies of organized business and other interests, and to use existing laws in a creative way to protect the poor, the disadvantaged, and indeed all of us (see Enrichment Study 17).

In the 1980s, environmentalists are focusing more on the unhealthful environments found indoors in factories and work places. They are forming coalitions with labor groups to improve working conditions. Environmentalists are also focusing more on seeing that existing environmental laws and regulations are enforced and on global issues such as acid deposition (Section 17-2) and rising levels of carbon dioxide in the atmosphere (Enrichment Study 3). The environmental movement is now moving into a more sophisticated and less visible phase. In many cases (except nuclear power), activists who once marched and demonstrated for a cleaner environment are being replaced by disciplined platoons of highly trained and dedicated environmental lawyers, scientists, and civil servants who are attempting to change the system from within. As Brock Evans, Washington director of the activist Sierra Club pointed out, "From now on the environmental movement will need fewer rabble-rousers like me, and more technicians. The struggles of the 1980s and 1990s will be within the bowels of the Environmental Protection Agency and in the courts."

By 1980 there were over 3,000 organizations throughout the world devoted to pollution control, wildlife conservation, and preservation of the human race. A large number of these organizations are based in the United States (see the Appendix for a list of some key environmental organizations). While many people sit on the sidelines, talking about how the system can't be changed, these groups are changing it. In 1980, some 5 to 8 million Americans belonged to at least one environmental group. Environmental causes are not mass movements yet, but they are growing. Political analysts indicate that dedicated political activity by only about 10 percent (perhaps less) of the population can bring about significant change. (Some estimate only 5 percent or less, but it probably takes an additional 5 percent to counteract the 5 percent who will organize against almost any movement.) Some industries have carried out massive ad campaigns depicting environmentalists as elitist, affluent, white, upper middle class individuals who want to lock up all the woods and to bankrupt the United States by overprotecting Americans from harmful air and water. The public, however, has not been persuaded by such unfounded, stereotyped images, and poll after poll has shown that public support for environmental protection is strong and widespread throughout the United States.

At the international level, Sweden and the People's Republic of China have set an example for the rest of the world. On most fronts, Sweden has moved into phase 4. It has reached zero population growth, instituted national land-use planning and extensive and sophisticated pollution control, protected large amounts of its shoreline for free public use, plans to phase out nuclear power and switch to renewable energy resources, and is now allocating 5 percent of its total budget for environmental programs (the United States allocates less than 2 percent). Sweden banned DDT and methyl mercury seed dressings (Enrichment Study 5) years ago, and Swedish research has alerted the world to a number of environmental dangers and their remedies. Some Swedish innovations include the pneumatic pipeline for solid waste removal and resource recovery (Enrichment Study 15), the Clivus Multrum waterless toilet (Section 16-6), and a three-way catalytic converter for controlling automobile emissions that U.S. companies said couldn't be developed (Section 17-6). Sweden, Norway, the Netherlands, and Canada are among the few affluent countries whose foreign aid to poor nations has increased over the past 15 years. Sweden, like any urbanized country, has serious social and environmental problems, but other nations clearly have many lessons to learn from Sweden's sustainable earth behavior.

The People's Republic of China, with the world's largest population, has moved into phase 3 in terms of population control. It apparently has the most effective and stringent population control program in the world (Section 8-3). Despite its massive population, China has managed to feed its population with a combination of small, decentralized communal farms, intermediate technology, and strict government control. China also has one of the most effective reforestation programs in the world. According to inventor and world thinker R. Buckminster Fuller (who has been around the world 45 times) and environmental expert Lester R. Brown, China has the strongest sense of environmental ethics of any nation in the world today. Of course, other nations either do not have or do not want the strong, centralized government control found in China. Also, China may fall into the trap of developing a highly industrialized society along the environmentally destructive paths followed by Western industrial nations. So far, however, China has set an important global example of environmental responsibility.

I am not suggesting that everything is going well in the world. We have only begun to recognize our predicament, much less decide on courses of action. But it is amazing how much progress has been made between 1968 and today (Section 1-6). Some cynics say that ecology is a fad. If it is, it will be the last fad. There will be much confusion and disagreement, and many early converts will drop out or oppose the environmental movement once they realize the fundamental economic, political, social, and ethical changes that it requires. But awareness and action are increasing.

20-2 The Four Levels of Environmental Awareness and Action

The First Level: Pollution There are four levels of awareness of the ecological crisis (see the accompanying box). At the first level we discover the symptom, *pollution*. In only a few years pollution has become a major issue for most U.S. citizens. Although this is very encouraging, it is also dangerous. As soon as we discover a problem, we want to fix blame. We are still engaged in an unhealthy, counterproductive phase of the environmental crisis—a "pollution witch hunt." We blame industry, government, technology, and the poor—anyone

---

Four Levels of Environmental Awareness

First level: Pollution. Discovering the symptoms.

Second level: Overpopullution. Seeing that population times per capita consumption times environmental impact equals ecosystem disruption and pollution (Section 1-5).

Third level: Spaceship earth. Seeing the problem as a complex mix of physical, social, political, and economic factors. Everything is connected to everything and our job is to run and preserve the ship by controlling everything and everybody.

Fourth level: Sustainable Earth. Seeing the problem as a complex mix of physical, social, political, economic, and ethical factors (Figure 1-5). Everyone and every living species is interconnected, and our job is to preserve ecological stability and diversity, and human dignity and freedom by cooperating with nature and by caring and sharing. Because we can never know how everything or even most things are interconnected, we must exercise restraint and humility as plain citizens of the earth—not as its masters.

---

but ourselves. Of course, we must point out and stop irresponsible acts of pollution by large and small organizations and resist being duped by slick corporate advertising. But we must at the same time change our own life-styles. We have all been drilling holes in the bottom of our boat. Arguing over who is drilling the biggest hole only diverts us from working together to keep the leaky boat from sinking.

Another danger in remaining at the pollution awareness level is that it leads people to see the crisis as a problem comparable to a "moon shot," and to look for a quick solution: Have technology fix us up, send me the bill at the end of the month, but don't ask me to change my way of living. Using technology and spending enormous amounts of money will be necessary, but they are not enough.

The problem at the pollution level is that individuals and industries see their own impacts as too tiny to matter. This is what human ecologist Garrett Hardin calls the *tragedy of the commons*. Individuals and industries tend to pollute common resources such as air and water that are not owned by anyone; laws must be passed and enforced to protect these resources from abuse.

The Second Level: Overpopullution   Many have already moved to the second level of awareness, the *overpopullution* level. The cause of pollution is not just people but their level of consumption and the environmental impact of various types of production, especially in more developed nations (Section 1-5 and Figure 1-5). At the overpopullution level the answers seem obvious. We must simultaneously reduce the number of people in both rich and poor nations and the level of consumption in rich nations. We also need to change to less harmful and wasteful consumption patterns, especially in the industrialized nations, which, with less than 30 percent of the world's population, account for about 90 percent of the environmental pollution.

The Third Level: Spaceship Earth   But these changes will not even start until a reasonable number of leaders and citizens move to a third plateau of awareness, the *spaceship earth* level. At this point we recognize that the earth has limits and that our life-support system is vulnerable. We are forced to recognize that all human beings depend on each other and on the same life-support system and that protecting and preserving the ecosphere that sustains all life must be our primary goal.

The spaceship earth level is a step in the right direction. But because it follows the "astronaut model" too closely, it is also a very dangerous world view. To protect astronauts and their life-support system, every natural function must be rigidly controlled in a programmed existence. Instead of novelty, spontaneity, joy, and freedom, the spaceship model is based on cultural homogenization, social regimentation, artificiality, monotony, sameness, and gadgetry. Using a spaceship crew as the ultimate model for solving problems poses a dire threat to individual human freedom and to the ecosphere.

This world view is also an upside-down view of reality and an expression of our arrogance toward nature. Our task is not to learn how to pilot spaceship earth or, as Teilhard de Chardin would have it, "to seize the tiller of the world." Our difficult—but crucial—task is to give up our fantasies of being all-powerful rulers of nature. We must learn anew that it is we who belong to the earth, not the earth to us.

The Fourth Level: Sustainable Earth   Recognizing our finiteness and interdependence and moving from a fron-

tier world view to a spaceship world view constitute an important step. But this step is not enough. Somehow we must move to the *sustainable earth* level, as first described in Section 3-4. At this level we finally see that the solution to our problems lies in working with nature and in selectively controlling relatively small parts of nature on the basis of ecological understanding. This approach is based on the principle that nature knows best. Control over the environment should be kept to a minimum by recognizing that (1) the role of humans is not to rule and control nature but, in the words of Aldo Leopold, "to be a plain member and citizen of nature"; (2) the ecosphere is so complex that its workings can never be fully understood, so that attempts at excessive control will sooner or later backfire (Section 6-3); (3) our major goal should be to preserve the ecological integrity, stability, and diversity of the ecosphere; and (4) all living species by virtue of their existence have an inalienable right to life in their natural environments so that the forces of biological evolution, not human technological control, should determine which species live or die.

The important differences between the spaceship and sustainable earth world views (Table 20-1) are the recognition of *freedom* (versus control), *humility* (versus the assumption of total knowledge and control), deliberate preservation of *diversity* (versus artificial simplification), and *sharing* (versus greed). In the words of Mahatma Gandhi, "There is enough for everybody's need but not for anybody's greed."

Making the transition to a sustainable earth society means that affluent nations must build a low-waste or low-entropy-producing society that emphasizes the reduced use and waste of matter and energy resources and the increased use of intermediate, decentralized technology (Section 1-5). Rich nations must also help poor nations to become more self-reliant and to develop appropriate technology that avoids the heavy resource use and heavy pollution now found in affluent nations. For more details on the meaning and challenges of developing a sustainable earth society, see the Guest Editorials at the end of this chapter by Richard A. Falk and William Ophuls.

Some may see the sustainable earth approach as "going back to nature." But this attitude is based on an idealized and romanticized view that nature's ways are somehow always kind, beautiful, and gentle. Such people do not know nature's harsh realities, confusing a desire to feel close to nature with living close to nature. A mass return to natural living would also mean death for billions of human beings. Long ago we exceeded the population carrying capacity for a world living at a low

Table 20-1 Stages of Cultural and Ecological Evolution

Characteristic	Stage			
	Primitive	Frontier	Spaceship	Sustainable Earth
Human relationship to nature	Humans in nature, but controlled by nature	Humans vs. nature: increased control over nature	Humans vs. nature: attempt at complete control	Humans and nature: very selective control with large portions of the earth in their natural state
Goals	Individual survival	Individual survival; high quality of life for self	Individual survival; high quality of life for everyone	Individual survival; high quality of life for everyone; survival of all living species in their natural habitats; preserving the integrity, stability, and diversity of the ecosphere
Method of reaching goals	Try to get enough food, clothes, and shelter to stay alive	Produce, use, and acquire as much as possible	Complete technological and social control of nature and people to avoid exceeding the limits of the earth	Selective control based on ecological understanding, diversity, cooperation, and caring to avoid exceeding the limits of the earth
Social units	Individual; tribe	Family; community; corporation; nation	Family; community; earth	Family; community; earth
Reward	Staying alive	Profit; efficiency; power	Survival; comfort; power	Survival; joy; purpose to life; working with nature
Population	Human reproduction to survive	Human reproduction determined by economic and social factors	Human reproduction controlled by the state	Human reproduction controlled by a combination of voluntary action, education, and mutually agreed upon laws
Environmental quality	Not always a meaningful idea	A free good to be used and abused at will	A basic concept of critical value	A basic concept of critical value
Sharing wealth and resources	Not always a meaningful idea	A poor idea; acquire as much as possible	Crucial for survival	Crucial for survival

technological level. This option is available to only a few in an overcrowded world that has lost its technological and social virginity.

But this does not mean we can't make our life-styles more harmonious with natural cycles and adopt a philosophy of enoughness. Important examples of low consumption, appropriate technology, and ecologically sane alternatives to economic growth at any cost can be seen in the myriad of fragile but crucial experiments now being carried out in America, western Europe, and some less developed nations. These activities include rural and urban communes, extended families, experiments in organic farming and appropriate technology, alternative nonprofit cooperative marketing groups, countermedia (such as *Mother Earth News, CoEvolution Quarterly*, the *Whole Earth Catalog, Organic Gardening*, and the *Journal of the New Alchemists*), voluntary simplicity (doing more with less), individuals and groups attempting to become more self-reliant, do-it-yourself neighborhood urban renewal, the global ecology and feminist movements, and free schools and clinics. From such attempts to break out of the conventional urban-industrial-high-technology trap will come diverse and meaningful alternatives. As in any transition period, many of these experiments will fail. But by searching for new meaning, a few experiments—like blades of grass sprouting up through cracks in asphalt—will survive to show others the way.

There is increasing evidence that we have only about 50 years—or one generation—to rid ourselves of our present high-waste, high-entropy world view and adopt and live by a low-waste, low-entropy world view. We don't really have any choice in this matter. We will either make this crucial transition by voluntarily reducing the rate at which we use matter and energy resources and produce environmental disorder or entropy (Figure 3-3), or the laws of matter and energy use (Chapter 3) operating through nature will do it for us in a harsh manner. The automatic backlash from stretching nature to its entropy limits could result in a massive dieback of humans—along with the extinction of many other living species. The more matter and energy resources a person, city, industry, or nation uses the more vulnerable it is to nature's backlash. Thus, the first people to succumb will probably be those in a high-energy, high-matter use society who don't know how to adjust quickly to a sudden drop in available matter and energy resources. People in less developed societies will have a better chance of survival because they have been forced to learn how to survive by using less energy and matter.

Some have criticized such a world view as being unnecessarily gloomy. Real gloom, however, consists in living in a dream world state as if the laws that govern the use of matter and energy could be violated. A world view and life-style based on the laws of matter and energy are the best way to avoid catastrophe in the difficult, but potentially exciting, years ahead. These laws show us that the way to survive in the new low-waste, low-entropy era—which we must enter—is to begin unhooking ourselves from dependence on large, centralized systems for our air, water, energy, or food. If possible, work for yourself or for a small, locally owned business where you live (the big, centralized, energy-intensive national and multinational corporations will probably be the first to collapse during a crisis). Learn to use organic gardening techniques to grow some of your own food in a small garden plot, solar greenhouse, or in window boxes. Invest some of your earnings into buying a year's supply of dehydrated food as a source of food during a crisis and/or as a way to beat inflation from rising food prices if a crisis doesn't occur (a win-win situation). Store water or, if possible, have your own well (with a standby hand-operated pump). Accumulate the tools and other items you would really need to survive on your own, instead of putting your limited funds into things that are merely wants. Get as much of your energy as possible from sources such as the sun, wind, water, or biomass (wood and crop wastes). Having your own sources of food, water, and energy will save you money in a world where the price of almost everything is rising and will give you a sense of self-reliance and security in an increasingly insecure world.

Sustainable Earth Tools

Thermodynamics: What we can't do with matter and energy resources in a finite world.
Cybernetics: What we can do in complex systems.
Politics: How to bring about or slow down change.
Economics: Systems of rewards for bringing about or inhibiting change.
Ethics: What we should do.

20-3 Sustainable Earth Ethics: Science, Economics, and Politics Are Not Enough

Sustainable Earth Tools Two major themes of this book have been the first and second laws of energy or thermodynamics (Chapter 3) and cybernetics (Section 6-2). The laws of thermodynamics tell us what we can't do in our closed, finite system, and cybernetics helps us understand some of the things we can do in complex, multivariable systems. Thermodynamics and cybernetics, we now see, become our first two tools for achieving a sustainable earth society (see the box on sustainable earth tools). Politics (Chapter 19), economics (Chapter 18), and ethics are additional tools for attaining such a society. Politics can help us bring about or slow down change, and economics can provide a system of rewards for encouraging or stifling change. We can and must develop sustainable earth politics (Section 19-4) and economics (Section 18-2), but once developed, how should they be used? Like science and technology, sustainable earth politics and economics can be used for good or evil—to enrich or to impoverish, to protect or to destroy, to free or to enslave. None of these important tools can tell us what we *should* do. We can move to a sustainable earth society only through a creative, synergistic interaction among thermodynamics, cybernetics, politics, economics, and ethics.

Ecological concern will be short-lived and ecological action crippled unless we deal with the attitudes and values that have led to environmental deterioration. The ecological crisis is a result of our attitudes toward nature, toward technology, and toward one another. Directly and indirectly, we continue environmentally destructive habits and behavior because of the way we view the world. Unless we unpack, reshape, and in many cases replace our cultural and psychological luggage, we will continue our self-defeating attempts to treat symptoms rather than adopting a new world view and a life-style that move us to cure the diseases of civilization. As the late E. F. Schumacher said, "Environmental deterioration does not stem from science or technology, or from a lack of information, trained people, or money for research. It stems from the lifestyle of the modern world, which in turn arises from its basic beliefs or its religion."

Attitudes Toward Nature The American attitude (and presumably that of most industrialized nations) toward nature can be expressed as eight basic beliefs:

1. Humans are the source of all value.

2. Nature exists only for our use.

3. Our primary purpose is to produce and consume. Success is based on material wealth.

4. Production and consumption must rise endlessly because we have a right to an ever increasing material level of living.

5. Matter and energy resources are unlimited.

6. We need not adapt ourselves to the natural environment since we can remake it to suit our own needs by means of science and technology.

7. A major function of the state is to help individuals and corporations exploit the environment to increase wealth and power. The most important nation-state is the one that can command and use the largest fraction of the world's resources.

8. The ideal person is the self-made individualist who does his or her own thing and hurts no one.

Although most of us probably would not accept all of these statements, we act individually, corporately, and governmentally as if we did—and this is what counts.

How did we get such attitudes toward nature? Historian Lynn White, Jr., among others, traces the Western ecological crisis to the Judeo-Christian concept that we should be "fruitful and multiply, fill the earth and subdue it, and have dominion over the fish of the sea and over the birds of the air and over every living thing" (Gen. 1:28).

Theologians and other scholars have been quick to point out that this theory treats the Judeo-Christian tradition as a monolithic structure instead of a rich diversity of beliefs operating in many different ways in the history of Western civilization. The Judeo-Christian tradition (or its misinterpretation) is merely one of the factors that have led to our present crisis of humans versus nature. The creation story and other portions of the Bible speak not only of dominion but also of responsibility, respect, and stewardship for nature.* In addition, the phrase "have dominion" can be construed to mean loving care, not greedy exploitation. The problem may not be in Christianity—or any religion—but in the failure of humans to practice Christianity or any religion.

White's thesis can also be contested on other grounds. Misuse and destructive exploitation of the land through overgrazing, soil erosion, and excessive deforestation have also occurred in non-Western, non-Judeo-Christian cultures. Instead of debating what is to blame for destructive attitudes toward nature, we should focus on how we can make them constructive.

Approaches to Sustainable Earth Ethics How can we change our attitude and thus our actions toward nature? There are three basic approaches: *ecological, humanistic,* and *theological.* Although the three overlap and essentially share the same goals, they differ in emphasis and in motivating force.

The *ecological* approach recognizes an immense web of life in which all our past, present, and future actions have effects, some of which are unpredictable. We can never do only one thing in nature; we can never fully understand the workings of nature; and we can never completely do our own thing without some effect now or in the future on other living species. This world view of interdependence, diversity, finiteness, and vulnerability should serve as a model for our actions in the world. In the words of Robert Cahn, "The main ingredients of an environmental ethic are caring about the planet and all of its inhabitants, allowing unselfishness to control the immediate self-interest that harms others, and living each day so as to leave the lightest possible footprints on the planet." We can use Aldo Leopold's guideline for putting such an ethic into practice: "A thing is right when it tends to preserve the integrity, stability, and beauty of the biotic community. It is wrong when it tends otherwise."

Arthur Purcell has put it another way: "A conservation ethic means simply a desire to get the most out of

---

*Gen. 2:15; Lev. 25:2–5; Deut. 8:17, 20:19–20, 22:6; Job 38; Pss. 8, 24:1–6, 29, 65:11–13, 67:6–7, 84:3, 104, 147, 148; Isa. 24:4–6, 35:1–2, 6–7, 55:9–13; Jer. 4:23–26; Hos. 4:1–3; Mal. 3:11–12; Matt. 6:12, 22–39; Luke 12:16–21, 16:1–2; Rev. 8:7–13.

what people use, and a recognition that the wasteful use of precious resources is harmful and detrimental to the quality of everyone's life. In a low-waste society, products will be manufactured in the most efficient ways possible, using the least amount of energy and materials, and relying heavily on low-pollution renewable energy sources such as the sun, the wind, and water. Consumers will expect products to be recyclable, durable, reusable, multiusable, standardized, and simple." For a further discussion of ecological ethics see William Ophul's Guest Editorial at the end of this chapter.

The *humanistic* theme is similar, emphasizing the ultimate responsibility we have for other humans on this planet. Because the welfare of our fellow passengers on this voyage of life is intimately tied to the proper functioning of the earth's life-support systems, human concern also demands a concern for nature.

The *theological* approach entails several different emphases. Ecological ethics must be based not only on the human-centered view that we endanger ourselves when we endanger the ecosphere but also on our obligation toward all life. This theme of a reverence for life was also developed earlier by Albert Schweitzer, the eminent theologian Paul Tillich, Paul Santmire, and ecologists Maston Bates and Aldo Leopold. Others disagree strongly and see our obligation to be toward God and humanity and not toward *all* life. René Dubos, Harold Schilling, and theologian Gabriel Fackré suggest that we adopt a stewardship ethic, in which we use, guide, cultivate, and cooperate with nature in a wise, creative, and respectful manner.

Theologians such as Harvey Cox and Dietrich Bonhoeffer have attacked the separation of the secular from the sacred. Instead of waiting for life after death, Christians must express their concern for others by responsible involvement in the world. But such involvement requires that we protect and maintain the integrity of the ecosphere, which sustains us all.

Some have suggested that the answer lies not in Western but in Eastern religions, which see humans *in* nature. For example, Taoism and Zen Buddhism include the idea of the harmony and unity of humans with nature, and Buddhism fosters reverence for all living creatures and an appreciation of the beauty of nature. But non-Western civilizations have also ruined the land through overgrazing, soil erosion, and excessive deforestation. It is not the religion that is to blame, but the failure of humans to put the religion into practice.

Which path is best? Will ecology, humanism, Western religion, or Eastern religion provide us with the direction that will help us cherish and preserve life? There seems to be no one way for all humans. History shows us men and women who have acted with ultimate concern for nature and human life by following each of these diverse teachings. As an unknown theologian once asked, "How dare we mere mortals restrict God or any religion to only one path?"

Shallow Environmentalism and Deep Ecology In 1973, the Norwegian ecophilosopher Arne Naess pointed out two different approaches to attempting to solve environmental problems, which he called "shallow environmentalism" and "deep ecology." *Shallow environmentalism* (also called *reformist environmentalism*) corresponds roughly to the spaceship earth world view discussed in Section 20-2. Its goal is to use technology, economics, and conventional politics to control population growth, pollution, and resource depletion. This is to be done without seriously questioning the economic, political, social, and ethical foundations of modern industrial society.

By contrast, *deep ecology* (also called *revolutionary ecology*) is based on (1) preserving the stability, integrity, and diversity of the ecosphere; (2) recognizing humans as plain citizens—not rulers—of nature; (3) recognizing the right of all species to live and blossom without interference or control by humans; (4) not wasting the earth's resources; and (5) controlling excessive pollution and ecosystem disruption. In other words, deep ecology corresponds roughly to the sustainable earth world view discussed above.

Some proponents of the deep ecology world view have sharply attacked those holding the shallow environmentalist world view. Such attacks, however, do not recognize that these latter people are responsible for most of the environmental reforms that have taken place since 1965. The shallow environmentalist world view also buys us time to make more sweeping changes in attitudes and actions and can lead its followers to the deep ecology world view, which calls for a total rethinking of the beliefs underlying modern industrial society. What we need is a combination of the ethical principles of the latter view and some of the successful tactics of the former.

Sustainable Earth Ethics The sustainable earth world view is based on replacing the eight attitudes toward nature that were listed earlier with the following ethical guidelines:

1. Humans are not the source of all value.

2. Nature does not exist primarily for human use but for all living species.

3. Our primary purpose is not to produce and consume but to help conserve and renew the earth's resources—replenish, not ravage, the earth.

4. Improving life quality, not ever increasing production and consumption of material things, must be our primary goal.

5. Earth resources are finite and must be cherished and renewed, not wasted.

6. Our relationship to nature must be that of humans *and* nature, a partnership with all living species based on ecological understanding and cooperation.

7. We must preserve ecological stability and integrity by preserving and encouraging physical, biological, and cultural diversity.

8. A major function of the state is to supervise long-range planning, to prevent individuals and corporations from exploiting or damaging the environment, and to preserve human freedom and dignity.

9. The ideal human goal is sharing and caring, not complete individualism and domination.

10. Each human being on this planet is unique and has a right to a basic share of the ecosphere's resources.

11. No individual, corporation, or nation has a right to an ever increasing share of the earth's finite resources.

If you study or follow humanism or any of the world's great religions, you will find nothing particularly new about this set of values. But we have now reached the point where we must face up to living, not just talking about, this new sustainable earth approach to life. The ecological crisis is forcing us to face the ultimate questions of life's meaning. Who are we? Where are we going? What should we do?

20-4 What We Must Do: A Sustainable Earth Program

We need a major long-range program for converting our present frontier rules to sustainable earth rules over the next 50 years, as outlined in the box at right. It will require a massive, organized effort of the world's best minds from all fields to set our priorities, to establish the

---

A Sustainable Earth Program

1. Bring about a value revolution—a caring and sharing explosion.

2. Identify the major causes of our ecological crisis.

3. Set up a worldwide ecological monitoring and early warning system. The Earthwatch monitoring system that resulted from the 1972 UN Conference on the Human Environment in Stockholm and the outstanding contributions of Lester Brown's Worldwatch Society (see Appendix) are excellent beginnings.

4. Begin to formulate the rules for living in a sustainable earth, dynamic, steady state world.

5. Identify short-range problems and take temporary actions to buy the necessary time.

6. Develop and begin putting into effect careful plans for the long-range transition to sustainable earth rules over the next 50 years. Each proposal should be evaluated for scientific, political, administrative, and economic feasibility, for ethical acceptability, and for effectiveness.

7. Move progressively as needed from voluntary methods to incentives to legal restrictions, also employing a massive awareness and persuasion program. The success of each phase should be monitored to determine when we must move to the next level in order to prevent catastrophe or deterioration of the environment and life quality.

---

rules for living on a finite planet, to produce social innovations along with technological innovations, and to find the short-term actions that will give us enough time to make fundamental changes in our global economic, political, technological, and ethical systems and institutions. Of course, enormous amounts of money will be necessary, but ecological awareness, conscience, and cooperative action by individual citizens will be even more essential. As shown in Figure 20-1, the driving force or imperative for implementing a sustainable earth

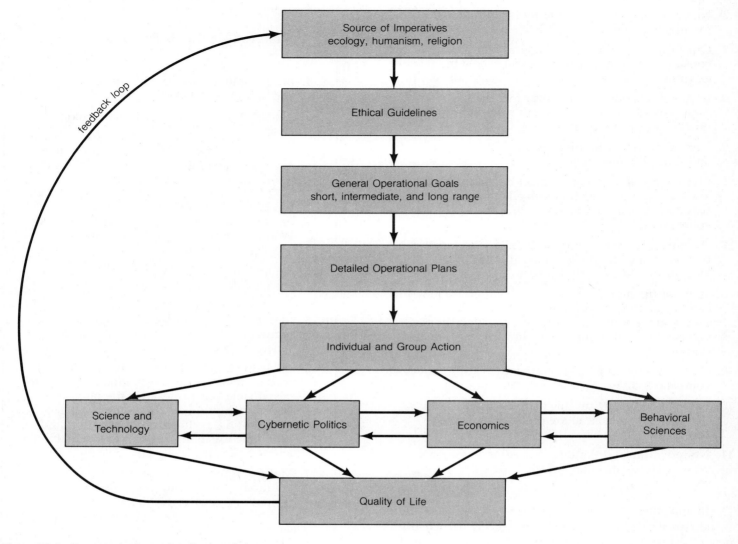

Figure 20-1 The organization and realization of change.

society is a world view based on ecology, humanism, or one of the world's religions.

Major Causes of the Environmental Crisis Many of the causes of the environmental crisis have already been identified:

1. *Overpopulation:* relative to food (in less developed countries) and relative to resource consumption and pollution (in more developed countries)

2. *Population distribution:* the population "implosion," or urban crisis

3. *Overconsumption and wasteful patterns of consumption:* the throwaway society; planned obsolescence; production of unnecessary and harmful items; consumption of more than one's fair share of resources; little recycling and reuse of essential matter resources; emphasis on acquisition of goods not essential for a life of dignity and quality

4. *Unwise use of technology:* failure to consider the impact of our activities on the environment; ignorance of the implications of the second law of thermodynamics; disregard for the ecological effects of technological innovations; blind faith in technology; overemphasis on big technology rather than appropriate technology

5. *Crisis in management:* failure of our political and economic systems; growth at any cost; a lack of long-range planning; misplaced priorities; refusal to establish sustainable earth priorities and leaders; frontier rather than sustainable earth politics and economics

6. *Simplification of ecosystems:* failure to conserve ecological diversity and species diversity; extinction of species; failure to recognize that everything is connected; cultural homogenization

7. *Me-first behavior:* tragedy of the commons; lack of responsibility for the world's present human population, for future generations, for other living species, and for the condition of the ecosphere; concentration only on the present; fatalism; technological optimism; the enemy-is-the-other-person mentality

All of these causes are connected in a complex, synergistic manner (Figure 1-5) that is not understood. All of these causes (and any others we will discover) must be dealt with in both short-range and long-range approaches and as a set of interlocking problems. Focusing almost exclusively on the symptoms of pollution, as we are now doing, at best buys a little time. If we go no further, even more serious and perhaps fatal future crises are assured (Enrichment Study 1). Fortunately, in a complex cybernetic system it is often easier to solve a large number of interlocking problems simultaneously than to solve a single problem by itself (see Enrichment Study 1).

Much more research remains to be done. How are the major causes interrelated (Figure 1-5)? How should each factor be weighted to incorporate present and future impacts and the time required for change?

Operational Plans We are in trouble, so what must we do? We must translate our general sustainable earth ethical guidelines into the following operational goals:

1. Stabilize and eventually lower world population by sharply decreasing the birth rate.

2. Decrease the flow of people from rural areas to urban areas. Defuse the population implosion.

3. Reduce consumption rates and the waste of matter and energy resources, and emphasize recycling and reuse of matter resources and improved energy efficiency.

4. Develop a responsive cybernetic governmental system based on global loyalty (Sections 19-5 and 19-6) and a sustainable earth economy (Section 18-2).

5. Bring about a sharing explosion: Redistribute the earth's resources and wealth more fairly.

6. Seek peace by disarmament, not armament. (The arms race is eventually a lose-lose game that threatens nuclear or ecological catastrophe by draining off and wasting material and human resources.)

7. Preserve ecological and cultural diversity by living in harmony with nature instead of trying to conquer it.

8. Bring about a caring explosion—learn to care about the earth and our fellow passengers, those here now as well as those to come.

No one, of course, knows how to translate these goals into detailed short-, intermediate-, and long-term plans, but this does not mean that we should not try. We must start somewhere. Tentative proposals by sustainable earth citizens and leaders must be drawn up so that they can be analyzed, debated, changed, and put into action before the momentum of events dangerously narrows our choices. Throughout this book I have presented basic principles and specific suggestions for solving what I see as the major global problems. These are offered not as final answers but as an effort to stimulate debate and prod others to come up with better proposals.

All of these or any other plans that can help solve our problems must be fed into our eco-socio-politico-cybernetic system of change (Figure 20-2).

20-5 What Can You Do?

Finally, it all comes down to what you and I are willing to do as individuals and in groups. Begin with yourself.

1. *You can evaluate the way you think the world works and sensitize yourself to the environment.* Stand up, look around, compare what is with what could and should be. Examine your room, your home, your school, your place of work, your street, and your city, state, nation, and world. What things around you really improve the quality of your life? What are your own environmental bad habits? What is your own world view? Are the assumptions upon which it is based a valid view of the real world?

2. *You can become ecologically informed.* Give up your frontier, or linear, thinking and immerse yourself in sustainable earth thinking. Don't fall into the "all growth is good" and "technology will save us" traps. Specialize in one particular area of the

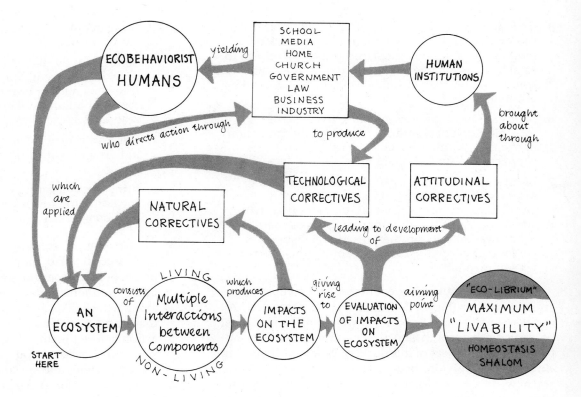

Figure 20-2 The how-to-make-it-to-year-2000-A.D. diagram. (Used by permission from John A. Ray, professor of physics, Linfield College, McMinnville, Oregon)

ECOBEHAVIORIST HUMANS

yielding

SCHOOL MEDIA HOME CHURCH GOVERNMENT LAW BUSINESS INDUSTRY

HUMAN INSTITUTIONS

brought about through

who directs action through

to produce

which are applied

TECHNOLOGICAL CORRECTIVES

ATTITUDINAL CORRECTIVES

NATURAL CORRECTIVES

leading to development of

LIVING

consists of

AN ECOSYSTEM

START HERE

Multiple Interactions between Components

NON-LIVING

which produces

IMPACTS ON THE ECOSYSTEM

giving rise to

EVALUATION OF IMPACTS ON ECOSYSTEM

aiming point

"ECO-LIBRIUM" MAXIMUM "LIVABILITY" HOMEOSTASIS SHALOM

ecological crisis and pool your specialized knowledge with others. Everyone doesn't need to be an ecologist, but you do need to "ecologize" your particular profession or job.

3. *You can choose a simpler life-style by reducing your energy and matter consumption and waste and entropy (pollution) production.* Go on an energy, matter, and entropy diet. For every high-energy use, high-waste, or high-entropy-producing thing you do (having a child, buying a car, living or working in an air conditioned building), give up a number of other things. Where possible, use low or intermediate technology instead of high-level technology. Such a life-style will be cheaper, and it may add more joy as you learn how to break through the plastic, technological membrane that separates many of us from nature and from one another.

4. *You can remember that environment begins at home.* Before you start converting others, begin by changing your own living patterns. Move closer to work, ride a bicycle to the shopping center or to work, refuse to buy beer and soft drinks in throwaway cans and bottles. If you become an ecological activist, be prepared for everyone to be looking for and pointing out your own ecological sins.

5. *You can avoid the four do-nothing traps of technological optimism, gloom-and-doom pessimism, fatalism,* and *extrapolation to infinity* ("If I can't change the entire world quickly, then I won't even try to change any of it"). While most people are talking about the difficulties of changing the system, others (such as Rachel Carson, Ralph Nader, and Martin Luther King, Jr.) have gone ahead and changed it.

6. *You can become politically involved on local and national levels.* Start or join a local environmental group, and also join national organizations (see the list in the Appendix). Become the ecosphere citizen of your block or school. Use positive synergy to amplify your efforts. The environment would improve noticeably if each of us made an annual donation to one or more politically active environmental organizations. In this way you are hiring professional lobbyists, lawyers, and experts to work for you. Better yet, volunteer your services to such organizations. Work to elect sustainable earth leaders and to influence officials once they are elected (Enrichment Study 17).

7. *You can do the little things.* Individual acts of consumption, litter, and so on have contributed to the mess. When you are tempted to say "This little bit won't hurt," multiply it by millions of others saying the same thing. Picking up a single beer

can, not turning on a light, joining a carpool, writing on both sides of a piece of paper, and not buying a grocery product with more packages inside of the outer package are all very significant acts. Each small act reminds us of ecological thinking and leads to other ecologically sound practices. Start now with a small, concrete, personal act, and then add more such acts. Little acts can be used to expand our awareness of the need for fundamental changes in our political, economic, and social systems over the next few decades. These acts also help us avoid psychological numbness when we realize the magnitude of the job to be done.

8. *You can work on the big polluters and big problems, primarily through political action.* Individual actions help reduce pollution, give us a sense of involvement, and help us develop a badly needed ecological consciousness. Our awareness must then expand to recognize that large-scale pollution and environmental disruption are caused by industries, municipalities, and big agriculture. Picking up a beer can is significant, but it does not mean we can allow uncontrolled strip mining of coal in South Dakota.

9. *You can start a counter J curve of awareness and action.* The world is changed by changing the two people next to you. For everything, big or little, that you decide to do, make it your primary goal to convince two others to do the same thing and

persuade them in turn to convince two others. Carrying out this doubling process only 28 times would convince everyone in the United States. After 32 doublings everyone in the world would be convinced.

10. *Don't make people feel guilty.* If a couple has several children or if neighbors are overconsuming, don't make them feel bad. Instead, find the things that each individual is willing to do to help the environment. There is plenty to do and no one can do everything. Use positive rather than negative reinforcement (win-win rather than win-lose games). We need to nurture, reassure, and understand rather than threaten one another.

Begin at the individual level and work outward. Join with others and amplify your actions. This is the way the world is changed. Envision the world as made up of all kinds of cycles and flows in an incredibly beautiful and diverse web of interrelationships and a kaleidoscope of patterns and rhythms whose very complexity and multitude of potentials remind us that cooperation, honesty, humility, and love must be the guidelines for our behavior toward one another and the earth.

Indifference is the essence of inhumanity.
George Bernard Shaw

Guest Editorial: The Challenge of Achieving a Sustainable Earth Society

Richard A. Falk

Richard A. Falk is Albert E. Milbank Professor of International Law and Practice at Princeton University. He is

a senior fellow of the Institute of World Order and has served as director of American participation in the World Order Models Project since its start in 1968. He has written hundreds of articles and a number of important books emphasizing the need for world order and describing how we can make the transition to a world order society. He is an example of an outstanding sustainable earth thinker and leader.

Barely noticed by Americans as yet, a remarkable development has occurred in the late 1970s and early 1980s. Throughout western Europe, Japan, and to a lesser extent North America, a militant struggle against reliance on nuclear energy has taken shape. This international opposition to nuclear power is virtually without precedent. The movement is growing in numbers and intensity. In West Germany, where as many as 15 million are actively associated with antinuclear citizens' groups, demonstrations have involved hundreds of thousands, caused large-scale combat with the police, and led to a virtual moratorium on the construction of new nuclear reactors. Two hundred thousand people took part in an antinuclear protest in Bilbao, Spain, during July 1977; weeks later in France, a demonstrator was killed in a clash with the police. The nuclear controversy is the first battleground on which the potency of sustainable earth as a challenge to the prevailing order has been revealed.

Of course, there are many strong beliefs on both sides of the nuclear debate. A social movement reveals its character by the outlook of its most committed adherents. In essence, I believe the struggle over nuclear power pits the forces of system maintenance against the forces of system change. Advocates of nuclear power believe, by and large, that if this technological energy solution can take place without disruption, the stability and prosperity of industrial civilization can be sustained and gradually spread to the rest of the world. Opponents, while skeptical of these claims, rest their case mainly on the convictions that nuclear power is too sinister a technology to entrust to human institutions, that its deployment threatens the sanctity of life and prospects for humane governance, and that more benign energy alternatives exist.

In the wider setting of global policy, the nuclear issue is a microcosm of contending world views on the most momentous challenge that has ever confronted the human species: learning to cope with the emergent realities of an *inevitable* social, economic, political, cultural, and ecological order of *planetary scale*. Institutions don't learn, only people learn. Individuals, especially those whose attitudes are not shaped by the roles they play in the existing system, can learn to reshape their expectations and behavior—although it is difficult. Often young people and artists play critical roles in cultural innovation, which is why these groups are so quickly perceived as threatening to guardians of the established order.

Throughout the world this process of challenge to existing structures and resistance to demands for change is taking place. Only in the Western world do we associate the impulse to achieve a sustainable earth society with the antinuclear movement. Throughout Asia, Africa, and Latin America the impulse is associated with the struggle to create independent and fair national societies that are able to meet the basic needs of their people. In the Third World trying to achieve a sustainable earth society means primarily struggling to establish social, economic, and political arrangements that allow the mass of a population to live free from misery and repression. It is not surprising that this struggle engenders powerful resistance from entrenched leaders eager to retain privileged positions of wealth and power. The realities of population growth make it seem impossible to keep the privileged sectors of society satisfied while binding the wounds of the poor. We witness, then, a strong tendency for moderate government to collapse and be replaced by authoritarianism of some form, whether it appeals to the left or right. The global rise of authoritarian government has an ominous bearing on the hopes for a new orientation toward reality—what we are calling a sustainable earth society.

In America and some other democracies, a series of discoveries are being made about the conditions for human development in our time. Such discoveries begin with individuals and communities. These include organic farming and eating, equality in social and economic relations, and planetary citizenship. The lure of voluntary simplicity emerges to displace the lure of affluence; global humanism supersedes traditional patriotism; decentralized images of organization with the emergence of appropriate technologies seize hold of the imagination.

Somewhere in this process belongs a utopian vision to guide the transition to a sustainable earth society. And utopias are born in creative, questing minds. Ursula Le Guin's fine book *The Dispossessed* exhibits the impulse to achieve such a cultural revolution. It also resists the temptation to depict a new Eden as an easy solution not beset by contradictions of its own; she has set forth, in her words, "an ambiguous utopia." Others are beginning to design just world order systems for the future. Rearrangements of power and wealth are taking shape that embody what must be done to provide self-sustaining development paths for the poor of the world and for humanity as a whole. An undertaking such as the World Order Models Project has this as its central ambition, linking scholars on major political systems and on cultures of the world in a continuing search for new political forms to make human governance, and hence a sustainable earth society, possible.

As in any period of transition, the evidence points in both directions. Virtually everywhere state power is growing and assuming more control over lives and destiny. At the same time even political leaders speaking from the pinnacles of state power are beginning to acknowledge that fundamental changes are necessary, although their roles discourage any appropriate actions. In fact, promises of a new world order, of human rights, of satisfaction of basic needs for everyone, and of nonmaterialist priorities are being made to the peoples of the world while the old order perfects neutron bombs and finds more fiendish means to torture its opponents. The mystification and hypocrisy of this gap between promise and performance are beginning to cast doubts in many minds as to whether it is any longer possible to leave the future in the hands of government. An impulse to act grows stronger as the case for change becomes more imperative. The challenge of developing a sustainable earth society is an invitation to join in the struggle to transform the values and institutions of this world so as to make us feel positive and joyful about the future of the planet and about our own gifted, tormented species.

1. What major global issues represent an attempt to come to grips with the concept of achieving a sustainable earth society?

2. Compare the approaches to achieving a sustainable earth society in more developed and less developed nations.

3. Do you agree that it may no longer be possible to leave the future in the hands of government? What are the alternatives?

Guest Editorial: The Politics of the Ecological Future

William Ophuls

William Ophuls is a writer and lecturer whose work on the politics of ecological transformation draws on an unusually broad and varied background—as an officer in the merchant marine and the U.S. Coast Guard; as a U.S. foreign service officer stationed in Washington, West Africa, and Japan; and as a political scientist teaching at Yale and Northwestern. In addition to numerous articles, he is the author of Ecology and the Politics of Scarcity: Prologue to a Political Theory of the Steady State *(1977, San Francisco: W. H. Freeman & Co.) which received awards from the American Political Science Association and the International Studies Association.*

The social and political implications of ecology are radical. We stand on the threshold of an ecological transformation of human culture that will bring epochal changes in every sphere of life. Life in the age of ecology now dawning will be as different from our own as the latter has been from the life of our medieval ancestors. However, in a curious fashion, our ecological future may closely resemble our past in many important respects—because both eras, unlike our own, have scarcity as their organizing principle.

The age of affluence has shaped all the institutions and beliefs of the modern world. Once humankind left behind the original affluent society of the hunter-gatherer for an agricultural existence (Chapter 2), the resulting scarcity of matter and energy that is a necessary consequence of such development created societies that, however admirable, were closed, hierarchical, and predominantly concerned with spiritual matters. When a combination of peculiar and unique factors—such as the "discovery" and greedy exploitation of the wealth found in the New World—suddenly lifted the burden of ecological scarcity from Europe, the political, social and economic structures of these countries were transformed or "modernized": They became comparatively open, egalitarian, and primarily concerned with material things.

The problem is that the whole process of economic development as we know it strongly resembles a chain letter: The first people to get in on the scheme get rich, but the latecomers (either classes within the nation or whole nations) do not do nearly so well, and the game can only go on for so long before exhausting its finite resources. We have now reached this point. What one historian has called "the 400-year boom" is about to collapse, returning us to the usual historical state of scarcity. The inevitable consequence is that all our values, practices, and institutions, which were created and nurtured in affluence, must now adapt.

We have certainly learned a thing or two during the abnormal age of affluence. This knowledge will stand us in good stead in coping with the reemergence of scarcity, and we need not simply revert to premodern existence with all its evils (although a combination of ecological heedlessness and nuclear warfare could well bring about such an undesirable outcome). In fact, we possess enough material wealth and technical understanding to create a semiutopian civilization, *but we shall have to change our values, practices, and institutions to take into account current ecological realities.*

The new political ethos can be summed up in two words—frugality and fraternity. Frugality means making a little go a long way. Fraternity means making this a cooperative instead of competitive venture. Nothing less than these actions will do: We must scale down our demands on the environment, yet we must at the same time ensure that the shrinking of the resource pie does not simply cause increased conflict or oppression, as the few try to force the many to maintain them in the style to which they have become accustomed.

Implicit in these new values are two ideas. First, selfish *individualism* has to go, for it is totally antithetical to both frugality and fraternity. But the *individual* need not be and must not be abandoned. Whatever the excesses of individualism, we surely have no wish to return to a state in which all but a tiny handful of people at the top of the social pyramid are considered worthless. Our task is therefore to find social structures for our future that continue to permit individuals to seek fulfillment but in ways that do not harm the community directly or indirectly. To borrow a word from the psychologist Carl Jung, we must find a way to transform individualism into *individuation*.

Second, and closely related to the above, we shall have to rediscover the ancient truth that the real purpose, meaning, and joy of life are not found in the things of this world, but rather in the limitless realm of the spirit. It is so simple: Since the artistic or intellectual frontier is endless, all we need to create a civilization more advanced than our own is a small amount of material well-being, not endless growth in the material realm; and since spiritual and cultural goods can be fully shared—indeed, only have real meaning when shared—we can participate in their creation and enjoyment fraternally in ways that simultaneously enhance our own self-development and the welfare of the community.

Utopia, of course, cannot be realized here on earth. But even if we must abandon certain gross forms of material progress, that does not mean that progress itself must end. To the contrary, we can turn the ecological crisis into a grand opportunity to build a better world than any that humankind has known thus far. Whether this happens is up to us.

Guest Editorial Discussion

1. What are some of the advantages and disadvantages of living in the age of scarcity that we are entering?

2. What things have we learned that might help us cope with the reemergence of scarcity?

3. How should we redefine progress in a sustainable earth society?

Discussion Topics

1. Do you believe that prophecies of ecological doom are useful? Why or why not? Cite examples.

2. Do you agree that "all effective action is fueled by hope"? Cite examples in your own life to support or deny this hypothesis.

3. As a class, list the rationalizations that we typically use to avoid thought, action, and responsibility.

4. Do you agree with the cartoon character Pogo that "we have met the enemy and he [or she] is us"? Why or why not? Criticize this statement from the viewpoint of the poor; from the viewpoint that large corporations and government are the really big polluters.

5. Distinguish carefully between the spaceship earth and sustainable earth world views.

6. Do you agree with the characteristics of the human cultural and ecological stages summarized in Table 20-1? Can you add other characteristics?

7. What are the useful results of the back-to-nature movement? What are its limitations?

8. Debate the following resolution: The Judeo-Christian tradition of Western civilization is the root of our ecological crisis.

9. Do you agree with the sustainable earth ethics listed in Section 20-3? Why or why not? Can you add others? Which ones do you try to follow?

10. Why is it so important to do the little things? Discuss this in terms of thermodynamics and cybernetics. Why are these actions not enough? As a class, make a list of all the little things you can do.

11. What products sold in a typical suburban shopping center are really essential for survival and for a meaningful life?

Readings

Barbour, Ian G., ed. 1973. *Western Man and Environmental Ethics*. Reading, Mass.: Addison-Wesley. Outstanding collection of essays.

Cahn, Robert. 1978. *Footprints on the Planet: A Search for an Environmental Ethic*. New York: Universe Books. One of the best books on environmental ethics and progress by a former member of the President's Council on Environmental Quality.

Cailiet, G., et al. 1971. *Everyman's Guide to Ecological Living*. New York: Macmillan. Superb summary of what you can do.

Caldwell, Lynton K., et al. 1976. *Citizens and the Environment: Case Studies of Popular Action*. Bloomington: Indiana

University Press. The best available summary of what citizens can do to improve the environment.

Callahan, Daniel. 1973. *The Tyranny of Survival.* New York: Macmillan. Magnificent analysis contrasting sustainable earth ethics and spaceship earth ethics.

Callenbach, Ernest. 1975. *Ecotopia.* Berkeley, Calif.: Banyan Tree Books. Stirring vision of what the world could be like in 1990 if we move to a sustainable earth society.

Devall, Bill. 1980. "Streams of Environmentalism." *Natural Resources Journal,* Spring, pp. 13–28. Excellent summary of deep ecology.

Elder, Frederick. 1970. *Crisis in Eden: A Religious Study of Man and Environment.* Nashville, Tenn.: Abingdon Press. Reply to Lynn White's charge that Christianity is the culprit. Calls for a theology of nature based on reverence for all life.

Elgin, Duane, and Arnold Mitchell. 1977. "Voluntary Simplicity (3)." *CoEvolution Quarterly,* Summer, pp. 4–27. Superb description of the trend toward sustainable earth life-styles.

Fackré, Gabriel. 1971. "Ecology and Theology." *Religion in Life,* vol. 40, 210–224. Superb overview.

Falk, Richard A. 1975. *A Study of Future Worlds.* New York: Free Press. Superb discussion of how to achieve a world order or sustainable earth society.

Fritsch, Albert J. 1980. *Environmental Ethics: Choices for Concerned Citizens.* New York: Anchor Books. Highly recommended.

Fritsch, Albert J., et al. 1977. *99 Ways to a Simple Lifestyle.* Bloomington: University of Indiana Press. Try to read this book and pass it on to others.

Fromm, Eric. 1968. *The Revolution of Hope: Toward a Humanized Technology.* New York: Harper & Row. Excellent analysis of hope, going beyond the typical superficial approach.

Gardner, John W. 1970. *The Recovery of Confidence.* New York: Norton. Hope as the driving force of human action.

Hardin, Garrett. 1977. *The Limits of Altruism: An Ecologist's View of Survival.* Bloomington: Indiana University Press. Superb and controversial discussion of environmental ethics.

Hayes, Denis. 1980. "The Unfinished Agenda." *Environment,* April, pp 6–13. Excellent overview of environmental progress since 1970 along with challenges for the 1980s.

Heilbroner, Robert L. 1974. *An Inquiry into the Human Prospect.* New York: Norton. Pessimistic view of our future.

Henderson, Hazel. 1978. *Creating Alternative Futures.* New York: Berkley. Excellent description of exciting experiments and trends that could lead to a sustainable earth society.

Johnson, Warren. 1978. *Muddling Toward Frugality.* San Francisco: Sierra Club Books. Very important and hopeful book showing how we might make it to a sustainable earth society.

Laszlo, Ervin. 1978. *Goals for Mankind.* Bergenfield, N.J.: New American Library. Highly recommended.

Livingston, John A. 1973. *One Cosmic Instant.* Boston: Houghton Mifflin. Superb and readable summary of human cultural evolution and relationship to nature.

Nicholson, Max. 1973. *The Big Change: After the Environmental Revolution.* New York: McGraw-Hill. Superb analysis of the major changes we must make within the next 50 years.

Odell, Rice. 1980. *Environmental Awakening: The New Revolution to Protect the Earth.* Cambridge, Mass.: Ballinger. Important book describing environmental progress since 1965.

Platt, John R. 1966. *The Step to Man.* New York: Wiley. Collection of essays by an ecosphere thinker.

Rifkin, Jeremy. 1980. *Entropy: A New World View.* New York: Viking. Very important book giving a nontechnical overview of the transition to a sustainable earth society based on the second law of energy.

Sessions, George. 1980. "Shallow and Deep Ecology: A Review of the Philosophical Literature." Paper prepared for Earthday X Colloquium at the University of Denver, Colorado. Available from the author, Department of Philosophy, Sierra College, Rocklin, Calif. 95677.

Soloman, Lawrence. 1978. *The Conserver Society.* Garden City, N.J.: Doubleday. Excellent discussion of a sustainable earth society.

Stivers, Robert L. 1976. *The Sustainable Society.* Philadelphia: Westminster. Excellent discussion of environmental ethics and a sustainable earth society.

Stokes, Bruce. 1981. *Helping Ourselves: Local Solutions to Global Problems.* New York: Norton. Superb examples.

Tiger, Lionel. 1979. *Optimism: The Biology of Hope.* New York: Simon & Schuster. Antidote for despair.

Valaskakis, Kimon, et al. 1979. *The Conserver Society: A Workable Alternative for the Future.* New York: Harper & Row. Very useful description of a sustainable earth society.

Watt, Kenneth E. F. 1974. *The Titanic Effect: Planning for the Unthinkable.* Stamford, Conn.: Sinauer. Superb overview of our problems and their possible solutions.

White, Lynn, Jr. 1967. "The Historical Roots of Our Ecologic Crisis." *Science,* vol. 155, 1203–1207. Important and controversial article with the thesis that the root cause of the ecological crisis lies in the Judeo-Christian tradition.

Worster, Donald. 1977. *Nature's Economy: The Roots of Ecology.* San Francisco: Sierra Club Books. Outstanding discussion of why we must work with—not against—nature.

Epilogue

This book is based on nine deceptively simple theses:

1. The ecological crisis is not only more complex than we think but more complex than we can ever think.

2. In Garrett Hardin's terms, the basic principle of ecology is "that everything and everyone are all interconnected." Truly accepting this and trying to learn how things and people are connected will require a basic change in our patterns of living. But because we can never completely know how everything is connected, we must function in the ecosphere with a sense of humility and creative cooperation rather than blind domination.

3. On a closed spaceship there are no consumers, only users of materials. We can never really throw anything away. This is a threat to a frontier society, but an opportunity for reuse, recycling, and conservation of matter resources in a sustainable earth society.

4. Because of the first law of thermodynamics we can't get anything for nothing, and because of the second law of thermodynamics almost every action we take has some undesirable impact on our environment, or life-support system. As a result, there can be no completely technological solution to pollution on a spaceship, although technology can help. If the number of passengers and their wasteful use of energy and materials continue to increase, the quality of life can only decline, eventually threatening survival for many human passengers and for nonhuman forms of life.

5. Because we have rounded the bend on the J curves of population, resource and energy use, and pollution, we could now seriously disrupt the earth's life-support systems.

6. The implication of these ideas is that each of us, and particularly those in the affluent middle and upper classes, must now give up certain things and patterns in our lives to prevent a continuing decrease in freedom and in the quality of life for all.

7. Our primary task must be to move from simplistic, linear thinking to circular, cybernetic thinking that is harmonious with the ecological cycles that sustain us; we must form a dynamic, diverse, adaptable, steady state, sustainable earth society that is in keeping with the fundamental rhythms of life.

8. Informed action based on hope rather than on pessimism, technological optimism, or apathy offers humankind its greatest opportunity to come closer to that elusive dream of peace, freedom, brotherhood, sisterhood, and justice for all.

9. It is not too late, if. . . . There is time—50 years—to deal with these complex problems if enough of us really care. It's not up to "them," but to "us." Don't wait.

Enrichment Studies

Enrichment Study 1

The Limits-to-Growth Debate: Projecting Alternative Futures

E1-1 Computer Modeling of Complex Systems

Simple Linear Models Individuals, businesses, and nations continually make plans based on what they think might or might not happen in the future. Certain assumptions are made and then used to project future events or trends. In other words, we use intuitive mental models to project alternative futures: "If such and such a trend continues for another x years, then so and so is likely to happen." It is very important to note that these are exploratory projections of what *might* happen—not predictions or forecasts of what *will* happen. If we use different sets of initial assumptions, we can get quite different results; there is no certainty that the assumptions we make and the model we use to process them are valid. For example, we might assume that if we save 10 percent of our earnings each year, we will have enough money to live on when we retire. However, if we assume that the rate of inflation grows at a faster rate than the interest on the money we set aside for retirement, then we will not have enough money to live on in later years. We also have to make assumptions about which trends will be the most important. For instance, if we assume that the inflation rate will not rise as fast as the investment interest rate, then we may end up with enough money to retire on after all.

Unfortunately, our minds can handle only a small number of variables and trends at one time. In addition, we are usually limited to very simple linear models based on extending (extrapolating) assumed trends as straight lines into the future. Linear extrapolation models can be useful for projecting alternative short-range futures, but they are rarely useful for projecting intermediate- and long-range futures. Even for the short term they are often useless or misleading; very sophisticated thinkers have gone wrong using linear extrapolation methods. In 1967 Herman Kahn and his associates at the Hudson Institute (a futuristic think tank) made projections for the world between 1967 and 2000. Their linear model failed to even mention the problems of population, pollution, and energy. Later projections mentioned these problems but declared them unimportant and easily solved, and they assumed that two trends, continuing economic growth and technological innovation, would be more important than all other trends. Such failures occur because most of the important world and national changes and problems result from a large number of variables and trends that interact in a complex and often nonlinear manner.

In complex systems the trend in one variable feeds back on another and can change the direction and intensity of one or both trends. The interaction of these two variables and trends can in turn affect another whole system of variables and trends. These can then feed back to affect the initial trends. It is very difficult to form a model and to understand such *multiple feedback loops* (Section 6-2, Figure 8-3).

The problem is complicated even further because of the *time delays* and *synergistic interactions* found in complex systems (Section 6-2). If you do something in a simple system (push a button), the response is usually immediate (the doorbell rings). In a complex system the result of an interaction of some variables and loops might not show up for decades. Further, two variables can interact synergistically so that the net result is greater than the sum of their individual effects. A combination of alcohol and sleeping pills (barbiturates) is much more dangerous than either drug acting alone.

Because of the multiple feedback loops, time lags, and synergistic interactions in our social and ecological systems, we have great difficulty in projecting useful future plans and in bringing about the changes we want. Using simple linear thinking, we devise a solution to a problem only to find that in the long run we have made matters worse, as shown in Table E1-1. We can write a formula to describe our attempts to change the world using intuitive linear thinking: STS = LTP (short-term

Table E1-1 Intuitive and Counterintuitive Solutions to Problems in Some Complex Systems

Problem	Intuitive Solution	Unexpected Result	Counterintuitive Solution
Bus or airplane company losing money	Raise fares	Number of passengers decreases, and the company loses more money than ever	Lower fares to attract new riders
City going bankrupt	Raise business and property taxes	Businesses and homeowners leave the city, reducing income from taxes and raising the city's deficit	Lower business and property taxes to hold existing businesses and residents and to attract new ones
People moving to the suburbs	Build freeways into the city so people can get to work	More people move to suburbs, freeways get crowded, taxes rise, businesses flee, jobs get scarcer, and poverty increases	Instead of freeways between suburbs and the city, build good city transportation systems; more people and businesses will stay, raising the tax base, providing more jobs, and combating poverty
Poor people living in slums	Clear slums and build high-rise, low-income housing	More poor people move in but can't get jobs or move again, so city has more poor people than before	Build low-density housing, improve cheap mass transportation within the city, and lower the tax rate so businesses will stay to provide more jobs for the poor
Poverty	Establish federal, state, and local government welfare agencies	More money is spent to run the agencies than is received by the poor	Allot to any person or family with an income below a certain level funds from the Internal Revenue Service to bring them up to the minimum level; the entire federal, state, and local welfare bureaucracy would be eliminated, and the welfare system would be administered through existing tax agencies based on annual income tax returns
Waste paper	Establish paper recycling campaign and centers	Scrap dealers are flooded so price drops; dealers finally stop buying scrap paper	Create a large demand for waste paper by having all government agencies buy at least 50% paper products made totally or partially from recycled paper
Supplies of oil and natural gas	Use government regulation to keep prices low for industries and consumers	Waste is encouraged, finite supplies are depleted more rapidly, prices eventually rise catastrophically but too late to maintain supply, and entire economy is disrupted	Deregulate prices and add energy tax so price rises will encourage conservation and help develop other energy sources; use income from energy taxes to develop new sources and to provide relief for the poor

solution equals long-term problem). To avoid this danger, we often have to develop a counterintuitive solution based on a better understanding of complex systems (Table E1-1).

Dynamic Computer Modeling A promising new method for making medium- and long-range future projections is the use of *system dynamics computer modeling*. As with any model, the key variables, trends, and weighting factors for each trend must first be assumed. In this case, however, there is an attempt to build into the model the interactions of key variables resulting from feedback loops, time delays, synergy, and other properties of complex systems. Such a model consists of a set of mathematical equations that attempt to simulate the multiple interactions and nonlinear relationships among variables—something that our simple linear models can't cope with. The equations are then fed into a computer. The computer's sole function is to help us deal with the enormous number of factors and interactions built into the model and then to trace their dynamic behavior. *The end result of any model, of course, is no better than the assumptions, data, and equations used in the model.* As with any model—mental or computer—feed garbage in and you get garbage out.

Computer models have three important advantages over intuitive linear models. First, computer models require that all assumptions, weighting factors, data, and other parts of the model be clearly specified in order to develop the mathematical equations. This allows other people to verify the model or identify points of disagreement so that new, improved models can be developed and tested. Linear models are often vague about assumptions and particularly about weighting factors.

Second, computer models attempt to simulate the real world by building in feedback loops and nonlinear relationships between interacting variables. These loops and relationships may be very crude simulations of reality, but they are an important advance over the even cruder mental models. Third, computer models are dynamic and can be easily changed and updated. We can change the assumptions, weighting factors, and feedback loops or update the data and have the computer quickly produce new alternative projections.

Since the 1960s a number of interdisciplinary teams of experts have developed system dynamics computer models of ponds, lakes, grasslands, and other natural systems and of industrial, agricultural, energy, economic, political, urban, and other social systems.

In recent years a number of teams have developed dynamic computer models to project alternative economic and environmental futures for the entire world and for various regions of the world. One of the most important and controversial of these world models was first developed by Jay Forrester. This was then refined by Dennis and Donella Meadows and the other members of their interdisciplinary team under the sponsorship of the Club of Rome, an association of prominent scientists, scholars, and industrialists from 25 nations. Known data were used to test the model between 1900 and 1970, and projections were then run to the year 2100. The Forrester-Meadows model was published in popularized form in the book *The Limits to Growth* (1972, New York: Universe Books). The projections of this model were so startling that few books in this century have generated more intense debate. By 1980 about 4 million copies of this popular and readable book had been printed in more than 20 languages.

E1-2   The Forrester-Meadows Model

Nature of the Model   Since the Forrester-Meadows model has been heavily criticized for making doomsday predictions, we should begin our discussion by emphasizing again that this model, as well as others, are *projections*—not predictions—of the future. In the authors' words:

> The project was not intended as a piece of futurology. It was intended to be, and is, an analysis of current trends, of their influence on one another, and of their possible outcomes. Our goal was to provide warnings of potential world crisis if these trends are allowed to continue, and thus offer an opportunity to make changes in our political, economic, and social systems to ensure that these crises do not take place.

The Forrester-Meadows model looks at the dynamic interaction of five major variables—population, pollution, natural resources, industrial output per capita, and food per capita. The model is *extremely crude* in that large multivariable subsystems have been lumped together into single systems. For example, all the hundreds of nonrenewable resources, which have different and undetermined depletion times (Chapter 12), are included under a single variable that assumes a supply large enough to last 250 years at 1970 usage rates. Likewise, the pollution variable represents only a "long-lived, globally distributed family of pollutants such as lead, mercury, asbestos, and stable pesticides and radioisotopes." As with any model, resource supplies, pollution levels, food production, population growth, and industrial growth were estimated from existing knowledge or from educated guesses by experts. For each variable a factor was used in the mathematical equations to indicate the intensity of its interaction with other variables. In addition, time-lag variables were introduced to simulate the long delays in feedback processes.* For example, even if every couple in the world decided today to have only enough children to replace themselves, it would still take 50 to 70 years for world population to stabilize because there are so many young people in today's population (Section 7-4).

Following are the six major assumptions of the Forrester-Meadows model: (1) a finite stock of exploitable, nonrenewable resources; (2) a finite amount of land that can be used to grow food (arable land); (3) a finite capacity for the environment to absorb pollutants; (4) a finite yield of food that can be obtained from each unit of arable land; (5) exponential growth of population, pollution, and industrial output as long as resource supplies

---

*The detailed assumptions, equations, and data underlying the model are found in the technical report (Meadows et al. 1974. *Dynamics of Growth in a Finite World*. Cambridge, Mass.: Wright-Alen) used to back up the more popular presentation in *The Limits to Growth*.

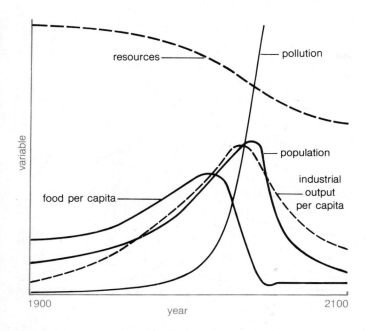

Figure E1-1 Projections of Forrester-Meadows world model assuming that, beginning in 1975, known reserves of resources were doubled and 75 percent of all nonrenewable resources were recycled. At a certain point the soaring pollution curve raises the death rate so that there is a sharp decline in world population. *(These are projections, not predictions.)* (After Meadows et al., *The Limits to Growth*, a Potomac Associates book published by Universe Books, New York, 1972. Used by permission)

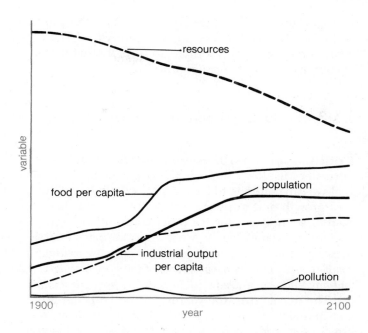

Figure E1-2 Projections of Forrester-Meadows world model assuming that all the policies listed in question 3 of the text were instituted in 1975. Finally, all variables stabilize. Population rises but then stabilizes, with an average world standard of living higher than today's. *(These are projections, not predictions.)* (After Meadows et al., *The Limits to Growth*, a Potomac Associates book published by Universe Books, New York, 1972. Used by permission)

and interactions with the variables in the system permit; and (6) forms of technological change (such as birth control, agricultural yield, and capital productivity) built into the model provided that there is money to pay for them and that environmental technology (such as resource recycling and pollution control) is also developed. The more assumptions and estimates made, the greater the uncertainty of the model, of course. But we need some model to project the future, and the only important question is whether this model is better than the intuitive linear ones we've been using up to now.

Projections of the Model   One of the nice things about dynamic computer models is that we can play with them. Let us ask some questions and see what answers the simulated projections give us:

Question 1. *What if the present J curves of population growth and industrial output continue?* Sometime after the year 2000, nonrenewable resources will be depleted; a population crash will follow as death rates rise due to a

scarcity of food and medical services (as shown earlier in Figure 6-9). This projection based on present trends, known as the "standard run," is used as a base for comparing the effects of adopting various policies and strategies.

Question 2. *Since resource depletion is a primary problem, what if we assume that technological advances will double all resource reserves and allow the recycling of 75 percent of all resources?* Pollution rises so sharply that death rates rise, leading to a severe population decline (Figure E1-1).

Question 3. *What happens if we set all of the following policies beginning in 1975: (1) Everyone has access to birth control, and couples average two children. (2) World industrial output per capita is stabilized at 1975 levels. (3) Resource consumption is reduced to one-fourth of 1970 values per unit of production. (4) Pollution is reduced to one-fourth of 1970 values per unit of production. (5) Consumption is shifted from material goods toward services such as education and health. (6) Capital is directed to food production, soil enrichment, and erosion prevention. (7) Industrial capital (such as factories and machines) is built to last much longer.* Finally, population rises and the standard of living improves (Figure E1-2).

Question 4. *What if we wait until the year 2000 instead of 1975 to put the policies of question 3 into effect?* The population rise depletes resources so severely that the population eventually drops (Figure E1-3).

E1-3   Evaluating Computer Models

Criticisms of the Forrester-Meadows Model If the Forrester-Meadows model is valid, it challenges the idea that we can continue to have exponentially rising industrial growth and population in a finite world. In other words, sooner or later we must confront the limits to growth on planet Earth. Most important, *the Forrester-Meadows model should destroy the myth of simple solutions to complex problems and the absurdity of thinking that variables and problems can be dealt with in isolation from one another.*

The debate over the validity of the Forrester-Meadows model has been intense. Many of the criticisms were anticipated and clearly acknowledged in *The Limits to Growth*. The authors warn us that their model is very crude, uses educated guesses for many important data, oversimplifies by grouping many variables into aggregates, and is a preliminary effort to project current patterns—*not* a prediction of the inevitable. Their challenge is not for scholars to necessarily "believe" in their model but to improve it and to develop other, more sophisticated models. The Forrester-Meadows model is one of the most tested computer models ever developed because it was clearly and thoroughly documented by its developers.

One observer reported finding an error in the Forrester-Meadows model that if corrected makes the curves less disastrous. The major criticism of the model, however, centers on the role of technology. The Forrester-Meadows model assumes major technological advances in finding and recycling resources, increasing food productivity, and controlling pollution, but it doesn't assume that technological innovations will increase exponentially on a J curve. As a result, the model does not assume that technology can solve every problem that might arise. Others, however, believe that technology can grow exponentially. Figure E1-4 shows a modified version of the Forrester-Meadows model using the assumptions of the technological optimist. In this case population rises and then levels off, natural resources are not depleted, pollution levels remain very low, and economic growth and the quality of life keep rising.

This result, of course, shouldn't be a surprise. The Forrester-Meadows model was designed to test the im-

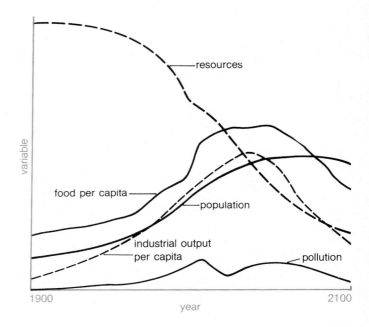

Figure E1-3 Projections of Forrester-Meadows world model assuming that all the policies listed in question 3 of the text are not instituted until the year 2000. Population rises to a much higher level than in Figure E1-2. During the delay in introducing policies, resources are severely depleted, and food and resource shortages begin to reduce population by raising the death rates. *(These are projections, not predictions.)* (After Meadows et al., *The Limits to Growth*, a Potomac Associates book published by Universe Books, New York, 1972. Used by permission)

plications of different assumptions. Different assumptions should yield different conclusions. The argument in this case is not over the model itself but over which assumptions should be used to give reasonable projections of the future. Neither model can tell us how good our assumptions are.

The Mesarovic-Pestel Model Another major criticism of the Forrester-Meadows model is that it treats the world as a single unit. In reality, the world is divided into rich, poor, and not-so-poor countries and regions, each area having its own economic, food, population, resource, and social problems (see Figure 7-15). To correct this possible defect, the Club of Rome sponsored the development of another computer model that divided the world into ten fairly homogeneous regions with a submodel developed for each region. In addition to considering the differences between areas, this approach can aid in developing specific plans for each region. This new model also included assumptions about the amount of econom-

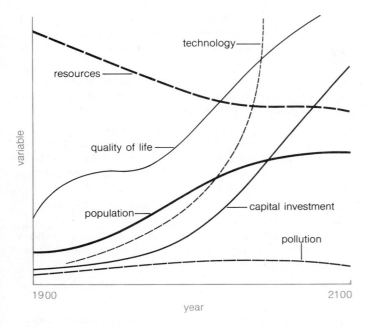

Figure E1-4 A modified version of the Forrester-Meadows model assuming that technology increases exponentially to provide essentially infinite resources, greatly reduced pollution, greatly increased food yields, and perfect birth control for everyone. Population rises but eventually levels off, resources are not depleted, pollution is kept at low levels, and economic growth and the quality of life keep rising. *(These are projections, not predictions.)* (Modified from Boyd, Robert. 1972. "World Dynamics: A Note," *Science*, vol. 177, 516–519).

ic aid that poor countries might receive from rich countries. The results of this model, issued under the direction of Mihajlo Mesarovic and Eduard Pestel, were presented in popular form in the book *Mankind at the Turning Point* (1974, New York: E. P. Dutton).

The primary conclusions of the Mesarovic-Pestel model are that (1) collapses of resource and food supplies and a sharp drop in population are projected before 2050, primarily in the poor regions of the world; (2) regional collapses can only be prevented by global cooperation among the ten regions, with rich nations using and wasting less resources and providing vast amounts of economic aid to the poor nations; (3) if any one region fails to cooperate and pursues its own path of rapid population growth or excessive resource use, then there will be a collapse in all regions in the long run; and (4) if rich nations delay in making massive economic aid available to poor nations, eventual solutions will be extremely difficult and expensive.

The Mesarovic-Pestel model did not project that all forms of economic growth must be halted to avoid global collapse, but it did lead its authors to call for a redistribution of economic growth, with less economic growth in the rich nations and more in the poor nations. In general, then, the conclusions of the Mesarovic-Pestel model at the global level do not differ significantly from those of the Forrester-Meadows model. Indeed, some reviewers found the second Club of Rome report even more pessimistic than the first. This model has also been criticized for the following reasons: (1) incorporating the assumptions of technological optimists; (2) being too simplistic politically and economically by assuming that all the problems of the poor countries can be solved by providing them with money rather than with appropriate technology and technical aid that will help them become more self-reliant; (3) emphasizing what the rich countries must do rather than what the poor nations must do, such as redistributing land to the poor and stabilizing population; (4) excluding or superficially treating the environmental disruption of the world's fisheries, forests, and air, water, and soil resources; and (5) having difficulty determining which of the model's conclusions were already built into the model and which were drawn from it.

Computer Models Are Not Cure-alls For critics to spend so much time complaining that the models aren't perfect seems unreasonable—it is like criticizing the first airplanes because they couldn't fly across the Atlantic at the speed of sound. Admittedly the models are crude, but they are vast improvements over the simplistic and often misleading models we have been using to help us make crucial decisions. The real challenge of the next decade is to develop better computer models at the global, regional, and national levels. One recent attempt to build upon and improve the Forrester-Meadows and Mesarovic-Pestel models was the Global 2000 model developed by the U.S. Council on Environmental Quality. Its conclusions are not significantly different than those from the two earlier models, as discussed by Gus Speth in his Guest Editorial at the end of Chapter 1.

At the same time, we must recognize that computer simulation models—no matter how good they become—cannot solve all our problems. They can demonstrate the danger of dealing with only one problem at a time, and they can help us to work with an unmanageable number of interacting variables. But these models cannot choose which assumptions to use or decide which projected alternative solutions are best. Human value judgments enter at every step. Are there some problems for which there are no technological solutions? When there is a technological solution, does it eliminate the problem or merely substitute one crisis for another? These are important questions. The vigorous debate between technological optimists and technological pessimists will and should continue so that we can examine these important questions more carefully and critically.

Computer models are very important tools, but they don't free us from the basic ethical and moral questions. How much do we really care about the others who inhabit the earth and about future generations? Do we really care about preserving our life-support system?

Concern for humanity must always form the chief interest of all technical endeavors in order that the creations of our minds shall be a blessing, not a curse, to humankind. Never forget that in the midst of your diagrams and equations.

Albert Einstein

Discussion Topics

1. Try to add to the examples of unexpected results and counterintuitive solutions shown in Table E1-1.

2. Explain the difference between a projection and a prediction of the future. Why is the Forrester-Meadows model not a prediction of the future?

3. What are some limitations of the Forrester-Meadows and the Mesarovic-Pestel models? What are their major strengths?

4. Debate the following resolution: The Forrester-Meadows and Mesarovic-Pestel models are useless, misleading gloom-and-doom approaches to the world's problems.

5. Discuss the fallacies of technological optimism and of technological pessimism. What assumptions underlie the position of each school? Which of these schools of thought, if either, do you support? Why?

Readings

Boughey, Arthur S. 1976. *Strategy for Survival: An Exploration of the Limits to Further Population and Industrial Growth.* Menlo Park, Calif.: W. A. Benjamin. Excellent introductory text explaining and evaluating computer models.

Boyd, Robert. 1972. "World Dynamics: A Note." *Science*, vol. 177, 516–519. By adding an exponentially growing technology function to the Forrester model, disaster is averted.

Clark, J., and S. Cole. 1975. *Global Simulation Models: A Comparative Survey.* New York: Wiley. Very useful comparison and evaluation of world models.

Cole, H. S. O., et al., eds. 1973. *Models of Doom: A Critique of The Limits to Growth.* New York: Universe Books. Detailed critical analysis of the Forrester-Meadows world model by a British systems analysis team. See also in this book the reply to their critique by Meadows et al., pp. 217–240.

Council on Environmental Quality. 1980. *The Global 2000 Report to the President*, vol. 2. Washington, D.C.: U.S. Government Printing Office. Superb model with projections of world food, population, land, water, energy, minerals, and pollution problems to the year 2000.

Dole, M. P. 1970. "Systems Analysis and Ecology." *Ecology*, vol. 51, 2–16. Good introduction.

Forrester, Jay W. 1971. "Counterintuitive Behavior of Social Systems." *Technology Review*, vol. 73, no. 3. Readable summary of results of the first world model.

Forrester, Jay W. 1971. *World Dynamics*. Cambridge, Mass.: Wright-Allen Press. Detailed description of the first world model.

Kahn, Herman, et al. 1976. *The Next 200 Years: A Scenario for America and the World.* New York: Morrow. A dazzling example of linear extrapolation by one of the world's foremost technological optimists. Unfortunately, the assumptions and the reasoning used to arrive at the conclusions generated by this simplistic model are not clearly specified.

Meadows, Donella H., et al. 1972. *The Limits to Growth*. New York: Universe Books. Popular description of the second world model.

Mesarovic, Mihajlo, and Eduard Pestel. 1974. *Mankind at the Turning Point.* New York: Sutton. Popular presentation of the regional model of the world. Compare it with *The Limits to Growth*.

Oltmans, Willem L. 1974. *On Growth*. New York: Putnam's. Useful collection of interviews of 70 of the world's great thinkers in many disciplines on the debate over the Forrester-Meadows model.

Starr, Chauncey, and Richard Rudman. 1973. "Parameters of Technological Growth." *Science*, vol. 182, 358–364. Strong presentation of the view that technology can grow exponentially and thus avert the problems projected by the Forrester-Meadows and Mesarovic-Pestel models.

Enrichment Study 2

Biomes: Major Land Ecosystems

In this enrichment study we will look briefly at the structure of plant and animal life in the major biomes, or land ecosystems, of the world (Figure 4-6), as introduced in Section 4-2. Biomes show that similar conditions of climate (Figure 4-7), and to some extent soil (Figure 4-9), lead to similar groupings of organisms. The relationship between biome type and average annual temperature and precipitation is shown in Figure E2-1. The fact that similar biomes are found in widely separated areas shows that different living organisms can develop similar adaptations to similar environmental conditions. Let's begin with the coldest biome below the Arctic Circle.

E2-1 Arctic and Alpine Tundras

Very few people want to spend much time in the *tundra*, an icy, treeless grassland found between the tree line and the Arctic Circle (*arctic tundra*) (Figure E2-2) and just above the timber line on mountaintops (*alpine tundra*). Only a few hardy plant and animal species can survive in its harsh climate of bitter cold (below $-5°C$, or $23°F$), low precipitation, and permanently frozen soil (permafrost). Even if trees could survive the cold air, they could not put down deep enough roots to grow. Summers last only a few weeks, just long enough to thaw a thin veneer of soil above the permafrost. During this short summer thaw, the normally frozen plain turns into a quagmire of puddles, bogs, and shallow lakes. Humans and other animals that enter this biome during the thaw are attacked by hordes of mosquitoes, deerflies, and blackflies.

The tundra landscape is covered with a mat of low-growing lichens, mosses, grasses, sedges, and in alpine tundra some small shrubs and mountain wildflowers. Most of the tundra's permanent animal residents are creatures that burrow under the snow, such as lemmings—small furry herbivores whose population rises rapidly and then crashes about every 4 years. Other small herbivores are the arctic hare, ermine, and snowy owl (which feeds on lemmings). The white coats of these animals help camouflage them from predators during the long winters. Large herbivores, such as caribou, reindeer, and musk oxen, slowly migrate south during the winter. Carnivores, such as white foxes and lynxes, and omnivores, such as grizzly and Kodiak bears, also inhabit this barren biome. During the short summer, large numbers of migrating birds, especially waterfowl, invade the tundra to feed on the swarms of insects.

The limiting factors in this ecosystem are severe cold and a shortage of radiant energy (sunlight). These factors allow only a few producer species and primary consumers to survive and make the tundra an extremely vulnerable ecosystem—it is easily disturbed and recovers very slowly. Even today marks of wagons that passed over the tundra 100 years ago are clearly visible. The fragility of this ecosystem is why many ecologists feared the construction and operation of the Alaskan oil and gas pipelines. Leaks of the hot oil could cause long-term ecosystem destruction and melt some of the permafrost, leading to severe erosion and possible shifting or sagging of the pipe in the mush. The pipes must also be constructed and maintained so they don't block the annual migration of caribou herds. Restricting the movement of these herds could cause overgrazing and thus destroy the food supply for the caribou and other tundra animals.

E2-2 Taiga and Temperate Rain Forest

Moving south from the tundra, we encounter the *taiga*, or *northern coniferous forest*, biome (also called the *boreal forest* biome). This large biome, containing many millions of acres, stretches across North America and Eurasia (where it extends across Sweden, Finland, Russia, and Siberia; see Figure 4-6). The climate of this biome is severe. Winters are long and extremely cold, but the

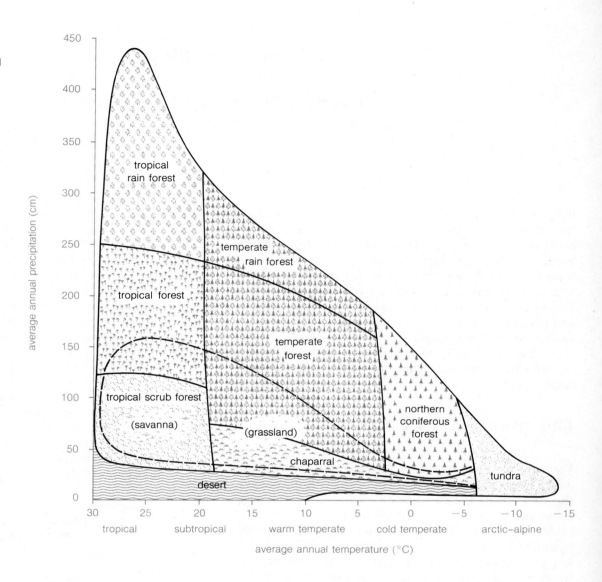

Figure E2-1 A greatly simplified summary of the relationship between biomes and climate.

summers are warmer and slightly longer than in the tundra. Lakes, ponds, and bogs are often found.

Taiga forests are dominated by a few species of needle-leafed, coniferous (cone-bearing) evergreen trees (Figure E2-3). The northernmost taiga are dominated by spruces, firs, short-needled pines (jack pine), and hemlock. Further south we may find long-needled pines and broad-leafed aspens, beeches, and poplars. Some of the most beautiful U.S. national parks are located in these coniferous forests, including Yosemite, Sequoia, Kings Canyon, and Yellowstone. The floors of these boreal forests are usually covered with a carpet of needles and leaf litter, interrupted by only a few small shrubs and plants that can survive the taiga's harsh climate and relatively infertile soil. Decomposition and decay of this forest floor litter are slow because of the cold.

Along the Pacific Coast of North America, with its heavy rainfall and mild winters, we find a variant of the taiga, which is dominated by Douglas fir, several species of pine, and the majestic redwoods. This variation is often called the *temperate rain forest*.

The principal large herbivores of these coniferous forests are moose, mule deer, caribou (which migrate down from the tundra during winter), and elk. Smaller herbivores include the snowshoe hare (which is white in winter and brown during the summer), red squirrels, and a variety of rodents, needle-eating caterpillars, beetles, wasps, mosquitoes, and biting flies. There is rela-

Figure E2-2 Tundra ponds in an expanse of Alaskan tundra. Only a few hundred different plant and animal species can survive the harsh winters, frozen or waterlogged soil, and short growing seasons.

U.S. Fish and Wildlife Service, USDI/Urban C. Nelson

Figure E2-3 A northern coniferous forest, or taiga.

Stephen L. Wolfe

tively little insect diversity, but a single insect pest can cause extensive damage to the huge stands of one or two species of coniferous trees. For example, the spruce budworm often causes major damage to taiga dominated by spruce.

Major predators in the taiga are the timber wolf, Canada lynx, and red fox, and to a lesser extent the marten, wolverine, mink, otter, ermine, and short-tailed weasel. Grizzly bears and black bears eat almost anything— leaves, buds, berries, fish, and occasionally mammals and the supplies of campers. Because of large-scale killing by farmers and ranchers, the timber wolf, which once inhabited most North American taiga, is now found primarily in Canada and Alaska. Wolf packs play an important ecological role by helping keep moose, caribou, and deer populations from getting too large. When wolf populations are killed off or driven away, the increased populations of moose and other plant eaters can devastate taiga vegetation.

The taiga is also threatened by heavy logging and fires caused by lightning and humans. Because coniferous trees are softwoods that grow faster than hardwoods, they have great economic value for lumber and paper pulp. When large areas are completely cleared of trees (clear-cutting) and not replanted properly, severe erosion and destruction of wildlife habitats occur (Section 10-4). At present, a large fraction of these northern forests remains as uncut wilderness areas. But pressures from our growing needs for wood and the use of these areas for recreation require that these biomes be protected and used with great care.

E2-3 Tropical Rain Forest

The most diverse of all terrestrial biomes is the *tropical rain forest*, which contains literally millions of different plant and animal species (Figure E2-4). Naturalist Marston Bates calls it a great green cathedral of towering evergreens, but he concedes that to many humans it is a humid hell. Tropical rain forests are found near the equator where there is plenty of moisture and heat—in the Amazon of South America, in the Congo Basin of Africa, and in Central America, India, and Southeast Asia (Figure 4-6).

The richness and variety of life in this biome stagger the imagination. It has more different kinds of organisms than any other biome, but there are fewer individuals of any one species in a given area. There may be 100 to 200 different species of trees per hectare (compared with 5

Figure E2-4 A tropical rain forest in Central America.

to 10 species of trees per hectare in temperate European and North American forests), but you may have to walk a long way to find two trees of the same species. This species diversity is in sharp contrast to that of the tundra and taiga, which are dominated by relatively few species. In the tropical rain forest, the different kinds of organisms living on or in a single tree can exceed the number of different species living in an entire taiga.

The diversity of the tropical rain forest results from its almost unchanging climate of high (but not excessive) temperatures and very heavy rainfall (Figure E2-1). Much of the year torrential rains fall at least once a day, and in the humid air, moisture drips constantly from vegetation. In addition, the stability of this biome has allowed numerous plant and animal species to evolve for long periods of time. Here the limiting factor is light, not temperature or water.

These forests consist of several layers of plant and animal life. The top layer is dominated by tall trees, reaching heights of 30 to 60 meters (100 to 200 feet), which form a massive canopy overhead so that the forest floor below is dark, cool, and steamy. With so little sunlight, the ground is relatively free of vegetation—in sharp contrast to the image presented in most jungle movies. Dense growth may be found, however, along river banks and at the edge of cleared areas. Decomposition is very rapid, and everything that falls to the ground is quickly carried off, consumed, or decomposed by armies of beetles, termites, ants, and other insects. Insects are often large in this ecosystem. In the Amazon forest there are moths with a wing span of almost 30 centimeters (1 foot) and spiders large enough to eat small birds that get trapped in their webs. Below the upper canopy a maze of thick woody vines (called lianas) hangs from the branches. The branches are also covered with thousands of species of epiphytes, or air plants (such as orchids), and strange pineapplelike plants called bromeliads. With no underground roots, epiphytes stay alive by getting minerals from falling leaves and the falling wastes of animals and by trapping pools of water in their flowers or leaves. These airborne pools are miniature ecosystems, containing entire communities of insects, spiders, and even tiny frogs.

The animal life in tropical forests is also quite varied, and it, too, occurs in layers. These forests literally swarm with insects, frogs, toads, and birds. Many species of colorful exotic birds, such as parrots, toucans, tanagers, manakins, and macaws, fly about in the forest canopy. They are joined by monkeys swinging and hopping about, and lemurs, snakes, opossums, and other mammals.

Humans have steadily been clearing tropical rain forests to get lumber and to plant crops (Sections 9-6 and 10-4). Once large areas are cleared, it is almost impossible for this diverse ecosystem to become reestablished, since these biomes are not suited for intensive agriculture. Most of the plant nutrients are in the trees and other forms of vegetation instead of in the soil. What few nutrients the soil does have are quickly washed or leached away by the torrential rains. In addition, some of the soils in these biomes are laterites (Figure 4-8). They contain iron and aluminum compounds that harden into concretelike, infertile slabs when baked in the sun.

E2-4 Temperate Deciduous Forest

If we have a somewhat cooler and drier climate, we encounter the *temperate deciduous forest* biome (Figures 4-6

and E2-5). At one time much of central Europe, eastern China, and eastern North America was covered by these magnificent forests. Today much of these forests has been cleared to obtain lumber and to plant crops. A few virgin stands still remain, often protected in state and national parks.

The climate of the deciduous forest is not as cold as that of the taiga and not as hot or wet as that of the tropical rain forest (Figure E2-1). There is abundant (but not excessive) rainfall, moderate temperatures that gradually change with the seasons, and a long growing season (4 to 6 months). As temperatures drop in the fall, the leaves on the trees exhibit a rainbow of colors before falling to the ground. The decomposition of this thick carpet of dead leaves (as well as logs) and the favorable climate produce a rich soil, which supports a much greater diversity of plant species than the taiga (although not as great as that of the rain forest).

Dominant tree species vary among deciduous forests, depending largely on local rainfall. In the more moist northern and mountainous regions (such as New England and the Lake States), we find various combinations of maples, birches, and beech. Oak and hickory (and at one time the American chestnut) dominate drier regions and are perhaps the most typical trees of this biome. Around 1900 the accidental importation of the chestnut blight fungus killed nearly all of the American chestnut. In the southern deciduous forests (the southern Appalachians) we find ash, yellow poplar, basswood, black cherry, and walnut. Further south we find the southern pine forest, containing longleaf, shortleaf, slash, and loblolly pines. In California, dry summer and fall months lead to a variation of the temperate deciduous forest, commonly called a *woodland*. It consists of scattered oak trees spread across rolling grassland and is largely used for ranchland or for growing wheat or barley.

Plant growth in a deciduous forest normally occurs in several layers, like those found in tropical rain forests. There is an umbrella-like canopy of tall trees, an understory of smaller hardwoods that can tolerate shade, a layer of deciduous and evergreen shrubs, a layer of herbs that cover the forest floor with colorful flowers in the spring, and finally a layer of lichens and mosses that grow primarily on rocks and fallen logs.

Animal life is far more varied than that occurring in coniferous forests. This results from the diversity of habitats available in the different layers and the variety of flowers, fruits, seeds, and other food available for herbivores. The resulting variety of herbivores, in turn, supports a large number of various carnivores. The domi-

Figure E2-5 A temperate deciduous forest: a stand of young timber in Virginia.

Forest Service, USDA/E. S. Shipp

nant herbivore of the deciduous forests in the eastern United States is the whitetail deer. Because its predators, such as the wolf, have largely been eliminated or driven out, the whitetail deer population often grows out of control. This normally leads to destruction of vegetation and mass starvation of the deer. Other animal species include the black bear, porcupine (now fairly rare), opossum, raccoon, striped skunk, chipmunk, gray squirrel, shrew, and cottontail rabbit. Where they have not been driven out, wolves, bobcats, gray foxes, and mountain lions feed on many of these smaller mammals. These forests are also inhabited by an abundance of quail, songbirds, frogs, salamanders, lizards, turtles, snakes, mice, and other rodents, including the beaver, the largest rodent in North America. The beaver plays an important ecological role in the deciduous forest. Its renowned dam-building activities create many new ponds and lakes. As these fill up with silt and vegetation, they are slowly replaced by highly fertile meadows. Predator birds, such as owls, ravens, hawks, and eagles, also play

an important ecological role by keeping down populations of small rodents. Reducing populations of these predator birds can lead to the destruction of vegetation by mushrooming rodent populations.

The temperate deciduous forest has been more drastically modified by human activity than any other forest biome. The fact that relatively few virgin stands of these important and diverse ecosystems still remain should be a clear warning to us in our often tragic attempts to dominate nature.

E2-5 Tropical and Temperate Grasslands

The grassland biome is found where rainfall is great enough to keep deserts from forming but low and erratic enough so that cycles of drought prevent forests from growing. Here we find a carpet of high and low grasses, mixed in some areas with small bushes and shrubs and even a few widely dispersed trees. Grasslands are found all over the world in both temperate and tropical climates. At one time more than 40 percent of the earth's surface was covered with grass. The *tropical grassland,* or *savanna,* biome occurs in areas with long dry seasons but warm temperatures throughout the year. Here, of course, the limiting factor is water. Savannas are found in southern Asia (especially India), Australia, and north and south of the tropical rain forests in Africa and South America (Figure 4-6). Savanna consists of broad expanses of tall grasses with scattered low, thorny trees and occasional small groves of trees (Figure E2-6). During the dry season, large areas of savanna often burn.

Because the savanna is open and covered with grass, it is usually populated by large herds of grazing, hoofed mammals. In Africa we find large herds of herbivores, such as wildebeest, zebra, and antelope. These swiftly running animals are preyed upon by large carnivores, such as the lion and cheetah (and in Asia the tiger). Australian savannas are populated with species of the herbivorous kangaroos and wallabies. The ability of the kangaroo (and the jack rabbit) to leap allows it to see above the tall grass and catch sight of approaching predators. Humans have had a tremendous impact on savannas through fire, agriculture, and hunting. As a result, the great herds of grazing animals and their predators are disappearing rapidly except in protected areas.

The *temperate grasslands* are the great plains and prairies of Canada and the United States (Figure E2-7), the pampas of South America, the veldts of Africa, and the steppes of Russia and central Asia. Here the winters are cold (compared to the savanna); summers are hot and dry; and with no natural windbreaks, the winds blow almost continuously. Moister grasslands are covered with tall grasses, while more arid grasslands have short grasses growing in a thick mat of stems and low-growing roots. The soils of the tall-grass prairie are among the richest in the world (Figure 4-8). This explains why most of the grasslands in Canada and the United States have been converted to vast fields of corn and wheat. It is difficult to find very much original or undisturbed grassland in these countries.

Before being overhunted and converted to agriculture, the Great Plains of North America were dominated by large herbivores, such as the bison, pronghorn antelope, elk, and wild horses. These grazing animals were preyed upon by the wolf, coyote, panther, and plains Indians. Today these herds have been replaced by domesticated cattle, sheep, and goats. Because they are confined, these animals often overgraze the land, especially in years of severe drought. The exposed soil is quickly blown away by the wind and the productivity of the grassland is destroyed.

Undisturbed temperate grasslands also contain numerous species of small herbivores, such as the prairie dog, ground squirrel, pocket gopher, and jack rabbit. The prairie dog plays an important ecological role in this biome. Its elaborate tunnels and burrows help aerate the soil, and its droppings enrich the soil. Settlers on the North American prairie, however, considered prairie dogs a nuisance, and the animals have now been largely eliminated and replaced by the ground squirrel.

Without a protective canopy of trees, grasslands are ecosystems under continual stress from the wind, sun, and large temperature fluctuations. Thus, they can easily be destroyed by humans. They can provide ample crops in good years, but during drought years crops fail. Without vegetation to hold it together, the precious topsoil can blow away. This happened in the 1930s when large areas of cultivated grassland in the United States became a "dust bowl." Large quantities of fertile soil particles blown from the parched midwestern grassland formed a dust cloud that covered the eastern United States with a thin layer of grit. Stringent soil conservation practices, as discussed in Section 16-6, must be used to keep us from experiencing this tragic lesson again.

E2-6 Tropical and Mediterranean Scrub and Woodland

In arid tropical climates we find the *thorn scrub* (Figure E2-8) and *thorn woodland* biomes. Such areas are found in much of Mexico, parts of Australia, and Africa just south of the Sahara Desert (Figure 4-6). As their names suggest, these biomes contain, respectively, small thorny plants and medium-sized trees. Grass or dense shrubs grow below the trees.

When a temperate area has a so-called Mediterranean climate—mild, damp winters but hot, dry summers—we encounter a biome known as *chaparral* (Figure E2-9), or *Mediterranean scrub and woodland.* This biome is found in Europe around the Mediterranean Sea, in southern Australia, and in parts of southern and central California (Figure 4-6). In Australia this biome is dominated by eucalyptus trees and scrub vegetation. In Europe and California the hillsides are covered with almost impenetrable growths of evergreen shrubs (such as manzanita in California). Oak and sycamore trees are also

Figure E2-6 A savanna, or tropical grassland, in East Africa.

Roger K. Burnard

Figure E2-7 A temperate grassland in Kansas.

National Park Service, USDI/Dr. W. G. Tomanek

Figure E2-8 African thorn scrubland.

Roger K. Burnard

Figure E2-9 Chaparral stand in the Cleveland National Forest in California.

Forest Service, USDA/D. F. Costello

found in more protected areas. The tough evergreen leaves of these shrubby plants have waxy coatings that reduce evaporation of water and help them survive long periods of drought. Other typical chaparral plants are holly, sumac, and poison sumac and ivy. Rabbits, quail, hawks, raccoons, coyotes, lizards, rattlesnakes, and the California condor also inhabit this biome.

Fire periodically sweeps through the chaparral, which plays an important ecological role in clearing out dead material and old growth and in allowing various fire-adapted species to reproduce. Many plants in this biome have become adapted to fire. But this cannot be said of the many humans who have built houses in the chaparral to take advantage of its favorable climate. The severe penalty for building a home in the chaparral is that it may burn along with the plants. Human inhabitants of the chaparral must also practice strict water conservation, as many Californians learned during the drought years of the late 1970s.

E2-7 Desert

Forest, grassland, desert: This is a sequence of increasing environmental stress. Desert ecosystems are found in areas with climates too dry to support grasslands. Deserts generally have less than 25 centimeters (10 inches) of rain annually, and even this meager supply comes unpredictably. Months or even years may go by with little or no rain. Then, a sudden downpour occurs. Unfortunately, much of the water evaporates rapidly and runs off of the relatively barren soil. Indeed, a high rate of evaporation characterizes a desert as much as its low input of moisture. Directly after a rainfall the plants and animals of the desert explode in an orgy of activity in order to capture and use as much of the scarce and short-lived resource as possible. Plants and animals in the desert must be able to adapt to this unreliable supply of water.

Deserts are found all over the world (Figure 4-6) and make up more than one-third of the earth's land surface. There are two general types of deserts: cold deserts and warm deserts. *Cold deserts* have cold winters (there may even be snow on the ground) and hot summers. Examples are found in Oregon, Utah, and Nevada. Many cold deserts are produced by rain shadows from mountain ranges. *Warm deserts* have warm to hot temperatures throughout the year. Typical warm deserts are found in Arizona, New Mexico, California, Texas (Figure E2-10),

northern Mexico, Africa (the Sahara), and Saudi Arabia. Both types of deserts lack water. In both types there are usually sharp fluctuations of temperature during the hot seasons, with the nights being cold.

Most people have a movie conception of deserts: endless stretches of barren sand dunes. While this is true of a few hot and very dry deserts, such as the Sahara, it is by no means typical. Most deserts consist of widely scattered thorny bushes and shrubs, perhaps a few succulents such as cacti (especially in the Western Hemisphere), and after rains some small flowers that carpet the desert floor. These desert plants use a number of strategies to get and conserve water. Cacti and other succulents have very shallow roots that extend over a wide area so that they can rapidly take up water when the rains come. Cacti can also store large amounts of water in their fleshy stems. Their lack of leaves also decreases loss of water by evaporation. Other desert plants, such as mesquite bushes, get water with their long taproots, which extend as far down as 30 meters (100 feet) to tap groundwater. The creosote bush has waxy leaves that reduce loss of water by evaporation.

Animals have also made adjustments to survive the rigors of desert life. Most desert animals are small and avoid the heat by coming out only at night, especially near dusk and dawn. During the day they find shade or live in burrows under the sand. These animals include a number of rodents (such as the kangaroo rat), lizards, snakes and other reptiles, owls, eagles, vultures, many small birds, and numerous insects.

In addition to avoiding the heat, desert animals must be able to get and conserve water. Some get it from the morning dew. Others, such as the kangaroo rat, never drink at all, obtaining water from the breakdown of their food in their bodies. The scales of reptiles and the exterior covering of insects prevent evaporation of water.

The desert biome shows increasing signs of human intervention. Climate is the major factor in forming deserts. But deforestation, overgrazing, and lack of proper soil conservation practices in agricultural areas have led to the spread of deserts in many parts of the world. With ample irrigation many deserts can be converted to (or back to) productive agricultural land. Unlike tropical rain forests, the desert soil is relatively fertile when provided with adequate water. But making deserts bloom is almost always an expensive process that requires a large input of energy. In the United States there are new threats to this biome. Hordes of motorcycles and dune buggies rip up the desert plants and soil. And plant thieves threaten the extinction of many types of cacti as they truck them

Figure E2-10 Warm desert in Big Bend National Park in Texas.

National Park Service, USDI

away for sale to city dwellers, who remain blissfully unaware of this degradation.

Nature sustains itself through three precious principles, which one does well to embrace and follow. These are gentleness, frugality, and humility.

Lao Tzu

Discussion Topics

1. Why would you expect similar biomes to be found at high altitudes and high latitudes?

2. Would you expect to find the same plant and animal species in an Alaskan tundra and in an Andean tundra? Why?

3. What are epiphytes and why are they most commonly found in the tropics and subtropics?

4. What natural biomes have had the greatest influence on the expansion of human culture? What harmful effects has this expansion had on these biomes?

Readings

Billings, W. D. 1970. *Plants, Man, and the Ecosystem*. 2nd ed. Belmont, Calif.: Wadsworth. Excellent detailed discussion of biomes.

Clapham, W. B., Jr. 1973. *Natural Ecosystems*. New York: Macmillan. See chapter 6 for an overview of biomes.

Cloudsley-Thompson, J. L. 1975. *Terrestrial Environments*. New York: Wiley. Superb detailed description of biomes.

Kucera, Clair L. 1978. *The Challenge of Ecology*. 2nd ed. St. Louis: Mosby. See chapter 8 for an excellent overview of biomes.

Wasserman, Aaron O. 1975. *Biology*. 2nd ed. Reading, Mass.: Addison-Wesley. See chapter 21 for a superb overview of biomes.

Are We Changing the World's Climate?

When it comes to global climate, the question is not "Will it change?" but "How will it change and over what length of time?" Natural changes in global, regional, and local climate have taken place throughout the earth's history. In recent years, however, concern has mounted that human activities may be influencing climate at the local and regional levels and perhaps even at the global level. In this enrichment study we will examine this important issue.

E3-1 Natural and Human-Related Climate Change

Past Climate Changes   One way to project how climate might change in the future is to see how it has changed in the past. Although official climate records have been kept for only the past 100 years, scientists have attempted to reconstruct climatic history for the past several hundred years by using tree rings, burial sites, records of grape harvests, sea ice, and other historical data. Scientists have also attempted to trace climate change even further back by examining the fossil evidence of climate-sensitive forms of life, such as pollens, beetles, and ocean plankton found in rock strata, cores from ice sheets, and sediments on the ocean bottom.

This detective work—which is, of course, preliminary and often speculative—indicates that eight great ice ages, or glacial periods, have occurred over the past 700,000 years, during which thick ice sheets spread southward over much of North America, Europe, and parts of Asia. Each glacial period lasted about 100,000 years and was followed by a warmer interglacial period lasting about 10,000 to 12,500 years (Figure E3-1). The last great ice age ended about 10,000 years ago and at its coldest point the mean temperature of the atmosphere near the earth was only about 5°C (9°F) cooler than the atmosphere today. During this period the average tem-

perature was up to tens of degrees cooler in higher altitudes and only slightly cooler in tropical areas.

For the past 10,000 years we have been enjoying the warmer temperatures (compared with those in the last ice age) of the latest interglacial period. During this period of favorable climate, agriculture began and spread rapidly throughout the world to support the increase in the world's population that the warmer weather allowed (Figure 8-4). If climatic history repeats itself and is not altered by human activities, we are due for a new ice age sometime within the next 2,500 years. Until recently it was assumed that the transition from an interglacial period to an ice age took place gradually over several thousand years. But analysis of pollen in cores of ice drilled from glaciers indicates that about 90,000 years ago the earth shifted from an interglacial period like that of today into a full ice age in less than 100 years. According to a more recent hypothesis, we could move from a warm period to an ice age within 10 to 20 years as a result of a *snowblitz*. Massive amounts of snow and ice could blanket many parts of the world during one winter and then not melt in the spring and summer because of a drop in mean global temperature. This increased snow and ice cover would reflect more sunlight, causing a further drop in mean air temperature and leading to more snow and ice each succeeding year. Within a decade or so much of North America, Europe, and eastern Asia could be covered with ice. Thus, by looking at the earth's long-term natural climate change, we can speculate that much of the world could return to more glacial conditions sometime within the next 10 to 2,500 years.

To make more accurate projections of how climate might change during the next 10 to 200 years, we need to look at what has happened during the present interglacial period—particularly during the past 100 years. Any recurring trends during these shorter time periods might give us clues about what might happen over the next few decades. Climate fluctuates between hot and cold during an interglacial period, but the swings are not enough to be called a 100,000-year great ice age. Instead we get a series of cooling periods called *little ice ages*, when glaciers spread southward for up to several hundred years before retreating. During the past 10,000 years, six to eight little ice ages—the last one occurring between 1550 and 1870—have occurred. The cooler atmospheric temperatures during a little ice age also alter global precipitation patterns, and these two factors change the parts of the world where certain foods can be grown. During the last little ice age, cereal cultivation ended in Iceland, vineyards were abandoned in England, and in 1816 New England had snow in June and fall frost starting in August—the "year without a summer." During a warming epoch about 6,000 years ago more rain fell in the arid subtropics, while the U.S. plains—now one of the world's major food-growing regions—were much drier. Thus, either a slight warming or a slight cooling of the atmosphere can cause a major shift in the world's food-growing regions.

Following the end of the last little ice age, the mean global temperature of the atmosphere rose by about 0.4° to 0.6°C between 1880 and 1940 and then dropped slightly between 1940 and 1965 (Figure E3-2). Between 1965 and 1975, however, the Southern Hemisphere warmed 0.2°C, while temperature in the Northern Hemisphere changed very little.

Predicting Future Climate Changes   How can we explain these trends and use them to predict what might happen over the next few decades? There is considerable disagreement on this issue. There are three major views: (1) We don't have enough knowledge and evidence either to explain these short-term (and perhaps random) swings or to use them as clues about future short-term changes; (2) it will get colder as we move into a new great ice age (or into a new little ice age) because of long-term natural trends (Figure E3-1) or a combination of natural trends and human activities; and (3) it will get warmer over the next century primarily because of human activities that counteract the natural and human-caused cooling trends.

In other words, experts are making three predictions about climate change in the next few decades: We can't tell what will happen, it will get colder, and it will get hotter. The experts also have three views on the effects of human activities on global climate: no effect, a small effect, and a major effect. Since these conclusions cover all the possibilities, you might wonder why we need experts. The problem is that climate change is an incredibly complex process, which is influenced by many factors interacting over short and long periods of time. Furthermore, it is only since the development of earth satellites and high-speed computers that we have had highly sophisticated tools even to study the problem.

The major factors determining the earth's overall climate are (1) the input of solar energy (Section 5-2); (2) the earth's rotation rate; (3) the chemical composition of the earth's atmosphere, which controls how much sunlight gets through and how rapidly heat is radiated back into space (Figure 5-4); (4) the properties of the oceans (which are vast heat reservoir and heat pumps) and their interactions with the atmosphere; and (5) the reflectivity (albedo), vegetation, and other surface characteristics of the land and sea. The difficulty is in learning how these factors interact and feed back on one another.

Climatologists have developed a number of dynamic mathematical models to predict the effects of changing one climatic factor (such as increased atmospheric dust from volcanic eruptions or human land-clearing and industrial activities) on other climatic factors. Despite these important advances, however, these models are still too crude to make reliable short- and long-term projections. Thus, the vigorous debate over conflicting

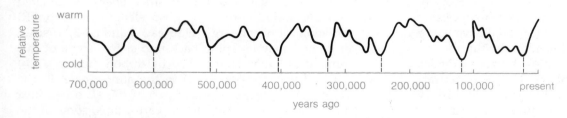

Figure E3-1   Estimated average atmospheric temperature through geological time. During the past 700,000 years eight great ice ages have occurred (dotted lines), each lasting around 100,000 years and followed by a warmer interglacial period lasting about 10,000 to 12,500 years. If natural climatic history repeats itself, we are due for another great ice age within the next 2,500 years.

hypotheses is a natural and healthy characteristic of science—especially when there is insufficient knowledge.

Why Worry about Climate Change? If the experts can't agree, then why should we worry about this issue? Why not wait until the smoke clears and we have a better understanding of climate change? Unfortunately, we can't afford this tempting luxury. Climate change is too important in human affairs to postpone action until it is more thoroughly understood from a scientific viewpoint.

Although climatologists disagree on how climate will change and on what the major causes of change are, they generally agree that we could well be in for some rather far-reaching changes in climate over the next century. Just a slight rise or fall in the mean global temperature of the atmosphere can trigger effects that could be with us for thousands of years.

If seasonal temperature and precipitation changes should come a few weeks earlier or later on a regular basis in various parts of the world, food production could be thrown into chaos. This in turn could lead to political and social disruption. With over 4.6 billion people to support and perhaps 8 billion within a few decades (Figure 7-8), there is little margin for error in knowing where the climate might be most favorable for food production in the future. Thus, climate change is not merely a scientific problem—it is also a political, economic, and ethical problem that demands our attention regardless of how little we know.

Climate and Human Activities A major thrust of this concern must be to determine the potential effect of human activities on climate. Until recently it was assumed that we had very little effect on global and regional climate compared with volcanic eruptions, sunspots, and other natural phenomena. Now we have evidence that human activities (1) may have been affecting local, regional, and even global climate since the discovery of fire; (2) are definitely affecting local climates now, especially in and near urban areas; and (3) could have major effects on regional and global climate in the future.

From Table E3-1 we see that most human activities tend to warm the lower atmosphere. This is in contrast to the natural trends, which according to climatic history may lead to cooling (Figure E3-1). Natural climate trends, however, take thousands to hundreds of thousands of years, whereas human activities could trigger climate changes within several decades to hundreds of years (Table E3-1). Thus, the interaction of human activities

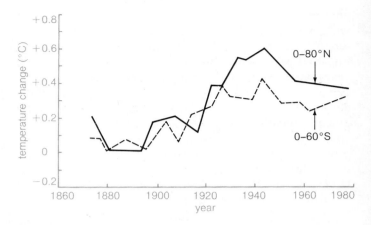

Figure E3-2 Changes in mean surface temperatures of the atmosphere in the Northern Hemisphere (solid line) and Southern Hemisphere (dotted line) between 1870 and 1975.

with natural climate trends could determine whether we descend into a new little ice age or a great ice age, have a much warmer climate, or maintain the relatively good weather we have had during the past several thousand years.

In the remainder of this Enrichment Study we will look more closely at the possible effects of increasing the amounts of carbon dioxide, particles, and heat in the atmosphere from human activities. The potential effects of freons on the ozone layer were discussed in Section 6-3.

E3-2 Carbon Dioxide and the Greenhouse Effect: Is the Atmosphere Warming?

The Greenhouse Effect Approximately 30 percent of the solar radiation reaching the earth is reflected back into space (Figure 5-4). Most of the remaining 70 percent is absorbed by the land, sea, and clouds. When the land and water bodies cool, the absorbed energy is radiated into the atmosphere as long-wavelength infrared (IR) radiation, or heat energy (Figures 5-4 and E3-3). Instead of immediately escaping back into space, some of this infrared radiation is absorbed by carbon dioxide (CO_2) gas and water vapor (H_2O) in the atmosphere. These chemical gatekeepers radiate part of the absorbed heat into space and part back to the earth; thus, some of the heat that would normally be lost to space fairly rapidly is reradiated to warm the lower atmosphere (Figure E3-3). This warming effect is sometimes called the **greenhouse effect,** because the atmosphere acts similarly to

Table E3-1 Climate and Human Activities

Human Activity	Probable Climatic Effect	Present Area of Impact	Estimated Years before Global Impact	Potential for Controlling
Release of carbon dioxide from burning fossil fuels	Warming of lower atmosphere (greenhouse effect) and cooling of upper atmosphere	Regional (variable)	10 to 50 years	Poor until fossil fuels used up
Diffusion of chlorofluorohydrocarbons (freons) into the stratosphere	Warming of lower atmosphere and cooling of upper atmosphere; reduction of stratospheric ozone, allowing more harmful ultraviolet radiation to reach the earth (Section 6-3)	Regional to global	Major impact within 20 to 30 years	Fair to poor
Land clearing (deforestation, agriculture, overgrazing, irrigation)	Warming or cooling of lower atmosphere because of changes in surface albedo (reflectivity) and warming because of carbon dioxide released from land clearing	Local, regional	Speculative, 20 to 200 years	Fair to poor
Release of particles (aerosols) from industry, burning of fossil fuels, and land clearing	May cool lower atmosphere by reflecting sunlight over water or heat lower atmosphere by absorbing sunlight over land	Local, regional	Unknown, but may have little global effect since most particles remain in atmosphere for only a few days	Fair (large particles) to poor (fine particles)
Release of heat from urbanization and burning of fossil and nuclear fuels faster than the heat can be radiated back into space	Direct warming of lower atmosphere	Local, regional	100 to 200 years	Poor

the glass in a greenhouse or a car window, which allows visible light to enter but hinders the escape of long-wavelength IR, or heat radiation.* The mean global atmospheric temperature today is about 10°C (18°F) higher than it would be without any CO_2 or water vapor in the atmosphere. The oceans, as part of the carbon cycle, dissolve an estimated one-third to one-half of all carbon dioxide injected into the atmosphere within a few years. Without this major sink, the average global concentration of CO_2 would probably be twice its present value.

Because of the large amount of water vapor and its relatively rapid rate of cycling (Section 15-2), humans can do little to upset the average water concentration in the atmosphere. However, the relatively small average concentration of CO_2 (about 0.03 percent) can be increased significantly as the earth's fossil fuels are burned up and as forests are cleared. When coal, oil, natural gas, wood, or any carbon-containing fuel is burned, CO_2, H_2O, and

*Strictly speaking, the term *greenhouse effect* is misleading. A greenhouse, or a closed car on a sunny day, not only traps heat energy but also reduces heat exchange with the wind and keeps the warmed air from rising and cooling. Even though technically inexact, the use of this term is widespread.

heat are released into the atmosphere. For example, burning 909 kilograms (1 ton) of coal releases about 2,700 kilograms (3 tons) of CO_2. Green plants and trees also remove some of the CO_2 from the atmosphere through photosynthesis (Section 5-4). However, when plants and trees are cut down and either burned as fuel or allowed to decay, CO_2 is added to the atmosphere. If plants are being removed from the earth faster than they are being replanted or faster than they regrow naturally, the amount of CO_2 released is greater than that removed by photosynthesis. Additional CO_2 can be released from decay in soil humus (Figure 4-8) that has been exposed to the sunlight when a forest or field is cleared of vegetation.

Increasing Carbon Dioxide Levels Measurements since 1958 show and estimates of past values suggest that average global concentrations of CO_2 have been increased 15 to 25 percent since the beginning of the industrial revolution (around 1800) with a sharp increase since 1940 and an even sharper rise since 1958. Since 1950 fossil fuel combustion is believed to have been the dominant source

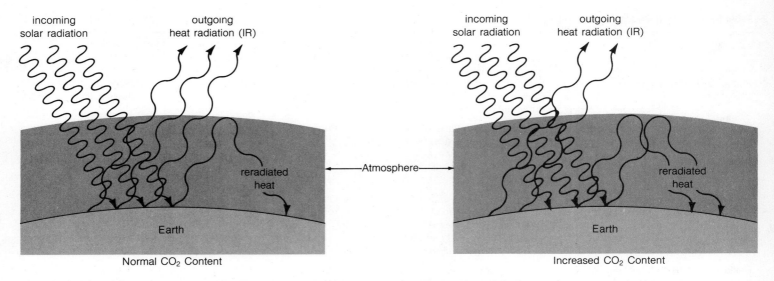

Figure E3-3 The greenhouse effect. Short-wavelength solar radiation strikes the earth and is transformed into long-wavelength IR, or heat radiation, some of which is absorbed and reradiated back to the earth by the CO_2 and water vapor in the atmosphere. Compared with CO_2, the average amount of water vapor in the air is so large that human activities do not significantly change its average global concentration. The average CO_2 content, however, can be significantly increased by burning wood and fossil fuels and clearing forests; this could lead to a warming of the earth's atmosphere.

of CO_2. Because of a lack of information, there is considerable debate over how much CO_2 deforestation has added in recent years; estimates range from 10 to as high as 50 to 60 percent of the CO_2 added from burning fossil fuels.

According to the greenhouse model, the increase in CO_2 between 1880 and 1975 should have increased the mean global atmospheric temperature by about 0.3°C (0.5°F) (Figure E3-4). Assuming that the use of fossil fuels continues to grow at the 1940 to 1973 average rate of 4 percent a year, that the oceans and plant life remove 50 percent of the total CO_2 added to the atmosphere, and that all other factors remain constant, then atmospheric CO_2 concentration should double the preindustrial (1800) level between 2020 and 2050, and by 2175 if annual fossil fuel use grows at a rate of 2 percent a year. A doubling of the 1800 CO_2 levels could raise the mean global temperature by 1.5°C to 4.5°C (3° to 8°F) with a 3°C (5°F) rise the most likely estimate. Perhaps even more significant, the projected temperature rise in the north polar region is expected to be about 2 to 3 times larger than the average global increase with temperature increases as much as 7°C to 10°C (13°F to 18°F). Some observers feel that the effects of doubling CO_2 levels in the atmosphere may be less than those predicted by currently accepted models, but this calculation has been disputed.

The increase in atmospheric CO_2 and the resulting temperature change could occur more rapidly or more slowly than these models predict. For example, as the lower atmosphere warms, some of the CO_2 now dissolved in the oceans could be released—like the dissolved CO_2 released when soda pop or beer warms up. This could accelerate the warming and release even more dissolved CO_2, so that the warming effect could be intensified. In addition, increased deforestation (Section 10-4) and the heat automatically released by the use of any form of energy could add to the warming effect as population and energy use continue to rise (see Section E3-4). There is also some evidence that if CO_2 levels rise rapidly, the ocean becomes less effective in removing CO_2.

Conversely, the warming of the atmosphere could evaporate more water from the ocean, producing more clouds, which could shield and cool the ocean surface. But whether clouds tend to warm or cool the earth depends on their altitude; low-level clouds tend to cool the atmosphere, and high-level clouds tend to warm the earth since water vapor is an infrared absorbant like CO_2. Higher CO_2 levels could also increase the rate of photosynthesis so that plants grow faster and thus remove more CO_2 from the atmosphere. This assumption, however, has been questioned; even if it is valid, such a phe-

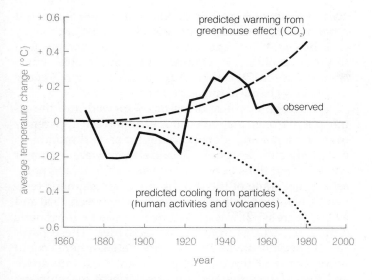

Figure E3-4 Comparison of observed (solid line) and predicted changes (dashed and dotted lines) in average atmospheric temperature. The dashed line shows the atmospheric warming predicted by models of carbon dioxide increase and the dotted line shows the atmospheric cooling predicted by models of increased concentration of atmospheric particles from volcanoes and human sources.

nomenon could be overcome by increased cloudiness and deforestation. In addition, the higher temperature resulting from a CO_2 buildup would increase the rate of plant respiration, thereby reducing the net production of CO_2.

The greenhouse model may have caused much of the 0.4° to 0.6°C (0.7° to 1.0°F) rise in mean atmospheric temperature between 1880 and 1940, but how can this model explain the approximately 0.3°C (0.4°F) drop in temperature in the Northern Hemisphere since 1940 (Figure E3-4)? This slight decline could be due to a natural cooling trend or a combination of natural and human factors (such as more dust in the air) that could counteract the CO_2 warming effect. The sharpest rise in CO_2 is expected between 1975 and 2000 (Figure E3-4). By 2000, if not sooner, many scientists predict that the CO_2 warming effect will overwhelm any natural or human-caused cooling effects. The apparent leveling off of the temperature in the Northern Hemisphere and the slight increase in temperature in the Southern Hemisphere (where human activity and human-generated particle pollution is lowest) (Figure E3-2) are cited as evidence that the CO_2 warming effect may be gradually overcoming cooling effects.

Possible Effects on Climate Why worry about all of this? At first thought a slightly warmer climate might seem desirable, resulting in longer growing seasons and milder winters that would save fuel and possibly increase crop productivity. But unfortunately along with benefits for some parts of the world there could be serious consequences in other areas, especially if such a change took place fairly rapidly over a few decades. No one knows exactly what would happen, but we can get some clues by looking at what happened during a period of slight warming (about 2°C) 4,000 to 8,000 years ago.

The major effect of a slight warming would be shifts in crop-growing regions plus changes and shifts in rainfall patterns, which make it difficult to know where to plant crops from year to year. Some arid regions, such as the Sahel area in Africa and the Sahara and Arabian deserts, might get more rain, while the midwestern breadbasket in the United States might become drier. The U.S. wheat and corn belt in Iowa and Indiana might shift northward into Saskatchewan in Canada, where the soils are poorer and less productive. Fish populations might move northward so that New England's fishing fleet would find the cod off Greenland instead of Nova Scotia. Some nations might eventually be able to grow more food than they do today. But for several decades there would probably be a sharp drop in global food production and distribution because many of the new crop-growing areas would have poor soils and not be organized to farm, irrigate, store, and distribute large amounts of grain.

According to present climate models, the effects at the poles would be even more drastic, since a 3°C (5°F) rise in mean global temperature would result in a 7° to 10°C (13° to 18°F) rise there. Sea levels would rise about 1 meter (3.3 feet) because of the thermal expansion of warmer ocean water. Most, if not all, of the floating Arctic ice pack would probably melt, which would have the benefit of opening the northwest and northeast passages to ships through most of the year. Since this ice pack is afloat, its melting would not raise the water level in oceans—just as melting a floating ice cube in a glass of water does not raise the water level. But the absence of polar ice would change ocean currents and trigger unpredictable changes in the climate of the Northern Hemisphere. Some of the land-based Antarctic glacial ice might melt slowly, but the increased evaporation of ocean water could also increase snowfall, building up the snow accumulation at the pole. The resulting stresses could cause the edges of the ice cap to break off and slide into the ocean, raising the sea level about 6 meters (20 feet) over 300 years. Despite stories in the popular press predicting that the world's major coastal cities and flood plains (which produce most of the world's food) will soon be flooded, this melting process, if it occurred, would probably take place slowly over tens to hundreds of years. If this happened, it would cause damages of nearly $1 trillion (in 1971 U.S. dollars) in the United States alone. Over the next 50 years the more likely immediate threat to the world from a global warming is the shift in food-growing regions and capacity during a time when the world's population is expected to at least double. Rainfall patterns would shift and some cropland would have to be abandoned and replaced with other land of unknown quality. Existing irrigation and drainage systems and food storage and transportation systems that cost many billions of dollars would also have to be rebuilt to reflect new rainfall patterns.

Thus, if we continue to burn fossil fuels and cut down much of the world's moist tropical forests (Section 10-4), we will be faced with a possible doubling of atmospheric carbon dioxide levels within 40 to 70 years. The burning of the world's proven reserves of oil and natural gas may not cause unacceptable climate changes, but if all global reserves of coal were burned, atmospheric CO_2 levels could increase eightfold. Burning the world's estimated reserves of shale oil and synfuels produced from coals (Section 14-3) could cause an even greater increase in CO_2 levels.

The solution to this potential global danger is to: (1) not shift to coal, shale oil, or synfuels as a major energy source over the next 50 years and rely more on either nuclear power (Section 14-3) or a combination of solar, wind, geothermal, and biomass energy and energy conservation (Sections 14-1, 14-6, 14-7, and 14-8);* or (2) use scrubbers to remove CO_2 from the stack gases of coal-burning power and industrial plants. The latter solution is technically feasible but would be expensive and require an energy input equal to about 43 percent of the energy found in a unit of coal.

E3-3 Particles in the Atmosphere: Is the Atmosphere Cooling?

Aerosols or particles of solids and liquids are constantly injected into the atmosphere in large quantities. Dust, soot, and other particles enter the atmosphere from active volcanoes, forest fires, dust storms, sea spray, and other natural sources. Humans also add particles by clearing land for agriculture and urbanization and through smokestack, chimney, and automobile emissions (Chapter 17). Unlike CO_2, particles differ markedly in size and chemical makeup (Figure 17-11).

The huge quantity of particles spewed into the atmosphere from a major volcanic eruption can apparently cause regional and global cooling for several months to a year after the eruption. Because there were no major volcanic eruptions between 1940 and 1970, it is hypothesized that some of the drop in mean atmospheric temperature in the Northern Hemisphere between 1940 and 1970 (Figure E3-2) was caused by increased atmospheric inputs of particles from human activities. These particles, especially those in the upper atmosphere, could reflect some of the incoming sunlight back into space and thus reduce the amount of solar heat reaching the earth's surface.

However, particles can either raise or lower atmospheric temperature depending on their size (Figure 17-11), composition, reflective properties, altitude, and the reflectivity of the earth's surface below. Over a dark surface, such as the ocean, particles tend to be net reflectors of incoming sunlight and cool the atmosphere. But over much of the land, which is lighter than the oceans, particles can absorb heat energy and radiate some of it back toward the earth, thus warming the atmosphere. In the atmosphere both the cooling and warming processes take place, and the net effect depends on the strength of each process and the altitude of the dust layer. If the layer is high enough, the cooling process probably dominates.

There is considerable evidence that the human input of atmospheric particles has increased over the past few decades, especially above cities and industrial regions in Europe and the United States. But we do not know whether human activities are a major source of this input compared with natural processes. Estimates of the human production of atmospheric dust range from 5 to 50 percent of the total input each year. Most large-particle emissions near the earth's surface have a residence time of days to a few weeks before they fall out or are washed out by rain. Although they can affect local weather patterns significantly, these particles are not a major factor in global climate. However, very small particles that rise in or are injected into the stratosphere have a residence time of 1 to 5 years and can affect global climate. It is argued that since most particles from human activities end up in the lower atmosphere, their climatic effects are primarily local. Thus, the overall effects of particles from

---

*To limit the CO_2 atmospheric increase to no more than about 50 percent above 1800 levels would require global fossil fuel use to peak and begin declining between 2000 and 2020.

natural and human sources on global climate are complex and still poorly understood.

E3-4 Heat: The Ultimate Pollutant

Cities and Heat Take a breath, raise your arm, turn on a light, drive a car, or heat or air condition your house or car, and you add heat to the atmosphere. According to the second law of energy (Section 3-3), whenever energy is used, some of it is degraded to heat energy, which flows into the atmosphere and is eventually radiated back into space (Figure 5-4). If human activities should produce energy faster than it can be radiated back into space, then the average temperature of the atmosphere will rise—just as an auditorium heats up when it is filled with people. Thus, as more and more people try to use more and more energy, this direct input of heat could cause atmospheric warming, first on a local and regional level, and eventually on a global level.

This heating effect is already occurring in large cities and urban areas. Anyone who lives or works in a city knows that it is warmer there than in nearby suburbs or rural areas. Day in and day out, cities emit vast quantities of heat through home and building heating and air conditioning, industrial plants, and automobiles. Concrete and brick buildings and asphalt pavements absorb heat during the day and release it slowly at night. Tall, closely spaced buildings slow down wind near the ground and reduce the rate of heat loss. Water rapidly runs off the paved surfaces in cities, in contrast to rural areas where water soaks into the soil and then slowly evaporates to cool the surrounding air. Thus, it is not surprising that a dome of heat hovers over a city, creating what is called an *urban heat island* (Figure E3-5). Not only is a city

warmer than rural areas, but it typically has lower visibility, more air pollution, less sun, less wind, and lower humidity (Table E3-2).

As urban areas grow and merge into vast urban regions (Figure 11-4), the heat domes from a number of cities can combine to form *regional heat islands*, which could affect regional climate. The prevailing winds that normally cleanse the center of the dome would already be polluted—thus raising air pollution levels under the large regional dome. In addition, summer heat levels in the center could become intolerable, and the use of millions of air conditioners would add even more heat to the atmosphere and increase the chances of power brownouts and blackouts.

Table E3-2 Comparison of Urban and Nearby Rural Climates

Variable	Urban Compared with Rural Levels
Temperature	
Annual mean	0.5 to 1.0°C higher
Winter average	1.0 to 2.0°C higher
Visibility	5 to 30 percent less
Pollutants	
Particulates	10 times more
Gases(sulfur dioxide, carbon dioxide, carbon monoxide)	5 to 25 times more
Solar radiation	15 to 20 percent less
Wind speed	
Annual mean	20 to 30 percent less
Calms (stagnant air)	5 to 20 percent more
Relative humidity	
Winter	2 percent less
Summer	8 percent less

Global Heating Because of the second energy law, each human on earth adds heat to the atmosphere continuously at about the same rate as a 100-watt light bulb. When we add the other direct and indirect uses of energy, each person in the world imposes a continuous average heat load onto the atmosphere equal to that of five 100-watt bulbs. In the United States average per capita energy use is so high (Section 13-2) that each American injects a continuous average heat load equivalent to a hundred 100-watt bulbs. As world population and energy use continue to increase, the resultant heat load could eventually affect global climate. Today the human input of heat is only about 0.01 percent of the input of energy from the sun. In other words, at present the sun's contribution to the atmospheric heat load is about 10,000 times that caused by human activities.

Global climate changes could occur when the human heat input reaches about 0.5 to 1.0 percent of that from the sun. If world energy use grows at about 5 percent a year, we could reach this level within 125 years. This could cause the mean atmospheric temperature to rise from 0.2° to 4.0°C, with 2 to 3 times this change at the earth's poles. Although such human-induced changes in global climate are not an immediate problem, they could occur within 100 years or perhaps sooner from the combined effects of direct inputs of heat and carbon dioxide (Section E3-2) from human activities.

E3-5 Needed: A Global Plan

By burning up the world's fossil fuels, cutting down the world's forests, and converting land to cropland, we appear to be carrying out a gigantic climate experiment with unknown and perhaps disastrous long-term results. Although we don't have an adequate understanding of global climate change, there may be a significant change, or at least unpredictable variations, over the next 20 to 100 years. Regardless of the causes of climate change, clearly one of the major tasks facing the world today is to develop plans for responding to either global heating or global cooling, as well as natural climate fluctuations such as droughts.

Because a major climate change would probably take place gradually over many years, there may be a dangerous tendency to delay planning and action. But to establish new food-growing regions and food distribution networks or to limit the burning of fossil fuels and forest clearing would take decades. Failure to make plans and to develop better models for predicting climate

change could easily doom millions of people to a premature death in the future.

We may be able to use fossil fuels (primarily coal if we run out of oil and natural gas) for another 30 to 50 years without drastic effects on climate. But after that period we must either shift to other energy sources, such as nuclear, solar, wind, and water power, that do not produce CO_2 (Chapters 13 and 14) or find ways to remove CO_2 from fossil fuel emissions. In addition, we must support a massive global research program to (1) find out more about the ability of the oceans and green plants to absorb CO_2 from the atmosphere; (2) learn the extent of global deforestation; (3) develop better models for predicting the effects of increased atmospheric CO_2, particles, heat, and cloudiness on global and regional climate; and (4) develop alternative ecological, agricultural, economic, social, and political plans to adapt to possible climate changes.

Such research is crucial, but it will take decades—perhaps after long-term and potentially harmful changes have already occurred. Because of this uncertainty, climatologist Stephen H. Schneider (see his Guest Editorial at the end of Chapter 4) has urged the world to store up several years of food as insurance against climate change and variability. In the Book of Genesis the pharaoh heeded Joseph's advice to store up food for the lean years. Hopefully, we will be wise enough to adopt a similar "genesis strategy."

When you understand all about the sun and all about the atmosphere and all about the rotation of the earth, you may still miss the radiance of the sunset.

Alfred North Whitehead

Discussion Topics

1. Trace all of the direct and indirect effects you had today on local and global climate. Classify these activities as essential, desirable, or frivolous.

2. Explain why most radiation returning to space has longer wavelengths (lower energy) than incoming solar radiation. Does this mean that less energy flows back than reaches the earth? Explain.

3. Criticize the following statements:
   a. A new ice age could spread across the United States by the year 2050.

b. Massive global flooding would occur if we melted the floating Arctic ice pack.

c. Massive global flooding near seacoasts could occur by the year 2050.

4. Explain how particles, depending on their size and location, cause the atmosphere (a) to cool, (b) to heat up.

5. Criticize the statement "We shouldn't worry about the heating up of the atmosphere from increased carbon dioxide levels because a warmer climate is more desirable."

6. What effect on the climate might each of the following have: (a) oil spills, (b) increased land under cultivation, (c) driving an air conditioned automobile, (d) switching on a light, (e) air conditioning your home or place of work, (f) strip mining, (g) using an electric dryer to dry hair or clothing, (h) switching from oil and coal power plants to nuclear power plants, (i) switching from fossil fuel and nuclear power plants to solar energy power plants?

7. Are the climate changes in urban areas shown in Table E3-2 desirable or undesirable in terms of human comfort and energy use during the winter and summer? Explain.

8. Criticize the statement "Human actions will not affect global climate for 100 to 200 years, so we need not be concerned with the problem now."

9. Debate the idea that we should set up a world food bank to store several years' food as insurance against climate change. How would you decide who gets this food in times of stress?

Readings

Allen, Richard. 1980. "The Impact of CO_2 on World Climate." *Environment*, vol. 22, no. 10, 6–38. Excellent overview.

Baes, C. F., Jr., et al. 1977. "Carbon Dioxide and Climate: The Uncontrolled Experiment." *American Scientist*, vol. 65, 310–320. Excellent overview of this important problem.

Bolin, Bert. 1977. "The Impact of Production and Use of Energy in Global Climate." In *Annual Review of Energy*. Vol. 2. Palo Alto, Calif.: Annual Reviews. Superb overview of potential effects of human activities on climate.

Bryson, Reid A., and Thomas J. Murray. 1977. *Climates of Hunger: Mankind and the World's Changing Weather*. Madison: University of Wisconsin Press. Excellent summary of why the world may be cooling.

Bryson, Reid A., and John E. Ross. 1972. "The Climate of the City." In Thomas R. Detwyler and Melvin G. Marcus, eds., *Urbanization and Environment*. North Scituate, Mass.: Duxbury. Superb summary of urban climate effects.

Calder, Nigel. 1974. *The Weather Machine: How Our Weather Works and Why It is Changing*. New York: Viking. Very readable overview with emphasis on global cooling.

Council on Environmental Quality. 1981. *Global Energy Futures and the Carbon Dioxide Problem*. Washington, D.C.: Council on Environmental Quality. Superb overview.

Elliot, W. P., and L. Machta, eds. 1977. *Proceedings of ERDA Workshop on Environmental Effects of Carbon Dioxide from Fossil Fuel Combustion*. Washington, D.C.: U.S. Department of Energy. Very useful, technical overview.

Holdren, John P. 1971. "Global Thermal Pollution." In J. P. Holdren and P. R. Ehrlich, eds., *Global Ecology*. New York: Harcourt Brace Jovanovich. Very clear summary of the calculations and principles involved in predicting the effects of human heat inputs on climate.

Kellogg, William W. 1977. "Global Influences of Mankind on the Climate." In John Gribbin, ed., *Climatic Change*. Cambridge: Cambridge University Press. Outstanding overview with emphasis on global warming.

Lamb, H. H. 1972. *Climate: Present, Past and Future*. Vol. 1. London: Methuen. Very useful discussion of climatic history.

Landsberg, H. E. 1970. "Man-Made Climatic Changes." *Science*, vol. 170, 1265–1274. Outstanding balanced summary. Good bibliography.

National Academy of Sciences. 1975. *Understanding Climatic Change: A Program For Action*. Washington, D.C.: National Academy of Sciences. Superb overview.

National Academy of Sciences. 1979. *Carbon Dioxide and Climate*. Washington, D.C.: National Academy of Sciences. Excellent overview.

Roberts, Walter Orr, and Henry Lansford. 1979. *The Climate Mandate*. San Francisco: W. H. Freeman. Superb discussion of climate and possible climatic effects of human activities.

SCEP (Study of Critical Environmental Problems). 1970. *Man's Impact on the Global Environment*. Cambridge, Mass.: MIT Press. Very useful and authoritative source.

Schneider, Stephen H. 1976. *The Genesis Strategy: Climate and Global Survival*. New York: Plenum Press. Outstanding overview of possible effects of human activities on climate, with a detailed plan for action.

Schneider, Stephen H., and Robert S. Chen. 1980. "Carbon Dioxide Warming and Coastline Flooding: Physical Factors and Climatic Impact." In Hollander, Jack M., ed. *Annual Review of Energy*. Vol. 5, pp. 107–140. Palo Alto, Calif.: Annual Reviews. One of the best summaries of the CO_2 problem and its possible effects.

Woodwell, George M. 1978. "The Carbon Dioxide Question." *Scientific American*, vol. 238, no. 1, 34–43. Superb overview with emphasis on effects of land-clearing activities.

Enrichment Study 4

Species Interactions in Ecosystems

In all ecosystems, different species constantly interact with one another. In this enrichment study we will look at the three major types of species interaction: *competition*, *predation*, and *symbiosis*. These interactions can affect both the structure (Chapter 4) and the function (Chapter 5) of ecosystems by changing the type and population size of species and by altering energy flows through food webs.

E4-1 Competition

When cattle and sheep are placed together on a limited grassland, they compete with each other for food (and for water when a drought occurs). **Competition** occurs when two or more species in the same ecosystem attempt to use the same scarce resources. The resource may be food, water, a place to live, sunlight, or anything that is needed for survival. If two or more species in an ecosystem have the same requirement for a resource, their ecological niches (Section 5-5) overlap. The greater the overlap, the greater the competition between the species. However, no two species in an ecosystem can indefinitely occupy exactly the same niche or exist on the same limited resource. This is called the **principle of competitive exclusion** (Gause's principle).

When the niches of different species overlap completely or to a large degree, one competitor may die out or become extinct (Section 10-7 and Enrichment Study 12). The species that wins has some competitive advantage. It may be able to reproduce its young faster, to obtain food or to defend itself more effectively, or to tolerate a greater range of variance in some limiting factor (Section 4-3).

Fortunately, extinction is not the only possible outcome of species competition. One species may merely move or migrate to another ecosystem where there is less competition. It may also remain in the same ecosystem and change its needs or behavior to remove or minimize niche overlap. Some species may be able to switch to a different source of food, eat or drink at a different time of day or night, or move to a different habitat in the same ecosystem. For example, the shag and cormorant are two similar species of fish-eating, cliff-nesting birds. When seen diving into the water for fish, they appear to compete for the same food. But the shag eats fish and eels found in the upper level of the ocean, while the cormorant feeds on bottom-dwelling fish and shrimp. Similarly, five different species of warbler birds found in Maine spruce forests coexist by feeding from different levels or parts of the trees. Sometimes such adaptations are made quickly or temporarily. In many cases, however, species undergo slow evolutionary adaptations that allow them to occupy different niches and thus avoid competition. Through such evolutionary changes, a greater diversity of species can develop in an ecosystem over a long period of time.

E4-2 Predation

The most obvious form of species interaction is **predation**. It occurs when an organism of one species (the predator) captures and feeds on an organism of another species (the prey). In most cases a predator species has more than one prey species. Likewise, a single prey species may have several different predators. Eagles, owls, and hawks eat rats, mice, rabbits, and other prey. Mountain lions and wolves eat squirrels, rabbits, deer, and other animals. We usually think of predation in terms of animal-animal interactions, but it can also involve plants. A cow can be classified as a predator when it eats grass (the prey), and carnivorous plants, like the Venus flytrap, catch and digest various insects.

Predation is the major way that energy and many materials are moved through and within an ecosystem. The ability of predators to find and feed on their prey determines the rate at which energy and various types of matter flow from one trophic level to another (Section 5-3).

Predation, along with competition, is a major factor in controlling the population size of various species in an ecosystem. In a stable ecosystem the ratio of a predator to its prey fluctuates around a fairly constant figure. Such periodic fluctuations of population size over a 90-year period are shown in Figure E4-1 for the lynx (the predator) and the snowshoe hare (the prey) in Canada. Note from the figure that when the lynx population is relatively high, the size of the rabbit population soon decreases. You might expect the rabbits to be wiped out completely, but as their numbers decrease, the lynx have a harder time finding them. Some of the lynx then die from a lack of food. This relieves the pressure on the rabbits, and their population size begins to rise again slowly.

In addition, as prey becomes scarce, predators are mostly limited to killing the old, the very young, and the sick prey. This means that the survivors tend to be the strongest and healthiest. Predation not only keeps a prey population stable, it also keeps it healthy. Once prey populations increase again, the predators have a better chance to find food and their numbers begin to grow—starting the cycle again. In nature, of course, cycles such as the one in Figure E4-1 are rarely so simple. Most ecosystems have elaborate food webs (Figure 5-8) in which most species are both prey for some species and predators to others.

Often hunting by humans is justified as means of population control of animals. Lions, wolves, and other natural predators of a species, such as the deer, may be killed off or driven out of an ecosystem. Then humans must act as hunters or predators to keep the deer population from exploding and destroying much of the vegetation. In other words, once natural predators have been removed, hunting may be necessary. But this can cause a serious problem. Human hunters usually don't kill the old, sick, and weak animals. Instead, they go after the strongest and healthiest ones—the animals most needed for reproduction. Thus, hunting can control a population, but the quality of the remaining population can be lowered.

E4-3 Symbiosis

Symbiosis, which means "living together," is an interaction in which two different species live in close physical contact, with one living on or in the other so that

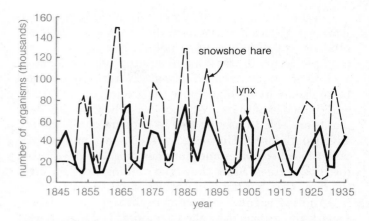

Figure E4-1 Predator-prey cycles are shown by the periodic fluctuations in the populations of the lynx (predator) and the snowshoe hare (prey) in Canada from 1845 to 1935.

one or both species benefit from the association. This interaction is an *ecological association* involving some transfer of energy or other ecological benefit. There are three types of symbiosis: *mutualism, commensalism,* and *parasitism*.

Mutualism is a symbiotic relationship between two different species in which both species benefit from the association. For example, a termite eats wood, but it cannot digest it without help, which is provided by a tiny protozoan living in the termite's gut. In the digestion process this microbe uses some of the nutrients to remain alive. Neither termites nor these microbes can live without each other. A newly hatched termite instinctively licks the anus of another termite in its closely packed colony to obtain a supply of protozoans for its gut.

Another mutualistic relationship exists in the nitrogen cycle (Figure 5-13) between legume plants (such as peas, clover, beans, and alfalfa) and *Rhizobium* bacteria that live in nodules on the roots of these plants. Large colonies of bacteria in these nodules "fix," or convert, gaseous nitrogen (N_2) to forms of nitrogen that can be used as nutrients by the plant and by the bacteria themselves.

Still another example of mutualism is the *lichen*. A lichen growing on a bare rock looks like a single plant, but it actually consists of two plant species living together. One is a type of alga, a green plant that makes food by photosynthesis. The other is a fungus that cannot make its own food. The algae provide food for themselves and the fungus, and the fungus provides shelter for the algae and absorbs water to keep them both from drying out in the hot sun.

In the second type of symbiosis, called **commensalism,** one species benefits from the association while the other is apparently neither helped nor harmed. One example occurs in tropical and subtropical forests. Here we find green plants called *epiphytes* (various orchids and bromeliads), living high above the ground on the trunks and branches of trees. With no roots, these so-called air plants are able to use the tree to get sunlight in the relatively dark forest. They also use their leaves and cupped petals to collect water and minerals that drip down from the tops of trees. Since they take nothing from the tree, the tree is neither harmed nor benefited.

Another example of commensalism occurs between a shark and a small fish called a remora. The remora uses a suction disk on the top of its head to attach itself to the underside of the shark. In this way it gets a free ride, free protection, and free food by eating floating scraps from the shark's meal. Apparently the shark is neither harmed nor benefited by this arrangement.

In **parasitism,** the third form of symbiosis, one species (the parasite) benefits and the other species (the host) is harmed. The parasite usually gets its nourishment from the host, either externally from skin, feathers, hair, or scales (ecoparasitism), or internally from the cells, tissues, and other parts of the host (endoparasitism). Examples of parasites are leeches (which suck blood from their victims), lice, ticks, fleas, bacteria, protozoans, fungi, and worms (such as tapeworms, hookworms, and pinworms). Human diseases caused by parasitic bacteria include typhoid fever, tuberculosis, cholera, syphilis, and gonorrhea (Enrichment Study 6). Diseases such as amoebic dysentery, African sleeping sickness, and malaria are caused by parasitic protozoans. Plants are also plagued by parasites. Parasite fungi cause wheat rust, corn leaf blight, Dutch elm disease, and other diseases that destroy a large part of plant species. By planting large fields of only one species, such as corn, humans help parasites wipe out an entire crop. A successful parasite may harm its host, but it does not kill the host. If the host dies, the parasite must also die or find a new host.

Like predation, parasitism helps regulate populations. Epidemics can spread rapidly and kill many members of a dense host population. Once the host population has been reduced, the parasites are less likely to find new hosts, and as they die off, the spread of the epidemic is slowed. In this way the two species tend to regulate each other's population density.

Parasitism, like predation, involves one species feeding on another. But there are significact differences between these two types of species interaction. Parasites are usually smaller than their host, whereas most predators are larger than their prey. Parasites tend to live in, on, or near their host and slowly consume only part of their host. In contrast, predators live apart from their prey and tend to kill and then consume most or all of their prey.

In this enrichment study we have seen how interactions between species are an important characteristic of ecosystems. These interactions, along with interactions between organisms and their environment, are the key to understanding energy flow and chemical cycling in ecosystems.

All things from eternity are of like form and come round in a circle.

Marcus Aurelius

Discussion Topics

1. Give three possible consequences of the ecological niches of two different species overlapping considerably.

2. Explain how predation and competition
   a. help control the population size of different species in an ecosystem.
   b. affect energy flow in an ecosystem.

3. Discuss the advantages and disadvantages of hunting by humans. Do you think hunting should be banned? Why or why not? What restrictions, if any, would you put on hunting? Why?

4. Explain how parasitism differs from predation.

5. Give an example not discussed in the text of commensalism, parasitism, and predation.

Readings

See the references at the end of Chapter 4.

Enrichment Study 5

Cadmium, Lead, and Mercury in the Environment

E5-1 Trace Elements in the Environment

About 40 of the 92 naturally occurring chemical elements are essential for most forms of plant and animal life. The 9 elements needed in relatively large quantities (hydrogen, oxygen, carbon, nitrogen, phosphorus, sulfur, magnesium, calcium, and potassium) are known as *macronutrients* (Section 5-4). Our bodies also contain trace amounts (less than 0.01 percent of the body) of at least 40 elements. Fourteen (and perhaps more) of these trace elements, known as *micronutrients*, are also necessary for life. They are iodine, fluorine, selenium, silicon, chromium, manganese, iron, cobalt, copper, zinc, molybdenum, tin, vanadium, and nickel. Unfortunately, a few of these micronutrients, along with other trace elements in the body and various radioactive isotopes (Section 14-3), can threaten human health when present in larger quantities.

From existing evidence, five metallic elements—cadmium, lead, mercury (in the form of methyl mercury), nickel (in the form of nickel carbonyl), and beryllium—are known hazards to humans (Table E5-1). The other four elements shown in Table E5-1 either are suspected to be health hazards or are not yet used in sufficient quantities to be of concern to the general public.

In this enrichment study we will examine the effects of three of these toxic metals—cadmium, lead, and mercury. These metals are special threats because they are widely used, nondegradable (Section 1-4), sometimes biologically magnified in food chains (Section 6-2), and cumulative poisons. Because of their persistence, these metals can accumulate in the body, gradually reaching harmful levels. For example, biological half-life in the human body is about 200 days for cadmium,* 1,460 days (4 years) for lead, and 70 days for mercury.

---

*Whole-body or biological half-life is the time required for half of a given quantity of an element to be excreted from the body. For example, after 200 days, half of a given input of cadmium still remains in the body.

E5-2 Cadmium

Cadmium is widely used in electroplating metals to prevent corrosion, in plastics and paints, and in nickel-cadmium batteries. It is also a contaminant in phosphate fertilizers. The evidence of cadmium's harmful effects is circumstantial and in some cases contradictory, but concern is growing. Japanese doctors found in 1955 that *itai-itai byo,* or "ouch-ouch" disease, was related to exposure to high levels of cadmium, although some scientists dispute this evidence. Ouch-ouch disease causes excruciating pain in the joints and slowly weakens the bones through loss of calcium. Even standing or coughing can break bones, and sufferers may eventually die as their entire bone structure withers away. Between 1955 and 1968 several hundred cases and at least 100 deaths were reported in northern Japan, mostly in people who ate rice and soybeans grown in fields contaminated by nearby mines and cadmium-using industries.

The real threat to most of us, however, may be exposure to low levels of cadmium over long periods of time. Because of its long biological half-life (200 days), cadmium gradually accumulates in our bodies. At birth the human body contains only about one-millionth of a gram of cadmium, but by age 50 a typical adult has 38,000 times this level.

Only about 2 percent of the cadmium we eat or drink stays in the body, but from 10 to 50 percent of the cadmium we inhale remains in the body. For this reason, tobacco smoke is the major source of cadmium for most people. Pack-a-day smokers carry about twice as much cadmium in their bodies as nonsmokers. People in the same room with smokers are also exposed to cadmium and other dangerous chemicals found in cigarette smoke (see Enrichment Study 6). Tests on mice indicate that pregnant women probably accumulate cadmium at a rate 2 to 3 times higher than other humans. Once in the body, cadmium accumulates primarily in the liver and kidneys and can cause irreversible damage to these organs.

Table E5-1 Sources and Health Effects of Some Widely Used Metals

Element	Sources	Health Effects
Class 1: Serious Threats Now		
Cadmium	Burning of coal; zinc mining; water pipes; tobacco smoke; rubber tires; plastics; superphosphate fertilizers	Heart and artery disease; high blood pressure; bone embrittlement; kidney disease; fibrosis of lungs; possibly cancer
Lead	Automobile exhaust (leaded gasoline); paints (made before 1940)	Brain damage; convulsions; behavioral disorders; death
Mercury (as methyl mercury)	Burning of coal; electrical batteries; many industrial uses	Nerve damage; death
Nickel (as nickel carbonyl)	Diesel oil; burning of coal; tobacco smoke; various chemicals; steel; gasoline additives	Lung cancer
Beryllium	Burning of coal; increasing industrial use (including nuclear power industry and rocket fuel)	Acute and chronic respiratory diseases; lung cancer; beryllosis
Class 2: Potential Hazards If Levels Increase		
Antimony	Industry; typesetting; enamelware	Heart disease; skin disorders
Arsenic	Burning of coal and oil; pesticides; mine tailings	Cumulative poison at high levels; possibly cancer
Selenium	Burning of coal, oil, and sulfur; some paper products	Possibly cancer; possibly tooth decay
Manganese	Metal alloys; smoke suppressant in power plants; possible gasoline additive in future	Nerve damage

Trace levels of cadmium in test animals and humans have also been linked to high blood pressure (hypertension), which makes heart attacks more likely. This effect may occur because cadmium is chemically similar to zinc and may replace zinc in the body. When zinc is replaced, fats accumulate in the circulatory system, leading to high blood pressure and heart trouble. Although strong circumstantial evidence links cadmium and high blood pressure, some evidence does not support this relationship.

We still have much to learn about the effects of cadmium on humans. But the widespread, increasing use of this metal (Table E5-1) and the evidence we have so far indicate the importance of controlling the cadmium content in cigarettes, air, food, and drinking water. In Sweden, most products containing cadmium have been banned since 1980.

E5-3   Lead

Lead Is Everywhere Some lead enters the ecosphere from natural sources, but most of the input by far comes from human activities. Lead has been used in pottery, batteries, solder, plumbing, cooking vessels, pesticides, and household paints, and is emitted into the atmosphere by lead smelters and the burning of coal and gasoline. As a result, lead levels have been increasing throughout the world, even in Greenland glaciers. As shown in Figure E5-1, the amount of lead in Greenland ice samples increased 500 percent between 800 B.C., when humans began mining and using lead, and 1750. Concentrations rose by another 400 percent between 1750 and 1940. This is the period of the industrial revolution, which spawned coal burning (which emits small amounts of lead) and lead smelters. An even sharper rise occurred between 1940 and 1967, when the number of automobiles burning leaded gasoline, which contains tetraethyl lead as an antiknock additive, increased sharply. The lead concentrations in Figure E5-1 are in parts per trillion and are therefore negligible. But these levels in remote Greenland dramatically illustrate that lead in the environment is widespread and that the level is increasing. Another indication of lead's growing presence is the threefold to fivefold increase in the concentration of lead in the open ocean since 1924, when leaded gasoline was introduced. Studies indicate that the average lead level in Americans may be 500 times that in Peruvians who lived 1,800 years ago.

Lead is one of the oldest known toxic metals. It may even have hastened the fall of Rome. In the second century B.C., the Roman ruling class suffered widespread sterility, stillbirths, and brain damage—possibly because of lead poisoning from the leaden wine and food vessels that only the rich could afford. Support for this theory comes from the high lead content found in the bones of some ancient Romans.

Airborne Lead   Today we are more democratic. Everyone is exposed to lead in air, drinking water, and food. In the United States 90 percent of this form of air pollution comes from the burning of leaded gasoline in cars, and another 5 percent from industrial smelters. Each day Americans inhale tiny particles of lead compounds emitted from automobile exhausts. Airborne lead also enters food when lead particles settle over agricultural and grazing areas, especially those near highways. Luckily, these lead particles are not absorbed into the plants; very careful washing can remove most of this contamination. As you might suspect, urban air has more lead than rural air, and urban dwellers have more lead in their blood than people living in rural areas.

Other Sources of Lead   Another source of lead in the human environment is earthenware pottery with lead glazes. Such pottery is particularly dangerous if used for acidic liquids such as orange and apple juice, which leach the lead out of the glaze. Modern pottery and china in the United States no longer have lead glazes, but any old or foreign-made pieces should be tested for lead content.

Lead is also a serious threat to workers in lead smelters, and battery plants and to people who do a lot of soldering.

Many house painters and perhaps some famous artists, such as Goya, probably died of lead poisoning from long-term exposure, since lead compounds have been widely used as paint pigments. Prior to 1940 lead was used in interior and exterior house paint in the United States. After 1940 lead-based paint was not used for interior painting, and since 1971 the lead content of paint in the United States has been sharply reduced by the Lead Poisoning Prevention Act of 1971. Nevertheless, young children living in pre-1940 houses and tenements often suffer lead poisoning, permanent brain damage, and hyperactivity from eating flaking paint and lead-containing dirt and dust.

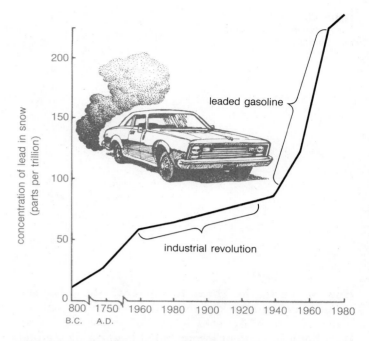

Figure E5-1   Average annual lead content in isolated Greenland glaciers has been increasing since 800 B.C. The actual data are a series of scattered points, and the curve represents the best average line through these points. In addition, there is considerable seasonal variation in lead levels.

Children may also take in lead by inhaling or eating street dust, by eating or chewing color pages from glossy magazines and gift wrapping paper, by eating or licking snow and icicles contaminated with lead from automobile exhaust, and by exposure to the clothes of members of the household who work with lead. An estimated 500,000 children are exposed to high levels of lead in the environment. In the United States, about 200 children die each year from lead poisoning. Another 12,000 to 16,000 children are treated for lead poisoning each year and survive. About 30 percent of those who survive suffer from palsy, partial paralysis, and permanent brain damage. Most cases of lead poisoning involve children between the ages of 1 and 3 who have *pica*. This abnormal craving for unnatural foods, including dirt, paper, putty, plastic, and paint chips, may result from a diet deficiency.

Recent research indicates that about half of the lead we ingest in our food probably comes from the lead-soldered seams in tin cans. Also, lead contamination in some samples of canned tuna exceeded natural background concentrations in the environment by a factor of 10,000.

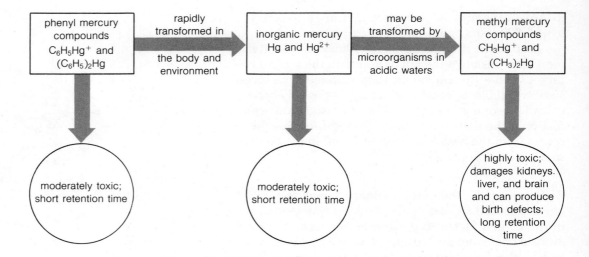

Figure E5-2 Some chemical forms of mercury and how they may be transformed.

phenyl mercury compounds $C_6H_5Hg^+$ and $(C_6H_5)_2Hg$

rapidly transformed in the body and environment

inorganic mercury Hg and Hg^{2+}

may be transformed by microorganisms in acidic waters

methyl mercury compounds CH_3Hg^+ and $(CH_3)_2Hg$

moderately toxic; short retention time

moderately toxic; short retention time

highly toxic; damages kidneys. liver, and brain and can produce birth defects; long retention time

How Serious Is the Threat to Humans? Lead is a cumulative poison. Luckily, most of the lead we inhale or ingest is usually excreted in the urine fast enough to keep the lead content in our blood below a dangerous level, except in cases of prolonged exposure at high concentrations. Children can absorb up to 50 percent of the lead they ingest and about 40 percent of the small particles of airborne lead we inhale each day is absorbed in our lungs. A small part of this daily lead intake gradually accumulates in our bones, replacing the calcium. Here it is normally insoluble and harmless. But under certain conditions, such as feverish illness, cortisone therapy, and old age, this accumulated lead can be released suddenly into the blood at toxic levels.

Considering the number of cars in the United States, it is not surprising that Americans have the highest average blood levels of lead in the world, although the Japanese may soon take over the number one spot. These blood levels, though significant, fall 25 to 50 percent below the threshold for classical lead poisoning—although this threshold is constantly being lowered. Indeed, some researchers are wondering whether there really is a safe threshold level for lead. Companies making lead additives for gasoline and other lead-using industries point out that no concrete evidence exists that airborne lead harms humans. But experiments with animals have indicated that low levels of lead can increase animal death rates at all ages by as much as one-quarter.

As with smoking, we can't establish a direct relationship between lead from automobiles and human health. But because of circumstantial and statistical evidence, a number of prominent scientists have urged that lead additives be banned from gasoline and tin cans and that

smelting, battery, and other industries that use lead be required to control lead emissions into the air and water.

In 1978 the EPA established a standard requiring that by 1982 airborne lead levels in the United States be limited to 1.5 micrograms of lead per cubic meter of air, based on a quarterly average. Currently, U.S. airborne lead levels average 2 to 4 micrograms, with concentrations as high as 6 micrograms in some large cities such as Los Angeles. The EPA has also established a standard to reduce the average lead content in gasoline. The EPA has, however, granted some delays in meeting this standard and companies making lead additives are challenging the EPA standard in the courts. These companies hope to sell lead additives for gasoline abroad where lead levels are not restricted.

E5-4 Mercury

Natural and Human Sources Get a tooth filled, flip a silent light switch, install an automatic furnace or air conditioner, use fluorescent or street lights, and you are depending on mercury—a chemical that has been used in various forms for over 27 centuries. It is also used in some paints, floor waxes, and furniture polishes, in antibacterial and antimildew agents, medicines, and fungicides for seeds, and in making plastics, paper, clothing, and camera film. Human input of mercury into the air and water has been increasing, especially by the burning of coal (which contains mercury as a trace contaminant) and by deliberate and accidental discharges into rivers, streams, and lakes. Yet, human inputs total only a fraction of the natural inputs from vaporization from the earth's crust and from the vast amounts naturally stored as bottom sediments in the ocean. It is dangerous to consume large amounts of pike, tuna, swordfish, and other large ocean species that contain high levels of mercury. But most, if not all, of this mercury comes from natural sources, and the danger has probably always been present. Although the human input into the ocean is insignificant, some lakes, rivers, bays, and estuaries near mercury-using industries are being threatened.

Mercury and Human Health Suppose you were taking your temperature with a mercury-filled thermometer and you accidentally bit it in half. Would the mercury you swallowed harm you? Actually, elemental mercury is not a dangerous poison unless vaporized and inhaled directly into the lungs. Almost all of the mercury you swallowed would pass out of your system in a few days. The real threat from mercury comes in an extremely toxic organic form known as methyl mercury (CH_3Hg^+). It stays in the body more than 10 times longer than metallic mercury, can attack the central nervous system, kidneys, liver, and brain tissue, and can cause birth defects. The major forms of mercury and the ways they are transformed are summarized in Figure E5-2.

Between 1953 and 1960, 52 people died and 150 suffered serious brain and nerve damage from methyl mercury discharged into Minamata Bay, Japan, by a nearby chemical plant. Most of the victims in this seaside village area ate fish contaminated with methyl mercury three times a day. In 1969, a New Mexico farm laborer fed seed grain treated with methyl mercury to his hogs. After he and his family ate this hog meat, three of his children became severely crippled. A fourth child, poisoned in his mother's womb, was born blind and mentally retarded. In Iraq in 1972, a large shipment of seed grain treated with methyl mercury was distributed to villagers, who fed it to animals and used it to bake bread. Four hundred and fifty-nine people died, and an estimated 6,530 were injured.

An unexpected discovery about mercury occurred in 1969, when two young Swedish scientists, Sören Jensen and Arne Jernelöv, duplicated stream bottom conditions in an aquarium and found that anaerobic (non-oxygen-requiring) bacteria dwelling in bottom mud could convert relatively harmless elemental mercury and inorganic mercury (II) salts into highly toxic methyl mercury (Figure E5-2). Fortunately, most waters apparently are not acidic enough to enable this transformation. However, we still know far too little about the complex chemistry of mercury in living systems and we may encounter some unexpected changes and effects in the future. In addition, the increases in acidity of many lakes from acid rain (Section 17-2) may aggravate this problem.

In summary, the danger from mercury is mainly a local problem arising in three special situations: (1) when humans eat food contaminated with methyl mercury seed dressings; (2) when methyl mercury used or formed in industrial processes enters natural waters; and (3) when inorganic mercury or organic phenyl mercury is converted into alkyl mercury compounds by microorganisms found in the bottom sediments of acidic waters. To guard against such situations, we need a global ban on mercury seed dressings and on the discharge of mercury by mercury-using industries. The technology for this control already exists.

Cadmium, lead, and mercury present us with a challenging paradox. Simultaneously, they are very important and very dangerous materials. So far we have been lucky, but adequate protection requires stringent controls on the negligent discharge of these valuable resources into the environment.

The ultimate end . . . is not knowledge, but action. To be half right on time may be more important than to obtain the whole truth too late.

Aristotle

Discussion Topics

1. Criticize the statement "Since we have always been exposed to background levels of metals from natural sources, the fear of toxic metals is ecohysteria."

2. Debate the following resolution: Because of their dangers, we should ban the use of cadmium, lead, mercury, nickel, and beryllium. How would your life be changed if such a ban were instituted?

3. Explain how lead might have been a factor in the downfall of Rome. Could this also happen in the United States? How does the present U.S. situation differ from that in early Rome?

4. Criticize the following statements:
   a. Because the average lead level in blood tends to be below the level for classical lead poisoning, there is no serious problem.
   b. There is no absolute proof that lead in gasoline has killed any Americans.

5. Should all metal additives be banned from gasoline? Explain.

6. Criticize the following statements:
   a. We are seriously polluting the ocean with mercury.
   b. Because we are not the major source of mercury pollution in the ocean, there is no cause for concern.
   c. We should no longer eat tuna fish and swordfish.
   d. Since metallic mercury is not highly toxic to humans, we have little to fear.
   e. Mercury poisoning is a global environmental problem.

7. Why do some experts consider cadmium our most serious toxic metal threat?

8. Debate the following resolution: Smoking should be banned by law in all enclosed public places and on all forms of mass transportation.

9. Contrast the threats from lead, mercury, and cadmium in terms of (a) source (water, air, or food), (b) pervasiveness (global, regional, or local), (c) severity of threat to human health, and (d) feasibility of control.

Readings

Council on Environmental Quality. 1971. *Toxic Substances.* Washington, D.C.: U.S. Government Printing Office. Excellent summary of pollution from lead, cadmium, mercury, and vanadium.

D'Itri, Patricia R., and Frank M. D'Itri. 1977. *Mercury Contamination.* New York: Wiley. Superb summary.

Frieden, Earl. 1972. "The Chemical Elements of Life." *Scientific American*, July, pp. 52–60. Excellent summary of positive and harmful effects of trace elements.

Goldwater, Leonard J. 1971. "Mercury in the Environment." *Scientific American*, vol. 224, no. 5, 15–21. Excellent summary.

Hiatt, V., and J.E. Huff. 1975. "The Environmental Impact of Cadmium." *International Journal of Environmental Studies*, vol. 7, no. 4, 277–285. Very good overview.

Jenkins, Dale W. 1972. "The Toxic Metals in Your Future— and Your Past." *Smithsonian*, vol. 3, no. 1, 62–69. Superb nontechnical summary.

McCaull, Julian. 1971. "Building a Shorter Life." *Environment*, vol. 13, no. 7, 3–41. Superb review of the cadmium problem.

Montague, Katherine, and Peter Montague. 1976. *No World without End: The New Threats to Our Biosphere.* New York: Putnam's. Excellent overview of threats from lead, mercury, cadmium, and other toxic metals.

National Academy of Sciences. 1980. *Lead in the Human Environment.* Washington, D.C.: National Academy of Sciences. Authoritative review.

National Science Foundation. 1977. *Lead in the Environment.* Washington, D.C.: National Science Foundation. Authoritative review.

Needleman, Herbert L. 1980. "Lead Exposure and Human Health: Recent Data on an Ancient Problem." *Technology Review*, March/April, pp. 39–45. Excellent overview.

Schroeder, Henry A. 1974. *The Poisons around Us: Toxic Metals in Food, Air, and Water.* Bloomington: Indiana University Press. Superb summary by an expert toxicologist.

Smith, W. Eugene, and Aileen M. Smith. 1975. *Minamata.* New York: Holt, Rinehart and Winston. Well-researched description of methyl mercury poisonings in Japan.

Williams, Michael. 1971. "Lead Pollution on Trial." *New Scientist*, September 9, pp. 578–580. Argues that lead pollution from automobiles is not a serious problem.

Enrichment Study 6

Environmental Health and Human Disease

A 32-year-old Indian peasant farmer is forced to stop working his tiny plot of irrigated land because of agonizing pains in his lower abdomen, fever, diarrhea, and general fatigue. He is infected with a parasite that causes schistosomiasis, or snail fever. Last month the youngest of his six malnourished children died from severe diarrhea, and next year his 30-year-old wife and two of his children will die from cholera. Meanwhile, thousands of kilometers away, a well-nourished infant in New York City has easily recovered from an attack of diarrhea. Before her eighth birthday, however, she will be without parents. Her mother, who has been a four pack a day smoker since age 16, will die of lung cancer at age 45. Her father, who also smokes heavily and who has been overweight for 20 years, will drop dead from a heart attack 3 days before his forty-eighth birthday. These are only a few examples of the complex and varied global picture of health that we will examine in this enrichment study.

E6-1 Types of Disease

Infectious and Noninfectious Diseases We become afflicted with a disease when there is an upset of the complex, delicate balance that is normally maintained between our bodies and the environment. The upset may result from factors in the physical environment (air, water, food, or sun), the biological environment (bacteria, viruses, plants, and animals, including humans), the social environment (work, leisure, and cultural habits and patterns), or any combination of these three sources.

Human diseases can be broadly classified as *infectious* and *noninfectious*. **Infectious disease** occurs when we are *host* to disease-causing living organisms (called *agents*), such as bacteria, viruses, and parasitic worms. Infectious diseases can be classified according to the method of transmission, as either vector-transmitted or non-vector-transmitted. **Vector-transmitted infectious diseases** (such as malaria, schistosomiasis, and African sleeping sickness) are carried from one person to another by some living organism (usually an insect), which is called the **vector.** Some of the major vector-transmitted infectious diseases found in the world today are shown in Table E6-1. **Non-vector-transmitted infectious diseases** (such as the common cold, tuberculosis, cholera, measles, mononucleosis, syphilis, and gonorrhea) are transmitted from person to person without an intermediate carrier. This transmission usually takes place by one or a combination of methods: (1) close physical contact with infected persons (syphilis, gonorrhea, mononucleosis, and leprosy); (2) contact with water, food, soil, clothing, bedding, or other vehicles contaminated by fecal material or saliva from infected persons (cholera, typhoid fever, and infectious hepatitis); or (3) inhalation of air containing tiny droplets of contaminated fluid expelled when infected persons cough, sneeze, or talk (common cold, influenza, and tuberculosis).

When an infectious disease (such as syphilis) is carried by many hosts without leading to a rapid and widespread death toll, it is *endemic* to the population. For example, mononucleosis is endemic in the U.S. population, and many high school and college students have it unknowingly. An *epidemic* occurs when a sudden, severe outbreak of an infectious disease (such as typhoid fever or influenza) affects many people in a population and leads to a large number of deaths. An infectious disease (such as influenza) becomes *pandemic* when it spreads worldwide to infect and kill a large number of people. Because of the extensive movement of people and food throughout the world, only strict sanitation and public health measures can protect against pandemics from non-vector-transmitted infectious diseases. Vector-transmitted infections can become pandemic only when the vector organisms (such as fleas and bats) are transferred throughout the world and can survive under a variety of climates and conditions.

Noninfectious diseases are those not relayed by a disease-causing organism and not transmitted from one person to another (excluding genetic diseases). Exam-

Table E6-1 Major Vector-Transmitted Infectious Diseases

Disease	Infectious Organism	Vector	Estimated Number of People Infected (millions)
Malaria	*Plasmodium* (parasite)	*Anopheles* (mosquito)	500*
Schistosomiasis	*Schistosoma* (trematode worm)	Certain species of freshwater snails	300
Filariasis (elephantiasis and onchocerciasis, or river blindness)	Several species of parasitic worms	Certain species of mosquitoes and blood-sucking flies (elephantiasis); female black flies (onchocerciasis)	250
Trypanosomiasis (African sleeping sickness and Chagas' disease)	*Trypanosoma* (parasites)	Tsetse fly (African sleeping sickness); kissing bugs (Chagas' disease)	100

*150 million new cases each year.

ples include cardiovascular (heart and blood vessel) disorders, cancer, diabetes, chronic respiratory diseases (bronchitis and emphysema, Section 17-3), allergies (asthma and hay fever), nerve and other degenerative diseases (cerebral palsy and multiple sclerosis), and genetic diseases (hemophilia and sickle cell anemia). Many of these diseases have several, often unknown causes* and tend to develop slowly and sometimes progressively over a number of years. Typically they are caused by (1) exposure to certain chemicals (some cancers and emphysema), ultraviolet energy from the sun (some forms of skin cancer), and pollen and other materials found in air, water, and food (asthma and hay fever); (2) inherited genetic traits (hemophilia); (3) a combination of environmental and genetic factors (emphysema); and (4) changes in body chemistry triggered by unknown causes (cerebral palsy and diabetes).

Acute and Chronic Diseases We can also classify diseases as either acute or chronic according to their effect and duration. An **acute disease** is an infectious disease (such as measles, whooping cough, typhoid fever) that normally lasts for a relatively short time before the victim either recovers or dies. A **chronic disease** is one that lasts for a long time (often for life) and may flare up periodically (malaria), become progressively worse (cancer and cardiovascular disorders), or disappear with age (child-

---

*Because of this, some diseases now classified as noninfectious (such as cancer) may later be found to be caused or triggered by viruses or other infectious organisms.

hood asthma). Chronic diseases may be infectious (malaria, schistosomiasis, leprosy, and tuberculosis) or noninfectious (cardiovascular disorders, cancer, diabetes, emphysema, and hay fever). Table E6-2 summarizes major characteristics of acute infectious diseases, chronic infectious diseases, and chronic noninfectious diseases.

The Social Ecology of Disease By studying Table E6-2 carefully we can see that the prevalence and mortality of the three categories of diseases differ between the more developed and the less developed nations. The populations of less developed nations tend to have a short average life span largely because of the complex interactions among poverty, malnutrition, and infectious diseases (Figure 9-2). Poor people in these nations are more likely to come into contact with infectious organisms because of contaminated water and food, crowding, and poor sanitation. The tropical or equatorial location of most poor nations also increases the chances of infection, because hot, wet climates and the absence of winter enable disease vectors (Table E6-1) to thrive year round. In addition, poor people—especially infants—tend to be more susceptible to these diseases because these people are more likely to be weakened by malnutrition (Section 9-1). Thus, *infectious diseases that the rich recover from tend to kill the poor.* For example, in 1967 through 1968, the mortality rate from whooping cough in some poor countries was 300 times higher than that in rich nations; from typhoid fever, 160 times higher; from diphtheria, 100 times higher; from dysentery, 76 times higher; and from measles, 55 times higher. Generally, most poor people

Table E6-2 Comparison of Acute Infectious, Chronic Infectious, and Chronic Noninfectious Diseases

Characteristic	Acute Infectious	Chronic Infectious	Chronic Noninfectious
Examples	Measles, typhoid fever, whooping cough, smallpox	Malaria, schistosomiasis, tuberculosis	Cardiovascular disorders, cancer, diabetes, emphysema
Cause	Living organism	Living organism	Usually several, often unknown environmental and/or genetic factors
Transmission	Usually non-vector	Vector and non-vector	Not transmitted directly but some may be transmitted genetically
Time for development (latent period)	Short (hours or days)	Long (usually years)	Long (usually years)
Duration	Usually brief (days)	Long (often for life)	Long (often for life)
Effects	Usually temporary or reversible	Usually irreversible	Usually irreversible
Age group	Children and adults	Middle- to old-age adults	Middle- to old-age adults
Prevalence	High in less developed nations, low in more developed nations	High in less developed nations, low in more developed nations	High, especially in more developed nations where longer life spans allow diseases to develop
Mortality	High in less developed nations, low in more developed nations	High in less developed nations, low in more developed nations	High in more developed nations
Prevention	Sanitation, clean drinking water, vaccination	Sanitation, clean drinking water, vaccination, vector control	Control of environmental factors such as smoking, diet, and exposure to polluted air, water, and food

don't live long enough to die from chronic noninfectious diseases, such as heart disease, cancer, or emphysema. Although the death certificates in poor nations (if filed) may list an infectious disease as the cause of death, the real underlying causes are poverty, malnutrition, and overpopulation.

One indicator of the prevalence of infectious diseases in a country is its infant mortality rate. In Finland, Denmark, Norway, and Sweden, which have the lowest infant mortality rates in the world, only about 1 infant out of every 100 born will die in the first year of life. In the United States, which ranks seventeenth in the world in infant mortality, about 1 infant in 77 will die in its first year. By contrast, in some parts of Africa the infant death toll is 1 in 5.

In most more developed nations, safe water supplies, public sanitation, adequate nutrition, and immunization have nearly stamped out many infectious diseases. In 1900 the infectious diseases pneumonia, influenza, tuberculosis, diarrhea, and enteritis were the leading causes of death in the United States. Today deaths from these diseases are very few; the major causes of death now are chronic noninfectious diseases, heart disease and cancer, which respectively accounted for 38 percent and 20 percent of all deaths in the United States in 1979.

Contrary to popular belief, the rise in the average life expectancy in the United States between 1900 and 1950 did not occur as a result of modern medicine. With the exceptions of whooping cough, polio, and influenza, the decline in death rates from infectious disease occurred primarily because of improved nutrition and better hygiene and sanitation. Indeed, since 1950 the rise in the average life expectancy in America has leveled off and today it has begun to drop for men. According to the U.S. Department of Health and Human Services the major cause of the rise in cancer and heart disease in the United States is the increased pollution in the environment since 1950. Let's now look more closely at some of the diseases that afflict the world.

E6-2 Vector-Transmitted Infectious Diseases: Malaria and Schistosomiasis

Malaria People in the United States and in most more developed countries tend to view malaria as a disease of the past. But *in the tropical and subtropical regions of the world, malaria is still the single most serious health problem—killing about 1.5 million people in 1978 and incapacitating many millions of people* (Figure E6-1). An estimated 2 billion people—half the world's population—live in malaria-infested regions. In Africa alone, malaria strikes an estimated 150 million people and kills more than 1 million children under age 14 annually.

Malaria's symptoms come and go; they include fever and chills, anemia, an enlarged spleen, severe abdominal pain and headaches, extreme weakness, and greater susceptibility to other diseases. It is caused by one of four species of protozoa (one-celled organisms) of the genus *Plasmodium*. The disease is transmitted from person to person by the bite of several species of *Anopheles* mosquito, which act as vectors (Figure E6-2). The *Plasmodium* protozoa circulate in the bloodstream of an infected person and can be ingested by a biting *Anopheles* mosquito. The protozoa multiply in the mosquito's stomach and develop into the sporozoite stage of their life cycle. When the infected mosquito bites another person, it injects the sporozoite form of the parasite into that person's bloodstream. The parasites multiply in the liver, change into a new stage of their life cycle, and then invade the blood cells, producing fever, chills, headache, and weakness. This newly infected host can now pass malaria on to others in the human-mosquito-human cycle (Figure E6-2). Malaria can also be transmitted when a person receives the blood of an infected person in a blood transfusion and when an infected drug user shares a needle with another user. For this reason heroin is usually "cut" with quinine, an antimalarial drug.

One way to control malaria is to administer antimalarial drugs, which protect people against infection from bites of *Anopheles* mosquitoes. For over 100 years quinine has been used to prevent and treat malaria, and today more effective drugs, such as chloroquine and primaquine, are being used. Antimalaria drugs are helpful, but they cannot be used effectively to rid an area of malaria. The cost is too high because people in infested areas would have to take the drugs continuously throughout their lives. In addition, new strains of carrier mosquitoes eventually develop that have genetic resistance to any antimalarial drug that is widely used.

Another approach is vector control—trying to get rid of the mosquito carriers by draining swamps and by spraying breeding areas with DDT and other pesticides (Enrichment Study 11). In the 1950s and 1960s the World Health Organization made great strides in reducing malaria in many areas, eliminating it in 37 countries by

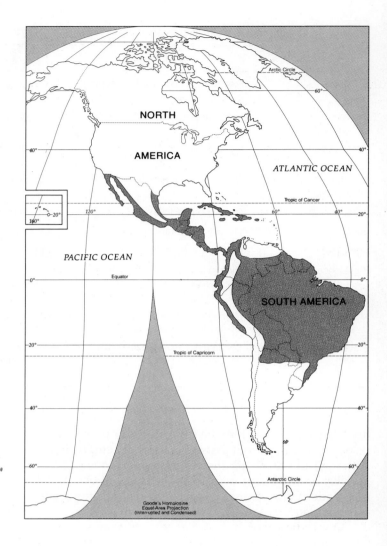

widespread spraying of DDT and the use of antimalarial drugs. In India malaria cases were cut from a 1947 high of 75 million to only 40,000 in 1966, and in Pakistan cases were reduced from 7 million in 1961 to only 9,500 in 1967. Since 1970, however, malaria has made a dramatic comeback in many parts of the world. By 1978 the number of cases in India had risen to 50 million and in Pakistan to 10 million. This tragic resurgence has occurred because of the following: (1) increased genetic resistance of mosquito carriers to DDT and other insecticides and to antimalarial drugs (Enrichment Study 11); (2) rising costs of pesticides and antimalarial drugs (between 1974 and 1975 the price of DDT tripled, primarily because of rising oil prices); (3) the spread of irrigation ditches, which provide new mosquito breeding grounds; (4) the physical

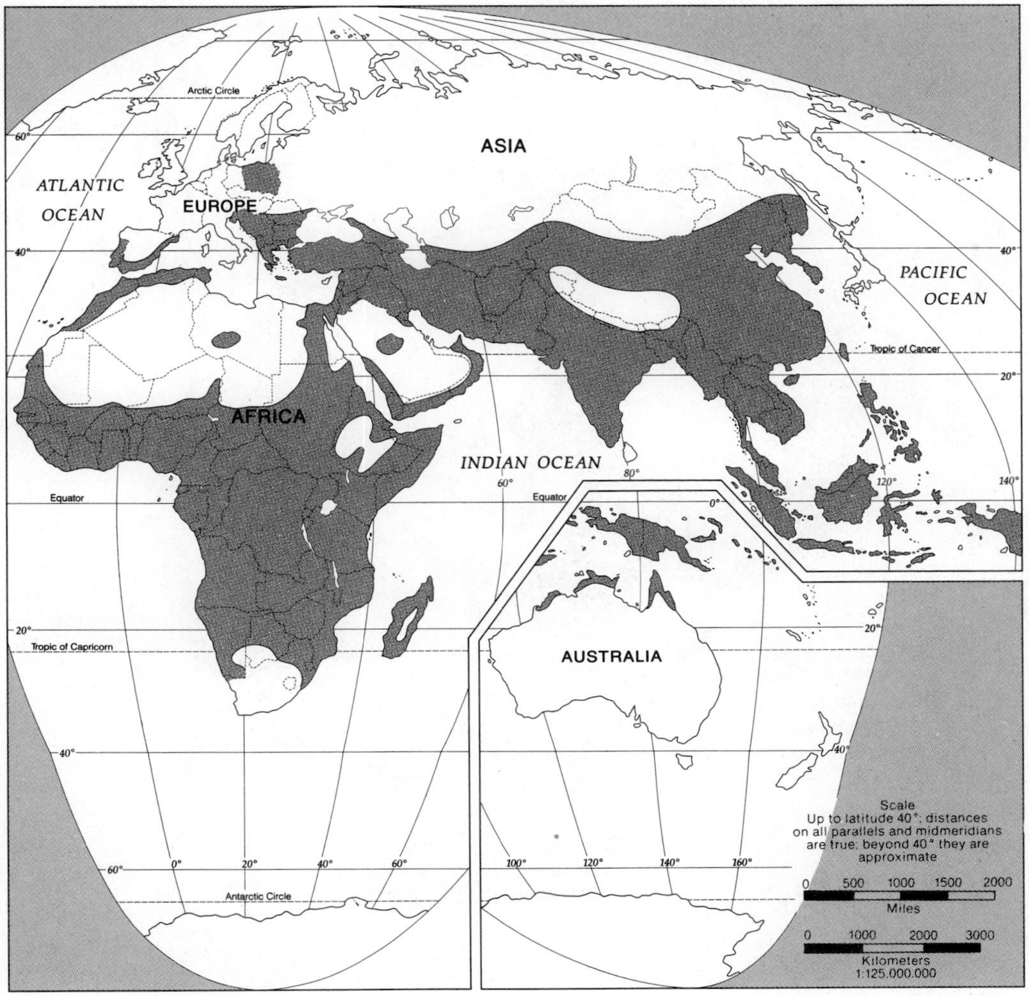

Figure E6-1 World distribution of malaria.

inability to reach and spray all mosquito-infested areas; and (5) reduction of budgets for malaria control due to the belief that the disease had been controlled.

Research is being carried out to develop biological controls for *Anopheles* mosquitoes and to develop anti-malarial vaccines, but so far such approaches are still in the early development stages. One promising form of biological control is the use of bacteria (*Bacillus sphaericus*) that kill mosquito larvae. Unfortunately, the amount of money being devoted to research on malaria and other tropical diseases is shockingly low when we consider that more people suffer and die from these diseases than all other diseases combined. The World Health Organization estimates that only 3 percent of the money spent each year on biomedical research is spent on tropical

diseases. The remaining 97 percent of the funds are spent primarily on cancer, heart disease, and genetic diseases, which are the major health problems of the more developed nations.

Schistosomiasis Schistosomiasis, like malaria, chronically afflicts hundreds of millions of people (Table E6-1), especially in Africa, South America, the Caribbean, the Middle East, and Asia. Humans are the major hosts, although other hosts include cattle, sheep, goats, cats, dogs, and some wild animals. Schistosomiasis is caused by the trematode worm *Schistosoma*, which is transmitted between human and animal hosts by tiny freshwater snails (Figure E6-3). The adult worms lodge in the hu-

Figure E6-2 The life cycle of malaria.

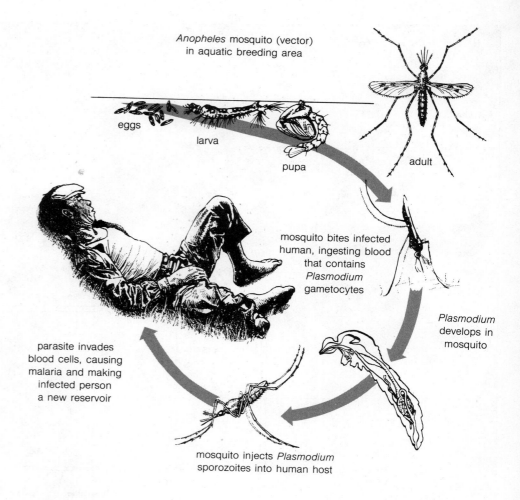

Anopheles mosquito (vector) in aquatic breeding area

eggs

larva

pupa

adult

mosquito bites infected human, ingesting blood that contains *Plasmodium* gametocytes

Plasmodium develops in mosquito

parasite invades blood cells, causing malaria and making infected person a new reservoir

mosquito injects *Plasmodium* sporozoites into human host

man host's veins and deposit eggs in surrounding organs and tissues, causing chronic inflammation, swelling, and pain. Though almost every organ in the body can be infected, the urinary bladder and the liver are especially susceptible. Victims suffer from cough, fever, enlargement of the spleen and liver, a general wasting away of the body, filling of the abdomen with fluid (which produces the characteristic pot belly), and constant pain. Victims are also more susceptible to other diseases and are often too weak to work. Mildly infected victims usually recover, but persons who are severely malnourished or severely infected may die (Figure E6-3).

Schistosoma eggs excreted in the urine and feces of the hosts often go directly into nearby streams, rivers, lakes, or irrigation canals. Once in the water the eggs hatch and, after developing into larvae, enter certain species of tiny snails that breed in the freshwater systems of warm and tropical climates. In the snails, the larvae multiply and change into another free-swimming larval

form, which in turn is released from the snail into the local water. These larval forms can burrow into the skin of new human hosts, who may be bathing, swimming, or wading in the water. Once inside the body, the larvae begin to grow into adult worms, which spread throughout the body and deposit their eggs. The urine and feces of these newly infected humans can then start the entire cycle again.

With schistosomiasis we encounter the problem of human trade-offs in less developed nations. To grow more food for their populations, these nations undertake massive irrigation projects. Irrigation ditches are ideal breeding places for the intermediate host snails. As workers urinate and wade in the ditches, schistosomiasis spreads widely. Farmers, weakened from the infection, produce less food even though more land is available.

Schistosomiasis can be reduced or even eradicated in an area by (1) preventing human excreta from reaching the snails through improved sanitation; (2) preventing

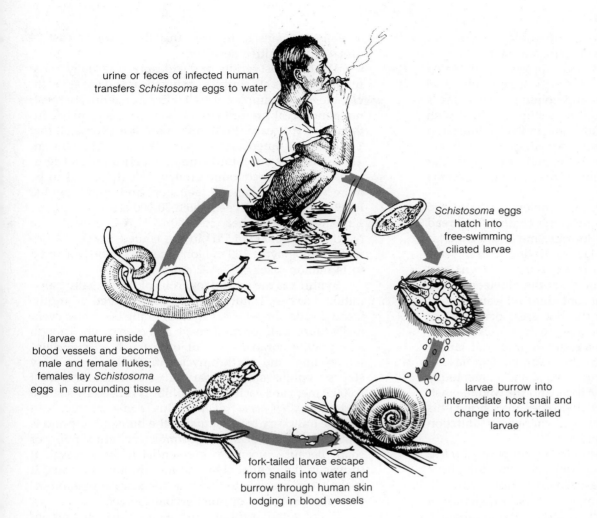

urine or feces of infected human transfers *Schistosoma* eggs to water

Schistosoma eggs hatch into free-swimming ciliated larvae

larvae mature inside blood vessels and become male and female flukes; females lay *Schistosoma* eggs in surrounding tissue

larvae burrow into intermediate host snail and change into fork-tailed larvae

fork-tailed larvae escape from snails into water and burrow through human skin lodging in blood vessels

people from swimming or washing in contaminated water; (3) protecting people who farm or fish in contaminated waters by the use of boots and protective clothing; (4) developing drugs to kill the worms in the body; and (5) killing the snails with chemicals. In practice, however, schistosomiasis is a very difficult disease to control. The first three approaches are either expensive or difficult to put into effect, or both. The fourth approach has had mixed success. Several drugs have been developed that can kill most of the worms in the human body. But so far none works on all people or on all species of the parasite, and all of the drugs are expensive or have serious side effects. So far, the fifth approach has had only limited success because the chemicals are too expensive for the almost continuous use that is required. In addition, the chemicals can kill fish, poison the water, and have other ecological and health side effects. However, there is some hope. Preliminary results indicate that the

dried, ground berries of the endod, used by villagers in Ethiopia as a detergent for washing clothes at streamside, may be effective in killing the snails without hurting other animals and plants.

Nevertheless, it seems clear that reducing the incidence of schistosomiasis in the less developed nations is going to be very difficult. In 1975 only about $8 million was devoted to schistosomiasis research throughout the world—less than one-hundredth of the world's cancer research budget.

E6-3 Non-Vector-Transmitted Infectious Diseases: Cholera and Sexually Transmitted Diseases

Cholera One of the most frightening infectious diseases is cholera—a term used to describe a collection of infections that result in severe diarrhea and dehydration. The bacteria causing cholera are transmitted from person to person through water and food supplies contaminated with sewage. Within a half day the infected individual suffers from severe diarrhea and vomiting, which leads to rapid dehydration. Unless the victim is treated with antibiotics that combat the infection and with fluids and salt that counter the effects of dehydration, the blood pressure falls, the skin shrivels up, and severe muscular cramps, coma, and death follow. This sequence of events occurs in 2 to 7 days.

Until the nineteenth century, cholera was confined to India. Throughout the nineteenth century, it spread to China, Japan, East Africa, Europe, and North America in a series of six pandemic plagues, lasting 10 to 20 years each and killing thousands in the affected towns and cities. It was not until the middle of the nineteenth century that people learned that contaminated water spread the dreaded disease. After the last great pandemic of 1865 through 1875, cholera was pushed back into its southern Asia homeland as a result of improved sanitation and vaccines. Since 1961, however, cholera has begun to march across continents for a seventh time; today it kills people all over Asia, Africa, and the Middle East. There is fear that an infected traveler may bring this dreaded scourge to Latin America, where poor sanitation would allow it to spread rapidly.

Cholera is a major threat to the urban poor who live in crowded, unsanitary conditions and who don't have access to vaccines. Even vaccination is not a cure-all, since cholera vaccine gives only a 50 percent chance of protection, and that protection lasts for only about 6 months. In most poor nations it is too difficult and expensive to vaccinate the entire population every 6 months. The only effective way to combat cholera (along with a host of other waterborne infectious diseases) is to improve water supplies and sanitation throughout the world—especially in the tropics. Tropical disease experts estimate that chlorinating and filtering water supplies and using fairly simple sanitation measures for sewage (such as pit latrines and simple privies) could reduce the incidence of cholera by 60 to 90 percent.

Sexually Transmitted Diseases **Sexually transmitted diseases** (STDs) include more than two dozen infectious diseases that are transmitted from person to person through sexual intercourse, kissing, and contact with the sexual organs of infected persons. The term *sexually transmitted disease* (STD) is now used instead of *venereal disease* (VD). VD refers primarily to gonorrhea and syphilis and fails to indicate that there are at least 24 diseases transmitted sexually.

The five most serious and widespread sexually transmitted diseases are syphilis, gonorrhea, and the as yet incurable herpes simplex virus 2 (HSV-2 or genital herpes), nongonococcal urethritis (NGU) in men, and pelvic inflammatory disease (PID) in women. It is estimated that 1 of every 20 Americans is affected by an STD each year. These diseases are found among Americans of all ages, races, and socioeconomic groups, but they tend to be more widespread among teenagers and young adults. In 1979 there were an estimated 70,000 cases of syphilis, 1 million of gonorrhea, 500,000 of HSV-2, 3 million of NGU, and 800,000 of PID in the United States. Worldwide there may be 100 million cases of gonorrhea and 5 to 14 million cases of HSV-2 per year.

Syphilis is the most dangerous of the sexually transmitted diseases. If not discovered and treated promptly, it can invade almost every system in the body and eventually cause widespread damage and even death. Though it is readily curable by antibiotics (such as penicillin, tetracycline, and erythromycin) if caught in the early stages, syphilis is the primary cause of death for at least 3,000 Americans each year. Syphilis is caused by a spiral bacterium, *Treponema pallidum*. This fragile organism can survive only very briefly outside the human body and is rapidly killed by heat, lack of moisture, antiseptics, or soap. Because moisture is essential to its survival, it thrives in the genital area, the mouth, and the anus. It is almost impossible to contract this disease without intimate heterosexual or homosexual contact.

If untreated, syphilis progresses through four increasingly serious phases over a period of up to 30 years. The primary stage usually develops about 3 weeks after infection (although it can appear as much as 3 months later). The first sign is a *chancre*, which occurs at the site of contact (either on the genitals, anus, mouth, or the cervix of some females). Initially the chancre feels like a bump under the skin but soon becomes an open sore or ulcer. Because the chancre is not painful or itchy and is often internal (especially in females), it may be ignored or go unnoticed. Even without treatment the sore disappears within a few days or weeks, and the victim often falsely assumes that the infection has been cured. During the primary stage the disease is highly contagious, and diagnosis is difficult unless patients tell their doctors of their suspicions. The spiral bacterium is hard to identify and is not detected in blood samples during this stage.

If not treated, the disease progresses to a second stage, which lasts up to 4 years. During this period the victim is still highly infectious; thus one carrier can directly or indirectly infect many other people. During this stage the disease may go unnoticed or not be treated properly because the symptoms (skin rash, sore throat, enlarged lymph nodes, mouth sores, swollen joints, fever, headache, pain in the bones, and patchy loss of hair from the scalp and eyebrows) vary with different individuals and are also characteristic of many other diseases. These symptoms may come and go over a 4-year period and will eventually disappear even without treatment. Diagnosis at this stage can be made only through blood tests. However, a single negative test does not mean that the person is not infected or has been cured. Treatment should not be terminated until there have been at least two negative blood tests.

If untreated, the disease then enters a third stage, known as the latent (or hidden) period, which usually lasts 5 years or more. The disease goes "underground," while the bacteria slowly infect and attack almost every organ in the body. During this period the person can still infect others, so that an undetected carrier can continue to spread the disease for almost 10 years. Diagnosis can be made through repeated blood tests, and treatment to prevent further damage is still possible during this phase.

A woman who is in the first, second, or early part of the third stage can transmit syphilis to her unborn child. This can lead to miscarriage, still birth, premature delivery, or fetal disorders. These effects can be prevented, however, through treatment of the mother, especially during the first 18 weeks of pregnancy. For this reason most states in the United States require serologic (serum) blood tests for syphilis in pregnant women.

Next the disease enters its fourth and final stage, which may last as long as 20 years. The infected person may deteriorate mentally and physically from heart damage, blindness, paralysis, and insanity. By this time the damage is irreversible, although the person is no longer infectious.

Gonorrhea is caused by the bacterium *Neisseria gonorrhoeae*, which usually attacks the mucous membranes of the genital organs and eyes. This organism also cannot live outside the body for any length of time and is almost without exception spread by intimate sexual activity. Unlike syphilis the incubation period for gonorrhea is very short—only about 2 to 5 days. For this reason, immediate diagnosis and treatment are needed.

The symptoms differ in men and women. Most infected men have a burning sensation during urination and a discharge of yellow pus from the urethra. This highly infectious discharge can be transferred accidentally to the eyes. Women often have slight or nonexistent early symptoms; thus they may be unaware of the disease and spread infection to any male sexual partners who do not use condoms or to homosexual partners. If untreated, gonorrhea usually causes bladder infection and painful and frequent urination. If untreated for a long time, it can eventually cause further damage, including sterility in both the male and female. An infected pregnant female can transmit the disease to her unborn child when it moves through the birth canal during delivery.

Infections from the traditional bacterial strains of gonorrhea can usually be cured with one or two shots of an antibiotic (such as penicillin, tetracycline, or ampicillin) or, in some cases, with sulfa drugs. Since 1976, however, world health officials have become alarmed about a new strain of gonorrhea bacteria that are not killed by penicillin. Apparently these new bacteria can secrete an enzyme (penicillinase) that destroys penicillin. This new strain is spreading slowly around the world. Another antibiotic, spectinomycin, can be used to treat the new strain. However, it is about 8 times more expensive than penicillin, does not knock out syphilis (as does penicillin), requires several applications, and could also meet bacterial genetic resistance as it becomes more widely used. At present, extensive research is being carried out to develop a vaccine to prevent gonorrhea.

Unlike for gonorrhea and syphilis, there is no known cure for **herpes simplex virus 2** (HSV-2 or genital herpes), which is spreading rapidly throughout the United States and the world. By 1980 an estimated 10 to 20 million Americans had HSV-2, and there are about half a million new cases each year. An estimated 30 percent of the sexually active U.S. population have been exposed to genital herpes. Because HSV-2 is caused by a virus—not a bacterium—it cannot be cured by antibiotics or any known medication. New drugs are being tested but so far the FDA has not licensed any drugs for the treatment of this illness.

HSV-2 is similar to herpes simplex virus 1 (HSV-1), which causes painful cold sores and fever blisters on the mouth, face, and lips. HSV-2, however, causes very painful red blisters on or near the genitals within 2 to 20 days after sexual activity with an infected partner. Herpes sores are sometimes confused with those of syphilis—a much more dangerous disease. Herpes blisters, however, are almost always painful, while those of syphilis are usually painless. In most cases an attack of these extremely painful herpes sores (somewhat like being burned with a soldering iron) will clear up within a week to 10 days. But they can then recur without warning throughout the entire life of about 2 out of 3 infected victims. Some individuals suffer attacks each month, while others may go for long periods without another outbreak. No one knows what triggers a new attack, but some investigators suspect that stress and the onset of menstruation may play a role. Since at present there is no cure, every time an outbreak recurs the carrier can infect others. Unfortunately, the disease can sometimes be transmitted even before the blisters appear. In some cases the attack may go undetected because the sores are deep within the vagina or male urethra. Another problem is that if victims touch a herpes sore and then rub their eyes, they can get an eye infection called herpes keratitis, which causes blindness for thousands of Americans each year.

Another serious problem is that female victims of this disease are 5 to 8 times more likely than usual to develop cervical cancer. Cervical cancer is nearly 100 percent curable if detected early. As a result, women with HSV-2 should have a Pap test for cervical cancer at least twice a year. In the male, HSV-2 may lead to cancer of the prostate. HSV-2 can also cause birth defects. During delivery a woman with an active infection has a good chance of passing the disease on to her baby. Three out of four infected infants will probably suffer brain damage or blindness, and some will die. This tragedy can be prevented by carefully monitoring an infected pregnant woman. If active sores are found near the time of delivery, the doctor may perform a cesarean delivery so that the baby won't pick up the infection as it passes through the birth canal.

Two newly discovered STDs that are spreading very rapidly are **nongonococcal urethritis** or NGU in men and **pelvic inflammatory disease** or PID in women. These diseases are usually caused by the bacterium *Chlamydia trachomatis*. Some experts expect *Chlamydia* infections (which were first incorrectly believed to be a new strain of penicillin-resistant gonorrhea) to become the most widespread STD in the world—a record presently held by gonorrhea. The symptoms of NGU and PID are similar to those of gonorrhea—sometimes a discharge from the penis and painful urination for men and fever and severe abdominal pain for women. PID can cause sterility in about one out of five infected women, especially in teenagers. If untreated, or if a woman is repeatedly infected, the scar tissue that forms in the fallopian tube can cause an ectopic pregnancy, where the fetus grows in the fallopian tube rather than in the uterus. This type of pregnancy can rupture the fallopian tube and in some cases can kill the mother. The infection can be passed on to newborn infants and cause a serious eye infection and pneumonia. In the male, if NGU is not treated or is treated improperly, it can cause infection in the prostate gland and the tube carrying sperm from the scrotum; it can also lead to sterility. Both NGU and PID are difficult to detect and are often improperly diagnosed as gonorrhea and then treated with penicillin (which works for gonorrhea, but not NGU or PID) rather than with tetracycline, which can cure all three of these diseases.

It is tragic that in an age when gonorrhea, syphilis, NGU, and PID can be cured they are still widespread. The best ways to minimize the possibility of contracting these diseases and others such as HSV-2 are (1) to refrain from sex (understandably not a very popular solution); (2) to have fewer sexual partners; (3) for the male to use a condom (Enrichment Study 8); and (4) to scrub the genitals with soap and water internally and externally immediately after sex. Anyone suspecting or finding symptoms of infection should seek immediate diagnosis and treatment from a physician or from the free clinics available in most areas.* Anyone who is sexually active with a number of partners should seriously consider having a medical examination and blood tests for these sexually transmitted diseases at least once a month.

E6-4 Chronic Noninfectious Diseases: Cancer

Effects and Nature of Cancer Cancer is a complex set of chronic noninfectious diseases. It is the only major cause of death in the United States whose incidence has continued to rise since 1900. Between 1900 and 1979, the death rate from cancer in the United States almost tripled. Between 1970 and 1976, the incidence of cancer (after adjustments are made for age and longer life spans of the population) increased about 10 percent. Today cancer strikes one in every four Americans and accounts for about one of every five deaths in the United States. In 1979 approximately 1 million Americans found out they had cancer. About 300,000 of these cases were skin cancers, usually treatable with no significant effect on life expectancy. The other 700,000 cases, however, were serious enough to kill about 400,000 Americans—an average of about 1,095 deaths each day. This death toll in only 1 year equals the total number of Americans killed during World War II, the Korean War, and the Vietnam War. In addition to death, cancer in the United States

---

*Anyone needing confidential information (you don't need to give your name) can call the national toll-free "hot line" (800-523-1885) from anywhere in the United States except Pennsylvania. In Pennsylvania call collect 215-567-6973, and in Philadelphia 567-6969.

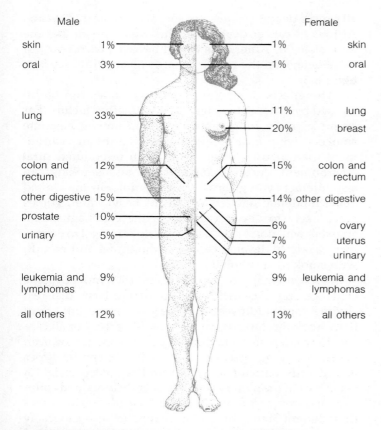

Male | | | Female
skin | 1% | 1% | skin
oral | 3% | 1% | oral
lung | 33% | 11% | lung
| | 20% | breast
colon and rectum | 12% | 15% | colon and rectum
other digestive | 15% | 14% | other digestive
prostate | 10% | |
urinary | 5% | 6% | ovary
| | 7% | uterus
| | 3% | urinary
leukemia and lymphomas | 9% | 9% | leukemia and lymphomas
all others | 12% | 13% | all others

Figure E6-4 Where fatal cancer strikes; percentage of all U.S. cancer deaths in 1977.

resulted in hospitalization costs and loss of productivity and earning power equal to at least $30 billion in 1979.

Cancer is the name for a group of more than 100 different diseases that strike people of all ages. It is characterized by the uncontrolled growth of cells in body tissues, which leads to the formation of tumors. *Benign tumors* grow slowly, never spread, and are enclosed within a fibrous capsule. By contrast, the *malignant tumors* that characterize cancer tend to grow rapidly, spread to other parts of the body (called *metastasis*), and are rarely encapsulated. Specific groups of cancers are named according to the types of cells affected. Cancer in the cells of the connective tissues, including bones, are called *sarcomas;* those in cells lining the body's internal and external surfaces (lungs, breasts, and skin) are called *carcinomas;* and those in cells that make up the blood-forming system are called *leukemias,* or *lymphomas.*

Although we still don't know exactly how cancers get started, most are probably related to exposure to radiation (X-rays, radioactivity, and the sun's ultraviolet rays) or to one or more chemicals called **carcinogens.** Cancer is usually a *latent disease*, having a typical time lag of 15 to 40 years between the initial cause and the appearance of symptoms. The long time lag, along with the number of different types of cancer, makes it extremely difficult to identify the specific cause of a particular cancer. The long time lag also prevents many people from taking simple precautions that would greatly decrease their chances of getting the disease. For instance, it is very difficult for high school and college students in good health to accept the fact that their smoking and eating habits *today* will be major factors determining whether they die from cancer during their thirties, forties, or fifties.

Incidence and Geography of Cancer Despite the similar features of all types of cancer, its incidence varies by age, sex, race, specific location in the body, geographic location, and ethnic or national origin. Cancer affects people of all ages but is mostly a disease of middle and old age. In the United States the incidence of cancer in men begins to increase sharply at 35 and peaks at 65. For women it rises rapidly at age 20 and peaks at age 60. Males and females in the United States have different incidences and death rates from the different types of cancer (Figure E6-4). The leading killer of males is lung cancer, and of females breast cancer. Cancer, primarily leukemia, also kills a large number of children. In the United States, cancer is second only to accidents as the leading cause of death in children between the ages of 5 and 14.

Cancer death rates also vary geographically between countries and within countries. The rates for breast cancer and bowel cancer are 4 to 5 times higher in the United States than in Japan, whereas stomach cancer rates in Japan are almost 7 times higher than in the United States. Figure E6-5 shows how the death rates for cancer vary in white males throughout the United States. Similar patterns have been found for white women and for black men and women. From Figure E6-5 we see that the highest cancer mortality rates are found in large cities and in the heavily industrialized states of the Northeast and Great Lakes regions.

Causes of Cancer We still can't relate most cancers to specific causes because of the complexity of the disease and its long latent period. Hereditary factors, environmental factors, and possibly viruses are believed to be involved. For example, the fact that mongoloid children

(Down's syndrome) have leukemia at 11 times the rate of normal children indicates that heredity can play a role. In addition, cancer of the female breast appears in some families more often than others. Heredity is apparently involved in only a small portion of observed cancers, perhaps 10 to 30 percent. So far only circumstantial evidence links viruses to some forms of cancer, but many scientists believe that viruses will eventually be implicated as factors in leukemia, cancer of the lymph nodes, and cervical cancer.

Most experts agree that environmental factors are responsible for 70 to 90 percent of all human cancers. This conclusion is reached primarily from differences in both the incidence and the distribution of different types of cancers throughout the world and within the United States (Figure E6-5). The environmental factors leading to 70 to 90 percent of all cancers include: (1) our lifestyles (whether we smoke, drink, and eat foods high in fat and low in fiber, and how much we are exposed to the sun); (2) our occupations (whether we are exposed to certain industrial chemicals);* (3) where we live (whether we live in a city, near an industrial area, or in an area with more sunshine)†; (4) our personal hygiene (people with poor sexual hygiene may be more susceptible to cancer of the cervix and penis); and (5) other factors as yet unidentified.

There is widespread agreement that the leading U.S. cause of cancer deaths (mostly from lung cancer) is cigarette smoking. Smoking has been linked to 80 to 90 percent of all lung cancers, and people who smoke heavily for decades increase their odds of dying from lung cancer 10- to 20-fold. Tobacco smoke also increases the chances of getting cancers of the mouth, throat, bladder, esophagus, and pancreas. Fortunately, people who quit smoking can greatly reduce this risk. About 10 years after they quit, smokers have about the same risk of cancer as those who never smoked.

It is estimated that if Americans stopped smoking cigarettes, this alone would eliminate 15 to 20 percent of

all cancer deaths (40 percent for males) within 20 years. At today's cancer death rate, this would mean that the lives of 46,000 Americans would be saved each year (for more details on the health hazards of smoking, see Section E6-5).

The effects of smoking on cancer rates can be increased by synergistic interaction with other factors. For example, more lung cancer is found among cigarette smokers living in a polluted industrial urban environment than among those living in an unpolluted rural environment. Alcohol consumption and smoking can also interact synergistically. For example, in the United States moderate smokers who drink heavily are 25 times more likely to develop cancer of the esophagus than smokers who don't drink. Heavy drinkers are 2 to 6 times more likely to develop cancer of the throat and mouth, with smoking multiplying the risk.

A second major cause of cancer is diet. Indeed, some evidence suggests that on a worldwide basis diet (excluding food additives) may be even more important than smoking, causing as much as 50 percent of all cancers in women and one-third of those in men. However, evidence linking specific dietary habits to specific types of cancer is difficult to obtain and is controversial. A small part of the dietary risk of cancer in developed countries may come from the increased use of food additives (Enrichment Study 10). But the major factors—especially in cancers of the breast, bowel (colon and rectum), liver, kidney, stomach, and prostate—may be the fats, fibers, nitrosamines, and nitrites in the diet. Bowel cancer, for example, is rare in most less developed countries and in more developed countries, like Japan, that have low-fat diets. But it is very common in countries such as the United States, Great Britain, Canada, and Denmark, where lots of high-fat beef is consumed. For instance, bowel cancer is the second largest cause of cancer deaths in the United Kingdom and the United States. It has been proposed that high incidences of bowel cancer may result from the low fiber content in Western diets, a by-product of the use of highly refined foods. So far, however, various studies have given conflicting results and the low-fiber hypothesis is still controversial. A high-fat, high-protein diet may also be a factor in cancers of the breast, prostate, testis, ovary, pancreas, and kidney. In addition, high levels of nitrate and nitrite preservatives may increase the risk of stomach cancer.

Diet has also been implicated in the very high incidence of stomach cancer in Japan. An important factor may be the large amounts of dried, salted, and smoked fish in the Japanese diet. Dried and salted fish contain nitrosamines, which are known carcinogens, and the

---

*Workers in the following groups tend to have higher incidences of various types of cancer: coal mining, asbestos (construction, shipbuilding), chemistry, foundries, pesticides production, textiles, newspaper printing, uranium and other metals mining, coke ovens, cadmium production, rubber industry, petroleum refining, furniture production, shoe production, leather production, and the plastics industry.

†Outdoor workers are particularly susceptible to skin cancer on the face, hands, and arms. White Americans who spend long hours in the sun greatly increase their chances of developing skin cancer and also tend to end up with wrinkled, dry skin by age 40. Most skin cancers can be cured, but they are painful and often leave disfiguring scars. Sunbathers can reduce this risk greatly and still get a tan (although more slowly) by using suntan lotions containing sunscreen agents, which block out most of the harmful ultraviolet rays of the sun.

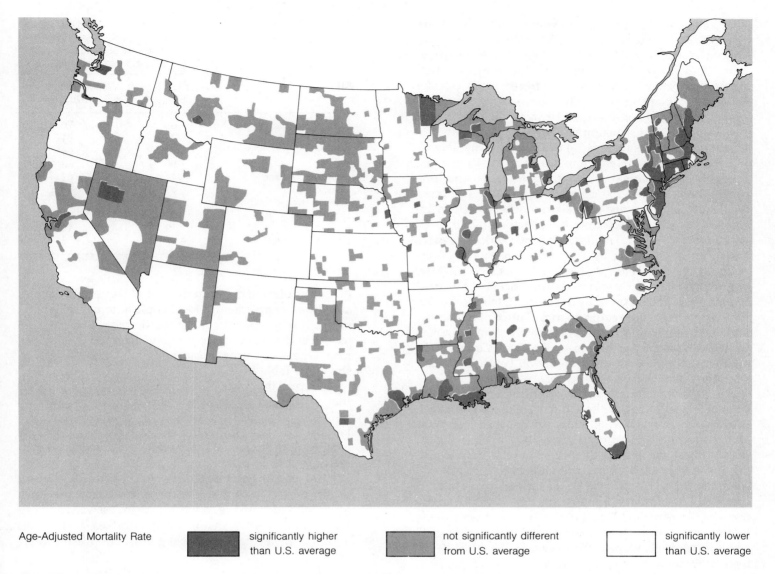

Age-Adjusted Mortality Rate [dark box] significantly higher than U.S. average [medium gray box] not significantly different from U.S. average [white box] significantly lower than U.S. average

Figure E6-5 Geographic patterns of cancer mortality rates for white males (at all body sites) in the United States, 1950–1969.

smoked fish contain polycyclic aromatic hydrocarbons, which cause cancer in test animals.

The third major cause of cancer is occupational exposure to carcinogens. Until 1978 the percentage of cancers in the United States that were related to occupation was estimated at 1 to 5 percent, a figure industry still likes to use. But in 1978 a study by the National Cancer Institute and the National Institute of Environmental Health estimated that at least 20 percent and perhaps as much as 38 percent of all cancers in the United States each year may be job related. The major job risk is ex-

posure to *asbestos*, which will probably kill 1.6 million of the 4 million heavily exposed workers over the next 30 to 35 years (an average of 67,000 deaths a year) through its relationship to lung cancer, stomach cancer, and cancer of the chest or stomach lining (mesothelioma).* In

*The already serious cancer risk from exposure to asbestos is greatly increased by smoking. An asbestos worker who smokes has 8 times the risk of dying from lung cancer as a coworker who doesn't smoke, and 92 times the risk of a person who neither works with asbestos nor smokes. For this reason, the Johns-Manville Corporation decided in 1977 not to hire smokers to work in their asbestos mines and plants.

all, 35 to 44 percent of deceased workers who were heavily exposed to asbestos since World War II died of lung cancer, stomach cancer, or mesothelioma—a death rate about 4 to 5 times higher than that for workers not exposed to asbestos. Asbestos is a major threat to asbestos miners and plant workers, auto mechanics (because of brake linings), steamfitters, carpenters, tile setters, and insulation and construction workers.

Other job risks include (1) exposure to *vinyl chloride* (2.3 million workers), which increases the risks of a rare liver cancer (hemangiosarcoma), brain cancer, and lung cancer, respectively, 200 times, 4 times, and 1.9 times; (2) exposure to *benzene* (2 million workers), which increases the risk of leukemia by a factor of 2 to 7; (3) exposure to *arsenic* (1.5 million workers), which increases the risk of lung cancer by a factor of 3 to 8; and (4) exposure to *coal tar pitch* and *coke oven emissions* (60,000 workers), which increases the risk of cancers of the lung, larynx, skin, and scrotum by a factor of 2 to 6. Reducing job-related exposure requires strict control of all mining and manufacturing processes that involve known or suspected carcinogens. If enforced, the Toxic Control Substances Act of 1975 (Section 16-6) will be an important factor in establishing such control.

At least 700 new chemicals are introduced to the environment each year in the United States. Testing each of these chemicals for its ability to cause cancer takes about 3 to 5 years and costs from $200,000 to $400,000 per chemical. Having the chemical industry pay for testing these chemicals before they are introduced would cost only 0.3 to 0.4 percent of the annual gross sales of the chemical industry. Some scientists, however, argue that environmentalists have become obsessed with trying to achieve a zero-risk society—a goal that is physically and economically impossible to obtain. Zero risk is, of course, impossible, but this should not prevent us from reducing the risks to workers and the general public as much as possible.

Opponents of stricter government control of worker exposure to potentially dangerous chemicals sometimes state that almost anything can cause cancer so why pick on one particular chemical. This is a highly misleading argument since most chemicals tested don't cause cancer. By 1977, only about half of the 1,500 chemicals that had been thoroughly tested were found to cause cancer in test animals, and only 26 (18 of these found in the workplace) had been directly linked to cancer in humans.

Diagnosis, Treatment, and Prevention   During the past two decades great strides have been made in the early

Table E6-3   Chances of Recovering from Cancer in the United States

Type of Cancer	Chance of Survival for 5 Years or More (percent)	
	Cases Diagnosed 1960–1963	Cases Diagnosed 1970–1973
Skin (melanoma)	55	70
Uterus	73	81
Breast	63	68
Prostate	50	63
Hodgkin's disease	41	67
Colon, rectum	43	49
Leukemia (childhood)	4	32
Stomach	12	13
Lung	9	11
Leukemia (acute)	1	3

diagnosis of cancer and in the use of surgery, radiation, and drugs as treatment. Most people automatically think of death when they hear the word *cancer*, but early detection and treatment have greatly increased the survival rates for many forms of cancer in the United States, as shown in Table E6-3.

Despite this important progress, Table E6-3 shows that we have had little success increasing the survival rates for the biggest cancer killers of children (acute leukemia) and adults (lung and stomach cancer). Cancer is a depressing subject, but the really good news is that as many as 40 to 50 percent of all cancers can be prevented. Each of us can greatly reduce the risks of developing cancer by trying to find work in a less hazardous environment, not smoking, not drinking excessively, and eating a diet that is low in animal fats, nitrates, and nitrites and high in vegetables, whole grains, and fresh fruits.

E6-5   Smoking: The Most Dangerous Form of Personal Pollution

The major factors that kill people in more developed nations are smoking, drinking, poor diet, lack of exercise, stress, environmental pollution, and automobiles. All these factors are related to life-style and come under our personal or social control. Of these factors, there is overwhelming evidence from more than 30,000 studies that cigarette smoking is the leading cause of preventable death and injury each year in the United States. During 1977 in the United States there were an estimated 320,000 premature deaths caused by cigarette smoking—more deaths in 1 year than all Americans killed in combat during World War II. About 225,000 of these smoking-related deaths were from heart disease, 80,000 from lung cancer, 22,000 from other cancers, and 19,000 from chronic pulmonary lung disease. During 1979 the cost of smoking in terms of medical services, loss of earnings and production, and the 13 percent of all residential fires related to smoking amounted to more than $27 billion in the United States—with much of this bill being paid for by nonsmokers because of increased medical and insurance costs.

Heavy smokers shorten their lives by an average of 5½ minutes for each cigarette they smoke. Thus, on a statistical basis, the average two-pack-a-day smoker will die 8 to 9 years before the average nonsmoker of the same age. According to a former secretary of the Department of Health and Human Services, "Today, there can be no doubt that smoking is truly slow-motion suicide." Compared with nonsmokers, heavy smokers under age 65 are 3 to 6 times more likely to die from coronary heart disease, 14 times more likely to die from lung cancer, 25 times more likely to die from chronic bronchitis and emphysema, 5 times more likely to die from cancer of the esophagus, 2.5 times more likely to die from ulcers, and much more likely to get cancer of the mouth, lip, larynx, pancreas, and urinary bladder. In addition, women under 50 who smoke are about 20 times more likely to have heart attacks than nonsmoking women, are more likely to develop facial wrinkles, and if pregnant are twice as likely to have a miscarriage.

There is some good news, however. Between 1964 (when the U.S. Surgeon General's first report on the health consequences of smoking appeared) and 1975, some 30 million Americans quit smoking and as many as 90 percent of all U.S. cigarette smokers say they would like to cut down or quit smoking. The proportion of smokers among the U.S. adult male population fell from 53 to 39 percent and among adult women from 34 to 29 percent. Educated Americans have kicked the habit in droves. Between 1964 and 1975, half of the U.S. college graduates who ever smoked stopped. Smokers can reduce their risks by quitting before disease symptoms appear. In such cases, the damage from previous smoking largely disappears within 10 years. Some people now smoke low-tar cigarettes to reduce the risks somewhat, but they often tend to smoke more, thus offsetting their advantage.

There is also some bad news. The United States is still the world's leading cigarette-smoking country, followed closely by Japan. The average number of cigarettes smoked per smoker and the total number of cigarettes smoked each year in the United States have continued to increase, although the percentage of the U.S. population that smokes has been declining. In 1965 Americans smoked 505 billion cigarettes—an average of 9,940 per smoker. By 1979 Americans puffed away a record 617 billion cigarettes worth $17 billion—an average of about 11,000 during 1979 for each of the 53 million American smokers. Much of this increase is due to a sharp rise in the number of teenagers who have begun smoking. A British government study showed that adolescents who smoke more than one cigarette have only a 15 percent chance of remaining nonsmokers. One out of five 12-year-olds in the United States now smokes, and among 12- to 18-year-olds, more females than males now smoke. As a result, there has been a fivefold increase in lung cancer among women between 1958 and 1976. By 1983, lung cancer is expected to overtake breast cancer as the leading cause of cancer deaths in women.

Another recent U.S. trend is an increasing concern for the rights of nonsmokers. Smoking can no longer be considered as a personal pollution that harms only the smoker. Nonsmokers, especially in a restaurant, car, bus, train, plane, classroom, office, or other closed area, are being exposed against their will to smoke that is not only irritating but also potentially dangerous. In closed areas, the particulate levels in the air as a result of smoking are typically 2 to 20 times higher than the level at which the Environmental Protection Agency issues an air quality alert, and long-term exposure is equivalent to a nonsmoker smoking one to ten cigarettes per day. Evidence of the harmful effects of smoke to nonsmokers is still preliminary and controversial, but there is agreement that smoke poses a definite risk to those suffering from heart disease, allergies, emphysema, and other respiratory diseases. A 1980 study indicated that nonsmoking spouses of heavy smokers are more than twice as likely to develop lung cancer as a nonsmoking spouse of a nonsmoker.

Nonsmokers in the United States have also become more assertive in insisting that they not be involuntarily exposed to irritating and potentially dangerous chemicals. By 1978 over 33 states had passed some kind of legislation protecting nonsmokers in public places—although many of these laws are poorly enforced. Airlines and many businesses have voluntarily set up separate smoking and nonsmoking areas, and some businesses are even refusing to hire smokers. In 1978 American tobacco companies raised strong protests because the Department of Health and Human Services proposed to spend $23 million in 1979 on an antismoking campaign. But these companies didn't point out that in 1977 the federal government provided the tobacco industry with

4 times this amount ($97 million) in tobacco price supports and export subsidies, or that the tobacco industry itself spent about 20 times more ($500 million, or an average of $1.4 million per day) to persuade people to start smoking or to smoke more.

An alarming trend is the increase in smoking in less developed nations, especially in cities and among the educated, who see it as a symbol of modernization and privilege. Smoking by the poor in these nations is also rising but is limited by a lack of money. Since poverty is a major global problem, it is shocking to realize that $85 to $100 billion are spent worldwide each year to buy 4 trillion cigarettes in spite of the well-established dangers of smoking. This amount equals the total annual income for 500 million of the poorest of the world's population and is about 5 times the aid that rich countries give to the poor countries each year. We find tobacco being planted on good cropland in India while nearby peasants starve, the United States shipping tobacco to less developed nations as part of its Food for Peace program, and governments actively supporting the growth and sale of tobacco. Indeed, of the world's five leading cigarette companies, four are government owned and run. The five major companies are, in order, the Chinese government monopoly, the British American Tobacco Company, the Soviet and Japanese government monopolies, and Philip Morris, Inc. As their people become hooked on cigarettes, governments become hooked on the income and taxes that increased sales provide. American tobacco companies faced with new antismoking campaigns see hundreds of millions of people in less developed nations as potential customers who need to be introduced through mass advertising to the joys of smoking.

How can we reduce this major threat to global health? A comprehensive program might include: (1) preventing young people from getting hooked on cigarettes; (2) banning all cigarette advertising or at least restricting it to simple black-and-white print ads, so that slick ads cannot be used to create the impression that smokers are young, attractive, sophisticated, healthy, and sexy; (3) passing and enforcing strict laws to protect nonsmokers in all public places and encouraging all offices and businesses to allow smoking only in designated areas; (4) eliminating all financial subsidies to the tobacco industry and offsetting the resulting loss of income and jobs by providing aid and subsidies that would allow farmers to grow more healthful crops, such as soybeans and vegetables; (5) requiring that all cigarettes not exceed certain levels of tar, nicotine, and other chemicals shown to be a threat to health; and (6) increasing research to develop tobacco substitutes and less harmful cigarettes so that those who choose to smoke or who cannot break this very addictive habit are exposed to fewer health risks.

Sweden hopes to lead the way by putting into effect a 25-year program so that children born after 1974 will become that country's first nonsmoking generation. Intensive education on the hazards of smoking will be introduced at all school levels beginning in kindergarten, no one under 16 will be allowed to buy cigarettes, the sale of cigarettes in vending machines will be banned, cigarette prices will be raised gradually, cigarette advertising will be phased out, and all cigarette packs must carry tar and nicotine levels along with 16 different warnings on the specific hazards of smoking.

Health and a good state of body are above all gold, and a strong body above infinite wealth.

Eccles. 40:15

Discussion Topics

1. Compare the social ecology of disease patterns in more developed and less developed countries. Why are infectious diseases more common in less developed countries? Why do so many infants and young children in less developed nations die from measles, diarrhea, and other common childhood diseases?

2. List diseases you or members of your family have had and classify them according to the type of disease and the probable mode of transmission. Which types of diseases are likely to be hereditary and thus make you or your offspring more susceptible to attack?

3. Discuss the life cycle, mode of transmission, effects, possible control, and side effects of control of malaria and schistosomiasis.

4. Should DDT and other pesticides be banned from use in malaria control? Why or why not? (See Enrichment Study 11.)

5. How can cholera be brought under better control? Why are there often outbreaks of cholera in an area hit by an earthquake, flood, or other natural disaster?

6. Explain why the incidences of gonorrhea and syphilis are rising even though both diseases can be prevented and cured.

7. Assume that you have contracted gonorrhea, syphilis, NGU, PID, or HSV-2 and that you have had the good sense to have it diagnosed and treated. Would you give the name and address of the person or persons with whom you had sexual contacts over the previous months to public health officials? Why or why not?

8. Analyze the incidence and types of cancer deaths in the area in which you live. Can you account for the high incidence of certain types of cancer?

9. Give some possible reasons why the death rate from breast cancer in the United States is almost 6 times higher than in Japan, while the death rate for stomach cancer in Japan is almost 7 times higher than in the United States.

10. Analyze your life-style and diet to determine your relative risks of developing some form of cancer before you reach age 55. Which type of cancer are you most likely to get? How could you significantly reduce your chances of getting this cancer?

11. Give your reasons for agreeing or disagreeing with each of the six proposals designed to reduce the health hazards of smoking.

Readings

Beattie, Edward J. 1980. *Toward the Conquest of Cancer.* New York: Crown. Superb analysis showing how 40 to 50 percent of cancers can be prevented and about 50 percent can be cured.

Benenson, A. S., ed. 1975. *Control of Communicable Diseases in Man.* 12th ed. Washington, D.C.: American Public Health Association. Basic reference.

Campbell, T. C. 1980. "Chemical Carcinogens and Human Risk Assessment." *Federation Proceedings*, vol. 39, no. 8, 2467–2484. Excellent overview.

Council on Environmental Quality. 1975. *Environmental Quality 1975.* Washington, D.C.: U.S. Government Printing Office. See pp. 1–42 for an excellent overview of cancer problems.

Eckholm, Erik. 1977. *The Picture of Health: Environmental Sources of Disease.* New York: Norton. Superb overview of environmental health problems throughout the world.

Eckholm, Erik. 1978. *Cutting Tobacco's Toll.* Washington, D.C.: Worldwatch Institute. Superb overview of smoking problems and possible solutions in the United States and throughout the world.

Eisenbud, Merril. 1979. *Environment, Technology, and Health: Human Ecology in Historical Perspective.* New York: New York University Press. Outstanding analysis.

Goldsmith, Edward. 1980. "The Ecology of Health." *The Ecologist*, vol. 10, nos. 6/7, 225–245. Eloquent summary of an ecological—as opposed to a modern medical—approach to health.

Gorman, James. 1979. *Hazards to Your Health: The Problem of Environmental Disease.* New York: New York Academy of Sciences. Superb overview.

Gregg, Sandee. 1980. "STDs." *SciQuest*, November, pp. 11–15. Excellent summary.

Hamilton, Richard. 1980. *The Herpes Book.* New York: Houghton-Mifflin. Very informative book.

Highland, Joseph, et al. 1980. *Malignant Neglect.* New York: Random House. Excellent discussion of cancer and the environment.

Humphrey, J. H. 1977. "The Challenge of Parasitic Diseases." *Bulletin of the Atomic Scientists*, March, pp. 46–53. Excellent overview of tropical diseases.

Marshall, Carter L. 1972. *Dynamics of Health and Disease.* New York: Appleton-Century-Crofts. Very good overview of disease.

Richards, Robert N. 1974. *Venereal Diseases and Their Avoidance.* Chicago: Holt, Rinehart and Winston. Excellent overview and well illustrated.

Richards, Victor. 1978. *Cancer, The Wayward Cell: Its Origins, Nature, and Treatment.* 2nd ed. Los Angeles: University of California Press. Outstanding summary.

Sartwell, Philip E. 1973. "Section III—Chronic Illness." In M. Rosenau, ed., *Preventive Medicine and Public Health.* 10th ed. New York: Appleton-Century-Crofts. Good overview of chronic illness.

Staff report. 1976. "Conference on Sexually Transmitted Diseases." *Bulletin of the New York Academy of Medicine*, vol. 52, no. 8, 64–86. Excellent in-depth review.

Stein, Jane. 1977. "Water for the Wealthy." *Environment*, vol. 19, no. 4, 6–14. Good overview of infectious waterborne diseases.

Stern, Edwin B., and James H. Price. 1977. *Human Sex and Sexuality.* New York: Wiley. Good overview of sexually transmitted diseases.

Strauss, Anselm L. 1975. *Chronic Illness and the Quality of Life.* St. Louis: Mosby. Good overview of selected chronic illnesses.

Weisburger, J. H. 1976. "Environmental Cancer." *Journal of Occupational Medicine*, vol. 18, no. 4, 245–252. Superb overview.

Enrichment Study 7

Population Control Methods

There is considerable debate over whether world population growth can be controlled by (1) economic development, (2) voluntary family planning programs, (3) beyond family planning programs (abortion, education, changing women's roles, economic incentives and disincentives, and involuntary control), or (4) some combination of these three methods. The economic development and family planning approaches were discussed in Sections 8-2 and 8-3. This enrichment study will examine beyond family planning methods for population control.

E7-1 Is Voluntary Family Planning Enough?

Voluntary family planning is an extremely important method for helping control world population growth, but many observers feel that it must be coupled with economic development and with methods that go beyond family planning (Section 8-2). This view is based on the beliefs that family planning programs alone will not be able to slow world population growth rapidly enough and that family planning is not really a method for population control.

Supporters of family planning point to a number of successes in reducing fertility rates over the past 25 years, as discussed in Section 8-3. They also point out that by 1978, 136 million women in the world were using some form of contraception. Critics, however, point out that after over 20 years of family planning efforts, only about two-thirds of the couples of reproductive age throughout the world were using any form of contraception in 1977. Critics use these data to show that family planning methods are too slow to have significant impact on world population growth. Supporters of family planning programs argue that this is not the fault of family planning programs but represents the failure of governments to provide enough funds and personnel to make such efforts more effective.

Another criticism of family planning is that it is not designed to be a method for population control. The announced aim of family planning is to help couples have the number of children they want when they want them. Without family planning most couples have more children than they want, but with family planning they still have more children than many observers feel can be supported by available resources. The problem is that many couples want so many children that world population will continue to grow at a relatively high rate, especially in less developed nations, unless economic development and beyond family planning methods are used.

E7-2 Voluntary Liberalized Abortion

Freedom of Choice or Murder? Liberalization of abortion laws and easy availability of abortion are often suggested as important additions to voluntary methods for fertility control. Abortion, however, is a highly emotional issue that does not lend itself to compromise or cool debate. Basically, the argument is between those who regard abortion as murder and those who believe that a woman should have the right to choose whether to bear a child. One side emphasizes the basic right of a pregnant woman to control her own body, while the other emphasizes the rights of the unborn child.

Proponents view antiabortion laws as a form of "compulsory pregnancy" that denies each woman the right to control her fertility according to her own beliefs and needs. Some people who vigorously oppose abortion on moral grounds label anyone who does not support their religious or moral belief as a "proabortionist." In fact, however, very few people are for abortion. Instead, they argue for reproductive freedom: no one should be forced to have an abortion, and at the same time no one should be forced to have a baby. Furthermore, they believe strongly that making abortion a crime imposes the religious or moral views of one group on other women who may not hold the same religious or moral views.

Some individuals, however, have strong moral and religious beliefs that view abortion as an act of murder and thus believe that the "right to life" of an unborn child should take precedence over a pregnant woman's "right to choose" whether to terminate her pregnancy. There is an inconclusive and controversial medical, theological, and legal debate about when life begins—at conception, at birth, or at some difficult-to-define point in between. Is the fetus only a piece of unborn living matter that is a potential human being, or is it human from the moment of conception? Some make the distinction between an embryo and a viable fetus (one sufficiently developed to survive outside the uterus). Because of incubators and modern medical techniques, survival is now possible after 28 weeks and in rare circumstances after 24 weeks. Neither the Catholic church nor any other Christian church, however, baptizes or demands that an aborted fetus less than seven months old be given proper burial and death rites. Indeed, the Catholic church permitted early abortions under some circumstances until a papal decree in 1969.

No court ruling will settle these ethical questions. Indeed, as legal restraints are removed, the ethical issues emerge even more strongly for the individual. To some religious leaders, forcing individuals to face up to these moral decisions rather than allowing them to hide behind legal reasons represents an improvement. More and more Catholics agree with Cardinal Cushing's statement that "Catholics do not need the support of civil law to be faithful to their own religious convictions." Most American Roman Catholics also believe it is wrong to impose their religious or moral beliefs on others.

The Extent of Abortion   In spite of strong antiabortion laws throughout human history, abortion has been and still is one of the most widely used methods of birth control in the world. With the wider distribution of birth control during the past decade, abortion is probably in fourth place on a worldwide basis, behind voluntary sterilization (approximately 92 million users), oral contraceptives (approximately 58 million users), and IUDs (about 52 million users). The total number of legal and illegal abortions throughout the world each year is estimated at about 40 million—about one abortion for every four live births. About half of these are performed illegally and represent a leading cause of death among women of childbearing age. From this it is clear that laws banning abortion have been among the most ineffective

laws of all time. The real issue then is not whether abortions will be done, but whether women will be allowed to have them legally and safely or illegally and unsafely. Compared with preventing an unwanted baby by contraception, abortion is an unhappy solution. But once a woman has conceived, making abortion a crime does not prevent it or even reduce it. All it does is to make abortion an unnecessarily expensive, dirty, and dangerous procedure that kills thousands of women each year—especially poor women who cannot afford to travel to a region where abortion is legal. In Colombia, for example, which has one of the strictest abortion laws in the world, the largest maternity hospital in Bogota must devote half its beds to cases of complications arising from illegal abortions. After a restrictive abortion law was passed in Romania in 1966, abortion-related deaths had risen sevenfold by 1977. In less developed nations illegal abortion is 20 to 200 times more dangerous than legal abortion. In the United States illegal abortion is 17 to 50 times more dangerous than legal abortion and 3 to 10 times more dangerous to the mother than having a baby.

Perhaps half of all illegal abortions are self-induced. Women swallow large and dangerous doses of chemicals such as quinine, which are sold as "home remedies." Should this method fail, they resort to a back-street abortionist or a knitting needle. Most poor women throughout the world still abort themselves with a sharpened stick. Infection is understandably a major killer. The most dangerous bacterium, *Clostridium welchii*, kills in only 12 hours unless medical treatment is provided immediately. Antibiotics decrease the risk but again must be given quickly; most are often not available in less developed nations.

Health and Psychological Risks   The most common modern procedure for legal abortion—vacuum aspiration—takes about 5 minutes, and in 1979 cost about $200 in a U.S. clinic. With this method, a legal abortion done under medical supervision within the first 12 weeks of pregnancy is 4 to 6 times safer than childbirth:

There has been much discussion and mixed evidence concerning the potential psychological problems associated with abortions. These problems are very real for some women, particularly those who are masochistic or acutely depressed. But legal abortion clinics in New York State have found psychological problems much rarer than expected. Apparently if legal and moral stigmas are removed, many women do not experience guilt feelings. In contrast, many problems can arise from being denied an abortion—broken careers, forced teenage marriages (which have very high divorce rates), abandoned and disturbed children, and "battered babies." Compared with wanted children, unwanted children born to women denied an abortion tend to have a higher incidence of illness, slightly poorer school marks, and poorer social adjustment.

Worldwide Abortion Liberalization One of the major social trends throughout the world during the past decade has been the legalization of abortion. Between 1965 and 1978, 30 countries removed major restrictions limiting or prohibiting abortion. During this same 13-year period, only five countries—Bulgaria, Czechoslovakia, Hungary, New Zealand, and Romania—enacted more restrictive abortion laws. By 1978, only 20 percent of the world's population lived in countries where abortion was prohibited or allowed only to save the life of the pregnant woman. In addition, some countries with restrictive abortion laws—such as South Korea, the Netherlands, and Taiwan—do not enforce the laws and have encouraged a substantial growth in abortion services. The three major reasons for the worldwide liberalization of abortion are (1) the awareness of how much death and illness are caused by illegal abortion, (2) court decisions (as is the case in the United States), and (3) the growth of women's movements, especially in more developed nations.

In 1973 the U.S. Supreme Court made a historic decision, stating that during the first three months (12 weeks) of pregnancy, the decision about having an abortion must be left up to a woman and her doctor. This decision thus made unconstitutional all antiabortion laws in the United States. A state may regulate but not deny abortions in the third through sixth months of pregnancy; after this period, each state can draw up its own statutes.

Between 1973 and 1979 the number of legal abortions in the United States doubled, increasing from almost 745,000 to over 1.54 million. Of the women who had legal abortions in 1978, about 75 percent were unmarried, 69 percent were white, and 31 percent were teenagers. In 1979, 30 percent of pregnant women in the United States chose to terminate their pregnancy by a legal abortion and an estimated 29 percent of the women who wanted legal abortions were unable to obtain them. In 1977 a nationwide survey showed that 77 percent of all Americans and 73 percent of all American Catholics polled believed that abortion should be legal either under any circumstances (22 percent of all Americans and 21 percent of American Catholics) or under certain circumstances. In addition, 70 percent of Americans polled in 1978 said they believed that federal funds should be used to pay for abortions in all (23 percent) or some (47 percent) circumstances.

In spite of widespread and increasing approval of reproductive freedom by Americans, a small but militant minority in the Catholic church and in right-to-life groups is still applying intense organized pressure against legal abortion with efforts to pass a constitutional amendment making abortion illegal. In 1977 the Supreme Court ruled that even though every woman has a legal right to an abortion, the government is not obliged to pay for it. Under intense pressure from antiabortion forces, Congress eliminated federal Medicaid funding for most abortions for the poor in 1977. In recent years, eight legal abortion clinics in Minnesota, Vermont, Nebraska, Iowa, and Ohio have been hit by fire, and another eight clinics have been vandalized. Although abortion is legal and the reproductive freedom this ruling allows is supported by most Americans, the intense ethical, religious, and political controversy over this issue has clearly not ended. In 1980 several congressional candidates who favored reproductive freedom were defeated. The main reason for this is that the antiabortion minority (only about 23 percent of the American public) is a highly vocal, organized, one-issue group that can help defeat individuals who oppose their view. By contrast, the 77 percent of the American public who favor reproductive freedom have a diverse range of other issues they consider more important. As a result, it is difficult to organize this majority view into an effective, single-issue voting bloc. In early 1981, antiabortionists in Congress were attempting to pass a law that would declare that life begins at the moment of fertilization. This would attempt to ban abortions by getting around the Supreme Court ruling without having to pass a constitutional amendment—a much more difficult process.

E7-3 Changes in Education, Women's Roles, and Family Structure

A Sustainable Earth Curriculum Education through both mass communication and formal education can play an important part in population control. In the United States a comprehensive sustainable earth education program should be designed for kindergarten through college that emphasizes human relationships to and responsibilities as citizens for the ecosphere. Special efforts should be directed at the preschool and elementary levels, where many values are introduced or at least heavily reinforced. Although there has been considerable improvement since 1970, some elementary school readers and other materials in the United States are still ecological disaster areas.

Instead of showing the typical American family with two or three children and two cars, we should introduce other models. Some families might have only Dick or only Jane, and we might introduce the couple down the street who married at the age of 30 and have a meaningful life with no children and a small car. There might be visits from Uncle George, a happy bachelor who rides a bicycle to work, and Aunt Sally, an unmarried woman who is a doctor, senator, executive, judge, or lawyer. We must display a diverse array of identity options to young children. We must destroy the myths that couples without children can't be happy and that unmarried persons, especially women, lead less fulfilling lives. Contrary to popular opinion, research studies comparing married and unmarried women indicate that personal fulfillment does not depend on marriage or parenthood.

Somehow we must be made aware that the quality, not the quantity, of parenthood is important. Some people have the ability and compassion to provide quality parenthood for more than two children, and these rare individuals should not be discouraged. But many couples should stop at two or one or none. In all education and persuasion programs, however, the emphasis *must* be on positive reinforcement and showing other options rather than on punishment and making people feel guilty.

Changes in Cultural Patterns To many, the birth of a child is an essential and fulfilling event. Psychiatrist Robert Coles recorded this statement about what a new child means to a poverty-stricken black mother:

> To me having a baby inside me is the only time I'm really alive. I know I can make something, do something, no matter what color my skin is, and what names people call me. When the baby gets born you can see the little one grow and get larger and start doing things, and you feel there must be some hope, some chance that things will get better.

But many women are trapped into motherhood as a role that society expects of them (see Section 8-2). It does little good, however, to talk about altering motivation toward childbearing without offering women the opportunity to become educated and to express their lives in work and other meaningful social roles. In most less developed nations women do not have equitable access to education. About 60 percent of the world's 1 billion illiterates are women, and almost everywhere males are giv-

en preference in education and vocational training. In subsistence agriculture societies in less developed nations women typically do more than half of the field work associated with growing food, gather firewood, haul water, take care of any children, do the housekeeping, and suffer the most malnutrition because men and children are given first claim to the limited food supplies. In most cases women are not paid for this vital and exhausting work.

The percentage of women in various occupations varies throughout the world, as shown in Table E7-1. About 50 percent of the world's work force in 1979 was female, including 69 percent in Sweden, 68 percent in the Soviet Union, 51 percent in the United States, and 1.8 percent in Algeria. In the United States most working women have clerical and service jobs and earn an average of 41 percent less than male workers, and in 1978 they accounted for only 2.3 percent of executives earning at least $25,000 per year. In 1979, women made up 85 percent of the elementary school teachers and 51 percent of the high school teachers; they made up only 10 percent of tenured college professors, 5 percent of school superintendents, and 1 percent of college presidents.

One very significant event has been the drive to recognize and guarantee women's rights in the United States and several other nations. This movement is important primarily in its recognition of human dignity and freedom, but it is also a crucial element in any successful effort to control U.S. population. Providing women with equal work opportunities causes a marked change in the family structure and can lead to later marriage and smaller families (as it has in the U.S.S.R. and China). A few governments have moved ahead of the United States in allowing men and women to participate on an equal basis in employment outside the home and work within the home. Cuba, China, and Sweden have made the sharing of housework by men and women official policy—although all three governments recognize that this policy is almost impossible to enforce. Sweden, France, and East Germany aid women who want to work outside the home by setting up essentially nationwide preschool care for children over age 3.

We must support and encourage efforts to eliminate male domination—an outdated frontier role. This will not be easy, but cultural patterns can change, and equality for women is a much-needed sustainable earth rule. It can be achieved through laws, education, and increasing the sensitivity of males to the conscious and unconscious ways in which women's rights are denied.

Family structure patterns may also be changing, especially in some more developed nations. Through much

Table E7-1 Percentage of Women in Selected Occupations throughout the World in 1977

Occupation	Soviet Union	United States	Sweden	Japan	India	Chile
Physicians	70	13	18	10	7	8
Lawyers	35	9	8	2	1	10
Members of national legislature	35	3	21	3	5	7
Managerial positions	32	20	11	5	2	9
Union members	60	21	33	28	12	—
Agricultural workers	44	16	26	50	20	3

of human cultural evolution, the predominant family pattern has been the *extended family*, consisting of the mother, father, grandfather, grandmother, children, grandchildren, and other relatives living together or at least nearby. During the past 50 years, the extended family in the United States has largely been replaced by the *nuclear family*, composed of the mother, father, and their children. Some observers feel that the nuclear family may be replaced by a *multiadult extended family*, consisting of networks of intimate friends who may or may not live together.

The possible cultural need for an extended family, coupled with the lack of age diversity in the nuclear family, may account in part for the thousands of experimental communes that have sprung up in the United States and western Europe in recent years. There is great variety among the estimated 3,000 communes formed in the United States since 1965. They range from rural to urban and religious to economic, and they share everything from income to beds and board.

Most communes are volatile, short-lived, and beset with problems. Desmond Morris observed that most rural communes don't last because people brought up in an urban society have in effect lost their "social virginity." At first, fugitives from a highly stimulating urban society find a return to simplicity satisfying. Eventually, however, disillusionment and boredom may set in. At this point the group either collapses from internal stress or stirs itself into economic or other activities that place it back into the rat race. One weakness of most rural and urban communal experiments is that they are structured horizontally around one age group or a common set of problems or interests rather than vertically, with an array of ages and interests. Often such diversity can provide more long-term social and economic stability.

The importance of communes must not be underestimated. Most represent attempts to break out of the small nuclear family and to return to the extended fam-

ilies that are more characteristic of our evolutionary past. In addition, they serve as important flesh-and-blood examples of alternatives to the urban-industrial life-style and temporary halfway houses for people suffering from cultural battle fatigue. We need to encourage these experiments, which are designed to help us establish a richer network of meaningful human relationships in a stressful urban world.

E7-4 Economic Incentives and Disincentives

There has been considerable interest in using economic incentives and disincentives to reduce population growth. There are two approaches: positive (or economic-reward) incentives and negative (or economic-penalty) approaches. *Positive incentives* include direct cash payments, savings certificates, free contraceptives, free abortion and sterilization, free health plans, free old-age pensions, and free education for individuals and couples who delay marriage or childbearing, limit their number of children, or agree to use contraceptives or to be sterilized.

Disincentives, or *negative incentives*, include elimination of income tax deductions for some or all children; elimination of welfare, health, maternity, housing, or educational benefits after more than the allotted number of children; and taxes on marriage, children, and child-related goods and services. All incentive approaches are based on the reasonable assumption that economic rewards and penalties provide effective motivation.

Positive incentives have the advantage of redistributing wealth to the poor, since they would have greater need and are more inclined to accept such rewards. Thus, incentives may be particularly useful in less developed countries, where most people are poor. In such countries a combination of small, immediate cash rewards plus an old-age security plan might simultaneously reduce population and raise economic well-being. It must be remembered that in these countries one of the main reasons for having children is to provide parents with security in their old age, which might be their thirties to fifties. Positive incentives are noncoercive in principle, but may be coercive in practice. Often the poor might have little choice but to accept them even though they strongly want to have children.

Economic disincentives that add taxes, eliminate child-related services, or increase the costs of children would be unjust to both the poor and the lower middle classes and to the children who would have to bear the brunt of reduced economic income. Children, however, are also penalized when parents plan poorly and have more children than they can support. Positive incentives appear particularly effective in less developed countries, but they might have little impact on middle and upper classes anywhere, for whom negative incentives or penalties might be more effective.

A diverse array of carefully planned incentive and disincentive programs must be tried on a pilot basis throughout the world over the next few decades. We need to know what types of incentives and disincentives will work. Because of vast cultural, economic, and political differences even within a single country, approaches will vary considerably. Instead of looking for the "one best incentive or disincentive," we need to develop a broader, integrated package of multiple economic incentives and disincentives at the individual, small-group, community, and national levels.

China is already using economic incentives and disincentives with apparent success (Section 8-3). Singapore provides abortion on demand at a cost of only $5 and uses several economic disincentives to discourage childbirth, including doubling the hospital fees for a second child and not providing maternity leave.

E7-5 Involuntary Population Control

Arguments for Coercion To most people the use of coercive measures for population control is either unthinkable or at best a last resort. Some believe that the world population situation is already bad enough to justify instituting some forms of involuntary control. They argue that our life-support system is already threatened by overpopulation or will be within 50 to 70 years. They also believe that voluntary and even extended voluntary methods either will not work or will be too slow. Garrett Hardin has argued that voluntary programs won't work

because individuals do not see their own actions as a threat to others—the "do-your-own thing" myth. The impact of people who voluntarily give up their right to breed or pollute can be minimized if they constitute a dwindling proportion of the total population. It is also argued that the various coercive proposals do not *completely* deny the individual freedom to have children. Instead they limit the number of children to one or two.

What Is Coercion? To draw a sharp line between voluntary and involuntary approaches to population control is impossible. Every day we engage in actions falling somewhere between the two approaches in other areas. We stop at red lights and pay taxes. We have coercive prohibitions of crime, coercive school attendance, restrictions on the number of wives or husbands we can have at one time, and a host of others. We surrender certain freedoms to do as we please to gain other, more important ones—to drive safely, to be free from certain diseases, and to live in a community providing education, fire and police protection, streets, parks, and other services.

So perhaps restricting the number of children that a couple can have is a justifiable limitation of individual liberty that protects the air, water, and land resources for present and future generations. Any involuntary approach, however, must be clearly justified and enforceable. Unenforceable legislation can be a disaster, as the United States learned during Prohibition and as India learned recently when it tried to coerce people to be sterilized (Section 8-3). Before any involuntary approach is used, several important questions must be answered: Is the approach really necessary for security, survival, or freedom? Does it represent the least possible coercion, have the fewest harmful consequences, and minimize injustice? How will it be enforced? Are there other alternatives?

Nearly all successful forms of social control are developed by employing those measures that appear to be fair. People resent compulsion less than unfairness in the distribution of rewards and punishments. For example, how would we punish people who had too many children? Would they be sent to jail? Fined? In either case, the "sins" of the parents could be passed on to innocent children.

Restricting Immigration One coercive approach to limiting the population of a particular country already exists: restricting immigration. For 200 years America had an open-door immigration policy, but beginning with laws passed in 1921 and 1924, quotas were set, and in 1965 even stricter immigration laws were enacted. In spite of this, legal immigration in the 1970s accounted for about 20 percent of the U.S. population growth each year, compared with 11 percent in the 1950s. The United States admits more immigrants than any other country in the world. In contrast, the Soviet Union, China, Japan, Hungary, Czechoslovakia, and several other countries admit almost no immigrants.

Whether to decrease further or even eliminate legal and illegal immigration into the United States is an extremely difficult and controversial question. Present immigration policies also pose several ethical dilemmas. One is the "brain drain," a policy that encourages trained and skilled persons in less developed nations to immigrate to the United States. An estimated one-third of the scientists in the United States today came from less developed countries. Currently about 7,000 of the 14,000 new physicians each year in the United States are immigrants, mostly from India, the Philippines, and other less developed nations. Thus, U.S. immigration policy deprives less developed countries of their most valuable resource—educated citizens—and is a reverse form of foreign aid from the poor nations to the rich nations. Should the United States eliminate all immigration or only that of trained personnel? These are agonizing questions for a country that has considered itself the "melting pot" of the world.

In this enrichment study we have seen that there are many possible approaches to controlling population, each with specific advantages and disadvantages. Because people and countries have exciting and necessary uniqueness and diversity, each approach must be analyzed in relation to the needs and political realities of each culture. We all have a role to play: the couples who decide to have one, two, or no children; the couples who believe they can truly provide *quality* parenthood for more than two children; those who find life can be meaningful without marriage; the druggist or storeowner who openly displays contraceptives; the newspaper executive who decides to accept ads for birth control; people who insist that each woman has a right to avoid birth by having an abortion; people who oppose abortion on moral grounds; the courageous politician who introduces or supports liberalized abortion or sex education laws; the insurance executive who insists that abortion costs be covered in health plans; and the leaders who insist that their country institute an official population stabilization policy.

If policies and programs can be designed to help women achieve their goals by means other than motherhood, two very important objectives can be met at once: raising the status of women and lowering the birth rate.

Kathleen Newland

Discussion Topics

1. Should abortion be a private decision between a woman and her physician? Is allowing the birth of an unwanted child immoral?

2. Should federal and state funds be used to provide abortion for the poor in the United States?

3. Debate the following resolution: The unrestricted freedom to reproduce is a universal human right.

4. Psychoanalyst Erik Erikson predicts that we are heading for the day when there will be "a fervent public conviction that the most deadly of all sins is the mutilation of a child's spirit." Do you agree with this? Balance this argument that every child has the inviolable right to be loved and wanted with the antiabortionists' claim that every fetus has the inviolable right to live.

5. Is the use of massive media advertising for smaller families a desirable form of population control? What about advertising for cigarettes? Milk? A balanced diet? Cancer prevention? What distinguishes "desirable" advertising from "undesirable" advertising? Is a media campaign for population control likely to be effective?

6. What are your beliefs and feelings about the feminist movement and the role of women in American society? Contrast the role of women in the United States with the roles of women in other cultures throughout the world. What are the attitudes and practices toward women in your student body? Faculty?

7. Discuss the idea that rural communes will never work for a significant portion of society in more developed regions because they do not provide the stimulus and diversity that modern people have become accustomed to.

8. What is freedom of choice? Do we ever really have freedom of choice? List examples of situations in which you do.

9. Make a list of all the things in your life that would be classified as coercive. In each case list the freedom or freedoms given up or diminished and those gained or increased. Then determine whether on balance that form of coercion is justified and useful. Are there any general guidelines that can be used in determining these issues?

10. Debate the issue that "doing your own thing" is one of the most naive, irresponsible, and dangerous ideas to come along. Relate this to your own life and life-style and to the second law of thermodynamics.

Readings

American Friends Service Committee. 1970. *Who Shall Live?* New York: Hill and Wang. Examines ethics of human control over life and death.

Augenstein, L. 1969. *Come Let Us Play God.* New York: Harper & Row. Good discussion of ethics of popluation control.

Callahan, Daniel. 1970. *Abortion: Law, Choice and Morality.* New York: Macmillan. Comprehensive survey of the abortion issue.

Callahan, Daniel. 1972. "Ethics and Population Limitation." *Science,* vol. 175, 487–494. Very good discussion of ethical issues of population control.

Connery, John. 1977. *Abortion: The Development of the Roman Catholic Perspective.* Chicago: Loyola University Press. Excellent overview.

Gray, Elizabeth Dodson. 1979. *Why the Green Nigger: Re-mything Genesis.* Wellesley, Mass.: Roundtable Press. Excellent discussion of women's rights and feminism and the environment.

Hardin, Garrett. 1974. *Mandatory Motherhood: The True Meaning of "Right to Life."* Boston: Beacon Press. Superb discussion of abortion issue.

Hardin, Garrett. 1978. *Exploring New Ethics for Survival.* 2nd ed. New York: Viking. Another superb contribution by this prominent human ecologist. Explores ethics of population control polices.

Jaffe, Frederick S. et al. 1980. *Abortion Politics.* New York: The Alan Guttmacher Institute. An outstanding balanced approach that attempts to provide a reasonable solution to this dilemma.

Kangas, L. W. 1970. "Integrated Incentives for Fertility Control." *Science,* vol. 169, 1278–1283. Superb analysis of incentive approach with call for a broader multifaceted approach.

Kanter, Rosabeth M. 1972. *Commitment and Community.* Cambridge, Mass.: Harvard University Press. One of the best analyses of communes and utopias.

NARAL Foundation. 1978. *Legal Abortion: Arguments Pro & Con.* Washington, D.C.: NARAL Foundation. Excellent summary.

Newland, Kathleen. 1977. *Women and Population Growth: Choice beyond Childbearing.* Washington, D.C.: Worldwatch Institute. Superb discussion of women's roles.

Newland, Kathleen. 1980. *Women, Men, and the Division of Labor.* Washington, D.C.: Worldwatch Institute. Excellent summary.

Pohlman, Edward A. 1971. *How To Kill a Population.* Philadelphia: Westminster. Excellent presentation of the case for using incentives for population control.

Polgar, Stephen. 1972. "Population History and Population Policies from an Anthropological Perspective." *Current Anthropology,* vol. 13, no. 2, 203–241. Most population control programs fail because they are not tailored to the cultural characteristics of each group.

Population Crisis Committee. 1979. "World Abortion Trends." *Population,* no. 9, 1–6. Excellent summary.

Sarvis, Betty, and Hyman Rodman. 1972. *The Abortion Controversy.* New York: Columbia University Press. Excellent balanced discussion.

Silverman, Anna C., and Arnold Silverman. 1971. *The Case against Having Children.* New York: McKay. Excellent discussion of alternatives to motherhood.

Tietze, Christopher, and Sarah Lewit. 1977. "Legal Abortion." *Scientific American,* vol. 236, no. 1, 21–27. Excellent discussion of the spread of legal abortion throughout the world.

Zero Population Growth. 1976. *The One Child Family.* Washington, D.C.: Zero Population Growth. Excellent pamphlet summarizing advantages of a one-child family.

Enrichment Study 8

Birth Control Methods Today and Tomorrow

The ideal contraceptive has yet to be found. Indeed, given the diversity of needs of people throughout the world, there will never be a perfect method for everyone. But we can list the desired characteristics of any contraceptive. It should be 100 percent effective, harmless, long lasting, easy to administer, cheap, and readily reversible, offer protection against sexually transmitted disease (STD), and be acceptable to local cultural, religious, and sexual attitudes.

E8-1 Today's Birth Control Methods

Types and Effectiveness Present methods of birth control can be divided into three basic types:

1. *Biological*

    abstention (no intercourse)

    rhythm method (no intercourse during woman's fertile period)

    coitus interruptus (withdrawal before male's climax)

2. *Mechanical*

    condom (protective sheath that covers penis)

    diaphragm (dome-shaped disk placed over woman's cervical opening before intercourse)

    intrauterine device (IUD) (small plastic or metal device inserted semipermanently into uterus)

    surgical sterilization (tubal ligation and vasectomy—obstructing the tubes that carry eggs and sperm, respectively)

3. *Chemical*

    douche (rinsing out the vagina with a chemical immediately after intercourse)

    spermicide (sperm-killing foams, jellies, and creams used before intercourse)

    oral contraceptives (the "pill") (hormonal control of woman's reproductive cycle)

IUD with slow-release hormone (hormonal control of woman's reproductive cycle)

Worldwide, the most widely used form of birth control in 1980 was sterilization (approximately 92 million users—65 million women and 35 million men), followed by oral contraceptives (approximately 58 million users), IUDs (approximately 52 million users), and condoms (about 37 million users). From this we can see that women have assumed the major burden for birth control. Part of this is a result of the sexist attitudes of many men and part is from the fact that women have more at stake in birth control because they are the ones—not men—who must bear the physical and emotional strain of carrying a child for 9 months and face the substantial risk of dying in childbirth. This occurs despite the fact that men need to take precautions to prevent unwanted pregnancy at all times, while strictly speaking women only need to protect themselves during certain days of the month.

Table E8-1 summarizes the effectiveness of these methods and others in the United States. This table presents the maximum theoretical effectiveness (based on the method itself) and the average actual effectiveness (based on actual use).

Couples with very strong motivation can and do use rhythm and withdrawal methods with surprising success. However, many others who use these methods or who rely only on douches are called mommy and daddy. Although effectiveness is obviously a major factor, choosing a method for birth control is a highly individual process influenced by possible side effects, cost, inconvenience, availability, education,* motivation, religious views, and the age of the user.

Cost comparisons should be made on a lifetime basis. If we assume sexual activity 100 times per year over

---

*Contraceptive education in less developed countries has its special problems. Government birth control workers visiting rural villages in Southeast Asia demonstrated condoms by pulling them over a stick. Returning weeks later, they found that the villagers had faithfully followed their instructions: By each sleeping mat couples had placed a condom over a piece of wood.

a 30-year period, then the least expensive method of contraception (excluding withdrawal and the rhythm method) is sterilization ($50 to $150 for a man and $350 to $750 for a woman in 1976). The most expensive method is the pill ($2,210 to $4,080 in 1976). Lifetime costs for condoms, the IUD, and the diaphragm fall between these two extremes.

By 1978, from about 77 percent of married women aged 15 to 44 in the United States were either surgically sterilized or used some form of contraception compared with only 38 percent in 1965. By 1980 about 6 million men in the U.S. had undergone vasectomies as a means of permanent birth control. For married women and men over age 25 surgical sterilization is now the most commonly used and fastest-growing birth control method among U.S. couples. For married women under 25 oral contraceptives are the most common form of birth control. Unwanted teenage pregnancy, however, remains a major problem in the United States, with 1 million female teenagers—one out of every ten—getting pregnant each year. In 1979, an estimated 80 percent of the 5 million sexually active teenagers in the United States did not use any form of birth control because of ignorance, unwillingness, or the unavailability of contraceptive devices. In addition, fewer than 10 percent of all U.S. teenagers are exposed to any valid formal sex education in the schools.

Benefits and Risks Table E8-2 summarizes some of the advantages and disadvantages of present birth control methods.

Despite widespread publicity about medical problems caused by the pill, such as blood clots, stroke, and heart attack, the risk to life up to age 30 is very low and is significantly lower than the death rate from pregnancy and birth. Indeed, in the United States all major forms of birth control involve much less risk than pregnancy (Figure E8-1 on page E69). The only exception is for women over 40 who are pill users and who smoke (Figure E8-1). The pill should also not be used by women of any age who are heavy smokers, are pregnant, or suffer from diabetes, high blood pressure, liver disease, breast cancer, cystic fibrosis, or obesity. It should also be discontinued at least 4 weeks prior to surgery to reduce the risk of blood clotting.

E8-2 Possible Birth Control Methods of the Future

Researchers throughout the world are at work trying to develop new and better methods of fertility control.

Table E8-1 Effectiveness of Birth Control Methods Used in the United States

Method	Theoretical Effectiveness (percentage)	Typical Effectiveness (percentage)
Extremely Effective		
Abortion	100	100
Sterilization		
Tubal ligation	99.96	99.5
Vasectomy	99.85	99.0 to 99.5
Highly Effective		
Oral contraceptive (various types)	100	98 to 99
IUD with slow-release hormones	100	98 to 99
IUD plus spermicide	99	98
Diaphragm plus spermicide	99	98
IUD		
Copper T	99	98
Older loops	98	94 to 97
Condom (good brand) plus spermicide	99.9	95
Effective		
Spermicide (vaginal foam)	97	90
Condom (good brand)	99	85 to 93
Diaphragm alone	98	85 to 87
Moderately Effective		
Spermicide (creams, jellies, suppositories)	90	75 to 80
Rhythm method based on temperature	95	80
Relatively Ineffective		
Condom (cheap brand)	85	70
Withdrawal	85	70
Rhythm method not based on temperature	90	Variable, but normally below 60
Unreliable		
Douche	—	40

Among some of the possibilities for the future are:

1. *Morning-after pill.* A synthetic hormone, diethylstilbestrol (DES), will prevent pregnancy if taken for 5 days within 72 hours after intercourse. It was approved in 1975 by the U.S. Food and Drug Administration for use

Table E8-2 Comparison of Birth Control Methods

Method	Causes or Technique	Advantages	Disadvantages
Abortion, self-induced or by an unqualified person	Trauma; chemical action on breaking the membranes starts premature labor	Sometimes effective; only alternative to birth for some	Mother may die of infection or bleed to death; fetus may be damaged
Abortion by a qualified physician Vacuum aspiration (during first 12 weeks of pregnancy)	Cervix dilated, embryo and placenta gently sucked out by vacuum pump	100% effective; simple and quick; does not require overnight hospital stay	Possible psychological effects and guilt feelings; does not prevent sexually transmitted disease (STD)
Dilation and curettage (D&C) (during first 12 weeks of pregnancy)	Surgical dilation (widening) of cervix followed by scraping of embryo and placenta from walls of uterus	100% effective; relatively simple 20- to 30-minute procedure	Classed as surgery; normally requires overnight hospital stay; 1 to 2% have complications; possible psychological effects and guilt feelings; does not prevent STD
Intraamniotic injections (after 16 weeks of pregnancy)	Needle inserted through abdominal wall into cavity of uterus; small amount of amniotic fluid withdrawn and replaced with salt solution; induces labor	100% effective	Same as D&C except more serious; slightly higher risk of complications
Sterilization Tubal ligation (female)	Fallopian tubes (which carry eggs from ovary to uterus) are cut and tied	99.5% effective; no inherent detrimental effects on sex life; may increase enjoyment of sex by removing fear of pregnancy; low lifetime cost	Surgical procedure; requires 4 to 6 days in hospital (a new, safer technique—laparoscopy—cuts normal hospital stay to 1 day); rarely reversible; moderate to high cost; does not prevent STD
Vasectomy (male)	Very small incision made in scrotum, a small section is removed from one of the tubes that carry the sperm, and the ends are tied	Essentially 100% effective after sperm counts become zero; simple, safe, 20-minute procedure; no hospitalization needed; no inherent effect on sex life; volume of ejaculate not measurably changed; may increase enjoyment of sex by removing fear of pregnancy; low lifetime cost; may reduce incidence of cervical cancer in females	Normally not reversible, but techniques are improving (new microsurgery techniques improve chances of reversing process to about 45%); possible (but unsubstantiated) increased susceptibility to some diseases, such as atherosclerosis (clogging of blood vessels); possible psychological effects; does not prevent STD
Oral contraceptive	Pill containing synthetic female hormones (estrogen and progestin) or just progestin (minipill), taken once a day, keeps ovary from releasing egg	98 to 99% effective; separate from intercourse; no loss of sensation; easy to take; regulates periods and decreases menstrual cramps	Possible side effects (nausea, weight gain, headaches, dizziness, tissue swelling, genital irritation), which usually disappear within a few months; should not be used by women suffering from blood-clotting disorders, diabetes, high blood pressure, liver disease, cystic fibrosis, breast cancer, or obesity; should not be used by heavy smokers, women over 40, or pregnant women; prescription needed; must be taken daily; periodic medical exam required; does not prevent STD; highest lifetime cost

Method	Cause or Technique	Advantages	Disadvantages
Intrauterine device (IUD)	Small plastic or plastic and metal device inserted through the vagina into the uterus; apparently causes a minor inflammation of the uterine lining that prevents the fertilized egg from implanting on the uterine wall	95 to 98% effective; constant protection; separate from intercourse; no loss of sensation; easily and quickly inserted; especially suitable for large-scale programs; moderate lifetime cost	Must be inserted and checked by physician; possible expulsion (expulsion rate less than 6% with new copper IUDs); possible side effects such as minor pain and bleeding (except for copper IUDs), which usually disappear within a few months; some cases of pelvic infection and perforation of uterus; can cause miscarriages and some complications if user becomes pregnant; normally recommended after 1 or more children but copper T usable by others; does not prevent STD (but may in the future)
IUD with slow-release hormone	Unlike pill, which acts throughout the body, hormone stays in uterus to prevent egg release; also normal IUD effect	Same as conventional IUD except even more effective (99%); must be replaced once a year in a doctor's office; avoids most of the side effects of the pill	Same as conventional IUD
Diaphragm plus spermicide	Flexible, hemispherical rubber dome used with spermicidal cream or jelly; inserted by woman into vagina to fit over cervix before intercourse; mechanically blocks sperm from reaching egg and spermatocide kills sperm	Highly effective (98%); no side effects; moderate lifetime cost	Messy; may interrupt sexual act (some new foams can be inserted several hours before intercourse); must be inserted correctly; must be fitted and prescribed by physician; requires high motivation; does not prevent STD
Condom	Thin sheath of rubber or animal skin worn tightly over the penis to keep sperm from entering vagina	70 to 93% effective; highly effective (95%) when a good brand is used jointly with vaginal foam, cream, or jelly; no side effects; used by male; no physician required; prevents STD	May be aesthetically unpleasant; may interrupt sexual act; dulls sensation; can break; demands high motivation; fairly high lifetime cost
Spermicides (foams, creams, jellies, suppositories)	Applicator used to squirt or insert preparations far into the vagina before intercourse; kills sperm	Foam 90% effective but creams, jellies, and suppositories only effective 75 to 80%; no side effects; no physician required; moderate lifetime cost; some types reduce STD in women	Messy; may interrupt sexual act; uncomfortable for a few users; does not prevent STD for males and only partially for females; pregnancy during, or several weeks after, discontinuance may increase birth defect and miscarriage chances
Rhythm	Intercourse limited to woman's nonfertile period; in calendar method, woman keeps a monthly record of her cycles; in temperature method, temperature taken daily on awakening (a 0.5 to 1.0°F rise occurs just before fertile period)	Temperature method moderately effective; no side effects; no physician needed; only accepted practice for Catholics; no cost except for thermometer	Both methods demand great care and motivation; hard to use; failure rate varies widely but is typically 40%; no sex for 11 days out of each 28-day period; cannot be used if woman has very irregular menstruation; fear of pregnancy may lessen sexual enjoyment; does not prevent STD

Table E8-2 Comparison of Birth Control Methods (continued)

Method	Cause or Technique	Advantages	Disadvantages
Withdrawal (coitus interruptus)	Male partner withdraws penis from vagina before ejaculation (oldest known contraceptive method)	No cost; no doctor needed; better than nothing	Works poorly (30% failure) because some sperm may escape before climax; demands very high motivation and self-control; may limit sexual gratification; does not prevent STD
Douche	Flushing of vagina with chemical immediately after intercourse to remove or destroy sperm	Slightly better than nothing; low cost	Poor method (60% failure) because sperm enter cervix within 90 seconds after ejaculation; does not prevent STD

in emergency situations, such as rape. Its use may be limited because of its side effects (intense nausea and vomiting) and its possible linkage to a rare vaginal cancer in daughters of women who have used it. Research is under way to find safer compounds.

2. *Abortion pill.* Prostaglandins that affect hormone actions are being used to abort pregnancies of 12- to 16-week duration. They are not considered as safe as saline injection and they have side effects, including nausea, vomiting, headache, and sometimes diarrhea.

3. *Long-lasting hormone injections.* Injections of Depo-Provera, a synthetic progestin, provide contraceptive protection for 3 months. It is being used in more than 70 nations throughout the world but approval has been denied for use in the United States after 10 years of debate because of a possible increased risk of breast cancer associated with its use. It may also cause permanent sterility, and long-term effects are unknown. Unlike the pill, it cannot be withdrawn if there are adverse side effects.

4. *Long-lasting hormone implants.* A continuous low dose of progestin can be released into the blood or into the uterus either by a pill in a biodegradable capsule that is implanted under the skin or by a ring that is inserted into the vagina. These implantations would release minute daily doses of only one hormone (not estrogen, which causes most side effects from the pill). The capsule could be removed at any time; otherwise, it would remain effective for 1 to 6 years. It has been widely tested on animals, and human trials are under way.

5. *Antipregnancy vaccine.* A vaccine that causes impregnated women to menstruate and thus to wash away the

fertilized ovum has been tested with animals and previously sterilized women with no adverse side effects. Further tests on fertile women are being carried out, but more work needs to be done to establish reliability and long-term safety.

6. *Male contraceptives.* Earlier male hormone pills tended to reduce sex drive. Recently, however, encouraging results were obtained in human tests using the steroid danazol (which suppresses sperm production) in combination with a monthly shot of a synthetic male hormone, testosterone (to ensure a healthy sex drive). Further testing is needed to establish reliability and long-term effects and to ensure that an egg will not be fertilized by a partially damaged sperm. Preliminary tests are also being carried out on a chemical analogue of a brain hormone that stops sperm production in rats. Gossypol, a derivative of cottonseed oil, has also been tested as a male contraceptive in China since 1978 and on animals in the United States. But data are still incomplete and it apparently can accumulate in the body and cause side effects such as nausea, gastric discomfort, reduced appetite, decreased sexual desire, weakness (probably from disturbances in potassium metabolism), and changes in electrocardiograms. If everything goes right, some type of male pill could be on the market by 1990, but probably no sooner than 2000.

7. *Reversible vasectomy for males.* Microsurgery techniques and implanted valves are being used to increase the possibility of reversing vasectomy, but success is still low (no more than 45 percent).

8. *Influencing brain chemistry.* Chemical research is under way to influence chemicals in the brain that trigger the

release of hormones which suppress ovulation in females or sperm formation in males. Preliminary trials in women are under way, but long-term effects and reliability are still unknown.

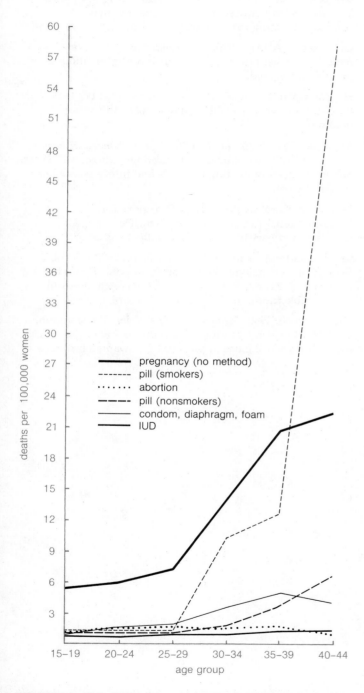

Figure E8-1 Risks of death from birth control and pregnancy in the United States.

9. *Use of sterilizing chemicals in drinking water or food.* There is very little chance of ever developing an acceptable drinking water or food contraceptive for mass use, even if such an approach became ethically acceptable. It would have to be effective and harmless in both low and high doses, because the amount ingested daily would vary considerably with water and food intake. It would have to be stable in solution and over a wide range of temperatures because of heat from cooking, sunlight exposure, and contact with pipes, valves, and other substances. It could have no side effects in humans even though used continuously throughout entire lifetimes, and it could not affect animals. Sterilization of animals through drinking treated water would upset natural and human food chains on which we depend.

Some important and promising research is under way, but we should not expect sensational advances. Considerable money (at least $10 million), extensive testing, and much time are required before a new chemical contraceptive can be developed and approved for general use. To make matters worse, there has been a decline in the funding of such research throughout most of the world. As a Ford Foundation study put it, "The future of the human race depends not upon the conquest of cancer but on the control of human reproduction."

The future of the earth is in our hands. How shall we decide?
Pierre Teilhard de Chardin

Discussion Topics

1. What types of contraceptive and abortion counseling and services are available on your campus? Should they be broadened or made more easily available? Interview college officials or have them talk to your class about this problem and their concerns.

2. Debate whether unmarried teenagers should have free access to birth control counseling and devices without parental permission. Try to get one or more parents who oppose this free access to talk with your class about their concerns.

3. Explain why putting a chemical in the water or in food supplies is probably not feasible technologically and is very undesirable ecologically and ethically. Would it work at all in most less developed countries?

4. Explain why even the "ideal contraceptive" will not completely solve the population problem. Why is there no purely technological solution to the population problem?

5. It is feasible that in the near future couples will be able to choose the sex of their child. What effects might this have on population control in the United States? In most less developed countries? What dangers might arise? Would you use this procedure if it was available? Why or why not?

6. It might be possible, using artificial insemination or genetic alteration, to improve human stock, just as we have bred better strains of plants and livestock. Discuss the pros and cons of doing this. Would you be in favor of it? Why or why not? Suppose we could breed a population who "love" one another in the best sense? Would you favor this? Why or why not?

Readings

Baldwin, Wendy H. 1976. "Adolescent Pregnancy and Childbearing—Growing Concerns for Americans." *Population Bulletin*, vol. 31, no. 2, 1–34. Excellent overview of this problem.

Djerassi, Carl. 1970. "Birth Control after 1984." *Science*, vol. 169, 941–955. Summary of what advances can be expected by a highly qualified researcher in this field. Shows why putting birth control agents in water supplies is not technologically or ecologically feasible, even if it were somehow viewed as ethically acceptable.

Djerassi, Carl. 1980. *The Politics of Contraception*. New York: Norton. Inside view by an expert of how drug companies and the government see the development of new contraceptive drugs and devices.

Guttmacher, Alan F. 1970. *Birth Control and Love*. New York: Bantam. Excellent description of birth control methods by a pioneer in the field.

Hardin, Garrett. 1970. *Birth Control*. New York: Pegasus. Excellent and very readable summary of birth control methods.

Koblinsky, Roy A. G., et al. 1976. *Reproduction and Human Welfare: A Challenge to Research*. Cambridge, Mass.: MIT Press. Superb analysis of existing methods and future possibilities for fertility control.

Korenbrot, Carol C. 1980. "New Directions for Contraception." *Technology Review*, Nov./Dec., pp. 53–62. Excellent summary of future possibilities.

Segal, Sheldon J., and Olivia S. Nordberg. 1977. "Fertility Regulation Technology: Status and Prospects." *Population Bulletin*, vol. 31, no. 6, 1–25. Excellent overview of existing and possible future methods of birth control.

Stokes, Bruce. 1980. *Men and Family Planning*. Washington, D.C.: Worldwatch Institute. Superb discussion of the male's role and responsibilities in preventing unwanted births.

Enrichment Study 9

Ecology and the Poor

Are family planning programs in the United States a form of "black genocide"? Is concern for the environment in the United States diverting funds from housing, jobs, health care, and other human needs? Are the rich countries exploiting the poor countries? In this enrichment study we will look briefly at these controversial issues.

E9-1 The Genocide Question

In the 1960s and early 1970s, some blacks charged that family planning programs in the United States are a form of black genocide. Birth control programs, which seem to be directed primarily at poor blacks, are viewed as a deliberate, government-sponsored plot to exterminate black people or at least to keep their population low.

In spite of these charges, there is no evidence that contraception, abortion, and sterilization have been used in a plot to exterminate black Americans. It is true, however, that there have been attempts since 1958 in some states, such as Mississippi, to enact compulsory sterilization bills, supposedly to deal with the problem of illegitimacy. But to date no compulsory birth control or sterilization laws have been enacted. Three and a half centuries of persecution of blacks have understandably left a legacy of mistrust and suspicion, however. Government policies emphasizing family planning primarily for the poor and the feeling among some Americans that the poor (especially the black poor) are the cause of U.S. population problems fuel these suspicions.

Other blacks reject the charge of genocide as a sensationalist tactic to scare mothers away from services they desperately need. Mary Treadwell, executive director of Pride, Inc., a black self-help organization in Washington, D.C., makes the following reply to charges of genocide:

> A few members of my community tell me that family planning and liberalized abortion are simply another white man's trick to foster racial genocide. They say we

need to reproduce as many black children as possible. There is no magic in a home where someone has reproduced five or more black babies and cannot manage economically, educationally, spiritually, nor socially to see that these five black babies become five highly trained black minds. . . . Wake up, brothers and sisters, power in America is mind power, not muscle power or number power. Black people cannot afford pregnancy as an ego trip.

These thoughts are echoed by black radical Julius Lester, who is also sensitive to women's rights. "Those black militants who tell women 'Produce black babies!' are telling black women to be slaves." U.S. Representative Shirley Chisholm has also rejected the genocide charge and called it "male rhetoric for male ears."

Although there is no evidence to support charges of genocide, blacks and other minority groups need to remain vigilant to be sure family planning programs are not misused. Such fears might be lessened if family planning efforts placed more emphasis on middle class Americans, involved blacks and other minorities in the design of family planning programs, and used blacks and other minority personnel in such programs whenever possible.

E9-2 Ecology as a Diversion from Other Human Needs

Most blacks, Chicanos, Indians, and other minorities in the United States criticize the environmental movement. They regard ecology as irrelevant to their most pressing needs—jobs, housing, health care, and education. They further claim that the environmental movement diverts attention and funds from the urgent problems of poverty and racism. As Tom Bradley, black mayor of Los Angeles, put it in a 1969 speech to the Sierra Club:

> Perhaps what the poor resent most of all is that our nation has been able to mobilize massive resources to

rehabilitate the entire Western world after World War II, put men on the moon, and engage in military adventures, but unable to mount a similar attack on poverty and racism. Concern over social pollutants is only generated when they affect the lives of middle and upper income citizens. High unemployment rates were acceptable until aircraft workers and aerospace scientists and engineers lost their jobs. Drug abuse was ignored until it was no longer confined to the ghetto. Now everyone is in an uproar because the dirt, smog, crowding, and noise that have long made up the slum dweller's daily environment have spread to affluent neighborhoods.

Vernon Jordan, president of the National Urban League, has accused the Environmental Protection Agency (EPA) of not insisting that enough minority workers be hired for the design, construction, and operation of the sewage treatment facilities funded by the federal government. He has also criticized the EPA for not adequately consulting with minorities on environmental problems that are crucial to inner-city residents.

The usual response to charges by minorities is that although they are true, it is also true that we all breathe the same air and drink the same water. Because we all live here together, we must all be concerned about the increasing population, pollution, and misuse of technology that threaten our life-support systems.

But do the poor and the rich really share the same air and water? It is not the rich who are forced by economic circumstances to live near polluting factories or in city slums. The average poor, inner-city dweller gets a much heavier dose of pollution than the person who lives in a higher-income neighborhood. Studies done in Chicago, Washington, D.C., Buffalo, St. Louis, Kansas City, and other cities all showed that the urban poor are exposed to more air pollution and have higher rates of illness and death from diseases associated with air pollution.

Lead poisoning occurs more often among ghetto residents, particularly children (see Enrichment Study 5). This is because so many of the poor are forced to live near freeways (where the air has a higher lead content from automobile emissions) and because many of the older houses in which the poor live still have lead water pipes and lead-based paints.

The National Advisory Commission on Civil Disorders summarized other environmental problems typically found in urban ghettos:

1. high population density

2. poor medical services

3. inadequate sanitation, garbage removal, street cleaning, snow removal, and other services

4. use of streets as recreation areas

5. infestation by rodents and other pests

6. little or no public transportation

7. uprooting by freeway construction

8. high noise levels (Enrichment Study 13)

9. electricity rates higher than in the suburbs

Increased exposure to pollution is not just a problem of the urban poor. Rural poor in Appalachia and other areas devastated by strip mining are the most likely to have nearby streams polluted by sediment and acid run-off and to be buried in landslides. Low- and middle-income workers in the mines, the textile industry, and factories are exposed to serious noise and health hazards, leading to loss of hearing, black lung, brown lung, lung cancer, and other forms of cancer (Enrichment Study 6). Migrant farm workers have higher DDT levels in their blood and run the risk of direct exposure to pesticides, such as parathion, that can kill. In 1970 DDT levels in the blood of black children were 2 to 3 times higher than those in white children in Charleston County, South Carolina. A recent study by the Environmental Protection Agency found that levels of potentially harmful PCBs (Enrichment Study 11) were 3 times higher in blacks than in whites.

It is dehumanizing and the cruelest of jokes to say that the poor are an important cause of pollution and population problems. Instead, it is the poor who are the chief sufferers from pollution. Pollution control will benefit everyone but will have the greatest benefits for the poor. Pollution control efforts must not be divorced from efforts to eradicate poverty.

E9-3 Rich versus Poor: A New International Economic Order

The rich nations have been charged with exploiting the poor nations by controlling international trade so that the poor countries are forced to sell their resources at a price far below their value. In this way the rich nations are accused of stripping the world of its fossil fuel and nonrenewable resources so that there won't be enough resources for the less developed nations in the future. This position was summarized by French economist and government official Pierre Jalée:

The peoples of the Third World extract ever more basic materials, minerals, and primary products and for these the imperialist buyers pay less and less. In return the people of the Third World are obliged to buy more and more of the manufactured goods they lack, and as these goods increase in price, and their income from exports falls, they have to cut back on their essential needs or else extract a larger volume of basic products the price of which then falls farther; there is no way out for them. . . . To ease their conscience, imperialist nations then give a pitiful amount of foreign aid with political and ideological strings attached, as a way of absolving themselves from the need to be aware of the exploitation of the Third World.

British economist Barbara Ward has pointed out that about 80 percent of the annual export earnings of the less developed nations comes from the export of 12 major raw materials (excluding oil). In 1974 the less developed nations received $30 billion for these materials, while the goods made from these raw materials, mostly by the more developed nations, were sold back to them for $200 billion. The less developed nations argue that such a distribution of profits is unfair. Any American president or member of Congress who allowed other nations to coerce the United States into selling its coal or other resources at very low prices would almost certainly be voted out of office. Likewise, Third World leaders would be foolish to allow the same thing to happen or should at least vigorously protest such a situation.

Efforts by rich nations to have poor nations control their population growth are also viewed with suspicion by many less developed countries. In 1972, UNESCO sponsored a Conference on Population and the Environmental Crisis that brought together prominent young scientists from 14 different countries. Their report viewed family planning aid offered by the United States and other affluent countries as a form of imperialism designed to help the affluent countries maintain their control over most of the world's resources.

When those who urge birth control on the Third World have themselves sterilized (for the price of a transistor radio, as is the case in some developing countries), then the Third World would begin to believe in the sincerity of those who urged population control for the world's good, rather than for the sake of continued dominance of one-third of the world over the other two-thirds.

The majority of less developed countries attending the UN Stockholm Conference on the Human Environment in 1972 discounted population as a major environmental problem and named poverty as the real human environmental problem. The message from the poor all over the world is "Help us out of our poverty by helping us become more self-reliant so we can earn a fair share of the world's income. Don't just send us pills, IUDs, and pollution and population experts." The suspicion, however, that population control aid from the rich to the poor nations is being used as a form of control may be blown out of proportion since population assistance amounts to less than 2 percent of all assistance to the poor nations. Some poor nations tend to view appropriate technology (Section 1-5) as part of a conspiracy by the rich nations to keep the poor nations permanently backward.

How valid are the charges of imperialism and exploitation? It can be argued that when more developed countries purchase raw materials from less developed countries, they provide funds that the less developed countries need for their own economic development. This argument may be reasonable in a world with infinite resources. But what advantage will it be for the poor nations to industrialize if the industrialized nations have significantly depleted the fuels, minerals, and other resources necessary for maintaining industrialization? The poor nations may find themselves priced out of the market for what is left.

The truth may lie somewhere between gross exploitation and true aid. It seems clear that the rich nations are not paying a just price for many resources. Average per capita GNP in the United States has been rising steadily, equaling about $9,700 in 1980. But the average per capita cost of raw materials in the United States is less than $150, a price only slightly higher than at the beginning of the century. Between 1945 and 1977, the United States gave to Third World countries about $4 billion in economic aid, $63 billion in loans through international agencies, $3.2 billion in trade concessions, and a great deal of advice and technical help. But this aid has mostly been for economic and political rather than humanitarian reasons and has amounted to only a token in comparison to the profits made from selling products made from raw materials bought cheaply from poor nations. According to Thomas Ehrlich, president of the International Development Corporation Agency, which is designed to coordinate U.S. foreign aid, "For every dollar the United States has paid into the World Bank as aid for less developed nations, about $2 has been spent by these nations in the U.S. economy." In addition, one out of every seven manufacturing jobs in the United States depends on foreign trade and one of every three farm acres is producing for export.

It is urgent that the rich nations heed the less developed nations' call for a *new international economic order*— a proposal designed to shift more of the world's wealth from the rich to the poor nations. This idea is summarized by Carlos Pérez, president of Venezuela:

> We aren't out to destroy the values or prosperity of the industrialized countries. What we want is for them to accept a new relationship in which our raw materials and our labor are given their proper value, which in turn will give us the opportunity to develop our economies.

This plan includes (1) a substantial increase in aid from industrialized nations to less developed nations with special emphasis on the extension of new credit at favorable terms; (2) removal of trade barriers that restrict less developed nations from selling their products to industrial nations; (3) increasing the prices of raw materials exported from poor to rich nations; (4) providing less developed nations with a greater say in the running of international lending institutions, such as the World Bank and the International Monetary Fund; and (5) relieving the poor nations from some of their $250 billion financial debt to the rich nations.

In addition to ethical and ecological reasons, rich nations have important economic reasons for achieving a new international world economic order. It would enhance the prospects for world peace and provide the rich nations with a larger and growing market. By 1979 Third World countries were already buying roughly one-third of all U.S. exports, and such purchases are expected to increase in the decades ahead.

The discussion in this enrichment study underscores the need for including the following cornerstones in the population and environmental plans of the United States and other affluent nations:

1. The issues of population, pollution, misuse of technology, poverty, dangerous working conditions, urbanization, and race and sex discrimination must all be tackled simultaneously in an integrated plan.

2. The United States, being the richest nation, the leading consumer of world resources, and one of the world's biggest polluters, must set the example for the rest of the world by controlling its population and its wasteful consumption of matter and energy resources.

3. The poor should be involved in the planning and execution of environmental programs.

4. The United States and other affluent nations must redistribute the world's wealth and resources more

justly and humanely to help achieve a sustainable earth economy (Section 18-2).

When people in half of the world are dying from too little to eat, and people in the other half are dying from too much to eat, there has to be something basically wrong in the global system of distribution.

Sydney Harris

Discussion Topics

1. Criticize the following statement: Since we all breathe the same air and drink the same water, we should all be concerned about the environment.

2. Debate the pros and cons of the following issues:
   a. Poverty, not population, must be the key issue for most blacks and members of other minorities.
   b. The environmental movement is a middle class diversion from the problems of poverty, war, and racism.
   c. The environmental movement has been taken over by the establishment.
   d. The environmental movement is a genocidal plot by whites to eliminate nonwhite minorities.

3. Debate the issue of whether the United States and other more developed countries are systematically and unjustly draining resources from less developed countries. What should be done? Why? How? What effects will this have on your life?

4. Does everyone have a right to some guaranteed basic share of the world's resources? Why or why not? In the long run, what are the economic, political, and ecological consequences of not redistributing the world's wealth?

Readings

Barnet, Richard J. 1980. *The Lean Years: Politics in an Age of Scarcity*. New York: Simon & Schuster. Superb overview of resource exploitation by the rich nations.

Blake, Judith. 1969. "Population Policy for Americans: Is the Government Being Misled?" *Science*, vol. 164, 522–529. Raises serious questions about focusing family planning on the poor as the basic U.S. population policy.

Chrisman, Robert. 1970. "Ecology Is a Racist Shuck."

Scanlan's, August. Reprinted in R. Buckhour et al., eds., *Toward Social Change: A Handbook for Those Who Will*, New York: Harper & Row. One of the most comprehensive and scathing attacks on the entire environmental movement by the editor of *The Black Scholar*.

Hallow, R. Z. 1969. "The Blacks Cry Genocide." *The Nation*, April 28, pp. 535–537. Good statement of genocide fears.

Hare, Nathan. 1970. "Black Ecology." *The Black Scholar*, April. Penetrating analysis of the environmental movement by a prominent black academician.

Lean, Geoffrey. 1978. *Rich World Poor World*. London: Allen & Unwin. Excellent discussion of the need for a new international world order.

Love, Sam. 1972. "Ecology and Social Justice: Is There a Conflict?" *Environmental Action*, August 5, pp. 3–6. Superb description of how the poor bear the brunt of pollution in the United States.

McCaull, Julian. 1976. "Discriminatory Air Pollution." *Environment*, vol. 18, no. 2, 26–32. Details on how the poor suffer most from air pollution.

Ryan, William. 1971. *Blaming the Victim*. New York: Pantheon. States that the poor suffer from the most damaging aspects of environmental degradation and then are unjustly blamed for causing it.

Singh, Joyt. 1977. *The New International World Order*. New York: Praeger. Excellent overview.

Smith, James Noel, ed. 1974. *Environmental Quality and Social Justice*. Washington, D.C.: Conservation Foundation. Superb collection of dialogues.

Ward, Barbara. 1979. *Progress for a Small Planet*. New York: Norton. Superb discussion of the urgent need for a new international world economic order by a distinguished economist and global thinker.

Weisbord, Robert G. 1975. *Genocide: Birth Control and the Black American*. New York: Two Continents. Superb analysis of this controversial issue.

Enrichment Study 10

The Food Additives Controversy

E10-1 Use of Food Additives in the United States

Give us this day our daily calcium proprionate (spoilage retarder), sodium diacetate (mold inhibitor), monoglyceride (emulsifier), potassium bromate (maturing agent), calcium phosphate monobasic (dough conditioner), chloramine T (flour bleach), aluminum potassium sulfate acid (baking powder ingredient), sodium benzoate (preservative), butylated hydroxyanisole (antioxidant), mono-isopropyl citrate (sequestrant); plus synthetic vitamins A and D.

Forgive us, O Lord, for calling this stuff BREAD.

Averill Park   J. H. Reed

This letter lists only a few of the up to 93 different chemicals that may be added to "enriched" bread. A **food additive** is a chemical that is deliberately added to a food in order to modify its characteristics.[†] Additives may be of natural origin, such as salt and spices, or they may be made synthetically, such as the preservative calcium proprionate and the controversial sweetener saccharin.

All food, of course, is just a mixture of chemicals, but today at least 2,800 different chemicals are deliberately added to foods in the United States, and at least another 3,000 are used in food-packaging materials. As Americans have consumed more and more convenience and processed foods, the use of deliberately added chemicals has grown rapidly, nearly quadrupling between 1960 and 1980. Each year the average American consumes about 55 kilograms (120 pounds) of sugar, 7 kilograms (15 pounds) of salt, and about 4.5 kilograms (10 pounds) of other additives. In 1979 the manufacturing of food additives (excluding sugar, starch, and salt) in the United States was a $1 billion business.

Additives are added to food for at least 45 different reasons—to enhance flavor, color, texture (for example, crunchiness), and appearance; to retard spoilage; to make foods safer for human consumption and easier to prepare; and to improve nutritional value. For example, vitamin A is added to margarine, vitamin C to fruit drinks, vitamin D to milk, iodine to salt (to prevent goiter), and B vitamins to breads and cereals (to replace some of those lost in the milling and processing of grains). Most additives, however, have no nutritional value. Table E10-1 summarizes the major classes of food additives.

There is a growing controversy over the safety of food additives and the need for additives that merely improve appearance and sales appeal. The most widely used groups of additives—coloring agents, natural and synthetic flavoring agents, and sweeteners—have the sole purpose of making food look and taste better. They contribute nothing to food safety, nutrition, or ease of preparation.

Although nothing in life can be guaranteed as being absolutely safe—and food additives are no exception—most of the additives in use are probably harmless or at least pose so little risk relative to their benefits (such as preventing food spoilage and food poisoning) that we accept their use. However, a handful of once widely used additives (such as red dyes no. 2 and no. 4) have been banned in the United States because of their potential harm to humans. In addition, most chemicals added to U.S. foods have not been adequately tested for links to cancer, genetic mutations, and birth defects. About three-fourths of all cases of cancer in the United States are believed to result from environmental factors—the air we breathe, the cigarettes we smoke, the water we drink, and the food we eat (Enrichment Study 6). Food

---

*Used by permission of the *Times-Union*, Albany, N.Y.

[†]Food additives should be distinguished from *food contaminants*, such as pesticides (Enrichment Study 11), minute amounts of drugs fed to animals, chemicals that seep into or are leached out of plastic packaging materials, radioactive isotopes (Section 14-3), insects, and bacteria, which inadvertently gain entry to food from the environment.

Table E10-1 Commonly Used Food Additives and Food Processes

Class	Function	Examples	Foods Typically Treated
Preservatives	To retard spoilage caused by bacterial action and molds (fungi)	Processes: drying, smoking, curing, canning (heating and sealing), freezing, pasteurization, refrigeration	Bread, cheese, cake, jelly, chocolate syrup, fruit, vegetables, meat
		Chemicals: salt, sugar, sodium nitrate, sodium nitrite, calcium and sodium propionate, sorbic acid, potassium sorbate, benzoic acid, sodium benzoate, citric acid, sulfur dioxide	
Antioxidants (oxygen interceptors, or freshness stabilizers)	To retard spoilage of fats (excludes oxygen or slows down the chemical breakdown of fats)	Processes: sealing cans, wrapping, refrigeration	Cooking oil, shortening, cereal, potato chips, crackers, salted nuts, soup, toaster tarts, artificial whipped topping, artificial orange juice, many other foods
		Chemicals: lethicin, butylated hydroxyanisole (BHA), butylated hydroxytoluene (BHT), propyl gallate	
Nutritional supplements	To increase nutritive value of natural food or to replace nutrients lost in food processing*	Vitamins, essential amino acids	Bread and flour (vitamins and amino acids), milk (vitamin D), rice (vitamin B_1), corn meal, cereal
Flavoring agents	To add or enhance flavor	Over 1,700 substances, including saccharin, monosodium glutamate (MSG), essential oils (such as cinnamon, banana, vanilla)	Ice cream, artificial fruit juice, toppings, soft drinks, candy, pickles, salad dressing, spicy meats, low-calorie foods and drinks, most processed heat-and-serve foods
Coloring agents	To add aesthetic or sales appeal, to hide colors that are unappealing or that show a lack of freshness	Natural color dyes, synthetic coal tar dyes	Soft drinks, butter, cheese, ice cream, cereal, candy, cake mix, sausage, pudding, many other foods
Acidulants	To provide a tart taste or to mask undesirable aftertastes	Phosphoric acid, citric acid, fumaric acid	Cola and fruit soft drinks, desserts, fruit juice, cheese, salad dressing, gravy, soup
Alkalis	To reduce natural acidity	Sodium carbonate, sodium bicarbonate	Canned peas, wine, olives, coconut cream pie, chocolate eclairs
Emulsifiers	To disperse droplets of one liquid (such as oil) in another liquid (such as water)	Lecithin, propylene glycol, mono- and diglycerides, polysorbates	Ice cream, candy, margarine, icing, nondairy creamer, dessert topping, mayonnaise, salad dressing, shortening
Stabilizers and thickeners	To provide smooth texture and consistency, to prevent separation of components, to provide body	Vegetable gum (gum arabic), sodium carboxymethyl cellulose, seaweed extracts (agar and algin), dextrin, gelatin	Cheese spread, ice cream, sherbet, pie filling, salad dressing, icing, dietetic canned fruit, cake and dessert mixes, syrup, pressurized whipped cream, instant breakfasts, beer, soft drinks, diet drinks
Sequesterants (chelating agents, or metal scavengers)	To tie up traces of metal ions that catalyze oxidation and other spoilage reactions in food, to prevent clouding in soft drinks, to add color, flavor, and texture	EDTA (ethylenediamine-tetraacetic acid), citric acid, sodium phosphate, chlorophyll	Soup, desserts, artificial fruit drinks, salad dressing, canned corn and shrimp, soft drinks, beer, cheese, frozen foods

*Adding small amounts of vitamins to breakfast cereals and other "fortified" and "enriched" foods in America is basically a sales gimmick used to raise the price unnecessarily for vitamin-conscious consumers. The manufacturer may add about ½¢ worth of vitamins to 340 grams (12 ounces) of cereal and then add 45 percent to the retail price. Vitamin pills are normally far cheaper sources of vitamins than fortified foods. The best way to get vitamins, however, is through a balanced diet.

additives probably make up only a small number of the cancer risks from environmental sources at present, but more and more new chemicals are being added and the amounts of presently used additives are increasing.

The extremes of this controversy range from "essentially all food additives are bad" and "we should eat only natural foods" to "there's nothing to worry about since there is no absolute proof that chemical X has ever harmed a human being." As usual, the truth probably lies somewhere between. Some additives are necessary and safe, but others are unnecessary, unsafe, or of doubtful safety. The pertinent questions to this issue are: (1) What food additives are necessary? (2) What food additives are safe? (3) How well are consumers protected from unnecessary, unsafe additives?

E10-2 Food Additive Safety: Natural versus Synthetic Foods

The presence of synthetic chemical additives does not necessarily mean a food is harmful, and the fact that a food is completely natural is no guarantee that it is safe. A number of natural, or totally unprocessed, foods contain potentially harmful and toxic substances.

Polar bear or halibut liver can cause vitamin A poisoning. Cabbage, lettuce, spinach, tea, and charcoal-grilled steak contain very small amounts of 3,4-benzopyrene, a known cancer-causing chemical also found in tobacco smoke and automobile exhausts.* Lima beans, sweet potatoes, cassava (yams), sugar cane, cherries, plums, and apricots contain glucosides, which our intestines convert to small amounts of deadly hydrogen cyanide. Eating cabbage, cauliflower, turnips, mustard greens, collard greens, or brussel sprouts can cause goiter in susceptible individuals. Certain amines that can raise blood pressure dramatically are found in bananas, various acid cheeses (such as Camembert), and some beers and wines. Although these are usually detoxified by the body, people taking tranquilizers can become seriously ill and even die because some tranquilizers inhibit or block the body chemicals that detoxify these compounds. Safrole (a flavoring agent once used in root beer) and a component of tarragon oil both cause liver tumors in rats. Aflatoxins produced by fungi that are sometimes found on corn and peanuts are extremely toxic to humans and are not legal in U.S. food at levels above 20 parts per billion.

---

*Since this chemical has been associated primarily with lung cancer, not stomach cancer, its presence in tobacco smoke and automobile exhausts is probably a much greater hazard than in foods.

Clams, oysters, cockles, and mussels can concentrate natural and artificial toxins in their bodies. In addition, natural foods can be contaminated with food-poisoning bacteria, such as *Salmonella* and the deadly *Clostridium botulinum*, through improper processing, food storage, or personal hygiene. The botulism toxin from *Clostridium botulinum* is one of the most toxic chemicals known. As little as one-ten-millionth of a gram can kill an adult, and it is estimated that 227 grams (half a pound) would be enough to kill every human being on earth.

Many synthetic food additives, such as vitamins, citric acid, and sorbitol, are identical to chemicals found in natural foods. *Whether natural or synthetic, a chemical is a chemical is a chemical, as long as it is pure.* It makes no difference whether you get vitamin C from eating oranges or from taking synthetic vitamin C tablets. It also makes no difference whether you are poisoned by a natural chemical or a chemical made by humans.

Because there are potentially harmful chemicals in both natural and synthetic foods, the question boils down to whether enough of a chemical is present to cause harmful effects, and whether the effects of a chemical are cumulative.Unfortunately, the answers are not simple because individuals vary widely in susceptibility. Some chemicals may be harmful at any levels, while others are harmful only above threshold levels (Figure 1-4). In addition, a chemical that has been thoroughly tested and found to be harmless by itself may interact synergistically (Section 6-2) with another chemical to produce a hazard. Of course, the more synthetic chemicals we add to our food, the greater the chances of a harmful synergistic interaction.

Testing a single food additive or drug may take up to 8 years and cost $200,000 to $1,000,000. Thus, to test the many thousands of natural and synthetic chemicals for possible synergistic interactions is essentially impossible. Thus, we face a cost-benefit analysis. Do the benefits of introducing a particular chemical into our food outweigh the risks? This involves scientific research, but it also involves economic, political, and ethical judgments that go far beyond science.

E10-3 Consumer Protection: FDA, the GRAS List, and the Delaney Clause

FDA and the GRAS List In the United States the safety of foods and drugs has been monitored by the Food and Drug Administration (FDA) since its establishment by the Food and Drug Act of 1906, which was amended and strengthened by the 1938 Food, Drug, and Cosmetic Act. Yet not until 1958 did federal laws require that the safety of any new food additive be established by the manufacturer and approved by the FDA *before* the additive was put into common use. Today a new additive must undergo extensive toxicity testing, which costs upwards of a million dollars per item. If the additive passes these tests and is approved for use by the FDA, it can be used only for specific purposes and in the minimal amount needed to do the job.

However, this law did not apply to the hundreds of additives that were already in use before 1958. Instead of making expensive time-consuming tests on additives such as salt, sugar, baking soda, and spices, the FDA drew up a list of the food additives in use in 1958 and circulated it among several hundred experts. These experts were asked to give their professional opinion on the safety of these substances. A few substances were deleted, and in 1959 a list of the remaining 415 substances was published as the "generally recognized as safe" or *GRAS* (pronounced "grass") *list*. Additives on the GRAS list could be forced off the market through the courts if the FDA later found them to be dangerous.

Most substances on the GRAS list have been used for years and presumably are safe or create small but acceptable risks relative to their benefits. Since 1958, however, further testing has led the FDA to ban several substances that were on the original GRAS list, including cyclamate sweeteners (1969), brominated vegetable oil (1970), and a number of food color dyes, such as red dye no. 2 (1976). In 1969 the FDA began a review of all of the 415 items on the GRAS list. By 1980 this long, complicated process had been completed. Some 373 of the additives were considered safe as currently used; 19 additives (including caffeine, BHA, and BHT) needed further study; 7 (including salt and 4 modified starches) can be used but only at restricted levels; and 18 were recommended for removal from the GRAS list. In addition to the GRAS review, the FDA announced that by 1982 it would review all other food additives approved for use since the original GRAS list.

As a regulatory agency, the FDA is caught in a crossfire between consumer groups and the food industry. It is criticized by consumer groups as being overly friendly to industry and for hiring a large proportion of its executives from the food industry—a practice the FDA contends is the only way it can get the most experienced food scientists. At the same time, the food industry complains that the FDA sometimes gives in too easily to demands from consumer groups. Both industry and consumer groups have criticized the agency for bureaucratic inefficiency.

Controversy over Food Color Additives   Although natural pigments and dyes exist, most artificial food colors are obtained from coal tar dyes. In 1900 about 100 artificial dyes were in use in the United States, but evidence began accumulating that many of them cause cancer in test animals. By 1980 only six coal tar dyes were still approved by the FDA, and even these had not been tested adequately for safety. Even with this small number, public exposure to coal tar food dyes can be extensive. The FDA estimates that by age 12, 10 percent of all U.S. children have eaten over 454 grams (1 pound) of these dyes. About half of the food additives that have been banned by the FDA have been coal tar dye food colorings.

Some manufacturers are using more natural food colorings such as carotene, paprika, and chlorophyll. But since even the safety of natural additives can't be guaranteed, critics ask why the risk of cancer or other health hazards should be taken for the sake of food coloring. In a 1976 Gallup poll, 59 percent of the women interviewed said they favored banning food additives used only to improve the appearance of food, even if there was no positive evidence of harm.

The Delaney Clause   One powerful weapon the FDA has is the *Delaney clause,** a 1958 amendment to the food and drug laws. It prohibits the deliberate use of any food additive that has been shown to cause cancer in animals or humans. The FDA must evaluate the evidence linking an additive to cancer; if the FDA finds there is a risk, however slight, it must ban the chemical. The amendment is absolute, allowing for no extenuating circumstances or consideration of benefits versus risks. Between 1958 and 1979, the FDA used this amendment to ban only nine chemicals.

Despite the fact that the Delaney clause has been used only a few times, it has been under intense attack since its passage. Critics say it is too rigid and is not needed, since the FDA already has the power to ban any chemical it deems unsafe. In general, the food industry would like to see it removed, while some scientists and politicians would like it to be modified to allow a consideration of benefits versus risks. Others criticize the law because it allows chemicals to be banned even if they

---

*Named after Representative James J. Delaney of New York, who fought long and hard to have this amendment passed despite great political pressure and lobbying by the food industry.

cause cancer in test animals at doses 10 to 1,000 times greater than the amount that a person might be expected to consume. These critics also argue that cancer tests in animals don't necessarily apply to humans.

Supporters of the Delaney amendment point out that since humans can't serve as guinea pigs, animal tests are the next best thing. Such tests don't prove that a chemical will cause cancer in humans, but they strongly suggest that there is a definite risk. Supporters also point out that the high doses of chemicals administered in animal tests are necessary to compensate for the relatively short life spans of test animals and for their relatively fast rates of metabolism and excretion. Besides not providing accurate information, tests using low doses would require thousands of test animals to demonstrate that an effect was not due to chance. Such tests would be prohibitively expensive. Supporters also favor the rigidity of the law. They argue that a carcinogen should be automatically banned because threshold levels for cancer-causing agents have not yet been established and carcinogens may be nonthreshold agents.

Indeed, instead of revoking the Delaney clause, some scientists feel it should be strengthened and expanded. Some even argue that the clause is too flexible—it gives the FDA too much discretion, including the right to reject the validity of well-conducted animal experiments that do show carcinogenicity. These critics cite the FDA's infrequent use of the clause as evidence that the law is too weak. It is also argued that the automatic nature of the law protects FDA officials from undue pressure from the food industry and politicians. If the FDA had to weigh benefits versus risks, political influence and lobbying by the food industry could prevent the ban of a dangerous chemical or at least delay its ban while it underwent years of study. The long delays and failure to ban other potentially harmful chemicals not covered by the Delaney clause illustrate this problem.

Supporters of the Delaney clause have suggested that it be expanded to allow the automatic banning of additives that cause birth defects or genetic mutations in animals or humans and additives that are converted into cancer-producing substances in animals or humans, even if the original additive itself has not been linked to cancer. To strengthen enforcement of the law, it has been recommended that FDA officials who fail to invoke the Delaney clause when there is sufficient scientific evidence to support a ban be subject to legal punishment.

What Can the Consumer Do? It is almost impossible for a consumer in an affluent nation to avoid all food additives. Indeed, as we have seen, many additives per-

form important functions, and there is no guarantee that natural foods will always be better and safer. However, in order to minimize risk, we can do the following:

1. Try to eat a balanced diet, consuming less sugar, salt, and animal fats and more vegetables, fresh fruits, and whole grains.

2. Become informed about additives (such as food colorings) and natural foods that have come under suspicion, and try to avoid them until their safety is established. Some additives may be needed to prevent food spoilage or food poisoning, but since many additives are unnecessary, why take the risk?

3. Exert political pressure to see that the FDA and similar agencies in other countries are adequately funded and staffed and that such agencies and food-manufacturing activities are carefully monitored.

4. Work politically to strengthen existing laws with the following requirements:
   a. All new and presently used additives should be reviewed and tested not only for toxicity and carcinogenic effects but also for their ability to induce birth defects and long-term genetic effects.
   b. All testing of additives should be by a third party, independent of the food industry.
   c. All additives (including specific flavors and colors) should be listed on the label or container of all foods.

5. Unnecessary additives should be banned unless extensive testing establishes that they are safe. It is difficult, however, to define what is unnecessary and then write this definition into an effective and enforceable law. Perhaps the only necessary additives would be those that add to the nutritive content of foods or that prevent foods from spoilage or contamination by harmful bacteria and molds.

The only certainty is that citizens in the wealthiest countries ingest a few thousand different chemical compounds, most of which have not been adequately tested for links to cancer, genetic mutations, birth defects, and behavioral problems.
Erik P. Eckholm

Discussion Topics

1. **a.** Using Table E10-1 and the label of a food in the grocery

store, try to classify the additives listed as (1) necessary and safe, (2) necessary and potentially harmful because of a lack of tests, (3) unnecessary but safe, or (4) unnecessary and potentially harmful. Compare evaluations of different common foods by other class members.

b. Compare brands to see if you can find ones that don't contain additives that are controversial, either because of safety or their usefulness.

c. Evaluate the additives found in baby foods and recommend whether they should be allowed or banned.

2. Explain the fallacies in the following statements:

a. All synthetic food additives should be banned, and we should all return to safe, nutritious natural foods.

b. All foods are chemicals, so we shouldn't worry about artificial chemical additives.

c. Since some natural foods contain harmful chemicals, we should not get so concerned about synthetic food additives.

d. Food additives are essential and without them we would suffer from malnutrition, food poisoning, and spoiled food.

3. What is the GRAS list? The Delaney clause? Describe weaknesses in both. Do you believe that the Delaney clause should be revoked, left as is, altered to allow an evaluation of risks and benefits, or strengthened and broadened? Give reasons for your position.

Readings

Benarde, Melvin A. 1971. *The Chemicals We Eat*. New York: American Heritage Press. Readable introduction to additives by a prominent health scientist. A moderate view, weighted somewhat toward the food industry.

Jacobson, Michael F. 1972. *Eater's Digest: The Consumer's Factbook of Food Additives*. Garden City, N.Y.: Doubleday. Outstanding moderate overview. Consult this paperback book to determine which additives you might want to avoid.

Mellinkoff, Sherman H. 1973. "Chemical Intervention." *Scientific American*, vol. 229, no. 3, 103–112. Excellent overview of overuse of drugs and food additives.

Staff report. 1977. "Should the Delaney Clause Be Changed? A Debate on Food Additive Safety, Animal Tests, and Cancer." *Chemical and Engineering News*, June 27, pp. 24–46. Superb debate by four experts on the Delaney clause.

Verrett, Jacqueline, and Jean Carper. 1974. *Eating May Be Hazardous to Your Health*. New York: Simon & Schuster. Excellent overview of the potential dangers of food additives and the problems of consumer protection.

Whelan, Elizabeth M., and Frederick J. Stare. 1976. *Panic in the Pantry*. New York: Atheneum. Excellent presentation advocating the use of food additives and the elimination of the Delaney clause.

Winter, Ruth A. 1978. *A Consumer's Dictionary of Food Additives*. New York: Crown. Extremely useful guide to additives, suggesting which ones you may wish to avoid.

Enrichment Study 11

Pest Control

Throughout most of recorded history, humans and pests have lived together in reasonable harmony. Most of the world's billion billion insects, rodents, and fungi do not interfere with humans, and many are crucial in cycling vital chemicals through the ecosphere, pollinating plants, building up soil fertility, and eating or killing pest species. Occasionally populations of pest species have grown rapidly and caused disease and famine. Most of the time, however, natural insect predators, disease, and parasites have kept pest populations under control. During the past 35 years this situation has begun to change. Today there is increasing reliance on a variety of synthetic chemicals, called pesticides, to kill insects, plants, rodents, fungi, and other unwanted organisms. **Pesticides** (or *biocides*) are chemicals devised to kill organisms that humans consider to be undesirable. Scientists have developed *insecticides* to kill unwanted insects; *herbicides* to kill unwanted plants; *fungicides* to kill unwanted fungi; *rodenticides* to kill rats, mice, gophers, and other rodents; and a number of other poisons to kill other pests. Since pesticides have both beneficial and harmful effects, their use presents us with a dilemma. In 1962, Rachel Carson's book *Silent Spring* dramatized the potential dangers of pesticides to food, wildlife, and humans and set off a controversy that still endures.* What are the benefits of and threats from pesticides? Do the benefits outweigh the risks? Are there alternatives other than using chemicals for controlling pests? In this enrichment study we will take a look at these important questions by concentrating on the two most widely used types of pesticides: insecticides and herbicides.

---

*Although some technical details of Rachel Carson's book have been shown to be in error by later research, its basic thesis that pesticides can contaminate and cause widespread damage to ecosystems has been established. Unfortunately, Carson's early death from cancer came before her book was recognized as one of the most important events in the history of environmental awareness and action in this century.

E11-1   Insecticides: Types and Properties

Chemicals against Insects: A Brief History The estimated 1 million different species of insects make up about 75 percent of the earth's known animal species. Only 5,000 to 15,000 of the 1 million insect species have become pests by human standards. Plants manufactured insect-killing and disease-resisting chemicals long before humans began their war against pests. These natural organic substances were probably the earliest insecticides extracted and used by humans. One of the oldest effective natural insecticides is a class of compounds known as *pyrethrins*, which are extracted from the pyrethrum flower, a member of the chrysanthemum family. Pyrethrins are particularly valuable because of their specificity for certain insects, their lack of toxicity to birds and animals, and their relatively rapid breakdown in the environment. Other insecticides derived from natural plant sources include nicotine (as nicotine sulfate) from tobacco, rotenone from the tropical derris plant, and even garlic oil, which has been used against the larvae of mosquitoes, houseflies, and other insects.

Some manufactured inorganic chemicals, especially highly toxic salts of arsenic, lead, mercury, copper, and zinc, have been used as insecticides for over a century. Although they are still used occasionally, many of them, such as lead arsenate, are permanently nondegradable in the environment. Tobacco produced today on soil that was treated with these deadly pesticides during the early part of this century is still contaminated with trace amounts of these dangerous metals (Enrichment Study 5).

The major revolution in insect control occurred in 1939 when Paul Mueller, a Swiss chemist, discovered that DDT (*dichlorodiphenyltrichloroethane*), a chemical known since 1874, was a powerful insecticide for many kinds of insects. During World War II it was demonstrated that DDT could be used to control *typhus* (a rickettsial infection transmitted by lice and fleas) and *malaria* (a protozoan infection transmitted by certain types of mosquitoes) (Enrichment Study 6). In 1948 Mueller was awarded the Nobel Prize for Physiology and Medicine for his discovery.

Increasing Use of Pesticides   The use of synthetic pesticides has grown enormously over the past 35 years. Worldwide, in 1979 about 2 billion kilograms (4 billion pounds) of pesticides were used—equal to about 0.5 kilogram (1 pound) of pesticides per year for every person on earth. Furthermore, the worldwide use of pesticides is projected to more than double between 1975 and 2000, with usage increasing four- to sixfold in the less developed nations. By 1979 about 1,400 different chemicals were registered in the United States with the Environmental Protection Agency for use in over 40,000 pesticide products. Between 1950 and 1979 pesticide production in the United States increased over sixfold and it had become a $4.2-billion-a-year business. About half of the pesticides produced in 1979 were used in the United States and half were exported to other nations. From 15 to 25 percent of these annual exports (primarily to less developed nations) involved pesticides that either have been banned in the United States or have not even been tested and approved for use in the United States. It was not until 1978 that the U.S. Congress passed a law requiring pesticide manufacturers to add a label to exported pesticides indicating possible health effects or the fact that the pesticide was not registered for use in the United States.

If the total amount of pesticides produced each year in the United States were blanketed over the entire U.S. land area, about 48 kilograms of pesticides would be deposited on each square kilometer of land (275 pounds per square mile). Fortunately, pesticide application is unevenly distributed. In 1979, only about 9 percent of all U.S. cropland (including pastures) was treated with insecticides, 22 percent with herbicides, and 1 percent with fungicides. About two-thirds of all insecticides applied each year in the United States are used on only two crops: cotton (50 percent to kill pests such as the boll weevil) and corn (17 percent to kill corn borers and other insects). Of the herbicides used each year in the United States, 45 percent is applied to corn and 17 percent to soybeans. The major applications of fungicides are to fruit crops (60 percent) and vegetables (26 percent). Despite such large-scale use, only about half of all U.S. farmers use any pesticides on their land. In addition, although the total use of pesticides is much greater on commercial crops, suburban lawns and gardens in the United States receive the heaviest doses of pesticides per unit of land area.

Types and Properties of Insecticides   The three main groups of synthetic insecticides are *chlorinated hydrocarbons, organophosphates,* and *carbamates* (Table E11-1). A fourth group, compounds made from toxic metals such as arsenic, lead, and mercury (Enrichment Study 5), are little used today. Most chemical pesticides are broad-spectrum poisons that kill all insects in an area that is sprayed—somewhat like a shotgun blast. This means that useful insects and predators that help control pest populations naturally are killed along with the target pests.

An important property of a pesticide is its *persistence,* or the length of time it remains active in the ecosphere. From Table E11-1 we can see that chlorinated hydrocarbons stay active for 2 to 15 years and are classified as *persistent pesticides.* Most organophosphate and carbamate insecticides remain active for a few hours to several months and are called *nonpersistent pesticides.* The lead and arsenic pesticides that were once used remain active for hundreds of years and are called *permanent pesticides.*

E11-2   The Case for Insecticides

Disease Control   By helping control major human diseases transmitted by insects, synthetic chemical pesticides have saved and extended the lives of millions of people. Some human diseases partly controlled by pesticides, especially DDT, are malaria (transmitted by the *Anopheles* mosquito), bubonic plague (rat flea), typhus (body lice and fleas), sleeping sickness (tsetse fly), and Chagas' disease (kissing bugs) (see Enrichment Study 6).

Malaria still threatens half of humankind and is the single most serious health problem in tropical and subtropical regions of the world (Figure E6-1). After malaria struck 250 million people and killed 2.5 million people in 1955, the World Health Organization launched a global program to wipe out malaria by widespread spraying with DDT and dieldrin and the use of antimalarial drugs. By 1965 the number of malaria cases throughout the world had dropped dramatically to 107 million. Thanks largely to DDT and dieldrin, over 1 billion people have been freed from the risk of malaria and the lives of at least 5 million were saved between 1947 and 1970. Thus, by helping to control malaria, typhus, and other diseases, DDT has probably saved more lives than any synthetic chemical substance in history.

Table E11-1 The Major Types of Insecticides

Type	Examples	Action on Insects	Persistence
Chlorinated hydrocarbons	DDT, DDE, DDD, aldrin, dieldrin, endrin, heptachlor, toxaphene, lindane, chlordane, kepone, mirex	Nerve poisons that cause convulsions, paralysis, and death	High (2 to 15 years)
Organophosphates	Malathion, parathion, Azodrin, Phosdrin, methyl parathion, Diazinon, TEPP, DDVP	Nerve poisons that inactivate the enzyme that transmits nerve impulses	Low to moderate (normally 1 to 12 weeks but some can last several years)
Carbamates	Carbaryl (Sevin), Zineb, maneb, Baygon, Zectran, Temik, Matacil	Nerve poisons	Usually low (days to 2 weeks)

But there is an important catch to this miracle story. By 1979, 61 species of malarial mosquitoes had become resistant to DDT and to dieldrin and other chlorinated hydrocarbon pesticides used to replace DDT. Thus, although DDT and several other chlorinated hydrocarbons deserve their reputation as givers of life, they are no longer effective in many parts of the world, with insecticide resistance appearing in 62 out of 107 countries where there is malaria (see Figure E6-1). As a result, malaria has made a dramatic comeback since 1970. Between 1970 and 1980 there was a 30- to 40-fold increase in malaria cases in many countries.

In spite of DDT's increasing ineffectiveness, about 15 percent of the total amount of DDT produced each year is used for malaria control in areas where mosquitoes have not become resistant. According to the World Health Organization, a wholesale ban on DDT and its substitutes where they are still useful would lead to large increases in human suffering, disease, and death.

Increased Crop Yields   The use of pesticides to protect food crops is an important factor in reducing starvation throughout the world, as discussed in Section 9-7. Each year pests, crop diseases, and weeds consume or destroy about 40 to 50 percent of the world's food supply (with 30 to 35 percent destroyed prior to harvest and 10 to 15 percent lost after harvest). Even in the United States, which has a sophisticated crop production and food storage system, about 39 percent (33 percent before harvest and 6 percent after harvest) of the food crops grown each year are destroyed by pests, crop diseases, and weeds.

Without the use of pesticides in the United States, the Department of Agriculture estimates that total production of crops, livestock, and forests would drop by 25 to 30 percent, and food prices would probably rise by 50 to 75 percent. Another estimate, however, indicates that U.S. preharvest crop losses due to pests and crop diseases would rise only 9 percent (from 33 to 42 percent) if pesticide use was completely banned, and human food loss would only be about 5 percent. No serious food shortage would occur, although the production of certain fruits and vegetables, such as apples, peaches, tomatoes, and onions, would be greatly reduced as long as consumers insist on buying only perfect-looking fruits and vegetables. Resistance to pesticides is increasingly rapidly among pests that devour major food crops. By 1980, the UN Food and Agricultural Organization estimated that at least 233 agricultural pests had become resistant to major pesticides.

There are alternatives to relying on chemical pesticides to control pests (Section E11-5), but proponents argue that using synthetic chemical pesticides has a number of advantages over other approaches. These include the following: (1) A variety of pesticides are available to control most pests at a reasonable cost; (2) pesticides act quickly and are effective against large pest populations; (3) reliable equipment is available to apply pesticides; and (4) an increasing number of narrow-spectrum, nonpersistent pesticides, especially herbicides, have been developed that can be used to control specific pests and diseases without widespread killing of other nonpest organisms.

E11-3   The Case against Insecticides

In view of the benefits of using pesticides, you may wonder why anyone would question their use. The answer is that pesticides also cause a number of undesirable and harmful side effects in ecosystems and nonpest living organisms, including humans. The major problems include (1) killing natural enemies of existing pests so that larger and more frequent doses of pesticides are needed to maintain control; (2) creating new pests by killing natural enemies of organisms that were previously kept under control; (3) genetic resistance of insects to pesticide chemicals so that heavier doses and eventually new and more toxic chemicals must be used; (4) regional and local contamination by movement of some persistent pesticides beyond their application sites; (5) biological magnification (Section 6-2) of some persistent pesticides in food chains; (6) decreased reproduction rates of some predatory birds because of food-chain magnification of persistent pesticides; (7) ecosystem simplification by disruption of food chains and normal predator-prey balances (Enrichment Study 4); (8) human deaths and illness from careless use and handling of highly toxic pesticides such as organophosphates; and (9) unknown but potentially harmful effects on humans (including cancer) from long-term exposure to low levels of persistent pesticides.

A very conservative estimate is that the environmental and social costs of pesticide use in the United States amount to a loss of at least $839 million each year. This includes 45,000 humans poisoned and 200 deaths from pesticides, $12 million in livestock losses, $135 million in honeybee poisonings and reduced pollination of vital crops, $70 million in losses of crops and trees, $11 million in fish and wildlife losses, and $14 million in miscellaneous losses. Honeybees and wild bees, which are vital to pollinate fruits, vegetables, forage crops, and natural plants, are very susceptible to poisoning by pesticides. Each year an estimated 20 percent of all honeybee colonies in the United States are killed by pesticides and another 15 percent of the colonies are damaged. A more complete accounting would probably yield total losses several times these estimates. Let's look at the major problems with pesticides in more detail.

Killing Natural Enemies, Creating New Pests, and Development of Genetic Resistance Sometimes pesticides have reduced pest populations and saved crops. But in many—perhaps most—cases farmers would have suffered smaller crop losses and saved money by rotating crops and letting natural enemies of the pests control their population. One reason for this is that most modern insecticides are broad-spectrum poisons that kill both the target pest species and a host of other organisms, often

including the target pest's natural predators. Without natural enemies and lots of food available, rapidly reproducing pest insects can make an even stronger comeback within a few days or weeks after being initially controlled. This forces farmers to use heavier doses and more frequent applications of the pesticide to keep the pest under control. This knocks out even more nontarget species and can aggravate the problem. U.S. crop losses from insect pests before harvest almost doubled between 1945 and 1977 in spite of a twelvefold increase in insecticide use—hardly a ringing endorsement for the effectiveness of pesticides. Widespread use of broad-spectrum pesticides can also create new pests and convert minor pests to major pests—the reverse of what such pesticides are supposed to do. Insects whose populations are kept under control by natural enemies can become new, major pests when their natural predators are killed off by insecticides. By 1970, 24 of California's 25 most serious insect pests were either pesticide created or pesticide aggravated. This is shocking but not surprising, since California uses 5 percent of all pesticides used each year in the world.

The most serious drawback to using chemicals to control pests is that nearly all species of insects are capable of developing genetic resistance to any chemical poison. As a group, insects are by far the most successful and adaptable animals that have ever evolved on earth. When an area is sprayed with insecticides, most of the insects present are killed. But a few survive because some trait carried in their genetic makeup (chromosomes) makes them less susceptible to the poison. These survivors then begin reproducing a new generation of insects that are more genetically resistant to the chemical poison used to wipe out most of their ancestors. Insects have short generation times and can spawn so many offspring that they can make rapid evolutionary changes. Thus, each succeeding generation has genetic traits that make it less susceptible to a chemical poison (Section 6-2). (For example, a generation for the boll weevil, a major cotton pest, lasts only 21 days, with each mating pair producing up to two dozen offspring.) This means that the widespread use of any chemical to control insects is eventually doomed to failure, typically within about five years. Worldwide, by 1979 at least 400 species of insects had strains resistant to one or more chemical pesticides. The more chemicals we use, the worse this problem will become. Of California's 25 most serious insect pests, 18 had become resistant to one or more insecticides by 1970.

The use of chemical poisons as the only or primary method for pest control is good business for companies that sell these chemicals. But this narrow approach merely hooks the farmer onto a chemical treadmill that costs more and more money to yield poorer and poorer results. When genetic resistance first develops, pesticide sales representatives urge farmers to apply heavier and more frequent doses of pesticides. This not only costs the farmers more money but also increases the rate at which genetic resistance develops. A new and typically more costly pesticide may be developed, but eventually insects can become resistant to entire classes of pesticides so that none are effective. Then pests having few natural enemies can devastate a crop.

This is precisely what happened to the cotton crop in southeastern Texas and northeastern Mexico in the 1960s. In the late 1950s the boll weevil, a major cotton pest, became resistant to DDT and carbamate pesticides, thus forcing a switch to organophosphates. The organophosphates wiped out natural enemies of cotton bollworms, a minor pest, and elevated it to major pest status. For a while, elevated doses of organophosphates helped control the boll weevil and bollworms but greatly increased production costs. Then in the mid-1960s the bollworm developed genetic resistance to the major organophosphate insecticide being used (methyl parathion) so that some growers were treating their fields 15 to 18 times each growing season at great cost and still suffering major crop losses. In Texas, the profits from the cotton industry dropped sharply, and in northeastern Mexico the entire multimillion-dollar cotton industry disappeared, prompting an economic depression.

Global Mobility and Biological Magnification of Persistent Pesticides Because DDT and other persistent pesticides are volatile, soluble in fats, and slow to degrade, they can be dispersed throughout the globe far beyond where they are applied. After being sprayed, airborne droplets of persistent pesticides are transported by the wind and brought down in distant areas by rain or snow. Persistent pesticides are also washed into streams and eventually into the oceans, where currents move them long distances. Migratory birds and fish that feed on species containing pesticide residues also help disperse pesticides to other areas. Depending on their persistence, DDT and other slowly degraded pesticides can circulate in local, regional, and global ecosystems for many years—in some cases for decades—after they are applied. As a result, there are traces of pesticides in the oceans, in the air and rain at the remote Eniwetok Atoll in the North Pacific Ocean, in the fatty tissues of penguins in the Antarctic, in your body, and just about everywhere.

Some persistent pesticides can be concentrated or biologically magnified in food chains (Figure 6-8). The concentration of DDT can be magnified hundreds, thousands, even millions of times above the levels found in the soil or water. Typical magnification factors for DDT in freshwater chains from water to fish-eating birds or humans are on the order of 75,000 to 150,000, while those in ocean food chains may be several million (see Figure 6-8). Land-based food chains such as DDT →leaf→ earthworm→ robin are shorter, with magnification factors of 10 to 100. Some evidence, however, indicates that DDT and other pesticides do not build up continuously in organisms because they eventually reach a level at which they are being excreted or degraded in amounts equal to their intake. A model of the movement and biological concentration of DDT in the ecosphere is shown in Figure E11-1.

Effects on Wildlife and Marine Organisms Insecticides, of course, are designed to kill plant-eating insects. But these chemicals can also kill other beneficial organisms at higher levels in the food chain, either by direct exposure or by biological magnification which concentrates the largest amounts in species at the top of food chains (Figures 6-8 and E11-1). Marine organisms in estuarine and coastal waters, especially shellfish, are vulnerable to minute concentrations of chlorinated hydrocarbons. Pesticides are also one of the factors involved in the increase in yearly fish kills in the United States, which went from an average of 200,000 to 400,000 per year in the 1960s to well over 1 million a year between 1970 and 1978.

There is considerable evidence that DDT and two chemicals into which it can break down (DDE and DDD) have been key factors in reducing populations of some species of predatory birds that eat at high levels in food chains. Species affected include peregrine falcons, pelicans, ospreys, prairie falcons, sparrow hawks, and Bermuda petrels. Such predatory birds control the populations of rabbits, ground squirrels, and other small mammals that may damage crops. In many cases the birds themselves are not poisoned. Instead the DDT and DDE apparently interfere with their calcium metabolism, making the shells of their eggs so thin that the eggs tend to break before the offspring hatch. In 1972, the Environmental Protection Agency banned the use of DDT for almost all purposes in the United States. Since that time, DDT, DDD, and DDE residues have dropped in many bird species, and by 1975 dramatic reproductive improvement had occurred in ospreys, brown pelicans, and prairie falcons.

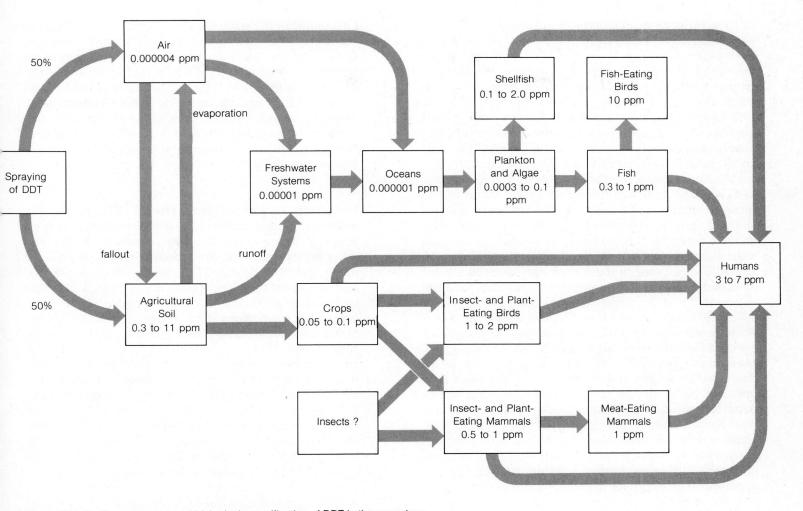

Figure E11-1 The movement and biological magnification of DDT in the ecosphere.

Ecosystem Simplification and Food-Chain Disruption
The buildup of persistent pesticides and other toxic substances in the ecosphere can have profound effects on the structure (Chapter 4) and function (Chapter 5) of ecosystems. One obvious effect of pesticides is that the ecosystem becomes simpler as pests are killed off. But broad-spectrum pesticides also destroy helpful organisms. As a result, food chains and webs are shortened and modified. Eliminating or reducing lower levels can weaken the entire structure, threatening specialized animals that feed at the top of the chain.

Short-Term Threats to Human Health The general public is rarely exposed to high levels of toxic pesticides.

By very conservative estimates, however, 500,000 farm workers, pesticide plant employees, and children worldwide become seriously ill and about 5,000 die each year from exposure to toxic pesticides. In the United States alone there are about 45,000 pesticide poisonings and about 200 deaths each year. These illnesses and deaths must be balanced against the illnesses and deaths prevented by the use of pesticides.

The number of pesticide-related illnesses among U.S. farm workers each year may be greatly underestimated because of poor records and a lack of reporting. Compared to the United States, pesticide-related illnesses and deaths occur much more frequently among farm workers in less developed nations, where educational levels are low and control over pesticide use is often lax.

The short-term toxic effects of different pesticides vary widely. Pesticide plant workers and convict volunteers exposed to high levels of DDT showed no short-term toxic effects. These studies, however, have been criticized as being poorly designed, and they tell us nothing about possible long-term effects. Between 1972 and 1976 the Environmental Protection Agency banned most uses of DDT and several other persistent chlorinated hydrocarbon pesticides (aldrin, dieldrin, heptachlor, and chlorodane) in the United States. Despite this ban, pesticide manufacturing companies continue vigorous efforts to have these chemicals reinstated for use, and most of these chemicals are still made in the United States and shipped to other countries where they have not been banned. Since 1972, there has been a switch to less persistent organophosphate and carbamate pesticides in the United States. Some of these chemicals (such as methyl parathion), however, are more toxic to humans than the chlorinated hydrocarbons they replaced.

In 1975 state officials found that 70 workers in a pesticide manufacturing plant in Hopewell, Virginia, had been poisoned by exposure to high levels of *kepone* (chlorodecone), a persistent, chlorinated hydrocarbon pesticide used as an ant and roach poison. The plant was operated under dangerous and illegal working conditions. Kepone dust filled the air, covered equipment, and was even found in the employees' lunch area. The plant—which was associated with Allied Chemical Company—was shut down and 29 plant workers were hospitalized with uncontrollable shaking, blurred speech, apparent brain and liver damage, loss of ability to concentrate, joint pain, and in some cases sterility. Exposed workers could also be more susceptible to cancer since kepone causes cancer in test animals. Doctors, however, have reduced this risk by finding a chemical that can remove most of the kepone from workers' bodies. Allied Chemical Company has paid out $13 million in damage suits, but this will not make these victims of unsafe working conditions healthy again.

Unfortunately, this was only the beginning of the kepone tragedy. Further investigation revealed that about 160 kilometers (100 miles) of the James River were contaminated with an estimated 46,500 kilograms (100,000 pounds) of kepone, which were dumped illegally between 1966 and 1975 by the manufacturer into the municipal sewage system. The kepone disrupted the bacterial decomposition processes in the sewage treatment plant and resulted in the discharge of untreated, kepone-laden sewage into the James River. Fish and shellfish taken from the river were contaminated with kepone, and between 1975 and 1980 more than 160 kilometers

(100 miles) of the river and its tributaries were closed to commercial fishing, resulting in a loss of jobs and millions of dollars. Bowing to pressure from the state's ailing fishing industry, the Virginia Board of Health lifted most of its ban on fishing in 1980, but still advised women and small children against eating fish from contaminated areas. This tragic incident, which has led to human misery and a loss of many millions of dollars, could have been prevented by an investment of only $200,000 by the company making kepone.

Long-Term Threats to Human Health   The real concern among a number of scientists is the possible effects on humans of long-term, low-level exposure to DDT and other persistent pesticides. These chemicals are soluble in fats and thus are stored for long periods of time in the fatty tissues of the human body. Even though DDT and most other persistent chlorinated hydrocarbon pesticides have been banned for most uses in the United States for several years, Americans will carry slowly declining levels of DDT in their bodies for decades. In 1971, Americans carried an average of about 8 ppm of DDT in their bodies. By 1977, the average level had dropped to about 3 ppm (Figure E11-1). Similarly, between 1971 and 1977 the average level of dieldrin in human fatty tissue dropped by about 50 percent. In contrast, concentrations of DDT in human fatty tissue and human food will almost certainly increase in less developed countries where DDT is still being used extensively.

People born after 1946 are the first generation to carry DDT in their bodies throughout their lifetime. Frankly, no one knows what effects, if any, such long-term exposure to low levels of DDT and related pesticides may be. The results will not be known for two to three decades, since the oldest people who have carried DDT and other persistent pesticides in their bodies since conception only reached the age of 35 in 1981. However, some disturbing but inconclusive evidence has emerged. DDT, aldrin, dieldrin, heptachlor, mirex, endrin, and 19 other pesticides have all been found to cause cancer, especially liver cancer, in mice. In addition, autopsies have shown that people who died from various cancers, cirrhosis of the liver, hypertension, cerebral hemorrhage, and softening of the brain had fairly high levels of DDT (and its breakdown products, DDE and DDD) and other chlorinated hydrocarbon pesticides in their fatty tissue. A National Academy of Sciences study indicated that up to 25 percent of the 1,400 different chemicals used in registered pesticides in the United States may cause cancer in human beings. Such *potential* long-term health effects of persistent pesticides on humans must be weighed against the short-term benefits of disease control and more food for the world's growing population.

E11-4 PCBs and Herbicides

Polychlorinated Biphenyls (PCBs) DDT is not the only persistent chemical that we carry in the fatty tissues of our bodies. Since 1966 scientists have found contamination from a widely used group of chemicals known as *polychlorinated biphenyls*, or *PCBs*, almost everywhere. PCBs are mixtures of about 70 different but closely related chlorinated hydrocarbon compounds (made like DDT of carbon, hydrogen, and chlorine). Since 1929 PCBs have been widely used as pesticide extenders; as softeners in plastics, paints, and rubber; as additives in adhesives, ink, and duplication paper; and as coolant and insulating fluids in large electrical transformers and capacitors.

Like DDT, PCBs are insoluble in water, soluble in fats, and very resistant to biological and chemical degradation. Thus, they have the ideal properties for persistence and magnification in food chains. Indeed, PCBs are more persistent than DDT. High levels of PCBs have been found in Antarctic penguins, fish-eating and predatory birds at the top of food chains, and in the milk of nearly one-third of nursing mothers who were tested in a 1975 survey by the Environmental Protection Agency. The EPA estimates that by 1976 at least 98 percent of all Americans had detectable levels of PCBs in their fatty tissues. PCBs have killed shrimp and game birds, have reduced the reproductive capacity of some birds and fish-eating mammals such as mink and seals, and may be twice as effective as DDT in thinning the eggshells of some birds.

What effects do PCBs have on people? There was little concern about PCBs until 1968, when about 1,100 Japanese came down with a painful skin disease and suffered liver damage after they had eaten rice oil accidentally contaminated with high levels of PCBs. There is some unsubstantiated evidence that these effects could have been caused by chlorinated dibenzofurans, found as impurities in most PCBs. Japan promptly banned all use of PCBs.

As with DDT, the long-term health effects on humans exposed to low levels of PCBs are unknown. But PCBs have been found to cause liver cancer in laboratory animals. In 1977 the EPA used the Toxic Substances Control Act of 1976 to ban the production, sale, and use of PCBs in the United States by July 1979—over 10 years after a similar ban was put into effect in Japan. But some 682 million kilograms (750,000 tons) of PCBs are still used in industrial equipment (primarily transformers and capacitors), and about 273 million kilograms (300,000 tons) have been disposed of in dumps and landfills. In 1978 a PCB-salvaging firm from Buffalo, New York, was convicted of dumping 125,000 liters (33,000 gallons) of PCB-contaminated oil along roadsides in North Carolina. These "midnight dumpers" went bankrupt and were sent to jail. By 1981, after 3 years of confusion and delay (partly because no county in the state wants a PCB disposal site), government officials in North Carolina had still not removed most of the PCB-contaminated soil from the roadsides, and many of the signs warning motorists of the danger had been torn down and not replaced. This PCB-contaminated oil could have been disposed of safely for $100,000. Instead, the state of North Carolina may have to spend between $2 and $12 million to remove and dispose of the contaminated soil (the second law again), and thousands of persons have been (and are still being) exposed to low levels of PCBs with unknown long-term effects.

In 1980, the Environmental Protection Agency, the Food and Drug Administration, and the Department of Agriculture proposed that all equipment (such as transformers and capacitors) that contain PCBs be removed from food and animal production facilities and agricultural chemical plants. This should help eliminate accidental contamination of human and other animal food supplies with PCBs leaking from such equipment. Despite these bans many decades will pass before the sediments of rivers, lakes, and oceans and the fatty tissues in our bodies will be free of these very persistent chemicals. One problem is that it is expensive to destroy PCBs. The only two known methods are incineration at temperatures of several thousand degrees and exposure to ozone and ultraviolet light. Neither of these methods can be used to eliminate the PCBs already found in your body and in other parts of the environment.

Herbicides: 2,4-D and 2,4,5-T Within the pesticide industry, herbicides are the fastest-growing and most profitable branch with sales of $1.3 billion in the United States in 1980. Two of the most widely used weed-killers are the phenoxy herbicides, 2,4-D (short for 2,4-dichlorophenoxyacetic acid) and 2,4,5-T (short for 2,4,5-trichlorophenoxyacetic acid). Luckily, these chemicals do not persist for a long time and do not build up in food chains.

The safety of 2,4-D was not seriously questioned until 1980, when the EPA called for a review of its health effects to determine whether it should be banned. The safety of 2,4,5-T, however, has been questioned for almost 20 years. The controversy over 2,4,5-T use began in the 1960s during the Vietnam war. It was used in high concentrations as an ingredient in Agent Orange, a 50-50 mixture of 2,4-D and 2,4,5-T sprayed to defoliate jungles in South Vietnam between 1962 and 1970. In 1965 and 1966 a study commissioned by the National Cancer Institute found that low levels of 2,4,5-T caused high rates of birth defects in laboratory animals. This report, however, was not released to the public until 1969. Because of these results and public pressure from environmentalists and health experts, the Vietnam defoliation program was halted in 1970. At the same time, the U.S. Department of Agriculture restricted the use of 2,4,5-T in household products and in or near parks, lakes, irrigation ditches, recreation areas, and homes and on all food crops except rice. Despite these restrictions, in 1976 about 2.3 million kilograms (5 million pounds) of 2,4,5-T were still being used in the United States, primarily for killing forest underbrush, brush on livestock grazing land, weeds in rice crops, and brush on rights-of-way areas near highways, utility lines, and railroad tracks.

Investigations have revealed that birth defects in animals were probably caused by a dioxin called TCDD. This chemical is apparently formed in minute quantities as an unavoidable contaminant during the manufacture of 2,4,5-T. TCDD is one of the most toxic substances known, killing laboratory animals in doses as small as a few parts per billion. In addition, it can cause leukemia, liver and lung diseases, birth defects, cancer, and miscarriages in laboratory animals even at low levels. There is also concern that TCDD, unlike 2,4,5-T, is a persistent chemical and may be accumulating in aquatic and possibly human food chains. There is conflicting evidence, however, on these claims. A study of 121 American chemical workers believed to have been exposed to TCDD in an industrial accident in 1949 found few long-term health effects. But five independent studies of European workers exposed to TCDD, 2,4-D, and 2,4,5-T showed a higher than expected incidence of several types of cancer. By 1980, more than 1,200 Vietnam veterans had filed claims with the U.S. Veterans Administration for disabilities based on exposure to Agent Orange. Conditions claimed to have been caused by Agent Orange included liver damage, muscular weakness, testicular cancer, numbness, loss of sex drive, skin disease (chloracne), sleep and mood disturbances, and birth defects in offspring. By 1980, the Veterans Administration had awarded 10 percent disability ($48 per month) to only three veterans for scars left by chloracne—a rash that develops after exposure to TCDD.

After over a decade of conflict, 2,4,5-T and a related herbicide (Silvex) were banned for use in the United States in 1979 because they may cause miscarriages and birth defects. This emergency ban was put into effect after an abnormally high incidence of miscarriages was found among women living in an area of Oregon where helicopters sprayed dioxin-contaminated 2,4,5-T to increase the productivity of commercial forests. Dow Chemical Company and ten other manufacturers of these herbicides fought this ban in court, but in 1979 the EPA ban was upheld by a U.S. district court judge. By 1980 a review was under way to determine whether the ban should become permanent. Dow Chemical Company, the chief manufacturer of 2,4,5-T, claims that 2,4,5-T is not the only source of TCDD in the environment so they should not be held liable for its harmful effects. They claim that TCDD is formed in minute quantities by combustion processes in everything from fossil-fuel power plant stack emissions to home fireplaces, cigarettes, charcoal grills, and automobile exhausts. The EPA, however, disputes this claim and notes that the Dow study may have revealed the formation of some types of dioxins during combustion but not the specific dioxin, TCDD, that is found in 2,4,5-T. They also argue that the evidence presented in the Dow study does not establish that the dioxins they found were actually formed in the combustion processes.

E11-5 Alternative Methods of Insect Control

The Ideal Approach The ideal method of pest control would (1) kill only the target pest (a rifle rather than a shotgun approach), (2) be nonpersistent, (3) not result in genetic resistance in the target organism, and (4) be cheap. Unfortunately, no pest control method meets all these criteria, and the widespread use of chemical pesticides will always lose effectiveness in the long run because of genetic resistance.

Fortunately, there are a number of alternatives to relying exclusively on conventional chemical pesticides to control insects (see the accompanying summary box).

Integrated Pest Management An increasing number of experts believe that our almost exclusive dependence on pesticides should be replaced with an integrated or ecological approach to pest management—usually called *integrated pest management* (IPM). In this method each crop and its pests are considered as an ecological system, and a control program is developed that integrates a variety of biological, chemical, and cultural methods in proper sequence and timing. The overall aim is not to eradicate but to keep pest populations just below the level producing economic loss. Fields are carefully monitored to check whether pests have reached an economically damaging level. When such a level is reached, farmers first use biological and cultural methods (see box). Pesticides are used only when absolutely necessary in small amounts and with different chemicals being used at different times to retard the development of genetic resistance.

Over the past 25 years more than two dozen integrated control programs have been highly successful. These experiments have indicated that a properly designed IPM program can reduce the use of conventional insecticides by 50 to 75 percent and at the same time increase yields and reduce overall costs. For example, an integrated pest management program with early-maturing varieties of cotton used 50 to 75 percent less insecticides, 80 percent less fertilizer, and 50 percent less irrigation water with higher yields and profits than those of conventional cotton varieties treated heavily with pesticides and fertilizer. Integrated pest management is proving so successful that by 1979 it was used on over one-third of all the cotton acreage in 14 major cotton-producing states. Integrated pest management, however, is complex and requires expert knowledge about each pest-crop situation. In addition, methods developed for a given crop in one area may not be applicable to other areas having slightly different growing conditions. Although the total costs of IPM are typically lower than the total costs of using pesticides, initial costs may be higher. Pesticide sales representatives offer farmers free advice, while highly trained IPM consultants must charge for their services.

We already have enough information to use IPM for a number of pests, but a crash research program and an extensive farmer education program are needed to make it the primary method for pest control. The Federal Insecticide, Fungicide, and Rodenticide Act passed in 1972 and amended in 1975 and 1980 is a step in the right direction. It directs the EPA to give priority to the development of biologically integrated alternatives for pest control and the distribution of educational materials for IPM to farmers. In 1978 the Secretary of Agriculture declared that "it is the policy of the U.S. Department of Agriculture to develop, practice, and encourage the use

of integrated pest management methods." However, it remains to be seen whether entrenched farm bureaucrats who are used to promoting pesticides will try to implement this important goal among the 1 million American farmers who use pesticides.

The use of pesticides in the United States can be greatly reduced by switching to integrated pest management over the next 20 years. But to make this transition possible, Congress should enact legislation along the following lines:

1. *Establish a corps of licensed integrated pest management advisors with training and licensing standards set by the EPA.* Free advice would be given to farmers to counteract the free and biased information given by pesticide sales representatives.

2. *Make pesticides available only by written and registered prescription.* Treat them as the dangerous drugs they are and allow them to be used only after approval by a licensed integrated pest management advisor.

3. *Require chemical companies to have all new pesticides tested to see if they cause cancers, birth defects, or genetic mutations in test animals, with all tests carried out by laboratories independent of the pesticide industry.* Testing laboratories would be approved and monitored by the Environmental Protection Agency. In 1978 the EPA began a safety assessment of the 40,000 registered pesticide products that contain at least 1,400 different chemical ingredients. But this massive project will not be complete until at least 1993. In 1980 the General Accounting Office accused the EPA of unnecessary foot-dragging in its assessment of the safety of pesticides.

4. *Streamline the lengthy administrative procedures the EPA must go through to cancel or deny registration of a pesticide it finds unsafe, and eliminate the rule passed in 1980 that allows Congress to veto any EPA rules and regulations dealing with pesticides.*

5. *Allow citizen participation and access to safety data about any registered or proposed pesticide products.*

6. *Prohibit the export to other nations of any pesticide that either is not registered for use in the United States or has been banned for use in the United States.* Exceptions would be allowed for emergency situations approved by the Environmental Protection Agency.

A major hindrance to the widespread use of integrated pest management is political pressure from powerful agricultural chemical companies that see little profit in such methods. As a result, this approach will have to be developed by federal and state financial support. To make the transition to integrated pest control a reality,

Alternative Methods of Insect Control

Cultural Control

For centuries farmers have modified the crop ecosystem to hinder pest species. Such methods include alternating between susceptible and nonsusceptible crops to reduce insect populations (crop rotation), adjusting planting times to avoid certain pests, spacing and locating crops to minimize damage, removing stalks and debris that serve as breeding places for insects, leaving strips of uncultivated land, planting hedgerows and alternating rows of different crops to set up barriers, and growing crops in areas where particular major pests don't exist. In southern Texas, for example, farmers were able to control boll weevils by switching to a rapidly maturing variety of cotton that blooms before the insects arrive. As a result, profits have risen because growers now use 75 percent less pesticide, 80 percent less fertilizer, and half as much water as they did 10 years ago. Unfortunately, farmers in more developed nations have abandoned many of these once widely used controls either because they are too much trouble or because the resultant yields are slightly less than yields from large fields of single crops sprayed frequently with pesticides (at least until pesticide resistance occurs).

Biological Control

Throughout human history natural predators, parasites, and plant diseases have kept most insect populations from becoming major pests. Today such natural biological control still keeps about 90 percent of the potential pests under control free of charge and without any help from us. Unfortunately, the widespread use of pesticides has reduced the effectiveness of natural biological control by killing off the natural predators of some pests. As a result, scientists have been trying to reintroduce or develop new natural predators, parasites, and pathogens (disease-causing bacteria and viruses), which can be used to combat specific insects. Worldwide there have been about 300 successful biological control projects carried out by humans compared to the 50,000 to 150,000 successes that nature accomplishes for us all the time. Human successes include using a species of ladybug to control the cottony-cushion scale insect that attacked citrus orchards in California, ladybugs and praying mantises to control aphids, tiny parasitic wasps to control alfalfa weevils and mealy bugs on apples, a bacterial agent (*Bacillus thuringiensis*) to control leaf-eating caterpillars, and viruses to help control the tussock moth (which infests Douglas fir trees) and the cotton bollworm. Scientists in the Soviet Union and China have also used a fungus to effectively control a number of forest and orchard insects. Obstacles to widespread use of biological agents include (1) difficulty in mass producing the agents, (2) getting the agents established in fields, (3) making them work consistently in fields with wide variations in temperature and moisture, (4) protecting the agents from pesticides, and (5) being sure that the agents themselves don't become pests. In addition, farmers find that pesticides are faster acting and simpler to apply than biological controls, and pesticide companies can make much larger profits by encouraging frequent spraying of pesticides than by encouraging natural biological control.

Genetic Control by Sterilization

Males of an insect pest species can be raised in the laboratory, sterilized by radiation or chemicals, and then released in an infested area to mate with fertile females. Since the mating produces no offspring, the insect population can be sharply reduced or eliminated if the ratio of sterile males to normal males is high enough. This method works best if (1) the females mate only once, (2) the infested area is isolated so that it can't be periodically reinfested with new nonsterilized males, and (3) the insect pest population has already been reduced to a fairly low level by weather, pesticides, or other factors. The sterile male technique has been used to eradicate the oriental fruit fly in Guam and the Mediterranean fruit fly on Capri. It has also been used to control the screwworm fly (a major livestock pest) in the southeastern and southwestern United States, although reinfestation from Mexico causes periodic resurgence of the pest in these areas. Major problems with this method are (1) the difficulty of providing a sufficient number of sterile male insects, (2) having sufficient knowledge of the mating times and behavior of each target insect, and (3) the possibility that laboratory-produced strains of sterile males may not be as sexually active as normal wild males.

Attractants

Sound, light, and sex attractant chemicals can be used to lure pests into traps containing toxic chemicals or to confuse male insects so they can't find mates. Chemical sex attractants (such as pheromones) can be very effective in reducing or eliminating pest populations that are already at low levels. Such chemicals are highly specific, active at very low concentrations, and essentially nontoxic, and they have low persistence. Sex attractants have been used to eradicate Ori-

ental fruit flies in some areas of Hawaii and are available commercially for use against 25 major pests including the pink bollworm, the cotton bollweed, the cabbage looper, and the bark beetle. Problems with this method are (1) difficulties in identifying and isolating the specific sex attractant for each pest species, (2) knowing the mating behavior of the target insect, and (3) coping with periodic reinfestation from surrounding areas. Genetic resistance will also develop if these chemicals are widely used.

Hormones

Extracted or synthetic chemical insect hormones, sometimes called "third-generation pesticides," can be used to prevent specific pest insects from reaching maturity and reproducing. Hormones found useful in this approach are the juvenile hormones (JH) and the molting hormones (MH). They must be present in certain amounts at each stage of development as shown in Figure E11-2. Although much testing still needs to be done, juvenile hormones are (1) often fairly easy to synthesize, (2) apparently break down rapidly (usually within a week), (3) aren't poisonous to animals, (4) can be used in small amounts, and (5) can often be tailored for a specific pest. Disadvantages of hormones include the following: (1) They take weeks rather than minutes to kill; (2) they are often ineffective with a large infestation; (3) they tend to be fairly expensive; (4) they sometimes break down chemically in the environment before they can act; (5) they must be applied at the right time in an insect's life cycle; and (6) they can sometimes affect other nontarget insect species. Without further testing it is unknown whether insects can develop tolerance to higher hormone levels or develop behavioral mechanisms to avoid exposure to these chemicals.

Resistant Crop Varieties

New varieties of plants resistant to insects, fungi, and diseases are continually being developed by plant breeders. To develop a resistant strain may take 10 to 20 years, however, and new insects or plant diseases can arise to which the plants are not resistant.

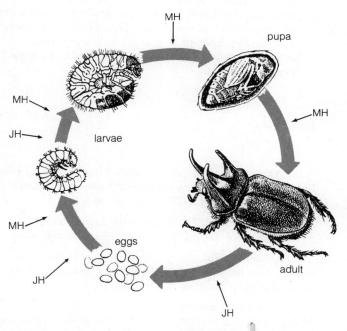

Figure E11-2 Juvenile hormones (JH) and molting hormones (MH) must be present at these typical stages of development in the life cycle of an insect. Synthetic hormones can be used to disrupt growth, development, and reproduction.

you and I will have to exert political pressure to counteract the lobbying power of pesticide manufacturing companies. In addition, we will have to accept the fact that a few holes or frayed leaves have nothing to do with the quality of fruits and vegetables. Indeed, we threaten our own health by forcing growers to use more and more pesticides to provide perfect-looking food.

We need to recognize that pest control is basically an ecological, not a chemical problem.
Robert L. Rudd

Discussion Topics

1. Explain how the use of insecticides can actually favor insects, the very targets they are supposed to hit, and threaten carnivores and higher animals, including humans.

2. How does genetic resistance to pesticides occur? Couldn't humans also develop genetic resistance to dangerous chemicals? What is the major advantage insects have over humans in this respect?

3. Criticize the following statement: "All commonly used pesticides are biologically concentrated through the food chain and this is their greatest hazard to humans."

4. Explain how DDT and other pesticides can threaten ecosystem stability. How might this be the most serious threat to humans in the long run?

5. Debate the following statement: "DDT poses no demonstrable threats to human health and indeed has probably saved more lives than any other single chemical in human history."

6. Criticize the following statement: "Since insecticides are used on only a small number of major crops in the United States, there is nothing to worry about."

7. How could the widespread use of DDT in the long run cause even greater outbreaks of malaria than before its use? Is there any evidence that this may be occurring (see Enrichment Study 6)?

8. DDT and a number of other pesticides have been banned in the United States except for a few essential purposes, but the United States still ships large quantities of DDT (and other banned pesticides) to other parts of the world. Debate the pros and cons of this practice.

9. Discuss the fallacy in the argument that in the controversy over DDT and other insecticides, we must choose between bugs and people.

10. Debate the pros and cons of banning the manufacture and use of 2,4,5-T as a herbicide in the United States. Check the recent literature to see what, if any, new restrictions have been placed on its use by the Environmental Protection Agency since this book was published.

11. List the major advantages and disadvantages of pest control by (a) natural predators and pathogens, (b) male sterilization, (c) sex attractants, (d) juvenile hormones, (e) resistant crop varieties, and (f) cultural methods.

12. Describe integrated pest management, list its major advantages and disadvantages, and outline what you must do if you wish this method to be widely used.

13. What are the advantages and disadvantages of each of the following policies to the farmer? To you? (a) Pesticides to be used by prescription only; (b) a corps of licensed integrated pest management advisors to provide free information to farmers and approve any use of pesticides; (c) screening of all pesticides by independent laboratories; (d) streamlining EPA procedures for banning a pesticide it finds unsafe; and (e) allowing citizens access to safety data about any registered or proposed pesticide project.

Readings

Adler, C. A. 1973. *Ecological Fantasies.* New York: Green Eagle Press. Argues that environmentalists have overdramatized the harmful effects of DDT and other pesticides.

Ahmed, A. Karim. 1976. "PCBs in the Environment." *Environment,* vol. 18, no. 2, 6–16. Excellent overview.

Carson, Rachel. 1962. *Silent Spring.* Boston: Houghton Mifflin. First major warning about pesticides. One of the more important books of this century.

Council on Environmental Quality. 1973. *Integrated Pest Management.* Washington, D.C.: U.S. Government Printing Office. Fine summary.

Dethier, V. G. 1976. *Man's Plague? Insects and Agriculture.* Princeton, N.J.: Darwin Press. Excellent presentation of pros and cons of pesticide use.

Entomological Society of America. 1975. *Integrated Pest Management: Rationale, Potential, Needs, and Implementation.* Washington, D.C.: Entomological Society of America. Excellent overview.

Environmental Protection Agency. 1975. *Production,*

Distribution, Use and Environmental Impact Potential of Selected Pesticides. Washington, D.C.: Environmental Protection Agency. Excellent source of data.

Goldstein, Jerome. 1978. *The Least Is Best Pesticide Strategy.* Emmaus, Pa.: J. G. Press. Excellent discussion of integrated pest management.

Huffaker, Carl B., ed. 1980. *New Technology of Pest Control.* New York: Wiley-Interscience. Authoritative review of integrated pest management.

Huffaker, Carl B., and P. S. Messenger. 1976. *Theory and Practice of Biological Control.* New York: Academic Press. Authoritative source.

Luck, Robert F., et al. 1977. "Chemical Insect Control—A Troubled Pest Management Strategy." *BioScience,* vol. 27, no. 9, 606–611. Excellent overview with examples of backlashes from the use of pesticides.

McEwen, F. L., and G. R. Stephenson. 1979. *The Use and Significance of Pesticides in the Environment.* Somerset, N.J.: Wiley-Interscience. Authoritative treatment.

Mellanby, K., and F. H. Perring. 1977. *Ecological Effects of Pesticides.* New York: Academic Press. Authoritative source.

Metcalf, Robert L., and John L. McKelvey, Jr., eds. 1976. *The Future for Insecticides.* New York: Wiley-Interscience. Collection of articles by experts on insecticides and alternative methods of pest control.

National Academy of Sciences. 1975. *Pest Control: An Assessment of Present and Alternative Technologies.* 5 vols. Washington, D.C.: National Academy of Sciences. Authoritative source.

Pimentel, David, et al. 1980. "Environmental and Social Costs of Pesticides: A Preliminary Assessment." *Oikos,* vol. 34, no. 2, 126–140. Superb overview.

Rudd, Robert L. 1975. "Pesticides in the Environment." In W. W. Murdoch, ed., *Environment: Resources, Pollution and Society.* 2nd ed. Sunderland, Mass.: Sinauer. Excellent overview.

van den Bosch, Robert. 1978. *The Pesticide Conspiracy.* New York: Doubleday. Pest management expert exposes political influence of pesticide companies in preventing widespread use of biological and integrated pest management.

Woodwell, G. M. 1970. "Effects of Pollution on the Structure and Physiology of Ecosystems." *Science,* vol. 168, 429–433. Superb reference on ecosystem simplification by pesticides and on biological magnification of pesticides and other chemicals.

Woodwell, G. M., et al. 1971. "DDT in the Biosphere: Where Does It Go?" *Science,* vol. 174, 1101–1107. Description of the movement of DDT throughout the entire ecosphere.

Wright, James W. 1970. "DDT: It Is Needed against Malaria, But for the Whole Environment?" *Smithsonian,* October, pp. 40–46. Excellent presentation of the case for DDT by a scientist with the World Health Organization. See also Enrichment Study 6.

Enrichment Study 12

Species Introduction and Species Extermination

Two major wildlife problems are ecological disruption, which occurs when an alien species is accidentally or deliberately introduced into an ecosystem, and human activities, which can lead to or hasten the extermination or near extermination of species (Section 10-7). When an alien species is introduced into an ecosystem it can upset the ecological balance by (1) taking over the ecosystem if the exotic species has no enemies, (2) killing or competing with existing species, or (3) causing a population explosion of one or more existing species by killing off their natural predators. Species extinction is a natural evolutionary process, but its acceleration due to human activities is neither natural nor desirable (Section 10-7). In this enrichment study we will look at several instances of species introduction and species extermination in order to gain a better insight into these problems.

E12-1 Accidental Introductions: The Lamprey, Alewife, and Norway Rat

The Sea Lamprey The accidental introduction of the sea lamprey into the Great Lakes in the United States is a classic example of what can happen when a natural environmental barrier to an ecosystem is removed. The sea lamprey *(Petromyzon marinus)* is a primitive, parasitic vertebrate with a slender eellike body and a round, sucking mouth, which enables it to climb rock walls and to prey on fish by attaching itself (Figure E12-1). It rips open wounds in its prey's skin with its rasping tongue and sharp, horny teeth and then sucks out blood and body fluids. If the attacked fish is not killed outright, it may die of bacterial and fungal infections that invade the gaping wounds. Even if the fish survives, the ugly scar makes it unsalable.

The sea lamprey originally ranged just off the Atlantic seaboard from Labrador to Florida, but it spawns in fresh water and easily adapts to fresh water. Over the centuries it moved into the St. Lawrence River and the

eastern end of Lake Ontario, but Niagara Falls had blocked it out of Lake Erie and the other Great Lakes. However, in 1829 the Welland Ship Canal gave both ships and the sea lamprey a way around the falls.

The Great Lakes contained no natural enemies of the sea lamprey. For a century it spread slowly throughout the lakes. This process was accelerated when the canal was deepened in 1932. Between 1940 and 1960, the rapidly growing population of the sea lamprey, along with overfishing and pollution, caused a 97 percent decrease in the multimillion-dollar Great Lakes whitefish-, sturgeon-, and trout-fishing industries.

In the early 1950s, the U.S. Fish and Wildlife Service, the Great Lakes Fisheries Departments, and the Canadian government declared war on the lamprey. First, they tried to trap adults in their spawning streams with electric fences with very limited success. Then after testing over 6,000 chemicals, scientists discovered a selective poison (trifluoromethylnitrophenol, or TFM) that in only minute amounts destroys sea lamprey larvae within 16

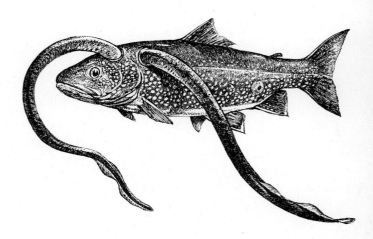

Figure E12-1 The sea lamprey attaches itself to a lake trout (or other fish), opens a hole in the skin, and sucks out blood and body fluids.

hours but is harmless to trout and sunfish and to the insect larvae, lake clams, and other food species of these game fish.

The application of this chemical to all lamprey-spawning tributaries to the Great Lakes cut the sea lamprey population 80 percent by 1962. Restocked with millions of lake trout since 1960, the Great Lakes fisheries' remaining enemy is pollution.

The Alewife Like sea lampreys, plankton-eating fish called alewives (*Alosa pseudoharengus*) used the Welland Canal to migrate from the Atlantic Ocean to the Great Lakes. Finding no natural predators, the alewife multiplied so fast that by 1965 they made up 90 percent of all fish in the upper Great Lakes—crowding out more desirable plankton-feeding fish, which in turn served as food for some larger fish.

By the early 1960s the sea lamprey was being brought under control with chemicals, but the more prolific alewife seemed ready to crowd out the millions of restocked trout. After considerable research, scientists decided to try biological control. They deliberately introduced into the Great Lakes the coho salmon (*Oncorhynchus kisutch*), which is big and highly adaptive, is itself a sport fish, and feeds on fish such as the alewife.

First released in the late 1960s, the cohos gobbled up the alewives, decreasing their population and allowing the trout population to grow. After about 3 years, 9- to 14-kilogram (20- to 30-pound) cohos were widely scattered throughout the lakes, much to the delight of sport fishing enthusiasts.

The lamprey-trout and alewife-coho stories are fascinating examples of how we can get into (and in some cases out of) trouble by interfering with an ecosystem. Because of our ignorance and greed, however, most interventions do not have happy endings.

The Norway Rat One of the most prolific animals on the planet is the Norway rat (*Rattus norvegicus*). By stowing away on ships, this destructive pest has spread around the world. It is especially adaptable to the human environment because it feeds on almost any type of garbage or food and enters almost any type of home, warehouse, garbage dump, barn, or other structure. In the United States alone, rats cause an estimated $2.5 billion in damage to property and food supplies each year. In addition, they carry many diseases, including trichinosis, typhus, and bubonic plague, and cause food poisoning (Enrichment Study 6).

The rat especially threatens the poor, who already have too little food and too many diseases. Their dwellings are often poorly built and thus are easily invaded. Slum dwellers often get infections from rat bites, and some babies have even been killed by rats—creating an environment of fear for children and parents.

The United States spends far too little on rat control, especially among the vulnerable poor. We might spend a fortune, however, and still not solve this problem. Poisons and traps are only partly successful because rats are so adaptable and so prolific and have no natural predators (excepts for cats) in cities. The only sure ways to control rats are to make buildings ratproof and to be extremely careful in disposing of and storing food.

E12-2 Deliberate Introductions: Food Crops, Carp, and the Water Hyacinth

Some Beneficial Introductions As we saw, the coho salmon appears to be a beneficial import. Other helpful species introductions in the United States include (1) the honeybee (from Europe), (2) Monterey pine, (3) wheat, rice, and most other food crops, (4) many game species, and (5) the mosquito fish, which helps control mosquitoes by eating both larvae and pupae. The ring-necked pheasant, introduced from England in 1790, has thrived particularly well in the corn and wheat belts of the Midwest. Modern agriculture and the draining of low-lying areas, however, are now destroying the habitat for this excellent game bird species.

The most important and successful deliberate introductions are the food crops. Some 70 of the 80 most important crops grown in the United States are introduced species. Scientists and other plant hunters have searched the world for plants to use for food and medicines. Plant breeders are becoming more and more sophisticated in crossbreeding varieties from all over the world to produce higher-yielding and more disease-resistant plants. The most recent Green Revolution (Section 9-7), which introduced new high-yield species of wheat and rice into some less developed nations, is an excellent example of this process.

There are also attempts in the United States to reintroduce certain disappearing species, such as the wild turkey. A plentiful food source in colonial days, this bird had lost three-quarters of its natural range to humans by 1920. In recent years the Pennsylvania game department has captured and then released these large game birds into habitats where they could thrive. There are now over

60,000 in Pennsylvania, and limited hunting is once again allowed. Pennsylvania turkeys are even being used to restock some other states. Of course, it is both cheaper and more foolproof to set aside and protect habitats for endangered species than to almost wipe them out and then try to reintroduce them (the second energy law again).

The European Carp People have been far less successful in deliberately introducing animals and nonfood plants (Table 10-4). Among many failures is the introduction of the European, or German, carp (*Cyprinus carpio*) into the United States. This Asiatic fish first gained favor in Europe in the 1800s. It could be kept in ponds, ate almost anything, grew large fast, was a good game fish, and prospered almost anywhere it was introduced. Spurred on by these glowing reports, American officials imported about 120 carp from Europe in 1876.

Within a few years millions of carp were well established in almost every waterway in the United States. In fact, they did too well and by 1900 the romance was over. By rooting in bottom sediments, they destroyed the spawning grounds and nests of native fish as well as the plants needed by waterfowl. Many desirable species of fish die off when oxygen is depleted by industrial, agricultural, and thermal water pollution (Section 16-4), but the carp thrives in these polluted habitats. To make matters worse, most Americans will not eat carp.

The carp is now so widespread in the United States that it cannot be eliminated. However, attempts have been made to control its population at great cost. The fish have been netted and also poisoned with rotenone, but rotenone also kills other fish species. Even if a chemical could be found that killed only carp, a few survivors could easily repopulate an area.

The Water Hyacinth If you visit Florida you may admire the beauty of mats of leaves and purple flowers that cover many freshwater lakes and streams. These water hyacinths (*Eichhornia crassipes*)—floating plants native to Central and South America—were brought to the United States in the 1880s for an exhibition in New Orleans. A woman brought one back to plant in her backyard in Florida. Within 10 years the colorful plant was a public menace. Unchecked by natural enemies and nourished by Florida's nutrient-rich waters, the water hyacinth (which can double its population in only 2 weeks) rapidly displaced native aquatic plants and took over. Today water hyacinths blanket at least 809 square kilometers (200,000 acres) of Florida canals and lakes and have spread to waterways in other southeastern states.

Unfortunately, the water hyacinths' surface beauty masks several serious problems. Their luxuriant growth chokes canals, bayous, and rivers, blocking boat passage and shading out many desirable native plants. In 1898 the U.S. Army Corps of Engineers tried unsuccessfully to use a mechanical cropper to remove these plants from navigable waters. Next they tried a chemical, sodium arsenite. This chemical was somewhat successful, but it was abandoned in the 1930s because the deadly arsenic found its way into the food of spray boat crews. In the mid-1940s a combination of mechanical removal and the herbicide 2,4-D (Enrichment Study 11) was used, but the water hyacinth continued to spread.

In recent years, scientists have brought in natural predators to help control the hyacinth. A species of weevil, which feeds only on hyacinths, has been brought from Argentina and introduced into Florida waters. Results look promising, but it is too early to evaluate this experiment. A species of water snail from Puerto Rico has also been introduced, but it is less effective than the weevil and can also feed on other, more desirable plants.

The grass carp, or white amur (*Ctenopharyngodon idellas*), brought in from the Soviet Union, is also being tried to control water hyacinths and other undesirable aquatic weeds. The grass carp, which resembles a big silver-colored goldfish and can weigh 45 kilograms (100 pounds), satisfies its huge appetite mostly by eating aquatic vegetation. This introduced fish species may solve the water hyacinth problems, but it could easily become a major pest itself. If its population grows, the grass carp may eat nearly every aquatic plant, including desirable species—making this cure worse than the original problem.

Although the water hyacinth has become a major problem in southeastern waterways, there is some good news. Preliminary research by the National Aeronautic and Space Administration (NASA) has shown that hyacinths can be used in several beneficial ways: (1) introduced in sewage treatment lagoons to absorb toxic chemicals, (2) converted by anaerobic fermentation to a biogas fuel similar to natural gas, (3) used as a mineral and protein supplement for cattle feed, and (4) used as a fertilizer and soil conditioner.

E12-3 Extermination: The Passenger Pigeon

Species can become extinct naturally, but *Homo sapiens* has accelerated the process (Section 10-7). Although

Figure E12-2   The extinct passenger pigeon. The last known living passenger pigeon died in the Cincinnati Zoo in 1914.

many examples of extermination (in contrast to natural extinction) could be cited, the passenger pigeon (Figure E12-2) is one of the most striking.

At one time the passenger pigeon (*Ectopistes migratorius*) was the most numerous bird on the North American continent. In the 1850s Alexander Wilson, a prominent ornithologist, watched a single migrating flock darken the sky for over 4 hours. He estimated that the flock was 386 kilometers (240 miles) long and 1.6 kilometers (1 mile) wide and contained over 2 billion birds.

By the early 1900s the passenger pigeon had disappeared forever. How could such a vast population become extinct in only a few decades? There are probably several reasons. First, many probably died of disease. Any infectious disease could have become epidemic since these birds nested in dense colonies. Second, passenger pigeons laid only 1 egg per nesting compared with 4 to 6 for robins and 8 to 12 for pheasants. Once flock size was reduced, it was hard for the species to recover. Third, millions of birds died in severe storms as they made their long fall migration from North America to Central and South America.

Two additional reasons for the extinction of the passenger pigeon involve people. Land clearing for farms and cities destroyed the habitats and food supply of the passenger pigeon's favorite breeding areas. As beech, maple, and oak trees were chopped down and burned, the supply of acorns and beech nuts dropped sharply. The pigeons had rigid migration patterns and could not adjust by moving to areas where food was more plentiful. The second human factor was hunting. Passenger pigeons were easy to shoot because they congregated in gigantic flocks. Sometimes a hunter could find 100 nests in a single tree. One trick involved capturing a pigeon alive, blinding it, and then tying it to a stake in a clearing as a "stool pigeon." Soon a curious flock would alight beside it and be shot or trapped by nets. Beginning around 1858 massive "shoots" and night "drives" were organized; killing passenger pigeons became a big business. Shotguns, fire, traps, artillery, and even dynamite were used. At least 1 billion birds were killed in Michigan alone, and one New York dealer sold about 18,000 birds a day. Their tasty meat became a fashionable dish in many posh restaurants. Within only a few years the massive breeding colonies had vanished. The last wild breeding colony was observed in 1896. The last wild pigeon was shot in 1907, and the last captive pigeon, a hen called Martha, died in 1914 in the Cincinnati Zoo.

E12-4   Endangered Species: The American Bison and the Blue Whale

The American Bison   Other species have been brought to the brink of extinction by *Homo sapiens*. The American bison (*Bison bison*), commonly called the buffalo, was once so numerous that in 1832 a traveler wrote, "As far as my eye could reach, the country seemed absolutely blackened by innumerable herds." In the middle 1800s an estimated 60 million bison roamed the prairies of North America.

For centuries the Plains Indians had depended on the bison without substantially reducing the herds. The meat was their staple diet. The skin was used for their tepees, moccasins, and clothes. The gut made their bowstrings, and the horns their spoons. Even the dried feces, called "buffalo chips" by white settlers, were used for fuel. Hunting on foot and armed only with lances and bows and arrows, or occasionally driving the bison over cliffs, the Indians maintained an ecological balance with the herds.

As white settlers moved westward after the Civil War, the balance became upset. Indians traded bison skins for steel knives and firearms and began killing bison in large numbers around 1825. But the real devastation resulted from other factors. First, as the railroads spread westward in the late 1860s, they employed professional hunters to provide the construction crews with bison for their basic food supply. The well-known railroad bison hunter "Buffalo Bill" Cody killed an estimated 4,280 bison in only 18 months—almost surely a world record.

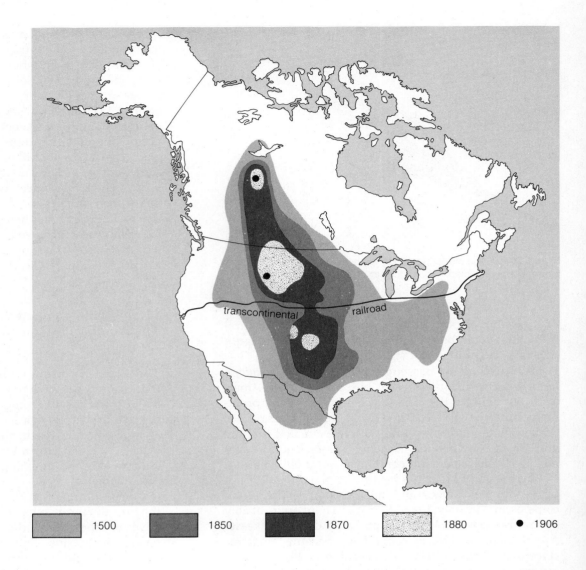

Figure E12-3 The shrinking range of the American bison, 1500–1906.

1500	1850	1870	1880	● 1906

transcontinental railroad

Second, millions of bison were shot for their hides by an army of hide hunters. Most of the meat from these carcasses went to waste—less than 1 percent was sold. At least 100,000 animals were slaughtered only for their tongues, which had become a delicacy. Once the flesh had rotted, "bone pickers" collected the skeletons and shipped them back to fertilizer plants.

A final and perhaps major factor in the near extinction of the bison was a deliberate policy of the U.S. government: subduing the fierce Plains Indians and taking over their lands by killing off their food supply, the bison. This early American form of biological warfare succeeded and nearly destroyed both the bison and certain Indian tribes. Figure E12-3 shows how the range of the

bison on the North American continent shrank as it was driven to a state of regional and ecological extinction and near biological extinction.

Between 1870 and 1875 at least 2.5 million animals were slaughtered each year, and in 1894 the last wild bison was shot by a Colorado rancher. From 250 animals that remained in captivity after this slaughter, herds have been built up and protected by laws. Today, several thousand American bison remain on ranges in the western United States.

The Blue Whale Humans seemingly have a passion to track down and kill large animal species. Not content with land animals, we have roamed the seas in search of earth's largest animal, the blue whale *(Balaenoptera musculus)* (Figure E12-4). This graceful, playful, gentle species has been hunted to near extinction for its oil, meat, and bone.

Whales, ranging in size from the 0.9-meter (3-foot) porpoise to the giant 15- to 30-meter (50- to 100-foot) blue, can be divided into two major groups, *toothed whales* and *baleen whales.* Toothed whales, such as the porpoise, sperm whale, and killer whale, feed mostly on squid, fish, octopuses, and other marine animals. Baleen whales, such as the blue, gray, humpback, and finback, have several hundred horny plates in their jaw that filter plankton from seawater.

The blue whale feeds primarily on tiny, shrimplike krill *(Euphausia superba)* filtered from seawater. Blue whales spend about 8 months of the year in Antarctic waters, where krill are abundant, and then migrate to warmer waters where their young are born.

Whales are hard to count, but 200,000 blue whales may once have roamed the Antarctic. By 1930 the annual catch of blue whales reached a peak of almost 30,000. Since then overexploitation has caused the annual catch to drop sharply until 1964, when it reached nearly zero. Only then did the International Whaling Commission protect the blue whale completely. Probably only a few hundred to a few thousand blue whales remain—perhaps too few for the species to recover. Within the next few decades they could pass from very endangered to extinct, even though they are protected.

This sharp decline can be attributed to a ruthless, greedy whaling industry as well as two unfortunate characteristics of blue whales. First, because they tend to congregate in the Antarctic feeding grounds, they can be caught in large numbers. Second, they multiply very slowly, taking up to 25 years to mature sexually and having one offspring every 2 to 5 years. Once the total population is reduced below a certain level, mates may no longer be able to find one another, and natural death rates may exceed natural birth rates until extinction occurs.

As the blue whale catch declined, the whaling industry shifted to smaller species of whales, especially the finback. Now the finback is also threatened, as are all but 3 of the 11 major species of whales that are hunted by the whaling industry. In 1900 an estimated 4.4 million whales swam the ocean. Today only about 1.1 million remain, with sperm, minke, and sei whales making up 90 percent of the total.

After World War II the 17 major whaling nations established the International Whaling Commission (IWC).

Figure E12-4   The blue whale.

It is supposed to regulate the annual harvest by limiting each catch in order to maintain a sustainable supply of all important species. On paper this is an excellent idea. The commission, however, is made up completely of whaling nations or nations such as the United States that once hunted whales. The big whaling nations—especially Japan and Russia (which sells most of its catch to Japan), which do 90 percent of the whale hunting—either block calls for bans and smaller quotas or ignore the quotas that are set. Nations with small whaling interests and without modern, efficient whaling fleets can do little more than watch the major whaling nations systematically strip the ocean and the world of these valuable species. The United States and a number of other nations have repeatedly called for a 10-year ban on all commercial whaling, and environmentalist groups such as the Greenpeace movement have used bold tactics to embarrass whaling nations and gain worldwide publicity and support for protecting whales.

In 1979 a glimmer of hope appeared when the International Whaling Commission adopted a selective moratorium that includes (1) halting whaling from factory ships on the high seas indefinitely except for the relatively numerous minke whales; (2) reducing the quota for the commercially valuable but jeopardized sperm whale by more than 75 percent; and (3) establishing a whale sanctuary in most of the Indian Ocean for 10 years. As a result of these actions, the large factory fleets of Russia and Japan may become too expensive to operate and Russia may abandon whaling altogether. These restrictions on whaling, however, are hard to enforce and do not apply to nations that are not members of the International Whaling Commission.

It is the responsibility of all who are alive today to accept the trusteeship of wildlife and to hand on to posterity, as a source of wonder and interest, knowledge, and enjoyment, the entire wealth of diverse animals and plants. This generation has no right by selfishness, wanton or international destruction, or neglect, to rob future generations of this rich heritage. Extermination of other creatures is a disgrace to humankind.

World Wildlife Charter

Discussion Topics

1. On balance do the benefits of the following factors outweigh their disadvantages? Explain each answer and give specific reasons: (a) the Welland Canal, (b) killing lampreys with chemicals, (c) controlling alewives in the Great Lakes by introducing the coho salmon, (d) introducing the European carp to America, (e) introducing the grass carp to America, (f) introducing major food crops, (g) introducing the ring-necked pheasant, (h) introducing the water hyacinth.

2. Outline a national policy for rat control. Why has there been so little interest in such a policy by political leaders? What role have you played in this behavior?

3. Should a ban be placed on the introduction of all new plant and animal species into the United States? Develop guidelines and criteria that should be met before any new species is introduced. Why haven't such guidelines been developed and enforced?

4. Discuss your gut-level reaction to the statement: "Who cares that the passenger pigeon is extinct and the buffalo, blue whale, whooping crane, bald eagle, grizzly bear, and a number of other species are nearly extinct. They are important only to a bunch of bird watchers, Sierra Clubbers, and other ecofreaks." Be honest about your reaction and then try to organize arguments for your position.

Readings

Dasmann, Raymond F. 1981. *Wildlife Biology.* 2nd ed. New York: Wiley. Superb textbook by an expert.

Ehrenfeld, D. W. 1970. *Biological Conservation.* New York: Holt, Rinehart and Winston. One of the best introductions to conservation of wildlife.

Fisher, J., N. Simon, and J. Vincent. 1969. *Wildlife in Danger.* New York: Viking. Fine overview.

Hunter, Robert. 1979. *Warriors of the Rainbow: A Chronicle of the Greenpeace Movement.* New York: Holt, Rinehart and Winston. Excellent account of this environmentalist group that has used bold tactics to prevent whaling.

Joffe, Joyce. 1970. *Conservation.* Garden City, N.Y.: Natural History Press. Outstanding overview of conservation of wildlife and other resources. Superb photographs.

Laycock, G. 1966. *The Alien Animals.* Garden City, N.Y.: Natural History Press. Basic reference on effects of introducing alien species.

Owen, Oliver S. 1980. *Natural Resource Conservation: An Ecological Approach.* 3rd ed. New York: Macmillan. Outstanding basic text. Highly recommended for the reader wanting more details.

Prance, Ghillean T., and Thomas S. Elias, eds. 1976. *Extinction Is Forever.* New York: Botanical Garden. Excellent collection of articles.

Radway, Allen K. 1980. *Conservation and Management of Whales.* Seattle: University of Washington Press. Superb discussion.

Roots, Clive. 1976. *Animal Invaders.* New York: Universe Books. Excellent discussion of good and bad results from introducing species to new areas.

Scheffer, Victor B. 1974. *A Voice for Wildlife.* New York: Scribner's. Excellent overview.

Enrichment Study 13

Noise Pollution

E13-1   Sonic Assault

In many urban areas in the United States, a chorus of garbage collectors announces the arrival of the day. For apartment dwellers, clanking pipes, flushing toilets, pets, television, and the sounds of the neighbors' children gradually blend in with the din of garbage disposals, dishwashers, vacuum cleaners, washers, and dryers. For suburbanites on their way to work, the freeway and subway sounds reach a crescendo punctuated by jackhammers, air compressors, bulldozers, wrecking balls, and riveting equipment used for street repair and construction projects.

Offices hum, roar, and clack with air conditioners, heaters, typewriters, and office machines, to say nothing of jangling telephones. Factories deafen their workers with industrial machinery. After a noisy trip home workers may then be greeted with blasts from power lawn mowers, motorbikes, or a rock group on the stereo. Later on some go to rock concerts, bars, or clubs, where the noise level can be 4 times greater than is permitted by law at an industrial plant. Finally, the night's sleep may be broken by barking dogs, passing jets, helicopters, sirens, trucks, motorcycles, and the rumble of air conditioners. Even those who take to the wilderness for solitude and renewal find their escape interrupted by trail bikes, snowmobiles, and jets.

At least 19 million Americans suffer acute hearing loss, and about 30 million—or 15 percent of the population—now have significant hearing loss. Furthermore, this number is rising fast. Industrial workers head the list, with 19 million hearing-damaged people out of a work force of 75 million. Equally disturbing is the fact that 5 million U.S. children under age 18 have impaired hearing. Noise now adversely affects the lives of 40 percent of the U.S. population. Indeed, it is estimated that if environmental noise continues at its present rate, by the year 2000 almost no one in the United States over age 10 will have normal hearing.

E13-2   Noise and Its Effects

Ranking Noise   What is noise? We usually define it as "unwanted sound." This is not a precise definition, because one person's favorite rock or disco group may be another person's earache. Instead we try to talk about noise in ways that can be measured. We need to distinguish between sound power or intensity and the pressure exerted on our eardrums from sound. The **decibel (db),** named for Alexander Graham Bell, is the unit used to measure either sound power or sound pressure. Sound pressure measurements in decibels can be made using a small sound pressure level meter (called a decibel meter) that can fit into a coat pocket. These measurements can then be converted to sound power levels by a mathematical equation if desired. The decibel scales for both sound power and sound pressure are logarithmic rather than linear but differ slightly from one another. The decibel scale for sound pressure ranges from 0 to 180 decibels, whereas the scale for sound power ranges from 0 to 90 decibels. Because they are logarithmic scales, a 10-fold increase in sound loudness or power occurs with a 10 db rise. A 10-fold increase in sound pressure represents a 20 db increase. Thus, a rise in sound pressure from 30 db (quiet rural area) to 60 db (normal restaurant conversation) represents a 32-fold rise in sound pressure on the ear and a 1,000-fold increase in sound loudness. An increase from 50 db (normal living room conversation) to 100 db (an outboard motor or subway) represents a 316-fold increase of sound pressure and a 100,000-fold increase in sound intensity.

The loudness and pressure of a sound, however, are only part of the problem, for sounds also have *pitch* (frequency). After correcting for the fact that high-pitched sounds annoy us more than low-pitched sounds, we can rank noise sources fairly well according to sound pressure (Table E13-1). The most common sound pressure scale weighted for high-pitched sounds is the A scale, whose units are written "dbA." Hearing loss begins with prolonged exposure (8 hours or more) to 80 to 90 dbA levels of sound pressure. Sound pressure becomes painful at around 120 dbA and can kill at 180 dbA. The U.S. Occupational Safety and Health Administration (OSHA)

Table E13-1 Effects of Common Sound Pressure Levels

Example	Sound Pressure in Decibels (dbA)	Effect with Prolonged Exposure
Jet takeoff (close range)	150	Eardrum rupture
Aircraft carrier deck	140	
Armored personnel carrier	130	
Thunderclap, textile loom, live rock music, discotheque, jet takeoff at 61 meters (200 feet), siren (close range), chain saw	120	Human pain threshold
Steel mill, riveting, automobile horn at 1 meter (3 feet)	110	
Jet takeoff at 305 meters (1,000 feet), subway, outboard motor, power lawn mower, motorcycle at 8 meters (25 feet), farm tractor, printing plant, jackhammer, garbage truck, farm tractor	100	Serious hearing damage (8 hours)
Busy urban street, diesel truck, food blender, cotton spinning machine	90	Hearing damage (8 hours), speech interference
Garbage disposal, clothes washer, average factory, freight train at 15 meters (50 feet), dishwasher	80	Possible hearing damage
Freeway traffic at 15 meters (50 feet), vacuum cleaner, noisy office or party	70	Annoying
Conversation in restaurant, average office, background music	60	Intrusive
Quiet suburb (daytime), conversation in living room	50	Quiet
Library	40	
Quiet rural area (nighttime)	30	
Whisper, rustling leaves	20	Very quiet
Breathing	10	
	0	Threshold of audibility

considers the following as safe time limits for exposure to various sound pressure levels: 90 dbA, 8 hours; 92 dbA, 6 hours; 95 dbA, 4 hours; 100 dbA, 2 hours; 105 dbA, 1 hour; 110 dbA, 30 minutes; 115 dbA, 15 minutes or less; and more than 115 dbA, no exposure at all. By comparing these safety limits with the levels that many people experience (Table E13-1), we can see why more and more Americans are being exposed to potentially damaging sound pressure levels.

Effects of Noise As with air pollution, it is hard to link noise directly with specific physiological and mental disorders, but noise is almost surely an important contributor to many of them. Excessive noise is a form of stress and can cause both physical and psychological damage. Noise effects fall into four general categories: annoyance, disruption of activity, partial or total loss of hearing, and physical or mental deterioration. Continued exposure to high sound levels destroys the microscopic hair cells (cochlear cells) in the fluid-filled inner ear, which convert sound energy to nerve impulses.

Hearing specialist and ear surgeon Samuel Rosen explains that in addition to causing psychic shock, sudden noise automatically constricts blood vessels, dilates pupils, tenses muscles, increases the heartbeat, and causes wincing, holding of breath, and stomach spasms. Constriction of the blood vessels can become permanent, increasing blood pressure and contributing to heart disease. Migraine headaches, gastric ulcers, and changes in brain chemistry can also occur. Some experiments have shown that during the last 3 months of pregnancy, a fetus stirs and convulses at loud noises. Research in the United States, England, and Japan has also revealed that the occurrence of birth defects, high blood pressure, and admissions to mental hospitals is more frequent among those who live around airports.

Although general urban noise and startling sounds are a serious problem, the noise levels people endure every day at their work are even more serious. Workers who run a high risk of temporary or permanent hearing loss include boilermakers, weavers, riveters, bulldozer and jackhammer operators, taxicab drivers, bus and truck drivers, mechanics, shop supervisors, bar and nightclub employees, and rock and disco band performers.

E13-3 What Can Be Done?

Noise is probably the easiest type of pollution to control. We have both the means and the money—all we need is the will. Noise control can be accomplished in three major ways: (1) reducing noise at its source, (2) substituting less noisy machines and operations, and (3) reducing the amount of noise entering the listener's ear. Machines don't have to be noisy. We already know how to produce quieter trucks, motorcycles, vacuum cleaners, and other machines. Likewise, houses and buildings can easily be insulated to reduce sound transfer.

The U.S.S.R. and many western European and Scandinavian countries are far ahead of the United States in what we might call the "quiet revolution." Several European countries have developed quiet jackhammers, pile drivers, and air compressors that do not cost much more than their noisy counterparts. These countries also muffle construction equipment noise by using small sheds and tents. Some countries use rubberized garbage trucks. A simple redesign of the tread can decrease the screech of truck tires at no cost to the consumer. The Swiss and West Germans have established maximum day and night sound pressure levels for various areas, and in 1960 the U.S.S.R. banned factory sound pressure levels above 85 dbA and residential levels above 30 dbA. Many countries have noise control specifications for homes and other buildings; noise control for an apartment house adds only about 5 percent to its cost.

Noise control provisions could easily be standardized and written into building codes if citizens insist on such laws. Likewise, noise control standards for cars, motorcycles, trucks, airplanes, home devices, and factories could be set and achieved with existing technology and some price increases. Rubberized wheels could be put on subway cars (as has been done in Montreal and Mexico City), and quiet garbage cans, vacuum cleaners, and office machines are available. Cars could have separate city and highway horns, as they do in France. Highways can be lowered to block out noise, and we can muffle the sounds from cities, houses, and roads with some of the best natural sound absorbers—trees. Airplane approach and takeoff patterns could be changed so that the smallest number of people are affected. Those who must work in noisy factories and areas should be told of the potential danger to their hearing and be required to wear earplugs or ear protectors, just as hard hats must be worn around construction sites.

Before 1970 there was little action in the United States to control noise. New York and California, in 1965 and 1967, respectively, were the first states to enact antinoise laws, but these laws have not been strictly enforced. New York City probably has campaigned harder against noise than any other American city. In 1969 it became the first city to establish an office of noise abate-

ment. Much of the push for this office came from the Citizens for a Quieter City. This group, founded and headed by Robert Alex Baron, is a model of what can be accomplished by citizen action. Cincinnati, Bloomington (Indiana), Chicago, and Memphis have enacted well-defined antinoise laws, but these codes are often not enforced. Palo Alto, California, has a rather stringent and well-enforced antinoise ordinance. You can get a ticket there for driving through town with a noisy muffler or for having a barking dog.

At the federal level, Congress passed the Noise Control Act of 1972. This act gave the Environmental Protection Agency (EPA) broad authority (1) to set maximum allowed sound pressure levels for construction equipment, transportation equipment (except aircraft), and all motors, engines, and electrical equipment manufactured after 1972; (2) to require all manufacturers to label their products according to the amount of noise they produce; and (3) to administer research on noise and noise control. By 1980 the EPA had issued noise-level regulations for air conditioners and some trucks and trains and had proposed others for buses, motorcycles, and garbage trucks. So far, however, enforcement of these regulations has been almost nonexistent because the 1972 law allows only fines rather than possible jail terms for violators.

Little progress was made between 1972 and 1980 in reducing aircraft noise, because of the adversary relationship between the EPA, which recommends regulations, and the Federal Aviation Administration (FAA), which has final authority. So far the FAA has refused to enact the regulations proposed by the EPA. Another factor hindering progress in noise pollution control is the fact that the already small amount of money spent each year on federal noise research has been sharply reduced since 1977. The EPA has proposed a national plan for noise control, but unless Congress strengthens the 1972 law, allows the EPA to regulate aircraft noise, and increases the amount of money appropriated for noise research, this plan will probably collect dust in bureaucratic files. A small step in the right direction occurred when Congress passed the Quiet Communities Act of 1978. It authorizes the EPA to develop programs to help state and local governments combat excessive noise. By 1980 the EPA had assisted 26 states in launching noise control programs.

The United States can make important progress in controlling noise pollution, but it appears that this will happen only if citizen pressure forces lawmakers to enact and enforce much tougher legislation. In turning down the noise, the United States has much to learn from its Soviet, European, and Scandinavian neighbors.

Air pollution kills us slowly but silently; noise makes each day a torment.

Robert Alex Baron

Discussion Topics

1. As a class or group project, try to borrow one or more sound pressure decibel meters from the physics or engineering department or from a local stereo or electronic repair shop. Make a community survey of sound pressure levels at several times of day and at several locations; plot the results on a map. Include measurements in a room with a stereo and at an indoor rock concert or nightclub at various distances from the speakers of the sound system. Correlate your findings with those in Table E13-1.

2. Debate the proposition that we have always had noise and we can get used to it.

3. Are there any noise-level regulations in your area? What specifications, if any, for noise control are written into the building codes? Are they adequate? What plans, if any, do local officials have for requiring noise controls on jackhammers, compressors, garbage trucks, garbage cans, and other noise makers? Are they aware that such devices are readily available?

Readings

Carmen, Richard. 1977. *Our Endangered Hearing*. Emmaus, Pa.: Rodale. Excellent overview of noise problems, effects, and possible solutions.

Environmental Protection Agency. 1974. *Noise Pollution: Now Hear This*. Washington, D.C.: Environmental Protection Agency. Very good overview of the problems.

Environmental Protection Agency. 1977. *Toward a National Strategy for Noise Control*. Washington, D.C.: U.S. Government Printing Office. Excellent plan for what the United States needs to do. Implementing this plan is the problem.

Kryter, Karl D. 1970. *The Effects of Noise on Man*. New York: Academic Press. Basic reference.

Lipscomb, David M. 1974. *Noise: The Unwanted Sound*. New York: Nelson-Hall. Authoritative review of the health hazards of excessive noise and methods for noise control.

Milne, Anthony. 1979. *Noise Pollution: Impact and Countermeasures*. New York: David & Charles. Superb basic reference.

Stevenson, Gordon M., Jr. 1972. "Noise and the Urban Environment." In Thomas R. Detwyler and Melvin G. Marcus, eds., *Urbanization and the Environment*. North Scituate, Mass.: Duxbury. Outstanding summary.

Thumann, Albert, and Richard K. Miller. 1976. *Secrets of Noise Control*. Atlanta: Fairmont Press. Very useful overview with good tips.

Enrichment Study 14

Urban Open Space and Land-Use Control

Most people agree that open space in or near urban areas should be preserved rather than destroyed. But translating this belief into action is another matter. One problem is the difficulty in defining open space. Another difficulty is that people are unaware of the many important functions of open space. In addition, there are the legal, political, and economic problems connected with preserving open space. Who is responsible for preserving open space? Where will the money needed to buy and maintain open space come from? What techniques can be used to hold off the developers and bulldozers? In this enrichment study we will look at the functions and types of urban open space and some methods for preserving more of these precious areas.

E14-1 The Case for Urban Open Space

What Is Urban Open Space? Urban open space has many meanings. To some people urban open space means large areas of woods, wildlife sanctuaries, and other natural areas that should be preserved near or within urban areas. To others it means moderate-sized areas set aside within urban areas for picnics, boating, swimming, baseball diamonds, playgrounds, zoos, and other forms of recreation. To other individuals it means small spaces within urban areas such as abandoned lots, dried-up creek beds, abandoned railroad beds, and other strips and patches of unused land that can be redeveloped as vest-pocket parks and playgrounds, bicycle and jogging trails, and other recreational or aesthetic uses. The term **urban open space**, then, can be used to describe any large, medium-sized, or small area of land or water in or near urban areas that can be used for recreational, aesthetic, or ecological functions.

Why Do We Need Urban Open Space? Urban open space performs important recreational, aesthetic, and ecological functions. Specifically, urban open space can provide (1) room for recreation, (2) pleasant, quiet, and beautiful places, (3) contact with natural diversity, (4) a better climate (green areas help moderate temperature extremes by absorbing and releasing water), (5) a decreased chance of floods (green areas and wetlands absorb water and slow runoff), (6) less air pollution (trees and plants can absorb some air pollutants), (7) less water pollution (forests and wetlands can help purify water), (8) less noise (trees and plants can block and absorb urban noise), (9) habitats for birds and other forms of wildlife that can live in or near urban areas, (10) physical and ecological buffer zones between and within urban areas, and (11) a means to block harmful patterns of urban growth and development.

Most people recognize the need for having open spaces available for recreational use. Many city dwellers also feel a need to experience trees, flowers, lakes, rivers, and other forms of natural diversity as a source of beauty and as a relief from the concrete and asphalt monotony of the urban environment. Most urban dwellers, however, are unaware of the important ecological functions that open spaces perform, such as moderating the urban climate and reducing air, water, and noise pollution.

E14-2 Big Open Space: Greenbelts and Wedges

One of the most ambitious efforts at preserving large open spaces in order to contain urban sprawl is the London greenbelt. In 1931, land was bought for a large belt of permanent open space surrounding London. More land was bought after World War II, so that today there is a 10- to 16-kilometer (6- to 10-mile) wide greenbelt around the city.

This example of long-range planning has preserved some land-use choices for London that most cities squandered long ago. But it has failed to halt growth; the sub-

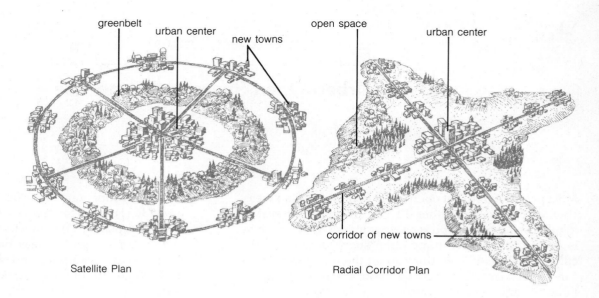

Figure E14-1 Two plans for preserving large blocks of urban open space.

Satellite Plan

Radial Corridor Plan

urbs have jumped the belt. The large belt has also been criticized as not being available to people, and there is increasing pressure to develop some of the space. As William Whyte pointed out, "Open space has to have a positive function. It will not remain open if it does not. People must be able to do things on it or with it—at the very least to be able to look at it."

Another way to preserve large open spaces near an urban area is to build a series of new towns beyond the central urban area. Among the possibilities are the *satellite plan*, where a ring of new towns connected by a beltway is built beyond a greenbelt, and a *radial corridor plan*, where new towns are built along corridors separated by wedges of open space (Figure E14-1). Reston, Virginia, and Columbia, Maryland, are successful examples of new towns planned and built to serve as satellites to Washington, D.C.

E14-3 Middle-Sized Open Space: Parks, Cluster Developments, and New Towns

Urban Parks Some cities have had the foresight to preserve open space in moderate- to large-sized *municipal parks*. Central Park in New York City and San Francisco's Golden Gate Park are two famous examples. Even though Central Park is now crisscrossed by six-lane roads and is crime infested at night, it is still heavily used. Cities that have large municipal parks must continually fight efforts to build freeways through them.

Unfortunately, cities that did not plan for such parks early in their development have little chance of securing such areas at a later date.

Cluster Developments Since World War II the typical pattern of a suburban housing development in the United States has been to bulldoze a patch of woods or land completely and build rows of houses, each house having a standardized yard (Figure E14-2). In recent years a new pattern, known as *cluster development* or *planned unit development* (PUD), has been used with increasing success to preserve moderate-sized blocks of open space. Houses, townhouses, condominiums, and garden apartments are built on a relatively small portion of the designated land area with the rest left as open space in its natural state and as recreation areas—playgrounds, tennis courts, swimming pools, and bike and bridle trails (Figure E14-3).

The cluster approach opens up some exciting possibilities, but it also has serious pitfalls. A real concern is that developers may use clusters to obtain unreasonably high population densities, thus bringing the evils of noise and crowding. After all, to the developer the advantage of this approach lies in the cluster, not the open space. Laws, careful supervision, and an ongoing maintenance fund must be used to ensure that the open space is carefully developed and maintained. Another problem is the design of community open spaces between buildings and the much smaller private spaces for individual occupants. The careful design of patios, walled gardens,

Figure E14-2 A typical suburban development tract.

courtyards, and other private open spaces is crucial to any successful cluster development.

New Towns Designing and building completely new towns is another method that can be used for preserving medium-sized blocks and open space within the towns. There are three types of new towns: (1) *satellite towns,* located relatively close to an existing large city (Figure E14-1); (2) *freestanding new towns,* located far from a major city; and (3) *"in-town" new towns,* located within existing urban areas. Typically, new towns are conceived for populations of 20,000 to 100,000. Some planners, however, believe that the new town concept can be expanded to "experimental cities" with an optimum size of 250,000. This size might provide the richer diversity of work and leisure opportunities needed for such ventures to be more independent from existing major cities.

The new town movement was originated in England around 1900 by Sir Ebenezer Howard. Since Howard's initial work, Great Britain has built 16 new towns and is building 15 more. New towns have also sprung up in Singapore, Hong Kong, Europe (especially Finland, Sweden, France, and the Netherlands), and North and South America.

The most widely acclaimed new town is Tapiola, Finland, about 11 kilometers (7 miles) from Helsinki. Designed in 1952, it is being built gradually in seven sections with an ultimate population of 80,000. Today it has a healthy economic and social mix of about 30,000 people and provides an almost 50-50 mix of more than 6,000 jobs for blue- and white-collar wage earners. Many of its residents work in Helsinki, but the long-range aim is for the town to be industrially and commercially independent. Tapiola is divided into several villages, which are separated by greenbelts. The town is a showplace of architectural diversity, since each village has been designed by an architect selected through competition. Each village has several neighborhoods clustered around a shopping and cultural center. Individual neighborhoods have a neighborhood center and contain a mix of high-rise apartments and single-family garden-type houses. As of 1971, 54 percent of the total area of Tapiola consisted of planned open space. Finland has drawn up plans for building six more new towns around Helsinki.

A major problem with new towns is that they can rarely succeed without massive government financial support. Private developers find such towns to be risky ventures. They must put up large amounts of money to buy the land and install the facilities, and then they must pay heavy taxes and interest charges for decades before any profit can be made. In the United States two privately developed new towns—Columbia, Maryland, and Reston, Virginia—have been in constant financial diffi-

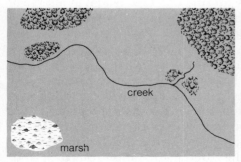

Undeveloped Land

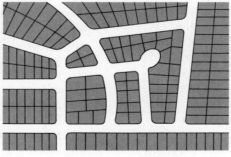

Typical Housing Development

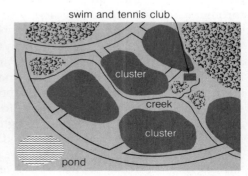

Cluster Housing Development

Figure E14-3 Tract and cluster development of the same land area.

culty since they were started over a decade ago, although their situations are gradually improving. In 1971 the U.S. Department of Housing and Urban Development (HUD) provided more than $300 million in federally guaranteed loans for developers to build 13 new towns.* By 1978 all 13 HUD-backed new towns were in financial trouble. By 1980 the department had to take title to 8 towns that went bankrupt. HUD has sold or transferred funding for some of these bankrupt communities and it won't provide loans for any more new towns. The agency, however, plans to continue loan guarantees for the 4 new towns (italicized in the footnote below) that it believes have a chance of survival in the long run. New towns can also draw the young and educated out of the large cities and hasten inner-city decay, as has happened to some extent in England.

E14-4   Small Open Spaces: Abandoned Strips and Patches of Land

The most overlooked and probably most important open spaces are the small strips and odd-shaped patches of unused land that dot urban areas. For example, utility rights-of-way, abandoned railroad beds and trolley lines, and dried-up canals, creek beds, and aqueducts can be reclaimed for walkways, bridle paths, and bike trails.

The Illinois Prairie Path is a walkway and bridle path running from Chicago to its western suburbs along an abandoned trolley line. Through his annual hikes, the late Supreme Court Justice William Douglas helped Americans discover the Chesapeake and Ohio Canal that runs for 296 kilometers (185 miles) between Washington, D.C., and Cumberland, Maryland. In Santa Barbara, California, dry creek beds, or arroyos, have been developed as bicycle paths and walkways. San Antonio, Texas, has rejuvenated much of the downtown area by making creative use of the San Antonio River, which runs through a 21-block area of the city.

Within cities, abandoned lots can be developed as vest-pocket parks and playgrounds. An outstanding example of such miniparks is Paley Park in midtown Manhattan. With 17 locust trees and vines of kudzu and ivy, it provides a refreshing refuge for about 3,000 people each day. Some cities are beginning to rediscover the ancient idea of rooftop gardens. A magnificent example is the Kaiser Center Roof Garden in Oakland, California.

*Maumelle, Ark.; Shenandoah, Ga.; Park Forest South, Ill.; St. Charles, Md.; Cedar Riverside and Jonathan, Minn.; Gananda and Riverton, N.Y.; Soul City, N.C.; Newfields, Ohio; Harbison, S.C.; Flower Mund and The Woodlands, Texas. (Italics explained in text.)

Abandoned lots cluttered with old car hulks, lumber piles, pipes, and piles of dirt and rocks can be used as "adventure playgrounds." Usually jampacked with children, these places look dangerous to parents. But fewer accidents occur there than in the more traditional and expensive playgrounds neatly laid out with swings, slides, and steel climbing bars.

E14-5   Land-Use Control: Getting and Keeping Urban Open Space

Method of Land-Use Control   Recognizing that open spaces can make an urban area a better place to live is an important first step. But such open spaces will not be preserved and used effectively unless citizens actively support private and government efforts to acquire and protect them.

Some methods for controlling how land is used include: (1) a public agency or benevolent foundation that purchases land and then holds, leases, or resells it for only specified uses; (2) zoning land so that it can be used only in certain ways; (3) taxing profits on land sales to discourage development; (4) giving tax breaks on land used or donated for agriculture, open space, or other specified purposes; (5) donation or purchase of development rights that leave the land in private ownership but prohibit the owner from developing it or using it for certain purposes; (6) assigning a land area a fixed number of development rights that can be transferred by sale among the various owners of the land area; and (7) controlling population growth and development by limiting building permits, sewer hookups, roads, schools, and other public services.

Direct Purchase   Obviously the surest way to save open space is by direct purchase. Federal, state, and local governments can buy up land and then hold it in reserve or sell or lease it with the stipulation that it be used for open space or only in certain ways. This approach has been widely used in Australia, Canada, Denmark, England, Germany, the Netherlands, Hong Kong, Israel, Norway, Sweden, and to a limited extent the United States. Public acquisition, however, has certain drawbacks: It is costly; it removes land from the tax base; and it requires public funds to cover operation and maintenance costs. Another problem is that owners often grossly inflate the price if they learn that the government wants to buy their land. Experience in Sweden and other countries shows that to avoid inflated prices the government must purchase the land 20 to 30 years before it is to be used, leased, or sold for controlled development.

Another problem is that the bureaucracy usually moves too slowly to buy up crucial areas that are threatened by immediate development. Private organizations such as the Nature Conservancy have performed a valuable public service by buying and holding threatened land in the United States until government purchase funds are available. Such organizations, however, have very limited funds.

Zoning and Tax Policies   Zoning land so it can be used only in certain ways is the most common method of land-use control in the United States. Local zoning boards, however, are often not concerned with open space preservation and are highly vulnerable to pressures from developers and other economic interests. Landowners who are suddenly offered high prices for their land pressure the board to have zoning restrictions changed or waived. Zoning that requires developers to use large lots for each house is a much-used technique. Although this plan gives an open feeling to a developed area, it leaves less usable open space than cluster development. Zoning decisions can also be challenged in court. Even if the decision is upheld, public funds must normally be used to pay legal costs and public officials can be tied up in drawn-out legal proceedings. Zoning is also so fragmented among different local governments that regional planning for open space preservation and use is usually out of the question. In California alone more than 1,400 separate government bodies make zoning decisions.

In spite of its disadvantages, zoning can be an effective land-use control if it is based on an ecological land-use plan (Section 11-5), is strictly enforced, and is supported by the public. One form of zoning, floodplain zoning, has been used effectively in a number of communities to exclude permanent buildings from natural floodplain areas. Often these areas are set aside for recreational uses or as wildlife preserves.

Zoning can be even more effective in preserving open space when it is coupled with taxation policies that discourage harmful forms of development. Vermont has enacted such an approach. A permit for a project is issued only if the developer provides extensive sewage treatment and landscaping. In addition, the higher the profit on the project and the shorter the time the developer holds the property, the higher the property taxes. In many states land is taxed on the basis of its highest potential use, which is usually high-density development. Faced with high tax bills, owners of agricultural

and undeveloped land are often forced to sell or develop their land. To relieve this pressure for development, about half of the states now base property taxes on *current* use of the land rather than on its highest *potential* use.

Another increasingly popular form of land-use control is preferential tax assessment. In this approach taxes are lowered on farmland, forests, historic sites, open spaces, and other land near urban areas that the state or community wishes to protect from intense development. To be effective, such tax breaks should be given only for land that is used by its present or a specified purpose for at least 10 years. By 1974 at least 33 states had adopted some form of preferential taxation, and other states are seriously considering the idea. But lowering the taxes on some land usually raises taxes for other landowners. This can place serious financial hardships on low- and middle-income property owners.

Donation or Purchase of Development Rights   In another method of controlling land use, landowners donate or sell certain development rights to a public agency and in return obtain lower tax rates. For example, owners might donate or sell the rights to develop their land, to cut down trees, or to use their land in certain ways. If farmland is worth $12,350 per hectare ($5,000 per acre) to a developer but only $3,700 per hectare ($1,500 per acre) as farmland, a public agency would pay the difference—$8,650 per hectare ($3,500 per acre)—for the development rights. This approach ensures that the land will continue to be used only as farmland (or for other specified purposes), but it still allows the original owners to keep the land. Landowners who donate these rights to a public agency can be given reduced property taxes, and their donation may be deductible as a charitable gift in computing federal and state income taxes.

This approach to land-use control normally costs less than direct purchase, does not remove the land from the tax base, and imposes no land maintenance costs on the community. To meet legal requirements, however, the development rights must be specifically described. Unfortunately, land most in need of protection normally has such a high value as developed land that the cost of purchasing development rights almost equals that of direct purchase. Another problem is that this approach can be difficult to enforce, especially when the land is transferred to heirs or sold to new owners.

Transferable Development Rights   Another relatively new approach is for a zoning board or other government agency to assign only a limited number of development rights for a given area of land, based on a master plan that shows zones where low-, medium-, and high-density development can take place. Initially each landowner is assigned the same number of development rights per square kilometer (or acre). Landowners, however, can sell and transfer their development rights for use in other zones where moderate- or high-density development is allowed. Thus, parts of the land area can be developed while other parts remain undeveloped, with total development not exceeding the assigned limit for the entire area. Owners of undeveloped land are compensated by being paid for their development rights and by paying lower taxes on their land. This approach preserves open space, historic sites, and other desirable land areas at no cost to the public, and it does not reduce the tax base. To be effective, however, zoning or other boards must have a sound master plan that does not assign too many rights to a given land area. As with the zoning approach, boards succumb to political pressure from developers to add more rights or to allow exceptions. So far this promising approach is still in its infancy. But if it proves to be successful, it could become a major method for land-use control in the United States.

No-Growth and Slow-Growth Policies   Between 1970 and 1979, at least 300 U.S. communities deliberately attempted to stop or slow local population growth and land development. Some communities have tried to stop growth altogether by allowing no more development or by establishing population size limits. Such schemes, however, merely tend to push growth elsewhere and are often thinly veiled ways to exclude minority and low-income individuals. Furthermore, such absolute approaches are usually banned by the courts as violating or denying the constitutional right of landowners to use their land in a reasonable manner.

A more common approach is to slow growth by regulating the rate of development over a specified number of years. Typically this is done by controlling the number of new housing permits, sewer hookups, or other public services. An example of this approach is found in Rampo, New York, a town 56 kilometers (35 miles) north of Manhattan. When its population soared from 35,000 to 77,000 in the 1960s, Rampo developed an 18-year plan to control the direction and rate of its growth. Each development proposal is rated by a point system, which is based on the availability of public services at the site and on inclusion of housing for minority and low-income

people. Projects without a sufficient number of points are not approved by the town board.

The Rampo program has been upheld in court on the basis that its limited rate of expansion is necessary to provide adequate public services and to protect public health, safety, and welfare. A similar 5-year plan for controlling the rate of growth in Petaluma, California—a small community 128 kilometers (80 miles) north of San Francisco—was ruled unconstitutional by a lower California court—a decision that was overturned later by the California Supreme Court and the U.S. Supreme Court. In general, courts tend to uphold a community's efforts to slow the rate of growth provided that the plan is temporary and makes a specific provision for minority and low-income housing.

Limiting the rate of growth, however, may only push growth to another area and create more adverse economic, environmental, and social effects. Controlling growth by not extending sewer lines may result in more septic tanks, which can cause more water pollution. Thus, acting to improve environmental quality by limiting growth in one area can have the opposite effect by causing a greater decrease in environmental quality elsewhere.

We have seen that each method for controlling and preserving open space has certain advantages and drawbacks. The key is to develop an ecological approach to land-use planning (Section 11-5) and then use a mix of flexible and creative land-use control methods to ensure that open space is preserved and used wisely.

I have a country but no town. . . .
Bulldozers cut my lawn.

John Ciardi

Discussion Topics

1. What kinds of open spaces appeal to you? Why? Compare your observations with those of others.

2. Make a class survey and draw a map identifying good and poor uses of open space in your area. Concentrate especially on small open spaces.

3. Develop and debate a master plan for acquiring and using open space in your area.

4. Debate the idea that cluster development should be required for all housing developments.

Readings

See also the readings for Chapter 11.

Burby, Raymond J., et al. 1976. *New Communities U.S.A.* Lexington, Mass.: Lexington Books. Excellent overview of new towns in the United States.

Council on Environmental Quality. 1974. *Land Use.* Washington, D.C.: U.S. Government Printing Office. Superb overview of methods for land-use control.

Dantzig, George B., and Thomas L. Saaty. 1973. *Compact City: A Plan for a Liveable Environment.* San Francisco: Freeman. Readable study of the feasibility of building a new city using a total systems approach.

League of Women Voters Education Fund. 1977. *Growth and Land Use: Shaping Future Patterns.* Washington, D.C.: League of Women Voters. Excellent summary of methods for land-use control.

Little, Charles E., and John G. Mitchell, eds. 1971. *Space for Survival: Blocking the Bulldozer in Urban America.* New York: Pocket Books. An excellent book on how to preserve open space.

Rudofsky, B. 1969. *Streets for People: A Primer for Americans.* New York: Doubleday. Superb analysis of how we should design and use streets.

Shomon, J.J. 1971. *Open Land for Urban America.* Baltimore: Johns Hopkins Press. Fine overview.

Wallace, David, ed. 1970. *Metropolitan Open Spaces and Natural Processes.* Philadelphia: University of Pennsylvania Press. Good collection of articles.

Whyte, William H. 1968. *The Last Landscape.* Garden City, N.Y.: Doubleday. Outstanding work on open space.

Enrichment Study 15

Solid Waste

As the gross national product of an affluent nation grows, so does one of its major gross national by-products—garbage, or solid waste. **Solid waste** is any usless, unwanted, or discarded material that is not a liquid or a gas. It is yesterday's newspaper and junk mail, today's dinner table scraps, raked leaves and grass clippings, nonreturnable bottles and cans, worn-out appliances and furniture, abandoned cars, animal manure, crop residues, food-processing wastes, sewage sludge from waste treatment plants (Section 16-6), fly ash from coal-burning electric power plants (Section 17-4), mining and industrial wastes, and an array of other cast-off materials.

Trying to dump, bury, or burn this resource-rich solid waste represents a squandering of the earth's finite mineral resources (Chapter 12), a massive energy waste (Chapter 13), and a staggering economic loss. Although some hazardous wastes must be isolated and stored, most of the things we throw away should not be regarded as solid wastes but as wasted solids that we need to either reuse or recycle (Section 12-1). In many cases (such as excessive packaging), it is material that we should not use in the first place.

In this enrichment study we will focus on the problem of what to do with solid waste, with emphasis on the *urban* and *municipal wastes* generated by households and commercial establishments and on *toxic and hazardous wastes* generated primarily by industries in the United States—the world's leading producer of solid waste.

E15-1 Solid Waste Production in the United States

Amount of Solid Waste Produced During 1978 each American directly or indirectly produced an average of about 18,000 kilograms (20 tons) of solid waste per year, or 49 kilograms (108 pounds) per day. To make matters worse, the amount of solid waste produced in the United States is growing by 2 to 4 percent annually—about 3 to 6 times faster than the population growth rate.

Sources of Solid Waste As seen from Figure E15-1, most solid waste is produced indirectly by agricultural, mining, and industrial activities. Animal, crop, and forest wastes from agricultural activities make up 56 percent of the total (Figure E15-1). This solid waste problem is discussed in Enrichment Study 16. The piles of rock, dirt, sand, and slag left behind from the mining and processing of energy resources (Section 10-5) and nonfuel mineral resources (Chapter 12) are the second largest source of solid waste in the United States (Figure E15-1).

Industry accounts for only about 6 percent of the waste produced each year. Much of this is scrap metal, plastics, slag, paper, sludge from sewage treatment plants, and fly ash from electric power plants. Ironically, the last two categories, sludge and fly ash, are increasing rapidly because of stricter water pollution (Section 16-6) and air pollution (Section 17-6) control laws. Fly ash wastes will increase dramatically in coming years if more and more coal is used to produce electricity (Section 14-2). The total amount of industrial solid waste produced each year is small compared with solid waste from agricultural and mining activities.

Hazardous and Toxic Wastes Some industrial waste consists of hazardous materials that are toxic, flammable, or explosive. In 1980 about 57 billion kilograms (63 million tons) of hazardous industrial wastes were produced in the United States by approximately 750,000 different producers. These wastes—which are growing at a rate of 3 percent a year—include a variety of toxic chemicals, such as acids, cyanides, pesticides (Enrichment Study 11), compounds of lead, mercury, arsenic, and cadmium (Enrichment Study 5), and radioactive materials (Section 14-3) that must be prevented from entering water and food supplies. Some of these substances can cause cancer and others are suspected of causing miscarriages and stillbirths. The Environmental Protection Agency estimates that only 10 percent of all these toxic and hazardous wastes are disposed of properly. About 50 percent are simply dumped into unlined ponds, 29 percent are disposed of in unsafe landfills, and about 9 percent are burned, recycled, or dumped at sea (a practice that became illegal in 1981). The rest is illegally dumped into municipal landfills, sewers, wells, unused land, or spread along the roadsides by "midnight dumpers."

The proper disposal, deactivation, or storage of hazardous industrial wastes is already a serious environmental problem and is expected to become even more serious in the future. The Toxic Substances Control Act of 1976 (Section 16-6) and the Resource Conservation and Recovery Act of 1976 require the Environmental Protection Agency (EPA) to identify toxic and hazardous wastes, to set standards for their management, and to issue guidelines and provide some financial aid to establish state programs and managing hazardous wastes. In 1980 the EPA issued regulations for the handling of hazardous wastes. These regulations are supposed to be fully implemented by 1990. They identify 46 hazardous chemicals and 89 chemical processes that will require disposal in federally approved hazardous waste dumps—if citizens can somehow be persuaded to allow the 50 to 150 such dumps needed by 1985 to be located near their communities. Another possibility under serious consideration is to destroy these wastes far away from population centers by incinerating them at sea in specially designed ships. Other chemicals will be added to the list in the future. All firms producing hazardous wastes are required to disclose where their waste will go and how it will be disposed of. Furthermore, all firms that store, treat, or dispose of hazardous wastes must apply to the EPA for a permit. To reduce illegal dumping, companies must use a manifest system to track waste shipments through every step en route to their destinations. Both the transporter and the waste disposal site operator are required to sign the manifest and return a signed copy to the company that produced the waste. In addition, disposal site operators will be responsible for waste 30 years after a site is closed.

Although these regulations are a step in the right direction, environmentalists point to several serious loopholes and difficulties. These include: (1) the slowness of the EPA to inventory and identify hazardous chemicals not presently on the fairly short list of such chemicals; (2) inadequate sampling and testing procedures to be used by waste producers to determine

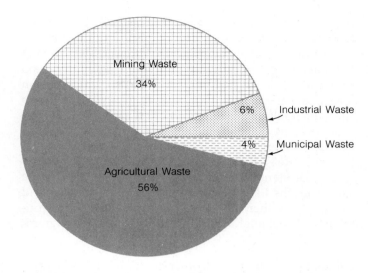

Figure E15-1 Sources of solid waste in the United States in 1978 as a percentage of the total wet weight produced.

whether their wastes are classified as hazardous under federal guidelines; (3) exclusion from the regulations of hazardous waste mixed with domestic sewage, thus allowing a company to bypass the regulations by dumping hazardous wastes down the sewer where they could overload or disrupt municipal sewage systems and pollute waterways; (4) exemption of recycled or reused hazardous wastes from regulation; (5) exemption of firms producing less than 1,000 kilograms (2,200 pounds) of hazardous wastes a month from the regulations [these small businesses produce only about 1 percent of the total hazardous wastes produced each year, but this still adds up to about 591 million kilograms (1.3 billion pounds) per year]; and (6) no requirement for states to regulate all the hazardous wastes identified by the EPA so that states with weaker programs could be used by industry as dumping grounds for certain unregulated wastes.

Even if these new laws are enforced, some of the hazardous wastes dumped in the past, when regulations were not as strict, will come back to haunt us, as occurred with the Love Canal nightmare (Section 6-3). By 1980 the EPA had estimated that there were 32,000 to 50,000 sites in the United States that contained hazardous wastes, with an estimated 1,000 to 2,000 of these sites believed to pose significant risks to human health and the environment. By late 1980, about 350 dumps had been identified by the EPA as almost sure pockets of hazardous wastes ticking away like chemical time bombs. The estimated cost for cleaning up past hazardous waste sites ranges from $28 billion to $55 billion. In 1980 Congress passed a bill setting up a $1.6 billion fund to clean up hazardous waste sites and spills, with about 87 percent of the money coming from industry through a system of federal fees or taxes imposed on the sales of certain chemicals. This law, however, provides no compensation for victims of exposure to hazardous wastes from dump sites and spills and no compensation for damage to personal property—a serious loophole vigorously opposed by environmental and consumer groups. In early 1981, President Reagan was considering shifting the responsibility for identifying and cleaning up hazardous waste sites from the EPA to several other federal agencies and to the states themselves—a move that many environmentalists feel might gut the hazardous waste program.

Urban Solid Wastes   Most discussions of solid waste emphasize the urban, or municipal, solid wastes produced by homes and businesses in or near urban areas, even though this source amounts to only about 4 percent of the total solid waste produced each year in the United States (Figure E15-1)—amounting to an average of about 1.4 to 2.3 kilograms (3 to 5 pounds) per person each day. There are several reasons for this emphasis. First, this solid waste is concentrated in highly populated areas, and for public health reasons it must be removed quickly and efficiently at great cost. In 1980 a whopping $5 billion—mostly as taxes—was spent to collect and dispose of urban solid waste in the United States. This process required about 10 percent of all the energy used in the United States during 1980. Over 80 percent of this cost is for labor to collect the waste. Between 1975 and 1985, collection and disposal costs are expected to at least double and perhaps triple as stricter waste disposal laws are phased in and enforced. The United States spends over $500 million each year just picking up litter—not surprising, since the litter Americans throw away on a single holiday weekend on streets, highways, and parks could fill a line of garbage trucks 69 kilometers (43 miles) long.

Second, this category of solid waste typically shows the fastest yearly rate of growth and is expected to almost double between 1978 and 1990. Third, the present methods for disposal of these wastes are inadequate, as discussed in the next section. Finally, we have more information on the amount and composition of this type of waste because most of it (at least two-thirds) is collected.

For these reasons and because solid waste from agricultural (Enrichment Study 16), mining (Sections 10-5 and 12-1), and industrial (Sections 16-1 and 17-1, and Enrichment Study 5) activities are discussed elsewhere in this book, the remainder of this enrichment study will be devoted to possible solutions to the problem of urban solid waste.

E15-2   Disposal of Urban Solid Waste: Dump, Bury, or Burn?

Present Solutions   What happens to the trash and garbage that is left on the curb for pickup in the United States? Most citizens and businesses couldn't care less where their trash is disposed of as long as they don't have to smell it, see it, or pay too much in taxes or weekly fees to have it taken away. Based on this "out of sight, out of mind" principle, local sanitation departments or privately owned services collect the wastes and then dump them on the land, bury them, or burn them. In 1978 about 62 percent of the collected urban solid waste was deposited in open dumps, 22 percent buried in sanitary landfills, 8 percent burned in municipal incinerators, 8 percent recycled, and a tiny fraction composted.* Table E15-1 lists the major advantages and disadvantages of these methods for solid waste disposal and resource recovery. In the past, the United States dumped some urban solid waste into the ocean, but since 1981, the Environmental Protection Agency has banned all ocean dumping of wastes except dredged materials.

It is important to distinguish four methods for land disposal of solid waste: (1) open dumps, (2) landfills, (3) sanitary landfills, and (4) secured landfills. An **open dump** is a land disposal site where solid and liquid wastes are deposited and left uncovered with little or no regard for control of scavenger, aesthetic, disease, air pollution, and water pollution problems. A **landfill** is a land waste disposal site that is located with little, if any, regard for possible pollution of groundwater and surface water due to runoff and leaching; waste is covered intermittently with a layer of earth to reduce scavenger, aesthetic, disease, and air pollution problems. In effect, it is a slightly upgraded version of the open dump. A **sanitary landfill** (Figure E15-2) is a land waste disposal site that is located to minimize water pollution from runoff and leaching; waste is spread in thin layers, compacted, and covered with a fresh layer of soil each day to minimize pests and aesthetic, disease, air pollution, and water pollution problems. A **secured landfill** is a land site for the storage of hazardous solid and liquid

---

Composting is the breakdown of organic matter in solid waste in the presence of oxygen by aerobic (oxygen-needing) bacteria to produce a humuslike end product, compost, which can be used as a soil conditioner.

Table E15-1 Comparison of Methods for Solid Waste Disposal and Resource Recovery

Method	Advantages	Disadvantages	1978 Operating Cost* (dollars per metric ton of waste)
Littering	Easy	Unsightly; very expensive to clean up; wastes resources	$44 to $4,400 to clean up[†]
Open dump	Easy to manage; low initial investment and operating costs; can be put into operation in a short period of time; can receive all kinds of wastes	Unsightly; breeds disease-carrying pests; foul odors; causes air pollution when wastes are burned; can contaminate groundwater and surface water through leaching and runoff; ecologically valuable marshes and wetlands may be erroneously considered "useless" and be filled (Section 10-6); wastes resources; difficult to find locations because of public opposition	$1.50 to $3.50
Sanitary landfill	Easy to manage; relatively low initial investment and operating costs; can be put into operation in a short period of time; if properly designed and operated, can minimize pest, aesthetic, disease, air pollution, and water pollution problems; methane gas produced by waste decomposition can be used as a fuel; can receive all kinds of wastes; can be used to reclaim and enhance the value of submarginal land[‡]	Can degenerate into an open dump if not properly designed and managed; requires large amount of land; difficult to find sites because of citizen opposition and rising land prices[§]; wastes resources; leaching may cause water pollution; filled land may settle; production of methane gas from decomposing wastes can create a fire or explosion hazard; obtaining adequate cover material may be difficult; hauling waste to distant sites is costly and wastes energy	$2 to $9
Incineration	Removes odors and disease-carrying organic matter; reduces volume of wastes by at least 80%; extends life of landfills; requires little land; can produce some income from salvaged metals and glass and use of waste heat to heat nearby buildings	High initial investment; high operating costs; frequent and costly maintenance and repairs; requires skilled operators; resulting residue and fly ash must be disposed of; causes air pollution unless very costly controls are installed; fine-particle air pollution (Section 17-4) even with pollution control; wastes some resources	$9 to $17
Composting	Converts organic waste to soil conditioner that can be sold for use on land; moderate operating costs; most disease-causing bacteria destroyed	Can be used only for organic wastes; wastes must be separated; limited market in U.S. for resulting soil conditioner; American solid waste with less organic waste is poorly suited for composting	$5 to $13
Resource recovery plant	High public acceptance; if designed and operated properly, produces little air and water pollution; reduces waste of resources; extends life of landfills; can produce income from salvaged metals, glass, and other materials and from sale of recovered energy for heating nearby buildings; may be easier to find a site than for landfill or conventional incinerator	High initial investment; high operating costs; technology for many operations not fully proven; requires markets for recovered materials or energy produced; costly maintenance and repair; requires skilled operators; can cause air pollution if not properly controlled; profitable only with high volume of waste; discourages low technology sustainable earth approach emphasizing reuse and decreased use and waste of resources (Table 12-2)	$8 to $15

*These costs vary widely with location, have been rising rapidly and do not include the costs of land, plant construction, and waste collection. Typical collection costs in urban areas range from $30 to $70 per metric ton of waste.
†Litter is so widely dispersed that labor and operating costs for collection are extremely high (the second energy law again).
‡In Virginia Beach, Virginia, a landfill known as Mount Trashmore is used as an amphitheater; near Chicago, a landfill is used as a ski slope.
§By 1980 about half of the cities in the United States had run out of available landfill sites, and most of the remainder will probably run out sometime between 1980 and 1990.

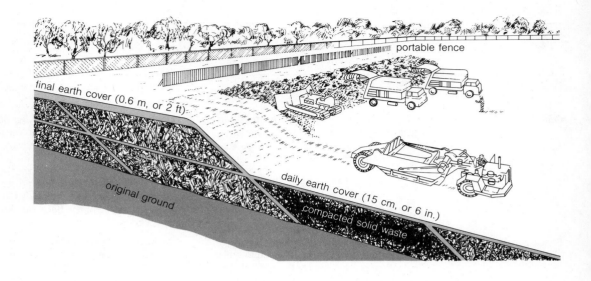

Figure E15-2 A sanitary landfill. Wastes are spread in a thin layer and then compacted with a bulldozer. A scraper (foreground) covers the wastes with a fresh layer of soil at the end of each day. Portable fences are used to catch and hold debris blown away by the wind.

portable fence

final earth cover (0.6 m, or 2 ft)

original ground

daily earth cover (15 cm, or 6 in.)

compacted solid waste

wastes, which are normally stored in containers and then buried; the site has restricted access, is continually monitored, and is located above geological strata that should prevent any wastes from leaching into groundwater.

The Resource Conservation and Recovery Act of 1976 requires that all open dumps throughout the United States be closed or upgraded by 1983 and forbids the creation of new open dumps. Unfortunately, this law does not clearly distinguish between landfills and sanitary landfills. As a result, many of the present sites designed as sanitary landfills are really landfills. Because of their unfavorable location, many of these landfills will cause water pollution problems, especially groundwater contamination.

Possible Future Methods One method for waste disposal that is being tested in several pilot plants is **pyrolysis**—the high-temperature decomposition of waste material in the absence of oxygen. The wastes are converted to oil, organic solids, char, gases such as methane, and inorganic materials. Some of these materials may be resold as fuel to offset the very high plant investment costs and the moderately high operating costs. This method, however, uses large amounts of energy to produce the high temperatures needed for waste decomposition, and pyrolysis plants can cause air pollution problems unless expensive controls are added.

Progress is also being made in developing biodegradable containers. The ideal food container is one that would be eaten along with its contents, such as an ice

cream cone, a taco shell, an apple skin, or a beer bottle made of pretzels. Edible containers could be common within the next 10 years, and some hotels and restaurants are already using nutritious containers that dissolve in water during cooking. Scientists also hope to develop plastics that are readily biodegradable by microorganisms or ones that decay when exposed to sunlight or rain. We must be cautious, however, about developing packaging that dissolves in water. The resulting chemicals must be carefully tested to be sure that in solving a solid waste problem we aren't creating an even worse water pollution problem. Everything must go somewhere (Section 3-1).

Improving Collection Because collection and hauling account for about 80 to 90 percent of the cost of solid waste disposal, new approaches are being developed to cut human labor costs. One improvement is the modern compaction truck, which uses hydraulic pressure to compress the waste as it is picked up. Even though such trucks can cost $50,000 to $80,000, their increased capacity and lower labor requirements save money. In spite of these advantages, these trash compactors and home "trash mashers" are ecologically unsound. By compacting mixed trash, they make it very difficult and expensive to dig up, separate, and recycle useful resources in the future when landfills may become urban mines. Home garbage disposal units reduce the volume of trash to be collected, but they are also undesirable from an ecological viewpoint. Food and organic wastes are ground up and flushed to a sewage treatment plant and then to water systems rather than being returned to the soil as compost.

A breakthrough in trash collection is "Son of Godzilla," a truck (resembling the mythical monster Godzilla) with a long mechanical arm used to pick up special 303-liter (80-gallon) hard plastic containers set on curbsides. The truck costs about 3 to 4 times more than a conventional truck, but after a few years a community can save money by using the Son of Godzilla approach. It costs about $65,000 a year to operate this truck, which requires only a driver, compared with about $98,000 a year for a conventional compaction truck with a crew of three. Scottsdale, Arizona, has used this method since 1969, saving the city at least $350,000 a year; Phoenix, Arizona, began using this system in 1978.

Even Son of Godzilla can't hold a candle to the pneumatic-type waste collection system used in a number of hospitals, apartment complexes, and housing developments, especially in Sweden. Occupants dump their trash into chutes, which is then sucked through a vacuum-powered pipeline to a central incinerator where the trash is burned. The heat generated can be used to melt snow and ice on sidewalks and roads, to generate electricity, and to warm buildings and residences as far as 3.2 kilometers (2 miles) away. Glass and metals can be sorted out for recycling before or after incineration. By 1978 at least 400 pneumatic collection systems were operating in Sweden, England, West Germany, France, and other parts of the world. The largest system in the world is found at the Disney World complex in Florida.

E15-3 Resource Recovery from Solid Waste

The Recycle Society Poor people in less developed countries have long recognized the need to recycle almost everything. Discarded glass, paper, plastic, rags, tin, bones, and other materials are collected by two groups: (1) the urban poor, who use these materials to make clothing, to build shacks, and for other survival purposes; and (2) people in the resource recovery (or secondary materials) business, who sell the materials to factories and other businesses for recycling. Unfortunately, most industrialized nations still recycle relatively little of the vast quantities of the world's material resources they use each year.

There are signs that affluent nations' emphasis on resource disposal rather than resource recovery is beginning to change. In the recycle society of the future, most of the waste and scrap in industrialized nations—which are now called secondary materials—would become the primary material resources, and virgin natural resources would become the backup, or secondary, material resources (Section 12-2). In 1976 Japan, which is heavily dependent on other nations for its resources, began implementing a national plan to require the recycling of wastes by all mining and manufacturing industries and by entire communities. In the United States, only 8 percent of the urban solid waste produced in 1978 was recycled. But this could change. The Resource Conservation and Recovery Act of 1976 provides some federal funds for demonstration plants for resource recovery and for state, regional, and local agencies to develop programs for resource recovery and resource conservation. The Environmental Protection Agency projects that the United States could recycle 25 percent of its urban solid waste by 1990. A more optimistic projection is that at least two-thirds of the material resources used in the United States each year could be recycled without important changes in life-styles.

However, recycling even 25 percent of the U.S. material resources will not occur as long as the subsidies, depletion allowances, and other economic and political factors favor the use of virgin resources over recycled resources (see Section 12-2). There is also disagreement over whether resources should be recycled by using a centralized, high technology approach or a decentralized, low technology approach.

Urban Resource Recovery Plants: The High Technology Approach As medium- and large-sized cities run out of sites for sanitary landfills, they are becoming increasingly interested in building a series of large-scale resource recovery plants capable of processing an entire city's mixed refuse for usable materials and energy. In this high technology approach, collection trucks or pneumatic pipelines would transport mixed urban waste to one or more highly automated resource recovery plants (Figure E15-3).

At each plant the mixed wastes would be shredded and then automatically separated to recover glass, iron, aluminum, and other valuable materials. The remaining paper, plastics, and other combustible waste could either be burned to produce steam, hot water, or electricity, which could be sold to nearby buildings and manufacturing plants, or converted by pyrolysis to a solid, liquid, or gaseous fuel, which could then be sold. Iron, steel, and other ferrous metals could be extracted by electromagnets; paper and plastic by using air to blow them into different chambers; and glass, garbage, aluminum,

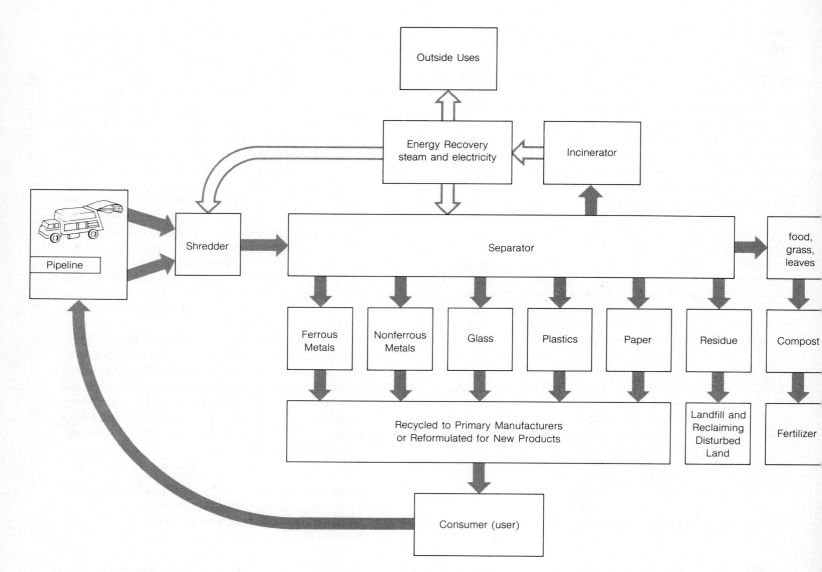

Figure E15-3 An urban resource recovery plant. At present, most plants are being built to burn trash in an incinerator to recover energy.

and other nonferrous metals by such methods as mechanical screens and flotation. Food waste, grass, leaves, and other organic wastes could be burned, sold as animal feed, or composted and thus recycled to the land as a soil conditioner. The recovered glass, iron, and aluminum could be sold to primary manufacturing for recycling or converted to new materials that could be sold. For example, glass could be returned to glass factories for remelting, processed into glass wool insulation, or mixed with recovered rubber to make highway paving materials. The incinerator residue, including par-

ticulates removed to prevent air pollution, could be used as landfill to reclaim damaged land or be processed into cinder blocks, bricks, or other building materials.

By 1980 there were 23 municipal resource recovery plants in operation in the United States; 33 others were either under construction (12) or in an advanced planning stage (21); and 54 other communities were seriously considering this approach. At this stage none are full-scale resource recovery plants like the one shown in Figure E15-3. Indeed, all of the 56 existing or planned plants are concerned exclusively or primarily with burning trash to recover energy, and only 8 of these plants are designed to separate iron, aluminum, and glass for recycling. Thus, most are merely sophisticated incinerators with equipment for heating recovery.

By 1977, Denmark was converting 60 percent of its wastes to energy, Switzerland 40 percent, and the Netherlands and Sweden each 30 percent—compared with less than 1 percent in the United States. According to optimistic estimates, the United States could convert 10 percent of its wastes to energy by 1990. Even if successful this would amount to only 2 percent of the total U.S. energy use projected for 1990. Burning paper products to obtain energy—as opposed to recycling paper—makes little ecological sense. First, there is usually a net energy loss because the energy used for collecting and handling the paper and for operating the incerator is often greater than the energy obtained from burning the paper. Second, recycling saves both energy and trees. Third, net energy losses and operating costs are much higher than expected because the incinerators require expensive maintenance and repairs.

The new high technology approach to materials and energy recovery shows promise, but it has a number of problems. These include the high cost of building such plants (up to $100 million), frequent maintenance, high operating costs, air pollution from fine particles (Section 17-4) and toxic metals (Enrichment Study 5), the large amount of waste needed each day to make the plant economical, and the lack of a steady market for recovered materials and energy. In Baltimore, a highly publicized garbage recycling and energy recovery plant built in 1972 had so many operating problems and air pollution violations that the company operating the $26 million plant shut it down and paid a $3 million fine. The city of Baltimore then had to spend at least $14 million to modify the plant before it could be reopened.

Source Separation: The Low Technology Approach
Most materials recovered in the United States today are recycled by source separation. In this simpler, small-scale approach, homes and businesses deposit recyclable waste materials (such as paper, glass, metals, and food scraps) into separate containers. Compartmentalized city collection trucks, private haulers and scrap dealers, or voluntary recycling or service organizations then pick up the segregated wastes. The recyclable wastes are then cleaned up if necessary and transported and sold to scrap dealers, compost plants (organic garbage), or manufacturing plants. By 1978 at least 218 U.S. cities had programs for the separate collection of recyclable materials, and there were more than 3,000 voluntary community recycling centers in operation.

This is an input approach where wastes are separated by each user, rather than being mixed and then separated by expensive resource recovery plants. Most cities already require trash to be deposited in certain types of containers. Requiring homes and businesses to segregate trash into four separate containers (glass, metal, paper, and organic garbage) would impose little hardship, cut refuse handling costs for the taxpayer, and not tie up taxpayer's money in expensive, unnecessary, and financially risky resource recovery plants. One study showed that source separation of all solid wastes in the average American household would only take about 16 minutes a week. By contrast, mixing wastes and then sending them off to landfills or resource recovery plants is an "out of sight, out of mind" approach that can encourage waste.

Proponents of waste separation also argue that the high technology approach hinders the recycling of paper and encourages the use of throwaway cans and bottles rather than returnable bottles. To be economical, large-scale resource recovery plants depend on a large daily input of aluminum and tin cans and burnable paper. Environmentally, it makes more sense to recycle paper and to ban throwaway cans for most purposes and use returnable bottles instead (Table 12-2). Indeed, proponents of large-scale resource recovery plants in the United States have opposed federal and state laws to ban or discourage the use of nonreturnable cans and bottles and to encourage paper recycling because removal of these materials from mixed urban refuse could make such plants unprofitable.

Recycling Paper The United States accounts for over a third of the world's production of paper and cardboard, with about 60 percent of this output being used for packaging. Each American uses directly or indirectly an average of about 273 kilograms (600 pounds) of paper per year—about 9 times the world average and about 46 times that in less developed nations. Yet the United States has the lowest paper recycling rate of the industrialized countries—explaining why paper makes up about one-third by weight of the urban solid waste produced each year. In 1919 the United States recycled 28 percent of its paper, and during World War II the recycling rate rose to 36 percent when paper drives and recycling were national priorities. Between 1966 and 1979, however, the paper recycling rate hovered around 20 percent, even though annual paper production increased by almost 50 percent. In other words, about 80 percent of the paper produced in the United States each year is eventually lost forever by being incinerated or buried in landfills. In contrast, Japan recycles nearly half of its paper, and many European countries recycle between 30 and 46 percent of theirs. In Sweden, the separation of wastepaper from all garbage in homes, shops, and offices has been required by law since 1980.

Each year about one billion trees are cut down to satisfy the enormous appetite for paper and paper products in the United States. Every Sunday edition of the *New York Times* consumes about 0.61 square kilometer (150 acres) of forest. To make the throwaway paper items used each year by McDonald's fast-food franchises in the United States consumes about 817 square kilometers (202,000 acres) of forest each year. Recycling a stack of newspapers only 0.9 meter (36 inches) high saves one tree. Most trees used to make paper are grown on tree farms especially for this purpose. Using recycling to reduce the need for these trees could allow much of this land to be used for recreational, grazing, or other purposes; recycling would also reduce the harmful environmental effects of clear-cutting (Section 10-4).

In addition to saving trees and land, recycling paper saves energy and can reduce air and water pollution from pulp mills. Recycling paper requires about 23 percent less energy than producing paper from virgin paper pulp. If one-half of the discarded paper were recycled, the United States would save enough energy to provide 10 million people with electrical power each year. Recycling paper to make high-quality finished products, however, causes more water pollution from the deinking and bleaching of the waste paper than producing such products from virgin pulp.

Having individual homes and businesses separate out paper for recycling is an important key to increased recycling. Otherwise the paper becomes so contaminated with other household and municipal trash that wastepaper dealers will not buy it. Such source separation is feasible primarily for newspapers from homes, corrugated boxes from commercial and industrial establishments, and printing and writing papers from offices. Slick paper magazines, magazine sections, and advertising supplements, however, cause contamination problems and must not be included. By 1978, over 100 cities required residences and businesses to separate out newspapers and cardboard for pickup and recycling. By 1978 about 500 American companies and organizations were separating and selling computer cards and high-grade office wastepaper for recycling. In addition, guidelines issued in 1976 require the source separation and recycling of (1) high-grade paper in federal office buildings with more than 100 workers, (2) newspaper from federal facilities housing more than 500 families, and (3) corrugated containers from federal establishments generating more than 11 metric tons (10 tons) of corrugated waste per month. Unfortunately, the value of wastepaper for recycling fluctuates wildly depending on demand; typically, it ranges from $11 to $220 per metric ton ($10 to $200 per ton). If wastepaper is burned in a resource recovery plant (Figure E15-3) instead of being recycled, however, it has an even lower value of $5.50 to $8.80 per metric ton ($5 to $8 per ton) based on its energy content.

A major national goal should be to recycle 35 percent of the paper used in the United States by 1985 and 50 percent by 1990. Economics plays a key role in preventing more paper recycling. Tax subsidies and other financial incentives (Section 12-2) make it cheaper to produce paper from trees than from recycling. For example, the capital gains of producers of virgin timber are taxed at only 30 percent, while the paper recycling industry pays the normal corporate rate of 48 percent. This means that American taxpayers are giving virgin timber producers over $100 million a year to encourage them to grow more pulp trees. In addition, a larger and more stable demand for recycled paper must be created. For example, all federal, state, and local government agencies might be required to buy paper products that contain a certain percentage of recycled paper fibers. In 1978, guidelines issued under the Resource Conservation and Recovery Act of 1976 require all federal agencies to buy products composed of the highest percentage of recycled materials practicable.

You can help by actively supporting legislation to accomplish 50 percent recycling of paper by 1990. You can also start and support recycling drives and centers in your community. Avoid buying and using rarely necessary paper throwaway products, such as paper towels, napkins, plates, cups, and diapers. Bring consumer pressure on manufacturers and store owners by refusing to buy goods that are excessively packaged. When given a choice between comparable goods, always buy the one that has the least packaging. This will not only reduce environmental pollution and energy use but also save you money. An increasing fraction of what we pay for products is for the packaging, which we throw away and then pay to have carted away for disposal. Refuse paper bags and wrapping for small items you purchase, and indicate why to salespersons and store managers. Take grocery or other bags back to the market and use them again. If you take your lunch, use a lunch box rather than a paper sack. Ask the local post office how to stop the flow of any junk mail you receive—a flow that wastes paper, time, and energy and results in higher postal rates. Write on both sides of paper and try to get local colleges and school systems to adopt this as a standard practice for all administrators, teachers, and students as an important lesson in ecological awareness.

E15-4 The Low-Waste Society: Going beyond Disposal and Recycling

Recycling can help reduce the use of matter and energy resources (Table E15-2) and decrease air pollution, water pollution, and solid waste. Thus, increasing the recycling rate of materials in solid waste in the United States from 8 percent to at least 50 percent by a combination of high technology resource recovery plants, low technology recycling based on waste separation by consumers, and economic incentives and policies that favor recycling should be an important national goal. But Americans must not be duped into making more and more throwaway items and then trying to recycle them at faster and faster rates. This still wastes finite matter resources, costs too much, and uses up large amounts of finite energy resources.

An even more fundamental goal of any national resource and solid waste management program should be to waste less resources by a combination of (1) reduced resource use per product (for example, smaller cars and thinner-walled containers), (2) reduced resource use per person (for example, fewer cars per family), (3) increased product lifetime (for example, longer-lived cars, tires, and appliances), and (4) increased product reuse by substituting products that can be reused in their original form (for example, refilling a returnable glass bottle) for throwaway items (for example, aluminum drink cans and nonreturnable bottles).

Reduced Resource Use per Product and per Person Large amounts of resources can be conserved by designing products so that minimum quantities of resources are used in their manufacture. For example, replacing the soldered three-piece steel can presently used with a two-piece drawn and ironed can would reduce the steel used per can by 25 to 30 percent; save large amounts of water; save enough energy to meet the annual electricity needs for about 3.5 million people; and reduce air pol-

Table E15-2 Energy Saved by Recycling Compared with Processing Virgin Materials

Material	Percentage of Energy Saved
Aluminum	97
Plastics (polyethylene)	97
Copper	88–95
Steel (100% scrap)	47
Newsprint	23
Glass containers	8

lution, water pollution, mining wastes, and urban solid waste.

You might think that large containers use more resources than small ones. But for most products using a larger package size means less packaging material per unit of weight or volume of product. For example, the 207-milliliter (7-ounce) returnable glass bottle requires about twice as much glass and energy per milliliter of soft drink as the 947-milliliter (32-ounce) size and produces about 50 percent more air pollution, water pollution, and solid waste.

The annual production of about 10 million vehicles consumes about 65 percent of all rubber used in the United States each year, 68 percent of the lead, 50 percent of the iron, 33 percent of the zinc, 20 percent of the steel, 13 percent of the nickel, 8 to 9 percent of the copper and aluminum, 7 percent of the copper, and 5 percent of the plastics. Each year in the United States 7 to 9 million cars are discarded. About 80 percent of these vehicles are eventually recycled, but redesigning automobiles to make them smaller and lighter would save much larger quantities of energy and matter resources and result in a greater reduction in air pollution, water pollution, solid waste, and land disruption. If all cars were reduced to 955 kilograms (2,100 pounds)—the weight of a typical subcompact sedan—the United States would save about 8.2 billion kilograms (9 million tons) of material resources each year.

Even greater resource savings could be accomplished if larger numbers of middle and upper class consumers in the United States and other countries used less resources per person. We need to analyze our life-styles and see which purchased items really increase the quality of our lives.

Designing Products for Longer Life In a high-consumption society built around planned obsolescence, many products seem to wear out or break down just about the time the consumer (or more accurately the "user") finishes paying for them. Designing products that last longer and that can be repaired easily with standardized parts and simple tools is a major way to reduce unnecessary resource use. For example, annual styling changes in cars and clothes rarely improve the product. They are merely schemes to persuade consumers that still-useful goods have become obsolete or unfashionable. A 1975 Louis Harris poll revealed, however, that 92 percent of the American people were willing to eliminate annual model changes in automobiles, and 90 percent were willing to eliminate yearly fashion changes in clothing.

If all vehicle tires were retreaded once, the demand for synthetic rubber would be cut by about one-third, tire disposal problems would be cut in half, and considerable amounts of energy would be saved. A retreaded tire typically has a lifetime from 30 to 90 percent as long as new tires, yet only about 20 percent of all vehicle tires produced in the United States are retreaded. Experts also believe that a 161,000-kilometer (100,000-mile) tire can be developed. If all new cars purchased after 1978 had such tires, and if these tires were retreaded once for an additional 43,200 kilometers (27,000 miles) of use, by 1990 the United States would save 23 million barrels of oil, 1.6 billion kilograms (1.75 million tons) of rubber, and $35 million in solid waste disposal costs per year.

The average useful life of automobiles in many countries is often around 20 years, but in the United States it is only about 10 years. If all cars sold in 1980 were designed for a 12-year lifetime, then by 1990 the United States would be saving 6.1 billion kilograms (6.7 million tons) of a variety of resources each year. At a 1973 international auto show in Frankfurt, Germany, Porsche displayed a car designed to have a 20-year life, but unfortunately the company assured the car industry that it had no intentions of producing such a car.

Reuse Reuse is different from recycling in that products are not reprocessed and refabricated but are used over and over again in their original form. The use of returnable beverage containers instead of throwaway cans and nonreturnable glass bottles is a prime example of reuse. Unfortunately, the trend in the United States has been to replace returnable beverage bottles with throwaway containers. In 1947 almost all soft drink and beer containers were refillable bottles with a refundable deposit required for each bottle. Even as late as 1960 almost all soft drinks and half of the beer were sold in refillable bottles. By 1979, however, about 75 percent of the nation's beer and soft drink containers were nonre-

turnable, throwaway bottles and cans. A major driving force behind this shift has apparently been the attempt of larger bottle and can manufacturing companies to expand their markets by driving smaller bottlers and breweries out of business. With refillable deposit bottles, the market area is determined by how far delivery trucks from local breweries and bottling plants can carry filled bottles and return with the empties. With throwaway containers, however, large companies can ship their products anywhere in the country and invade the small territories once dominated by local brewers and soft drink companies.

In 1979 Americans purchased 80 billion one-way beverage containers. About 15 percent of these containers were collected and recycled, but most were thrown away. About 4 billion of these were tossed along roadsides and trails to make up about 35 percent of the total litter by item (and about 50 percent by volume). The remaining 64 billion cans and bottles made up almost 10 percent by weight of the total urban solid wastes discarded in 1979.

Of the 30 billion aluminum cans made in 1979, about 8.4 billion—or 30 percent—were recycled in over 2,500 recycling centers set up by the aluminum industry. This saved matter and energy resources and recovered aluminum worth $69 million. About 2 to 3 percent of the throwaway glass bottles were crushed, melted, and remade into new bottles. But less matter and energy resources would be wasted by refilling returnable glass bottles. It takes about 3 times as much energy to make throwaway steel cans and glass bottles and 3.6 times more energy to make throwaway aluminum cans than it does to make returnable glass bottles that can be refilled an average of 19 times before being lost or broken. Recycling glass bottles and aluminum cans merely adds to this energy imbalance, since recycled glass bottles require 3.2 times as much energy and recycled aluminum cans require about 3.8 times as much energy as using refillable glass bottles.

There are two major approaches to shifting the emphasis from throwaway beverage containers back to refillable bottles. One is to ban nonreturnable beverage containers, as has been done in Denmark, and to require that all beverages be supplied in standardized bottle sizes that can be refilled by any bottler. The second approach, which has been adopted in Sweden and Norway and in six states in the United States, is to require deposits on all beverage bottles and cans to discourage the use of throwaways. In 1972, Oregon became the first state to pass a "bottle bill" requiring mandatory deposits on all beverage containers. In 1973 Vermont followed suit and by 1978 four other states—Michigan, Maine, Connecticut, and Iowa—had passed similar legislation despite intense and misleading lobbying efforts by can and bottle manufacturers—a powerful lobby that also includes steel and aluminum companies, metalworkers' unions, supermarket chains, and major brewers and soft drink bottlers. Since 1977 all beverage containers sold on federal property have been required to carry a deposit. Contrary to the dire predictions made by the can and bottle lobby to scare voters, the Oregon and Vermont bottle bills have been smashing successes in reducing beverage container litter by 67 to 83 percent, saving matter and energy resources, creating a net gain of jobs, and saving consumers' money. It is still too early to evaluate the effects of the bottle bills in the other four states.

The Environmental Protection Agency estimates that by 1980 a national container deposit law would (1) reduce roadside beverage container litter by 60 to 70 percent; (2) reduce total urban solid waste by 1 percent; (3) save

---

A Suggested Plan for Achieving a Low-Waste Society in the United States

1. Place primary emphasis on reducing resource waste and use by enacting and enforcing legislation to
   a. remove all subsidies, preferential transportation charges, depletion allowances, and tax breaks for primary-materials industries,
   b. require mandatory deposits on all beverage containers with a gradual shift to a complete ban on all nonreturnable beverage containers,
   c. require the sale price of all manufactured products to incorporate the costs of disposal or recycling,
   d. give tax breaks on comparable products that use less resources per unit or that last longer,
   e. standardize package sizes for each item and add a tax for excess packaging,
   f. require standardized, easily replaceable, interchangeable parts for products,
   g. add an extraction tax on all virgin materials if resource conservation goals are not being achieved,
   h. establish a massive education program to make citizens aware of the need to use and waste fewer resources, and
   i. allow taxpayers to deduct the cost of appliance repairs from their taxable income.

2. Increase the recycling of material resources to at least 50 percent and ideally 75 percent by
   a. requiring all households and businesses to separate trash into recyclable components,
   b. labeling all products to show the amount and type of recycled materials,
   c. requiring local, state, and federal agencies to buy materials composed of the highest percentage of recycled material,
   d. giving tax breaks to all manufacturers using recycled materials for production,
   e. placing a tax on synthetic fertilizer to encourage composting and the use of animal waste as fertilizer (Enrichment Study 16), and
   f. providing financial and tax breaks for high technology resource recovery plants with emphasis on units that can operate economically without burning valuable paper and other resources for energy and without having to recover large amounts of glass, steel, and aluminum from throwaway containers.

3. Require all landfills to be upgraded to sanitary landfills that meet strict location and operation standards, and severely limit the use of marshes, bays, and estuaries for solid waste disposal.

4. Enforce existing laws governing the disposal and treatment of hazardous wastes, and take those actions necessary to prevent all existing hazardous waste disposal sites from contaminating groundwater or surface water systems.

5. Require all manufacturers to label all products with adequate disposal instructions and to note clearly the presence of any toxic substances that might be released or formed as a result of incineration or burial in a landfill.

6. Carefully integrate this low-waste resource plan with those for population control, energy resources, land use, and pollution control.

$25 million to $50 million a year in waste disposal costs; (4) reduce annual glass consumption by 40 percent, annual aluminum consumption by 10 percent, and yearly steel consumption by 2 percent; (5) save enough energy to provide the annual electrical needs for 2 to 7.5 million people or to heat from 660 thousand to 2.5 million three-bedroom brick houses each year; (6) produce a net increase of 80,000 to 100,000 jobs;* and (7) save consumers at least $1 billion annually.

Efforts have been made since 1975 to pass a national beverage container deposit bill. By 1980, however, the bottle and can lobby had prevented such a bill from being passed by Congress, even though surveys show that at least 70 percent of the Americans polled would support such legislation. The president of the Adolph Coors Brewing Company—the only major brewer to support container legislation—estimated that the container lobby is spending $20 million a year to defeat bottle bill legislation at the state and national levels.

With such an irresistible array of environmental and economic benefits and overwhelming public support, political pressure on Congress by citizens should be enough to ensure passage of a national bottle bill, despite organized lobbying against such a law. Start action today as discussed in Enrichment Study 17. Meanwhile you can help conserve resources by (1) never buying beverages in nonreturnable bottles or cans, (2) picking up and returning all throwaway cans and bottles you find to recycling centers, and (3) working to have nonreturnable beverage cans and bottles banned in your state and on your campus.

Achieving a Low-Waste Society in the United States The problems of solid waste and resource waste will continue to mount until the United States changes from its linear, or throwaway, resource use system to a low-waste, or sustainable earth, resource system that reduces the use and waste of matter and energy resources and attempts to convert most solid waste to solid resources (Table 12-2). The accompanying box on page E125 lists a suggested plan for helping achieve a low-waste society in the United States.

Any plan for conserving and recovering the mineral resources we now waste will by necessity involve a complex mixture of approaches. But the important point is that such a plan can be implemented if informed citizens become politically involved.

---

*There would be a decrease in the number of jobs in the throwaway container manufacturing and supply industries. However, a larger number of normally higher paying jobs would be created in the returnable beverage filling, distribution, and retailing industries.

Waste is a human concept. In nature nothing is wasted, for everything is part of a continuous cycle. Even the death of a creature provides nutrients that will eventually be reincorporated in the chain of life.

Dennis Hayes

Discussion Topics

1. List the advantages and disadvantages of each of the following methods for waste disposal: (a) open dumping, (b) sanitary landfill, (c) incineration, and (d) composting.

2. How is solid waste collected and disposed of in your community? Does the community have any open dumps or hazardous waste disposal sites? Are the land waste disposal sites in the community true sanitary landfills or merely landfills?

3. Explain why the solid waste problem in the United States can be viewed primarily as an economic and political problem. What actions or changes would you make to correct this situation?

4. List possible ecological problems with each of the following: (a) home trash compactors, (b) having everyone put their trash in plastic bags, (c) developing plastic bottles that dissolve in water, and (d) sink garbage disposal units.

5. Why is there so little recycling in the United States? How would you correct this?

6. List the advantages and disadvantages of the high technology (resource recovery plant) and the low technology (source separation) approaches to recycling. Would you favor requiring all households and businesses to separate recyclable materials? Defend your answer.

7. What is the basic limitation of recycling? What thermodynamic and other alternatives are available (see Section 12-2)?

8. Does your school or city have a paper, can, or glass recycling program? If not, consider starting one as a class community project. Does your school or local government specify that a certain fraction of all paper purchases contain recycled fiber? Why not? Do the teachers in your school expect everyone to write on both sides of paper? Why not start a campaign to have this practice adopted in all local colleges and in the local public school system?

9. Debate the following resolution: All nonreturnable beverage containers should be banned.

10. Is your state contemplating a law to ban nonreturnable bottles and require deposits on all beer and beverage

containers similar to the Oregon law? If not, why not start a statewide campaign for such a law?

11. Does your school sell drinks in throwaway cans or bottles? Why not campaign for the use of returnable bottles in all school drink machines?

12. Debate the idea that a recycling tax (say $100) be added as a deposit on all automobiles to be returned when an automobile is delivered to an official recycling center.

13. Debate the following resolution: All depletion allowances and special tax breaks for primary-materials industries should be removed.

14. How would implementing the principles suggested for achieving a low-waste society in the U.S. affect your life-style?

15. Compare the throwaway, recycling, and sustainable earth (or low-waste) approaches to waste disposal and resource recovery and conservation for (a) glass bottles, (b) "tin" cans, (c) aluminum cans, (d) paper, (e) plastics, (f) leaves, glass, and food wastes, and (g) cars (See Table 12-2).

Readings

Barnhart, Benjamin J. 1978. "The Disposal of Hazardous Wastes." *Environmental Science & Technology*, vol. 12, no. 10, 1132–1136. Good overview.

Berry, Stephen R. 1972. "Recycling, Thermodynamics and Environmental Thrift." *Bulletin of the Atomic Scientists*, May, pp. 8–15. Recycling is not always the answer and must be coupled with other approaches.

Brown, Michael. 1979. *Laying Waste: The Poisoning of America by Toxic Wastes*. New York: Pantheon. Very critical attack with detailed discussion of the Love Canal disaster.

Citizens' Advisory Committee on Environmental Quality. 1976. *A New Look at Recycling Waste Paper*. Washington, D.C.: Citizens' Advisory Committee on Environmental Quality. Excellent discussion of paper recycling problems and possibilities.

Environmental Protection Agency. 1976. *Decision-Makers Guide in Solid Waste Management*. Washington, D.C.: U.S. Government Printing Office. Superb analysis of advantages and disadvantages for the major methods of solid waste collection, disposal, and high technology resource recovery.

Environmental Protection Agency. 1977. *Fourth Report to Congress: Resource Recovery and Waste Reduction*. Washington, D.C.: Environmental Protection Agency. Superb analysis of solid waste disposal, high and low technology resource recovery, and resource conservation in the United States.

Environmental Protection Agency. 1980. *Damages and Threats Caused by Hazardous Material*. Washington, D.C.: Environmental Protection Agency. Authoritative overview.

Franchot, Peter. 1978. *Bottles and Cans: The Story of the Vermont Deposit Law*. Washington, D.C.: National Wildlife Federation. Excellent summary.

Hamer, John. 1974. "Solid Waste Technology." *Editorial Research Reports*, vol. 2, no. 8, 643–660. Outstanding overview of solid waste disposal and resource recovery.

Hayes, Dennis. 1978. *Repairs, Reuse, Recycling—First Steps toward a Sustainable Society*. One of the best available overviews of resource recovery and conservation.

Kasper, William C. 1974. "Power from Trash." *Environment*, vol. 16, no. 2, 34–39. Fine review of energy available from burning trash.

League of Women Voters. 1972. *Recycle*. Washington, D.C.: League of Women Voters. Excellent reference on the economics and politics of a national plan for recycling. Good bibliography.

Purcell, Arthur H. 1980. *The Waste Watchers: A Citizen's Handbook for Conserving Energy and Resources*. New York: Anchor Press/Doubleday. Superb guide for achieving a low-waste society.

Randers, Jorgen, and Dennis L. Meadows. 1972. "The Dynamics of Solid Waste." *Technology Review*. March–April, pp. 20–32. Computer simulation of various proposed solutions to solid waste problem.

Rose, David J., et al. 1972. "Physics Looks at Waste Management." *Physics Today*, February, pp. 32–41. Outstanding evaluation of alternative solutions.

Seaborg, Glenn T. 1974. "The Recycle Society of Tomorrow." *The Futurist*, June, pp. 108–115. Very readable and stirring vision of what a society based on recycling and resource conservation would be like.

Small, W. E. 1971. *Third Pollution: The National Problem of Solid Waste Disposal*. New York: Praeger. Somewhat dated but still a very good analysis of solid waste problems and possible solutions. Good bibliography.

Enrichment Study 16

Controlling Eutrophication and Agricultural Water Pollution

Two related water pollution problems are cultural eutrophication—the overloading of lakes and estuaries with excess plant nutrients, such as nitrates and phosphates (Figure 6-10)—and the runoff of fertilizer and animal wastes from land to nearby lakes and streams. In this enrichment study we will look briefly at these water pollution problems and their possible solutions.

E16-1 Controlling Cultural Eutrophication

Ecological Succession, Natural Eutrophication, and Cultural Eutrophication All lakes undergo a normal aging process by which they gradually fill up with solid material from the surrounding watershed. The species comprising the aquatic community and their populations change as the lake fills in (Figure E16-1). This process is called *ecological succession* (Section 6-1) and the end result is the conversion of the lake into a bog (Figure 6-2).

As part of its natural aging process, a lake receives nutrients, such as phosphorus (in the form of phosphates), carbon, and nitrogen (in the form of nitrates or ammonia), from its surroundings—by drainage from the surrounding land basin, from bottom sediments, and from the residing organisms. This process is called *eutrophication*, or *natural eutrophication*, as discussed in Section 16-3. We need to distinguish carefully between *eutrophication*, the degree of nutrient enrichment, and *succession*, a complex aging process that depends not only on nutrient enrichment but also on many other variables (Figure E16-1).

We also need to distinguish between natural eutrophication and cultural eutrophication. As discussed in Section 16-3, *cultural eutrophication* is the speeding up of natural nutrient enrichment as a result of human activities. As shown in Figure 6-10, the main sources of this acceleration are (1) inorganic fertilizer runoff, (2) effluents from sewage treatment plants and, to a lesser degree, from septic tanks, (3) runoff from livestock feedlots, (4) synthetic detergents, (5) air pollution deposits primarily

from internal combustion engines, and (6) land runoff from cultivation, construction, mining, and poor soil conservation practices. All of these, plus natural inflow, work together to overload a lake ecosystem with nutrients, as discussed earlier in Sections 6-3 and 16-3.

Controlling Cultural Eutrophication What can we do to save lakes from accelerated eutrophication? There are two basic categories of solutions: output approaches (which treat the symptoms) and input approaches (which treat the causes), as summarized in the accompanying box.

As with any illness, we need to treat both the symptoms and the causes and at the same time use preventive medicine to keep healthy lakes from getting sick. Figure E16-2 illustrates a comprehensive approach to controlling lake eutrophication. Not all the controls would be needed in all areas. Instead, a particular approach or combination of approaches must be carefully chosen for each situation. For example, because phosphorus is the limiting factor in most freshwater lakes,* its control should be emphasized. In some lakes and in coastal waters and estuaries, nitrogen is the limiting factor; the emphasis should be in reducing inputs of nitrogen, primarily from fertilizer runoff, sewage treatment plants, and soil erosion.

The Detergent Controversy Until 1945 soap was used to wash clothes in the United States. But in areas with hard water (which contains ions of calcium, magnesium, or iron), soap leaves a greasy, grayish film (the soap curd). Around 1945 chemists invented synthetic deter-

---

*This is based on the *limiting factor principle* (Section 4-3), which states that when a number of chemicals or nutrients are needed for the growth of a particular species (such as algae), then the one in smallest supply will limit or stop growth. For example, one unit of growth for a typical species of algae requires 106 atoms of carbon, 16 atoms of nitrogen, and 1 atom of phosphorus. In this case phosphorus is normally the limiting factor, and growth should be controlled by managing the input of phosphorus, not nitrogen or carbon.

gents, which contain chemicals (such as sodium tripolyphosphate), to prevent the oily film from forming. This fact plus massive advertising by detergent manufacturers caused detergents to almost completely replace soap for cleaning laundry.

Most laundry detergents sold in the United States in the early 1970s contained about 12 percent phosphorus by weight and accounted for about 50 percent of the phosphorus (as phosphates) in domestic wastewater. These phosphates were released into lakes directly or indirectly in the effluents discharged from secondary sewage treatment plants that do not remove phosphates (Figure 16-9). By 1977 the average phosphorus content of detergents in the United States had dropped to about 5 percent and accounted for about 35 percent of the phosphorus in wastewater in regions that did not have a phosphate detergent ban.

For lakes where phosphorus is the limiting factor, the best approach to minimizing cultural eutrophication is to drastically reduce the input of phosphorus. But how should this be done? Should we ban or limit phosphates in detergents? Or should we remove phosphates from wastewater at treatment plants? To no one's surprise, the detergent industry favors the second plan, and city governments and consumer groups favor the first. Banning or limiting phosphates in detergents is faster and cheaper than upgrading sewage plants (Section 16-6). Such a ban could cut phosphate inputs into lakes where phosphorus is the limiting factor by 30 to 70 percent in a single stroke. Removing phosphates in a sewage treatment plant, however, is not prohibitively expensive and would cost only about 1¢ per person per day.

By 1980 six states (Michigan, Wisconsin, Vermont, Indiana, New York, and Minnesota) had banned almost all phosphate-containing detergents, household cleaners, and water conditioners, and Canada required a reduction in phosphate in these products. Bans have also been in effect in Chicago, Miami, Akron, and other U.S. cities. The ban of phosphate detergents in Syracuse, New York, caused the phosphate content of nearby Lake Onondaga to drop 57 percent in only 1½ years. Other studies show that the point source control of phosphate inputs enables lakes to recover rapidly from eutrophication.

Eliminating phosphates from detergents, however, is not without its problems. The substitute may be worse. For example, a promising substitute, trisodium nitrilotriacetate (NTA), was banned in 1970 by the U.S. Surgeon General because of evidence that it might cause urinary tract cancer in rats and mice. Some highly alkaline replacements, especially carbonates and silicates, can irritate the eyes, skin, and respiratory tract. Of course, all detergents are harmful if swallowed and should always be kept out of reach of small children.

Another approach is to return to the use of soap. Approximately 60 percent of the U.S. population lives in areas where soap works well because the water is soft or only slightly hard. People who live in areas with moderately to very hard water (check with local water officials) could use soap with a water softener, such as washing soda.* Clothes will not be quite as bright because

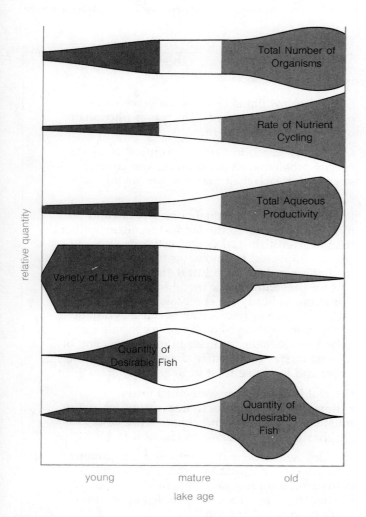

Figure E16-1 The changes in a lake as it undergoes natural aging through ecological succession.

relative quantity

Total Number of Organisms

Rate of Nutrient Cycling

Total Aqueous Productivity

Variety of Life Forms

Quantity of Desirable Fish

Quantity of Undesirable Fish

young   mature   old

lake age

*The procedure is as follows: First strip the detergents from your clothes by washing them in hot water containing about 4 tablespoons of washing soda. From then on wash a normal load of clothes with 1 cup of pure soap flakes or powder plus 2 to 4 tablespoons of washing soda, depending on the hardness of your water.

modern automatic washers are not designed for soap, even with added water softeners. In old-fashioned wringer washers, the water squeezed out of the cloth flushed some of the oily film off the surface of the cloth. An automatic washer's spin cycle forces water through the clothes by centrifugal force and traps the soap curd in the cloth fibers. Even so, soap will work if you are not hooked on having your clothes sparkling white. Maybe someone can design an automatic washer that can use soap.

A new development could restore soap at least partially to its earlier place in the laundry room. In 1972 scientists at the U.S. Department of Agriculture's Research Service formulated a modified soap that performs in hard water and at low washing temperatures as well as or better than today's detergents, but so far it is not available commercially.

A Success Story—Lake Washington's Rebirth What can citizens do to help clean up lakes plagued with cultural eutrophication? A great deal, as shown by the success of Seattle's citizens in cleaning up Lake Washington and nearby Puget Sound. In 1952 W. T. Edmondson, a prominent zoologist and pollution expert, began studying pollution in Lake Washington. He found that algal growth had been stimulated by ten sewage treatment plants that had been built around the lake since 1941. Puget Sound waters were also extensively polluted by large volumes of raw sewage added daily. Both the lake and the sound were unsafe for swimming.

Edmondson's research and James R. Ellis's civic leadership sparked one of the most outstanding pollution cleanups in the nation, which began in 1953. After several years of careful study, a citizens' committee began to tackle the problem politically. They proposed a single

---

Summary of Methods for Controlling Cultural Eutrophication

Output Approaches

1. Bypass the lake by diverting wastewater to fast-moving streams or to the ocean. This is not possible in most places. Where it is possible it may transfer the problem from a lake to a nearby estuary system.

2. Dredge lake sediments to remove excess nutrient buildup. This is impractical in large, deep lakes and not very effective in shallow lakes. Also, dredging often reduces local water quality, and the dredged material must go somewhere— usually the ocean.

3. Remove or harvest excess weeds, debris, and rough fish. Difficult and expensive in large lakes with present technology.

4. Control nuisance plant growth with herbicides and algicides. The direct addition of such toxic substances as well as magnification in the food chain may upset the ecosystem (Enrichment Study 11).

Input Approaches

1. Remove phosphates from sewage treatment plant effluents before they reach the lake. Eliminates most point sources by removing phosphates from industrial and municipal sewage.

2. Ban or set low limits (less than 4 percent) on phosphates in detergents. Decreases phosphate input by 30 to 70 percent.

3. Conduct research to define the critical nutrients, special problems, characteristics, and control strategy for each major lake, slow-moving river, and estuarine region.

4. Recover and recycle valuable phosphate and nitrogen nutrients to the land as fertilizers rather than overfertilizing lakes and estuaries. Will require improved technologies for transporting treated sewage to agricultural and forest areas and for preventing toxic metal buildup in the soil (Enrichment Study 5). The basic problem here is economic, not technological, because synthetic fertilizer is so cheap. Perhaps a tax should be added to synthetic fertilizer to make recycling of natural wastes competitive. Funds could go to a water and land-use trust fund.

5. Control land use near watershed areas. Ultimately any program to improve water quality must control the use and abuse of the land and emphasize soil conservation (Section 16-6).

6. Use deliberate, carefully controlled enrichment to increase lake or estuarine productivity for cultivating desirable fish and shellfish, and harvest algae as a food for people (aquaculture and mariculture, Section 9-5).

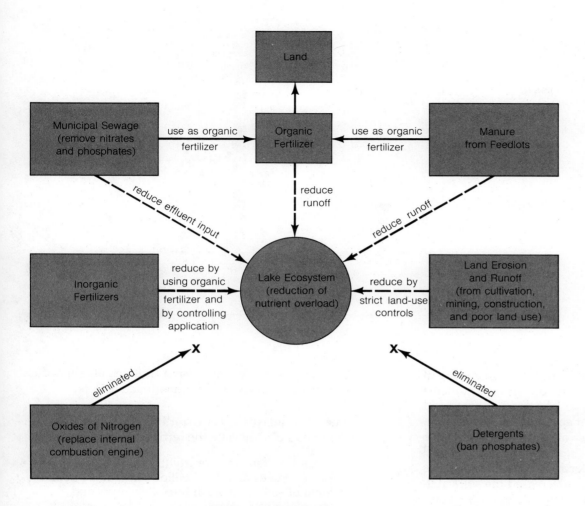

Land

Municipal Sewage (remove nitrates and phosphates) → use as organic fertilizer → Organic Fertilizer ← use as organic fertilizer ← Manure from Feedlots

reduce runoff

reduce effluent input

reduce runoff

Inorganic Fertilizers → reduce by using organic fertilizer and by controlling application → Lake Ecosystem (reduction of nutrient overload) ← reduce by strict land-use controls ← Land Erosion and Runoff (from cultivation, mining, construction, and poor land use)

X

eliminated

Oxides of Nitrogen (replace internal combustion engine)

X

eliminated

Detergents (ban phosphates)

governmental unit that would deal with all the pollution sources in the entire drainage basin. After extensive lobbying, they persuaded the legislature to pass a bill in 1957 permitting the formation of METRO, the Municipality of Metropolitan Seattle. After an intensive 6-week campaign—in which 5,000 men, women, and children rang doorbells, citizen speakers gave over 300 talks, and endorsements were obtained from more than 200 civic, community, and professional organizations—the voters approved METRO in 1958.

More sewers and two big new treatment plants were built to eliminate all sewage discharges into Lake Washington and all raw sewage discharge into Puget Sound. The results were dramatic. Phosphate and nitrate levels in both bodies of water dropped sharply, and the beaches of both are now open.

The Lake Washington success cannot necessarily be transferred to other areas (such as the Great Lakes) for several reasons. First, industrial pollution was not a significant factor in Seattle. Second, surrounding areas were essentially urban or forested rather than agricultural; thus, nutrients were not very concentrated in the runoff. Third, a convenient dumping ground, Puget Sound, was available. Nevertheless, this success story is a dramatic example of what organized, informed, and dedicated action by ordinary citizens can do.

E16-2 Controlling Agricultural Water Pollution

Modern agriculture in the United States is a major polluter of water systems, accounting for 30 to 50 percent of all water pollution. The major factor is the runoff of fertilizer and manure from the land to nearby water systems (Figure E16-3).

The U.S. Fertilizer Problem During the last several decades the use of inorganic, or synthetic, fertilizer in

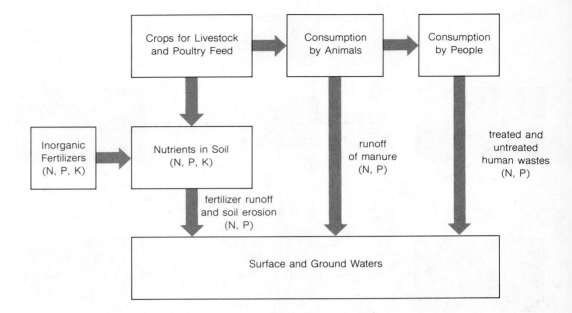

Figure E16-3 Water pollution by synthetic fertilizer runoff, feedlot runoff, and human wastes, all of which contain nitrogen (N), phosphorus (P), and/or potassium (K) compounds.

the world has skyrocketed. It seems logical that some of this increasing input of nitrogen and phosphorus nutrients into the soil is running off into lakes and streams and leaching into groundwater. But several questions remain.

What happens to fertilizer after it is applied to the ground? How much of it ends up in surface and ground waters? How are fertilizers affecting eutrophication? Has the widespread use of fertilizer decreased the soil's ability to hold nutrients? Unfortunately, the movement and chemistry of nitrogen and phosphorus in the soil are extremely complex and poorly understood. They vary considerably according to soil type, topography, weather, and time of fertilizer application. And once nitrates and phosphates reach the water, it is hard to determine their original sources.

As with any problem with conflicting and inconclusive information, opposing schools of thought have arisen among environmentalists and agriculturalists (see Table E16-1). There is probably some truth in both viewpoints. More research, more careful evaluation of existing data, and more cooperation between agriculturalists and environmentalists may eventually lead to a realistic plan of action.

In short, the degree of water pollution from fertilizers is unknown. It is probably serious only in heavily farmed areas near lakes in which nitrogen is the limiting factor and in farming areas where excess nitrate levels have built up in groundwater that serves as the domestic water supply. More serious sources of nitrates and phos-phates appear to be soil erosion, municipal and industrial sewage, and manure from animal feedlots.

Some Solutions to the Fertilizer Problem A wide range of solutions can alleviate the fertilizer problem:

1. Extend soil erosion control (Section 16-6). In the United States about 3.6 billion kilograms (4 billion tons) of sediment wash into waterways and reservoirs each year.

2. Prohibit spreading of nitrogen or phosphorus fertilizer on frozen soils or on land near surface water supplies that slopes more than 5 percent, unless erosion is controlled.

3. Establish ideal fertilizer amounts for each type of crop and soil, and circulate the information among farmers.

4. Rotate crops and plant nitrogen-fixing legume crops, such as clover and alfalfa, to decrease leaching of nitrates into groundwater.

5. Leave crop residues on soil surfaces to reduce erosion.

6. Use slow-release nitrogen fertilizers.

7. Decrease the amount of phosphorus in fertilizers.

8. Increase research on soil chemistry (especially the movement of nitrogen and phosphate in soil systems) and study ways to remove nitrates from drinking water in home and farm systems.

Table E16-1 Summary of the Debate on the Use of Synthetic Fertilizers

Environmentalist Position	Agriculturalist Position
Fertilizer runoff contributes 30 to 50% of the nitrates in ground and surface waters.	Nitrogen fertilizers undoubtedly contribute nitrates to groundwater systems in some localities, but the data are too scanty and conflicting to make generalizations. Amounts vary considerably with conditions and locations and are usually less than 30 to 50%. Excess nitrates more often come from treated sewage, soil erosion, food processing, and feedlot wastes.
Widespread fertilizer use deteriorates the soil's ability to hold nitrogen.	Nitrogen is naturally lost by erosion, leaching, volatilization, denitrification, and harvesting crops. The purpose of fertilizer is to replace this lost nitrogen. Without its widespread use, soils would be depleted to a much greater extent.
Fertilizer runoff is a major cause of eutrophication.	Although some nitrates in fertilizer can run off, phosphorus (the main cause of eutrophication) is strongly held by soil particles so that relatively little is lost. Municipal and industrial wastes and detergents are the main cause of eutrophication. Fertilizers could contribute in estuarine areas where nitrogen is the limiting agent and where agricultural use of land is heavy.
The situation in Great Britain and the Netherlands differs from that in the United States. These countries have no large lakes, and rivers there are short and fast flowing.	U.S. eutrophication problems due to fertilizer use are not serious. No serious problems have been reported in Great Britain and the Netherlands, where fertilizer use is 3 and 11 times U.S. usage, respectively.
Americans are increasing the danger of being poisoned by excessive nitrate concentrations in public water supplies and wells. If children under 4 months of age are exposed to nitrate levels exceeding the public health limit (10 milligrams of nitrate per liter), they can get sick and even die from methemoglobinemia.	In several surveys less than 1 percent of public water supplies exceeded the safe limit, but a number of rural wells did, especially in California, Missouri, Illinois, Minnesota, and Wisconsin. Between 1944 and 1972, 41 infants died from methemoglobinemia in the United States (versus 80 in Europe). All cases but one involved poisoning from rural wells, usually from septic tank or feedlot runoff, and most cases occurred between 1945 and 1950.
The fertilizer runoff problem is so serious that we should ban or sharply reduce the use of fertilizer in the United States.	With increasing use and no program for control, fertilizer runoff could become a serious problem in some areas. Control should be based on reducing excess application by farmers, applying at the right time, and reducing use in highly critical watershed or groundwater basin areas. If fertilizer use was banned, food prices could rise considerably, soil fertility would decline sharply, and much additional land would have to be cultivated to feed the U.S. population. Much of this would be marginal land prone to soil erosion, which could add more nitrates than the fertilizer on existing cropland. This could also use up land that should be reserved for recreation and wildlife habitats (Sections 10-3 and 10-7).

9. Prohibit or limit fertilizer use in critical areas where it contributes to surface and ground water pollution.

10. If problems are not under control by 1983, put a tax on each unit of fertilizer, with funds being used for the control of water pollution and land erosion.

The U.S. Manure Problem Some consider manure to be one of the major agricultural pollution problems in the United States. In earlier times it was a highly prized fertilizer, and it is still in some countries. Because synthetic fertilizers now cost so little, some feedlot operators can't sell manure, give it away, burn it, or find enough land on which to spread it.

The annual output of animal manure in the United States today is equivalent to the wastes from a human population of 2 billion people—about 10 times the actual U.S. population. At least half (and in many areas a much larger portion) of these wastes are recycled by being spread on the land. But much of the rest, especially in some areas, could be a potential hazard to surface and ground water—not to mention the problems of odor, dust, and flies.

Twenty years ago U.S. feedlots were rare, and an average steer roamed and fed on an open range with its waste naturally recycled to the soil. Today at least half of the 125 million steers (as well as hogs and poultry) are crowded into feedlots holding 1,000 or more animals. Near Greeley, Colorado, almost 100,000 head of cattle are penned on only 1.3 square kilometers (320 acres) of land.

State and federal regulations now limit the sites on which feedlots can be built, but some existing operations are located on hillsides so that fluid wastes drain easily into the waterways below. Serious water pollution can occur when rains flush a large amount of waste into nearby streams in a short time. Another important source of excess nitrates in lakes and streams near feedlots may be gaseous ammonia from animal manure decomposing on the feedlot surface.

Solutions to the Manure Problem The animal manure problem in one sense is not one of control but one of waste management. Controlling inputs into water courses will temporarily relieve local situations and buy needed time. But manure is a valuable resource that belongs on the land, not in the water. Some solutions are as follows:

1. Recycle manure to the land. Unless either the use of manure is subsidized by tax incentives or synthetic fertilizers are taxed, this method will probably not be adopted by industrialized agriculture because many feedlots are located near big cities (to cut livestock hauling costs), where land for recycling the manure is not available.

2. Recycle processed manure as livestock feed. Experiments have shown that this processed animal by-product can be used as an excellent poultry and livestock feed. This cuts operating costs and returns proteins, vitamins, and other valuable nutrients to the animals. Care must be taken to ensure that contaminants, such as pesticides (Enrichment Study 11) and toxic metals (Enrichment Study 5), do not build up to dangerous levels through recycling and that infectious diseases are not spread.

3. Convert animal manure to oil. New, relatively simple chemical processes now in the pilot stage can convert animal manure to a low-sulfur, heavy oil that could be used for generating electricity. This process, however, is expensive and normally requires such a large input of energy that the net energy yield is very low or even negative (Section 13-3).

4. Require structures around all feedlots that would intercept and divert runoff so that manure does not flow directly into surface water sources.

5. Divert runoff into retention basins from which the water can be pumped for application to cropland or forest land. Unfortunately, when retention basins are too small or poorly designed, they can overflow into nearby water courses during heavy rains. Design and operation should be regulated by state permit.

6. Treat manure to eliminate offensive odor and to make it less desirable as a breeding ground for flies and vermin.

7. Set up oxygenation stations (air bubblers) in ponds, lakes, and streams so that they can absorb more manure (an expensive plan).

8. Prohibit the spreading of manure on frozen land or on land located near waterways that slopes more than 5 percent.

9. Establish state and federal regulations on the location, operation, and pollution control of feedlots.

10. Use rural land-use zoning to set aside areas for feedlots where odors and some water pollution can be tolerated.

11. To reduce the animals' need for hay, place plastic tabs in their stomachs to replace roughage. In trial studies this has reduced daily manure output up to 40 percent from that of animals fed conventionally.

12. Dehydrate manure to remove odors, bag it, and sell it to home gardeners.

As with many complex environmental problems, we must not be trapped into a simplistic approach. Each situation involving fertilizer use and manure has unique characteristics, and a carefully developed, multifaceted approach must be used.

Today in the United States everybody is downwind or downstream from somebody or something else.
William D. Ruckelshaus

Discussion Topics

1. Although eutrophication and ecological succession are often used interchangeably, they are really different concepts. Explain the differences.

2. Explain how eating steak or any form of meat may contribute to eutrophication somewhere, even if not in your own area.

3. Explain why building expensive primary and secondary sewage treatment plants (Section 16-6), although necessary, may hasten the deterioration of water quality through cultural eutrophication. What are some solutions to this dilemma?

4. Explain what is meant by the statement: "The problem

with Lake Erie is not that it is dead but that it is too much alive."

5. Is eutrophication always bad? Compare its beneficial and harmful effects. Debate the idea that we should deliberately manipulate the degree of eutrophication to keep aquatic ecosystems at stages most useful to us.

6. Explain some possible problems and ecological side effects of the following proposed solutions to cultural eutrophication: (a) directing wastewater to the ocean, (b) dredging lake sediments, (c) harvesting excess weeds and fish, (d) using herbicides and algicides to control excessive plant growth, and (e) placing a total ban on the use of phosphate detergents in the United States.

7. Debate the following statements:

   a. Fertilizer runoff is one of the major causes of eutrophication.

   b. Using fertilizer makes the soil less able to hold nitrogen.

   c. We are in increasing danger of being poisoned by nitrates in our water supplies.

   d. Fertilizer use in the United States should be banned or sharply reduced.

   e. Because Great Britain and the Netherlands, which use 3 to 11 times as much fertilizer per acre as the U.S. does, are not having any serious eutrophication problems, there is no cause for concern in the United States.

8. Debate the idea that a tax should be added to each unit of synthetic fertilizer used in the United States and put into a land and water use trust fund. What implications would this have for the farmer? For you? For foreign trade and the U.S. balance of payments? What are the possible consequences of not doing this?

9. Debate the idea that we should return completely or at least to a large degree to organic farming in the United States (see Section 9-7). What might be some political, economic, and ecological implications of such a decision?

10. Debate the following resolution: Large animal feedlots in the United States should be prohibited.

11. Debate the concept that landowners such as farmers or feedlot owners have the right to do as they please with the land they own. Assume first that you are not a landowner, and then assume that you have valuable land holdings that will be affected by new environmental laws.

Readings

Aldrich, S. R. 1972. "Some Effects of Crop Production on Environmental Quality." *BioScience*, vol. 22, no. 2, 90–95.

Contains an excellent summary of the contributions of agriculture to water pollution, a response to Commoner's charges on agricultural pollution, and an appeal for cooperation rather than polarization.

American Society of Agricultural Engineers. 1976. *Managing Livestock Wastes.* St. Joseph, Mo.: American Society of Agricultural Engineers. Very useful summary.

Commoner, Barry. 1971. *The Closing Circle: Nature, Man and Technology.* New York: Knopf. See chapter 6 on eutrophication and chapter 5 on the nitrate problem.

Edmondson, W. T. 1973. "Lake Washington." In Charles R. Goldman et al., eds., *Environmental Quality and Water Development.* San Francisco: Freeman. Excellent summary of this success story by one of its planners.

Edmondson, W. T. 1975. "Fresh Water Pollution." In William W. Murdoch, ed., *Environment: Resources, Pollution and Society.* Sunderland, Mass.: Sinauer. Fine summary of eutrophication by an expert.

Grundy, R. D. 1971. "Strategies for Control of Man-made Eutrophication." *Environmental Science & Technology*, vol. 5, no. 12, 1184–1190. Excellent overview.

Hasler, Arthur D. 1970. "Man-Induced Eutrophication of Lakes." In S. Fred Singer, ed., *Global Effects of Environmental Pollution.* New York: Springer-Verlag. Superb summary by a prominent limnologist.

Hutchinson, G. Evelyn. 1973. "Eutrophication." *American Scientist*, July, pp. 269–279. Outstanding summary.

Lee, G. Fred, et al. 1978. "Eutrophication of Water Bodies: Insights for an Age-Old Problem." *Environmental Science & Technology*, vol. 12, no. 8, 900–908. Superb overview.

Loehr, Raymond C., ed. 1977. *Food, Fertilizer, and Agricultural Residues.* Ann Arbor, Mich.: Ann Arbor Publishers. Excellent series of papers on agricultural pollution, problems, and possible solutions.

Loehr, Raymond C., et al. 1979. *Best Management Practices for Agriculture and Silviculture.* Ann Arbor, Mich.: Ann Arbor Science Publishers. Authoritative source.

National Academy of Sciences. 1969. *Eutrophication: Causes, Consequences, and Correction.* Washington, D.C.: National Academy of Sciences. Authoritative treatment of eutrophication. Excellent bibliography.

National Academy of Sciences. 1972. *Accumulation of Nitrate.* Washington, D.C.: National Academy of Sciences. Balanced view of the nitrate problem. Good bibliography.

Soil Conservation Society of America. 1971. "A Primer of Agricultural Pollution." Reprint from *Journal of Soil Conservation*, March–April. 7515 Northeast Ankeny Road, Ankeny, Iowa 50021. Very readable summary.

Stanford, G., et al. 1970. *Fertilizer Use and Water Quality.* U.S.

Department of Agriculture, Agricultural Research Service, ARS 41–168. Washington, D.C.: U.S. Government Printing Office. Excellent summary of fertilizer problems and ongoing research.

Stoker, H. S., and Spencer L. Seager. 1976. *Environmental Chemistry: Air and Water Pollution.* 2nd ed. Glenview, Ill.: Scott, Foresman. See chapter 9 for a superb summary of the phosphate detergent problem.

Viets, Frank G., Jr. 1971. "Water Quality in Relation to Farm Use of Fertilizer." *BioScience,* vol. 21, no. 10, 460–467. Basic arguments against Commoner's position by a prominent agriculturalist.

Wadleigh, C. H. 1968. *Wastes in Relation to Agriculture and Forestry.* U.S. Department of Agriculture Miscellaneous Pub. No. 1065. Washington, D.C.: U.S. Government Printing Office. One of the best summaries.

Wadleigh, C. H., and Clarence S. Britt. 1970. "Issues in Food Production and Clean Water." In T. L. Willrich and G. E. Smith, eds., *Agricultural Practices and Water Pollution.* Ames: Iowa State University Press. Superb introduction to agricultural pollution problems.

Enrichment Study 17

How to Influence Elected Officials

E17-1 Why Is Writing Letters Important?

Do you know the names of your congressional representatives and senators? Do you write them opposing or supporting special environmental legislation or complimenting them for a particular stand they took? Do you belong to Common Cause, the citizens' lobby? Have you sent donations to the League of Women Voters, Ralph Nader's Center for Responsive Law, the Environmental Defense Fund (EDF), the Legal Defense Fund (LDF), the Center for Public Law and Social Policy, the Natural Resources Defense Council (NRDC), or some other group working on your behalf? (See the list of organizations in the Appendix.) Have you established a public interest research group (PIRG) on your campus? If you have answered no to more than two of these five questions, you have yet to become a sustainable earth citizen, and you are missing out on opportunities to practice much-needed cybernetic politics (Section 19-4).

Writing your elected representatives in the correct way is an extremely important action. You may be thinking, "What can my one letter or one vote do?" But this response merely reveals that you don't appreciate the importance of positive synergy, lag times, the threshold effect, and other aspects of cybernetic politics. Letters supporting or opposing a particular position can slowly accumulate until a threshold is crossed; elected officials are forced to recognize that if they don't vote in a certain way for the people they represent, they are likely not to be reelected. Consider what happened when ordinary citizens and environmental groups organized to defeat the SST against overwhelming corporate and presidential power. Senator Clinton Anderson, chairperson of the Aeronautical and Space Sciences Committee and an ardent supporter of the SST, voted against the SST much to everyone's surprise. His explanation was, "I read my mail. This morning my letters and telegrams opposed the SST by a whopping 78 to 8 margin."

Although writing letters is always important, it is not enough if you want to practice cybernetic politics. To be effective, we need a J curve of letters. This means organizing and persuading others to write letters. For every letter we write, we should get two other people to write letters, too, and ask them to get two others, and so on. This is what a J curve, or positive synergy, is all about—not 1, 2, 3, 4, 5, . . . , but 1, 2, 4, 8, 16, . . . Carrying out this doubling process only 28 times would convince everyone in the United States.

E17-2 How Does the Legislative Process Work?

The first thing to know is that the standard outline you learned in your government course (a bill is introduced, approved by committee, approved by the House and Senate, signed into law, and implemented) is much too simple. There are three major aspects of congressional legislation that you need to understand more fully: (1) the committees, (2) the conference committee, and (3) the appropriations process.

Committees When a bill is introduced, it must go to the proper committee. Many bills could go to any of several committees, and the chair of one may be friendly to the bill, whereas the chair of another may be determined to kill it. Thus, which committee is chosen can greatly determine a bill's chance of passage. Generally jurisdictional disputes are solved by compromise, but if a compromise can't be worked out, the Senate or House parliamentarian may decide.

A bill's chance of passing depends not only on which committee it goes to but also on when it is introduced. Congress operates on a 2-year cycle composed of two 1-year sessions. Any bill still pending at the end of the first session automatically carries over to the second. But any

Writing Effective Letters

1. Address the letter properly:

   a. The president:

   The President
   The White House
   1600 Pennsylvania Ave., N.W.
   Washington, D.C. 20500

   Dear Mr. President:

   Telephone: (202) 456-1414

   b. Your senators:

   The Honorable _____
   United States Senate
   Washington, D.C. 20510

   Dear Senator _____ :

   Telephone (202) 224-3121

   c. Your representative:

   The Honorable _____
   House of Representatives
   Washington, D.C. 20515

   Dear Representative _____ :

   Telephone: (202) 224-3121

2. Always concentrate on your own representatives, but also write the chair or members of the committee that is holding hearings on legislation that interests you. Try to write the original committee chair and members, the conference committee members, and the chair and members of the correct appropriations committee.

3. Be brief (a page or less), cover only one subject, come quickly to the point, write the letter in your own words and express your own views. Don't sign and send a form or mimeographed letter. Make the letter personal, and don't say you are writing for some organization (the representative should already know the official position of organized bodies).

4. Identify the bill by number (for example, "H.R. 123" or "S. 313") or name if possible, and ask the representative or senator to do something specific (cosponsor, support, or oppose it). You can get a free copy of any bill or committee report by writing to the House Document Room, U.S. House of Representatives, Washington, D.C. 20515, or the Senate Document Room, U.S. Senate, Washington, D.C. 20510.

5. Give specific reasons for your position. If pertinent, mention the bill's impact on the member's district.

bill introduced late in the second session is not carried over and has a slim chance of passage; so, the entire process must be repeated if the bill is to be passed in the next cycle. Some members of Congress use this fact to please constituents without really helping them. With much fanfare and publicity they introduce or cosponsor bills late in the second session that they know will not pass.

The committee structure often gets blamed for congressional inaction. But in spite of its need for reform (see Section 19-5), the committee system is a very important review process by which experts examine and analyze a bill before passing it on. Much bad legislation is filtered out in committee, and good ideas are often strengthened and made more workable.

Conference Committees In the long and tortuous path toward enactment, most bills change substantially. Rarely does any important bill pass both House and Senate in identical form, but a bill cannot become law until both houses agree on it. This is where conference committees come in.

The leaderships of both houses appoint members (almost always the chair and senior members of the committees that originally handled the legislation) to the conference committee, which meets secretly on neutral ground to "horse trade" until they reach a final agreement. No press, public, or even congressional staff members are allowed, and no minutes are taken. The resulting conference report is submitted to both houses for take-it-or-leave-it approval, with no amendments

6. If you have expert knowledge, share it. You may give your representative much-needed information.

7. Be courteous and reasonable. Don't be rude, make threats, or berate. Don't pretend that you have vast political influence. Don't begin on the righteous note of "as a citizen and taxpayer."

8. Don't become a constant penpal. Quality at the right time, rather than quantity, is what counts.

9. Follow up. Telegrams are particularly useful in the last few days before a vote. You can send a Public Opinion Telegram of 15 words (not counting your name or the recipient's address) to the president, vice president, U.S. senator, or representative from anywhere in the country for $2.50—a superb investment in your future. A member of Congress (or his or her staff) can also be reached by telephone through the capitol switchboard at (202) 224-3121.

10. Include your name and return address.

11. If you don't have time to write or send a telegram, make a phone call. As with letters, be polite, concise, and specific. Introduce yourself as a constituent, and ask to speak to the staff member who works on the issue that you are concerned about.

12. Use positive reinforcement. After the vote write your representative a short note of thanks. A general rule here (as well as for life in general) is to give at least two compliments for every criticism.

13. If you are going to Washington, consider visiting your representative to lobby for your position. But go prepared or you can destroy your credibility and effectiveness. An alternative is to become a contributing member of Common Cause and/or environmental groups that have full-time professional lobbyists working for you. These organizations exist only by individual support (see the Appendix for a list).

14. Remember that getting a bill passed is only the first step. You need to follow up by writing the president to be sure that he or she doesn't veto the bill or refuse to spend all the money appropriated by Congress. Finally, write the federal agency (see addresses in the Appendix) charged with carrying out the program, asking it to establish effective regulations or to be more active in enforcing the law. Even more important is monitoring and influencing action at the state and local levels, where all federal and state laws are either ignored or enforced. As Thomas Jefferson once said, "The execution of laws is more important than the making of them."

allowed. The conference can sometimes strengthen a bill or just as easily undo or critically weaken it.

Appropriations Suppose a strong bill is passed. If it takes money to put it into effect, it must then be reviewed by the Appropriations Committee or one of its specialized subcommittees to determine how much money will be appropriated. Congress may authorize a high level of spending for a bill, but the Appropriations Committee determines how much will actually be spent—sometimes so little as to nullify the legislation. The chairpersons of the appropriations subcommittees can be and often are the most powerful people in Congress.

But the appropriations fight doesn't even end here. The president can issue public statements about improv-

ing the environment and then quietly refuse to release the money appropriated by Congress.

E17-3 How to Write Elected Officials

The best guide for writing to Congress, called *When You Write to Washington*, is issued annually by the League of Women Voters.* The accompanying box lists suggested rules for writing elected officials.

---

*The pamphlet, which includes an annual list of all committee members and chairpersons, can be obtained from the League of Women Voters, 1730 M St., N.W., Washington, D.C. 20005.

Remember that most members of Congress are hard-working men and women trying to do a difficult job. They are buffeted from all sides by conflicting viewpoints, which are essential for revealing all facets of a problem. However, managing these differing attitudes does not ease the job of finding the best way for the country and world while still getting reelected.

E17-4   Rules for Effective Political Action

Writing letters is essential. But to use positive synergy, we need to support national lobbying organizations (see the Appendix) and join or form a local ongoing organization or temporary task force on a particular issue. It is particularly important that we support professional citizens' lobby groups at the national level to counteract the massive lobbying activities of industry and other vested interests.

John Gardner has summarized the basic rules for effective action by organizations:

1. Have a full-time continuing organization.

2. Limit the number of targets and hit them hard. Most groups dilute their efforts by taking on too many issues.

3. Get professional advisers to provide you with accurate, effective information and arguments.

4. Increase positive synergy by forming alliances with other organizations on a particular issue.

5. Have effective communication that will state your position in an accurate, concise, and moving way.

6. Persuade and use positive reinforcement—don't attack. Try to find allies within the institution, and compliment individuals and organizations when they do something you like.

7. Organize for action—not just for study, discussion, or education. Minimize regular meetings, titles, and minutes. Have a group coordinator, a series of task forces with a project leader, press and communications contact, legal and professional advisers, and a *small* group of dedicated workers. A small cadre can accomplish more than a large, unwieldy group. Work in small groups but always keep in mind the Abilene paradox: "People in groups tend to agree on courses of action which, as individuals, they know are stupid."

8. Don't work exclusively at the national level. Concentrate much of your effort at the state and particularly at the local level.

College students should also be sure that an active public interest research group (PIRG) is formed on their campus and as a statewide network. This is one of the tunnel-effect ideas (Section 19-4) developed by Ralph Nader and Donald Ross. College student organizations and actions are rarely sustained and often lack professional expertise and adequate funds to mount a consistent and effective effort. Just when the most work is needed, students may be on spring break or summer vacation or in the midst of exam week.

PIRG is a simple plan that tunnels through these problems. In effect, most of the colleges in a state join in a synergistic effort to hire a state cadre of full-time professionals and experts to work on issues selected by a governing board of students elected from each campus. In other words, you hire professionals to work on issues for you full-time, and use student and faculty volunteers as needed and as available.

The real tunnel effect, however, is in the financing of PIRG. A majority of the students on a campus petition the student senate and/or board of regents or trustees to increase activity or incidental fees by a few dollars per year (typically about $3). Normally this money is automatically collected and used to hire a staff of lawyers, scientists, or other experts to work full-time on behalf of the students on local and state issues. Students who do not wish to support PIRG may get their money back at an announced time after registration, but special effort is required to do this.

I know that the great tragedies of history often fascinate people with approaching horror. Paralyzed, they cannot make up their minds to do anything but wait. So they wait and one day Gorgon devours them. But I should like to convince you that the spell can be broken, and that there is only an illusion of impotence, that strength of heart, intelligence and courage are enough to stop fate and sometimes reverse it. One has merely to will this, not blindly, but with a firm and reasoned will.

Albert Camus

Readings

Alderson, George, and Everett Sentman. 1979. *How You Can Influence Congress: The Complete Handbook for the Citizen Lobbyist.* New York: E. P. Dutton. Superb guide.

Cagle, Carol W. 1972. "It's a Wonder That Congress Does

Anything!" *Environmental Action*, January 8, pp. 11–14. Superb outline of how Congress operates.

Gardner, John W. 1972. *In Common Cause.* New York: Norton. Outstanding book on citizen action by the founder and former leader of Common Cause, the citizens' lobby.

Green, Mark J., et al. 1972. *Who Runs Congress?* New York: Bantam/Grossman. See especially chapter 9, "Taking on Congress: A Primer for Citizen Action." An outstanding book.

League of Women Voters. Annual. *When You Write to Washington.* League of Women Voters, 1730 M St., N.W., Washington, D.C. 20005. The best guide on how to write elected officials.

Morris, David, and Karl Hess. 1975. *Neighborhood Power: The New Localism.* Boston: Beacon Press. Excellent guide for local action.

Nader, Ralph, and Donald Ross. 1971. *Action for a Change: A Student's Manual for Public Interest Organizing.* New York: Grossman. How to form a PIRG group.

Peters, Charles. 1980. *How Washington Really Works.* Boston: Addison-Wesley. Superb and revealing guide.

Pezzuti, Thomas. 1974. *You Can Fight City Hall and Win.* Los Angeles: Sherbourne Press. Fact-filled guide.

Robertson, James, and John Lewallen, eds. 1975. *The Grass Roots Primer: The Spare Time, Low Cost, At Home Guide to Environmental Action.* New York: Scribner's. Superb guide.

Ross, Donald K. 1973. *A Public Citizen's Action Manual.* New York: Grossman. Superb guide.

Smith, Dorothy. 1979. *In Our Own Interest (A Handbook for the Citizen Lobbyist in State Legislatures).* Seattle: Madrona. Outstanding handbook.

Appendix

Periodicals, Environmental Organizations, and Government Agencies

Periodicals

The following is a list of journals that will aid the intelligent citizen in keeping well informed and up-to-date on environmental problems. Those marked with an asterisk are recommended as basic reading. Since subscription prices tend to change, they are not given.

American Forests, published monthly by the American Forestry Association, 1319 18th St., N.W., Washington, D.C. 20036. Popular treatment, "seeks to promote an enlightened public appreciation of natural resources."

Audubon, published bimonthly by the National Audubon Society, 950 Third Ave., New York, N.Y. 10022. Conservationist viewpoint; covers more than bird-watching. Good popularizer of environmental concerns; well-produced, sophisticated graphics.

BioScience, published monthly by the American Institute of Biological Sciences, 1401 Wilson Blvd., Arlington, Va. 22209. Official publication of AIBS; gives major coverage to biological aspects of the environment, including population. Style ranges from semipopular to technical. Features and news sections attentive to legislative and governmental issues.

*Bulletin of the Atomic Scientists, published 10 times a year by the Educational Foundation for Nuclear Science. Address inquiries to *Bulletin of the Atomic Scientists*, 935 East 60th St., Chicago, Ill. 60637. In recent years has increased coverage of environmental issues, particularly in relation to nuclear power and nuclear testing and fallout.

Catalyst for Environmental Quality, published quarterly at 274 Madison Ave., New York, N.Y. 10016. High-level, popular treatment; substantial articles on all aspects of environment, including population control. Reviews books and films suited to environmental education.

Ceres, published bimonthly by the Food and Agricultural Organization of the United Nations (FAO), UNIPUB, Inc., 650 First Avenue, P.O. Box 433, New York, N.Y. 10016. Contains articles on the population-food problem.

*The CoEvolution Quarterly, published quarterly by The CoEvolution Quarterly, P.O. Box 428, Sausalito, Calif. 94965.

Covers a wide range of environmental and self-sufficiency topics. Also publishes *The New Whole Earth Catalog* (1980).

*Conservation Foundation Letter, published monthly by the Conservation Foundation, 1717 Massachusetts Avenue, N.W., Washington, D.C. 20036. Usual issue 12 pages long. Good summaries of key issues.

Cry California, published quarterly by California Tomorrow, Monadnock Building, 681 Market St., San Francisco, Calif. 94105. Frequently contains environmental articles that have application to all states.

Design and Environment, published quarterly by RC Publications, 6400 Goldsboro Rd., N.W., Washington, D.C. 20034. A new journal devoted to the interaction between technology and environment.

*Earth Shelter Digest, published six times a year by Earth Shelter Digest, 479 Fort Road, St. Paul, Minn. 55102. Gives the latest information on earth-sheltered (underground) housing.

*The Ecologist, published ten times a year by Ecosystems Ltd., 73 Molesworth St., Wadebridge, Cornway PL27 7DS, United Kingdom. Wide range of articles on environmental issues from an international viewpoint.

Ekistics, published monthly by the Athens Center of Ekistics, 24 Strat Syndesmou St., Athens 136, Greece. Reviews the problems and science of human settlements. Reflects ideas of such planners as Constantine Doxiadis, R. Buckminster Fuller, and the late John McHale.

The Energy Consumer, published monthly by U.S. Department of Energy, Office of Consumer Affairs, 86082 Washington, D.C. 20585. Free publication. Gives summaries of energy developments, government programs, and publications.

*Environment, published ten times a year by Environmental Magazine, P.O. Box 3066, St. Louis, Mo. 63130. Seeks to put environmental information before the public. Excellent in-depth articles on key issues.

Environmental Abstracts, published twice monthly by the Environment Information Center, Inc., 124 East 39th St., New York, N.Y. 10016. Compilation of environmental abstracts; basic bibliographic tool. Too expensive for individual subscription but should be available in your library.

Environmental Action, published monthly by Environmental Action, Inc., Room 731, 1346 Connecticut Ave., N.W., Washington, D.C. 20036. Political orientation. Excellent coverage of environmental issues from legal, political, and social action viewpoints.

Environmental Education Journal, published quarterly by Heldreth Publications, 4000 Albemarle St., N.W., Washington, D.C. 20016. Good for teachers.

Environmental Science & Technology, published monthly by the American Chemical Society, 1155 16th St., N.W., Washington, D.C. 20036. Emphasis on water, air, and solid waste chemistry. Basic reference to keep up-to-date on technological developments.

EPA Journal, published monthly by the Environmental Protection Agency. Order from U.S. Government Printing Office, Washington, D.C. 20402. Broad coverage of environmental issues and updates on EPA activities.

Family Planning Perspectives, published bimonthly by Planned Parenthood-World Population, Editorial Offices, 666 Fifth Ave., New York, N.Y. 10019. Free on request. Usual issue over 50 pages long. Well produced, detailed and informative, wide ranging, liberal attitude. Useful to anyone concerned with population problems.

The Futurist, published bimonthly by the World Future Society, P.O. Box 19285, Twentieth Street Station, Washington, D.C. 20036. Covers wide range of societal problems, including environmental, population, and food issues. A fascinating and readable journal.

Impact of Science on Society, published quarterly by UNESCO, 317 East 34th St., New York, N.Y. 10016. Essays on the social consequences of science and technology.

Journal of the New Alchemists, published by New Alchemy Institute, P.O. Box 432, Woods Hole, Mass. 02543. Articles on appropriate technology, alternative energy, and self-sufficient living alternatives.

Living Wilderness, published quarterly by the Wilderness Society, 1901 Pennsylvania Ave., N.W., Washington, D.C. 20006. Strong statement of "wild areas" viewpoint.

Mother Earth News, published six times per year by Mother Earth News, Inc., P.O. Box 70, Hendersonville, N.C. 28739. Superb articles on organic farming, alternative energy systems, and alternative life-styles.

National Parks and Conservation Magazine, published monthly by National Parks and Conservation Association, 1701 18th St., N.W., Washington, D.C. 20009. Good coverage of parks and wildlife issues.

National Wildlife, published bimonthly by the National Wildlife Federation, 1412 16th St., N.W., Washington, D.C. 20036. Good summaries of issues with wildlife emphasis. Action oriented with a "Washington report."

Natural History, published ten times a year by the American Museum of Natural History, Central Park West at 79th St., New York, N.Y. 10024. Popular; wide school and library circulation. Regularly concerned with environment.

Nature, published weekly by Macmillan Journals, Ltd., Brunel Road, Basingstoke, Hamshire, England. British equivalent to *Science*, enjoys outstanding reputation.

New Scientist, published monthly at 128 Long Acre, London, W.C. 2, England. Excellent general science journal with extensive coverage of environmental issues.

Not Man Apart, monthly publication of Friends of the Earth, 1245 Spear Street, San Francisco, Calif. 94105. Excellent capsule summaries of information and a few in-depth articles on national and international environmental issues.

Organic Gardening & Farming Magazine, published monthly by Rodale Press, Inc., 33 E. Minor St., Emmaus, Pa. 18049. The best guide to organic gardening.

Population and Vital Statistics Report, published quarterly by the United Nations. Available from UN Publications Sales Section, New York, N.Y. 10017. Latest world figures.

Population Bulletin, published bimonthly by the Population Reference Bureau, 1337 Connecticut Ave., N.W., Washington, D.C. 20036. Nontechnical articles on mortality, migration, age structure, fertility rates. Highly recommended.

Population Bulletin, published irregularly by the United Nations. Available from UN Publications Sales Section, New York, N.Y. 10017. Statistical summaries. English and French editions.

Population Crisis, published irregularly by the Population Crisis Committee, Suite 550, 1120 19th St., N.W., Washington, D.C. 20036. Free on request, usual issue 4 pages long.

Rain, published by Rain, 2270 N.W. Irving, Portland, Oreg. 97210. A very comprehensive journal of appropriate technology.

Resources, published three times a year by Resources for the Future, Inc., 1755 Massachusetts Ave., N.W., Washington, D.C. 20036. Free on request; each issue 24 pages long. Devoted to findings and conjectures from recent research into resource development and use.

Science, published weekly by the American Association for the Advancement of Science, 1515 Massachusetts Ave., N.W., Washington, D.C. 20036. A basic resource. Probably the single best source for key environmental articles.

Science for Society—A Bibliography, published annually by the American Association for the Advancement of Science, Education Department, 1515 Massachusetts Avenue, N.W., Washington, D.C. 20005. Bibliography on environment.

*Science News, published weekly by Science Service, Inc., 1719 N St., N.W., Washington, D.C. 20036. Good popular summaries of scientific developments, including environmental topics.

*Scientific American, published monthly at 415 Madison Ave., New York, N.Y. 10017. Outstanding journal for the intelligent citizen who wants to keep up with science. Many general articles on environment and ecology.

*The Sierra Club Bulletin, published monthly by the Sierra Club, 530 Bush St., San Francisco, Calif. 94108. Excellent coverage of a wide range of environmental problems and of citizen action. Beautiful photographs.

*Technology Review, published nine times a year at the Massachusetts Institute of Technology. Address inquiries to *Technology Review*, Room E219–430, M.I.T., Cambridge, Mass. 02139. Not specialized or always technical, but addressed to a sophisticated audience. In recent years has devoted more than half its pages to environmentally related material; also strong on issues of science policy.

UNESCO Courier, published monthly by the United Nations Educational, Scientific, and Cultural Organization in Paris; available from UNESCO Publications Center, 317 East 34th St., New York, N.Y. 10016. A magazine for the general reader; frequently attentive to environmental issues.

*Worldwatch Papers, a series of reports designed to serve as an early warning system on major environmental problems. Published by Worldwatch Institute, 1776 Massachusetts Ave., N.W., Washington, D.C. 20036. Highly recommended.

Environmental Organizations

For a more detailed list of national, state, and local organizations, see *Conservation Directory*, published annually by the National Wildlife Foundation, 1412 16th St., N.W., Washington, D.C. 20036. For a list of world organizations, see Thaddeus C. Trzyna and Eugene V. Coan, eds., *World Directory of Environmental Organizations*, San Francisco: Sequoia Institute, 1976. In the following list, an asterisk indicates that the organization is politicially active.

American Forestry Association, 1319 18th St., N.W., Washington, D.C. 20036. Focuses on forest and soil conservation, although active in air and water pollution concerns. Doesn't lobby directly, but pushes indirectly for preserving and creating parklands. Publishes *American Forests*.

Center for Environmental Education, Inc., 2100 M St., N.W., Washington, D.C. 20037. Dedicated to encouraging informed citizen involvement. Also sponsors the Whale Protection Fund (WPF).

Center for Renewable Resources, 1001 Connecticut Ave., N.W., Washington, D.C. 20036. Offers technical assistance to grassroots organizers, conducts policy research, and provides educational materials.

Center for Science in the Public Interest, 1755 S St., N.W., Washington, D.C. 20009. Group of public interest scientists concerned especially with energy, environmental, food, and nutrition issues. Publishes many informative reports.

Center for the Study of Responsive Law, P.O. Box 19367, Washington, D.C. 20036. A research organization working in the public interest; areas investigated include problems of the environment. Publishes research reports from the Ralph Nader study groups.

Citizens Energy Project, 1110 6th St., N.W., Suite 300, Washington, D.C. 20001. Emphasis on research and education, alternative energy, nuclear power, and appropriate technology.

Clean Water Action Project, 1341 G St., N.W., Suite 200, Washington, D.C. 20005. National citizen action organization advocating strict pollution control and safe drinking water.

*Common Cause, 2030 M St., N.W., Washington, D.C. 20036. One of the most important citizen groups in the country; a citizens' lobby with over 100,000 members who lobby hard on a broad range of political issues. Try to join this group. It is working for you.

The Conservation Foundation, 1717 Massachusetts Ave., N.W., Washington, D.C. 20036. Active in conservation, analysis of the ecological impact of foreign aid, and conservation education in the schools. Publishes *Conservation Foundation Letter*.

*Consumer Action Now, 317 Pennsylvania Ave., S.W., Washington, D.C. 20003. Emphasis on energy conservation, solar energy, and conservation.

Critical Mass Energy Project, 215 Pennsylvania Ave., S.E., Washington, D.C. 20003. Sponsors national conferences on issues such as nuclear energy, alternative energy sources, and legislative and citizen activities; publishes monthly newspaper promoting safe and efficient energy.

Defenders of Wildlife, 1244 19th St., N.W., Washington, D.C. 20036. Tries to preserve all forms of wildlife. Research, education, lobbying.

Ducks Unlimited, P.O. Box 66300, Chicago, Ill. 60666. Has acquired or protected over 2 million acres of vital breeding habitats for migrating waterfowl.

*Environmental Action, Inc., Room 731, 1346 Connecticut Ave.,

N.W., Washington, D.C. 20036. Nonprofit organization that evolved from Earth Day 1970. Lobbies for effective legislation for environmental reform. Publishes *Environmental Action.*

Environmental Defense Fund, Inc., 475 Park Ave. South, New York, N.Y. 10016. A public benefit organization composed of scientists, lawyers, and laypersons; works to link law and science in defense of the environment before courts and regulatory agencies. Other offices at 1525 18th St., N.W., Washington, D.C. 20036; 2606 Dwight Way, Berkeley, Calif. 97404.

The Environmental Law Institute, Suite 620, 1346 Connecticut Ave., N.W., Washington, D.C. 20036. The institute, a joint project of the Conservation Foundation and the Public Law Education Institute, conducts a wide program of research and education in environmental law.

*Environmental Policy Center, 317 Pennsylvania Ave., S.E., Washington, D.C. 20003. Lobbying for water policy and all aspects of energy development.

*Friends of the Earth, 318 Massachusetts Ave., N.E., Washington, D.C. 20002. Vigorous membership lobbying group that has also brought lawsuits. Active on a variety of issues. Monthly newspaper. Its political arm, the League of Conservation Voters, raises funds for congressional candidates who have a sound environmental record.

The Fund for Animals, Inc., 1765 P St., N.W., Washington, D.C. 20036. Dedicated to preserving wildlife and promoting humane treatment of animals.

Institute for Local Self-Reliance, 1717 18th St., N.W., Washington, D.C. 20009. Research and education; promotion of appropriate technology for communities.

The Izaak Walton League of America, 1800 North Kent St., Suite 806, Arlington, Va. 22209. A membership organization with local chapters and state divisions. Promotes conservation and wise use of renewable natural resources and development and protection of high-quality outdoor recreation opportunities. Monthly magazine.

John Muir Institute for Environmental Studies, 743 Wilson St., Napa, Calif. 94558. Purpose is environmental research and education.

Keep America Beautiful, 99 Park Ave., New York, N.Y. 10016. National public service organization. Conducts a public education program to combat litter as a necessary first step toward solving broader environmental problems and a program to increase knowledge of solid waste disposal techniques. Organization provides assistance, materials, and advice for grass roots efforts by some 7,000 community groups and 32 statewide affiliates.

*League of Conservation Voters, 317 Pennsylvania Ave., S.E., Washington, D.C. 20003. This nonpartisan organization is a national campaign committee working to promote the

election of legislators pledging to seek a healthy environment. Publicizes roll call votes on environmental issues. Political arm of Friends of the Earth.

*League of Women Voters of the United States, 1730 M St., N.W., Washington, D.C. 20036. An outstanding membership organization with local and state leagues working for political responsibility through an informed and active citizenry. Played a central role in bringing water pollution to the public's attention. Publications on political and environmental issues. Research and education by the League of Women Voters Education Fund (same address).

National Audubon Society, 950 Third Ave., New York, N.Y. 10022; and 1511 K Street, N.W., Washington, D.C. 20005. Research and lobbying. Operates 40 wildlife sanctuaries across the country and provides a wide variety of ecology education services. Publishes *Audubon* and *Audubon Field Notes.*

National Parks and Conservation Association, 1701 18th Street, N.W., Washington, D.C. 20009. Research and lobbying. Urges acquisition and protection of public parklands. Now active in general environmental issues, such as resource management, pesticides, and pollution. Led coalition against Everglades jetport. Publishes *National Parks and Conservation Magazine.*

National Recreation and Park Association, 1601 N. Kent St., Arlington, Va. 22209. A membership organization active in recreation and park development, conservation, and beautification. Publishes helpful booklets and a monthly magazine, *Parks and Recreation.*

National Wildlife Federation, 1412 16th St., N.W., Washington, D.C. 20036. Research and education. Encourages citizen and governmental action for conservation. Publishes *National Wildlife* and a comprehensive annual conservation directory.

Natural Resources Defense Council, Inc., 122 East 42nd St., New York, N.Y. 10017; and 1725 I St., N.W., Suite 600, Washington, D.C. 20006. Dedicated to protecting America's natural resources and improving environmental quality.

The Nature Conservancy, Suite 800, 1800 N. Kent St., Arlington, Va. 22209. A membership organization with state chapters seeking to preserve natural areas. Often acquires endangered property and holds it for later resale to public agencies.

People's Business Commission, Suite 1010, 1346 Connecticut Ave., Washington, D.C. 20036. Research and education on energy, economics, and health policies.

Population Crisis Committee, Suite 550, 1120 19th St., N.W., Washington, D.C. 20036. Promotes public understanding and action on the world population crisis. Publishes *Population Crisis.*

Population Reference Bureau, 1337 Connecticut Ave., N.W.,

Washington, D.C. 20036. Clearinghouse for data concerning the effects of the worldwide population explosion. Publishes *Population Bulletin*.

The Public Citizen, 1346 Connecticut Ave., N.W., Washington, D.C. 20036. Ralph Nader's political action and lobbying organization.

Public Interest Research Group, P.O. Box 19312, Washington, D.C. 20036. Organizes research and education in environmental issues.

Resources for the Future, 1775 Massachusetts Ave., N.W., Washington, D.C. 20036. Conducts programs of research and education in the development, conservation, and use of natural resources and on the quality of the environment through its own staff and through grants to other institutions. Publishes *Resources*.

Scientists' Institute for Public Information, 355 Lexington Ave., New York, N.Y. 10017; and 1256 National Press Building, Washington, D.C. 20045. Utilizes scientists of all disciplines in public information programs dealing with many social issues, and serves as national coordinating body for local scientific information committees.

*Sierra Club, 530 Bush St., San Francisco, California 94108; and 330 Pennsylvania Avenue, S.E., Washington, D.C. 20003. Membership group devoted to protecting the nation's scenic resources. Provides films, manuals, exhibits, and speakers; publishes books and a monthly bulletin. Sierra Club's Washington Office is an effective lobbying operation.

Solar Lobby, 1028 Connecticut Ave., N.W., Washington, D.C. 20036. Lobbying for solar energy.

Union of Concerned Scientists, 1025 15th St., N.W., Washington, D.C. 20005 and 1384 Massachusetts Ave., N.W., Cambridge, Mass. 02238. Lobbying, research, and education with special emphasis on nuclear power safety.

The Wilderness Society, 1901 Pennsylvania Ave., N.W., Washington, D.C. 20006. A large membership organization, its main goal is protection of wild lands and acquisition of additional wilderness and primitive areas by the federal government. Played a leading role in opposing oil development in the Alaskan Arctic. Publishes *Living Wilderness*.

Wildlife Society, Suite 611, 7101 Wisconsin Ave., N.W., Washington, D.C. 20014. Major concern is wildlife preservation, but its base is broadening.

Worldwatch Institute, 1776 Massachusetts Ave., N.W., Washington, D.C. 20036. Research, early warning, and education on major environmental problems. Publishes several *Worldwatch Papers* each year.

World Wildlife Fund, 1319 18th St., N.W., Washington, D.C. 20036. Research and education on endangered species. Habitat acquisition.

*Zero Population Growth, 1346 Connecticut Ave., N.W., Washington, D.C. 20036. Primary emphasis is on family planning, population stabilization, and voluntary sterilization, but is expanding its concern. Has local chapters and a correspondence group that monitors the media and directs letters to advertisers and others. Active lobbying group based in Washington.

Addresses of U.S. Government Agencies

Bureau of Land Management
Interior Building, Room 5660
Washington, D.C. 20240

Bureau of Mines
2401 E St., N.W.
Washington, D.C. 20241

Bureau of Outdoor Recreation
Interior Building, Room 4410
Washington, D.C. 20240

Bureau of Reclamation
Interior Building, Room 7654
Washington, D.C. 20240

Council on Environmental Quality
722 Jackson Place, N.W.
Washington, D.C. 20006

Department of Agriculture
Washington, D.C. 20250

Department of Energy
Washington, D.C. 20545

Department of the Interior
Interior Building
Washington, D.C. 20240

Department of Transportation
400 7th St., S.W.
Washington, D.C. 20590

Environmental Protection Agency
401 M St., S.W.
Washington, D.C. 20460

Federal Power Commission
825 N. Capitol St., N.E.
Washington, D.C. 20426

Fish and Wildlife Service
Department of the Interior
18th & C Sts., N.W.
Washington, D.C. 20240

Food and Drug Administration
Department of Health and Human Services
5600 Fishers Lane
Rockville, Md. 20852

Forest Service
500 12th St., S.W.
Washington, D.C. 20250

Geological Survey
Reston, Va. 22092

Government Printing Office
Washington, D.C. 20402

National Academy of Sciences
2101 Constitution Ave., N.W.
Washington, D.C. 20418

National Center for Appropriate Technology
P.O. Box 3838
Butte, Mont. 59701

National Oceanic and Atmospheric Administration
14th and Constitution Ave., N.W.
Washington, D.C. 20235

National Park Service
Department of the Interior
Washington, D.C. 20240

National Solar Heating and Cooling Information Center
P.O. Box 1607
Rockville, Md. 20850
[Call toll free for information on solar energy: (800) 523-2929 anywhere in the United States except Pennsylvania; (800) 462-4983 in Pennsylvania.]

National Technical Information Service (NTIS)
Department of Commerce
5285 Port Royal Rd.
Springfield, Va. 22161
(Sells publications of government-sponsored research.)

Nuclear Regulatory Commission
1717 H St., N.W.
Washington, D.C. 20555

Solar Energy Research Institute (SERI)
6536 Cole Blvd.
Golden, Colo. 80401

Water Resources Council
2120 L St., N.W.
Washington, D.C. 20423

Glossary

Abiotic   nonliving.

Abortion   expulsion or extraction of a fetus from the womb before the twentieth week of pregnancy.

Abyssal zone   bottom zone of the ocean. Compare *bathyal zone, euphotic zone.*

Acid rain   rain and snow that becomes acidic primarily by the formation of weak solutions of sulfuric acid (H_2SO_4) and nitric acid (HNO_3) when the water vapor in the air reacts with the air pollutants sulfur dioxide (SO_2) and nitrogen dioxide (NO_2).

Acute disease   an infectious disease (such as measles, whooping cough, typhoid fever) that normally lasts for a relatively short time before the victim either recovers or dies.

Aerobic organism   organism that requires oxygen to live.

Aerosols   liquid and solid particles suspended in air.

Age-sex pyramid   a horizontal bar graph comparing the proportions of males and females in different age groups in the population.

Age-specific birth rate   number of live births to women in a specific age group (such as 25–29) per 1,000 females in that age group at midyear.

Age-specific death rate   number of deaths in a specific age group per 1,000 individuals in that age group at midyear.

Age structure (age distribution)   number or percentage of persons at each age level in a population.

Agricultural waste   waste material produced from the raising of plants and animals for food. These materials include manure, plant stalks, hulls, leaves, and fertilizer runoff.

Air pollution   air that contains one or more chemicals in high enough concentrations to harm humans, other animals, vegetation, or materials.

Air quality criterion   amount of air pollution and length of exposure at which a specific adverse effect to health or welfare takes place.

Air quality standard   prescribed level of a pollutant in the outside air that should not be exceeded during a specified time in a specified geographic area.

Airshed   a region that shares a common air supply. Because of the nature of air, an airshed is not a precise physical division like a watershed but a political convenience for dealing with air problems that cross municipal and state lines.

Albedo   fraction of the incident light that strikes a surface or body that is reflected from it. A measure of the reflectivity of the earth and its atmosphere.

Alga (algae)   simple one-celled or many-celled plant, usually aquatic, capable of carrying on photosynthesis.

Algae bloom   population explosion of algae in surface waters.

Alpha particle   form of radiation consisting of a helium nucleus containing two protons and two neutrons and no electrons outside the nucleus.

Alveoli   tiny sacs at the end of the bronchiole tubes in the lungs, numbering in the hundreds of millions. Oxygen in the air passes through their walls to combine with hemoglobin in the blood, and carbon dioxide passes from the blood back through the alveoli walls for exhaling.

Ambient air   surrounding outdoor air.

Ambient quality standard   maximum level of a specific pollutant allowed in the air, water, soil, or food. May vary from region to region depending on conditions. Compare *emission standard.*

Amino acids   basic building block molecules of proteins. Each different type of protein molecule consists of a long chain of certain amino acid molecules held together by chemical bonds.

Anaerobic organism   organism that does not require oxygen to live.

Animal feedlot   confined area where hundreds or thousands of livestock animals are fattened for sale to slaughterhouses and meat processors.

Appropriate (soft) technology   technology that is small, simple, decentralized, inexpensive, and people centered. It conserves matter and energy resources and produces as little pollution as possible. See Table 1-5. Compare *high (hard) technology.*

Aquaculture   deliberate growing and harvesting of fish and shellfish in land-based ponds.

Aquifer   permeable layers of underground rock or sand that hold or transmit groundwater.

Area strip mining   surface mining by cutting deep trenches. Used on flat or rolling terrain.

Arithmetic population density   the average number of people per square kilometer or other unit of area based on the total land area of the portion of the world under consideration.

Artesian well   a water well drilled into a pressurized aquifer where the hydraulic pressure is so great that the water flows freely out of the well without pumping.

Asthma   see *Bronchial asthma.*

Atmosphere   the gaseous envelope of air surrounding the earth.

Atoms   extremely small particles that are the basic building blocks of all matter.

Attractant   sound, light, or sex lure used in pest control to confuse pests so they can't find mates or to draw them into traps containing toxic chemicals.

Autotrophic organism   an organism that uses solar energy to photosynthesize organic food substances and other organic chemicals from carbon dioxide and water. Compare *heterotrophic organism*.

Background radiation   radiation in the environment from naturally radioactive materials and from cosmic rays entering the atmosphere.

Bacteria   smallest living organisms; with fungi, they comprise the decomposer level of the food chain.

Bathyal zone   middle or open-water zone in an ocean below the level of light penetration. Compare *abyssal zone, euphotic zone*.

Benzo(α)pyrene (or 3,4-benzopyrene)   aromatic hydrocarbon, which under certain circumstances has produced cancer in test animals.

Beta particle   swiftly moving electron emitted by a radioactive substance. Strontium-90 and carbon-14 emit beta particles.

Biochemical oxygen demand (BOD)   amount of oxygen dissolved in water needed by microorganisms to break down organic waste matter in water.

Biocide   any agent that kills living organisms.

Biodegradable   capable of being broken down by bacteria into basic elements and compounds. Most organic wastes and paper are biodegradable.

Biofuels   gas or liquid fuels (such as ethyl alcohol) made from biomass (plants and trees).

Biogas   a mixture of methane (CH_4) and carbon dioxide (CO_2) gases produced when anaerobic bacteria break down plants and organic waste (such as manure).

Biogeochemical cycles   mechanisms by which chemicals such as carbon, oxygen, phosphorus, nitrogen, and water are moved through the ecosphere to be renewed over and over again. The three major types are gaseous, sedimentary, and hydrologic.

Biological control   pest control that uses natural predators, parasites, or disease-causing bacteria and viruses (pathogens).

Biological extermination   biological extinction of a species that is caused or hastened by human activities.

Biological extinction   complete disappearance of a species because of failure to adapt to environmental change.

Biological half-life   time required for half

the amount of a substance (such as a drug or radioactive tracer) in a living organism to be eliminated, whether by excretion, metabolic decomposition, or other natural process.

Biological magnification   buildup in concentration of some substance, such as DDT or some radioactive isotopes, in successively higher trophic levels of the food chain or web.

Biological methylation   conversion of elemental mercury and inorganic mercury salts into highly toxic methyl mercury by microorganisms. Term can also be applied to other metals that undergo similar reactions.

Biomass   total dry weight of all living organisms that can be supported at each trophic level in a food chain; total dry weight of all living organisms in a given area; plant and animal matter that can be used in any form as a source of energy.

Biome   a large terrestrial ecosystem characterized by distinctive types of plants and animals and maintained under the climatic conditions of the region.

Biosphere   see *ecosphere*.

Biota   all living organisms, both plant and animal, of a region or period.

Biotic   living.

Biotic (reproductive) potential   the maximum rate at which a population can reproduce with unlimited resources and ideal environmental conditions.

Birth control (fertility control)   all methods of conception control plus abortion.

Blue-green algae   type of tiny, floating green plants that often causes surface waters to appear like pea soup. See *alga*.

Brackish water   form of saline water typically found inland that contains 1,000 to 4,000 ppm of dissolved solids. See *saline water, salted water, seawater*.

Breeder reactor   nuclear reactor that produces more nuclear fuel than it consumes by converting nonfissionable uranium-238 into fissionable plutonium-239.

Broad-spectrum pesticide   chemical that kills more than the target species.

Bronchial asthma   a respiratory disease characterized by a narrowing of the bronchial passages and excessive mucus secretion that obstructs the flow of air to the lungs. This brings about recurrent episodes of shortness of breath, prolonged coughing, and difficulty in breathing.

Bronchiole tubes   tiny ducts or tubes that are subdivisions of the main bronchus tubes and that lead to the alveoli.

Bronchus   one of the two large tubes entering the lungs, which divide and subdivide into the bronchiole tubes and eventually lead to the alveoli.

Brown air city   popular name for a photochemical smog city, such as Los Angeles, Tokyo, Sydney, Mexico City, or Buenos Aires. Typically a young, automobile-dominated city in a dry climate where a major pollutant is yellow brown nitrogen dioxide (NO_2), formed from internal combustion engine exhaust.

Calorie   amount of energy required to raise the temperature of 1 gram of water 1°C.

Cancer   a group of more than 100 different diseases that strike people of all ages and races; characterized by uncontrolled growth of cells in body tissue.

Carbamates   major chemical group of nerve poison pesticides, including Sevin, Zireb, and others.

Carbon monoxide (CO)   gaseous molecule containing one atom of carbon and one atom of oxygen formed by the incomplete combustion of fossil fuels, especially in the internal combustion engine.

Carcinogen   a chemical or form of radiation (energy) that either directly or indirectly causes a form of cancer.

Carnivore   meat-eating organism.

Carrying capacity   maximum population that a given ecosystem can support indefinitely under a given set of environmental conditions.

Chemical cycles   see *biogeochemical cycles*.

Chlorinated hydrocarbon insecticides   synthetic, organic nervous system poisons containing chlorine, hydrogen, and carbon. Highly stable and fat soluble, they tend to be recycled through food chains, thereby affecting nontarget organisms. Members include DDT, aldrin, dieldrin, endrin, chlordane, heptachlor, toxaphene, and BHC.

Chronic bronchitis   disease characterized by inflammation of the bronchial passages, excessive secretions of mucus, and recurrent coughing. It appears to be aggravated by air pollution, particularly sulfur oxides.

Chronic disease   disease that lasts for a long time (often for life) and that (1) may flare up periodically (malaria), (2) become progressively worse (cancer), or (3) disappear with advancing age (childhood asthma). Chronic diseases may be infectious (malaria, tuberculosis) or noninfectious (cardiovascular disorders, diabetes, hay fever).

Cilia tiny hairs lining the lungs that continually undulate and sweep foreign matter out of the lungs.

Clear-cutting removing all trees from an area.

Climate the average of daily atmospheric conditions (weather) over a relatively long period of time.

Climax ecosystem (climax community) a relatively stable stage of ecological succession; a mature ecosystem with a diverse array of species and ecological niches, capable of using energy and cycling critical chemicals more efficiently than simpler, immature ecosystems.

Climax species species that dominates an ecosystem, usually at a mature stage of ecological succession.

Closed system system in which energy but not matter is exchanged between the system and its environment. For all practical purposes, the earth is a closed system. Compare *isolated system, open system.*

Coal a solid, combustible organic material containing 55 to 90 percent carbon mixed with small amounts of hydrogen, oxygen, nitrogen, and sulfur compounds.

Coal gasification a process in which solid coal is converted to either low-heat-content industrial gas or high-heat-content synthetic natural gas (SNG).

Coal liquefaction a process in which solid coal is converted to synthetic crude oil by the addition of hydrogen (hydrogenation).

Coastal wetlands shallow shelves that are normally wet or flooded and that extend back from the freshwater-saltwater interface. They consist of a complex maze of marshes, bays, lagoons, tidal flats, and mangrove swamps.

Cogeneration the production of two useful forms of energy from the same process. For example, in a factory steam produced for industrial processes or space heating is first run through turbines to generate electricity, which can be used by the industry or sold to power companies.

Coitus interruptus withdrawal of penis in sexual intercourse before ejaculation.

Combustion burning. Any very rapid chemical reaction in which heat and light are produced.

Commensalism a symbiotic relationship between two different species in which one species benefits from the association while the other is apparently neither helped nor harmed. See *mutualism, parasitism, symbiosis.*

Commons natural resources, especially land, reserved for common use. Many experts in environmental law also treat rivers, lakes, oceans, and the atmosphere as commons.

Community (natural) group of plant and animal populations living and interacting in a given locality.

Competition two or more species in the same ecosystem attempting to use the same scarce resources.

Composting breakdown of organic matter in solid waste in the presence of oxygen by aerobic (oxygen-needing) bacteria to produce a humuslike end product, which can be used as a soil conditioner.

Concentration amount of a chemical or pollutant in a particular volume or weight of air, water, soil, or other medium.

Condom thin sheath of rubber or animal skin worn tightly over the penis to mechanically prevent sperm from entering vagina.

Conservation of genetic information preservation of most or perhaps all species of life in at least some of their natural habitats since they might prove essential to human or other forms of life.

Consumer organism that lives off other organisms. Generally divided into primary consumers (herbivores), secondary consumers (carnivores), and microconsumers (decomposers).

Consumptive use water lost to the air by evaporation and transpiration after being drawn from a lake, river, or reservoir for use by humans. Compare *degrading use, net use, withdrawal use.*

Contour strip mining surface mining by cutting out a series of contour bands on the side of a hill or mountain. Used primarily for coal. Usually the most destructive form of strip mining.

Control rods neutron-absorbing rods that are raised or lowered in the core of a nuclear reactor to control the rate of nuclear fission.

Cooling tower large tower used to transfer the heat in cooling water from a power or industrial plant to the atmosphere either by direct evaporation (wet, or evaporative, cooling tower) or by convection and conduction (dry cooling tower).

Cost-benefit analysis an attempt to compare the costs of pollution control or some other project with the costs of pollution damage (dollar and otherwise) from an activity or project in an attempt to minimize the total costs and still reduce harmful environmental effects to an acceptable level.

Critically endangered species a species that will become biologically extinct without direct human intervention and protection.

Crude birth rate number of live births per 1,000 persons in the population at the midpoint of a given year.

Crude death rate number of deaths per 1,000 persons in the population at the midpoint of a given year.

Crude migration rate difference between the number of people leaving and the number entering a given country or area per 1,000 persons in its population at midyear.

Cultural eutrophication overnourishment of aquatic ecosystems with plant nutrients due to human activities such as agriculture, urbanization, and industrial discharge. See *eutrophication.*

Cybernetic system see *homeostatic (cybernetic) system.*

DDT *d*ichloro*d*iphenyl*t*richloroethane, a chlorinated hydrocarbon that has been widely used as a pesticide.

Decibel (db) unit used to measure either sound power or sound pressure.

Deciduous trees trees that lose their leaves during part of the year.

Decomposer bacterium or fungus that causes the chemical disintegration (rot or decay) of organic matter.

Deep-well injection disposal of liquid wastes by pumping them under pressure into underground cavities and pore spaces.

Defoliation stripping of leaves from plants, especially by use of chemical sprays.

Degradable pollutant pollutant that can be decomposed, removed, or consumed and thus reduced to an acceptable level either by natural processes or by human-engineered processes. Those that are broken down rapidly are called rapidly degraded, or nonpersistent, pollutants, and those broken down slowly are called slowly degradable, or persistent, pollutants. Compare *nondegradable pollutant.*

Degrading use water contaminated by dissolved salts, other chemicals, or heat before it is returned to the hydrological cycle. Compare *consumptive use, net use, withdrawal use.*

Demographic transition the transition from a condition of high birth and death rates to substantially lower birth and death rates for a given country or region. Supposedly it is brought about by economic development.

Demography science of vital and social statistics of populations, such as births, deaths, diseases, and marriages.

Dependency load ratio of the number of old and young dependents in a population to the work force.

Depletion curve plot of the supply and production rate of a nonrenewable resource as a function of time. Used to predict when the supply might run out or become scarce. See also *depletion time.*

Depletion time the time required to use up a certain fraction (usually 80 percent) of the known or estimated supply of a resource according to various assumed rates of use. See also *depletion curve.*

Desalination purification of salt or brackish water by removing the dissolved salts.

Detergent synthetic, organic, liquid, or water-soluble cleaning agent that has wetting-agent and emulsifying-agent properties. Unlike soap, detergents are not manufactured from fats and oils.

Detritus food chain transfer of energy from one trophic level to another by decomposers. Compare *grazing food chain.*

Deuterium (hydrogen-2) isotope of the element hydrogen with a nucleus containing one proton and one neutron, thus having a mass number of 2. Compare *tritium.*

Developed nation see *more developed nation.*

Developing nation see *less developed nation.*

Diaphragm flexible, hemispherical rubber dome inserted into the vagina to fit over the cervix during intercourse to prevent conception.

Dieback see *population crash.*

Dilation and curettage (D & C) method of abortion by surgically widening the cervix and then scraping the embryo and placenta from walls of the uterus.

Disinfection sewage treatment to remove water coloration and to kill disease-carrying bacteria and some (but not all) viruses.

Dissolved oxygen (DO) extent to which oxygen occurs dissolved in water or wastewater. It is usually expressed as a concentration in parts per million or as a percentage of saturation.

Diversity physical or biological complexity of a system. In many cases it leads to ecosystem stability.

Doubling time number of years it takes for a population to double in size.

Douche flushing the vagina with a liquid; ineffective as a method of contraception.

Dredging surface mining of seabeds, primarily for sand and gravel.

Dry steam steam that is so hot that no water droplets are mixed with it.

Dynamic equilibrium state state in a closed system that is maintained in balance by the dynamic flow of energy through the system and the cycling of critical chemicals within the system.

Dynamic steady state dynamic state of an open system where the input and output of matter and energy of the system are balanced by a steady flow. Any living organism can be described as an open system in a dynamic steady state.

Ecological backlash unexpected and often undesirable side effects from changing or stressing an ecosystem.

Ecological efficiency (food chain efficiency) the percent transfer of useful energy from one trophic level to another in a food chain.

Ecological equivalents species that occupy the same or similar ecological niches in similar ecosystems located in different parts of the world. For example, cattle in North America and kangaroos in Australia are both grassland grazers.

Ecological niche description of a species' total structural and functional role in an ecosystem.

Ecological succession change in the structure and function of an ecosystem; replacement of one kind of community of organisms with a different community over a period of time. See *primary succession, secondary succession.*

Ecology study of the relationships of living organisms with each other and with their environment; study of the structure and function of nature.

Economic growth rate of increase of an economy's real output or income over time. Frequently expressed as total or per capita GNP over a period of time.

Economics the study of principles and customs that affect the production, consumption, growth, and distribution of material wealth for human needs.

Ecosphere (biosphere) total of all the various ecosystems on the planet along with their interactions. The sphere of air, water, and land in which all life is found.

Ecosphere share concept that each human being is automatically entitled to a basic share of the world's resources in the form of basic food, shelter, and clothing.

Ecosystem self-sustaining and self-regulating community of organisms interacting with one another and with their environment.

Efficiency see *first law energy efficiency* and *second law energy efficiency.*

Effluent any substance, particularly a liquid, that enters the environment from a point source. Generally refers to wastewater from a sewage treatment or industrial plant.

Effluent charge fee levied by a public agency on a producer of waste for each unit of waste discharged.

Electromagnetic energy energy that can move through a vacuum in the form of waves (such as visible light).

Electromagnetic spectrum span of energy ranging from high-energy gamma waves to the low-energy radio waves.

Electron fundamental particle found moving around somewhere outside the nucleus of an atom. Each electron has one unit of negative charge (-1) and has extremely little mass.

Electrostatic precipitator device for removing particulates from smokestack emissions by causing the particles to become electrostatically charged and then attracting them to an oppositely charged plate, where they are precipitated out of the air.

Emergency core cooling system (ECCS) system designed to flood the core of a nuclear reactor instantaneously with large amounts of water to prevent meltdown if the core overheats.

Emigration the process of leaving one country to take up permanent residence in another.

Emission standard maximum amount of a

pollutant that is permitted to be discharged from a single polluting source.

Emissivity   total amount of degraded heat energy flowing from the earth back into space.

Emphysema   see *pulmonary emphysema.*

Endangered species   species in immediate danger of biological extinction or extermination.

Energy   ability or capacity to do work or produce a change by pushing or pulling some form of matter.

Energy crisis   a shortage or catastrophic price rise for one or more forms of useful energy or a situation in which energy use is so great that the resultant pollution and environmental degradation threaten human health and welfare.

Energy flow   in ecology, the one-way transfer of energy through an ecosystem; more specifically, the way in which energy is converted and expended at each trophic level.

Energy pyramid   figure representing the loss or degradation of useful energy at each step in a food chain. About 80 to 90 percent of the energy in each transfer is lost as waste heat, and the resulting shape of the energy levels is that of a pyramid.

Energy quality   ability of a form of energy to do useful work. High-quality energy (such as high-temperature heat, fossil fuels, and nuclear fuel) is concentrated, whereas low-quality energy (such as low-temperature heat) is dispersed or diluted.

Entropy   measure of disorder or energy not available for useful work.

Environment   aggregate of external conditions that influence the life of an individual organism or population.

Environmental resistance   limiting factors that tend to regulate the maximum allowable size, or carrying capacity, of a population.

EPA   Environmental Protection Agency, the agency responsible for federal efforts to control air and water pollution, radiation and pesticide hazards, ecological research, and solid wastes disposal.

Epilimnion   warm, less dense top layer in a stratified lake. Compare *hypolimnion, thermocline.*

Essential amino acid   one of the eight (nine for children) chemical building blocks for proteins that cannot be made in the human body and must be included in the diet for good health.

Estuarine zone   area near the coastline that consists of estuaries and coastal saltwater wetlands.

Estuary   area in which the sea and a river valley meet and in which tidal ebb and flow rhythmically counter the usual flow of water from the mouth of a river into the sea.

Euphotic zone   surface layer of an ocean, lake, or other body of water through which light can penetrate; thus, the zone of photosynthesis. Compare *abyssal zone, bathyal zone.*

Eutrophic lake   a lake with a large or excessive supply of plant nutrients (nitrates and phosphates).

Eutrophication (natural)   an excess of plant nutrients in an aquatic ecosystem supporting a large amount of aquatic life that can deplete the oxygen supply. See also *cultural eutrophication.*

Evapotranspiration   combination of evaporation and transpiration of water into the atmosphere from living plants and soil.

Evolution   the process by which a population of a species changes its characteristics (genetic makeup) over the course of time.

Exponential growth   geometric growth by doubling; yields a J curve.

Exponential reserve index   estimated number of years until known world reserves of a nonrenewable resource will be 80 percent depleted if consumed at a rate increasing by a given percentage each year. Compare *static reserve index.*

External combustion engine   engine (for example, the steam engine) in which combustion occurs outside the cylinder or cylinders.

External cost   cost of production or consumption that must be borne by society and not by the producer.

Externality   external cost or benefit.

Extinction   see *biological extermination, biological extinction.*

Extrinsic limiting factor   factor that can regulate population growth and size by operating from outside a population. Examples are food supply, climate, and disease. Compare *intrinsic limiting factor.*

Family planning   voluntary planning and action by individuals to have the number of children they want, when and if they want them.

Fauna   animal populations of a region.

Feedback   signal sent back into a self-regulating, or homeostatic, system so that the system will respond.

Feedback loop   return to the input of part of the output of a homeostatic system, which is then processed by the system.

Fermentation (anaerobic)   process in which carbohydrates are converted in the absence of oxygen to hydrocarbons (such as methane).

Fertile isotopes   isotopes of elements that can be converted by the absorption of fast-moving neutrons into isotopes that will undergo nuclear fission.

Fertilizer   substance that makes the land or soil capable of producing more vegetation or crops.

First energy law   see *first law of thermodynamics.*

First law energy efficiency   the ratio of the useful work or energy output of a device to the work or energy input that must be supplied to get the output. This ratio is normally multiplied by 100 so that the efficiency can be expressed as a percentage.

$$\text{first law energy efficiency (\%)} = \frac{\text{useful work or energy (or work) output}}{\text{energy (or work) input}} \times 100$$

First law of thermodynamics (energy)   in any ordinary chemical or physical change, energy is neither created nor destroyed, but merely changed from one form to another. You can't get something for nothing, you can only break even, or there is no such thing as a free lunch.

Fissionable isotopes   isotopes of elements that are capable of undergoing nuclear fission.

Floodplain   land next to a river that becomes covered by water when the river overflows its banks.

Flora   plant population of a region.

Fluidized-bed combustion   using a flowing stream of hot air to suspend a mixture of powdered coal and limestone so that the coal burns more efficiently. In addition, the limestone removes about 90 to 95 percent of the sulfur in the coal.

Fly ash   small, solid particles of ash and soot generated when coal, oil, or waste materials are burned.

Food additive   a chemical deliberately added

to a food, usually to enhance its color, flavor, shelf life, or nutritional characteristics.

Food chain sequence of transfers of energy in the form of food from organisms in one trophic level to those in another when one organism eats or decomposes another. See *detritus food chain, grazing food chain*.

Food contaminant a chemical, such as a pesticide, which inadvertently gains entry to food from the environment.

Food web complex, interlocking series of food chains.

Fossil fuel remains of dead plants and animals of a previous geologic area that can be burned to release energy. Examples are coal, crude oil, and natural gas.

Freons chlorofluorocarbon compounds composed of atoms of carbon, chlorine, and fluorine.

Fuel any substance that can be burned, be fissioned in a chain reaction, or undergo nuclear fusion to produce heat.

Fuel rod metal rod containing fissionable isotopes that is inserted into the core of a nuclear reactor.

Fungicide substance or mixture of substances intended to prevent or kill fungi.

Fungus simple or complex organism without chlorophyll. The simpler forms are one-celled; the higher forms have branched filaments and complicated life cycles. Examples are molds, yeasts, and mushrooms.

Gamma rays high-energy electromagnetic waves with very short wavelengths, produced during the disintegration of some radioactive elements. Like X rays, they readily penetrate body tissues.

Gaseous cycle biogeochemical cycle with the atmosphere as the primary reservoir. Examples include the oxygen and nitrogen cycles.

Gasohol vehicle fuel consisting of a mixture of gasoline and ethyl or methyl alcohol (usually contains 10 to 20 percent alcohol by volume).

Gene pool total genetic information possessed by a given reproducing population.

General fertility rate average number of live births per 1,000 women in the reproductive age group (ages 15 to 44 in the United States and 15 to 49 in most nations).

Genetic control see *sterile male technique*.

Genetic damage damage by radiation or chemicals to reproductive cells, resulting in mutations that can be passed on to future generations in the form of fetal and infant deaths and physical and mental deformities.

Genocide deliberate extermination of all members of a race or nation.

Geometric growth see *exponential growth*.

Geothermal energy heat energy produced when rocks lying below the earth's surface are heated to high temperature by energy from the decay of radioactive elements in the earth and from magma.

Gonococcus bacterium that causes gonorrhea.

Gonorrhea disease caused by gonococcus and transmitted by sexual contact.

Gray air city popular name for an older industrial smog city, such as London, Chicago, Baltimore, Birmingham, Philadelphia, or Pittsburgh, that depends heavily on burning coal and oil. Major pollutants are particulates and sulfur oxides that produce a gray haze.

Grazing food chain transfer of energy in the form of food from one organism to another when green plants (producers) are eaten by plant eaters (herbivores), which in turn may be eaten by meat eaters (carnivores). Compare *detritus food chain*.

Green revolution popular term for the greatly increased yield resulting from the introduction of new, scientifically bred or selected varieties of a grain (rice, wheat, maize) which with high enough inputs of fertilizer and water can give increased yields per area of land planted.

Greenhouse effect trapping of heat in the atmosphere. Incoming short-wavelength solar radiation penetrates the atmosphere, but the longer-wavelength outgoing radiation is absorbed by water vapor, carbon dioxide, and ozone in the atmosphere and reradiated to earth, causing a rise in atmospheric temperature.

Gross national product (GNP) total market value of all goods and services produced in a definite area (usually a nation) during a specific time period (usually a year).

Gross national quality (GNQ) gross national product (GNP) minus the negative (harmful) products and services. Should be a measure of those items that contribute to the quality of life.

Gross primary productivity total rate at which green plants convert solar energy by photosynthesis into chemical energy or biomass. See also *net primary productivity*.

Groundwater water beneath the surface of the ground that is in a saturated zone.

Growth rate (population) percentage of increase or decrease of a population. It is the number of births minus the number of deaths per 1,000 population, plus net migration, expressed as a percentage.

Habitat place where an organism or community of organisms naturally lives or grows.

Half-life length of time taken for one-half the atoms in a given amount of a radioactive substance to decay into another isotope. The definition has been extended to refer to biological half-life, or the length of time it takes for half of any substance in a biological system (such as mercury in the brain) to be broken down or excreted.

Hardness condition of water caused by dissolved salts of calcium, magnesium, and iron, such as bicarbonates, carbonates, sulfates, chlorides, and nitrates.

Heat form of kinetic energy that flows from one body to another as a result of a temperature difference between the two bodies.

Heat island horizontal pocket of relatively warm air surrounded by cooler air. Often found over city centers and industrial complexes.

Heat pump device that uses mechanical or electrical energy to transfer heat from a cooler region to a warmer one or vice versa. Heat pumps work on the same principle as do air conditioners and refrigerators.

Heavy metals group of metallic elements with relatively high atomic weights, such as mercury, iron, cobalt, cadmium, lead, nickel, zinc, and a number of others.

Heavy oil (bitumen) a black, high sulfur, tarlike oil found mixed with clay, sand, and water in swampy deposits of tar sands.

Heavy water water (D_2O) in which all of the hydrogen atoms have been replaced by deuterium (D).

Herbicide chemical that injures or kills plant life by interfering with normal growth.

Herbivore plant-eating organism.

Heterotrophic organism organism that cannot manufacture its own food and must consume organic food compounds found in other plants and animals. Compare *autotrophic organism*.

High (hard) technology   technology that is complex, centralized, expensive, and machine centered and that sometimes wastes matter and energy resources and produces large amounts of pollution. See Table 1-5. Compare *appropriate (soft) technology*.

Holistic   view that nature can be understood only by looking at it as a general complex system of parts and wholes.

Homeostatic plateau   maintenance of some constant value or steady state in a homeostatic system, for example, the maintenance of human body temperature within a relatively narrow range.

Homeostatic (cybernetic) system   self-regulating living system in which control of key variables or responses is maintained by information feedback, allowing the system to accommodate new conditions.

Human ecology   interdisciplinary study of the relations between the human community and its environment. It crosses traditional academic and scientific boundaries and represents an attempt to integrate scientific, behavioral, sociological, political, economic, and ethical functions in human relationships to the environment.

Humus   complex mixture of decaying organic matter and inorganic compounds in the soil that serves as a major source of plant nutrients and increases the soil's capacity to absorb water.

Hydrocarbons   class of organic compounds containing carbon (C) and hydrogen (H). They often occur as air pollutants from unburned or partially burned gasoline and evaporation of industrial solvents, especially from refineries. In the presence of sunlight and oxides of nitrogen they can form photochemical smog.

Hydroelectric plant   electric power plant in which the energy of falling water is used to spin a turbine generator to produce electricity.

Hydrological cycle   biogeochemical cycle that moves and recycles water in various forms through the ecosphere.

Hydropower   electrical energy produced by falling water.

Hydrosphere   water portion of the earth (including water vapor in the air), as distinguished from the solid, gaseous, and living parts.

Hypolimnion   bottom layer of cold water in a lake. Compare *epilimnion, thermocline*.

Hypothetical resources   deposits of a resource that can be reasonably expected to exist in areas where deposits have been found in the past. Compare *speculative resources, undiscovered resources*.

Identified resources   specific bodies of mineral-bearing deposits whose existence and location are known. Compare *conditional resources, reserves*.

Immigration   the process of entering one country from another to take up permanent residence.

Incineration   the controlled process by which combustible wastes are burned and changed into gases.

Industrial smog   air pollution, primarily from sulfur oxides and particulates, produced by the burning of coal and oil in households, industries, and power plants.

Inertia   the ability of an ecosystem (or any system) to resist being disturbed or altered.

Infant mortality rate   number of deaths of infants under one year of age in a given year per 1,000 live births in the same year.

Infectious disease   disease resulting from presence of disease-causing organisms or agents, such as bacteria, viruses, and parasitic worms. See also *non-vector-transmitted infectious disease, vector-transmitted infectious disease*.

Information feedback   information sent back into a homeostatic system so that the system can respond to a new environmental condition.

Inland freshwater wetlands   swamps, marshes, and bogs found inland beyond the coastal saltwater wetlands.

Inorganic compounds   substances that consist of chemical combinations of two or more elements except those used to form organic compounds.

Inorganic fertilizer   synthetic plant nutrients produced by humans. Examples are ammonium sulfate, calcium nitrate. Compare *organic fertilizer*.

Insecticide   substance or mixture of substances intended to prevent, destroy, or repel insects.

Integrated pest management (IPM)   combination of natural, biological, chemical, and cultural controls designed specifically for a specific pest problem.

Internal combustion engine   type of engine that uses a series of explosions within cylinders to drive pistons.

Internal costs   costs of production that are directly paid by the user or producer.

Intrauterine device (IUD)   small plastic or metal device inserted into the uterus to prevent conception. Very effective.

Intrinsic limiting factor   factor, such as social stress, that operates within a population to regulate population growth and size. Compare *extrinsic limiting factor*.

Inversion   see *thermal inversion*.

Ions   species of atoms with either negative or positive electrical charges.

Isolated system   system in which neither matter nor energy is exchanged between the system and its environment. Compare *closed system, open system*.

Isotopes   two or more forms of a chemical element that have the same number of protons but different numbers of neutrons in their nuclei.

IUD   see *intrauterine device*.

J curve   curve with the shape of the letter J that depicts exponential or geometric growth (1, 2, 4, 8, 16, 32, . . .).

Juvenile hormone   chemical that controls the ability of an insect to pass through its life stages. Some are being used as pesticides.

Kerogen   a rubbery, solid mixture of hydrocarbons that is intimately mixed with a limestonelike sedimentary rock. When the rock is heated to between 782°C and 982°C (800°F and 1,000°F), the kerogen is vaporized and much of the vapor can be condensed to yield shale oil, which can be refined to give petroleumlike products. See also *oil shale, shale oil*.

Kilocalorie (kcal)   unit of energy equal to 1,000 calories. See *calorie*.

Kilowatt   unit of power equal to 1,000 watts. See *watt*.

Kinetic energy   energy that matter has because of its motion.

Kwashiorkor   nutritional deficiency (malnutrition) disease that occurs in infants and very young children when they are weaned from mother's milk to a starchy diet that is relatively high in calories but low in protein.

Landfill　a land waste disposal site that is located without regard to possible pollution of groundwater and surface water due to runoff and leaching; waste is covered intermittently with a layer of earth to reduce scavenger, aesthetic, disease, and air pollution problems. Compare *open dump, sanitary landfill, secured landfill.*

Laterite　soil found in some tropical areas in which an insoluble concentration of metals, such as iron and aluminum, are present; soil fertility is generally poor.

Law of conservation of energy　see *first law of thermodynamics.*

Law of conservation of matter　in any ordinary physical or chemical change, matter is neither created nor destroyed but merely changed from one form to another.

Leaching　extraction or flushing out of dissolved or suspended materials from soil, solid waste, or another medium by water or other liquids as they percolate downward through the medium to groundwater. Compare *runoff.*

Lentic system　a nonflowing or standing body of fresh water, such as a lake or pond.

Less developed nation　nation that, compared with more developed nations, typically has (1) a low average per capita income, (2) a high rate of population growth, (3) a large fraction of its labor force employed in agriculture, (4) a high level of adult illiteracy, and (5) a weak economy and financial base because only a few items are available for export.

Limiting factor　factor such as temperature, light, water, or a chemical that limits the existence, growth, abundance, or distribution of an organism.

Limiting factor principle　the existence, growth, abundance, or distribution of an organism can be determined by whether the levels of one or more limiting factors fall above or below the levels required by the organism.

Limnetic zone　open-water surface layer of a lake through which sunlight can penetrate.

Limnology　scientific study of physical, chemical, and biological conditions in lakes, ponds, and streams.

Lithosphere　crust of the earth.

Littoral zone　area on or near the shore of a body of water.

Lotic system　a flowing body of fresh water, such as a river or stream.

Macronutrient　chemical needed in a relatively large quantity to sustain life in an organism. Carbon, hydrogen, nitrogen, and oxygen are examples.

Magma　molten rock material within the earth's interior.

Magnetohydrodynamic (MHD) generation　energy-conversion technique that generates electricity directly from high-temperature ionized gases that are passed through a magnetic field.

Malnutrition　situation in which quality of diet is inadequate and fails to meet an individual's minimum daily requirements for proteins, fats, vitamins, minerals, and other specific nutrients required for good health.

Malthusian overpopulation　a condition where the population size of the world or a given portion of the world tends to outrun the ability of people to produce or buy food so that poor health and death from starvation and disease begins to restore the balance. Compare *neo-Malthusian overpopulation.*

Malthusian theory of population　theory (first published by Thomas Malthus) that population tends to increase as a geometric progression while food tends to increase as an arithmetic progression. The conclusion is that human beings are destined to misery and poverty unless population growth is controlled.

Marasmus　a nutritional deficiency disease that results from a diet that is low in both calories and protein.

Mariculture　deliberate cultivation of fish and shellfish in estuarine and coastal areas. Compare *aquaculture.*

Mass number　relative number giving the approximate mass of an isotope of an atom. It is the sum of the number of neutrons and protons in the nucleus.

Mass transit　transportation systems (such as buses, trains, and trolleys) that use vehicles that carry large numbers of people.

Matter　anything that has mass and occupies space.

Megalopolis　see *urban region.*

Megawatt　a unit of electrical power equal to 1,000 kilowatts, or one million watts. A gigawatt is a billion watts.

Meteorology　science of the earth's atmosphere.

Methyl mercury　(CH_3Hg^+) deadly form of mercury that can apparently be formed by microscopic organisms from less harmful elemental mercury and inorganic mercury salts.

Metropolitan area　city in the United States of 50,000 or more people plus its surrounding counties and suburbs that are an integral part of the city's economic and social life.

Microconsumer　see *decomposer.*

Micronutrient　chemical that is needed in only a small quantity to sustain life in an organism. Copper, nickel, and at least 20 other chemicals are in this group.

Microorganism　generally, any living thing of microscopic size; includes bacteria, yeasts, simple fungi, some algae, slime molds, and protozoans.

Mineral　either a chemical element or a chemical compound (combination of chemical elements).

Mineral resource　a nonrenewable chemical element or compound that is used by humans. Mineral resources are classified either as metallic (such as iron and tin) or nonmetallic (such as fossil fuels, sand, and salt).

Moderator　substance such as water or graphite used in the core of a nuclear reactor to slow down neutrons so they can cause nuclear fission.

Molecule　a chemical combination of two or more atoms of different chemical elements.

Monoculture　cultivation of a single crop (such as maize or cotton) to the exclusion of other crops on a piece of land.

More developed nation　nation that, compared with less developed nations, typically has (1) a high average per capita income, (2) a low rate of population growth, (3) a small fraction of its labor force employed in agriculture, (4) a low level of adult illiteracy, and (5) a strong economy.

Mortality　the death rate.

Multiple use　a principle for managing a forest so that it is used not for a single purpose but for a variety of purposes, including timbering, mining, recreation, grazing, wildlife preservation, and soil and water conservation.

Municipal waste　combined residential and commercial waste materials generated in a given municipal area.

Mutagen　any substance capable of increasing the rate of genetic mutation of living organisms.

Mutagenic capable of producing harmful genetic mutations.

Mutation process of change in the genetic material that determines the characteristics of a species. Mutations caused by chemical compounds are generally regressive; that is, they produce bizarre, grotesque, or unviable forms of the parent organism.

Mutualism a symbiotic relationship between two different species that benefits both species. See *commensalism, parasitism, symbiosis*.

Natural controls those natural forces that operate to keep population in check. These include famine, disease, plagues, pestilence, and environmental changes.

Natural eutrophication see *eutrophication*.

Natural gas natural deposits of gases consisting of 50 to 90 percent methane (a hydrocarbon with the chemical formula CH_4) and small amounts of other, more complex hydrocarbons such as propane (C_3H_8) and butane (C_4H_{10}).

Natural increase (or decrease) difference between the crude birth rate and crude death rate in a given population in a given period of time.

Natural resource see *resource*.

Natural selection the mechanism for evolutionary change in which individual organisms in a single population die off over a period of time because they cannot tolerate a new stress and are replaced by individuals whose genetic traits allow them to cope with the stress and to pass these adaptive traits on to their offspring.

Negative feedback flow of information into a system that causes the system to counteract the effects of an input or change in external conditions. Compare *positive feedback*.

Negative income tax plan for guaranteeing a minimum level of income through payments to families with incomes below a certain level.

Negative synergy (antagonistic effect) the interaction of two or more factors so that the net effect is less than that resulting from adding their independent effects.

Neo-Malthusian overpopulation situation in the world or a given country or region in which a relatively small number of people use highly polluting resources at such a fast rate that the resulting pollution can threaten the health and survival of humans and other species and disrupt the natural processes that cleanse and replenish the air, water, and soil. Compare *Malthusian overpopulation*.

Neritic zone portion of the ocean that includes the estuarine zone and the continental shelf.

Net birth rate total number of births during a given time period.

Net death rate total number of deaths during a given time period.

Net energy see *net useful energy*.

Net increase total population growth in a given time period, obtained by subtracting net or total death rate from net or total birth rate.

Net migration in a given population, the difference between the number of persons entering and leaving through migration during a given time period.

Net primary productivity rate at which plants produce usable food or chemical energy (usable biomass). Obtained by subtracting the rate of respiration from the gross primary productivity. See also *gross primary productivity*.

Net use total amount of water withdrawn for human use minus the water lost to the air by evaporation and transpiration (consumptive use). See *consumptive use, degrading use, withdrawal use*.

Net useful energy total useful energy of a resource as it is found in nature minus the useful energy needed to find, extract, and process the resource, upgrade energy quality, meet environmental and safety requirements, and deliver the energy to the user *minus* the useful energy lost as a result of the second energy law and the uses of unnecessarily inefficient and wasteful energy systems.

net useful energy	=	total useful energy	−	useful energy to find, prepare, upgrade, and deliver the energy in a useful form	−	useful energy lost and wasted

Neutron elementary particle present in all atomic nuclei (except hydrogen-1). It has no electric charge and a relative mass of 1.

Niche see *ecological niche*.

Nitrate (NO_3^-) negatively charged chemical group consisting of one nitrogen and three oxygen atoms. A major component of some chemical fertilizers.

Nitrite (NO_2^-) negatively charged chemical group consisting of one nitrogen and two oxygen atoms. It can be poisonous when it combines with hemoglobin in infants.

Nitrogen fixation process in which bacteria and other soil microorganisms convert atmospheric nitrogen into nitrates, which become available to growing plants.

Nitrogen oxides (NO_x) air pollutants that consist primarily of nitric oxide (NO) and nitrogen dioxide (NO_2) produced by the reaction of the nitrogen (N_2) and oxygen (O_2) in air at the high temperatures found in internal combustion engines and furnaces.

Nondegradable pollutant pollutant that is not broken down by natural purifying mechanisms, including inorganic substances, salts of heavy metals, sediments, some bacteria and viruses, and some synthetic organic chemicals. Compare *degradable pollutant*.

Noninfectious disease illness not caused by a disease-causing organism and that, except for genetic diseases, is not transmitted from one person to another. Examples include heart disease, bronchitis, cancer, diabetes, asthma, multiple sclerosis, and hemophilia.

Nonmetropolitan area any area in the United States in which most inhabitants are not an integral part of the economic and social life of a city of at least 50,000 people.

Nonpoint source source of pollution in which wastes are not released at one specific, identifiable point but from a number of diffuse points.

Nonrenewable resource resource that can be used up or at least depleted to such a degree that further recovery is too expensive. Compare *renewable resource*.

Nonspontaneous process any process that requires an outside input of energy to occur. Compare *spontaneous process*.

Nonthreshold pollutant substance or condition harmful to a particular organism at any level or concentration.

Non-vector-transmitted infectious disease disease that is transmitted from person to person without an intermediate nonhuman live carrier. The transmission usually takes place by (1) close physical contact with infected persons (syphilis, gonorrhea, mononucleosis); (2) contact with water, food, soil, clothing, bedding, or other substance contaminated by fecal material or saliva from infected persons (cholera, typhoid fever); or (3) inhalation of air containing tiny droplets of contaminated fluid, which are expelled when infected persons cough, sneeze, or talk (common cold, influenza).

Nuclear energy   energy released when atomic nuclei undergo fission or fusion.

Nuclear fission   process in which the nucleus of a heavy element splits into two or more nuclei of lighter elements, with the release of neutrons and substantial amounts of energy. The most important fissionable materials are uranium-235 and plutonium-239.

Nuclear fusion   process in which the nuclei of two light, nonradioactive elements (such as hydrogen isotopes) are forced together at ultrahigh temperatures to form the nucleus of a slightly heavier element (such as helium) with the release of substantial amounts of energy.

Nucleus   the extremely tiny center of an atom that contains one or more positively charged protons and in most cases one or more neutrons with no electrical charge. The nucleus contains most of an atom's mass.

Nutrient   element or compound that is an essential raw material for organism growth and development. Examples are carbon, oxygen, nitrogen, phosphorus, and the dissolved solids and gases in water.

Nutritional (physiological) population density   number of persons per unit of area of cultivated land.

Ocean thermal gradients   temperature difference between warm surface waters and cold bottom waters in an ocean. If the difference is large enough, this storage of solar heat could be tapped as a source of energy.

Oil   see *petroleum*.

Oil shale   an underground formation of limestonelike sedimentary rock (marlstone) that contains a rubbery, solid mixture of hydrocarbons known as kerogen. See also *kerogen, shale oil*.

Oligotrophic lake   a lake with a low supply of plant nutrients.

Omnicide   killing of everyone (probably through global nuclear war).

Omnivore   animal such as a human that can use both plants and other animals as food sources.

OPEC   the Organization of Petroleum Exporting Countries, 13 nations that aim at developing common prices and policies for marketing crude oil extracted within their boundaries.

Open dump   land disposal site where wastes are deposited and left uncovered with little or no regard for control of scavenger, aesthetic, disease, air pollution, or water pollution problems. Compare *landfill, sanitary landfill, secured landfill*.

Open pit mining   surface mining of materials that creates a large pit. Used primarily for stone, sand, gravel, iron, and copper.

Open sea (oceanic zone)   the part of the ocean that is beyond the continental shelf.

Open system   system in which energy and matter are exchanged between the system and its environment. A living organism is an example. Compare *closed system, isolated system*.

Optimum population   level of population that allows most, if not all, of the world's or a region's population to live with reasonable comfort and individual freedom.

Oral contraceptive (the pill)   combination of synthetic female hormones (such as estrogen and progesterone), which are taken once a day (or less frequently with some newer types) to prevent conception by inhibiting the release of eggs from the ovaries.

Ore   mineral containing constituent, usually a metal, which can be mined and worked.

Organic compounds   molecules that typically contain atoms of the elements carbon and hydrogen; carbon, hydrogen, and oxygen; or carbon, hydrogen, oxygen, and nitrogen.

Organic farming   a method of producing crops and livestock naturally by using organic fertilizer (manure, legumes, composting, crop residues), crop rotation, and natural pest control (good bugs that eat bad bugs, plants that repel bugs, and environmental controls such as crop rotation) instead of using artificial fertilizer and synthetic pesticides and herbicides.

Organic fertilizer   animal manure or other organic material used as a plant nutrient. Compare *inorganic fertilizer*.

Organophosphates   diverse group of nonpersistent synthetic chemical insecticides that act chiefly by breaking down nerve and muscle responses; examples are parathion and Malathion.

Overfishing   harvesting so many fish of a species that there is not enough breeding stock left to repopulate the species for the next year's catch.

Overnutrition   diet so high in calories, saturated (animal) fats, salt, sugar, and processed foods and so low in vegetables and fruits that the consumer runs high risks of suffering from diabetes, hypertension, heart disease, and other health hazards. Compare *malnutrition*.

Overpopulation   see *Malthusian overpopulation, neo-Malthusian overpopulation*.

Oxidants   measure of the presence of oxidizing chemicals, such as ozone, in the ambient air. An indicator of photochemical smog.

Oxygen-demanding waste   organic water pollutants that are usually degraded by bacteria if there is sufficient dissolved oxygen (DO) in the water. See also *biochemical oxygen demand*.

Ozone (O_3)   highly reactive molecule made up of three atoms of oxygen that forms a layer high in the atmosphere. This layer filters out harmful ultraviolet radiation, thus protecting life on earth. It is also formed at the earth's surface as a damaging component of photochemical smog.

Ozone layer   layer of gaseous ozone (O_3) in the upper atmosphere that protects life on earth by filtering out harmful ultraviolet radiation from the sun.

PAN   group of chemicals (photochemical oxidants) known as *peroxyacylnitrates* that are found in photochemical smog.

Parasitism   a symbiotic relationship between two different species in which one species (the parasite) benefits and the other species (the host) is harmed. See *commensalism, mutualism, symbiosis*.

Particulates   solid particles or liquid droplets suspended or carried in the air.

Pathogen   any organism that produces disease.

PCBs (*polychlorinated biphenyls*)   mixture of at least 50 widely used compounds containing chlorine that can be biologically magnified in the food chain with unknown effects.

Pedalfers   soils found in the hot, wet rain forest and in biomes such as the temperate rain forest, deciduous (leaf-dropping) forest, taiga or coniferous (evergreen and cone-bearing) forest, and tundra, which have cool to very cold climates with moderate to high precipitation.

Pedocals   soils found in biomes such as grassland, shrubland (savanna), and desert, which have climates with moderate to low precipitation (semiarid to arid) and moderate to high temperatures.

Pesticide any chemical designed to kill weeds, insects, fungi, rodents, and other organisms that humans consider to be undesirable; examples are chlorinated hydrocarbons, carbamates, and organophosphates.

Petrochemicals chemicals made from natural gas or petroleum.

Petroleum (crude oil) dark, greenish-brown, foul-smelling liquid containing a complex mixture of hydrocarbon compounds plus small amounts of oxygen, sulfur, and nitrogen compounds and found in natural underground reservoirs.

pH numeric value that indicates the relative acidity or alkalinity of a substance on a 0 to 14 scale with the neutral point at 7.0. Values lower than 7.0 indicate the presence of acids and greater than 7.0 the presence of alkalis (bases).

Photochemical oxidants see *photochemical smog.*

Photochemical smog complex mixture of air pollutants (oxidants) produced in the atmosphere by the reaction of hydrocarbons and nitrogen oxides under the influence of sunlight. Three of the most harmful photochemical oxidants are *ozone* (O_3), *peroxyacylnitrates* (PAN), and various aldehydes.

Photosynthesis complex process that occurs in the cells of green plants whereby sunlight is used to combine carbon dioxide (CO_2) and water (H_2O) to produce oxygen (O_2) and simple sugar or food molecules, such as glucose ($C_6H_{12}O_6$).

Photovoltaic conversion process by which radiant (solar) energy is converted directly into electrical energy using a solar cell.

Phytoplankton free-floating, mostly microscopic aquatic plants.

Plankton microscopic floating plant and animal organisms of lakes, rivers, and oceans.

Plasma "gas" of charged particles (ions) of elements that exists only at such high temperatures (40 million to several billion degrees Celsius) that all electrons are stripped from the atomic nuclei.

Point source source of pollution that involves discharge of wastes from an identifiable point, such as a smokestack or sewage treatment plant.

Pollution undesirable change in the physical, chemical, or biological characteristics of the air, water, or land that can harmfully affect the health, survival, or activities of humans or other living organisms.

Pollution charges effluent or emission charges per unit of pollutant released during a particular time period.

Pollution rights sale on the open market of a limited number of rights to pollute up to a specific amount in a given place over a particular time period.

Population group of individual organisms of the same kind (species)

Population control all methods for conception and birth control plus regulation of migration and natural or deliberate changes in economic, political, or social conditions in order to bring about either population growth or decline.

Population crash (dieback) extensive deaths resulting when a population exceeds the ability of the environment to support it.

Population density number of organisms in a particular population per square kilometer or other unit of area. See also *nutritional (physiological) population density.*

Population distribution variation of population density over a given country, region, or other area.

Positive feedback feedback where the information sent back into a homeostatic system causes the system to change continuously in the same direction; as a result, the system can go out of control. Compare *negative feedback.*

Positive synergy interaction of two or more factors so that the net effect is greater than that resulting from adding their independent effects.

Potential energy stored energy that an object possesses due to its position, condition, or composition.

Power rate at which work is done or energy is expended.

Predation situation in which an organism of one species (the predator) captures and feeds on an organism of another species (the prey).

Predator organism that lives by killing and eating other organisms.

Primary air pollutant chemical that has been added directly to the air and occurs in a harmful concentration. Compare *secondary air pollutant.*

Primary succession ecological succession that begins on an area (such as bare rock, lava, or sand) that has not been previously occupied by a community of organisms.

Primary treatment (of sewage) mechanical treatment in which large solids, like old shoes and sticks of wood, are screened out, and suspended solids in the sewage settle out as sludge. Compare *secondary treatment, tertiary treatment.*

Primate any mammal of the order Primates, including humans, the apes, monkeys, lemurs, tarsiers, and marmosets.

Prime reproductive age years between ages 20 and 29, during which most women have most of their children.

Principle of competitive exclusion (Gause's principle) no two species in an ecosystem can indefinitely occupy exactly the same niche or exist on the same limited resources.

Producer organism that synthesizes its own organic substances from inorganic substances, such as a plant.

Profundal zone a lake's deep-water region that is not penetrated by sunlight.

Pronatalist refers to cultural attitudes and values that favor motherhood and large families.

Protein-calorie malnutrition combination of undernutrition and malnutrition.

Pulmonary emphysema lung disease in which the alveoli enlarge and lose their elasticity, thus impairing the transfer of oxygen to the blood.

Pyramid of biomass diagram representing the biomass, or total dry weight of all living organisms, that can be supported at each trophic level in a food chain.

Pyramid of numbers figure representing the number of organisms of a particular type that can be supported at each trophic level from a given input of solar energy at the producer trophic level in a food chain.

Pyrolysis high-temperature decomposition of material in the absence of oxygen.

Radioactive waste radioactive end products of nuclear power plants or processes.

Radioactivity property of certain chemical elements of spontaneously emitting radiation from unstable atomic nuclei. The emitted radiation may damage organisms. See *radioisotope*.

Radioisotope isotope of an element whose nuclei are capable of spontaneously emitting radiation in the form of alpha particles, beta particles, or gamma rays.

Range of tolerance the range or span of conditions that must be maintained for an organism to stay alive and grow, develop, and function normally.

Rankine engine vapor cycle engine consisting of a closed tube containing a fluid that is heated externally by a low-grade gasoline or kerosene fuel (an external combustion engine). The fluid (sometimes water) is transformed into vapor, which expands to drive pistons or spin turbines. The liquid is condensed and reused. The steam engine is an example.

Rare species species that is not presently in danger of biological extinction but is subject to risk because of its low numbers in widely separated subpopulations.

Rate of natural increase (or decrease) measure of population change obtained by finding the difference between the crude birth rate and the crude death rate.

Recycle to collect and remelt a resource so it can be used again, as when used glass bottles are collected, melted down, and made into new glass bottles. Compare *reuse*.

Renewable resource resource that potentially cannot be used up because it is constantly or cyclically replenished. Either it comes from an essentially inexhaustible source (such as solar energy from the sun), or it can be renewed by natural or human-devised cyclical processes if it is not used faster than it is renewed. Compare *nonrenewable resource*.

Replacement level of fertility fertility rate of 2.11 children per woman (in the United States) which will supply just enough births to replace the parents and compensate for premature deaths, assuming proper age structure and no net effect of migration.

Reproductive age ages 15 to 44, when most women have all of their children.

Reproductive potential see *biotic potential*.

Reserves amount of a particular resource in known locations that can be extracted at a profit with present technology and prices. Compare *conditional resources, identified resources*.

Resilience the ability of an ecosystem (or any system) to restore its structure and function following a natural or human-induced stress.

Resistant crop variety plant variety that is genetically bred to be resistant to certain insects, fungi, and diseases.

Resource (natural) anything needed by an organism or group of organisms. See also *mineral resource, nonrenewable resource, renewable resource*.

Resource recovery extraction of useful materials or energy from waste materials. This may involve recycling or conversion into different and sometimes unrelated products or uses. Compare *reuse, recycling*.

Resources total amount of a particular resource material that exists on earth.

Respiration complex process that occurs in the cells of plants and animals in which food molecules such as glucose ($C_6H_{12}O_6$) combine with oxygen (O_2) and break down into carbon dioxide (CO_2) and water (H_2O), releasing usable energy.

Reuse to reuse a product over and over again, as is done with returnable glass bottles, which are washed and refilled. Compare *recycle*.

Rhythm method method of birth control based on abstention from sexual intercourse during a woman's fertile period.

Runoff lateral movement of nutrients and soil to surface waters. Compare *leaching*.

Rural area an area in the United States containing up to 2,500 people.

S curve leveling off of an exponential or J curve.

Saline water any water containing more than 1,000 ppm of dissolved solids of any type. Includes inland brackish water, salted water, and seawater. See *brackish water, salted water, seawater*.

Salinity amount of dissolved salts in a given volume of water.

Salted water water having 4,000 to 18,000 ppm of dissolved salts. See *brackish water, saline water, seawater*.

Sanitary landfill land waste disposal site that is located to minimize water pollution from runoff and leaching; waste is spread in thin layers, compacted, and covered with a fresh layer of soil each day to minimize pest, aesthetic, disease, air pollution, and water pollution problems. Compare *landfill, open dump, secured landfill*.

Saprophytic obtaining food by absorbing the products of organic breakdown and decay.

Saprotrophic organisms tiny organisms—such as bacteria, fungi, termites, and maggots—that break down the bodies and complex chemicals in dead animals and plants into simpler chemicals.

Scrubber common antipollution device that uses a liquid spray to remove pollutants from a stream of air.

Seawater water having 18,000 to 35,000 ppm of dissolved solids. See *brackish water, saline water, salted water*.

Second energy law see *second law of thermodynamics*.

Second law energy efficiency ratio of the minimum amount of useful energy (or work) needed to perform a task to the actual amount of useful energy (or work) used

$$\text{second law energy efficiency (\%)} = \frac{\text{minimum amount of useful energy (or work)}}{\text{actual amount of useful energy (or work) needed to perform a task}} \times 100$$

Second law of thermodynamics (law of energy degradation) (1) In all conversations of heat energy to work, some of the energy is always degraded to a more dispersed and less useful form, usually heat energy given off at a low temperature to the surroundings, or environment, *or* you can't break even in terms of energy quality. (2) Any system and its surroundings (environment) as a whole spontaneously tend toward increasing randomness, disorder, or entropy, *or* if you think things are mixed up now, just wait.

Secondary air pollutant harmful chemical formed in the atmosphere through a chemical reaction among air components. Compare *primary air pollutant*.

Secondary materials uniformly segregated and processed waste materials from a recycling or resource recovery plant, which are sold to manufacturers for use in making basic products.

Secondary succession ecological succession that begins on an area (such as abandoned farmland, a new pond, or land disrupted by fire) that had previously been occupied by a community of organisms.

Secondary treatment (of sewage) second step in most waste treatment systems, in which bacteria are used to break down the organic parts of sewage wastes. It is usually accomplished by bringing the sewage and bacteria together in trickling filters or in the activated sludge process. Compare *primary treatment, tertiary treatment.*

Secured landfill   a land site for the storage of hazardous solid and liquid wastes, which are normally placed in containers and then buried underground; the location has restricted access, is continually monitored, and is located above geologic strata that should prevent any wastes from being leached into groundwater. Compare *landfill, open dump, sanitary landfill.*

Sediment   soil particles, sand, and minerals washed from the land into aquatic systems as a result of natural and human activities.

Sedimentary cycle   biogeochemical cycle with materials primarily moved from land to sea and back again. Examples include the phosphorus and sulfur cycles.

Selective cutting   cutting only certain mature or diseased trees in a forest. Used especially in diverse climax forests.

Septic tank   underground tank that receives wastewater directly from a home. The bacteria in the sewage decompose the organic wastes, and the sludge settles to the bottom of the tank. The effluent flows out of the tank into the ground through drains.

Shale oil   a low-sulfur, very viscous, petroleumlike liquid that is obtained when kerogen in shale oil rock is vaporized at high temperatures and then condensed. Shale oil can be refined to yield petroleum products. See also *kerogen, oil shale.*

Shelter wood cutting   cutting only a small stand of trees in a forest area to allow light penetration.

Silviculture   cultivation of forests.

Single-cell protein (SCP)   form of protein made from oil by the action of microorganisms.

Slash-and-burn agriculture   practice of clearing a patch of forest overgrowth, burning the residue, and planting crops. The patch is abandoned after 2 or 3 years to prevent depletion of soil fertility. Used in many tropical areas.

Sludge   solid matter settling to the bottom of sedimentation tanks in a sewage treatment plants that must be disposed of by digestion or other methods or recycled to the land.

Smog   originally a combination of *fog* and *smoke*; now applied also to the photochemical haze produced by the action of sun and atmo-sphere on automobile and industrial exhausts. Compare *industrial smog, photochemical smog.*

Social cost   cost to society of a particular act. It can include economic and noneconomic costs passed on to society by a user or producer. See *external cost.*

Social density   number of social interactions between individuals of the same species in a given area.

Society   group of people living together in a region as a community and sharing the same general living system and cultural beliefs.

Soil   complex mixture of small pieces of rock, minerals (inorganic compounds), organic compounds, living organisms, air, and water. It is a dynamic body that is always changing in response to climate, vegetation, local topography, parent rock material, age, and human use and abuse.

Soil horizons   layers that make up a particular type of soil (see Figure 4-8).

Solar cell   device that converts radiant energy from the sun directly into electrical energy by the photovoltaic process.

Solar collector   device for collecting radiant energy from the sun and converting it into heat.

Solar energy   direct radiation or energy from the sun plus indirect forms of energy—such as wind, falling or flowing water (hydropower), ocean thermal gradients, and biomass—that are produced when solar energy interacts with the earth.

Solid waste   any unwanted or discarded material that is not a liquid or a gas.

Sonic boom   loud sound produced by the shock wave of an aircraft traveling at supersonic speed; the shock wave is continuously produced but sounds explosive at any single point on the ground.

Spaceship earth   metaphor for the earth as a finite ecosystem in which resources must be husbanded and the ever-changing balance between humans and their environment preserved if life is to survive.

Species   a group of plants or animals that breed or are bred together but not successfully with members outside their group. This results in a natural population or group of populations that transmit specific characteristics from parents to offspring.

Species diversity   ratio between the number of species in a community and the number of individuals in each species. (For example, low diversity occurs when there are few species but many individuals per species.)

Speculative resources   deposits that are thought to be in areas that have not been examined and tested for resources. Compare *hypothetical resources, undiscovered resources.*

Spermatocide   chemical that inactivates or kills sperm.

Spontaneous process   any process that can occur naturally without an outside input of energy; for example, water flowing downhill or heat energy flowing from hot to cold. Compare *nonspontaneous process.*

SST   supersonic transport plane that can fly at speeds greater than sound.

Stability   persistence of the structure of a system (such as an ecosystem, community, or organism) over time.

Static reserve index   estimated number of years until known world reserves of a nonrenewable resource will be 80 percent depleted if consumed at today's rate with no increase. Compare *exponential reserve index.*

Stationary population   stable population that does not increase or decrease in size.

Steady state   see *dynamic steady state.*

Steam engine   see *Rankine engine.*

Sterile male technique   form of pest control in which vast numbers of sterilized males are released to mate unsuccessfully with normal insects and thus reduce the population.

Sterilization   any surgical, chemical, or radiological procedure by which an individual is made incapable of reproduction.

Strip mining   mining in which the earth's surface is stripped away.

Subeconomic resources   known supplies of resources that cannot be recovered profitably with present prices and technology. Compare *identified resources, reserves.*

Subsidence   sinking down of part of the earth's crust due to underground excavations, such as a coal mine.

Succession   see *ecological succession.*

Sulfur dioxide (SO₂)   heavy, colorless gas that is very toxic to plants and fairly toxic to humans. It is produced by burning coal and by smelting and other industrial processes.

Sulfur oxides (SOₓ)   sulfur dioxide (SO_2) and sulfur trioxide (SO_3), which are produced when coal or oil containing small amounts of sulfur is burned. They are common air pollutants. SO_2 can react with oxygen in the air to produce SO_3, which can react with water vapor to produce *sulfuric acid* (H_2SO_4).

Sulfuric acid (H₂SO₄) corrosive acid; often produced from the reaction of sulfur trioxide with water vapor in the air. See *sulfur oxides*.

Surface mining the process of removing the overburden of topsoil, subsoil, and other strata so that underlying mineral deposits can be removed. See *area strip mining, contour strip mining, dredging, open-pit mining*.

Surroundings (environment) everything outside of a specified system or collection of matter.

Sustained yield principle for managing a forest in which there is a balance between new planting and growing and the amount of wood removed by cutting, pests, disease, and fire so that a forest is not depleted.

Symbiosis interaction in which two different species live in close physical contact, with one living on or in the other so that one or both species benefit from the association. See *commensalism, mutualism, parasitism*.

Synergistic effect an effect that occurs when two or more substances or factors interact to produce effects that they could not produce by acting separately. See *negative synergy, positive synergy*, and *synergy*.

Synergy interaction in which the total effect is greater than or less than the sum of two effects taken independently. See *negative synergy, positive synergy*.

Synfuels fuels such as synthetic natural gas (SNG) and synthetic fuel oil produced from coal or sources other than natural gas or crude oil.

Syphilis infectious disease transmitted by sexual contact; potentially crippling or deadly.

System collection of matter under study.

Tar sands (oil sands) enormous swamps that contain fine clay and sand mixed with water and highly variable amounts of a black, high-sulfur, molasseslike tar known as heavy oil, or bitumen, which is about 83 percent carbon. The heavy oil can be extracted from the tar sand by heating and flotation and then purified and upgraded to synthetic crude oil. See *heavy oil*.

Temperature the relative hotness or coldness of a substance. It is a measure of the average kinetic energy of all the atoms and molecules in a sample of matter.

Ten percent law only about 10 percent of the chemical energy available at one trophic level gets transferred in usable form to the bodies of the organisms at the next trophic level in a food chain or food web.

Teratogen substance that, if taken by a pregnant female, causes malformation of the developing fetus. The drug thalidomide is a powerful teratogen.

Territory area that an organism (such as a lion) will defend against intruders of the same species (other lions).

Tertiary treatment (of sewage) removal from wastewater of traces of organic materials and dissolved solids that remain after *primary* and *secondary treatment*.

Tetraethyl lead form of lead added to gasoline to reduce engine knock; considered a major source of the lead that is now accumulating in our bodies.

Thermal inversion layer of cool air trapped under a layer of warm air thus reversing the normal situation. If prolonged, it often allows air pollution levels to rise to harmful levels.

Thermal pollution increase in air or water temperature that disturbs the climate or ecology of an area.

Thermocline fairly thin layer in a lake that separates an upper warmer zone *(epilimnion)* from a lower colder zone *(hypolimnion)*.

Thermodynamic efficiency measure of the ability of an engine or process to convert energy to useful work, or the ratio of useful energy to total energy input. Its limit is determined by the second law of thermodynamics.

Threatened species species that is still abundant in its geographic range but is threatened with biological extinction because of a decline in numbers.

Threshold effect phenomenon in which no effect is observed until a certain level or concentration is attained. See *threshold pollutant*.

Threshold pollutant substance that is harmful to a particular organism only above a certain concentration, or threshold level.

Time delay delay between the time an information signal or stimulus is received by a homeostatic system and the time when the system makes a corrective action by negative feedback.

Tolerance limit point at and beyond which a chemical or physical condition (such as heat) becomes harmful to a living organism.

Total fertility rate projection of the average number of children a woman will have from ages 15 to 44 in the United States and ages 15 to 49 in most other countries, if she continues at the same reproductive rate as women in their reproductive years do today.

Toxic substances substances (chemicals) that can cause serious illness or death.

Transpiration direct transfer of water from the leaves of living plants to the atmosphere.

Trickling filter bed of rocks or stones. Sewage is trickled over the bed so that bacteria can break down the organic wastes. The bacteria collect on the stones through repeated use of the filter.

Tritium (hydrogen-3) isotope of the element hydrogen with a nucleus containing one proton and two neutrons, thus having a mass number of 3. Compare *deuterium*.

Trophic level level where energy in the form of food is transferred from one organism to another in a food chain or food web.

Troposphere lower layer of the atmosphere that contains about 95 percent of the earth's air. It extends about 8 to 12 kilometers (5 to 7 miles) above the earth's surface.

Tubal ligation method of female sterilization by cutting and tying fallopian tubes.

Tundra a thin layer of topsoil found on top of permafrost.

Turbidity in meteorology, any condition in the atmosphere that reduces its transparency to radiation, especially visible radiation.

Ultraviolet (UV) radiation electromagnetic radiation with wavelengths somewhat shorter than those for visible light but longer than those for X rays.

Undernutrition situation in which there is an insufficient quantity or calorie intake of food needed to meet an individual's minimum daily energy requirement.

Undiscovered resources resource supplies that are believed to exist. See *hypothetical resources, speculative resources*.

Upwelling region area adjacent to a continent where ocean bottom waters rich in nutrients are brought to the surface.

Urban area any place in the United States with a population of 20,000 or more.

Urban growth increase in size of an urban population.

Urban open space any large, medium-sized, or small area of land or water in or near an urban area that is used for a recreational, aesthetic, or ecological function.

Urban region (megalopolis) large zone of metropolitan areas separated only by occasional topographical barriers and containing at least 1 million people.

Urban waste general term used to categorize the entire waste stream from an urban area. It is sometimes used in contrast to "rural waste."

Urbanization the proportion of the total population concentrated in an urban area.

Vacuum aspiration modern method of abortion in which the cervix is dilated and the embryo and placenta are gently sucked out by a vacuum pump.

Vasectomy method of male sterilization in which small sections of the vas tubes are removed, and the tubes are retied. Reversible in some cases.

Vector living organism (usually an insect) that carries an infectious disease from one host (person) to another.

Vector-transmitted infectious disease disease carried from one host (person) to another by some living organism (usually insect), which is called a vector. Examples include malaria, schistosomiasis, and African sleeping sickness.

Water cycle see *hydrologic cycle*.

Water logging saturation of soil with irrigation water so the water table rises close to the surface.

Water pollution degradation of a body of water by some substance or condition to such a degree that the water doesn't meet specified standards or cannot be used for a specific purpose.

Water table level below the earth's surface at which the ground becomes saturated with water.

Watershed land area from which water drains toward a common watercourse in a natural basin.

Watt unit of power or rate at which electrical work is done.

Wavelength distance between the crest (or trough) of one wave and that of the next.

Weather day-to-day variation in atmospheric conditions.

Wetland any area that is regularly wet or flooded and where the water table stands at or above the land surface for at least part of the year. Coastal wetlands extend back from estuaries and include salt marshes, tidal basins, marshes and mangrove swamps. Inland freshwater wetlands consist of swamps, marshes, and bogs.

Wilderness area where the earth and its community of life are undisturbed by humans and where humans themselves are temporary visitors.

Withdrawal use total amount of water taken out of a lake, river, or reservoir. Compare *consumptive use, degraded use, net use.*

Yield takeoff dramatic and sudden increase in the yield per acre of a selected crop. See *green revolution*.

Zero population growth (ZPG) state in which the birth rate (plus immigration) equals the death rate (plus emigration) so that population is no longer growing. Also the name of an important organization dedicated to achieving this goal.

Index